CONTEMPORARY FAMILY LAW

Fifth Edition

■ ■ ■

Douglas E. Abrams
Associate Professor of Law
University of Missouri School of Law

Naomi R. Cahn
Harold H. Greene Professor of Law
The George Washington University Law School

Catherine J. Ross
Fred C. Stevenson Research Professor of Law
The George Washington University Law School

Linda C. McClain
Robert B. Kent Professor of Law
Boston University School of Law

AMERICAN CASEBOOK SERIES®

WEST
ACADEMIC
PUBLISHING

American Casebook Series is a trademark registered in the U.S. Patent and Trademark Office.

© West, a Thomson business, 2006
© 2009, 2012 Thomson Reuters
© 2015 LEG, Inc. d/b/a West Academic
© 2019 LEG, Inc. d/b/a West Academic
    444 Cedar Street, Suite 700
    St. Paul, MN 55101
    1-877-888-1330

Printed in the United States of America

ISBN: 978-1-64020-591-8

To my parents, Barbara and Saul D. Abrams, who led our family.

D.E.A.

To my parents, Paul and Elissa Cahn, and to Louisa, Abigail,
and Tony, for always teaching me about family.

N.R.C.

To the three men in my life:
In loving memory of my father, Alexander I. Ross,
a pioneer in paternal custody, and

To my husband Jon and son Daniel, with love and thanks.

C.J.R.

To my father, Robert C. McClain, Esq., for sparking my interest in law.

L.C.M.

PREFACE

The profound changes that have transformed family law over the past several decades are arguably unmatched in any other area of the law. The pace of change appears to be accelerating because questions that have been at the core of this book since it first appeared in 2006—and that may have appeared merely theoretical to some readers at that time—now dominate the agenda in courts, legislatures, and public discussion.

This book captures the rapid evolution of doctrine, introduces students to continually shifting policy debates, and explores issues central to family law practice. Solid grounding in legal analysis and reasoning is indispensable to family law study and practice because court decisions, statutes, and administrative regulations are every lawyer's basic legal tools regardless of specialty. Command of doctrine in fields like family law carries lawyering only so far, however, because much of today's doctrine will be tomorrow's history. By conveying a solid sense of the rapid trajectory of ongoing doctrinal change, this book provides students a foundation for anticipating, understanding, and participating in continuing developments in law school and throughout their careers.

Policy study is particularly central to family law because the legislature's broad discretionary standards compel practitioners and judges to grapple with policy concerns when they apply doctrine to the lives of individuals who summon the law's protection. It is impossible to determine the "best interests" of a child or an "equitable" division of a couple's marital assets, for example, without weighing public policy.

Policy considerations will also help shape future doctrinal evolution in contentious areas that largely went unmentioned in family law courses only a relatively short time ago—areas such as the decline of marriage as an institution and the growing class divide in family structure, marriage by same-sex couples, assisted reproductive technology and different pathways to parenthood, joint custody of children, domestic violence, cohabitants' rights and obligations, and indeed the very definition of "family" itself. Because many family law policy issues now sharpen political debate (the so-called "culture wars" or "war over the family"), the book encourages students and their teachers to analyze not only what the law is, but also what the law should be. To help inform this analysis, notes in several chapters introduce interdisciplinary and international materials.

Themes and chapter organization. Four themes unify the chapters. The first theme, appearing in virtually every chapter, is that family structures are diverse and that family law addresses this diversity in various ways. Such diversity includes not only various forms of adult-adult intimate relationships, encompassing marital and nonmarital heterosexual and same-sex relationships, but also various forms of parent-child relationships, arising from multiple pathways to parenthood and changing relationships among the important adults in a child's life.

The second theme is that federal and state constitutional law have become increasingly integrated into familial rights and responsibilities through such issues as the right to marry, parents' rights to control their children's upbringing, and other rights based on individual and family privacy, and through reform of marriage, divorce, and parentage laws in light of emerging equal protection doctrine.

Third, the book pays particular attention to the ways various biases—such as express and implicit distinctions based on gender, ethnicity, cultural diversity, sexual orientation, race, and class—have affected family law's development and application.

The fourth theme concerns the importance of collaboration among family lawyers and other professionals who can serve their clients, including marriage counselors, mental health professionals, child psychologists, and forensic accountants. The book's interdisciplinary materials explore non-legal issues that arise in domestic relations practice; the purpose is not to provide expertise, but to accustom students to general concepts in preparation for career-long collaboration with other professionals amid the high emotions that often accompany family disputes.

Based on these themes, the book offers a distinct approach to several family law issues. For example, we devote separate sections or entire chapters to legal ethics, alternative dispute resolution, and private ordering in marriage and divorce. And, although family law casebooks often treat alimony and property distribution together, we consider them in separate chapters to underscore their distinctive practical and theoretical aspects. Finally, we devote two chapters to child custody arrangements, which produce some of family law's most acrimonious legal disputes; the first custody chapter treats the initial custody decision, and the second explores disputes that frequently continue after the initial custody decision, including legal battles over visitation and international disputes governed by the Hague Convention.

Recognizing the importance of practical skills training, each chapter includes questions and exercises that invite classroom resolution. These problems place students in the roles envisioned by the Preamble of the Model Rules of Professional Conduct: advisor, advocate, negotiator, and evaluator.

Chapter authorship. The authors divided responsibility for the individual chapters. Each author takes responsibility for the content of the chapters we authored, though we all benefited from an active collaboration in which authors commented on each other's drafts.

Chapter authorship is as follows:

Professors Cahn, McClain, and Ross co-authored Chapter 1 (Marriage and Family in Contemporary America).

Professors Cahn and Ross jointly authored Chapter 3 (Social and Economic Rights and Obligations).

Professors Cahn and McClain jointly authored Chapter 4 (Nonmarital Couples).

Professor McClain authored Chapters 2 (Entering Marriage), 8 (Divorce), and 16 (Private Ordering in Marriage and Divorce).

Professor Ross authored Chapters 9 (Division of Marital Property at Dissolution), 12 (Child Custody), and 13 (Visitation and Post-Dissolution Custody Disputes).

Professor Cahn authored Chapters 5 (Establishing Parenthood), 10 (Alimony), and 17 (Locations of Family Law Litigation).

Professor Abrams authored Chapters 6 (Adoption), 7 (Civil and Criminal Remedies for Family Injury), 11 (Child Support), 14 (Ethics), and 15 (Alternative Dispute Resolution).

To help students and faculty remain current in family law, we anticipate periodic supplements on major developments provided to users as a courtesy, Internet updates, and new editions. Because student and faculty readers are truly collaborators in our joint project, we invite your comments and suggestions for improvement or for teaching the material. Your input will benefit the next generation of family law practitioners and the families whose lives they touch.

Gratitude. Writing a book, like teaching in the classroom, is a team effort that thrives on valuable contributions from others. Our team includes many terrific people who deserve to share the credit. We continue to benefit from the contributions of everyone who assisted and supported us in preparing this book's earlier editions. With this, as with previous editions, we have benefited from thoughtful feedback from many faculty across the country who use this casebook.

We owe a special debt of gratitude to Editorial Consultant Judith Helfman, whose expert editorial assistance on the first edition's manuscript went well above and beyond all reasonable expectations and continues to be reflected in each edition. And we thank Dean David Meyer for his contributions to earlier editions, starting with the First.

As always, we have incurred many debts as we prepared the Fifth Edition. Deans R. Lawrence Dessem, Gary Myers, and Lyrissa Lidsky at

Missouri and Dean Blake Morant at George Washington University generously continued the support those institutions have provided since we began the First Edition. Former Dean Maureen O'Rourke and Dean Angela Onwuachi-Willig at Boston University School of Law supported Professor McClain's participation in the Fourth Edition as well as in this Fifth Edition. Professor G. Ray Warner at St. John's graciously helped refine the sections on bankruptcy law, Professors Karen Brown (George Washington), Roberta Kwall (DePaul) and Margaret Ryznar (Indiana) helped with analysis of the 2017 tax law changes, and Professor Todd Peterson (George Washington) provided useful feedback on Chapter 17. Law students at George Washington University—Priom Ahmed, Danielle Bereznay, Dana Florkowski, Maryam Gueye, Kaitlin Kinsella, Amy Lopez, Miranda Millerick, Olivia Soloperto, and Aimee Registe—provided excellent research support for the Fifth Edition. Reference Librarian Mary Kate Hunter at George Washington provided the superb help and attention to detail that Professors Cahn and Ross have come to rely on. They also received valuable support from several administrative assistants at George Washington University. Professor McClain acknowledges the valuable research support provided by the librarians at Boston University School of Law, and, especially, that of her faculty liaison, Stefanie Weigmann, Assistant Director for Research, Faculty Assistance, and Technology. In addition, BU Law students Kellie Desrochers, Brittany Hacker, and Katherine N. ("Nina") Jones provided excellent research and editorial assistance.

Working with the West Academic editors and their staff in preparing each edition has been a pleasure. We particularly thank James Cahoy, Staci Herr, Louis Higgins, Laura Holle, Ryan Pfeiffer, Daniel Buteyn, and Jennifer Schlagel.

We also thank our own families for enriching our appreciation of the meaning of family law and the challenges and rewards of family life, and for supporting our work on this book. Finally, we thank the family law students we have taught throughout our careers. Classroom give-and-take with these thoughtful students has helped refine our own thoughts about the important issues that this book treats. Many of our students enroll in the course because they plan to devote their professional energies to family law after graduation. Others expect to practice family law as part of a broader general practice, to enter government service, or to serve on bar association committees, law revision commissions and similar bodies committed to improving family law in the public interest. To whatever stops and destinations their career paths lead, our students make us proud that we were their teachers.

DOUGLAS E. ABRAMS
NAOMI R. CAHN
CATHERINE J. ROSS
LINDA C. MCCLAIN

May 2019

Guidance regarding deleted material and citations:

We have used one set of three asterisks to indicate that we have omitted one or more words, sentences, or paragraphs from cases and other materials excerpted in the book. Brackets similarly indicate deleted material. In some lead cases we have omitted footnotes and citations to minor state cases without so specifying to eliminate distractions for readers. Numbered footnotes are from the original materials and retain the original numbering. Footnotes designated "Editors' Note" and indicated by a letter rather than a number indicate that the casebook authors added the note.

Throughout, we use a modified Bluebook style that enables readers to find the materials on which we rely. When citing statutes, three of the authors reference online citations. In contrast, Professor Ross has followed bluebook citation for federal and state statutes, citing the most recent published statute and updating it when the legislature has made changes not yet reflected in the published code. So, some of the dates may seem old, but you may rest assured the language cited is current as we go to press.

ACKNOWLEDGMENTS

Alstott, Anne L., *Updating The Welfare State: Marriage, The Income Tax, And Social Security In The Age Of Individualism*, 66 TAX L. REV. 695 (2013). Copyright 2013 by Anne L. Alstott and the Tax Law Review, New York University. Reprinted by permission.

American Law Institute, Principles of the Law of Family Dissolution: Analysis and Recommendations, §§ 2.03(1)(b), 2.03(c), 2.03 (Comment b. (iii), Illustration 13), 2.08, 2.17 (4), 6.03 (Comments and Illustrations). Copyright 2002 by the American Law Institute, Philadelphia, Pennsylvania. Reprinted with permission. All rights reserved.

Atwood, Barbara, Representing Children Who Can't or Won't Direct Counsel: Best Interests Lawyering or No Lawyer at All?, 53 ARIZ. L. REV. 381 (2011). Reprinted by permission.

Brinig, Margaret F., Does Mediation Systematically Disadvantage Women?, 2 WM. & MARY J. WOMEN & L. 1 (1994). Copyright by The College of William and Mary. Reprinted by permission.

Cahn, Naomi & Jana Singer, Adoption, Identity and the Constitution: The Case For Opening Closed Records, 2 U. PA. J. CONST. L. 150 (1999). Copyright by The University of Pennsylvania Journal of Constitutional Law. Reprinted by permission.

Calvert, Cynthia Thomas, Family Responsibilities Discrimination: Litigation Update 2010 (2010). Copyright by The Center for WorkLife Law. Reprinted by permission of The Center for WorkLife Law.

Cammett, Ann, Deadbeats, Deadbrokes, and Prisoners, 18 GEO. J. POVERTY LAW & POL'Y 127, 128–31 (2011). Copyright 2011 by Ann Cammett. Reprinted by permission.

Doherty, William J. and Leah Ward Sears, Second Chances: A Proposal to Reduce Unnecessary Divorce (Institute for American Values, 2011). Copyright 2011 by Institute of American Values. Reprinted by permission of the Institute for American Values.

Fedders, Barbara, Race and Market Values in Domestic Infant Adoption, 88 N.C. L. REV. 1687, 1689–95 (2010). Copyright 2010 by Barbara Fedders. Reprinted by permission.

Galston, William, What About the Children?, BLUEPRINT MAGAZINE, May 21, 2002. Copyright by Blueprint Magazine. Reprinted by permission Blueprint Magazine.

Garrison, Marsha, Is Consent Necessary? An Evaluation of the Emerging Law of Cohabitant Obligation, 52 UCLA L. REV. 815, 817–819

(2005). Copyright 2005 UCLA Law Review, Los Angeles, California. Reprinted by permission.

_____, Lawmaking for Baby Making: An Interpretive Approach To the Determination of Legal Parentage. 113 HARV. L. REV. 835, 845–852 (2000). Reprinted by permission of the Harvard Law Review Association and William S. Hein Company.

Glennon, Theresa, Still Partners? Examining the Consequences of Post-Dissolution Parenting, 41 FAM. L. Q. 105 (2007). Reprinted by permission of the author and the American Bar Association.

Goldfarb, Sally, Reconceiving Civil Protection Orders for Domestic Violence: Can Law Help End the Abuse?, 29 CARDOZO L. REV. 1487 208–216 (2008). Reprinted by permission of the author.

Hollinger, Joan Heifetz, Adoption in America Today, Conference Draft (2015). Reprinted by permission of the author.

Kay, Herma Hill, From the Second Sex to the Joint Venture: An Overview of Women's Rights and Family Law in the United States During the Twentieth Century, 88 CAL. L. REV. 2048–2049, 2062–2064, 2088, 2090, 2093 (2000). Copyright 2000 by the California Law Review, Berkeley, California. Reprinted in all editions by permission of the University of California, Berkeley.

Kisthardt, Mary Kay, Re-thinking Alimony: The AAML's Considerations for Calculating Alimony, Spousal Support or Maintenance, 21 J. AM. ACAD. MATRIMONIAL L. 61 (2008). Copyright American Academy of Matrimonial Lawyers. Reprinted by permission.

Kohn, Laurie S., Engaging Men as Fathers: The Courts, the Law, and Father Absence in Low-Income Families, 35 CARDOZO L. REV. 511, 512–57 (2013). Copyright 2013 by Yeshiva University. Reprinted by permission.

Krawiec, Kimberly D., Altruism and Intermediation in the Market for Babies, 66 WASH. & LEE L. REV. 203, 204–05, 226, 230–31, 247–49, 255–56 (2009). Copyright by 2009 by Washington and Lee University School of Law. Reprinted by permission.

Lande, John & Forrest S. Mosten, Collaborative Lawyers' Duties to Screen the Appropriateness of Collaborative Law and Obtain Clients' Informed Consent to Use Collaborative Law, 25 OHIO ST. J. ON DISP. RESOL. 347, 349–70, 393–406, 411 (2010). Copyright 2010 by John Lande, Forrest S. Mosten, and the *Ohio State Journal on Dispute Resolution*. Reprinted by permission.

McClain, Linda C., Class Handout Used in Family Law Class, Boston University School of Law (2019). Reprinted by permission of the author.

Mnookin, Robert H., Divorce Bargaining: The Limits on Private Ordering, 18 U. MICH. J. L. REF. 1015, 1015–16 (1985). Reprinted with the permission of LexisNexis.

Mnookin, Robert H. & Lewis Kornhauser, Bargaining in the Shadow of the Law, 88 YALE L.J. 950 (1979). Copyright by Robert H. Mnookin. Reprinted by permission.

Neely, Richard, The Primary Caretaker Parent Rule: Child Custody and the Dynamics of Greed, 3 YALE L. & POL'Y REV. 177 (1984). Copyright 1984 Yale Law and Policy Review, New Haven, Connecticut. Reprinted by permission.

Rebouché, Rachel, A Case Against Collaboration, 76 MD. L. REV. 547, 551–53 (2017). Reprinted by permission.

Ross, Catherine J., From Vulnerability to Voice: Appointing Counsel for Children in Civil Litigation, 64 FORD. L. REV. 1615–1616 (1996). Copyright 1996 Fordham Law Review, New York, New York. Reprinted by permission.

Schepard, Andrew I., Children, Courts, and Custody: Interdisciplinary Models for Divorcing Families 45–46, 167–169 (2004). Copyright 2004 Cambridge University Press, New York, New York. Reprinted by permission.

Semple, Noel, Judicial Settlement-Seeking in Parenting Cases: A Mock Trial, 2013 J. DISP. RESOL. 301, 324–27. Copyright 2013 by Noel Semple and the *Journal of Dispute Resolution*. Reprinted by permission.

Singer, Jana B., Dispute Resolution and the Postdivorce Family: Implications of a Paradigm Shift, 47 FAM. CT. REV. 363, 363–365 (2009). Copyright by Association of Family and Conciliation Courts. Reproduced with the permission of Blackwell Publishing Ltd.

Sorensen, Elaine, Child Support Plays an Increasingly Important Role for Poor Custodial Families, http://www.urban.org/UploadedPDF/412272-child-support-plays-important-role.pdf (2010). Copyright 2010 by the Urban Institute. Reprinted by permission.

Starnes, Cynthia Lee, THE MARRIAGE BUYOUT: THE TROUBLED TRAJECTORY OF U.S. ALIMONY LAW (2014). Copyright NYU Press. Reprinted by permission.

Steinberg, Jessica K., In Pursuit of Justice? Case Outcomes and the Delivery of Unbundled Legal Services, 18 GEO. J. ON POVERTY L. & POL'Y 453, 453–56, 458, 461–63, 465–70 (2011). Copyright by Jessica K. Steinberg. Reprinted by permission.

Waggoner, Lawrence, The Uniform Probate Code's Elective Share: Time for a Reassessment, 37 UNIV. OF MICH. J. L. REF. 1 (2003).

Copyright 2003 University of Michigan Journal of Law Reform, Ann Arbor, Michigan. Reprinted by permission.

Wallace, Monica Hof, Child Support Savings Accounts: An Innovative Approach to Child Support Enforcement, 85 N.C. L. REV. 1155, 1158–64 (2007). Copyright 2007 by the North Carolina Law Review Association. Reprinted by permission.

Wasserman, Rhonda, Parents, Partners, and Personal Jurisdiction. 1995 UNIV. OF ILL. L. REV. 813–815. Copyright 1995 The Board of Trustees of the University of Illinois, Champaign, Illinois.

Zainaldin, Jamil S., The Emergence of a Modern American Family Law: Child Custody, Adoption, and the Courts, 1796–1851, 73 Nw U. L. Rev. 1035 (1979). Reprinted by special permission of Northwestern University School of Law, *Northwestern University Law Review.*

SUMMARY OF CONTENTS

TABLE OF CONTENTS

Table of Cases

The principal cases are in bold type.

CONTEMPORARY FAMILY LAW

Fifth Edition

CHAPTER 1

MARRIAGE, FAMILY AND PRIVACY IN CONTEMPORARY AMERICA

■ ■ ■

Over the past half-century, family life—and family law—have been transformed. No-fault divorce is now available in every state, marriage between same-sex couples is now legal in every state, there are a growing number of pathways to becoming a legal parent, children born outside of marriage have virtually all of the same legal rights as children born within marriage, and women and men are equally eligible for child custody and alimony. Social science research confirms that "nothing short of a revolution has occurred in family life" in the United States since the middle of the twentieth century. Suzanne M. Bianchi, *Family Change and Time Allocation in American Families*, 638 Annals 21, 21 (2011).

Revolutions are often accompanied by periods of confusion and tumult, and that is certainly true of the revolution in family life. Regardless of whether you think the social and demographic changes of the last half-century are positive or negative developments (or have a split verdict on the changes), it is undeniable that the family is central to many contemporary political and legal debates. The assertion that the family—and, in particular, the marital family—is a basic social institution recurs in political rhetoric and judicial opinions. Family policy dominates the front pages of our newspapers, debates about judicial appointments, political elections, and congressional actions. Of course, family law and policy also vitally affect the day-to-day lives of adults and children. In prominent coverage, social commentators warn that the nuclear family is receding and becoming quickly eclipsed by a variety of less conventional family forms. Indeed, the law governing family life increasingly seeks to protect different types of families rather than holding out one model of family life as the ideal.

The rapidity of social change is striking. In 1960, for example, 65% of children in the United States were reared in the same kind of family, consisting of married parents, with a stay-at-home mother and a breadwinning father at work, and another 18% lived with married parents who both worked. Philip Cohen, *Family Diversity is the New Normal for America's Children*, Council on Contemporary Families (Sept. 4, 2014). By contrast, there is no one "typical" or "normal" family today. Only 22% of children live in a "married male-breadwinner family," while approximately one-third of children live with married parents who are both employed. Twenty-three percent of children live with a single mother. *Id.* Many individuals are choosing to marry later, or to forgo marriage altogether for a widening array of nontraditional alternatives. The number of households headed by single mothers has grown significantly since 1960. Almost 40% of all births are to unmarried women. There is considerable geographic and demographic variation in this rate throughout the U.S., based on such factors as age and race. Centers for Disease Control and Prevention, *Births: Final Data for 2017,* 67:8 National Vital Statistics Report 1, 5–6 (Nov. 7, 2018).

Moreover, the Census Bureau has found a shift toward what it calls "nonfamily" households. U.S. Census Bureau, *Historical Household Tables* (2018). These households—consisting of single adults living alone or with others not related by marriage, birth, or adoption—already comprise more than one-third of all households, and their numbers have grown rapidly over the past decade. This increase in the number of nonfamily households, moreover, does not fully capture the growing frequency of different types of living arrangements. Some households classified by the Census Bureau as "family households" (because they contain two or more people related by birth, adoption, or marriage) nevertheless contain broader intimate groupings that the Bureau does not recognize as "families"—for instance, unmarried partners living with a child who is related by birth or adoption to only one partner. Thus, even the ranks of "family households" include a growing number of what might be called "nonfamily families." Increasingly, family members (and family ties) are "spread among more than one household;" for example, divorced or nonmarital fathers may retain ties to children who live with their mother and the mother's new romantic partner. *See* Katharine Silbaugh, *Distinguishing Households From Families*, 43 Fordham Urban L. J. 1071 (2016). Household membership also fluctuates over the life cycle, as young adults return home ("boomerang" families) or aging parents move in and out. *Id.*

Changes in the patterns and forms of family life have attracted intense, very public, and sometimes acrimonious discussion. Nonetheless, legislation and administrative policy concerning the family have shown a sustained trend toward permitting individuals greater freedom to define the content and terms of their own relationships. The shift toward legislatures and courts viewing premarital agreements as consistent with public policy allows married couples greater freedom to set the economic terms of their relationship, including if it ends in divorce, rather than have such terms supplied by family law doctrines of marital property and alimony. While these trends point to deregulation in the area of intimate relationships, family law continues to regulate family life in many ways, from defining who is a legal parent to setting the terms for entering and exiting marriage and specifying the rights and responsibilities of family members.

Family law is dynamic, in part because family life and family structure are dynamic. This casebook invites students to consider evolution in family law itself, evaluating continuity as well as transformation in such areas as the laws regulating marriage and nonmarriage, as well as the parent-child relationship.

This Chapter sets the stage for learning about contemporary family law. It begins with a detailed overview of the dramatic changes in family structure that have occurred in the last half-century and the growing class-based differences in patterns of family life. It also introduces debates about the definition and future of marriage in the face of the growing separation of marriage and parenthood.

The Chapter then examines the relationship between families and the law. To do so, this Chapter focuses on the contours of family privacy and liberty, beginning with constitutional limits on defining family. The Chapter then considers such limits on governmental regulation of adult decision-making about reproduction and intimate sexual relationships. There are several reasons for this introductory focus on privacy and liberty. First, the constitutional right to privacy is closely entwined with the rights and obligations of family members and of the entity of the family itself. Second, this focus introduces students to the significant role constitutional law plays in family law by delineating the limits of governmental regulation of the family and its members. Third, an examination of the right of privacy introduces the central characters that recur throughout family law—the family unit itself, the individual, the married couple, the unmarried couple, spouses, parents, children, and the state and federal governments. Fourth, this Chapter emphasizes tensions that run throughout family law. As you read the majority, concurring, and dissenting opinions in the Supreme Court's family privacy decisions, you will see the intense disagreements that family law issues evoke. These disagreements are seen in debates over public policy and have practical significance for client representation.

The final section of the Chapter provides an overview of family law practice, previewing the intellectually challenging and emotionally complex issues that family lawyers face. Parallel to the evolution in substantive law are significant shifts in how attorneys and the legal system itself address family law disputes.

Whether or not you ultimately practice family law, understanding the subject is an important component of a well-rounded legal education (even beyond its value for the bar exam). This course is rich in human challenges and emotions, and its lessons are useful. Family law (and traffic violations) are among the most common points of contact between most individuals and the justice system. Because everyone is somehow involved with one or more families, your friends, family members, and clients will likely ask you, either formally or informally, about subjects covered in this course. Since family law overlaps with so many other areas of substantive law, ranging from tax to real property to corporate to poverty law, you are likely to use what you learn in this course regardless of what area of legal practice you eventually enter.

PROBLEM 1-1

In studying the relationship between family life and family law, here are several orienting questions. Please think about the following questions and briefly summarize your responses.

1. **What is a family?** In defining "family," consider whether there are, or should be, differences between the following:

(a) a personal or social definition, that is, how people might answer when asked who they consider to be part of their "family;" and

(b) a legal definition for determining who is eligible for governmental benefits (e.g., tax deductions or credits or housing) based on family status and also who is legally obligated to other persons based on family status (e.g., parental obligations to children).

2. **What should the relationship be between families and the law?** For example,

(a) should the government have a role in supporting particular family forms and determining what rights and responsibilities attach to different family structures? If so, why? If not, why not?

(b) Should family status be the basis for various legal benefits and obligations? If not, then what, if any, legal consequences should flow from family membership?

You may want to revisit your response to the questions in this Problem at the end of the course.

1. THE AMERICAN FAMILY TODAY

The structure of the family has changed dramatically over the past century as individuals live longer, marry at a later age (if at all), have fewer children, increasingly separate marriage and parenthood and, over the life course, have children with more than one partner. Family life in America comprises a diversity of family forms, including: marital families with opposite-sex and same-sex spouses, families formed by remarriage, nonmarital couples, single parents, and couples who live apart and are committed to one another (often called "living apart together," or "LATs"). Just under half of all children are raised in a family with two married parents in their first marriage, although another 22% live with either remarried or cohabiting parents. Pew Research Center, The American Family Today (2015). More than 40% of people between the ages of 19–29 have at least one step-sibling. Jens Manuel Krogstad, *5 Facts About the Modern American Family*, Pew Research Center (April 30, 2014). Increased longevity has also created a growing segment of older adults who may form new household units and whose adult children and young grandchildren may interact with them as both sources and consumers of emotional and financial support.

Multigenerational family households (composed of either two or more adult generations or grandparents and grandchildren) are also increasing. In 2016, "a record 64 million people, or 20% of the U.S. population, lived with multiple generations under one roof." D'Vera Cohn & Jeffrey S. Passel, *A Record 64 Million Americans Live in Multigenerational Households*, Pew Research Center (April 5, 2018). This type of household increased sharply during the Great Recession of 2007–2009, and the number of such households continues to grow, despite improvements in the U.S. economy. *Id.* at 1. Another upward trend is in "skipped generation" households, in which grandparents are caring for their grandchildren.

The median age of first marriage in the United States continues to increase. In 2018, it was 29.8 for men and 27.8 for women. Press Release, U.S. Census Bureau, U.S. Census Bureau Releases 2018 Families and Living Arrangements Tables (Nov. 14, 2018). By contrast, in 1960, the median age at first marriage was 20.3 for women and 22.8 for men. On the other hand, in 1890, the median age at first marriage was 22.0 for women and 26.1 for men. U.S. Census Bureau, *Table MS-2. Estimated Median Age of First Marriage By Sex, 1890 to the Present* (Nov. 14, 2018).

In 2016, 18 million Americans were in cohabiting relationships. This percentage has increased 29% since 2007. Renee Stepler, *Number of U.S. adults cohabiting with a partner continues to rise, especially among those 50 and older*, Pew Research Center (Apr. 6, 2017). Many of those households include children. Approximately 35% of all unmarried parents are cohabiting. Gretchen Livingston, *The Changing Profile of Unmarried Parents*, Pew Research Center (April 25, 2018). Children today are far more likely than children 50 years ago to live with an unmarried parent.

The likelihood of marrying, of having children only within marriage, and remaining married is not evenly distributed across social and economic groups. Over the past fifty years, a class divide has appeared in family behavior, which has consequences for children.

Well into the 1960s, those who were moderately educated and those who were more highly educated had comparable rates of marriage and marital happiness. That has changed. College graduates are more likely to be married and to raise their children in a two-parent family and less likely to get divorced. June Carbone and Naomi Cahn, Marriage Markets: How

Inequality is Remaking the American Family 16–19 (2014). Indeed, "[t]he marriage gap has varied directly with the earnings gap." Andrew J. Cherlin, Labor's Love Lost: The Rise and Fall of the Working-Class Family in America 19 (2014).

More affluent families tend to be headed by stably partnered parents who enjoy comparatively high levels of relationship quality and stability. Working-class and poor families face higher levels of family instability and single parenthood and lower levels of relationship quality. Further, compared with earlier decades, there is a growing investment gap—or "spending gap"—between what parents in the richest families and parents in other families spend on their children's education, child care, and other goods. Claire Cain Miller, *The Relentlessness of Modern Parenting*, N.Y. Times (Dec. 25, 2018). Parents across class divides express support for a labor intensive and financially expensive model of "intensive parenting" as the best way to rear children, but less affluent families lack the resources to enact that model. *Id.*

Trends in fertility, the frequency of assortative mating (similarly educated individuals forming families with one another), and rates of education can contribute to variations in earnings between households. Laurie DeRose et al., *Introduction*, in Unequal Family Lives 1, 2 (Naomi Cahn et al. eds., 2018).

Educational attainment—closely linked to income and earning potential—increasingly predicts marital stability and happiness. Marital stability is correlated with marrying for the first time at a later age and waiting to have children. The decline in the divorce rate that began in the 1970s is "concentrated among people with college degrees," while "for the less educated, divorce rates are closer to those of the peak divorce years." Claire Cain Miller, *The Divorce Surge Is Over, But the Myth Lives On*, N.Y. Times, Dec. 2, 2014, at A3. Yet even for those who are college educated, the income level of the family of origin is correlated with marriage rates; at some colleges, those from the top 20% of income are almost 40% more likely to marry than those from the bottom 20%. Kevin Carey, *The Ivy League Students Least Likely to Get Married,* N.Y. Times (March 29, 2018).

These marriage trends are nationwide, but they also differ across urban, suburban, and rural communities: residents of urban counties are less likely to be married than residents of suburban and rural counties. Race and ethnicity play some part in this marriage gap, since urban areas have "a larger share of black residents, who are typically less likely to be married than other racial groups." Gretchen Livingston, *Family Life Is Changing in Different Ways Across Urban, Suburban, and Rural Communities in the U.S.*, Pew Research Center (June 19, 2018). However, the gap also holds when looking at white urban residents. *Id.*

The rate of cohabitation is higher among persons with lower educational and income levels than for college graduates, as is the rate of childbirth before or outside of marriage. Children reared in stable married parent families have the best chance of upward intergenerational mobility, while children in communities with more single mothers have less mobility. DeRose, *Introduction, supra*, at 13. Married parents are typically better off financially than unmarried parents, but there are also significant economic and racial differences between cohabiting and single (or solo) unmarried parents. Compared with cohabiting parents, solo parents are more likely to be in poverty and are more likely to be black. Eighty-one percent are mothers, compared with 19% solo fathers. Livingston, *Family Life, supra.*

Sociologist Sara McLanahan and her colleagues on the Fragile Families and Child Wellbeing Study use the term "fragile families" to refer to the family structure of "families formed by unmarried parents." Sara S. McLanahan & Irwin Garfinkel, *Fragile Families: Debates, Facts, and Solutions, in* Marriage at the Crossroads: Law, Policy, and the Brave New World of Twenty-First-Century Families 142 (Martha Garrison & Elizabeth S. Scott, eds., 2012). More than 40% of all births in the United States are to unmarried mothers; the study found that "a majority of unmarried parents appear to be in committed relationships at the time of their child's birth." *Id.* at 145. The "most important predictor" of a father's "parental investment" is whether he lives with his child, but only about 35% of couples who cohabited when their child was born were still living together by the time their child turned five. *Id.* at 147–148. Among "nonresident fathers," only about 35% maintain "regular contact" with their children. *Id.* at 148.

Legal challenges by same-sex couples to their exclusion from marriage also spurred legal commentators—and judges—to consider the purpose and continuing importance of marriage. For example, in *United States v. Windsor*, 133 S. Ct. 2675 (2013), which is discussed in Chapter 2, dissenting Justice Alito argued that the Court should not resolve a "debate between two competing views of marriage," which he labeled as the "traditional" or "conjugal" view and the new, "consent-based" view. *Id.* at 2718. The former vision of marriage is as "an exclusively opposite-sex institution and as one inextricably linked to procreation and biological kinship." The latter view "primarily defines marriage as the solemnization of mutual commitment—marked by strong emotional attachment and sexual attraction—between two persons;" "gender differentiation is not relevant to this vision." *Id.*

Indeed, some commentators have challenged the privileged place accorded to marriage in family law and policy. Some urge that the law should recognize a broader range of close personal relationships in addition to marriage—including adult relationships that are not sexual and long-term caretaking relationships—and accord these relationships legal protections resembling those accorded to marital families. *See, e.g.*, Maxine

Eichner, The Supportive State: Families, Government, and America's Political Ideals 104–107 (2010). Others suggest that society does not need marriage as a legal category. They argue that family law should focus on the caretaker/dependent relationship, and that the "economic subsidies and privilege" currently attached to marriage should shift to that "core" relationship. Martha Albertson Fineman, The Autonomy Myth: A Theory of Dependency 123 (2004).

NOTES AND QUESTIONS

1. *The fertility rate and the fertility gap.* The year 2016 marked a record low in the United States for the number of babies born per 1000 women of childbearing age. See Claire Cain Miller, *The Fertility Rate Is Down, Yet More Women Are Mothers*, N.Y. Times (Jan. 18, 2018). The declining fertility rate has some interesting patterns. Since the 1990s, "the biggest increases in motherhood" have been "in groups of women with higher education." *Id.* One study found that 86% of women with professional degrees have had a child by age 44, up from 65% in the 1990s. Also increasing, across economic and racial groups, is motherhood by women who have never married. *Id.*

2. *The risks of divorce are not randomly distributed.* "Your chances of divorce may be much lower than you think" because the "background characteristics of people entering a marriage have major implications for their risk of divorce." Elizabeth Marquardt et al., State of Our Unions: Marriage in America 2012 74, The National Marriage Project (2012). Several factors affect the "percentage point decreases in the risk of divorce * * * *during the first ten years of marriage.*" For example, college graduates are 25% less likely to divorce than those who did not complete high school, and having an annual income over $50,000 diminishes the risk of divorce by 30% when compared to a person with an annual income below $25,000. *Id.* Delaying childbearing until marriage (including having a child in the first seven months of marriage) decreases the likelihood of divorce by 24%, as does waiting until age 25 to marry (versus before the age of 18). *Id.* Chapter 8 will discuss these disparities in greater detail.

3. *Unequal family structures and "fragile families."* If, as some have argued, one primary function of marriage is to provide a stable setting for raising children, how concerned should society be about the existence of class-correlated family structures? Should government play a role in encouraging marriage, at least for couples who have, or plan to have, children? If so, on what basis and by what means? Would it be better to focus, on inculcating a norm of "responsible parenthood"? If so, how would you define that norm? How might public policy help "fragile families"? Should family law develop a new legal status that focuses on the relationship between unmarried co-parents to respond to the increasing separation of marriage and parenthood? *See, e.g.,* Merle Weiner, A Parent-Partner Status for Family Law (2015). We discuss parenthood questions more fully in Chapter 5.

4.   *Is marriage still important or is it "obsolete"?* Amidst the demographic changes discussed above, public opinion is divided over the role of marriage and its importance to society. In a 2010 survey, for example, almost 40% of Americans responded "yes" when asked if marriage was becoming obsolete. Pew Research Center, *The Decline of Marriage and Rise of New Families* 1 (Nov. 18, 2010). Nonetheless, most Americans (two-thirds) believe "that more single women raising children on their own [is] bad for society, and 48% said the same about more unmarried couples raising children." Livingston, *Changing Profile, supra.* Love, followed by commitment, are the primary reasons people identify for getting married; having children is an important reason for just less than half. Abigail Geiger and Gretchen Livingston, *8 Facts About Love and Marriage in America* (Feb. 13, 2019). "Marriage aside, three-quarters (76%) of adults in the 2010 survey said that their family "is the most important element of their life at this time," and another 22% said family is one of the most important elements of their life. Pew, *The Decline of Marriage, supra,* at 5. How do you view the relationship between marriage and parenthood? As you read the next Section of this Chapter, consider how the law treats families that do not resemble the idealized nuclear family.

2. FAMILIES AND THE LAW: PUBLIC LAW

The law affects the family in many different ways. Areas of law that have an impact on family life and well-being include tax and bankruptcy law, education and employment law, federal benefits laws, and zoning law in addition to the laws conventionally labeled "family law," such as regulation of the formation and dissolution of the family as a legal unit (as in the law of marriage and parentage) and the rights and responsibilities of family members. As you will see throughout this book, local, municipal, state, federal, and even international law affect or regulate families in various ways. This Section focuses on how federal constitutional law shapes the definition and regulation of the family. The readings introduce recurrent tensions over how to view family privacy.

A. THE PURPOSES OF FAMILY LAW

The law's response to family change might depend on the law's goals with respect to affecting families. In an article that remains influential decades after it appeared, Professor Carl Schneider identified five distinct functions of family law. Carl Schneider, *The Channelling Function in Family Law*, 20 Hofstra L. Rev. 495, 497–98 (1992). The following excerpt describes those functions and provides illustrations of each.

LINDA C. MCCLAIN,
THE FUNCTIONS OF FAMILY LAW
(2019).[a]

Professor Schneider's list of the functions of family law provides a helpful starting point for considering what different ends family law pursues and how they may sometimes be in tension with each other. This is not a canonical list, by which I mean Schneider's list is not akin to a "doctrine," but it offers a useful guide as we consider the relationship between families and the law and why families are subject to constitutional protection as well as regulation.

A.   The "protective function": a basic duty of law is to provide protection for individuals from harm by other individuals. In the context of the family, we think particularly of the state's interest in protecting adult partners and children from abuse and of fostering children's best interests. Protecting from economic harm (e.g., laws of property distribution upon family dissolution) is another example.

B.   The "facilitative function": the law helps people to arrange and live their lives in ways that they choose. Family law does this by allowing people to enter into enforceable contracts and by validating their private choices. A few examples are premarital agreements (before a couple marries) as well as parenting plans (when parents divorce or separate). Other examples are the various procedures that state family law provides for adults to become legally recognized parents (e.g., by consenting to a partner's use of assisted reproductive technology or by a voluntary acknowledgement of parenthood).

C.   The "arbitral function": family law helps people resolve their conflicts. Upon divorce, the courts decide between the parties on disputes involving property, spousal maintenance, child custody and child support. States that offer civil union and domestic partnership status also afford access to such rules concerning dissolving an adult relationship.

Unmarried parents may also ask a court to determine custody and support.

D.   The "expressive function": this function "works by deploying the law's power to impart ideas through words and symbols." This function has two related aspects: "first, to provide a voice in which citizens may speak and, second, to alter the behavior of people the law addresses." We encounter this when we consider the symbolic dimensions of marriage. Schneider has argued, elsewhere, that in listing grounds for a fault-based divorce, divorce law expresses an ideal of proper marital behavior: good

---

[a]   *Editors' Note:* This excerpt is adapted from Linda McClain, *Love, Marriage, and the Baby Carriage: Revisiting the Channelling Function of Family Law,* 28 Card. L. Rev. 2133 (2007). All quotes in this excerpt are from the original article by Professor Schneider.

spouses are faithful, not cruel, and live together. What message, for example, does the law express about marriage by permitting no-fault divorce?

E. The "channelling function": the law develops and "(more often) supports social institutions which are thought to serve desirable ends." Channelling features centrally in discussion and debate about the social institution of marriage and its purposes; parenthood is Schneider's other example of an important social institution. In the constitutional battle over same-sex marriage, one argument offered in defense of state marriage laws defining marriage as only the union of one man and one woman was that the primary purpose of marriage was to properly "channel" the reproductive sexual conduct of men and women to ensure paternal investment in children and support of the child's mother.

NOTES AND QUESTIONS

1. *Are there more?* As Professor McClain notes, this list is not exhaustive. What additional functions might family law serve? Consider, for example, the "private welfare function" of families—the role of families in providing care and material support for their members and the related assumption that families, rather than government, should meet these dependency needs. *See, e.g.,* McClain, *The Channelling Function, supra,* at 2175.

2. *Social institutions and socially productive behaviors.* Marriage and parenthood, some observe, are the two "pillars" or anchors of family law. Silbaugh, *Distinguishing Households from Families, supra,* at 1082. What other socially desirable institutions or relationships are supported by family law?

B. DEFINING THE FAMILY

By deciding what groups constitute a family, the law has a significant impact on the benefits of, and restrictions on, different familial structures. As you read the following case and notes, consider what purposes are served by the East Cleveland ordinance. Consider also how the Court views the purposes of families.

MOORE V. CITY OF EAST CLEVELAND
Supreme Court of the United States, 1977.
431 U.S. 494.

takeaway: the ordinance violated substantive due process because it intruded too far upon the "sanctity of the family."

MR. JUSTICE POWELL announced the judgment of the Court, and delivered an opinion in which MR. JUSTICE BRENNAN, MR. JUSTICE MARSHALL and MR. JUSTICE BLACKMUN joined.

East Cleveland's housing ordinance, like many throughout the country, limits occupancy of a dwelling unit to members of a single family.

facts

§ 1351.02.[1] But the ordinance contains an unusual and complicated definitional section that recognizes as a "family" only a few categories of related individuals. § 1341.08.[2] Because her family, living together in her home, fits none of those categories, appellant stands convicted of a criminal offense. The question in this case is whether the ordinance violates the Due Process Clause of the Fourteenth Amendment.

I

Issue = grandmother was not allowed for her grandson to live with her.

Appellant, Mrs. Inez Moore, lives in her East Cleveland home together with her son, Dale Moore, Sr., and her two grandsons, Dale, Jr., and John Moore, Jr. The two boys are first cousins rather than brothers; we are told that John came to live with his grandmother and with the elder and younger Dale Moores after his mother's death.

In early 1973, Mrs. Moore received a notice of violation from the city, stating that John was an "illegal occupant" and directing her to comply with the ordinance. When she failed to remove him from her home, the city filed a criminal charge. Mrs. Moore moved to dismiss, claiming that the ordinance was constitutionally invalid on its face. Her motion was overruled, and upon conviction she was sentenced to five days in jail and a $25 fine. * * *

II

the city's argument

The city argues that our decision in *Village of Belle Terre v. Boraas,* 416 U.S. 1 (1974), requires us to sustain the ordinance attacked here. Belle Terre, like East Cleveland, imposed limits on the types of groups that could occupy a single dwelling unit. Applying the constitutional standard announced in this Court's leading land-use case, *Euclid v. Ambler Realty*

---

[1]   All citations by section number refer to the Housing Code of the city of East Cleveland, Ohio.

[2]   Section 1341.08 (1966) provides:

" 'Family' means a number of individuals related to the nominal head of the household or to the spouse of the nominal head of the household living as a single housekeeping unit in a single dwelling unit, but limited to the following:

"(a)   Husband or wife of the nominal head of the household.

"(b)   Unmarried children of the nominal head of the household or of the spouse of the nominal head of the household, provided, however, that such unmarried children have no children residing with them.

"(c)   Father or mother of the nominal head of the household or of the spouse of the nominal head of the household.

"(d)   Notwithstanding the provisions of subsection (b) hereof, a family may include not more than one dependent married or unmarried child of the nominal head of the household or of the spouse of the nominal head of the household and the spouse and dependent children of such dependent child. For the purpose of this subsection, a dependent person is one who has more than fifty percent of his total support furnished for him by the nominal head of the household and the spouse of the nominal head of the household.

"(e)   A family may consist of one individual."

Co., 272 U.S. 365 (1926),[6] we sustained the Belle Terre ordinance on the ground that it bore a rational relationship to permissible state objectives.

But one overriding factor sets this case apart from *Belle Terre.* The ordinance there affected only unrelated individuals. It expressly allowed all who were related by "blood, adoption, or marriage" to live together, and in sustaining the ordinance we were careful to note that it promoted "family needs" and "family values." 416 U.S. at 9. East Cleveland, in contrast, has chosen to regulate the occupancy of its housing by slicing deeply into the family itself. This is no mere incidental result of the ordinance. On its face it selects certain categories of relatives who may live together and declares that others may not. In particular, it makes a crime of a grandmother's choice to live with her grandson in circumstances like those presented here.

When a city undertakes such intrusive regulation of the family, neither *Belle Terre* nor *Euclid* governs; the usual judicial deference to the legislature is inappropriate. "This Court has long recognized that freedom of personal choice in matters of marriage and family life is one of the liberties protected by the Due Process Clause of the Fourteenth Amendment." *Cleveland Bd. of Educ. v. LaFleur,* 414 U.S. 632, 639–40 (1974). A host of cases, tracing their lineage to *Meyer v. Nebraska,* 262 U.S. 390, 399–401 (1923), and *Pierce v. Soc'y of Sisters,* 268 U.S. 510, 534–35 (1925), have consistently acknowledged a "private realm of family life which the state cannot enter." *Prince v. Massachusetts,* 321 U.S. 158, 166 (1944). *See, e.g., Roe v. Wade,* 410 U.S. 113, 152–53 (1973); *Stanley v. Illinois,* 405 U.S. 645, 651 (1972); *Griswold v. Connecticut,* 381 U.S. 479 (1965); *Poe v. Ullman,* 367 U.S. 497, 542–44, 549–53 (1961) (HARLAN, J. dissenting); *cf. Loving v. Virginia,* 388 U.S. 1, 12 (1967). Of course, the family is not beyond regulation. But when the government intrudes on choices concerning family living arrangements, this Court must examine carefully the importance of the governmental interests advanced and the extent to which they are served by the challenged regulation.

When thus examined, this ordinance cannot survive. The city seeks to justify it as a means of preventing overcrowding, minimizing traffic and parking congestion, and avoiding an undue financial burden on East Cleveland's school system. Although these are legitimate goals, the ordinance before us serves them marginally, at best. For example, the ordinance permits any family consisting only of husband, wife, and unmarried children to live together, even if the family contains a half dozen licensed drivers, each with his or her own car. At the same time it forbids

---

[6]   *Euclid* held that land-use regulations violate the Due Process Clause if they are "clearly arbitrary and unreasonable, having no substantial relation to the public health, safety, morals, or general welfare." 272 U.S. at 395. Later cases have emphasized that the general welfare is not to be narrowly understood; it embraces a broad range of governmental purposes. But our cases have not departed from the requirement that the government's chosen means must rationally further some legitimate state purpose.

an adult brother and sister to share a household, even if both faithfully use public transportation. The ordinance would permit a grandmother to live with a single dependent son and children, even if his school-age children number a dozen, yet it forces Mrs. Moore to find another dwelling for her grandson John, simply because of the presence of his uncle and cousin in the same household. We need not labor the point. Section 1341.08 has but a tenuous relation to alleviation of the conditions mentioned by the city.

III

City argues that the constitutional right only extends to the "nuclear family"

The city would distinguish the cases based on *Meyer* and *Pierce*. It points out that none of them "gives grandmothers any fundamental rights with respect to grandsons," and suggests that any constitutional right to live together as a family extends only to the nuclear family—essentially a couple and their dependent children.

To be sure, these cases did not expressly consider the family relationship presented here. They were immediately concerned with freedom of choice with respect to childbearing, e.g., *LaFleur, Roe v. Wade, Griswold*, or with the rights of parents to the custody and companionship of their own children, *Stanley v. Illinois*, or with traditional parental authority in matters of child rearing and education. But unless we close our eyes to the basic reasons why certain rights associated with the family have been accorded shelter under the Fourteenth Amendment's Due Process Clause, we cannot avoid applying the force and rationale of these precedents to the family choice involved in this case.

Understanding those reasons requires careful attention to this Court's function under the Due Process Clause. Mr. Justice HARLAN described it eloquently:

> Due process has not been reduced to any formula; its content cannot be determined by reference to any code. The best that can be said is that through the course of this Court's decisions it has represented the balance which our Nation, built upon postulates of respect for the liberty of the individual, has struck between that liberty and the demands of organized society. If the supplying of content to this Constitutional concept has of necessity been a rational process, it certainly has not been one where judges have felt free to roam where unguided speculation might take them. The balance of which I speak is the balance struck by this country, having regard to what history teaches are the traditions from which it developed as well as the traditions from which it broke. That tradition is a living thing. A decision of this Court which radically departs from it could not long survive, while a decision which builds on what has survived is likely to be sound. No formula could serve as a substitute, in this area, for judgment and restraint.

... [T]he full scope of the liberty guaranteed by the Due Process Clause cannot be found in or limited by the precise terms of the specific guarantees elsewhere provided in the Constitution. This 'liberty' is not a series of isolated points pricked out in terms of the taking of property; the freedom of speech, press, and religion; the right to keep and bear arms; the freedom from unreasonable searches and seizures; and so on. It is a rational continuum which, broadly speaking, includes a freedom from all substantial arbitrary impositions and purposeless restraints, . . . and which also recognizes, what a reasonable and sensitive judgment must, that certain interests require particularly careful scrutiny of the state needs asserted to justify their abridgment.

Poe v. Ullman, [367 U.S.] at 542–43 [(HARLAN, J., dissenting)].

Substantive due process has at times been a treacherous field for this Court. There are risks when the judicial branch gives enhanced protection to certain substantive liberties without the guidance of the more specific provisions of the Bill of Rights. * * * [T]here is reason for concern lest the only limits to such judicial intervention become the predilections of those who happen at the time to be Members of this Court. That history counsels caution and restraint. But it does not counsel abandonment, nor does it require what the city urges here: cutting off any protection of family rights at the first convenient, if arbitrary boundary—the boundary of the nuclear family.

Appropriate limits on substantive due process come not from drawing arbitrary lines but rather from careful "respect for the teachings of history [and] solid recognition of the basic values that underlie our society." *Griswold,* 381 U.S. at 501 (HARLAN, J. concurring). Our decisions establish that the Constitution protects the sanctity of the family precisely because the institution of the family is deeply rooted in this Nation's history and tradition. It is through the family that we inculcate and pass down many of our most cherished values, moral and cultural.

Ours is by no means a tradition limited to respect for the bonds uniting the members of the nuclear family. The tradition of uncles, aunts, cousins, and especially grandparents sharing a household along with parents and children has roots equally venerable and equally deserving of constitutional recognition. Over the years, millions of our citizens have grown up in just such an environment, and most, surely, have profited from it. Even if conditions of modern society have brought about a decline in extended family households, they have not erased the accumulated wisdom of civilization, gained over the centuries and honored throughout our history, that supports a larger conception of the family. Out of choice, necessity, or a sense of family responsibility, it has been common for close relatives to draw together and participate in the duties and the satisfactions of a common home. Decisions concerning child rearing, which *Yoder*, *Meyer*, *Pierce* and other cases have recognized as entitled to constitutional protection, long have been shared with grandparents or other relatives who occupy the same household indeed who may take on major responsibility for the rearing of the children. Especially in times of adversity, such as the death of a spouse or economic need, the broader family has tended to come together for mutual sustenance and to maintain or rebuild a secure home life. This is apparently what happened here.[16]

Whether or not such a household is established because of personal tragedy, the choice of relatives in this degree of kinship to live together may not lightly be denied by the State. *Pierce* struck down an Oregon law requiring all children to attend the State's public schools, holding that the Constitution "excludes any general power of the State to standardize its children by forcing them to accept instruction from public teachers only." 268 U.S. at 535. By the same token the Constitution prevents East Cleveland from standardizing its children—and its adults—by forcing all to live in certain narrowly defined family patterns.

Reversed.

MR. JUSTICE BRENNAN, with whom MR. JUSTICE MARSHALL joins, concurring.

I join the plurality's opinion. I agree that the Constitution is not powerless to prevent East Cleveland from prosecuting as a criminal and jailing a 63-year-old grandmother for refusing to expel from her home her now 10-year-old grandson who has lived with her and been brought up by her since his mother's death when he was less than a year old. I do not question that a municipality may constitutionally zone to alleviate noise and traffic congestion and to prevent overcrowded and unsafe living conditions, in short to enact reasonable land-use restrictions in furtherance of the legitimate objectives East Cleveland claims for its ordinance. But the zoning power is not a license for local communities to enact senseless and arbitrary restrictions which cut deeply into private areas of protected family life. East Cleveland may not constitutionally define "family" as essentially confined to parents and the parents' own children. The plurality's opinion conclusively demonstrates that classifying family patterns in this eccentric way is not a rational means of achieving the ends East Cleveland claims for its ordinance, and further that the ordinance unconstitutionally abridges the "freedom of personal choice in matters of . . . family life [that] is one of the liberties protected by the Due Process Clause of the Fourteenth Amendment." *LaFleur*, 414 U.S. at 639–40. I write only to underscore the cultural myopia of the arbitrary boundary

---

[16] We are told that the mother of John Moore, Jr., died when he was less than one year old. He, like uncounted others who have suffered a similar tragedy, then came to live with the grandmother to provide the infant with a substitute for his mother's care and to establish a more normal home environment.

drawn by the East Cleveland ordinance in the light of the tradition of the American home that has been a feature of our society since our beginning as a Nation—the "tradition" in the plurality's words, "of uncles, aunts, cousins, and especially grandparents sharing a household along with parents and children." The line drawn by this ordinance displays a depressing insensitivity toward the economic and emotional needs of a very large part of our society.

In today's America, the "nuclear family" is the pattern so often found in much of white suburbia. The Constitution cannot be interpreted, however, to tolerate the imposition by government upon the rest of us of white suburbia's preference in patterns of family living. The "extended family" that provided generations of early Americans with social services and economic and emotional support in times of hardship, and was the beachhead for successive waves of immigrants who populated our cities, remains not merely still a pervasive living pattern, but under the goad of brutal economic necessity, a prominent pattern—virtually a means of survival—for large numbers of the poor and deprived minorities of our society. For them compelled pooling of scant resources requires compelled sharing of a household.

The "extended" form is especially familiar among black families. We may suppose that this reflects the truism that black citizens, like generations of white immigrants before them, have been victims of economic and other disadvantages that would worsen if they were compelled to abandon extended, for nuclear, living patterns. Even in husband and wife households, 13% of black families compared with 3% of white families include relatives under 18 years old, in addition to the couple's own children.[8] In black households whose head is an elderly woman, as in this case, the contrast is even more striking: 48% of such black households, compared with 10% of counterpart white households, include related minor children not offspring of the head of the household.

I do not wish to be understood as implying that East Cleveland's enforcement of its ordinance is motivated by a racially discriminatory purpose: The record of this case would not support that implication. But the prominence of other than nuclear families among ethnic and racial minority groups, including our black citizens, surely demonstrates that the "extended family" pattern remains a vital tenet of our society. It suffices that in prohibiting this pattern of family living as a means of achieving its objectives, appellee city has chosen a device that deeply intrudes into family associational rights that historically have been central, and today remain central, to a large proportion of our population.

Moreover, to sanction the drawing of the family line at the arbitrary boundary chosen by East Cleveland would surely conflict with prior

---

[8]   R. Hill, The Strengths of Black Families 5 (1972).

decisions that protected "extended" family relationships. For the "private realm of family life which the state cannot enter," recognized as protected in *Prince*, 321 U.S. at 166, was the relationship of aunt and niece. * * *

[The concurring opinion of STEVENS, J., and the dissenting opinions of BURGER, C.J., STEWART, J. (joined by REHNQUIST, J.), and WHITE, J., are omitted.]

NOTES AND QUESTIONS

1. *Family definition and the limits of legal regulation.* What family relationship is not considered a "family" for purposes of the East Cleveland housing ordinance? Under what circumstances are grandparent-headed households permissible under the ordinance? Does the ordinance allow an engaged couple to live together? Does it matter if a child lives with them?

2. *Rationales for the ordinance.* The city offered various justifications for the ordinance, none of which the Court found persuasive. Do you agree? What ideas does Justice Powell's opinion express about family privacy? What role do history and tradition play in the Court's evaluation of the ordinance? Do you think the Court's analysis of the family "prioritize[s] formal ties of consanguinity and affinity above other types of affiliations"? Melissa Murray, Obergefell v. Hodges *and Nonmarriage Inequality*, 104 Cal. L. Rev. 1207, 1237 (2016).

3. *The decline and rise of multigenerational family households.* Both the majority and concurring opinions refer to a long tradition of extended families sharing a household. In 1950, 21% of the U.S. population lived in multigenerational family households. By 1980, a few years after *Moore*, the percentage had declined to a low of 11%; by 2016, it had risen to 20% (64 million Americans). Cohn & Passel, *A Record Number of Americans Live in Multigenerational Households, supra*. In addition, an estimated 3.2 million Americans live in households made up of grandparents and grandchildren. *Id.* Out of concern for the opioid crisis leading to an "unprecedented" number of grandparents and other relatives stepping in to care for children, Senator Susan Collins proposed the "Supporting Grandparents Raising Grandchildren Act" to create an advisory council to support such grandparents by providing information and coordinating federal resources. The bill, S. 1091, enjoyed bipartisan support and became a law in July, 2018. Pub. L. No. 115–196, 132 Stat. 1511 (2018).

4. *The (in)visibility of race in* Moore. Justice Powell's opinion nowhere mentions race, while Justice Brennan's concurring opinion explicitly notes the higher rates of extended families headed by an "elderly woman" (such as Mrs. Moore) among "black families" than among white families. What role did race play in *Moore*? Consider the views of Professor Robert Burt, writing two years after the decision was issued:

> At first glance, the East Cleveland ordinance might appear anti-black and constitutionally suspect on that ground. But Mr. Justice Brennan

observed that "the record . . . would not support [an] implication [of racially discriminatory purpose]. Mr. Justice Stewart, in a footnote to his dissenting opinion, explains why: "In point of fact, East Cleveland is a predominantly Negro community, with a Negro City Manager and City Commission." * * * The plurality did not consider that the purpose of the ordinance was quite straightforward: to exclude from a middle-class, predominantly black community, that saw itself as socially and economically upwardly mobile, other black families most characteristic of lower-class ghetto life. * * * The Court in *Moore* myopically saw the case as a dispute between "a family" and "the state" rather than as a dispute among citizens about the meaning of "family."

Robert A. Burt, *The Constitution of the Family*, 1979 Sup. Ct. Rev. 329, 388–89, 391 (1979). Other scholars contend that, given the racial context in which the case unfolded, *Moore* cannot be understood merely in terms of class. *See* R.A. Lenhardt, *The Color of Kinship*, 102 Iowa L. Rev. 2071 (2017); R.A. Lenhardt & Clare Huntington, *Foreword: Moore Kinship: Celebrating the 40th Anniversary of Moore v. East Cleveland*, 85 Fordham L. Rev. 2551 (2017).

5.   *Are roommates family?* The Court mentions *Village of Belle Terre v. Boraas,* in which the Court upheld the constitutionality of a zoning ordinance that prevented more than two unrelated persons from living together in the same household. In 2015, a Pennsylvania court upheld an ordinance that permitted residency of "a group of persons living as a single household unit using housekeeping facilities in common, but not to include more than three persons unrelated by blood, marriage or adoption." *Schwartz v. Philadelphia Zoning Bd. of Adjustment,* 126 A.3d 1032, 1034 (Pa. Commw. Ct. 2015). Most states have upheld similar zoning restrictions.

PROBLEM 1-2

Imagine that you are the head of a city's housing department, and that the city council has recently enacted an ordinance that limits occupancy of a dwelling unit to a single "family." You are responsible for drafting a definition of "family" for purposes of this ordinance. (Someone else is defining the definition of "dwelling unit.")

(a)   Will you use a definition of "family" or "household unit"? If the former, how do you define "family"? Does a family include grandparents? Heterosexual or same-sex cohabitants? Cohabitants who have lived together for a certain period of time? Cohabitants with children? Three roommates attending your law school? Two friends who team up to help each other as they age? Two unmarried mothers and their children who share family expenses and childcare? Is a family limited by biology or contract? How does your definition handle "foster children, communes, students, seniors, single parents and their children, people with disabilities, formerly incarcerated people, and people rehabilitating from substance abuse"? Kate Redburn, *Zoned Out: How Zoning*

Law Undermines Family Law's Functional Turn 31 (Oct. 28, 2018), Yale L. J. (forthcoming).

(b)   As an alternative to defining family, you are considering residential limits based only on square feet per resident. What are the benefits and dangers of such an ordinance?

PROBLEM 1-3

Jan and Dan Rose are a married couple with one child. For years, they have been close friends with another couple, Josh and Jules Green, who have three children, and a third couple, LeRoy and Lee Lilac, who are married without children. In September, this group of 10 intentionally came together as a family when Jan and Dan purchased a 6,000 square foot, nine-bedroom home on two acres of land in an affluent residential neighborhood in the Town of Tranquil. Only Jan and Dan are listed on the mortgage, but the group has pooled money into a household bank account to share the cost of mortgage payments, groceries, and utilities. The residents of the house take turns cooking dinner and engage in regular routines, such as a weekly family night for activities like charades and talent shows. After a coalition of neighbors complained to the zoning board that, although the group of 10 seem to be "nice people," they violate the neighborhood's zoning for single-family homes, the board determined that the arrangement does not meet the ordinance's definition of family—"those related by blood, marriage, civil union, or legal adoption." Jan and Dan come to your law office after receiving a "cease and desist" notice from the board that they must discontinue their current living arrangement or vacate the neighborhood. They ask you to represent them before the Zoning Board of Appeals and, if they lose that appeal, then in a court action. What are your strongest arguments on their behalf? What do you anticipate will be the strongest arguments made on behalf of upholding the zoning board's ruling?

PROBLEM 1-4

For purposes of defining who is a "close family member" of a U.S. citizen or lawful permanent resident and eligible to enter the United States on a family-based immigrant visa, suppose that the State Department has proposed the following definition:

> *a close familial relationship is defined as a parent (including parent-in-law), spouse, child, adult son or daughter, son-in-law, daughter-in-law, and sibling. For all relationships, half or step status is included (e.g., "half-brother" or "step-sister"). "Close familial relations" do not include any other "extended" family members, such as first- or second-cousins.*

You are a member of the Office of Legal Counsel at the State Department. What other categories of relationships might be included? Should they be included? Why or why not?

3. FAMILIES AND THE LAW: THE RIGHT OF PRIVACY

Moore's plurality opinion discusses the "basic reasons why certain rights associated with the family have been accorded shelter under the Fourteenth Amendment's Due Process Clause." The decisions in this Section explore the evolution of the right to privacy with respect to the constitutional liberty of families and unmarried adults. Some arguments supporting a right to family and personal privacy rely on the Fourteenth Amendment, but the Justices have also found this right elsewhere in the Constitution. As you read this Section, try to sort out the sources of the rights being discussed.

The origins of the right to privacy within the family are often traced to *Meyer v. Nebraska*, 262 U.S. 390 (1923) and *Pierce v. Society of the Sisters*, 268 U.S. 510 (1925). These decisions, which concerned parents' rights to make decisions about their children's education, contained frequently-quoted language concerning parents' Fourteenth Amendment substantive due process liberty interest in the "care, custody and control" of their children.

Meyer struck down a state statute that barred teaching in the German language to children who had not yet reached the eighth grade. Although the case involved the appeal of a teacher who had been convicted of teaching in the German language, the Court stressed the Fourteenth Amendment liberty interests of parents who wanted their children to study German:

> While this Court has not attempted to define with exactness the liberty thus guaranteed, the term has received much consideration and some of the included things have been definitely stated. Without doubt, it denotes not merely freedom from bodily restraint but also the right of the individual to contract, to engage in any of the common occupations of life, to acquire useful knowledge, to marry, establish a home and bring up children, to worship God according to the dictates of his own conscience, and generally to enjoy those privileges long recognized at common law as essential to the orderly pursuit of happiness by free men.

Meyer, 262 U.S. at 399.

Decided just two years after *Meyer*, *Pierce* overturned an Oregon statute that provided that parents could satisfy the state's compulsory education law only by enrolling their children in public schools. A coalition of sectarian and nonsectarian independent schools challenged the statute as a threat to their businesses. As in *Meyer*, no parent or child was a party to the action. The Court nonetheless applied the earlier decision, which, it held, made it "entirely plain" that the statute "unreasonably interferes with the liberty of parents and guardians to direct the upbringing and education of children under their control." The Court further stated: "The child is not the mere creature of the state; those who nurture him and direct his destiny have the right, coupled with the high duty, to recognize and prepare him for additional obligations." *Pierce*, 268 U.S. at 534–35.

A third decision, *Prince v. Massachusetts*, 321 U.S. 158 (1944), in which an aunt and her niece challenged the application of Massachusetts' child labor laws to the distribution of religious publications on the street, is frequently cited along with *Meyer* and *Pierce* as recognizing family privacy. Justice Rutledge wrote in *Prince*:

> It is cardinal with us that the custody, care and nurture of the child reside first in the parents, whose primary function and freedom include preparation for obligations the state can neither supply nor hinder. And it is in recognition of this that [our] decisions have respected the private realm of family life which the state cannot enter.

Id. at 166. However, this often-quoted statement is dicta The Court held that neither the family, nor parenthood, nor religious exercise were "beyond regulation" and upheld the Massachusetts law as applied to the child's distribution of religious literature, rejecting the aunt's parental liberty claim, as well as the aunt's and the child's separate claims based on religious exercise. The Court emphasized the state's *parens patriae* authority to foster children's healthy development and protect them from harm.

A. THE RIGHT TO CONTRACEPTION

The decisions discussed above provided the early framework for the Supreme Court's reexamination of family privacy in the 1960s. The issue first returned to the Court in the context of whether a married couple had a constitutional right to obtain contraception, and if so, where the source of that right could be found.

GRISWOLD V. CONNECTICUT
Supreme Court of the United States, 1965.
381 U.S. 479.

MR. JUSTICE DOUGLAS delivered the opinion of the Court.

Appellant Griswold is Executive Director of the Planned Parenthood League of Connecticut. Appellant Buxton is a licensed physician and a professor at the Yale Medical School who served as Medical Director for the League at its Center in New Haven—a center open and operating from November 1 to November 10, 1961, when appellants were arrested.

[handwritten margin note: takeaway: An implied "right of privacy" exists within the Bill of Rights that prohibits a state from preventing married couples from using contraception]

facts

They gave information, instruction, and medical advice to married persons as to the means of preventing conception. They examined the wife and prescribed the best contraceptive device or material for her use. * * *

The statutes whose constitutionality is involved in this appeal are §§ 53–32 and 54–196 of the General Statutes of Connecticut (1958 rev.). The former provides:

statute at issue

> Any person who uses any drug, medicinal article or instrument for the purpose of preventing conception shall be fined not less than fifty dollars or imprisoned not less than sixty days nor more than one year or be both fined and imprisoned.

Section 54–196 provides:

> Any person who assists, abets, counsels, causes, hires or commands another to commit any offense may be prosecuted and punished as if he were the principal offender.

The appellants were found guilty as accessories and fined $100 each, against the claim that the accessory statute as so applied violated the Fourteenth Amendment. * * *

We think that appellants have standing to raise the constitutional rights of the married people with whom they had a professional relationship * * * [b]y reason of a criminal conviction for serving married couples in violation of an aiding-and-abetting statute. * * *

* * *

Coming to the merits, we are met with a wide range of questions that implicate the Due Process Clause of the Fourteenth Amendment. Overtones of some arguments suggest that *Lochner* v. *New York*, 198 U.S. 45 [(1905)], should be our guide. But we decline that invitation. * * * We do not sit as a super-legislature to determine the wisdom, need, and propriety of laws that touch economic problems, business affairs, or social conditions. This law, however, operates directly on an intimate relation of husband and wife and their physician's role in one aspect of that relation. *Key*

The association of people is not mentioned in the Constitution nor in the Bill of Rights. The right to educate a child in a school of the parents' choice—whether public or private or parochial—is also not mentioned. Nor is the right to study any particular subject or any foreign language. Yet the First Amendment has been construed to include certain of those rights.

By *Pierce* v. *Society of Sisters* [268 U.S. 510 (1925)], the right to educate one's children as one chooses is made applicable to the States by the force of the First and Fourteenth Amendments. By *Meyer* v. *Nebraska*, [262 U.S. 390 (1923)], the same dignity is given the right to study the German language in a private school. In other words, the State may not, consistently with the spirit of the First Amendment, contract the spectrum of available knowledge. The right of freedom of speech and press includes not only the right to utter or to print, but the right to distribute, the right to receive, the right to read and freedom of inquiry, freedom of thought, and freedom to teach—indeed the freedom of the entire university community. Without those peripheral rights the specific rights would be less secure. And so we reaffirm the principle of the *Pierce* and the *Meyer* cases.

In *NAACP* v. *Alabama*, 357 U.S. 449, 462 [(1958)], we protected the "freedom to associate and privacy in one's associations," noting that freedom of association was a peripheral First Amendment right. * * * In other words, the First Amendment has a penumbra where privacy is protected from governmental intrusion. In like context, we have protected forms of "association" that are not political in the customary sense but pertain to the social, legal, and economic benefit of the members. * * *

* * *

The foregoing cases suggest that specific guarantees in the Bill of Rights have penumbras, formed by emanations from those guarantees that help give them life and substance. *See Poe* v. *Ullman*, 367 U.S. 497, 516–22 [(1961) (DOUGLAS, J., dissenting)]. Various guarantees create zones of privacy. The right of association contained in the penumbra of the First Amendment is one, as we have seen. The Third Amendment in its prohibition against the quartering of soldiers "in any house" in time of peace without the consent of the owner is another facet of that privacy. The Fourth Amendment explicitly affirms the "right of the people to be secure in their persons, houses, papers, and effects, against unreasonable searches and seizures." The Fifth Amendment in its Self-Incrimination Clause enables the citizen to create a zone of privacy which government may not force him to surrender to his detriment. The Ninth Amendment provides: "The enumeration in the Constitution, of certain rights, shall not be construed to deny or disparage others retained by the people."

The Fourth and Fifth Amendments were described in *Boyd* v. *United States*, 116 U.S. 616, 630 [(1886)], as protection against all governmental invasions "of the sanctity of a man's home and the privacies of life." We recently referred in *Mapp* v. *Ohio*, 367 U.S. 643, 656 [(1961)], to the Fourth Amendment as creating a "right to privacy, no less important than any other right carefully and particularly reserved to the people."

We have had many controversies over these penumbral rights of "privacy and repose." These cases bear witness that the right of privacy which presses for recognition here is a legitimate one.

The present case, then, concerns a relationship lying within the zone of privacy created by several fundamental constitutional guarantees. And it concerns a law which, in forbidding the use of contraceptives rather than regulating their manufacture or sale, seeks to achieve its goals by means having a maximum destructive impact upon that relationship. Such a law cannot stand in light of the familiar principle, so often applied by this Court, that a "governmental purpose to control or prevent activities constitutionally subject to state regulation may not be achieved by means which sweep unnecessarily broadly and thereby invade the area of protected freedoms." *NAACP v. Alabama*, 377 U.S. [288], 307 [(1964)]. Would we allow the police to search the sacred precincts of marital bedrooms for telltale signs of the use of contraceptives? The very idea is repulsive to the notions of privacy surrounding the marriage relationship.

We deal with a right of privacy older than the Bill of Rights—older than our political parties, older than our school system. Marriage is a coming together for better or for worse, hopefully enduring, and intimate to the degree of being sacred. It is an association that promotes a way of life, not causes; a harmony in living, not political faiths; a bilateral loyalty, not commercial or social projects. Yet it is an association for as noble a purpose as any involved in our prior decisions.

Reversed.

MR. JUSTICE GOLDBERG, whom THE CHIEF JUSTICE and MR. JUSTICE BRENNAN join, concurring.

I agree with the Court that Connecticut's birth-control law unconstitutionally intrudes upon the right of marital privacy, and I join in its opinion and judgment. * * * [T]he concept of liberty protects those personal rights that are fundamental, and is not confined to the specific terms of the Bill of Rights. My conclusion that the concept of liberty is not so restricted * * * embraces the right of marital privacy though that right is not mentioned explicitly in the Constitution is supported both by numerous decisions of this Court, referred to in the Court's opinion, and by the language and history of the Ninth Amendment. In reaching the conclusion that the right of marital privacy is protected, as being within the protected penumbra of specific guarantees of the Bill of Rights, the Court refers to the Ninth Amendment. I add these words to emphasize the relevance of that Amendment to the Court's holding.

* * *

This Court, in a series of decisions, has held that the Fourteenth Amendment absorbs and applies to the States those specifics of the first eight amendments which express fundamental personal rights. The language and history of the Ninth Amendment reveal that the Framers of the Constitution believed that there are additional fundamental rights, protected from governmental infringement, which exist alongside those fundamental rights specifically mentioned in the first eight constitutional amendments. The Ninth Amendment reads, "The enumeration in the

Constitution, of certain rights, shall not be construed to deny or disparage others retained by the people." * * *

* * *

While this Court has had little occasion to interpret the Ninth Amendment,[6] "[i]t cannot be presumed that any clause in the constitution is intended to be without effect." *Marbury* v. *Madison*, 1 Cranch 137, 174 [(1803)]. * * * The Ninth Amendment to the Constitution may be regarded by some as a recent discovery and may be forgotten by others, but since 1791 it has been a basic part of the Constitution which we are sworn to uphold. To hold that a right so basic and fundamental and so deeprooted in our society as the right of privacy in marriage may be infringed because that right is not guaranteed in so many words by the first eight amendments to the Constitution is to ignore the Ninth Amendment and to give it no effect whatsoever. Moreover, a judicial construction that this fundamental right is not protected by the Constitution because it is not mentioned in explicit terms by one of the first eight amendments or elsewhere in the Constitution would violate the Ninth Amendment, which specifically states that "[t]he enumeration in the Constitution, of certain rights shall not be construed to deny or disparage others retained by the people."

* * * [T]he Ninth Amendment shows a belief of the Constitution's authors that fundamental rights exist that are not expressly enumerated in the first eight amendments and an intent that the list of rights included there not be deemed exhaustive. As any student of this Court's opinions knows, this Court has held, often unanimously, that the Fifth and Fourteenth Amendments protect certain fundamental personal liberties from abridgment by the Federal Government or the States. The Ninth Amendment simply shows the intent of the Constitution's authors that other fundamental personal rights should not be denied such protection or disparaged in any other way simply because they are not specifically listed in the first eight constitutional amendments. * * *

* * *

In determining which rights are fundamental, judges are not left at large to decide cases in light of their personal and private notions. Rather, they must look to the "traditions and [collective] conscience of our people" to determine whether a principle is "so rooted [there] * * * as to be ranked as fundamental." *Snyder* v. *Massachusetts*, 291 U.S. 97, 105 [(1934)]. The inquiry is whether a right involved "is of such a character that it cannot be denied without violating those 'fundamental principles of liberty and justice which lie at the base of all our civil and political institutions' . . ."

---

[6] This Amendment has been referred to as "The Forgotten Ninth Amendment," in a book with that title by Bennett B. Patterson (1955). * * * As far as I am aware, until today this Court has referred to the Ninth Amendment only in [three cases]. * * *

Powell v. Alabama, 287 U.S. 45, 67 [(1932)]. "Liberty" also "gains content from the emanations of . . . specific [constitutional] guarantees" and "from experience with the requirements of a free society." *Poe* v. *Ullman*, 367 U.S. 497, 517 [(1961) (Douglas, J., dissenting)].

I agree fully with the Court that, applying these tests, the right of privacy is a fundamental personal right, emanating "from the totality of the constitutional scheme under which we live." Id. at 521. Mr. Justice Brandeis, dissenting in *Olmstead* v. *United States*, 277 U.S. 438, [478 [(1928)], comprehensively summarized the principles underlying the Constitution's guarantees of privacy:

> * * * The makers of our Constitution undertook to secure conditions favorable to the pursuit of happiness. They recognized the significance of man's spiritual nature, of his feelings and of his intellect. They knew that only a part of the pain, pleasure and satisfactions of life are to be found in material things. They sought to protect Americans in their beliefs, their thoughts, their emotions and their sensations. They conferred, as against the government, the right to be let alone—the most comprehensive of rights and the right most valued by civilized men.

The Connecticut statutes here involved deal with a particularly important and sensitive area of privacy—that of the marital relation and the marital home. * * *

I agree with MR. JUSTICE HARLAN's statement in his dissenting opinion in Poe, 367 U.S. at 551–52:

> Certainly the safeguarding of the home does not follow merely from the sanctity of property rights. The home derives its pre-eminence as the seat of family life. And the integrity of that life is something so fundamental that it has been found to draw to its protection the principles of more than one explicitly granted Constitutional right. . . . Of this whole 'private realm of family life' it is difficult to imagine what is more private or more intimate than a husband and wife's marital relations.

The entire fabric of the Constitution and the purposes that clearly underlie its specific guarantees demonstrate that the rights to marital privacy and to marry and raise a family are of similar order and magnitude as the fundamental rights specifically protected.

Although the Constitution does not speak in so many words of the right of privacy in marriage, I cannot believe that it offers these fundamental rights no protection. * * *

* * *

Although the Connecticut birth control law obviously encroaches upon a fundamental personal liberty, the State does not show that the law serves any "subordinating [state] interest which is compelling" or that it is "necessary . . . to the accomplishment of a permissible state policy." The State, at most, argues that there is some rational relation between this statute and what is admittedly a legitimate subject of state concern—the discouraging of extra-marital relations. It says that preventing the use of birth-control devices by married persons helps prevent the indulgence by some in such extra-marital relations. The rationality of this justification is dubious, particularly in light of the admitted widespread availability to all persons in the State of Connecticut, unmarried as well as married, of birth-control devices for the prevention of disease, as distinguished from the prevention of conception. But, in any event, it is clear that the state interest in safeguarding marital fidelity can be served by a more discriminately tailored statute, which does not, like the present one, sweep unnecessarily broadly, reaching far beyond the evil sought to be dealt with and intruding upon the privacy of all married couples. * * * The State of Connecticut does have statutes, the constitutionality of which is beyond doubt, which prohibit adultery and fornication. These statutes demonstrate that means for achieving the same basic purpose of protecting marital fidelity are available to Connecticut without the need to "invade the area of protected freedoms." *NAACP* [*v. Alabama*], 377 U.S. [288,] 307 [(1964)].

* * *

In sum, I believe that the right of privacy in the marital relation is fundamental and basic—a personal right "retained by the people" within the meaning of the Ninth Amendment. Connecticut cannot constitutionally abridge this fundamental right, which is protected by the Fourteenth Amendment from infringement by the States. I agree with the Court that petitioners' convictions must therefore be reversed.

MR. JUSTICE HARLAN, concurring in the judgment.

I fully agree with the judgment of reversal, but find myself unable to join the Court's opinion. * * *

* * *

In my view, the proper constitutional inquiry in this case is whether this Connecticut statute infringes the Due Process Clause of the Fourteenth Amendment because the enactment violates basic values "implicit in the concept of ordered liberty," *Palko v. Connecticut*, 302 U.S. 319, 325 [(1937)]. * * * I believe that it does. While the relevant inquiry may be aided by resort to one or more of the provisions of the Bill of Rights, it is not dependent on them or any of their radiations. The Due Process Clause of the Fourteenth Amendment stands, in my opinion, on its own bottom.

* * *

MR. JUSTICE WHITE, concurring in the judgment.

In my view this Connecticut law as applied to married couples deprives them of "liberty" without due process of law, as that concept is used in the Fourteenth Amendment. I therefore concur in the judgment of the Court reversing these convictions under Connecticut's aiding and abetting statute.

* * * Surely the right invoked in this case, to be free of regulation of the intimacies of the marriage relationship, "come[s] to this Court with a momentum for respect lacking when appeal is made to liberties which derive merely from shifting economic arrangements." *Kovacs v. Cooper*, 336 U.S. 77, 95 [(1949) (FRANKFURTER, J., concurring)].

The Connecticut anti-contraceptive statute deals rather substantially with this relationship. * * *

An examination of the justification offered, however, cannot be avoided by saying that the Connecticut anti-use statute invades a protected area of privacy and association or that it demands the marriage relationship. The nature of the right invaded is pertinent, to be sure, for statutes regulating sensitive areas of liberty do, under the cases of this Court, require "strict scrutiny" * * *.

[T]he State claims but one justification for its anti-use statute. [T]he statute is said to serve the State's policy against all forms of promiscuous or illicit sexual relationships, be they premarital or extramarital, concededly a permissible and legitimate legislative goal.

Without taking issue with the premise that the fear of conception operates as a deterrent to such relationships in addition to the criminal proscriptions Connecticut has against such conduct, I wholly fail to see how the ban on the use of contraceptives by married couples in any way reinforces the State's ban on illicit sexual relationships. * * *

* * *

MR. JUSTICE BLACK, with whom MR. JUSTICE STEWART joins, dissenting.

I agree with my Brother STEWART's dissenting opinion. And like him I do not to any extent whatever base my view that this Connecticut law is constitutional on a belief that the law is wise or that its policy is a good one. In order that there may be no room at all to doubt why I vote as I do, I feel constrained to add that the law is every bit as offensive to me as it is my Brethren of the majority and my Brothers HARLAN, WHITE and GOLDBERG who, reciting reasons why it is offensive to them, hold it unconstitutional. There is no single one of the graphic and eloquent strictures and criticisms fired at the policy of this Connecticut law either by the Court's opinion or by those of my concurring Brethren to which I cannot subscribe—except their conclusion that the evil qualities they see in the law make it unconstitutional.

Had the doctor defendant here, or even the nondoctor defendant, been convicted for doing nothing more than expressing opinions to persons coming to the clinic that certain contraceptive devices, medicines or practices would do them good and would be desirable, or for telling people how devices could be used, I can think of no reasons at this time why their expressions of views would not be protected by the First and Fourteenth Amendments, which guarantee freedom of speech. * * * The Court talks about a constitutional "right of privacy" as though there is some constitutional provision or provisions forbidding any law ever to be passed which might abridge the 'privacy' of individuals. But there is not.

* * *

* * * I like my privacy as well as the next one, but I am nevertheless compelled to admit that government has a right to invade it unless prohibited by some specific constitutional provision. For these reasons I cannot agree with the Court's judgment and the reasons it gives for holding this Connecticut law unconstitutional.

* * *

* * * My disagreement with the Court's opinion holding that there is such a violation here is a narrow one, relating to the application of the First Amendment to the facts and circumstances of this particular case. But my disagreement with Brothers HARLAN, WHITE and GOLDBERG is more basic. I think that if properly construed neither the Due Process Clause nor the Ninth Amendment, nor both together, could under any circumstances be a proper basis for invalidating the Connecticut law. * * *

The due process argument which my Brothers HARLAN and WHITE adopt here is based, as their opinions indicate, on the premise that this Court is vested with power to invalidate all state laws that it consider to be arbitrary, capricious, unreasonable, or oppressive, or this Court's belief that a particular state law under scrutiny has no "rational or justifying" purpose, or is offensive to a "sense of fairness and justice." If these formulas based on "natural justice," or others which mean the same thing, are to prevail, they require judges to determine what is or is not constitutional on the basis of their own appraisal of what laws are unwise or unnecessary. The power to make such decisions is of course that of a legislative body. * * * But perhaps it is not too much to say that no legislative body ever does pass laws without believing that they will accomplish a sane, rational, wise and justifiable purpose. * * *

* * *

I realize that many good and able men have eloquently spoken and written, sometimes in rhapsodical strains, about the duty of this Court to keep the Constitution in tune with the times. The idea is that the Constitution must be changed from time to time and that this Court is charged with a duty to make those changes. For myself, I must with all deference reject that philosophy. The Constitution makers knew the need for change and provided for it. Amendments suggested by the people's elected representatives can be submitted to the people or their selected agents for ratification. That method of change was good for our Fathers, and being somewhat old fashioned I must add it is good enough for me.
* * *

* * *

MR. JUSTICE STEWART, whom MR. JUSTICE BLACK joins, dissenting.

Since 1879 Connecticut has had on its books a law which forbids the use of contraceptives by anyone. I think this is an uncommonly silly law. As a practical matter, the law is obviously unenforceable, except in the oblique context of the present case. As a philosophical matter, I believe the use of contraceptives in the relationship of marriage should be left to personal and private choice, based upon each individual's moral, ethical, and religious beliefs. As a matter of social policy, I think professional counsel about methods of birth control should be available to all, so that each individual's choice can be meaningfully made. But we are not asked in this case to say whether we think this law is unwise, or even asinine. We are asked to hold that it violates the United States Constitution. And that I cannot do.

In the course of its opinion the Court refers to no less than six Amendments to the Constitution: the First, the Third, the Fourth, the Fifth, the Ninth, and the Fourteenth. But the Court does not say which of these Amendments, if any, it thinks is infringed by this Connecticut law.

* * *

What provision of the Constitution, then, does make this state law invalid? The Court says it is the right of privacy 'created by several fundamental constitutional guarantees'. With all deference, I can find no such general right of privacy in the Bill of Rights, in any other part of the Constitution, or in any case ever before decided by this Court.

At the oral argument in this case we were told that the Connecticut law does not "conform to current community standards." But it is not the function of this Court to decide cases on the basis of community standards. * * * If, as I should surely hope, the law before us does not reflect the standards of the people of Connecticut, the people of Connecticut can freely exercise their true Ninth and Tenth Amendment rights to persuade their elected representatives to repeal it. That is the constitutional way to take this law off the books.

NOTES AND QUESTIONS

1. *Classic impact litigation. Griswold* offers a classic example of well-crafted impact litigation and a stark reminder of the rapidity of social change. By the 1950s, Connecticut was the only state that still imposed an absolute ban on contraceptive devices. Some doctors in private practice apparently ignored the law and offered advice to their married patients, who could obtain birth control in neighboring states. Other doctors followed the law. Single persons and people too poor to afford private medical care had no options. Estelle Griswold, who had just become the executive director of the Planned Parenthood League of Connecticut, enlisted the help of two Yale professors, C. Lee Buxton of the Medical School and Fowler Harper who taught family law at the Law School. They enlisted well-chosen patients for the initial suit, entitled *Poe v. Ullman*, 367 U.S. 497 (1961). Jane Poe, a 25-year-old housewife, was a patient of Dr. Buxton's. Admitted to the emergency room for complications of pregnancy, she had had a stroke, which left her partially paralyzed, with a damaged kidney and speech impairment. Her pregnancy led to a stillbirth. Dr. Buxton believed she could not survive another pregnancy. Two other married couples were also named plaintiffs. One couple had already lost three children in infancy, all of whom had been born with genetic problems. The other had been advised that blood tests indicated that they would not be able to have a healthy child.

In the initial round of litigation in the Connecticut courts, the plaintiffs sought a declaratory judgment that would allow birth control clinics for married patients, but did not raise the privacy argument.

They lost in the Connecticut courts, and the Supreme Court declined to reach the merits on the ground that no realistic threat of criminal prosecution existed. *See Poe v. Ullman*, 367 U.S. 497 (1961). However, two *Poe* dissenters, Justices Douglas and Harlan, emphasized the married couple's right to privacy. Regrouping, the plaintiffs decided to open one clinic in New Haven, which led, within ten days, to Dr. Buxton's arrest and closure of the clinic. In this new procedural posture, the defense relied heavily on the thinking of the *Poe* dissenters, leading to the result in *Griswold. See* Catherine G. Roraback, Griswold v. Connecticut: *A Brief Case History*, 16 Ohio N.U. L. Rev. 395 (1989).

2. *Constitutional grounding for the right to privacy.* You have read all six opinions issued in *Griswold*, four supporting the right to privacy in the marital relationship, and two opposed. Which constitutional amendments did the supporters rely on to find a constitutional right to privacy? What constitutional standards and level of scrutiny did they apply? Did they apply the correct level of scrutiny? What are the essential differences between Justice Douglas's opinion for the Court and the two concurrences? Do the dissenters disagree with the majority about the text of the Constitution, the role of the Court, or both?

3. *Contours and strength of the right to privacy.* How far does the right to privacy expounded in *Griswold* extend? What questions does *Griswold* leave unanswered? How solid is the jurisprudential basis for the right to privacy set forth in the majority and concurring opinions? How strong is the right to privacy within the family? Outside the context of a "family"?

4. Griswold *as a poverty case.* Legal scholar Cary Franklin argues that, while *Griswold* is known primarily for its role in the line of the Court's reproductive rights cases, it should also be recognized as an important part of the Warren Court's poverty cases. While Connecticut's law did not target any particular group, Franklin explains that it "had special bite for low income women," since its "most tangible and direct regulatory effect was to prevent the opening of birth control clinics," which provided contraception and counseling to women who lacked access to private physicians. Cary Franklin, Griswold *and the Public Dimension of the Right to Privacy,* 124 Yale L.J. Forum (March 2015).

5. *The right to privacy for families on public welfare.* In 1971, the Supreme Court decided *Wyman v. James,* 400 U.S. 309 (1971). Barbara James, a public welfare recipient, refused to allow her caseworker to visit her home, explaining that she would provide any information relevant to her continued receipt of welfare, but without a home visit. At the time, New York state law required home visits to public welfare recipients once every three months to verify information concerning eligibility for welfare, provide professional counseling, and prevent welfare fraud. Moreover, New York law specified that a child would be eligible for aid only "if his home situation is one in which his physical, mental and moral well-being will be safeguarded and his religious faith preserved and protected." *Id.* at 312. The *James* majority distinguished between a true Fourth Amendment search and the "visitation" at issue, which it found neither forced nor compelled, nor sanctionable with criminal penalties. Even if the home visit was a search in some sense, the majority held it not unreasonable under the Fourth Amendment. The majority upheld termination of Ms. James's welfare benefits because of her refusal to comply with the home visit requirement.

In dissent, Justices Marshall and Brennan criticized the argument that the home visit was justified "to protect dependent children from 'abuse' and 'exploitation.'" *Id.* at 341 (Marshall, J., dissenting). "These are heinous crimes," the dissent continued, "but they are not confined to indigent households. Would the majority sanction, in the absence of probable cause, compulsory visits to all American homes for the purpose of discovering child abuse? Or is this Court prepared to hold as a matter of constitutional law that a mother, merely because she is poor, is substantially more likely to injure or exploit her children?" *Id.* at 342.

As these questions show, family privacy means different protections for various kinds of families. Jacobus tenBroek identified this problem more than 40 years ago. *See* Jacobus tenBroek, *California's Dual System of Family Law: Its Origin, Development and Present Status* (pts. 1 & 3), 16 Stan. L. Rev. 257

(1964), 17 Stan. L. Rev. 614 (1965). Professor Jill Elaine Hasday argues that "the poor are . . . noticeably absent from the family law canon," and that "the exclusion of welfare law from the family law canon has helped obscure the sharp bifurcation in family law between the legal principles and presumptions governing poor families and the legal principles and presumptions governing other families." Jill Elaine Hasday, Family Law Reimagined 195–196 (2014). Do the decisions you have read so far in this Chapter support this statement?

Another tension concerning family privacy is that the family exists as a legal entity, yet the individual members within a family also have rights and interests. How should family law address this tension? The Supreme Court revisited some of the questions left unanswered in *Griswold* in the following decision, which arose out of a lecture at Boston University in 1967.

EISENSTADT V. BAIRD

Supreme Court of the United States, 1972.
405 U.S. 438.

MR. JUSTICE BRENNAN delivered the opinion of the Court.

Appellee William Baird was convicted at a bench trial in the Massachusetts Superior Court, under Massachusetts General Laws Ann., c. 272, § 21, first, for exhibiting contraceptive articles in the course of delivering a lecture on contraception to a group of students at Boston University and, second, for giving a young woman a package of Emko vaginal foam at the close of his address. The Massachusetts Supreme Judicial Court unanimously set aside the conviction for exhibiting contraceptives on the ground that it violated Baird's First Amendment rights, but by a four-to-three vote sustained the conviction for giving away the foam. * * * [T]he Court of Appeals for the First Circuit vacated the dismissal and remanded the action with directions to grant the writ discharging Baird. We affirm.

Massachusetts General Laws Ann., c. 272, § 21, under which Baird was convicted, provides a maximum five-year term of imprisonment for "whoever . . . gives away . . . any drug, medicine, instrument or article whatever for the prevention of conception," except as authorized in § 21A. Under § 21A, "[a] registered physician may administer to or prescribe for any married person drugs or articles intended for the prevention of pregnancy or conception. [And a] registered pharmacist actually engaged in the business of pharmacy may furnish such drugs or articles to any married person presenting a prescription from a registered physician." As interpreted by the State Supreme Judicial Court, these provisions make it a felony for anyone, other than a registered physician or pharmacist acting in accordance with the terms of § 21A, to dispense any article with the intention that it be used for the prevention of conception. The statutory scheme distinguishes among three distinct classes of distributees—first, married persons may obtain contraceptives to prevent pregnancy, but only from doctors or druggists on prescription; second, single persons may not obtain contraceptives from anyone to prevent pregnancy; and, third, married or single persons may obtain contraceptives from anyone to prevent, not pregnancy, but the spread of disease. This construction of state law is, of course, binding on us.

The legislative purposes that the statute is meant to serve are not altogether clear. In *Commonwealth v. Baird*, the Supreme Judicial Court noted only the State's interest in protecting the health of its citizens: "[T]he prohibition in § 21," the court declared, "is directly related to" the State's goal of "preventing the distribution of articles designed to prevent conception which may have undesirable, if not dangerous, physical consequences." In a subsequent decision, the court, however, found "a second and more compelling ground for upholding the statute"—namely, to protect morals through "regulating the private sexual lives of single persons." The Court of Appeals, for reasons that will appear, did not consider the promotion of health or the protection of morals through the deterrence of fornication to be the legislative aim. Instead, the court concluded that the statutory goal was to limit contraception in and of itself—a purpose that the court held conflicted "with fundamental human rights" under *Griswold v. Connecticut*, where this Court struck down Connecticut's prohibition against the use of contraceptives as an unconstitutional infringement of the right of marital privacy.

We agree that the goals of deterring premarital sex and regulating the distribution of potentially harmful articles cannot reasonably be regarded as legislative aims of §§ 21 and 21A. And we hold that the statute, viewed as a prohibition on contraception per se, violates the rights of single persons under the Equal Protection Clause of the Fourteenth Amendment.

* * *

The basic principles governing application of the Equal Protection Clause of the Fourteenth Amendment are familiar. * * *

The question for our determination in this case is whether there is some ground of difference that rationally explains the different treatment accorded married and unmarried persons under [the Massachusetts statute].[7] For the reasons that follow, we conclude that no such ground exists.

First. Section 21 stems from Mass. Stat. 1879, c. 159, § 1, which prohibited without exception, distribution of articles intended to be used as contraceptives. In *Commonwealth v. Allison*, 227 Mass. 57, 62 (1917), the

---

[7] Of course, if we were to conclude that the Massachusetts statute impinges upon fundamental freedoms under *Griswold*, the statutory classification would have to be not merely *rationally related* to a valid public purpose but *necessary* to the achievement of a *compelling* state interest. But . . . we do not have to address the statute's validity under that test because the law fails to satisfy even the more lenient equal protection standard.

Massachusetts Supreme Judicial Court explained that the law's "plain purpose is to protect purity, to preserve chastity, to encourage continence and self restraint, to defend the sanctity of the home, and thus to engender in the State and nation a virile and virtuous race of men and women." Although the State clearly abandoned that purpose with the enactment of § 21A, at least insofar as the illicit sexual activities of married persons are concerned, the court reiterated in *Sturgis v. Attorney General*, that the object of the legislation is to discourage premarital sexual intercourse. Conceding that the State could, consistently with the Equal Protection Clause, regard the problems of extramarital and premarital sexual relations as "[e]vils . . . of different dimensions and proportions, requiring different remedies," *Williamson v. Lee Optical Inc.*, 348 U.S. 483, 489 (1955), we cannot agree that the deterrence of premarital sex may reasonably be regarded as the purpose of the Massachusetts law.

It would be plainly unreasonable to assume that Massachusetts has prescribed pregnancy and the birth of an unwanted child as punishment for fornication, which is a misdemeanor under Massachusetts General Laws Ann., c. 272, § 18. Aside from the scheme of values that assumption would attribute to the State, it is abundantly clear that the effect of the ban on distribution of contraceptives to unmarried persons has at best a marginal relation to the proffered objective. What Mr. Justice Goldberg said in *Griswold*, 381 U.S. at 498 (concurring opinion), concerning the effect of Connecticut's prohibition on the use of contraceptives in discouraging extramarital sexual relations, is equally applicable here. "The rationality of this justification is dubious, particularly in light of the admitted widespread availability to all persons in the State of Connecticut, unmarried as well as married, of birth-control devices for the prevention of disease, as distinguished from the prevention of conception." * * * Nor, in making contraceptives available to married persons without regard to their intended use, does Massachusetts attempt to deter married persons from engaging in illicit sexual relations with unmarried persons. Even on the assumption that the fear of pregnancy operates as a deterrent to fornication, the Massachusetts statute is thus so riddled with exceptions that deterrence of premarital sex cannot reasonably be regarded as its aim.

Moreover, §§ 21 and 21A on their face have a dubious relation to the State's criminal prohibition on fornication. As the Court of Appeals explained, "Fornication is a misdemeanor [in Massachusetts], entailing a thirty dollar fine, or three months in jail. Violation of the present statute is a felony, punishable by five years in prison. We find it hard to believe that the legislature adopted a statute carrying a five-year penalty for its possible, obviously by no means fully effective, deterrence of the commission of a ninety-day misdemeanor." * * * [W]e, like the Court of Appeals, cannot believe that in this instance Massachusetts has chosen to expose the aider and abetter who simply gives away a contraceptive to 20 times the 90-day sentence of the offender himself. * * *

Second. * * * The Supreme Judicial Court in *Commonwealth v. Baird* held that the purpose of the amendment [enacting Section 21A] was to serve the health needs of the community by regulating the distribution of potentially harmful articles. It is plain that Massachusetts had no such purpose in mind before the enactment of § 21A. As the Court of Appeals remarked, "Consistent with the fact that the statute was contained in a chapter dealing with 'Crimes Against Chastity, Morality, Decency and Good Order,' it was cast only in terms of morals. * * * Nor did the Court of Appeals "believe that the legislature [in enacting § 21A] suddenly reversed its field and developed an interest in health. Rather, it merely made what it thought to be the precise accommodation necessary to escape the *Griswold* ruling."

Again, we must agree with the Court of Appeals. If health were the rationale of § 21A, the statute would be both discriminatory and overbroad. * * *. If there is need to have a physician prescribe (and a pharmacist dispense) contraceptives, that need is as great for unmarried persons as for married persons." * * *

* * *

But if further proof that the Massachusetts statute is not a health measure is necessary, * * *. [T]he statute is redundant in light of the] federal and state laws *already* regulating the distribution of harmful drugs. * * *

Third. [May] the Massachusetts statute * * * nevertheless[ ] be sustained simply as a prohibition on contraception? * * * The Court of Appeals went on to hold:

> To say that contraceptives are immoral as such, and are to be forbidden to unmarried persons who will nevertheless persist in having intercourse, means that such persons must risk for themselves an unwanted pregnancy, for the child, illegitimacy, and for society, a possible obligation of support. Such a view of morality is not only the very mirror image of sensible legislation; we consider that it conflicts with fundamental human rights. In the absence of demonstrated harm, we hold it is beyond the competency of the state.

We need not and do not, however, decide that important question in this case because, whatever the rights of the individual to access to contraceptives may be, the rights must be the same for the unmarried and the married alike.

If under *Griswold* the distribution of contraceptives to married persons cannot be prohibited, a ban on distribution to unmarried persons would be equally impermissible. It is true that in *Griswold* the right of privacy in question inhered in the marital relationship. Yet the marital couple is not an independent entity with a mind and heart of its own, but an association of two individuals each with a separate intellectual and emotional makeup. If the right of privacy means anything, it is the right of the individual, married or single, to be free from unwarranted governmental intrusion into matters so fundamentally affecting a person as the decision whether to bear or beget a child.

On the other hand, if *Griswold* is no bar to a prohibition on the distribution of contraceptives, the State could not, consistently with the Equal Protection Clause, outlaw distribution to unmarried but not to married persons. In each case the evil, as perceived by the State, would be identical, and the underinclusion would be invidious. * * *

* * * We hold that by providing dissimilar treatment for married and unmarried persons who are similarly situated, Massachusetts General Laws Ann., c. 272, §§ 21 and 21A, violate the Equal Protection Clause.

* * *

MR. JUSTICE POWELL and MR. JUSTICE REHNQUIST took no part in the consideration or decision of this case.

MR. JUSTICE DOUGLAS, concurring.

While I join the opinion of the Court, there is for me a narrower ground for affirming the Court of Appeals. This to me is a simple First Amendment case, that amendment being applicable to the States by reason of the Fourteenth.

Under no stretch of the law as presently stated could Massachusetts require a license for those who desire to lecture on planned parenthood, contraceptives, the rights of women, birth control, or any allied subject, or place a tax on that privilege. * * *

Baird addressed an audience of students and faculty at Boston University on the subject of birth control and overpopulation. His address was approximately one hour in length and consisted of a discussion of various contraceptive devices displayed by means of diagrams on two demonstration boards, as well as a display of contraceptive devices in their original packages. In addition, Baird spoke of the respective merits of various contraceptive devices; overpopulation in the world; crises throughout the world due to overpopulation; the large number of abortions performed on unwed mothers; and quack abortionists and the potential harm to women resulting from abortions performed by quack abortionists. Baird also urged members of the audience to petition the Massachusetts Legislature and to make known their feelings with regard to birth control laws in order to bring about a change in the laws. At the close of the address Baird invited members of the audience to come to the stage and help themselves to the contraceptive articles. We do not know how many accepted Baird's invitation. We only know that Baird personally handed one woman a package of Emko Vaginal Foam. He was then arrested and indicted (1) for exhibiting contraceptive devices and (2) for giving one such device away. The conviction for the first offense was reversed, the Supreme Judicial Court of Massachusetts holding that the display of the articles was essential to a graphic representation of the lecture. But the conviction for the giving away of one article was sustained. * * *

Had Baird not "given away" a sample of one of the devices whose use he advocated, there could be no question about the protection afforded him by the First Amendment. A State may not "contract the spectrum of available knowledge." However noxious Baird's ideas might have been to the authorities, the freedom to learn about them, fully to comprehend their scope and portent, and to weigh them against the tenets of the "conventional wisdom," may not be abridged. Our system of government requires that we have faith in the ability of the individual to decide wisely, if only he is fully apprised of the merits of a controversy.

* * *

It is irrelevant to the application of these principles that Baird went beyond the giving of information about birth control and advocated the use of contraceptive articles. The First Amendment protects the opportunity to persuade to action whether that action be unwise or immoral, or whether the speech incites to action.

In this case there was not even incitement to action. There is no evidence or finding that Baird intended that the young lady take the foam home with her when he handed it to her or that she would not have examined the article and then returned it to Baird, had he not been placed under arrest immediately upon handing the article over.

First Amendment rights are not limited to verbal expression. The right to petition often involves the right to walk. The right of assembly may mean pushing or jostling. Picketing involves physical activity as well as a display of a sign. A sit-in can be a quiet, dignified protest that has First Amendment protection even though no speech is involved. * * * Putting contraceptives on display is certainly an aid to speech and discussion. Handing an article under discussion to a member of the audience is a technique known to all teachers and is commonly used. * * * But passing one article to an audience is merely a projection of the visual aid and should be a permissible adjunct of free speech. * * *

I do not see how we can have a Society of the Dialogue, which the First Amendment envisages, if time-honored teaching techniques are barred to those who give educational lectures.

MR. JUSTICE WHITE, with whom MR. JUSTICE BLACKMUN joins, concurring in the result.

In *Griswold*, we reversed criminal convictions for advising married persons with respect to the use of contraceptives. As there applied, the Connecticut law, which forbade using contraceptives or giving advice on the subject, unduly invaded a zone of marital privacy protected by the Bill of Rights. The Connecticut law did not regulate the manufacture or sale of such products and we expressly left open any question concerning the permissible scope of such legislation.

Chapter 272, § 21, of the Massachusetts General Laws makes it a criminal offense to distribute, sell, or give away any drug, medicine, or article for the prevention of conception. Section 21A excepts from this prohibition registered physicians who prescribe for and administer such articles to married persons and registered pharmacists who dispense on medical prescription.

Appellee Baird was indicted for giving away Emko Vaginal Foam, a "medicine and article for the prevention of conception. . . ." * * * The gravamen of the offense charged was that Baird had no license and therefore no authority to distribute to anyone. As the Supreme Judicial Court of Massachusetts noted, the constitutional validity of Baird's conviction rested upon his lack of status as a "distributor and not . . . the marital status of the recipient." * * *

* * * Had Baird distributed a supply of the so-called "pill," I would sustain his conviction under this statute. Requiring a prescription to obtain potentially dangerous contraceptive material may place a substantial burden upon the right recognized in *Griswold*, but that burden is justified by a strong state interest. * * *

Baird, however, was found guilty of giving away vaginal foam. * * * Due regard for protecting constitutional rights requires that the record contain evidence that a restriction on distribution of vaginal foam is essential to achieve the statutory purpose, or the relevant facts concerning the product must be such as to fall within the range of judicial notice.

Neither requirement is met here. * * *

That Baird could not be convicted for distributing Emko to a married person disposes of this case. * * *

MR. CHIEF JUSTICE BURGER, dissenting.

The judgment of the Supreme Judicial Court of Massachusetts in sustaining appellee's conviction for dispensing medicinal material without a license seems eminently correct to me and I would not disturb it. It is undisputed that appellee is not a physician or pharmacist and was prohibited under Massachusetts law from dispensing contraceptives to anyone, regardless of marital status. To my mind the validity of this restriction on dispensing medicinal substances is the only issue before the Court * * *. * * * [E]veryone seems to agree that if Massachusetts has validly required, as a health measure, that all contraceptives be dispensed by a physician or pursuant to a physician's prescription * * *.

* * *

NOTES AND QUESTIONS

1. *Extending the privacy doctrine: from the marital unit to the individual. Eisenstadt* confronted two questions that *Griswold* left unanswered. First, was the right to privacy restricted to the confines of marriage? Second, did the right to sexual privacy attach only to a couple, or also to the individuals who might comprise a couple? As with the debate over whether the nature of marriage should be centered on procreation and child-rearing or on autonomous adult commitment and self-definition, commentators differ on whether or not they see *Eisenstadt's* shift away from the privacy of the married couple toward the privacy rights of individuals (whether married or unmarried) as a positive development. Khiara M. Bridges, *Privacy Rights and Public Families*, 34 Harv. J.L. & Gender 113, 142 (2011) ("*Eisenstadt* alters the base of the right to privacy to one that is closer to (individual) decisional autonomy and (individual) bodily integrity").

2. *Equal Protection.* To answer the questions *Griswold* left open, the Court turned to yet another constitutional provision, which it had not considered in *Griswold*: the Equal Protection Clause. Does the application of the Equal Protection Clause affect the level of scrutiny the Court must apply, or the terms of the analysis? If *Griswold* had not opted for substantive due process analysis, would equal protection have also been a sound basis for that decision? What classification would have provided a basis for an equal protection decision? How does usage of the Equal Protection Clause affect the meaning of privacy?

3. *Narrower grounds.* Justice Douglas suggested that *Eisenstadt* could have been resolved as a speech case. Chief Justice Burger, dissenting, argued that the case could have been construed more narrowly as involving the practice of medicine without a license. If the Court had used Justice Douglas's approach, what questions would have been answered, or left unanswered? If the Court had followed Chief Justice Burger's lead, would it have had sufficient factual findings or would a remand have proved necessary? If the Court had all the necessary findings, which questions would it have been able to resolve, and which would have remained for another day?

4. *What standard of review is used in fundamental liberty cases?* You may have been confused about what standard of review the Court applied in the cases you have just read about fundamental liberties, beginning with *Moore.* James E. Fleming and Linda C. McClain observe that in *Moore,* and in prior and subsequent cases involving the Supreme Court's "constitutional

family law about the regulation of marriage and parental rights and responsibilities," the Court "engages in a 'two-step' ": step one—"a declaration that something is 'fundamental' and 'private'—[is quickly followed by] step two—a clarification that it is neither absolute nor beyond regulation." James E. Fleming and Linda C. McClain, Ordered Liberty: Rights, Responsibilities, and Virtues 249, 254–257 (2013). In *Moore*, for example, Justice Powell draws on Justice Harlan's approach to substantive Due Process and applies "something approximating what we now call intermediate scrutiny, not what we now call strict scrutiny." *Id.* at 257. Subsequent Supreme Court cases involving "constitutional" family law also draw on Justice Harlan's approach to Due Process liberty, as you will see in later chapters. As you read this book, keep your eye on what standard of review the Court uses and how courts analyze the regulation of marriage and of the parent-child relationship.

5. *The legacy of* Eisenstadt? Susan Frelich Appleton argues that *Eisenstadt* promised to (1) dethrone marriage by moving toward more inclusive notions of relationships that count as family; (2) gesture toward a more liberatory vision of sexual freedom; and (3) promote the understanding that restricting access to contraception had a disproportionate impact on women compared to men. Susan Frelich Appleton, *The Forgotten Family Law of* Eisenstadt v. Baird, 28 Yale J. L. & Feminism 1 (2017). She concludes that that promise remains unfulfilled, pointing to, among other things, marriage's continuing role as the "template" for adult relationships, public policies such as abstinence-only sex education, and the continuing controversy over women's access to and use of contraception, evident in the numerous challenges to the requirement in the Affordable Care Act that employers' insurance plans cover contraception. *Id.* In *Burwell v. Hobby Lobby*, 542 U.S. 692 (2014), the Supreme Court upheld a challenge brought by three for-profit closely-held corporations to ACA's contraceptive mandate on the ground that it violated their right to free exercise of religion under the Religious Freedom Restoration Act. For more discussion of reproductive rights, see Chapter 3.

PROBLEM 1-5

Pick the Justice whose *Griswold* opinion you find most interesting. If you were a clerk for that Justice, and you also received the briefs in *Eisenstadt* as a hypothetical, would you advise your Justice to revise his opinion? How and why? You might be interested to know that Justice Stephen Breyer was a law clerk to Justice Goldberg during the 1964 Term and wrote the first draft of Goldberg's concurring opinion in *Griswold*.

B. THE RIGHT TO LIBERTY "IN MATTERS PERTAINING TO SEX"

The Supreme Court has revisited the scope of family and personal privacy several times since the beginning of the 21st century. The major doctrinal developments have involved the interpretation of "liberty" under the Due Process Clause of the Fourteenth Amendment with respect to same-sex intimate sexual relationships, the topic to which we now turn.

Because *Griswold* and *Eisenstadt* concerned the right to contraception, neither of them initially appeared to have any application to the privacy rights that might inhere in intimate relationships between persons of the same sex. In *Bowers v. Hardwick,* the Court considered whether the right of privacy recognized in *Griswold* protects sexual intimacy between same-sex partners. 478 U.S. 186 (1986). In a 5–4 opinion that immediately proved controversial, the Court upheld a Georgia law that criminalized sodomy between consenting adults. The Court embraced a narrow test for recognizing "fundamental rights" under the Constitution: to qualify for heightened judicial protection under substantive due process, a claimed liberty must be " 'deeply rooted in this Nation's history and tradition' " or " 'implicit in the concept of ordered liberty,' such that 'neither liberty nor justice would exist if [it] were sacrificed.' " *Id.* at 191–92. *Bowers* dismissed as "at best, facetious" the suggestion that "homosexual conduct" could qualify for constitutional protection under this test. *Id.* at 194. The five-Justice majority distinguished earlier precedents protecting family privacy as centering on procreation: "[n]o connection between family, marriage, or procreation on the one hand and homosexual activity on the other has been demonstrated." *Id.* at 191.

In 2003, the Supreme Court once again considered a challenge to a state sodomy law. In this case, a Texas law specifically criminalized only same-sex sodomy. *Lawrence v. Texas* expressly overturned *Bowers,* drawing upon both *Griswold* and *Eisenstadt.* As you read the case, consider which lines of analysis prove most important.

LAWRENCE V. TEXAS
Supreme Court of the United States, 2003.
539 U.S. 558.

JUSTICE KENNEDY delivered the opinion of the Court.

* * *

The question before the Court is the validity of a Texas statute making it a crime for two persons of the same sex to engage in certain intimate sexual conduct.

In Houston, Texas, officers of the Harris County Police Department were dispatched to a private residence in response to a reported weapons disturbance. They entered an apartment where one of the petitioners, John Geddes Lawrence, resided. The right of the police to enter does not seem to have been questioned. The officers observed Lawrence and another man, Tyron Garner, engaging in a sexual act. The two petitioners were arrested, held in custody over night, and charged and convicted before a Justice of the Peace [of violating a Texas statute making it a crime to engage in oral or anal sex with a person of the same sex. On appeal, they argued that the Texas statute violated the Due Process and Equal Protection Clauses of the Fourteenth Amendment.]

* * *

II

* * *

There are broad statements of the substantive reach of liberty under the Due Process Clause in earlier cases, * * * but the most pertinent beginning point is our decision in *Griswold v. Connecticut,* 381 U.S. 479 (1965).

In *Griswold* the Court invalidated a state law prohibiting the use of drugs or devices of contraception and counseling or aiding and abetting the use of contraceptives. The Court described the protected interest as a right to privacy and placed emphasis on the marriage relation and the protected space of the marital bedroom.

After *Griswold* it was established that the right to make certain decisions regarding sexual conduct extends beyond the marital relationship. In *Eisenstadt v. Baird,* 405 U.S. 438 (1972), the Court invalidated a law prohibiting the distribution of contraceptives to unmarried persons[:]

> "It is true that in *Griswold* the right of privacy in question inhered in the marital relationship. . . . If the right of privacy means anything, it is the right of the *individual,* married or single, to be free from unwarranted governmental intrusion into matters so fundamentally affecting a person as the decision whether to bear or beget a child."

Id. at 453.

* * *

In *Carey v. Population Services Int'l,* 431 U.S. 678 (1977), the Court [invalidated] a New York law forbidding sale or distribution of contraceptive devices to persons under 16 years of age. * * * Both *Eisenstadt* and *Carey,* as well as the holding and rationale in *Roe* [*v. Wade,* 410 U.S. 113 (1973) (striking down a Texas law banning abortion)], confirmed that the reasoning of *Griswold* could not be confined to the protection of rights of married adults. This was the state of the law with respect to some of the most relevant cases when the Court considered *Bowers v. Hardwick* [478 U.S. 186 (1986) (upholding a Georgia anti-sodomy law against a nearly identical constitutional challenge)].

* * *

The Court began its substantive discussion in *Bowers* as follows: "The issue presented is whether the Federal Constitution confers a fundamental right upon homosexuals to engage in sodomy and hence invalidates the laws of the many States that still make such conduct illegal and have done so for a very long time." That statement, we now conclude, discloses the Court's own failure to appreciate the extent of the liberty at stake. To say that the issue in *Bowers* was simply the right to engage in certain sexual conduct demeans the claim the individual put forward, just as it would demean a married couple were it to be said marriage is simply about the right to have sexual intercourse. The laws involved in *Bowers* and here are, to be sure, statutes that purport to do no more than prohibit a particular sexual act. Their penalties and purposes, though, have more far-reaching consequences, touching upon the most private human conduct, sexual behavior, and in the most private of places, the home. The statutes do seek to control a personal relationship that, whether or not entitled to formal recognition in the law, is within the liberty of persons to choose without being punished as criminals.

This, as a general rule, should counsel against attempts by the State, or a court, to define the meaning of the relationship or to set its boundaries absent injury to a person or abuse of an institution the law protects. It suffices for us to acknowledge that adults may choose to enter upon this relationship in the confines of their homes and their own private lives and still retain their dignity as free persons. When sexuality finds overt expression in intimate conduct with another person, the conduct can be but one element in a personal bond that is more enduring. The liberty protected by the Constitution allows homosexual persons the right to make this choice.

Having misapprehended the claim of liberty there presented to it, and thus stating the claim to be whether there is a fundamental right to engage in consensual sodomy, the *Bowers* Court said: "Proscriptions against that conduct have ancient roots." In academic writings, and in many of the scholarly *amicus* briefs filed to assist the Court in this case, there are fundamental criticisms of the historical premises relied upon by the majority and concurring opinions in *Bowers*. We need not enter this debate in the attempt to reach a definitive historical judgment, but the following considerations counsel against adopting the definitive conclusions upon which *Bowers* placed such reliance.

At the outset it should be noted that there is no longstanding history in this country of laws directed at homosexual conduct as a distinct matter. * * * [E]arly American sodomy laws were not directed at homosexuals as such but instead sought to prohibit nonprocreative sexual activity more generally. This does not suggest approval of homosexual conduct. It does tend to show that this particular form of conduct was not thought of as a separate category from like conduct between heterosexual persons.

* * *

[T]he longstanding criminal prohibition of homosexual sodomy upon which the *Bowers* decision placed such reliance is as consistent with a general condemnation of nonprocreative sex as it is with an established tradition of prosecuting acts because of their homosexual character.

The policy of punishing consenting adults for private acts was not much discussed in the early legal literature. We can infer that one reason for this was the very private nature of the conduct. Despite the absence of prosecutions, there may have been periods in which there was public criticism of homosexuals as such and an insistence that the criminal laws be enforced to discourage their practices. But far from possessing "ancient roots," *Bowers*, 478 U.S. at 192, American laws targeting same-sex couples did not develop until the last third of the 20th century. * * *

* * *

[T]he Court in *Bowers* was making the broader point that for centuries there have been powerful voices to condemn homosexual conduct as immoral. The condemnation has been shaped by religious beliefs, conceptions of right and acceptable behavior, and respect for the traditional family. For many persons these are not trivial concerns but profound and deep convictions accepted as ethical and moral principles to which they aspire and which thus determine the course of their lives. These considerations do not answer the question before us, however. The issue is whether the majority may use the power of the State to enforce these views on the whole society through operation of the criminal law. "Our obligation is to define the liberty of all, not to mandate our own moral code." *Planned Parenthood of Southeastern Pa. v. Casey*, 505 U.S. 833, 850 (1992).

[O]ur laws and traditions in the past half century are of most relevance here. These references show an emerging awareness that liberty gives substantial protection to adult persons in deciding how to conduct their private lives in matters pertaining to sex. "[H]istory and tradition are the starting point but not in all cases the ending point of the substantive due process inquiry." *County of Sacramento v. Lewis*, 523 U.S. 833, 857 (1998) (KENNEDY, J., concurring).

This emerging recognition should have been apparent when *Bowers* was decided. In 1955 the American Law Institute promulgated the Model Penal Code and made clear that it did not recommend or provide for "criminal penalties for consensual sexual relations conducted in private." ALI, Model Penal Code 2.13.2, cmt. 2, p. 372 (1980). * * *

In *Bowers* the Court referred to the fact that before 1961 all 50 States had outlawed sodomy, and that at the time of the Court's decision 24 States and the District of Columbia had sodomy laws. [T]hese prohibitions often were being ignored, however. Georgia, for instance, had not sought to enforce its law for decades. * * *.

* * *

* * * The 25 States with laws prohibiting the relevant conduct referenced in the *Bowers* decision are reduced now to 13, of which 4 enforce their laws only against homosexual conduct. * * *

Two principal cases decided after *Bowers* cast its holding into even more doubt. * * * The *Casey* decision again confirmed that our laws and tradition afford constitutional protection to personal decisions relating to marriage, procreation, contraception, family relationships, child rearing, and education. [*Planned Parenthood of Southeastern Pa. v. Casey*, 505 U.S. 833, 851 (1992).] In explaining the respect the Constitution demands for the autonomy of the person in making these choices, we stated as follows:

> "These matters, involving the most intimate and personal choices a person may make in a lifetime, choices central to personal dignity and autonomy, are central to the liberty protected by the Fourteenth Amendment. At the heart of liberty is the right to define one's own concept of existence, of meaning, of the universe, and of the mystery of human life. Beliefs about these matters could not define the attributes of personhood were they formed under compulsion of the State."

[*Id.*] Persons in a homosexual relationship may seek autonomy for these purposes, just as heterosexual persons do. The decision in *Bowers* would deny them this right.

The second post-*Bowers* case of principal relevance is *Romer v. Evans,* 517 U.S. 620 (1996). There the Court struck down class-based legislation directed at homosexuals as a violation of the Equal Protection Clause. *Romer* invalidated an amendment to Colorado's constitution which named as a solitary class persons who were homosexuals, lesbians, or bisexual either by "orientation, conduct, practices or relationships," and deprived them of protection under state antidiscrimination laws. We concluded that the provision was "born of animosity toward the class of persons affected" and further that it had no rational relation to a legitimate governmental purpose. *Id.* at 634.

* * *

The foundations of *Bowers* have sustained serious erosion from our recent decisions in *Casey* and *Romer*. * * *

* * *

* * * In his dissenting opinion in *Bowers*, Justice STEVENS came to these conclusions:

"Our prior cases make two propositions abundantly clear. First, the fact that the governing majority in a State has traditionally viewed a particular practice as immoral is not a sufficient reason for upholding a law prohibiting the practice; neither history nor tradition could save a law prohibiting miscegenation from constitutional attack. Second, individual decisions by married persons, concerning the intimacies of their physical relationship, even when not intended to produce offspring, are a form of 'liberty' protected by the Due Process Clause of the Fourteenth Amendment. Moreover, this protection extends to intimate choices by unmarried as well as married persons."

478 U.S. at 216. Justice STEVENS' analysis, in our view, should have been controlling in *Bowers* and should control here.

Bowers was not correct when it was decided, and it is not correct today. It ought not to remain binding precedent. *Bowers v. Hardwick* should be and now is overruled.

The present case does not involve minors. It does not involve persons who might be injured or coerced or who are situated in relationships where consent might not easily be refused. It does not involve public conduct or prostitution. It does not involve whether the government must give formal recognition to any relationship that homosexual persons seek to enter. The case does involve two adults who, with full and mutual consent from each other, engaged in sexual practices common to a homosexual lifestyle. The petitioners are entitled to respect for their private lives. The State cannot demean their existence or control their destiny by making their private sexual conduct a crime. Their right to liberty under the Due Process Clause gives them the full right to engage in their conduct without intervention of the government. "It is a promise of the Constitution that there is a realm of personal liberty which the government may not enter." *Casey*, [505 U.S.] at 847. The Texas statute furthers no legitimate state interest which can justify its intrusion into the personal and private life of the individual.

Had those who drew and ratified the Due Process Clauses of the Fifth Amendment or the Fourteenth Amendment known the components of liberty in its manifold possibilities, they might have been more specific. They did not presume to have this insight. They knew times can blind us to certain truths and later generations can see that laws once thought necessary and proper in fact serve only to oppress. As the Constitution endures, persons in every generation can invoke its principles in their own search for greater freedom.

The judgment of the Court of Appeals for the Texas Fourteenth District is reversed, and the case is remanded for further proceedings not inconsistent with this opinion.

It is so ordered.

JUSTICE O'CONNOR, concurring in the judgment.

* * * I joined *Bowers,* and do not join the Court in overruling it. Nevertheless, I agree with the Court that Texas' statute banning same-sex sodomy is unconstitutional. Rather than relying on the substantive component of the Fourteenth Amendment's Due Process Clause, as the Court does, I base my conclusion on the Fourteenth Amendment's Equal Protection Clause.

The Equal Protection Clause of the Fourteenth Amendment "is essentially a direction that all persons similarly situated should be treated alike." *Cleburne v. Cleburne Living Ctr., Inc.,* 473 U.S. 432, 439 (1985). Under our rational basis standard of review, "legislation is presumed to be valid and will be sustained if the classification drawn by the statute is rationally related to a legitimate state interest." [*Id.*] at 440.

* * * We have consistently held, however, that some objectives, such as "a bare . . . desire to harm a politically unpopular group," are not legitimate state interests. *Dep't of Agric. v. Moreno,* 413 U.S. 528 (1973)[; *see also Cleburne,* 473 U.S.] at 44647; *Romer v. Evans,* [517 U.S. 620 (1996)]. When a law exhibits such a desire to harm a politically unpopular group, we have applied a more searching form of rational basis review to strike down such laws under the Equal Protection Clause.

We have been most likely to apply rational basis review to hold a law unconstitutional under the Equal Protection Clause where, as here, the challenged legislation inhibits personal relationships. * * *

* * *

The Texas statute makes homosexuals unequal in the eyes of the law by making particular conduct—and only that conduct—subject to criminal sanction. * * *

* * *

Moral disapproval of a group cannot be a legitimate governmental interest under the Equal Protection Clause because legal classifications must not be "drawn for the purpose of disadvantaging the group burdened by the law." [*Romer,* 517 U.S.] at 633. Texas' invocation of moral disapproval as a legitimate state interest proves nothing more than Texas' desire to criminalize homosexual sodomy. * * *

* * *

That this law as applied to private, consensual conduct is unconstitutional under the Equal Protection Clause does not mean that other laws distinguishing between heterosexuals and homosexuals would similarly fail under rational basis review. Texas cannot assert any legitimate state interest here, such as national security or preserving the traditional institution of marriage. Unlike the moral disapproval of same-sex relations—the asserted state interest in this case—other reasons exist to promote the institution of marriage beyond mere moral disapproval of an excluded group.

A law branding one class of persons as criminal based solely on the State's moral disapproval of that class and the conduct associated with that class runs contrary to the values of the Constitution and the Equal Protection Clause, under any standard of review. * * *

JUSTICE SCALIA, with whom THE CHIEF JUSTICE and JUSTICE THOMAS join, dissenting.

* * *

[N]owhere does the Court's opinion declare that homosexual sodomy is a "fundamental right" under the Due Process Clause; nor does it subject the Texas law to the standard of review that would be appropriate (strict scrutiny) if homosexual sodomy *were* a "fundamental right." Thus, while overruling the *outcome* of *Bowers,* the Court leaves strangely untouched its central legal conclusion: "[R]espondent would have us announce . . . a fundamental right to engage in homosexual sodomy. This we are quite unwilling to do." Instead the Court simply describes petitioners' conduct as "an exercise of their liberty"—which it undoubtedly is—and proceeds to apply an unheard-of form of rational-basis review that will have far-reaching implications beyond this case.

* * *

Our opinions applying the doctrine known as "substantive due process" hold that the Due Process Clause prohibits States from infringing *fundamental* liberty interests, unless the infringement is narrowly tailored to serve a compelling state interest. We have held repeatedly, in cases the Court today does not overrule, that *only* fundamental rights qualify for this so-called "heightened scrutiny" protection—that is, rights which are " 'deeply rooted in this Nation's history and tradition.' " All other liberty interests may be abridged or abrogated pursuant to a validly enacted state law if that law is rationally related to a legitimate state interest.

* * *

* * * Not once does [the majority] describe homosexual sodomy as a "fundamental right" or a "fundamental liberty interest," nor does it subject the Texas statute to strict scrutiny. Instead, having failed to establish that the right to homosexual sodomy is " 'deeply rooted in this Nation's history and tradition,' " the Court concludes that the application of Texas's statute to petitioners' conduct fails the rational-basis test, and overrules *Bowers'* holding to the contrary. * * *

* * *

* * * [A]n "emerging awareness" is by definition not "deeply rooted in this Nation's history and tradition[s]," as we have said "fundamental right" status requires. Constitutional entitlements do not spring into existence because some States choose to lessen or eliminate criminal sanctions on certain behavior. * * *

IV

I turn now to the ground on which the Court squarely rests its holding: the contention that there is no rational basis for the law here under attack. This proposition is so out of accord with our jurisprudence—indeed, with the jurisprudence of *any* society we know—that it requires little discussion.

The Texas statute undeniably seeks to further the belief of its citizens that certain forms of sexual behavior are "immoral and unacceptable," *Bowers*, [478 U.S.] at 196—the same interest furthered by criminal laws against fornication, bigamy, adultery, adult incest, bestiality, and obscenity. *Bowers* held that this *was* a legitimate state interest. The Court today reaches the opposite conclusion. * * * This effectively decrees the end of all morals legislation. If, as the Court asserts, the promotion of majoritarian sexual morality is not even a *legitimate* state interest, none of the above-mentioned laws can survive rational-basis review.

V

Finally, I turn to petitioners' equal-protection challenge, which no Member of the Court save Justice O'CONNOR embraces: On its face 21.06(a) applies equally to all persons. Men and women, heterosexuals and homosexuals, are all subject to its prohibition of deviate sexual intercourse with someone of the same sex. To be sure, 21.06 does distinguish between the sexes insofar as concerns the partner with whom the sexual acts are performed: men can violate the law only with other men, and women only with other women. But this cannot itself be a denial of equal protection, since it is precisely the same distinction regarding partner that is drawn in state laws prohibiting marriage with someone of the same sex while permitting marriage with someone of the opposite sex.

* * *

Justice O'CONNOR simply decrees application of "a more searching form of rational basis review" to the Texas statute. The cases she cites do not recognize such a standard, and reach their conclusions only after finding, as required by conventional rational-basis analysis, that no conceivable legitimate state interest supports the classification at issue. * * *

This reasoning leaves on pretty shaky grounds state laws limiting marriage to opposite-sex couples. Justice O'CONNOR seeks to preserve them by the conclusory statement that "preserving the traditional institution of marriage" is a legitimate state interest. But "preserving the traditional institution of marriage" is just a kinder way of describing the State's *moral disapproval* of same-sex couples. * * *

* * *

Let me be clear that I have nothing against homosexuals, or any other group, promoting their agenda through normal democratic means. Social perceptions of sexual and other morality change over time, and every group has the right to persuade its fellow citizens that its view of such matters is the best. * * *

One of the benefits of leaving regulation of this matter to the people rather than to the courts is that the people, unlike judges, need not carry things to their logical conclusion. The people may feel that their disapprobation of homosexual conduct is strong enough to disallow homosexual marriage, but not strong enough to criminalize private homosexual acts—and may legislate accordingly. The Court today pretends that it possesses a similar freedom of action, so that that we need not fear judicial imposition of homosexual marriage, as has recently occurred in Canada * * *. See *Halpern v. Toronto*, [[2003] 65 O.R. (3d) 161] (Ontario Ct. App.). [T]he Court says that the present case "does not involve whether the government must give formal recognition to any relationship that homosexual persons seek to enter." Do not believe it. More illuminating than this bald, unreasoned disclaimer is the progression of thought displayed by an earlier passage in the Court's opinion, which notes the constitutional protections afforded to "personal decisions relating to *marriage,* procreation, contraception, family relationships, child rearing, and education," and then declares that "[p]ersons in a homosexual relationship may seek autonomy for these purposes, just as heterosexual persons do." Today's opinion dismantles the structure of constitutional law that has permitted a distinction to be made between heterosexual and homosexual unions, insofar as formal recognition in marriage is concerned. If moral disapprobation of homosexual conduct is "no legitimate state interest" for purposes of proscribing that conduct; and if, as the Court coos (casting aside all pretense of neutrality), "[w]hen sexuality finds overt expression in intimate conduct with another person, the conduct can be but one element in a personal bond that is more enduring," what justification could there possibly be for denying the benefits of marriage to homosexual couples exercising "[t]he liberty protected by the Constitution?" Surely not the encouragement of procreation, since the sterile and the elderly are allowed to marry. This case "does not involve" the issue of homosexual marriage only if one entertains the belief that principle and logic have nothing to do with the decisions of this Court. Many will hope that, as the Court comfortingly assures us, this is so.

* * *

NOTES AND QUESTIONS

1. *What is the holding of* Lawrence? On what basis does the Court overrule *Bowers v. Hardwick*? Does the Court's opinion in *Lawrence* offer guidance about the scope of constitutional liberty and how to define the right being infringed by Texas's law? What role, for example, do history and tradition play in defining "liberty"?

Some scholars argue that *Lawrence* is surprisingly opaque. While it "purported to correct *Bowers'* erroneously parsimonious level of generality about what rights are fundamental," it did not make explicit its own "theory for thinking about levels of generality" or unenumerated rights. Eric Berger, Lawrence's *Stealth Constitutionalism and Same-Sex Marriage Litigation,* 21 Wm. & Mary Bill of Rts. J. 765, 776–777 (2013). Some courts adopted Justice Scalia's view that *Lawrence* found no fundamental right and invalidated the Texas law solely on the ground that it failed rational-basis review. *See, e.g., Standhardt v. Superior Court,* 77 P.3d 451, 457 (Ariz. Ct. App. 2003). Others have read the majority opinion as striking down the Texas sodomy law on the ground that it violated a fundamental privacy right relating to family or intimate association. *See Lowe v. Swanson,* 663 F.3d 258, 262 (6th Cir. 2011), *cert. denied,* 132 S. Ct. 2383 (2012) (noting conflict in interpreting *Lawrence*); *see also* Laurence H. Tribe, Lawrence v. Texas: *The "Fundamental Right" That Dare Not Speak Its Name,* 117 Harv. L. Rev. 1893 (2004).

Professors Fleming and McClain conclude (as Justice O'Connor claimed) that *Lawrence* applied "rational basis scrutiny with 'bite.' " They observe that, although the majority opinion does not explicitly invoke Justice Harlan (as Justice Powell did in *Moore, supra*), *Lawrence* follows Harlan's approach to substantive due process by "carefully scrutinizing a statute without laboring any compulsion to articulate a rigid formula or framework that will substitute for making reasoned judgments." Fleming & McClain, Ordered Liberty, *supra,* at 266.

2. *Criminal law, "desuetude," and decriminalization.* Professor Cass Sunstein suggests that *Lawrence* is best understood as an exceptional response to the fact that sodomy laws, like the contraception laws struck down in *Griswold*, had fallen into desuetude and were "hopelessly out of touch with existing [popular] convictions." Cass R. Sunstein, *What Did* Lawrence *Hold? Of Autonomy, Desuetude, Sexuality, and Marriage,* 55 Sup. Ct. Rev. 27, 27 (2003). The same was true of the laws challenged in *Griswold* and *Eisenstadt.* Professor Melissa Murray argues that many constitutional law cases that are part of the family law canon, such as *Griswold, Eisenstadt,* and *Lawrence* (and *Loving v. Virginia* (1967), which you will read in Chapter 2), are *criminal law* cases with constitutional dimensions: the Court put limits on the state's ability to use the criminal law to regulate sexuality and marriage and signal disapproval. *See* Melissa Murray, *Strange Bedfellows: Criminal Law, Family Law, and the Legal Construction of Intimate Life,* 94 Iowa L. Rev. 1253, 1272–73 (2009). What tools does the state have other than criminal law to promote norms about sexuality and marriage?

3.   *Were* Bowers *and* Lawrence *examining the same questions?* It is often said that the question the Court asks largely determines the result it reaches. How did the Court frame the question before it in *Bowers?* In *Lawrence?*

4.   *Individual or familial privacy? Griswold* appeared to ground the right of privacy in the intimate associational bond between married partners, while *Eisenstadt* emphasized the rights of single persons as individuals. What about *Lawrence's* analysis of liberty? Professor David Meyer contends that the expansion of the right of privacy in *Lawrence* is based on "a broadening conception of family," rather than on a broader conception of protection for sexual liberty; "the Court ultimately appeared to link constitutional protection to contemporary society's acceptance of the legitimacy of the family bonds constructed by gays and lesbians." David D. Meyer, *Domesticating* Lawrence, 2004 U. Chi. L. Forum 453, 454–55. If that is a correct reading, does *Lawrence* "domesticate" liberty and gay and lesbian sexuality by treating same-sex sexual intimacy as the same as heterosexual sexual intimacy and, thus, worthy of protection only to the degree of that similarity? *See* Katherine M. Franke, *The Domesticated Liberty of* Lawrence v. Texas, 104 Col. L. Rev. 1399 (2004). What type of privacy is protected post-*Lawrence?*

5.   *"The end of all morals legislation"?* What stance do the different opinions take on whether moral disapproval is a sufficient basis for criminal sanction? Is *Lawrence*, as Scalia warns, the end of all "morals" legislation, including criminal laws prohibiting "fornication, bigamy, adultery, adult incest, bestiality, and obscenity"? In Chapter 2, we will examine the import of *Lawrence* for traditional state restrictions on who may marry.

6.   Lawrence *and marriage.* The majority expressly states that the case "does not involve whether the government must give formal recognition to any relationship that homosexual persons seek to enter." In other words, the case involves a right to be free *from* unwarranted governmental intrusion in the form of criminal prosecution; it does not involve a right *to* governmental recognition of an intimate relationship as a source of benefits or entitlements. Is this reasoning persuasive? Or do you find more persuasive Justice Scalia's widely-publicized warning (in dissent) about the majority's disclaimer: "Do not believe it." Certainly, as Justice Scalia's dissent predicted, *Lawrence's* willingness to protect private intimacy between same-sex partners led some lower courts to reconsider the constitutionality of laws banning same-sex marriage, as you will see in Chapter 2.

7.   *Equal protection, "animus," and moral disapproval.* Justice Kennedy draws on *Romer v. Evans* (an opinion he also authored) as one precedent undermining *Bowers.* Justice O'Connor reads *Romer* and earlier equal protection cases on which *Romer* relied as supporting a "more searching form of rational basis review" (short of formal intermediate scrutiny) when laws show a "desire to harm a politically unpopular group." *Romer* and these other cases identify the constitutional wrong of singling out a group for discriminatory treatment based on moral disapproval, "animus," or a "bare desire to harm." *Romer v. Evans*, 517 U.S. 620, 632–634 (1996). As mentioned

in Note 1 (above), some commentators describe this "more searching form" of review as "rational basis plus" or "rational basis with bite," although the Court does not refer to it in this way.

4. THE STATUS AND CONDITIONS OF FAMILY LAW PRACTICE

Family law practice involves intellectually challenging and emotionally complex issues that are at the core of contemporary life. Historically, however, family law has not always enjoyed such a high reputation. When the first family law, or "domestic relations," casebooks were published in the 1890s, both legal academics and attorneys in "elite legal practice" viewed the field of family law with suspicion and even disdain. These views were based on beliefs about the field's "conceptual untidiness, its unscientific nature," and "its gendered character," given "the inescapable presence of women as wives, as sexual beings, of dishonored husbands suing for compensation, and of dependent children." Hendrik Hartog, Man and Wife in America: A History 289 (2000).

Much of this perception of family law as a low status field of practice stemmed from broader societal forces beyond the control of individual domestic relations lawyers. Divorce carried a profound stigma, which sometimes reflected adversely on the lawyers who practiced in the area. Major law firms rarely handled divorce cases, creating a vacuum that left the field to lawyers who sometimes found themselves excluded from prestigious firms because of religion, ethnicity, race or gender. Sanford N. Katz, *Prologue*, 33 Fam. L.Q. 435, 435 (1999). The traditional low status of family law practice, however, also derived from some processes within the field. By the 1930s and 1940s, divorce procedure was "rotten to the core" because couples often colluded to obtain divorces that would otherwise not have been obtainable in the era of strict, fault-based divorce law. Lawrence M. Friedman, *A Dead Language: Divorce Law and Practice Before No-Fault*, 86 Va. L. Rev. 1497, 1536 (2000). As elaborated in Chapter 8, one impetus for the no-fault divorce revolution was the pressing need to stem this pervasive corruption.

As major changes to substantive family law began in the late 1950s and 1960s, and accelerated in the 1970s, perceptions of family law practice improved. In 1958, the American Bar Association recognized family law as a specialty. Katz, *supra,* at 436. Beginning in 1969, states adopted no-fault divorce legislation and equitable property distribution laws. *Id.* at 437–38. Courts also initiated reform efforts and moved away from adversary proceedings toward alternative dispute resolution. *Id.* at 439. Meanwhile, the family law bar developed aspirational guidelines for family law attorneys to resolve conflict in ways that minimized the adverse impact on children and made post-divorce co-parenting possible. American Academy of Matrimonial Lawyers, *Bounds of Advocacy* (adopted in 1991; revised in

2000). Such changes enhanced the image and reputation of lawyers who specialized in family law.

These developments coincided with broad social and political change, including the rise of the women's and children's rights movements, and the federal government's involvement with child support policy and enforcement and child welfare legislation. Another significant development was a series of Supreme Court decisions (some of which you read earlier in this chapter) that applied the Due Process and Equal Protection Clauses, along with other constitutional provisions, to limit state regulation of the family. With this increased constitutionalization of family law doctrine, family law issues became more and more central to cultural and political debates throughout the nation.

Contemporary family law cases require a breadth of knowledge even beyond an awareness of how constitutional law shapes doctrine. Family law practitioners today need to develop some expertise in areas ranging from tax to contracts to retirement planning as well as psychology. *See* Mary E. O'Connell & J. Herbie DiFonzo, *The Family Law Education Reform Project Final Report*, 44 Fam. Ct. Rev. 524, 525 (2006).

So too, perhaps the most significant change for family court judges over the last fifty years is the expanded "breadth of potential legal issues encountered today in family law cases." Natalie Anne Knowlton, *The Modern Family Court Judge: Knowledge, Qualities and Skills for Success*, 53 Fam. Ct. Rev. 203, 204 (2015). The contemporary intellectual rigor of family law and the complex human situations that family law practitioners face mean that "family law is—and must be—a collaborative enterprise" because the practice "poses special challenges and requires judges and attorneys, as well as other professionals like psychologists and social workers, to study and work together." Sandra Day O'Connor, *Remarks: The Supreme Court and the Family*, 3 U. Pa. J. Const. L. 573, 573, 576 (2001).

As you will see in later chapters, one "special challenge" routinely facing family lawyers is the raw emotion that characterizes many domestic relations proceedings. Parties contemplating dissolution seek help from lawyers at fragile moments in their lives. "Family law lawyers very often, and not surprisingly, see clients at their worst. The very subject matter of family law cases, *i.e.*, children, money, and personal conflict, are of such great importance to our clients, that clients often lose sight of their better judgment." Alan C. Eidsness & Lisa T. Spencer, *Confronting Ethical Issues in Practice*, 45 Fam. L.Q. 21 (2011). Among other factors, this emotional dimension may contribute to many of the distinctive professional and ethical challenges that family lawyers frequently face, a matter explored in Chapter 14.

The client's familial relationship may have been marked by conflicts over parenting, significant power imbalance between the spouses or partners, ongoing personal strife, and even physical confrontation or assault. Neither spouse nor partner may ever have consulted a lawyer before, except to make a will or close on a home purchase. Most adults have never entered a courtroom except to serve jury duty or plead to a traffic violation, but parties to a dissolution face legal proceedings with high stakes for themselves and the persons closest to them.

The client's emotional vulnerability may affect the lawyer-client relationship. For example, a demoralized client, bent on establishing innocence and the other party's guilt for the family's breakup, may misinterpret the lawyer's more dispassionate focus on tangible factors in a no-fault regime, usually dominated by the property and child-related issues. The client may resist the lawyer's explanations of why emotion-laden court presentations will likely backfire.

In a typical year, approximately five million domestic relations cases enter the state court systems; that number is dominated, in most states, by divorce cases, followed by civil protection orders and child support cases. National Center for State Courts, *Court Statistics* (2018). There is, however, "a stark dichotomy in our family courts between the wealthy and the poor," because some "litigants with abundant resources" are able to "engage interdisciplinary teams of professionals to help them navigate the system," while "many more parents lack the financial means to obtain even the most basic services necessary to address critical legal, mental health and dispute resolution issues impacting their family." Peter Salem & Michael Saini, *A Survey of Beliefs and Priorities About Access to Justice of Family Law: The Search for A Multidisciplinary Perspective*, 55 Fam. Ct. Rev. 120, 121 (2017). One study found that 80–90% of family law cases in some courts involve at least one self-represented (*pro se)* litigant, and in many cases, neither party is represented by a lawyer. Natalie Ann Knowlton, *Cases Without Counsel: Research on Self-Representation Experiences In Family Court,* Institute for the Advancement of the American Legal System (May 2016), at 1. Family law practice and the legal system are adjusting to this new reality through *pro se* clinics, standardized filing forms, informational court websites and other measures. Chapter 14 discusses another recent innovation, unbundled legal services, in which a lawyer provides an explicitly limited scope of representation.

A. THE LEGAL SYSTEM'S APPROACH
TO FAMILY LAW DISPUTES

The following article summarizes some of the major changes that have occurred over the last few decades in how the legal system handles family disputes. Many of these changes implicate alternative dispute resolution methods, the subject of Chapter 15.

JANA SINGER,
DISPUTE RESOLUTION AND THE POSTDIVORCE FAMILY: IMPLICATIONS OF A PARADIGM SHIFT

47 Fam. Ct. Rev. 363, 363–365 (2009).

Over the past [few] decades, there has been a paradigm shift in the way the legal system handles most family disputes—particularly disputes involving children. This paradigm shift has replaced the law-oriented and judge-focused adversary model with a more collaborative, interdisciplinary, and forward-looking family dispute resolution regime. It has also transformed the practice of family law and fundamentally altered the way in which disputing families interact with the legal system. Although this "velvet revolution" in family conflict resolution offers many potential benefits for children and for parents, it also poses a number of challenges—both for families and for the judicial system. * * *

ELEMENTS OF THE PARADIGM SHIFT

The paradigm shift in family dispute resolution encompasses a number of related components. The first component is a profound skepticism about the value of traditional adversary procedures. An overriding theme of recent divorce reform efforts is that adversary processes are ill suited for resolving disputes involving children. Relatedly, social science suggests that children's adjustment to divorce and separation depends significantly on their parents' behavior during and after the separation process: the higher the levels of parental conflict to which children are exposed, the more negative the effects of family dissolution. Armed with these social science findings, academics and court reformers have argued that family courts should abandon the adversary paradigm, in favor of approaches that help parents manage their conflict and encourage them to develop positive postdivorce co-parenting relationships.

Family courts across the country have embraced this insight and have adopted an array of nonadversary dispute resolution mechanisms designed to avoid adjudication of family cases. This rejection of adversary procedures has moved beyond divorce-related custody disputes—where court-connected mediation is now the norm—to the more public arena of state-initiated child welfare proceedings, where family group conferencing and other problem-solving approaches have begun to supplant more traditional adjudicative models. An increasing number of family lawyers have also rejected the adversary paradigm, in favor of a collaborative law model under which lawyers pledge at the outset of their representation not to take a client's case to trial. * * *

A second element of the paradigm shift in family dispute resolution is the belief that most family disputes are not discrete legal events, but ongoing social and emotional processes. This de-legalization of family disputes began with the shift from fault-based to no-fault divorce; more recently, it has become one of the basic tenets of the movement for unified family courts. Thus recharacterized, family disputes call *not* for zealous legal approaches, but for interventions that are collaborative, holistic, and interdisciplinary, because these are the types of interventions most likely to address the families['] underlying dysfunction and emotional needs. Understanding family conflict as primarily a social and emotional process, rather than a legal event, also reduces the primacy of lawyers in handling these disputes and enhances the role of nonlegal professionals in the family court system.

Third, this new understanding of family disputes has led to a reformulation of the goal of legal intervention in the family. Traditionally, legal intervention was a backward-looking process, designed primarily to assign blame and allocate rights; under the new paradigm, by contrast, judges assume the forward-looking task of supervising a process of family reorganization. As Andrew Schepard has noted, family court judges no longer function primarily as fault finders or rights adjudicators, but rather as ongoing conflict managers.

The therapeutic jurisprudence movement embodies this forward-looking orientation. From a therapeutic perspective, legal intervention in the family strives not merely to resolve disputes, but to improve the material and psychological well-being of individuals and families in conflict. Problem-solving judges embrace this therapeutic role by attempting to understand and address underlying family dynamics and by using judicial authority "to motivate individuals to accept needed services and to monitor their compliance and progress."

Fourth, to achieve these therapeutic goals, family courts have adopted systems that deemphasize third-party dispute resolution in favor of capacity-building processes that seek to empower families to resolve their own conflicts. Consistent with this philosophy, jurisdictions across the country have instituted mandatory divorce-related parenting education and other programs designed to enhance litigants' communication and problem-solving skills. Similarly, the American Law Institute's (ALI) Principles of the Law of Family Dissolution endorses individualized parenting plans as an alternative to judicial custody rulings and urges the adoption of court-based programs that facilitate these voluntary agreements. A number of jurisdictions have made such parenting plans a central feature of their divorce and custody regimes. More recently, a number of family courts have added parenting coordinators to their staffs; these quasi-judicial officials assist high-conflict families to develop concrete parenting plans and to resolve ongoing parenting disputes that arise under these plans.

A fifth component of the paradigm shift is an increased emphasis on predispute planning and preventive law. Familiar examples include the increased acceptance and enforceability of prenuptial agreements and domestic partnership contracts. Parenting plans that include a mechanism for periodic review or a process for resolving future disagreements are similarly designed to minimize the need for future court intervention. [Some states allow prebirth parentage orders for] a nonbiologically related adult who anticipates caring for the child. * * * Perhaps more ambitiously, a few states have considered broad-based premarriage education requirements as a prerequisite for obtaining a marriage license, and the federal government has invested substantial resources in public and private marriage education programs aimed especially at low-income partners. More generally, scholars and advocates of preventive law have urged individuals to use legal mechanisms to anticipate and plan for family transitions such as the formation and dissolution of intimate partnerships. This emphasis on publicly supervised private ordering creates a hybrid model that expands the role of family courts and lawyers beyond their traditional dispute-resolution function. It also extends the time frame during which families interact with the legal system.

Taken together, these developments hold considerable promise for families. Non-adversary dispute resolution procedures offer families a mode of conflict resolution that is both more enduring and less destructive of ongoing relationships than adversary litigation.

Nonadversary processes are also more amenable to direct participation by family members—a particularly important feature, given the high percentage of family litigants who are not represented by counsel. Similarly, judicial interventions that successfully build capacity and enhance problem-solving skills should allow families to avoid the financial and emotional drain of future encounters with the legal system. On a more theoretical level, the paradigm shift in family dispute resolution appropriately rejects the mythology of the private family, a mythology that characterizes "normal" families as fully autonomous and self-sufficient and that labels families that seek—or are subject to—state intervention as dysfunctional or inadequate. The new paradigm recognizes instead that family and state governance are intertwined and that most families need public support in order to function effectively.

NOTES AND QUESTIONS

1. *Questions and concerns about the paradigm shift.* What are the different elements of the paradigm shift that Singer identifies? How does the paradigm shift fit with the strong protection for family privacy explored earlier in the Chapter? Singer herself identifies several concerns about the paradigm shift. One, explored later in this book, is the evident tension between (a) the "clean break" philosophy that undergirds no fault-divorce and economic distribution at divorce, and (b) the law's growing commitment to post-divorce shared parenting, which often requires close and continuing contact between

co-parents. Singer, *Dispute Resolution, supra,* at 367. What other questions or concerns might you want to consider?

2. *Challenges faced by the court system in implementing the new paradigm.* Even some of the most ardent supporters of the "velvet revolution" toward a problem-solving, interdisciplinary, collaborative model observe that the combination of severe budget cuts and a burgeoning docket in family courts poses challenges for translating the family law revolution into practice, so that its benefits extend to persons without money or lawyers. Rebecca Love Kourlis et al., *IIALS' Honoring Families Initiative Courts and Communities Helping Families in Transition Arising From Separation or Divorce,* 51 Fam. Ct. Rev. 351, 353, 367 (2013). In later work, Professor Singer (with Professor Jane Murphy) notes the risk of a "process gap" in the experiences of rich and poor litigants in family court. Jane C. Murphy & Jana B. Singer, Divorced from Reality (2015).

3. *The "reasonable" family lawyer?* As Professor Singer suggests, there has been a movement toward conflict management among family lawyers. Indeed, "empirical research indicates that most family lawyers try to be reasonable. Moreover, many modern family lawyers function not only as legal advocates and counselors but also as (non-therapeutic) family counselors, advising clients about dealing with spouses and children." John Lande, *The Revolution in Family Law Dispute Resolution*, 24 J. Am. Acad. Matrimonial Law. 411, 426–27 (2012); *see* Linda C. McClain, *Is There a Way Forward in the "War Over the Family?"*, 93 Tex. L. Rev. 705, 735–37 (2015) (discussing research finding that divorce lawyers employ a "reasonable lawyer" model, which generally views the zealous advocacy model as inapt for family law disputes) (citing Lynn Mather et al., Divorce Lawyers at Work 111 (2001)).Why might this movement serve the best interests of dissolution clients and their families?

PROBLEM 1-6

Your client, Jamie, is hurt and upset by the proposed divorce initiated by her spouse, Beni. Beni and Jamie have two young children. The couple has little money. What advice might you give about the divorce process? What are the different roles you might assume?

B. FAMILY LAW PRACTICE

Studies of job satisfaction among lawyers typically find that family lawyers have one of the highest job satisfaction scores, despite the emotional intensity frequently experienced by family law practitioners in their client representation. Lawrence R. Richard, *Psychological Type and Job Satisfaction Among Practicing Lawyers in the United States*, 29 Cap. U. L. Rev. 979, 1014, 1057 (2002). This result may stem largely from the nature of contemporary family law practice. Family law is a people-oriented practice, whose lawyers help one family at a time. Family law is typically practiced in smaller firms, or in smaller departments within larger firms. Unlike lawyers in larger corporate firms, domestic relations lawyers typically do not have high hourly-billing demands and have a great deal of autonomy. Indeed, a four-state study of lawyers found that: "Experiences of autonomy (including authenticity), relatedness [connection] to others, and competence most strongly predicted attorney well-being." Lawrence S. Krieger & Kennon M. Sheldon, *What Makes Lawyers Happy?: A Data-Driven Prescription to Redefine Professional Success*, 83 Geo. Wash. L. Rev. 554, 617 (2015).

Family law lawyers can also apply their legal training in an intellectually satisfying variety of meaningful public and private roles. In the public arena, family lawyers participate *pro bono* in family law associations and in law reform activities. Family lawyers are also active in national and local debates about such questions as work/family balance, abortion and other procreative issues, children's rights and obligations, and adoption and access to rapidly evolving assisted reproductive technologies.

In individual disputes, family lawyers may act in a variety of roles. In addition to representing a client, family lawyers (along with some other specially-trained professionals) may serve as advisors, facilitators, or decision makers in such roles as:

(1) Mediator—A neutral third party who meets with the parties, with or without counsel, seeking to facilitate voluntary settlement.

(2) Arbitrator—A third-party decision maker to whom the parties agree to submit a dispute for binding resolution; nonbinding arbitration may also be ordered by a court to facilitate settlement or case management.

(3) Guardian Ad Litem (GAL)—An advisor appointed by the court to represent the child's interests in a role that has several possible meanings (discussed in Chapter 12 and 13).

(4) Parent Educator—An instructor for divorcing parents in a classroom setting who teaches about post-divorce matters involving child custody and visitation.

(5) Parent Coordinator—An attorney who provides intensive case management for high-conflict families with children.

(6) Divorce Counselor—An attorney who advises someone about what type of attorney and legal representation he or she needs in a family dissolution process.

GALs do not have to be attorneys. They may be volunteers who lack professional expertise but receive special training. Other roles listed above may be filled by persons who have professional training outside the law.

As you learn about the substance of family law in the remaining chapters, you will also see how family lawyers increasingly retain, interact with or serve on, teams that include other professionals, such as doctors, mental health professionals, social workers, and accountants. You will also encounter some of the ethical questions that arise in the practice of family law along with the professional skills necessary to become a family law practitioner.

CHAPTER 2

ENTERING MARRIAGE

■ ■ ■

States regulate the institution of marriage by determining who may marry, how they may marry, what the legal benefits and obligations of marriage are, and when a marriage may be legally terminated. This Chapter concerns the requirements for entering marriage. By limiting who may marry, lawmakers have sought to define and reinforce foundational social values relating to citizenship, morality, childrearing, gender, sexuality, and race. Long ago, the Supreme Court stated that marriage, which "create[s] the most important relation in life, * * * having more to do with the morals and civilization of a people than any other institution, has always been subject to the control of the legislature." *Maynard v. Hill,* 125 U.S. 190, 205 (1888). As this chapter explains, understandings of the permissible boundaries of that governmental "control" have changed over time, due both to evolving understandings of marriage and significant developments in constitutional law.

On the one hand, the basic procedural rules about how to marry have remained largely unchanged for most of American history. A formal marriage requires the parties to obtain a marriage license and exchange vows of commitment (or solemnize their marriage) in a civil or religious ceremony. A handful of states also recognize informal marriage (also called common-law marriage), which permits competent parties to marry simply by expressing their mutual intentions to be married, by living together, and by establishing a community reputation as a married couple.

On the other hand, the rules about *who* may marry reflect both continuity and change. Continuity is evident in the requirement, in every state, that to enter a valid marriage, a prospective spouse currently be unmarried, not have a close familial relation with the intended partner, give consent to the marriage, and be at least a specified minimum age. In this chapter, you will read about two dramatic changes in state restrictions on who may marry. First, in *Loving v. Virginia,* 388 U.S. 1 (1967), the Supreme Court struck down Virginia's law banning interracial marriage (antimiscegenation law) and, by implication, similar laws in fifteen other states. Second, in 2015, the Court's struck down the remaining state laws that barred marriage by same-sex couples. *Obergefell v. Hodges,* 576 U.S. ___, 135 S. Ct. 2584 (2015).

As this chapter explains, since the second half of the twentieth century, courts have recognized significant constitutional limitations on governmental power over intimate and family life, bounding state regulation of marriage. Chapter 1 introduced this development by tracing the evolution of the "right to privacy" and of interpretations of "liberty" under the Due Process Clause. These constitutional developments opened new lines of challenge to traditional marriage regulation. So, too, as Chapter 3 will detail, the 1970s ushered in a new understanding of the Equal Protection Clause that limited the government's ability to enforce gender roles through family law and helped to dismantle the gender hierarchy of traditional marriage. These twin constitutional developments have required states to articulate strong public policy reasons for marriage laws that had once seemed natural and self-evident.

A trend toward "deregulation" of marriage is also apparent. As state legislatures have scaled back restrictions on entry into marriage, they have also made exit easier through liberalized divorce laws, as you will learn in Chapter 8.

The following materials introduce the ebb and flow of marriage regulation. The Chapter opens with the substantive rules that govern who is eligible to marry and who they may marry, beginning with two Supreme Court decisions that overturned restrictions on the right to marry. We then examine the evolving scope of the fundamental right to marry by considering the Supreme Court's decision, in *Obergefell*, that two persons of the same sex have a constitutional right to marry. The Chapter then turns to other restrictions, such as those on bigamous, incestuous, and under-age marriages, and the justifications for, and challenges to, such restrictions. One area of recent state legislative activity concerns "child marriage" and whether to raise the minimum age for marriage. The Chapter examines the requirement of consent to marriage, as well as the bases for annulling a marriage.

Finally, the Chapter reviews the procedural rules about how eligible parties may enter into marriage, contrasts these rules with informal (common-law) marriage, and introduces some equitable doctrines that enable courts to save apparent marriages when parties fail to comply with such rules. It explains the doctrine of annulment. As you read these materials, consider whether the law appropriately navigates the tensions between the conception of marriage as a public institution and as a private sphere of intimate freedom.

1. SUBSTANTIVE REQUIREMENTS FOR ENTRY INTO MARRIAGE

Recognizing the practical difficulties with rigid enforcement of marriage restrictions in a frontier society, state law took a largely permissive attitude toward marriage formation during America's first century or so. On the one hand, to be a marriage, the relationship between one man and one woman had to be "legally constituted" or "legally recognized." Hendrik Hartog, Man and Wife in America: A History 23 (2000). On the other, state law widely permitted couples to form marriages on their own without formalities, so that often "[t]he boundary between the legally constituted and the non- or illegally constituted was porous and fuzzy." *Id.*

For most of the 1800s, states showed little or no interest in the physical or mental health of persons embarking on marriage. By the 1930s, however, 26 states "would restrict the marriages of those infected with syphilis and gonorrhea," and 41 states "would use eugenic categories to restrict the marriage of 'lunatics,' 'imbeciles,' idiots,' and the 'feebleminded.' " Peggy Pascoe, What Comes Naturally: Miscegenation Law and the Making of Race in America 138 (2009). These terms sound shocking today, but at that time they were medical terms of art used unabashedly by physicians and lawmakers alike.

Within a few decades, blood tests became a "standard legal requirement" for persons seeking to marry. *Id.* During the same period, states raised the minimum legal age for marriage to ensure that the partners possessed sufficient maturity to fulfill their marital obligations. Some states had barred interracial marriage (anti-miscegenation laws) since colonial times, or the Civil War era; by the 1930s, many more states had such laws, premised on now-discredited theories about race. *Id.* at 85–93, 115–19.

After World War II, the tide of public regulation of marriage turned again. Many state legislatures rolled back age restrictions, abandoned mandatory health screening, and slowly repealed various gatekeeping regulations aimed at maintaining the moral purity of marriage. For example, until 1991, Louisiana law barred subsequent marriage between an adulterer and his or her "accomplice in adultery." La. Civ. Code Ann. art. 161 (repealed 1991).

A. FREEDOM TO MARRY THE PERSON ONE LOVES: RACE

The Supreme Court's recognition in *Griswold v. Connecticut* (a principal case in Chapter 1) of a constitutional right of privacy within marriage contributed to the trend toward greater deregulation. 381 U.S. 479 (1965). The trend was also fueled through the political process. By the mid-1960s, for example, most states had repealed their anti-miscegenation laws. In 1948, in a pioneering decision, the California Supreme Court held that the state's anti-miscegenation law violated the fundamental right to marry and the Equal Protection Clause of the U.S. Constitution. *Perez v.*

Lippold, 198 P.2d 17 (Cal. 1948). In the years following *Brown v. Board of Education,* 347 U.S. 483 (1954), which held that separate but equal in public education violated the Equal Protection Clause, a number of states repealed their laws. However, 16 states retained such laws when the Supreme Court heard our next case. This was the first Supreme Court decision to strike down a state restriction on who could marry.

takeaway: A state may not restrict marriages between persons solely on the bars of race under the equal protection and due process clauses of the 14th Amendment.

LOVING V. VIRGINIA

Supreme Court of the United States, 1967.
388 U.S. 1.

MR. CHIEF JUSTICE WARREN delivered the opinion of the Court.

* * *

In June 1958, two residents of Virginia, Mildred Jeter, a Negro woman, and Richard Loving, a white man, were married in the District of Columbia pursuant to its laws. Shortly after their marriage, the Lovings returned to Virginia and established their marital abode in Caroline County. At the October Term, 1958, of the Circuit Court of Caroline County, a grand jury issued an indictment charging the Lovings with violating Virginia's ban on interracial marriages. On January 6, 1959, the Lovings pleaded guilty to the charge and were sentenced to one year in jail; however, the trial judge suspended the sentence for a period of 25 years on the condition that the Lovings leave the State and not return to Virginia together for 25 years. He stated in an opinion that:

> "Almighty God created the races white, black, yellow, malay and red, and he placed them on separate continents. And but for the interference with his arrangement there would be no cause for such marriages. The fact that he separated the races shows that he did not intend for the races to mix."

After their convictions, the Lovings took up residence in the District of Columbia [and thereafter filed suit challenging the validity of their convictions on the ground that Virginia's law banning interracial marriage violated the Equal Protection and Due Process Clauses of the U.S. Constitution]. * * *

* * *

Virginia is now one of 16 States which prohibit and punish marriages on the basis of racial classifications. Penalties for miscegenation arose as an incident to slavery and have been common in Virginia since the colonial period. The present statutory scheme dates from the adoption of the Racial Integrity Act of 1924, passed during the period of extreme nativism which followed the end of the First World War. The central features of this Act, and current Virginia law, are the absolute prohibition of a "white person" marrying other than another "white person," a prohibition against issuing marriage licenses until the issuing official is satisfied that the applicants' statements as to their race are correct, certificates of "racial composition" to be kept by both local and state registrars, and the carrying forward of earlier prohibitions against racial intermarriage.

I.

In upholding the constitutionality of these provisions in the decision below, the Supreme Court of Appeals of Virginia referred to its 1955 decision in *Naim v. Naim*, [87 S.E.2d 749 (1955),] as stating the reasons supporting the validity of these laws. In *Naim*, the state court concluded that the State's legitimate purposes were "to preserve the racial integrity of its citizens," and to prevent "the corruption of blood," "a mongrel breed of citizens," and "the obliteration of racial pride," obviously an endorsement of the doctrine of White Supremacy. The court also reasoned that marriage has traditionally been subject to state regulation without federal intervention, and, consequently, the regulation of marriage should be left to exclusive state control by the Tenth Amendment.

While the state court is no doubt correct in asserting that marriage is a social relation subject to the State's police power, the State does not contend in its argument before this Court that its powers to regulate marriage are unlimited notwithstanding the commands of the Fourteenth Amendment. * * * Instead, the State argues that the meaning of the Equal Protection Clause, as illuminated by the statements of the Framers, is only that state penal laws containing an interracial element as part of the definition of the offense must apply equally to whites and Negroes in the sense that members of each race are punished to the same degree. Thus, the State contends that, because its miscegenation statutes punish equally both the white and the Negro participants in an interracial marriage, these statutes, despite their reliance on racial classifications do not constitute an invidious discrimination based upon race. * * *

Because we reject the notion that the mere "equal application" of a statute containing racial classifications is enough to remove the classifications from the Fourteenth Amendment's proscription of all invidious racial discriminations, we do not accept the State's contention that these statutes should be upheld if there is any possible basis for concluding that they serve a rational purpose. * * * [In cases] involving distinctions not drawn according to race, the Court has merely asked whether there is any rational foundation for the discriminations, and has deferred to the wisdom of the state legislatures. In the case at bar, however, we deal with statutes containing racial classifications, and the fact of equal application does not immunize the statute from the very heavy burden of justification which the Fourteenth Amendment has traditionally required of state statutes drawn according to race.

* * *

There can be no question but that Virginia's miscegenation statutes rest solely upon distinctions drawn according to race. The statutes proscribe generally accepted conduct if engaged in by members of different races. Over the years, this Court has consistently repudiated "[d]istinctions between citizens solely because of their ancestry" as being "odious to a free people whose institutions are founded upon the doctrine of equality." *Hirabayashi v. United States*, 320 U.S. 81, 100 (1943). At the very least, the Equal Protection Clause demands that racial classifications, especially suspect in criminal statutes, be subjected to the "most rigid scrutiny," *Korematsu v. United States*, 323 U.S. 214, 216 (1944), and, if they are ever to be upheld, they must be shown to be necessary to the accomplishment of some permissible state objective, independent of the racial discrimination which it was the object of the Fourteenth Amendment to eliminate. * * *

There is patently no legitimate overriding purpose independent of invidious racial discrimination which justifies this classification. * * * There can be no doubt that restricting the freedom to marry solely because of racial classifications violates the central meaning of the Equal Protection Clause.

II.

These statutes also deprive the Lovings of liberty without due process of law in violation of the Due Process Clause of the Fourteenth Amendment. The freedom to marry has long been recognized as one of the vital personal rights essential to the orderly pursuit of happiness by free men.

Marriage is one of the "basic civil rights of man," fundamental to our very existence and survival. *Skinner v. State of Oklahoma*, 316 U.S. 535, 541 (1942). To deny this fundamental freedom on so unsupportable a basis as the racial classifications embodied in these statutes * * * is surely to deprive all the State's citizens of liberty without due process of law. The Fourteenth Amendment requires that the freedom of choice to marry not be restricted by invidious racial discriminations. Under our Constitution, the freedom to marry, or not marry, a person of another race resides with the individual and cannot be infringed by the State.

These convictions must be reversed. It is so ordered.

[The concurring opinion of STEWART, J., is omitted.]

NOTES AND QUESTIONS

1. *Constitutional scrutiny of state restrictions on marriage and family.* How are liberty and equality both at issue in restrictions on marriage? What role do the Fourteenth Amendment Equal Protection and Due Process Clauses play in the Court's holding? As you will see in Section C, *Loving's* twin holdings

played a central role in constitutional litigation over state bans on marriage by same-sex couples.

2.   *The* Loving *case. Loving* is one of the best-known constitutional law cases and has become "part of mainstream culture," with the story of Mildred Jeter and Richard Loving recently depicted both in the HBO documentary, *The Loving Story* (2012) and the Hollywood film, *Loving* (2016). *See* R.A. Lenhardt et al., *Foreword: Fifty Years of* Loving v. Virginia *and the Continued Pursuit of Racial Equality*, 86 Ford. L. Rev. 2625, 2727 (2018). Richard Loving and Mildred Jeter grew up together in rural Central Point, Virginia. They fell in love as teenagers with no intention of becoming civil rights pioneers. Professor Robert Pratt, who grew up nearby and knew their families, recounts the origins of their landmark case:

> Mildred did not know that interracial marriage was illegal in Virginia, but Richard did. This explains why, on June 2, 1958, he drove them across the Virginia state line to Washington, D.C., to be married. With their union legally validated by the District of Columbia, Mr. and Mrs. Loving returned to Central Point to live with Mildred's parents; however, their marital bliss was short-lived. Five weeks later, on July 11, their quiet life was shattered when they were awakened early in the morning as three law officers "acting on an anonymous tip" opened the unlocked door of their home, walked into their bedroom, and shined a flashlight in their faces. Caroline County Sheriff R. Garnett Brooks demanded to know what the two of them were doing in bed together. Mildred answered, "I'm his wife," while Richard pointed to the District of Columbia marriage certificate that hung on their bedroom wall. "That's no good here," Sheriff Brooks replied. He charged the couple with unlawful cohabitation, and then he and his two deputies hauled the Lovings off to a nearby jail in Bowling Green.

Robert A. Pratt, *Crossing the Color Line: A Historical Assessment and Personal Narrative of* Loving v. Virginia, 41 How. L.J. 229, 236 (1998). After their convictions and banishment from their home state, they spent five years of exile in Washington, D.C. but wanted to return to Virginia. In 1963, after Mildred Loving wrote to Attorney General Robert F. Kennedy about their situation, the ACLU took the case. It filed suit on the Lovings' behalf, and Virginia lawyers Bernard Cohen and Philip Hirschkop (a recent law graduate) argued the case before the Supreme Court. At oral argument, Cohen stated: "No matter how we articulate this, no matter which theory of the due process clause, * * * no one can articulate it better than Richard Loving, when he said to me: 'Mr. Cohen, tell the court I love my wife, and it is just unfair that I can't live with her in Virginia.' " Landmark Briefs and Arguments of the Supreme Court of the United States, Vol. 64, 971 (Philip B. Kurland & Gerhard Casper eds.,1975).

After the Supreme Court unanimously ruled in their favor, the Lovings returned to Central Point with their three children. Tragically, Richard was killed by a drunk driver shortly after the couple's 17th wedding anniversary in 1975. For the next 33 years, until her death in 2008, Mildred continued to live "in the same house that Richard built for her," generally seeking to avoid the limelight their case generated. "All we ever wanted was to get married, because we loved each other," she told Professor Pratt in 1994. "I married the only man I had ever loved, and I'm happy for the time we had together." Pratt, *Crossing the Color Line, supra,* at 243–44. For additional background, *see* Phyl Newbeck, Virginia Hasn't Always Been for Lovers: Interracial Marriage Bans and the Case of Richard and Mildred Loving (2004); Peter Wallerstein, Tell the Court I Love My Wife: Race, Marriage, and the Law—An American Story (2002).

In 2007, on the 40th anniversary of the Court's decision, Mildred Loving released a public statement that affirmed her belief in the right of couples to marry regardless of race, sex, or sexual orientation and spoke of generational changes as the "older generation's fears and prejudices have given way." Mildred Loving, Loving for All (June 12, 2007).

3. *Public attitudes about interracial marriage, then and now.* Between 1948, when California's high court struck down California's miscegenation law in *Perez, supra,* and 1965, 13 states (largely in the west) repealed their laws barring interracial marriage, but public support for the laws remained substantial. Pascoe, What Comes Naturally, *supra* at 238. A 1965 Gallup poll showed that 72% of Southern whites and 42% of Northern whites favored laws banning interracial marriage. In general, should courts consider public opinion in determining whether state laws violate the fundamental due process or equal protection right to marry? Why or why not?

In June 2017, on the 50th anniversary of *Loving,* the Pew Research Center released a report showing "more than a fivefold increase" from 1967 to 2015 in the percentage of "all U.S. newlyweds [who] had a spouse of a difference race or ethnicity"—from 3% to 17%. *Intermarriage in the U.S. 50 Years After Loving v. Virginia,* Pew Research Center (May 16, 2017). Overall, "one-in-ten married people in 2015—not just those who recently married—had a spouse of a different race or ethnicity," translating into "11 million people who were intermarried" in the United States. *Id.* at 5. The report also noted "shifting societal norms as Americans have become more accepting of marriages involving spouses of different races and ethnicities, even within their own families." *Id.* at 7.

The Pew report found that some forms of intermarriage are more common than others. "The most common racial or ethnic pairing among newlywed intermarried couples is one Hispanic and one white spouse (42%). Next most common are one white and one Asian spouse (15%) and one white and one multiracial spouse (12%)." *Id.* at 9. "The share of recently married blacks with a spouse of a different race or ethnicity has more than tripled, from 5% in 1980 to 18% in 2016." *Id.* at 11. White newlyweds have also "experienced a rapid increase in intermarriage, with rates rising from 4% to 11%," but "remain the least likely of all major racial or ethnic groups to marry someone of a different race or ethnicity." *Id.* at 5.

Media coverage of *Loving* at 50 featured human interest stories about the experiences of currently married interracial couples, as well as couples who married—or attempted to marry—before or around the time the Lovings did. *See, e.g.*, Sheryl Gay Stolberg, *The Faces of Intermarriage, 50 Years after Loving*, N.Y. Times (July 6, 2017) (collecting readers' responses to question: "Has being in an interracial relationship united or divided your family?"); Hans Lo Wang & Marisa Penalize, *Interracial Marriages Face Pushback 50 Years After Loving*, NPR Morning Edition (June 12, 2017).

Do the Pew Report's findings mirror your own perception of trends and attitudes toward intermarriage? Do you think *Loving* has affected these trends and attitudes?

B. CAN THE RIGHT TO MARRY BE ABRIDGED?

The next decision, *Zablocki v. Redhail*, illustrates that the scope of a "fundamental right" may not be clear. The standard of constitutional review is also sometimes ambiguous and defies a rigid formula or framework.

Zablocki began in September 1974, when the Milwaukee County Clerk refused to issue a marriage license to Roger Red Hail because he had failed to support a daughter he had fathered three years earlier, while he was still in high school. Indigent and unemployed, he had paid none of his $109 monthly child support obligation since admitting paternity two years earlier. As you read *Zablocki*, consider carefully the different ways in which the various Justices understand the "right to marry."

ZABLOCKI V. REDHAIL
Supreme Court of the United States, 1978.
434 U.S. 374.

MR. JUSTICE MARSHALL delivered the opinion of the Court.

At issue in this case is the constitutionality of a Wisconsin statute, Wis. Stat. § 245.10(1), (4), (5) (1973), which provides that members of a certain class of Wisconsin residents may not marry, within the State or elsewhere, without first obtaining a court order granting permission to marry. The class is defined by the statute to include any "Wisconsin resident having minor issue not in his custody and which he is under obligation to support by any court order or judgment." The statute specifies that court permission cannot be granted unless the marriage applicant submits proof of compliance with the support obligation and, in addition, demonstrates that the children covered by the support order "are not then and are not likely thereafter to become public charges." * * *

[Roger Red Hail was ineligible to marry under the statute because he was more than $3,700 in arrears on his child support obligations and, even if he had made all mandated payments, his daughter would still have qualified as a public charge. After the state denied Red Hail a marriage license, he sued and a three-judge federal district court held the statute unconstitutional.]

* * *

II.

In evaluating § 245.10(1), (4), (5) under the Equal Protection Clause, "we must first determine what burden of justification the classification created thereby must meet, by looking to the nature of the classification and the individual interests affected." *Mem'l Hosp. v. Maricopa County*, 415 U.S. 250, 253 (1974). Since our past decisions make clear that the right to marry is of fundamental importance, and since the classification at issue here significantly interferes with the exercise of that right, we believe that "critical examination" of the state interests advanced in support of the classification is required. *Scrutiny*

The leading decision of this Court on the right to marry is *Loving v. Virginia*, 388 U.S. 1 (1967). In that case, an interracial couple who had been convicted of violating Virginia's miscegenation laws challenged the statutory scheme on both equal protection and due process grounds. The Court's opinion could have rested solely on the ground that the statutes discriminated on the basis of race in violation of the Equal Protection Clause. But the Court went on to hold that the laws arbitrarily deprived the couple of a fundamental liberty protected by the Due Process Clause, the freedom to marry. * * *

Although *Loving* arose in the context of racial discrimination, prior and subsequent decisions of this Court confirm that the right to marry is of fundamental importance for all individuals. Long ago, in *Maynard v. Hill*, 125 U.S. 190 (1888), the Court characterized marriage as "the most important relation in life," and as "the foundation of the family and of society, without which there would be neither civilization nor progress." In *Meyer v. Nebraska*, 262 U.S. 390 (1923), the Court recognized that the right "to marry, establish a home and bring up children" is a central part of the liberty protected by the Due Process Clause, and in *Skinner v. Oklahoma ex rel. Williamson*, [316 U.S. 535, 541 (1942),] marriage was described as "fundamental to the very existence and survival of the race."

More recent decisions have established that the right to marry is part of the fundamental "right of privacy" implicit in the Fourteenth Amendment's Due Process Clause. In *Griswold v. Connecticut*, 381 U.S. 479 (1965), the Court observed:

> "We deal with a right of privacy older than the Bill of Rights—older than our political parties, older than our school system. Marriage is a coming together for better or for worse, hopefully enduring, and intimate to the degree of being sacred. It is an

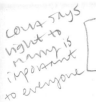

association that promotes a way of life, not causes; a harmony in living, not political faiths; a bilateral loyalty, not commercial or social projects. Yet it is an association for as noble a purpose as any involved in our prior decisions."

Id. at 486.

* * *

It is not surprising that the decision to marry has been placed on the same level of importance as decisions relating to procreation, childbirth, child rearing, and family relationships. As the facts of this case illustrate, it would make little sense to recognize a right of privacy with respect to other matters of family life and not with respect to the decision to enter the relationship that is the foundation of the family in our society. The woman whom appellee desired to marry had a fundamental right to seek an abortion of their expected child or to bring the child into life to suffer the myriad social, if not economic, disabilities that the status of illegitimacy brings. Surely, a decision to marry and raise the child in a traditional family setting must receive equivalent protection. * * *

By reaffirming the fundamental character of the right to marry, we do not mean to suggest that every state regulation which relates in any way to the incidents of or prerequisites for marriage must be subjected to rigorous scrutiny. To the contrary, reasonable regulations that do not significantly interfere with decisions to enter into the marital relationship may legitimately be imposed. *See Califano v. Jobst,* [434 U.S. 47, 55 n.12 (1977)]. The statutory classification at issue here, however, clearly does interfere directly and substantially with the right to marry.

Under the challenged statute, no Wisconsin resident in the affected class may marry * * * without a court order * * *. Some of those in the affected class, like appellee, will never be able to obtain the necessary court order, because they either lack the financial means to meet their support obligations or cannot prove that their children will not become public charges. These persons are absolutely prevented from getting married. Many others, able in theory to satisfy the statute's requirements, will be sufficiently burdened by having to do so that they will in effect be coerced into forgoing their right to marry. And even those who can be persuaded to meet the statute's requirements suffer a serious intrusion into their freedom of choice in an area in which we have held such freedom to be fundamental.[12]

---

[12] The directness and substantiality of the interference with the freedom to marry distinguish the instant case from *Califano v. Jobst.* [*Editors' Note:* The U.S. Supreme Court heard oral arguments for *Jobst* and *Zablocki* on the same day, October 4, 1977.] In *Jobst,* [434 U.S. 47 (1977),] we upheld sections of the Social Security Act providing, *inter alia,* for termination of a dependent child's benefits upon marriage to an individual not entitled to benefits under the Act. As the opinion for the Court expressly noted, the rule terminating benefits upon marriage was not "an attempt to interfere with the individual's freedom to make a decision as important as

III.

When a statutory classification significantly interferes with the exercise of a fundamental right, it cannot be upheld unless it is supported by sufficiently important state interests and is closely tailored to effectuate only those interests. Appellant asserts that two interests are served by the challenged statute: the permission-to-marry proceeding furnishes an opportunity to counsel the applicant as to the necessity of fulfilling his prior support obligations; and the welfare of the out-of-custody children is protected. We may accept for present purposes that these are legitimate and substantial interests, but, since the means selected by the State for achieving these interests unnecessarily impinge on the right to marry, the statute cannot be sustained.

* * * Even assuming that counseling does take place—a fact as to which there is no evidence in the record—this interest obviously cannot support the withholding of court permission to marry once counseling is completed.

With regard to safeguarding the welfare of the out-of-custody children, appellant's brief does not make clear the connection between the State's interest and the statute's requirements. At argument, appellant's counsel suggested that, since permission to marry cannot be granted unless the applicant shows that he has satisfied his court-determined support obligations to the prior children and that those children will not become public charges, the statute provides incentive for the applicant to make support payments to his children. This "collection device" rationale cannot justify the statute's broad infringement on the right to marry.

First, with respect to individuals who are unable to meet the statutory requirements, the statute merely prevents the applicant from getting married, without delivering any money at all into the hands of the applicant's prior children. More importantly, regardless of the applicant's ability or willingness to meet the statutory requirements, the State already has numerous other means for exacting compliance with support obligations, means that are at least as effective as the instant statute's and yet do not impinge upon the right to marry. Under Wisconsin law, whether the children are from a prior marriage or were born out of wedlock, court-determined support obligations may be enforced directly via wage assignments, civil contempt proceedings, and criminal penalties. And, if the State believes that parents of children out of their custody should be responsible for ensuring that those children do not become public charges,

marriage." The Social Security provisions placed no direct legal obstacle in the path of persons desiring to get married, and—notwithstanding our Brother REHNQUIST's imaginative recasting of the case [in dissent]—there was no evidence that the laws significantly discouraged, let alone made "practically impossible," any marriages. Indeed, the provisions had not deterred the individual who challenged the statute from getting married * * *.

this interest can be achieved by adjusting the criteria used for determining the amounts to be paid under their support orders.

There is also some suggestion that § 245.10 protects the ability of marriage applicants to meet support obligations to prior children by preventing the applicants from incurring new support obligations. But the challenged provisions of § 245.10 are grossly underinclusive with respect to this purpose, since they do not limit in any way new financial commitments by the applicant other than those arising out of the contemplated marriage. The statutory classification is substantially overinclusive as well: Given the possibility that the new spouse will actually better the applicant's financial situation, by contributing income from a job or otherwise, the statute in many cases may prevent affected individuals from improving their ability to satisfy their prior support obligations. And, though it is true that the applicant will incur support obligations to any children born during the contemplated marriage, preventing the marriage may only result in the children being born out of wedlock, as in fact occurred in appellee's case. Since the support obligation is the same whether the child is born in or out of wedlock, the net result of preventing the marriage is simply more illegitimate children.

The statutory classification * * * thus cannot be justified by the interests advanced in support of it. The judgment of the District Court is, accordingly,

Affirmed.

* * *

MR. JUSTICE STEWART, concurring in the judgment.

* * *

I do not agree with the Court that there is a "right to marry" in the constitutional sense. That right, or more accurately that privilege, is under our federal system peculiarly one to be defined and limited by state law. A State may not only "significantly interfere with decisions to enter into [the] marital relationship," but may in many circumstances absolutely prohibit it. Surely, for example, a State may legitimately say that no one can marry his or her sibling, that no one can marry who is not at least 14 years old, that no one can marry without first passing an examination for venereal disease, or that no one can marry who has a living husband or wife. But, just as surely, in regulating the intimate human relationship of marriage, there is a limit beyond which a State may not constitutionally go.

The Constitution does not specifically mention freedom to marry, but it is settled that the "liberty" protected by the Due Process Clause of the Fourteenth Amendment embraces more than those freedoms expressly enumerated in the Bill of Rights. And the decisions of this Court have made clear that freedom of personal choice in matters of marriage and family life is one of the liberties so protected.

It is evident that the Wisconsin law now before us directly abridges that freedom. The question is whether the state interests that support the abridgment can overcome the substantive protections of the Constitution.

* * *

* * * The Wisconsin law makes no allowance for the truly indigent. The State flatly denies a marriage license to anyone who cannot afford to fulfill his support obligations and keep his children from becoming wards of the State. We may assume that the State has legitimate interests in collecting delinquent support payments and in reducing its welfare load. We may also assume that, as applied to those who can afford to meet the statute's financial requirements but choose not to do so, the law advances the State's objectives in ways superior to other means available to the State. The fact remains that some people simply cannot afford to meet the statute's financial requirements. To deny these people permission to marry penalizes them for failing to do that which they cannot do. Insofar as it applies to indigents, the state law is an irrational means of achieving these objectives of the State.

As directed against either the indigent or the delinquent parent, the law is substantially more rational if viewed as a means of assuring the financial viability of future marriages. * * * But the State's legitimate concern with the financial soundness of prospective marriages must stop short of telling people they may not marry because they are too poor or because they might persist in their financial irresponsibility. * * * A legislative judgment so alien to our traditions and so offensive to our shared notions of fairness offends the Due Process Clause of the Fourteenth Amendment.

* * *

MR. JUSTICE POWELL, concurring in the judgment.

* * * I write separately because the majority's rationale sweeps too broadly in an area which traditionally has been subject to pervasive state regulation. The Court apparently would subject all state regulation which "directly and substantially" interferes with the decision to marry in a traditional family setting to "critical examination" or "compelling state interest" analysis. Presumably, "reasonable regulations that do not significantly interfere with decisions to enter into the marital relationship may legitimately be imposed." The Court does not present, however, any principled means for distinguishing between the two types of regulations. * * *

I.

On several occasions, the Court has acknowledged the importance of the marriage relationship to the maintenance of values essential to organized society. "This Court has long recognized that freedom of personal choice in matters of marriage and family life is one of the liberties protected by the Due Process Clause of the Fourteenth Amendment." *Cleveland Bd. of Educ. v. LaFleur*, 414 U.S. 632, 639–40 (1974). * * *

Thus, it is fair to say that there is a right of marital and familial privacy which places some substantive limits on the regulatory power of government. But the Court has yet to hold that all regulation touching upon marriage implicates a "fundamental right" triggering the most exacting judicial scrutiny.

The principal authority cited by the majority is *Loving v. Virginia*. Although *Loving* speaks of the "freedom to marry" as "one of the vital personal rights essential to the orderly pursuit of happiness by free men," the Court focused on the miscegenation statute before it. * * * Thus, *Loving* involved a denial of a "fundamental freedom" on a wholly unsupportable basis—the use of classifications "directly subversive of the principle of equality at the heart of the Fourteenth Amendment. . . ." It does not speak to the level of judicial scrutiny of, or governmental justification for, "supportable" restrictions on the "fundamental freedom" of individuals to marry or divorce.

In my view, analysis must start from the recognition of domestic relations as "an area that has long been regarded as a virtually exclusive province of the States." *Sosna v. Iowa*, 419 U.S. 393, 404 (1975). The marriage relation traditionally has been subject to regulation, initially by the ecclesiastical authorities, and later by the secular state. As early as *Pennoyer v. Neff*, 95 U.S. 714, 734–35 (1878), this Court noted that a State "has absolute right to prescribe the conditions upon which the marriage relation between its own citizens shall be created, and the causes for which it may be dissolved." The State, representing the collective expression of moral aspirations, has an undeniable interest in ensuring that its rules of domestic relations reflect the widely held values of its people.

> "Marriage, as creating the most important relation in life, as having more to do with the morals and civilization of a people than any other institution, has always been subject to the control of the legislature. That body prescribes the age at which parties may contract to marry, the procedure or form essential to constitute marriage, the duties and obligations it creates, its effects upon the property rights of both, present and prospective, and the acts which may constitute grounds for its dissolution."

Maynard v. Hill, 125 U.S. 190, 205 (1888).

State regulation has included bans on incest, bigamy, and homosexuality, as well as various preconditions to marriage, such as blood tests. Likewise, a showing of fault on the part of one of the partners traditionally has been a prerequisite to the dissolution of an unsuccessful union. A "compelling state purpose" inquiry would cast doubt on the network of restrictions that the States have fashioned to govern marriage and divorce.

II.

State power over domestic relations is not without constitutional limits. The Due Process Clause requires a showing of justification "when the government intrudes on choices concerning family living arrangements" in a manner which is contrary to deeply rooted traditions. Due process constraints also limit the extent to which the State may monopolize the process of ordering certain human relationships while excluding the truly indigent from that process. * * *

The Wisconsin measure in this case does not pass muster under either due process or equal protection standards. * * * The opinion of the Court amply demonstrates that the asserted counseling objective bears no relation to this statute. * * *

The so-called "collection device" rationale presents a somewhat more difficult question. * * * To the extent this restriction applies to persons who are able to make the required support payments but simply wish to shirk their moral and legal obligation, the Constitution interposes no bar to this additional collection mechanism. The vice inheres, not in the collection concept, but in the failure to make provision for those without the means to comply with child-support obligations. * * *

* * *

[The statute] tells the truly indigent, whether they have met their support obligations or not, that they may not marry so long as their children are public charges or there is a danger that their children might go on public assistance in the future. Apparently, no other jurisdiction has embraced this approach as a method of reducing the number of children on public assistance. Because the State has not established a justification for this unprecedented foreclosure of marriage to many of its citizens solely because of their indigency, I concur in the judgment of the Court.

* * *

MR. JUSTICE REHNQUIST, dissenting.

I substantially agree with my Brother POWELL's reasons for rejecting the Court's conclusion that marriage is the sort of "fundamental right" which must invariably trigger the strictest judicial scrutiny. I disagree with his imposition of an "intermediate" standard of review, which leads him to conclude that the statute, though generally valid as an "additional collection mechanism" offends the Constitution by its "failure to make provision for those without the means to comply with child-support obligations." * * * I would view this legislative judgment in the light of the traditional presumption of validity. [Under the "rational basis test," the statute] is a permissible exercise of the State's power to regulate family life and to assure the support of minor children, despite its possible imprecision in the extreme cases envisioned in the concurring opinions.

* * *

[The concurring opinions of BURGER, C.J., and STEVENS, J., are omitted.]

NOTES AND QUESTIONS

1. *Basis for the constitutional right to marry.* The Constitution's text does not specifically mention marriage or family. On what basis do *Loving* and *Zablocki* conclude that personal choices concerning marriage implicate individual "liberty" and thus warrant especially sensitive constitutional protection? Is it because the ability to marry one's chosen partner is essential to personal "happiness," as *Loving* might be read to suggest? Or is it because our country has a deeply-rooted social tradition of honoring freedom of choice in marriage, as Justice Powell suggests in his *Zablocki* concurrence? What is the significance of the choice between these rationales?

2. *What is the scope of the right to marry?* Like *Loving*, *Zablocki* has served as a building block in arguments about the existence of a fundamental right to marry—most recently, in challenges to the one man-one woman definition of marriage, discussed below. Does the *Zablocki* majority provide guidance about how to determine the scope of that right? What about Justice Powell's concurring opinion?

3. *What level of scrutiny?* What guidance does *Zablocki* give lower courts about how to evaluate a law that implicates a fundamental liberty, such as marriage? Does *Zablocki* instruct courts regarding what level of scrutiny applies to restrictions on marriage? What test does the majority apply?

4. *The interference/regulation distinction.* *Zablocki* distinguishes between statutes that "interfere directly and substantially" with the choice to marry—which require heightened constitutional scrutiny—and "reasonable regulations that do not significantly interfere" with free choice—which do not require such scrutiny. Is this a useful distinction? Into which category do you think most substantive marriage prohibitions fall? What about most formal requirements, such as the requirements to secure a license and have a ceremony officiated by a qualified person? Justice Powell criticizes the majority's differentiation among marriage regulations as unprincipled, but agrees that not all marriage restrictions should be subject to heightened scrutiny. Does he offer a principled basis for exempting "bans on incest, bigamy, and homosexuality, as well as various preconditions to marriage, such as blood tests"?

The interference/regulation distinction surfaced in *Viet Anh Vo v. Gee*, 301 F. Supp. 3d 661 (E.D. La. 2017), in which the plaintiff (Viet Anh Vo), a naturalized U.S. citizen born in an Indonesian refugee camp to Vietnamese parents and a resident of Louisiana since he was three months old, was denied a marriage license because he could not produce a verified birth certificate. Because neither Indonesian nor Vietnamese authorities recognized his birth, they never issued him a birth certificate. Louisiana provided a waiver of the birth certificate requirement only for a U.S. citizen born in the U.S. or one of its territories. The plaintiff provided the clerk with other official documents, including a Louisiana state driver's license and a social security number, but the clerk refused to issue the license. *Id.* at 663–64.

A federal district court concluded the requirement violated the plaintiff's due process rights "by denying him the fundamental right to marry." *Id.* at 666. The court observed that "[t]he current birth certificate provisions completely bar the Plaintiff from obtaining a marriage license;" under *Zablocki*, "even though states may impose reasonable regulations on marriage, [the Court] applies a strict scrutiny test when regulations 'interfere directly and substantially with the right to marry.'" *Id.* The district court also concluded that Louisiana's rule violated the Equal Protection Clause by distinguishing between U.S. citizens based on their national origin. *Id.* at 665–66.

5. *More on* Zablocki. Milwaukee Legal Services, which brought Roger Red Hail's challenge as part of its law reform efforts to benefit low-income persons, documented that in 1974, in Milwaukee County alone, the clerk denied marriage licenses to 660 applicants under Wisconsin's "permission to marry" law. Red Hail was a citizen both of the Oneida tribe and the U.S. (his last name is misspelled in the Court's opinion), and he "grew up in a close-knit but poor Indian family." The child support order set in his case ($109 per month) was "shockingly high" even given the high degree of discretion judges had at the time; by comparison, the minimum wage in Wisconsin for minors (like Red Hail) at the time was $1.45 per hour. Tonya L. Brito et al., *Chronicle of a Debt Foretold: Zablocki v. Red Hail, in* The Poverty Law Canon: Exploring the Major Cases (Marie A. Failinger & Ezra Rosser, eds. 2016). As Chapter 11 will discuss, the problem of setting realistic child support awards in the case of low-income parents remains, even though states now have child support guidelines.

6. *Prison marriages.* In *Turner v. Safley,* 482 U.S. 78 (1987), Missouri prison inmates challenged a state regulation that permitted an inmate to marry only with permission of the prison superintendent and only for "compelling reasons," such as pregnancy or childbirth. The Court applied *Zablocki* to strike down the regulation:

> It is settled that a prison inmate "retains those [constitutional] rights that are not inconsistent with his status as a prisoner or with the legitimate penological objectives of the corrections system." The right to marry, like many other rights, is subject to substantial restrictions as a result of incarceration. Many important attributes of marriage

remain, however, after taking into account the limitations imposed by prison life. First, inmate marriages, like others, are expressions of emotional support and public commitment. [Second], many religions recognize marriage as having spiritual significance * * *. Third, most inmates eventually will be released * * * and therefore most inmate marriages are formed in the expectation that they ultimately will be fully consummated. Finally, marital status often is a precondition to the receipt of government benefits (*e.g.*, Social Security benefits), property rights * * * and other, less tangible benefits (*e.g.*, legitimation of children born out of wedlock). These incidents of marriage * * * are unaffected by the fact of confinement or the pursuit of legitimate corrections goals.

Id. at 95–96.

Because the state's legitimate interests in prison security and inmate rehabilitation could be served equally effectively by alternative means having less restrictive effect on inmates' freedom to marry, the Court held that the regulation failed constitutional scrutiny even under the more deferential "reasonable relationship" test typically used to review correctional policies.

Is the Court's willingness to find a "constitutionally protected marital relationship in the prison context" consistent with Justice Powell's suggestion in *Zablocki* that the right of marriage extends where societal traditions have honored free choice?

C. THE FREEDOM TO MARRY THE PERSON ONE LOVES: GENDER

This Section considers the evolving scope of the fundamental right to marry by examining the dramatic change concerning whether same-sex couples may enter into civil marriage. The landmark decision, *Obergefell v. Hodges*, 135 S. Ct. 2584 (2015) (below), recounts some of this history.

1. Challenges to the One Man-One Woman Definition of Marriage

Until 2004, no state permitted couples of the same sex to marry. Early judicial decisions reasoned that the constitutional right to marry simply had no application to same-sex couples because marriage necessarily assumed a union of one man and one woman. For example, in 1971, an adult male couple in Minnesota sued after a clerk refused to issue them a marriage license. They contended that Minnesota's law did not expressly prohibit "same-sex marriages," but the Minnesota Supreme Court held that a "sensible reading of the statute" was that the legislature intended the "common usage" of "union between persons of the opposite sex." It further observed that such a union was as "old as the Book of Genesis." *Baker v. Nelson*, 191 N.W.2d 185, 185–86 (Minn. 1971), *appeal summarily dismissed*, 409 U.S. 810 (1972).

In subsequent years, courts continued to reject challenges by same-sex couples, made under the federal or state constitutions. *See, e.g., Dean v. District of Columbia*, 653 A.2d 307, 333 (D.C. 1995). In 1993, however, the Hawaii Supreme Court found that excluding same-sex couples from marriage was a form of sex discrimination subject to strict scrutiny under the Hawaii Constitution and remanded for consideration of whether the state had compelling grounds for that exclusion. *Baehr v. Lewin*, 852 P.2d 44, 57 (Haw. 1993). While the litigation was pending, the state passed a constitutional amendment leaving it to the legislature to define marriage. Voters approved the amendment in 1998.

In 1996, citing recent developments in Hawaii as a spur to action, Congress enacted the Defense of Marriage Act ("DOMA"). DOMA had two essential provisions. First, it stated that, for purposes of federal benefits, marriage was defined as applying only to unions between a man and a woman, regardless of whether the marriage was lawful in the state where the marriage was performed. The Supreme Court struck down this provision in *United States v. Windsor*, 570 U.S. 744, 133 S. Ct. 2675 (2013) (discussed below). The second DOMA provision made explicit that states had the authority to refuse to recognize marriages between same-sex couples that were valid in other states. Many states also enacted their own versions of DOMA, either by statute, constitutional amendment, or referenda.

Hoping to avoid adverse decisions in the federal courts, advocates for the right of same-sex couples to marry raised state constitutional claims in state courts. A significant victory came in 2003 in Massachusetts, shortly after the U.S. Supreme Court's ruling in *Lawrence v. Texas* (which you read in Chapter 1), and drew on that decision. *Goodridge v. Dep't of Pub. Health*, 798 N.E.2d 941 (Mass. 2003).[a] The state's highest court held that the state constitution required that two persons of the same sex be allowed to marry each other.

The court invoked a familiar family law concept about the state's role in marriage: "In a real sense, there are three partners to every civil marriage: two willing spouses and an approving State. * * * [T]he terms of the marriage—who may marry and what obligations, benefits, and liabilities attach to civil marriage—are set by the Commonwealth." *Id.* at 954. The court stressed that the plaintiffs' challenge concerned access to "civil marriage," not religious marriage.

The court concluded that three legislative rationales offered by Massachusetts for excluding same-sex couples from marriage did not survive constitutional challenge under rational basis review: "(1) providing

---

[a] *Editors' Note:* As discussed in Chapter 4, a constitutional challenge in Vermont led to the Vermont legislature creating civil unions for same-sex couples. Baker v. State, 744 A.2d 864 (Vt. 1999).

a 'favorable setting for procreation'; (2) ensuring the optimal setting for child rearing, * * * defined as 'a two-parent family with one parent of each sex'; and (3) preserving scarce State and private financial resources." *Id.* at 961. *Goodridge* also rejected arguments made by some *amici* that including same-sex couples in marriage would "destroy the institution of marriage as it has historically been fashioned." The court explained that "civil marriage is an evolving paradigm," and "[a]larms about the imminent erosion of the 'natural' order of marriage were sounded over the demise of antimiscegenation laws, the expansion of the rights of married women, and the introduction of 'no-fault' divorce." Yet "[m]arriage has survived all of these transformations, and we have no doubt that marriage will continue to be a vibrant and revered institution." *Id.* at 966–67.

Goodridge emphasized the numerous tangible benefits that flow from marriage and its unique emotional and symbolic importance. The state supreme court drew on *Lawrence* for the conclusion that denying marriage to same-sex couples lacked any legitimate public purpose and was therefore unconstitutional. *Id.* at 948, 959. In 2004, after the Massachusetts legislature amended the law in light of the court's ruling, Massachusetts became the first state in which same-sex couples could marry. After *Goodridge*, some state high courts upheld prohibitions against same-sex couples marrying (*e.g., Hernandez v. Robles*, 855 N.E.2d 1 (N.Y. 2006)); others struck down such laws (*e.g., Varnum v. Brien*, 764 N.W.2d 862 (Iowa 2009)). Without the spur of judicial ruling, some states (such as New Hampshire), also amended their marriage laws to allow same-sex couples to marry.

In 2008, Proposition 8 was placed on the ballot to nullify the California Supreme Court's decision that the state's ban on marriage by same-sex couples violated the couples' fundamental state constitutional right to marry. *In re Marriage Cases*, 183 P.3d 384 (Cal. 2008). (As a result, for a few weeks in October 2008, same-sex couples were able to marry in California.) In November 2008, voters approved Proposition 8, which amended the state's constitution to reinstate the ban on marriage by same-sex couples.

Same-sex couples launched a new attack in federal court, this time grounding their complaint in the federal Constitution. Prominent lawyers David Boies and Ted Olson, who had famously squared off in *Bush v. Gore*, 531 U.S. 98 (2000), teamed up to represent the plaintiffs. When California's Attorney General declined to defend the statute, the federal district court allowed persons who had been influential in passing Proposition 8 to intervene as its defenders (the court called them the "proponents").

The lower court held that Proposition 8's ban on marriage of same-sex couples denied due process and equal protection under the Fourteenth Amendment. *Perry v. Schwarzenegger*, 704 F. Supp. 2d 921, 1003–04 (N.D.

Cal. 2010). The Ninth Circuit affirmed. *Perry v. Brown,* 671 F.3d 1052 (9th Cir. 2012). The U.S. Supreme Court, however, held that the proponents lacked standing to defend Proposition 8, and it declined to address the merits. *Hollingsworth v. Perry,* 570 U.S. 693 (2013) (vacating 9th Cir. opinion).

The Court did reach the merits in *United States v. Windsor,* 570 U.S. 744 (2013), decided on the same day as *Hollingsworth. Windsor* involved a challenge to Section 3 of DOMA:

> In determining the meaning of any Act of Congress, or of any ruling, regulation, or interpretation of the various administrative bureaus and agencies of the United States, the word 'marriage' means only a legal union between one man and one woman as husband and wife, and the word 'spouse' refers only to a person of the opposite sex who is a husband or a wife.

1 U.S.C. § 7 (1996). Plaintiff Edith Windsor had been involved in a decades-long relationship with another woman, Thea Spyer, whom she ultimately married in Canada. They resided in New York, which recognized their marriage. When Spyer died, she left an estate on which federal taxes were due unless the beneficiary (Windsor) was her spouse. Citing DOMA, the IRS required Windsor to pay $363,053 in estate taxes on the ground that, under federal law, she was not Spyer's "surviving spouse." Windsor sued and prevailed in the lower federal courts as well as before the Supreme Court. *Windsor v. United States,* 833 F. Supp. 2d 394 (S.D.N.Y. 2012), *aff'd,* 699 F.3d 169 (2d Cir. 2012), *aff'd, United States v. Windsor,* 570 U.S. 744 (2013).

In the majority opinion, Justice Kennedy drew on his prior opinion in *Romer v. Evans,* 517 U.S. 620 (1996) (discussed in Chapter 1) and concluded that DOMA was unconstitutional. His *Windsor* opinion also referred to the significance of marriage and how DOMA undermines the "dignity" marriage confers:

> This status is a far-reaching legal acknowledgment of the intimate relationship between two people, a relationship deemed by the State worthy of dignity in the community equal with all other marriages. It reflects both the community's considered perspective on the historical roots of the institution of marriage and its evolving understanding of the meaning of equality.

> * * *

> DOMA's principal effect is to identify a subset of state-sanctioned marriages and make them unequal. The principal purpose is to impose inequality * * *. By this dynamic DOMA undermines both the public and private significance of state-sanctioned same-sex marriages; for it tells those couples, and all

the world, that their otherwise valid marriages are unworthy of federal recognition. This places same-sex couples in an unstable position of being in a second-tier marriage. The differentiation demeans the couple, whose moral and sexual choices the Constitution protects, see *Lawrence*, and whose relationship the State has sought to dignify. And it humiliates tens of thousands of children now being raised by same-sex couples. [It] makes it even more difficult for the children to understand the integrity and closeness of their own family and its concord with other families in their community and in their daily lives.

Windsor, 570 U.S. at 769, 772.

Justice Scalia dissented in *Windsor,* as he had in *Lawrence*, predicting that the *Windsor* majority opinion would readily be used to challenge state restrictions on marriage. 570 U.S. at 777–78, 798–99 (Scalia, J., dissenting). By the time *Obergefell v. Hodges,* the decision you are about to read, reached the Supreme Court, most lower federal courts that had considered such challenges had held, based on either equal protection or due process, that same-sex couples had a right to marry and to state recognition of their out-of-state marriages. *See Obergefell,* 135 S. Ct. at 2608–09 (Appendix A to Opinion of the Court).

In November 2014, a Circuit split finally developed when the Sixth Circuit rejected challenges to the marriage laws in four states. *DeBoer v. Snyder,* 772 F.3d 388 (6th Cir. 2014). The Supreme Court granted certiorari in the case (now named *Obergefell v. Hodges*) on two questions: "(1) whether the Fourteenth Amendment requires a State to license a marriage between two people of the same sex and (2) whether the Fourteenth Amendment requires a State to recognize a same-sex marriage licensed and performed in a State which does grant that right."

On June 26, 2015, the anniversary of the decisions in both *Lawrence* and *Windsor*, the Court announced its ruling.

2.   The *Obergefell* Decision

OBERGEFELL V. HODGES
Supreme Court of the United States, 2015.
576 U.S. ___, 135 S. Ct. 2584.

Takeaway: Same-sex marriage bans violate both the 14th Amendment Substantive Due Process and Equal Protection Clauses.

JUSTICE KENNEDY delivered the opinion of the Court.

The Constitution promises liberty to all within its reach, a liberty that includes certain specific rights that allow persons, within a lawful realm, to define and express their identity. The petitioners * * * seek to find that liberty by marrying someone of the same sex and having their marriages

Liberty to define + express their identity

deemed lawful on the same terms and conditions as marriages between persons of the opposite sex.

These cases come from Michigan, Kentucky, Ohio, and Tennessee, States that define marriage as a union between one man and one woman. The petitioners are 14 same-sex couples and two men whose same-sex partners are deceased. The respondents are state officials responsible for enforcing the laws in question. The petitioners claim the respondents violate the Fourteenth Amendment by denying them the right to marry or to have their marriages, lawfully performed in another State, given full recognition.

* * *

II

Before addressing the principles and precedents that govern these cases, it is appropriate to note the history of the subject now before the Court.

A

[T]he annals of human history reveal the transcendent importance of marriage. The lifelong union of a man and a woman always has promised nobility and dignity to all persons, without regard to their station in life. Marriage is sacred to those who live by their religions and offers unique fulfillment to those who find meaning in the secular realm. Its dynamic allows two people to find a life that could not be found alone, for a marriage becomes greater than just the two persons. Rising from the most basic human needs, marriage is essential to our most profound hopes and aspirations.

The centrality of marriage to the human condition makes it unsurprising that the institution has existed for millennia and across civilizations. Since the dawn of history, marriage has transformed strangers into relatives, binding families and societies together. * * * There are untold references to the beauty of marriage in religious and philosophical texts spanning time, cultures, and faiths, as well as in art and literature in all their forms. It is fair and necessary to say these references were based on the understanding that marriage is a union between two persons of the opposite sex.

That history is the beginning of these cases. The respondents say it should be the end as well. To them, it would demean a timeless institution if the concept and lawful status of marriage were extended to two persons of the same sex. Marriage, in their view, is by its nature a gender-differentiated union of man and woman. This view long has been held—and continues to be held—in good faith by reasonable and sincere people here and throughout the world.

The petitioners acknowledge this history but contend that these cases cannot end there. Were their intent to demean the revered idea and reality of marriage, the petitioners' claims would be of a different order. * * * To the contrary, it is the enduring importance of marriage that underlies the petitioners' contentions. * * * Far from seeking to devalue marriage, the petitioners seek it for themselves because of their respect—and need—for its privileges and responsibilities. And their immutable nature dictates that same-sex marriage is their only real path to this profound commitment.

* * * Petitioner James Obergefell, a plaintiff in the Ohio case, met John Arthur over two decades ago. They fell in love and started a life together, establishing a lasting, committed relation. In 2011, however, Arthur was diagnosed with amyotrophic lateral sclerosis, or ALS. * * * Two years ago, Obergefell and Arthur * * * resolv[ed] to marry before Arthur died. [T]hey traveled from Ohio to Maryland, where same-sex marriage was legal. It was difficult for Arthur to move, and so the couple were wed inside a medical transport plane as it remained on the tarmac in Baltimore. Three months later, Arthur died. Ohio law does not permit Obergefell to be listed as the surviving spouse on Arthur's death certificate. By statute, they must remain strangers even in death, a state-imposed separation Obergefell deems "hurtful for the rest of time." He brought suit to be shown as the surviving spouse on Arthur's death certificate.

[Descriptions of the remaining named plaintiffs are omitted.]

B

The ancient origins of marriage confirm its centrality, but it has not stood in isolation from developments in law and society. The history of marriage is one of both continuity and change. That institution * * * has evolved over time.

For example, marriage was once viewed as an arrangement by the couple's parents based on political, religious, and financial concerns; but by the time of the Nation's founding it was understood to be a voluntary contract between a man and a woman. As the role and status of women changed, the institution further evolved. Under the centuries-old doctrine of coverture, a married man and woman were treated by the State as a single, male-dominated legal entity. See 1 W. Blackstone, Commentaries on the Laws of England 430 (1765). As women gained legal, political, and property rights, and as society began to understand that women have their own equal dignity, the law of coverture was abandoned. These and other developments in the institution of marriage * * * were not mere superficial changes. Rather, they worked deep transformations in its structure, affecting aspects of marriage long viewed by many as essential. * * *

These new insights have strengthened, not weakened, the institution of marriage. Indeed, changed understandings of marriage are characteristic of a Nation where new dimensions of freedom become apparent to new generations, often through perspectives that begin in pleas or protests and then are considered in the political sphere and the judicial process.

This dynamic can be seen in the Nation's experiences with the rights of gays and lesbians. Until the mid-20th century, same-sex intimacy long had been condemned as immoral by the state itself in most Western nations, a belief often embodied in the criminal law. [M]any persons did not deem homosexuals to have dignity in their own distinct identity. A truthful declaration by same-sex couples of what was in their hearts had to remain unspoken. * * *

For much of the 20th century, moreover, homosexuality was treated as an illness. When the American Psychiatric Association published the first Diagnostic and Statistical Manual of Mental Disorders in 1952, homosexuality was classified as a mental disorder, a position adhered to until 1973. Only in more recent years have psychiatrists and others recognized that sexual orientation is both a normal expression of human sexuality and immutable.

In the late 20th century, following substantial cultural and political developments, same-sex couples began to lead more open and public lives and to establish families. * * *

This Court first gave detailed consideration to the legal status of homosexuals in *Bowers v. Hardwick* (1986). There it upheld the constitutionality of a Georgia law deemed to criminalize certain homosexual acts. Ten years later, in *Romer v. Evans* (1996), the Court invalidated an amendment to Colorado's Constitution that sought to foreclose any branch or political subdivision of the State from protecting persons against discrimination based on sexual orientation. Then, in 2003, the Court overruled *Bowers*, holding that laws making same-sex intimacy a crime "demea[n] the lives of homosexual persons." *Lawrence v. Texas.*

Against this background, the legal question of same-sex marriage arose. * * *

* * * In 2003, the Supreme Judicial Court of Massachusetts held the State's Constitution guaranteed same-sex couples the right to marry. See *Goodridge v. Department of Public Health*. After that ruling, some additional States granted marriage rights to same-sex couples, either through judicial or legislative processes.[b] [I]n *United States v. Windsor* (2013), this Court invalidated DOMA to the extent it barred the Federal

---

[b] *Editors' Note:* Justice Kennedy here refers to Appendix B, attached to his opinion, "State and Federal Judicial Decisions Addressing Same-Sex Marriage." *Obergefell,* 135 S. Ct. at 2611. Appendix A, also attached to his opinion, lists "State Legislation and Judicial Decisions Legalizing Same-Sex Marriage." *Id.* at 2608–10. These appendices are omitted here.

Government from treating same-sex marriages as valid even when they were lawful in the State where they were licensed. * * *

* * *

III   *14th Amendment Protection*

Under the Due Process Clause of the Fourteenth Amendment, no State shall "deprive any person of life, liberty, or property, without due process of law." The fundamental liberties protected by this Clause include most of the rights enumerated in the Bill of Rights. In addition these liberties extend to certain personal choices central to individual dignity and autonomy, including intimate choices that define personal identity and beliefs. See, *e.g., Eisenstadt v. Baird* (1972); *Griswold v. Connecticut* (1965).

The identification and protection of fundamental rights is an enduring part of the judicial duty to interpret the Constitution. That responsibility, however, "has not been reduced to any formula." *Poe v. Ullman* (1961) (Harlan, J., dissenting). Rather, it requires courts to exercise reasoned judgment in identifying interests of the person so fundamental that the State must accord them its respect. See *ibid.* * * * History and tradition guide and discipline this inquiry but do not set its outer boundaries. See *Lawrence.* That method respects our history and learns from it without allowing the past alone to rule the present.

The nature of injustice is that we may not always see it in our own times. The generations that wrote and ratified the Bill of Rights and the Fourteenth Amendment did not presume to know the extent of freedom in all of its dimensions, and so they entrusted to future generations a charter protecting the right of all persons to enjoy liberty as we learn its meaning. * * *

Right to marry is protected

Applying these established tenets, the Court has long held the right to marry is protected by the Constitution. In *Loving v. Virginia* (1967), which invalidated bans on interracial unions, a unanimous Court held marriage is "one of the vital personal rights essential to the orderly pursuit of happiness by free men." The Court reaffirmed that holding in *Zablocki v. Redhail* (1978), which held the right to marry was burdened by a law prohibiting fathers who were behind on child support from marrying. The Court again applied this principle in *Turner v. Safley* (1987), which held the right to marry was abridged by regulations limiting the privilege of prison inmates to marry. Over time and in other contexts, the Court has reiterated that the right to marry is fundamental under the Due Process Clause. * * *

It cannot be denied that this Court's cases describing the right to marry presumed a relationship involving opposite-sex partners. * * *

* * * In defining the right to marry [earlier] cases have identified essential attributes of that right based in history, tradition, and other

constitutional liberties inherent in this intimate bond. See, *e.g., Lawrence; Turner; Zablocki; Loving; Griswold.* And in assessing whether the force and rationale of its cases apply to same-sex couples, the Court must respect the basic reasons why the right to marry has been long protected. See, *e.g., Eisenstadt; Poe* (Harlan, J., dissenting).

[F]our principles and traditions * * * demonstrate that the reasons marriage is fundamental under the Constitution apply with equal force to same-sex couples.

A first premise of the Court's relevant precedents is that the right to personal choice regarding marriage is inherent in the concept of individual autonomy. This abiding connection between marriage and liberty is why *Loving* invalidated interracial marriage bans under the Due Process Clause. * * *

Choices about marriage shape an individual's destiny. * * *

The nature of marriage is that, through its enduring bond, two persons together can find other freedoms, such as expression, intimacy, and spirituality. This is true for all persons, whatever their sexual orientation. See *Windsor.* * * *

A second principle * * * is that the right to marry is fundamental because it supports a two-person union unlike any other in its importance to the committed individuals. * * * Suggesting that marriage is a right "older than the Bill of Rights," *Griswold* described marriage [as] * * * "an association for as noble a purpose as any involved in our prior decisions."

* * * The right to marry thus dignifies couples who "wish to define themselves by their commitment to each other." *Windsor.* Marriage responds to the universal fear that a lonely person might call out only to find no one there. It offers the hope of companionship and understanding and assurance that while both still live there will be someone to care for the other.

As this Court held in *Lawrence,* same-sex couples have the same right as opposite-sex couples to enjoy intimate association. [I]t does not follow that freedom stops there. Outlaw to outcast may be a step forward, but it does not achieve the full promise of liberty.

A third basis for protecting the right to marry is that it safeguards children and families and thus draws meaning from related rights of childrearing, procreation, and education. See *Pierce v. Society of Sisters* (1925); *Meyer v. Nebraska* (1923). The Court has recognized these connections by describing the varied rights as a unified whole: "[T]he right to 'marry, establish a home and bring up children' is a central part of the liberty protected by the Due Process Clause." *Zablocki.* * * * By giving recognition and legal structure to their parents' relationship, marriage allows children "to understand the integrity and closeness of their own family and its concord with other families in their community and in their daily lives." *Windsor*. Marriage also affords the permanency and stability important to children's best interests.

As all parties agree, many same-sex couples provide loving and nurturing homes to their children, whether biological or adopted. * * * Most States have allowed gays and lesbians to adopt, either as individuals or as couples, and many adopted and foster children have same-sex parents. This provides powerful confirmation from the law itself that gays and lesbians can create loving, supportive families.

Excluding same-sex couples from marriage thus conflicts with a central premise of the right to marry. Without the recognition, stability, and predictability marriage offers, their children suffer the stigma of knowing their families are somehow lesser. They also suffer the significant material costs of being raised by unmarried parents, relegated through no fault of their own to a more difficult and uncertain family life. The marriage laws at issue here thus harm and humiliate the children of same-sex couples. See *Windsor*.

That is not to say the right to marry is less meaningful for those who do not or cannot have children. An ability, desire, or promise to procreate is not and has not been a prerequisite for a valid marriage in any State. * * *

Fourth and finally, this Court's cases and the Nation's traditions make clear that marriage is a keystone of our social order. * * *

* * *

For that reason, just as a couple vows to support each other, so does society pledge to support the couple, offering symbolic recognition and material benefits to protect and nourish the union. Indeed, while the States are in general free to vary the benefits they confer on all married couples, they have throughout our history made marriage the basis for an expanding list of governmental rights, benefits, and responsibilities. These aspects of marital status include: taxation; inheritance and property rights; rules of intestate succession; spousal privilege in the law of evidence; hospital access; medical decision-making authority; adoption rights; the rights and benefits of survivors; birth and death certificates; professional ethics rules; campaign finance restrictions; workers' compensation benefits; health insurance; and child custody, support, and visitation rules. Valid marriage under state law is also a significant status for over a thousand provisions of federal law. See *Windsor*. The States have contributed to the fundamental character of the marriage right by placing that institution at the center of so many facets of the legal and social order.

There is no difference between same- and opposite-sex couples with respect to this principle. Yet by virtue of their exclusion from that institution, same-sex couples are denied the constellation of benefits that the States have linked to marriage. This harm results in more than just material burdens. Same-sex couples are consigned to an instability many opposite-sex couples would deem intolerable in their own lives. As the State itself makes marriage all the more precious by the significance it attaches to it, exclusion from that status has the effect of teaching that gays and lesbians are unequal in important respects. It demeans gays and lesbians for the State to lock them out of a central institution of the Nation's society. Same-sex couples, too, may aspire to the transcendent purposes of marriage and seek fulfillment in its highest meaning.

The limitation of marriage to opposite-sex couples may long have seemed natural and just, but its inconsistency with the central meaning of the fundamental right to marry is now manifest. With that knowledge must come the recognition that laws excluding same-sex couples from the marriage right impose stigma and injury of the kind prohibited by our basic charter.

Objecting that this does not reflect an appropriate framing of the issue, the respondents refer to *Washington v. Glucksberg* (1997), which called for a " 'careful description' " of fundamental rights. They assert the petitioners do not seek to exercise the right to marry but rather a new and nonexistent "right to same-sex marriage." *Glucksberg* did insist that liberty under the Due Process Clause must be defined in a most circumscribed manner, with central reference to specific historical practices. Yet while that approach may have been appropriate for the asserted right there involved (physician-assisted suicide), it is inconsistent with the approach this Court has used in discussing other fundamental rights, including marriage and intimacy. *Loving* did not ask about a "right to interracial marriage"; *Turner* did not ask about a "right of inmates to marry"; and *Zablocki* did not ask about a "right of fathers with unpaid child support duties to marry." Rather, each case inquired about the right to marry in its comprehensive sense, asking if there was a sufficient justification for excluding the relevant class from the right. * * *

That principle applies here. If rights were defined by who exercised them in the past, then received practices could serve as their own continued justification and new groups could not invoke rights once denied. This Court has rejected that approach, both with respect to the right to marry and the rights of gays and lesbians. See *Loving*; *Lawrence*.

The right to marry is fundamental as a matter of history and tradition, but rights come not from ancient sources alone. They rise, too, from a better informed understanding of how constitutional imperatives define a liberty that remains urgent in our own era. Many who deem same-sex marriage to be wrong reach that conclusion based on decent and honorable religious or philosophical premises, and neither they nor their beliefs are disparaged here. But when that sincere, personal opposition becomes enacted law and public policy, the necessary consequence is to put the imprimatur of the State itself on an exclusion that soon demeans or stigmatizes those whose own liberty is then denied. Under the Constitution, same-sex couples seek in marriage the same legal treatment as opposite-sex couples, and it would disparage their choices and diminish their personhood to deny them this right.

The right of same-sex couples to marry that is part of the liberty promised by the Fourteenth Amendment is derived, too, from that Amendment's guarantee of the equal protection of the laws. The Due Process Clause and the Equal Protection Clause are connected in a profound way, though they set forth independent principles. Rights implicit in liberty and rights secured by equal protection may rest on different precepts and are not always co-extensive, yet in some instances each may be instructive as to the meaning and reach of the other.

* * *

The Court's cases touching upon the right to marry reflect this dynamic. In *Loving* the Court invalidated a prohibition on interracial marriage under both the Equal Protection Clause and the Due Process Clause. * * * The reasons why marriage is a fundamental right became more clear and compelling from a full awareness and understanding of the hurt that resulted from laws barring interracial unions.

The synergy between the two protections is illustrated further in *Zablocki*. * * * Each concept—liberty and equal protection—leads to a stronger understanding of the other.

Indeed, in interpreting the Equal Protection Clause, the Court has recognized that new insights and societal understandings can reveal unjustified inequality within our most fundamental institutions that once passed unnoticed and unchallenged. * * * Notwithstanding the gradual erosion of the doctrine of coverture, * * * invidious sex-based classifications in marriage remained common through the mid-20th century. These classifications denied the equal dignity of men and women. One State's law, for example, provided in 1971 that "the husband is the head of the family and the wife is subject to him; her legal civil existence is merged in the husband, except so far as the law recognizes her separately, either for her own protection, or for her benefit." Ga. Code Ann. § 53–501 (1935). Responding to a new awareness, the Court invoked equal protection principles to invalidate laws imposing sex-based inequality on marriage. Like *Loving* and *Zablocki*, these precedents show the Equal Protection Clause can help to identify and correct inequalities in the institution of marriage, vindicating precepts of liberty and equality under the Constitution.

* * *

In *Lawrence* the Court acknowledged the interlocking nature of these constitutional safeguards in the context of the legal treatment of gays and lesbians. Although *Lawrence* elaborated its holding under the Due Process Clause, it acknowledged, and sought to remedy, the continuing inequality that resulted from laws making intimacy in the lives of gays and lesbians a crime * * *.

[handwritten margin note: Equal Protection Clause also protects same-sex marriage]

This dynamic also applies to same-sex marriage. It is now clear that the challenged laws burden the liberty of same-sex couples, and it must be further acknowledged that they abridge central precepts of equality. [S]ame-sex couples are denied all the benefits afforded to opposite-sex couples and are barred from exercising a fundamental right. Especially against a long history of disapproval of their relationships, this denial to same-sex couples of the right to marry works a grave and continuing harm. The imposition of this disability on gays and lesbians serves to disrespect and subordinate them. And the Equal Protection Clause, like the Due Process Clause, prohibits this unjustified infringement of the fundamental right to marry. See, *e.g., Zablocki*.

These considerations lead to the conclusion that the right to marry is a fundamental right inherent in the liberty of the person, and under the Due Process and Equal Protection Clauses of the Fourteenth Amendment couples of the same-sex may not be deprived of that right and that liberty. The Court now holds that same-sex couples may exercise the fundamental right to marry. [T]he State laws challenged by Petitioners in these cases are now held invalid to the extent they exclude same-sex couples from civil marriage on the same terms and conditions as opposite-sex couples.

IV

There may be an initial inclination in these cases to proceed with caution—to await further legislation, litigation, and debate. The respondents warn there has been insufficient democratic discourse before deciding an issue so basic as the definition of marriage. * * *

Yet there has been far more deliberation than this argument acknowledges. There have been referenda, legislative debates, and grassroots campaigns, as well as countless studies, papers, books, and other popular and scholarly writings. There has been extensive litigation in state and federal courts. * * * As more than 100 *amici* make clear in their filings, many of the central institutions in American life * * * have devoted substantial attention to the question. This has led to an enhanced understanding of the issue * * *.

Of course, the Constitution contemplates that democracy is the appropriate process for change, so long as that process does not abridge fundamental rights. * * *

The dynamic of our constitutional system is that individuals need not await legislative action before asserting a fundamental right. * * * An individual can invoke a right to constitutional protection when he or she is harmed, even if the broader public disagrees and even if the legislature refuses to act. The idea of the Constitution "was to withdraw certain subjects from the vicissitudes of political controversy, to place them beyond the reach of majorities and officials and to establish them as legal principles to be applied by the courts." *W. Va. Bd. of Ed. v. Barnette* (1943). This is why "fundamental rights may not be submitted to a vote; they depend on the outcome of no elections." *Ibid.*

* * *

This is not the first time the Court has been asked to adopt a cautious approach to recognizing and protecting fundamental rights. In *Bowers*, a bare majority upheld a law criminalizing same-sex intimacy. That approach might have been viewed as a cautious endorsement of the democratic process, which had only just begun to consider the rights of gays and lesbians. * * * Although *Bowers* was eventually repudiated in *Lawrence*, men and women were harmed in the interim, and the substantial effects of these injuries no doubt lingered long after *Bowers* was overruled. Dignitary wounds cannot always be healed with the stroke of a pen.

A ruling against same-sex couples would have the same effect—and, like *Bowers*, would be unjustified under the Fourteenth Amendment. The petitioners' stories make clear the urgency of the issue they present to the Court. * * *

* * * Were the Court to stay its hand to allow slower, case-by-case determination of the required availability of specific public benefits to same-sex couples, it still would deny gays and lesbians many rights and responsibilities intertwined with marriage.

The respondents also argue allowing same-sex couples to wed will harm marriage as an institution by leading to fewer opposite-sex marriages * * * because licensing same-sex marriage severs the connection between natural procreation and marriage. That argument, however, rests on a counterintuitive view of opposite-sex couple[s'] decision-making processes regarding marriage and parenthood. Decisions about whether to marry and raise children are based on many personal, romantic, and practical considerations; and it is unrealistic to conclude that an opposite-sex couple would choose not to marry simply because same-sex couples may do so. * * *. Indeed, * * * these cases involve only the rights of two consenting adults whose marriages would pose no risk of harm to themselves or third parties.

Finally, it must be emphasized that religions, and those who adhere to religious doctrines, may continue to advocate with utmost, sincere conviction that, by divine precepts, same-sex marriage should not be condoned. * * * The Constitution, however, does not permit the State to bar same-sex couples from marriage on the same terms as accorded to couples of the opposite sex.

V

These cases also present the question whether the Constitution requires States to recognize same-sex marriages validly performed out of State. * * *

Being married in one State but having that valid marriage denied in another is one of "the most perplexing and distressing complication[s]" in the law of domestic relations. *Williams v. North Carolina* (1942). Leaving the current state of affairs in place would maintain and promote instability and uncertainty. For some couples, even an ordinary drive into a neighboring State to visit family or friends risks causing severe hardship in the event of a spouse's hospitalization while across state lines. In light of the fact that many States already allow same-sex marriage—and hundreds of thousands of these marriages already have occurred—the disruption caused by the recognition bans is significant and ever-growing.

* * * The Court * * * hold same-sex couples may exercise the fundamental right to marry in all States. It follows that the Court also must hold—and it now does hold—that there is no lawful basis for a State to refuse to recognize a lawful same-sex marriage performed in another State on the ground of its same-sex character.

* * *

No union is more profound than marriage, for it embodies the highest ideals of love, fidelity, devotion, sacrifice, and family. In forming a marital union, two people become something greater than once they were. As some of the petitioners in these cases demonstrate, marriage embodies a love that may endure even past death. It would misunderstand these men and women to say they disrespect the idea of marriage. Their plea is that they do respect it, respect it so deeply that they seek to find its fulfillment for themselves. Their hope is not to be condemned to live in loneliness, excluded from one of civilization's oldest institutions. They ask for equal dignity in the eyes of the law. The Constitution grants them that right.

The judgment of the Court of Appeals for the Sixth Circuit is reversed.

CHIEF JUSTICE ROBERTS, with whom JUSTICE SCALIA and JUSTICE THOMAS join, dissenting.[c]

Petitioners make strong arguments rooted in social policy and considerations of fairness. They contend that same-sex couples should be allowed to affirm their love and commitment through marriage, just like opposite-sex couples. That position has undeniable appeal * * *.

But this Court is not a legislature. Under the Constitution, judges have power to say what the law is, not what it should be. * * * Although the policy arguments for extending marriage to same-sex couples may be compelling, the legal arguments for requiring such an extension are not. The fundamental right to marry does not include a right to make a State change its definition of marriage. And a State's decision to maintain the meaning of marriage that has persisted in every culture throughout human history can hardly be called irrational. In short, our Constitution does not enact any one theory of marriage. The people of a State are free to expand marriage to include same-sex couples, or to retain the historic definition.

Today, however, the Court takes the extraordinary step of ordering every State to license and recognize same-sex marriage. Many people will rejoice at this decision, and I begrudge none their celebration. But for those who believe in a government of laws, not of men, the majority's approach is deeply disheartening. Supporters of same-sex marriage have achieved considerable success persuading their fellow citizens—through the democratic process—to adopt their view. That ends today. Five lawyers have closed the debate and enacted their own vision of marriage as a matter of constitutional law. Stealing this issue from the people will for many cast a cloud over same-sex marriage, making a dramatic social change that much more difficult to accept.

The majority's decision is an act of will, not legal judgment. The right it announces has no basis in the Constitution or this Court's precedent. [T]he Court invalidates the marriage laws of more than half the States and orders the transformation of a social institution that has formed the basis of human society for millennia, for the Kalahari Bushmen and the Han Chinese, the Carthaginians and the Aztecs. Just who do we think we are?

* * *

* * * There is no serious dispute that, under our precedents, the Constitution protects a right to marry and requires States to apply their marriage laws equally. The real question in these cases is what constitutes "marriage," or—more precisely—*who decides* what constitutes "marriage"?

* * *

---

[c] *Editors' Note:* Internal divisions of Parts and subparts within each dissent have been omitted in the interests of brevity.

As the majority acknowledges, marriage "has existed for millennia and across civilizations." For all those millennia, across all those civilizations, "marriage" referred to only one relationship: the union of a man and a woman. * * *

This universal definition of marriage as the union of a man and a woman is no historical coincidence. Marriage * * * arose in the nature of things to meet a vital need: ensuring that children are conceived by a mother and father committed to raising them in the stable conditions of a lifelong relationship. * * *

The premises supporting this concept of marriage are so fundamental that they rarely require articulation. [F]or the good of children and society, sexual relations that can lead to procreation should occur only between a man and a woman committed to a lasting bond.

Society has recognized that bond as marriage. And by bestowing a respected status and material benefits on married couples, society encourages men and women to conduct sexual relations within marriage rather than without. * * *

This singular understanding of marriage has prevailed in the United States throughout our history. * * *

The Constitution itself says nothing about marriage, and the Framers thereby entrusted the States with "[t]he whole subject of the domestic relations of husband and wife." *Windsor* (quoting *In re Burrus* (1890)). There is no dispute that every State at the founding—and every State throughout our history until a dozen years ago—defined marriage in the traditional, biologically rooted way. * * * Even when state laws did not specify this definition expressly, no one doubted what they meant. * * *

This Court's precedents have repeatedly described marriage in ways that are consistent only with its traditional meaning * * *

* * *

* * * Stripped of its shiny rhetorical gloss, the majority's argument is that the Due Process Clause gives same-sex couples a fundamental right to marry because it will be good for them and for society. * * *

* * * Petitioners do not contend that their States' marriage laws violate an *enumerated* constitutional right, such as the freedom of speech protected by the First Amendment. * * * They argue instead that the laws violate a right *implied* by the Fourteenth Amendment's requirement that "liberty" may not be deprived without "due process of law."

* * *

* * * Our precedents have * * * insisted that judges "exercise the utmost care" in identifying implied fundamental rights, "lest the liberty

protected by the Due Process Clause be subtly transformed into the policy preferences of the Members of this Court." *Washington v. Glucksberg* (1997) * * *.

The need for restraint in administering the strong medicine of substantive due process is a lesson this Court has learned the hard way. * * *

* * * In a series of early 20th-century cases, most prominently *Lochner* [*v. New York,* 198 U.S. 45 (1905)], this Court invalidated state statutes that presented "meddlesome interferences with the rights of the individual," and "undue interference with liberty of person and freedom of contract." * * *

* * *

Eventually, the Court recognized its error and vowed not to repeat it. * * * Thus, it has become an accepted rule that the Court will not hold laws unconstitutional simply because we find them "unwise, improvident, or out of harmony with a particular school of thought." *Williamson v. Lee Optical of Okla., Inc.* (1955).

[O]ur modern substantive due process cases have stressed the need for "judicial self-restraint." * * *

* * * Expanding a right suddenly and dramatically is likely to require tearing it up from its roots. * * * The only way to ensure restraint in this delicate enterprise is "continual insistence upon respect for the teachings of history, solid recognition of the basic values that underlie our society, and wise appreciation of the great roles [of] the doctrines of federalism and separation of powers." *Griswold* (Harlan, J., concurring in judgment).

B

The majority['s] * * * aggressive application of substantive due process breaks sharply with decades of precedent and returns the Court to the unprincipled approach of *Lochner.* ⟹ Return to Lochner-era?

* * *

[T]he majority * * * relies primarily on precedents discussing the fundamental "right to marry." * * * These cases [*Loving, Zablocki,* and *Turner*] do not hold, of course, that anyone who wants to get married has a constitutional right to do so. They instead require a State to justify barriers to marriage as that institution has always been understood. * * *

None of the laws at issue in those cases purported to change the core definition of marriage as the union of a man and a woman. * * *

In short, the "right to marry" cases stand for the important but limited proposition that particular restrictions on access to marriage *as traditionally defined* violate due process. These precedents say nothing at all about a right to make a State change its definition of marriage, which is the right petitioners actually seek here. * * *

2

The majority suggests that "there are other, more instructive precedents" informing the right to marry. * * * [T]his reference seems to correspond to a line of cases discussing an implied fundamental "right of privacy." *Griswold.* * * * In the Court's view, such [criminal] laws [banning contraception] infringed the right to privacy in its most basic sense: the "right to be let alone." *Eisenstadt v. Baird;* see *Olmstead v. United States* (1928) (Brandeis, J., dissenting).

The Court also invoked the right to privacy in *Lawrence,* which * * * relied on the position that criminal sodomy laws, like bans on contraceptives, invaded privacy by inviting "unwarranted government intrusions" that "touc[h] upon the most private human conduct, sexual behavior . . . in the most private of places, the home."

* * * [T]he marriage laws at issue here involve no government intrusion. * * * Same-sex couples remain free to live together, to engage in intimate conduct, and to raise their families as they see fit. No one is "condemned to live in loneliness" by the laws challenged in these cases— no one. [T]he laws in no way interfere with the "right to be let alone."

The majority also relies on Justice Harlan's influential dissenting opinion in *Poe v. Ullman* (1961) * * * But * * * Harlan's opinion makes clear that courts implying fundamental rights * * * exercise not only "judgment" but "restraint." * * *

In sum, the privacy cases provide no support for the majority's position, because petitioners do not seek privacy. Quite the opposite, they seek public recognition of their relationships, along with corresponding government benefits. * * *

* * *

* * * The truth is that today's decision rests on nothing more than the majority's own conviction that same-sex couples should be allowed to marry because they want to, and that "it would disparage their choices and diminish their personhood to deny them this right." * * *

* * *

One immediate question invited by the majority's position is whether States may retain the definition of marriage as a union of two people. Cf. *Brown v. Buhman,* 947 F. Supp. 2d 1170 (Utah 2013), appeal pending, No. 14–4117 (CA10). [T]he majority * * * offers no reason at all why the two-person element of the core definition of marriage may be preserved while the man-woman element may not. Indeed, from the standpoint of history and tradition, a leap from opposite-sex marriage to same-sex marriage is much greater than one from a two-person union to plural unions, which have deep roots in some cultures around the world. * * *

It is striking how much of the majority's reasoning would apply with equal force to the claim of a fundamental right to plural marriage. * * * [W]hy would there be any less dignity in the bond between [sic] three people * * *? * * *

* * * Expanding marriage to include same-sex couples, the majority insists, would "pose no risk of harm to themselves or third parties." * * *

[T]his assertion of the "harm principle" sounds more in philosophy than law. * * * As Judge Henry Friendly once put it, echoing Justice Holmes's dissent in *Lochner*, the Fourteenth Amendment does not enact John Stuart Mill's On Liberty any more than it enacts Herbert Spencer's Social Statics. * * * And it certainly does not enact any one concept of marriage.

* * *

The majority * * * fails to provide even a single sentence explaining how the Equal Protection Clause supplies independent weight for its position * * *. [T]he marriage laws at issue here do not violate [that] Clause, because distinguishing between opposite-sex and same-sex couples is rationally related to the States' "legitimate state interest" in "preserving the traditional institution of marriage." *Lawrence* (O'Connor, J., concurring in judgment).

* * *

* * * Over and over, the majority exalts the role of the judiciary in delivering social change. * * *

The Court's accumulation of power * * * comes at the expense of the people. And they know it. Here and abroad, people are in the midst of a serious and thoughtful public debate on the issue of same-sex marriage. * * *

But today the Court puts a stop to all that. By deciding this question under the Constitution, the Court removes it from the realm of democratic decision. There will be consequences * * *.

* * *

* * * The majority offers a cursory assurance that it does not intend to disparage people who, as a matter of conscience, cannot accept same-sex marriage. That disclaimer is hard to square with the very next sentence, in which the majority explains that "the necessary consequence" of laws codifying the traditional definition of marriage is to "demea[n] or stigmatiz[e]" same-sex couples. * * *

* * *

I respectfully dissent.

JUSTICE SCALIA, with whom JUSTICE THOMAS joins, dissenting.

I join THE CHIEF JUSTICE'S opinion in full. I write separately to call attention to this Court's threat to American democracy.

The substance of today's decree is not of immense personal importance to me. The law can recognize as marriage whatever sexual attachments and living arrangements it wishes, and can accord them favorable civil consequences, from tax treatment to rights of inheritance.

* * * It is of overwhelming importance, however, who it is that rules me. Today's decree says that my Ruler, and the Ruler of 320 million Americans coast-to-coast, is a majority of the nine lawyers on the Supreme Court. The opinion in these cases is the furthest extension * * * of the Court's claimed power to create "liberties" that the Constitution and its Amendments neglect to mention. This practice of constitutional revision by an unelected committee of nine, always accompanied * * * by extravagant praise of liberty, robs the People of the most important liberty they asserted in the Declaration of Independence and won in the Revolution of 1776: the freedom to govern themselves.

I

* * *

The Constitution places some constraints on self-rule—constraints adopted *by the People themselves* when they ratified the Constitution and its Amendments. * * * Aside from these limitations, those powers "reserved to the States respectively, or to the people" can be exercised as the States or the People desire. These cases ask us to decide whether the Fourteenth Amendment contains a limitation that requires the States to license and recognize marriages between two people of the same sex. Does it remove *that* issue from the political process?

Of course not. * * *

* * * When the Fourteenth Amendment was ratified in 1868, every State limited marriage to one man and one woman, and no one doubted the constitutionality of doing so. That resolves these cases. [T]he public debate over same-sex marriage must be allowed to continue.

But the Court ends this debate, in an opinion lacking even a thin veneer of law. Buried beneath the mummeries and straining-to-be-memorable passages of the opinion is a candid and startling assertion: No matter *what* it was the People ratified, the Fourteenth Amendment protects those rights that the Judiciary, in its "reasoned judgment," thinks the Fourteenth Amendment ought to protect.

This is a naked judicial claim to legislative—indeed, *super-legislative*—power; a claim fundamentally at odds with our system of government. * * * A system of government that makes the People subordinate to a committee of nine unelected lawyers does not deserve to be called a democracy.

* * * And to allow the policy question of same-sex marriage to be considered and resolved by a select, patrician, highly unrepresentative panel of nine is to violate a principle even more fundamental than no taxation without representation: no social transformation without representation.

[this should not be decided by SCOTUS]

[W]hat really astounds is the hubris reflected in today's judicial Putsch. The [majority is] entirely comfortable concluding that every State violated the Constitution for all of the 135 years between the Fourteenth Amendment's ratification and Massachusetts' permitting of same-sex marriages in 2003. They have discovered in the Fourteenth Amendment a "fundamental right" overlooked by every person alive at the time of ratification, and almost everyone else in the time since. * * *

The opinion is couched in a style that is as pretentious as its content is egotistic. It is one thing for separate concurring or dissenting opinions to contain extravagances * * * of thought and expression; it is something else for the official opinion of the Court to do so. Of course the opinion's showy profundities are often profoundly incoherent. "The nature of marriage is that, through its enduring bond, two persons together can find other freedoms, such as expression, intimacy, and spirituality." (Really? Who ever thought that intimacy and spirituality [whatever that means] were freedoms? And if intimacy is, one would think Freedom of Intimacy is abridged rather than expanded by marriage. Ask the nearest hippie. * * *) * * * The world does not expect logic and precision in poetry or inspirational pop-philosophy; it demands them in the law. * * *

JUSTICE THOMAS, with whom JUSTICE SCALIA joins, dissenting.

* * *

The majority's decision today [is] largely based on a constitutional provision guaranteeing "due process" before a person is deprived of his "life, liberty, or property." I have elsewhere explained the dangerous fiction of treating the Due Process Clause as a font of substantive rights. *McDonald v. Chicago* (2010) (THOMAS, J., concurring in part and concurring in judgment). It distorts the constitutional text, which guarantees only whatever "process" is "due" before a person is deprived of life, liberty, and property. * * *

* * *

As used in the Due Process Clauses, "liberty" most likely refers to "the power of locomotion, of changing situation, or removing one's person to whatsoever place one's own inclination may direct; without imprisonment or restraint, unless by due course of law." 1 W. Blackstone, Commentaries on the Laws of England 130 (1769) (Blackstone). That definition is drawn from the historical roots of the Clauses and is consistent with our Constitution's text and structure. * * *

* * *

* * * In the American legal tradition, liberty has long been understood as individual freedom *from* governmental action, not as a right *to* a particular governmental entitlement.

* * *

[P]etitioners have been left alone to order their lives as they see fit.

* * * Nor have the States prevented petitioners from approximating a number of incidents of marriage through private legal means, such as wills, trusts, and powers of attorney.

Instead, the States have refused to grant them governmental entitlements. Petitioners claim that as a matter of "liberty," they are entitled to access privileges and benefits that exist solely *because of* the government. * * * But receiving governmental recognition and benefits has nothing to do with any understanding of "liberty" that the Framers would have recognized.

To the extent that the Framers would have recognized a natural right to marriage that fell within the broader definition of liberty, it would * * * have included a right to engage in the very same activities that petitioners have been left free to engage in—making vows, holding religious ceremonies celebrating those vows, raising children, and otherwise enjoying the society of one's spouse—without governmental interference. [S]uch conduct was understood to predate government, not to flow from it. * * * Petitioners misunderstand the institution of marriage when they say that it would "mean little" absent governmental recognition.

* * *

* * * As a philosophical matter, liberty is only freedom from governmental action, not an entitlement to governmental benefits. [A]s a constitutional matter, it is likely even narrower * * *, encompassing only freedom from physical restraint and imprisonment. * * *

* * *

[T]he majority's decision [also] threatens the religious liberty our Nation has long sought to protect.

* * *

* * * In our society, marriage is not simply a governmental institution; it is a religious institution as well. Today's decision might change the former, but it cannot change the latter. It appears all but inevitable that the two will come into conflict, particularly as individuals and churches are confronted with demands to participate in and endorse civil marriages between same-sex couples.

The majority appears unmoved by that inevitability. * * *

* * *

[H]uman dignity cannot be taken away by the government. Slaves did not lose their dignity (any more than they lost their humanity) because the government allowed them to be enslaved. Those held in internment camps did not lose their dignity because the government confined them. * * * The government cannot bestow dignity, and it cannot take it away. * * *

JUSTICE ALITO, with whom JUSTICE SCALIA and JUSTICE THOMAS join, dissenting.

Until the federal courts intervened, the American people were engaged in a debate about whether their States should recognize same-sex marriage. The question in these cases, however, is not what States *should* do about same-sex marriage but whether the Constitution answers that question for them. It does not. * * *

* * *

[T]he Court['s] * * * argument is that the fundamental purpose of marriage is to promote the well-being of those who choose to marry. * * *

This understanding of marriage, which focuses almost entirely on the happiness of persons who * * * marry, is shared by many people today, but it is not the traditional one. For millennia, marriage was inextricably linked to the one thing that only an opposite-sex couple can do: procreate.

* * *

While, for many, the attributes of marriage in 21st-century America have changed, those States that do not want to recognize same-sex marriage have not yet given up on the traditional understanding. * * * It is far beyond the outer reaches of this Court's authority to say that a State may not adhere to the understanding of marriage that has long prevailed, not just in this country and others with similar cultural roots, but also in a great variety of countries and cultures all around the globe.

* * *

Today's decision * * * will be used to vilify Americans who are unwilling to assent to the new orthodoxy. [T]he majority compares traditional marriage laws to laws that denied equal treatment for African-

Americans and women. The implications of this analogy will be exploited by those who are determined to stamp out every vestige of dissent.

* * * I assume that those who cling to old beliefs will be able to whisper their thoughts in the recesses of their homes, but if they repeat those views in public, they will risk being labeled as bigots and treated as such by governments, employers, and schools.

[T]he Nation will experience bitter and lasting wounds.

* * *

NOTES AND QUESTIONS

1. *What is marriage? Why does marriage matter?* How do the majority and the dissenters answer these basic questions? Are you persuaded by dissenting Chief Justice Roberts' argument that the "vital need" to ensure responsible procreation explains the one man-one woman definition of marriage? How does the majority opinion address this argument?

Consider how each opinion uses history and tradition in defining marriage. Is it relevant, for example, how the Kalahari Bushmen or the Aztecs defined marriage? Or that, over the millennia, marriage was often *polygamous* in form? *See* Richard A. Posner, *The Chief Justice's Dissent Is Heartless*, Slate (June 27, 2015) (characterizing as "nonsense" Chief Justice Roberts' assertion that, "for millennia * * * 'marriage' referred to only one relationship: the union of a man and a woman").

2. *What is the scope of the fundamental right to marry?* The majority opinion and the dissenting opinions provide different frameworks for defining the fundamental right to marry. Which opinion do you find more persuasive on the question of whether the petitioners are asserting a fundamental right or a new right without basis in the Constitution?

3. *Liberty and equality.* How do the different opinions view the relationship between liberty and equality—and the Fourteenth Amendment Due Process and Equal Protection Clauses—with respect to understanding the scope of the fundamental right to marry?

4. *The level of scrutiny and Equal Protection.* By the time *Obergefell* reached the Supreme Court, some federal appellate courts had struck down state laws barring same-sex couples from marriage on the basis that, under the Equal Protection Clause, classifications based on sexual orientation required heightened scrutiny—either intermediate scrutiny (which courts apply to classifications based on sex) or strict scrutiny (which courts apply to classifications based on race and to fundamental rights). Those courts ruled that such classifications could not survive challenge under any level of heightened scrutiny. *See, e.g., Baskin v. Bogan*, 766 F.3d 648 (7th Cir. 2014); *Latta v. Otter*, 771 F.3d 456 (9th Cir. 2014). Some judges had also concluded that state laws barring same-sex couples form marrying warranted heightened

scrutiny because they are a form of sex discrimination. *See id.* at 479–87 (Berzon, J., concurring).

Although the *Obergefell* majority opinion does not explicitly address these issues, it does refer to sexual orientation as "immutable." A trait's immutability is one of four criteria generally used to determine whether a classification is suspect (or quasi-suspect) such that it requires heightened scrutiny under the Equal Protection Clause.

5. *Who decides?* Chief Justice Roberts asserts that "our Constitution does not enact any one theory of marriage," and thus that "[t]he people of a State are free to expand marriage to include same-sex couples, or to retain the historic definition." Is this position compatible with recognition of a fundamental right to marry?

Does it matter whether the Court rules at the very beginning of public debate or after the debate has played out for some time and a solid majority of Americans support allowing same-sex couples to marry? *See* Justin McCarthy, *Record-High 60% of Americans Support Same-sex Marriage*, Gallup (May 19, 2015) (reporting, one month before *Obergefell* ruling, that 60% of Americans believed that marriages between same-sex couples should be recognized by law as valid, up from 55% in 2014, and 27% in 1996, first year question asked). For example, suppose this case had reached the Court in 2004, when only one state allowed same-sex couples to marry and a majority of Americans (55%) did *not* believe same-sex marriage should be valid? *Id.* Is it realistic to suggest that the Court in *Obergefell* was leading social change rather than following or consolidating it?

6. *Marriage, "dignity," and family diversity.* In declaring that "[n]o union is more profound than marriage," and in stressing the "costs [to children] of being raised by unmarried parents," what messages does Justice Kennedy's majority opinion send about family diversity and relationships other than marriage?

7. *Obergefell's impact.* In the month *Obergefell* was decided, 390,000 same sex-couples were married (38% of all same-sex couples). By October 2015, there were 486,000 married same-sex couples (45% of all same-sex couples). Gary J. Gates & Taylor N.T. Brown, *Marriage and Same-Sex Couples After Obergefell*, The Williams Institute (Nov. 2015). Two years after *Obergefell*, a Gallup survey found that "10.2 % of lesbian, gay, bisexual, or transgender adults in the U.S. are married to a same-sex spouse." David Masci et al., *Five Facts about Same-Sex Marriage*, Pew Research Center (June 26, 2017). This percentage marks an increase from the 7.9 % rate in the months prior to *Obergefell*. "[M]ost same-sex cohabiting couples (61%) are now married, up from 38% before the ruling." *Id.*

8. *The "same terms and conditions."* *Obergefell* holds that states must offer same-sex couples civil marriage "on the same terms and conditions as opposite-sex couples." As discussed further in Chapter 5, in *Pavan v. Smith*, 582 U.S. ___, 137 S. Ct. 2075, 2077 (2017) (per curiam), the Court held that the

Arkansas Department of Health's refusal to place on the child's birth certificate the name of the female spouse of a woman who gives birth is "differential treatment" that "infringes *Obergefell's* commitment to 'provide same-sex couples the constellation of benefits that the States have linked to marriage.'"

9. *Religious liberty: a clash of rights?* The dissenters warn that *Obergefell* leaves serious questions about the religious liberty of people who adhere to a traditional understanding of marriage. Do you agree? What role should religious convictions about marriage play in determining the scope of the fundamental right to marry?

In the years since *Obergefell*, a number of high-profile controversies over religious liberty or conscience objections have arisen as same-sex couples have exercised—or attempted to exercise—their right to marry. The brief discussion that follows provides a sense of the range of these contexts in which these conflicts arise.

(a) *Marriage licenses and solemnization.* As states have amended their marriage laws to extend civil marriage to same-sex couples (both before and after *Obergefell),* such laws commonly protect a form of religious liberty that would seem to go without saying under the First Amendment: clergy are not obligated to perform a marriage ceremony that conflicts with the religious beliefs of the religious organization to which they belong. But what about town clerks who argue that their religious beliefs about traditional marriage preclude them from issuing marriage licenses? Or public officials authorized to perform civil marriage ceremonies who object to doing so based on their beliefs?

Most states made efforts "to implement complete marriage equality promptly after *Obergefell* issued." Carl Tobias, *Implementing Marriage Equality in America,* 65 Duke L. J. 25, 33 (2015). Thus, state attorneys general advised clerks that *Obergefell's* language made clear "that marriage licenses must be issued to same-sex couples on the same terms and condition as opposite sex couples." *See* The Hon. Steve Womack et al., 2015 WL 490123 (2015) (Letter from Office of the Attorney General, Mississippi).

The most visible example of a clerk refusing to do so was Kim Davis, County Clerk for Rowan County, Kentucky, who expressed the view that civil marriage law—if defined to include two men or two women—was "not of God" and that to issue licenses would violate her Apostolic Christian faith. Alan Blinder & Tamar Lewin, *Clerk in Kentucky Chooses Jail Over Deal on Same-Sex Marriage,* N.Y. Times (Sept. 3, 2015). Davis appealed a federal district court's order that she allow such licenses to be issued, but her appeal of that ruling was rendered moot because the Kentucky legislature provided her relief by revising the law concerning marriage license forms. *Miller v. Davis,* 667 Fed. Appx. 537, 2016 WL 3755870 (6th Cir. 2016). Henceforth, county clerks shall "make available" the forms (rather than "issuing" them), and there is no longer a requirement that their names or signature appear on the form. Ky. Rev. Stat. Ann. § 402.100 (West 2019).

Several states now have laws providing for recusal of public officials who assert that their religious beliefs prevent them from issuing marriage licenses to, or solemnizing marriages of, same-sex couples. *See, e.g.,* N.C. Gen. Stat. § 51–5.5 (2019). The Fourth Circuit dismissed a challenge to North Carolina's recusal law on the grounds that the plaintiffs lacked standing to bring their claim. *Ansley v. Warren,* 861 F.3d 512 (4th Cir. 2017). Mississippi has a recusal provision in its "Protecting Freedom of Conscience from Government Discrimination Act" (H.B. 1523). Miss. Code Ann. § 11–62–5(8)(a) (West 2019). Mississippi's law protects a wide range of public officials and employees, religious persons and organizations, and for-profit corporations from governmental "discrimination" if they act—or refuse to act—in many contexts based on "sincerely held religious beliefs or moral convictions" that (1) marriage "is or should be recognized as the union of one man and one woman," (2) "sexual relations are properly reserved to such a marriage," and (3) being "male" or "female" is immutably fixed at birth by one's biological sex. The second protected belief would include, for example, disapproval of nonmarital sexual relations and cohabitation between heterosexual as well as same-sex couples, while the third addresses beliefs about transgender persons.

In *Barber v. Bryant,* 193 F. Supp. 3d 677 (S.D. Miss. 2016), federal district judge Carlton W. Reeves preliminarily enjoined H.B. 1523, on the ground that it violated the Establishment Clause of the First Amendment and the Fourteenth Amendment Equal Protection Clause. Judge Reeves held that by enacting H.B. 1523, Mississippi granted "special rights to citizens who hold one of three 'sincerely held religious beliefs or moral convictions' reflecting disapproval of lesbian, gay, transgender, and unmarried persons," thus putting its "thumb on the scale to favor some religious beliefs over others." *Id.* at *688.

The Fifth Circuit reversed the injunction on the ground that the plaintiffs lacked standing, and the U.S. Supreme Court rejected plaintiffs' petition for certiorari. *Barber v. Bryant,* 860 F.3d 345 (5th Cir. 2017), *cert. denied,* 138 S. Ct. 652 (2018). As a practical matter, since Mississippi law (even without H.B. 1523) does not protect LGBT persons against discrimination, it is not clear what type of injury would trigger "standing" that would allow a successful challenge to H.B. 1523—perhaps a county clerk's office refusing to issue marriage licenses to same-sex couples. *See* Samantha Allen, *SCOTUS Lets HB 1523, America's Most Anti-LGBT Law, Stay in Place,* Daily Beast (Jan. 11, 2018).

(b) *Wedding-related goods and services.* Approximately 20 states and the District of Columbia include "sexual orientation" among the categories protected by public accommodations laws, which prohibit discrimination by businesses open to the public that provide goods and services. *See State Maps of Laws and Policies: Public Accommodations,* Human Rights Campaign (2019). In recent years, some business owners have declined to provide wedding-related goods and services (including cakes, flowers, photography, and wedding and reception sites) to same-sex couples based on their religious beliefs that marriage is between one man and one woman. Generally, most state courts and administrative tribunals hearing such cases have ruled that merchants who refused to provide such goods and services violated the state law and had rejected arguments that such laws unconstitutionally infringed upon, and failed to reasonably accommodate, the business owner's free exercise of religion or freedom of speech.

On June 4, 2018, the U.S. Supreme Court announced its much-anticipated opinion in the closely-watched case of Colorado baker (or "cake artist"), Jack Phillips. *Masterpiece Cakeshop, Ltd. v. Colorado Civil Rights Commission,* 584 U.S. ___, 138 S. Ct. 1719 (2018). In 2012, Phillips, owner of Masterpiece Cakeshop, declined to bake a cake for Charlie Craig and David Mullins's wedding reception because of his store policy, based on his religious beliefs, not to prepare wedding cakes for same-sex couples. The couple filed charges with the Colorado Civil Rights Division under the Colorado Antidiscrimination Act ("CADA"). Both an Administrative Law Judge and the Colorado Civil Rights Commission ruled (1) that Phillips violated CADA and (2) that denying Phillips an exemption did not violate his free exercise of religion. The Colorado Court of Appeals affirmed. *Craig v. Masterpiece Cakeshop,* 370 P.3d 272 (Colo. Ct. App. 2015), *rev'd,* 584 U.S. ___ (2018).

In a narrowly-written majority (7–2) opinion, Justice Kennedy reversed the Colorado Court of Appeals because the CCRC showed "hostility" toward Phillips's religious beliefs and this hostility was "inconsistent with the First Amendment's guarantee that our laws be applied in a manner that is neutral toward religion." *Id.* at 1732. Justice Kennedy focused particularly on a critical remark one Commissioner made about the appeal to religious beliefs to justify discrimination and on the contrast between the Commission's treatment of Phillips and of three other bakers who refused to create a requested cake expressing disapproval of same-sex marriage. *Id.* at 1729–32.

Justice Kagan (joined by Justice Breyer) concurred, pointing out how the CCRC could have applied CADA against Phillips in a manner "untainted by any bias against a religious belief." *Id.* at 1732–34. Justice Ginsburg (joined by Justice Sotomayor) dissented, arguing that Colorado officials did not show hostility toward Phillips. *Id.* at 1748–49. In a concurring opinion, Justice Gorsuch disagreed with both Kagan and Ginsburg, arguing no "after-the-fact maneuvering by our colleagues could save the Commission." *Id.* at 1737.

As the following excerpt indicates, the majority opinion did not, as some feared, call into question the legitimacy of state antidiscrimination law. Nor did the Court rule that such laws violated the Constitution unless they provide broad conscience-based exemptions. In setting aside the Commission's order against Phillips on the ground of "hostility, the Court postponed to "later cases" how best to resolve the many "difficult" and "delicate" questions the case raised. The following excerpt gives a sense of the majority opinion:

> Our society has come to the recognition that gay persons and gay couples cannot be treated as social outcasts or as inferior in dignity and worth. For that reason the laws and the Constitution can, and in some instances must, protect them in the exercise of their civil rights. The exercise of their freedom on terms equal to others must be given

great weight and respect by the courts. At the same time, the religious and philosophical objections to gay marriage are protected views and in some instances protected forms of expression. As this Court observed in Obergefell v. Hodges, 576 U.S. ___ (2015), "[t]he First Amendment ensures that religious organizations and persons are given proper protection as they seek to teach the principles that are so fulfilling and so central to their lives and faiths." Nevertheless, while those religious and philosophical objections are protected, it is a general rule that such objections do not allow business owners and other actors in the economy and in society to deny protected persons equal access to goods and services under a neutral and generally applicable public accommodations law. See Newman v. Piggie Park Enterprises, Inc., 390 U.S. 400, 402 n.5 (1968) (per curiam) * * *.

When it comes to weddings, it can be assumed that a member of the clergy who objects to gay marriage on moral and religious grounds could not be compelled to perform the ceremony without denial of his or her right to the free exercise of religion. This refusal would be well understood in our constitutional order as an exercise of religion, an exercise that gay persons could recognize and accept without serious diminishment to their own dignity and worth. Yet if that exception were not confined, then a long list of persons who provide goods and services for marriages and weddings might refuse to do so for gay persons, thus resulting in a community-wide stigma inconsistent with the history and dynamics of civil rights laws that ensure equal access to goods, services, and public accommodations.

It is unexceptional that Colorado law can protect gay persons, just as it can protect other classes of individuals, in acquiring whatever products and services they choose on the same terms and conditions as are offered to other members of the public.

* * *

The outcome of cases like this in other circumstances must await further elaboration in the courts, all in the context of recognizing that these disputes must be resolved with tolerance, without undue disrespect to sincere religious beliefs, and without subjecting gay persons to indignities when they seek goods and services in an open market.

Masterpiece Cakeshop, 138 S. Ct. at 1727–28, 1732.

On June 27, 2018, Justice Kennedy announced his retirement. Since Kennedy authored all of the Court's prior landmark gay rights opinions, including *Lawrence v. Texas* and *Obergefell,* that news introduced further uncertainty about the resolution of "future cases," should they reach a post-Kennedy Supreme Court. *See* Adam Liptak, *In Influence If Not in Title, This Has Been the Kennedy Court,* N.Y. Times (June 27, 2018). Kennedy's replacement by Judge Brett Kavanaugh added to that uncertainty.

10. *Same-sex marriage in global context.* In 2000, the Netherlands became the first country to legalize same-sex marriage. As this book goes to press, 27 out of 195 countries have enacted laws permitting same-sex couples to marry. Elisa Tang, *Here are the 27 Countries Where Same-sex Marriage Is Officially Legal,* CNN (June 22, 2018); *see also* Pew Research Center, *Gay Marriage Around the World* (Dec. 8, 2017). As chapter 4 discusses, in some countries alternative legal statuses (such as registered partnerships) are available.

2. POLYGAMY: THE NEXT FRONTIER?

Does the Court's evolving interpretation of the scope of the fundamental right to marry warrant reconsideration of the prohibition on plural marriage? Every jurisdiction in the United States prohibits *bigamy,* or legal marriage to more than one person. Some state prohibitions extend further, as our principal case (from Utah) will illustrate. As you read this Section, consider whether Chief Justice Roberts is right that the majority's reasoning in *Obergefell* immediately provokes the question of "whether States may retain the definition of marriage as a union of two people." 135 S. Ct. at 2621.

A. INTRODUCTION: POLYGAMY IN HISTORICAL AND CONTEMPORARY CONTEXT

Although *polygamy* means marriage to more than one spouse, polygamy historically has most often taken the form of *polygyny,* the marriage of one man to more than one woman. Far less common is *polyandry,* the marriage of one woman to more than one man. Almost "85 per cent of societies in the anthropological record permit men to marry multiple wives," and plural marriage is often "positively associated with status, wealth or nobility." Joseph Henrich et al., *The Puzzle of Monogamous Marriage,* 367 The Royal Society 657 (2012). A United Nations report indicates that in 2009, "at the national level, polygamy was legal or generally accepted in 33 or legal for some group of people in 41 countries, 18 of which were in Africa and 21 in Asia." *See Population Facts: World Marriage Patterns,* United Nations Department of Economic and Social Affairs: Population Division (Dec. 2011). Demographic and health surveys conducted between 2000 and 2010 reveal that "in 26 countries with data on polygamy, between 10 percent and 53 percent of women aged 15–49 had co-wives." *Id.* at 4.

In the American experience, polygamy is most closely associated with the Church of Jesus Christ of Latter-Day Saints, also referred to (until recently) as the Mormon Church. *See* Julia Jacobs, *Stop Saying "Mormon," Church Leader Says. But Is the Real Name Too Long?,* N.Y. Times (Aug. 18, 2018). In 1831, founder Joseph Smith announced plural marriage as a religious principle. The practice continued under Brigham Young's leadership, but in 1890, the Church leadership announced a new divine revelation "withdrawing the command to practice plural marriage." *Polygamy: Latter-day Saints and the Practice of Plural Marriage,* The Church of Jesus Christ of Latter-day Saints: Newsroom (n.d.). At that time, Congress had criminalized polygamy in the U.S. territories and ultimately compelled Utah to prohibit the practice as a condition of statehood.

Reynolds case

In *Reynolds v. United States,* 98 U.S. 145 (1878), the Court upheld the criminalization of polygamy against a claim that it punished religious conduct in violation of the First Amendment. It was here that "the Court first staked out a national commitment to monogamy as constitutive of life in civilized societies." Mark A. Brandon, States of Union: Family and Change in the American Constitutional Order 205 (2013). The Court reasoned that the Free Exercise Clause entitled polygamists to *believe* in polygamy as a tenet of their faith but not to *act* on that belief if the conduct would otherwise be "in violation of social duties or subversive of good order." *Reynolds,* 98 U.S. at 164. The Court asserted: "Polygamy has always been odious among the northern and western nations of Europe, and, until the establishment of the Mormon Church, was almost exclusively a feature of the life of Asiatic and of African people." *Id.* The Court further stated that "polygamy leads to the patriarchal principle, * * * which, when applied to large communities, fetters the people in stationary despotism"—a principle that "cannot long exist in connection to monogamy." *Id.* at 166.

Reynolds reasoning

The Church of Jesus Christ of Latter-Day Saints has prohibited the practice of polygamy for over 100 years. However, an estimated 30,000 to 100,000 persons in breakaway groups, such as the Fundamentalist Church of Jesus Christ of Latter-Day Saints ("FLDS"), continue to practice polygamy, clustered mostly in rural settlements in Western states such as Arizona and Utah. Philip L. Kilbride & Douglas R. Page, Plural Marriage For Our Times: A Reinvented Option? 3 (2012). The practice of polygamy may also be growing among some African-American and immigrant Muslim families in East Coast cities and beyond. Adrienne D. Davis, *Regulating Polygamy: Intimacy, Default Rules, and Bargaining for Equality,* 110 Colum. L. Rev. 1955, 1974 (2010).

Distinct from polygamy is *polyamory,* or having more than one consensual sexual or emotional relationship at once. No comprehensive statistics are available, but a 2016 study found that "one in five people in the U.S. engage in some form of consensual nonmonogamy throughout their lives." Samantha Cooney, *What Monogamous Couples Can Learn From Polyamorous Relationships, According to Experts,* Time (Aug. 27, 2018).

For more than half a century, law enforcement officials have generally refrained from vigorous pursuit or prosecution of polygamists. There have been some highly publicized exceptions. For example, Utah prosecuted

Thomas Green after multiple television appearances discussing his plural marriages—including at least one to a 13-year-old girl. *See State v. Green*, 99 P.3d 820 (Utah 2004) (upholding Green's conviction for criminal nonsupport of his 25 children and four counts of bigamy). In 2011, a Texas jury convicted Warren Jeffs, then-president of FLDS, to life in prison plus twenty years for sexually assaulting two girls who he claimed were his "spiritual wives." *Polygamous Leader Warren Jeffs Sentenced to Life in Prison*, CNN (Aug. 10, 2011). (Jeffs had also been on the FBI's Ten Most Wanted List for fleeing after charges of arranging polygamous marriages with underage girls.) Utah's attorney general has an official policy of declining to enforce Utah's bigamy statute against consenting adults, and of prosecuting only cases that involve inducing marriage under false pretenses or another crime or a relationship with a person under 18. *See, e.g., Brown v. Buhman*, 947 F. Supp. 2d 1170, 1216 (D. Utah 2013), *vacated as moot*, 822 F.3d 1151 (10th Cir. 2016), *cert. denied*, 137 U.S. 828 (2017) (describing policy).

Polygamy has also become more publicly visible through popular representation on television, first, in the fictional HBO series *Big Love* and second, in the reality television show *Sister Wives*, about Kody Brown and his multiple wives. After *Sister Wives* premiered in 2010, Utah prosecutors began a criminal investigation. Although they declined to prosecute, they stated that Brown and his wives were "committing crimes every night on television." *See Brown*, 947 F. Supp. 2d at 1179. Subsequently, the Browns (with the aid of law professor Jonathan Turley) sued in federal district court, challenging the constitutionality of Utah's bigamy law on numerous grounds, including "liberty" under the Fourteenth Amendment's Due Process Clause and the free exercise of religion under the First Amendment. *Id.* at 1176.

Several years before the Browns brought their federal challenge, Utah's highest court—in our next case—rejected a challenge to the bigamy law brought under both the Utah and federal constitutions. As you read the majority and dissenting opinions, consider which you find more persuasive in interpreting decisions such as *Lawrence* and whether *Obergefell* bears on the constitutional issues raised by Mr. Holm.

B. CONTEMPORARY CONSTITUTIONAL CHALLENGES TO THE BAR ON POLYGAMY

> ### STATE V. HOLM
> Supreme Court of Utah, 2006.
> 137 P.3d 726.

[handwritten: TAKEAWAY: entering into more than one marriage is bigamy and is NOT protected under Utah Law or the US Constitution]

DURRANT, JUSTICE:

In this case, we are asked to determine whether Rodney Hans Holm was appropriately convicted for bigamy and unlawful sexual conduct with a minor. * * * *[handwritten: Issue]*

BACKGROUND

Holm was legally married to Suzie Stubbs in 1986. Subsequent to this marriage, Holm, a member of the Fundamentalist Church of Jesus Christ of Latter-day Saints (the "FLDS Church"), participated in a religious marriage ceremony with Wendy Holm. Then, when Rodney Holm was thirty-two, he participated in another religious marriage ceremony with then-sixteen-year-old Ruth Stubbs, Suzie Stubbs's sister. After the ceremony, Ruth moved into Holm's house, where her sister Suzie Stubbs, Wendy Holm, and their children also resided. By the time Ruth turned eighteen, she had conceived two children with Holm, the second of which was born approximately three months after her eighteenth birthday.

* * *

At trial, Ruth Stubbs testified that although she knew that the marriage was not a legal civil marriage under the law, she believed that she was married. Stubbs's testimony included a description of the ceremony she had participated in with Holm. Stubbs testified that, at the ceremony, she had answered "I do" to the following question:

> Do you, Sister [Stubbs], take Brother [Holm] by the right hand, and give yourself to him to be his lawful and wedded wife for time and all eternity, with a covenant and promise on your part, that you will fulfill all the laws, rites and ordinances pertaining to this holy bond of matrimony in the new and everlasting covenant, doing this in the presence of God, angels, and these witnesses, of your own free will and choice?

Stubbs testified that she had worn a white dress, which she considered a wedding dress; that she and Holm exchanged vows; that Warren Jeffs, a religious leader in the FLDS religion, conducted the ceremony; that other church members and members of Holm's family attended the ceremony; and that photographs were taken of Holm, Stubbs, and their guests who attended the ceremony.

Stubbs also testified about her relationship with Holm after the ceremony. She testified that she had moved in with Holm; that Holm had provided, at least in part, for Stubbs and their children; and that she and Holm had "regularly" engaged in sexual intercourse at the house in Hildale, Utah. Evidence was also introduced at trial that Holm and Stubbs "regarded each other as husband and wife."

* * *

[Holm was convicted of one count of bigamy and three counts of unlawful sexual contact with a 16- or 17-year-old based on his relationship with Ruth Stubbs.] * * * The trial court sentenced Holm to up to five years in state prison on each conviction, to be served concurrently, and imposed a $3,000 fine. Both the prison time and the fine were suspended in exchange for three years on probation, one year in the county jail with work release, and two hundred hours of community service.

Holm appealed his conviction on all charges. * * *

* * *

ANALYSIS

* * *

I.   WE AFFIRM HOLM'S CONVICTION FOR BIGAMY

Holm was convicted pursuant to Utah's bigamy statute, which provides that "[a] person is guilty of bigamy when, knowing he has a husband or wife or knowing the other person has a husband or wife, the person purports to marry another person or cohabits with another person." Utah Code Ann. § 76–7–101 (2003). The jury weighing the case against Holm indicated on a special verdict form its conclusion that Holm had both "purported to marry another person" and "cohabited with another person" knowing that he already had a wife.

* * * First, Holm argues that his conviction under the "purports to marry" prong of the bigamy statute was improper as a matter of statutory interpretation. Specifically, Holm argues that he did not "purport to marry" Ruth Stubbs, as that phrase is used in the bigamy statute, because the word "marry" in subsection 76–7–101(1) refers only to legal marriage and neither Holm nor Stubbs contemplated that the religious ceremony solemnizing their relationship would entitle them to any of the legal benefits attendant to state-sanctioned matrimony. * * *

* * *

* * * We hold that the term "marry," as used in the bigamy statute, includes both legally recognized marriages and those that are not state-sanctioned because such a definition is supported by the plain meaning of

the term, the language of the bigamy statute and the Utah Code, and the legislative history and purpose of the bigamy statute.

First, the common usage of "marriage" supports a broader definition of that term than that asserted by Holm. The dictionary defines "marry" as "to join in marriage according to law or custom," or "to unite in close and [usually] permanent relation." * * *

* * *

Second, when we look, as we must, at the term "marry" in the context of the bigamy statute, as well as statutes in the same chapter and related chapters of the Utah Code, it is clear that the Legislature intended "marry" to be construed to include marriages that are not state-sanctioned. * * * Specifically, the bigamy statute does not require a party to enter into a second marriage (however defined) to run afoul of the statute; cohabitation alone would constitute bigamy pursuant to the statute's terms.

* * *

Third, although we need not look at other interpretive tools when the meaning of the statute is plain, our construction of "marry" is supported by the legislative history and purpose of the bigamy statute. * * * [T]he well-documented legislative history of this State's attempts to prevent the formation of polygamous unions supports our conclusion that the bigamy statute was intended to criminalize both attempts to gain legal recognition of duplicative marital relationships and attempts to form duplicative marital relationships that are not legally recognized. This court has previously recognized that the legislative purpose of the bigamy statute was to prevent "all the indicia of marriage repeated more than once." *State v. Green*, 99 P.3d 820 (Utah 2004). In *Green*, we allowed an unsolemnized marriage to serve as a predicate marriage for purposes of a bigamy prosecution. If an unlicensed, unsolemnized union can serve as the predicate marriage for a bigamy prosecution, we are constrained to conclude that an unlicensed, solemnized marriage can serve as a subsequent marriage that violates the bigamy statute.

* * *

Applying the definition of "marry" outlined above to the facts presented in this case, there can be no doubt that Holm purported to marry Stubbs. * * *

* * *

* * * The crux of marriage in our society, perhaps especially a religious marriage, is not so much the license as the solemnization, viewed in its broadest terms as the steps, whether ritualistic or not, by which two individuals commit themselves to undertake a marital relationship. Certainly Holm, as a result of his ceremony with Stubbs, would not be

entitled to any legal benefits attendant to a state-sanctioned marriage, but there is no language in the bigamy statute that implies that the presence of or desire for such benefits should be determinative of whether bigamy has been committed. Holm, by responding in the affirmative to the question placed to him by his religious leader, committed himself to undertake all the obligations of a marital relationship. The fact that the State of Utah was not invited to register or record that commitment does not change the reality that Holm and Stubbs formed a marital bond and commenced a marital relationship. The presence or absence of a state license does not alter that bond or the gravity of the commitments made by Holm and Stubbs.

Accordingly, we hold that Holm's behavior is within the ambit of our bigamy statute's "purports to marry" prong.[7] Having so concluded, we now turn to Holm's arguments attacking the constitutional legitimacy of his bigamy conviction. * * *

B. The Utah Constitution Does Not Shield Holm's Polygamous Behavior from State Prosecution

It is ironic indeed that Holm comes before this court arguing that the Utah Constitution, despite its express prohibition of polygamous marriage, actually provides greater protection to polygamous behavior than the federal constitution, which contains no such express prohibition. * * *

* * *

* * * [T]he Utah Constitution offers no protection to polygamous behavior and, in fact, shows antipathy towards it by expressly prohibiting such behavior. Specifically, article III, section 1, entitled "Religious toleration-Polygamy forbidden," states as follows: "First:—Perfect toleration of religious sentiment is guaranteed. No inhabitant of this State shall ever be molested in person or property on account of his or her mode of religious worship; but polygamous or plural marriages are forever prohibited." This language, known commonly as the "irrevocable ordinance," unambiguously removes polygamy from the realm of protected free exercise of religion. * * *

* * *

---

[7] Because we conclude that Holm's behavior violates the "purports to marry" prong of the bigamy statute, we need not reach Holm's arguments relating to the validity of the cohabitation prong. As indicated above, the jury convicted Holm under both prongs of the bigamy statute, and if, as we conclude, Holm was properly convicted pursuant to the "purports to marry" prong of the bigamy statute, it is of no consequence whether the cohabitation prong was properly applied to him.

C. Holm's Conviction Does Not Offend the Federal Constitution

* * *

Although the United States Supreme Court, in *Reynolds v. United States*, 98 U.S. 145 (1879), upheld the criminal prosecution of a religiously motivated polygamist as nonviolative of the Free Exercise Clause, Holm contends on appeal that his federal free exercise right is unduly infringed upon by his conviction in this case. Holm argues that *Reynolds* is "nothing more than a hollow relic of bygone days of fear, prejudice, and Victorian morality," and that modern free exercise jurisprudence dictates that no criminal penalty can be imposed for engaging in religiously motivated polygamy. * * *

* * * *Reynolds*, despite its age, has never been overruled by the United States Supreme Court and, in fact, has been cited by the Court with approval in several modern free exercise cases, signaling its continuing vitality. * * * As we noted in *Green*, the United States Supreme Court held in *Employment Division, Department of Human Resources v. Smith*, 494 U.S. 872 (1990), that a state may, even without furthering a compelling state interest, burden an individual's right to free exercise so long as the burden is imposed by a neutral law of general applicability. * * * In *Green*, we concluded that Utah's bigamy statute is a neutral law of general applicability and that any infringement upon the free exercise of religion occasioned by that law's application is constitutionally permissible.

* * *

Holm [further] argues that the State of Utah is foreclosed from criminalizing polygamous behavior because the freedom to engage in such behavior is a fundamental liberty interest * * *.

In arguing that his behavior is constitutionally protected as a fundamental liberty interest, Holm relies primarily on the United States Supreme Court's decision in *Lawrence v. Texas*, 539 U.S. 558 (2003). In that case, the United States Supreme Court struck down a Texas statute criminalizing homosexual sodomy, concluding that private, consensual sexual behavior is protected by the Due Process Clause of the Fourteenth Amendment. Holm argues that the liberty interest discussed in *Lawrence* is sufficiently broad to shield the type of behavior that he engages in from the intruding hand of the state. Holm misconstrues the breadth of the *Lawrence* opinion.

Despite its use of seemingly sweeping language, the holding in *Lawrence* is actually quite narrow. Specifically, the Court takes pains to limit the opinion's reach to decriminalizing private and intimate acts engaged in by consenting adult gays and lesbians. In fact, the Court went out of its way to exclude from protection conduct that causes "injury to a person or abuse of an institution the law protects." * * *

In marked contrast to the situation presented to the Court in *Lawrence*, this case implicates the public institution of marriage, an institution the law protects, and also involves a minor. In other words, this case presents the exact conduct identified by the Supreme Court in *Lawrence* as outside the scope of its holding.

[T]he behavior at issue * * * raises important questions about the State's ability to regulate marital relationships and prevent the formation and propagation of marital forms that the citizens of the State deem harmful.

* * *

The dissent states quite categorically that the State of Utah has no interest in the commencement of an intimate personal relationship so long as the participants do not present their relationship as being state-sanctioned. On the contrary, the formation of relationships that are marital in nature is of great interest to this State, no matter what the participants in or the observers of that relationship venture to name the union. * * *

* * *

[M]arital relationships serve as the building blocks of our society. The State must be able to assert some level of control over those relationships to ensure the smooth operation of laws and further the proliferation of social unions our society deems beneficial while discouraging those deemed harmful. The people of this State have declared monogamy a beneficial marital form and have also declared polygamous relationships harmful. * * *.

[T]his case features another critical distinction from *Lawrence*; namely, the involvement of a minor. Stubbs was sixteen years old at the time of her betrothal, and evidence adduced at trial indicated that she and Holm regularly engaged in sexual activity. * * *.

* * * *Lawrence* does not prevent our Legislature from prohibiting polygamous behavior. * * *

* * *

* * * Accordingly, we affirm the judgment of the trial court.

DURHAM, CHIEF JUSTICE, concurring in part and dissenting in part:

I join the majority in upholding Holm's conviction for unlawful sexual conduct with a minor. As to the remainder of its analysis, I respectfully dissent. * * *

The majority upholds Holm's criminal bigamy conviction based solely on his participation in a private religious ceremony because the form of that ceremony—though not its intent—resembled what we think of as a wedding, a ritual that serves to solemnize lawful marriages and in which the parties formally undertake the legal rights, obligations, and duties that belong to that state-approved institution. In resting its conclusion on that basis, the majority, in my view, ignores the legislature's intent that the concept of marriage in Utah law be confined to a legally recognized union. I also believe that the majority's reasoning fails to distinguish between conduct that has public import of a sort that the state may legitimately regulate and conduct of the most private nature.

* * *

I. INTERPRETATION OF "PURPORTS TO MARRY" IN SECTION 76–7–101

The majority concludes that Holm may be found guilty of "purport[ing] to marry another person" while already having a wife because he entered a religious union with Ruth Stubbs that the two of them referred to as a "marriage," even though neither believed, represented, or intended that the union would have the legal status of a state-sanctioned marriage. * * *

* * *

I do not believe it is appropriate to interpret the term "marry" when it appears in a state statute as providing what is essentially an anthropological description of human relationships. To do so is to ignore the fact that the law of our state and our nation has traditionally viewed marriage as denoting a legal status as well as a private bond.

* * *

As for the "cohabits" prong of section 76–7–101, the majority fails to explain why the breadth of that provision should conclusively determine our interpretation of the parallel "purports to marry" prong. [A]nother Utah Code provision * * * explains that Utah "recognize[s] as marriage only the legal union of a man and a woman as provided in this chapter." As a matter of simple grammatical extrapolation, if only a "legal union of a man and a woman" is "marriage," then "purporting to marry," must be purporting to enter into such a legal union.

* * *

The majority claims that "[t]he crux of marriage in our society, perhaps especially a religious marriage, is not so much the license as the solemnization" [and] alludes to the sanctification such a commitment receives when the partners participate in a religious ceremony in accord with their faith. Undoubtedly, a couple may feel it is their commitment before God that gives their relationship its legitimacy or permanence. However, it is beyond dispute that such private commitments alone, even when made before God, do not constitute "marriage" in our state or in our legal system. * * *

* * *

I next address the majority's treatment of Holm's state and federal constitutional claims and explain why I consider Holm's conviction for engaging in private religiously motivated conduct unconstitutional.

II. STATE CONSTITUTIONAL CLAIMS

* * *

B. Religious Freedom Claim

Holm essentially argues that the State may not subject him to a criminal penalty under a generally applicable criminal law for his religiously motivated practice of polygamy because imposing that penalty is inconsistent with our constitution's protection of religious freedom. The State does not dispute the sincerity of Holm's religious motivation * * *. * * *

* * *

* * * I believe that governmental burdens on religiously motivated conduct should be subject to heightened scrutiny * * *.

* * *

Applying heightened scrutiny, I conclude that imposing criminal penalties on Holm's religiously motivated entry into a religious union with Ruth Stubbs is an unconstitutional burden under our constitution's religious freedom protections. * * * I do not believe that any of the strong state interests normally served by the Utah bigamy law require that the law apply to the religiously motivated conduct at issue here—entering a religious union with more than one woman.

* * *

[T]he State has emphasized its interest in "protecting" monogamous marriage as a social institution. I agree that the state has an important interest in regulating marriage, but only insofar as marriage is understood as a legal status. In my view, the criminal bigamy statute protects marriage, as a legal union, by criminalizing the act of purporting to enter a second legal union. Such an act defrauds the state and perhaps an innocent spouse or purported partner. * * *

However, I do not believe the state's interest extends to those who enter a religious union with a second person but who do not claim to be legally married. For one thing, the cohabitation of unmarried couples, who live together "as if" they are married in the sense that they share a household and a sexually intimate relationship, is commonplace in contemporary society. Even outside the community of those who practice polygamy for religious reasons, such cohabitation may occur where one person is legally married to someone other than the person with whom he or she is cohabiting. Yet parties to such relationships are not prosecuted under the criminal bigamy statute, the criminal fornication statute, or, as far as I am aware, the criminal adultery statute, even where their conduct violates these laws.

* * *

The second state interest served by the bigamy law * * * is in preventing "marriage fraud," whereby an already-married individual fraudulently purports to enter a legal marriage with someone else, "or attempts to procure government benefits associated with marital status." * * * This interest is simply not implicated here, where no claim to the legal status of marriage has been made.

In *Green*, the court cited "protecting vulnerable individuals from exploitation and abuse" as the third state interest served by the bigamy statute. The court concluded that this was a legitimate state interest to which the criminal bigamy statute was rationally related * * *. The court rested this conclusion on the idea that perpetrators of other crimes "not unusually attendant to the practice of polygamy"—such as "incest, sexual assault, statutory rape, and failure to pay child support"—could be prosecuted for bigamy in the absence of sufficient evidence to support a conviction on these other charges. [R]eviewing this assessment in light of the heightened scrutiny I believe is called for here, I cannot conclude that the restriction that the bigamy law places on the religious freedom of all those who, for religious reasons, live with more than one woman is necessary to further the state's interest in this regard. * * *

* * *

* * * The State of Utah has criminal laws punishing incest, rape, unlawful sexual conduct with a minor, and domestic and child abuse. Any restrictions these laws place on the practice of religious polygamy are almost certainly justified. However, the broad criminalization of the religious practice itself as a means of attacking other criminal behavior is not.

* * *

III. FOURTEENTH AMENDMENT DUE PROCESS CLAIM

* * *

The majority also offers the view that "[t]he state must be able to . . . further the proliferation of social unions our society deems beneficial while discouraging those deemed harmful." The Supreme Court in *Lawrence*, however, rejected the very notion that a state can criminalize behavior merely because the majority of its citizens prefers a different form of personal relationship. * * *

* * *

I am concerned that the majority's reasoning may give the impression that the state is free to criminalize any and all forms of personal relationships that occur outside the legal union of marriage. While under *Lawrence* laws criminalizing isolated acts of sodomy are void, the majority seems to suggest that the relationships within which these acts occur may still receive criminal sanction. Following such logic, nonmarital cohabitation might also be considered to fall outside the scope of federal constitutional protection. Indeed, the act of living alone and unmarried could as easily be viewed as threatening social norms.

In my view, any such conclusions are foreclosed under *Lawrence*. Essentially, the Court's decision in *Lawrence* simply reformulates the longstanding principle that, in order to "secure individual liberty, ... certain kinds of highly personal relationships" must be given "a substantial measure of sanctuary from unjustified interference by the State." *Roberts v. U.S. Jaycees*, 468 U.S. 609, 618 (1984). Whether referred to as a right of "intimate" or "intrinsic" association, as in *Roberts*, a right to "privacy," as in *Griswold v. Connecticut*, a right to make "choices concerning family living arrangements," as in *Moore v. City of East Cleveland* (plurality), or a right to choose the nature of one's personal relationships, as in *Lawrence*, this individual liberty guarantee essentially draws a line around an individual's home and family and prevents governmental interference with what happens inside, as long as it does not involve injury or coercion or some other form of harm to individuals or to society. * * *

* * *

* * * I agree with the majority that because Holm's conduct in this case involved a minor, he is unable to prevail on his individual liberty claim under the Due Process Clause. However, I disagree with the majority's implication that the same result would apply where an individual enters a private relationship with another adult.

* * *

NOTES AND QUESTIONS

1.   *Why monogamy?* Are there persuasive contemporary justifications for barring plural marriage? Does *Holm's* majority opinion persuade you? How about the arguments in *Reynolds* about the relationship between the form of marriage and government?

2.   *How does* Obergefell *inform the scope of the right to marry?* If *Holm* had been decided after *Obergefell*, would its outcome have been different? Justice Kennedy identified four principles and traditions that show why marriage is "fundamental," and concluded that they apply equally to opposite-sex and same-sex couples. Review these principles and consider whether they

apply to plural marriages. Should polygamy's ancient roots support a due process argument that the freedom to enter polygamous marriages is implicit in the fundamental right to marry, or should the consistent ban in the United States point in the other direction?

Should public opinion about polygamy play any role in a constitutional challenge to the ban? In 2017, Gallup reported a "record high" of Americans finding polygamy morally acceptable, since it began measuring such opinion in 2003, but that record high was just 17%. Andrew Dugan, *Moral Acceptance of Polygamy at Record High—But Why?*, Gallup (July 28, 2017).

3.   *The liberty claim.* Do you find the majority or the dissent in *Holm* more persuasive in their analysis of *Lawrence* with respect to Mr. Holm's liberty claim under the Due Process Clause? Does *Lawrence* rule out basing the prohibition of polygamy on moral judgments about it? On what basis, besides tradition and morality, might polygamy be distinguished from monogamous marriage?

4.   *Polygamy and harm.* Is polygamy so closely associated with inherent harms that the state is justified in prohibiting it with both criminal and civil sanctions? In 2011, after a lengthy trial considering substantial evidence, the British Columbia Supreme Court upheld the constitutionality of Canada's criminal polygamy ban, concluding that polygamy was linked with higher rates of domestic violence and sexual abuse for women and girls, higher rates of infant mortality, the internalization by children of "harmful gender stereotypes," and "higher levels of conflict, emotional stress and tension" arising from "rivalry and jealously among co-wives." The court found a host of "pressing and substantial" state interests in monogamy and also found that Canada's international treaty obligations required it to eliminate polygamy. *In re Constitutional Question Act, R.S.B.C. 1986, c 68* (Brit. Colum. S. Ct. 2011).

Even if states have a compelling interest in preventing the types of harms found by the British Columbia court, would that interest justify banning all forms of plural marriage? Jonathan Turley contends that the harms that courts and critics of polygamy identify are present only in the "most extreme forms of polygyny" and that prohibiting polygamy impermissibly rests on moral disapproval. Jonathan Turley, *The Loadstone Rock: The Role of Harm in the Criminalization of Plural Unions*, 64 Emory L. J. 1905, 1909 (2015); *cf.* Elizabeth F. Emens, *Monogamy's Law: Compulsory Monogamy and Polyamorous Existence*, 29 N.Y.U. Rev. L. & Soc. Change 277, 283 (2004) (arguing that polyamory is a form of ethical nonmonogamy and involves relationships free from coercion or exploitation). What do you think?

Further, is it defensible to prohibit polygamy while tolerating multiple-partner intimacy outside marriage and the practice of "serial monogamy," in which persons marry multiple partners in succession?

5.   *The outcome of the* Sister Wives *case.* In 2013, Utah federal district court Judge Clark Waddoups ruled that the Utah bigamy statute's "cohabitation prong" violated the federal Constitution. *Brown,* 947 F. Supp. 2d

at 1234. In ruling in favor of the Browns' free exercise claim, Judge Waddoups applied heightened scrutiny. *Id.* at 1222. He declined to apply heightened scrutiny to their due process claim, but, invoking *Lawrence*, concluded that the statute violated Due Process under rational basis review. *Id.* at 1222–25.

Judge Waddoups substantially agreed with, and quoted from, Chief Justice Durham's *Holm* dissent. Judge Waddoups concluded that Utah could save its statute by striking the cohabitation prong and by narrowing the statute's construction along the lines that Durham proposed: defining bigamy as "the fraudulent or otherwise impermissible possession of two purportedly valid marriage licenses for the purpose of entering into more than one purportedly legal marriage." *Id.* at 1234.

In 2016, however, the Tenth Circuit vacated Judge Waddoups's opinion, ruling that he erred by reaching the merits of the Browns' claims about Utah's bigamy statute because the case was moot. *Brown v. Buhman*, 822 F.3d 1151 (10th Cir. 2016). Even assuming that the Brown family had standing to challenge Utah's law when they filed their lawsuit, they no longer suffered any "credible threat of prosecution" once the Utah County Attorney Office (UCAO) closed its investigation of the Browns and adopted an official policy (identical to that of the Utah Attorney General) that it "will bring bigamy prosecutions only against persons (1) who induce a partner to marry through misrepresentation or (2) who are suspected of committing a collateral crime such as fraud or abuse." *Id.* at 1155. The UCAO had found "no evidence of any crime by the Browns." *Id.* at 1159. Further, the Browns had moved from Utah to Nevada and indicated their intent to remain in Nevada. Thus, the Tenth Circuit concluded, Judge Waddoups should have granted the County Attorney's motion to dismiss the case as moot. In 2017, the U.S. Supreme Court denied the Browns' petition for certiorari. 137 U.S. 828 (2017).

What are the symbolic or practical effects of leaving Utah's bigamy law on the books but having law enforcement authorities enforce it only in limited circumstances?

6. *Utah's amended bigamy law.* On March 28, 2017, Utah's governor signed into law a bill modifying Utah's definition of the criminal offense of bigamy (as a third degree felony). The definition now reads: "A person is guilty of bigamy when, knowing the person has a husband or wife or knowing the other person has a husband or wife, the person purports to marry and cohabitates with the other person." H.B. 99, 2017 Gen. Sess (Utah 2017) (enacted at Chap. 442 of 2017 Utah Laws 2577). The new law also enhances the penalty for bigamy (making it a second degree felony) if the accused is also convicted of inducing marriage or bigamy under false pretenses, or of fraud, domestic abuse, child abuse, sexual abuse, human trafficking, or human smuggling. *Id.* How does this new legislative definition compare with the statutory definition in *Holm*? With Justice Waddoups' proposed construction of Utah's statute?

In April 2019, the Governor of Utah signed legislation repealing Utah's law that treated fornication (voluntary sexual intercourse between unmarried persons) as a criminal offense. S.B. 43, 63rd Leg., Gen. Sess (Utah 2019) (to be printed at 2019 Utah Laws 420) (repealing Utah Code Ann. § 76–7–104 (2019)). Will this repeal have any impact on the construction of Utah's bigamy law?

7.   *Evaluating free exercise claims to polygamy.* In 1878, *Reynolds* grounded its rejection of the Free Exercise claim partly on a distinction between religious belief (which the Court said the Constitution protected) and religiously motivated conduct (which the Court held was outside Free Exercise protection). In 1990, in *Emp't Div. v. Smith*, 494 U.S. 872 (1990), the Court held that government is not required to show a "compelling state interest" when a neutral, generally applicable law has an impact on religiously-motivated conduct. By comparison, when a law targets or shows hostility toward a particular religion, heightened scrutiny is appropriate. *See Church of Lukumi Babalu Aye v. City of Hialeah*, 508 U.S. 520 (1993) (applying strict scrutiny). Do you think laws barring plural marriage target particular religious groups?

8.   *Criminal and civil prohibitions against bigamy.* States typically maintain both criminal and civil prohibitions against bigamy. Civil law classifies bigamous marriages as void. Chief Justice Durham's dissent suggests that consenting adults might have a fundamental constitutional right to cohabit in a self-described polygamous religious "marriage" for which they did not seek legal recognition. But suppose they did seek legal recognition for a second or third marriage? In *Adgeh v. Oklahoma*, 434 Fed. Appx. 746 (10th Cir. 2011), the Tenth Circuit (citing *Reynolds*) summarily rejected as "frivolous" a man's claim that Oklahoma's bigamy law violated his legal right to have more than one wife and his First Amendment religious liberty. However, as Problem 2-1 indicates, *Obergefell* has spurred new constitutional challenges along these lines.

PROBLEM 2-1

Inspired by the Supreme Court's decision in *Obergefell* (particularly Chief Justice Roberts' dissent), Nathan Collier, legally married to Victoria Collier under Montana law, applied for a second marriage license to legally wed Christine Collier. He considered Christine his second wife and wed her in a religious ceremony in 2007, but did not then sign a marriage license because he wanted to avoid bigamy charges. *See Montana Man Seeks License for Second Wife*, CBS/AP News (July 1, 2015).

After county clerk officials declined to issue the license, the three sued in federal district court, challenging Montana's bigamy law. The complaint liberally employed language from the *Obergefell* majority opinion to allege that the four principles that show why marriage is "fundamental" apply equally to plural marriage. The federal district court dismissed the Colliers' complaint on the ground that they lacked standing to challenge Montana's law, since (similar to *Brown*) they failed to demonstrate "injury in fact," such as a credible threat of prosecution under Montana's bigamy law. *Findings and*

Recommendations of U.S. Magistrate Judge, Collier et al v. Fox et al., 2015 WL 12804521 (D. Mont. Dec. 8, 2015).

In 2016, the Colliers filed an amended complaint, once again challenging Montana's criminal law but also alleging that "denial of marriage licensure to polygamous marriage contracts denies equal protection of the law." *Complaint, Collier et al. v. Fox*, CV-15-83-SPW-CSO (D. Mont. Apr. 13, 2016). The relief they seek includes an order that defendants "issue a State-issued marriage license to Christine and Nathan Collier." *Id.* at ¶ 87, 105. The Colliers also argued that Montana's laws violate their free exercise of religion. *Id.* at ¶ 63.

A federal magistrate judge concluded that the Colliers lacked standing to challenge the criminal law, because of no credible threat of prosecution. *Collier v. Fox,* 2018 WL 1247411 (D. Mont. Feb. 22, 2018). The court also rejected the Colliers' argument that state laws barring polygamy violated the U.S. Constitution, observing that "although *Reynolds* is almost 140 years old, it is not antiquated and is still valid, binding authority." *Id.* at *8. On the other hand, the court concluded that the Colliers *did* have standing to challenge Montana's civil marriage laws prohibiting bigamous marriages because Nathan and Christine had applied for, and been denied, a marriage license. The Colliers argued that such law treated "polygamous families" unequally. *Id.* at *7.

If you were the judge assigned to hear the Colliers' challenge to Montana's civil marriage laws, how would you rule? What type of questions would you ask the Colliers and Montana public officials at a hearing or oral argument? Would your ruling depend on whether the Colliers practiced polygamy for religious reasons, or as a lifestyle choice not tethered to religious belief?

PROBLEM 2-2

If you were a state legislator considering revising your state's civil and criminal bigamy laws, what sorts of revisions would you recommend? (1) Would you support, for example, a law that allows persons to enter into legal marriage with more than one person, with all the benefits and obligations accorded "spouses" under state laws? (2) Would you support a law that allows people to enter into such marriage only if all parties were at least 18 years old and all parties consented? (3) Would you revise the criminal law to define more specifically when bigamy is a crime subject to prosecution?

3. INCESTUOUS MARRIAGE

Another long-standing restriction on who may marry is the prohibition of incestuous marriage—marriage between two people who are within a specified degree of family relationship. Incestuous sexual conduct is also punishable as a crime, although two states (New Jersey and Rhode Island) have no criminal prohibition for consensual contact between related adults. *See* Jennifer M. Collins, Ethan J. Leib & Dan Markel, *Punishing Family Status*, 88 B.U. L. Rev. 1327, 1343 & n.83 (2008). Ohio prohibits such sexual conduct when one person is the other's "natural or adoptive parent," stepparent, guardian, custodian, or in loco parentis, but does not list other family relationships. Ohio Rev. Code Ann. § 2907.03 (2019).

State marriage laws prohibit issuing marriage licenses to specified categories of relatives and treat incestuous marriages as void. There is no universal agreement among the states, however, about which family relationships qualify as sufficiently close to trigger the incest bar. The definition of incest sometimes varies within a jurisdiction depending upon whether the statute provides for criminal or civil sanctions. *See* National District Attorneys Association, Statutory Compilation Regarding Incest Statutes (Mar. 2013).

At its core, the crime of incest in all states includes marriage between specified close family members—including parent and child, grandparent and grandchild, and siblings. Moving outward from that core, however, more variation appears. Many, but not all, states treat relations by affinity (i.e., by marriage) the same as relations by consanguinity (i.e., by blood)— so that marriage would be denied, for instance, to a stepfather and stepdaughter. Likewise, most states treat relations created by adoption in the same manner as relations created by blood—so that marriage would be denied, for instance, to adoptive siblings. For example, the Missouri criminal incest statute provides that a "person commits the crime of incest if he marries or purports to marry or engages in sexual intercourse or deviate sexual intercourse with a person he knows to be, without regard to legitimacy: (1) His ancestor or descendant by blood or adoption; or (2) His stepchild, while the marriage creating that relationship exists; or (3) His brother or sister of the whole or half-blood; or (4) His uncle, aunt, nephew or niece of the whole blood." Mo. Stat. § 568.020(1) (2019).

When it comes to marriage of first cousins, the states are split nearly evenly. Not quite half the states prohibit such marriages in all circumstances; a handful prohibit them except for marriages between cousins incapable of procreation, and a substantial minority allow first-cousin marriages without restriction. Missouri's marriage law provides that all attempted marriages between "parents and children, including grandparents and grandchildren of every degree, between brothers and sisters of the half as well as the whole blood, between uncles and nieces, aunts and nephews, first cousins" are "presumptively void," thereby going beyond the reach of the criminal prohibition to prohibit marriages between first cousins, as well. *Id.* at § 451.020.

The following decision, *Smith v. State*, considers the public interests justifying incest laws. The court does so in the context of a criminal prosecution of an uncle-niece relationship close to the core of the incest prohibition. As you read the decision, consider whether the interests that the court pinpoints are sufficient to support incest regulations—both criminal and civil—that are closer to the periphery of the taboo, such as a marriage of first cousins. Note that *Smith* was decided before both *Lawrence* and *Obergefell*. Do either of those decisions require states to offer a stronger justification for traditional incest laws?

SMITH V. STATE
Court of Criminal Appeals of Tennessee, 1999.
6 S.W.3d 512.

HAYES, J.

* * *

On March 13, 1997, the appellant entered a guilty plea to one count of incest[1] and was sentenced to three years supervised probation. [She was subsequently sentenced to prison when she violated the conditions of her probation]. * * *

* * *

[A]ppellant's sole assignment of error is whether [Tennessee's criminal incest statute] is unconstitutional under the protections provided by the Constitution of the State of Tennessee. Specifically, the appellant relies upon the Court of Appeals decision in *Campbell v. Sundquist,* 926 S.W.2d 250, 262 (Tenn. App.), *perm. to appeal denied* (Tenn. 1996) (finding the Homosexual Practices Act unconstitutional), for the proposition that "an adult's right to engage in consensual and noncommercial sexual activities in the privacy of that adult's home is a matter of intimate personal concern which is at the heart of Tennessee's protection of the right to privacy."

The right to privacy is addressed within the context of due process guaranties. [After discussing the constitutional standard applicable to suspect classes and fundamental rights, the court continues] if no fundamental right or suspect class is affected, the court must determine whether there is some rational basis to justify a classification set out in a statute. There is no dispute that the challenged statutory provision does not involve a suspect class, thus, our initial determination remains whether the appellant's right to privacy encompasses a guaranteed protected "fundamental right" to engage in incestuous sexual activity.

* * *

---

[1] The indictment charged and it is not disputed that the appellant was involved in an incestuous relationship with her paternal uncle. The appellant does not deny this relationship. We are able to glean from the sparse record before us that the incestuous relationship began while the appellant was still a minor and continued into her majority. Her uncle was in his mid-thirties when the relationship began. No children were born as a result of this relationship. The appellant's brief indicates that she suffers from various psychological disorders and was eighteen years old when charged with this offense.

* * * It is clear from the precedent established by the Supreme Court that the constitutional right of privacy places limits on a state's right to interfere with a person's most basic decisions regarding family and parenthood.

[T]here is no general endorsement of an "all-encompassing 'right of privacy.'" * * * Rather, if the right cannot be logically deduced from the text of the Constitution, "the court must look to the traditions and collective conscience of our people to determine whether a principle is so rooted as to be ranked as fundamental." [*Griswold v. Connecticut*, 381 U.S. 479, 493 (1965) (Goldberg, J., concurring in the judgment).] * * *

* * *

Incest is the sexual intercourse or marriage between persons related to each other in any of the degrees of consanguinity or affinity that is prohibited by law.[9] The taboo against incest has been a consistent and almost universal tradition with recorded proscriptions against incest existing as early as 1750 B.C.[10] The incest taboo has been characterized as one of the most important human cultural developments and is found in some form in all societies. Being primarily cultural in origin, the taboo is neither instinctual nor biological and has little to do with actual blood ties. Anthropologists and sociologists claim the significance of the incest taboo is twofold: (1) the restriction forces family members to go outside their families to find sexual partners, requiring people to pursue relationships outside family boundaries that help form important economic and political alliances, and (2) to maintain the stability of the family hierarchy by protecting young family members from exploitation by older family members in positions of authority and by reducing competition and jealous friction among family members.

Although the ban on incest was widely followed in all societies, incest was not a common law crime in England; rather, punishment was left solely to the ecclesiastical courts. The ecclesiastical courts followed the interdiction of Levitical law which prohibited marriages between persons more closely related than fourth cousins unless a dispensation was procured from the Church of Rome; no distinction was made between persons related by affinity or consanguinity. In 1540, after England's separation from the Church of Rome, legislation was enacted to correct "an

---

[9]　Tenn. Code Ann. § 39–15–302 provides:

"(a) A person commits incest who engages in sexual penetration as defined in § 39–13–501, with a person, knowing such person to be, without regard to legitimacy:

(1) The person's natural parent, child, grandparent, grandchild, uncle, aunt, nephew, niece, stepparent, stepchild, adoptive parent, adoptive child; or

(2) The person's brother or sister of the whole or half-blood or by adoption."

[10]　Discovered in 1901, the Code of Hammurabi, a Babylonian king, punished the incestuous relationship between mother and son by burning of both parties at the stake. See Sara Robbins, Law: A Treasury of Art and Literature 20–22 (1990).

unjust law of the bishop of Rome" relating to the degrees in which marriages were permitted. The revised statutes limited prohibitions against marriage to relatives closer than first cousins. The ecclesiastical courts proclaimed the statute to be a return to "God's law."

The English tradition prohibiting incest within certain degrees was adopted by the American colonists. American jurisprudence, however, deviated from the ecclesiastical law in two respects: the majority of American jurisdictions extended the proscriptions beyond that of first cousins while others only imposed criminal penalties where the relationship was consanguineous. Specific to our concern, Tennessee has traditionally recognized the proscription against incest as a punishable offense. *See, e.g.*, Ch. 23, Section 18, Code of Tennessee (1829). * * *. Regardless of the manner of the proscription, the crime of incest is governed by specific statutes in every American jurisdiction. There is nothing to suggest a movement away from the historical treatment of incest; Tennessee, as other states, continues to condemn it as a grave public wrong.

To conclude that there exists a "fundamental right" to engage in an incestuous relationship, this court would be called upon to contradict centuries of legal doctrine and practice[,] which this court declines to do. The evidence is plain; the incest taboo is deeply rooted in Anglo-American history and traditions. Although one does have a general right to privacy, this right does not, by itself, warrant the sweeping conclusion that all intimate and personal decisions are so protected. Accordingly, * * * the asserted "right" to participate in adult consensual incest is not a fundamental liberty interest protected by the Tennessee Constitution.

In the absence of a fundamental right, a rational basis test is used to examine the statute's constitutional validity. A legislative enactment will be deemed valid if it bears a real and substantial relationship to the public's health, safety, morals or general welfare and it is neither unreasonable nor arbitrary.

There is little doubt that the prohibition against incest is directly reflective of the moral concerns of our society. Some argument has been made that this is an inadequate rationale to support the ban. The law, however, is constantly based on notions of morality, and if all laws representing essentially moral choices are to be invalidated, the courts would be very busy. *Bowers v. Hardwick.* * * * [C]riminal statutes prohibiting incestuous relationships reflect the belief that incest is a wrong against the public largely because of its potential to destabilize the family, traditionally regarded as society's most important unit.

* * *

The prohibition against incest is aimed at the protection of children and of the family unit. Society is concerned with the integrity of the family because society cannot function in an orderly manner when age distinctions, generations, sentiments, and roles in families are in conflict. The state has a legitimate and rationally based objective in prohibiting sexual relations between those related within the proscribed degrees of kinship to promote domestic peace and purity. We conclude that the state, in the exercise of its legislative function, may legitimately proscribe against acts which threaten public order and decency, including prohibitions against interfamilia[l] sexual relations. Our pronouncements of these principles are consistent with and not contrary to deeply rooted traditions. We, therefore, hold that Tenn. Code Ann. § 39–15–302 does not violate the Constitution of the State of Tennessee.

* * *

NOTES AND QUESTIONS

1.　*The impact of* Lawrence *and* Obergefell. *Smith* relies directly on *Bowers v. Hardwick* for two propositions: first, that traditional social consensus defines the scope of fundamental privacy rights, so that traditional penalties for incest are subject only to rational-basis review; and, second, that the state's interest in enforcing popular notions of morality provides a sufficient basis for incest prohibitions. Do these premises require reconsideration after *Lawrence*, which overruled *Bowers* and in which dissenting Justice Scalia predicted "the end of all morals legislation," including incest laws? If Texas may not criminalize private, consensual sexual conduct between two persons of the same sex, on what basis may Tennessee punish appellant Smith? Is disgust sufficient? *See* Courtney Megan Cahill, *Same-Sex Marriage, Slippery Slope Rhetoric, and the Politics of Disgust: A Critical Perspective on Contemporary Family Discourse and the Incest Taboo,* 99 Nw. U. L. Rev. 1543, 1549 (2005).

Courts in Tennessee and elsewhere have rejected the suggestion that *Lawrence* protects incestuous relations. *See, e.g., Beard v. State,* 2005 WL 1334378 (Tenn. Crim. App. 2005) ("the *Lawrence* decision does not establish a new constitutional right" to engage in incest and "in no way alters our holding in *Smith* [*v. State*]"); *People v. McEvoy,* 154 Cal. Rptr. 3d 914, 924 (Ct. App. 2013) (the state's "interests in protecting the integrity of the family unit and protecting against inbreeding are sufficiently important to justify [its] incest prohibition"); *State v. Freeman,* 801 N.E.2d 906 (Ohio. Ct. App. 2003) (distinguishing *Lawrence* because incest involves "injury to persons"). Do you think that *Obergefell* renders state bars on incestuous marriage vulnerable? For discussion, *see* Andrew J. Pecoraro, *Exploring the Boundaries of* Obergefell, 58 Wm. & Mary L. Rev. 2063 (2017).

2.　*More on* Lawrence: *age, consent, and public policy. Smith* involved an incestuous relationship that began when the appellant was a minor. Do concerns about intrafamilial sexual exploitation justify statutes punishing the *minor*, who is the object of the law's concern and who, as a matter of law, is incapable of consenting to sexual activity or being a party to a contract?

Would punishment be justified in the case of a relationship that, at all times, allegedly involved consent by the adult participants? In 2005, Michigan prosecutors charged a 46-year-old man and his 24-year-old daughter for engaging in what police, prosecutors, and the parties described as a consensual relationship. The woman had not known her father until they met when she was an adult; they later moved in together and had a child. Christy Arboscello, *Father, Daughter Face Incest Charge*, Detroit Free Press, Dec. 9, 2005, at 6.

In upholding incest convictions against fathers for conduct involving an adult daughter, courts have distinguished *Lawrence* based on doubts about both the presence and validity of consent. *See State v. Freeman*, 801 N.E.2d at 906, 909–10 (while mutual consent was "undisputed" in *Lawrence*, 20-year old daughter disputed father's claim that sexual act was consensual, rather than forced); *People v. Scott*, 68 Cal. Rptr. 3d 592, 595 (Ct. App. 2007) (18-year old daughter); *see also Lowe v. Swanson*, 663 F.3d 258, 264 (6th Cir. 2011), *cert. denied*, 132 S. Ct. 2383 (2012) (in a case involving father and 22-year-old stepdaughter, describing the stepparent-stepchild relationship as one in which a person "might be injured or coerced or where consent might not easily be refused," quoting *Lawrence*). *See also* Brett H. McDonnell, *Is Incest Next?*, 10 Cardozo Women's L.J. 337, 354–55 (2004) (observing that "[m]ost actual prosecutions for incest involve a father's contact with an under-age daughter, which can clearly still be criminalized under *Lawrence*").

In *People v. McEvoy*, the court upheld a brother's conviction for incest and assault based on a sexual encounter with his sister, rejecting his argument that concerns about vulnerability did not apply to a sexual relationship between an adult sister and her adult brother. 154 Cal. Rptr. 3d at 921. The court observed that the state's concerns about "the destructive influence of intra-family, extra-marital sexual contacts" and protecting persons "who may not be in a position to freely consent to sexual relationships with family members" were "at play in a sexual relationship between siblings." *Id.*

3.   *Interstate recognition of incestuous marriages.* In most states, an attempted marriage between persons falling within the prohibited class of incest statutes is both a crime and void for all civil purposes. Nevertheless, the general rule of marriage recognition is that a state will recognize as valid a marriage legally contracted in another state, unless recognition would offend very strong public policies of the recognizing state. Consequently, states will sometimes—though not always—recognize the validity of an incestuous marriage legally undertaken elsewhere. *See, e.g., Ghassemi v. Ghassemi*, 998 So.2d 731, 747 (La. Ct. App. 2008) ("Louisiana does not have a strong public policy against recognizing a marriage between first cousins performed in a state or country where such marriages are valid"). Does such recognition undermine a state's bars on incestuous marriage?

4. *Construing the purposes and scope of state incest laws.* In *Nguyen v. Holder*, 21 N.E.3d 1023, 1025 (N.Y. 2014), the court considered whether New York's prohibition of marriage between "an uncle and niece or an aunt and nephew" should be read to include marriage between "a half uncle and half niece (or half aunt and half nephew)." At issue was whether a Vietnamese immigrant could become a permanent United States resident by virtue of her marriage in 2000 to her uncle, a U.S. citizen, or whether her marriage was invalid. The court observed that, while the prohibition on brother-sister marriage included "of either the whole or the half blood," the uncle-niece/aunt-nephew prohibition did not. *Id.* New York's incest law, the court reasoned, serves two purposes: (1) "it reflects long-held and deeply-rooted values" and (2) "it is also concerned with preventing genetic diseases and defects." *Id.* at 1021. Why do you think the court concluded that those purposes did not require barring half uncle/half niece marriages?

5. *Health risks of incestuous procreation.* It is often said that special risks of genetic defects relating to intrafamily child-bearing support laws banning incest. *Smith* downplayed this concern, but it is evidently a significant basis for some states' incest laws that prohibit marriages between first cousins, unless they are incapable of reproduction due to age or other condition. *See, e.g.,* Ariz. Rev. Stat. Ann. § 25–101 (2019) (first cousins may marry if both are 65 or older or, if under 65, proof is offered to judge that one of the cousins "is unable to reproduce"); Ind. Code § 31–11–1–2 (2019) (if both are "at least 65").

Procreation between close relatives indisputably elevates the risk of passing on some medical conditions associated with recessive genes, but scientific evidence suggests that the risks are quite small in pairings of first cousins. *See* Robin Bennet et al., *Genetic Counseling and Screening of Consanguineous Couples and Their Offspring: Recommendations of the National Society of Genetic Counselors*, J. Genetic Counseling 11, 97–118 (2002). Professor Sanford Levinson argues that the "standard 'genetic' argument that is often trotted out with regard to adult incest * * * is riddled with holes," and might even be dismissed as "bogus." Sanford Levinson, *Thinking About Polygamy*, 42 San Diego L. Rev. 1049, 1052 (2005). Does the evidence suggesting only modest genetic risks warrant rethinking incest laws such as Arizona's or Indiana's, or is modest risk sufficient to satisfy rational basis review?

6. *Application to adoptive and stepfamily relationships.* The incest statute at issue in *Smith*, like those in many other states, includes parent-child and sibling relationships founded on adoption within the scope of prohibited incestuous relations. Adoption "creates one parent-child relationship and disrupts another," so "states could proscribe two kinds of relationships: (1) those between adopted parents and children; or (2) those between biological parents and their subsequently adopted children." Naomi Cahn, *Perfect Substitutes or the Real Thing?*, 52 Duke L.J. 1077, 1139–40 (2003).

State laws are more varied with respect to stepfamily relationships. Stepfamily relations were once broadly included within the scope of incest laws, but many states have since eliminated coverage of step-relations. Where these prohibitions still exist, they are clearly not founded on genetic concerns about a couple's offspring. Do prohibitions on marriage between persons related to one another only by an adoption or step relationship survive *Lawrence?* If so, on what rationale?

If state laws include step or adoptive relationships in their definition of prohibited incestuous marriage, should some relationships be treated differently than others? For example, should courts construe the prohibition as inapplicable where neither marriage partner created the step or adoptive relationship, as in the case of stepsiblings who meet as adults after the marriage of one's father and the other's mother? What if, instead, the prospective marriage partners became stepsiblings as children and grew up in the same household? Would state prohibition of these marriages be constitutional? Might these situations differ from, for example, a stepfather's effort to marry his stepdaughter?

7. *"Accidental" incest.* In 2008, newspapers reported the story of twin siblings who had been adopted into different families at birth but who met years later as adults and, unaware of their genetic ties, fell in love and married one another. Once they learned of their common origin, they annulled their marriage. A British legislator, who described their story as a "terrible tragedy," used the case to illustrate the need for legislation mandating that children conceived through assisted reproductive technology (ART) be informed of their genetic parents. *See Separated Twins Marry, Then Are Forced to Break Up,* Boston Globe (Jan. 12, 2008). Criminal incest statutes usually provide a defense for persons who were reasonably unaware of the incestuous relationship, but should pairings of adults sharing an unknown genetic connection be considered "incest" that would absolutely create a void marriage under a marriage statute? *See* Naomi Cahn, *Accidental Incest: Drawing the Line—or the Curtain?—for Reproductive Technology,* 32 Harv. J. Gender & L. 109 (2009). To reduce incest risks arising from the use of ART, would states be justified in limiting the number of children conceived from gametes (sperm or egg) provided by a single donor? Or in requiring that children born through the use either of donor sperm or donor eggs be provided with identifying information about their donor once they reach the age of 18?

PROBLEM 2-3

In 2013, Henry married Wilma in Springfield, Missouri. At the time of their marriage, Henry had sole custody of a 15-year-old son, Sam, and Wilma had sole custody of a 12-year-old daughter, Darla. Six years later, when Darla was 18 years old, Wilma died. If Henry and Darla were now to marry one another in Missouri, what would be the legal implications? If they cohabited without formally marrying, would that change the legal implications? Could Darla and Sam marry in Missouri? In answering, refer to the Missouri incest statutes recited above. Would it affect your answers if Henry had adopted Darla in 2013?

4. MINIMUM AGE AT MARRIAGE

To marry, each spouse must be of sufficient age to have the capacity to consent to marriage. What is that age? Answers have varied over time— and continue to evolve. The English common law treated 12 for females and 14 for males as the ages of presumptive marital consent. In 1753, concerned over young people marrying against their parents' wishes, Parliament passed Hardwicks's Marriage Act (later repealed), which treated as void marriages entered into by persons under 21 without parental consent. Vivian E. Hamilton, *The Age of Marital Capacity: Reconsidering Civil Recognition of Adolescent Marriage*, 92 B.U. L. Rev. 1817, 1824–28 (2012).

In the United States, states "adopted the English age of legal majority—twenty-one—as the statutory age of presumptive marital consent, when individuals' marriages no longer required parental consent." However, most states also "failed to explicitly repudiate the English common law ages of presumptive marital consent" (12 for females and 14 for males). *Id.* at 1829. Those common law ages have left their traces in state law. For example, *In re Marriage of J.M.H.*, 143 P.3d 1116, 1120 (Colo. Ct. App. 2006), a Colorado appeals court held that, because Colorado's minimum-age statute—requiring judicial approval for any marriage of a minor under the age of 16—did not expressly mention common law (or informal) marriage, "it appears that Colorado has adopted the common law age of consent for marriage as fourteen for a male and twelve for a female, which existed under English common law." Accordingly, the court held that a lower court was wrong to have invalidated the common-law marriage of a man to a 15-year-old girl on the ground that they failed to obtain judicial approval. The Colorado legislature swiftly responded to that holding by enacted a statute setting a minimum age of 18 for common-law marriage.

By the 1970s, as states lowered the age of majority from 21 to 18 in other contexts (such as the right to vote), many states lowered the presumptive age of marital consent to 18. Similar to the proposed Uniform Marriage and Divorce Act (1970) (UMDA), most states adopted a graduated approach: they set the minimum age for marriage at 18 years, but allowed minors to marry with parental or judicial consent. Most states permit a minor who is 16 or 17 years old to marry with approval either from a parent or a court. Many states also permit minors under 16 to marry with approval both from a parent *and* a court. Hamilton, *The Age of Marital Capacity, supra,* at 1832. In Nevada, for example, a court may authorize such a marriage "in extraordinary circumstances," if there is parental consent and the court finds that the marriage will serve the minor's "best interests." Nev. Rev. Stat. § 122.025 (2019). The statute indicates that "pregnancy alone" does not satisfy the best interests test, nor may a court require that a minor be pregnant to authorize a marriage. *Id.* Historically, a minor female's pregnancy provided a sufficient circumstance to allow a marriage, and still does in some jurisdictions. *See, e.g., State Department of Human Resources v. Lott*, 16 So.3d 104 (Ala. Ct. Civ. App. 2009) (finding that marriage of pregnant 13-year-old female to 19-year-old male satisfied the contemplated terms for an exception to the minimum age). Finally, in some jurisdictions, the relevant statute gives no minimum age below which minors may not marry, provided that the parties have parental and/or judicial consent. *See, e.g.*, Mass. Gen. Laws ch. 207, § 25 (2019).

It was formerly common for states to distinguish by sex in setting marriage age, setting a lower age for females than for males. These distinctions have been invalidated on equal protection grounds, but they linger on in the statutes of a handful of states. *See, e.g.*, Miss. Code Ann. § 93–1–5(d) (2019) (fixing minimum age for marriage at 17 for boys and 15 for girls). In 2018, the New Hampshire legislature raised the minimum age of marriage from 13 for girls and 14 for boys, to 16 for both. N.H. Rev. Stat. § 457:4 (2019).

The Equal Protection Clause permits states to discriminate based on age, so long as there is a rational basis for the lines states draw. In 1982, the Second Circuit held that "the right of minors to marry has not been viewed as a fundamental right deserving strict scrutiny." *Moe v. Dinkins*, 669 F.2d 67, 68 (2d Cir. 1982). Applying the rational basis test, the court held that the state's age restrictions on marriage plainly served "New York's important interest in promoting the welfare of children by preventing unstable marriages among those lacking the capacity to act in their own best interests." *Id.* In 2003, the Nevada Supreme Court rejected the argument that a state law authorizing a minor to marry by obtaining the consent of only one parent violates an objecting parent's fundamental right to participate in basic childrearing decisions. *See Kirkpatrick v. Eighth Jud. Dist. Ct.*, 64 P.3d 1056 (Nev. 2003).

If the premise of age restrictions is that most minors lack capacity to give informed consent to marriage, who, then, should safeguard their interests? The requirement that, below a specified age, a judge approve a marriage license, even after the minor's parent consents, reflects a social consensus that, as the minor's age diminishes, the state becomes less trusting of the parents' good judgment in the matter. Indeed, at some point, the question melds into one of child abuse, although states disagree on the tipping point.

Concern about minors being forced or pressured into marriage, as well as about the consequences of early marriage, has spurred many state legislatures to debate whether to raise the minimum age of marriage; several have done so. *See* Meghan McCann and Sarah Hill, *How Young Is Too Young?*, State Legislatures Magazine (July/Aug. 2018). In particular, groups such as Unchained at Last and the Tahirih Justice Center have sought to raise public awareness about the "real and persistent problem" in the U.S. of girls being pressured or forced into marriage by parents or other adults and have urged state legislatures to pass laws that better protect children from such marriages. *Falling Through the Cracks: How Laws Allow Child Marriage to Happen in Today's America,* Tahirih Justice Center (August 2017). Both groups have studied state records about the incidence of marriage by minors. Fraidy Reiss, *America's Child Marriage Problem,* N.Y. Times (Oct. 13, 2105). Although such data alone does not reveal anything about the circumstances under which such minors married, these groups argue, based on their experience working with victims of forced marriage, that many likely married against their will. *Id.* Fraidy Reiss, founder of Unchained at Last, has testified before state legislatures about her coercive betrothal in her teens to a man she barely knew, followed by harassment, stalking, and death threats until she finally divorced her husband after 15 years of marriage. Samuel G. Freedman, *Woman Breaks Through Chains of Forced Marriage, and Helps Others Do the Same,* N.Y. Times (Mar. 20, 2016).

Media accounts of the prevalence of very young girls marrying—and of parents crossing state lines to take advantage of more permissive state laws—have also spurred legislative action in some states. A series of news articles found that approximately 1,000 15-year old girls got married in Missouri between 1999 and 2015; of these, more than 300 married men 21 or older—some men were in their 30s, 40s, and 50s. At the time, Missouri law provided no minimum age for marriage, as long as at least one parent consented. As one story pointed out: "Assuming they had premarital sex, those grooms would be considered rapists" under Missouri law, which defines statutory rape as occurring when any person 21 or older has sex with someone under 17 outside of marriage. One Idaho father brought his pregnant daughter, on her 15th birthday, to Missouri to marry her 24-year old boyfriend. The father was subsequently sentenced in Idaho for felony injury to a child (including taking her across state lines to marry). Eric Adler, *Hundreds of Missouri's 15-Year-Old Brides May Have Married Their Rapists,* Kansas City Star (Mar. 11, 2018). In 2018, the Missouri legislature raised the minimum age of marriage to 16 (with the consent of a parent or guardian). The law also forbids issuing a marriage license to individuals 21 or older planning to marry someone 16 or younger. Mo. Ann. Stat. § 451.090 (2019); *see* Eric Adler, *Missouri Governor Signs Law Banning Marriage of 15 Year Olds,* Kansas City Star (July 13, 2018).

As states have revised upward their minimum age of marriage laws in the last several years, they have taken a range of approaches. Some state laws simply provide that no marriage license shall be issued to any individual under 18, with no exceptions. *See, e.g.,* Del. Code Ann. tit. 13, § 123 (2019), as amended by 2018 Del. Laws Ch. 235; N.J. Stat. Ann. 37:1–6 (2019). Some other states have set the minimum age of marriage at 18, unless a minor has been emancipated by court order. *See, e.g.*, Chap. 543, 2016 Va. Acts 972; Chap. 933, 2017 Tex. Gen. Laws 3775.

Other states have raised the minimum age, but not all the way to 18. For example, Florida, which was among the states with the most marriages involving minors, raised the minimum age from 16 to 17 provided there is parental consent and "the older party is not more than 2 years older than the younger party to the marriage." Chap. 81, 2018 Fla. Laws 1143. The statute eliminated judicial discretion to allow marriage of a minor at any age in the case of pregnancy. *See* Anjali Tsui, *Florida Moves to Ban Marriage Before the Age of 17,* PBS Frontline (Mar. 9, 2018) (reporting analysis of state and county marriage records). Some states have raised the minimum age and also increased the findings the judge must make before approving a proposed marriage by a minor. The following statute, enacted by the New York legislature in 2017, is illustrative. Prior to this revision, New York permitted 16 year olds to marry with parental consent and minors under 16 to marry with judicial approval and consent. It prohibited marriage below the age of 14.

[Section 1 requires that the town or city clerk obtain from each of the parties applying for a marriage license (a) a signed and verified statement or affidavit providing, among other information, their age, and (b) provide documentary proof of age.]

2. If it appears from the affidavits and statements so taken, and from the documentary proof of age presented, that the persons for whose marriage the license in question is demanded are legally competent to marry, the said clerk shall issue such license.

3. If it shall appear upon an application * * * that either party is at least seventeen years of age but under eighteen years of age, then the town or city clerk before he shall issue a license shall require:

(a) the written consent to the marriage from both parents of the minor or minors or such as shall then be living, or if the parents of both are dead, then the written consent of the guardian or guardians of such minor or minors. [The consent of one parent is sufficient if the other parent has been missing for at least a year, and the consent of the custodial parent is sufficient if the parents are divorced or had their marriage annulled. If there is no living parent or guardian (to the minor's knowledge), consent must be obtained from the person responsible for the minor's care.] The parents, guardians, or other persons whose consent it shall be necessary to obtain and file with the town or city clerk before the license shall issue, shall personally appear and acknowledge or execute the same before the town or city clerk, or some other officer authorized to administer oaths and take acknowledgments * * *; and

(b) the written approval of a justice of the supreme court or of a judge of the family court * * * to be attached to or endorsed upon the application, before the license is issued. The application for such approval may be made by either minor party to the proposed marriage and shall be heard by the judge at chambers. The justice * * * or the judge * * * shall appoint an attorney for the child for each minor party immediately upon the application for approval. The attorney for the child must have received training in domestic violence including a component on forced marriage. * * * Before issuing any approval, the justice of the supreme court or the judge of the family court shall:

(i) provide notification to each minor party of his or her rights, including but not limited to, rights in relation to termination of the marriage, child and spousal support, domestic violence services and access to public benefits and other services, which notification shall be developed by the office of court administration, in consultation with the office for the prevention of domestic violence;

(ii) with respect to each party, including a minor party, conduct a review of related decisions in court proceedings initiated pursuant to [New York's child abuse and neglect law], all warrants issued under [such law], and reports of the statewide computerized registry of orders of protection * * *, and reports of the sex offender registry * * *; and

(iii) have an in camera interview, separately with each minor party, and make the following written affirmative findings:

A. that it is the minor's own will that the minor enter into the marriage;

B. that the minor is not being compelled by force, threat, persuasion, fraud, coercion or duress; and

C. that the marriage will not endanger the mental, emotional or physical safety of the minor.

In making such findings, the court shall consider, among other relevant factors, the age difference between the parties intending to be married, whether there is a power imbalance between the parties intending to be married, whether the parties are incapable of consenting to a marriage for want of understanding, whether there is a history of domestic violence between the parties and whether there is a history of domestic violence between a party and either parties' or legal guardians' family members. The wishes of the parents or legal guardians of the minor intending to be married shall not be the sole basis for approval under this subdivision.

Upon the approval of the justice of the supreme court or the judge of the family court of the application to marry, each minor party shall have all the rights of an adult, including the right to enter into a contract, except for those specific constitutional and statutory age requirements such as, but not limited to, voting, use of alcoholic beverages, and other health or safety statutes relevant to him or her because of his or her age.

* * *

§ 3. Section 15–a of the domestic relations law, as amended by chapter 126 of the laws of 1984, is amended to read as follows:

§ 15–a. Marriages of minors under seventeen years of age

Any marriage in which either party is under the age of seventeen years is hereby prohibited. * * *

An Act to Amend the Domestic Relations Law, to Increase the Age of Consent for Purposes of Marriage to the Age of Seventeen, 2017 N.Y. Laws ch. 35 (codified at N.Y. Dom. Rel. Law § 13–b, 15, 15–a (2019)).

NOTES AND QUESTIONS

1. *The role of judicial discretion.* Does New York's new law provide sufficient guidance to a judge about how to make the necessary findings to approve a minor's application for marriage? For example, how do you think a judge would determine that a minor was "not being compelled by force, threat, persuasion, fraud, coercion, or duress"? Connecticut's amended marriage law requires a probate court to make similar findings in the case of minors who are "at least sixteen years of age but under eighteen years of age." 2017 Conn. Acts 17–54 (codified at Conn. Gen. Stat. 46b–20a (2019)).

2. *Age of marriage, harms, and religious liberty.* When the New Jersey legislature passed a bill raising the minimum age of marriage to 18, with no exceptions, then-Governor Chris Christie vetoed it, stating that its "absolute ban" on marriages for people under age 18, without any "exceptions," would "violate the cultures and traditions of some communities in New Jersey based on religious traditions." https://www.njleg.state.nj.us/2016/Bills/A3500/3091_V1.pdf. When Governor Phil Murphy signed the new law, in June 2018, Fraidy Reiss (who wrote the bill) hailed it as a human right victory "for girls and women across New Jersey." Press coverage noted that the law had been passed without any religious exceptions, even though some religious groups had requested them. In his signing statement, Governor Murphy said: "Studies have consistently showed that minors who enter into marriage—particularly

young women—are less likely to graduate from high school and college and more likely to suffer domestic abuse and live in poverty." Susan K. Livio, *New Jersey Bans Child Marriages. New Law Raises Minimum Age to 18*, NJ.com (June 20, 2018). One reason that supporters of a bright line rule of 18 give is the lack of legal resources available to minors in situations of domestic violence.

3. *Is minimum age a solution to forced marriage?* Would raising the minimum age to 18 solve the problem of forced marriage of minors? Reiss, for example, recounts that her family forced her into marriage when she was 19, above the legal age of consent. *The Joy of Leaving an Arranged Marriage—and the Cost*, NPR (June 25, 2014). Should states consider measures other than minimum age requirements to protect against such marriages?

4. *"Child marriage" as a human rights issue*. UNICEF describes child marriage as a "human rights violation" that is "all too common." *Child Marriage*, UNICEF (Mar. 2018). International human rights reports identify "child marriage" as a worldwide problem that disproportionately affects girls. *See* Nisha Varia, *Ending Child Marriage: Meeting the Global Development Goals' Promise to Girls*, Human Rights Watch World Report: 2016 33 (2016). Do you think that it is appropriate to frame the issue of child marriage *within the United States* as one of human rights? For such an argument, see Nicholas Kristof, *11 Years Old a Mom, and Pushed to Marry Her Rapist in Florida*, N.Y. Times (May 26, 2017).

PROBLEM 2-4

Imagine that you are a legislator in a state that is considering whether to change its minimum age of marriage law. Would you support doing so? If so, which approach (of those discussed above) would you favor? What are the relative pros and cons of a bright line rule (e.g., prohibiting any marriages below 18) versus an approach such as New York's? Would you propose a law prohibiting marriage by a minor if the marriage partner was more than a specified number of years older?

PROBLEM 2-5

Suppose, again, that you are a state legislator considering proposals to reform your state's age of marriage law. During a hearing, one witness (a legal scholar) urges that the legislature raise the minimum age of marriage to 21 or 22, allowing 18 to 20-year-olds to marry only with judicial consent. The witness offers the following evidence in support: Studies indicate that one risk factor for marital instability and divorce is early marriage. For marriages entered into before age 18, the divorce rate is nearly 70%; by age 25, it is less than 30%. Divorce rates start to level off only for marriages entered into at age 22 or older. Studies of the brain suggest that adolescent development of emotional maturity continues well into the 20s. Psychologists also find that, into the early 20s, young people's commitments and relationships are in flux as they explore their identities. The witness argues that young people entering into marriage may have the cognitive skills to understand the nature of marriage and consent, but that they lack the identity and relationship skills to make a marriage succeed. *See* Hamilton, *The Age of Marital Capacity, supra*, at 1850– 61. Would you support that proposal?

5. CONSENT TO MARRIAGE

Marriage is both a contract and a status. In the United States, a valid marriage has always required the spouses' mutual consent. Each party must have the mental capacity to consent. Setting a minimum age for marriage, as we have seen, reflects concerns over the presence of such capacity, but concerns over consent apply to adults as well. Thus, any expression of consent must be voluntary and free from duress or fraud. The following decision, discussing the essentials of consent, also illustrates the serious consequences that flow from failure to satisfy the elements that establish capacity to marry: the marriage may be void from its inception and subject to annulment. Section 6 will provide further detail about grounds for annulment, the consequences of annulling a marriage, and the difference between annulment and divorce.

IN RE ESTATE OF SANTOLINO

Superior Court of New Jersey, Chancery Division, 2005.
895 A.2d 506.

LYONS, J.

The issue before the court is may a court annul a marriage after the death of one party to the marriage. * * *

The decedent and the petitioner first met in January 2000, when the petitioner moved into the decedent's home as a tenant. On or about March 11, 2004, the decedent was admitted to Trinitas Hospital. During his hospitalization, he was diagnosed with lung cancer. He was released from the hospital on April 1, 2004, at which time he returned to his Elizabeth residence. The petitioner and the decedent were married on April 27, 2004, in the Elizabeth Municipal Court. At the time of the marriage, the decedent was 81½ years old, and the petitioner was 46 years old. He was readmitted to Trinitas Hospital on May 11, 2004, where he expired on May 20, 2004. No will of the decedent has ever been found.

[His sister claims] that the marriage to the petitioner is a nullity pursuant to N.J.S.A. 2A:34–1. * * * Counsel for the petitioner has filed the instant motion to dismiss * * * claiming * * * that * * * the death of the decedent terminated the marriage, and the validity of the marriage, therefore, can no longer be questioned.

* * *

A survey of the law in other states shows that the prevailing rule continues to provide that a void marriage may be annulled after the death of one of the parties in the absence of a statute to the contrary. * * *

* * *

N.J.S.A. 2A:34–1(d) provides that an annulment may be granted

"where the parties, or either of them, lacked capacity to marry due to want of understanding because of mental condition, or the influence of intoxicants, drugs, or similar agents; or where there was a lack of mutual assent to the marital relationship; duress; or fraud as to the essentials of marriage; and has not subsequently ratified the marriage."

The clause can be broken down into (1) inability to give consent; (2) lack of mutual assent; (3) duress; and (4) fraud as to the essentials of the marriage. Respondent argues that her brother did not have the mental capacity to give his consent and that the marriage constituted a fraud as to its essentials.

* * * The plain language of subsection d does not preclude a posthumous cause of action for lack of consent and further does not require that the action be brought only by one of the parties to the marriage. * * *

* * *

* * * With regard to capacity to consent, the courts of this state have held that where there is a lack of capacity to consent, the incapacitated party is not capable of contracting the marriage and the marriage is void ab initio.

In this case, Mr. Santolino was 81 1/2 years old; he was hospitalized on March 4, 2004 and diagnosed with lung cancer; he was released on April 1, only to be readmitted on May 11, where he expired on May 20. Respondent argues that during this time, Mr. Santolino was heavily medicated, was undergoing chemotherapy, required the daily assistance of an in-home nurse and was hooked up to an oxygen tank during his wedding to the petitioner. Under this factual setting, an argument certainly can be made that Mr. Santolino lacked the capacity to consent to the marriage.

* * *

FRAUD AS TO THE ESSENTIALS OF THE MARRIAGE:

Respondent's third argument for annulling the marriage is that it was the product of a fraud as to the essentials of the marriage. The courts have defined "fraud in the essentials" to include a number of different factual scenarios in which one spouse omits to mention or misrepresents an issue so material that it goes to the very essence of the marriage relationship constituting grounds for annulment. * * * However, a determination of whether a spouse's fraud goes to the essentials of a marriage warranting an annulment must be decided on a case-by-case basis since what is essential to the relationship of the parties in one marriage may be of considerably less significance in another. [The court dismisses this claim without prejudice due to the sister's failure to plead particular facts.]

CONCLUSION:

Based upon the foregoing analysis, petitioner's motion to dismiss is * * * granted without prejudice as to the claim of fraud in the essentials of the marriage; and denied without prejudice as to the claims of inability to consent and as to those permitted under the court's general equity jurisdiction. * * *

NOTES AND QUESTIONS

1. *"Void" versus "voidable" marriages.* The New Jersey statute in *Santolino* lists both impotence and mental incapacity as grounds establishing the "nullity" of a marriage. But, in a part of the opinion you did not read, the court distinguishes between the two grounds. Impotence creates a voidable marriage, which a court may nullify only if the other spouse requests annulment; mental incapacity renders a marriage void *ab initio* (from the beginning), regardless of the parties' wishes, and a third party may bring an action, even after the death one (or both) of the spouses. What public policies are served by allowing third parties to challenge a marriage? *Santolino's* disparate treatment of the two marriage defects illustrates the distinction between marriages that are "void" and ones that are merely "voidable. "Void" marriages are ones that offend very strong public policies; because of the state's overriding policy objection, such marriages are considered to be absolutely void even without a request for annulment. Because the union has no legal effect, no formal dissolution is required, although parties often find it advisable to obtain a judicial declaration of invalidity to avoid any uncertainty and to address any issues of property (as discussed in Section 6) or child custody. "Voidable" marriages, by contrast, offend weaker public policies relating to marriage formation. A "voidable" marriage is considered legally valid *unless* and *until* one party seeks annulment in court.

Most states regard purported bigamous and incestuous marriages as void. Traditionally, states also treated marriage between two persons of the same sex as void, but such treatment is unconstitutional after the Supreme Court's ruling in *Obergefell*. Most states treat as merely voidable a marriage in which at least one party is underage or lacks physical capacity, or a marriage that was induced by fraud or duress. *See, e.g.,* Del. Code Ann. tit. 13, § 101 (2019); Wyo. Stat. Ann. § 20–2–101 (2019).

The categories of "void" and "voidable" marriages may vary from jurisdiction to jurisdiction. For example, the District of Columbia, unlike New Jersey, treats lack of mental capacity as creating a voidable, not a void, marriage. *In re Estate of Randall*, 999 A.2d 51, 54 (D.C. 2010).

2. *Mental capacity to marry—and divorce.* Courts have held that to give valid consent to marriage, a party must be capable of "understand[ing] the rights, duties, and responsibilities of marriage at the time of the marriage contract." *Nave v. Nave*, 173 S.W.3d 766, 774–75 (Tenn. Ct. App. 2005). A party who enters marriage without capacity to consent but later regains mental competence can validate the marriage by ratifying the decision to marry. Statutes and case law also recognize the possibility that a party might lose mental capacity temporarily "because of the influence of alcohol, drugs or other incapacitating substances." Del. Code Ann. tit. 13, § 1506(a)(1) (2019).

Challenging questions arise when a party entering into marriage or seeking to end a marriage suffers from dementia or Alzheimer's disease. Several decisions have nullified those marriages, typically at the behest of the party's adult child or legal guardian. *See, e.g., Brown v. Watson*, 2005 WL 1566541 (Tenn. Ct. App. July 5, 2005). On the other hand, in *In re Marriage of Greenway*, 158 Cal. Rptr. 3d 364 (Ct. App. 2013), the court concluded that a 76-year-old husband's diagnosis of mild dementia was not sufficient to find that he lacked mental capacity to *end* his marriage. Questions of competence also arise when an adult is under a guardianship. In *Guardianship of O'Brien*, a ward with a mental disorder sought to marry, and his guardians (his parents) objected. 847 N.W.2d 710 (Minn. Ct. App. 2014). The court reasoned that "marriage is a fundamental civil right," so an adult ward who wishes to marry must be allowed to do so, provided he "understands the meaning, rights, and obligations of marriage." *Id.* at 714–15. In *Bakhtiar v. Saghafi*, 75 N.E.3d 801 (Ohio. Ct. App. 2016), the reviewing court concluded that the trial court did not err in granting the divorce petition of an 81-year woman who, both prior to and after being adjudged incompetent, had clearly indicated her intention to divorce.

3. *Mutual assent.* To enter into a valid marriage, competent parties must demonstrate their mutual assent to be married. With mixed success, parties sometimes seek to avoid an attempted marriage by claiming that it was undertaken in jest or without serious thought. A still-discussed example is singer Britney Spears' 55-hour marriage, begun on January 3, 2004, to a childhood friend, Jason Alexander, at an all-night wedding chapel in Las Vegas. Sam Lanky, *Britney Spears' Shotgun Wedding Turns 10: Remember 55 Magical Hours*, Rolling Stone (Jan. 3, 2014). Later that day, Spears signed papers seeking to annul the marriage on the ground that she "lacked understanding of her actions to the extent that she was incapable of agreeing to the marriage because the Plaintiff and Defendant did not know each other['s] likes and dislikes, each other['s] desires to have or not to have children, and each other['s] desires as to State of residency." She alleged that "[u]pon learning of each other['s] desires, they are so incompatible that there was a want of understanding of each other['s] actions in entering into this marriage." Compl. for Annulment, ¶ 8, *Spears v. Alexander*, No. D311371 (Clark Co., Nev. Dist. Ct. Jan. 5, 2004).

A Las Vegas district court agreed. Finding "no meeting of the minds in entering into this marriage contract," it granted Spears an annulment within hours. *Id.* ¶ 9 (Decree of Annulment). Should the court have so easily released her from the obligations of marriage? She did not, for example, claim that her judgment was impaired when she obtained a marriage license and exchanged vows. A handful of other decisions have allowed parties to annul a marriage undertaken on a dare or "in jest," *see, e.g., Davis v. Davis*, 175 A. 574 (Conn. 1934), but not all courts are so indulgent.

As a general matter, how compliant should courts be when an adult seeks to annul a marriage for lack of mutual assent? Should the answer be influenced by the length of the marriage, or by whether the marriage has produced minor dependent children?

4.   *Fraud.* A party's consent to marriage is legally ineffective if induced by fraud. Such a marriage is voidable by the party so induced, and may be annulled. In most jurisdictions, however, the fraud must relate to "the essence of the marriage." *See, e.g.,* 13 Del. Code § 1506(a)(4) (2019). *Santolino* recognizes that "the essentials of the marriage" vary from case to case, depending upon the values and priorities of the individuals involved. This recognition resembles the way courts define "material" fraud under the common law of torts. *See, e.g., Coldwell Banker Whiteside Assocs. v. Ryan Equity Partners*, 181 S.W.3d 879, 888 (Tex. Ct. App. 2006) (to recover for real estate fraud, "[a] fact is material if it would likely affect the conduct of a reasonable person concerning the transaction in question").

Traditionally, however, courts defined "the essentials of the marriage" in narrower terms. As one early decision put it: "[f]alse representations as to fortune, character, and social standing are not essential elements of the marriage, and it is contrary to public policy to annul a marriage for fraud or misrepresentations as to personal qualities." *Bielby v. Bielby*, 165 N.E. 231, 233 (Ill. 1929). Some modern courts still agree with this test. For example, where a man falsely led his fiancée to believe that he was "a well-educated millionaire with expertise in real estate and finance," for example, a California appellate court held that "the fraud * * *, as a matter of law, was not of the type that constitutes an adequate basis for granting an annulment." *In re Marriage of Meagher*, 31 Cal. Rptr. 3d 663, 664, 669 (Ct. App. 2005). A Michigan court noted that " '[f]raudulent representations of wealth, or connections, or health, or temper and disposition' " do not justify annulment and held that a wife's "fraudulent conduct in failing to inform [her husband] that she remained romantically involved with another man" was insufficient. *Chudnow v. Chudnow*, 2001 WL 672571, at *1 (Mich. Ct. App. Apr. 27, 2001). The court reasoned that a misrepresentation qualifies as " 'subversive of the true essence of the marriage relationship' " only if the misrepresentation demonstrates that the "party has no intention of ever fulfilling his or her marriage 'vows' or that such are impossible." *Id.* at * * 1–2. Thus, as long as the wife intended ultimately to abandon her adulterous relationship, her fraud did not concern the essentials of the marriage.

In another instance, a California court denied an annulment where a woman alleged that her husband had "created an entirely false portrait of his character, nature, previous conduct, behavior, and past," by saying, among things, that he was a former partner in a major accounting firm and a war hero who had won the Congressional Medal of Honor. *Summers v. Renz*, 2004 WL 2384845 (Cal. Ct. App. Oct. 26, 2004). She further alleged that after ten years of marriage, she learned that he had attempted to murder his first wife by shooting her as she slept and was suspected of arson and other violent crimes. The court found that "the fraud did not go to the essence of the marriage relationship," reasoning that " 'Husband'[s] criminal record played no part at all in the marriage until Wife became aware of it * * * six months following their tenth wedding anniversary,' " and that " '[d]uring the first ten years of their marriage, by Wife's own admission, Husband lived up to Wife's expectations.' " *Id.* at *9 n.3 (quoting trial court's opinion).

Do these courts' tests for what goes to "the essentials" of a marriage make sense? What public policies are served by such rules? Would you favor permitting annulment any time a misrepresentation *actually* led the other party to agree to marry? Why or why not?

5. *Fraud about reasons for marrying.* Courts sometimes grant an annulment where one prospective spouse misrepresents the reasons for marrying and the other prospective spouse relies on that misrepresentation. In *Desta v. Anyaoha*, 371 S.W.3d 596, 598–99 (Tex. Ct. App. 2012), the court found sufficient evidence that the wife, an Ethiopian citizen, fraudulently induced the husband, a U.S. resident, to marry her based on misrepresentations that "she loved him and wanted a long-term relationship, marriage, and children" when her true goal was to come to the United States and to get a green card (which would allow her to remain in the United States). A few days after obtaining her green card, the wife moved out, taking her belongings and leaving no note. *Id.* at 599. Although the Texas statute did not require a showing that the fraud affected the "essentials of a marital relationship," would that have made a difference? *Compare In re Marriage of Joel and Roohi*, 404 P.3d 1251 (Colo. Ct. App. 2012) (granting husband an annulment because wife's fraudulent misrepresentations that she married him because she loved him, rather than to obtain legal residency, went to the essentials) *with Golopapenko v. Karpachev*, 923 N.E.2d 1093 (Mass. Ct. App. 2010) (granting divorce instead of annulment because claims of fraudulent motive for marrying were based on "bald accusations' "). Professor Kerry Abrams argues that while, in some of these immigrant fraud cases involving "green card marriages," the "essentials of the marriage" test need not be stretched far to make the case for an annulment (as when a person never intended to have "procreative sexual relations with the spouse"), in others courts stretch the test to allow annulment. She reasons that some " 'green card marriages' would appear to be little different from marriages where a person marries for money or social standing," which, under a traditional "essentials" test," would not suffice. Kerry Abrams, *The End of Annulment*, 16 J. Gender, Race & Justice 681, 692–95 (2013).

PROBLEM 2-6

The reality television show *Married at First Sight* describes itself as "an extreme social experiment" in which "brave" singles "yearning for a life-long partnership" agree to marry a complete stranger the moment they meet. The couple is matched by four relationship experts. The show follows them through their wedding until several weeks later, when they must decide whether to remain married. Can participants in this show give legally valid consent to these marriages?

6. ANNULMENT

With stories such as that of the annulment of Britney Spears's 55-hour marriage (discussed earlier in this chapter) and of other celebrities and athletes seeking annulments, consumers of popular culture might understandably have the impression that annulments are simply quick divorces for quickly regretted marriages. A decree of annulment, however, is something quite different (or at least is supposed to be): a declaration recognizing that the marriage attempted by the parties never came into existence at all because of a fatal impediment at the time of formation. As one Texas judge recently explained, in dissent:

> Both an annulment and a divorce dissolve a marriage, but differences between the two procedures potentially impact the rights' in significant and lasting ways. A divorce does not make the marriage void ab initio; an annulment might make the marriage so and arguably might affect the ability of one of the spouses to maintain status as a permanent resident of the United States of America if that status was obtained based on the marriage that was later annulled. The Texas Legislature has provided for divorce under various scenarios arising after the parties' marriage and also for annulment under very narrow sets of circumstances arising before or at the time of the parties' marriage. The two legal remedies are not interchangeable.

Manjlai v. Manjlai, 447 S.W. 3d 376, 382 (Tex. App. 2014), *review denied*, No. 14–0139 (Tex. April 17, 2015) (Frost, C.J., dissenting).

Historically, the canon law doctrine of annulment recognized several such impediments to marriage (for example, fraud, duress, and bigamy). John Witte, Jr., From Sacrament to Contract: Marriage, Religion, and the Law in the Western Tradition 31–35 (1997). Protestant reformers attacked canon law, but also retained some of these impediments. *Id.* at 71–72. In England, the doctrine of annulment allowed the English ecclesiastical courts, though allowing no divorce, to permit exit from some failed marriages with the possibility of "remarriage." This distinctive nature of annulment was carried over into civil law in the United States, where it remains available in cases of marriages deemed to have been void or voidable from the start.

Although annulment and divorce have different histories and are conceptually distinct, as statutes and case law have intervened to provide for property and support rights in cases of annulment, annulment is coming increasingly to resemble divorce for most practical purposes.

A. GROUNDS FOR ANNULMENT

To obtain an annulment, a petitioner must show that the marriage suffers from a serious defect dating back to its inception rendering it "void" or "voidable." Section 5 introduced the distinction between "void" and "voidable" marriages. As a general matter, void marriages violate core marriage prohibitions, for example, bigamous and incestuous marriages, and are void from their inception. Voidable marriages are valid unless and until one of the spouses seeks annulment. Grounds that make a marriage voidable typically include fraud, being below the minimum age of marriage, or lacking the proper mental or physical capacity. *See* Alaska Stat. § 25.05.031 (2019); D.C. Code Ann. § 46–403 (2019). As Section 5 explained, however, there is some variation among states about what fits into the void and voidable categories.

B. EFFECTS OF ANNULMENT

Given the theory upon which annulment is premised—that a legal impediment rendered the marriage defective from the very beginning—an annulment clears the way for the parties to marry other persons, but traditionally could also result in very harsh consequences. If the marriage was deemed never to have existed, early law saw no basis for affording either party the economic or social protections that come with marriage. Thus, even a destitute and defrauded wife would have no claim for alimony. *See, e.g., Knott v. Knott*, 51 A. 15 (N.J. Ch. 1902). A child born during the putative marriage was retroactively deemed "illegitimate." *See, e.g., Eisenberg v. Eisenberg*, 160 A. 228, 230 (Pa. Super. Ct. 1932).

The obvious injustice of this legal regime generated strong pressure for change. Many states adopted statutes providing that children born during a later-annulled marriage retain their status as "legitimate." And some courts early on resorted to equitable devices, such as estoppel or constructive trust, to justify some economic provision in annulment for unwitting participants in a void marriage. *See, e.g., Speiss v. Speiss*, 183 N.W. 822, 824 (Minn. 1921). Even today, some states with no other legal framework for relief rely on the Putative Spouse Doctrine (discussed below, in Section 9) to mitigate the economic hardships that can attend annulment. Over the years, however, many states have regularized relief by enacting statutes that expressly authorize courts to provide alimony or property distribution in cases of annulment. Minnesota's statute, for instance, borrowing language taken from section 208(e) of the UMDA, 9A U.L.A. 186–87 (1998), provides simply that the statutory "provisions * * * relating to property rights of the spouses, maintenance, support and custody of children on dissolution of marriage are applicable to proceedings for annulment." Minn. Stat. § 518.03 (2019).

Some courts have arrived at the same result even when the governing statutes are much less explicit. For example, in *Splawn v. Splawn*, 429 S.E.2d 805 (1993), the Supreme Court of South Carolina considered whether the family court had subject-matter jurisdiction to equitably distribute property of a bigamous marriage. The parties, Nathaniel and Louvenia Splawn, married in April, 1961. In 1990, the wife brought divorce proceedings on the grounds of cruelty. The court denied the petition for lack of proof, but ordered that the property of the parties be equitably distributed, 60% to the wife and 40% to the husband. When the husband then filed for divorce on the basis of a one-year separation and sought enforcement of the equitable distribution order, the wife answered that she had recently learned that the husband had a previous, undissolved marriage (entered into in 1955). She argued both that the husband was not entitled to divorce from a void marriage and that, because the marriage was void, the Family Court lacked jurisdiction to make an equitable distribution order. *Id.* at 806. The Supreme Court of South Carolina rejected her argument, citing its own prior cases holding that S.C. Code Ann. § 20–7–420(6) (1985) vests Family Court with jurisdiction to consider and rule upon *all* matters in annulment actions. In response to the wife's argument that "the public policy of this State will be violated by rewarding one who may *willfully* commit bigamy with the protections and benefits of the equitable distribution statute," the court answered that the South Carolina statute "accords Family Courts discretion to consider misconduct, fault, and 'such other relevant factors' as it deems appropriate. Accordingly, where a spouse knowingly commits bigamy, the Family Court shall consider such bad conduct in determining the equitable distribution." *Splawn*, 429 S.E.2d at 807.

The South Carolina statute upon which the court relied, however, did not specifically authorize courts to divide property and award alimony in cases of annulment. Rather, it granted the Family Court exclusive jurisdiction over all family law matters (including annulment) and, in a later subsection, over all questions relating to family support or property rights. S.C. Code § 20–7–420(6) & (30) (repealed in 2008). The current statute provides that the Family Court has exclusive jurisdiction "to hear and determine actions for the annulment of marriage" but likewise makes no specific reference to property distribution in the case of an annulled marriage. S.C. Code Ann. § 63–3–530 (2019).

NOTES AND QUESTIONS

1. *The convergence of annulment and divorce.* The South Carolina court's willingness, in *Splawn*, to construe the South Carolina statute to authorize the recognition of support and property rights within void marriages reflects the convergence of the laws of annulment and divorce in recent years. If the legal consequences of marriage in terms of alimony and property attach to void marriages, are these marriages "void" in any real sense?

2. *Revival of alimony following annulment.* One possible continuing distinction between annulment and divorce concerns the legal consequences for parties outside the putative marriage. In some states, the ex-spouse's alimony obligation, previously terminated because of the recipient's remarriage, may be "revived" if the recipient's remarriage is later annulled. Revival is available even in some states, like South Carolina, that would permit the recipient to seek alimony from the second "spouse" incident to the annulment. In some jurisdictions, alimony revival depends on whether the subsequent marriage is classified as "void" or "voidable." If void, the obligor's duty is revived on the theory that the second marriage never came into existence; if the later marriage is merely voidable, the duty is not revived on the theory that the marriage was legally valid until annulled. *See, e.g., Watts v. Watts*, 547 N.W.2d 466 (Neb. 1996). In some other states, the matter is simply decided case-by-case according to general considerations of equity. *See, e.g., Joye v. Yon*, 586 S.E.2d 131 (S.C. 2003) (holding that courts should look to general equitable considerations in deciding whether an earlier alimony obligation should be revived). The UMDA similarly takes the position that in deciding whether to give full retroactive effect to an annulment decree, courts should be permitted to consider the interests of third parties and all other "relevant circumstances." *See* UMDA § 208(e), 9A U.L.A. 186–87 (1998). If retroactive effect is withheld, there may be no meaningful legal difference between an annulment and a divorce.

3. *Labels may still matter.* In *Manjlai, supra,* 447 S.W.3d at 380–81, a wife prevailed on her suit for annulment on the ground that her husband, in the United States from Pakistan on a visitor's visa, used fraud to induce her to marry. She alleged his sole reason for marrying her was to obtain a green card for himself and his family and obtain certain material benefits. She testified that she realized the fraud after learning that he had engaged in an Islamic ceremony terminating their marriage. *Id.* The dissenting judge, quoted earlier in this Section, found the evidence insufficient to sustain an annulment, because there was no material, false promise to induce marriage and husband's immigration status was known to wife at the time of the wedding. *Id.* at 382. The judge also stressed the serious consequences to the husband that flowed from granting the wife an annulment rather than, as she sought in the alternative, a divorce: "[w]hether the marriage is dissolved by annulment or divorce arguably might determine whether the marriage is void ab initio and whether [husband] may maintain his status as a permanent resident." *Id.* at 384. The dissent cautioned: "[I]t is important not to allow an annulment under circumstances in which a divorce is the proper remedy because doing so may

wipe out valuable rights and create precedent that undercuts the statute's unambiguous language prescribing a narrow set of circumstances under which annulment is available." *Id.*

4. *Religious versus civil annulments.* Annulment carries religious significance for adherents of certain faiths. Roman Catholics, for example, must annul a marriage before they marry again in the Church. Annulments for these purposes are granted under religious law by religious authorities. Although the civil law of annulment has roots in ecclesiastical law, it is now a purely secular matter. Canonical annulments have no legal effect on the validity of a civil marriage, and religious authorities retain autonomy to decide for themselves whether to give effect to civil judgments concerning annulment or divorce.

7. MARRIAGE FORMALITIES

States generally prescribe two formal requirements to establish a valid ceremonial marriage: the parties must obtain a marriage license and the marriage must be solemnized in a ceremony conducted by a qualified officiant. These requirements serve important purposes, but they are meant to reflect what most marrying parties would normally expect to do. States do not expect parties to consult a lawyer to determine how to get married.

Statutes set out the basic requirements for obtaining a marriage license. Ordinarily, parties must submit an application providing personal information about their identities, marital histories, age, and other information needed to determine their eligibility to marry. A Minnesota statute, for example, provides:

Application for a civil marriage license shall be made by both of the parties upon a form provided for the purpose and shall contain the following information:

(1) the full names of the parties and the sex of each party;

(2) their post office addresses and county and state of residence;

(3) their full ages;

(4) if either party has previously been married, the party's married name, and the date, place and court in which the civil marriage was dissolved or annulled or the date and place of death of the former spouse;

(5) if either party is a minor, the name and address of the minor's parents or guardian;

(6) whether the parties are related to each other, and, if so, their relationship;

(7) address of the parties after the civil marriage is entered into to which the local registrar shall send a certified copy of the civil marriage certificate;

(8) the full names the parties will have after marriage and the parties' Social Security numbers. * * *

* * *

Minn. Stat. Ann. § 517.08(1a) (2019).

The legal requirements for the second formality, solemnization, are typically flexible and forgiving, as the following excerpt from the UMDA illustrates.

UNIFORM MARRIAGE AND DIVORCE ACT
9A U.L.A. 182 (1998).

§ 206. Marriage

(a) A marriage may be solemnized by a judge of a court of record, by a public official whose powers include solemnization of marriages, or in accordance with any mode of solemnization recognized by any religious denomination, Indian Nation or Tribe, or Native Group. Either the person solemnizing the marriage, or, if no individual acting alone solemnized the marriage, a party to the marriage, shall complete the marriage certificate form and forward it to the [appropriate county or municipal] clerk.

(b) If a party to a marriage is unable to be present at the solemnization, he may authorize in writing a third person to act as his proxy. If the person solemnizing the marriage is satisfied that the absent party is unable to be present and has consented to the marriage, he may solemnize the marriage by proxy. If he is not satisfied, the parties may petition the [appropriate] court for an order permitting the marriage to be solemnized by proxy.

(c) Upon receipt of the marriage certificate, the [designated] clerk shall register the marriage.

(d) The solemnization of the marriage is not invalidated by the fact that the person solemnizing the marriage was not legally qualified to solemnize it, if either party to the marriage believed him to be so qualified.

NOTES AND QUESTIONS

1. *Rationale for requiring a ceremony.* Given the very loose requirements for a valid ceremony, what is the purpose of requiring solemnization at all?

2. *Forgiveness of failure to satisfy all required formalities.* Some jurisdictions require strict compliance with licensing requirements. Emphasizing the need to avoid uncertainty with respect to who is legally

married, these jurisdictions have held that ceremonial marriages undertaken without a valid marriage license are legally ineffective. *See Stovall v. City of Memphis*, 2004 WL 1872896 (Tenn. Ct. App. Aug. 20, 2004); *Betemariam v. Said*, 48 So. 3d 121 (Fla. Dist. Ct. App. 2010).

Other jurisdictions, however, are more forgiving of inadvertent failures to satisfy all of the formal requirements for legal marriage. For example, a New York court held that a couple was legally married despite their failure to obtain a marriage license; the couple participated in a Hindu marriage ceremony attended by 275 family members and friends, followed by an event at a reception hall; the bride wore white, gifts were received, and thank you notes were sent. *Persad v. Balram*, 724 N.Y.S.2d 560 (Sup. Ct. 2001).

A Connecticut court explained the strong presumption of validity:

> Marriage is strongly favored by the law, and existing marriages are presumed to be valid and that presumption has been described by the courts as very strong. It is a presumption that grows stronger with the passage of time, is especially strong when the legitimacy of children is involved, and can only be negated by disproving every reasonable possibility that it is valid.

Hassan v. Hassan, 2001 WL 1329840, at *8 (Conn. Super. Ct. Oct. 9, 2001).

3.   *Limits to indulging the presumption of validity?* If parties fail to satisfy *both* formal requirements for marriage—i.e., obtaining a license and solemnizing their marriage—may the court excuse the failure and uphold the marriage as valid? In *Pinkhasov v. Petocz*, 331 S.W.3d 285 (Ky. Ct. App. 2011), the court held these two requisites to be "inviolable." "While every presumption will be indulged to support finding a legally valid civil marriage, parties may not disregard statutorily mandated solemnities." In *Pinkhasov*, the parties asked a rabbi to perform a Jewish marriage ceremony, but did not wish "for any civil marriage license or marriage certificate to be secured, executed, or filed." The rabbi understood that they sought to avoid civil marriage because neither was an American citizen and each wanted to remain legally free to marry an American citizen to gain the legal privileges such a marriage would carry. *Id.* at 288. Thus, despite the parties' Jewish wedding ceremony, the court concluded that the parties had never legally married.

4.   *Qualified officiants and the question of Universal Life Church ministers. Persad* (discussed in Note 1) is representative of the highly deferential approach taken by many courts (and section 206(a) of the UMDA) in determining the qualifications of persons to officiate at marriage ceremonies. That deference, however, is neither absolute nor universal. Some states consider a marriage performed by an unauthorized officiant to be voidable and a few even hold them to be void. *See Dodrill v. Dodrill*, 2004 WL 938476 (Ohio Ct. App. Apr. 28, 2004).

One recurring issue has been the validity of marriages officiated by ministers of the Universal Life Church (ULC). On its website, the ULC offers "instant ordination" to perform legal weddings and other ceremonies.

Universal Life Church. A non-denominational church originating in Modesto, California in 1962, the ULC claims to have ordained over 20 million ministers and has no set doctrines other than "adherence to the doctrine of religious freedom: Do only that which is right." A perusal of a newspaper's weekly wedding announcements usually reveals a number performed by a ULC minister, often by a friend or family member who got ordained for that purpose. Joanna Grossman, *Can Universal Life Ministers Officiate at Weddings? In Some States, the Answer Is No*, Verdict, Nov. 1 & 22, 2011 (two-part series).

Some courts have concluded that a ULC minister is not a "minister" qualified to perform valid weddings, as contemplated by state marriage laws. *See Ranieri v. Ranieri*, 539 N.Y.2d 382, 388 (App. Div. 1989). In *Oswald v. Oswald*, 963 N.Y.S.2d 762 (App. Div. 2013), however, a New York appellate court declined to follow cases from "a quarter-century ago" (such as *Ranieri*) and concluded it was time to address the issue "anew." The decision creates an evident split among New York courts.

By contrast, some jurisdictions expressly hold that ULC ministers are empowered to officiate at weddings. *See In re Will of Blackwell*, 531 So.2d 1193 (Miss. 1988) (concluding that the ULC was "enough of a religious body" and the officiant "enough of a spiritual leader" to validate the marriage).

5. *Marriage formalities and destination weddings.* A court generally will defer to the laws of a jurisdiction where a marriage took place and treat the marriage as valid so long as it was entered into validly in that state or country. In *Ponorovskaya v. Steciklow*, the court applied that rule to decline to recognize a marriage entered into in Mexico because the parties failed to comply with Mexico's legal requirements for a valid civil marriage, such as obtaining a marriage license. 45 Misc.3d 597 (N.Y. Sup. Ct. 2014). The parties filled out a planning questionnaire that Dreams Tulum Resort (the site of their wedding) provided to all couples planning a wedding. Where the form asked, "Your ceremony will be: A) Civil; B) Religious/symbolic," they crossed out the words "civil" and "Religious" and wrote, in capital letters, "SYMBOLIC." *Id.* at 599. When one party later sought a divorce, the court held there was no marriage, observing that neither party "expected, or could have expected that their marriage was valid in Mexico." The court advised that couples who seek to have weddings in foreign locations often "opt to have a civil ceremony in New York either before or after they have their symbolic wedding" to ensure a legal marriage. *Id.* at 546.

6. *Marriage by proxy.* Consistent with section 206(b) of the UMDA, several states permit marriage by proxy when one party is unable to be present at the ceremony. One state, Montana, permits "double proxy" solemnization at which *both* spouses are absent. Gail Schontzler, *E-wedding in Montana Unites Couple Thousands of Miles Away*, Bozeman Daily Chron., Dec. 23, 2005. In *Tshiani v. Tshiani*, the court concluded that a marriage by proxy or by telephone does not violate Maryland's public policy, and honored a foreign marriage where one party participated by phone. 56 A.3d 311, 322 (Md. Ct. Spec. App. 2012).

A California statute provides that "[n]o particular form for the ceremony of marriage is required for solemnization of the marriage, but the parties shall declare, in the presence of the person solemnizing the marriage and necessary witnesses, that they take each other as husband and wife." Cal. Fam. Code § 420(a) (2014). California also explicitly permits "a member of the Armed Forces of the United States who is stationed overseas and serving in a conflict or a war" to participate in a valid marriage ceremony by proxy. *See* Cal. Fam. Code § 420(b) (2014). What sorts of circumstances should validate a proxy marriage?

In *Tshiani,* the court observed that "distant marriages are becoming more and more common," especially for military personnel, and "may be a couple's only option," due to factors like "modern employment commitments" uprooting a person from home for long periods. 56 A.3d at 322. Are there still good reasons to insist upon physical "presence" in our increasingly mobile society? *See* Andrea B. Carroll, *Reviving Proxy Marriage*, 76 Brooklyn L. Rev. 455 (2011); Adam Candeub & Mae Kuykendall, *Modernizing Marriage*, 44 U. Mich. J.L. Ref. 735 (2011) (advocating reform to permit use of videoconferencing).

7. *Premarital waiting periods; marriage education; covenant marriage.* Most states require a short waiting period (typically 72 hours) between the issuance of a marriage license and the marriage ceremony. In efforts to reduce marital instability and divorce, nine states have enacted legislation providing incentives to couples to obtain premarital counseling, by waiving waiting periods and/or lowering license fees for couples who complete an approved educational program. *See* Alan J. Hawkins, *A Proposal for a Feasible, First-Step Legislative Agenda for Divorce Reform*, 26 BYU J. Pub. L. 220 (2012); *see also* Matthew J. Astle, *An Ounce of Prevention: Marital Counseling Laws as an Anti-Divorce Measure*, 38 Fam. L.Q. 733 (2004). Should more states pass such laws?

A number of states offer couples who plan to marry published materials containing legal and other information about marriage, sometimes including guidance about marital dynamics and the skills and knowledge important to successful marriage. *See, e.g.,* The Alabama Marriage Handbook: Keys to a Healthy Marriage (Oct. 2011). A basic premise is that relationship skills can be learned and will help couples navigate inevitable conflicts. The federal government itself currently maintains a National Healthy Marriage Resource Center and funds efforts to promote "healthy marriage" and "responsible fatherhood."

What do you think of these educational efforts? Are they the proper business of government? Do states have an interest in ensuring that couples entering into a marriage contract understand its terms? Are such efforts likely to be helpful? In Chapter 8, you will read about various proposals to promote marital stability and deter divorce, including "covenant marriage," available in Arizona, Arkansas, and Louisiana.

8. *Health screening.* As noted in Section 1, at one time, states scrutinized the health of applicants for a marriage license to determine their

suitability for marriage and refused to permit persons with specified conditions—venereal disease or epilepsy, for example—to marry. To the extent that states continue to mandate blood tests and screening for disease, the mandate is now typically only to inform the marital partners about their health status, not to police access to marriage. Michigan's statute represents the contemporary trend:

> (1) An individual who is applying for a marriage license shall be advised through the distribution of written educational materials by the county clerk regarding prenatal care and the transmission and prevention of sexually transmitted infection and HIV infection. The written educational materials must describe the availability to the applicant of tests for both sexually transmitted infection and HIV infection. The information must include a list of locations where HIV counseling and testing services funded by the department are available. * * *

* * *

> (3) If either applicant for a marriage license undergoes a test for HIV or an antibody to HIV, and if the test results indicate that an applicant is HIV infected, the physician or his or her designee [or other listed medical personnel, such as a certified nurse midwife or certified nurse practitioner or the person administering the test or his or her designee] immediately shall inform both applicants of the test results, and shall counsel both applicants regarding the modes of HIV transmission, the potential for HIV transmission to a fetus, and protective measures.

* * *

Mich. Comp. L. § 333.5119 (2019). Under the above law, a county clerk "shall not issue a marriage license" to an applicant unless the application indicates the applicant has received the educational materials and testing site information mentioned above in section (1). *Id.* at § 333.5119 (2).

PROBLEM 2-7

Anthony and Roberta obtained a marriage license and participated in a marriage ceremony. The minister signed the marriage license at the ceremony, but the parties never filed it with the county clerk's office, as required by state law. Anthony claims that the couple lived together for two months following the ceremony before separating.

Roberta insists that the parties never intended to file the marriage license or become legally married. She alleges that Anthony told her that his mother and daughter knew that the couple had a sexual relationship and believed he would go to hell if he did not marry her. Thus, she claims Anthony proposed a "fake" ceremony to be performed by his cousin and represented to her that the marriage would not be valid. Roberta states that, following the ceremony, she took possession of the marriage license and burned it. She alleges that the license was destroyed with Anthony's full knowledge and consent. She further claims that the parties never lived together as husband and wife. In the alternative, Roberta asserts that, if the court does find the parties were legally married, the marriage should be annulled and declared void. She claims that, at the time of the ceremony, she was emotionally vulnerable due to the recent death of her husband and that she relied on Anthony's misrepresentations that the marriage would not be valid.

If you were the trial judge, would you find a valid marriage? Which factual disputes, if any, would you need to resolve in order to decide?

PROBLEM 2-8

If you were on a law reform commission tasked with revising your state's laws about marriage formalities, would you support a law that allowed laypersons to become a "minister for a day" for purposes of performing a wedding ceremony? Would you offer any other proposal concerning who may solemnize marriages? Of what relevance would it be to you that there is an evident upward trend in couples having a friend officiate at their wedding? *See* Rainesford Stauffer, *Why More Couples Are Getting Married by a Friend*, Atlantic (Apr. 10, 2019).

8. COMMON-LAW MARRIAGE

The preceding section considered the consequences of noncompliance with the formal requirements of licensure and solemnization. At one time, defects in a formal marriage were of less concern because "common-law marriage" stood as a backstop in most states to validate such marriages. Even without solemnization or a license, parties could contract a valid common-law marriage simply by (1) living together and (2) holding themselves out as married with (3) the mutual intention to be married. Once formed, a common-law marriage was valid for all legal purposes, and could be dissolved only through formal divorce.

For much of American history, common-law marriage was widely practiced and permitted as a necessary response to frontier conditions. Professor Nancy Cott explains:

> Despite stipulation of appropriate marriage ceremonies, informal marriage was common and validated among white settlers from the colonial period on. The dispersed patterns of settlement and the insufficiency of officials who could solemnize vows meant that couples with community approval simply married themselves. Acceptance of this practice testified to the widespread belief that the parties' consent to marry each other, not the words said by a minister or magistrate, mattered most. Neighbors' awareness of the couple's cohabitation and reciprocal economic contributions

figured a great deal in establishing that a marriage existed between a man and a woman, but consent was the first essential.

Nancy Cott, Public Vows: A History of Marriage and the Nation 30–31 (2000).

Professor Ariela Dubler suggests that additional public policies propelled the widespread embrace of the doctrine of common-law marriage in the eighteenth and nineteenth centuries. Common law marriage:

> provided judges with a way to privatize the financial dependency of economically unstable women plaintiffs. By declaring a woman to be a man's wife or widow at common law, courts shielded the public fisc from the potential claims of needy women, effectively deflecting those claims inward to a particular private, family unit. In addition, holding a couple married at common law avoided branding their children with the legal status of illegitimacy.

> Moreover, common law marriage * * * allowed judges to efface the potentially threatening nature of nonmarital domestic relationships by labeling them marriages. Common law marriage thus transformed potentially subversive relationships—subversive in their disregard for the social and legal institution of marriage—into completely traditional relationships.

Ariela R. Dubler, *Wifely Behavior: A Legal History of Acting Married*, 100 Colum. L. Rev. 957, 969 (2000).

Beginning in the late 1800s, the tide turned against common-law marriage and most states have enacted legislation abolishing the institution. Today, couples may enter into a common-law marriage in only a small number of jurisdictions: Colorado, District of Columbia, Iowa, Kansas, Montana, Rhode Island, South Carolina, and Texas. Utah and Oklahoma recognize common-law marriages under limited circumstances. *See* 50 State Statutory Survey: Common Law Marriage, 0080 Surveys 20 (Westlaw Edge 2018); Nat'l Conf. of State Legislatures, *Common Law Marriage by State* (2014). Similarly, New Hampshire will treat the surviving party as the deceased's spouse when two persons cohabit and acknowledge each other as spouses, and are generally reputed as such, for at least three years and until the death of one of them. N.H. Rev. Stat. § 457:39 (2019).

In 2003, a Pennsylvania lower court claimed to abolish the doctrine of common-law marriage in the state prospectively. The opinion captures common concerns about the doctrine:

> Many sound reasons exist to abandon a system that allows the determination of important rights to rest on evidence fraught with inconsistencies, ambiguities and vagaries. The circumstances creating a need for the doctrine are not present in today's society.

A woman without dependent children is no longer thought to pose a danger of burdening the state with her support and maintenance simply because she is single, and the right of a single parent to obtain child support is no longer dependent upon his or her marital status. Similarly, the marital status of parents no longer determines the inheritance rights of their children. Access to both civil and religious authorities for a ceremonial marriage is readily available in even the most rural areas of the Commonwealth. The cost is minimal, and the process simple and relatively expedient. Under Pennsylvania's statutory scheme, the fee for the issuance of a license is $3.00.

PNC Bank Corp. v. Workers' Comp. App. Bd., 831 A.2d 1269, 1279 (Pa. Cmmw. Ct. 2003). The Pennsylvania legislature subsequently amended the law to declare that no common-law marriages may be contracted after January 1, 2005. *See* 23 Pa. Cons. Stat. § 1103 (2019). Common-law marriages entered into before that date, however, will continue to be valid. Thus, in *In re Estate of Carter*, 159 A.3d 970 (Pa. Super. Ct. 2017), the court held that a surviving spouse satisfied his burden of showing that he and the deceased entered into a common-law marriage before January 1, 2005. Notably, in reversing the trial court, the reviewing court concluded that the same-sex couple had the capacity to marry even though they exchanged vows in 1996, when Pennsylvania law did not permit them to marry legally (Pennsylvania enacted a "defense of marriage" law in 1996, soon after the federal DOMA). Citing *Obergefell v. Hodges,* 135 S. Ct. 2584 (2015), the court reasoned that the lower court could not deny them the right to marry based on now-invalidated laws.

Do you agree with *PNC Bank* that common-law marriage has outlived its utility? What are the potential social costs of abolishing common-law marriage? Would there be any benefits in retaining and even reviving it?

Despite the abolition of common-law marriage in most states, conflict-of-laws rules provide for upholding a common-law marriage as valid throughout the United States, provided that the parties created it in a state that recognized the institution when the marriage was formed. In addition, common-law marriages created before statutory abolition (e.g., 2017 in Alabama, 2005 in Pennsylvania, and 1997 in Georgia) remain valid. *See, e.g., In re Estate of Love*, 618 S.E.2d 97 (Ga. Ct. App. 2005). Accordingly, the institution of common-law marriage is of continuing relevance, even in states that do not permit creation of such marriages within their borders.

In re Estate of Hunsaker

Supreme Court of Montana, 1998.
968 P.2d 281.

Nelson, J.

Anne Barnett (Anne) appeals from the July 17, 1997 Findings of Fact, Conclusions of Law and Order of the District Court for the First Judicial District, Broadwater County, determining that she was not the common-law wife of decedent Maurice L. Hunsaker (Maurice) and was therefore not an heir to his estate. * * *

Factual and Procedural Background

Sometime in 1985, Maurice and Anne met at a restaurant where Anne worked as a waitress. At that time, Anne was married to Raymond Price; Maurice had never married. Maurice and Anne became close friends initially, but they did not share an intimate relationship until sometime later. Anne separated from her husband in December 1986 and was divorced on February 30, 1987.

After Anne separated from her husband, she moved into a mobile home that Maurice bought for her. Maurice and Anne moved her personal effects into the mobile home the week prior to Christmas 1986. Anne testified that Maurice gave her a gift on every day of that week and that, on Christmas Day, Maurice gave her an engagement ring along with a matching wedding band and asked her to marry him. Anne wore the engagement ring at times, but she did not wear the wedding band. Anne stated that she never wore the wedding band because she did not believe that she had the right to wear it since she and Maurice did not have a formal wedding ceremony.

Maurice stayed nights with Anne at the mobile home until October 1987, when they moved into Maurice's house near Toston. The title and mortgage on the house were in Maurice's name alone. Maurice and Anne lived together in the house until Maurice's death on September 27, 1996.

* * *

Leonard Lambott (Lambott), a Toston area farmer and grain-elevator operator who knew Maurice and Anne for many years, testified at the bench trial on this matter that a sign in front of the house read, "Hunsakers, Home of the Classics" (referring to Maurice's and Anne's classic car collection). Lambott further testified that the message on the telephone answering machine, recorded by Anne, stated, "this is the Hunsaker residence."

Anne testified that she and Maurice purchased a large grandfather clock together and displayed the clock in the living room of the house. Maurice had the pendulum of the clock engraved with an "H" for Hunsaker in the center of the pendulum and an "M" for Maurice intertwined with the left side of the "H" and an "A" for Anne intertwined with the right side of the "H." Anne stated that she and Maurice were proud of the clock and showed it to people who came to the house.

* * *

* * * Anne and Maurice kept separate bank accounts. Because Maurice had poor credit, Anne purchased many personal items for Maurice and he bought many items with Anne's credit. Anne testified that Maurice generally reimbursed her for these purchases.

Maurice and Anne owned shares of stock in two companies as joint tenants. They also owned a time-share condominium at Island Park, Idaho as joint tenants. Maurice listed Anne as the secondary beneficiary to his sister on his Department of Veterans Affairs life insurance policy. Anne was listed as Maurice's spouse on the Designation of Beneficiary forms for that policy. Although most of one form was filled in by Maurice, Anne testified that she filled in the word "spouse" on that form. Maurice had another life insurance policy that listed Shorland as the sole beneficiary.

Maurice and Anne filed separate income tax returns each year listing themselves as single instead of married. Anne testified that they filed as single persons because Maurice told her that he was in trouble with the IRS and that he did not want to get her involved with his financial problems. Anne testified that she did not know that she could have filed as married filing jointly. Gary Spitzer (Spitzer), the accountant who prepared Maurice's income tax returns until 1993, testified that Maurice did not indicate to him that Maurice was married.

Steven Shapiro (Shapiro), a Montana City attorney who represented Maurice in several matters starting in the fall of 1993, testified that he once introduced Anne to a mediator as "Annie Hunsaker, Morrie's wife." Shapiro stated that neither Maurice nor Anne corrected his introduction. Shapiro sent Christmas cards to Maurice and Anne and addressed the cards to "Maurice and Anne Hunsaker." * * *

* * *

Anne testified that she felt that she was married to Maurice during their relationship. She also testified that she thought that Maurice felt married to her.

* * *

Lee Stokes, a Bozeman attorney, represented a client that was purchasing land from Maurice and two of his brothers and their spouses. He testified that, in trying to make sure that the title to the land was clear, he asked Maurice if he had any premarital agreements with Anne and that Maurice responded that Anne was not his wife and that he did not involve her in business.

Shorland testified that Maurice called Anne his "sweetheart," but not his wife. Shorland also testified that he was close enough to Maurice that if Maurice had been married, he would have told Shorland. * * *

Maurice was listed as Anne's "significant other" on two hospital consent forms that Anne signed. One of the consent forms initially listed Maurice as Anne's "husband." However, the word "husband" was crossed out and replaced with "significant other" [based on information Anne provided.]

On September 25, 1997,[d] Maurice contacted Stonecipher about preparing a will. Stonecipher testified that Maurice told him that Anne was his "common-law wife" and that he wanted to leave everything to her. Stonecipher further testified that Maurice said that he did not have a will and that his family would "eat [Anne] alive" if he died without a will leaving his estate to her. Because Stonecipher usually does not prepare wills, he and Maurice decided to speak again the following week to make arrangements for the preparation of a will. However, two days after their initial conversation and before a will could be drafted, Maurice died. He was 63 years old. At the time of his death, Maurice had five surviving brothers and one surviving sister. One brother, Harper Hunsaker, died shortly after Maurice.

* * *

[T]he District Court * * * concluded that Anne was not Maurice's common-law wife. The court therefore ruled that Anne was not an heir to Maurice's estate and it denied Anne's petition to be named personal representative of that estate. * * *

Standard of Review

* * *

We * * * conclude that, although substantial evidence exists to support the District Court's findings of fact, the District Court misapprehended the effect of the evidence.

Discussion

* * *

We have long held that the party asserting that a common-law marriage exists has the burden of proving: (1) that the parties were competent to enter into a marriage; (2) that the parties assumed a marital relationship by mutual consent and agreement; and (3) that the parties confirmed their marriage by cohabitation and public repute. *Matter of*

---

 d *Editors' Note:* The court's opinion is inconsistent about whether Maurice died in September 1996 or September 1997. In addition, the court states that Anne separated from her first husband on February 30, 1987, a non-existent date. Nevertheless, the errors appear to be immaterial to the court's decision.

Estate of Alcorn [supra, at] 630. The party asserting the existence of a common-law marriage must prove all three elements. Public policy generally favors the finding of a valid marriage.

[W]e first consider whether Maurice and Anne were competent to enter into a marriage. [A] party may not enter into a marriage prior to the dissolution of an earlier marriage. Thus, Anne was not competent to enter into a marriage with Maurice, as a matter of law, until her dissolution of marriage from Price was finalized on February 30, 1987. After Anne's divorce was finalized, the record shows that both she and Maurice were competent to enter into marriage. Thus, Anne has carried her burden as to this element.

Second, we consider whether Maurice and Anne assumed a marital relationship by mutual consent and agreement. The mutual consent of the parties does not need to be expressed in any particular form. Mutual consent can be implied from the conduct of the parties. This Court has stated that the mutual consent "must always be given with such an intent on the part of each of the parties that marriage cannot be said to steal upon them unawares."

In *Alcorn*, Kathee, who asserted that she was common-law married to Fred, proved that she and Fred mutually consented and agreed to marriage. Fred gave Kathee a wedding ring that he designed. The ring contained two interlocking horseshoes made with Yogo sapphires, which reflected the couple's shared interest in horses. Kathee testified that Fred designed the ring and gave her a matching bracelet. The couple also used the interlocking horseshoe design at their home by cementing horseshoes into the walkway leading to their house and etching their names below the horseshoes. Kathee also testified that she and Fred agreed that they were husband and wife. The combination of these factors led to our holding in that case that they mutually consented and agreed to a marriage.

Similar evidence found in the record in the case at bar shows that Maurice and Anne agreed to a marital relationship. Anne wore an engagement ring that Maurice gave her. While we recognize that Anne did not wear the accompanying wedding band, she explained that she did not wear the wedding band only because they did not have a "formal" wedding ceremony.

Likewise, the grandfather clock engraved with Maurice's and Anne's initials that they prominently displayed in their home has the same effect as the horseshoe design in the walkway in *Alcorn*. Both of these displays are evidence that the parties living together in the home mutually consented and agreed to a marital relationship. Finally, Anne testified that she felt married to Maurice. Anne also testified that she believed that Maurice felt married to her. The engraving on the pendulum of the grandfather clock is evidence of this in that Maurice considered Anne a

Hunsaker. Thus, the effect of the evidence in the record is that Anne carried her burden of proving that she and Maurice mutually consented and agreed to a marital relationship.

Finally, we consider whether Anne proved that she and Maurice confirmed their marriage by cohabitation and public repute. There is no dispute that Maurice and Anne lived together for almost nine years. As to public repute, we consider how the public views the couple. Relevant to this inquiry is whether the couple held themselves out to the community as husband and wife. A common-law marriage does not exist if the parties have kept their marital relationship secret.

In *Alcorn*, the record was clear that Fred and Kathee lived together for nine years. That, in turn, led us to focus in that case on whether Fred and Kathee established a common-law marriage by public repute. We noted that Kathee never changed her last name to Fred's last name; that she did not list Fred as a beneficiary on her life insurance, health insurance, or retirement forms; that she filed her tax returns as a single person during the term of her relationship with Fred; that Fred stated in his will, which left Kathee one-half of the net value of his ranch and all of his household furniture and goods, that he was single; that two of Fred's friends testified that Fred told them that he was not married to Kathee, and that Fred indicated to an attorney who drafted three wills for him, that he was single.

Nevertheless, we held in *Alcorn* that Fred and Kathee held themselves out to be husband and wife. In support of this holding, we set out that they spent all of their free time together, that Kathee wore the wedding ring that Fred gave her, that they regularly hosted people at the house, that Kathee spent time with Fred and cared for him during an extensive illness, that Kathee's family referred to Fred as "Uncle Fritz," that several witnesses testified that they considered Fred and Kathee to be married, and that Fred and Kathee held themselves out as a married couple to those witnesses.

In the case at bar, the record shows that Anne and Maurice held themselves out as a married couple and, therefore, had a reputation as such. The sign in the front of their home and the pendulum of the grandfather clock are evidence that Maurice and Anne held themselves out as husband and wife to those who visited their home. The answering machine message is evidence that Maurice and Anne held themselves out as husband and wife to those who called their home. Maurice's brother Richard stated in a petition filed with the District Court that Anne was Maurice's "surviving spouse." One witness testified that Maurice called Anne "my wife." An attorney who represented Maurice thought that Maurice and Anne were married. * * * The cumulative effect of this evidence is that Maurice and Anne held themselves out to the community as husband and wife and, consequently, had a reputation as a married couple.

* * *

* * * The party asserting the existence of a common-law marriage must * * * prove that the three elements of common-law marriage all existed at one time. The record in the instant case reflects that although Anne could not prove an exact date when all three elements were satisfied, there was a period of time, prior to Maurice's death, when all three elements of common-law marriage existed.

In sum, although there was substantial evidence to support the District Court's findings of fact, our review of the record leads us to the conclusion that the court misapprehended the effect of the evidence.

Accordingly, we hold that the District Court erred in ruling that the evidence presented did not establish that Anne was the common-law wife of Maurice.

Reversed and remanded for further proceedings consistent with this opinion.

GRAY, J., dissenting.

* * * It is my view that the Court has merely substituted its judgment for that of the District Court in weighing conflicting evidence and determining the credibility of the witnesses. * * *

* * *

* * * Anne's testimony that she "felt" married to Maurice, and that she "believed" he "felt" married to her, reflects how she and Maurice felt; it does not rise to mutual consent and agreement to a marital relationship. I daresay that many people who live together in an emotionally and physically monogamous relationship "feel" married. That is a far cry, however, from parties actually mutually consenting and agreeing to enter into a marital relationship. * * *

* * *

NOTES AND QUESTIONS

1.   *Capacity to marry.* As with any marriage, parties to a common-law marriage must have legal capacity to marry. Thus, no common-law marriage can be created where the relationship would be bigamous, incestuous, or violative of some other substantive prohibition. *See, e.g., Johnson v. Jackson,* 261 F. Supp. 3d 1206 (M.D. Ala. 2017) (rejecting Jackson's attempt to recover under Johnson's auto insurance as a surviving spouse because he could not provide a record of divorce from a prior marriage; Jackson failed to satisfy "capacity to marry" element required under Alabama law). Similarly, no

common-law marriage can occur where one party is mentally incapable of giving consent, or suffers from some other incapacity. Where the incapacity or impediment to marriage is later removed, most courts insist upon post-removal acts that establish the requisite elements of common-law marriage. *See, e.g., Thomas v. 5 Star Transportation,* 770 S.E.2d 183 (S.C. Ct. App. 2015) (finding that a relationship was not converted to common-law marriage when impediment of one partner's marriage to someone else was removed by divorce; the other partner did not know of the impediment and could not agree to continue the relationship once it was removed).

In light of the capacity requirement, when do you think the Hunsakers' marriage began (if at all)? To determine Anne's status as an heir, pinning down a specific date of marriage formation may have been unnecessary. In many cases, however, the timing of marriage creation will dramatically affect the parties' entitlements to share in property acquired during the relationship.

2. *Present agreement to marry.* The issue did not arise in *Hunsaker,* but some decisions specify that the agreement to marry must be a "present agreement," that is, that the parties must agree to marry today, not a week or a month from now. Could Anne have had a present intention to be married even though she mistakenly believed that nothing short of a formal marriage could legally bind the parties? *Hunsaker* appears to say yes. *Compare Callen v. Callen,* 620 S.E.2d 59, 63 (S.C. 2005) ("A party need not understand every nuance of marriage or divorce law, but he must at least know that his [intentions and] actions will render him married as that word is commonly understood."). Would it be better to require a written agreement to marry?

3. *Weighing the evidence.* The Montana Supreme Court is one of the nation's most liberal courts in its willingness to find the elements of common-law marriage satisfied. Other jurisdictions demand stronger proof of the parties' mutual intentions. Many courts require that, while circumstantial evidence is permitted, the elements of common-law marriage must be proved by "clear and convincing evidence." *E.g., Cochran v. Chapman,* 81 So.3d 344 (Ala. Ct. Civ. App. 2011); *In re Estate of Duffy,* 707 S.E.2d 447 (S.C. Ct. App. 2011).

In *Luis v. Gaugler,* 185 A.3d 497 (R.I. 2018), the Supreme Court of Rhode Island vacated a Family Court judgment (reached after an 11-day trial) that there was clear and convincing evidence that Kevin Gaugler and Angela Luis were married at common law during their 23-year relationship. The Family Court ruled that Angela's request for a divorce should be granted and denied Kevin's motion to dismiss because they were never married. Based on a review of the record, the state high court concluded that the trial judge misconceived the *weight* of the evidence in finding a "present and mutual intent to be husband and wife," despite the parties' "consistently oscillating representations" about their relationship and " 'cherry pick[ing]' how they would portray their relationship based on how it would immediately benefit them." Thus, the record did not support "their serious intent to be husband and wife." *Id.* at 506.

4.   *Holding out as married.* In addition to capacity to marry and present agreement, states also require evidence that the parties "held themselves out," or established a community "reputation," as a married couple. The evidence consulted in *Hunsaker* is typical—e.g., the understandings of neighbors, business associates, and family members, filing status on tax returns, real estate deeds or leases, loan applications, and other official documents, use of a common name, and the intermingling of financial affairs. In contemporary America, it is not difficult for parties to hold themselves out as married if they truly wish to do so.

The absence of "holding out" is often persuasive evidence that the parties never actually regarded one another as spouses. *See, e.g., Earlham Savings Bank v. Morrell*, 837 N.W.2d 681 (Iowa Ct. App. 2013) (observing that holding out is "considered to the acid test of a common law marriage," and that the couple's statements to a few individuals that they were common-law married "cannot be considered general and substantial, let alone clear, consistent, and convincing"). What if there was powerful evidence of the cohabiting parties' mutual intention to be married—a written contract, for instance—but they kept their understanding private? *Hunsaker* and other decisions suggest no common-law marriage could be found for want of public "holding out." What is the purpose of insisting on evidence of "holding out," at least where the other elements of common-law marriage are clearly met?

5.   *Common-law marriage preceding or following a formal marriage.* Occasionally, a party to a formal marriage seeks to prove that the couple established a common-law marriage before the wedding ceremony. The fact that the parties entered into a formal marriage, however, might undercut the argument that they had a preexisting understanding that they were already married. This circumstance may impose an extra burden on the party seeking to prove present agreement, but it is not necessarily determinative. *Estate of Antonopoulos*, 993 P.2d 637, 648 (Kan. 1999) (finding sufficient evidence of common-law marriage where, five years before their ceremonial marriage, parties moved in together and "Nick gave Barbara rings in a private ceremony witnessed by Barbara's two young daughters").

Parties have also claimed to establish common-law marriages with a former spouse following a divorce and reconciliation. Courts, however, have demanded proof of a new agreement to marry, cohabitation, and holding out after the dissolution of the formal marriage. In an Iowa case, for example, a woman claimed that she and her husband had divorced solely "as a means for her to qualify for various forms of public assistance, including financial aid, to enable her to attend college." *In re Marriage of Martin*, 681 N.W.2d 612, 615 (Iowa 2004). The parties resumed living together for the next ten years, however, frequently holding themselves out as married; when they ultimately separated, even their teenage daughter was "surprised" to learn that they had previously divorced. Nevertheless, the Iowa Supreme Court agreed that the facts—especially the couple's inconsistency in the way they described their relationship to others and the man's specifically refusing the woman's request to remarry formally—showed no mutual intent to be married following their divorce. *See id.* at 618.

PROBLEM 2-9

John Smith and Judy Jones, domiciliaries of Missouri, decided to attend a weekend dog show in Pueblo, Colorado. John and Judy had both divorced their respective spouses a few years earlier. Colorado recognizes common-law marriages created in that state, but Missouri abolished common-law marriage nearly a century ago.

While they were in Colorado for the dog show, John and Judy agreed to become husband and wife, and they told several of their Colorado friends about the agreement. John gave Judy a wedding ring, and she put it on her finger. They registered at a Pueblo hotel as "Mr. and Mrs. John Smith." At the end of the weekend, they returned home to St. Louis, where they have lived for the past two months and have told other friends about their agreement.

Must Missouri recognize the Smiths as married?

9. THE PUTATIVE SPOUSE DOCTRINE

Our final topic addresses the question: what happens if a court finds a defect in marriage formation that is too big to forgive (such as where one party is at all times married to another)? The putative spouse doctrine provides an equitable remedy for an innocent spouse who has relied in good faith on a mistaken belief in the validity of the marriage. It does *not* validate the defective marriage. The attempted marriage remains void, but the doctrine provides for relief that may closely resemble the relief the party would have received if the attempted marriage had ended in divorce. Where the doctrine does not apply (either on the facts of the case or because the relevant jurisdiction does not recognize the doctrine), the parties are left to whatever relief the jurisdiction affords cohabiting, nonmarital partners (discussed in Chapter 4).

In *Williams v. Williams,* the Nevada Supreme Court considered for the first time whether to adopt the putative spouse doctrine. As you read the decision, consider what functions the doctrine serves and whether it might undermine other policies distinguishing between valid and invalid marriages.

WILLIAMS V. WILLIAMS
Supreme Court of Nevada, 2004.
97 P.3d 1124.

PER CURIAM.

This is a case of first impression involving the application of the putative spouse doctrine in an annulment proceeding. Under the doctrine, an individual whose marriage is void due to a prior legal impediment is treated as a spouse so long as the party seeking equitable relief participated in the marriage ceremony with the good-faith belief that the ceremony was legally valid. A majority of states recognize the doctrine when dividing property acquired during the marriage, applying equitable principles, based on community property law, to the division. However, absent fraud, the doctrine does not apply to awards of spousal support. While some states have extended the doctrine to permit spousal support awards, they have done so under the authority of state statutes.

We agree with the majority view. Consequently, we adopt the putative spouse doctrine in annulment proceedings for purposes of property division and affirm the district court's division of the property. However, we reject the doctrine as a basis of awarding equitable spousal support. Because Nevada's annulment statutes do not provide for an award of support upon annulment, we reverse the district court's award of spousal support.

FACTS

On August 26, 1973, appellant Richard E. Williams underwent a marriage ceremony with respondent Marcie C. Williams. At that time, Marcie believed that she was divorced from John Allmaras. However, neither Marcie nor Allmaras had obtained a divorce. Richard and Marcie believed they were legally married and lived together, as husband and wife, for 27 years. In March 2000, Richard discovered that Marcie was not divorced from Allmaras at the time of their marriage ceremony.

In August 2000, Richard and Marcie permanently separated. In February 2001, Richard filed a complaint for an annulment. Marcie answered and counterclaimed for one-half of the property and spousal support as a putative spouse. In April 2002, the parties engaged in a one-day bench trial to resolve the matter.

At trial, Richard testified that had he known Marcie was still married, he would not have married her. He claimed that Marcie knew she was not divorced when she married him or had knowledge that would put a reasonable person on notice to check if the prior marriage had been dissolved. Specifically, Richard stated that Marcie should not have relied on statements from Allmaras that he had obtained a divorce because Marcie never received any legal notice of divorce proceedings. In addition, Richard claimed that in March 2000, when Marcie received a social security check in the name of Marcie Allmaras, Marcie told him that she had never been divorced from Allmaras. Marcie denied making the statement.

Marcie testified that she believed she was not married to her former husband, John Allmaras, and was able to marry again because Allmaras told her they were divorced. Marcie further testified that in 1971, she ran into Allmaras at a Reno bus station, where he specifically told her that they were divorced and he was living with another woman. According to Marcie, she discovered she was still married to Allmaras during the course of the annulment proceedings with Richard. * * *

During the 27 years that the parties believed themselves to be married, Marcie was a homemaker and a mother. From 1981 to 1999, Marcie was a licensed child-care provider for six children. During that time, she earned $460 a week. At trial, Marcie had a certificate of General Educational Development (G.E.D.) and earned $8.50 an hour at a retirement home. She was 63 years old and lived with her daughter because she could not afford to live on her own.

* * *

The district court found that Marcie had limited ability to support herself. The district court also concluded that both parties believed they were legally married, acted as husband and wife, and conceived and raised two children. Marcie stayed home to care for and raise their children. Based upon these facts, the district court granted the annulment and awarded Marcie one-half of all the jointly-held property and spousal support. * * * Richard timely appealed the district court's judgment.

DISCUSSION

Annulment

A marriage is void if either of the parties to the marriage has a former husband or wife then living. Richard and Marcie's marriage was void because Marcie was still married to another man when she married Richard. * * * An annulment proceeding is the proper manner to dissolve a void marriage and resolve other issues arising from the dissolution of the relationship.

* * *

Putative spouse doctrine

Under the putative spouse doctrine, when a marriage is legally void, the civil effects of a legal marriage flow to the parties who contracted to marry in good faith. That is, a putative spouse is entitled to many of the rights of an actual spouse. A majority of states have recognized some form of the doctrine through case law or statute. States differ, however, on what exactly constitutes a "civil effect." The doctrine was developed to avoid depriving innocent parties who believe in good faith that they are married from being denied the economic and status-related benefits of marriage, such as property division, pension, and health benefits.

The doctrine has two elements: (1) a proper marriage ceremony was performed, and (2) one or both of the parties had a good-faith belief that there was no impediment to the marriage and the marriage was valid and proper. "Good faith" has been defined as an "honest and reasonable belief that the marriage was valid at the time of the ceremony." Good faith is presumed. * * * However, when a person receives reliable information that an impediment exists, the individual cannot ignore the information, but instead has a duty to investigate further. Persons cannot act " 'blindly or without reasonable precaution.' " Finally, once a spouse learns of the impediment, the putative marriage ends.

We have not previously considered the putative spouse doctrine, but we are persuaded by the rationale of our sister states that public policy supports adopting the doctrine in Nevada. Fairness and equity favor recognizing putative spouses when parties enter into a marriage ceremony in good faith and without knowledge that there is a factual or legal impediment to their marriage. Nor does the doctrine conflict with Nevada's policy in refusing to recognize common-law marriages or palimony suits. In the putative spouse doctrine, the parties have actually attempted to enter into a formal relationship with the solemnization of a marriage ceremony, a missing element in common-law marriages and palimony suits. As a majority of our sister states have recognized, the sanctity of marriage is not undermined, but rather enhanced, by the recognition of the putative spouse doctrine. We therefore adopt the doctrine in Nevada.

We now apply the doctrine to the instant case. The district court found that the parties obtained a license and participated in a marriage ceremony on August 26, 1973, in Verdi, Nevada. The district court also found that Marcie erroneously believed that her prior husband, Allmaras, had terminated their marriage by divorce and that she was legally able to marry Richard. * * *

* * * The district court was free to disregard Richard's testimony, and substantial evidence supports the district court's finding that Marcie did not act unreasonably in relying upon Allmaras' representations. The record reflects no reason for Marcie to have disbelieved him and, thus, no reason to have investigated the truth of his representations. * * * We conclude that the district court did not err in finding that Marcie entered into the marriage in good faith. She therefore qualifies as a putative spouse. We now turn to the effect of the doctrine on the issues of property division and alimony.

Property division

* * *

* * * In this case, the district court treated the parties' property as quasi-community property and equally divided the joint property between the parties. Substantial evidence supports the district court's division, and we affirm the district court's distribution of the property.

Spousal support

States are divided on whether spousal support is a benefit or civil effect that may be awarded under the putative spouse doctrine. Although some states permit the award of alimony, they do so because their annulment statutes permit an award of rehabilitative or permanent alimony. * * *

* * *

Nevada statutes do not provide for an award of alimony after an annulment. Thus, the cases in which alimony was awarded pursuant to statute are of little help in resolving this issue. * * *

* * *

The putative spouse doctrine did not traditionally provide for an award of spousal support. Extensions of the doctrine have come through statute or findings of fraud and bad faith. As neither is present in this case, we decline to extend the doctrine to permit an award of spousal support when both parties act in good faith. * * *

CONCLUSION

* * * We adopt the putative spouse doctrine and conclude that common-law community property principles apply by analogy to the division of property acquired during a putative marriage. However, the putative spouse doctrine does not permit an award of spousal support in the absence of bad faith, fraud or statutory authority. Therefore, we affirm that portion of the district court's order equally dividing the parties' property and reverse that portion of the order awarding spousal support.

NOTES AND QUESTIONS

1.   *Good faith and termination of putative spouse status.* As *Williams* states, finding "good faith" for these purposes requires a fact-intensive inquiry. A party may not recover if he or she remains willfully blind to red flags warning of serious defects in the marriage. And, if the party undertook the putative marriage in good-faith ignorance of its invalidity, subsequent discovery of the impediment terminates the party's status as a putative spouse. Accordingly, any property or support rights cease to accrue after the truth comes to light. *See* UMDA § 209, 9A U.L.A. at 192 ("Any person who has cohabited with another to whom he is not legally married in the good faith belief that he was married to that person is a putative spouse *until knowledge of the fact that he is not legally married terminates his status and prevents acquisition of further rights*") (emphasis added). Some jurisdictions do not recognize the putative spouse doctrine, but they may have other forms of equitable relief available to allow financial distribution. *See, e.g., Thomas, supra,* 770 S.E.2d at 191–92.

2.   *Property and support rights.* Contrary to *Williams,* many states do allow putative spouses to recover alimony or spousal support, as well as an equitable distribution of community or marital property. *See Choa Yang Xiong*

v. Xiong, 800 N.W.2d 187 (Minn. Ct. App. 2011). The UMDA also takes this approach. *See* UMDA § 209 ("A putative spouse acquires the rights conferred upon a legal spouse, including the right to maintenance following termination of his status, whether or not the marriage is prohibited * * * or declared invalid."). What basis exists for forcing a marriage-like division of property between putative spouses? What principle—equitable or otherwise—might support withholding future support from putative spouses while according them a spouse-like property distribution? *Williams* pointed to decisions, some of them quite old, reasoning that in the absence of a valid marriage there could be no basis for imposing an ongoing obligation of support. *See Williams*, 97 P.3d at 1130–31.

3. *Putative common-law marriage. Williams* limits the scope of Nevada's putative spouse doctrine to cases in which one party relies in good faith on a defective *ceremonial* marriage. *Accord* 750 Ill. Comp. Stat. Ann. § 5/305 (2019) (modifying UMDA provision by limiting relief to "[a]ny person, having gone through a marriage ceremony, who has cohabited with another"). This limit would exclude the possibility of a putative common-law marriage, as for example where one party genuinely but mistakenly believed the couple had succeeded in establishing a valid common-law marriage. Why limit relief to putative ceremonial marriages? A very small number of states—particularly those few that continue to recognize common-law marriage—extend the putative spouse doctrine to defective common-law marriages. *See, e.g., In re Estate of Marson*, 120 P.3d 382 (Mont. 2005).

CHAPTER 3

SOCIAL AND ECONOMIC RIGHTS AND OBLIGATIONS

■ ■ ■

This Chapter chronicles the profound changes that have taken place over time in the relationship of gender to American family life. The first two sections of the Chapter address the changing legal, economic, and domestic status of women and men, and the remaining sections turn to various types of interspousal obligations. As you study this ongoing evolution, consider whether social change prompted legal change, whether legal change prompted social change, or whether each helped prompt the other.

1. CHANGING VIEWS ON THE LEGAL, SOCIAL, AND ECONOMIC STATUS OF WOMEN

A. THE COMMON LAW

Until the mid-nineteenth century, American and British women's legal rights—or lack of rights—depended heavily on the commentaries of Sir William Blackstone, which defined a married woman and man as one person under the law. Blackstone continued to hold considerable influence in the United States throughout most of the nineteenth century, when most lawyers entered the profession by "reading law"—that is, by reading Blackstone (and American commentaries written by James Kent and Joseph Story). Here is what Blackstone wrote in 1765:

WILLIAM BLACKSTONE,
COMMENTARIES ON THE LAWS OF ENGLAND
Vol. 1, 442–45 (1765).

By marriage, the husband and wife are one person in law: that is, the very being or legal existence of the woman is suspended during the marriage, or at least is incorporated and consolidated into that of the husband; under whose wing, protection, and *cover*, she performs every thing; and is therefore called in our law-French a *feme-covert, foemina viro co-operta*; is said to be *covert-baron*, or under the protection and influence of her husband, her *baron*, or lord; and her condition during her marriage is called her *coverture*. Upon this principle, of a union of person in husband

and wife, depend almost all the legal rights, duties, and disabilities, that either of them acquire by the marriage. I speak not at present of the rights of property, but of such as are merely *personal*. For this reason, a man cannot grant any thing to his wife, or enter into covenant with her: for the grant would be to suppose her separate existence; and to covenant with her, would be only to covenant with himself: and therefore it is also generally true, that all compacts made between husband and wife, when single, are voided by the intermarriage. * * * And a husband may also bequeath any thing to his wife by will; for that cannot take effect till the coverture is determined by his death. The husband is bound to provide his wife with necessaries by law, as much as himself: and, if she contracts debts for them, he is obliged to pay them; but, for any thing besides necessaries, he is not chargeable. Also if a wife elopes, and lives with another man, the husband is not chargeable even for necessaries; at least if the person who furnishes them, is sufficiently apprized of her elopement. If the wife be indebted before marriage, the husband is bound afterwards to pay the debt; for he has adopted her and her circumstances together. If the wife be injured in her person or her property, she can bring no action for redress without her husband's concurrence, and in his name, as well as her own: neither can she be sued without making the husband a defendant. There is indeed one case where the wife shall sue and be sued as a feme sole, *viz.* where the husband has abjured the realm, or is banished: for then he is dead in law; and the husband being thus disabled to sue for or defend the wife, it would be most unreasonable if she had no remedy, or could make no defence at all. In criminal prosecutions, it is true, the wife may be indicted and punished separately; for the union is only a civil union. But, in trials of any sort, they are not allowed to be evidence for, or against, each other: partly because it is impossible their testimony should be indifferent; but principally because of the union of person. * * *

But, though our law in general considers man and wife as one person, yet there are some instances in which she is separately considered; as inferior to him, and acting by his compulsion. And therefore any deeds executed, and acts done, by her, during her coverture, are void; except it be a fine, or the like manner of record, in which case she must be solely and secretly examined, to learn if her act be voluntary. She cannot by will devise lands to her husband, unless under special circumstances; for at the time of making it she is supposed to be under his coercion. And in some felonies, and other inferior crimes, committed by her, through constraint of her husband, the law excuses her: but this extends not to treason or murder.

The husband also, by the old law, might give his wife moderate correction. For, as he is to answer for her misbehaviour, the law thought it reasonable to intrust him with this power of restraining her, by domestic chastisement, in the same moderation that a man is allowed to correct his apprentices or children; for whom the master or parent is also liable in some cases to answer. But this power of correction was confined within reasonable bounds, and the husband was prohibited from using any violence to his wife. * * * But, with us, in the politer reign of Charles the second, this power of correction began to be doubted: and a wife may now have security of the peace against her husband; or, in return, a husband against his wife. Yet the lower rank of people, who were always fond of the old common law, still claim and exert their ancient privilege: and the courts of law will still permit a husband to restrain a wife of her liberty, in the case of any gross misbehaviour.

These are the chief legal effects of marriage during the coverture; upon which we may observe, that even the disabilities, which the wife lies under, are for the most part intended for her protection and benefit. So great a favourite is the female sex of the laws of England.

NOTES AND QUESTIONS

1. *Rationale.* Blackstone's approach to marriage and the status of women was based primarily on an economic rationale. "Marriage was an arrangement of property for the propertied and their children, who were the conduits for family wealth. In Blackstone's rendition of marital unity, women and men approached marriage as theoretical equals to a contract. After marriage, nothing remained of that equality because of the very nature of the contract." Norma Basch, *Invisible Women: The Legal Fiction of Marital Unity in Nineteenth-Century America*, 5 Feminist Stud. 346, 350 (1979). Was Blackstone's approach relevant to the life circumstances of the vast majority of British and American spouses, who were not members of a landed gentry?

2. *Disabilities or protection?* Blackstone asserted that married women's disabilities were intended for their "protection and benefit." What support did Blackstone provide for this proposition?

3. *Coverture in America.* Professor Linda McClain points out that, in early America, the "colonists' rejection of hierarchy and insistence upon equality in politics did not extend to rejection of these rules of family governance. All free women, married or unmarried, lacked the right to participate formally in democratic self-government." Moreover, she notes that "African Americans held in slavery" did not even have "legal access to marriage" nor to other forms "of protection of family life." Linda McClain, The Place of Families: Fostering Capacity, Equality and Responsibility 57 (2006).

B. FAMILY NAMES

Family surnames can tell much about the social and economic status of a married couple. Based on the modern Anglo-American tradition, most women adopt their husband's last name, but this has not always been the case. In medieval England, for example, the family might adopt the woman's surname if she inherited property. Deborah J. Anthony, *A Spouse by Any Other Name,* 17 Wm. & Mary J. Women & L. 187, 192 (2010). Based on common law, men and women could generally change their names in any manner although, under the law of coverture, it was customary for a married woman to use her husband's last name. This custom did not become law until the middle of the nineteenth century, primarily as a result of judicial decisionmaking; apparently only one state—Hawaii—enacted a law (since repealed) mandating that a woman adopt her husband's name upon marriage. Elizabeth F. Emens, *Changing Name Changing: Framing Rules and the Future of Marital Names,* 74 U. Chi. L. Rev. 761, 771–73 (2007). Nonetheless, until the 1970s, some state laws still required that a married woman use her husband's last name in order to vote.

In traditional Latino culture, individuals are referred to by a combination of two surnames, one from each parent. When a woman marries, she retains her father's surname and adds her husband's father's last name to create her own surname. The couple's children are then given each parent's current surnames, hyphenated, free-standing, or separated by the letter "y," meaning "and," to create their surnames. Yvonne M. Cherena Pacheco, *Latino Surnames: Formal and Informal Forces in the United States Affecting the Retention and Use of the Maternal Surname,* 18 T. Marshall L. Rev. 1, 10–11 (1992).

In mainland China, women typically do not change their surnames when they get married. But the father's name usually passes on to his children. In Hong Kong and Taiwan, women generally add their husbands' surname before their names.

In contemporary America, most jurisdictions permit people to change any part of their names at will, provided the change does not defraud, misrepresent, or interfere with the rights of others. Most states allow a woman either to maintain her name or to accept her husband's last name, but other alternatives are not as easily accessible.

For men, changing a name upon marriage is still more difficult in many states than it is for women. Beth D. Cohen, *A Name of One's Own: The Spousal Permission Requirement and the Persistence of Patriarchy,* 46 Suffolk U. L. Rev. 1, 4 (2013). In 2007, California enacted the Name Equality Act, which allows parties in a marriage or domestic partnership to choose their own names through an application for a marriage license or a domestic partnership certificate. Nine states have statutes explicitly allowing a husband to take his wife's surname. Anthony, *supra,* at 204. In other states, however, if a couple chooses to adopt an entirely new name, they may be faced with the costs of a filing fee, running upwards of $100, an appearance in court, running between $200 and $500, and the expense of publishing a legal notice in the newspaper to inform creditors of this name change. These costs can deter many couples from exploring such options.

Notwithstanding the financial cost and the traditional expectation that a woman adopt her husband's last name at the time of marriage, some contemporary couples are making different choices. Among these options are the following:

a.   One spouse adds the other spouse's last name via hyphen;

b.   Both spouses hyphenate their surnames, each adding the other's surname;

c.   One spouse takes the other's name;

d.   One spouse uses birth name as middle name;

e.   One spouse takes the other's name socially, but keeps the birth name professionally; or

f.   Both jointly select a new name that may use both of their birth surnames or be completely different.

The change of surname, even in the traditional case of a woman adopting her husband's family name, is not automatic upon marriage, and while a name change may not be financially costly, it can be time consuming. After obtaining a marriage certificate, a woman must then take affirmative steps to change her driver's license, Social Security card, passport, and voter's registration, each of which requires official documentation of the name change. Also, written notice of the name change must be given to banks, employment offices, insurance companies, hospitals, credit card administrators, utility offices, the post office, property records, creditors, and other such organizations. Once the proper documentation is received, the name changes will be made without cost.

While there are no legal barriers to one spouse keeping or changing a name upon marriage, approximately 80% of American women still adopt their husband's surname upon marriage, and only 3% of men change theirs. Claire Cain Miller & Derek Willis, *Maiden Names, on the Rise Again*, N.Y. Times (June 27, 2015); *see* Emily Fitzgibbons Shafer & MacKenzie A. Christensen, *Flipping the (Surname) Script: Men's Nontraditional Surname Choice at Marriage*, 39 J. Fam. Issues 3055, 3063 (2018). Higher income urban women appear most likely to retain their own names. Miller & Willis, *supra*. When a woman keeps her name—or even when she hyphenates it—researchers believe this "increases the likelihood that others will think of the man as less dominant—as weaker in the household." Christine Kitchener, *Why Don't More Men Take Their Wives' Last Names?*, The Atlantic (Jul. 25, 2018).

While there is less information concerning same-sex unions, it appears far less common for gay and lesbian couples to assume common names.

Emens, *supra*, at 785–90. Same-sex couples may decide to change their names in order to create a shared family identity. *See generally* Vicki Valosik, *For Same-Sex Couples, Changing Names Takes on Extra Significance*, Atlantic (Sep. 27, 2013).

In 2018, Oregon became the first state to allow its residents to choose a non-binary—or gender X—identity for their driver's licenses; Oregon also does not require a court order for a change of gender assignment and name on a birth certificate. Elise Herron, *Starting Next Week, Oregon Will Let You Change the Name and Gender on Your Birth Certificate in Just Two Easy Steps*, Willamette Week (Dec. 27, 2017).

Issues involving the surnames to be given to a child are discussed in Chapter 12.

NOTE AND QUESTIONS

Reasons for name changes. A variety of explanations for contemporary approaches to name changes upon marriage have been offered, including "social norms." *See* Suzanne Kim, *Marital Naming/Naming Marriage: Language and Status in Family Law*, 85 IND. L.J. 893, 928 (2010). What norms encourage the status quo? Why do you think name changes differ for same-sex couples?

PROBLEM 3-1

The Columbia state legislature is concerned about the custom of name changing, in which the vast majority of women continue to change their names upon marriage. It is also concerned about the lack of name commonality in families in which one partner's name does not change. It is considering legislation that would impose uniformity on all married couples. Among the options it is considering are requiring couples: 1) to hyphenate their names; 2) to choose one partner's name as the name for all members of the family; 3) to choose a new name to apply to all members of the family; or 4) to prevent name changes upon marriage. Which, if any, of the options seems best? Why? How would each of these options affect public perceptions of the couple and of each individual? If you were a legislator, how would you vote?

C. WOMEN'S CONTEMPORARY LEGAL STATUS

This Section describes the movement toward women's equality within the law, providing a brief history of the law affecting women's rights.

American constitutional law was slow to shed Blackstone's view of women's social and economic status. The Fourteenth Amendment, which became part of the Constitution in 1868, barred states from denying "any person" equal protection of the laws. Consider whether its framers intended the Equal Protection Clause to protect women, particularly because women could not vote at that point.

For decades, the Supreme Court did not think so. When the Amendment was barely five years old, the Court denied the claims (under the Fourteenth Amendment's Privileges and Immunities Clause) of a married woman who sought admission to the Illinois Bar. *Bradwell v. Illinois*, 83 U.S. 130 (1873). Justice Joseph B. Bradley, concurring in *Bradwell*, explained that "[t]he paramount destiny and mission of woman are to fulfill the noble and benign offices of wife and mother. This is the law of the Creator." *Id.* at 141 (Bradley, J., concurring). Justice Bradley's discussion left no room for gender equality as we conceive it today:

> Man is, or should be, woman's protector and defender. The natural and proper timidity and delicacy which belongs to the female sex evidently unfits it for many of the occupations of civil life. The constitution of the family organization, which is founded in the divine ordinance, as well as in the nature of things, indicates the domestic sphere as that which properly belongs to the domain and functions of womanhood. The harmony, not to say identity, of interests and views which belong, or should belong, to the family institution is repugnant to the idea of a woman adopting a distinct and independent career from that of her husband.

> *Id.*

The Court remained inhospitable to gender equity well into the 1960s. In *Hoyt v. Florida*, the Court, applying rational basis scrutiny to an equal protection claim, upheld a state statute that granted women (but not men) an absolute exemption from jury service. 368 U.S. 57 (1961). "Despite the enlightened emancipation of women from the restrictions and protections of bygone years, and their entry into many parts of community life formerly considered to be reserved to men," wrote Justice John M. Harlan, "woman is still regarded as the center of home and family life." *Id.* at 61–62. The court overruled *Hoyt* in 1975. *Taylor v. Louisiana*, 419 U.S. 522 (1975).

In the excerpt below, Herma Hill Kay traces the trajectory of Equal Protection jurisprudence during the last half of the twentieth century.

HERMA HILL KAY,
FROM THE SECOND SEX TO THE JOINT VENTURE: AN OVERVIEW OF WOMEN'S RIGHTS AND FAMILY LAW IN THE UNITED STATES DURING THE TWENTIETH CENTURY
88 Calif. L. Rev. 2017, 2048–49, 2062–64, 2088, 2090, 2093 (2000).

* * *

The movement of twentieth century family law in the United States has been away from a patriarchal model and toward a more egalitarian one. * * *

F.   The Reemergence of the Women's Movement in the 1960s: Focus on Civil Rights, the Birth Control Pill, and N.O.W.

The period of the 1960s was one of extraordinary social and political ferment in the United States. In 1960, the Federal Drug Administration approved the first birth control pill for contraceptive use, thus for the first time providing women with a reliable method of controlling their fertility. African-American students began their lunch counter sit-ins in Greensboro, North Carolina in February 1960, adding a new element to the civil rights movement. * * *

Responding to the efforts of liberals and African Americans under the leadership of the Reverend Martin Luther King, Jr., and pressured by the Birmingham riots in April and May of 1963, President Kennedy sent a civil rights bill to Congress on June 19, 1963. It was enacted in 1964 after his assassination made Lyndon Johnson President. The Civil Rights Act of 1964, meant to redress the situation of African Americans, contained an unexpected bonus for women. Title VII of the Act, as originally drafted, forbade discrimination in employment based on "race, color, religion, or national origin." As enacted, however, it also applied to discrimination based on "sex." These favorable federal laws and comparable state laws may have facilitated the entry of women into the labor force in dramatically increased numbers: between 1960 and 1980, the number of women workers almost doubled, from 23 million in 1960 to 45.5 million in 1980. * * *

* * *

I.   Constitutional Campaigns for Women's Equality and Self-Determination

1.   *Ruth Bader Ginsburg and the Equal Protection Clause*

During the 1970s, while the state legislatures were occupied with divorce reform, abortion reform, and ratification of the [proposed Equal Rights Amendment to the Constitution ("ERA"), which ultimately failed to become federal law, falling three states short when the ratification period expired on June 30, 1982], a quiet campaign was underway in the federal courts to create a secure place for women in the United States Constitution. This campaign was conceived, implemented, and carried out by the Women's Rights Project of the American Civil Liberties Union, under the leadership of [then] law professor Ruth Bader Ginsburg. When the campaign began, the United States Supreme Court's interpretation of the Equal Protection Clause consisted of a two-tier review process: claims were tested either under the deferential or "rational relationship" standard, or under the "strict scrutiny" standard. The first standard was said to be "offended only if the classification rests on grounds wholly irrelevant to the achievement of the State's objective. . . . A statutory discrimination will not be set aside if any state of facts reasonably may be conceived to justify it."

[*McGowan v. Maryland*, 366 U.S. 420, 425 (1961)]. The higher standard was reserved for "suspect classifications" such as race or national origin, as well as where "fundamental interests," such as voting, were involved. In such cases, the government was required to show a much closer fit between ends and means: that it was pursuing a "compelling" state interest and that the classification was necessary to promote that interest. * * *

Equal protection claims brought by women had been relegated to the lower tier of this approach and were decided under the "rational relationship" standard [as in *Hoyt*]. Not surprisingly, most of these claims were unsuccessful. * * * [T]he feminist strategists of the ACLU undertook the ambitious task of changing the Court's interpretation of the Equal Protection Clause to make sex, like race, a "suspect classification." Their argument received its first hearing in the Supreme Court in *Reed v. Reed*, 404 U.S. 71 (1971), and resulted in the creation of a new tier of review, one that came to be known as an "intermediate" standard. Two years later, in *Frontiero v. Richardson*, 411 U.S. 677 (1973), the Court came within one vote of classifying sex as a "suspect classification." Ginsburg later described her strategy in choosing cases to bring before the Court as "basic education," explaining that the 1970s cases ... all rested on the same fundamental premise: that the law's differential treatment of men and women, typically rationalized as reflecting "natural" differences between the sexes, historically had tended to contribute to women's subordination— their confined "place" in man's world—even when conceived as protective of the fairer, but weaker and dependent-prone sex. Ginsburg's strategy succeeded brilliantly. When she left the academy to accept appointment to the federal bench in 1980, the intermediate scrutiny standard was well established and, with it, women's enhanced ability to assert constitutional claims for equality.

* * *

III. Challenges for the Twenty-First Century

[Historian] Carl Degler characterized the differing attitudes of nineteenth-and early twentieth-century men and women toward their work:

> Although women have been a part of the industrial system in the United States virtually from its inception, their relation to that system has always been different in certain fundamental ways from that of men. From the outset woman's employment was shaped around the family, while man's work, in a real sense, shaped the family. The family moved, lived, and functioned as man's work decreed; woman's employment, on the other hand, ceased when the family began, and from then on, as we have seen,

it adjusted to the needs of the family, for the family was a woman's first responsibility.[466]

As the twenty-first century opens, this observation has lost much of its force for a relatively small, but growing, number of career women working in the professions, politics, and business. These women come from all racial and ethnic backgrounds and all socioeconomic classes. Unlike many of their mothers and grandmothers, they do not expect to forego family life to take on full-time careers, nor do they derive their identities from their husbands or companions. They are no longer the "second" sex. Their influence as trend-setters has not yet spread to all women, but their example as role models is powerful.

* * *

The other side of this story—its impact on men—has as yet been only imperfectly explored. * * * As women sought to break down barriers to their own participation in the public sphere, some men sought expression for their nurturing capacities in the private sphere.

* * *

NOTES AND QUESTIONS

1.   *Are we there yet?* As Professor Kay notes, full equality has been difficult to achieve. Some have heralded "the end of men" based on facts like the majority of college graduates are women, and women are increasingly likely to outearn their husbands. *See* Hanna W. Rosin, The End of Men: And the Rise of Women (2012). On the other hand, while it is true that the gender wage gap decreased in the sixties and seventies, and that women have become more likely than men to graduate from college, progress on closing the gender wage gap began to slow in the 1990s. Moreover, for female college graduates, the gender wage gap has increased, and "it takes a master's degree for a woman to catch up with a man with a BA." June Carbone, Nancy Levit, & Naomi Cahn, Shafted (forthcoming 2020). Why such differing interpretations of the same phenomenon?

2.   *The standard.* Although the Court "held in *Craig v. Boren* (1976) that sex-based state action would trigger intermediate rather than strict scrutiny under the Equal Protection Clause[,] Craig never explained why it would be inappropriate to require strict scrutiny, which would demand compelling state interests and narrow tailoring to further those interests." Jill Elaine Hasday, *Women's Exclusion from the Constitutional Canon*, 2013 U. Ill. L. Rev. 1715, 1726 (2013). Should regulation of gender discrimination depend on the Court's application of equal protection, or should regulation depend on legislative action?

---

[466] Carl N. Degler, *At Odds* 395 (1980).

In *United States v. Virginia*, 518 U.S. 515 (1996), Justice Ginsburg considered the constitutionality of Virginia's same-sex military college. In striking down the school's gender-based admission policy, the Court held that it:

> has carefully inspected official action that closes a door or denies opportunity to women (or to men). To summarize the Court's current directions for cases of official classification based on gender: Focusing on the differential treatment or denial of opportunity for which relief is sought, the reviewing court must determine whether the proffered justification is "exceedingly persuasive." The burden of justification is demanding and it rests entirely on the State. The State must show "at least that the [challenged] classification serves 'important governmental objectives and that the discriminatory means employed' are 'substantially related to the achievement of those objectives.'" The justification must be genuine, not hypothesized or invented *post hoc* in response to litigation. And it must not rely on overbroad generalizations about the different talents, capacities, or preferences of males and females.

The Court found no such "exceedingly persuasive" justification for Virginia's continuation of a sex-segregated school.

It is that constitutional standard that the Court applied in the next case, in which it considered a challenge to immigration laws that distinguished between the conferral of citizenship by nonmarital mothers and fathers.

SESSIONS V. MORALES-SANTANA

Supreme Court of the United States, 2017.
137 S. Ct. 1678.

JUSTICE GINSBURG delivered the opinion of the Court.

This case concerns a gender-based differential in the law governing acquisition of U.S. citizenship by a child born abroad, when one parent is a U.S. citizen, the other, a citizen of another nation. The main rule [a]pplicable to married couples requires a period of physical presence in the United States for the U.S.-citizen parent. [T]he requirement is five years prebirth, § 1401(g) (2012 ed.). That main rule is rendered applicable to unwed U.S.-citizen fathers by § 1409(a). Congress ordered an exception, however, for unwed U.S.-citizen mothers. Contained in § 1409(c), the exception allows an unwed mother to transmit her citizenship to a child born abroad if she has lived in the United States for just one year prior to the child's birth.

* * *

B

Respondent Luis Ramón Morales-Santana moved to the United States at age 13, and has resided in this country most of his life. Now facing deportation, he asserts U.S. citizenship at birth based on the citizenship of his biological father, José Morales, who accepted parental responsibility and included Morales-Santana in his household.

José Morales was born in Guánica, Puerto Rico, on March 19, 1900. * * * After living in Puerto Rico for nearly two decades, José left his childhood home on February 27, 1919, 20 days short of his 19th birthday, therefore failing to satisfy § 1401(a)(7)'s requirement of five years' physical presence after age 14. He did so to take up employment as a builder-mechanic for a U.S. company in the then-U.S.-occupied Dominican Republic.

By 1959, [ ] he was living with Yrma Santana Montilla, a Dominican woman he would eventually marry. In 1962, Yrma gave birth to their child, respondent Luis Morales-Santana. [ ] Yrma and José married in 1970, and [ ] José was then added to Morales-Santana's birth certificate as his father. * * * In 1975, when Morales-Santana was 13, he moved to Puerto Rico, and by 1976, the year his father died, he was attending public school in the Bronx, a New York City borough. * * *

C

In 2000, the Government placed Morales-Santana in removal proceedings based on several convictions for offenses under New York State Penal Law, all of them rendered on May 17, 1995. Morales-Santana ranked as an alien despite the many years he lived in the United States, because, at the time of his birth, his father did not satisfy the requirement of five years' physical presence after age 14. [He challenged this determination.] Relying on this Court's post-1970 construction of the equal protection principle as it bears on gender-based classifications, the [Second Circuit] held unconstitutional the differential treatment of unwed mothers and fathers. [W]e consider the matter anew.

II

Because [the statute] treats sons and daughters alike, Morales-Santana does not suffer discrimination on the basis of *his* gender. He complains, instead, of gender-based discrimination against his father, who was unwed at the time of Morales-Santana's birth and was not accorded the right an unwed U.S.-citizen mother would have to transmit citizenship to her child.

* * *

III

[The relevant statutes] date from an era when the lawbooks of our Nation were rife with overbroad generalizations about the way men and women are. See, *e.g., Hoyt v. Florida,* 368 U.S. 57, 62 (1961) (women are the "center of home and family life," therefore they can be "relieved from the civic duty of jury service"). Today, laws of this kind are subject to review under the heightened scrutiny that now attends "all gender-based classifications"[. S]ee, *e.g., United States v. Virginia,* 518 U.S. 515, 555–56 (1996) (state-maintained military academy may not deny admission to qualified women).

Laws granting or denying benefits "on the basis of the sex of the qualifying parent," our post-1970 decisions affirm, differentiate on the basis of gender, and therefore attract heightened review under the Constitution's equal protection guarantee. *Califano v. Westcott,* 443 U.S. 76 (1979) (holding unconstitutional provision of unemployed-parent benefits exclusively to fathers). cf. *Reed v. Reed,* 404 U.S. 71, 74, 76–77 (1971) (holding unconstitutional a probate-code preference for a father over a mother as administrator of a deceased child's estate).

* * *

The defender of legislation that differentiates on the basis of gender must show "at least that the [challenged] classification serves important governmental objectives and that the discriminatory means employed are substantially related to the achievement of those objectives." *Virginia,* 518 U.S. at 533. Moreover, the classification must substantially serve an important governmental interest *today,* for "in interpreting the [e]qual [p]rotection [guarantee], [we have] recognized that new insights and societal understandings can reveal unjustified inequality . . . that once passed unnoticed and unchallenged." *Obergefell v. Hodges,* 135 S.Ct. 2584 (2015). Here, the Government has supplied no "exceedingly persuasive justification," for [the statute's] "gender-based" and "gender-biased" disparity.

1

History reveals what lurks behind § 1409. Enacted in the Nationality Act of 1940 (1940 Act), § 1409 ended a century and a half of congressional silence on the citizenship of children born abroad to unwed parents. During this era, two once habitual, but now untenable, assumptions pervaded our Nation's citizenship laws and underpinned judicial and administrative rulings: In marriage, husband is dominant, wife subordinate; unwed mother is the natural and sole guardian of a nonmarital child.

Under the once entrenched principle of male dominance in marriage, the husband controlled both wife and child. * * * Through the early 20th century, a male citizen automatically conferred U.S. citizenship on his alien wife. A female citizen, however, was incapable of conferring citizenship on her husband; indeed, she was subject to expatriation if she married an alien. The family of a citizen or a lawfully admitted permanent resident enjoyed statutory exemptions from entry requirements, but only if the citizen or resident was male. And from 1790 until 1934, the foreign-born child of a married couple gained U.S. citizenship only through the father.

* * *

In the 1940 Act, Congress discarded the father-controls assumption concerning married parents, but codified the mother-as-sole-guardian perception regarding unmarried parents. * * *

2

For close to a half century, as earlier observed, this Court has viewed with suspicion laws that rely on "overbroad generalizations about the different talents, capacities, or preferences of males and females." *Virginia,* 518 U.S. at 533. In particular, we have recognized that if a "statutory objective is to exclude or 'protect' members of one gender" in reliance on "fixed notions concerning [that gender's] roles and abilities," the "objective itself is illegitimate." *Mississippi Univ. for Women,* 458 U.S. at 725.

* * * Laws according or denying benefits in reliance on "[s]tereotypes about women's domestic roles," the Court has observed, may "creat[e] a self-fulfilling cycle of discrimination that force[s] women to continue to assume the role of primary family caregiver." *Nevada Dept. of Human Resources v. Hibbs,* 538 U.S. 721, 736 (2003). Correspondingly, such laws may disserve men who exercise responsibility for raising their children. In light of the equal protection jurisprudence this Court has developed since 1971, § 1409(a) and (c)'s discrete duration-of-residence requirements for unwed mothers and fathers who have accepted parental responsibility is stunningly anachronistic.

B

[The Government] maintains that the statute [ensures] a connection between the child to become a citizen and the United States [a rationale that does not survive] heightened scrutiny.

* * *

In sum, the Government has advanced no "exceedingly persuasive" justification for § 1409(a) and (c)'s gender-specific residency and age criteria. Those disparate criteria, we hold, cannot withstand inspection under a Constitution that requires the Government to respect the equal dignity and stature of its male and female citizens.

* * * The gender-based distinction infecting §§ 1401(a)(7) and 1409(a) and (c), we hold, violates the equal protection principle, as the Court of Appeals correctly ruled.

It is so ordered.

JUSTICE GORSUCH took no part in the consideration or decision of this case.

JUSTICE THOMAS, with whom JUSTICE ALITO joins, concurring in the judgment in part. [omitted]

NOTES AND QUESTIONS

1. *Remedy*. Although the Court held the statute unconstitutional, it did not give Morales-Santana the relief he sought. Instead, the Court decided that it could not give him "the special treatment" received by children of U.S.-citizen mothers because the longer physical-presence requirement applicable to children of married parents "must hold sway. Going forward, Congress may address the issue and settle on a uniform prescription that neither favors nor disadvantages any person on the basis of gender." *Morales-Santana*, 137 S. Ct. at 1701.

2. *Justifications*. What gender-based stereotypes does the Court identify and dismiss? Do you think there are any constitutionally justifiable reasons for distinguishing between married and unmarried parents? Nonmarital mothers and fathers?

2. WORK AND FAMILY: DOMESTIC AND ECONOMIC ROLES

A. INTRODUCTION

A significant portion of women have always worked for wages—including single mothers, women from low-income families, and women of color. Indeed, poor and African-American women have historically participated in the labor market at far higher rates than have white, middle-class women, and have confronted the family-work dilemma throughout their working lives. For example, in 1900, 26% of married black women were in the labor force, compared to 3.2% of comparable white women. Evelyn Nakano Glenn, *Cleaning Up/Kept Down: A Historical Perspective on Racial Inequality in "Women's Work,"* 43 Stan. L. Rev. 1333, 1337 (1991). Today, a high proportion of women of all races and social classes participate in the work force. Indeed, women now constitute approximately 50% of all workers. Not only do more women work outside the home, but this group includes both married and unmarried women with children. Women have, however, still not achieved pay parity with men regardless of their particular job.

Working mothers remain far more likely than working fathers to be interested in part-time, rather than full-time work. Kim Parker & Wendy Wang, *Modern Parenthood*, Pew Res. CTR. (Mar. 14, 2013). Moreover, there is an ongoing debate in contemporary culture over whether mothers of young children should work outside the home at all, or whether they should stay home. Indeed, only 16% of the public believe that a mother who works full-time is best for a young child, while 42% believe that a mother who works part-time is best, and 33% say it's best for the child if the mother is not in the paid labor force. *Id.*

In the past generation, the federal government has adopted laws and policies designed to facilitate women's participation and equal treatment in the workplace. The Family and Medical Leave Act of 1993 (FMLA), 29 U.S.C. §§ 2601 *et seq.* (2019), recognized the importance of having both mothers and fathers care for children. The Act's advocates hoped to promote a more gender-neutral allocation of work and family roles between parents, based on a belief that the law can and does significantly affect families by helping change gender expectations within the home. Other laws aim to eliminate discrimination against pregnant women and caregivers.

This Section first describes women's employment status, then discusses allocation of domestic work within the family, and, finally, reviews the applicable federal law supporting work and family roles.

As the next reading shows, some occupational segregation remains, and women still earn less than men in most occupations.

U.S. DEPARTMENT OF LABOR, U.S. BUREAU OF LABOR STATISTICS HIGHLIGHTS OF WOMEN'S EARNINGS IN 2016
(2017).

Introduction

In 2016, women who were full-time wage and salary workers had median usual weekly earnings that were 82 percent of those of male full-time wage and salary workers. In 1979, the first year for which comparable earnings data are available, women's earnings were 62 percent of men's. Most of the growth in women's earnings relative to men's occurred in the 1980s and 1990s. Since 2004, the women's-to-men's earnings ratio has remained in the 80 to 83 percent range.

* * *

Asian women and men earned more than their White, Black, and Hispanic counterparts in 2016. Among women, Whites ($766) earned 85 percent as much as Asians ($902); Blacks ($641) earned 71 percent, and Hispanics ($586) earned 65 percent. In comparison, White men ($942) earned 82 percent as much as Asian men ($1,151); Black men ($718) earned 62 percent as much; and Hispanic men ($663), 58 percent.

* * *

Women and men working full time in management, business, and financial operations occupations had higher median weekly earnings than workers in any other major occupational category in 2016 ($1,099 for women and $1,491 for men). Within management, business, and financial operations occupations, women who were chief executives ($1,876) and computer and information systems managers ($1,680) had the highest median weekly earnings in 2016. Among men, those who were chief executives ($2,419) and architectural and engineering managers ($2,265) earned the most.

The occupational distributions of female and male full-time workers differ significantly. Compared with men, relatively few women work in construction, production, or transportation occupations, and women are far more concentrated in administrative support jobs.

Women also are more likely than men to work in professional and related occupations. In 2016, 30 percent of women worked in professional and related occupations, compared with 19 percent of men. Within the professional category, though, the proportion of women employed in the higher paying jobs is much smaller than the proportion of men employed in them. In 2016, 10 percent of women in professional and related occupations were employed in the relatively high-paying computer (median weekly earnings of $1,325 for women and $1,518 for men) and engineering ($1,207 for women and $1,529 for men) fields, compared with 46 percent of men.

* * *

Median weekly earnings for mothers of children under age 18 ($756) were little different from the earnings for women without children under 18 ($746). Earnings for fathers with children under 18 were $1,013, compared with $861 for men without children under 18.

* * *

Women are more likely than men to work part time—that is, less than 35 hours per week on a sole or main job. Women who worked part time made up 25 percent of all female wage and salary workers in 2016. In comparison, 12 percent of men in wage and salary jobs worked part time.

NOTES AND QUESTIONS

1. *Continuing gender equity issues.* Although women have made great progress toward pay equity, substantial unexplained differentials persist. One study of physicians, for example, found that "[m]ale specialists earn an average

of $358,000 per year, while females earn $263,000—a pay difference of 36 percent." Alexa Lrdieri, *Report: Despite Physician Salary Increases, Wage Gaps Still Exist,* U.S. News (Apr. 11, 2018).

2.   *Accounting for the pay gap.* A number of factors account for the gender wage gap.

> Much of the gap is attributable to the fact that men and women work in different jobs, but a significant chunk (41.1 percent!) cannot be explained by characteristics of women or their jobs. Over time, the gender gap has narrowed—it was 59 cents on the dollar in the early 1970s—but the pace of convergence has slowed to a crawl in recent years.

THE SHRIVER REPORT: A WOMAN'S NATION CHANGES EVERYTHING 58 (Heather Boushey and Ann O'Leary, eds., 2009). Moreover, men work longer hours than women, which contributes to the gap. Claudia Goldin, *A Grand Gender Convergence: Its Last Chapter,* 104 AM. ECON. REV. 1091 (2014).

3.   *Beyond equity.* Husbands are still expected to fulfill the breadwinner role; more than 70% of Americans believe "it is very important for a man to be able to support a family financially to be a good husband or partner," while less than half that say it is "very important for a woman to do the same to be a good wife or partner." Kim Parker & Renee Stepler, *Americans See Men as the Financial Providers, Even as Women's Contributions Grow,* PEW RES. CTR. (Sept. 20, 2017). Nonetheless, while only 13% of married women in 1980 earned as much, or more than, their husbands, by 2017, that was true of 31% of married or cohabiting women. *Id.* What impact might this have on family roles?

4.   *Who does the caregiving?* While men's participation in household work has increased over the past several decades, women remain most likely to perform child-care responsibilities. Indeed, data from the American Time Use Survey found that in households with children under the age of 18, women spent twice as much time per day caring for children as a primary household activity compared to men. Bureau of Labor Statistics, *American Time Use Survey—2017 Results* Tbl. 1 (2018). Women also spent more than three times as much time in housework as men and more than twice as much time in food preparation and cleanup, while men spent slightly more than twice as much time as women in lawn and garden care. *Id.*

5.   *Elder care.* Elder care is another critical activity for many families. Approximately "40 million family caregivers" deliver "an estimated 37 billion hours of care to an adult with limitations in daily activities," with an "estimated economic value of [ ] approximately $470 billion." Susan Reinhard et al., *Valuing the Invaluable: 2015 Update,* AARP Pub. Pol'y Inst. (2015). As the age of childbearing rises, parents in the "sandwich generation" may need to care for both their children and for their parents at the same time.

B. THE LAW

Two federal laws, the Family and Medical Leave Act and the Pregnancy Discrimination Act, are designed to eliminate discrimination based on family-related issues. Each is discussed in this Section. In addition, existing sex discrimination laws may be useful in helping family caregivers achieve parity in the workplace, as addressed in the last article in this Section. Finally, as the Section makes clear, other sources of law may be useful as well.

1. The Family and Medical Leave Act

The FMLA entitles eligible employees to take up to 12 weeks of unpaid leave from work for medical reasons related to a spouse, child, or parent. The FMLA is often used for parental leave, but it also can be used for leave to care for a sick family member. Eligibility is defined partly by whether the Act covers the individual's employer. The Act does not reach private employers with fewer than 50 employees at any one workplace, but does apply to all public agencies and to both public and private elementary and secondary schools.

The following Department of Labor regulations summarize the scope and purposes of the FMLA.

DEPARTMENT OF LABOR COVERAGE UNDER THE FAMILY AND MEDICAL LEAVE ACT

29 C.F.R. §§ 825.100–101; 122 (2018).

§ 825.100   The Family and Medical Leave Act.

(a) The Family and Medical Leave Act of 1993, as amended, (FMLA or Act) allows "eligible" employees of a covered employer to take job-protected, unpaid leave, or to substitute appropriate paid leave if the employee has earned or accrued it, for up to a total of 12 workweeks in any 12 months [to engage in specified family caretaking]* * * In certain cases, FMLA leave may be taken on an intermittent basis rather than all at once, or the employee may work a part-time schedule.

(b) An employee on FMLA leave is also entitled to have health benefits maintained while on leave as if the employee had continued to work instead of taking the leave. * * *

(c) An employee generally has a right to return to the same position or an equivalent position with equivalent pay, benefits and working conditions at the conclusion of the leave. The taking of FMLA leave cannot result in the loss of any benefit that accrued prior to the start of the leave. * * *

§ 825.101   Purpose of the Act.

(a) FMLA is intended to allow employees to balance their work and family life by taking reasonable unpaid leave for medical reasons, for the birth or adoption of a child, for the care of a child, spouse, or parent who has a serious health condition, for the care of a covered servicemember with a serious injury or illness, or because of a qualifying exigency * * *. The Act is intended to balance the demands of the workplace with the needs of families, to promote the stability and economic security of families, and to promote national interests in preserving family integrity. It was intended that the Act accomplish these purposes in a manner that accommodates the legitimate interests of employers, and in a manner consistent with the Equal Protection Clause of the Fourteenth Amendment in minimizing the potential for employment discrimination on the basis of sex, while promoting equal employment opportunity for men and women.

(b) The FMLA was predicated on two fundamental concerns—the needs of the American workforce, and the development of high-performance organizations. Increasingly, America's children and elderly are dependent upon family members who must spend long hours at work. When a family emergency arises, requiring workers to attend to seriously-ill children or parents, or to newly-born or adopted infants, or even to their own serious illness, workers need reassurance that they will not be asked to choose between continuing their employment, and meeting their personal and family obligations or tending to vital needs at home.

(c) The FMLA is both intended and expected to benefit employers as well as their employees. A direct correlation exists between stability in the family and productivity in the workplace. FMLA will encourage the development of high-performance organizations. When workers can count on durable links to their workplace they are able to make their own full commitments to their jobs. The record of hearings on family and medical leave indicate the powerful productive advantages of stable workplace relationships, and the comparatively small costs of guaranteeing that those relationships will not be dissolved while workers attend to pressing family health obligations or their own serious illness.

* * *

§ 825.122   Definitions of covered servicemember, spouse, parent, son or daughter

(a) Covered servicemember * * *

(b) *Spouse, as defined in the statute,* means a husband or wife. For purposes of this definition, husband or wife refers to the other person with whom an individual entered into marriage as defined or recognized under state law for purposes of marriage in the State in which the marriage was entered into or, in the case of a marriage entered into outside of any State, if the marriage is valid in the place where entered into and could have been entered into in at least one State. This definition includes an individual in a [ ] common law marriage that either: (1) Was entered into in a State that recognizes such marriages; or (2) If entered into outside of any State, is valid in the place where entered into and could have been entered into in at least one State.

(c)   Parent. Parent means a biological, adoptive, step or foster father or mother, or any other individual who stood in loco parentis to the employee when the employee was a son or daughter as defined in paragraph (c) of this section. This term does not include parents "in law."

(d)   Son or daughter. For purposes of FMLA leave taken for birth or adoption, or to care for a family member with a serious health condition, son or daughter means a biological, adopted, or foster child, a stepchild, a legal ward, or a child of a person standing in loco parentis * * *.

* * *

(3)   Persons who are "in loco parentis" include those with day-to-day responsibilities to care for and financially support a child, or, in the case of an employee, who had such responsibility for the employee when the employee was a child. A biological or legal relationship is not necessary.

––––––––

The FMLA only provides unpaid leave. The United States is the only one among 41 of the most developed countries that does not mandate any paid leave for new parents, and it is in the small minority of countries that do not provide paid leave for new fathers. OECD, *Key Characteristics of Parental Leave Systems* 3, 6 (2017).

NOTES AND QUESTIONS

1.   *Limitations of the FMLA.* The FMLA is designed to protect individuals dealing with family illness or child care, but many limitations prevent a large percentage of employees from invoking its benefits. Employees are eligible only if they have already worked for the employer for a full year, and only if the employer employs at least 50 employees within one general worksite. What kinds of common worksites might not be covered? In addition, the employee must prove that he or she, or a family member, suffers from a serious medical condition (other than in situations of birth and adoption). The leave is unpaid, so taking time off can severely strain a family in need of support, and many covered persons cannot afford to take time off from work. Slightly less than 60% of employees, and less than 20% of workplaces, are actually covered by the FMLA. Jacob Klerman, Kelly Daley, & Alyssa Pozniak, Family and Medical Leave in 2012: Executive Summary (2012).

2.   *Leave-taking.* In 2012, 16% of eligible employees had taken leave under the FMLA during the previous year. The median length of leave was ten

days, with less than one-fifth of all leaves exceeding 60 days. Women are one-third more likely than men to take leave and almost twice as many women as men report an unmet need for leave. Of those who took leave, 54.6% took time off because of their own sickness. Even though the FMLA does not require compensated leave, 66% of leave takers received some compensation during their time away from work. Jacob Klerman, Kelly Daley, & Alyssa Pozniak, Family and Medical Leave in 2012: Technical Report (2014).

3. *Paid leave in the United States.* Some states (California, Massachusetts, New Jersey, New York, Rhode Island, and Washington State) along with Washington, D.C., have enacted legislation that provides paid leave for new parents, meaning that "one in four Americans now lives in a state that provides benefits to new parents." Deborah Widiss, *Single Parents and Family Leave* (2019).

4. *Institutional constraints modify individual preferences about sharing responsibilities.* While young people, both men and women, prefer an egalitarian relationship, they end up making more "gendered work-family decisions" when they confront gendered institutional constraints at work. David S. Pedulla & Sarah Thébaud, *Can We Finish the Revolution? Gender, Work-Family Ideals, and Institutional Constraint*, 80 AM. SOC. REV. 116 (2015). These constraints include a lack of workplace flexibility and the absence of government policies—like those available in other countries—that support an egalitarian "dual-earner, dual-caregiver" family arrangement. Pedulla and Thébaud conclude that the persistent norms about male roles, including the male breadwinner ideal, and the "negative social consequences" when men take advantage of policies that support parenting and family obligations, will make men less likely than women to take advantage of institutional changes, at least in the absence of policies that aim "more explicitly to destabilize overwork norms" for men than those being contemplated in the United States today. *Id.* at 133. What government or employer policies might support individuals who seek more egalitarian families?

2. The Pregnancy Discrimination Act (PDA) and Other Protections for New Mothers

In 1978, Congress amended Title VII of the Civil Rights Act of 1964 to add the Pregnancy Discrimination Act (PDA). The PDA, 42 U.S.C. § 2000e(k), provides:

> The terms "because of sex" or "on the basis of sex" include, but are not limited to, because of or on the basis of pregnancy, childbirth, or related medical conditions; and women affected by pregnancy, childbirth, or related medical conditions shall be treated the same for all employment-related purposes, including receipt of benefits under fringe benefit programs * * *. This subsection shall not require an employer to pay for health insurance benefits for abortion, except where the life of the mother would be endangered

if the fetus were carried to term, or except where medical complications have arisen from an abortion * * *.

The PDA prohibits employers from treating pregnant employees differently from nonpregnant employees. If, for example, an employer provides temporary disability benefits, those benefits must be available for pregnancy. *See generally* Enforcement Guidance on Pregnancy Discrimination and Related Issues, EEOC (2015). In 2015, the Supreme Court reiterated that the PDA does not grant pregnant employees any special treatment, but that a pregnant employee can show discrimination when an employer treats her less favorably than other employees for no justifiable reason. *Young v. United Parcel Service,* 575 U.S. ___, 135 S. Ct. 1338 (2015).

As a result of the Affordable Care Act, employers are required to provide a "reasonable" break time for mothers who are nursing. *Fact Sheet #73: Break Time for Nursing Mothers under the FLSA,* U.S. Dep't of Labor (Apr. 2018). The requirement generally does not cover employees who are ineligible for overtime pay, so many professional and executive employees are not included (for example, many teachers and lawyers).

PROBLEM 3-2

Ace Employer offers neither temporary disability benefits nor a parental leave program. Amy is a pregnant employee who has sued Ace alleging that it must provide her with disability benefits for pregnancy and then 16 weeks of paid leave once the baby is born. You are counsel to Ace. What advice do you give about the lawsuit and policies? Does the Act mandate that an employer which does not otherwise offer temporary disability benefits make them available for pregnancy?

PROBLEM 3-3

Beta Employer offers pregnant employees up to 10 weeks of paid pregnancy-related medical leave for pregnancy and childbirth as part of its short-term disability insurance. Beta also offers new mothers six weeks of parental leave. A male employee has sued Beta, alleging that this policy is discriminatory as it gives to 16 weeks of leave to women and no leave to men. You are counsel to Beta. What advice do you give about the lawsuit and the policies?

3. Discrimination Based on Family Responsibilities

There has been increasing attention given to family responsibilities discrimination (FRD) based on family caregiving, a form of treatment not directly addressed by the PDA or the FMLA. Family caregiving may take the form of child or elder care, and it implicates financial issues within the household:

FRD is employment discrimination because of an employee's caregiving obligations. When employees sue their employers for FRD, the cases include complaints of discrimination based on pregnancy, motherhood, fatherhood, care for family members who are sick or have disabilities, and care for aging or ill parents. * * *.

The number of employees who have caregiving responsibilities has increased, and the failure of the workplace to adjust to this reality has significantly increased FRD litigation.

- FRD cases have risen 269% over the last decade—a period when federal employment discrimination cases decreased. * * *

- Employees win 67% of the FRD cases that go to trial—a far higher rate than other employment cases—and employees prevail in 52% of all FRD cases that are filed.

- Employees in FRD cases were awarded almost half a billion dollars in verdicts and settlements in the last decade ($477,009,417 in 2006–2015), which is more than double the amount of the previous decade. This amount is likely a vast understatement of the real amount because it does not include confidential settlement agreements.

- FRD cases have been brought by white, black, Latino, and Asian American employees. How FRD is experienced can vary by the employees' race/ethnicity, and 8% of FRD cases include allegations of race discrimination.

- FRD is found in every industry and at every level within companies. Claims for FRD have been filed in every state. * * *

A pregnant employee's supervisor refuses to let her take a break as her doctor directed. A father who occasionally stays home with his sick child is excluded from meetings and punished for infractions other employees commit without consequences. A mother of young children isn't considered for promotion. A male employee is fired when he asks for leave to take his elderly parents to the doctor. Each of these situations may be the result of family responsibilities discrimination.

* * *

No federal statute expressly prohibits employment discrimination based on family responsibilities, although several state and local laws do. As a result, most caregiver cases are brought using a patchwork of claims under federal and state anti-discrimination and leave laws.

* * *

Several states and 90 local jurisdictions have passed legislation that addresses family responsibilities discrimination in employment. * * *

Cynthia Thomas Calvert, *Caregivers in the Workplace: Family Responsibilities Discrimination: Litigation Update 2016* (2016).

NOTES AND QUESTIONS

1. *The motherhood penalty.* Studies have shown that the "motherhood penalty" is alive and well. "Experimental research has documented that employers are less likely to hire mothers compared with childless women, and when employers do make an offer to a mother, they offer them lower salaries than they do other women. Fathers, in contrast, do not suffer a penalty compared with other men." AAUW, The Simple Truth about the Gender Wage Gap 9 (2014). Indeed, "[e]ach child chops 4 percent off a woman's hourly wages, . . . Men's earnings increase by 6 percent when they become fathers, after controlling for experience, education, marital status and hours worked." Natalie Kitroeff & Jessica Silver-Greenberg, *Pregnancy Discrimination is Rampant Inside America's Biggest Companies*, NY Times (June 15, 2018). While there is no doubt that the motherhood penalty is alive and well, some scholars suggest that it does not affect all women equally. Some sociological studies have shown, for example, that motherhood has little or no wage consequence for black and Latina mothers, that black working mothers are viewed more favorably than black stay-at-home moms in comparison to their white counterparts, and that women of color also enjoy more household help from Latino and black men, an advantage that promotes mothering and market work. Asmara M. Tekle, *The "Non-Maternal Wall" and Women of Color in High Governmental Office*, 35 T. Marshall L. Rev. 169, 175–78 (2010). What attitudes might account for these preferences?

2. *Formal legal protection for working parents?* The federal Equal Employment Opportunity Commission ("EEOC") has issued an Enforcement Guidance that specifies some of the situations under which family caregivers may experience discrimination, such as asking female job applicants about their marital or caregiving responsibilities, but not asking men the same questions. The EEOC Enforcement Guide notes that, while caregiver status is not protected by federal equal employment law, employees may nonetheless have a claim "when an employer discriminates based on sex or another characteristic protected by federal law." Such situations include: 1) when an employer denies "job opportunities to women—but not men—with young children, or [reassigns] a woman recently returned from pregnancy-related medical leave or parental leave to less desirable work based on the assumption that, as a new mother, she will be less committed to her job;" 2) denies "a male caregiver leave to care for an infant but grant[s] such leave to a female caregiver;", or 3) discriminates "against a Latina working mother based on stereotypes about working mothers and hostility towards Latinos generally."

EEOC, *Enforcement Guidance on Pregnancy Discrimination and Related Issues* (2015). Some states explicitly provide protection from discrimination for family caregivers; would you support such a statute at the federal level? Why?

3.   *Class, women, and work.* Work-family conflict is pervasive. Indeed, not only do "[l]ow-income families struggle with exceptionally high levels of work-family conflict," but also women who do not have "high school degrees report higher levels of work-family conflict than do college graduates." Joan C. Williams & Heather Boushey, The Three Faces of Work-Family Conflict 11 (2010). What might account for these higher levels?

3. INTERSPOUSAL SUPPORT OBLIGATIONS

As you read the following materials, consider the nature of the reciprocal obligations of spouses.

A. THE GENERAL SUPPORT OBLIGATION

"general "support" obligation

At common law, the husband was required to support the wife, and he had the corresponding right to her "domestic services." To enforce the support obligation, a wife might seek to force her husband to provide her with money or might use the "necessaries doctrine" to induce third parties to extend credit to her.

1.   The Traditional View of Support Obligations

This classic case shows how courts interpreted the support duty, and provides insight into the traditional status of wives.

McGUIRE V. McGUIRE
Supreme Court of Nebraska, 1953.
59 N.W.2d 336.

Opinion by MESSMORE, JUSTICE.

The plaintiff, Lydia McGuire, brought this action in equity in the district court for Wayne County against Charles W. McGuire, her husband, as defendant, to recover suitable maintenance and support money, and for costs and attorney's fees. Trial was had to the court and a decree was rendered in favor of the plaintiff.

The district court decreed that the plaintiff was legally entitled to use the credit of the defendant and obligate him to pay for certain items in the nature of improvements and repairs, furniture, and appliances for the household in the amount of several thousand dollars; required the defendant to purchase a new automobile with an effective heater within 30 days; ordered him to pay travel expenses of the plaintiff for a visit to each of her daughters at least once a year; that the plaintiff be entitled in the future to pledge the credit of the defendant for what may constitute necessaries of life; awarded a personal allowance to the plaintiff in the sum of $50 a month; awarded $800 for services for the plaintiff's attorney; and as an alternative to part of the award so made, defendant was permitted, in agreement with plaintiff, to purchase a modern home elsewhere.

[The defendant appealed.]

* * *

The record shows that the plaintiff and defendant were married in Wayne, Nebraska, on August 11, 1919. At the time of the marriage the defendant was a bachelor 46 or 47 years of age and had a reputation for more than ordinary frugality, of which the plaintiff was aware. She had visited in his home and had known him for about 3 years prior to the marriage. After the marriage the couple went to live on a farm of 160 acres located in Leslie precinct, Wayne County, owned by the defendant and upon which he had lived and farmed since 1905. The parties have lived on this place ever since. The plaintiff had been previously married. Her first husband died in October 1914 * * *. * * *

* * *

The plaintiff testified that she was a dutiful and obedient wife, worked and saved, and cohabited with the defendant until the last 2 or 3 years. She worked in the fields, did outside chores, cooked, and attended to her household duties such as cleaning the house and doing the washing. For a number of years she raised as high as 300 chickens, sold poultry and eggs, and used the money to buy clothing, things she wanted, and for groceries. She further testified that the defendant was the boss of the house and his word was law; that he would not tolerate any charge accounts and would not inform her as to his finances or business; and that he was a poor companion. The defendant did not complain of her work, but left the impression to her that she had not done enough. On several occasions the plaintiff asked the defendant for money. He would give her very small amounts, and for the last 3 or 4 years he had not given her any money nor provided her with clothing, except a coat about 4 years previous. The defendant had purchased the groceries the last 3 or 4 years, and permitted her to buy groceries, but he paid for them by check. * * * For the past 4 years or more, the defendant had not given the plaintiff money to purchase furniture or other household necessities. Three years ago he did purchase an electric, wood-and-cob combination stove which was installed in the kitchen, also linoleum floor covering for the kitchen. The plaintiff further testified that the house is not equipped with a bathroom, bathing facilities, or inside toilet. The kitchen is not modern. She does not have a kitchen sink. * * * The plaintiff has had three abdominal operations for which the defendant has paid. She selected her own doctor, and there were no restrictions placed in that respect. When she has requested various things for the home or personal effects, defendant has informed her on many

[handwritten margin note: the work that the wife completed)]

occasions that he did not have the money to pay for the same. She would like to have a new car. * * * The plaintiff further testified that she had very little funds, possibly $1,500 in the bank which was chicken money and money which her father furnished her * * *. * * *

It appears that the defendant owned 398 acres of land with 2 acres deeded to a church, the land being of the value of $83,960; that he has bank deposits in the sum of $12,786.81 and government bonds in the amount of $104,500; and that his income, including interest on the bonds and rental for his real estate, is $8,000 or $9,000 a year. * * *

* * *

The defendant assigns as error that the decree is not supported by sufficient evidence; that the decree is contrary to law; that the decree is an unwarranted usurpation and invasion of defendant's fundamental and constitutional rights; * * *. * * *

* * *

In the case of *Earle v. Earle*, 43 N.W. 118 [Neb. 1889], the plaintiff's petition alleged, in substance, the marriage of the parties, that one child was born of the marriage, and that the defendant sent his wife away from him, did not permit her to return, contributed to her support and maintenance separate and apart from him, and later refused and ceased to provide for her support and the support of his child. The court stated that it was a well-established rule of law that it is the duty of the husband to provide his family with support and means of living—the style of support, requisite lodging, food, clothing, etc., to be such as fit his means, position, and station in life—and for this purpose the wife has generally the right to use his credit for the purchase of necessaries. The court held that if a wife is abandoned by her husband, without means of support, a bill in equity will lie to compel the husband to support the wife without asking for a decree of divorce.

* * *

In the case of *Polster v. Polster*, 123 S.W. 81 [Mo. App. 1909], the evidence disclosed that the husband drank considerably, came home under the influence of intoxicating liquor, abused his wife, and struck her with his fist several times, on occasion blacking one of her eyes. He became enamored of another woman and went with her frequently, telling persons he was a single man and intended to marry her. He spent money entertaining her and gave her presents. The evidence was held sufficient to render his wife's condition in life intolerable. The court said * * * that while there may not be an abandonment of the wife by the husband from a physical point of view, there is an abandonment of the obligation resting upon the husband to provide for the support of the wife. * * *

* * *

There are also several cases, under statutes of various states, in which separate maintenance was refused the wife, where the husband and wife were living in the same house. These cases are to the effect that it is an indispensable requirement of a maintenance statute that the wife should be living separate and apart from her husband without her fault, and that therefore, a wife living in the same house with her husband, occupying a different room and eating at a different time, was not entitled to separate maintenance.

* * *

In the instant case the marital relation has continued for more than 33 years, and the wife has been supported in the same manner during this time without complaint on her part. The parties have not been separated or living apart from each other at any time. In the light of the cited cases it is clear, especially so in this jurisdiction, that to maintain an action such as the one at bar, the parties must be separated or living apart from each other.

The living standards of a family are a matter of concern to the household, and not for the courts to determine, even though the husband's attitude toward his wife, according to his wealth and circumstances, leaves little to be said in his behalf. As long as the home is maintained and the parties are living as husband and wife it may be said that the husband is legally supporting his wife and the purpose of the marriage relation is being carried out. Public policy requires such a holding. It appears that the plaintiff is not devoid of money in her own right. She has a fair-sized bank account and is entitled to use the rent from the 80 acres of land left by her first husband, if she so chooses.

* * *

Reversed and remanded with directions to dismiss.

YEAGER, JUSTICE, dissenting.

I respectfully dissent. * * *

* * *

At the time of the marriage plaintiff had a one-third interest in 80 acres of land left by her former husband. Later this interest was transferred to her two daughters. At the time of trial she had a bank account jointly with one of her daughters in the amount of $5,960.22.

* * *

As long as she was able plaintiff made a garden, raised chickens, did outside chores, and worked in the fields. From the sale of chickens and eggs she provided groceries, household necessities, and her own clothing. These things she is no longer able to do, but notwithstanding this the defendant does no more than to buy groceries. He buys her no clothing and does not give her any money at all to spend for her needs or desires. Only one incident is mentioned in the record of defendant ever buying plaintiff any clothing. He bought her a coat over 3 years before the trial.

* * *

There is and can be no doubt that, independent of statutes relating to divorce, alimony, and separate maintenance, if this plaintiff were living apart from the defendant she could in equity and on the facts as outlined in the record be awarded appropriate relief.

* * *

If relief is to be denied to plaintiff under this principle it must be denied because of the fact that she is not living separate and apart from the defendant and is not seeking separation.

In the light of what the decisions declare to be the basis of the right to maintain an action for support, is there any less reason for extending the right to a wife who is denied the right to maintenance in a home occupied with her husband than to one who has chosen to occupy a separate abode?

If the right is to be extended only to one who is separated from the husband equity and effective justice would be denied where a wealthy husband refused proper support and maintenance to a wife physically or mentally incapable of putting herself in a position where the rule could become available to her.

* * *

NOTES AND QUESTIONS

1.   *The husband's rights and obligations.* As a result of coverture, a woman retained few, if any, property rights during marriage. Yet to some extent, law purportedly protected a wife from her inescapable economic dependency. In exchange for the wife's duty to provide household, sexual, and other services to her husband, the law imposed a duty of support on the husband. Alicia Brokars Kelly, *Money Matters in Marriage: Unmasking Interdependence in Ongoing Spousal Economic Relations*, 47 U. Louisville L. Rev. 113, 151–52 (2008). What rights does *McGuire* grant one spouse concerning claims against the other spouse during the course of the ongoing marriage? See Mary Anne Case, *Enforcing Bargains in an Ongoing Marriage*, 35 Wash. U.J.L. & Pol'y 225, 228 (2011).

2.   *The domestic curtain.* If courts fail to intervene to enforce one spouse's obligation to support the other, whose authority does this failure enhance? How meaningful was the wife's entitlement to "support"? Could a

wife easily leave the marital household, a prerequisite for invoking the necessaries doctrine? What collateral consequences might she suffer if she left? Why were courts reluctant to intervene? Professor Twila Perry notes that in intact marriages even today, "the expectation is that each married couple will work out the definition of 'support' in their own marriage. * * * There is a strong belief that judicial intervention into disputes of such nature would violate principles of marital autonomy [and] hopelessly entangle the courts in the day-to-day marital relationship." Twila Perry, *The Essentials of Marriage: Reconsidering the Duty of Support and Services*, 15 Yale J.L. & Feminism 1, 14 (2003). A divorce filing shatters this expectation and raises the prospect of intrusive judicial scrutiny of the family's finances, matters treated in Chapters 9–11.

2.   The Necessaries Doctrine

To compensate for the wife's legal disabilities during marriage and as part of the husband's duty to support his wife, the "necessaries doctrine" allowed her to buy necessities from a third party using her husband's credit. If the husband refused to pay, the creditor could sue the husband for the debt. The traditional necessaries doctrine provided merchants and other creditors with a guarantee that they could collect payment for goods or services purchased by a wife. Theoretically, this doctrine would help induce merchants to sell to women on credit, confident that the law implied a contract between the husband and the merchant even if the husband refused to pay. However, many merchants were unwilling to extend credit to women because this logic broke down in practice. First, the definition of what constituted a "necessary" depended on "the family's social position and [was] limited by the husband's ability to pay." Note, *The Unnecessary Doctrine of Necessaries*, 82 Mich. L. Rev. 1767, 1773–75 (1984). Indeed, uncertainty about whether a particular purchase involves necessities continues to inhibit practical application of the doctrine. A layperson might expect that courts would find food, clothing and shelter to be quintessential necessities. No such bright line rule exists, however. *See generally* Restatement (Third) of Restitution and Unjust Enrichment § 22 (2011).

Second, "the wife had to be cohabiting with her spouse or living apart through no fault of her own when the sale occurred, and the creditor had to rely on the husband's, not the wife's, credit—it was very difficult to know, before going to court, whether the doctrine of necessaries would apply." *Id.* In addition, a "merchant could collect for necessaries from a recalcitrant husband only if the merchant sued the husband and won. Litigation would be costly, and the doctrine of necessaries gave merchants no guarantee of success." Jill Elaine Hasday, *The Canon of Family Law*, 57 Stan. L. Rev. 825, 846 (2004). The doctrine was most useful when the husband was an economically stable member of the community. Elizabeth Katz, *Criminal Law in a Civil Guise: The Evolution of Family Courts and Support Laws*, 86 Chi. L. Rev. ___ (forthcoming 2019).

Some courts and legislatures have abolished the necessaries doctrine, explaining that the common-law notion that a husband must provide for his wife's needs is no longer warranted. *See, e.g., Wal Mart Stores, Inc. v. Holmes,* 7 A.3d 13, 29 (Md. 2010). Nonetheless, most states retain the doctrine in some form. *See* Hasday, *supra,* at 847.

Those states that have retained the doctrine have made it gender neutral. These states have adopted two different approaches.

The first approach is to make one spouse primarily responsible for payment of his or her own debts for necessaries before seeking reimbursement from the other spouse. For example, in *Cheshire Med. Ctr. v. Holbrook,* 663 A.2d 1344 (N.H. 1995), the court modified the traditional common law doctrine instead of abolishing it: the medical provider was required to seek payment from the individual who incurred the debt before pursuing payment from the spouse. Similarly, Ohio provides that each spouse is required to support that "spouse out of the person's property or by the person's labor. If a married person is unable to do so, the spouse of the married person must assist in the support so far as the spouse is able." Ohio Rev. Code Ann. § 3103.03 (2018); *see Embassy Healthcare v. Bell,* Slip Opinion No. 2018-Ohio-4912.

As a variation of the first approach, Pennsylvania requires that "where debts are contracted for necessaries by either spouse for the support and maintenance of the family, it shall be lawful for the creditor in this case to institute suit against the husband and wife for the price of such necessaries and, after obtaining a judgment, have an execution against the spouse contracting the debt alone; and, if no property of that spouse is found, execution may be levied upon and satisfied out of the separate property of the other spouse." 23 Pa. Cons. Stat. Ann. § 4102 (2018).

The second approach makes the spouses jointly and severally liable for each other's debts for necessaries. In Illinois, the "expenses of the family and of the education of the children shall be chargeable upon the property of both husband and wife, or of either of them, in favor of creditors therefor, and in relation thereto they may be sued jointly or separately." 750 Ill. Comp. Stat. 65/15(a) (1) (2018).

NOTES AND QUESTIONS

1.   *Still necessary?* The necessaries doctrine originated at a time when wives were under a legal disability. Does it still serve a purpose today by appropriately protecting dependents and promoting moral obligations during marriage? *See* Hanoch Dagan, *Restitution and Relationships,* 92 B.U. L. Rev. 1035, 1046 (2012). As you will see in Chapter 9, courts struggle at divorce with how to allocate debts acquired during the marriage.

2.   *Useful to whom?* In recent years, providers of health care and elder care have used the doctrine of necessaries to ensure bills are paid. For example,

in *Hickory Creek at Connersville v. Estate of Combs*, 992 N.E.2d 209 (Ind. Ct. App. 2013), a long-term care facility sued the husband's estate to recover for debts incurred by the decedent's wife. The court outlined the doctrine as follows:

> When, however, there is a shortfall between a dependent spouse's necessary expenses and separate funds, the law will impose limited secondary liability upon the financially superior spouse by means of the doctrine of necessaries. The liability is characterized as "limited" because its outer boundaries are marked by the financially superior spouse's ability to pay *at the time the debt was incurred*. It is "secondary" in the sense that it exists only to the extent that the debtor spouse is unable to satisfy his or her own personal needs or obligations.

Id. at 212.

3. *Medicaid.* Medicaid, which has complex rules for determining eligibility, directs that spouses have a reciprocal duty to support each other. Its "spousal impoverishment rules" are governed by both state and federal statutes and regulations rather than by local family law, such as a state's interpretation of the doctrine of necessaries. *See Spousal Impoverishment*, Medicaid.gov, (2019).

4. *Child support obligations in intact families.* When parties divorce or have a nonmarital child, the court is involved in a close, sometimes highly intrusive, inquiry into the parents' financial condition in order to determine child support obligations. (These obligations are discussed in Chapter 11.) This close inquiry contrasts starkly with the law's hands-off attitude concerning child support while the family remains intact.

The assumption, grounded in constitutional family privacy and autonomy doctrines, prevails as long as the parents provide at least a minimal level of child support sufficient to defeat a neglect petition in the juvenile or family court. This minimal level may be considerably lower than what the child support guidelines would require based on parental income and the child's needs and what observers would regard as adequate support. The tolerated level may also stem from recognition that the remedies available for neglect—which may include the child's temporary or permanent removal from the home for foster placement or other state custody—would not necessarily help the child if the bar were set higher. Concerning neglect generally, see Douglas E. Abrams, Susan Mangold, and Sarah H. Ramsey, Children and the Law—Doctrine, Policy and Practice, ch. 4 (6th ed. 2017).

PROBLEM 3-4

Sam and Irene have been married for 25 years, and they have one child in high school who lives at home, and another in college in a different state. Sam recently bought five shirts that he needs for both work and social events, two ties for business meetings, a convertible, and a brand-new, top-of-the-line computer. Because of his high blood pressure, he has been hospitalized several times. When he finds himself without enough money to cover all these expenses, who is responsible for any parts of Sam's debt under the different approaches outlined above?

B. SPOUSAL PROPERTY DISTRIBUTION UPON DEATH

When a spouse dies without a will, a state's laws of intestacy establish how the property should be distributed, and spouses are favored recipients. For example, the Uniform Probate Code provides that the decedent's entire estate is left to the surviving spouse if the spouses only have joint children. Unif. Probate Code §§ 2–201 to 2–214.

When people write wills, they typically leave their assets to family members, generally to spouses. In community property states, regardless of what the will provides, the surviving spouse is entitled to one-half of the property accumulated during the marriage. But in common-law title states, the surviving spouse may be entirely left out of the will. The traditional protection for the surviving spouse in these states was either dower, under which a widow was entitled to a life interest in one-third of her husband's real property, or curtesy, through which a widower acquired a life interest in all of his wife's real property if children were born into the marriage.

Dower and curtesy no longer exist in virtually all jurisdictions, but almost all non-community property states have replaced them with the statutory elective share. The elective share typically allows a surviving spouse to elect to receive one-third of the estate of the deceased spouse, even if the decedent has written a will that leaves nothing to the surviving spouse (importantly for family lawyers, the elective share can be waived through marital agreement). Unlike dower and curtesy, the elective share typically applies to all property, not just real estate; it is gender neutral; and it provides for full ownership, not just a life estate.

NOTES AND QUESTIONS

1.   *Wills and the protection of spouses.* Professor Lawrence Waggoner questions whether the elective share provides sufficient protection:

> One plausible theory of the elective share is the marital sharing theory. Under that theory, marriage is viewed as an economic partnership, a view that imports a goal of equalizing the marital assets. Another plausible theory is the support theory, that the elective share is a means of continuing the decedent's duty of support beyond the grave. The traditional elective share statute implements neither theory. * * * Regarding the partnership theory, one-third or one-half of the decedent's estate might be significantly less than the amount necessary to equalize the marital assets when those assets are disproportionately titled in the decedent's name and considerably in excess of the amount necessary to do so when those assets are

already titled equally or are disproportionately titled in the survivor's name. Regarding the support theory, one-third or one-half might be significantly less than the amount necessary to satisfy the survivor's support needs in a smaller estate and considerably in excess of those needs in a larger estate.

Lawrence A. Waggoner, *The Uniform Probate Code's Elective Share: Time for a Reassessment*, 37 U. Mich. J.L. Reform 1, 3 (2003). Indeed, outside of the community property states, a surviving spouse may receive less protection at death than does a divorcing spouse under the property distribution and spousal maintenance statutes of those same states. *See* Laura A. Rosenbury, *Two Ways to End a Marriage: Divorce or Death*, 2005 Utah L. Rev. 1227 (2005). Does any theory convince you that the elective share is justified or should be reformed? For other proposals, see Carla Spivack, *Let's Get Serious: Spousal Abuse Should Bar Inheritance*, 90 Or. L. Rev. 247 (2011).

2.   *Wills and protection of children.* Except in Louisiana, a parent can disinherit his or her marital or nonmarital child for any reason or no reason at all, no matter how young the child and no matter how much the child needs continued support. This majority rule is contrary to the rule that prevails in most other developed nations.

Louisiana follows the civil law rule, which prohibits parents from disinheriting their minor or adult children, except in narrow circumstances that establish "just cause" for disinheritance. "Just cause" is established where the child attempted to murder or committed an act of violence against the parent, refused after reaching majority to contact the parent for two years, married while a minor without the parent's consent, or was convicted of a crime carrying the death penalty or life imprisonment. *See* La. Civ. Code Ann. art. 1621 (2018). Even in Louisiana, however, children over the age of 23 do not have the right to inherit, unless they, "because of mental incapacity or physical infirmity, are permanently incapable of taking care of their persons." La. Civ. Code Ann. art. 1493(A) (2018).

Should the law permit parents to disinherit their children? Should children, especially if they are minors when their parent dies, receive an elective share? Why have states not protected children in the same way as spouses?

3.   *What if there is no will and no spouse?* Although state intestacy laws generally apply only to a spouse, several states grant intestacy succession rights to the surviving members of couples who have another legally recognized status, such as a civil union or domestic partnership. *See, e.g.*, Vt. Stat. Ann. tit. 15, § 1204 (2018).

When it comes to descendants, equal protection requires equal treatment of marital and nonmarital children, at least where a court entered a filiation order concerning the nonmarital child during the father's lifetime. *See Lalli v. Lalli*, 439 U.S. 259 (1978); *Trimble v. Gordon*, 430 U.S. 762 (1977). Intestacy laws provide that the children take equally, without regard to their age or other condition. Under what circumstances might this "sibling parity" cause hardship to minor children? How might a parent avoid this hardship?

4.   MEDICAL DECISIONMAKING FOR ONE'S SPOUSE

Most spouses consult each other about major medical decisions and in emergencies may be asked to make medical decisions for each other. Later in this Section we will explore a variety of issues concerning assumptions about who makes medical decisions within family units. We begin, however, with the constitutional doctrine governing women's constitutional right to make decisions about whether to bear children.

A.   THE RIGHT OF MARRIED WOMEN TO CONTROL THEIR PREGNANCIES

The Supreme Court considered the extent to which spouses maintain separate identities and discrete privacy interests in the context of abortion in the following case. The joint opinion you are about to read established the current legal standard for assessing the constitutionality of regulations affecting the availability of abortion. Look for the standard the case established as you read.

PLANNED PARENTHOOD OF SOUTHEASTERN PENNSYLVANIA V. CASEY

Supreme Court of the United States, 1992.
505 U.S. 833.

JUSTICE O'CONNOR, JUSTICE KENNEDY, and JUSTICE SOUTER announced the judgment of the Court and delivered the opinion of the Court with respect to Parts I, II, III, V-A, [and] V-C * * *.

I

* * *

At issue in these cases are five provisions of the Pennsylvania Abortion Control Act * * *. The Act requires * * * [that] a married woman seeking an abortion must sign a statement indicating that she has notified her husband of her intended abortion. § 3209. The Act exempts compliance * * * in the event of a "medical emergency," which is defined in § 3203 of the Act. * * *

Before any of these provisions took effect, the petitioners, who are five abortion clinics and one physician representing himself as well as a class of physicians who provide abortion services, brought this suit seeking declaratory and injunctive relief. Each provision was challenged as unconstitutional on its face. The District Court entered a preliminary injunction against the enforcement of the regulations, and, after a 3-day bench trial, held all the provisions at issue here unconstitutional, entering a permanent injunction against Pennsylvania's enforcement of them. The Court of Appeals for the Third Circuit affirmed in part and reversed in part, upholding all of the regulations except for the husband notification requirement. We granted certiorari.

* * *

II

* * *

Our law affords constitutional protection to personal decisions relating to marriage, procreation, contraception, family relationships, child rearing, and education. *Carey v. Population Services International*, 431 U.S. [678, 685 (1977)]. Our cases recognize "the right of the *individual*, married or single, to be free from unwarranted governmental intrusion into matters so fundamentally affecting a person as the decision whether to bear or beget a child." *Eisenstadt v. Baird*, 405 U.S. 438, 453 (1972) (emphasis in original). Our precedents "have respected the private realm of family life which the state cannot enter." *Prince v. Massachusetts*, 321 U.S. 158, 166 (1944). These matters, involving the most intimate and personal choices a person may make in a lifetime, choices central to personal dignity and autonomy, are central to the liberty protected by the Fourteenth Amendment. At the heart of liberty is the right to define one's own concept of existence, of meaning, of the universe, and of the mystery of human life. Beliefs about these matters could not define the attributes of personhood were they formed under compulsion of the State.

These considerations begin our analysis of the woman's interest in terminating her pregnancy but cannot end it, for this reason: though the abortion decision may originate within the zone of conscience and belief, it is more than a philosophic exercise. Abortion is a unique act. It is an act fraught with consequences for others: for the woman who must live with the implications of her decision; for the persons who perform and assist in the procedure; for the spouse, family, and society which must confront the knowledge that these procedures exist, procedures some deem nothing short of an act of violence against innocent human life; and, depending on one's beliefs, for the life or potential life that is aborted. Though abortion is conduct, it does not follow that the State is entitled to proscribe it in all instances. That is because the liberty of the woman is at stake in a sense unique to the human condition and so unique to the law. The mother who carries a child to full term is subject to anxieties, to physical constraints, to pain that only she must bear. That these sacrifices have from the beginning of the human race been endured by woman with a pride that ennobles her in the eyes of others and gives to the infant a bond of love cannot alone be grounds for the State to insist she make the sacrifice. Her suffering is too intimate and personal for the State to insist, without more, upon its own vision of the woman's role, however dominant that vision has been in the course of our history and our culture. The destiny of the woman must be shaped to a large extent on her own conception of her spiritual imperatives and her place in society.

* * *

V

* * *

C

Section 3209 of Pennsylvania's abortion law provides, except in cases of medical emergency, that no physician shall perform an abortion on a married woman without receiving a signed statement from the woman that she has notified her spouse that she is about to undergo an abortion. The woman has the option of providing an alternative signed statement certifying that her husband is not the man who impregnated her; that her husband could not be located; that the pregnancy is the result of spousal sexual assault which she has reported; or that the woman believes that notifying her husband will cause him or someone else to inflict bodily injury upon her. A physician who performs an abortion on a married woman without receiving the appropriate signed statement will have his or her license revoked, and is liable to the husband for damages.

The District Court heard the testimony of numerous expert witnesses, and made detailed findings of fact regarding the effect of this statute. These included:

"273.   The vast majority of women consult their husbands prior to deciding to terminate their pregnancy. . . .

* * *

"279.   The 'bodily injury' exception could not be invoked by a married woman whose husband, if notified, would, in her reasonable belief, threaten to (a) publicize her intent to have an abortion to family, friends or acquaintances; (b) retaliate against her in future child custody or divorce proceedings; (c) inflict psychological intimidation or emotional harm upon her, her children or other persons; (d) inflict bodily harm on other persons such as children, family members or other loved ones; or (e) use his control over finances to deprive [her] of necessary monies for herself or her children. . . .

* * *

"281.   Studies reveal that family violence occurs in two million families in the United States. This figure, however, is a conservative one that substantially understates * * * the actual number of families affected by domestic violence. In fact, researchers estimate that one of every two women will be battered at some time in their life. . . .

* * *

"289.   Mere notification of pregnancy is frequently a flashpoint for battering and violence within the family. The number of battering incidents is high during the pregnancy and often the worst abuse can be associated with pregnancy. . . . The battering husband may deny parentage and use the pregnancy as an excuse for abuse. . . .

* * *

* * * The vast majority of women notify their male partners of their decision to obtain an abortion. In many cases in which married women do not notify their husbands, the pregnancy is the result of an extramarital affair. Where the husband is the father, the primary reason women do not notify their husbands is that the husband and wife are experiencing marital difficulties, often accompanied by incidents of violence [citations omitted].

[T]he District Court's findings reinforce what common sense would suggest. In well-functioning marriages, spouses discuss important intimate decisions such as whether to bear a child. But there are millions of women in this country who are the victims of regular physical and psychological abuse at the hands of their husbands. Should these women become pregnant, they may have very good reasons for not wishing to inform their husbands of their decision to obtain an abortion. * * *

The spousal notification requirement is thus likely to prevent a significant number of women from obtaining an abortion. It does not merely make abortions a little more difficult or expensive to obtain; for many women, it will impose a substantial obstacle. We must not blind ourselves to the fact that the significant number of women who fear for their safety and the safety of their children are likely to be deterred from procuring an abortion as surely as if the Commonwealth had outlawed abortion in all cases.

Respondents attempt to avoid the conclusion that § 3209 is invalid by pointing out that it imposes almost no burden at all for the vast majority of women seeking abortions. They begin by noting that only about 20 percent of the women who obtain abortions are married. They then note that of these women about 95 percent notify their husbands of their own volition. Thus, respondents argue, the effects of § 3209 are felt by only one percent of the women who obtain abortions. Respondents argue that since some of these women will be able to notify their husbands without adverse consequences or will qualify for one of the exceptions, the statute affects fewer than one percent of women seeking abortions. For this reason, it is asserted, the statute cannot be invalid on its face. We disagree with respondents' basic method of analysis.

The analysis does not end with the one percent of women upon whom the statute operates; it begins there. Legislation is measured for consistency with the Constitution by its impact on those whose conduct it affects. * * * The proper focus of constitutional inquiry is the group for whom the law is a restriction, not the group for whom the law is irrelevant.

Respondents' argument itself gives implicit recognition to this principle, at one of its critical points. Respondents speak of the one percent of women seeking abortions who are married and would choose not to notify their husbands of their plans. By selecting as the controlling class women who wish to obtain abortions, rather than all women or all pregnant women, respondents in effect concede that § 3209 must be judged by reference to those for whom it is an actual rather than an irrelevant restriction. Of course, as we have said, § 3209's real target is narrower even than the class of women seeking abortions identified by the State: it is married women seeking abortions who do not wish to notify their husbands of their intentions and who do not qualify for one of the statutory exceptions to the notice requirement. * * * [Section] 3209 * * * will operate as a substantial obstacle to a woman's choice to undergo an abortion. It is an undue burden, and therefore invalid.

This conclusion is in no way inconsistent with our decisions upholding parental notification or consent requirements [for minors]. Those enactments, and our judgment that they are constitutional, are based on the quite reasonable assumption that minors will benefit from consultation with their parents and that children will often not realize that their parents have their best interests at heart. We cannot adopt a parallel assumption about adult women.

We recognize that a husband has a "deep and proper concern and interest . . . in his wife's pregnancy and in the growth and development of the fetus she is carrying." *Danforth, supra,* at 69. With regard to the children he has fathered and raised, the Court has recognized his "cognizable and substantial" interest in their custody. *Stanley v. Illinois,* 405 U.S. 645, 651–652 (1972) [additional citations omitted]. If these cases concerned a State's ability to require the mother to notify the father before taking some action with respect to a living child raised by both, therefore, it would be reasonable to conclude as a general matter that the father's interest in the welfare of the child and the mother's interest are equal.

Before birth, however, the issue takes on a very different cast. It is an inescapable biological fact that state regulation with respect to the child a woman is carrying will have a far greater impact on the mother's liberty than on the father's. The effect of state regulation on a woman's protected liberty is doubly deserving of scrutiny in such a case, as the State has touched not only upon the private sphere of the family but upon the very bodily integrity of the pregnant woman. The Court has held that "when the wife and the husband disagree on this decision, the view of only one of the two marriage partners can prevail. Inasmuch as it is the woman who physically bears the child and who is the more directly and immediately affected by the pregnancy, as between the two, the balance weighs in her favor." *Danforth, supra,* at 71. This conclusion rests upon the basic nature of marriage and the nature of our Constitution: "the marital couple is not an independent entity with a mind and heart of its own, but an association of two individuals each with a separate intellectual and emotional makeup. If the right of privacy means anything, it is the right of the *individual,* married or single, to be free from unwarranted governmental intrusion into matters so fundamentally affecting a person as the decision whether to bear or beget a child." *Eisenstadt v. Baird,* 405 U.S. at 453 (emphasis in original). The Constitution protects individuals, men and women alike, from unjustified state interference, even when that interference is enacted into law for the benefit of their spouses.

There was a time, not so long ago, when a different understanding of the family and of the Constitution prevailed. In *Bradwell v. State,* 16 Wall. 130 (1873), three Members of this Court reaffirmed the common-law principle that "a woman had no legal existence separate from her husband, who was regarded as her head and representative in the social state; and, notwithstanding some recent modifications of this civil status, many of the special rules of law flowing from and dependent upon this cardinal principle still exist in full force in most States." *Id.* at 141 (BRADLEY, J., joined by SWAYNE and FIELD, JJ., concurring in judgment). Only one generation has passed since this Court observed that "woman is still regarded as the center of home and family life," with attendant "special responsibilities" that precluded full and independent legal status under the Constitution. *Hoyt v. Florida,* 368 U.S. 57, 62 (1961). These views, of course, are no longer consistent with our understanding of the family, the individual, or the Constitution.

In keeping with our rejection of the common-law understanding of a woman's role within the family, the Court held in *Danforth* that the Constitution does not permit a State to require a married woman to obtain her husband's consent before undergoing an abortion. 428 U.S., at 69. The principles that guided the Court in *Danforth* should be our guides today. For the great many women who are victims of abuse inflicted by their husbands, or whose children are the victims of such abuse, a spousal notice requirement enables the husband to wield an effective veto over his wife's decision. [T]he notice requirement will often be tantamount to the veto found unconstitutional in *Danforth.* The women most affected by this law—

those who most reasonably fear the consequences of notifying their husbands that they are pregnant—are in the gravest danger.

The husband's interest in the life of the child his wife is carrying does not permit the State to empower him with this troubling degree of authority over his wife. The contrary view leads to consequences reminiscent of the common law. A husband has no enforceable right to require a wife to advise him before she exercises her personal choices. If a husband's interest in the potential life of the child outweighs a wife's liberty, the State could require a married woman to notify her husband before she uses a postfertilization contraceptive. Perhaps next in line would be a statute requiring pregnant married women to notify their husbands before engaging in conduct causing risks to the fetus. After all, if the husband's interest in the fetus' safety is a sufficient predicate for state regulation, the State could reasonably conclude that pregnant wives should notify their husbands before drinking alcohol or smoking. Perhaps married women should notify their husbands before using contraceptives or before undergoing any type of surgery that may have complications affecting the husband's interest in his wife's reproductive organs. And if a husband's interest justifies notice in any of these cases, one might reasonably argue that it justifies exactly what the *Danforth* Court held it did not justify—a requirement of the husband's consent as well. A State may not give to a man the kind of dominion over his wife that parents exercise over their children.

Section 3209 embodies a view of marriage consonant with the common-law status of married women but repugnant to our present understanding of marriage and of the nature of the rights secured by the Constitution. Women do not lose their constitutionally protected liberty when they marry. The Constitution protects all individuals, male or female, married or unmarried, from the abuse of governmental power, even where that power is employed for the supposed benefit of a member of the individual's family. These considerations confirm our conclusion that § 3209 is invalid.

* * *

[The opinion of STEVENS, J., concurring in part and dissenting in part, is omitted.]

JUSTICE BLACKMUN, concurring in part, concurring in the judgment in part, and dissenting in part. I join Parts I, II, * * *, V-A, [and] V-C * * * of the joint opinion of JUSTICES O'CONNOR, KENNEDY, and SOUTER.

* * *

A State's restrictions on a woman's right to terminate her pregnancy also implicate constitutional guarantees of gender equality. State restrictions on abortion compel women to continue pregnancies they otherwise might terminate. By restricting the right to terminate pregnancies, the State conscripts women's bodies into its service, forcing women to continue their pregnancies, suffer the pains of childbirth, and in most instances, provide years of maternal care. The State does not compensate women for their services; instead, it assumes that they owe this duty as a matter of course. This assumption—that women can simply be forced to accept the "natural" status and incidents of motherhood—appears to rest upon a conception of women's role that has triggered the protection of the Equal Protection Clause. The joint opinion recognizes that these assumptions about women's place in society "are no longer consistent with our understanding of the family, the individual, or the Constitution."

* * *

* * * If there is much reason to applaud the advances made by the joint opinion today, there is far more to fear from THE CHIEF JUSTICE [REHNQUIST]'s opinion.

* * *

Even more shocking than THE CHIEF JUSTICE's cramped notion of individual liberty is his complete omission of any discussion of the effects that compelled childbirth and motherhood have on women's lives. The only expression of concern with women's health is purely instrumental—for THE CHIEF JUSTICE, only women's *psychological* health is a concern, and only to the extent that he assumes that every woman who decides to have an abortion does so without serious consideration of the moral implications of her decision. In short, THE CHIEF JUSTICE's view of the State's compelling interest in maternal health has less to do with health than it does with compelling women to be maternal.

Nor does THE CHIEF JUSTICE give any serious consideration to the doctrine of *stare decisis*. For THE CHIEF JUSTICE, the facts that gave rise to *Roe* are surprisingly simple: "women become pregnant, there is a point somewhere, depending on medical technology, where a fetus becomes viable, and women give birth to children." This characterization of the issue thus allows THE CHIEF JUSTICE quickly to discard the joint opinion's reliance argument by asserting that "reproductive planning could take virtually immediate account of" a decision overruling *Roe*.

* * *

But, we are reassured, there is always the protection of the democratic process. While there is much to be praised about our democracy, our country since its founding has recognized that there are certain fundamental liberties that are not to be left to the whims of an election. A woman's right to reproductive choice is one of those fundamental liberties. Accordingly, that liberty need not seek refuge at the ballot box.

* * *

CHIEF JUSTICE REHNQUIST, with whom JUSTICE WHITE, JUSTICE SCALIA, and JUSTICE THOMAS join, concurring in the judgment in part and dissenting in part.

* * *

We first emphasize that Pennsylvania has not imposed a spousal *consent* requirement of the type the Court struck down in *Planned Parenthood of Central Missouri v. Danforth*, 428 U.S. at 67–72. Missouri's spousal consent provision was invalidated in that case because of the Court's view that it unconstitutionally granted to the husband "a veto power exercisable for any reason whatsoever or for no reason at all." *Id.* at 71. But the provision here involves a much less intrusive requirement of spousal *notification*, not consent. Such a law requiring only notice to the husband "does not give any third party the legal right to make the [woman's] decision for her, or to prevent her from obtaining an abortion should she choose to have one performed." *Hodgson v. Minnesota*, 497 U.S. 417, 496 (1990) (KENNEDY, J., concurring in judgment in part and dissenting in part). * * * Petitioners * * * argue that the real effect of such a notice requirement is to give the power to husbands to veto a woman's abortion choice. The District Court indeed found that the notification provision created a risk that some woman who would otherwise have an abortion will be prevented from having one. For example, petitioners argue, many notified husbands will prevent abortions through physical force, psychological coercion, and other types of threats. But Pennsylvania has incorporated exceptions in the notice provision in an attempt to deal with these problems. For instance, a woman need not notify her husband if the pregnancy is the result of a reported sexual assault, or if she has reason to believe that she would suffer bodily injury as a result of the notification. * * *

The question before us is therefore whether the spousal notification requirement rationally furthers any legitimate state interests. We conclude that it does. First, a husband's interests in procreation within marriage and in the potential life of his unborn child are certainly substantial ones. The State itself has legitimate interests both in protecting these interests of the father and in protecting the potential life of the fetus, and the spousal notification requirement is reasonably related to advancing those state interests. By providing that a husband will usually know of his spouse's intent to have an abortion, the provision makes it more likely that the husband will participate in deciding the fate of his unborn child, a possibility that might otherwise have been denied him. * * *

The State also has a legitimate interest in promoting "the integrity of the marital relationship." 18 Pa. Cons. Stat. § 3209(a) (1990). This Court has previously recognized "the importance of the marital relationship in our society." * * * *Danforth, supra* at 69. In our view, the spousal notice requirement is a rational attempt by the State to improve truthful communication between spouses and encourage collaborative decisionmaking, and thereby fosters marital integrity. * * * The Pennsylvania Legislature was in a position to weigh the likely benefits of the provision against its likely adverse effects, and presumably concluded, on balance, that the provision would be beneficial. Whether this was a wise decision or not, we cannot say that it was irrational. We therefore conclude that the spousal notice provision comports with the Constitution.

* * *

[The opinion of SCALIA, J., concurring in part and dissenting in part, is omitted.]

NOTES AND QUESTIONS

1.   *Understanding* Casey. Why did Pennsylvania seek to require that only married women, and not single women, notify the man most interested in the pregnancy? If the Court had upheld that provision of the statute, and the statute were being crafted today, should the state distinguish between married couples and cohabitants given the profound rise in cohabitation?

2.   *Autonomy for teenage girls. Casey* defended its holding against anticipated arguments that it was inconsistent with the Court's earlier decisions upholding statutes that require parental notice or consent before a pregnant minor may have an abortion. In *Bellotti v. Baird*, 443 U.S. 622 (1979) (plurality opinion), for example, the plurality identified three factors that have traditionally justified distinguishing the rights of minors from those of adults: (i) the "peculiar vulnerability" of children; (ii) their presumed "inability to make critical decisions in an informed, mature manner"; and (iii) the significance of the "parental role in child rearing."

Despite these distinguishing factors, *Bellotti* found that deference to parental authority is not always appropriate in the abortion context: "[T]he unique nature and consequences of the abortion decision make it inappropriate 'to give a third party an absolute, and possibly arbitrary, veto over the decision of the physician and his patient to terminate the patient's pregnancy, regardless of the reason for withholding the consent.'" *Id.* at 643 (citing *Danforth, supra*, at 74 (1976)). *Bellotti* thus held that, to protect pregnant minors from such absolute and arbitrary vetoes, parental consent and notification statutes must provide for a judicial bypass procedure—a procedure enabling the pregnant minor to go directly to court to obtain permission for an abortion without first consulting with or notifying her parents. If the minor can persuade the court that she is "mature enough and well enough informed to make her abortion decision, in consultation with her physician, independently of her parents' wishes," or that an abortion would be in her best interests, the court must authorize the operation. *Bellotti*, 443 U.S. at 643–44. *Casey* noted that "the vast majority of women consult their husbands prior to deciding to terminate their pregnancy." 505 U.S. at 888. So too, the majority of pregnant minors consult with their parents upon learning they are pregnant. Some adolescents, however, find that their circumstances render parental consultation an unreasonable option. *See, e.g., In re Doe*, 33 A.3d 615, 615 (Pa. 2011) (minor seeking judicial authorization cites belief that her mother would "throw her out" as basis for failure to reveal her pregnancy to a parent).

Judicial bypass procedures are extremely important safeguards for minors who, because of an abusive home life or other reasons, cannot discuss their pregnancy with their parents without endangering themselves. Applying *Casey's* approach by only considering the impact of a "parental involvement" statute on the "minors who prefer not to notify their parents of the decision to have an abortion," the Seventh Circuit upheld an Illinois law that provided a bypass procedure but did not expressly grant the state's courts the power to waive parental consent. *Zbaraz v. Madigan*, 572 F.3d 370 (7th Cir. 2009). In 2013, the state's highest court upheld the same statute against a challenge based on the state constitution. *Hope Clinic for Women, Ltd. v. Flores*, 991 N.E.2d 745 (Ill. 2013).

B. *CASEY'S* VITALITY

Until 2007, one principle remained sacrosanct in the jurisprudence of abortion rights: statutes regulating access to abortion must contain a "health exception" to preserve the mother's life. *Ayotte v. Planned Parenthood of N. New England*, 546 U.S. 320, 326–28 (2006). In 2007, however, the Court upheld the Partial-Birth Abortion Ban of 2003, 18 U.S.C. § 1531 (2011) (the "Act"), by a 5–4 vote even though it did not contain an exception for treatment needed to preserve the pregnant woman's health. *Gonzales v. Carhart*, 550 U.S. 124 (2007) (often referred to as *Carhart II*).

Justice Kennedy's opinion for the majority in *Gonzales* stated at the outset that the majority was bound by *Casey* and was following *Casey's* precepts. First, the Court stated it was applying *Casey's* "undue burden" standard, under which the Court would not overturn state regulations unless they imposed an undue burden on the woman's ability to choose an abortion by placing a "substantial obstacle" in her path. *Casey*, 505 U.S. at 863–74, 878. Second, Justice Kennedy emphasized: "a premise central to [*Casey's*] conclusion—that the government has a legitimate and substantial interest in preserving and promoting fetal life—would be repudiated were the Court now to [strike down the Act]." *Casey*, Justice Kennedy explained, "struck a balance" that the Court would apply, using a "rational basis" analysis. *Gonzales*, 550 U.S. at 145–46.

The majority opinion shared its view of how women as a group respond to motherhood and to the termination of pregnancies in terms many had thought long put to rest: "While we find no reliable data to measure the phenomenon, it seems unexceptionable to conclude some women come to regret their choice to abort the infant life they once created and sustained. * * *" *Id.* at 159. As you will see below, the opinion suggested that women were not capable of informed choice when it came to emotionally fraught decisions such as whether and how to terminate a pregnancy. Justices Thomas and Scalia, who joined Justice Kennedy's opinion, wrote separately to underscore their "view that the Court's abortion jurisprudence, including *Casey* and *Roe v. Wade*, has no basis in the Constitution." *Id.* at 169.

Dissenting, Justice Ginsburg (joined by justices Stevens, Souter and Breyer) took issue with the majority's view of women and its treatment of *Casey*. Justice Ginsburg wrote, in part:

> Today's decision is alarming. It refuses to take *Casey* * * * seriously. It tolerates, indeed applauds, federal intervention to ban nationwide a procedure found necessary and proper in certain cases by the American College of Obstetricians and Gynecologists (ACOG). * * * And, for the first time since *Roe*, the Court blesses a prohibition with no exception safeguarding a woman's health.

> * * *

> As *Casey* comprehended, at stake in cases challenging abortion restrictions is a woman's "control over her [own] destiny." 505 U.S. at 869 (plurality opinion). "There was a time, not so long ago," when women were "regarded as the center of home and family life, with attendant special responsibilities that precluded full and independent legal status under the Constitution." * * * Those views, this Court made clear in *Casey*, "are no longer consistent with our understanding of the family, the individual, or the Constitution." Women, it is now acknowledged, have the talent, capacity, and right "to participate equally in the economic and social life of the Nation." *Id.* at 856. * * * Thus, legal challenges to undue restrictions on abortion procedures do not seek to vindicate some generalized notion of privacy; rather, they center on a woman's autonomy to determine her life's course, and thus to enjoy equal citizenship stature. * * *

> * * *

> Ultimately, the Court admits that "moral concerns" are at work, concerns that could yield prohibitions on any abortion. * * *

> Revealing in this regard, the Court invokes an antiabortion shibboleth for which it concededly has no reliable evidence: Women who have abortions come to regret their choices, and consequently suffer from "severe depression and loss of esteem".[7]

---

[7]   The Court is surely correct that, for most women, abortion is a painfully difficult decision. * * *. But "neither the weight of the scientific evidence to date nor the observable reality of 33 years of legal abortion in the United States comports with the idea that having an abortion is any

Because of women's fragile emotional state and because of the "bond of love the mother has for her child," the Court worries, doctors may withhold information about the nature of the intact D & E procedure.[8] The solution the Court approves, then, is *not* to require doctors to inform women, accurately and adequately, of the different procedures and their attendant risks. Cf. *Casey* * * *.

This way of thinking reflects ancient notions about women's place in the family and under the Constitution—ideas that have long since been discredited. * * *

Eliminating or reducing women's reproductive choices is manifestly *not* a means of protecting them. When safe abortion procedures cease to be an option, many women seek other means to end unwanted or coerced pregnancies.

* * *

* * * The Court's hostility to the right *Roe* and *Casey* secured is not concealed. * * * Instead of the heightened scrutiny we have previously applied, the Court determines that a "rational" ground is enough to uphold the Act * * *

————

Subsequently, federal Courts of Appeals concluded that, taken together, *Casey* and *Gonzales* supported the constitutionality of government regulations that might "encourage the patient to choose childbirth over abortion" so long as the state does not put unduly burdensome obstacles in the way of a woman who, nonetheless, chooses abortion or create a barrier that deprives her of the liberty to choose. *E.g., Richmond Med. Ctr. for Women v. Herring*, 570 F.3d 165 (4th Cir. 2009).

Numerous states began to test the boundaries of that doctrine. From 2011 through 2014, states enacted 231 abortion restrictions—"more than the total number enacted in the entire previous decade." Heather D. Boonstra & Elizabeth Nash, *A Surge of State Abortion Restrictions Puts Providers—and the Women They Serve—in the Crosshairs*, 17 Guttmacher Pol'y Rev. 1 (Winter 2014); Elizabeth Nash & Rachel Benson gold, *In Just the Last Four Years, States Have Enacted 231 Abortion Restrictions*, Guttmacher Inst. (Jan. 5, 2014). Those statutes took a variety of forms, including regulating abortion clinics and those who staff them, and

————

more dangerous to a woman's long-term mental health than delivering and parenting a child that she did not intend to have * * *."

[8]   Notwithstanding the "bond of love" women often have with their children, * * * not all pregnancies, this Court has recognized, are wanted, or even the product of consensual activity. See *Casey* ("[O]n an average day in the United States, nearly 11,000 women are severely assaulted by their male partners. Many of these incidents involve sexual assault").

imposing waiting periods between counseling and the procedure that may be as long as 72 hours.

And, although *Casey* stated that a legal requirement aimed at promoting informed consent to abortion must be must be truthful, not misleading, and relevant so it would promote "mature and informed" decisions by the patient, some state laws required doctors to deliver false or misleading messages designed to discourage abortions, *Casey*, 505 U.S. at 882–83. States increasingly mandate that doctors and abortion clinics deliver specific, even scripted, messages to pregnant women who ask about abortion, including messages that are misleading and deceptive. For example, the clinic may be required to inform the woman of a "purported link between abortion and breast cancer" or the risk of mental health problems following abortion. *An Overview of Abortion Laws*, Guttmacher Inst. (Mar. 1, 2019). Utah, for example, requires doctors to tell women that abortions achieved through medication rather than surgery are "reversible," although no scientific studies support that claim. Laura Bassett, *Utah Forces Doctors to Tell Women Some Abortions Are Reversible*, Huffington Post (Mar. 27, 2017). While the Supreme Court has not considered the legality of those required messages, in 2018 it overturned a California statute that required "prolife" clinics to provide their clients with accurate information about their right to an abortion and where they could find appropriate resources, including state funding. The Court considered the case as one involving the free speech rights of those who operated unlicensed "life advocacy" clinics. *Nat'l Inst. of Family & Life Advocates v. Becerra*, 138 S. Ct. 2361 (2018).

A Texas statute, which had resulted in the closing of most of the abortion clinics in the state, reached the Supreme Court during the 2015 term. The Supreme Court took advantage of the opportunity to elaborate on the meaning of the standard established in *Casey* for the first time since it decided *Casey*. The Court's opinion in *Whole Woman's Health v. Hellerstedt*, 136 S. Ct. 2292 (2016), explicated the meaning of the "undue burden" test laid out in *Casey,* applied the test, and made *Casey*'s continued vitality clear.

Hellerstedt reviewed the constitutionality of two provisions of the Texas abortion statute: a requirement that doctors staffing abortion centers have admitting privileges at a nearby hospital, and that the centers meet all the requirements for ambulatory surgical centers, most of which were unnecessary for surgical abortion procedures and were inapplicable to medical abortions (in which the patient is given pills to take at home). *Hellerstedt*, 136 S. Ct. at 2300, 2311, 2316–18.

Reversing the Fifth Circuit and resolving a division among the lower courts, *Hellerstedt*'s five-Justice majority (per Justice Breyer) held that the provisions violated a woman's right to decide to have an abortion, and clarified the meaning of the "undue burden" test set out in *Casey*. In *Casey*, the Court explained, "a plurality of the Court concluded that there 'exists' an 'undue burden' on a woman's right to decide to have an abortion, and consequently a provision of law is constitutionally invalid if the '*purpose* or *effect*' of the provision '*is to place a substantial obstacle*' in the path of a woman seeking an abortion before the fetus attains viability.' (Emphasis added). * * * '[u]nnecessary health regulations that have the purpose or effect of presenting a substantial obstacle to a woman seeking an abortion impose an undue burden on the right.' " *Id.* at 2300 (*quoting Casey*, 505 U.S. at 878). Chief Justice Roberts and justices Thomas and Alito dissented.

The majority concluded that evidence showed that abortion is "much safer, in terms of minor and serious complications, than many common medical procedures not subject to such intense regulation * * *" as Texas imposed on abortions (including colonoscopies, vasectomies, plastic surgery and even "childbirth"). *Id.* at 2302 (Breyer, J.), 2320 (Ginsburg, J. *concurring.*).

Hellerstedt held that both the admitting privileges and the ambulatory surgical center standards requirements were "medically unnecessary" (in the "virtual absence of any health benefit"). The Court reasoned that an unnecessary medical regulation clearly does not offer "medical benefits sufficient to justify the burdens on access" to abortion that it imposes. Therefore, each regulation "places a substantial obstacle in the path of a previability abortion, each imposes an undue burden," and each violates the Constitution. 136 S. Ct. at 2300.

Justice Breyer's majority opinion clearly states that the Fifth Circuit misunderstood the applicable law when it applied rational basis review. The appellate court expressly directed the lower courts not to attempt to balance the benefits of legislation that regulates abortion against the burdens on women who seek access to abortion. *Id.* at 2309.

Hellerstedt clarifies that *Casey* requires:

(1) that "courts consider the burdens a law imposes on abortion access together with the benefits those laws confer"; and

(2) that courts perform their "*independent constitutional duty to review factual findings where constitutional rights are at stake,*" and not defer to legislatures by applying the rational basis review that is appropriate when considering, for example, "economic legislation."

Id. at 2309–10.

The Court did not establish a bright line at which a burden becomes "undue." The challenged regulations served no medical purpose because abortions in Texas were already very safe, with low complication rates and virtually no mortality, and because (as the state essentially conceded at oral argument) the regulations were unlikely to improve the health of even one woman. The "substantial obstacle" was also clear: the number of abortion clinics in Texas had been reduced from 40 to 7 or 8, and large areas of the state did not have even one clinic. Resulting impediments (including long travel distance, weeks-long waits, and overcrowded facilities) not only failed to promote women's health, they in fact undermined it—as established in numerous amicus briefs—by leading to later abortions (requiring surgical rather than medical approaches) with greater risk of complications, and greater risk that women would seek to self-abort or resort to illegal providers. *See id.* at 2316–18; (Ginsburg, J., concurring) at 2321.

The opinion also addressed how courts should calculate the "large fraction" of women affected, an enterprise that replicated *Casey*'s discussion of which women were affected by the Pennsylvania spousal notification requirement overturned in that case (pages 214–216: the "real target" and "proper focus of constitutional inquiry" is "married women seeking abortions who do not wish to notify their husbands of their intentions and who do not qualify for one of the statutory exceptions . . ."). So too in *Hellerstedt*, the Court rejected the state's argument that the appropriate denominator for considering the regulations' impact was all the women in Texas of child-bearing age. No, the Court held, the women affected are those "for whom [the provision] is an actual rather than an irrelevant restriction." *Id.* at 2320 (quoting *Casey*). *Hellerstedt* does not tell us what fraction amounts to a "large fraction" once the correct denominator is applied. However, if the denominator is defined correctly to capture only the women whose access to abortion is actually affected, the fraction is unlikely to be large.

The lower federal courts have not applied *Hellerstedt* uniformly. Some courts seek "to cabin *Hellerstedt* in a variety of unpersuasive ways," Professor Leah Litman concludes, even "recycling—occasionally with success—many of the arguments that *Hellerstedt* rejected." Leah Litman, *Unduly Burdening Women's Health: How Lower Courts Are Undermining* Whole Woman's Health v. Hellerstedt, 116 Mich. L. Rev. Online 50 (2017). One approach states have adopted is to frame their purpose as protecting fetal—rather than maternal—life. *Id.*

Since *Hellerstedt*, many states have continued to press the boundaries of what amounts to an undue burden, continuing the trend that had begun before that case reached the Supreme Court. These new laws continue the approaches that preceded *Hellerstedt*, including precisely the provisions that the Court overturned in that case. *An Overview of Abortion Laws*, Guttmacher Inst. (Mar. 1, 2019). States, including Texas, have also recently imposed so-called fetal burial laws that are being challenged in court. *Whole Woman's Health v. Hellerstedt*, 338 F. Supp. 3d 606 (W.D. Tex.

2018), *appeal filed sub nom Whole Woman's Health v. Smith* (5th Cir. Sept. 7, 2018); Manny Fernandez, *Federal Judge Rejects a Texas Law Requiring Cremation of Fetal Tissue*, N.Y. Times, Sept. 6, 2018, at A16. In the first quarter of 2019 alone, as this book goes to press, the pace of state legislative efforts to ban abortions by passing statutes that clearly violate the central tenets of *Roe v. Wade* accelerated, with new laws banning abortions as early as six weeks into pregnancy when a fetal heartbeat can be heard, often a point when many women do not yet realize they are pregnant. Elizabeth Nash et al., *Radical Attempts to Ban Abortion Dominate State Policy Trends in the First Quarter of 2019*, Guttmacher Inst. (Apr. 2019). Niraj Chokshi, *Ohio Is Third State to Enact a Heartbeat Abortion Ban*, N.Y.Times, Apr. 16, 2019. However, a handful of states, including New York, have enacted or are considering legislation reaffirming a woman's right to an abortion until fetal viability, in apparent anticipation of continued attacks on *Roe v. Wade*, Nash, *supra*, at 4.

NOTES AND QUESTIONS

1. *Images of gender.* What are the views of women in the *Gonzales* majority opinion, in Justice Ginsburg's dissent, and in the various abortion restrictions discussed above? How do those views compare with the views expressed in *Casey*?

2. *Vitality of* Roe v. Wade. What phrase in the *Hellerstedt* opinion's summary of the test *Casey* created signals that *Roe v. Wade* remains important?

3. *Waiting periods.* What burdens are imposed by a statutory waiting period of 24, 48, or 72 hours between consultation and the procedure? Should the availability of abortion clinics in proximity to the woman's home affect the analysis?

4. *Compelled medical treatment?* If the value of a potential life is balanced against the mother's health and autonomy interest under *Gonzales*, can the state's interest in the fetus be used to impose unwanted medical care or procedures on pregnant women? For example, can the state force a woman to accept extraordinary measures to preserve her life after she is brain dead in order to bring the fetus to term? *See* Margo Kaplan, *"A Special Class of Persons": Pregnant Women's Right to Refuse Medical Treatment after* Gonzales v. Carhart, 13 U. Pa. J. Const. L. 145 (2010).

Pregnant women who refuse medical care, including procedures that could lead to the mother's death, have been forced to undergo cesarean sections; women have also been sentenced to prison after the loss of an unborn and not yet viable fetus, as in the case of one mother who fell down the stairs, triggering a miscarriage. Researchers have documented 793 arrests and forced interventions between the decision in *Roe v. Wade* and the fall of 2014, with the pace of arrests accelerating in recent years. Lynn M. Paltrow & Jeanne Flavin, *Arrests of and Forced Interventions on Pregnant Women in the United*

States, 1973–2005: Implications for Women's Legal Status and Public Health, 38 J. Health Pol. Pol'y & L. 299 (April 2013). Courts that uphold these practices take the view that the state's interest in saving the unborn child outweighs the mother's physical liberty. *Id.* Is this an accurate interpretation of *Casey*?

5. THE DELEGATION OF MEDICAL DECISIONMAKING FOR INCOMPETENT ADULTS

Decisions about childbearing and abortion, discussed in the last Section, "are deeply tied to relational circumstances, beliefs, and values," writes Professor Sonia Suter. "So too," she explains, "are decisions about how to spend one's final time on earth—whether to be aggressive in pursuing all treatment options, no matter how uncertain; to choose palliative care over treatment; or to choose some combination. These decisions * * * impact, in deep and lasting ways, how one relates to and is remembered by one's family." Sonia M. Suter, *The Politics of Information: Informed Consent in Abortion and End-of-Life Decision Making*, 39 Am. J.L. & Med. 7, 18–19 (2013). In contrast to the multiple informed consent statutes aimed at abortion before and after *Casey*, statutes regulating informed consent at the end of life are "more recent" and "fewer." *Id.* at 19.

Competent adults are generally presumed to have an autonomy interest in participating in end-of-life decisions involving their own care. A variety of circumstances arise, however, in which once-competent adults become unable to make or express their own decisions about medical care due to temporary or permanent incapacity. These situations may involve terminal illnesses, emergencies, or other crises. At such times, another adult who is close to the patient generally has legal power to make decisions on the patient's behalf, with the presumption that the surrogate decision maker is likely to be aware of the individual's values and preferences. The surrogate is entitled to the same information from medical providers that would have been available to the patient. *Id.* at 31.

This Section considers the default legal presumptions about the hierarchy of relationships—such as spouse, parent, or domestic partner—that lead to a presumption that one person should make decisions on behalf of another in the absence of express, written instructions from the incapacitated patient. The Section also discusses the legal requirements for designating one's own surrogate decisionmaker.

Because advancing medical technology frequently enables doctors to save patients who in the past certainly would not have survived, disputes over end-of-life decisionmaking have become more common. Such disputes can often lead to bitter feuds and costly litigation involving the incapacitated person's parents, spouse, children, doctors, and even the government. End-of-life decisions are increasingly common, and are increasingly likely to be governed by "complex legal rules that treat decisions about medical treatment at the end of life differently than other important decisions about medical treatment." Lois Shepherd, *The End-of-Life Law*, 92 N.C. L. Rev. 1693, 1695 (2014).

Florida law, like that of many other states, provides that when a person is incapacitated, his or her spouse is the default medical decisionmaker, unless the person previously designated an alternative surrogate. Fla. Stat. Ann. § 765.401 (West 2016). The case of Terri Schiavo, a young Florida woman who had spent 15 years in a persistent vegetative state, attracted national attention when her husband sought to remove her feeding tube over her parents' objections. The initial guardianship appointment of her husband, Michael, had been undisputed in the trial court. Jay Wolfson, Guardian Ad Litem for Theresa Schiavo, *A Report to Governor Jeb Bush and the Sixth Judicial Circuit in the Matter of Theresa Marie Schiavo*, at 8 (Dec. 1, 2003), http://abstractappeal.com/schiavo/WolfsonReport.pdf. Later, as the Florida District Court of Appeal observed, her parents, the Schindlers, "attempted to bring suit as the 'natural guardians' * * * even though they kn[e]w she [was] an adult, married daughter with an appointed legal guardian [her husband] and a pending guardianship proceeding." *In re Guardianship of Schiavo*, 792 So.2d 551, 555 (Fla. Dist. Ct. App. 2001). Michael asked that the trial court judge be substituted as surrogate decision maker. *Id.* at 557.

The conflicting claims of parents, *qua* parents, and spouses on behalf of incapacitated adults never became the focus of legal arguments in the *Schiavo* case, but the issue raises intriguing questions. If you were a trial court judge in a state that made no default provision, what factors might you consider in deciding whether an incapacitated adult's spouse or parents should make decisions on the patient's behalf?

The highly publicized *Schiavo* case, and other cases involving intra-family disputes over medical decisionmaking, highlight the importance of executing advance medical directives, including living wills and health care proxies. A living will is a written document that states a person's wishes regarding life-sustaining medical care in the event that he or she becomes incompetent. In a living will, a person may, for example, direct that she not be given life-sustaining artificial nutrition and hydration in the event that she is in a persistent vegetative state with no reasonable expectation of recovery. Links to sample living wills for each state can be found at http://www.uslivingwillregistry.com/. A health care proxy, or health care power of attorney, is a written document appointing another person to make health care decisions for the signer in the event that the signer becomes incapacitated. The appointed decisionmaker (called a "proxy" or a "surrogate") is expected to implement the patient's own wishes as reflected in a living will or through "prior expressions or other indicia of the patient's values and preferences regarding end-of-life decisions." Norman L. Cantor, *Twenty-Five Years After Quinlan: A Review of the Jurisprudence of Death and Dying,* 29 J.L. Med. & Ethics 182, 189 (2001). Both kinds of documents are forms of advance directives.

Despite the importance of living wills, only a small proportion of Americans appear to have executed these documents, though exact numbers are not available. The most recent studies indicate that about one in three adults in the United States have executed some form of advance directive. Yadav et al., *Approximately One in Three US Adults Completes Any Type of Advance Directive For End-Of-Life Care,* 36 Health Aff. 1244 (2017) (meta-analysis of studies published from 2011–2016).

The relatively low rate of executing advance directives has persisted despite educational and legal efforts to encourage individuals to leave instructions and the approval of Medicare payments to physicians for time spent in counselling patients about end of life planning that became effective in 2016. *Id.* at 1245. People may be reluctant to prepare such documents because the process conjures up the basic human fear of confronting one's own mortality and the forms may be too complex for many people to understand. Perhaps not surprisingly, patients 65 and older were more likely to complete advance directives, as are patients in hospice care.

Even when the patient has executed a living will, family members and doctors operate under the constraint of legal presumptions that "continued life" is "almost always * * * in a person's best interests." Shepherd, *supra,* at 1699. Advance directives may prove difficult to apply to the facts, and, some studies suggest, are "routinely ignored." *Id.* at 1707. Studies indicate that "many people want their health care agents to take their 'instructions' in living wills as 'suggestions'—and to have leeway to respond as they think appropriate" if it becomes necessary to exercise their powers as surrogate. *Id.*

When patients have not designated a trusted person to make decisions for them in the event they become incapacitated, most states award decisionmaking power to a family member by statute. The vast majority of states have enacted default surrogate consent laws. American Bar Association, *Health Care Decision-Making* (Feb. 27, 2019) (including state-by-state summaries and forms).

Spouses are normally the default decision makers under these statutes, usually followed in descending order of priority by the patient's adult children, parents, adult siblings, and other blood relatives. Of course, a default provision is only that. For example, in a state that provides for spouses to be default decisionmakers, a married person may still execute an advance directive appointing someone other than the spouse to make decisions in the event of incapacity. Courts may appoint specific guardians in contested cases.

At least one-third of the states allow a "close friend" to be recognized by statute as the person who makes medical decisions for an incapacitated person, but usually place friends at or near the bottom of the statutory hierarchy. A close friend may be just that and no more, or may be an intimate partner in either a heterosexual or same-sex relationship. *See, e.g.*, 755 Ill. Comp. Stat. 40/25 (2018) (a "close friend" who may be a same sex or heterosexual cohabitant may serve only if six other categories of persons in order of priority are unavailable); Miss. Code § 41-41-211 (West 2018) (recognizing a person "who has exhibited special care and concern for the patient, who is familiar with the patient's values * * *", but only after four other categories of persons).

PROBLEM 3-5

A woman who regularly seeks medical care is married to an observant Christian Scientist who will not seek medical assistance under any circumstances. She consults you as an attorney to ask whether she and her husband should execute health care proxies. What factors might you advise her to consider?

6. CONFIDENTIAL RELATIONSHIP: EVIDENTIARY PRIVILEGES

The statutory presumption that married adults would entrust to their spouses decisions about whether to prolong life through extraordinary medical interventions discussed above reflects the understanding that marriage involves a special level of reciprocal trust. That vision of the marital relationship is both reflected in and promoted by the federal law of evidence, which protects confidential communications between spouses. The federal marital evidentiary privilege was created by the Supreme Court under common law principles.

The First Circuit summarized the doctrine in 2014:

> The common law recognizes two related but distinct marital privileges: (1) the spousal testimony privilege, which allows one spouse to refuse to testify adversely against the other in criminal or related proceedings [commonly referred to as the adverse testimonial privilege]; and (2) the marital communications privilege, which permits a defendant to refuse to testify, and allows a defendant to bar his spouse or former spouse from testifying, as to any confidential communications made during their marriage.

> The marital communications privilege exists to promote marital harmony and stability by "ensur[ing] that spouses . . . feel free to communicate their deepest feelings to each other without fear of eventual exposure in a court of law." [citations omitted]. Indeed, the protection of marital confidences is "regarded as so essential to the preservation of the marriage relationship as to outweigh

[handwritten margin note: 2 common law marital privileges (from evidence)]

the disadvantages to the administration of justice which the privilege entails." *Wolfle v. United States*, 291 U.S. 7, 14 (1934).

However, this privilege, like others, "is not limitless, and courts must take care to apply it only to the extent necessary to achieve its underlying goals." [citations omitted]

United States v. Breton, 740 F.3d 1, 9–10 (1st Cir. 2014).

In order to assert the marital privilege, three conditions must be satisfied: (i) a valid marriage must have existed at the time the communication was made; (ii) the "utterances or expressions" for which the privilege is asserted must be "intended by one spouse to convey a message to the other"; and (iii) "the communication must have been made in confidence, which is presumed." *In re Reserve Fund Sec. & Derivative Litig.*, 275 F.R.D. 154, 157 (S.D.N.Y. 2011).

In *Trammel v. United States*, 445 U.S. 40 (1980), the Supreme Court held that a husband could not prevent his wife from testifying against him in a criminal trial after she had been threatened with prosecution as a co-conspirator. The Court restricted the scope of the long-recognized common-law spousal privilege by holding that a wife could voluntarily testify against her husband over his assertion of the adverse testimony privilege. The Court reasoned that by the time one spouse is prepared to turn on the other in the witness box, "there is probably little in the way of marital harmony for the privilege to preserve." *Id.* at 52. *Trammel* preserved the adverse testimonial privilege where both spouses asserted it, and also left the privilege covering confidential marital communications intact. Do you agree with the Court's reasoning? Is testimony truly voluntary when, as in Elizabeth Trammel's case, an individual who is a co-conspirator must choose between incriminating her spouse and incarceration?

NOTES AND QUESTIONS

1. *Comparative law on the scope of intrafamily privilege*. Compare the American approach to spousal testimony with that of European civil law countries, including France and Germany, where communications among a broad group of family members are protected from compelled testimony. *In re Grand Jury*, 103 F.3d 1140, 1162 (3d Cir. 1997) (Mansmann, J., dissenting). In France, any recipient of a subpoena may refuse to testify if related "by blood or by marriage in the direct line of one of the parties or his [or her] spouse, even though divorced." Catherine J. Ross, *Implementing Constitutional Rights for Juveniles: The Parent-Child Privilege in Context*, 14 Stan. L. & Pol'y Rev. 85, 91 (2003). Similarly, German law provides extensive safeguards against compulsory testimony by family members. The right to refuse to testify in either civil or criminal matters begins with a couple's engagement to marry and continues after divorce, reaching relatives by blood and marriage "to the third degree." *Id.*

2.   *When does the marital privilege end?* Wigmore asks whether the testimonial privilege continues after divorce: "After the grave cause for dissolution—adultery, desertion, crime or the like—has come to pass, and the parties have been * * * solemnly freed, by judicial decree, * * * is there any longer, either in fact or in policy, a marital peace which must be kept inviolable?" 8 J. Wigmore, Evidence § 2237, at 238 (McNaughton rev. ed. 1961). As Professor Wigmore suggests, the modern justification for the spousal privilege—the preservation of marital harmony—cannot be said to apply after divorce under common law. Some states, however, have enacted statutes that preserve the privilege for confidential communications even after the end of the marriage, as provided in some other countries. *See, e.g.*, Mich. Comp. Laws § 600.2162(4) (2010) (the privilege covers "a married person or a person that has been previously married"). What policy considerations might justify preserving the privilege after divorce?

3.   *A parent-child privilege?* A parent-child testimonial privilege can be traced back to ancient Jewish and Roman law, which "entirely barred family members from testifying against one another based on a desire to promote the solidarity and trust that support the family unit." *Grand Jury*, 103 F.3d at 1162. While there appears to be no express prohibition against a parent-child privilege in the American common law, most federal and state courts that have considered recognizing such a privilege have declined to do so. Furthermore, the Supreme Court has never granted review of a case involving an asserted parent-child privilege.

Professor Ross argues that courts have failed to distinguish among three kinds of confidences: (1) testimony concerning confidences from a minor child to a parent; (2) testimony concerning confidences from adult children to parents; and (3) testimony concerning confidences from parents to their children, and have failed to distinguish all three from testimony not based on confidences at all. Ross, *supra*, at 86, 93, 94. She argues that recognition of what she calls the "essential parent-child privilege," covering confidential communications from a minor child to a parent, is necessary before minors can meaningfully exercise their established constitutional rights, including the right to counsel and the right to be silent in the face of interrogation. *Id.* at 102. Parental advice and mediation may be the most effective means of preserving these rights or guaranteeing that any waiver by a minor is truly informed and intelligent. *Id.* at 107.

4.   *Evidentiary privilege for cohabitants?* In the United States, the marital privilege has historically been limited to those who are legally married. Should the spousal privilege be confined to married couples, or should the privilege be extended to protect the confidential communications of cohabitants, whether heterosexual or same-sex couples, who choose not to marry? Some statutes governing civil unions, when they were offered as an exclusive alternative to marriage for same-sex couples, expressly extended the evidentiary privilege to domestic partners. *See* Elizabeth Kimberly Penfil, *In the Light of Reason and Experience: Should Federal Evidence Law Protect Confidential Communications Between Same-Sex Partners?*, 88 Marq. L. Rev.

815, 834 (2005). What social policy considerations do you think should come into play, and what factors might a court examine to determine if the testimonial privilege should be recognized for a particular unmarried couple?

5.   *Domestic violence may abrogate the privilege.* The opinion in *Breton v. United States*, excerpted above, continues: "courts have long recognized an exception to the privilege when one spouse commits an offense against the other, thereby harming the marital relationship and thwarting the privilege's purpose." 740 F.3d at 10. This means that the testimonial privilege is inapplicable where one of the spouses is charged with abusing a member of the family—whether the spouse who is called to testify or children who are part of the household.

7.   FEDERAL LAW AND FAMILY FINANCES

Beyond the dignitary and emotional benefits of marriage, we have already seen that the legal status of marriage offers a number of concrete benefits, such as the right of support, inheritance rights, hospital visiting access, and spousal privilege in court proceedings. In this Section we turn to aspects of federal law affecting a family's finances that are tied to marital status or to how many children are in the household.

Society has long distinguished between the married and unmarried and has promulgated statutes and regulations designed to create "material benefits to protect and nourish the union" and its offspring. *Obergefell v. Hodges,* 135 S. Ct. at 2601. In *Obergefell* Justice Kennedy summarized the "expanding list of governmental rights, benefits, and responsibilities" tied to marriage under state and federal law. In addition to those listed above, he points to taxation regimes, campaign finance restrictions, workers' compensation benefits and health insurance as being "aspects of marital status." *Id.* By controlling access to valid marriage, the states regulate "a significant status for over a thousand provisions of federal law" affecting financial well-being. *Id.*

We can only touch on a few of these, focusing on taxation and social security. But we begin with a discussion of the precarious financial position in which many families with children find themselves.

A.   THE FINANCIAL INSTABILITY OF THE AMERICAN FAMILY

Many families in the United States are on thin ice financially, especially families with children. In an influential book published in 2004 when she was a Harvard Law School professor, Elizabeth Warren documented some of the economic pressures American families were experiencing even before the recession that began in 2008. Elizabeth Warren & Amelia Warren-Tyagi, The Two-Income Trap: Why Middle Class Parents Are Going Broke (2004). The book documented the real decline in the family's purchasing power and level of financial security in the last thirty-five years, and concluded that any unanticipated misfortune (such as a health crisis, a fire, or loss of a job) could push a person or a family into bankruptcy. Families with children experience a great deal of financial pressure and often have little discretionary disposable income. Warren and her co-author argued that "having a child is the single best predictor that a woman will end up in financial collapse." *Id.* at 6. The authors found that married couples with children are more than twice as likely to file for bankruptcy as childless couples, and a divorced woman raising a child is nearly three times as likely to file for bankruptcy as a woman who never had children, as is, presumably, a single mother. *Id.* at 6.

A spate of studies show that working- and middle-class families are walking a financial tightrope. One 2018 study described the "fiscal vertigo" confronting American families, especially once they have children. Alissa Quart, Squeezed: Why Our Families Can't Afford America 3 (2018). Middle-class life, including rent or mortgage payments, health care (even for those with insurance), child care and, for the ambitious, a public college education costs 30% more than it did twenty years ago. *Id.* Middle class parents, Alissa Quart concluded, "can't afford life in America." *Id.* at 245.

Social science data helps to explain why.

- *Wage stagnation and decline.* "Between 2000 and 2012, median incomes fell from roughly $68,642 to $62,241. Since 2000, incomes have been stagnating across the income scale—not just at the median. In essence, the vast majority of those who sustain a living through employment are not earning more money." Joseph Nathan Cohen, Financial Crisis in American Households: The Basic Expenses That Bankrupt the Middle Class 5 (2017). "Stable, well compensated jobs are disappearing. Wages have barely outpaced living costs. People save less, borrow more, and go bankrupt more often than a generation ago." *Id.* at 1.

- *Rent burden.* Studies show that increasing rent between 2001 and 2015 "affected the ability of American households to use financial services, accumulate savings and transition to home ownership" as well as to meet basic needs. Seventeen percent of renters were "severely rent burdened"—spending 50 percent or more of their income on rent. Rents increased by roughly 19% from 2001 to 2015, far outpacing changes in income. *American Families Face a Growing Rent Burden,* Pew Charitable Trusts (Apr. 19, 2018).

- *Limited savings.* In 2017 the Federal Reserve reported that 44 percent of all Americans "could not cover an unexpected $400 emergency expense." Press Release, Federal Reserve

Board Issues Report on the Economic Well-Being of U.S. Households (May 19, 2017). Indeed in 2018 more than one-third of all American households surveyed (including homeowners as well as renters) reported they had access to less than $1,000 in the event of an emergency. Taylor Tepper, *Most Americans don't have enough savings to cover a $1K emergency*, Bankrate (Jan,18, 2018).

- *Unstable earnings.* Income volatility has increased due to layoffs, cuts in hours, and irregular hours—jobs are simply less stable. Christian E. Weller, *Working-Class Families Are Getting Hit From All Sides*, Ctr. for Am. Progress (July 26, 2018).

As noted above, these challenges are particularly hard on parents. According to figures released by the federal government, the average cost of raising a child in a middle income ($59,200 to $107,400) married-couple family from birth to age 17 in 2015 was $233,610, not counting college tuition. Mark Lino et al., *Expenditures on Children by Families, 2015* (2017). For higher income families earning more than $106,800 (in 2015 dollars, the most recent available figures), the estimated cost per child will be $372,210. *Id.* at 24. The cost of raising a child varies considerably, not only by household income, but also by what region of the country the parents live in, the number of children in the family, and individual choices. The average higher income (over $107,400, average $185,400) family throughout the United States can expect to spend $372,210 raising a child to age 17, again, before counting college expenses. *Id.* at 24. But a high income family in the urban northeast of the United States can expect to spend $407,490 in 2015 dollars. *Id.* at 25.

Most observers believe that to be a very conservative estimate. Although the government reports that housing is the biggest component of the cost of raising children, official calculations omit the cost of big-ticket items, such as college tuition and salaries foregone by parents who stay at home to care for children. *Id.*

Furthermore, if a 26-year-old parent who earns about $30,000 a year withdraws from the job market for five years to take care of a child, that will result in a lifetime reduction of earnings by 19 percent, or $467,000. Darla Mercado, *Forget college tuition. Annual child-care costs exceed $20,000 in these states*, CNBC.com (Aug. 28, 2018). At higher income levels, the results are even starker. In 2014 it was estimated that a parent making $45,000 a year who stays home with a child until the child begins school, and then returns to work part-time until the child graduates from high school, would sacrifice more than $800,000 in lost wages (counting normal inflation and raises). Ron Lieber, *Child Care Accounts, Limited*, N.Y. Times, Nov. 8, 2014, at B1.

Federal studies indicate that families with one child spend approximately 26 percent of their income on the child; with two children, the average family spends about 39% of its income on the children. Lino, *supra,* at 18. Studies by economists using different methods estimate that families spend between 31 and 47 percent of their income raising two children. *Id.* at 18. The proportion of income spent by single parents, most of whom fall in the lowest income group, is about the same as for married parents with similar incomes. *Id.* at iii, 5.

The highest proportion of expenses associated with raising children are housing (especially if the family seeks a good school district) and food. *Id.* at 3, 9, 11. As children age, they cost more to provide for, but when families have more than one child, economies of scale kick in (for housing, passing down clothing, etc.) *Id.* at 14.

However, in 2018 if a family paid to send a child who is not yet in school to a child care center or a family care center in someone's home, or hired a nanny, the costs were higher than they have ever been. *This is how much child care costs in 2018,* care.com (July 17, 2018). One-third of American families spent 20% or more of their annual household income on child care, and nearly one in five spends a quarter of their income for child care. *Id.* Child care for one year may cost more than college tuition. *Id.* For example, the Farhar family in Bath, Michigan pays $23,200 a year to place two children in center-based care; for comparison, state residents pay about $40,000 total for all four years at the University of Michigan, including tuition, books, and room and board. Mercado, *supra.* In Massachusetts, the most expensive state for child care, the average annual cost of child care for two children is $34,381, roughly the same amount that out-of-state students pay for a year's tuition at the University of Massachusetts. *Id.* Many private colleges cost far more.

Most other industrialized countries subsidize or provide free child care, and many other expenses associated with raising a child, including paid parental leave, after school activities, and highly subsidized post-secondary education. Maxine Eichner, *The Privitized American Family,* 93 Notre Dame L. Rev. 213, 221 (2017). In the United States most two-parent households depend on two incomes just to make ends meet, and sometimes the cost of childcare is so prohibitive that it forces one parent to leave the labor market, jeopardizing the family's economic well-being.

The federal tax code, which could be a tool for helping working parents, fails to provide much relief. The code allows (but does not require) employers to offer their employees a tax-advantaged dependent care account, which primarily benefits families in higher income brackets. Margot L. Crandall-Hollick, Cong. Research Serv., R44993, Child and Dependent Care Tax Benefits: How they Work and Who Receives Them (2018) (summary). The dependent care account funds are deducted from the worker's gross income and reduce the worker's taxable income. A family can put up to $5,000 a year into the account, an amount that will not cover a full-time worker's day care expenses in most parts of the country. The amount—which has not increased since the program was enacted in 1981—does not vary based on how many children or aging parents the wage-earner supports. Lieber, *supra*. A second provision is only partly refundable, resulting in only 13% of families with children claiming the credit, and receiving an average benefit of $500 to $600. Crandall-Hollick, *supra*.

NOTES

1.   *Household debt and bankruptcy.* Financial instability is often linked to marital instability. Families with children, as you have seen, often experience a great deal of financial pressure and often have little discretionary income. People struggling with crushing rates of debt often file for bankruptcy.

2.   *Rising household debts.* According to the Federal Reserve, in 2018 the average household debt was roughly $50,000 with significant regional variation, with the total national household debt reaching its highest level ever, at $13.9 trillion. Fed'l Reserve Bank of N.Y., *Quarterly Report on Household Debt and Credit* (Aug. 2018) at 20 and Summary. Note that these are not primarily debts for consumer items; they include home mortgages, car loans, and student loans.

Declining housing prices have been an on-going problem in many parts of the country for the last decade. The proportion of "underwater" mortgages—mortgages that are higher than the current market value of the house—fell significantly in 2018, officially below 10%. Elina Tarkazikis, *12 cities with the most underwater homeowners*, National Mortgage News (May 30, 2018). But some observers have concluded that the "national 'effective' negative equity rate" was nearly 25% of homeowners at the end of 2017. *Id.* A significant number of homeowners owe at least double what their home is worth today. *Id.* Filing for bankruptcy is one way out of this dilemma.

Bankruptcy affects husbands and wives in intact marriages differently. Men continue to be more likely to manage the family finances generally, but the pattern shifts when families are in financial trouble. When families seek credit counseling or bankruptcy, the wives are often in charge of trying to salvage the family finances. Stephen Roll & Stephanie Moulton, *The Impact of Credit Counseling on Consumer Outcomes: Evidence from a National Demonstration Program* 10 (2016), https://www.fdic.gov/news/conferences/consumersymposium/2016/documents/roll_paper.pdf. Many husbands continue to feel that their failure to be a "good provider" undermined their "identities as husbands, as fathers, as men," as social scientists reported at least forty years ago. Warren & Warren-Tyagi, *supra*, at 11; *see* Jessie Barnard, *The Good Provider Role: Its Rise and Fall*, 36 Am. Psych. 2 (1981). The economic impact on a former spouse when a divorced person files for bankruptcy will be discussed in Chapter 9.

3.   *Joint liability for debt.* While it is possible for married persons to maintain separate credit accounts, many spouses contract to be jointly responsible for obligations by co-signing for loans, credit cards, or lines-of-credit attached to the family home. Each spouse is fully liable for joint debts contracted during the marriage, and the liability continues both during marriage and after the marriage ends. If one spouse runs up bills based on credit that was established jointly, each spouse may be individually liable for joint debts contracted during the marriage, and the liability continues both during the marriage and after the marriage ends. If one spouse runs up bills based on credit that was established jointly, each spouse may be individually liable for the entire amount. *See Margaret M. Mahoney, The Equitable Distribution of Marital Debts,* 79 UMKC L. Rev. 445 (2010). (Joint and several liability for taxes will be discussed below.) In addition, each spouse may be held responsible for expenses construed as necessary for family support, as discussed in Section 3 of this Chapter. The division of marital debt upon divorce will be discussed in Chapter 9.

B.   TAXES AND FAMILY FORMS

People who live and work in the United States pay a variety of federal, state, and local taxes. Some are paid without reference to family status or income: for example, state and local sales tax and car registration fees. Some of the taxes primarily deducted from paychecks take family status into account, while others do not. The rate at which one's income is taxed varies depending on earnings as well as family status (married or unmarried), as you will see below. Other taxes collected from the paycheck—those that cover social security and other forms of social insurance—fall on individuals regardless of marital status, but may result in varying levels of benefits depending on marital status and whether the payor has dependent children at the time benefits are triggered.

Persons who are legally married have the option of filing their federal income tax returns jointly or separately. Depending on a number of factors, the option chosen will produce a marriage "bonus" or a marriage "penalty." A marriage penalty results whenever a couple pays higher federal income taxes as a result of their marital status than they would if they had remained single and each filed individually. *See, e.g.,* Margaret Ryznar, *A Practical Solution to the Marriage Penalty,* 44 Pepp. L. Rev. 647 (2016) (describing the problem and proposing a separate filing status for two-income married couples). Penalties are highest when two wage-earners earn roughly equal incomes. A marriage bonus, on the other hand, occurs whenever a married couple pays lower federal income taxes than would two unmarried individuals each filing separately. Bonuses are highest when only one spouse is in the paid labor market and earns all the household income. Thus, couples in "traditional" marriages, with one primary breadwinner (usually the husband), reap the most benefits under the current system.

A married person may not file as an unmarried person, but may elect to file as "married-filing separately," which triggers a different, generally disadvantageous, calculation of taxes owed. As a result, the vast majority of married couples choose to file joint federal income tax returns. Professor Boris Bittker famously called joint returns an offer "that could not be refused." Boris Bittker, *Federal Income Taxation and the Family*, 27 Stan. L. Rev. 1389, 1409 n.55 (1975). For decades, commentators and politicians lamented the marriage penalty and made various attempts to alleviate the financial burden it imposes on married taxpayers. Lawrence Zelenak, *Doing Something About Marriage Penalties: A Guide for the Perplexed*, 54 Tax L. Rev. 1, 2 (2000). Modest reforms, beginning in 2001 and extended through 2017 alleviated but did not fully eliminate the marriage penalty/bonus for high-income earners. 2005 TNT 108–16 [Part 1 of 5] n. 1; *see* Margaret Ryznar, *To Work or Not to Work? The Immortal Tax Disincentives for Married Women*, 13 Lewis & Clark L. Rev. 921 (2009); American Taxpayer Relief Act of 2012. Pub. L. No. 112–240, 126 Stat. 2313.

Even with those legislative modifications, the nonpartisan Congressional Research Service ("CRS") concluded in 2013 that "[m]arriage penalties remain at the high and low income levels, and could also apply to those with children * * * [T]he current system is likely to encourage rather than discourage marriage and favors married couples over singles." Jane G. Gravelle, Cong. Research Serv., RL33755, Federal Income Tax Treatment of the Family (2013) (summary). However, the CRS observed that "there is no reason to expect that unmarried individuals are penalized in the aggregate," as opposed to in particular cases. On average, "singles who live together are * * * being penalized relative to married couples," but all of these patterns also depend on the source and division of income, as well as the presence of children in the household. *Id.* at 23.

A federal tax overhaul passed in 2017 but many of its provisions will expire in less than a decade. Tax Cuts and Jobs Act of 2017, Pub. L. No. 115–97, 131 Stat. 2054. The new tax code continued the marriage bonus/penalty approach, and returned its structure to the period before Congress attempted temporary "fixes." Reed Shuldiner, *Marginal Rates Under the TCJA*, 159 Tax Notes 1911, 1911, 1917 (2018). As before, the "marriage penalty will be largest for equal-earner couples * * * [the marriage bonus will increase the more uneven the earnings of the two individuals, and it will be largest for single-earner couples." *Id.* at 1914. The new law that went into effect in 2018 "greatly expanded the marriage bonus region and correspondingly shrank the marriage penalty." *Id.* at 1915. Under the current law, the marriage penalty is only triggered where the couple's "combined taxable-income exceeds $600,000" and the dollar amount of the penalty is one-quarter of what it was under prior law. *Id.* at 1916. Unmarried taxpayers reach the highest tax bracket (37%) when they earn $100,000 less than the income that brings married couples into the highest bracket. *Id.* at 1915.

Low-wage earners face a different set of tax issues based on marriage. These taxpayers are affected by another part of the Internal Revenue Code, the Earned Income Tax Credit ("EITC"), an antipoverty program that provides a fully refundable tax credit worth a percentage of earnings on a sliding scale that declines and is phased out once income reaches a certain level. The rate depends on both income and the number of children in the family under the age of 19 (or 24 if they are full-time students). The EITC is available regardless of marital status, focusing instead on the number of children in the family unit, with declining payments per child, up to a maximum of three children as of 2018. Even though the maximum income to qualify for the EITC is about $5,000 higher for married couples than for single parents, when two low-wage earners who earn roughly the same amount of money marry, they may find that their combined income eliminates their eligibility for the EITC, creating a different sort of marriage penalty. *Id.* at 7. The EITC, the largest cash assistance program for low-income families in the United States, reached more than 27 million households in 2017. Those families received an average credit of over $2,488. *Statistics for Tax Returns with EITC*, Internal Revenue Service (2018). In addition, a growing number of states (29 in 2018) have enacted a state EITC that supplements the federal refund. Solana Rice et al., *Prosperity Now Scorecard, Whose Bad Choices? How Policy Precludes Prosperity and What We Can Do About It*, Prosperity Now (2018) 9.

The author of the next article considers whether the current demographics of the American family and the decline of marriage require a fundamental rethinking of the income tax system. More broadly, the article challenges the assumption that marriage is a bright line status that should control access to certain government benefits and burdens. As you read, consider the changing portrait of families set out in Chapter 1, as well as the discussion of the economic and caring responsibilities within marriage in this Chapter.

ANNE L. ALSTOTT,
UPDATING THE WELFARE STATE: MARRIAGE, THE INCOME TAX, AND SOCIAL SECURITY IN THE AGE OF INDIVIDUALISM
66 Tax L. Rev. 695, 695, 697–99, 702–08, 720–21, 727–29, 748–49, 752–58 (2013).

I.   Introduction

* * *

[T]he federal income tax and the Social Security system continue to define "family" based on formal marriage, and our textbooks treat the economic vulnerability of the married woman as the central problem of gender in tax policy design. In this Article, I argue that the growing gap between legal fiction and social reality undermines the ability of the tax-and-transfer system to achieve any of a range of objectives—whether fostering individual freedom, aiding the poor, or shoring up the traditional family.

* * *

* * * I initially focus on a central feature of the income tax: joint filing. Later, I consider implications of the new individualism for a second key component of the welfare state: the spousal benefit in Social Security.

My thesis is that the new individualism has rendered obsolete legal doctrines and policy analyses that treat formal marriage as the proxy for family life. * * *

* * * Once we recognize that marriage is no longer the organizing institution for work and family life, and once we understand that marriage has become heterogeneous, the principle of "equal taxation of equal-earning married couples" no longer packs the same normative punch. Similarly, once we recognize that gender equality in married couples has increased, that most wives work outside the home [increasingly matching or exceeding their husband's earnings], and that single mothers bear the greatest burden of gendered roles, the most vulnerable player is no longer the nonworking wife but the working (but low-earning) single mother.

Much like joint filing, the spousal benefit in Social Security tracks a social reality that no longer exists. The spousal benefit, along with other provisions, protects wives in traditional marriages when husbands/breadwinners retire, die, or become disabled. At the same time, the spousal benefit, combined with the payroll tax, penalizes working wives and rewards traditional gender roles. But the framing of the social problem has gone askew here as well. Two-earner marriages are the norm rather than the exception. And while women today are economically vulnerable by virtue of their lower wages and care responsibilities, they are often divorced or never-married single mothers rather than widows or dependent wives.

* * *

[T]he income tax and Social Security both stand in need of major reform.

* * * Liberal individualism militates in favor of individual filing in the income tax and individual benefits, with optional joint-and-survivor annuities, in Social Security. By contrast, welfarist traditions endorse the aggregation of income at the household level in order to measure well-being. * * *

* * *

A.   The Federal Income Tax and the Joint Return

* * *

[Under the] federal income tax enacted in 1913 [e]ach individual paid income taxes on his or her own income, without regard to family relationships. By 1948, however, a series of milestone cases had revealed the weaknesses of individual filing in the era of mid-twentieth-century marriage.

* * *

The middle- and upper-class push for income-splitting reflected cultural conditions as well as legal design. Most women had little income of their own: They married young, had children early, and worked primarily in the home thereafter. Marriage typically lasted for life, and couples expected to share in their good or bad fortune together, making it irrelevant, in practical terms, whether the couple called it "his money" or "her money." Thus, the stage was set for income-splitting as a device that would reduce taxes for a wide swath of American families.

[Following several lawsuits over whether a married couple could split a single income between two people, in] 1948, Congress solved the problem by extending income-splitting to couples in all states. The vehicle for income-splitting was the joint rate schedule, which adopted tax brackets for married couples filing jointly that were twice as wide as those for single individuals. The new joint filing system equalized the tax burden on married couples with equal incomes: Under the new regime, a couple with $10,000 of total income would owe the same tax, regardless of how the income was divided between spouses and whether the couple lived in a community property state. * * *

* * *

* * * By 1969, the first inklings of demographic change had appeared: The divorce rate and age at first marriage began to climb upward, and wives began to enter the workplace in record numbers. * * * Congress reacted to complaints that income-splitting favored the married couple over the single man by adjusting the rate schedules so that the marginal-rate brackets for married couples were no longer twice as wide as those for single taxpayers.

* * * The 1969 legislation created the first "marriage penalty" for some couples. The 1969 compromise persists to this day: Husbands and wives with divergent earnings still claim a marriage bonus, but two-earner couples with similar earnings pay a marriage penalty.

The marriage penalty/bonus problem is [tax experts agree] insoluble. The well-known "trilemma" holds that an income tax cannot simultaneously impose progressive marginal tax rates, assess equal taxes on married couples with equal earnings, and maintain marriage neutrality (so that the total income taxes paid by two unmarried individuals neither increase nor decrease when the couple marries).

Individual filing permits a progressive income tax to be marriage neutral but imposes unequal tax burdens on equal-earning couples. By contrast, income-splitting sacrifices marriage neutrality in order to impose progressive rates and keep tax burdens even across couples. The result is that any system of joint filing inevitably creates a marriage bonus, a marriage penalty, or both, as our income tax has done since 1969.

Feminist scholars have pointed out that joint filing with progressive marginal rates tends to reward traditional gender roles while penalizing two-earner couples, because the largest marriage bonuses are claimed by couples with one working and one nonworking spouse. Compounding the gender inequity, joint filing tends to discourages wives' employment, because the first dollar of wives' wages is taxed at the (higher) marginal rate established by the husband's earnings. (Importantly, this pathology of joint filing * * * is true in any system of joint filing when, culturally, the wife is understood to be what economists bluntly term the "secondary worker.")

* * *

[T]he treatment of marriage followed a similar path in the Social Security system.

B.   The Social Security System and the Spousal Benefit

* * * As originally enacted in 1935, Social Security provided only for benefits for workers, but an amendment in 1939 added supplementary benefits for wives and surviving widows.

The spousal benefit persists today. Husbands now are eligible as well as wives, although the great majority of claimants are women, due to women's generally lower earnings and fewer years in the workforce. In 2011, the Social Security system paid about $761 per month to two million wives and husbands solely because they were (or had been) married to a qualifying retired worker.

A spouse is eligible for a spousal benefit if she is married to a retired worker entitled to a Social Security retirement benefit. Divorced spouses are entitled to the benefit if the marriage lasted ten years. The spousal benefit equals 50% of the retired worker's benefit.

For example, suppose that Abner retires at age 66 and is entitled to an average Social Security monthly benefit of $1300. His wife, Betty, would be entitled to claim a spousal benefit equal to one-half that amount, or $650, even if she had never worked for wages. Spouses who can also claim benefits as workers, based on their own work records, receive the higher of their own benefit or the spousal benefit. Thus, if Betty's own earnings record entitled her to $800 per month, Social Security would pay her that amount. But if Betty's earnings were low enough that her benefit was below $650, she would still receive the $650 entitlement based on her marital status.

Spousal benefits linked to formal marriage made eminent good sense in the era of mid-twentieth-century marriage. The aim of Social Security * * * is to protect workers and their dependents against major income shocks. * * *

But the spousal benefit, like joint filing, rewards some couples at the expense of others. [B]eneficiaries must pay a payroll tax to participate in the system. The combined tax-benefit "deal" is particularly good for couples with traditional gender roles: They receive 150% of the worker's retirement benefit after paying taxes on 100% of the husband's salary. By contrast, two-earner couples pay a higher price (taxes on two salaries) and may not, in the end, collect more than 150% of the higher earner's retirement benefit.

Many two-earner couples thus pay incremental taxes for no incremental benefit. To see why, return to Abner and Betty. If Betty has a record of low wages relative to Abner's, she may well be entitled to a retired worker's benefit of less than 50% of Abner's benefit. In that case, she will take the spousal benefit. The spousal benefit raises the total payment to the couple (compared to their earned benefits alone). But the two-earner couple has paid taxes on Betty's earnings without, in the end, earning any incremental coverage at retirement.

* * *

Today, * * * [t]he decline in marriage, continued high divorce rates, and nonmarital child-bearing and rearing have created new vulnerabilities not captured by rules that presume that formally- and long-married wives are the principal dependents whose needs should be served.

* * *

Today, the gendered division of labor falls heavily on the rising proportion of single mothers, who bear a heavy burden of care work along with paid employment. * * * Even during the * * * recession [that began in 2008], two-thirds of single mothers work[ed] outside the home.

[III.] C. The Tightening Link Between Marriage and Class

* * *

* * * In 2011, more than half of unmarried-couple households had incomes at or below the fortieth percentile of the income distribution. In neat symmetry, more than 50% of married couples had incomes at or above

the sixtieth income percentile, and more than 30% had incomes at or above the eightieth percentile.

Bolstering the association between lasting marriage and higher income, divorce rates fall with income and with educational attainment * * *.

* * *

IV. Updating the Income Tax: Joint Filing and the New Individualism

The new individualism poses serious policy challenges for the income tax. [F]ormal marriage no longer demarcates family life. Many people form and dissolve relationships outside marriage—and they bear and rear children outside marriage as well. The growing heterogeneity of marriage means that even among married couples, the law cannot infer that traditional activities are taking place: Married couples today may or may not rear children, conform to traditional gender roles, expect to remain married for the long-term, or expect to share their economic fortune "for better or worse."

* * *

In this Part, I argue that the new demographics of the family render joint filing obsolete—whatever one's views about the sanctity and desirability of marriage.

[R]ecall the two major problems that income-splitting solved in 1948. First, the income-splitting joint return provided a reasonably accurate assessment of individuals' family status and, thus, a reasonable measure of well-being derived from shared income and relational commitments from others. Second, joint filing prevented tax-motivated transfers of assets and income between husbands and wives.

[J]oint filing no longer serves either purpose particularly well.

* * * What kind of tax policy would make the most sense?

Begin with the easy conclusion: Joint filing is an exceptionally poor tool for encouraging people to marry and stay married. After all, joint filing does not necessarily favor marriage. Its penalties and bonuses are a complex function of rate brackets and the division of income in the couple. Some couples face marriage penalties, including couples in the EITC income range * * *

* * *

[V.] B.   Gender Inequality and Social Security

* * *

As traditionally understood, * * * Social Security faces a policy dilemma: The program can only protect economically-vulnerable wives if it sacrifices gender equity for working wives. Repealing the spousal benefit would remove the penalty on working wives, who would then claim the full benefit of their incremental payroll taxes. But doing so would leave many wives worse off, in terms of the total benefit received. Worst off would be homemakers and homemaker-breadwinner couples.

But * * * [t]he percentage of women claiming benefits solely as workers (that is, with no marital claim) is now nearly 50%. The percentage of elderly women claiming Social Security only as wives has plummeted since 1960, from about a third to less than 10%. As of 2011, only three million of thirty-six million retirees claim Social Security as wives and husbands rather than as retired workers.

* * *

* * * In the mid-twentieth century, almost all women were wives and almost all men were husbands, and both groups mostly occupied prescribed roles. In that world, gender inequality burdened wives and benefitted husbands, and abandoned wives and widows were the object of great (and deserved) social concern. Today, by contrast, the new individualism situates gender inequality elsewhere. Women continue to earn lower wages than men, due in part to discriminatory employment structures. Mothers earn lower wages than childless women, due to the structure of child care. Single mothers often live in poverty, due to low wages, child care responsibilities, and the absence of financial and hands-on support from absent fathers.

* * *

As we think about true innovation in Social Security, [several] issues (at least) should be pressing. First, the issue of generational transition should be in the forefront of our thinking. * * * Phase-outs and other transitional mechanisms will be essential if we are to tailor programs to changing social reality.

Second, the de-institutionalization of marriage invites a deeper rethinking of the mission of Social Security (and social insurance more generally). As formal marriage wanes in importance as a social category, we need new ways of thinking about the life course and the catastrophes against which the state should insure individuals. What are the major events that can leave an individual economically and socially vulnerable today? Divorce, low wages, a childhood in poverty, non-marital births?

* * *

VI. Conclusion

* * *

Once we abandon the fiction that joint filing represents a sound (or even tenable) approach to taxing the family, new challenges and opportunities arise. * * *

[H]ousehold filing * * * would require new rules and technology for defining the household and monitoring entry and exits. But a tax system capable of aggregating income at the household level (even reasonably well) would mark a major advance in the ability to administer the EITC and other tax-based transfer programs * * *. Aggregating income at the household level—across the board or only for purposes of certain rules—would provide Congress with a new tool for social policy. But the costs include a loss of privacy * * * .

[M]arriage [might be used] as a "tag" for class privilege or ability (respectively) in order to redistribute income fairly * * * . While a marriage tax seems unlikely to be a political centerpiece for either party, policymakers could at a minimum remove tax advantages to marriage, which—in light of the new individualism—map rather closely onto tax advantages for the social elite.

Finally, the * * * demise of mid-twentieth-century marriage and the changing burden of gender inequality should prompt the repeal of the spousal benefit in Social Security and the redesign of the system to address the situation of single parents and the diversity of modern families.

* * *

NOTES AND QUESTIONS

1. *A comparative perspective.* Most other industrialized countries, including Canada, Australia, Japan, and Sweden, require or allow each person to file taxes as an individual. Of the 11 OECD countries that allow joint filing, two nations also permit unmarried partners to file jointly. In the United States, however, the tax code treats married people differently than single people, regardless of whether they file separately or jointly. Do you agree with Alstott that requiring married persons to file joint returns (or penalizing them if they elect not to) no longer makes sense as a matter of sociological realism or social policy? If so, do you think filing as individuals or as households would be preferable? What are the advantages and disadvantages of each approach?

2. *Tax policy as social policy.* Should the tax code prefer the married to the unmarried couple? Or vice versa? Single parents to people without children? On what grounds? Should it matter whether the members of the married couple are of childbearing age, have never been married, or are members of the AARP and have each been married multiple times?

3.   *Other benefits covered by Social Security*. "Social Security" is often used as shorthand for monthly cash payments to retirees. However, it is actually part of a broader social insurance plan that also protects workers' spouses (and ex-spouses). The social security system provides disability payments and survivors' benefits to spouses and dependent children, regardless of the insured's age at the time of death.

4.   *Joint legal accountability for tax filings*: *The "innocent spouse" doctrine*. Filing a joint income tax return exposes each spouse to joint and several liability for the other's tax deficiencies. Joint and several liability means that the Internal Revenue Service can collect from one spouse any tax deficiency that is subsequently determined, even if the deficiency was caused entirely by the other spouse. *See, e.g.,* Amy C. Christian, *Lurking Marriage Penalty*, Nat'l L.J., Aug. 23, 1999, at A14. The agency may collect the entire amount of the deficiency from either spouse, but it will often choose to pursue one spouse over the other "because prospects of recovering from the other spouse are poor (e.g., the other spouse is judgment-proof, has no attachable income stream or the other spouse's whereabouts are unknown)." Lily Kahng, *Innocent Spouses: A Critique of the New Tax Laws Governing Joint and Several Tax Liability*, 49 Vill. L. Rev. 261, 264 (2004).

The "innocent spouse" doctrine creates an exception—albeit a very limited one—to the seemingly harsh joint and several liability regime. I.R.C. § 6015(b)–(c), (f) (2018). Relief from the consequences of joint return liability under § 6015(b) is available only in a small number of cases. Innocent spouses must prove: (1) that they neither knew nor had reason to know of the understatement of tax on the return; and (2) that when all the facts and circumstances are taken into account, it would be inequitable to hold them liable for the unpaid taxes, interest, and penalties. In evaluating the equities, courts generally examine whether the innocent spouse significantly benefited from the understatement of tax. To gain relief under § 6015(b), innocent spouses must prove both elements, a task that is usually onerous and often impossible.

For taxpayers who are divorced, legally separated, or no longer living together, § 6015(c) provides an alternate form of relief from joint and several liability—"proportionate relief." Kahng, *supra*, at 267. Spouses seeking proportionate relief elect to limit their liability to their allocable share of the tax deficiency. *Id.* Proportionate relief is not available if the I.R.S. can demonstrate that the "innocent spouse" had actual knowledge of the understatement at the time he or she signed the joint return. *Id.* at 268–69. Innocent spouses who cannot gain relief under § 6015(b) or (c) may seek "equitable relief" under § 6015(f) if, "taking into account all the facts and circumstances, it is inequitable to hold the individual liable for any unpaid tax or any deficiency (or any portion of either)." The odds against being awarded innocent spouse status are high. In 2010, only 7,683 of the more than 50,000 petitioners were recognized as innocent spouses, while another 6,383 received partial relief. Charles Delafuente, *Some Advice for Wary Spouses: Consider Filing a Separate Return*, N.Y. Times, Feb. 13, 2011, at Business-12.

CHAPTER 4

NONMARITAL COUPLES

■ ■ ■

Nonmarital cohabitation has become increasingly widespread over the past half century. Because family law has traditionally focused on the marital family, nonmarital families have presented challenges for the domestic relations field. This Chapter examines legal doctrines concerning the rights and responsibilities between nonmarital couples. Such matters appear regularly in a family lawyer's caseload.

In 1970, the number of households in the United States made up of cohabiting (nonmarital) opposite-sex couples was about 500,000. Susan Brown, Families in America 52–53 (2017). By 2016, that number had grown to more than 8 million, including about 3 million households with children; there were also approximately 400,000 same-sex cohabiting couples. Jennifer Ortman, *Changes to the Household Relationship Data in the Current Population Survey* (Jan. 11, 2017) (statistics not available for number of same-sex cohabitants with children).

Almost two-thirds (65%) of women between the ages of 19 and 44 have cohabited, and most women have cohabited before their first marriage. Wendy D. Manning & Bart Stykes, Twenty-five Years of Change in Cohabitation in the U.S., 1987–2013 1 (2015).

According to the U.S. Census Bureau, cohabitation is more common among adults 34 years or younger than among older adults, and married men and women are more likely to have a college degree than are cohabitants. Jonathan Vespa, Jamie M. Lewis & Rose M. Kreider, *America's Families and Living Arrangements: 2012* 18 (2013). Couples may choose to cohabit, temporarily or permanently, for various reasons. Indeed, cohabiters are "not a monolith," and cohabitation "serves different purposes for different groups." Brown, *supra*, at 56.

For example, couples may cohabit for financial reasons, such as sharing living expenses or because they are not financially ready to marry. Or they may cohabit to determine if they are compatible. Laura Tach & Sarah Halpern-Meekin, *Why They Cohabit: Couples' Reasons for Cohabitation and Relationship Quality* 9–10 (2014). Another reason couples cohabit is to provide a prelude or trial period before marriage. Indeed, most marriages now begin with cohabitation. Erez Aloni, *Registering Relationships,* 87 Tul. L. Rev. 573, 582 (2013).

Cohabitation can also be a response to pregnancy (often unintended) or the birth of a child; the phenomenon of "shotgun cohabitation" is analogous to the "shotgun weddings" more common in earlier generations. Caroline Kitchener, *The Age of 'Shotgun Cohabitation,'* The Atlantic (Apr. 25, 2018) (discussing research). One recent study found that "thirty-five percent of all unmarried parents are now cohabiting." Gretchen Livingston, *The Changing Profile of Unmarried Parents*, Pew Research Center (Apr. 25, 2018). Establishing legal parenthood, child support, custody, and visitation issues concerning nonmarital children are discussed in Chapters 5, 11, 12, and 13.

Couples may also prefer cohabitation because they fear divorce, or because they have ethical or other personal objections to the institution of marriage. Divorced and widowed individuals also often choose cohabitation as a prelude or alternative to marriage.

Cohabitants are less likely than married couples to pool their income or share their finances, such as through opening joint bank accounts or making significant purchases together. Isabel Sawhill, Generation Unbound: Drifting into Sex and Parenthood Without Marriage 21 (2014). There is some evidence that, the longer unmarried couples live together, the more likely they are to open joint bank accounts.

A first cohabiting union is more than twice as likely to dissolve as a first marriage, and after five years, less than half of women in their first cohabitating union remain in that relationship. Steven Ruggles & Sheela Kennedy, *Trends in Union Instability in the United States, 1980s–2010s* Table 1 (Minn. Population Center, Working Paper No. 2015-1). Yet cohabiting unions also mirror the patterns of the diverging destinies concerning marriage introduced in Chapter 1; women with a college education are more likely to transition into marriage than are women with less education. Janet Chen-Lan Kuo & R. Kelly Raley, *Diverging Patterns of Union Transition among Cohabitors by Race-Ethnicity and Education: Trends and Marital Intentions*, 53 Demography 921 (2016).

The reason that cohabiting unions are more likely to dissolve than marriage appears to be related to age rather than the cohabitation itself. In other words, the age when the marriage or cohabitation starts is a better predictor of dissolution than is the actual living-together status. Arielle Kuperberg, *Age at Coresidence, Premarital Cohabitation, and Marriage Dissolution: 1985–2009*, 76 J. Marr. & Fam. 352 (2014). The increasing popularity of cohabitation may also be a factor in the impact premarital cohabitation has on divorce. A few decades ago, couples who cohabited before marrying faced "higher odds of divorce" than those who did not, but "the association between premarital cohabitation and the risk of divorce has been negligible for couples who married after 1998." Brown, Families in America, *supra,* at 59.

Unlike marriage, in which a set of status-based laws establishes spousal rights and obligations, cohabitants have historically been subject to comparatively few laws governing their rights and obligations during their relationships or upon termination. Indeed, historically, cohabitation was a crime in many states. But as cohabitation has become more prevalent and more socially acceptable, laws concerning cohabitation have changed markedly. A spur to such change was the pursuit by cohabitants of various theories to establish legal claims against each other. There is, however, no uniformity among the states on the legal treatment of cohabitation.

Instead, states have developed three basic approaches. The first, and most common, allows cohabitants to assert legal and equitable claims. A second, available in a minority of jurisdictions, allows the assertion of status-based claims. A third approach, taken by a handful of states, accords no relief at all. *See* Albertina Antognini, *Against Nonmarital Exceptionalism,* 51 UC Davis L. Rev. 101, 122 (2018). States in this third category typically view recognizing such claims as contrary to public policy favoring formal marriage and abolishing common law marriage.

In addition, as discussed at the end of the Chapter, some states have also developed alternative approaches, such as according legal recognition to nonmarital couples who enter into a state-recognized domestic partnership or a civil union. With the advent of civil marriage equality for same-sex couples, some states no longer offer these statuses; but, in a small number of states, domestic partnerships and civil unions are still available to same-sex and (in some states) opposite-sex couples. Colorado has established a new status, a designated beneficiary agreement, which is not tied to cohabitation or to being in an intimate, marriage-like relationship. By contrast, other states do not permit or recognize such statuses, even if validly entered into in another state.

This Chapter surveys varying approaches to the economic obligations of nonmarital partners, discusses other aspects of nonmarital cohabitation, and then considers the rights and responsibilities that arise when cohabitants enter into a formal legal status, such as a domestic partnership or civil union. As you read the material in this Chapter, consider whether and how the variety of reasons that people cohabit should shape legal responses to it. Consider also what role marriage plays as courts, legislatures, and commentators design legal remedies between cohabitants.

1. INTENT (CONTRACT-BASED AGREEMENTS)

When relationships between cohabitants end, the parties must disentangle their formerly intertwined lives. As this Section shows, courts use a variety of bases for establishing that the parties may assert economic claims against each other. In a minority of states, however, courts decline to recognize any such claims or remedies to the extent that they grow out of the cohabitation relationship itself. As you read these materials, consider the arguments made for each approach and what role you think the law should play.

A. ESTABLISHING OR REJECTING RIGHTS?

1. Opening the Door to Claims by Cohabitants

☆ *Marvin v. Marvin*, set out below, is a landmark opinion because it is one of the earliest cases to recognize legal property and support rights arising from cohabitation, sometimes informally called "palimony." *Marvin* dominated the headlines because it involved a high-profile defendant, movie star Lee Marvin, who was best known for his Academy Award-winning role in *Cat Ballou* (1965). Marvin was at the height of his popularity when he separated from his wife, Betty Marvin, and began living with Michelle Triola, the plaintiff in this case. When Michelle Triola died in 2009, her obituary reported that, due to her lawsuit, "[p]alimony became a dictionary entry." Elaine Woo, *Michelle Triola Marvin Dies at 75; Her Legal Fight with Ex-Lover Lee Marvin Added 'Palimony' to the Language*, L.A. Times (Oct. 31, 2009). Triola stated that she believed her lawsuit "got the subject of people living together out of the closet" and encouraged people to discuss openly "what they want out of a relationship." *Id.*

As you read *Marvin* and the cases that follow, consider the evolution of courts' treatment of nonmarital relationships.

> **MARVIN V. MARVIN**
> Supreme Court of California, 1976.
> 557 P.2d 106.

Takeaway: A couple who live together but are not married may form an agreement related to their finances and assets. [handwritten margin note]

TOBRINER, J.

During the past 15 years, there has been a substantial increase in the number of couples living together without marrying.[1] Such nonmarital relationships lead to legal controversy when one partner dies or the couple separates. * * *

We conclude: (1) The provisions of the Family Law Act [which apply to divorcing couples] do not govern the distribution of property acquired during a nonmarital relationship; such a relationship remains subject solely to judicial decision. (2) The courts should enforce express contracts between nonmarital partners except to the extent that the contract is explicitly founded on the consideration of meretricious sexual services. (3)

---

[1] "The 1970 census figures indicate that today perhaps eight times as many couples are living together without being married as cohabited ten years ago." (Comment, *In re Cary: A Judicial Recognition of Illicit Cohabitation*, 25 Hastings L.J. 1226 (1974)).

In the absence of an express contract, the courts should inquire into the conduct of the parties to determine whether that conduct demonstrates an implied contract, agreement of partnership or joint venture, or some other tacit understanding between the parties. The courts may also employ the doctrine of quantum meruit, or equitable remedies such as constructive or resulting trust, when warranted by the facts of the case.

* * *

1.   *The factual setting of this appeal.*

* * *

Plaintiff avers that in October of 1964 she and defendant "entered into an oral agreement" that while "the parties lived together they would combine their efforts and earnings and would share equally any and all property accumulated as a result of their efforts whether individual or combined." Furthermore, they agreed to "hold themselves out to the general public as husband and wife" and that "plaintiff would further render her services as a companion, homemaker, housekeeper and cook to . . . defendant."

Shortly thereafter plaintiff agreed to "give up her lucrative career as an entertainer [and] singer" in order to "devote her full time to defendant . . . as a companion, homemaker, housekeeper and cook;" in return defendant agreed to "provide for all of plaintiff's financial support and needs for the rest of her life."

Plaintiff alleges that she lived with defendant from October of 1964 through May of 1970 and fulfilled her obligations under the agreement. During this period the parties as a result of their efforts and earnings acquired in defendant's name substantial real and personal property, including motion picture rights worth over $1 million. In May of 1970, however, defendant compelled plaintiff to leave his household. He continued to support plaintiff until November of 1971, but thereafter refused to provide further support.

On the basis of these allegations plaintiff asserts two causes of action. The first, for declaratory relief, asks the court to determine her contract and property rights; the second seeks to impose a constructive trust upon one half of the property acquired during the course of the relationship.

* * * Since the parties had stipulated that defendant's marriage to Betty Marvin did not terminate until the filing of a final decree of divorce in January 1967, the trial court treated defendant's motion as one for judgment on the pleadings augmented by the stipulation.

After hearing argument the court granted defendant's motion and entered judgment for defendant. * * * [Plaintiff appealed].

2. *Plaintiff's complaint states a cause of action for breach of an express contract.*

* * *

Defendant first and principally relies on the contention that the alleged contract is so closely related to the supposed "immoral" character of the relationship between plaintiff and himself that the enforcement of the contract would violate public policy. He points to cases asserting that a contract between nonmarital partners is unenforceable if it is "involved in" an illicit relationship. A review of the numerous California decisions concerning contracts between nonmarital partners, however, reveals that the courts have not employed such broad and uncertain standards to strike down contracts. The decisions instead disclose a narrower and more precise standard: a contract between nonmarital partners is unenforceable only *to the extent* that it *explicitly* rests upon the immoral and illicit consideration of meretricious sexual services.

* * *

Although the past decisions hover over the issue in the somewhat wispy form of the figures of a Chagall painting, we can abstract from those decisions a clear and simple rule. The fact that a man and woman live together without marriage, and engage in a sexual relationship, does not in itself invalidate agreements between them relating to their earnings, property, or expenses. Neither is such an agreement invalid merely because the parties may have contemplated the creation or continuation of a nonmarital relationship when they entered into it. Agreements between nonmarital partners fail only to the extent that they rest upon a consideration of meretricious sexual services. Thus the rule asserted by defendant, that a contract fails if it is "involved in" or made "in contemplation" of a nonmarital relationship, cannot be reconciled with the decisions.

[All case law cited by defendant] involved consideration that *was* expressly founded upon [ ] illicit sexual services. In *Hill v. Estate of Westbrook*, [213 P.2d 727 (Cal. Ct. App. 1950)], the woman promised to keep house for the man, to live with him as man and wife, and to bear his children; the man promised to provide for her in his will, but died without doing so. Reversing a judgment for the woman based on the reasonable value of her services, the Court of Appeal stated that the action is predicated upon a claim which seeks, among other things, the reasonable value of living with decedent in meretricious relationship [sic] and bearing him two children. * * *

* * *

* * * [A] contract between nonmarital partners, even if expressly made in contemplation of a common living arrangement, is invalid only if sexual acts form an inseparable part of the consideration for the agreement. In sum, a court will not enforce a contract for the pooling of property and earnings if it is explicitly and inseparably based upon services as a paramour. The Court of Appeal opinion in *Hill*, however, indicates that even if sexual services are part of the contractual consideration, any *severable* portion of the contract supported by independent consideration will still be enforced.

The principle that a contract between nonmarital partners will be enforced unless expressly and inseparably based upon an illicit consideration of sexual services not only represents the distillation of the decisional law, but also offers a far more precise and workable standard than that advocated by defendant. * * *

[I]n the present case a standard which inquires whether an agreement is "involved" in or "contemplates" a nonmarital relationship is vague and unworkable. Virtually all agreements between nonmarital partners can be said to be "involved" in some sense in the fact of their mutual sexual relationship, or to "contemplate" the existence of that relationship. Thus defendant's proposed standards, if taken literally, might invalidate all agreements between nonmarital partners, a result no one favors. Moreover, those standards offer no basis to distinguish between valid and invalid agreements. By looking not to such uncertain tests, but only to the consideration underlying the agreement, we provide the parties and the courts with a practical guide to determine when an agreement between nonmarital partners should be enforced.

* * *

In summary, we base our opinion on the principle that adults who voluntarily live together and engage in sexual relations are nonetheless as competent as any other persons to contract respecting their earnings and property rights. Of course, they cannot lawfully contract to pay for the performance of sexual services, for such a contract is, in essence, an agreement for prostitution and unlawful for that reason. But they may agree to pool their earnings and to hold all property acquired during the relationship in accord with the law governing community property; conversely they may agree that each partner's earnings and the property acquired from those earnings remains the separate property of the earning partner. So long as the agreement does not rest upon illicit meretricious consideration, the parties may order their economic affairs as they choose, and no policy precludes the courts from enforcing such agreements.

In the present instance, plaintiff alleges that the parties agreed to pool their earnings, that they contracted to share equally in all property acquired, and that defendant agreed to support plaintiff. The terms of the contract as alleged do not rest upon any unlawful consideration. We therefore conclude that the complaint furnishes a suitable basis upon which the trial court can render declaratory relief. The trial court consequently erred in granting defendant's motion for judgment on the pleadings.

* * *

3.   *Plaintiff's complaint can be amended to state a cause of action founded upon implied contract or theories of equitable relief.*

[Although plaintiff's claim rested on an express contract, the court addresses whether a nonmarital partner who renders services may recover based on an implied contract.] * * * We have examined the reasons advanced to justify this denial of relief, and find that none have merit.

First, we note that [prior] cases denying relief do not rest their refusal upon any theory of "punishing" a "guilty" partner. Indeed, to the extent that denial of relief "punishes" one partner, it necessarily rewards the other by permitting him to retain a disproportionate amount of the property. Concepts of "guilt" thus cannot justify an unequal division of property between two equally "guilty" persons.

Other reasons advanced in the decisions fare no better. The principal argument seems to be that "[e]quitable considerations arising from the reasonable expectation of . . . benefits attending the status of marriage . . . are not present [in a nonmarital relationship]." *Vallera v. Vallera*, [134 P.2d 761, 763 (Cal. 1943)]. But, although parties to a nonmarital relationship obviously cannot have based any expectations upon the belief that they were married, other expectations and equitable considerations remain. The parties may well expect that property will be divided in accord with the parties' own tacit understanding and that in the absence of such understanding the courts will fairly apportion property accumulated through mutual effort. We need not treat nonmarital partners as putatively married persons in order to apply principles of implied contract, or extend equitable remedies; we need to treat them only as we do any other unmarried persons.

The remaining arguments advanced from time to time to deny remedies to the nonmarital partners are of less moment. There is no more reason to presume that services are contributed as a gift than to presume that funds are contributed as a gift; in any event the better approach is to presume, as Justice Peters suggested, "that the parties intend to deal fairly with each other." *Keene v. Keene*, [371 P.2d 329, 339 (Cal. 1962) (Peters, J., dissenting)].

The argument that granting remedies to the nonmarital partners would discourage marriage must fail; as *Cary* pointed out "with equal or greater force the point might be that the pre-1970 rule was calculated to cause the income-producing partner to avoid marriage and thus retain the benefit of all of his or her accumulated earnings." Although we recognize the well-established public policy to foster and promote the institution of marriage, perpetuation of judicial rules which result in an inequitable distribution of property accumulated during a nonmarital relationship is neither a just nor an effective way of carrying out that policy.

In summary, we believe that the prevalence of nonmarital relationships in modern society and the social acceptance of them, marks this as a time when our courts should by no means apply the doctrine of the unlawfulness of the so-called meretricious relationship to the instant case. As we have explained, the nonenforceability of agreements expressly providing for meretricious conduct rested upon the fact that such conduct, as the word suggests, pertained to and encompassed prostitution. To equate the nonmarital relationship of today to such a subject matter is to do violence to an accepted and wholly different practice.

* * *

* * * The mores of the society have indeed changed so radically in regard to cohabitation that we cannot impose a standard based on alleged moral considerations that have apparently been so widely abandoned by so many. Lest we be misunderstood, however, we take this occasion to point out that the structure of society itself largely depends upon the institution of marriage, and nothing we have said in this opinion should be taken to derogate from that institution. The joining of the man and woman in marriage is at once the most socially productive and individually fulfilling relationship that one can enjoy in the course of a lifetime.

We conclude that the judicial barriers that may stand in the way of a policy based upon the fulfillment of the reasonable expectations of the parties to a nonmarital relationship should be removed. As we have explained, the courts now hold that express agreements will be enforced unless they rest on an unlawful meretricious consideration. We add that in the absence of an express agreement, the courts may look to a variety of other remedies in order to protect the parties' lawful expectations.

The courts may inquire into the conduct of the parties to determine whether that conduct demonstrates an implied contract or implied agreement of partnership or joint venture or some other tacit understanding between the parties. The courts may, when appropriate, employ principles of constructive trust or resulting trust. Finally, a nonmarital partner may recover in quantum meruit for the reasonable value of household services rendered less the reasonable value of support received if he can show that he rendered services with the expectation of monetary reward.[25]

---

[25] Our opinion does not preclude the evolution of additional equitable remedies to protect the expectations of the parties to a nonmarital relationship in cases in which existing remedies prove inadequate; the suitability of such remedies may be determined in later cases in light of the factual setting in which they arise.

NOTES AND QUESTIONS

1. *Law, morals, and social change.* What role does the growing rate of cohabitation play in the court's opinion? How does the court view the relationship between law and morality? Law and social change? Do you agree?

2. *Cohabitation and marriage.* How does the court view the relationship between cohabitation and the institution of marriage? Do you find its analysis of the likely impact upon marriage of giving remedies to cohabitants persuasive? As you read the different legal responses to cohabitation, consider the various functions of family law noted in Chapter 1. What *expressive* message will the law send about marriage if it allows or does not allow remedies between cohabitants? Will marriage's *channeling* function be affected by affording cohabitants property rights? Does *Marvin* further family law's *protective* function?

3. *Cohabitation and the prohibition on bigamy.* Why was the fact that the defendant was married during much of the cohabitation period not a bar to plaintiff's claim? Is recognizing economic claims between people arising out of an intimate relationship when one or both of them is married to someone else consistent with the legal prohibition on bigamy, discussed in Chapter 2?

4. *Marvin's ending.* On remand in 1979, the trial court ruled that Marvin and Triola had not executed an express contract. The court also dismissed the plaintiff's *quantum meruit* causes of action, and found that the parties' conduct did not demonstrate an implied contract. The trial court nonetheless awarded the plaintiff $104,000 "for purposes of rehabilitation so that she may have the economic means to re-educate herself and to learn new, employable skills or to refurbish those utilized, for example, during her most recent employment [so] that she may return from her status as companion of a motion picture star to a separate, independent but perhaps more prosaic existence." *Marvin v. Marvin*, No. C 23303, 5 Fam. L. Rep. (BNA) 3077, 3085 (Cal. Super. Ct. 1979). In 1981, however, the California appellate court reversed the rehabilitation award, finding that it was based on the plaintiff's need and the defendant's wealth, and was not rooted in a "recognized underlying obligation in law or in equity." *Marvin v. Marvin*, 176 Cal. Rptr. 555, 559 (Cal. Ct. App. 1981). Had you been the trial court judge, what would you have ruled?

5. *Is cohabitation required?* The New Jersey Supreme Court indicated that it is not, in *Devaney v. L'Esperance*, 949 A.2d 743 (N.J. 2008). *Devaney* involved a 20-year relationship between a married man and his unmarried girlfriend. The court held that cohabitation was "one of many factors" to consider in a palimony claim, but was not an indispensable element. The claiming party was required to prove a "marital-type" relationship, in which the parties committed to each other and fulfilled the other's financial, emotional, physical, and social needs, and agreed to forego other relationships. Should cohabitation be required as a basis for recovery between nonmarital couples?

PROBLEM 4-1

You are an attorney in a jurisdiction that follows *Marvin*, and you've just met with a new client, Shelly. Shelly has recently begun living with Devon, and has asked you to draft a cohabitation agreement. What issues do you need to address in order to draft the agreement? How would *Marvin* shape your drafting of the agreement?

2.   Rejecting Economic Claims Between Cohabitants

Although most states have accepted the *Marvin* approach, not all have done so. One notable example, discussed in the first subsection, is Illinois, while the second subsection addresses other states that do not permit such claims.

a.   The Illinois Approach to Economic Claims Between Cohabitants

The year after *Marvin* was decided, the Supreme Court of Illinois decided not to recognize marriage-like property or support rights between unmarried cohabitants for reasons of public policy. *Hewitt v. Hewitt*, 394 N.E.2d 1204 (Ill. 1979). The court concluded that allowing such rights would grant "legal status to a private arrangement substituting for the institution of marriage" and might undercut the state's goal of promoting marriage and the legislature's abolition of common law marriage. *Id.* at 1209–10. In light of *Hewitt*, lower courts in Illinois rejected other claims by cohabitants, including claims for loss of consortium, *Medley v. Strong*, 558 N.E.2d 244, 248 (Ill. App. Ct. 1990), and equitable interest in shared property, *Ayala v. Fox*, 564 N.E.2d 920, 922 (Ill. App. Ct. 1990). However, in 2014, an Illinois appellate court declined to follow *Hewitt*, citing to various changes in Illinois law since *Hewitt*. *Blumenthal v. Brewer*, 24 N.E.3d 168, 182 (Ill. App. Ct. 2014). That appellate court ruling provided the Supreme Court of Illinois, nearly four decades after deciding *Hewitt*, the occasion to revisit its ruling. As you read the following case, consider whether you find the analysis in the majority or the dissenting opinion more persuasive.

BLUMENTHAL V. BREWER
Supreme Court of Illinois, 2016.
69 N.E.3d 834.

JUSTICE KARMEIER.

In this case we are called on to consider the continued viability and applicability of our decision in *Hewitt v. Hewitt*, 94 N.E.2d 1204 (Ill. 1979), which held that Illinois public policy, as set forth in this State's statutory prohibition against common-law marriage, precludes unmarried cohabitants from bringing claims against one another to enforce mutual property rights where the rights asserted are rooted in a marriage-like relationship between the parties.

[handwritten: facts]

[This is] an action brought by Dr. Jane E. Blumenthal for partition of the family home she shared and jointly owned with Judge Eileen M. Brewer. The couple had maintained a long-term, domestic relationship and raised a family together but had never married. Blumenthal sought partition of the residence when the relationship ended and she moved out.

* * * Brewer counterclaimed for various common-law remedies, including sole title to the home as well as an interest in Blumenthal's ownership share in a medical group so that the couple's overall assets would be equalized now that the couple had ended their relationship. Blumenthal moved to dismiss [the counterclaim based on *Hewitt*]. The circuit court agreed * * *. * * *

The appellate court, however, * * * rebuffed *Hewitt's* holding as outmoded and ill-considered, * * * vacated the circuit court's dismissal * * * and remanded * * * Brewer's counterclaim * * *.

* * *

[handwritten: identical relationship to a married couple]

[T]he focus of this appeal was premised on the couple's domestic relationship, which Brewer characterized as "identical in every essential way to that of a married couple." * * * Counts I, II, IV, and V all pertained directly to * * * how the party's respective rights and interests in [their Chicago home] should be ascertained and valued and how the property should be divided. Count I sought imposition of a constructive trust based on unjust enrichment. Cou[n]t II argued that the house should be divided based on principles of equitable division. Count IV asserted that in allocating the value of the house, the court should factor in amounts expended by Brewer to maintain it after a certain date. Invoking principles of *quantum meruit,* [C]ount V claimed that apportionment of the home's value should take into account the value of Brewer's time in making sure the property was adequately secured, maintained, and repaired. Count III sought a constructive trust over the annual net earnings or the sale of Blumenthal's share of her medical practice, or in the alternative, restitution of funds that Blumenthal used from the couple's joint account to purchase the medical practice.

* * *

ANALYSIS

Blumenthal's central argument on this appeal is that the circuit court's order * * * should not have been disturbed because it was mandated by this court's decision in *Hewitt* and the prohibition against common-law marriage set forth in section 214 of the MDA [the Illinois Marriage and Dissolution of Marriage Act]. Blumenthal asserts that * * * the appellate court misread *Hewitt,* improperly reinstated common-law marriage in contravention of Illinois law, and usurped public policy determinations that properly belong to the legislature. * * *

Counterclaim Count III

[C]ount III * * * requests that the court impose a "Constructive Trust on Blumenthal's Medical Practice to Remedy Unjust Enrichment Or, in the Alternative, for Restitution." * * *

According to count III, "[t]hroughout the course of their relationship, Brewer and Blumenthal commingled their savings and investments." It was the funds from this joint account that went toward the purchase of Blumenthal's ownership interest in her medical practice group, Gynecologic Specialists of Northwestern, S.C. (GSN). Brewer contends that she allowed Blumenthal to use their joint account for this investment with the reasonable understanding and expectation that she, Brewer, would continue to benefit from the earnings derived from GSN. Once the couple ended their relationship in 2008, these financial benefits ceased, and Blumenthal retained the entire interest in the medical group, thereby keeping all of the earnings from the medical practice. * * * Brewer claims that Blumenthal is unjustly enriched [and] requests that this court create a constructive trust from Blumenthal's share of the annual net earnings of the medical group or any portion of the proceeds from any sale of Blumenthal's interest in the group that was attributable to Brewer's earnings or inheritance during their relationship and that this court award her the annual net earnings of GSN attributable to her as well as * * * this portion of the proceeds from any sale of Blumenthal's interest in GSN.

" 'A constructive trust is one raised by operation of law as distinguished from a trust created by express agreement * * *.' " *Suttles v. Vogel,* 533 N.E.2d 901 (1988). [It] is an equitable remedy, which may be imposed where the person in possession of the property would be unjustly enriched if he or she were permitted to retain that property. * * *

[The court accepts Blumenthal's argument that Illinois's Medical Corporation Act and Medical Practice Act "prohibit Brewer, a licensed attorney, from being a beneficiary of a constructive trust created on her ownership interest in GSN, unless Brewer is also a licensed doctor," which she is not.]

In the alternative, Brewer requests the common-law remedy of restitution for an undisclosed amount of funds she deposited into the couple's joint account since the year 2000, which was used to purchase Blumenthal's ownership interest in GSN. * * * Brewer requests this court uphold the appellate court's review of the longstanding public policy in Illinois barring unmarried, cohabiting partners from seeking common-law property rights if the claims are not independent from the parties' relationship.

To understand [that] public policy * * *, we must * * * review * * * Illinois's statutory prohibition of common-law marriage and * * * *Hewitt.* * * *

Common-law marriages are invalid in Illinois and have been since the early part of the last century. The prohibition is statutory and unequivocal. Section 214 of the [MDA] expressly provides that "[c]ommon law marriages contracted in this State after June 30, 1905 are invalid."

* * * In *Hewitt,* * * * this court undertook an extensive and in-depth public policy analysis with respect to the statutory change by which common-law marriages were abolished.

At issue in *Hewitt* was whether public policy barred the granting of common-law relief to plaintiff Victoria Hewitt, who was in a cohabiting, marriage-like relationship with the defendant, Robert Hewitt. Victoria and Robert commenced their relationship in 1960, while they were attending college in Iowa. After Victoria became pregnant, Robert proclaimed to Victoria "that they were husband and wife and would live as such, no formal ceremony being necessary, and that he would 'share his life, his future, his earnings and his property' with her." *Hewitt,* 394 N.E.2d at 1205. The parties immediately began holding themselves out as a married couple. Relying on Robert's promises, Victoria began to assist in paying for Robert's education and establishing a dental practice, helping him earn more than $80,000 annually and accumulate large amounts of property, owned either jointly with Victoria or separately.

After several years together, the relationship became sour, and Victoria filed for divorce, which the circuit court dismissed because the parties were never married. Victoria filed an amended complaint that sought an equitable one-half share of the parties' assets, based upon theories of implied contract, constructive trust, and unjust enrichment, which resulted from their "family relationship." The circuit court dismissed [Victoria's] complaint [because] "Illinois law and public policy require such claims to be based on a valid marriage." *Hewitt,* 394 N.E.2d at 1205. The appellate court reversed, giving considerable weight to the fact that the parties had held themselves out as a couple for over 15 years and lived "a most conventional, respectable and ordinary family life." *Hewitt v. Hewitt,* 380 N.E.2d 454 (1978). * * *Adopting the reasoning of *Marvin,* [it] held that the amended complaint stated a cause of action on an express oral contract * * *. [Robert Hewitt appealed.]

[In considering] whether the granting of common law relief to the plaintiff, an unmarried cohabitant, was barred by public policy, we * * * acknowledge[ed]:

> "* * *There are major public policy questions involved in determining whether * * * it is desirable to accord some type of legal status to claims arising from [unmarried cohabitants']

relationships. Of substantially greater importance than the rights of the immediate parties is the impact of such recognition upon our society and the institution of marriage." *Hewitt*, 77 Ill. 2d at 57–58.

In our view, the legislature intended marriage to be the only legally protected family relationship under Illinois law, and permitting unmarried partners to enforce mutual property rights might "encourage formation of such relationships and weaken marriage as the foundation of our family-based society." *Id*. at 58. This court was concerned that permitting such claims might raise questions about support, inheritance rights, and custody of nonmarital children.[1] We noted that the situation between the unmarried couple was "not the kind of arm's length bargain envisioned by traditional contract principles, but an intimate arrangement of a fundamentally different kind." *Id*. at 61. Because the question concerned changing the law governing the rights of parties in the delicate area of marriage-like relationships, which involves evaluations of sociological data and alternatives, this court decided that the underlying issue was best suited to the superior investigative and fact-finding facilities of the legislative branch in the exercise of its traditional authority to declare public policy in the domestic relations field. Accordingly, this court [rejected Victoria's claims.] We reasoned that an opposite outcome * * * would effectively reinstate common-law marriage and violate the public policy of this state since 1905 * * *.

Notably, * * * we emphatically rejected the holding in *Marvin* on which the appellate court relied. * * * [We] recognized that cohabitation by the unmarried parties may not prevent them from forming valid contracts about independent matters, for which sexual relations do not form part of the consideration and do not closely resemble those arising from conventional marriages. However, that was not the type of claim Victoria brought * * *.

The facts of the present case are almost indistinguishable from *Hewitt*, except, in this case, the parties were in a same-sex relationship. During the course of their long-term, domestic relationship, Brewer alleges that she and Blumenthal had a relationship that was "identical in every essential way to that of a married couple." Although the parties were not legally married, they acted like a married couple and held themselves out as such. [They] exchanged rings as a symbol of their commitment to each other, executed wills and trusts, each naming the other as the sole beneficiary of

---

[1]　The *Hewitt* court also questioned and considered the history of whether granting legal rights to cohabiting adults would encourage "what have heretofore been commonly referred to as 'illicit' or 'meretricious' relationships" which could weaken the institution of marriage. *Hewitt*, 77 Ill.2d at 58. Today, this court does not share the same concern or characterization of domestic partners who cohabit, nor do we condone such comparisons. Nonetheless, as explained herein, a thorough reading of *Hewitt* makes clear that the core reasoning and ultimate holding of the case did not rely nor was dependent on the morality of cohabiting adults.

her assets, and appointed each other as fiduciary for financial and medical decision making. [They] also began to commingle their personal and financial assets, which allowed them to purchase investment property as well as the Chicago home where they raised their three children. Much like in *Hewitt,* Brewer alleges that she contributed to Blumenthal's purchase of an ownership interest in the medical group GSN, helping Blumenthal earn the majority of income for the parties and "thereby guaranteeing the family's financial security." Because Blumenthal was able to earn a high income, Brewer was able to devote more time to raising the couple's children and to attend to other domestic duties. Once Blumenthal's and Brewer's relationship ended, Brewer, like Victoria Hewitt, brought suit seeking various common-law remedies to equalize their assets and receive an interest in Blumenthal's business.

* * * *Hewitt* did no more than follow the statutory provision abolishing common-law marriage, which embodied the public policy of Illinois that individuals acting privately by themselves, without the involvement of the State, cannot create marriage-like benefits. *Hewitt* clearly declared the law on the very issue in this case. Yet, the appellate court * * * declined to follow our ruling * * *. This was improper. Under the doctrine of *stare decisis,* * * * [this court] *"alone can overrule and modify its previous opinion* * * *."* * * *

The appellate court was also ill advised to adopt the reasoning in *Marvin,* given that in *Hewitt* we unquestionably rejected *Marvin.* [T]his court noted that during the time *Marvin* was being decided the Illinois legislature adopted the civil-law concept of the putative spouse * * *.[a] * * * This enactment * * * provided specific evidence of the General Assembly's intent to depart from *Marvin's* pure contract theory. [W]e felt judicial policy making in this area to be inappropriate in light of the "recent and unmistakeable legislative judgment disfavoring the grant of mutual property rights to knowingly unmarried cohabitants." * * *

When considering the property rights of unmarried cohabitants, our view of *Hewitt's* holding has not changed. As in *Hewitt,* the issue * * * cannot appropriately be characterized solely in terms of contract law, nor is it limited to considerations of equity or fairness as between the parties in such marriage-like relationships. These questions undoubtedly involve some of the most fundamental policy concerns in our society. Permitting such claims, as sought by Brewer, would not only impact the institution of marriage but also raise questions pertaining to other family-related issues. * * *

---

[a] *Editors' Note:* Chapter 2 explained this concept, pp. 173–178.

* * * The rationale, analysis, or distinctions that can be drawn from the following appellate court cases are helpful in explaining why we reject Brewer's invitation to overrule *Hewitt* and hold that it remains good law.

[The court discusses previous cases. For example, in *Spafford v. Coats*, 455 N.E.2d 241 (1983), Donna Spafford sought a constructive trust on various vehicles, because, although she purchased or paid the down payment for them from her own funds, they were titled in the name of her cohabiting partner, Richard Coats, so that insurance premiums would be less. The circuit court ruled against Spafford, citing *Hewitt*. The appellate court reversed, holding that their nonmarital, cohabiting relationship did not preclude creating that trust because Spafford's claims were "substantially independent" of that relationship and "not based on rights arising from their cohabitation"—she "paid for the motor vehicles herself."

In *Costa v. Oliven* (849 N.E.2d 122 (2006), *appeal denied*, 857 N.E.2d 670 (2006)), Eugene Costa sued Catherine Oliven for the imposition of a constructive trust upon real, personal, and intellectual property owned by Oliven. Costa alleged that, during their 24 year "quasi-marital relationship," he had "assumed the role of stay-at-home dad, nurturing and home-schooling their daughter" and maintained "an efficient household in order to enable the defendant to work full time." He alleged that, during that time, Oliven took sole title to almost every asset and possession that was acquired through the couple's joint efforts and labor. Oliven successfully argued that Costa's claims were unenforceable based on section 214 of the MDA and *Hewitt*.]

We find that the facts of the case before us today are not only factually similar to *Hewitt*, but also [to] *Costa*. According to Brewer's counterclaim, one of the ways Blumenthal and Brewer's domestic relationship was identical to that of a married couple was * * * their decision to "commingle [ ] their personal property and their finances." * * * [Their decision] * * * demonstrates that the funds were economically dependent on the parties' marriage-like relationship.

For about eight years, Brewer never objected to the arrangement, nor does the counterclaim allege that she tried to earmark or record which funds of hers were going specifically toward the purchase of GSN, as if she were a business partner. This was unquestionably because Blumenthal and Brewer wanted to live like a married couple. Both * * * voluntarily contributed to the joint account * * *. The parties' arrangement was made possible because Brewer, like the plaintiff in *Costa*, agreed to forgo advancing her own legal career in order for Blumenthal to pursue entrepreneurial endeavors including the purchase of an ownership interest in GSN. [Their] purchase of GSN * * * was an investment for the family, which included Blumenthal, Brewer, and their children * * * not an investment between business partners. Nor was it the kind of arm's-length bargain envisioned by traditional contract principles. Rather, [it] was an arrangement of a fundamentally different kind, * * * intimately related and dependent on Brewer's marriage-like relationship with Blumenthal.

Additionally, Brewer's claim for restitution in count III is distinguishable from *Spafford*. * * * Brewer does not allege that she contributed substantially all of the funds for the purchase of GSN [or] * * * a specific amount [or] that she and Blumenthal somehow attempted to keep their contributions separate. Rather, the purchase came after many years of the former domestic partners living together, raising a family, and depositing funds in their joint account as well as making certain family purchases out of the joint account. * * * [T]he purchase of Blumenthal's ownership interest in GSN was dependent on the parties' relationship, because the purchase was made for the family's financial security. * * *

* * * We find that Brewer failed to * * * show[ ] that count III * * * has an independent economic basis apart from the parties' [marriage-like] relationship. * * *

* * *

Next, Brewer respectfully asks this court to affirm the appellate court's [holding] that former cohabitants who * * * live in a marriage-like relationship may bring common-law property claims. [B]rewer argu[es] [that] various post-*Hewitt* legislative enactments in Illinois * * * indicate that the state's public policy has shifted dramatically in regards to unmarried couples and their children [and] now contradicts *Hewitt's* rule. We disagree.

[The legislative enactments discussed are: (1) adopting, in 1984, a no-fault ground of divorce based on irreconcilable differences; (2) the Illinois Parentage Act of 1984, which extends "[t]he parent and child relationship, including support obligations" to "every child and to every parent, regardless of the marital status of the parents;" (3) amending the Probate Act of 1975 to extend intestate inheritance rights to nonmarital children and similarly amending the Illinois Pension Code concerning survivor's benefits; (4) recognizing the rights of unmarried couples (and individuals) to adopt children; (5) the Illinois Religious Freedom and Civil Union Act (2011), which gave legal status to civil unions, available to both opposite-sex and same-sex couples; (5) the Religious Freedom and Marriage Fairness Act (2014), allowing same-sex couples to marry in Illinois; (6) the Illinois Parentage Act of 2015; and (7) in 2016, substantially revising the MDA.]

These post-*Hewitt* amendments demonstrate that the legislature knows how to alter family-related statutes and does not hesitate to do so when and if it believes public policy so requires. Nothing in these post-*Hewitt* changes, however, can be interpreted as evincing an intention by the legislature to change the public policy concerning the situation presently before this court. To the contrary * * * for almost four decades since *Hewitt* * * * the statutory prohibition against common law marriage set forth in [the MDA] has remained completely untouched and unqualified. * * *

* * * If this court were to recognize the legal status desired by Brewer, we would infringe on the duty of the legislature to set policy in the area of domestic relations. [T]he legislative branch is far better suited to declare public policy in the domestic relations field due to its superior investigative and fact-finding facilities * * *. * * *

* * *

We also reject Brewer's argument that changes in law since *Hewitt* demonstrate that the "legislature no longer considers withholding protection from nonmarital families to be a legitimate means of advancing the state's interest in marriage." To the contrary, * * * the current legislative and judicial trend is to uphold the institution of marriage. Most notably, * * * the United States Supreme Court in *Obergefell v. Hodges,* 135 S. Ct. 2584, 2604–05 (2015), held that same-sex couples cannot be denied the right to marry. [T]he Court found that "new insights [from the developments in the institution of marriage over the past centuries] have strengthened, not weakened, the institution of marriage." For the institution of marriage has been a keystone of our social order * * *. [T]he Court invalidated any state legislation prohibiting same-sex marriage because excluding same-sex couples from marriage would be excluding them "from one of civilization's oldest institutions." *Id.* at 2608.

[N]othing in [*Obergefell*] can fairly be construed as requiring states to confer on non-married, same-sex couples common law rights or remedies not shared by similarly situated non-married couples of the opposite sex. * * * Indeed, now that the centrality of the marriage has been recognized as a fundamental right for all, it is perhaps more imperative than before that we leave [this policy determination] to the legislative branch * * *.

* * *

Due Process and Equal Protection Claims

* * *Brewer [also] argues that the continued application of *Hewitt*'s rule would violate the Illinois and federal constitutional guarantees of due process and equal protection. Brewer claims that * * * preventing unmarried domestic partners the ability to bring common-law claims available to all other persons, solely because they are in a marriage-like relationship, does not rationally advance a legitimate governmental purpose and that it deliberately seeks to penalize unmarried partners for exercising their constitutionally protected right to enter into an intimate relationship. * * * *equal protection + due process arguments*

We disagree * * *. *Hewitt* only disallows unmarried cohabitants who live in a marriage-like relationship from accessing, under the guise of an implied contract, the rights and protections specified in the MDA. [I]ndividuals can enter into an intimate relationship, but the relationship itself cannot form the basis to bring common-law claims. Thus, *Hewitt*'s holding does not prevent or penalize unmarried partners from entering into intimate relationships. Rather, it acknowledges the legislative intent to provide certain rights and benefits to those who participate in the institution of marriage.

* * *

The State's interest in the creation, regulation, and dissolution of the marriage relationship is beyond question. * * *

Since marriage is a legal relationship that all individuals may or may not enter into, Illinois does not act irrationally or discriminatorily in refusing to grant benefits and protections under the MDA to those who do not participate in the institution of marriage. [U]nmarried individuals may make express or implied contracts with one another, and such contracts will be enforceable if they are not based on a relationship indistinguishable from marriage. * * * We, therefore, reject Brewer's claims.

* * * The judgment of the circuit court dismissing Brewer's counterclaim in full is affirmed. * * *

JUSTICE THEIS, concurring in part and dissenting in part:

I agree * * * with the majority's holding that count III of the counterclaim cannot proceed on a constructive trust theory. I disagree with the majority's holding that count III cannot proceed on a restitution theory.

* * *The doctrine of *stare decisis* is not an inexorable command and this court will depart from it and discard a prior case when there is good cause to do so. * * * [T]here is good cause to overrule *Hewitt*. The court's decision in that case was clouded by an inappropriate and moralistic view of domestic partners who cohabit and founded upon legal principles that have changed significantly.

* * * [Hewitt] etched into the Illinois Reports the arcane view that domestic partners who choose to cohabit, but not marry, are engaged in "illicit" or "meretricious" behavior at odds with foundational values of "our family-based society." *Hewitt*, 394 N.E.2d at 1207. [Justice Theis points out that "meretricious" means "of or relating to a prostitute."]

* * *Though the majority assures that "this court does not share the same concern or characterization of domestic partners who cohabit, nor do we condone such comparisons," its disavowal of *Hewitt* * * * occur[s] only in a footnote. Elsewhere, the majority borrows troubling language from that case. * * * [Similar to *Hewitt*], the majority states that the parties'

investment into Blumenthal's medical practice was not "the kind of arm's-length bargain envisioned by traditional contract principles," but rather "an arrangement of a fundamentally different kind, which * * * is intimately related and dependent on Brewer's marriage-like relationship with Blumenthal." * * *

* * * The majority assertion that *Hewitt*'s "core reasoning and ultimate holding * * * did not rely nor was dependent on the morality of cohabiting adults" is plainly incorrect because the court's discussion of the role of the legislature in setting public policy on domestic relations and the prohibition of common law marriage comes as an even-if afterthought. Insulating the institution of marriage from the "changing mores of our society" was the clear impetus for our holding in that case. *Hewitt,* 394 N.E.2d 1204.

* * * In 1979, Illinois still criminalized cohabitation. * * * [T]he prohibition against cohabitation was repealed in 1990. * * * The Second Restatement of Contracts [in 1981] * * * ceased to define all bargains between people in intimate relationships as illegal. * * *

* * *

Obviously, Illinois's common-law marriage ban is still in effect. Parallel statutes are in effect across the country, * * * but only Georgia and Louisiana have rulings similar to *Hewitt.* Courts in a vast majority of the remaining states, as well as the District of Columbia, that have chosen not to recognize common-law marriages also have chosen to recognize claims between former domestic partners like Blumenthal and Brewer.[b]

The recognition of claims between domestic partners has not revived the doctrine of common-law marriage in jurisdictions that have abolished it. * * *

In light of this wave of authority, the Restatement (Third) of Restitution and Unjust Enrichment now contains a new section that provides former domestic partners with an avenue "to prevent unjust enrichment upon the dissolution of the relationship." Restatement (Third) of Restitution and Unjust Enrichment § 28(1) (2011).

Illinois is a clear outlier on this issue. * * * *Hewitt* must be overruled because it is outmoded and out of touch with contemporary experience and opinions on cohabitation.

Additionally, * * * the legal landscape that formed the background for [*Hewitt*] has changed significantly. [Justice Theis points to the Supreme Court of Illinois eliminating any "conclusive presumption" against custody

---

[b]   *Editors' Note:* Justice Theis supports the statement in the text with a long string citation of cases from numerous states, omitted here.

because of a custodial parent's cohabitation and to the statutory changes mentioned in the majority opinion.] * * *

* * * Simply because the legislature has taken some action in the domestic relations arena does not mean that this court cannot act as well. The legislature is undoubtedly well equipped to declare public policy on domestic relations. Courts, however, are better equipped than the legislature to help parties divide joint assets using familiar legal and equitable rules. * * *

For more than a century and a half, Illinois courts have adjudicated property disputes between family members. Generally, courts have held that, when people live together in a family setting, contributions between them are presumed gratuitous and not compensable absent an express or implied contract. * * * Thus, seen in the light of established Illinois law, claims like Brewer's claim are nothing new.

More importantly, claims like Brewer's claim do not implicate the MDA and, thus, do not undermine the public policy of Illinois, as expressed in the prohibition of common-law marriage, that individuals themselves cannot create marriage-like benefits. Although the parties had what the majority terms a "marriage-like relationship," Brewer does not seek "marriage-like benefits" or "marriage-like rights" in count III. She simply asks to bring the same common-law claims available to other people. She should be allowed to do so. The fact that Brewer and Blumenthal were once domestic partners should be no impediment. Admittedly, such claims may be difficult to plead and prove * * *, but that is a matter for the trial court.

Hewitt's flaws, both linguistic and legal, have become more apparent with time. Our holding there is a court-made rule that this court should overrule. I believe that count III of Brewer's amended complaint should be remanded for the trial court to determine whether she has pleaded a cognizable cause of action. For these reasons, I dissent.

NOTES AND QUESTIONS

1.   *What's the right approach?* Do you find the majority or dissent more persuasive on *Hewitt's* viability in light of various legislative and other changes since *Hewitt*? If you were an Illinois state legislator, would you support legislation to permit economic claims between nonmarital cohabitants? *See* Stefani L. Ferrari, *Cohabitation in Illinois: The Need for Legislative Intervention,* 93 Chi.-Kent L. Rev. 561 (2018) (proposing such legislation). Or would you revisit the state's ban on common-law marriages and permit such marriages to address the issue?

2.   *Changing "mores" and* Marvin. Is the *Blumenthal* dissent persuasive in contending that the majority opinion is reaffirming *Hewitt's* "moralistic view of cohabitation"? *Marvin* (page 256) rested in part on recognizing society's changing "mores" about cohabitation as well as changing patterns of family

life. In reaffirming *Hewitt*, does the *Blumenthal* majority ignore those changing "mores" and expectations about intimate partnerships? In light of such changes, should marriage continue to be the dividing line for economic rights arising from such partnerships?

3. *The impact of* Obergefell. What role does *Obergefell* play in the majority's adherence to *Hewitt*? Are commentators correct that *Obergefell* gives states a constitutional rationale for privileging marriage over nonmarital relationships and denying nonmarital parties remedies when their relationships dissolve? *See* Melissa Murray, Obergefell v. Hodges *and Nonmarriage Inequality,* 104 Calif. L. 1207 (2016); Courtney G. Joslin, *The Gay Rights Canon and the Right to Nonmarriage,* 97 B.U. L. REV. 425 (2017). Does denying such remedies violate the constitutional liberty of individuals to form and live in nonmarital relationships? Should the fact that a couple could marry, but did not, bar them from making a binding agreement to share assets?

b. *Rejecting Economic Claims Between Cohabitants: Other States*

Several other state courts also reject *Marvin*. For example, in *Williams v. Ormsby,* 966 N.E.2d 255, 263 (Ohio 2012), the court denied a cohabitant's attempt to enforce an agreement to share equally proceeds on a home titled in her partner's name, declaring that "palimony is not recognized by Ohio statute or common law, and Ohio does not permit a division of assets or property based on cohabitation."

In *Davis v. Davis,* 643 So.2d 931, 936 (Miss. 1994), the Supreme Court of Mississippi considered whether Elvis Davis was entitled to share in the more than $5 million that Travis Davis accumulated during their 13-year cohabitation. They were the parents of a daughter. Elvis used Travis's surname during their relationship. Travis referred to Elvis as his wife in his will and on his tax forms and set up a marital trust for her. The couple separated after Travis announced he was marrying his secretary. After the separation, he bought Elvis a new house, car, furniture, and appliances.

Elvis contended that the two "had formed a partnership based on [an] oral agreement to live as husband and wife," with Elvis taking care of the home and Travis taking care of his business. She sought equitable distribution of the assets accumulated during the "alleged partnership" from their joint efforts. *Id.* at 933. Travis denied there was any agreement "which might be construed as forming the basis of a partnership or joint venture," and described her as a "mistress." *Id.* The court found that Elvis failed to prove the existence of a business partnership or that she played an active role in building Travis' business assets.

As did the *Blumenthal* court, the Supreme Court of Mississippi stressed that the Mississippi legislature had abolished common-law marriage and had not extended marital rights to those who "choose merely to cohabit." Noting that Elvis had declined at least one marriage proposal from Travis, the court concluded:

> When opportunity knocks, one must answer its call. Elvis Davis failed to do so and thus her claim is all for naught. * * * [C]ohabitation is still prohibited by statute. Elvis was well-compensated during and after the relationship. We see no reason to advocate any form of "palimony" when the legislature has not so spoken.

Id. at 936. A decade later, the Mississippi Supreme Court reaffirmed that if "a man and woman cohabit without the benefit of marriage, they do so at their own peril." *Nichols v. Funderburk*, 883 So.2d 554, 558 (Miss. 2004).

NOTES AND QUESTIONS

1. *Really different?* In *Cates v. Swain*, 215 So. 3d 492 (Miss. 2014), one woman (Swain) sued her female partner (Cates) based on unjust enrichment. Swain had given Cates $34,000 to purchase a new home and moved out when the relationship deteriorated. The court granted relief; it distinguished *Davis* because the plaintiff there sought equitable division of property "based upon a relationship," while Swain's claim was "for unjust enrichment based upon her monetary contributions" to Cates's purchase of a home retained by Cates after Swain moved out. *Id.* Do you find that distinction persuasive?

2. *Cohabitation and incentive effects.* What do you think are the incentive effects of permitting (as in *Marvin*) or denying (as in *Blumenthal* and *Davis*) economic claims between nonmarital partners? Will refusal to enforce cohabitation agreements lead cohabitants to marry or to enter into contracts that can be severed from the cohabitation?

B. TYPES OF CLAIMS

When they permit cohabiting couples to assert various claims against each other, states vary concerning the acceptability of each type of claim. A party may allege breach of an express contract, that is, that the other party has violated an agreement whose terms the parties have explicitly set out. Some jurisdictions allow recovery only where the parties have executed an express contract.

Some states require that contracts between cohabitants be in writing. *See, e.g.*, Minn. Stat. § 513.075 (2019); Tex. Bus & Com. Code Ann. § 26.01 (2019); *Posik v. Layton*, 695 So.2d 759 (Fla. Dist. Ct. App. 1997) (holding that a nonmarital support agreement must be in writing). The New Jersey Legislature amended its statute of frauds to require that palimony agreements be 1) in a writing signed by the person against whom enforcement is sought, and 2) "made with the independent advice of counsel for both parties." N.J. Stat. Ann. § 25:1–5h (2019); *Maeker v. Ross*, 62 A.3d

310 (N.J. Super. Ct. App. Div. 2013) (observing that legislative reform was to prevent accidental palimony).

Nonmarital couples may also use theories other than express contract. Parties often seek judgments based on implied contract, restitution, or unjust enrichment, through several methods. An implied-in-fact contract is an agreement that the parties presumably intended to make, either by tacit understanding or by their assumptions. In contrast, an implied-in-law contract is an obligation imposed by law because of the parties' conduct, because of some special relationship between them, or because one of them would be otherwise unjustly enriched.

Remedies may include the imposition of a constructive trust when one party has contributed consideration financially or in the form of labor to the other party's acquisition or improvement of the property. Brewer, as we saw above, unsuccessfully asserted such a trust with respect to the earnings of her former partner Blumenthal's medical practice, although the plaintiff in *Spafford* (discussed in *Blumenthal*) successfully obtained a constructive trust on vehicles purchased with her money. Alternatively, some jurisdictions allow parties to recover through a resulting trust, which a court can impose as a means of transferring title when circumstances indicate that the parties actually intended that the defendant hold property on behalf of ("in trust for") the plaintiff. A resulting trust arises, for example, where the defendant holds title, but the plaintiff provided some or all of the money used to purchase the property.

A *quantum meruit* suit allows an unmarried cohabitant to seek the value of services rendered or benefits received by the other. *See* Kristine L. Tungol, *Cause of Action by Same-Sex or Heterosexual Unmarried Cohabitant to Enforce Agreement or Understanding Regarding Support or Division of Property on Dissolution of Relationship*, 35 Causes of Action 2d 295 §§ 15–17 (2018).

The Restatement of Restitution and Unjust Enrichment (mentioned by the *Blumenthal* dissent) suggests a case-by-case approach when analyzing the appropriateness of these remedies. As the Restatement's Comments note, the existence of a remedy and the amount of relief depend on a number of factors defining the individual relationship. *See* Restatement (Third) of Restitution & Unjust Enrichment § 28 cmts. c–e (2011).

PROBLEM 4-2

Assume Ms. Brewer had come to your office at the time that she and Dr. Blumenthal moved in together. She tells you Blumenthal promises to take care of her while they are living together, and that if they ever break up, Blumenthal will continue to pay all Brewer's expenses for the same number of years as they live together. She wants to know what steps she can take to protect herself and to enforce the agreement if they should ever break up. What do you tell Ms. Brewer?

PROBLEM 4–3

You are a law clerk for a judge with the following case on the docket. Terry and Dee lived together in a committed relationship for nearly 18 years and are the parents of two children. Each party is the biological parent of one child, and each child was legally adopted by the other party. Their relationship began before their state's law allowed same-sex couples to marry and recently ended. Terry has now brought an action for various equitable remedies and for damages based on breach of an alleged oral "joint venture/partnership" agreement under which would share in assets, including Dee's retirement contributions and earnings, in exchange for Terry leaving her full-time job to care for the parties' children.

Terry's complaint alleges that before they had children, both Terry and Dee were employed full-time, earning a salary and retirement benefits. Based on this alleged oral "joint venture/partnership" agreement, they pooled their salaries to meet their shared expenses and purchased a house as joint tenants with rights of survivorship. Terry alleges that, after their first child was born, they agreed that, given the costs of child care, Terry would leave her full-time job and assume part-time work so she could be home with the child (later, children) and perform other non-financial services for the benefit of the family and for the parties' partnership and/or joint venture, while Dee would continue to work full-time to support the family/joint venture/partnership financially. They agreed that they would share equally in all financial and non-financial contributions made by each of them and that all of their contributions were for their mutual benefit.

Terry seeks contract damages for breach of the parties' oral agreement contract and equitable remedies, including unjust enrichment and a constructive trust on a portion of Dee's pension. Your judge asks you for a bench memo explaining the legal issues raised by this case, what factual development is necessary, and how Terry's claims should be resolved. How would your memo differ depending upon whether your judge sits in California or Illinois?

2. STATUS-BASED PROPERTY RIGHTS

When a marriage ends, the spouses have claims against each other based on their status and, unlike the *Marvin* line of cases discussed above, need not plead a contractual or equitable claim. As Chapter 16 discusses, if they have entered into a premarital agreement limiting economic sharing during marriage and any economic claims at divorce that otherwise arise under marriage law, they may assert that contract at divorce. When a nonmarital cohabitation relationship ends, what rights, if any, should the cohabitants have in the absence of an enforceable agreement or other equitable claim?

A. CASE LAW

As *Marvin* and *Blumenthal* suggest, the term "meretricious relationship" traditionally denoted an illicit sexual relationship. In Washington state, however, the term came to describe more benignly an informal, marriage-like relationship giving rise to legal property and support rights regardless of the existence of any type of contract or other type of equitable claim. In 2007, the Washington Supreme Court, recognizing the term's traditional "negative connotations," substituted "committed intimate relationship" for "meretricious relationship." *See Olver v. Fowler*, 168 P.3d 348, 350 n.1 (Wash. 2007); *see also Walsh v. Reynolds*, 335 P.3d 984 (Wash. Ct. App. 2014) (using terms "committed intimate relationship" and "equity relationship" interchangeably). The next unpublished decision (decided before *Olver* and so still using the term "meretricious relationship") illustrates Washington's approach and provides an example of a successful claim by a cohabitant.

> **FLEMING V. SPENCER**
> Court of Appeals of Washington, 2002.
> 110 Wash. App. 1017.

PER CURIAM.

Norman Spencer appeals the trial court's decision to award certain real property to Sheila Fleming, his companion for many years. He argues that a meretricious relationship did not exist between them and that the trial court erred in distributing the property to her at the end of their relationship. Because we conclude that they had a meretricious relationship and that the trial court did not abuse its discretion in awarding the property to Fleming, we affirm.

FACTS

Spencer and Fleming met and became intimate in 1982, while Spencer was separated but not yet divorced from his wife. He moved into Fleming's cottage in the summer of 1983. That same year, he purchased real property in Sultan with borrowed money for the down payment and the balance carried on a real estate contract. * * * When Spencer and his wife formally divorced in July 1985, he received the Sultan property in the decree. According to the trial court's findings, however, Spencer 'paid off' the property entirely by the joint earnings of [Fleming and Spencer].

From 1984 to 1991, Spencer and Fleming lived at the Sultan property without interruption. In 1991, however, Spencer went to work in Alaska for about a year. He returned in 1992 and lived with Fleming at the property until 1995, when he went back to Alaska for work purposes. By 1996 or 1997, he returned to live at the property with Fleming. * * * [Fleming] enrolled in the Thomas Cooley Law School for one year between 1996 to 1997 and lived in Michigan during that time. During law school, she accumulated $27,000 in student loans. She returned to Sultan and worked at her sister's child care business until opening her own child care business on the Sultan property in 1999. Spencer and Fleming remodeled the property for this purpose. The couple filed joint income tax returns throughout the 1990s, and in 1994, named each other executor and heir to any property remaining after specific bequests. In October 1994, Spencer quitclaimed the Sultan property to Fleming to shelter it from a potential lawsuit. Over six years later [sic], however, Spencer had Fleming quitclaim the property back to him in December 1998.

As stated many times in the record, the parties ceased being intimate in 1997. They continued to live together, but in separate parts of the house. According to Fleming, Spencer had become religious and felt that he was still married to his first wife[.] * * * Yet, they continued to file joint income tax returns until 1999.

In the summer of 1999, Spencer would not let Fleming clear a field on the Sultan property for horses and a garden. A few months later, Fleming sought out her attorney. She sued Spencer for dissolution of their meretricious relationship. * * *

* * *

After the trial, the court found that Spencer and Fleming maintained a meretricious relationship from 1983 to 1997 and distributed the property acquired during that time frame. Spencer appeals.

DISCUSSION

I.   Meretricious Relationship

Spencer first argues that there was no meretricious relationship. * * *

A meretricious relationship is a stable, marital-like relationship in which both parties cohabit knowing that a lawful marriage does not exist. To determine whether such a relationship exists, courts look at five factors: (1) continuous cohabitation; (2) duration of the relationship; (3) purpose of the relationship; (4) pooling of resources; and (5) intent of the parties. These factors are neither exclusive nor hypertechnical but merely a means to examine all relevant evidence. Ultimately, a court decides whether a meretricious relationship exists on a case-by-case basis.

Continuous Cohabitation: The trial court found that Spencer and Fleming commenced living together in 1983 when Spencer moved into Fleming's cottage after separating from his wife. In the winter of 1984, however, Spencer moved to the Sultan property. Fleming followed and permanently resided with Spencer, at about the same time Spencer formally divorced his wife. They lived together until 1991, when Spencer went to work in Alaska for about a year. He returned to the Sultan property in 1992 but went back to Alaska in 1995 to work for a short while. Meanwhile, from 1996 to 1997, Fleming attended Thomas Cooley Law School in Lansing, Michigan. After she returned to Sultan in 1997, they ceased being intimate and began living in separate rooms of the house. Based on these facts, it appears that except for career-related absences, they continuously cohabited from 1985 to 1997.

Duration of the Relationship: Spencer and Fleming met and became intimate in 1982. Their intimacy lasted until 1997. During this 15-year period, they remained apart from each other only for work and school related reasons. There is no evidence in the record that they dated other people while in this relationship. We conclude that the duration of their relationship was sufficiently long enough to support a stable, marital-like relationship.

Purpose of the Relationship: It is reasonable to infer from the trial court's findings that the purpose of the parties' relationship included friendship, companionship, intimacy, and mutual support. Such a purpose is marital-like.

Pooling of Resources: The pooling of resources and services for joint projects demonstrates a marital-like commitment also. According to the trial court's findings, Spencer and Fleming maintained joint bank accounts, commingled their earnings, and paid bills together. They even submitted joint income tax returns. With respect to the Sultan property, they paid off the real estate contract with joint earnings and remodeled the house three times, the latest remodel for the child care business. We conclude that they sufficiently pooled resources to imitate a marital-like relationship.

Intent of the Parties: Finally, a mutual intent to form a meretricious relationship is another factor to support the existence of such a relationship. As late as January 1994, Spencer and Fleming signed wills naming each other executor and heir to any remaining property after specific bequests. In October 1994, Spencer granted a quitclaim deed for the Sultan property to Fleming to shelter it from a potential lawsuit arising out of a construction job. Six years later [sic], in December 1998, Fleming quitclaimed the property back to Spencer. Granted, they discussed marriage three times to no avail. Nonetheless, the above facts demonstrate that the parties had a mutual intent to form a stable, marital-like relationship based on trust. Viewing the above factors as a whole, we must conclude that the parties had a meretricious relationship between 1983 and 1997. Spencer argues, however, that a meretricious relationship cannot commence when one party is married to another person.

* * * [E]quitable claims based on a meretricious relationship do not depend on whether the parties can legally marry each other. This is so because comparing a meretricious relationship to marriage is a mere analogy and to literally define it as equivalent to marriage would result in a common law marriage, contrary to precedent. In fact, this court has distributed property based on a meretricious relationship even when the parties purchased such property while one party was still married to a former spouse. Therefore, Spencer and Fleming could have commenced a meretricious relationship before he obtained a formal divorce.

After determining that a meretricious relationship exists, the trial court evaluates the interest each party has in the property acquired during the relationship. We review the trial court's decision on this matter under the abuse of discretion standard. There is a rebuttable presumption that property acquired during such a relationship belongs to both parties. A party may rebut this presumption with evidence demonstrating that he acquired the property in question with funds that would otherwise be characterized as separate property if he was married. Although a party may have taken sole title to the property, that fact alone does not rebut the presumption of common ownership.

Spencer argues that the trial court did not have authority to award the Sultan property to Fleming because he acquired it before the meretricious relationship and because a quitclaim deed from Fleming granted title to the Sultan property to him after the relationship ended. Based upon the analysis above, however, we have already determined that the parties commenced their meretricious relationship in 1983, before acquiring the Sultan property. Furthermore, title alone does not rebut the presumption of common ownership * * *. We conclude that the trial court did not abuse its discretion in finding that the Sultan property was subject to distribution at the end of the parties' meretricious relationship.

* * *

Spencer assigns error to the trial court's distribution of the property, indicating that it was not just and equitable. * * * In making the distribution, the trial court should prevent one party from being unjustly enriched and may look to the dissolution statute for guidance. * * * [W]e cannot say that the trial court abused its discretion.

* * *

In summary, we conclude that Spencer and Fleming did have a meretricious relationship commencing in 1983. The trial court did not abuse its discretion by including the Sultan property in the distribution and eventually awarding it to Fleming with an equalizing payment to Spencer.

* * *

NOTES AND QUESTIONS

1.　*Evaluating commitment.* How is marriage relevant to determining whether the parties had a "meretricious (or, now, a "committed intimate") relationship," or to determining what economic claims they have against each other? Do you agree with the court's result, based on the test for finding such a relationship?

2.　*Cohabitant rights surviving death.* In 2007, the Washington Supreme Court held that the property rights acquired by partners survive the death of one or both partners. *Olver,* 168 P.3d at 355–56, 357. Six years later, in *In re Estate of Langeland,* 312 P.3d 657 (Wash. Ct. App. 2013), the decedent's daughter and the woman with whom he "lived in a committed intimate relationship" asserted competing claims for the decedent's estate. The Washington Court of Appeals held that the decedent's girlfriend should enjoy the "presumption that all income and property acquired during the relationship are jointly owned." *Id.* at 660, 663.

3.　*More on determining "marriage-like relationships."* Similar to Washington, Alaska allows "marital-like property distribution" following a cohabiting relationship. *Boulds v. Nielsen,* 323 P.3d 58, 64 (Alaska 2014). So, too, conduct is pertinent to determining intent. The Supreme Court of Alaska summarized the types of evidence that courts consider in determining explicit and implicit intent to share property in a marriage-like relationship. *Id.* at 63. Many of the factors involve economic behavior, including making "joint financial arrangements such as joint savings or checking accounts, or jointly titled property," and contributing "to the payment of household expenses." *Id.* Other factors include whether they "held themselves out as husband and wife" or "have raised children together." *Id.* The court emphasized that "simply living together is not sufficient to demonstrate [the intent] to share property as though married," and "parties who intend to share some property do not presumptively intend to share all property." *Id.* at 64. But the court also concluded that "when the parties have demonstrated through their actions that they intend to share their property in a marriage-like relationship, a court does not need to find specific intent by each cohabitant as to each piece of property." *Id.* How do you think courts should determine parties' intent about economic sharing?

4.　*The Canadian approach.* In Canada, when cohabiting couples separate, "spousal support" is available in all the provinces except Quebec. Quebec law restricts spousal support to married couples. "Family" property distribution is also available in a few provinces and territories. Robert Leckey, *Developments in Family Law: The 2012–2013 Term,* 64 Sup. Ct. L. Rev. (2d) 241, 246 (2014).

B.　MODEL LEGISLATION

The American Law Institute (ALI), an organization of American judges, attorneys, and teachers, recommends that where unmarried couples have cohabited for a substantial period, the law should treat them the same way that it treats married couples upon termination of the relationship. In its *Principles of the Law of Family Dissolution* ("Principles"), the ALI sets out model rules for "domestic partners" that are designed to govern financial claims between parties in a nonmarital relationship.

AMERICAN LAW INSTITUTE, PRINCIPLES OF THE LAW OF FAMILY DISSOLUTION: ANALYSIS AND RECOMMENDATIONS
916–18, 937–38 (2002).

§ 6.03   Determination That Persons Are Domestic Partners

(1) For the purpose of defining relationships to which this Chapter applies, domestic partners are two persons of the same or opposite sex, not married to one another, who for a significant period of time share a primary residence and a life together as a couple.

(2) Persons are domestic partners when they have maintained a common household, as defined in Paragraph (4), with their common child, as defined in Paragraph (5), for a continuous period that equals or exceeds a duration, called the *cohabitation parenting period,* set in a rule of statewide application.

(3) Persons not related by blood or adoption are presumed to be domestic partners when they have maintained a common household, as defined in Paragraph (4), for a continuous period that equals or exceeds a duration * * * set in a rule of statewide application. * * *

(4) Persons *maintain a common household* when they share a primary residence only with each other and family members; or when, if they share a household with other unrelated persons, they act jointly, rather than as individuals, with respect to management of the household.

* * *

(6) When the requirements of Paragraph (2) or (3) are not satisfied, a person asserting a claim under this Chapter bears the burden of proving that for a significant period of time the parties shared a primary residence and a life together as a couple, as defined in Paragraph (7). Whether a period of time is significant is determined in light of all the Paragraph (7) circumstances of the parties' relationship and, particularly, the extent to which those circumstances wrought change in the life of one or both parties.

(7) Whether persons share a life together as a couple is determined by reference to all the circumstances, including:

(a) the oral or written statements or promises made to one another, or representations jointly made to third parties, regarding their relationship;

(b) the extent to which the parties intermingled their finances;

(c) the extent to which their relationship fostered the parties' economic interdependence, or the economic dependence of one party upon the other;

(d) the extent to which the parties engaged in conduct and assumed specialized or collaborative roles in furtherance of their life together;

(e) the extent to which the relationship wrought change in the life of either or both parties;

(f) the extent to which the parties acknowledged responsibilities to each other, as by naming the other the beneficiary of life insurance or of a testamentary instrument, or as eligible to receive benefits under an employee benefit plan;

* * *

(h) the emotional or physical intimacy of the parties' relationship;

(i) the parties' community reputation as a couple;

(j) the parties' participation in a commitment ceremony or registration as a domestic partnership;

* * *

(l) the parties' procreation of, adoption of, or joint assumption of parental functions toward a child;

(m) the parties' maintenance of a common household, as defined by Paragraph (4).

§ 6.04 Domestic-Partnership Property Defined

(1) Except as [otherwise] provided in * * * this section, property is domestic-partnership property if it would be marital property * * * had the domestic partners been married to one another during the domestic-partnership period.

(2) The domestic-partnership period

(a) starts when the domestic partners began sharing a primary residence, unless either partner shows that the parties did not begin sharing life together as a couple until a later date, in which case the domestic-partnership period starts on that later date, and

(b) ends when the parties ceased sharing a primary residence.

For the purpose of this Paragraph, parties who are the biological parents of a common child began sharing life together as a couple no later than the date on which their common child was conceived.

* * *

NOTES AND QUESTIONS

1. *Status or commitment?* Does either § 6.03 of the Principles or *Fleming* require any particular form of commitment between the parties? Might property acquired during any cohabiting relationships become subject to distribution? Professor Marsha Garrison argues that commitment should be legally significant:

> Marital commitment explains why married couples have legal obligations to each other when unmarried couples do not. Unmarried couples, like their married counterparts, may establish a home, family, and life together; they may be sexually faithful to each other and may share the expectation that their relationship will endure. But they have not publicly and mutually agreed to assume the legally binding obligations of marriage. Indeed, they have decided not to publicly assume those obligations.

> * * * [C]ourts and legislatures in a number of other industrialized nations [are] fashioning a "conscriptive" model that bases cohabitant obligation on status. The conscriptive model imposes on the cohabiting couple that has chosen to avoid marriage some or all of the obligations the couple would have incurred had they chosen to marry. Several Canadian provinces, for example, now impose a support obligation on cohabitants who have lived together for periods ranging from one to three years. All of the Australian states have adopted legislation that extends marital property rights to cohabitants who have a common child or have lived together for at least two years. * * *

> Only one American high court has thus far adopted a conscriptive approach to cohabitant obligation, but the American Law Institute has recently urged the states to abandon contract in favor of the conscriptive alternative.

Marsha Garrison, *Is Consent Necessary? An Evaluation of the Emerging Law of Cohabitant Obligation*, 52 UCLA L. Rev. 815, 817–19 (2005). Do you agree with Professor Garrison's characterization of the ALI and Washington approaches to enforcing cohabitation agreements? In the absence of some form of commitment, either through marriage or express contract, why should cohabitants be entitled to any form of property distribution or support from each other after they are no longer cohabiting? *See Collins v. Wassell*, 323 P.3d 1216, 1233–40 (Haw. 2014) (Pollack, J., dissenting) (pointing out difficulties in determining, in the absence of an express agreement, whether cohabitants intended to have a premarital economic partnership). *See* Kaiponanea T.

Matsumura *Consent to Intimate Relationships,* 96 N.C. L. Rev. 1013 (2018) (arguing for a consent-based inquiry).

2. *Protections through the Principles.* What types of rights between cohabitants do the Principles address? Should they grant all of the incidents of marriage to cohabiting couples? Professor Cynthia Grant Bowman believes cohabitants should have more rights:

> [The Principles] provide[ ] only divorce-style remedies upon dissolution of the relationship * * *. [M]y proposal extends far beyond the divorce remedies that may be of use only to relatively well-off couples, those who have property or income to share after separating their households. It treats the couple as though they were married, thus entitling them, among other things, to the right to inheritance, rights against third parties (such as suits for negligent infliction of emotional distress and for loss of consortium), rights against the government (such as social security survivors benefits, workers compensation, and taxation as a coupled unit), and rights in the private sphere (such as eligibility for family health insurance, next-of-kin status in hospitals, and the like).

Cynthia Grant Bowman, *Social Science and Legal Policy: The Case of Heterosexual Cohabitation,* 9 J.L. Fam. Stud. 1, 45–46 (2007). Do you agree with her proposal?

3. *A new Uniform Law on cohabitants' economic rights?* The Uniform Law Commission ("ULC"), which drafted the Uniform Commercial Code ("UCC") as well as several uniform laws related to family law, such as the Uniform Marriage and Divorce Act (discussed in Chapter 8) and the Uniform Parentage Act (2017) (discussed in Chapter 5), is drafting a uniform (or model) law on the economic rights of unmarried cohabitants. *See* Uniform Law Commission, *Drafting Committee on the Rights of Unmarried Cohabitants* (2019).

PROBLEM 4-4

Katherine and Richard began living together as unmarried intimate partners in 2014 in a house that Richard owned. In 2015, they moved to a new home, which Richard put in his own name, telling Katherine that "it was easier to place [the house] in his name because he had equity in another house and because they were not married." Katherine did not contribute funds for the house, but she helped plan, build, and improve the house and the grounds. While they cohabited, Katherine made about $250,000, which she placed in an account in Richard's name as protection from her creditors. The couple agreed that Katherine would be responsible for all the shopping, cooking, and landscaping, while Richard would run his automotive business. After their cohabitation ended in 2019, Katherine sued Richard to obtain half of the property and money they accumulated while living together from 2014 to 2019. What would be the result in a jurisdiction following *Marvin*? In a jurisdiction following *Blumenthal* and similar cases? In a jurisdiction that has adopted the ALI Principles?

3.   OTHER INCIDENTS OF NONMARITAL COHABITATION

Nonmarital cohabitants do not receive the same legal protections as married cohabitants. First, a handful of states (Idaho, Illinois, Minnesota, and North Carolina) still have criminal laws prohibiting "fornication" (sexual intercourse) between unmarried couples or, as in Michigan, cohabitation. *See* Mich. Comp. Laws § 750.335 (2019) ("Any man or woman, not being married to each other, who lewdly and lasciviously associates and cohabits together, and any man or woman, married or unmarried, who is guilty of open and gross lewdness and lascivious behavior, is guilty of a misdemeanor").

Subsequent to *Lawrence v. Texas*, 539 U.S. 558 (2003) (included in Chapter 1), some state courts held that fornication laws were unconstitutional. *Hobbs v. Smith*, 2006 WL 3103008 (N.C. Super. Ct. Aug. 25, 2006) (unreported opinion by trial court judge that North Carolina's fornication statute is unconstitutional under *Lawrence*); *Martin v. Ziherl*, 607 S.E.2d 367, 370 (Va. 2005) (finding "no principled way to conclude . . . that the Virginia statute criminalizing intercourse between two unmarried persons does not improperly abridge a personal relationship that is within the liberty interest of persons to choose").

When the Utah legislature was debating revising Utah's definition of bigamy (see Chapter 2), the impact of *Lawrence* on Utah's fornication law arose. The Utah Attorney General's office stated that, while adultery and fornication (defined as voluntary sexual intercourse between unmarried persons) were listed as misdemeanors in Utah's criminal law, "we don't prosecute them since *Lawrence v. Texas*." The spokesperson added: "For whatever reason, the Legislature has chosen to leave them on the books anyway." Nate Carlisle, *Orgies Appear to be Legal in Utah, and Other Notes from Polygamy Bill Hearing*, Salt Lake Tribune (Feb. 8, 2017). In April 2019, the Governor of Utah signed legislation repealing Utah's law that treated fornication as a criminal offense. S.B. 43, 63rd Leg., Gen. Sess (Utah 2019) (to be printed at 2019 Utah Laws 420) (repealing Utah Code Ann. § 76–7–104 (2019)).

In 2018, Massachusetts enacted the Negating Archaic Statutes Targeting Young Woman Act (known as the "NASTY Woman Act"), which repealed old criminal laws in Massachusetts prohibiting adultery, fornication, contraception, and abortion. The governor called the laws " 'antiquated, inappropriate,' and in some cases harmful." Bob Salsberg, *Massachusetts First to Repeal Long Dormant Ban on Abortion*, U.S. News: Best States (Jul. 27, 2018). In 2016, Florida repealed its 1868 law, which was similar to the Michigan statute quoted above. Although the Florida law was rarely enforced, the penalty was 60 days in jail and a $500 fine (the original penalty was up to two years in prison and a $300 fine). The 1868 law, as originally written, did not apply to same-sex partners. Gray Rohrer, *Shacking Up Now Legal in Florida After Gov. Scott Signs Bill*, Orlando Sentinel (Apr. 6, 2016).

One reported reason for the Florida repeal was the prohibition's impact on older people who, in the words of one legislator, were " 'living together, but it makes more sense financially or for whatever reason like Social Security to not be married. I don't think that they want to be considered to be violating the law." *Id.* The Florida legislature amended but left in force part of Section 798.02's prohibition, which now provides "If any man or woman, married or unmarried, engages in open and gross lewdness and lascivious behavior, they shall be guilty of a misdemeanor of the second degree . . . ." Fla. Stat. § 798.02 (2019).

As noted in Chapter 8, criminal adultery laws (which concern extramarital sexual conduct by a married person) have survived constitutional challenge post-*Lawrence*. Just over twenty states still have such laws. *See* Deborah L. Rhode, *Why Is Adultery Still a Crime?*, L.A. Times (May 2, 2016).

Another difference between marriage and cohabitation is that federal law does not treat nonmarital cohabitants as married. Thus, for example, nonmarried couples may not file joint federal tax returns; each person must file as a single person. *Cf. Sullivan v. Commissioner*, 256 F.2d 664, 666 (4th Cir. 1958) (holding that a legal separation prevents parties from filing jointly). The Internal Revenue Code does not specifically address the status or rights of unmarried cohabitants. Under I.R.C. § 6013(a), however, only a couple deemed to be married under applicable law can file a joint tax return. As explained below, in Section 4, the I.R.S. will not treat persons in domestic partnerships or civil unions as married for purposes of federal law. The tax treatment of married and divorcing couples is discussed in Chapters 3, 9, and 10.

Third, in many states, nonmarital cohabitants do not have the same tort claims as married couples, an issue more fully discussed in Chapter 7. Increasingly in recent years, plaintiffs have sought to recover for loss of consortium in the absence of a formal, legally recognized family relationship. The Massachusetts Supreme Judicial Court offered the following rationale for refusing to allow recovery by an unmarried female cohabitant after her male partner of more than ten years was severely injured:

> A loss of consortium claim presupposes a legal right to consortium of the injured person. While [the two partners] * * * well may have a "stable, significant romantic relationship," * * * they chose not

to marry and, consequently, have neither the obligation nor the "benefit of the rules of law that govern property, financial, and other matters in a marital relationship." To recognize a right to recover for loss of consortium by a person who could have but has declined to accept the correlative responsibilities of marriage undermines the "deep interest" that the Commonwealth has that the integrity of marriage "is not jeopardized."

Fitzsimmons v. Mini Coach of Boston, Inc., 799 N.E.2d 1256, 1257 (Mass. 2003). Other jurisdictions have agreed. *See, e.g., Milberger v. KBHL, LLC*, 486 F. Supp. 2d 1156, 1160–65 (D. Haw. 2007) (applying Hawaii law).

Not all courts agree with this policy analysis, however. In 2003, as a matter of first impression, the Supreme Court of New Mexico held that "a claim for consortium is not limited to married partners." *Lozoya v. Sanchez*, 66 P.3d 948 (N. M. 2003). New Mexico's approach is, however, a minority view. *See Vance v. Farmers Ins. Co.*, 1 Wash. App. 2d 1007, 2017 WL 4883353, at *4 (Wash. Ct. App. 2017), *review denied*, 412 P.3d 1260 (Wash. 2018) (describing New Mexico as only state permitting loss of consortium claims for unmarried cohabitants; rejecting such claims in Washington).

On the other hand, certain types of legal protections applicable to marital partners or family members also apply to nonmarital cohabitants. For example, as Chapter 7 explains, the domestic abuse statutes of many states generally include unmarried persons who reside together or who have a child in common (even if they are not living together) as among the "family or household members" who may seek a civil protection order against abuse. Some states also include persons in a dating relationship. See, e.g., Mass. Gen. Laws, ch. 209A, § 1 (2019).

In addition, premarital cohabitation may be relevant to property distribution upon divorce (as discussed further in Chapter 9). In *Matter of Munson and Beal*, 146 A.3d 153, 158 (N.H. 2016), the New Hampshire Supreme Court held that trial courts "may consider premarital cohabitation when formulating an equitable distribution of marital property," and deciding whether to depart from the statutory presumption that "an equal division is an equitable division of property."

Similarly, the Hawaii Supreme Court held that if a cohabiting couple forms a "premarital economic partnership" and their relationship "matures into marriage," the family court, "determining an equitable distribution of the marital estate," should consider contributions that either party made during the partnership." *Collins v. Wassell*, 323 P.3d 1216, 1225–26 (Haw. 2014).

NOTE AND QUESTIONS

Wrongs and rights. Would recognizing the relational injury to long-term cohabitants really undermine the state's interest in the integrity of marriage?

Are there other reasons to deny recovery? What if the claimants had been prevented from legally marrying at the time of the injury?

4. DOMESTIC PARTNERSHIPS, CIVIL UNIONS, AND OTHER LEGAL STATUSES

Adults who want formal recognition of their relationships may be able to enter into domestic partnerships, civil unions, or a reciprocal beneficiary or designated beneficiary status. These new statuses developed in different contexts and offer a range of benefits. Initially designed as a constitutional remedy for the exclusion of same-sex couples from marriage, civil unions provide nearly all the benefits and obligations linked to marriage under state law. Domestic partnerships may offer the same benefits and obligations as marriage or may offer fewer. Reciprocal beneficiary status (available in Hawaii) provides a limited number of rights, while the designated beneficiary status (available in Colorado) allows parties to choose from among legal incidents. Some of these legal arrangements are available only to intimate partners who would be eligible to marry; others are more broadly available, for example, to adult siblings or other adults who are not eligible to marry.

The impetus for states to create these new forms of relationships often came from advocates for LGBT equality. Consequently, some (but not all) states ceased to offer them once state law allowed same-sex couples to marry. States are still working through the impact on these statuses in the wake of *Obergefell v. Hodges,* 135 S. Ct. 2594 (2015). The availability of marriage in all fifty states has led to a decline in the use of these statuses.

This Section introduces these legal statuses by briefly explaining: 1) their histories; 2) the legal incidents each confers; 3) the criteria for eligibility to enter into each; and 4) the process for entering and exiting each of them. As you read this Section, consider whether a need exists to offer adults differing options for formalizing their intimate and family relationships and whether and how states should offer such options.

A. DOMESTIC PARTNERSHIPS

1. The History of Domestic Partnerships

The earliest domestic partnership laws date from the mid-1980s. Ordinances in several cities (for example, Berkeley, Cambridge, Iowa City, San Francisco, and Santa Monica) explained the purpose of such laws in language resembling this Ann Arbor, Michigan, ordinance: "Many persons today share a life as families in enduring and committed relationships apart from marriage ... The city of Ann Arbor has an interest in strengthening and supporting all caring, committed, and responsible family forms." Ann Arbor Code ch. 110, § 9:86 (2015). Domestic partner status provided "public" recognition to relationships formed by unmarried gay men and lesbians. Some municipal laws offered that status to unmarried heterosexual couples as well. Some ordinances required that employers within the city provide employment-related benefits, such as family health insurance. Barbara J. Cox, *Alternative Families: Obtaining Traditional Family Benefits Through Litigation, Legislation, and Collective Bargaining*, 2 Wis. Women's L. J. 1 (1986).

California established the first statewide domestic partnership law in 1999. Working within the constraint of California's "defense of marriage act" ("DOMA") (a ballot initiative (Proposition 8) approved by voters in 2000 limiting marriage to the union of one man and one woman), the legislature expanded the scope of the domestic partnership law several times. The California Domestic Partner Rights and Responsibilities Act of 2003, which took effect on January 1, 2005, declared that registered domestic partners "shall have the same rights, protections, and duties under law" as "are granted to and imposed upon spouses." Cal. Fam. Code, § 299.3 (2005). This included parental rights and responsibilities. Domestic partner status was (and remains) available not only to same-sex couples, but also to opposite-sex partners when one or both are over age 62. In subsequent federal litigation over the exclusion of same-sex couples from civil marriage, a federal district court concluded that California's creation of "two separate and parallel institutions"—marriage for opposite-sex couples and domestic partnerships for same-sex couples—"to provide couples with essentially the same rights and obligations of marriage"— violated federal due process by denying plaintiffs the fundamental right to marry without justification. *Perry v. Schwarzenegger*, 704 F.2d 921, 994 (N.D. Cal. 2010), *aff'd*, *Perry v. Brown*, 671 F. 3d 1052 (9th Cir. 2012), *vacated for lack of standing*, *Hollingsworth v. Perry*, 570 U.S. 693 (2013).

The first Fortune 500 company offered benefits to an employee's same-sex partner in 1990, and the majority of large corporations now do so. Human Rights Campaign, *Resources: Benefits* (2018). Some companies offered these benefits only to employees with same-sex partners, since they could not marry. Other companies have made the benefits available to employees with opposite-sex partners. A 2017 study found that, since *Obergefell*, "a growing number of employers are requiring same-sex couples to be married before an employee's partner can receive health care benefits." Stephen Miller, *Employers Are Dropping Domestic Partner Health Care Benefits*, Society for Human Resource Management (Aug. 18, 2018). Critics argue that such policies unduly pressure couples to marry and fail to acknowledge the changing shape of contemporary families.

2.   Legal Incidents: What? Who? How? Why?

Domestic partnership statutes vary in the extent to which the incidents linked to this status resemble the legal status of marriage.

Similar to California, several other states created a domestic partnership status with most or all of the rights and responsibilities tied to marriage under state law (for example, Nevada, Oregon, and Washington). Other states created domestic partnerships laws (for example, Maine, Maryland, New Jersey, New York) offering only a small subset of those rights and responsibilities. Municipal domestic partnership ordinances are modest in scope.

Some state domestic partnership laws are available only to same-sex couples and (as in California) to heterosexual "seniors." Why include these seniors? By contrast, Nevada's law is available to same-sex and to opposite-sex couples, and it offers domestic partners essentially the same responsibilities and obligations as spouses. Are there good arguments for following Nevada's example and opening up this status more broadly to opposite-sex couples? In recent years, lawmakers in California have introduced bills to expand domestic partnerships to opposite-sex couples. *See* 2019 CA S.B. 30 (NS) (introduced December 3, 2018). Would you support such legislation?

How people may enter into or exit a domestic partnership varies. In some states, in contrast to persons seeking to marry, persons seeking to register as domestic partners typically must satisfy certain criteria, such as sharing a residence and making a commitment to be responsible for each other, and the like. *See, e.g.,* Nev. Rev. Stat. § 122A.100.1–100.2 (2019) (two persons must file statement declaring that they "have chosen to share one another's lives in an intimate and committed relationship of mutual caring"; to be eligible to register as domestic partners, "both persons must have a common residence"). Some statutes do not require these conditions. Domestic partnership laws often have analogies to marriage requirements, such as ones specifying minimum age, absence of marriage or partnership with someone else, and not being within a prohibited degree of relationship. *See* Nev. Rev. Stat. § 122.100A.2. *See also* Or. Rev. Stat. § 106.315 (2019) ("Prohibited and void domestic partnerships") (same). As discussed in Chapter 2, Section 5, a number of state legislatures have passed or are considering legislation that would raise the minimum age of marriage. If a state also permits civil unions or domestic partnerships, such higher minimum age laws will also apply to such statuses.

At the exit stage, the most expansive domestic partnership laws mandate termination procedures analogous to those for dissolving marriage, with the court having jurisdiction over financial and child-related matters. In Nevada, for example, parties may also use a "simplified termination proceeding" if they have been registered as domestic partners five years or less, have no minor children, no community or joint property (or have reached agreement about it), and are waiving a right to future support. *Domestic Partnerships in Nevada, supra.*

3. Why Does the Label Matter?

Much is in a name—and a legal status.

First, in the pre-*Obergefell* era in which many states barred same-sex marriage by a statutory or constitutional DOMA, calling an alternative legal status "domestic partnership"—rather than marriage—provided a way to avoid running afoul of those prohibitions. Thus, Nevada's domestic partnership law states: "A domestic partnership is not a marriage for the purposes of. . . the Nevada Constitution [its DOMA]." Nev. Rev. Stat. § 122a.510 (2009).

Second, married couples are eligible for federal benefits, but couples in domestic partnerships and civil unions are not. *See, e.g.*, T.D. (Treasury Determination) 9785, 2016–38 I.R.B. (2016), which defines "spouse," "husband" and "wife" to exclude registered domestic partnerships and civil unions if the relationship is not recognized as a marriage in the state in which the parties entered into the domestic partnership or civil union.

Third, these comparatively new legal statuses have raised challenging questions about whether one state will recognize a status entered into lawfully in another state. In 2017, the Nevada legislature amended its domestic partnership law to provide that a legal union (other than marriage) that "was validly formed in another jurisdiction" and "is substantially equivalent" to a domestic partnership (as defined in Nevada's law) "must be recognized" in Nevada whether or not it has the name "domestic partnership." The law eliminated the requirement that, for such recognition, out-of-state couples had to register their relationship with the Nevada Secretary of State. *See* Nev. Rev. Stat. § 122.100A.500 (2019); Nevada Secretary of State: Domestic Partnerships.

Courts have struggled with the interstate recognition issue. As the Supreme Court of Vermont observed, *Obergefell* held that "there is no lawful basis for a State to refuse a lawful same-sex *marriage* performed in another State on the ground of its same-sex character," but "uncertainty remains as to whether *Obergefell* requires other states to recognize and dissolve civil unions established in Vermont," because marriage and civil unions remain "legally distinct entities." *Solomon v. Guidry*, 155 A.3d 1218, 1121 (Vt. 2016).

In *Gardenour v. Bondelie*, 60 N.E.3d 1109 (Ind. Ct. App. 2016), the court held that a domestic partnership registered in California was equivalent to marriage for determining a child's legal parent under Indiana law. After moving to Indiana, the female domestic partners "agreed to co-parent a child," and one partner gave birth after using artificial insemination. After an Indiana trial court terminated their domestic partnership, the partner who gave birth contended that the trial court erred in treating their domestic partnership as establishing a spousal relationship similar to marriage; in recognizing the relationship in

Indiana; and in recognizing the other partner as a legal parent for establishing custody, parenting time, and child support. *Id.* at 1111. The appellate court held that, as matter of comity, the trial court correctly treated the "foreign" domestic partnership as the equivalent of marriage under Indiana law. Turning to parental rights, comity also supported treating the women similarly to married couples who have a child "via artificial insemination." *Id.* at 1119.

4. The Future of Domestic Partnerships

States have differed concerning the fate of domestic partnerships once state law allowed same-sex couples marry. Domestic partnership status is still available in some states (for example, California and Nevada) and in the District of Columbia. *See Marriage, Domestic Partnerships, and Civil Unions: An Overview of Relationship Recognition for Same-Sex Couples Within the United States,* National Center for Lesbian Rights (2017). Other states have ceased to allow any new domestic partnerships. *Id.* For example, in 2018, Wisconsin announced that no new domestic partnerships could be formed after April 1, 2018. Christopher Sean Krimmer, *Imminent Demise: Register for Domestic Partnership Status Before It Disappears on April 1,* Inside Track: State Bar of Wisconsin (Feb. 7, 2018). Some states will continue to recognize existing domestic partnerships; others have taken the approach that existing domestic partnerships would convert to marriage unless they were dissolved (for example, Washington). *See* Wash. Rev. Code §§ 26.020, 26.60.100 (2019).

B. CIVIL UNIONS

1. The Development of Civil Unions

Civil unions emerged independently from domestic partnerships. They developed first in Vermont when its supreme court held that the state constitution's Common Benefits Clause (its analogue to the U.S. Constitution's Equal Protection Clause) required that the benefits, protections, and obligations linked to marriage under Vermont law must be made available to same-sex couples. *Baker v. State,* 744 A.2d 864 (Vt. 1999). The court directed the legislature to fashion a remedy consistent with the decision.

The Vermont legislature declined to extend marriage to same-sex couples, but created a new legal status, the "civil union," which accorded to same-sex couples who entered into it the same array of benefits and protections accorded to married couples. Vt. Stat. Ann. Tit. 15, § 23 (1999). The legislature found that the rationale for recognizing and supporting marriage, "to encourage close and caring families, and to protect all family members from the economic and social consequences of abandonment and divorce, focusing on those who have been especially at risk," also applied to other families (including those formed by same-sex couples). An Act Relating to Civil Unions, 2000 Vt. ALS 91. The legislature explained that it limited "marriage" to "a union between a man and a woman" to respect longstanding social institutions and religious tradition.

Several years later, in the wake of *Goodridge v. Department of Public Health*, 798 N.E. 2d 941 (Mass. 2003) (discussed in Chapter 2), the Massachusetts legislature sought an advisory opinion from the high court about whether permitting same-sex civil unions would be an acceptable remedy for the decision's holding that prohibiting marriage by same-sex couples violated the state constitution. The court ruled that the proposed civil unions would not suffice, since "to preserve the traditional historic nature and meaning" of civil marriage for opposite-sex couples while recognizing only civil unions for same-sex couples would be a form of "second-class citizenship." *Opinions of the Justices to the Senate*, 802 N.E.2d 565 (Mass. 2004).

When same-sex couples challenged New Jersey's marriage law, its high court followed the approach of Vermont rather than Massachusetts. *Lewis v. Harris*, 908 A. 2d 196 (N.J. 2006), The court held that the New Jersey constitution entitled same-sex couples to the rights *of* marriage; however, it was up to the legislature to determine whether the remedy also required the right *to* marry. The New Jersey legislature responded with a civil union bill.

Connecticut and New Hampshire created civil union statutes without the spur of a judicial ruling mandating a remedy. In subsequent years, a number of other state legislatures also created civil unions without such a spur.

2. What Are Civil Unions? Who May Enter into Them?

Generally, a civil union is a legal status that provides a same-sex couple with the same benefits, protections, and obligations available to spouses under state law. This equivalence stems from the origin of the civil union in Vermont and New Jersey as a constitutional remedy to the exclusion of same-sex couples from marriage. As other states enacted civil union statutes without the impetus of a judicial ruling, they also tended to use marriage as the benchmark for the legal incidents of a civil union. Thus, to enter a civil union, parties must meet the minimum age, not be too closely related to each other, and not be in a civil union or marriage with another person. *See, e.g.*, 750 Ill. Comp. Stat. 75/25 (2019) ("Prohibited civil unions").

To dissolve a civil union, the partners must follow the statutory procedures for ending a marriage. Some states (e.g., Colorado) require the parties to consent to the jurisdiction of that state's courts for any proceedings related to the civil union (such as dissolution), even if one or both parties no longer reside in the state. Depending on the state, however, they may not need to follow the same solemnization requirements. In addition, as with laws that extended civil marriage to same-sex couples, civil union laws often explicitly include provisions protecting religious freedom. For example, the Illinois Religious Freedom Protection and Civil Union Act, enacted in 2011, provides that religious bodies are "free to choose whether or not to solemnize or officiate a civil union." 750 Ill. Comp. Stat. 75/1 (2019).

Who may enter into a civil union? Initially, civil unions were available only to same-sex couples. However, several states have made civil unions available to same-sex and opposite-sex couples. For example, the Illinois Religious Freedom Protection and Civil Union Act defines civil unions as "a legal relationship between 2 persons, of either the same sex or opposite sex." *Id.* at § 10. Concerns about senior citizens who would lose important federal benefits if they married were one motive for this feature of the law. Colorado and Hawaii's laws also do not limit civil unions to same-sex couples. Colo. Rev. Stat. § 14–15–101 (2019); Haw. Rev. Stat. § 572B (2019).

3.   The Future of Civil Unions

After the Vermont legislature created civil unions, some legal scholars described them as a "way station": civil unions afforded same-sex couples a remedy for their exclusion from the benefits and obligations of marriage law while allowing an opportunity for those opposed to, or uncomfortable with, same-sex couples marrying to become accustomed to the ability of same-sex couples establishing formal, legally recognized relationships. *See, e.g.,* William Eskridge Jr., Equality Practice: Civil Unions and the Future of Gay Rights (1st ed. 2002). In fact, in several states that started with civil unions, such as Vermont and New Hampshire, the legislature subsequently enacted a civil marriage law. One reason for this move to marriage was because employers, hospital personnel, and others did not treat couples in civil unions equally to couples who were married. Some argued that civil unions did not have the same symbolic or expressive value as marriage. Also, couples in civil unions found that their relationships were not as portable as marriages; states that recognized out-of-state marriages might not give legal effect to an out-of-state civil union.

As is true with domestic partnerships, states varied in what they did with civil unions once they recognized the rights of same-sex couples to marry. *See* John G. Culhane, United States v. Windsor *and the Future of Civil Unions and Other Marriage Alternatives,* Vill. L. Rev. Online 27 (2013) In Hawaii and Illinois, the civil union continues to be available to both same-sex and opposite-sex couples. *See* 750 Ill. Comp. Stat. 75/10 (2019); Haw. Rev. Stat. § 572B–2 (2019); State of Hawaii Dep't of Health, About Civil Unions. In Illinois, for example, couples in a civil union may keep it or voluntarily convert it to a marriage. *See, e.g.,* 750 Ill. Comp. Stat. 75/65.

In some states, couples in a civil union were automatically converted into or merged into a civil marriage unless they dissolved their relationship. For example, the Delaware legislature approved a civil union law in 2011. In 2013, it enacted a civil marriage law automatically converting civil unions to marriages by 2014, unless civil union partners themselves married or dissolved their unions. *See* Del. Code Ann. tit. 13, § 218 (2019) (originally enacted in 2013). In other states, such as Vermont, couples in a civil union may remain in existing civil unions, but no new civil unions may be formed. *Marriage, Domestic Partnerships, and Civil Unions, supra.*

NOTES AND QUESTIONS

1. The *changing legal landscape.* The landscape of civil unions and domestic partnerships has changed rapidly over the past several decades. In the wake of *Obergefell,* it is likely to continue to change, as states consider what to do with these statuses. *See Marriage, Domestic Partnerships, and Civil Unions, supra.*

2. *Second-class citizenship or family law pluralism?* Some advocates of LGBTQ equality criticize the elimination of domestic partnerships when marriage becomes available, arguing that there should be options for couples other than marriage, with its blending of church and state. *See* Daniel D'Addario, *Gay Marriage's Gay Holdouts: The Progressive Who Thinks This Is the Wrong Fight,* Salon (March 27, 2013) (interviewing law Professor Nancy Polikoff). Professor Melissa Murray argues that "there was an earlier moment in the gay rights movement when domestic partnership was an end unto itself," an "innovation," and even a "paradigm shift" in the "legal understanding and recognition of intimate relationships and the conferral of public and private benefits;" marriage equality litigation then "transformed" it "into a second-rate marriage substitute." Melissa Murray, *Paradigms Lost: How Domestic Partnership Went from Innovation to Injury,* 37 N.Y.U. Rev. L. & Soc. Change 291 (2013); *see* Kaiponanea T. Matsumura, *A Right Not to Marry,* 84 Fordham L. Rev. 1509 (2016). What do you think? Should states, municipalities, and companies continue to offer benefits to those in civil unions and domestic partnerships? Do you see the value in a two-track system, in which couples (whatever their gender) have the option of civil marriage or civil union/domestic partnerships? Why might a couple choose a legal status alternative to marriage?

3. *Registered partnerships, PACs, and other statuses in Europe.* As discussed in Chapter 2, as of early 2019, marriage is available to same-sex couples in twenty-seven countries. In eighteen European countries, same-sex couples may enter into a registered (or "civil") partnership by registering their relationship with the relevant public authority in their country of residence. *See* European Comm'n., Marriage, Civil Partnerships, and Property Issues

(2017). In five countries, opposite-sex couples may also become registered partners. *Id.* Countries take a range of approaches to whether those statuses remain available once same-sex couples are allowed to marry. *See id.* For example, in Sweden, when marriage for same-sex partners was recognized in 2009, registered partnerships were abolished. However, partnerships entered into prior to that date continue to exist. *Id.* By contrast, in the Netherlands, partners (same- or opposite-sex) have a choice of two formal living arrangements: (1) marriage; or (2) a registered partnership. Individuals can also sign a cohabitation agreement or live together without signing any formal agreement. *See* Marriage, Registered Partnership and Cohabitation Agreements, Govt. of the Netherlands (2015). In France, where marriage became available to same-sex couples in 2013, couples may still enter into the *pacte civil de solidarité* (PACS), a contract available to two adults, of different or of the same gender, for the purposes of organizing their life in common. Created in 1999, the PACS offers a subset of the benefits and obligations of marriage. *See* Laurence Francoz Terminal, *Registered Partnerships in France*, in The Future of Registered Partnerships: Family Recognition Beyond Marriage? 153–184 (Jens M. Scherpe & Andy Haward, eds., 2018). While the marriage rate is still double that of PACS, 95% of those entering into PACS are heterosexual couples. Alex Ledsom, *Why Straight French Couples are choosing to PACS Instead of Getting Married,* Culture Trip (Nov. 22, 2017) (reporting 95% figure).

C. RECIPROCAL AND DESIGNATED BENEFICIARIES

Two additional new legal statuses warrant discussion. The first is reciprocal beneficiaries status, which originated in Hawaii and provides a small subset of the legal benefits linked to marriage. Haw. Rev. Stat. § 572C–1 to –7 (2019). The second, designated beneficiaries, is a more comprehensive status created by the Colorado legislature in 2009. Colo. Rev. Stat. Ann. § 15–22–104 to –06 (2019).

The "Designated Beneficiary Agreement" (DBA) form set out below lists the sixteen "rights or protections" available under Colorado law to persons who enter into a DBA. In completing the form, each party (identified as Party A and Party B) must indicate whether they are *granting* or *withholding* each of the rights or protections listed below by putting their initials either on the "grant" or "withhold" line for each right. The statute further provides that it shall be presumed that each party grants all rights and protections to the other party unless a party withholds specifics rights or protections by initialing on the appropriate spaces on the form. Colo. Rev. Stat. Ann. § 15–22–106–1.

The DBA must be signed and dated by the parties, acknowledged by a notary public, and filed with the county clerk and recorder of the county in which one of the designated beneficiaries resides to be effective. The DBA is not limited to partners in a romantic or cohabiting relationship. Any two persons may enter into a DBA as long as they are 18 years of age, competent to enter into a contract, unmarried, not party to another DBA, and "voluntarily entered [the] agreement without force, fraud or duress." *See* Colorado Bar Association, Colorado's Designated Beneficiary Agreement Act (n.d.) Legal scholar John Culhane argues that lawmakers who proposed the DBA and parties who have entered DBAs view it as a useful form of advance planning that provides a comparatively inexpensive form of "one-stop shopping." John Culhane, The Designated Beneficiary Agreement—Colorado's Successful Experiment (forthcoming 2020). The Legislative Declaration about the DBA stressed the private welfare function of such planning: "The power of individuals to care for one another and take action to be personally responsible for themselves and their loved ones is of tremendous societal benefit, enabling self-determination and reducing reliance on public programs and services." Colo. Rev. Stat. § 15–22–102 (1) (D).

DESIGNATED BENEFICIARY AGREEMENT

We, _____, who resides at _____, referred to as party A, and _____, who resides at _____, referred to as party B, hereby designate each other as the other's Designated Beneficiary with the following rights and protections, granted or withheld as indicated by our initials:

To grant one or more of the rights or protections specified in this form, initial the line to the left of each right or protection you are granting.

To withhold a right or protection, initial the line to the right of each right or protection you are withholding.

To **grant** a right or protection, initial:			To **withhold** a right or protection, initial:	
Party A:	Party B:		Party A:	Party B:
		The right to acquire, hold title to, own jointly, vivos or at death real or personal property as a joint tenant with me with right of survivorship or as a tenant in common with me;		
_____	_____		_____	_____
		The right to be designated by me as a beneficiary, payee, or owner as a trustee named in an inter vivos or testamentary trust for the purposes of a nonprobate transfer on death;		
_____	_____		_____	_____

The right to be designated by me as a beneficiary and recognized as a dependent in an insurance policy for life insurance;

_____   _____   _____   _____

The right to be designated by me as a beneficiary and recognized as a dependent in a health insurance policy if my employer elects to provide health insurance coverage for designated beneficiaries;

_____   _____   _____   _____

The right to be designated by me as a beneficiary in a retirement or pension plan;

_____   _____   _____   _____

The right to petition for and have priority for appointment as a conservator, guardian, or personal representative for me;

_____   _____   _____   _____

The right to visit me in a hospital, nursing home, hospice, or similar health care facility in which a party to a designated beneficiary agreement resides or is receiving care;

_____   _____   _____   _____

The right to initiate a formal complaint regarding alleged violations of my rights as a nursing home patient as provided in section 25–1–120, Colorado Revised Statutes;

_____   _____   _____   _____

The right to act as a proxy decision-maker or surrogate decision-maker to make medical care decisions for me pursuant to section 15–18.5–103 or 15–18.5–104, Colorado Revised Statutes;

_____   _____   _____   _____

The right to notice of the withholding or withdrawal of life-sustaining procedures for me pursuant to section 15–18–107, Colorado Revised Statutes;

_____   _____   _____   _____

The right to challenge the validity of a declaration as to medical or surgical treatment of me pursuant to section 15–18–108, Colorado Revised Statutes;

_____   _____   _____   _____

The right to act as my agent to make, revoke, or object to anatomical gifts involving my person pursuant to the "Revised Uniform Anatomical Gift Act", part 2 of article 19 of title 15, Colorado Revised Statutes;

_____   _____   _____   _____

The right to inherit real or personal property from me through intestate succession;

_____   _____   _____   _____

The right to have standing to receive benefits pursuant to the "Workers' Compensation Act of Colorado", article 40 of title 8, Colorado Revised Statutes, in the event of my death on the job;

_____   _____   _____   _____

The right to have standing to sue for wrongful death in the event of my death; and

_____   _____   _____   _____

The right to direct the disposition of my last remains pursuant to article 19 of title 15, Colorado Revised Statutes.

_____   _____   _____   _____

This Designated Beneficiary Agreement is effective when received for recording by the county clerk and recorder of the county in which one of the designated beneficiaries resides. This designated beneficiary agreement will continue in effect until one of the designated beneficiaries revokes this agreement by recording a revocation of designated beneficiary form with the county clerk and recorder of the county in which this agreement was recorded or until this agreement is superseded in part or in whole by a superseding legal document.

See Colo. Rev. Stat. § 15–22–106.

NOTES AND QUESTIONS

1.   *Real differences?* During oral argument in *Obergefell*, Justice Alito asked about two groups of people, the first, "a same-sex couple who have been together for 25 years, and they get married either as a result of a change in State law or as a result of a Court decision," and the second, "unmarried siblings" who have "lived together for 25 years" and whose "financial relationship is the same as the same-sex couple. They share household expenses and household chores in the same way. They care for each other in the same way." He asked: "Is there any reason why the law should treat the groups differently?" Transcript of Oral Argument at 33, Vol. 1, *Obergefell v. Hodges*, 135 S. Ct. 2584, April 28, 2015. How would you answer his question?

2.   *Who benefits?* Note that each partner to a DBA can make different choices concerning which rights to grant. Beyond siblings and adult intimate partners, who else might benefit from the designated beneficiary status? *See* Naomi Cahn, *The New Kinship*, 100 Geo. L.J. 367 (2012). Why do you think the Colorado legislature limits DBA agreements to persons who are unmarried and allows parties to enter into only one DBA? Would removing these restrictions make the DBA more useful?

3.   *Why not?* Why do you think more states have not adopted the designated beneficiary status? Do you think there would be demand for such a status in other states? Professor Culhane finds that, despite the promise the DBA holds as a flexible form of life planning, the frequency of using the DBA has declined since 2009. There was an initial demand—particularly by same-sex partners—for the DBA, but the number of new DBAs declined dramatically after Colorado offered civil unions (in 2013) and then civil marriage (2015). Very few opposite-sex parties have entered into DBAs. Culhane, The Designated Beneficiary Agreement, *supra*.

PROBLEM 4-5

In an essay about the DBA, Professor Culhane gives the following description of two people whom he interviewed:

> April and May Berjian[c] sat across from me in the well-appointed conference room of a major financial planning company in downtown Philadelphia. The sisters, now seventy-six and eighty years of age, have been "life partners" in the truest sense of that term. Since the

---

[c]   *Editors' Note:* Professor Culhane explains that the sisters requested anonymity, and so their names have been changed to honor that request.

younger of the two, May, was born, they have lived in the same home. Raised in what they described as a strict but loving home, they never married—and shocked their parents when, in their twenties, they moved out and bought their own home together, in an effort to gain some distance and independence. From early adulthood on, they have been financially interdependent. And * * * they share a deep emotional connection, finishing each other's sentences in the way usually associated with identical twins, and seemingly choreographing their every movement and expression.

They have spent a pile of money making sure that, once one of them becomes incapacitated and dies, the other will be protected to the maximum extent permissible under law. * * * [But, w]hen the first of them dies, the other will be hit with enormous federal and state estate tax bills, the payment of which might require the survivor to move out of the home they share, and will, in any event, compromise her current lifestyle. But if * * * the sisters had been married, the bill would be zero because surviving spouses are exempt from the tax. The state doesn't swoop in and take its cut until the second spouse's death. * * *

John C. Culhane, *After Marriage Equality, What's Next for Relationship Recognition?*, 60 S.D.L. Rev. 375, 386–87 (2015).

Which of the legal forms for adult relationships discussed in this Chapter might be appropriate for these two sisters? Is it legally appropriate to distinguish between these sisters and spouses or other sexually intimate partners?

PROBLEM 4-6

You are a member of the Columbia State legislature, trying to decide whether to adopt a civil union, domestic partnership, and/or a Designated Beneficiary law in your state. Which of your constituencies might favor each law? Who might be against the laws? How will you vote?

CHAPTER 5

ESTABLISHING PARENTHOOD

■ ■ ■

Parents have a constitutionally protected right to care for their children. While parentage has historically been associated with marriage, the determination of legal parentage has become more complex with the rising number of nonmarital couples having children and the increasing use of assisted reproductive technology to create children. The need to identify the legal parents is a critical issue throughout family law. When couples split up or have never lived together, courts must decide issues including custody and visitation and assign financial responsibility for supporting children. Later chapters will discuss how decisions are made about each of these issues in detail.

This Chapter focuses on whom the law recognizes as parents. It explores the laws conferring parenthood, including an examination of the role of marriage, biology, and function in identifying those entitled to exercise parental rights. It also discusses the movement in some states to recognize more than two parents. It concludes by discussing the possibility of disestablishing parentage.

1. MARITAL AND NONMARITAL PARENTS

At common law, marriage determined parenthood: a husband and wife were presumed to be the father and mother of children born into the marriage. Lord Mansfield's Rule, expounded in *Goodright v. Moss*, stated that "it is a rule, founded in decency, morality, and policy, that [the spouses] . . . shall not be permitted to say after marriage, that they have had no connection, and therefore that the offspring is spurious." 98 Eng. Rep. 1257, 1258 (K.B. 1777). The rule effectively barred either spouse from testifying that the husband was not the child's father. The marital presumption rule appears to pre-date *Goodright,* and to be drawn from Roman law, which presumed that marriage established the identity of the father. *See* Jane C. Murphy, *Legal Images of Fatherhood: Welfare Reform, Child Support Enforcement, and Fatherless Children*, 81 Notre Dame L. Rev. 325, 331 (2005). Marriage thus guaranteed parental rights to the husband, and his paternity was virtually irrebuttable, absent proof of impotence, sterility, or his non-access to his wife for the relevant time period.

Courts also refused to apply the marital presumption when a child with African-American features was born to a white couple. Evidence, such as the white husband's impotence or imprisonment during the child's conception or even physical comparison, could be admitted to rebut the presumption. *See* Zanita E. Fenton, *Bastards! . . . . and the Welfare Plantation*, 17 J. Gender Race & Just. 9, 18 (2014).

The marital presumption exists in some form in virtually all states today, and it is applicable to all marriages, regardless of the gender of the spouses. The presumption has, however, diminished in strength; for example, the spouses and the biological parent have the opportunity to rebut the presumption in most states. When the parents are not married to each other, state laws establish how nonmarital partners can establish their rights. Until comparatively recently, issues of maternity were straightforward, but the law of paternity has always been more complicated. Parentage laws are evolving to respond to changing demographics. One out of every four parents who lives with a child is unmarried, approximately one-third of all nonmarital parents are cohabiting, and just over half of nonmarital parents are single mothers, while 12% are single fathers. Gretchen Livingston, *The Changing Profile of Unmarried Parents,* Pew Social Trends (April 25, 2018).

A. THE CONSTITUTIONAL FRAMEWORK

At English common law and in colonial America, nonmarital children had no legally recognized relationship with either biological parent, and the parents had no recognized familial relationship with the child. Most states did not enact laws recognizing that "illegitimate" children were part of their mothers' families until the end of the nineteenth century. If both parents were slaves, their offspring were nonmarital, since marriage between slaves was not legally binding.

As the Supreme Court explained, "the mother was regarded as the child's natural and sole guardian. At common law, the mother, and only the mother, was 'bound to maintain [a nonmarital child] as its natural guardian.'" *Sessions v. Morales-Santana,* 137 S. Ct. 1678, 1691 (2017)(internal citation omitted)(a principal case in Chapter 3).

Unless they had "legitimated" their children, fathers could not exercise parental powers and, in effect, were defined as nonparents. In determining the constitutional rights of parents, because the Constitution does not define who qualifies as a parent, "that definition must come from the Court." Michael J. Higdon, *Constitutional Parenthood*, 103 Iowa L. Rev. 1483, 1492 (2018).

Beginning with the Supreme Court's 1972 decision in *Stanley v. Illinois*, 405 U.S. 645 (1972), and culminating in the 1989 decision of *Michael H. v. Gerald D.*, 491 U.S. 110 (1989) (reprinted below), the

Supreme Court issued a number of opinions considering the rights of putative fathers.

In *Stanley*, the Court struck down an Illinois statute that made children of nonmarital fathers wards of the state following the death of the mother. Petitioner Stanley sought the right to raise his three children following the death of their mother, Joan, with whom he had lived on and off for 18 years. Illinois argued it had an interest in the " 'moral, emotional, mental, and physical welfare of the minor and the best interest of the community.' " 405 U.S. at 652. The Court disagreed with the State, and struck down the statute as violative of the Fourteenth Amendment's due process and equal protection clauses, finding that Illinois had incorrectly presumed that all nonmarital fathers were unfit. While a landmark case, *Stanley* requires only that nonmarital fathers receive procedural justice concerning their parental rights.

The rights of a putative father were defined more clearly in *Quilloin v. Walcott*, 434 U.S. 246 (1978). A mother had raised her nonmarital child without the presence of the biological father. When her husband, the child's stepfather, attempted to adopt the child, the biological father, Quilloin, attempted to block it. The Georgia statute required only the mother of a nonmarital child to approve the adoption. The Supreme Court held that *Stanley* did not require Georgia to grant Quilloin a veto because he had not shouldered significant responsibility for the child's upbringing.

The Supreme Court reached a different result in *Caban v. Mohammed*, 441 U.S. 380 (1979). Abdiel Caban, the father, had lived with and had a relationship with his two nonmarital children prior to ending his relationship with the children's mother, Maria Mohammed. The Court held that Caban could block the adoption by the children's new stepfather and struck down a New York statute that, like the *Quilloin* statute, only required the mother's consent for adoption of a nonmarital child. The Court held that the statute violated equal protection because Caban's "substantial relationship" with his children was different from Quilloin's "failure to act as a father." *Id.* at 389 n.7.

In *Lehr v. Robertson*, 463 U.S. 248 (1983), the nonmarital father challenged his daughter's adoption by the mother's new husband. Under the applicable New York law, biological fathers were entitled to notice of an adoption under certain circumstances, including after registration with a putative father registry. Lehr did not, however, fall within the categories of men entitled to notice. Although Lehr challenged the New York statutory scheme as a violation of his due process right to a relationship with his child, the Supreme Court upheld the law. The Court held that the biological relationship between a father and child does not warrant constitutional protection unless the father had developed a substantial relationship with the child. The Court stated:

court: an unwed father had to be participating in raising the child

The difference between the developed parent-child relationship that was implicated in *Stanley* and *Caban* * * * is both clear and significant. When an unwed father demonstrates a full commitment to the responsibilities of parenthood by "com[ing] forward to participate in the rearing of his child," *Caban*, 441 U.S. at 392, his interest in personal contact with his child acquires substantial protection under the due process clause. At that point it may be said that he "act[s] as a father toward his children." *Id.* at 389, n.7. But the mere existence of a biological link does not merit equivalent constitutional protection. The actions of judges neither create nor sever genetic bonds. "[T]he importance of the familial relationship, to the individuals involved and to the society, stems from the emotional attachments that derive from the intimacy of daily association, and from the role it plays in 'promot[ing] a way of life' through the instruction of children as well as from the fact of blood relationship." *Smith v. Org. of Foster Families for Equal. & Reform*, 431 U.S. 816, 844 (quoting *Wisconsin v. Yoder*, 406 U.S. 205, 231–33 (1972)).

463 U.S. at 261.

Dissent:

Dissenting Justices White, Marshall, and Blackmun characterized the putative father's rights quite differently. They noted that Lehr had attempted to establish a relationship with his child but that the mother had concealed her location from him, thereby thwarting him in his efforts to visit. *Id.* at 268–69 (White, J. dissenting):

> A "mere biological relationship" is not as unimportant in determining the nature of liberty interests as the majority suggests.

> * * * The "biological connection" is itself a relationship that creates a protected interest. * * *

> Lehr was entitled to due process, and the right to be heard is one of the fundamentals of that right, which "has little reality or worth unless one is informed that the matter is pending and can choose for himself whether to appear or default, acquiesce or contest." *Schroeder v. City of New York*, 371 U.S. 208, 212 (1962).

> * * *

> No state interest is substantially served by denying Lehr adequate notice and a hearing. * * *

> * * * [I]n my view the failure to provide Lehr with notice and an opportunity to be heard violated rights guaranteed him by the Due Process Clause * * *. * * *

Id. at 271–72, 275–76.

1.   The Marital Presumption

These decisions provided the framework for the Supreme Court's consideration of the following case involving the constitutionality of the marital presumption. The case is focused on a nonmarital man's claims to be recognized as a father to a child born to a married woman whose husband also claimed fatherhood. As you read the case, consider the basis of each man's claim to be the father and the reasons for establishing the marital presumption and for retaining it today.

[handwritten: ✶ At issue]

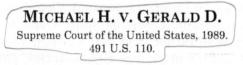

MICHAEL H. V. GERALD D.

Supreme Court of the United States, 1989.
491 U.S. 110.

[handwritten: ✶Holding: the presumption that a child's mother's husband is the father of the child if the child was born during the marriage does not violate the child's biological father's due process rights.]

JUSTICE SCALIA announced the judgment of the Court and delivered an opinion, in which THE CHIEF JUSTICE joins, and in all but footnote 6 of which JUSTICE O'CONNOR and JUSTICE KENNEDY join.

Under California law, a child born to a married woman living with her husband is presumed to be a child of the marriage. Cal. Evid. Code Ann. § 621 (West Supp. 1989). The presumption of legitimacy may be rebutted only by the husband or wife, and then only in limited circumstances. The instant appeal presents the claim that this presumption infringes upon the due process rights of a man who wishes to establish his paternity of a child born to the wife of another man, and the claim that it infringes upon the constitutional right of the child to maintain a relationship with her natural father.

[handwritten left margin: PRESUMPTION OF LEGITIMACY]
[handwritten left margin: the issue →]
[handwritten right margin: Scalia's reasoning: the Cali. presumption does not violate Michael's due process rights bc he wasn't denied a state-created interest.]

I

The facts of this case are, we must hope, extraordinary. On May 9, 1976, in Las Vegas, Nevada, Carole D., an international model, and Gerald D., a top executive in a French oil company, were married. The couple established a home in Playa del Rey, California, in which they resided as husband and wife when one or the other was not out of the country on business. In the summer of 1978, Carole became involved in an adulterous affair with a neighbor, Michael H. In September 1980, she conceived a child, Victoria D., who was born on May 11, 1981. Gerald was listed as father on the birth certificate and has always held Victoria out to the world as his daughter. Soon after delivery of the child, however, Carole informed Michael that she believed he might be the father.

[handwritten right margin: facts]

In the first three years of her life, Victoria remained always with Carole, but found herself within a variety of quasi-family units. In October 1981, Gerald moved to New York City to pursue his business interests, but Carole chose to remain in California. At the end of that month, Carole and Michael had blood tests of themselves and Victoria, which showed a 98.07% probability that Michael was Victoria's father. In January 1982, Carole

[handwritten bottom: Majority: A biological father may have a constitutionally protected interest in visitation with his child.]

visited Michael in St. Thomas, where his primary business interests were based. There Michael held Victoria out as his child. In March, however, Carole left Michael and returned to California, where she took up residence with yet another man, Scott K. Later that spring, and again in the summer, Carole and Victoria spent time with Gerald in New York City, as well as on vacation in Europe. In the fall, they returned to Scott in California.

In November 1982, rebuffed in his attempts to visit Victoria, Michael filed a filiation action in California Superior Court to establish his paternity and right to visitation. In March 1983, the court appointed an attorney and guardian ad litem to represent Victoria's interests. Victoria then filed a cross-complaint asserting that if she had more than one psychological or *de facto* father, she was entitled to maintain her filial relationship, with all of the attendant rights, duties, and obligations, with both. In May 1983, Carole filed a motion for summary judgment. During this period, from March through July 1983, Carole was again living with Gerald in New York. In August, however, she returned to California, became involved once again with Michael, and instructed her attorneys to remove the summary judgment motion from the calendar.

For the ensuing eight months, when Michael was not in St. Thomas he lived with Carole and Victoria in Carole's apartment in Los Angeles and held Victoria out as his daughter. In April 1984, Carole and Michael signed a stipulation that Michael was Victoria's natural father. Carole left Michael the next month, however, and instructed her attorneys not to file the stipulation. In June 1984, Carole reconciled with Gerald and joined him in New York, where they now live with Victoria and two other children since born into the marriage.

In May 1984, Michael and Victoria, through her guardian ad litem, sought visitation rights for Michael *pendente lite*. To assist in determining whether visitation would be in Victoria's best interests, the Superior Court appointed a psychologist to evaluate Victoria, Gerald, Michael, and Carole. The psychologist recommended that Carole retain sole custody, but that Michael be allowed continued contact with Victoria pursuant to a restricted visitation schedule. The court concurred and ordered that Michael be provided with limited visitation privileges *pendente lite*.

On October 19, 1984, Gerald, who had intervened in the action, moved for summary judgment on the ground that under Cal. Evid. Code § 621 there were no triable issues of fact as to Victoria's paternity. This law provides that "the issue of a wife cohabiting with her husband, who is not impotent or sterile, is conclusively presumed to be a child of the marriage." Cal. Evid. Code Ann. § 621(a) (West Supp. 1989). The presumption may be rebutted by blood tests, but only if a motion for such tests is made, within two years from the date of the child's birth, either by the husband or, if the natural father has filed an affidavit acknowledging paternity, by the wife.

On January 28, 1985, having found that affidavits submitted by Carole and Gerald sufficed to demonstrate that the two were cohabiting at conception and birth and that Gerald was neither sterile nor impotent, the Superior Court granted Gerald's motion for summary judgment, rejecting Michael's and Victoria's challenges to the constitutionality of § 621. The court also denied their motions for continued visitation pending the appeal under Cal. Civ. Code § 4601, which provides that a court may, in its discretion, grant "reasonable visitation rights . . . to any . . . person having an interest in the welfare of the child." It found that allowing such visitation would "violat[e] the intention of the Legislature by impugning the integrity of the family unit."

On appeal, Michael asserted, *inter alia*, that the Superior Court's application of § 621 had violated his procedural and substantive due process rights. Victoria also raised a due process challenge to the statute, seeking to preserve her *de facto* relationship with Michael as well as with Gerald. She contended, in addition, that as § 621 allows the husband and, at least to a limited extent, the mother, but not the child, to rebut the presumption of legitimacy, it violates the child's right to equal protection. Finally, she asserted a right to continued visitation with Michael under § 4601. After submission of briefs and a hearing, the California Court of Appeal affirmed the judgment of the Superior Court and upheld the constitutionality of the statute. It interpreted that judgment, moreover, as having denied permanent visitation rights under § 4601 * * *.

* * * Michael and Victoria both raise equal protection and due process challenges. We do not reach Michael's equal protection claim, however, as it was neither raised nor passed upon below.

II

The California statute that is the subject of this litigation is, in substance, more than a century old. * * * In their present form, the substantive provisions of the statute are as follows:

"§ 621.   Child of the marriage; notice of motion for blood tests

"(a) Except as provided in subdivision (b), the issue of a wife cohabiting with her husband, who is not impotent or sterile, is conclusively presumed to be a child of the marriage.

"(b) Notwithstanding the provisions of subdivision (a), if the court finds that the conclusions of all the experts, as disclosed by the evidence based upon blood tests performed pursuant to Chapter 2 (commencing with Section 890) of Division 7 are that the husband is not the father of the child, the question of paternity of the husband shall be resolved accordingly.

"(c) The notice of motion for blood tests under subdivision (b) may be raised by the husband not later than two years from the child's date of birth.

"(d) The notice of motion for blood tests under subdivision (b) may be raised by the mother of the child not later than two years from the child's date of birth if the child's biological father has filed an affidavit with the court acknowledging paternity of the child.["]

* * *

III

We address first the claims of Michael. At the outset, it is necessary to clarify what he sought and what he was denied. California law, like nature itself, makes no provision for dual fatherhood. Michael was seeking to be declared *the* father of Victoria. The immediate benefit he evidently sought to obtain from that status was visitation rights. But if Michael were successful in being declared the father, other rights would follow—most importantly, the right to be considered as the parent who should have custody, a status which "embrace[s] the sum of parental rights with respect to the rearing of a child, including the child's care; the right to the child's services and earnings; the right to direct the child's activities; the right to make decisions regarding the control, education, and health of the child; and the right, as well as the duty, to prepare the child for additional obligations, which includes the teaching of moral standards, religious beliefs, and elements of good citizenship." 4 California Family Law § 60.02[1][b] (C. Markey ed. 1987) (footnotes omitted). All parental rights, including visitation, were automatically denied by denying Michael status as the father. While Cal. Civ. Code Ann. § 4601 places it within the discretionary power of a court to award visitation rights to a nonparent, the Superior Court here, affirmed by the Court of Appeal, held that California law denies visitation, against the wishes of the mother, to a putative father who has been prevented by § 621 from establishing his paternity.

Michael raises two related challenges to the constitutionality of § 621. First, he asserts that requirements of procedural due process prevent the State from terminating his liberty interest in his relationship with his child without affording him an opportunity to demonstrate his paternity in an evidentiary hearing. We believe this claim derives from a fundamental misconception of the nature of the California statute. While § 621 is phrased in terms of a presumption, that rule of evidence is the implementation of a substantive rule of law. California declares it to be, except in limited circumstances, *irrelevant* for paternity purposes whether a child conceived during, and born into, an existing marriage was begotten by someone other than the husband and had a prior relationship with him. * * * [T]he conclusive presumption not only expresses the State's substantive policy but also furthers it, excluding inquiries into the child's paternity that would be destructive of family integrity and privacy.[1]

* * *

Michael contends as a matter of substantive due process that, because he has established a parental relationship with Victoria, protection of Gerald's and Carole's marital union is an insufficient state interest to support termination of that relationship. This argument is, of course, predicated on the assertion that Michael has a constitutionally protected liberty interest in his relationship with Victoria.

It is an established part of our constitutional jurisprudence that the term "liberty" in the Due Process Clause extends beyond freedom from physical restraint. *See, e.g., Pierce v. Soc'y of Sisters,* 268 U.S. 510 (1925); *Meyer v. Nebraska,* 262 U.S. 390 (1923). * * * In an attempt to limit and guide interpretation of the Clause, we have insisted not merely that the interest denominated as a "liberty" be "fundamental" (a concept that, in isolation, is hard to objectify), but also that it be an interest traditionally protected by our society.[2] As we have put it, the Due Process Clause affords only those protections "so rooted in the traditions and conscience of our people as to be ranked as fundamental." *Snyder v. Massachusetts,* 291 U.S. 97, 105 (1934) (CARDOZO, J.). * * *

* * * Michael reads the landmark case of *Stanley v. Illinois,* 405 U.S. 645 (1972), and * * * subsequent cases * * * as establishing that a liberty interest is created by biological fatherhood plus an established parental relationship—factors that exist in the present case as well. We think that distorts the rationale of those cases. As we view them, they rest not upon such isolated factors but upon the historic respect—indeed, sanctity would not be too strong a term—traditionally accorded to the relationships that develop within the unitary family.[3] In *Stanley,* for example, we forbade the

---

[1]   In those circumstances in which California allows a natural father to rebut the presumption of legitimacy of a child born to a married woman, *e.g.,* where the husband is impotent or sterile, or where the husband and wife have not been cohabiting, it is more likely that the husband already knows the child is not his, and thus less likely that the paternity hearing will disrupt an otherwise harmonious and apparently exclusive marital relationship.

[2]   We do not understand what Justice BRENNAN has in mind by an interest "that society traditionally has thought important . . . without protecting it." The protection need not take the form of an explicit constitutional provision or statutory guarantee, but it must at least exclude (all that is necessary to decide the present case) a societal tradition of enacting laws *denying* the interest. Nor do we understand why our practice of limiting the Due Process Clause to traditionally protected interests turns the Clause "into a redundancy[.]" Its purpose is to prevent future generations from lightly casting aside important traditional values—not to enable this Court to invent new ones.

[3]   Justice BRENNAN asserts that only a "pinched conception of 'the family' " would exclude Michael, Carole, and Victoria from protection. We disagree. The family unit accorded traditional respect in our society, which we have referred to as the "unitary family," is typified, of course, by the marital family, but also includes the household of unmarried parents and their children. Perhaps the concept can be expanded even beyond this, but it will bear no resemblance to traditionally respected relationships—and will thus cease to have any constitutional significance—if it is stretched so far as to include the relationship established between a married woman, her

destruction of such a family when, upon the death of the mother, the State had sought to remove children from the custody of a father who had lived with and supported them and their mother for 18 years. As Justice Powell stated for the plurality in *Moore v. East Cleveland*, 431 U.S. 494, 503 (1977): "Our decisions establish that the Constitution protects the sanctity of the family precisely because the institution of the family is deeply rooted in this Nation's history and tradition."

Thus, the legal issue in the present case reduces to whether the relationship between persons in the situation of Michael and Victoria has been treated as a protected family unit under the historic practices of our society, or whether on any other basis it has been accorded special protection. We think it impossible to find that it has. In fact, quite to the contrary, our traditions have protected the marital family (Gerald, Carole, and the child they acknowledge to be theirs) against the sort of claim Michael asserts.[4]

The presumption of legitimacy was a fundamental principle of the common law. Traditionally, that presumption could be rebutted only by proof that a husband was incapable of procreation or had had no access to his wife during the relevant period. As explained by Blackstone, nonaccess could only be proved "if the husband be out of the kingdom of England (or, as the law somewhat loosely phrases it, *extra quatuor maria* [beyond the four seas]) for above nine months. . . ." 1 Blackstone's Commentaries 456 (J. Chitty ed. 1826). And, under the common law both in England and here, "neither husband nor wife [could] be a witness to prove access or nonaccess." James Schouler, A Treatise on the Law of the Domestic Relations § 225, at 306 (3 ed. 1882); A Century of Family Law: 1857–1957, at 158 [R.H. Graveson & F.R. Crane eds., 1957). The primary policy rationale underlying the common law's severe restrictions on rebuttal of the presumption appears to have been an aversion to declaring children illegitimate, thereby depriving them of rights of inheritance and succession, and likely making them wards of the state. A secondary policy concern was the interest in promoting the "peace and tranquility of States and families," Schouler, *supra* § 225, at 304, a goal that is obviously impaired by facilitating suits against husband and wife asserting that their children are illegitimate. Even though, as bastardy laws became less harsh,

---

lover, and their child, during a 3-month sojourn in St. Thomas, or during a subsequent 8-month period when, if he happened to be in Los Angeles, he stayed with her and the child.

4   Justice BRENNAN insists that in determining whether a liberty interest exists we must look at Michael's relationship with Victoria in isolation, without reference to the circumstance that Victoria's mother was married to someone else when the child was conceived, and that that woman and her husband wish to raise the child as their own. See *post*, at 2353. We cannot imagine what compels this strange procedure of looking at the act which is assertedly the subject of a liberty interest in isolation from its effect upon other people-rather like inquiring whether there is a liberty interest in firing a gun where the case at hand happens to involve its discharge into another person's body. The logic of Justice BRENNAN's position leads to the conclusion that if Michael had begotten Victoria by rape, that fact would in no way affect his possession of a liberty interest in his relationship with her.

"[j]udges in both [England and the United States] gradually widened the acceptable range of evidence that could be offered by spouses, and placed restraints on the 'four seas rule' . . . [,] the law retained a strong bias against ruling the children of married women illegitimate." Michael Grossberg, Governing the Hearth: Law and the Family in Nineteenth Century America 202 (1985).

We have found nothing in the older sources, nor in the older cases, addressing specifically the power of the natural father to assert parental rights over a child born into a woman's existing marriage with another man. Since it is Michael's burden to establish that such a power (at least where the natural father has established a relationship with the child) is so deeply embedded within our traditions as to be a fundamental right, the lack of evidence alone might defeat his case. But the evidence shows that even in modern times—when, as we have noted, the rigid protection of the marital family has in other respects been relaxed—the ability of a person in Michael's position to claim paternity has not been generally acknowledged. * * *

Moreover, even if it were clear that one in Michael's position generally possesses, and has generally always possessed, standing to challenge the marital child's legitimacy, that would still not establish Michael's case. As noted earlier, what is at issue here is not entitlement to a state pronouncement that Victoria was begotten by Michael. It is no conceivable denial of constitutional right for a State to decline to declare facts unless some legal consequence hinges upon the requested declaration. What Michael asserts here is a right to have himself declared the natural father and thereby to obtain parental prerogatives.[5] * * * What counts is whether the States in fact award substantive parental rights to the natural father of a child conceived within, and born into, an extant marital union that wishes to embrace the child. We are not aware of a single case, old or new, that has done so. This is not the stuff of which fundamental rights qualifying as liberty interests are made.[6]

---

[5]   According to Justice BRENNAN, Michael does not claim-and in order to prevail here need not claim-a substantive right to maintain a parental relationship with Victoria, but merely the right to "a hearing on the issue" of his paternity. *Post*, at 2359, n. 12. "Michael's challenge . . . does not depend," we are told, "on his ability ultimately to obtain visitation rights." *Post*, at 2354. To be sure it does not depend upon his ability ultimately to *obtain* those rights, but it surely depends upon his *asserting a claim* to those rights, which is precisely what Justice BRENNAN denies. We cannot grasp the concept of a "right to a hearing" on the part of a person who claims no substantive entitlement that the hearing will assertedly vindicate.

[6]   Justice BRENNAN criticizes our methodology in using historical traditions specifically relating to the rights of an adulterous natural father, rather than inquiring more generally "whether parenthood is an interest that historically has received our attention and protection." There seems to us no basis for the contention that this methodology is "nove[l.]" For example, in *Bowers v. Hardwick*, 478 U.S. 186 (1986), we noted that at the time the Fourteenth Amendment was ratified all but 5 of the 37 States had criminal sodomy laws, that all 50 of the States had such laws prior to 1961, and that 24 States and the District of Columbia continued to have them; and we concluded from that record, regarding that very specific aspect of sexual conduct, that "to claim that a right to engage in such conduct is 'deeply rooted in this Nation's history and tradition' or

* * *

In *Lehr v. Robertson,* a case involving a natural father's attempt to block his child's adoption by the unwed mother's new husband, we observed that "[t]he significance of the biological connection is that it offers the natural father an opportunity that no other male possesses to develop a relationship with his offspring," 463 U.S. at 262, and we assumed that the Constitution might require some protection of that opportunity, *id.* at 262–65. Where, however, the child is born into an extant marital family, the natural father's unique opportunity conflicts with the similarly unique opportunity of the husband of the marriage; and it is not unconstitutional for the State to give categorical preference to the latter. * * *

* * *

IV

We have never had occasion to decide whether a child has a liberty interest, symmetrical with that of her parent, in maintaining her filial relationship. We need not do so here because, even assuming that such a right exists, Victoria's claim must fail. Victoria's due process challenge is, if anything, weaker than Michael's. Her basic claim is not that California has erred in preventing her from establishing that Michael, not Gerald, should stand as her legal father. Rather, she claims a due process right to maintain filial relationships with both Michael and Gerald. This assertion merits little discussion, for, whatever the merits of the guardian ad litem's belief that such an arrangement can be of great psychological benefit to a child, the claim that a State must recognize multiple fatherhood has no support in the history or traditions of this country. Moreover, even if we were to construe Victoria's argument as forwarding the lesser proposition that, whatever her status vis-à-vis Gerald, she has a liberty interest in maintaining a filial relationship with her natural father, Michael, we find that, at best, her claim is the obverse of Michael's and fails for the same reasons.

* * *

'implicit in the concept of ordered liberty' is, at best, facetious." *Id.* at 194. In *Roe v. Wade,* 410 U.S. 113 (1973), we spent about a fifth of our opinion negating the proposition that there was a longstanding tradition of laws proscribing abortion. *Id.* at 129–41.

We do not understand why, having rejected our focus upon the societal tradition regarding the natural father's rights vis-à-vis a child whose mother is married to another man, Justice BRENNAN would choose to focus instead upon "parenthood." Why should the relevant category not be even more general—perhaps "family relationships"; or "personal relationships"; or even "emotional attachments in general"? Though the dissent has no basis for the level of generality it would select, we do: We refer to the most specific level at which a relevant tradition protecting, or denying protection to, the asserted right can be identified. If, for example, there were no societal tradition, either way, regarding the rights of the natural father of a child adulterously conceived, we would have to consult, and (if possible) reason from, the traditions regarding natural fathers in general. But there is such a more specific tradition, and it unqualifiedly denies protection to such a parent.

The judgment of the California Court of Appeal is *Affirmed*.

JUSTICE O'CONNOR, with whom JUSTICE KENNEDY joins, concurring in part.

I concur in all but footnote 6 of Justice SCALIA's opinion. This footnote sketches a mode of historical analysis to be used when identifying liberty interests protected by the Due Process Clause of the Fourteenth Amendment that may be somewhat inconsistent with our past decisions in this area. * * *

JUSTICE STEVENS, concurring, in the judgment.

* * *

Under the circumstances of the case before us, Michael was given a fair opportunity to show that he is Victoria's natural father, that he had developed a relationship with her, and that her interests would be served by granting him visitation rights. On the other hand, the record also shows that after its rather shaky start, the marriage between Carole and Gerald developed a stability that now provides Victoria with a loving and harmonious family home. In the circumstances of this case, I find nothing fundamentally unfair about the exercise of a judge's discretion that, in the end, allows the mother to decide whether her child's best interests would be served by allowing the natural father visitation privileges. Because I am convinced that the trial judge had the authority under state law both to hear Michael's plea for visitation rights and to grant him such rights if Victoria's best interests so warranted, I am satisfied that the California statutory scheme is consistent with the Due Process Clause of the Fourteenth Amendment.

I therefore concur in the Court's judgment of affirmance.

JUSTICE BRENNAN, with whom JUSTICE MARSHALL and JUSTICE BLACKMUN join, dissenting.

In a case that has yielded so many opinions as has this one, it is fruitful to begin by emphasizing the common ground shared by a majority of this Court. Five Members of the Court refuse to foreclose "the possibility that a natural father might ever have a constitutionally protected interest in his relationship with a child whose mother was married to, and cohabiting with, another man at the time of the child's conception and birth." Five Justices agree that the flaw inhering in a conclusive presumption that terminates a constitutionally protected interest without any hearing whatsoever is a *procedural* one. Four Members of the Court agree that Michael H. has a liberty interest in his relationship with Victoria, and one assumes for purposes of this case that he does.

In contrast, only one other Member of the Court fully endorses Mr. Justice SCALIA's view of the proper method of analyzing questions arising under the Due Process Clause. Nevertheless, because the plurality opinion's exclusively historical analysis portends a significant and unfortunate departure from our prior cases and from sound constitutional decisionmaking, I devote a substantial portion of my discussion to it.

I

Once we recognized that the "liberty" protected by the Due Process Clause of the Fourteenth Amendment encompasses more than freedom from bodily restraint, today's plurality opinion emphasizes, the concept was cut loose from one natural limitation on its meaning. This innovation paved the way, so the plurality hints, for judges to substitute their own preferences for those of elected officials. Dissatisfied with this supposedly unbridled and uncertain state of affairs, the plurality casts about for another limitation on the concept of liberty.

It finds this limitation in "tradition." Apparently oblivious to the fact that this concept can be as malleable and as elusive as "liberty" itself, the plurality pretends that tradition places a discernible border around the Constitution. The pretense is seductive; it would be comforting to believe that a search for "tradition" involves nothing more idiosyncratic or complicated than poring through dusty volumes on American history. * * *

Even if we could agree, moreover, on the content and significance of particular traditions, we still would be forced to identify the point at which a tradition becomes firm enough to be relevant to our definition of liberty and the moment at which it becomes too obsolete to be relevant any longer. The plurality supplies no objective means by which we might make these determinations. Indeed, as soon as the plurality sees signs that the tradition upon which it bases its decision (the laws denying putative fathers like Michael standing to assert paternity) is crumbling, it shifts ground and says that the case has nothing to do with that tradition, after all. "[W]hat is at issue here," the plurality asserts after canvassing the law on paternity suits, "is not entitlement to a state pronouncement that Victoria was begotten by Michael." But that is precisely what is at issue here, and the plurality's last-minute denial of this fact dramatically illustrates the subjectivity of its own analysis.

It is ironic that an approach so utterly dependent on tradition is so indifferent to our precedents. * * *

It is not that tradition has been irrelevant to our prior decisions. Throughout our decisionmaking in this important area runs the theme that certain interests and practices—freedom from physical restraint, marriage, childbearing, childrearing, and others—form the core of our definition of "liberty." Our solicitude for these interests is partly the result of the fact that the Due Process Clause would seem an empty promise if it did not protect them, and partly the result of the historical and traditional importance of these interests in our society. In deciding cases arising under the Due Process Clause, therefore, we have considered whether the concrete limitation under consideration impermissibly impinges upon one of these more generalized interests.

Today's plurality, however, does not ask whether parenthood is an interest that historically has received our attention and protection; the answer to that question is too clear for dispute. Instead, the plurality asks whether the specific variety of parenthood under consideration—a natural father's relationship with a child whose mother is married to another man—has enjoyed such protection.

If we had looked to tradition with such specificity in past cases, many a decision would have reached a different result. Surely the use of contraceptives by unmarried couples, or even by married couples * * * and even the right to raise one's natural but illegitimate children, were not "interest[s] traditionally protected by our society," at the time of their consideration by this Court. * * *

* * * In the plurality's constitutional universe, we may not take notice of the fact that the original reasons for the conclusive presumption of paternity are out of place in a world in which blood tests can prove virtually beyond a shadow of a doubt who sired a particular child and in which the fact of illegitimacy no longer plays the burdensome and stigmatizing role it once did. Nor, in the plurality's world, may we deny "tradition" its full scope by pointing out that the rationale for the conventional rule has changed over the years, as has the rationale for Cal. Evid. Code Ann. § 621[1]; instead, our task is simply to identify a rule denying the asserted interest and not to ask whether the basis for that rule—which is the true reflection of the values undergirding it—has changed too often or too recently to call the rule embodying that rationale a "tradition." Moreover, by describing the decisive question as whether Michael's and Victoria's interest is one that has been "traditionally *protected by* our society," (emphasis added), rather than one that society traditionally has thought important (with or without protecting it), and by suggesting that our sole function is to "*discern* the society's views," (emphasis added), the plurality acts as if the only purpose of the Due Process Clause is to confirm the importance of interests already protected by a majority of the States. Transforming the protection afforded by the Due Process Clause into a redundancy mocks those who, with care and purpose, wrote the Fourteenth Amendment.

In construing the Fourteenth Amendment to offer shelter only to those interests specifically protected by historical practice, moreover, the

[handwritten margin note: Dissent says that the plurality is ignoring modern science (blood tests)]

---

[1]   See *In re Marriage of Sharyne and Stephen B.*, 124 Cal.App.3d 524, 528–531, 177 Cal.Rptr. 429, 431–433 (1981) (noting that California courts initially justified conclusive presumption of paternity on the ground that biological paternity was impossible to prove, but that the preservation of family integrity became the rule's paramount justification when paternity tests became reliable).

plurality ignores the kind of society in which our Constitution exists. We are not an assimilative, homogeneous society, but a facilitative, pluralistic one, in which we must be willing to abide someone else's unfamiliar or even repellent practice because the same tolerant impulse protects our own idiosyncrasies. Even if we can agree, therefore, that "family" and "parenthood" are part of the good life, it is absurd to assume that we can agree on the content of those terms and destructive to pretend that we do. In a community such as ours, "liberty" must include the freedom not to conform. The plurality today squashes this freedom by requiring specific approval from history before protecting anything in the name of liberty.

* * *

II

The plurality's reworking of our interpretive approach is all the more troubling because it is unnecessary. This is not a case in which we face a "new" kind of interest, one that requires us to consider for the first time whether the Constitution protects it. On the contrary, we confront an interest—that of a parent and child in their relationship with each other— that was among the first that this Court acknowledged in its cases defining the "liberty" protected by the Constitution, *see, e.g., Meyer v. Nebraska,* 262 U.S. 390, 399 (1923); *Skinner v. Oklahoma,* 316 U.S. 535, 541 (1942); *Prince v. Massachusetts,* 321 U.S. 158, 166 (1944), and I think I am safe in saying that no one doubts the wisdom or validity of those decisions. Where the interest under consideration is a parent-child relationship, we need not ask, over and over again, whether that interest is one that society traditionally protects.

Thus, to describe the issue in this case as whether the relationship existing between Michael and Victoria "has been treated as a protected family unit under the historic practices of our society, or whether on any other basis it has been accorded special protection," is to reinvent the wheel. The better approach—indeed, the one commanded by our prior cases and by common sense—is to ask whether the specific parent-child relationship under consideration is close enough to the interests that we already have protected to be deemed an aspect of "liberty" as well. On the facts before us, therefore, the question is not what "level of generality" should be used to describe the relationship between Michael and Victoria, but whether the relationship under consideration is sufficiently substantial to qualify as a liberty interest under our prior cases.

On four prior occasions, we have considered whether unwed fathers have a constitutionally protected interest in their relationships with their children. *See Stanley v. Illinois,* 405 U.S. 645 (1972); *Quilloin v. Walcott,* 434 U.S. 246 (1978); *Caban v. Mohammed,* 441 U.S. 380 (1979); and *Lehr v. Robertson,* 463 U.S. 248 (1983). Though different in factual and legal circumstances, these cases have produced a unifying theme: although an unwed father's biological link to his child does not, in and of itself, guarantee him a constitutional stake in his relationship with that child, such a link combined with a substantial parent-child relationship will do so.[2] "When an unwed father demonstrates a full commitment to the responsibilities of parenthood by 'com[ing] forward to participate in the rearing of his child,' . . . his interest in personal contact with his child acquires substantial protection under the Due Process Clause. At that point it may be said that he 'act[s] as a father toward his children.'" *Lehr*, 463 U.S. at 261. This commitment is why Mr. Stanley and Mr. Caban won; why Mr. Quilloin and Mr. Lehr lost; and why Michael H. should prevail today. Michael H. is almost certainly Victoria D.'s natural father, has lived with her as her father, has contributed to her support, and has from the beginning sought to strengthen and maintain his relationship with her.

Claiming that the intent of these cases was to protect the "unitary family," the plurality waves *Stanley, Quilloin, Caban,* and *Lehr* aside. In evaluating the plurality's dismissal of these precedents, it is essential to identify its conception of the "unitary family." If, by acknowledging that *Stanley* et al. sought to protect "the relationships that develop within the unitary family," the plurality meant only to describe the kinds of relationships that develop when parents and children live together (formally or informally) as a family, then the plurality's vision of these cases would be correct. But that is not the plurality's message. Though it pays lipservice to the idea that marriage is not the crucial fact in denying constitutional protection to the relationship between Michael and Victoria, the plurality cannot mean what it says.

The evidence is undisputed that Michael, Victoria, and Carole did live together as a family; that is, they shared the same household, Victoria called Michael "Daddy," Michael contributed to Victoria's support, and he is eager to continue his relationship with her. Yet they are not, in the plurality's view, a "unitary family," whereas Gerald, Carole, and Victoria do compose such a family. The only difference between these two sets of relationships, however, is the fact of marriage. The plurality, indeed, expressly recognizes that marriage is the critical fact in denying Michael a constitutionally protected stake in his relationship with Victoria: no fewer than six times, the plurality refers to Michael as the "*adulterous* natural father" (emphasis added) or the like. However, the very premise of *Stanley* and the cases following it is that marriage is not decisive in answering the question whether the Constitution protects the parental relationship under consideration. These cases are, after all, important precisely because they involve the rights of *unwed* fathers. It is important to remember, moreover,

[margin note:] ✱ Dissent: Marriage is not decisive

---

[2]   The plurality's claim that "[t]he logic of [my] position leads to the conclusion that if Michael had begotten Victoria by rape, that fact would in no way affect his possession of a liberty interest in his relationship with her," *ante*, at 2342, n. 4, ignores my observation that a mere biological connection is insufficient to establish a liberty interest on the part of an unwed father.

that in *Quilloin, Caban,* and *Lehr,* the putative father's demands would have disrupted a "unitary family" as the plurality defines it; in each case, the husband of the child's mother sought to adopt the child over the objections of the natural father. Significantly, our decisions in those cases in no way relied on the need to protect the marital family. Hence the plurality's claim that *Stanley, Quilloin, Caban,* and *Lehr* were about the "unitary family," as that family is defined by today's plurality, is surprising indeed.

The plurality's exclusive rather than inclusive definition of the "unitary family" is out of step with other decisions as well. This pinched conception of "the family," crucial as it is in rejecting Michael's and Victoria's claims of a liberty interest, is jarring in light of our many cases preventing the States from denying important interests or statuses to those whose situations do not fit the government's narrow view of the family. * * *

* * *

IV

The atmosphere surrounding today's decision is one of make-believe. Beginning with the suggestion that the situation confronting us here does not repeat itself every day in every corner of the country, moving on to the claim that it is tradition alone that supplies the details of the liberty that the Constitution protects, and passing finally to the notion that the Court always has recognized a cramped vision of "the family," today's decision lets stand California's pronouncement that Michael—whom blood tests show to a 98 percent probability to be Victoria's father—is not Victoria's father. When and if the Court awakes to reality, it will find a world very different from the one it expects.

JUSTICE WHITE, with whom JUSTICE BRENNAN joins, dissenting.

California law, as the plurality describes it, tells us that, except in limited circumstances, California declares it to be "*irrelevant* for paternity purposes whether a child conceived during, and born into, an existing marriage was begotten by someone other than the husband" (emphasis in original). This I do not accept, for the fact that Michael H. is the biological father of Victoria is to me highly relevant to whether he has rights, as a father or otherwise, with respect to the child. Because I believe that Michael H. has a liberty interest that cannot be denied without due process of the law, I must dissent.

I

Like JUSTICES BRENNAN, MARSHALL, BLACKMUN, AND STEVENS, I do not agree with the plurality opinion's conclusion that a natural father can never "have a constitutionally protected interest in his relationship with a child whose mother was married to, and cohabiting with, another man at the time of the child's conception and birth." Prior cases here have recognized the liberty interest of a father in his relationship with his child. In none of these cases did we indicate that the father's rights were dependent on the marital status of the mother or biological father. The basic principle enunciated in the Court's unwed father cases is that an unwed father who has demonstrated a sufficient commitment to his paternity by way of personal, financial, or custodial responsibilities has a protected liberty interest in a relationship with his child.

* * *

In the case now before us, Michael H. is not a father unwilling to assume his responsibilities as a parent. To the contrary, he is a father who has asserted his interests in raising and providing for his child since the very time of the child's birth. In contrast to the father in *Lehr*, Michael had begun to develop a relationship with his daughter. There is no dispute on this point. Michael contributed to the child's support. Michael and Victoria lived together (albeit intermittently, given Carole's itinerant lifestyle). There is a personal and emotional relationship between Michael and Victoria, who grew up calling him "Daddy." Michael held Victoria out as his daughter and contributed to the child's financial support. (Even appellee concedes that Michael has "made greater efforts and had more success in establishing a father-child relationship" than did Mr. Lehr.) The mother has never denied, and indeed has admitted, that Michael is Victoria's father. * * *

[handwritten margin note: * Michael H. is a willing father]

* * *

II

* * *

As the Court has said: "The significance of the biological connection is that it offers the natural father an opportunity that no other male possesses to develop a relationship with his offspring. If he grasps that opportunity and accepts some measure of responsibility for the child's future, he may enjoy the blessings of the parent-child relationship and make uniquely valuable contributions to the child's development." *Lehr*, 463 U.S. at 262. It is as if this passage was addressed to Michael. Yet the plurality today recants. Michael eagerly grasped the opportunity to have a relationship with his daughter (he lived with her; he declared her to be his child; he provided financial support for her) and still, with today's opinion, his opportunity has vanished. He has been rendered a stranger to his child.

* * *

NOTES AND QUESTIONS

1. *Conflicting rights.* In *Michael H.,* Justice Brennan argued that the Court should determine whether a liberty interest exists without reference to the facts that Carole was married to someone else when Victoria was conceived, and that Carole and Gerald wished to raise Victoria. Is this position reasonable? Is Justice Scalia's response that this position "leads to the conclusion that if Michael had begotten Victoria by rape, that fact would in no way affect his possession of a liberty interest in his relationship with her" persuasive? Is Justice Brennan correct in alleging that the opinion ultimately relies on a traditional view of marriage? *See* June Carbone & Naomi Cahn, *Which Ties Bind? Redefining the Parent-Child Relationship in an Age of Genetic Certainty,* 11 Wm. & Mary Bill Rts. J. 1011, 1042 (2003).

2. *Finding the father.* Professor Melissa Murray argues that "the bulk of the plurality's decision focused not on the parent-child relationship between Victoria and Michael, or Michael's rights as a biological father, but on the marital relationship between Carole and Gerald." Melissa Murray, *What's So New About the New Illegitimacy?,* 20 Am. U.J. Gender Soc. Pol'y & L. 387, 410 (2012). Professor Janet L. Dolgin goes a step further, arguing that after *Michael H.,* "[a] biological father does protect his paternity by developing a social relationship with his child, but this step demands the creation of a family, a step itself depending upon an appropriate relationship between the man and his child's mother." Janet L. Dolgin, *Just a Gene: Judicial Assumptions About Parenthood,* 40 UCLA L. Rev. 637, 650, 671 (1993). Why do you think Michael fought so hard to establish a parental relationship with Victoria?

3. *Children's interests in identifying their biological fathers.* Beyond the possibility of additional financial resources, a child might have several interests. First, knowing the identity of the father helps the child obtain information about medical history and genetic heritage. Second, it might benefit the child to establish a parental relationship. Moreover, *society* may have interests in ensuring that children receive adequate financial resources from their fathers, thereby decreasing their need for public assistance. Some suggest that societal interests might also favor fathers playing a parenting role in their children's lives, issues discussed further in Chapters 12 and 13.

4. *Paternity testing.* Prior to the advent of reliable blood tests, paternity was sometimes determined by family resemblance. Beginning in the 1980s, the Human Leukocyte Antigen (HLA) blood-test system, which detects antigens on white blood cells, was used in conjunction with red blood cell tests to disprove paternity. Today, DNA testing can establish or disestablish paternity at a greater than 99% accuracy rate. Does the statutory presumption that decided *Michael H.* make sense now that paternity can be established with virtual certainty? Following the Supreme Court's opinion, California amended the marital presumption and allows the presumed parent or the child's guardian *ad litem* to file a paternity action within two years of the child's birth. Cal.

Fam. Code § 7541(b) (2019). What arguments do you see for the two-year limitation?

5.   *Dual paternity.* Should the law ever recognize that a child could have two fathers in addition to a mother? This is the Louisiana dual paternity solution. Louisiana recognizes that a child may have both a biological and a "legal" father. *See Smith v. Cole*, 553 So.2d 847, 854 (La. 1989). The focus, however, is child support, not custody. Josh Gupta-Kagan, *Non-Exclusive Adoption and Child Welfare*, 66 Ala. L. Rev. 715, 747 (2015). Some legal scholars observe that having several fathers is "a social reality but not a legal category," given "our knowledge of the existence of multiple fathers, whether birthfathers, stepfathers, psychological fathers or other categories." Nancy E. Dowd, *Multiple Parents/Multiple Fathers*, 9 J. L. Fam. Stud. 231, 231 (2007). Should the law accord legal rights to all of these individuals? As discussed below, some states have recognized the possibility of three parents.

2. Parentage and Infants

From *Stanley* to *Michael H.*, the Supreme Court's nonmarital father decisions concerned children who were at least a few years old when the dispute arose. Subsequently, states confronted recurring issues concerning the rights of nonmarital parents to infants.

Indeed, many transfers of children to nonrelative adoptive parents occur at birth or within days (but not years) thereafter. What are the nonmarital father's constitutional rights to veto an adoption at the child's birth, when the nonmarital father will not have had any opportunity yet to "develop a relationship" with the child? What are the nonmarital father's constitutional rights where the biological mother, seeking to thwart his efforts to develop the requisite relationship with the child, places the baby for adoption after hiding the child from the father, after untruthfully asserting that she does not know the father's identity or whereabouts, after refusing to name the father, after forging his signature on consent documents, or after knowingly naming the wrong man? *See* David D. Meyer, *Family Ties: Solving the Constitutional Dilemma of the Faultless Father*, 41 Ariz. L. Rev. 753 (1999).

The Supreme Court confronted some of these issues in *Adoptive Couple v. Baby Girl,* 570 U.S. 637, 637–639 (2013). Christy Maldonado and Dusten Brown, a member of the Cherokee nation, were engaged when, in early 2009, Maldonado told Brown, who was then serving in the U.S. Army, that she was pregnant. He asked her to move up the date of the wedding and refused to provide any financial support until after they married. She broke off the engagement and ultimately terminated contact with him before the child (known as "Baby Veronica") was born. Prior to Veronica's birth, Maldonado asked Brown, via text message, if he would rather pay child support or relinquish his parental rights. He responded, via a text message to Maldonado, that he relinquished his parental rights. The mother, who was not Indian, sought to place the child for adoption and found Matt and Melanie Capobianco, who supported her emotionally and financially during the pregnancy and were in the delivery room when she gave birth in September, 2009. The Capobiancos filed adoption papers shortly afterwards,

> but did not serve or otherwise notify Father of the adoption action until January 6, 2010, approximately four months after Baby Girl was born and days before Father was scheduled to deploy to Iraq. On that date outside of a mall near his base, a process server presented Father with legal papers entitled "Acceptance of Service and Answer of Defendant," which stated he was not contesting the adoption of Baby Girl and that he waived the thirty day waiting period and notice of the hearing. Father testified he believed he was relinquishing his rights to Mother and did not realize he consented to Baby Girl's adoption by another family until after he signed the papers. Upon realizing that Mother had relinquished her rights to Appellants, Father testified, "I then tried to grab the paper up. [The process server] told me that I could not grab that [sic] because . . . I would be going to jail if I was to do any harm to the paper."

Adoptive Couple v. Baby Girl, 570 U.S. 637, 645 (2013).

Under South Carolina law, a nonmarital father can establish parental rights under several different circumstances, including when he has: 1) "openly lived with the child or the child's mother" for six months and "openly held himself out to be" the father during this period; or 2) provided "a fair and reasonable sum" to support the child or the mother's pregnancy. S.C. Code § 63–9–310(A)(5) (2018). Brown had not complied with any of the listed requirements.

The Court held that the federal Indian Child Welfare Act (ICWA), 25 U.S.C. §§ 1901–1963 (2018), did not prevent the adoption of Veronica over the objection of her biological father, a member of the Cherokee Nation. Although the case focused on the impact of federal law respecting preservation of parental rights for Native Americans, it shows the importance to unmarried men of establishing paternity pursuant to state law if they ever want to claim any of the rights associated with parenthood, including the ability to consent—or to withhold consent—to an adoption.

The majority opinion by Justice Alito opined that the Court need not decide whether Brown was a "parent" under the ICWA but, assuming for the sake of argument that he was, the Act did not bar termination of his parental rights because he had never had "custody" of the child. 133 S. Ct. at 2557. The majority stressed that this reading was consistent with the ICWA's aim of addressing the "unwarranted removal of Indian children from Indian families due to the cultural insensitivity and biases of social workers and state courts"—a goal not implicated in this case. *Id.* at 666.

Justice Sotomayor vehemently dissented, joined in full by Justices Ginsburg and Kagan and, in large part, by Justice Scalia, who also authored his own, brief dissent. Justice Sotomayor stated: *Dissent*

> Although the Constitution does not compel the protection of a biological father's parent-child relationship until he has taken steps to cultivate it, this Court has nevertheless recognized that "the biological connection . . . offers the natural father an opportunity that no other male possesses to develop a relationship with his offspring." *Lehr v. Robertson* (1983). Federal recognition of a parent-child relationship between a birth father and his child is consistent with ICWA's purpose of providing greater protection for the familial bonds between Indian parents and their children than state law may afford.

Id. at 669–670 (Sotomayor, J. dissenting).

Upon remand, the South Carolina Supreme Court promptly ordered the family court to finalize the adoption petition. *Adoptive Couple v. Baby Girl*, 746 S.E.2d 51 (S.C. 2014).

NOTES AND QUESTIONS

1.   *Who is the parent?* Consider what actions the father needed to take under South Carolina law to be deemed a parent entitled to withhold consent to an adoption. Do these seem appropriate requirements, or should his biological connection to the child have been sufficient? Did the mother deal fairly with the father?

2.   *Showing respect.* In his dissent, Justice Scalia charged that the opinion "needlessly demeans the rights of parenthood. It has been the constant practice of the common law to respect the entitlement of those who bring a child into the world to raise that child. . . . This father wants to raise his daughter, and the statute amply protects his right to do so. There is no reason in law or policy to dilute that protection." *Adoptive Couple*, 133 S. Ct. at 2571–72 (Scalia, J. dissenting). Does the decision "demean" the rights of all parents, both mothers and fathers? Do the statutory rights of the ICWA sufficiently distinguish this case from *Michael H*, where Justice Scalia ruled against an unmarried father? Justice Sotomayor alleged that because the majority focused on pre-existing custody rights instead of other parental rights, the majority's opinion would not protect a noncustodial father even if he had "actively participated in the[ ] child's upbringing." *Id.* at 2578 (Sotomayor, J. dissenting). For commentary on the differing approaches to father's rights, *see Indian Child Welfare Act—Termination of Parental Rights*—Adoptive Couple v. Baby Girl, 127 Harv. L. Rev. 368, 370 (2013).

B. STATUTORY APPROACHES TO RECOGNIZING MARITAL AND NONMARITAL PARENTS

While *Michael H.* articulated constitutional parameters for protecting the rights of marital and nonmarital parents, it did not resolve all issues concerning legal parenthood. As *Adoptive Couple* shows, states remain free to develop their own distinct systems for determining the parents. This Section explores the approach of the Uniform Parentage Act before turning to other state efforts to recognize parenthood.

1. The Uniform Parentage Act: Marital and Nonmarital Parents

In 1973, the National Conference of Commissioners on Uniform State Laws (now known as the Uniform Law Commission) promulgated the Uniform Parentage Act (UPA), a then-revolutionary set of laws for determining parentage that was designed to establish more consistency between states. Nineteen states adopted the UPA. Michael Morgan, *The New Uniform Parentage Act*, 25 Fam. Adv. 11 (2002). The UPA reflected Supreme Court rulings that banned discrimination based on illegitimacy in a variety of circumstances. The UPA was substantially revised in 2002 and again in 2017 to account for changing family structures and scientific developments in parentage, including advances in genetic testing and reproductive technology; and its language became gender neutral, as seen in the following excerpt from the most recent version.

the statute determines parentage

UNIFORM PARENTAGE ACT
(2017).

* * *

SECTION 201. ESTABLISHMENT OF PARENT-CHILD RELATIONSHIP. A parent-child relationship is established between an individual and a child if:

(1) the individual gives birth to the child[, except as otherwise provided in [Article] 8];

(2) there is a presumption under Section 204 of the individual's parentage of the child, unless the presumption is overcome in a judicial proceeding or a valid denial of parentage is made under [Article] 3;

(3) the individual is adjudicated a parent of the child * * *;

(4) the individual adopts the child;

(5) the individual acknowledges parentage of the child under [Article] 3, unless the acknowledgment is rescinded under Section 308 or successfully challenged under [this Act]; [or]

(6) the individual's parentage of the child is established under [the assisted reproduction provisions of this Act]; or

(7) the individual's parentage of the child is established under [the surrogacy Article].

* * *

SECTION 204. PRESUMPTION OF PARENTAGE.

(a) An individual is presumed to be a parent of a child if:

(1) except as otherwise provided [under state law]:

(A) the individual and the woman who gave birth to the child are married to each other and the child is born during the marriage, whether the marriage is or could be declared invalid;

(B) the individual and the woman who gave birth to the child were married to each other and the child is born not later than 300 days after the marriage is terminated by death, [divorce, dissolution, annulment, or declaration of invalidity, or after a decree of separation or separate maintenance], whether the marriage is or could be declared invalid; or

(C) the individual and the woman who gave birth to the child married each other after the birth of the child, whether the marriage is or could be declared invalid, the individual at any time asserted parentage of the child, and:

(i) the assertion is in a record filed with the [state agency maintaining birth records]; or

(ii) the individual agreed to be and is named as a parent of the child on the birth certificate of the child; or

(2) the individual resided in the same household with the child for the first two years of the life of the child, including any period of temporary absence, and openly held out the child as the individual's child.

(b) A presumption of parentage under this section may be overcome, and competing claims to parentage may be resolved, only by an adjudication [ ] or a valid denial of parentage [ ].

* * *

SECTION 608. ADJUDICATING PARENTAGE OF CHILD WITH PRESUMED PARENT.

* * *

(b) A presumption of parentage under Section 204 cannot be overcome after the child attains two years of age unless the court determines:

(1) the presumed parent is not a genetic parent, never resided with the child, and never held out the child as the presumed parent's child; or

(2) the child has more than one presumed parent.

* * *

NOTES AND QUESTIONS

1. *When to decide.* The UPA establishes a two-year limitation on parenthood disestablishment, but offers some exceptions. What is the basis for the exceptions?

2. *Presumptions, presumptions.* What are the different ways in which an individual can become a "presumed" parent? The law has multiple potential bases for determining parenthood, including contract, intent, marriage, or biology, or a standard that considers only the child's best interests. Should the bases for defining parenthood be the same for mothers and fathers?

3. *Holding out.* Section 204 allows an individual to establish parentage if the person lived with the child and "held out" the child as the individual's child for the first two years of the child's life. For example, a California court held that a man could seek to establish paternity based on claims that the child called him "Dada," and had visited him frequently. *Jason P. v. Danielle S.*, 226 Cal. App. 4th 167 (2014). The case, which attracted a great deal of media attention because of the acting career of the plaintiff, Jason Patric, raises important questions about what type of evidence should satisfy the "holding out" claim.

4. *Gender neutrality.* The UPA is gender-neutral. For further discussion, *see* Jessica Feinberg, *Consideration of Genetic Connections in Child Custody Disputes Between Same-Sex Parents: Fair or Foul?*, 81 Missouri L. Rev. 331 (2016). In 2017, the Supreme Court struck down gender-based disparities in immigration laws, finding no important government purpose "in the obsolescing view that 'unwed fathers [are] invariably less qualified and entitled than mothers' to take responsibility for nonmarital children." *Morales-Santana, supra,* at 1692.

PROBLEM 5-1

Jean was two months pregnant when she met Ken. Jean informed Ken that her ex-boyfriend, Lenny, was the father. Two months after Jean gave birth, she married Ken. No father is listed the birth certificate. How can Ken become the presumed father?

2. State Efforts to Protect Parents: Voluntary Parentage Registration Systems

There are some options for voluntarily acknowledging parentage. First, a number of states created putative father registries after *Lehr* upheld their general constitutionality. When a man believes he is or may be a child's father, these statutes place the burden on him to register (usually with the state department of health or similar agency) if he wishes to claim paternity and receive notice of a prospective adoption.

The New York registry statute at issue in *Lehr* did not establish a time limit within which the putative father must register to preserve his claim of right. In some states, however, the statute requires him to register before the child is born or within a specified short period after birth. *See, e.g.*, Ariz. Rev. Stat. § 8–106.01B (2018)(any time before the child's birth but not later than 30 days after birth). Failure to register within the specified period may constitute waiver not only of the right of notice but also of the right to contest an adoption. *See, e.g., id.* § 8–106.01E.

Registries have not proven as effective as their proponents had hoped because many men never learn of the registry's existence. Most nonmarital fathers are not lawyers, and it is not normal practice to consult a lawyer about childbirth or becoming a father. A few states have amended their registry statutes to maximize publicity in places likely to be frequented by nonmarital fathers, such as hospitals, local health departments and other such health facilities, motor vehicle department offices, and schools and universities. Regardless of the extent of publicity, however, the putative father's lack of knowledge of the registry's existence does not necessarily excuse noncompliance with the registration provisions. Noncompliance is likewise not typically excused because the nonmarital father asserts he did not know about the pregnancy or the birth. Indeed, part of the Virginia putative father registry statute provides: "Any man who has engaged in sexual intercourse with a woman is deemed to be on legal notice that a child may be conceived * * *." Va. Code § 63.2–1250(E) (2018).

Another problem is that, even if men know about the registries, they may not know where or how to register. Each state has enacted its own registry procedures, without reach or effect in other states. Assume two teenagers conceive a child while on summer vacation in state A, and then return to their homes in states B and C respectively. With the help of her parents, the teenage mother in state C then places the child for adoption in state D, asserting that she does not know the father's identity or whereabouts. Each of these states may have its own putative father registry.

As part of their participation in the federal public welfare system, states are also required to improve their systems for establishing paternity, primarily as a means to facilitate the collection of child support. Federal law mandates that states establish procedures for a "simple civil process for voluntarily acknowledging paternity," including hospital-based systems. 42 U.S.C. § 666(a)(5)(C)(i), (ii) (2018); *see* Jessica Dixon Weaver, *Overstepping Ethical Boundaries? Limitations on State Efforts to Provide*

Access to Justice in Family Courts, 82 Fordham L. Rev. 2705, 2719–21 (2014). All states now have this second option for establishing parentage:

> The signed document, known as a Voluntary Acknowledgement of Paternity ("VAP"), is recorded with the vital records office and, if not rescinded within sixty days, becomes a final legal judgment that can be challenged only on grounds of fraud, duress, or material mistake of fact. Today, VAPs are the primary means of establishing parentage in children born to unwed mothers.

Katharine K. Baker, *The DNA Default and Its Discontents: Establishing Modern Parenthood*, 96 B.U. L. Rev. 2037, 2049 (2016).

The UPA (2017) expands the potential use of these voluntary acknowledgements by renaming them "acknowledgments of parentage." UPA Sec. 301. In addition to the potential alleged genetic father, such an acknowledgement can also be used by " 'an intended parent' " of a child who is born through assisted reproduction or a " 'presumed parent' (which, most commonly, will be the woman's spouse—male or female)." Courtney G. Joslin, *Nurturing Parenthood Through the UPA (2017)*, 127 Yale L.J. Forum 589, 604 (2018). Nevada, for example, has adopted comparable legislation providing for a "voluntary acknowledgement of parentage." Nev. Rev. Stat. Ann. § 126.053 (2018). Nonetheless, although federal law conditions state receipt of federal funds for public welfare and child support programs on the availability of a voluntary acknowledgment procedure for the unmarried male partner of a woman who gives birth, it does not have a similar requirement for the nonmarital female partner. See Jessica Feinberg, *A Logical Step Forward: Extending Voluntary Acknowledgments of Parentage to Female Same-Sex Couples*, 30 Yale J.L. & Fem. 97 (2018).

NOTES AND QUESTIONS

1. *Failure to register*. G.W. was born in July 2010. Although the biological father, R.M., attended the child's birth and visited regularly, he did not file notice with the paternity registry, sign a birth certificate, or sign a paternity affidavit. The mother suspended R.M.'s visitation with the child in 2011, and married J.U. R.M. filed a paternity suit, and J.U. subsequently filed a petition for adoption. The court found that R.M.'s failure to register not only waived his right to notice, but also that such failure constituted implied consent to the adoption. *In re G.W.*, 983 N.E.2d 1193 (Ind. Ct. App. 2013). Should the failure to register constitute an absolute bar, given that the father had established a relationship with the child? Why should a court construe a putative registry requirement so strictly?

2. *Registry failure*. Baby Girl T was the result of a sexual relationship between Shasta B. Tew and Ramsey Shaud. Before the child's birth, Shaud filed a petition to establish paternity and notified Utah's Vital Records office of his efforts. Tew sought to place the child for adoption. The Vital Records office informed the adoption agency that there was no father listed in the

registry, a mere forty-five minutes before the office affirmatively entered Shaud's notice on the registry. The Utah Supreme Court held that a notice of paternity proceedings must be considered registered when it is received—not registered—by the state registry. *In re Baby Girl T.*, 298 P.3d 1251, 1260 (Utah 2012).

3. *Noticing what?* A system of interstate cooperation, which would enable putative fathers to search the registries of all states after registering in their own state, might help provide actual notice to men who truly want to assert their parental rights. In 2013, spurred in part by the Court's decision in *Adoptive Couple v. Baby Girl, supra,* Congress considered legislation, including the Protecting Adoption and Promoting Responsible Fatherhood Act of 2013, to establish a national paternity registry. H.R. 2439, 113th Cong. (2013); S. 1203, 113th Cong. (2013). Should Congress create a national or federal putative father registry to enhance and connect state registries? *See, e.g.,* Mary Beck, *A National Putative Father Registry,* 36 Cap. U. L. Rev. 295 (2007).

4. *Preglimony?* Before the establishment of paternity, should a man have any responsibility towards his pregnant partner? *See* Shari Motro, *Preglimony,* 63 Stan. L. Rev. 647 (2011) (arguing that the law should move towards recognizing such an obligation). In deciding parentage-related issues, should state statutes consider the nonmarital father's relationship with the pregnant woman? *See, e.g.,* Kan. Stat. § 59–2136(e) (2018)(evidence relating to identifying the father includes whether the mother was cohabiting with him at the time of conception and his willingness to support the mother during her pregnancy).

PROBLEM 5-2

You are a state legislator. In light of *Lehr, Michael H.,* and *Adoptive* Girl, would you vote to enact the following statutory provisions?

1.   In an adoption case, the juvenile court may terminate the rights of a child's unmarried father if it finds: a) that termination is in the best interests of the child; b) it appears by clear and convincing evidence that the child's unmarried mother has voluntarily terminated her rights; and c) the child's father, knowing he is the child's father, has provided no financial or emotional support to the mother during the pregnancy or at the birth of the child.

2.   Any individual with a good faith claim to biological parentage shall be able to prove at any time that he or she is the parent of any child and shall then be designated the legal parent of that child.

PROBLEM 5-3

After you complete the Family Law course, a friend confides that she has had intercourse with a man, that she is now pregnant, and does not intend to marry the man. Your friend tells you that she has not yet told the man that he is the father. She asks whether she should encourage the man to register with the putative father registry, and what the legal consequences would be if he did register. What questions do you have for her? What advice would you provide to her?

C. THE MARITAL PRESUMPTION TODAY

The marital presumption has been challenged in several different ways. First, at divorce, husbands have questioned whether they are indeed the biological fathers of children born into the marriage, arguing that they are not responsible for child support in the absence of proof of such a connection. States vary as to whether they permit such challenges. Second, the marital presumption has historically been used to identify the father and mother. The next case shows the Supreme Court addressing how the marital presumption applies to a same-sex couple. It is one part of the struggle of same-sex couples for parental recognition *See* Douglas NeJaime, *The Nature of Parenthood*, 126 Yale L.J. 2260 (2017).

[handwritten: TAKEAWAY: the Constitution entitles same-sex couples to civil marriage on the same terms and conditions as opposite-sex couples.]

> ### PAVAN V. SMITH
> Supreme Court of the United States, 2017.
> 582 U.S. ___, 137 S. Ct. 2075.

PER CURIAM.

As this Court explained in *Obergefell v. Hodges*, 576 U.S. ___ (2015), the Constitution entitles same-sex couples to civil marriage "on the same terms and conditions as opposite-sex couples." *Id.*, at (slip op., at 23). In the decision below, the Arkansas Supreme Court considered the effect of that holding on the State's rules governing the issuance of birth certificates. When a married woman gives birth in Arkansas, state law generally requires the name of the mother's male spouse to appear on the child's birth certificate—regardless of his biological relationship to the child. According to the court below, however, Arkansas need not extend that rule to similarly situated same-sex couples: The State need not, in other words, issue birth certificates including the female spouses of women who give birth in the State. Because that differential treatment infringes *Obergefell*'s commitment to provide same-sex couples "the constellation of benefits that the States have linked to marriage," *id.*, at (slip op., at 17), we reverse the state court's judgment. *[handwritten: R Holding]*

[handwritten: facts] The petitioners here are two married same-sex couples who conceived children through anonymous sperm donation. Leigh and Jana Jacobs were married in Iowa in 2010, and Terrah and Marisa Pavan were married in New Hampshire in 2011. Leigh and Terrah each gave birth to a child in Arkansas in 2015. When it came time to secure birth certificates for the newborns, each couple filled out paperwork listing both spouses as parents—Leigh and Jana in one case, Terrah and Marisa in the other. Both

times, however, the Arkansas Department of Health issued certificates bearing only the birth mother's name.

The department's decision rested on a provision of Arkansas law, Ark. Code § 20–18–401 (2014), that specifies which individuals will appear as parents on a child's state-issued birth certificate. "For the purposes of birth registration," that statute says, "the mother is deemed to be the woman who gives birth to the child." § 20–18–401(e). And "[i]f the mother was married at the time of either conception or birth," the statute instructs that "the name of [her] husband shall be entered on the certificate as the father of the child." § 20–18–401(f)(1). There are some limited exceptions to the latter rule—for example, another man may appear on the birth certificate if the "mother" and "husband" and "putative father" all file affidavits vouching for the putative father's paternity. *Ibid.* But as all parties agree, the requirement that a married woman's husband appear on her child's birth certificate applies in cases where the couple conceived by means of artificial insemination with the help of an anonymous sperm donor. * * * see also Ark. Code § 9–10–201(a) (2015) ("Any child born to a married woman by means of artificial insemination shall be deemed the legitimate natural child of the woman and the woman's husband if the husband consents in writing to the artificial insemination").

The Jacobses and Pavans brought this suit in Arkansas state court against the director of the Arkansas Department of Health—seeking, among other things, a declaration that the State's birth-certificate law violates the Constitution. The trial court agreed, holding that the relevant portions of § 20–18–401 are inconsistent with *Obergefell* because they "categorically prohibi[t] every same-sex married couple . . . from enjoying the same spousal benefits which are available to every opposite-sex married couple." App. to Pet. for Cert. 59a. But a divided Arkansas Supreme Court reversed that judgment, concluding that the statute "pass[es] constitutional muster." 2016 Ark. 437, 505 S. W. 3d 169, 177. In that court's view, "the statute centers on the relationship of the biological mother and the biological father to the child, not on the marital relationship of husband and wife," and so it "does not run afoul of *Obergefell.*" *Id.,* at 178. Two justices dissented from that view, maintaining that under *Obergefell* "a same-sex married couple is entitled to a birth certificate on the same basis as an opposite-sex married couple." 505 S. W. 3d, at 184 (Brill, C. J., concurring in part and dissenting in part); accord, *id.,* at 190 (Danielson, J., dissenting).

The Arkansas Supreme Court's decision, we conclude, denied married same-sex couples access to the "constellation of benefits that the Stat[e] ha[s] linked to marriage." *Obergefell,* 576 U. S., at (slip op., at 17). As already explained, when a married woman in Arkansas conceives a child by means of artificial insemination, the State will—indeed, *must*—list the name of her male spouse on the child's birth certificate. See § 20–18–

401(f)(1); see also § 9–10–201; *supra,* at 2. And yet state law, as interpreted by the court below, allows Arkansas officials in those very same circumstances to omit a married woman's female spouse from her child's birth certificate. See 505 S. W. 3d, at 177–178. As a result, same-sex parents in Arkansas lack the same right as opposite-sex parents to be listed on a child's birth certificate, a document often used for important transactions like making medical decisions for a child or enrolling a child in school. See Pet. for Cert. 5–7 (listing situations in which a parent might be required to present a child's birth certificate).

Obergefell proscribes such disparate treatment. As we explained there, a State may not "exclude same-sex couples from civil marriage on the same terms and conditions as opposite-sex couples." 576 U. S., at (slip op., at 23). Indeed, in listing those terms and conditions—the "rights, benefits, and responsibilities" to which same-sex couples, no less than opposite-sex couples, must have access—we expressly identified "birth and death certificates." *Id.,* at (slip op., at 17). That was no accident: Several of the plaintiffs in *Obergefell* challenged a State's refusal to recognize their same-sex spouses on their children's birth certificates. See *DeBoer* v. *Snyder,* 772 F. 3d 388, 398–399 (CA6 2014). In considering those challenges, we held the relevant state laws unconstitutional to the extent they treated same-sex couples differently from opposite-sex couples. See 576 U. S., at (slip op., at 23). That holding applies with equal force to § 20–18–401.

Echoing the court below, the State defends its birth-certificate law on the ground that being named on a child's birth certificate is not a benefit that attends marriage. Instead, the State insists, a birth certificate is simply a device for recording biological parentage—regardless of whether the child's parents are married. But Arkansas law makes birth certificates about more than just genetics. As already discussed, when an opposite-sex couple conceives a child by way of anonymous sperm donation—just as the petitioners did here—state law requires the placement of the birth mother's husband on the child's birth certificate. See *supra,* at 2. And that is so even though (as the State concedes) the husband "is definitively not the biological father" in those circumstances.

* * *

Arkansas has thus chosen to make its birth certificates more than a mere marker of biological relationships. The State uses those certificates to give married parents a form of legal recognition that is not available to unmarried parents. Having made that choice, Arkansas may not, consistent with *Obergefell,* deny married same-sex couples that recognition.

The petition for a writ of certiorari and the pending motions for leave to file briefs as *amici curiae* are granted. The judgment of the Arkansas

Supreme Court is reversed, and the case is remanded for further proceedings not inconsistent with this opinion.

It is so ordered.

JUSTICE GORSUCH, with whom JUSTICE THOMAS and JUSTICE ALITO join, dissenting.

Summary reversal is usually reserved for cases where "the law is settled and stable, the facts are not in dispute, and the decision below is clearly in error." *Schweiker* v. *Hansen*, 450 U.S. 785, 791 (1981) (Marshall, J., dissenting). Respectfully, I don't believe this case meets that standard.

To be sure, *Obergefell* addressed the question whether a State must recognize same-sex marriages. But nothing in *Obergefell* spoke (let alone clearly) to the question whether § 20–18–401 of the Arkansas Code, or a state supreme court decision upholding it, must go. The statute in question establishes a set of rules designed to ensure that the biological parents of a child are listed on the child's birth certificate. Before the state Supreme Court, the State argued that rational reasons exist for a biology based birth registration regime, reasons that in no way offend *Obergefell*—like ensuring government officials can identify public health trends and helping individuals determine their biological lineage, citizenship, or susceptibility to genetic disorders. In an opinion that did not in any way seek to defy but rather earnestly engage *Obergefell*, the state Supreme Court agreed. And it is very hard to see what is wrong with this conclusion for, just as the state court recognized, nothing in *Obergefell* indicates that a birth registration regime based on biology, one no doubt with many analogues across the country and throughout history, offends the Constitution. To the contrary, to the extent they speak to the question at all, this Court's precedents suggest just the opposite conclusion. See, *e.g.*, *Michael H.* v. *Gerald D.*, 491 U.S. 110, 124–125 (1989); *Tuan Anh Nguyen* v. *INS*, 533 U.S. 53, 73 (2001). Neither does anything in today's opinion purport to identify any constitutional problem with a biology based birth registration regime. So whatever else we might do with this case, summary reversal would not exactly seem the obvious course.

What, then, is at work here? If there isn't a problem with a biology based birth registration regime, perhaps the concern lies in this particular regime's exceptions. For it turns out that Arkansas's general rule of registration based on biology does admit of certain more specific exceptions. Most importantly for our purposes, the State acknowledges that § 9–10–201 of the Arkansas Code controls how birth certificates are completed in cases of artificial insemination like the one before us. The State acknowledges, too, that this provision, written some time ago, indicates that the mother's husband generally shall be treated as the father—and in this way seemingly anticipates only opposite-sex marital unions.

Dissent: Argues birth certificates are about biology

But if the artificial insemination statute is the concern, it's still hard to see how summary reversal should follow for at least a few reasons. First, petitioners didn't actually challenge § 9–10–201 in their lawsuit. Instead, petitioners sought and the trial court granted relief eliminating the State's authority under § 20–18–401 to enforce a birth registration regime generally based on biology. On appeal, the state Supreme Court simply held that this overbroad remedy wasn't commanded by *Obergefell* or the Constitution. And, again, nothing in today's opinion for the Court identifies anything wrong, let alone clearly wrong, in that conclusion. [ ] Third, further proof still of the state of the law in Arkansas today is the fact that, when it comes to adoption (a situation not present in this case but another one in which Arkansas departs from biology based registration), the State tells us that adopting parents are eligible for placement on birth certificates without respect to sexual orientation.

Given all this, it seems far from clear what here warrants the strong medicine of summary reversal. Indeed, it is not even clear what the Court expects to happen on remand that hasn't happened already. . . .

I respectfully dissent.

NOTES AND QUESTIONS

1.   *Stated reasons.* Is Arkansas's birth certificate law, as the state claimed, a "biology based birth registration system"? How does each opinion answer this question? Was *Michael H* such a system, as Justice Gorsuch appears to assert? For commentary on the decision and an earlier one requiring states to give full faith and credit to adoption decrees issued to a same-sex couple from a second state, see Joanna L. Grossman, *Summarily Reversed: Arkansas's Attempt to Flout* Obergefell v. Hodges *Is Blocked*, Verdict (June 29, 2017).

2.   *Moving forward. Per curiam* means "by the court." After this decision, how would you redraft the Arkansas law cited in the Court's opinion?

3.   *Becoming the parent.* Should the marital presumption apply upon a child's birth or after some time period has passed without the filing of a divorce? *See* Joanna L. Grossman, *The New Illegitimacy: Tying Parentage to Marital Status for Lesbian Coparents*, 20 Am. U. J. Gender Soc. Pol'y & L. 671 (2012). Consider whether application of the marital presumption should be based on assumptions concerning biology or marital unity. Why does this distinction matter?

PROBLEM 5-4

Yolanda and Vera lived together in New York and decided to have a child together. In November of 2018, Yolanda gave birth to Sam, and only her name is on the birth certificate. In January, 2019, Yolanda and Vera married. They separated and sought a divorce a month later. Vera seeks parenting rights.

You are the judge to whom this case has been assigned. Can Vera claim parental rights? *See Paczkowski v. Paczkowski*, 128 A.D.3d 968 (N.Y. App. Div. 2015).

2. BEYOND MARRIAGE

The traditional bases for establishing parenthood based on marriage and biology have been challenged in a variety of ways. This Section explores some of the additional means for conferring legal parentage, including assisted reproductive technology and functioning as a parent.

A. ASSISTED REPRODUCTIVE TECHNOLOGY

While most children are born through conventional reproductive acts (sexual intercourse either inside or outside of a marital relationship), an increasing number are born through assisted reproductive technology (ART), including the use of donor sperm and eggs and both genetic and gestational surrogacy.

1. Introduction

The following classic article provides an overview of ART and parentage determinations.

MARSHA GARRISON,
LAW MAKING FOR BABY MAKING: AN INTERPRETIVE
APPROACH TO THE DETERMINATION OF LEGAL PARENTAGE
113 Harv. L. Rev. 835, 845–52 (2000).

I.   The Revolution in Reproduction * * *

A. *Artificial Insemination*

Artificial insemination (AI) is the oldest and most popular means of technological conception. An estimated 20,000 to 30,000 children are born in the United States each year following AI with sperm provided by donors (AID) * * *. AI first came into widespread use during the 1950s. Until the 1980s, it was almost invariably sought by married couples * * *

* * * With AID, [ ] only the wife is genetically related to the child. Thus, under prevailing law at the time AID came into widespread use, her husband's parental status was unclear.

During the 1970s, the states began to enact legislation that clarified the AID child's legal parentage. The 1973 Uniform Parentage Act (UPA), for example, provided that "[i]f, under the supervision of a licensed physician and with the consent of her husband, a wife is inseminated artificially with semen donated by a man not her husband, the husband is treated in law as if he were the natural father of a child thereby conceived."

As of 1998, fifteen states had adopted the UPA or a virtually identical standard, and fifteen others had enacted similar statutes that varied by eliminating the licensed physician requirement.

Although the AID statutes resolved the status issue that courts initially confronted, they failed to resolve a host of other legal questions that might arise from the use of AID—and which increasingly do. The status issues posed by AID today reflect a shift in its usage. Advances in the treatment of male infertility have markedly reduced the number of married couples who seek AID, while a remarkable change in parenting norms has greatly expanded the number of would-be parents who seek AID for reasons unrelated to infertility: many of these new AID applicants are single women who wish to achieve pregnancy but have no male partner; others are parties to a surrogate parenting agreement; and an occasional applicant wishes to become pregnant using sperm from a deceased partner. Many of these new users continue to employ sperm banks and physician assistance in order to ensure donor screening and anonymity, but others rely on known donors and perform AID at home without physician involvement.

* * *

B.   *In Vitro Fertilization*

While AI avoids sex, in vitro fertilization (IVF) moves the entire process of conception outside the body. In IVF, ovarian stimulation is followed by the collection of eggs ready for fertilization. The process of fertilization takes place in vitro in a laboratory; some or all of the resulting preembryos are then implanted into the uterus or fallopian tubes. The first IVF birth occurred in 1978 in Great Britain. Since then, tens of thousands of children conceived through IVF have been born in the United States alone.

Like AI, IVF was originally employed by married couples with infertility problems; thus the first IVF baby, Louise Brown, was conceived using Mrs. Brown's ova in combination with her husband's sperm. But as with AI, the uses of IVF have expanded. Because IVF takes the process of conception outside the body, it permits the use of donated eggs (the analog to AID); this practice has expanded dramatically because IVF success rates for older women substantially increase when the eggs of younger women are employed. IVF also permits the use of another woman to gestate the fetus; although less common than IVF with donated ova, this practice, too, has increased. The net result is a confusing array of "parents"; for example, would-be parents A and B might obtain sperm from Man C and eggs from Woman D, then have a doctor implant the resulting preembryos in Woman E to be carried to term. And, as with AI, today's IVF users are not necessarily married couples with fertility problems. A and B might be a gay couple, or A and B might be simply A, a single man or woman.

The parenting possibilities created by IVF present a host of legal issues. . . .

* * *

C. Pregnancy for Another: The Various Forms of Surrogacy

Surrogacy—bearing a child for someone else—stands in contrast to AI and IVF in that it requires no technology at all. The Biblical Sarah, Rachel, and Leah all made use of surrogates—their handmaids—in order to produce children for their husbands; conception was achieved sexually rather than technologically. Modern surrogacy, however, invariably involves conception through AI. In the case of gestational surrogacy, in which the woman who gives birth is not genetically related to the child she bears, IVF is employed as well.

Modern surrogacy also differs from that of Biblical times in its reliance on contract. Biblical surrogacy involved an informal understanding between the infertile woman, her husband, and her handmaid, but surrogacy today is almost invariably conducted on the basis of a formal, written document specifying rights and obligations. Surrogacy today is also commercial: contracts almost always require payments both to the woman who will bear the child and to a service that has brokered the arrangement.

Commercial, contract surrogacy emerged in the United States in the late 1970s. Although its use has spread, the number of surrogate births remains small in comparison to those obtained through AI and IVF alone[.].

Public attention became focused on surrogacy as a result of the widely-publicized case of *In re Baby M*, involving the legality of an agreement by a "surrogate" mother to relinquish the child she had conceived through AI to the sperm donor and his wife in return for $10,000. Perhaps because of the media attention, state legislatures reacted to surrogacy with greater speed than they have reacted to AI and IVF. * * *

* * * With gestational surrogacy, it is possible for a child to have three "mothers"—one who is genetically related to the child, one who gave birth to the child, and one who planned the pregnancy and intended the child to be hers. It is also possible for a child to have three "fathers"—one related to the child genetically, one married to the woman who gave birth to it, and one who planned the pregnancy and intended it to be his. Current law, even in states with statutes governing surrogacy, typically fails to offer clear (or even murky) answers as to the rights and obligations of these various parties.

* * *

NOTES AND QUESTIONS

1.   *Infertility rates.* Assisted reproductive technology is fueled in part by significant rates of adult infertility, a condition that most experts define as being unable to get pregnant after at least one year of trying. The U.S. Centers for Disease Control and Prevention reports that more than 10% of women (7.3 million) between the ages of 15–44 have received infertility services at some time in their lives. CDC, *FastStats: Infertility* (2016).

ART has also assumed greater importance as more and more women have postponed having children until their 30s and 40s. About 20% of women in the United States now have their first child after age 35, and about one-third of couples have fertility problems when the woman is over 35. CDC, Infertility FAQs (2019). The average age for patients who use ART is 36. CDC, 2016 Assisted Reproductive Technology National Summary Report Figure 9 (2018).

2.   *Sparse legal regulation.* Despite the substantial health risks to children of ART, it is lightly regulated, and remains "bound only by the ethics of the fertility specialist and the financial and emotional limits of the infertile couple." Jennifer L. Rosato, *The Children of ART (Assisted Reproductive Technology): Should the Law Protect Them From Harm?*, 2004 Utah L. Rev. 57, 62.

Federal law regulates ART in the Fertility Clinic Success Rate and Certification Act of 1992, Pub. L. No. 102–493, 106 Stat. 3146 (codified as amended at 42 U.S.C. §§ 263a–1 to 7 (2018)). Without establishing standards of practice, the Act requires fertility clinics to provide information about their success rates, which the U.S. Centers for Disease Control and Prevention publishes. Federal law also requires that donor gametes undergo tests for some diseases, such as HIV. An increasing number of states have ART statutes.

PROBLEM 5-5

The Victorian Law Reform Commission recommended changes to existing ART legislation in Australia. The Commission suggested, among other things, amendments that:

1.   would prohibit ART treatment unless a woman is "in the circumstances in which she finds herself, unlikely to become pregnant other than by a treatment procedure";

2.   would presume that people who have been convicted for sexual and serious violent offences, or who have had child protection orders entered against them, may not have access to ART treatment; and

3.   would permit physicians or civil authorities who believe that a child born as a result of ART would be at risk of abuse or neglect to petition a clinical ethics committee, which would have authority to decide whether to prohibit ART treatment.

See Victorian Law Reform Commission, Assisted Reproductive Technology & Adoption Final Report (2007).

What problems do you see if Congress or a state legislature sought to enact these restrictions?

2. Donor Gametes

In each of the various ART methods discussed in Professor Garrison's article, the genetic material may belong to the intended parents, or it may have been "donated" by another person. This latter form of reproduction is often called "collaborative" or "third-party" reproduction, because it typically involves people who are not seeking parenthood, but who provide gametes (sperm or eggs) or embryos, or who assist in gestating an embryo. ART separates genetics from gestation.

Where a husband and wife use their own sperm and egg to conceive a child that is carried by the wife, of course, the wife is the child's mother by both gestation and genetics, and the husband is the father by genetics and presumption. In collaborative reproduction, however, biology can be more complicated and less dispositive in determining parentage. Most states have laws terminating the legal status of an unknown sperm donor; a significant number do the same for an unknown egg donor and some address embryo donors. Consequently, no legal relationship generally exists between unknown donors and recipients. The legal consequences of choosing a known donor can be quite different. A known sperm or egg donor seek to establish a relationship with the child and assert paternity or maternity.

The UPA, portions of which you have read earlier, seeks to produce a measure of clarity. Consider the identity of the parents in light of the UPA provisions set out below relating to sperm, egg, or embryo donation, and surrogacy contracts.

UNIFORM PARENTAGE ACT
(2017).

SECTION 102. DEFINITIONS. In this [act]

* * *

(4) "Assisted reproduction" means a method of causing pregnancy other than sexual intercourse. The term includes:

(A) intrauterine [ ] insemination;

(B) donation of gametes;

(C) donation of embryos; [and]

(D) in-vitro fertilization and transfer of embryos * * *

* * *

(9) "Donor" means an individual who provides gametes intended for use in assisted reproduction, whether or not for consideration. The term does not include:

(A) a woman who gives birth to a child conceived by assisted reproduction[, except as otherwise provided in [Article 8, concerning surrogacy]; or

(B) a parent under [Article 7, concerning assisted reproduction] or an intended parent under [Article] 8 (surrogacy)].

* * *

SECTION 702. PARENTAL STATUS OF DONOR. A donor is not a parent of a child conceived by assisted reproduction.

SECTION 703. PARENTAGE OF CHILD OF ASSISTED REPRODUCTION. An individual who consents under Section 704 to assisted reproduction by a woman with the intent to be a parent of a child conceived by the assisted reproduction is a parent of the child.

SECTION 704. CONSENT TO ASSISTED REPRODUCTION.

(a) Except as otherwise provided in subsection (b), the consent described in Section 703 must be in a record signed by a woman giving birth to a child conceived by assisted reproduction and an individual who intends to be a parent of the child.

(b) Failure to consent in a record as required by subsection (a), before, on, or after birth of the child, does not preclude the court from finding consent to parentage if:

(1) the woman or the individual proves by clear-and-convincing evidence the existence of an express agreement entered into before conception that the individual and the woman intended they both would be parents of the child; or

(2) the woman and the individual for the first two years of the child's life, including any period of temporary absence, resided together in the same household with the child and both openly held out the child as the individual's child * * *.

SECTION 705. LIMITATION ON SPOUSE'S DISPUTE OF PARENTAGE.

(a) Except as otherwise provided in subsection (b), an individual who, at the time of a child's birth, is the spouse of the woman who gave birth to the child by assisted reproduction may not challenge the individual's parentage of the child unless:

(1) not later than two years after the birth of the child, the individual commences a proceeding to adjudicate the individual's parentage of the child; and

(2) the court finds the individual did not consent to the assisted reproduction, before, on, or after birth of the child, or withdrew consent under [this Act].

(b) A proceeding to adjudicate a spouse's parentage of a child born by assisted reproduction may be commenced at any time if the court determines:

(1) the spouse neither provided a gamete for, nor consented to, the assisted reproduction;

(2) the spouse and the woman who gave birth to the child have not cohabited since the probable time of assisted reproduction; and

(3) the spouse never openly held out the child as the spouse's child.

(c) This section applies to a spouse's dispute of parentage even if the spouse's marriage is declared invalid after assisted reproduction occurs.

NOTE AND QUESTIONS

1. *Questions about the UPA.* If the man "donates" sperm by having sexual intercourse with a woman, what law determines the man's rights and obligations with respect to the child?

2. *Knowing—or not?* Does the UPA distinguish between donors who are known to the donee and anonymous donors? Should it?

3. *The marital presumption.* The marital presumption generally provides that where a child is born to a married woman, the other spouse is the parent. If a woman is inseminated with a donor's sperm without her spouse's knowledge, is the spouse the "parent" of the child and thus liable for child support?

3. Surrogacy

In traditional, or genetic, surrogacy, a woman agrees to carry to term in her womb and bear a child for another person or couple, and contributes her egg to conception. The sperm with which the egg is fertilized may be that of the intended father or that of a sperm donor selected by the intended parent(s). By contrast, a woman is a "gestational surrogate" when she carries the embryo created from the egg of another woman, who may be the intended mother or an egg donor. A genetic surrogate thus has both a genetic and gestational connection to the embryo she is carrying, but a gestational surrogate has no genetic connection.

Although the number of children born through traditional surrogacy is not known, approximately 2.3% of all recent reproductive technology cycles involve gestational surrogacy; almost 9000 children were born through gestational surrogacy from 2009–2013. Over half of these cycles

(50.2%) were performed in California, Connecticut, Texas, and Illinois; California had the highest number of gestational carrier cycles in the country. Nationally, just over half (50.2%) of gestational carrier cycles used donor eggs, so that means they had intending parents, a donor, and a surrogate. Kiran Perkins et al., *Trends and Outcomes of Gestational Surrogacy in the U.S.*, 106 Fertility & Sterility 435 (2016).

Surrogacy has been assailed as baby selling; "the strong intuition that one who gives birth to a baby is that baby's mother supports the baby selling narrative." Sheryl Colb, *Considering a New York Bill to Legalize Compensated Surrogacy,* Verdict (Nov. 8, 2017). Another criticism is that surrogacy exploits women who act as surrogates or commodifies their reproductive capacity.

On the other hand, it has resulted in the births of healthy children to some who would not otherwise have been able to have a child, possibly because the parents were gay, or one or both of the parents was infertile, or the intended mother was unable to carry a child to term, or the intended parents were fearful of gestation or of transmitting a genetic disease or defect through natural conception and childbirth.

The *Baby M* saga, described briefly in the Marsha Garrison article, involved a genetic surrogate who sought to retain her parental rights. The case dominated the headlines for months as it worked its way through the New Jersey court system in the late 1980s. The New Jersey Supreme Court delivered its unanimous opinion declaring surrogacy illegal when the child was nearly two years old. *In re Baby M*, 537 A.2d 1227 (N.J. 1988). The protracted litigation demonstrated the profound human emotions that may attend surrogate motherhood, and also the strains that surrogacy imposes on legal doctrines developed based on traditional assumptions about conception and birth.

Because no state had surrogacy legislation at the time, *Baby M's* bases for decision were traditional law and policies regulating contracts, adoption, custody, visitation and termination of parental rights. In the wake of *Baby M*, a number of states enacted surrogacy legislation. In part, because of the ethical, religious and moral questions surrounding surrogacy, however, not all states have done so.

In the more than thirty years since *Baby M*, surrogacy has become increasingly accepted in many states, although some states (and countries) prohibit paying a woman to serve as a surrogate. In 2018, New Jersey itself reversed course, with the governor signing new legislation permitting and regulating gestational surrogacy. *See* New Jersey Gestational Carrier Agreement Act, 2018 N.J. Sess. Law Serv. Ch. 18 (West).

Among the other states with legislation, no one approach has prevailed. For example, some states declare all surrogacy agreements unenforceable. *See, e.g.,* Neb. Rev. Stat. § 25–21,200 (2018). Other states deny enforcement where the surrogate is compensated. *See, e.g.,* Ky. Rev. Stat. § 199.590(4) (2018). Some states have exempted surrogacy agreements from baby-selling statutes See, e.g., Ala. Code § 26–10A–34(c) (2018). Some states permit only gestational surrogacy while other jurisdictions permit both gestational and genetic (traditional) surrogacy. *See* UPA Art. 8 Comment. For an overview of approaches to surrogacy, see Alex Finkelstein et al., Surrogacy Law and Policy in the U.S.: A National Conversation Informed by Global Lawmaking, Columbia (May 2016). In a thorough review of the enforceability of gestational surrogacy contracts, the Iowa Supreme Court upheld their validity, finding that they did not violate the state ban on baby-selling, and that any payments were for the gestational carrier's services, rather than for the baby. *P.M. v. T.B.,* 907 N.W.2d 522 (Iowa 2018).

A state may decide to limit surrogacy to situations where the intending mother "cannot physically gestate a pregnancy to term," or gestation poses a risk to the health of the intending mother or the child. Fla. Stat. Ann. § 742.15 (2018). New Hampshire restricts who may act as a surrogate, N.H. Rev. Stat. § 168–B:9 (2018)., and Virginia sets out requirements for advance judicial approval of the agreement. Va. Code § 20–160 (2018). Some states allow only married couples to serve as the intending parents. E.g., Fla. Stat. § 742.15 (2018); Va. Code § 20–156 (2018).

The Uniform Parentage Act of 2017 includes provisions that a state seeking to legitimate surrogacy can adopt.

UNIFORM PARENTAGE ACT
(2017).

* * *

SECTION 801. DEFINITIONS. In this [article]:

(1) "Genetic surrogate" means a woman who is not an intended parent and who agrees to become pregnant through assisted reproduction using her own gamete, under a genetic surrogacy agreement as provided in this [article].

(2) "Gestational surrogate" means a woman who is not an intended parent and who agrees to become pregnant through assisted reproduction using gametes that are not her own, under a gestational surrogacy agreement as provided in this [article].

(3) "Surrogacy agreement" means an agreement between one or more intended parents and a woman who is not an intended parent in which the woman agrees to become pregnant through assisted reproduction and which provides that each intended parent is a parent of a child conceived under the agreement. Unless otherwise specified, the term refers to both a gestational surrogacy agreement and a genetic surrogacy agreement.

SECTION 802. ELIGIBILITY TO ENTER GESTATIONAL OR GENETIC SURROGACY AGREEMENT.

(a) To execute an agreement to act as a gestational or genetic surrogate, a woman must:

    (1) have attained 21 years of age;

    (2) previously have given birth to at least one child;

    (3) complete a medical evaluation related to the surrogacy arrangement by a licensed medical doctor;

    (4) complete a mental-health consultation by a licensed mental-health professional; and

    (5) have independent legal representation of her choice throughout the surrogacy arrangement regarding the terms of the surrogacy agreement and the potential legal consequences of the agreement.

(b) To execute a surrogacy agreement, each intended parent, whether or not genetically related to the child, must:

    (1) have attained 21 years of age;

    (2) complete a medical evaluation related to the surrogacy arrangement by a licensed medical doctor;

    (3) complete a mental-health consultation by a licensed mental health professional; and

    (4) have independent legal representation of the intended parent's choice throughout the surrogacy arrangement regarding the terms of the surrogacy agreement and the potential legal consequences of the agreement.

SECTION 803. REQUIREMENTS OF GESTATIONAL OR GENETIC SURROGACY AGREEMENT: PROCESS. A surrogacy agreement must be executed in compliance with the following rules:

* * *

    (3) Each intended parent, the surrogate, and the surrogate's spouse, if any, must be parties to the agreement.

    (4) The agreement must be in a record signed by each party listed in paragraph (3).

    (5) The surrogate and each intended parent must acknowledge in a record receipt of a copy of the agreement.

    (6) The signature of each party to the agreement must be attested by a notarial officer or witnessed.

(7) The surrogate and the intended parent or parents must have independent legal representation throughout the surrogacy arrangement regarding the terms of the surrogacy agreement and the potential legal consequences of the agreement, and each counsel must be identified in the surrogacy agreement.

(8) The intended parent or parents must pay for independent legal representation for the surrogate.

(9) The agreement must be executed before a medical procedure occurs related to the surrogacy agreement, other than the medical evaluation and mental health consultation required by Section 802.

SECTION 804. REQUIREMENTS OF GESTATIONAL OR GENETIC SURROGACY AGREEMENT: CONTENT.

(a) A surrogacy agreement must comply with the following requirements:

(1) A surrogate agrees to attempt to become pregnant by means of assisted reproduction.

(2) [T]he surrogate and the surrogate's spouse or former spouse, if any, have no claim to parentage of a child conceived by assisted reproduction under the agreement.

(3) The surrogate's spouse, if any, must acknowledge and agree to comply with the obligations imposed on the surrogate by the agreement.

(4) [T]he intended parent or, if there are two intended parents, each one jointly and severally, immediately on birth will be the exclusive parent or parents of the child, regardless of number of children born or gender or mental or physical condition of each child.

(5) [T]he intended parent or, if there are two intended parents, each parent jointly and severally, immediately on birth will assume responsibility for the financial support of the child, regardless of number of children born or gender or mental or physical condition of each child.

(6) The agreement must include information disclosing how each intended parent will cover the surrogacy-related expenses of the surrogate and the medical expenses of the child. * * *

(7) The agreement must permit the surrogate to make all health and welfare decisions regarding herself and her pregnancy. This [act] does not enlarge or diminish the surrogate's right to terminate her pregnancy.

(8) The agreement must include information about each party's right under this [article] to terminate the surrogacy agreement.

(b) A surrogacy agreement may provide for:

(1) payment of consideration and reasonable expenses; and

(2) reimbursement of specific expenses if the agreement is terminated under this [article].

* * *

SECTION 811. GESTATIONAL SURROGACY AGREEMENT: ORDER OF PARENTAGE.

(a) [B]efore, on, or after the birth of a child conceived by assisted reproduction under a gestational surrogacy agreement, a party to the agreement may commence a proceeding in the [appropriate court] for an order or judgment:

(1) declaring that each intended parent is a parent of the child and ordering that parental rights and duties vest immediately on the birth of the child exclusively in each intended parent;

(2) declaring that the gestational surrogate and the surrogate's spouse or former spouse, if any, are not the parents of the child;

* * *

NOTES AND QUESTIONS

1. *Legal involvement?* What roles do lawyers play in the negotiation process? Who can pay their fees? Do the intending parents need to do anything other than execute the agreement to become the legal parents?

2. *Surrogate requirements.* Why do you think the surrogate's spouse (if any) must sign the agreement? What is the purpose of the eligibility requirements for the surrogate?

3. *Potential limits on the class of intended parents.* Should the UPA additionally require that surrogacy is permitted only where the intended parents can provide a convincing reason for turning to surrogacy, such as they are infertile? Where pregnancy might endanger the intended mother's health? Where one intended parent is genetically related to the child?

4. *Questions about judicial oversight.* Should the state permit surrogacy agreements only where a court, after a hearing, gives prior approval to the agreement? If the answer is yes, (a) who should be required to join in the petition to the court? (b) what factors should the court consider in determining whether to grant approval? (c) should the court appoint a guardian *ad litem* for the anticipated child? (d) should the court order an inspection and evaluation of the intended parents' household, similar to the procedures that precede court approval of an adoption?

PROBLEM 5-6

You are an attorney at a law firm with an active surrogacy practice. You currently have cases with the following issues. How will you resolve each one, assuming the UPA applies?

1. Your clients, the intending parents, have just learned that the surrogate, with whom they have entered into an UPA-compliant contract, no longer wants to give up the baby. They seek your advice.

2. The intending parents are concerned that the surrogate (your client) with whom they entered into an agreement is pregnant with triplets. They have asked her to "selectively reduce" the pregnancy so she is only carrying twins. The surrogate tells you she has refused to do so and seeks your advice about whether she may do so under the contract.

PROBLEM 5-7

You are a state senator in a state that is considering surrogacy legislation for the first time. You sit on the Families and Children Committee, which is considering adopting either the UPA (excerpted above) or the following bill.

BILL

1. Surrogate parenting contracts are hereby declared contrary to the public policy of this state, and are void and unenforceable.

2. "Surrogate parenting contract" shall mean any agreement, oral or written, in which:

    (a) a woman agrees either to be inseminated with the sperm of a man who is not her husband or to be impregnated with an embryo that is the product of an ovum fertilized with the sperm of a man who is not her husband; and

    (b) the woman agrees to, or intends to, surrender or consent to the adoption of the child born as a result of such insemination or impregnation.

Would you vote to send either bill to the floor as currently drafted? If not, how would you amend the bill in committee?

B. DE FACTO PARENTHOOD

Adults and children may develop strong ties in the absence of formal legal parenthood. For example, when unmarried couples raise one partner's children together, the children often regard both adults as their parents; in many states, however, only one adult has a legal claim to parenthood after the couple breaks up. In jurisdictions that recognize equitable claims to parenthood based on the role a third party has played in the child's life, a biological "stranger" may have standing to claim parenthood. Courts may find a basis for an equitable parenting claim in the common law, the best interests of the child standard or in the express provisions of state statutes. *See* Pamela Laufer-Ukeles & Ayelet Blecher-Prigat, *Between Function and Form: Towards a Differentiated Model of Functional Parenthood*, 20 Geo. Mason L. Rev. 419, 423–24 (2013). States vary in the labels they assign to third parties who claim parenthood, and there are technical distinctions as well. The terms include: (i) "parent by estoppel" or "equitable parent"; (ii) de facto parent; or (iii) functional parent. Many courts use the terms "de facto parent" and "equitable parent" interchangeably, although in other states, the terms may each have s distinct set of rights.

Through its de facto parentage statute, a child in the District of Columbia may have more than two legal parents so long as the existing parents agree with the third party's assumption of parenting responsibilities. D.C. Code § 16–831.01 (2018). Such a designation may arise from birth; in that situation, a de facto parent must have lived in the same household as the child when the child was born or adopted, taken on full and permanent responsibilities as a parent, and held him or herself out as the child's parent, with the agreement of the child's parents. *Id.* Even a de facto parent who did not live in the same household as the child at the time of birth or adoption can still claim parental status based on an alternative set of legal claims. In New York, if a nonmarital partner shows by clear and convincing evidence that the parties entered into a pre-conception agreement to conceive and to raise the child together, the non-biological, non-adoptive partner has standing, as a parent, to seek visitation and custody, although the court retains discretion on whether to grant those rights. *Brooke S.B. v. Elizabeth A.C.C.*, 61 N.E.3d 488 (N.Y. 2016). These issues are discussed further in Chapter 13.

C. ADOPTION

Adoption provides an additional means of becoming a parent. Adoption creates the legal parent-child relationship between the child and the adoptive parents, and terminates the child's legal relationship with the biological parents. There are more than 100,000 adoptions each year in the United States; less than 25% of them conform to the traditional model of a baby placed by a nonmarital mother with a married couple. The following excerpt provides a brief exploration of the kind of families formed through adoption; legal issues involving adoption are explored in much greater detail in Chapter 6.

JOAN HOLLINGER, ADOPTION IN AMERICA TODAY
Conference Draft (2015).

Adoptive families are the product of law, not blood. Through a highly regulated process culminating in a judicial proceeding, the state creates the status of parent and child "in all respects" between individuals who are not biogenetically related and severs the child's legal relationship to the biological parents and their families. Once an adoption decree has been issued, the adoptive family becomes the legal equivalent of the biogenetic family. The adoptee receives a new birth certificate with the names of her adoptive parents substituted for the names of the woman and man, if any, listed as her parents at birth.

Perhaps half of all adoptions are by stepparents; many others are by grandparents or other relatives, some of whom have served as state-licensed kinship caregivers for children separated from abusive or neglectful parents. Many other children placed in state-supervised out-of-home care are adopted by their previously unrelated foster parents. It is estimated that less than twenty-five percent of adoptions conform to the traditional model of an infant being placed at birth by an unwed mother and adopted by an infertile married couple who were "legal strangers" to the child.

An increasing number and percentage of adoptive families have been formed by same-sex couples where one partner or spouse is the biological parent of a child and the other partner or spouse legitimates their status as the "second parent" of the child through a second parent or stepparent adoption. In addition, many same-sex couples are jointly adopting children who have been in public foster care agencies, including children with special needs who might otherwise not have the benefit of being raised in a stable family setting. Based on data from the U.S. Census and the National Survey of Family Growth, the Williams Institute estimates that approximately 220,000 children were living in households headed by same-sex couples as of 2013; of these, at least 22,000 were adopted children.

Although a few states prohibit adoption by unmarried couples, every state allows single men or women, regardless of their sexual orientation, to adopt children through the state's foster care system. Even after *Obergefell v. Hodges*, for the tens of thousands of married and unmarried same-sex couples who have children through assisted reproduction and who want to establish joint legal parentage of their children with their same-sex partners, adoption will remain the most appropriate option for the non-biogenetic parent to become one of the child's legal parents. A second parent adoption (often called a stepparent adoption when couple is married) is a legal procedure that allows a same-sex co-parent to adopt his or her partner's or spouse's biological or adopted child. Second parent adoption protects children in same-sex parent families by giving the child the legal, economic and emotional security of having two legal parents with equal responsibilities for the child's care and support. Second parent adoption also protects the rights of both parents, by ensuring that each of them will continue to have a legally recognized parental relationship to their child if they separate or if the biological (or original adoptive parent) dies or becomes incapacitated.

Intercountry adoptions are the most prominent example of families being formed across ethnic and racial lines. Annual adoptions by U.S. citizens of children from other countries—primarily China, Russia, South Korea and Guatemala—tripled between the 1980s and 2004, to nearly 23,000 per year. Since the U.S. became an active party to the Hague Convention on Intercountry Adoption in 2008, however, and largely because of political conflicts between the U.S. and the primary as well as many other sending countries, the number of intercountry adoptions has fallen precipitously to fewer than 7,500 in fiscal year 2013. * * *

NOTES AND QUESTIONS

1. *Openness, round 1.* Once an adoption is finalized, the biological parents are no longer the child's legal parents. Nonetheless, some states recognize the enforceability of contracts between the adoptive and biological parents providing for ongoing contact. Such contact might range from occasional photo exchanges to visits. Is this equivalent to establishing different categories of parenthood, such as legal parenthood and parenthood lite?

2. *Openness, round 2.* An adopted individual is given a new birth certificate, showing the names of the adoptive parents. States are increasingly likely to allow adopted individuals to access their original birth certificates, recognizing that this can help them develop positive identities as well as provide potentially useful health information. *See* Evan B. Donaldson Adoption Institute, *For the Records, II, An Examination of the History and Impact of Adult Adoptee Access to Original Birth Certificates* (2010). Should such a right be granted to all adoptees?

3. *Openness, round 3. Obergefell* still has not eliminated all restrictions on joint adoptions by nonmarital couples. *See* Melissa Murray, Obergefell v. Hodges *and Nonmarriage Inequality*, 104 Cal. L. Rev. 1207, 1253 (2016).

PROBLEM 5-8

Two of your longtime friends, John and Judy Jones, stop by your family law office seeking your advice. They have been married for seven years, and both are in their late 20s. They are childless, and they have been trying unsuccessfully to conceive a child for the past two years. They are thinking about whether to adopt a child or to attempt some form of surrogacy arrangement. What would you advise concerning the relative merits of each avenue to parenthood?

D. THREE PARENTS

A growing number of jurisdictions have recognized the possibility of three parents either through legislation or through common law decisions.

The revised Uniform Parentage Act provides states with an option for including a provision allowing for more than two parents. UPA § 613 (2017).

A lesbian couple might agree that one of them will use donor sperm, and that both of them will be the parents of any child. D.C. Code § 16–909(e)(1) (2018). If they use a known semen donor, they might also sign an agreement with him that recognizes him as a parent. D.C. Code § 16–909(e)(2) (2018). The resulting child will have three parents.

In 2013, California adopted the following provisions, which directly addresses parental rights in families with three parents. It is similar to the standard in the Uniform Parentage Act. UPA § 613.

CAL. FAMILY CODE

7601. (a) "Parent and child relationship" as used in this part means the legal relationship existing between a child and the child's natural or adoptive parents incident to which the law confers or imposes rights, privileges, duties, and obligations. The term includes the mother and child relationship and the father and child relationship.

(b) This part does not preclude a finding that a child has a parent and child relationship with more than two parents.

(c) For purposes of state law, administrative regulations, court rules, government policies, common law, and any other provision or source of law governing the rights, protections, benefits, responsibilities, obligations, and duties of parents, any reference to two parents shall be interpreted to apply to every parent of a child where that child has been found to have more than two parents under this part.

* * *

[7612.] (c) In an appropriate action, a court may find that more than two persons with a claim to parentage under this division are parents if the court finds that recognizing only two parents would be detrimental to the child. In determining detriment to the child, the court shall consider all relevant factors, including, but not limited to, the harm of removing the child from a stable placement with a parent who has fulfilled the child's physical needs and the child's psychological needs for care and affection, and who has assumed that role for a substantial period of time. A finding of detriment to the child does not require a finding of unfitness of any of the parents or persons with a claim to parentage.

NOTES AND QUESTIONS

1. *But when?* Notwithstanding the potential breadth of the California statute, the legislative history has been interpreted to mean that its

application should "be narrow in scope and to apply only in 'rare cases' in which a child 'truly has more than two parents' who are parents 'in every way.' (In those rare cases, the Legislature sought to protect the child from the 'devastating psychological and emotional impact' that would result from '[s]eparating [the] child from a parent.'" *In re Donovan L., Jr.,* 244 Cal. App. 4th 1075, 1090 (2016). In *Donovan,* the court refused to recognize the biological father as a third parent to a child conceived during the marriage of the mother and her husband. By contrast, in a case eerily similar to *Michael H,* a California court found that a child had two fathers and a mother. A married woman, C.P., became involved with a co-worker, C.A., and she became pregnant. C.P. remained with her husband, but C.A. established a strong relationship with the child, including overnight visits and even making informal child support payments to the mother. The court did note it was "a 'rare' case where, pursuant to statutory authority, each of three parents should be legally recognized as such, to prevent detriment to their child." *C.A. v. C.P.,* 29 Cal. App. 5th 27 (Ct. App. 2018).

2. *Making laws.* Three-parent families have also been established by legislation in other jurisdictions, including the Canadian province of British Columbia. Family Law Act, S.B.C. 2011, c 25, s 30.

3. *Just how many?* Who benefits from three-parent families? Under the California statute, how many parents might a child have? A fundamental issue in these families is "equality—can and should the principle of equal parental status survive the recognition of more than two adults as legal parents?" June Carbone & Naomi Cahn, *Parents, Babies, and More Parents,* 92 Chi.-Kent L. Rev. 9, 10 (2017). Custody and visitation are discussed further in Chapters 12 and 13.

PROBLEM 5-9

Sean and Kip, an unmarried couple, decide to have a child together. A female friend, Amanda, offers to help them by serving as a gestational surrogate. Amanda is inseminated using a donor's eggs and Sean's sperm. They have not drafted a written agreement regarding their arrangement. When the child is born, Amanda and Sean's names are on the birth certificate. Sean and Kip take the child into their home, and they both provide daily care for the child. Amanda does not provide day-to-day care or financial support, but she occasionally visits. Five years later, Sean and Kip separate. Sean begins limiting Kip's access to the child. Assume that their state does not explicitly allow more than two parents. Can Kip establish any parental rights to the child?

PROBLEM 5-10

Sarah, who is single, asks her friend, Tim, to provide her with sperm so that she can have a child. Tim agrees to do so. When Ella is born, Sarah serves as the primary caretaker, and Tim, who lives in a different city, makes frequent visits. Should the two enter into any type of agreement to ensure the long-term stability of this situation?

Sarah subsequently marries Alan. Sarah wants to make sure that Alan has some parenting rights, although she wants to continue Tim's involvement. What steps might the three take? *See* Martha M. Ertman, Love's Promises: How Formal and Informal Contracts Shape All Kinds of Families (2015).

E. DISESTABLISHING PARENTHOOD

In most of the parenthood cases in this Chapter, individuals were fighting over the right to become a parent. In some cases, however, the question is how to disestablish parental rights. This problem may arise when a child has been conceived through rape. It may also arise when an individual is a presumed parent but subsequently discovers that person has no genetic relationship to the child, or when an individual claims no intent to become a parent.

1. Children Conceived Through Rape

Approximately 25,000 or more children are conceived through rape each year. More than half the states provide special means for terminating the parental rights of rapists. Some states require a criminal conviction before permitting termination, while others allow for termination without the requirement of a conviction, although they may mandate that the assault be established by a clear and convincing evidence. A number of states also allow the mother of a child conceived through rape to place the child for adoption without the consent of her attacker. Leslie Berkseth, Kelsey Meany, & Marie Zisa, *Rape and Sexual Assault*, 18 Geo. J. Gender & L. 743, 801 (2017).

In 2015, Congress enacted the Rape Survivor Child Custody Act, which authorizes governmental grants to states that have "a law that allows the mother of any child that was conceived through rape to seek court-ordered termination of the parental rights of her rapist with regard to that child, which the court is authorized to grant upon clear and convincing evidence of rape." 34 U.S.C.A. § 21303 (2018).

The UPA includes a provision addressing these issues.

SECTION 614. PRECLUDING ESTABLISHMENT OF PARENTAGE BY PERPETRATOR OF SEXUAL ASSAULT.

(a) In this section, "sexual assault" means [cite to this state's criminal rape statutes].

(b) In a proceeding in which a woman alleges that a man committed a sexual assault that resulted in the woman giving birth to a child, the woman may seek to preclude the man from establishing that he is a parent of the child.

(c)   This section does not apply if:

(1)   the man described in subsection (b) has previously been adjudicated to be a parent of the child; or

(2)   after the birth of the child, the man established a bonded and dependent relationship with the child which is parental in nature.

(d)   Unless Section 309 or 607 applies, a woman must file a pleading making an allegation under subsection (b) not later than two years after the birth of the child. The woman may file the pleading only in a proceeding to establish parentage under this [act].

(e)   An allegation under subsection (b) may be proved by:

(1)   evidence that the man was convicted of a sexual assault, or a comparable crime in another jurisdiction, against the woman and the child was born not later than 300 days after the sexual assault; or

(2)   clear-and-convincing evidence that the man committed sexual assault against the woman and the child was born not later than 300 days after the sexual assault.

(f)   Subject to subsections (a) through (d), if the court determines that an allegation has been proved under subsection (e), the court shall:

(1)   adjudicate that the man described in subsection (b) is not a parent of the child;

(2)   require the [state agency maintaining birth records] to amend the birth certificate if requested by the woman and the court determines that the amendment is in the best interest of the child; and

(3)   require the man pay to child support, birth-related costs, or both, unless the woman requests otherwise and the court determines that granting the request is in the best interest of the child.

Consider why rapists whose rights have been terminated still have an obligation to pay child support as the UPA permits. *See* Jennifer S. Hendricks, *The Wages of Genetic Entitlement: The Good, the Bad, and the Ugly in the Rape Survivor Child Custody Act*, 112 Nw. U.L. Rev. Online 75, 80 (2017)(addressing this issue).

2.   "Tricked Paternity"

This issue arises most frequently in the context of "tricked fathers" or "paternity fraud" cases, which are generally brought under one of two factual scenarios. In the first, the father alleges that the mother misrepresented her use of birth control and he had no intention of becoming a parent. The second scenario, which happens with increasing frequency, occurs when a man believes he is the genetic father, and that later turns out to be untrue. *See Dier v. Peters*, 815 N.W.2d 1, 4 (Iowa 2012). This discovery may occur during divorce or child support proceedings, often long after the child's birth.

In the 1990s, Congress passed child support legislation reflecting the advancement in scientific technologies and requiring states to provide genetic testing of all parties in contested paternity actions upon request. *See* 42 U.S.C. 666(a) (2018). While divorce is the legal process for dissolving marriage, an adult family relationship, disestablishment procedures provide a legal method for parents to dissolve the relationship with a child. *See* Vanessa S. Browne-Barbour,

States vary significantly in their approach to parenthood disestablishment. Consider the following:

> [I]n Arkansas, a man who signs a Voluntary Acknowledgment of Paternity ("VAP") can disestablish paternity based on a genetic test, and can even be relieved of past-due child support, but a man who is divorced cannot disestablish paternity because Arkansas considers the divorce decree to bar future litigation under res judicata and public policy reasons. Georgia's [ ] laws are just the reverse: a man can disestablish paternity after an adjudication, but if he signs a VAP, he can disestablish paternity only by showing fraud, mistake, or duress within a certain time frame. Furthermore, in Texas, a man who is adjudicated the father or who signs a VAP without a genetic test can now petition to terminate parental rights within two years of discovering he has been defrauded and is not the biological father.

Susan Ayres, *Paternity Un(Certainty): How the Law Surrounding Paternity Challenges Negatively Impacts Family Relationships and Women's Sexuality*, 20 J. Gender Race & Just. 237, 248–49 (2017).

––––––––––

The following case shows how the Texas statute affects these cases.

> ## IN RE C.E.
> Court of Appeals of Texas, 2012.
> 391 S.W.3d 200.

[handwritten marginalia: TAKEAWAY: A man who, without genetic testing, relied on misrepresentations that he was a child's biological father when he acknowledged paternity and agreed to pay child support may obtain genetic testing to disestablish paternity.]

JANE BLAND, JUSTICE.

* * *

The child who is the subject of this suit, C.E., was born to Stephanie Garcia in 1995, and was sixteen years old at the time of the hearing. At the time C.E. was born, Garcia was dating Ehrhardt. Shortly after C.E.'s birth, Ehrhardt signed a birth certificate acknowledging C.E. as his biological child.

In 2001, after the Office of the Attorney General [OAG] petitioned to establish the parent-child relationship and set child support, Ehrhardt signed an agreed child support review order. [CSRO] The trial court adjudicated Ehrhardt the father of C.E. and entered an agreed CSRO setting current child support in the amount of $206.00 per month.

In June 2011, the OAG filed a petition to modify the CSRO, seeking an order increasing Ehrhardt's monthly support obligation. The following month, Ehrhardt petitioned to terminate the parent-child relationship under Texas Family Code section 161.005(c). Section 161.005(c) permits a man to terminate the parent-child relationship if paternity previously was established without the benefit of genetic testing and a misrepresentation caused the man to believe that he fathered the child. Ehrhardt's verified petition alleged he previously had been adjudicated the father of C.E., but that his paternity was never confirmed with genetic testing. He further alleges that he discovered that Garcia had a relationship with another man the month before Garcia revealed she was pregnant. He averred that he mistakenly believed that he was C.E.'s biological father "based on misrepresentations that led him to that conclusion."

* * * Ehrhardt testified that th[e other] man was of a different ethnicity than him and that, as C.E. had grown, he noticed "a lot of differences" in "facial features and stuff like that." Ehrhardt never discussed the matter at C.E.'s birth and conceded that Garcia had never expressly told him that he was C.E.'s father.

Garcia did not testify. When asked by the trial court whether she would like to testify at the hearing, Garcia replied "I know he is the father. . . . And I mean, if—whatever needs to be done, . . . I'm willing to do whatever . . . whatever it takes to get this settled."

The trial court issued an order denying genetic testing, finding that testing was not warranted because Ehrhardt had failed to make a prima facie showing under section 161.005(c).

Ehrhardt contends that he produced sufficient evidence to set forth a prima facie case for termination under section 161.005(c). The OAG replies that Ehrhardt failed to identify any misrepresentation causing him to believe that he fathered C.E. and, in particular, a misrepresentation contemporaneous with the 2001 agreed CSRO-the proceeding in which Ehrhardt consented to paternity.

Texas Family Code section 161.005(c) permits a father to sue to terminate his parental rights under certain circumstances. TEX. FAM.CODE ANN. § 161.005(c). With exceptions inapplicable here, section 161.005(c) provides:

[A] man may file a suit for termination of the parent-child relationship between the man and a child if, without obtaining genetic testing, the man signed an acknowledgment of paternity of the child . . . or was adjudicated to be the father of the child in a previous proceeding under this title in which genetic testing did not occur. The petition must be verified and must allege facts showing that the petitioner:

(1) is not the child's genetic father; and

(2) signed the acknowledgment of paternity or failed to contest parentage in the previous proceeding because of the mistaken belief, at the time the acknowledgment was signed or on the date the court order in the previous proceeding was rendered, that he was the child's genetic father based on misrepresentations that led him to that conclusion.

Id. Section 161.005 requires that a man consent to paternity based on a mistaken belief—at the time he acknowledged paternity—that he fathered the child. And a man must believe that he is the father based on a misrepresentation.

* * * If the trial court finds that the man has established a prima facie case for termination, the trial court shall order the petitioner and child to submit to genetic testing. * * *

Ehrhardt's petition tracks the statutory language * * *

Although Ehrhardt's verified petition does not point to any particular misrepresentation, circumstantial evidence adduced at the pretrial hearing supports the allegations in his petition. At the pre-trial hearing, Ehrhardt's counsel asked him to list two reasons why he felt misled to believe that C.E. was his biological child. In reply, Ehrhardt testified, "[W]hen she was born, there was a comparison of the—to me in her features. I believed a lot of it." But as C.E. grew, C.E. and Ehrhardt no longer resembled one another. In addition to testimony regarding C.E.'s appearance, Ehrhardt raised doubts about C.E.'s parentage based on Garcia's relationship with another man. In 1995, Ehrhardt discovered photos of Garcia and another man. Garcia admitted to having a sexual relationship with the man. The following month, Garcia announced that she was pregnant with C.E. and sought child support from Ehrhardt as the child's father. C.E. later mentioned that Ehrhardt might not be her father. The hearing adduced circumstantial evidence that Garcia may have misrepresented Ehrhardt's paternity in naming him the father in the birth certificate and the child support proceeding because another possible father exists, and that Ehrhardt acknowledged paternity based on these representations, without undergoing paternity testing.

The statute asks for a prima facie showing of a misrepresentation causing Ehrhardt to believe that he fathered the child. We conclude that a verified petition alleging that a misrepresentation caused Ehrhardt to believe that he was C.E.'s biological father coupled with circumstantial evidence that a misrepresentation as to paternity was made constitutes a prima facie case for genetic testing under Texas Family Code section 161.005(c).

We reverse the judgment of the trial court and remand for further proceedings consistent with this opinion.

NOTES AND QUESTIONS

1. *Protecting interests.* What are the parenting interests at stake in *C.E.?* What about the child's interests? Should a father be able to disestablish paternity when a child is 16? Consider that one of the reasons that Ehrhardt believed he was not the father was that the child's features appeared to be that of a different "ethnicity." This type of claim after birth has occurred for centuries, and it was sometimes the cause for divorce among white married couples during the antebellum period—when, for example, the white wife gave birth to a child of mixed race. *See* Loren Schweninger, Families in Crisis in the Old South 23 (2012).

2. *Continuing the parental relationship.* The statute provides for counseling for any party, as well as an option for continued visitation with the child after the parent-child relationship has been terminated. Tex. Fam. Code Sec. 161.005(m)(2018).

3. *Contracts, doctors, and avoiding parental obligations.* Consider what happened to William Marotta, who responded to an ad for a sperm donor on "Craigslist" posted by a lesbian couple. *State, ex rel., Sec'y Dep't for Children & Families v. W.M.*, No. 2012DM2686, 2016 WL 8293872, at *1 (Kan. Dist. Ct. 2016).

Although the three of them signed an agreement establishing that Marotta's role was limited to sperm donation and did not include parenthood, a lower Kansas court decided that the agreement was unenforceable and that Marotta was, nonetheless, liable for child support. In effect, the contract was not effective because the parties had not used a licensed physician (the mother inseminated herself). An appellate court reversed the lower court's opinion, finding the mother's partner to be the second parent. How would the 2017 UPA have affected the outcome?

Should the establishment of parenthood turn on whether sperm has been provided to a licensed physician, as required by an earlier version of the UPA? Should individuals be able to determine, by contract, whether they must assume parental rights?

4. *No contracts, no rights.* Professor Katharine Baker has suggested that mothers should be able to enter into binding contracts with men concerning their parental support obligations, making fatherhood, unlike motherhood, a voluntary status. Katharine Baker, *Bargaining or Biology? The History and Future of Paternity Law and Parental Status*, 14 Cornell J.L. Pub. Pol'y 1 (2004). And Professor Melanie Jacobs questions why a man who has no intent to become a father may, nonetheless, be adjudicated the legal father. Melanie B. Jacobs, *Intentional Parenthood's Influence: Rethinking Procreative*

Autonomy and Federal Paternity Establishment Policy, 20 Am. U.J. Gender Soc. Pol'y & L. 489, 492 (2012). Do such outcomes seem appropriate and consistent with existing case law? Do they recognize the realities of parenting and the interests of the child?

PROBLEM 5-11

Molly Simmons has requested your legal advice. She recently gave birth to a healthy daughter, Susan. Her pregnancy, however, was utterly unexpected. She had begun a relationship with Richard Prentice. Before engaging in sexual intercourse, they had extensively discussed birth control options because Molly did not want to get pregnant. Richard told her that he had had a vasectomy, so pregnancy should not be a concern. Based on that representation, they entered into a sexual relationship.

She did not find out that she was pregnant until her fourth month. She was unwilling to have an abortion after her first trimester, so she carried the child to term. What obligations does she now have with respect to Richard? How might a court rule?

CHAPTER 6

ADOPTION

■ ■ ■

Chapter 5 covered assisted reproductive technology, one method that brings children into the family without the sexual intimacy between spouses or nonmarital partners that otherwise attends family creation. This Chapter concerns a second method, adoption.

1. HISTORICAL BACKGROUND AND THE CONTEMPORARY LANDSCAPE

A. HISTORICAL BACKGROUND

Formal adoption did not exist at common law. A child might be transferred informally from one household to another, sometimes as an indentured servant or an apprentice to a family that agreed to provide care and education, perhaps in return for needed labor. But neither indenture nor apprenticeship severed the legal relationship between biological parent and child and replaced it with a legal relationship with other parents. "These arrangements were highly contractual; the terms of obligation set out on both sides. * * * Masters may have agreed to certain parent-like obligations—feeding, housing, and moral education in the case of apprentices. They did not, however, understand themselves to be acquiring a relation but rather an employee (in the case of indenture) or a trainee (in the case of apprenticeship)." Carol Sanger, *Bargaining for Motherhood: Postadoption Visitation Agreements*, 41 Hofstra L. Rev. 309, 311 (2012).

Private legislative bills sometimes approved adoption of a particular child, substituting the adoptive parents for the biological parents. Such private bills, however, were rare. Legislation providing general processes for adoption by court order, the model maintained by every state today, did not appear until the mid-19th century.

JAMIL S. ZAINALDIN,
THE EMERGENCE OF A MODERN AMERICAN FAMILY LAW:
CHILD CUSTODY, ADOPTION, AND THE COURTS, 1796–1851
73 Nw. U. L. Rev. 1038, 1042–45 (1979).

[U]nlike most historical phenomena, the first instance of departure from the traditional model of adoption can be isolated by location, day, and year. On April 2, 1847, the Massachusetts House of Representatives ordered that the Committee on the Judiciary consider "the expediency of providing by law for the adoption of children." On May 13, 1851, the Committee reported to the House "A Bill for the Adoption of Children." There seems to have been little or no opposition. Eleven days later the Massachusetts legislature passed the first general "Act to Provide for the Adoption of Children" in America.

The Massachusetts adoption statute of 1851 was the first *modern* adoption law in history. It is notable for two reasons. First, it contradicted the most fundamental principles of English domestic relations law, and overruled centuries of English precedent and legislation which prohibited the absolute, permanent, and voluntary transfer of parental power to third persons. Second, the traditional status of adoption allocated benefits between the giver and taker, while the Massachusetts statute distinguished the adoptee as the prime beneficiary. The heart of the adoption transaction became the judicially monitored transfer of rights with due regard for the *welfare of the child* and the *parental qualifications* of the adopters.

Within the next twenty-five years, more than a score of states would enact some form of adoption law, and in most cases the Massachusetts statute served as a model. Strangely, it would seem, the passage of the first Massachusetts act attracted little public attention. Little or no debate over the issue occurred in the legislature, apparently no social reform movements advocated passage of the law, and, when the law did appear, few newspapers bothered to take note of the event. And for several years after the passage of the statute, few adopters took advantage of the law. There is, then, no clear explanation for why the legislature passed the law when it did. Nor at first glance would there seem to be any explanation for the casual reception accorded such an apparently radical statute.

The new law may have been part of the larger legislative trend of substituting private enactments with general statutes. Private laws granting divorce, legitimacy, incorporation, and change of name were becoming particularly cumbersome in the 1840s. And there is ample evidence that children throughout the United States were being "adopted" through private acts, especially those concerning change of name. A contemporary of the nineteenth century—and an advocate of statutory adoption—thought that the law would secure important rights to the adopters. A modern commentator, however, suggests that the first general adoption statute may have evolved out of a desire to protect the perceived right of inheritance of nonlegally adopted children.

Just why the Massachusetts legislature moved in 1851 may never be known. Perhaps all of these reasons prompted the lawmakers to action. At once they endeavored to protect the child and to endow his standing in the family with status, while conferring upon adopters the rights and duties of parents. The discretionary proceeding in the probate court was perceived as the soundest, most efficient method for effecting adoption.

B. THE CONTEMPORARY LANDSCAPE

"Some experts estimate that 100 million Americans have either been personally touched by adoption within their families or know someone who is or has adopted." Jo Jones & Paul Placek, Nat'l Council For Adoption, *Adoption: By the Numbers* ii (2017). Adopted children represent about 2.5% of children living with a parent-householder in the United States today, and courts grant more than a million child adoption petitions each decade. Nat'l Council For Adoption, *Adoption Factbook V*, at 5 (Nat'l Council For Adoption, Elisa A. Rosman et al. eds., 2011), http://www.adoptioncouncil. org/resources/adoption-factbook (last visited Mar. 23, 2019) ("Adoption Factbook").

"[T]he total number of all adoptions taking place in the U.S. has fallen, from a count of 133,737 adoptions in 2007 to 110,373 (41,023 related adoptions and 69,350 unrelated adoptions) in 2014." Jones & Placek, *supra* at ii. Despite the decline, the numbers remain sizable and adoption law remains a specialized family law field for attorneys, whether in private practice representing parties in individual adoptions, or in the public policy arena advancing systemic law reform in the best interests of children.

Adoption today is "the legal equivalent of biological parenthood." *Smith v. OFFER*, 431 U.S. 816, 844 n.51 (1977). "A decree of adoption severs forever every part of the biological parent and child relationship," and creates a new legal parent-child relationship between the child and the adoptive parents. *J.R. v. S.P.*, 89 N.E.3d 438, 441 (Ind. Ct. App. 2017). When a biological parent's marital or nonmarital partner (the child's stepparent) is the adoptive parent, the parent-child relationship continues with the custodial biological parent, and the adoption permanently displaces only the biological parent whose parental rights the court has terminated.

As the adoptee's legal parents, adoptive parents acquire the status, rights, and obligations of parenthood and family autonomy discussed elsewhere in this book, including the Fourteenth Amendment substantive due process right to direct the child's upbringing free from unreasonable government intervention. The adopted child assumes the status, rights, and obligations of a biological child of the adoptive parents. The new reciprocal parent-child relationship affects application of a variety of federal and state laws, including tax laws, workers' compensation laws, Social Security, public assistance laws, inheritance laws, and family leave laws.

[handwritten margin note: adoption today is the legal equivalent of biological parenthood]

[handwritten margin note: what the legal parents gain]

2. HOW MAY A CHILD BE ADOPTED?

In most states today, the juvenile or family court holds exclusive original jurisdiction to decide adoption petitions, though some states instead vest adoption jurisdiction in the probate court or surrogate's court. A child is adopted only when the court enters a final decree approving the adoption. This Section explores the adoption process.

Three steps mark the court's approval decision. The child must be available for adoption; the prospective adoptive parent must be within the adoption act's enumeration of persons eligible to adopt; and the court must find that the prospective adoption would be in the best interests of the child.

[handwritten margin note: 3 steps required for adoption]

A. PUBLIC AGENCIES, PRIVATE AGENCIES, AND PRIVATE PLACEMENTS

Adults may adopt children domestically or internationally. As Professor Fedders' excerpt below discusses, children may be adopted (1) through the public child welfare system which has custody of foster children who have either been removed from their biological parents for abuse or neglect, or whose parents have died, been imprisoned, or abandoned them; (2) through a nongovernmental for-profit or non-profit agency to which the biological parents have transferred custody of a child for adoptive placement; or (3) through an independent transfer (a "private placement") arranged directly between the adoptive and biological parents, often with the assistance of a lawyer or other intermediary.

BARBARA FEDDERS,
RACE AND MARKET VALUES IN
DOMESTIC INFANT ADOPTION

88 N.C. L. Rev. 1687, 1689–95 (2010), reprinted in Race in Transnational
and Transracial Adoption (Vilna Bashi Treitler ed., 2014).

Adoptive parents seeking to adopt a child who has been voluntarily placed by her birth parents may choose to work through an agency or to participate in an independent adoption. Agencies provide services often unavailable to those who adopt independently. For example, the more than 2,000 licensed adoption agencies nationwide provide pre- and post-adoption counseling to birth parents and also obtain medical and social histories of birth parents and their families for adoptive parents. Agencies arrange all contact and communication between adoptive and birth parents. They can typically offer an expectant birth mother and father several prospective adoptive parents, from which the birth parents can choose. Agencies can also find an adoptive family for a child whose birth parents do not want to be involved in the selection.

In independent adoptions, which are lawful in nearly every state, birth parents and adoptive parents find each other without the assistance of an agency. Most states also allow intermediaries, typically attorneys, to establish connections between adoptive and birth parents; the range of functions they may employ and the costs they may charge are regulated by statute and vary from state to state. A handful of states permit advertising by adoptive parents, birth parents, agencies, and/or adoption intermediaries.

* * *

Compared with adoptions from the public child-welfare system, private adoptions are extremely expensive. Agency adoptions are estimated to range from $4,000 to $100,000; the numbers are similar for independent adoptions. * * *

NOTES AND QUESTIONS

1.   *Race.* The public and private adoption markets are marked by sharp distinctions. "[The] state-run domestic market—comprised nearly entirely of older, minority, and special needs children—is one of the few sectors of the domestic baby trade not lacking in supply." Kimberly D. Krawiec, *Altruism and Intermediation in the Market for Babies*, 66 Wash. & Lee L. Rev. 203, 230 (2009). Professor Fedders notes that "the demand for white infants exceeds their supply." Fedders, *supra* at 1688. What factors account for the contemporary shortage of white adoptable children without special needs? The role of money in public and private adoptions is explored below ("Baby Selling").

2.   *Agency matching.* By the middle of the twentieth century, social workers believed that the happiness and fulfillment of adoptive families required matching adoptive parents and adoptees. "Matching became one of the principal strategies for lessening the stigma of adoption * * *. This included attempts to match people of the same ethnic, religious, and racial origins, so that the family would look like a biologically formed family." Naomi R. Cahn, *Perfect Substitutes or the Real Thing?*, 52 Duke L.J. 1077, 1148–49 (2003).

"Many vestiges of this matching strategy still exist" in the 21st century. *Id.* at 1149. "[A]gencies and social workers connect people looking to adopt with minors in need of a home through a highly discretionary matching process to which courts give legal effect." Dov Fox, *Race Sorting in Family Formation*, 49 Fam. L.Q. 55, 56 (2015).

In light of society's general commitment to end officially sanctioned discrimination, what state interests support continued discriminatory treatment of prospective adoptive parents who would otherwise be fit parents for a child who is available for adoption?

3.   *Special-needs adoptions.* In 2014, special-needs children comprised 88.5% of unrelated domestic adoptions, more than twice the 2007 percentage.

See Jo Jones & Paul Placek, Nat'l Council For Adoption, *Adoption: By the Numbers* 4 (2017). The definition of "special needs" differs from state to state, but all states' definitions include older children; children of racial or ethnic minority groups; children with siblings who should be placed together if possible; and children with behavioral, developmental, mental health, or medical challenges dating from birth, from physical or sexual or emotional abuse inflicted by their biological parents or other caretakers, or from the trauma of removal from the biological parents.

Psychologists recognize that children freed for adoption, feeling "the overwhelming and essential nature of belonging in a family," thrive best in permanent adoptive homes rather than in prolonged foster care or in institutional placement. Susan Livingston Smith et al., *A Family for Life: The Vital Need to Achieve Permanency for Children in Care* 4 (Donaldson Adoption Inst. 2013). (Foster care is the temporary placement of an abused or neglected child in the home of state-licensed adults when the legal parents or other caretakers cannot care for the child.)

For want of available adoptive homes, however, many special-needs children are deprived of permanency. Children awaiting adoption are disproportionately minorities and older children who have been in substitute care for most of their lives. *See* U.S. Dep't of Health and Human Servs., *The AFCARS Report # 25, Preliminary FY 2017 Estimates As of Aug. 10, 2018* (2018).

To facilitate adoption of special-needs children, federal and state laws provide financial assistance for parents who wish to adopt but may be unable to afford the sustained medical, maintenance, and special services that these children sometimes require. Eligibility for tax credits and other public assistance generally depends on the adoptive parents' financial circumstances and the child's special needs. "Adoption assistance helps many families adopting children from the welfare system—the vast majority of whom are foster parents (54%) or relatives (31%)—who have very low incomes." Georgia Deoudes, *The Vital Role of Adoption Subsidies* 1 (Donaldson Adoption Inst. 2012).

4. *The Internet and social media.* The Internet and social media continue to revolutionize many aspects of American life, including the process for adopting children. Official federal and state agency websites, for example, provide photographs and profiles of children who await adoption. Adults seeking to adopt also frequently use the Internet and social media to locate birth mothers and arrange private placements. *See, e.g.,* Tiffany Smart, *Ten Tips for Navigating an Open Adoption with Social Media* (2014); Nicole Pelletiere, WSB-TV, *Couple Adopt Baby Through Instagram*, July 18, 2018. What advice would you give a friend or client who is considering whether to use the Internet and social media to identify a prospective adoptive child?

A NOTE ON THE INTERSTATE COMPACT
ON THE PLACEMENT OF CHILDREN

State adoption laws and practices vary in sometimes significant ways. In the absence of national uniformity, persons seeking advantages from comparatively favorable provisions or processes may move a child from one state to another for placement. In 2007, about 14,000 children entered or left states for adoption, implicating the Interstate Compact on the Placement of Children, which all states have enacted since it was first proposed in 1960. *See* Adoption Factbook, *supra*, at 8–94; Am. Public Human Servs. Ass'n, *Text of Interstate Compact on the Placement of Children* (2018).

The Compact seeks to protect children who are moved between states for foster care or adoption, and to maximize their opportunity for a placement that serves their best interests. The Compact applies to both agency adoptions and private adoptions.

The Compact prohibits individuals and entities, except specified close relatives of a child, from bringing or sending the child into another state for foster or adoptive placement unless the sender complies with the Compact's terms and the receiving state's child placement laws. Before placing a child, senders must notify the receiving state's compact administrator, who must investigate and, if satisfied, notify the sending state that the proposed placement does not appear contrary to the child's best interests. The child may not be sent or brought into the receiving state until notification is given. The sending agency retains jurisdiction over the child in matters relating to custody, supervision, care, and disposition until the child is adopted, reaches majority, becomes self-supporting, or is discharged with the receiving state's concurrence. The sending agency also retains financial responsibility to support and maintain the child during the placement period.

The Compact recites two penalties for sending or bringing a child across state lines in violation of its provisions. Violations are punishable under either state's child placement laws, and may also be grounds for suspending or revoking a license to place or care for children. The Compact does not specify whether violation may also be a ground for dismissing the adoption petition, and only a few decisions have entered dismissal orders. Should dismissal be a potential remedy for violation?

Where a lawyer representing a party to the adoption overlooks or violates the Compact, the lawyer may face professional discipline, sanctions under the state civil procedure code's bad-faith pleading rule, or reduction of fees otherwise awardable. *See, e.g., Matter of Adoptive Child R.*, 828 N.Y.S.2d 846, 850 (Fam. Ct. 2006) (citing decisions). Counsel's noncompliance may be unintentional because many lawyers (like many law enforcement officials) do not know about the Compact's existence or operation.

B. CONSENT AND NOTICE

1. Consent

The Biological Parent's Consent

[handwritten: ⊕ key rule]

The general rule is that the court may not order an adoption unless the biological parent's rights have been terminated either voluntarily or involuntarily. The biological parent may give voluntary, knowing consent to adoption (or, as some statutes call it, "release," "relinquishment," or "surrender"). Most states specify that a biological parent may not execute a consent until the child is born. In some states, however, this specification applies only to the biological mother; the biological father may consent before or after the child's birth. Why would states distinguish between mothers and fathers in this respect?

[handwritten left margin: difference in states]

A biological parent may execute a specific consent (authorizing adoption only by particular persons named in the consent), or a general consent (authorizing adoption by persons chosen by the agency, an authorized intermediary, or the court). To preserve confidentiality, general consents are normally used in adoptions in which a child placement agency is the intermediary.

If a parent has not executed a voluntary consent, a court may terminate parental rights involuntarily, such as when the court determines that the biological parent is incompetent, has severely abused the child, or has abandoned or otherwise neglected the child for a specified period. If the biological parent is incompetent, the court may appoint a guardian of the parent's person, with authority to consent in the parent's stead.

The biological mother has traditionally held the right to veto an adoption by withholding her consent, unless consent was excused by operation of law. The right applied regardless of whether the mother was married to the father at conception and birth. Before *Stanley v. Illinois*, 405 U.S. 645 (1972), however, the nonmarital father held no right to notice of the child's impending adoption, and no right to veto the adoption under the federal Constitution, or under the constitutions or statutes of most states. By conferring federal due process and equal protection rights on the nonmarital father with respect to the child, *Stanley* and its progeny raise the specter that the father whose rights the court has not terminated (including a father who cannot be located) may appear sometime in the future and contest the adoption. Chapter 5 briefly discusses the *Stanley* line of decisions.

Because a biological parent's valid consent to adoption may terminate the parent-child relationship, statutes prescribe formalities designed to emphasize the profound consequences of consent. In almost all states, consent must be in writing. The adoption act may specify that the consent

[handwritten bottom: ⊕ biological parent's consent MUST be in writing]

be signed before a judge, notary, or other designated officer. A specified number of witnesses may be required, and the consent may have to be under oath. Failure to comply with one or more of these formalities leaves the consent's validity open to question and may invalidate the adoption. *See, e.g., In re Adoption of C.B.M.,* 992 N.E.2d 687, 693–94 (Ind. 2013). Why might a court approve the adoption despite technical failure to comply with consent formalities?

The Adoptee's or Agency's Consent

In most states, consent to the adoption must also be secured from the child if he or she is over a specified age. *See, e.g.,* Cal. Fam. Code § 8602 (2018) (twelve or older). Some statutes authorize the court to dispense with the child's consent for good cause. *See, e.g.,* Idaho Code Ann. § 16–1504(1) (2018) ("Consent to adoption is required from: (a) The adoptee, if he is more than twelve (12) years of age, unless he does not have the mental capacity to consent.").

Why should older adoptees' consent be a condition of adoption? Should the court have authority to dispense with this consent in appropriate cases? Should the court consider the wishes of a child who is below the minimum age of consent, and if so, how can the court ascertain these wishes?

Where a child is in the custody of a public or private child placement agency, the agency's consent to the adoption may also matter. In a few states, agency refusal to consent divests the court of authority to grant the adoption. Many states make the agency's consent a prerequisite to adoption, but authorize judicial scrutiny by providing that the agency may not unreasonably withhold consent. *See, e.g., Adoption of Paisley,* 178 A.3d 1228, 1235 (Me. 2018) (state agency unreasonably withheld its written consent to the two-year-old child's adoption by her licensed foster parents, with whom the girl had lived for most of her life). Even where the consent statute seemingly makes agency consent mandatory, many decisions hold that the agency's refusal to consent is persuasive only. The court may grant the adoption if it finds that the agency's refusal to consent is contrary to the best interests of the child.

A Minor Biological Parent's Consent

What if one or both unmarried biological parents are themselves minors? In most states, a minor parent's decision is "regulated exactly the same as an adult's decision. In only fifteen states are there different or additional requirements for a minor's decision * * *. In four states, a minor must be provided independent legal counsel. In another four states, a court must appoint a guardian ad litem for the minor parent. In five states, a minor's parent must consent" to the minor's decision. Malinda L. Seymore, *Sixteen and Pregnant: Minors' Consent in Abortion and Adoption,* 25 Yale

J.L. & Fem. 99, 129 (2013). To help reduce the adoption's vulnerability to later collateral attack, the adoptive parents' counsel may wish the minor to acknowledge her consent in open court.

Revoking Consent

revocation

In many states, a biological parent may revoke consent to adoption within the first few days after execution, or within the first few hours or days after the child's birth. The court may then have authority to determine whether revocation is in the best interests of the child, and whether the consent was procured by fraud or duress. *See, e.g., Thompson v. Brunck*, 545 S.W.3d 830 (Ark. Ct. App. 2018) (granting biological mother's motion to withdraw her consent to child's adoption as procured by fraud).

Professor Elizabeth J. Samuels concludes that the brief windows (considerably shorter than the approximate six-week windows afforded by most European nations) stem from policy choices to "value an increase in infant adoptions over the goal of encouraging careful deliberation" by the biological parent, usually the mother. Elizabeth J. Samuels, *Time to Decide? The Laws Governing Mothers' Consents to the Adoption of Their Newborn Infants*, 72 Tenn. L. Rev. 509, 511–12, 513 (2005).

Whose interests are at stake when the state establishes the length of time within which a biological parent may revoke consent to an adoption? Do the brief windows established in many states satisfactorily accommodate these interests? Should the window be longer where the biological mother is herself a minor, or should the law seek to vindicate the various interests when she is presented with the relinquishment agreement in the first instance?

2. Notice

The right to give or withhold consent to the adoption must be distinguished from the right to notice of the adoption proceeding. A person with the right to consent, such as a biological parent, may veto the adoption by withholding consent.

Notice of the adoption proceeding must be provided to persons whose consent to the adoption is required, including nonmarital fathers who have preserved their rights under the putative father registry or similar state laws. The state's adoption act, however, may also require notice to other persons, who may address the court concerning the best interests of the child, but who may not veto the adoption.

To expedite the adoption process, some states provide that notice of the adoption proceeding need not be given to persons who have executed valid consents to adoption. Do these provisions excusing notice make good sense?

C. ELIGIBILITY TO ADOPT

B.L. v. J.S., set out below, concerns the second step in the adoption process, the prospective adoptive parents' eligibility to adopt. The child was available for adoption once the trial court, after granting the biological parents notice and opportunity to be heard, entered an order terminating their parental rights. Eligibility depended on interpretation of Kentucky's adoption act.

[handwritten: ↖ issue of eligibility to adopt]

B.L. v. J.S.
Court of Appeals of Kentucky, 2014.
434 S.W.3d 61.

[handwritten: Takeaway: step-relatives qualify as relatives for purposes of adopting a child not officially placed for adoption beforehand.]

JONES, JUDGE:

This case arises from a Judgment of Adoption entered by the Franklin Circuit Court granting the adoption of a minor child, B.L. (Minor Child), to Appellees J.S. and J.S. (Adoptive Parents) and the resulting termination of Appellant's (Biological Father) parental rights with respect to Minor Child. * * * [W]e AFFIRM.

I. BACKGROUND

Minor Child was born on December 15, 2007, to A.R. (Biological Mother) and Biological Father. Biological Mother and Biological Father lived together on and off after Minor Child's birth. Biological Father was incarcerated several times after Minor Child's birth. He was last incarcerated on February 9, 2011, and remained in custody throughout the remainder of the time period at issue.

On April 14, 2011, Biological Mother gave birth prematurely to R.J.P., Minor Child's half-brother. After R.J.P. showed severe signs of drug withdrawal and his meconium drug screen tested positive for cocaine, methadone, and several other drugs, the Cabinet for Health and Family Services (the Cabinet) was alerted.

[handwritten: ↖ baby had signs of drug withdrawal at birth]

On April 21, 2011, the Cabinet filed a * * * Juvenile Neglect Petition for both children. The petition listed Biological Father as the biological father of Minor Child, but only Biological Mother was listed as a person responsible for neglecting Minor Child. Biological Father was properly served with a copy of the petition in jail. *[handwritten: ⋆ Juvenile Neglect Petition]*

* * * During the hearing [on April 29, 2011], Biological Mother stipulated to neglect * * *. The Cabinet placed the children with the Adoptive Parents in June of 2011. *[handwritten: ← kids go to adoptive parents]*

[The Adoptive Parents were the children's step great-aunt and step great-uncle. The trial court held various dispositional hearings, [and] ultimately * * * award[ed] custody of Minor Child to the Adoptive Parents. The Adoptive Parents filed a Petition to Adopt Minor Child.]

* * *

* * * After oral argument, the trial court denied Biological Father's motion to dismiss * * *. The trial court specifically found that "considering the fact that [Biological Father] was incarcerated during the entirety of the neglect case, and continues to be incarcerated, without the ability to take custody of, or care for [Minor Child], the trial court does not believe that the proceedings in the neglect case have any effect on the adoption petition that [Biological Father] seeks to dismiss."

A final hearing on the adoption petition was held on February 11, 2013. * * * Biological Father testified that he was aware of Biological Mother's drug use while caring for Minor Child; that he had previously used drugs while caring for Minor Child; that he had been incarcerated at least three of the five years of Minor Child's life; that he would be eligible for parole in March 2013 but he had no expectation that he would be granted parole; that he did not have employment lined up when he was released from prison; that he would likely have to live in a halfway house upon release; and that he had not participated in any medical or education choices for Minor Child. Biological Father also testified that he planned to pursue custody of Minor Child after his release from prison; that he had sent cards to Minor Child; that his mother had been in contact with Minor Child and sent him gifts; and that he had provided some supplies for Minor Child, such as diapers, on occasion prior to his incarceration. Biological Mother did not present any evidence.

The Adoptive Parents also testified and presented testimony from the Cabinet. * * * The trial court eventually * * * issued a Judgment of Adoption on March 21, 2013. It is from that Judgment that Biological Father appeals.

* * *

III. ANALYSIS

* * *

* * * [W]e see no error that the trial court committed in approving the adoption * * *. The trial court concluded that given Biological Father's and Biological Mother's respective situations, there was no likelihood of a successful, reasonably prompt reunification with Minor Child that would be in the child's best interests.

C.   Requisite Familial Relationship

Biological Father's final assignment of error is the circuit court erred by granting the petition for adoption because the Adoptive Parents did not have the requisite familial relationship to adopt Minor Child pursuant to KRS 199.470. This statute states, in relevant part:

(4)   No petition for adoption shall be filed unless prior to the filing of the petition the child sought to be adopted has been placed for adoption by a child-placing institution or agency, or by the cabinet, or the child has been placed with written approval of the secretary; but no approval shall be necessary in the case of:

(a)   A child sought to be adopted by a stepparent, grandparent, sister, brother, aunt, uncle, great-grandparent, great aunt, or great uncle;

[The court found that Minor Child was not placed for adoption by the Cabinet, which issued a report recommending the adoption only after the adoption petition was filed. The applicable statute provides that "[a]ny person who is eighteen (18) years of age and who is a resident of this state or has resided in this state for twelve (12) months next before filing may file a petition for leave to adopt a child * * *."] Therefore, Biological Father argues that since a step great-aunt and step great-uncle are not a group of individuals specifically listed in the above statute, the Adoptive Parents should not have been permitted to file a petition for adoption and therefore the trial court erred by granting the adoption.

* * *

Though the statute does list specific persons who may adopt as relatives, it *does not* mandate that those persons be blood relatives and there are no other applicable statutes defining relatives for purposes of adoption as only blood relatives. * * *

Also persuasive is the fact that relatives related only by marriage are consistently considered "relatives" for purposes of child placement in other contexts. * * *

It is our view in the absence of an express requirement that the relatives listed in KRS 199.470(4)(a) be blood relatives of the child, there is no error in allowing a great-aunt and great-uncle related by marriage to file a petition to adopt without placement for adoption by the Cabinet. Therefore, we find no reversible error in the trial court's decision to grant the adoption based on KRS 199.470. * * *

D.   THE BEST INTERESTS STANDARD

The final step in the adoption process is the court's determination whether the prospective adoption would be in the best interests of the child.

Only about 1% of adoptions annually are contested, but one or more of the following issues sometimes arise. Depending on the state adoption act's terms, some of these issues may also affect the prospective adoptive parents' eligibility to adopt.

Low-Income Persons

Adoption may be in the child's best interests regardless of the adoptive parents' income. Adoption seeks "to provide the *best* home that is available. By that is not meant the wealthiest home, but the home which * * * the court deems will best promote the welfare of the particular child." *State ex rel. St. Louis Children's Aid Soc'y v. Hughes*, 177 S.W.2d 474, 477 (Mo. 1944) (emphasis in original).

Same-Sex Couples

In 2016, in a suit by married same-sex couples, a federal district court struck down, on Fourteenth Amendment equal protection grounds, a Mississippi statute that barred "couples of the same gender" from adopting children. *Campaign for Southern Equality v. Miss. Dep't of Human Services*, 175 F. Supp. 3d 691 (S.D. Miss. 2016). Mississippi had been the only state with an express statutory ban, and the state did not appeal the decision.

One member of a same-sex marriage or nonmarital relationship may wish to file a "second parent" or "co-parent" petition to adopt the other's child, who may have been born or adopted before the relationship began. A same-sex couple may also seek to adopt a child of biological parents other than either petitioning spouse or partner.

In *Obergefell v. Hodges*, 135 S. Ct. 2584 (2015), a principal decision in Chapter 2, the Court held that same-sex couples have Fourteenth Amendment substantive due process and equal protection rights to marry. The Court decided only the issue presented—namely, the right to marry— and not whether the Constitution guarantees same-sex couples, or gays and lesbians generally, other rights or other protections against discrimination.

One study found that 60% of public and private adoption agencies accept applications from gays and lesbians, that some adoption agencies actively reach out to gays and lesbians, and that about 40% of adoption agencies have placed children with gay or lesbian parents. The study concluded that the numbers are probably higher because most agencies do not maintain statistics on their clients' sexual orientation, and because many applicants may hide their sexual orientation for fear that agencies would hold it against them. *See* Evan B. Donaldson Adoption Inst., *Expanding Resources for Children* 11 (2006).

Resistance continues, however. Some private adoption agencies cite their religious or moral objections for refusing to place children with same-sex couples. *See, e.g.*, Mark Strasser, *Conscience Clauses and the Placement of Children*, 2013 Utah L. Rev. 985. At least nine states (including Alabama, Mississippi, Michigan, North Dakota, South Dakota, Texas, and Virginia) have enacted legislation that permits such refusal. *See* Lawrence Hurley, *Gay Adoption Fight Looms After Supreme Court's Cake Ruling*, Reuters, June 4, 2018.

On the other hand, statutes in at least nine states (California, Maryland, Massachusetts, New Jersey, Nevada, New York, Oregon, Rhode Island, and Wisconsin) prohibit discrimination based on sexual orientation in adoption, foster care, or both. *Id.* Some states reportedly even take affirmative measures to encourage LGBT individuals to adopt foster children who await adoption. One of these states is Connecticut, whose Governor recently tweeted: "On any given day in our state, over 4,000 children are living in foster care. We want to spread the message that ALL families are valued as potential foster and adoptive families." Avery Anapol, *Connecticut Recruiting LGBT Families to Adopt Children As Other States Ban Same-Sex Couples*, The Hill, May 18, 2018.

With a future challenge to religious-objection adoption statutes likely to reach the Supreme Court, the Court sent mixed signals in its narrowly-reasoned decision in *Masterpiece Cakeshop, Ltd. v. Colorado Civil Rights Comm'n*, 138 S. Ct. 1719 (2018), as Chapter 2 discusses. On the one hand, the Court recognized the basic legitimacy of state laws protecting against discrimination based on sexual orientation; on the other, the Court insisted that persons who had religious objections to such laws were entitled to have their beliefs considered in a neutral and respectful way.

"Adoption by same-sex couples is increasingly seen as acceptable by Americans and adoptions are on the rise among lesbian and gay (LG) people." Rachel H. Farr & Abbie E. Goldberg, *Sexual Orientation, Gender Identity, and Adoption Law*, 56 Fam. Ct. Rev. 374, 374 (2018). Nearly 27,000 same-sex couples in the U.S. are raising 58,000 adopted or foster children. Anthony Giambrone, *Equality in Marriage May Not Bring Equality in Adoption*, The Atlantic, May 26, 2015. The bulk of these children have special needs and thus might otherwise be denied permanency in long-term foster care. *Id.*

When the child's availability for adoption and the parents' eligibility to adopt are established, adoptive placement depends on the best interests inquiry. The number of studies on gay and lesbian parenting is comparatively limited, but

> social science research concludes that children reared by gay and
> lesbian parents fare comparably to those of children raised by
> heterosexuals on a range of measures of social and psychological

adjustment. * * * [V]irtually every valid study reaches the same conclusion: The children of gays and lesbians adjust positively and their families function well. The limited research on gay/lesbian adoption points in the same direction.

Donaldson Adoption Inst., *Expanding Resources for Children, supra* at 11.

Single Persons

Most state adoption acts permit a single person to adopt a child who is available for adoption, but require married couples to petition jointly unless the petitioner is the child's stepparent. In some states, two unmarried adults may not be eligible jointly to adopt a child even if neither adult is a biological parent of the child. *See, e.g., In re Jason C.*, 533 A.2d 32 (N.H. 1987).

Adoption by single persons can be in the best interests of some children. "[S]ingle adoptive parents are * * * most likely to adopt older children than infants, and * * * tend[ ] to adopt 'special needs' children who [are] older, minority, and/or handicapped." W. Bradford Wilcox & Robin Fretwell Wilson, *Bringing Up Baby: Adoption, Marriage, and the Best Interests of the Child*, 14 Wm. & Mary Bill of Rts. J. 883, 884 n.4 (2006).

Grandparents or Other Relatives

Grandparents or other relatives may seek to adopt a child whose biological parents have died, have had their parental rights terminated voluntarily or involuntarily, or have become unable to care for the child because of the parents' disability, substance abuse, or other cause. Courts show a marked inclination to honor a biological parent's wish to place a child with fit relatives whom the parent has named, but the best interests of the child remain determinative.

Some state statutes create a preference or rebuttable presumption in favor of relatives who petition to adopt a child. The court, however, retains final authority to determine the best interests of the child and, where appropriate, to order adoption by other persons.

In *In re K.E.*, 809 S.E.2d 531 (W. Va. 2018), for example, the court denied adoptive placement of one-year-old twins with their paternal grandparents after termination of parental rights for drug abuse. The court determined that despite the statutory preference for grandparent placement, such placement was contrary to the twins' best interests. The twins were born drug dependent, and the grandparents lived only two houses away from the terminated parents and could not prevent the parents' continued access to the children. The court ordered the state agency to transition the twins gradually to their foster parents' custody in another county.

What policies underlie statutes that grant preferences or rebuttable presumptions in favor of relatives? Are these statutes generally a good idea?

Foster Parents

A substantial number of adoptions each year are by the child's foster parents. At one time, public and private child placement agencies often required prospective foster parents to agree in writing not to seek to adopt foster children placed in their homes. In the past generation or so, however, courts have refused to enforce no-adoption agreements where adoption by the foster parents was in the best interests of the child. Why might enforcement of no-adoption agreements be contrary to the best interests of the child?

Some state adoption acts now even grant a preference to foster parents who have cared for the child for a specified period, though the court retains authority to grant or deny the adoption petition in the best interests of the child. *See, e.g.*, N.Y. Social Servs. L. § 383(3) (2018) (preference for foster parents who have cared for the child continuously for one year or more). Courts may grant the foster parents' adoption petition even where a competing petitioner is the child's blood relative. *See, e.g., In re K.E., supra.*

What policies underlie foster parent preference statutes? Why can so many foster parents adopt their foster children when they become available for adoption?

Stepparents

A stepchild is not available for adoption by the stepparent until the court terminates the parental rights of the noncustodial biological parent by consent or in a contested proceeding. Most stepparent adoptions involve stepfathers adopting their spouses' marital or their partners' nonmarital children. An uncontested stepparent adoption generally gives the law's imprimatur to an existing family circumstance.

The best-interests-of-the-child standard determines the outcome when the biological custodial parent dies, the other fit biological parent has no parental rights or consents to termination, and the surviving stepparent wishes to adopt the child. If no competing petition is filed, the court is likely to approve the adoption unless the stepparent appears unfit. Nonetheless, the stepparent is considered a legal stranger to the child. The stepparent's position would appear most tenuous where the adoption act grants preference to a close relative. On the other hand, the stepparent's position would appear stronger if the child has resided with him for a significant period and if a change of circumstances would likely cause the child emotional harm.

The Petitioners' Ages

Young petitioners. In most states, a person must be 18 or older to adopt a child, unless he or she is the child's stepparent or is married to an adult petitioner. *See, e.g.,* Md. Code Ann., Fam. Law § 5–331 (2018). A few states establish a higher minimum age or set other requirements. *See, e.g.,* Ga. Code Ann. § 19–8–3 (2018) (petitioner must be "at least 25 years of age or * * * married and living with his spouse," and "at least ten years older than the child"). In states that establish no minimum age, courts determine on a case-by-case basis whether adoption by a minor would be in the best interests of the child. What factors should the court consider as it proceeds to this determination?

Older petitioners. Adoption statutes do not establish a maximum permissible age for adoptive parents. In *In re A.C.G.,* 894 A.2d 436 (D.C. 2006), for example, the court held that the best interests of a sexually abused 10-year-old girl warranted adoption by her 78-year-old great aunt, who had made financial arrangements for the girl and had arranged for two family members well known to the child, aged 67 and 41, to care for her if the aunt died or became disabled. The court found that removing the girl from the aunt's care would likely have had a severe negative impact on the girl because the aunt had cared for her since she was two months old. Where the petitioners are the child's grandparents or other older relatives, the factors discussed above may affect the outcome.

Persons with Disabilities

Several state adoption acts prohibit discrimination based on a prospective adoptive parent's physical disability. *See, e.g.,* Wis. Stat. Ann. § 48.82(5) (2018) ("Although otherwise qualified, no person shall be denied the [right to adopt a child] because the person is deaf, blind or has other physical handicaps."). What factors should the court consider when deciding whether granting an adoption petition filed by a person with disabilities would be in the best interests of the child?

Separate Adoptive Placements of Siblings

Neither the U.S. Supreme Court nor any state supreme court has articulated a constitutional right of "sibling association"—a child's right not to be separated from siblings by foster care or adoption in separate homes, or the child's right to maintain visitation with siblings after separation. *See, e.g., In re Meridian H.,* 798 N.W.2d 96, 107 (Neb. 2011). Nor does any federal or state statute confer a right on siblings to be placed together in foster care or adoption.

Sibling bonds remain a relevant (and indeed, weighty) factor for the court to consider in determining the child's best interests, but these bonds are not determinative. In *Adoption of Paisley*, 178 A.3d 1228 (Me. 2018), for example, the state agency favored permanent placement of the two-year-old child with the adoptive parents of two of the child's five biological siblings. The court held that the agency unreasonably withheld its written consent to the child's adoption by her licensed foster parents, with whom the girl had lived for most of her life.

The federal Fostering Connections to Success and Increasing Adoptions Act of 2008 requires states, as a condition for receiving federal funding for foster care maintenance and adoption assistance, to make "reasonable efforts" to place siblings together in the same foster or adoptive home. When common placement is impossible, state authorities must provide for frequent visitation, except where visitation is "contrary to the health, safety or well-being of one or more of the children." 42 U.S.C. § 671 (2018).

The federal Act establishes "a clear preference to place siblings together whenever possible," *In re Doe*, 416 P.3d 937, 941 (Idaho 2018), but the Act only influences application of the best interests standard, without displacing the standard as a matter of law. As a practical matter, the Act does not drive the result in particular cases because withholding of federal funding remains an unlikely prospect.

For a substantial number of children, separation from siblings begins with separate foster care placements. *See* Marie K. Cohen, *Lack of Will to Keep Siblings Together in Foster Care; But There Is a Way* (Donaldson Adoption Inst. 2015). The child welfare system encourages foster co-placement of siblings, but sibling separation happens frequently. "Only about 40 percent of these children are placed with a sibling, and often visitation between siblings, placed separately while they are in foster care, is not maintained on a regular basis." Randi Mandelbaum, *Delicate Balances: Assessing the Needs and Rights of Siblings in Foster Care to Maintain Their Relationships Post-Adoption*, 41 N.M. L. Rev. 1, 6 (2011). Separate foster placements often ripen into permanency with separate adoption by the foster parents. *See, e.g., Adoption of Paisley, supra.*

Should courts and child welfare agencies normally strive to keep siblings together in adoption whenever possible? Why might separate foster placement or separate adoption sometimes be in the best interests of the child?

NOTE AND QUESTIONS

The investigation, home study, and probationary period. In agency adoptions and private placements alike, judicial determination of the child's best interests depends significantly on at least one investigation or study of the prospective adoptive home by public authorities. In some states, courts may waive this requirement for good cause. Some states do not impose the requirement where the prospective adoptive parent is the child's stepparent or other close relative. What purposes do investigations or home studies serve?

In agency adoptions, the agency must make an investigation or home study before placing the child with the prospective adoptive parents, with the child sometimes placed in foster care in the interim. The agency must follow up with a further investigation or study shortly after placement.

In private placements, however, no investigation or home study normally takes place until after the placement, and sometimes not until long afterwards. Concern about lax regulation of private placements has led some states to require that, at least where the prospective adoptive parent is not the child's stepparent or other relative, a notice to adopt must be filed and an investigation or home study must be conducted before transfer of the child. Transfer may not be made until the parents are certified as qualified. *See, e.g.,* N.Y. Dom. Rel. L. §§ 115, 115–c, 115–d (2018). These requirements recognize that because of the child's need for continuity, a meaningful post-transfer study may not be possible.

Except in stepparent adoptions or other unusual circumstances, the adoption does not become final until the child has been in the adoptive parents' custody for a probationary period which, depending on the state, may range from three months to a year. The court issues the final adoption order if circumstances warrant after a final home investigation. Should states require home investigations and probationary periods in stepparent adoptions?

PROBLEM 6-1

Section 1–102 of the Uniform Adoption Act (UAA) creates broad eligibility to adopt, and thus directs focus on application of the best interests of the child standard and other statutory requirements: "Subject to this [Act], any individual may adopt or be adopted by another individual for the purpose of creating the relationship of parent and child between them." If a prospective adoptive parent is married, his or her spouse must join the petition. UAA § 3–301(b).

Under Section 1–102, "[n]o one is categorically excluded * * * from being considered as a prospective adoptee or as a prospective adoptive parent." The drafters are explicit that "[m]arital status, like other general characteristics such as race, ethnicity, religion, or age, does not preclude an individual from adopting." *Id.* § 1–102 cmt. Eligible parties may adopt only where the Act's many requirements are satisfied. For example, a child would become available for adoption only where the biological parents consent to a direct adoptive placement, relinquish their parental rights to an agency, or have their parental rights terminated by a court. The court may approve the adoption only if it finds that the prospective adoptive parents are fit to adopt and that the adoption would be in the best interests of the child.

If you were a state legislator, would you vote to enact Section 1–102 of the UAA in your state?

PROBLEM 6-2

You are the juvenile court judge hearing a contested adoption proceeding involving three-year-old twins who are available for adoption because the court has terminated the parental rights of both biological parents for their persistent unremedied drug abuse. The contestants, each eligible to adopt, are the children's foster parents and the children's aunt and uncle. What general factors would you consider to determine which petition to grant in the best interests of the children? What weight would you give to testimony by the aunt and uncle that they need to adopt the twins because they cannot conceive biological children, and because adoption would help shore up their shaky marriage?

A NOTE ABOUT "EQUITABLE ADOPTION"

Suppose an adult intends to adopt a child but fails to complete the adoption process and secure an adoption decree. The child continues to live in the adult's household, and the adult raises and educates the child and holds the child out as a member of the family. If the adult dies intestate (that is, without leaving a valid will), may the child inherit from the adult?

More than half the states recognize the judicially created equitable adoption doctrine, which enables courts to enforce agreements to adopt where the adult negligently or intentionally failed to complete the adoption process. The agreement may be with the child, the child's biological parent, or someone *in loco parentis*.

Most claimants invoking the equitable adoption doctrine have sought to share in the intestate adult's estate. Indeed, some courts have restricted the doctrine to intestacy cases. *See, e.g., In re Scarlett Z.-D.*, 28 N.E.3d 776, 792 (Ill. 2015). But other courts have also applied the doctrine in suits to recover damages for the adult's wrongful death, to recover support from the adult, to establish adoptive status under inheritance tax laws, or to recover life insurance, workers' compensation, Social Security, or other benefits following the adult's death. The adult might also seek to invoke the doctrine, for example, in suits seeking workers' compensation benefits for the child's death, inheritance from the child, or damages for the child's wrongful death. Should courts be more willing to invoke the doctrine in a suit by the putative adoptee than in a suit by the putative adoptor?

Equitable adoption does not confer adoptive status but, in accordance with the maxim that equity regards as done that which ought to be done, confers the benefit the claimant seeks. Most decisions that recognize equitable adoption require proof of (1) the adult's express or implied agreement to adopt the child, (2) the child's reliance on the agreement, (3) performance by the child's biological parents in relinquishing custody, (4) performance by the child in living in the adults' home and acting as their child, and (5) partial performance by the adults in taking the child into their home and treating the child as their own. *See, e.g., McMullen v. Bennis*, 20 So.3d 890, 891–92 (Fla. Dist. Ct. App. 2009).

Some states refuse to recognize the equitable adoption doctrine on the ground that establishing the parameters of adoption law is for the legislature. *See, e.g., In re Estate of Scherer*, 336 P.3d 129, 135 (Wyo. 2014). In states that do recognize the doctrine, the judicial embrace has been only lukewarm. Most recognizing jurisdictions require that the claimant prove the agreement to adopt by a heightened standard of proof, such as clear and convincing evidence. *See, e.g., In re Estate of Duke*, 352 P.3d 863, 890 (Cal. 2015). What explains the lukewarm judicial embrace?

3. ISSUES IN CONTEMPORARY ADOPTION LAW AND POLICY

This section presents five prominent issues that influence adoption law and policy—transracial adoption, Native American adoption, religious identity, international adoption, and baby selling.

A. TRANSRACIAL ADOPTION

The term "transracial adoption" literally describes any adoption in which the adoptive parents and child are of different races. The lion's share of the public debate about domestic transracial adoption, however, has concerned adoption by white parents of black or biracial children, though (according to U.S. Census Bureau definitions) racial differences may also involve an adopted child who is Native American, Asian, Pacific Islander, or a member of another group listed in the Bureau's race question.

This subsection 3.A treats Americans' transracial adoption of American children. Subsection 3.D below treats Americans' adoption of foreign nations' children, which frequently involves transracial pairings.

1. Historical Background

The first recorded adoption in the United States of a black or biracial child by white parents took place in 1948. *See* Joyce A. Ladner, Mixed Families: Adopting Across Racial Boundaries 59 (1977). The numbers of such adoptions began to increase, though some states criminalized transracial adoptions as unlawful race mixing before the end of official racial segregation in the 1960s. The numbers fell after the National Association of Black Social Workers, in 1972, condemned transracial adoption as "cultural genocide":

> * * * Black children should be placed only with Black families whether in foster care or for adoption. Black children belong, physically, psychologically and culturally in Black families in order that they receive the total sense of themselves and develop a sound projection of their future. Human beings are products of their environment and develop their sense of values, attitudes and self concept within their family structures. Black children in white

homes are cut off from the healthy development of themselves as Black people.

Our position is based on:

1.   the necessity of self-determination from birth to death, of all Black people.

2.   the need of our young ones to begin at birth to identify with all Black people in a Black community.

3.   the philosophy that we need our own to build a strong nation.

The socialization process for every child begins at birth. Included in the socialization process is the child's cultural heritage which is an important segment of the total process. This must begin at the earliest moment; otherwise our children will not have the background and knowledge which is necessary to survive in a racist society. This is impossible if the child is placed with white parents in a white environment.

Nat'l Ass'n of Black Social Workers, *Position Paper* (Apr. 1972), in Rita James Simon & Howard Altstein, Transracial Adoption 50–52 (1977) (reaffirmed by the NABSW in 2003).

The Howard M. Metzenbaum Multiethnic Placement Act of 1994 (MEPA), Pub. L. No. 103–382, 553(a)(1), was a federal funding statute that sought to encourage transracial adoption by ending the practice of matching adoptive parents with children of the same race in foster care and adoptive placement. MEPA prohibited states and private agencies from delaying or denying an adoptive placement "solely on the basis of race."

Experience quickly demonstrated that the word "solely" actually encouraged race matching by permitting agencies and courts to consider the potential adoptive family's financial status and other cultural, ethnic, and social factors. Congress amended MEPA in the Removal of Barriers to Interethnic Adoption Provisions of the Small Business Job Protection Act of 1996, Pub. L. No. 104–188. As amended, MEPA prohibits private and public child placement agencies from denying any person the opportunity to become an adoptive or foster parent, or from delaying or denying the placement of a child for adoption or into foster care, "on the basis of the race, color, or national origin of the adoptive or foster parent, or the child." 42 U.S.C. § 1996b(1) (2018). The amended Act applies to any agency that receives federal funds, and makes violations actionable under Title VI of the Civil Rights Act of 1964. *Id.* § 1996b(2).

After the 1996 amendments, many states with "statutes explicitly *requiring* race-matching in adoption or foster care modified their statutory law * * * to, at least ostensibly, preclude such practices. As a result, by the mid-2000s it had become significantly more rare for public institutions (and courts) to rely explicitly on race in adoption or foster care determinations, a decline that is reflected in the case law." Katie Eyer, *Constitutional Colorblindness and the Family*, 162 U. Pa. L. Rev. 537, 580 (2014) (emphasis in original).

2. The Ongoing Debate

More than two decades after MEPA, "transracial adoption remains a subject of recurring public debate." Twila L. Perry, *Race, Color, and the Adoption of Biracial Children*, 17 J. Gender, Race & Just. 73, 73 (2014).

Professor Ruth-Arlene W. Howe, for example, argues that "African-American children are not well served when race is off the table," because race-neutrality means that foster or prospective adoptive parents cannot be evaluated concerning whether they are " 'racially and culturally competent to help prepare the child for the challenges that he will encounter because of his appearance.' To deny the reality that continuing racial hostilities and inequalities abound in our society because of a belief that society is 'color blind' is irresponsible and unethical." Ruth-Arlene W. Howe, *Race Matters in Adoption*, 42 Fam. L.Q. 465, 469 (2008).

Professor Randall Kennedy, however, calls race matching "a destructive practice in *all* its various guises, from moderate to extreme." Randall Kennedy, Interracial Intimacies: Sex, Marriage, Identity, and Adoption 402, 416 (2003) (emphasis in original). He argues for "a system under which children in need of homes may be assigned to the care of foster or adoptive parents as quickly as reasonably possible, *regardless* of perceived racial differences," a system that he says would benefit not only "vulnerable children," but also "American race relations." *Id.* (emphasis in original). Professor Kennedy favors a system under which "race would not be allowed to play any part in the selection of adoptive families, unless there was some compelling justification substantiated by specific evidence directly relevant to the case at hand." *Id.*

The Donaldson Adoption Institute concludes that by mandating "an unyielding color-blindness," MEPA runs counter to sound adoption practice and often the best interests of children. *See* Susan Smith et al., Donaldson Adoption Inst., *Finding Families for African American Children: The Role of Race & Law in Adoption From Foster Care* 7 (2008). The Institute's comprehensive report criticizes MEPA for inhibiting agencies from assessing a family's readiness and capacity to help a transracially adopted child cope with being "different," develop a positive racial/ethnic identity, and face discrimination. *Id.* at 6–7.

The Donaldson Institute recommends that Congress reinstate the original MEPA standard that race may be one factor, but not the sole factor, considered in determining whether to approve a transracial adoption. *Id.*

NOTE AND QUESTIONS

In *Palmore v. Sidoti*, 466 U.S. 429 (1984), a principal case in Chapter 12, the white divorced mother lost custody of her young daughter after she began cohabiting with a black man, whom she later married. On the motion to modify the order granting custody to the mother, the trial court found neither biological parent unfit but placed the girl with the biological father because "it is inevitable that [she] will, if allowed to remain in her present situation and attains school age and thus more vulnerable to peer pressures, suffer from the social stigmatization that is sure to come." *Id.* at 431 (quoting the trial court).

Palmore held that the decision modifying custody violated equal protection. "It would ignore reality to suggest that racial and ethnic prejudices do not exist or that all manifestations of those prejudices have been eliminated. * * * The Constitution cannot control such prejudices but neither can it tolerate them. Private biases may be outside the reach of the law, but the law cannot, directly or indirectly, give them effect." *Id.* at 433.

The Supreme Court has not considered whether *Palmore* prohibits judicial enforcement of race matching in adoption cases, which raise child placement issues at least as profound as issues raised in custody disputes between biological parents. Under what circumstances, if any, should race be a permissible consideration in adoption? Should the child's age matter?

B. NATIVE AMERICAN ADOPTION

Congress' rejection of race matching in child placement and adoption in MEPA stands in contrast to the lawmakers' recognition of tribal identity in the Indian Child Welfare Act of 1978 (ICWA), Pub. L. No. 95–608 (codified as amended at 25 U.S.C. §§ 1901–1963 (2016)). MEPA expressly exempts the ICWA from its provisions.

The ICWA provides that "[i]n any adoptive placement of an Indian child under State law, a preference shall be given, in the absence of good cause to the contrary, to a placement with (1) a member of the child's extended family; (2) other members of the Indian child's tribe; or (3) other Indian families." *Id.* § 1915(b). By thus expressly recognizing children as tribal resources, the ICWA seeks to protect the best interests of Indian children, and to promote the security, survival and stability of Indian families and tribes. *Id.* §§ 1901(1), (3); 1902.

Professor Barbara Atwood reports that the ICWA has produced "greater respect for tribal authority over the placement of Indian children and an expansion of tribal family preservation programs," while decreasing the rate at which Indian children are removed from their homes and the rate of placement with non-Indian caregivers. Barbara Atwood, *The Voice of the Indian Child: Strengthening the Indian Child Welfare Act Through Children's Participation*, 50 Ariz. L. Rev. 127, 128 (2008).

In *Adoptive Couple v. Baby Girl*, 570 U.S. 637 (2013), discussed in Chapter 5, the ICWA's preferences were not determinative. Instead, the child was placed for adoption with the adoptive parents who had raised her for the first 27 months of her life. The Court rested its decision on the fact that the biological father of Native American heritage had never had custody of the child. The Court found that the lack of "continued custody" did not trigger the ICWA's provisions. The dissent argued that the majority failed to honor the Act's purposes by narrowly focusing on one provision.

The continued force of the statutory preferences will be left to future cases in which the biological parent has had prior custody or in which competing petitions for adoption are filed, neither of which was present in *Adoptive Couple*. Professor Atwood criticizes the *Adoptive Couple* decision as "an unwise retreat from the Supreme Court's earlier embrace of the Indian Child Welfare Act (ICWA). Animated by understandable empathy for the adoptive parents, Justice Alito's majority opinion devalues the Indian identity of the child * * * and her relationship with her Indian father. In so doing, the majority's opinion undermines the very goals that the ICWA was meant to achieve." Barbara Ann Atwood, *Hard Facts, Muddled Law: Deciphering the Baby Veronica Decision*, B.U. L. Rev. Annex (2013).

In late 2018, a Texas federal district court struck down the ICWA's mandatory placement preferences for violating Fifth Amendment equal protection. *See Brackeen v. Zinke*, 338 F. Supp.3d 514 (N.D. Tex. Oct. 4, 2018). The U.S. Court of Appeals for the Fifth Circuit has stayed the decision pending appeal.

C. RELIGIOUS IDENTITY

By statute in some states and case law in others, courts are mandated or authorized to consider the religion of the prospective adoptive parents and of the child (or the child's biological parents) in determining whether to approve the adoption under the best interests standard. Religious matching raises two fundamental questions:

a. *Religious differences.* The first question is whether the court may deny an adoption on the ground that the adoptive parents and the child (or the child's biological parents) are of different religions. Courts generally hold that where the statute requires religious matching when "feasible" or "practicable," or confers a preference based on religion without creating an inflexible rule requiring matching, agencies and courts may consider religion in determining the best interests of the child. *See, e.g.*, Md. Code Ann., Fam. Law § 5–520(a) (2018) ("In placing a minor child for adoption

* * *, a licensee shall give preference to persons of the same religious belief as that of the child or the child's parents unless the parents specifically indicate a different choice.").

Where the child is too young to express a religious belief, courts consider the biological parents' religious preferences for the child, but these preferences too are not determinative. *See, e.g., Cooper v. Hinrichs*, 140 N.E.2d 293, 297 (Ill. 1957). Religious differences are less significant where the biological parents consent to adoption by a petitioner of a different faith. *See, e.g., Adoption of Anonymous*, 261 N.Y.S.2d 439 (Fam. Ct. 1965).

Should the child's age affect the weight the court gives to the adoptive parents' different religion? Should the feasibility or practicability of religious matching depend on the availability of adoptive parents who share the faith of the child or the biological parents?

b. *Belief in a Supreme Being.* The second fundamental religious-matching question is whether a court may deny an adoption because a prospective adoptive parent does not believe in a Supreme Being. Some decisions consider a parent's nonbelief in God as indicating inability or unwillingness to direct the child's religious and moral upbringing. But *In re Adoption of E*, 279 A.2d 785 (N.J. 1971), is typical of decisions holding that without other facts, a court may not find failure to believe in God controlling. "Sincere belief in and adherence to the tenets of a religion may be indicative of moral fitness to adopt in a particular case," but morality does not lie "in the exclusive province of one or of all religions or of religiosity in general." *Id.* at 792–93.

Religious-matching statutes invite challenges that they violate the First Amendment by establishing a religion or by prohibiting the free exercise of religion. Where religious matching is merely one factor but not dispositive, courts reject these challenges on the ground that the statute seeks only to determine the best interests of the child. *See, e.g., Dickens v. Ernesto*, 281 N.E.2d 153 (N.Y. 1972). Some decisions have held, however, that courts violate the First Amendment when they invoke religious matching as the sole ground for denying an adoption. *See, e.g., Adoption of E*, 279 A.2d at 793–96; *Orzechowski v. Perales*, 582 N.Y.S.2d 341, 347–48 (Sup. Ct. 1992).

D. INTERNATIONAL ADOPTION

Largely unknown before the end of World War II, international (or transnational or intercountry) adoptions by Americans of children from other nations began in earnest with returning troops and with media coverage of the plight of orphaned or abandoned refugee children during and immediately after the global conflict. The Korean and Vietnam wars increased Americans' interest, but by then international adoption was no longer a product solely of war. *See* Robyn Brown, *Intercountry Adoption Processes and Their Continuing Complexities* 2 (U.S. DOJ 2018).

More than 40% of children adopted across national borders today come to the United States. Abby Budiman & Mark Hugo Lopez, *Amid Decline In International Adoptions to U.S., Boys Outnumber Girls For the First Time* 4 (Pew Research Center 2017). Americans' interest in international adoption appears to result, at least partly, from the contemporary shortage of readily adoptable children in the United States because of abortion, contraception, and single mothers' greater desire to keep their newborns. Interest also stems from Americans' frequent desire to avoid domestic transracial adoption, restrictive domestic agency guidelines, or open adoption arrangements that permit biological mothers to maintain contact with their adopted children. Concerning this last reason, however, Professor Malinda L. Seymore observes growing interest among American adoptive parents in openness in international adoptions. Malinda L. Seymore, *Openness In International Adoption*, 46 Colum. Hum. Rts. L. Rev. 163, 166–67 (2015).

International adoption continues to generate spirited worldwide debate. To many supporters, this adoption "serv[es] the most fundamental human rights of the most helpless of humans—the rights of children to the kind of family love and care that will enable them to grow up with a decent chance of living a healthy and fulfilling life." Elizabeth Bartholet, *International Adoption: Thoughts on the Human Rights Issues*, 13 Buff. Hum. Rts. L. Rev. 151, 151 (2007). But Professor Bartholet recognizes that international adoption "will never be more than a very partial solution for the problems of the homeless children of the world":

> The best solution * * * would be to solve the problems of social and economic injustice that prevent so many birth parents from being able to raise their children themselves. But given the realities of today's world, and the existence of so many children who will not be raised by their birth parents, international adoption does provide a very good solution for virtually all of those homeless children lucky enough to get placed.

Id. at 158.

Critics charge, however, that "[f]rom a position of social justice, [the] ethical appropriateness of only intervening to remove children from institutions for intercountry adoption must be questioned when we are doing little to address the issues that separate all children, with or without disabilities, from their families." Patricia Fronek et al., *Intercountry Adoption: Privilege, Rights and Social Justice,* in The Intercountry Adoption Debate Dialogues Across Disciplines 348, 361 (Robert L. Ballard, et. al. eds., 2015).

NOTES

1. *The downward trend.* International adoptions today account for nearly 15% of United States adoptions of children annually. The numbers of U.S. visas issued annually for international adoptees peaked in 2004, however, and have declined ever since. The U.S. State Department reports that in 2017, "[t]he overall number of adoptions to the United States * * * was 4,714, a decline of 658 from the previous year." *See* U.S. Dep't of State, *FY 2017 Annual Report on Intercountry Adoptions* 2 (2018). China remains the single greatest source of foreign children adopted by Americans, with South Korea now in second place. *Id.* Tbl. 1.

Ethiopia previously occupied second place, but in early 2018 the Ethiopian Parliament banned adoptions of that nation's children by foreigners. *See* U.S. Dep't of State, Bureau of Consular Affairs, *Ethiopia Adoption Notice: Ethiopia Passes Legislation Banning Intercountry Adoption*, Jan. 11, 2018. The parliamentary action stems from concern that many of the nation's previously adopted children have been victims of "various crimes and social crisis in the country they grew up in," and have been left "vulnerable to identity crisis, psychological problems, and violation of rights." With the ban in place, children can "grow up in Ethiopian culture, custom, social values and practices of their birth place." *See* Bijan Hosseini, CNN, *Ethiopia Bans Foreign Adoption*, Feb. 3, 2018.

Ethiopia is typical of some traditional "sending" nations that have restricted or terminated adoptions by foreigners because "[i]n some cases, * * * requirements and procedures in place were insufficient to prevent unethical practices, such the sale and abduction of children, coercion or manipulation of birth parents, falsification of documents and bribery." UNICEF, *Intercountry Adoption*, http://www.unicef.org/media/media_41918.html (June 26, 2015; reissued Feb. 27, 2018). The recent declines in U.S. international adoptions may also be partly due to increased State Department regulation aimed at combatting abuses overseas. Arthur C. Brooks, *Let's Restart the Adoption Movement*, N.Y. Times, Nov. 17, 2017.

2. *A changing profile.* In earlier years, most international adoptees coming to the U.S. were infants or toddlers. More recently, however, increasing numbers of international adoptees have been older children and adolescents with special needs that are often undisclosed to their American adoptive parents. "Children born in other areas of the world may have different health problems from those of children raised in the United States. Children may have been exposed to vaccine-preventable diseases that are rare in the United States. Some children are adopted from countries with high rates of diseases, such as tuberculosis, hepatitis, and HIV/AIDS." Centers for Disease Control and Prevention, *International Adoption: Health Guidance and the Immigration Process*, Jan. 8, 2018.

Professor Barbara Stark observes that for American adults unable to conceive, gestational surrogacy can provide a less expensive, less risky alternative to international adoption. Barbara Stark, *When Genealogy Matters:*

Intercountry Adoption, International Human Rights, and Global Neoliberalism, 51 Vand. J. Transnat'l L. 159, 202–03 (2017).

3. *Domestic enabling legislation.* The Hague Convention on Protection of Children and Co-operation in Respect of Intercountry Adoption, which entered into force in 1995, recognizes adoption as a positive alternative for children who are unable to remain with their biological families but are unlikely to be adopted in their own nations. But the Convention also seeks "to prevent the abduction, the sale of, or traffic in children," and to ensure that international adoption is "in the best interests of the child with respect to his or her fundamental rights." Hague Convention, 1870 U.N.T.S. 182–183. As of March 2018, 98 nations were contracting parties to the Convention. Ryan Hanlon, *Reflection: Ten Years After the United States Joins the Hague Convention* 1 (Nat'l Council For Adoption 2018).

The United States formally ratified the Hague Convention in 2007. The U.S. State Department has promulgated implementing and enforcement regulations requiring, among other things, that prospective adoptive parents receive pre-adoption training and counseling concerning the child's cultural, racial, religious, ethnic and linguistic background. U.S. Dep't of State, Final Rules, 22 C.F.R. Pts. 96–98 (2018). The Child Citizenship Act of 2000, Pub. L. No. 106–395, 114 Stat. 1631, confers United States citizenship automatically on thousands of foreign-born children who do not acquire citizenship at birth, including certain children adopted by American citizens.

E. BABY SELLING

Amid intense competition in the private adoption market, states have enacted statutes prohibiting baby selling and baby brokering by biological parents and adoption intermediaries. The statutes can operate against lawyers who act as intermediaries in private-placement adoptions by bringing together biological mothers (often unmarried teens) and prospective adoptive parents. The policy underlying these prohibitions is that adoption should not be a commercial transaction for profit, but many observers believe that these statutes frequently fail to prevent "under the table" payments by would-be adoptive parents who are desperate for healthy adoptable babies.

As you read *State v. Brown*, examine the quoted statute that defines permissible payments. Why are baby selling prosecutions few and far between?

State v. Brown

Supreme Court of Kansas, 2001.
35 P.3d 910.

McFarland, C.J.:

* * *

Defendant operated an escort service named "Blaze" out of her home in Wichita. Upon hearing that a former employee, Samantha Pruitt, had given birth to a child in Oklahoma and was considering putting the child up for adoption, defendant told her to wait. Defendant then went to Oklahoma and brought the mother and child to her home.

Defendant made arrangements for another employee (Teresa Lawrence) and Tina Black to acquire the child from Pruitt in exchange for a new car, $800, and a cell phone. Defendant was to receive half of the cash as compensation for her part in putting the deal together. The transfer of the child took place, but none of the agreed-upon compensation was paid or delivered. Pruitt became dissatisfied with the delay and complained to a friend who happened to be the girlfriend of a police officer.

Ultimately, Pruitt and the police officer reported the incident. In cooperation with the Wichita Police Department, Pruitt made a monitored telephone call to the defendant, wherein the following was said:

"Pruitt: So uh . . . what happened to the money that I was supposed to get and the car and cell phone. What did they. . . .

"Brown: Hey, you can get all that when you get the fucking uh . . . uh . . . birth certificate.

"Pruitt: . . . did they just . . . but what about you . . . your half of the money, did they give it all to you?

"Brown: Not yet they haven't. They're waiting for the birth certificate. I get to wait just like you get to wait.

"Pruitt: Yeah.

"Brown: You know, you produce what you're suppose and everything will go cool. All you have to go over you fucking . . . boyfriend's house and get it out of the garage . . . he has to wait 21 days . . . that's bullshit."

The conversation then disintegrated into name calling.

It was further stipulated: "None of the money was intended for any bill or expense incidental to birth or adoption proceedings." Ultimately, the child was found and taken into protective custody.

* * *

The Statute

K.S.A. 59–2121 provides:

"(a) Except as otherwise authorized by law, no person shall request, receive, give or offer to give any consideration in connection with an adoption, or a placement for adoption, other than:

(1) Reasonable fees for legal and other professional services rendered in connection with the placement or adoption not to exceed customary fees for similar services by professionals of equivalent experience and reputation where the services are performed, except that fees for legal and other professional services as provided in this section performed outside the state shall not exceed customary fees for similar services when performed in the state of Kansas;

(2) reasonable fees in the state of Kansas of a licensed child-placing agency;

(3) actual and necessary expenses, based on expenses in the state of Kansas, incident to placement or to the adoption proceeding;

(4) actual medical expenses of the mother attributable to pregnancy and birth;

(5) actual medical expenses of the child; and

(6) reasonable living expenses of the mother which are incurred during or as a result of the pregnancy.

"(b) In an action for adoption, a detailed accounting of all consideration given, or to be given, and all disbursements made, or to be made, in connection with the adoption and the placements for adoption shall accompany the petition for adoption. Upon review of the accounting, the court shall disapprove any such consideration which the court determines to be unreasonable or in violation of this section and, to the extent necessary to comply with the provisions of this section, shall order reimbursement of any consideration already given in violation of this section.

"(c) Knowingly and intentionally receiving or accepting clearly excessive fees or expenses in violation of subsection (a) shall be a severity level 9, nonperson felony. Knowingly failing to list all consideration or disbursements as required by subsection (b) shall be a class B nonperson misdemeanor."

* * *

Discussion

* * *

Defendant draws our attention to the fact that in K.S.A. 59–2121(a) the prohibited conduct is that "no person shall request, receive, give or offer to give any consideration in connection with an adoption," followed by six exceptions thereto. However, subsection (c) speaks only of "[k]nowingly and intentionally receiving or accepting clearly excessive fees." Thus, she argues, the legislature has only criminalized the prohibited conduct of receiving or accepting such fees. From there she contends that as she did not actually receive or accept the agreed upon fee, she did not violate K.S.A. 59–2121(c). Defendant treats "accepting" and "receiving" as being synonymous. We disagree. "Receive" is listed in subsection (a), but "accept" is not. One must conclude that the legislature intended to criminalize more than "receiving" excessive fees by adding "accepting." Otherwise "accepting" would be a redundant term pulled from the air rather than subsection (a).

[T]he purpose of K.S.A. 59–2121 is to discourage the marketing of children by limiting the profitability of such activity. The welfare of children lies at the heart of the legislation. The fact that defendant had not yet received the money she bargained for in brokering the child when law enforcement officials stepped in does not change the nature of the transaction. The child had changed hands pursuant to the deal defendant brokered. Defendant sold Pruitt's child * * *.

* * *

We conclude such conduct constituted "[k]nowingly and intentionally receiving or accepting clearly excessive fees or expenses in violation of subsection (a)," as set forth in K.S.A. 59–2121(c).

The judgment [of conviction] is affirmed.

NOTES AND QUESTIONS

1. *Child support arrearages.* A custodial biological parent's spouse or partner may petition the court to adopt the child. The court may grant the petition after terminating the non-custodial biological parent's parental rights. By creating a new parent-child relationship, adoption excuses the terminated biological parent from any future obligations to pay child support, but not from obligation to pay support that came due before the adoption. *See, e.g., Adoption of Marlene,* 822 N.E.2d 714 (Mass. 2005).

To secure the non-custodial biological parent's consent to termination of parental rights, may the custodial biological parent and the new spouse agree to waive the right to receive past child support that the non-custodial parent owes? The Kansas baby selling statute remains silent on the question, but other baby selling statutes frequently respond in the affirmative, provided that the court finds waiver to be in the best interests of the child. *See, e.g.,* S.C. Code § 16–3–1060 (2018). In a stepparent adoption, why might an agreement to waive the terminated non-custodial parent's support arrearages be in the best interests of the child?

2. *Questions about baby selling.* Would everyone, including the child, have been better off if the state had encouraged Samantha Pruitt to consent to adoption by a devoted couple willing to pay her for the child? Do you agree with one judge who called baby selling a victimless crime: "Even if baby selling does exist, what's so horrible about that? If the child is going to a home with good parents who can give it all the love and security it will ever need, why should we care if the parents paid $50,000 for the privilege? The child is happy, the parents are happy, so what is the harm?" *Newborn Fever: Flocking to An Adoption Mecca,* Time, Mar. 12, 1984, at 31.

If the thought of buying and selling babies offends sensibilities, does money already count for too much under the contemporary adoption system? Prospective adoptive parents of modest means may be able to afford only adoption through a public adoption agency that primarily places foster children, many of whom have special needs. Financially comfortable prospective parents have access both to private adoption agencies and to private-placement adoption, "so prospective adopters with enough money to explore the possibilities are able * * * to find their way to a healthy newborn." Elizabeth Bartholet, Family Bonds: Adoption, Infertility, and the New World of Child Production 73–74 (1999). Consider also these thoughts about market forces that help define the adoption process:

KIMBERLY D. KRAWIEC,
ALTRUISM AND INTERMEDIATION IN THE MARKET FOR BABIES
66 Wash. & Lee L. Rev. 203, 204–05, 226, 247–49, 255–56 (2009).

Few proposals generate the moral outrage engendered by a suggestion that babies—or, more accurately but less vividly, parental rights—should be traded on the open market. More than anything else, baby selling flies in the face of our deeply held convictions that some items are too priceless to ever be bought and sold. Throughout the world, in fact, baby selling is formally prohibited. And throughout the world babies are bought and sold each day.

* * *

[T]he baby market is big business. * * *

Contrary to popular belief, the prime driver of the adoption market has always been economics. * * *

In the adoption market, the primary legal restriction on the baby trade is the ban against baby selling. Although both international law and the laws of all fifty states prohibit "baby selling"—the relinquishment of parental rights in exchange for payment—few states specifically cap or otherwise restrict permissible payments for medical, living, and other expenses of birth parents, allowing some latitude to those eager to evade such restrictions. Therefore, birth parents are paid cash for the relinquishment of their child and, in some cases, the amount paid might approximate the parents' opportunity costs, equaling what would be earned in a free market. At the same time, because such payments must be justified as reasonable living or other expenses, the restriction could very well deter very large payments and act as a de facto price-fixing agreement that prevents particularly desirable birth parents from collecting the full value for their services.

Compensation to Baby Market Intermediaries, in contrast, is not similarly restricted and * * * the relatively small share of the profits garnered by birth parents has prompted calls for controls on intermediary activity in the adoption market. This is particularly true in the international adoption market, where the disparity between total fees paid by adoptive parents and the amounts rendered to birth parents may be vast.

* * *

Baby Market Intermediaries in the adoption sector, such as state-licensed adoption agencies, long have sought to protect their market positions through active agitation for prohibitions against baby selling, with exceptions for their own activities. Those efforts have met with mixed success in restricting the business of private agencies and brokers that enjoy the political support of lawmakers, whose constituents value the larger supply and shorter waiting times associated with private adoption. These anti-competitive efforts, however, have been quite successful in deterring independent market entry by birth parents, nearly all of whom are funneled into the baby trade through a Baby Market Intermediary, rather than as direct suppliers.

* * * Contrary to the common assumption that baby selling bans perform an important normative function by delineating those items that society views as irreducible to monetary valuation, * * * society appears to have no problem attaching price tags to children. * * *

[B]anning the baby market is politically infeasible in the United States. Consumer demand is simply too strong and too deeply felt, and unlikely to be sated through substitutes. In addition, baby market consumers and intermediaries are too economically and politically powerful and have too much at stake in the baby market to permit its abandonment.

NOTE

Despite the "moral outrage" that Professor Krawiec discusses, Judge Richard A. Posner argues that a regulated free market in adoptable infants would serve the best interests of many of the children involved. *See* Richard A. Posner & Elizabeth Landes, *The Economics of the Baby Shortage*, 7 J. Legal Stud. 323 (1978). Judge Posner finds that the existing adoption system countenances baby selling, marked by "a high black-market price conjoined with an artificially low price for babies obtained from adoption agencies and through lawful independent adoptions." Richard A. Posner, *The Regulation of the Market in Adoptions*, 67 B.U. L. Rev. 59, 65 (1987). He argues that a regulated market, with adoptions effective only on court approval, would be an antidote to the "the painful spectacle of mass abortion and illegitimacy in a society in which, to a significant extent, children are not available for adoption by persons unwilling to violate the law." *Id.* at 71.

4. THE AFTERMATH OF ADOPTION

A. POST-ADOPTION DISPUTES

Adoption is a stable method of family creation because "the rate of failed adoptions is quite small compared to the rate of failed marriages." Barbara Bennett Woodhouse, *Waiting for Loving: The Child's Fundamental Right to Adoption*, 34 Cap. U. L. Rev. 297, 319 (2005). "Studies consistently report that only a small percentage of completed adoptions dissolve—probably between 1 and 5 percent." U.S. Dep't of Health & Hum. Servs., *Adoption Disruption and Dissolution*, https://www.childwelfare.gov/pubPDFs/s_disrup.pdf#page=5&view=Dissolutions (last visited Mar. 23, 2019).

An adoption may be questioned, however, when the child manifests severe physical or emotional problems previously unknown to the adoptive parents. Adoption law faces its greatest challenge when an adoptive parent sues to annul an adoption or to recover damages for negligence or fraudulent misrepresentation by an adoption agency or other intermediary.

Adoption codes normally establish a short period within which finalized adoptions may be challenged. *See, e.g.*, Md. Ann. Code, Fam. Law § 5–353 (2018) (one year). The period is not tolled during the child's minority because tolling would defeat the short period's purpose, which is to produce finality and protect children from the emotional trauma occasioned by disrupted lives.

Limitations statutes, however, frequently reach only challenges for procedural irregularities or defects in the adoption proceeding itself. A few states expressly create a limitations period that also covers fraud challenges. *See, e.g.*, Colo. Rev. Stat. § 19–5–214(1) (2018).

Where the adoption code's statute of limitations reaches only procedural irregularities or defects, courts may permit challenges for fraud or other substantive irregularity under the state's civil procedure statute or rules relating to vacatur of final judgments generally. *See, e.g., Green v. Sollenberger*, 656 A.2d 773 (Md. 1995); Justin Owens, *Challenging Post-Adoption Decrees and the Convoluted Applications of State Courts*, 31 J. Am. Acad. Matrim. Law. 209 (2018). Under general limitations doctrines, the limitations period for a fraud claim may be tolled until the defrauded party discovered or should reasonably have discovered the fraud that accompanied the adoption. *See, e.g., McAdams v. McAdams*, 109 S.W.3d 649, 651–53 (Ark. 2003).

Burr v. Board of County Commissioners, 491 N.E.2d 1101 (Ohio 1986), was the first decision to impose civil liability on an adoption intermediary for nondisclosure of information about the adopted child's physical or mental condition. Several jurisdictions now permit recovery for fraud or negligence, or both. The measure of compensatory damages sought is normally the extraordinary costs of raising the child in light of the fraudulently or negligently concealed physical or mental condition.

Lawsuits will likely continue because today's adoption dockets include greater numbers of foster children and international adoptees with emotional or physical disabilities. Complete information about a foster child is sometimes unavailable because of poor record keeping, rapid turnover of social welfare agency personnel, and frequent movement of the child from home to home. Private adoption agencies frequently do not receive full information from foster care authorities. International adoptees may have been anonymously abandoned by their parents, or may have come from poorly administered orphanages that did not maintain adequate medical histories.

Adoptive parents may seek to annul the adoption rather than merely recover damages. Annulment makes the adoption a nullity from the outset, and thus frees the adoptive parents from the rights and obligations that adoption creates; a damage action, on the other hand, leaves the adoption intact but awards compensatory or punitive damages, or both, for the defendant's fraud or negligence.

A court is particularly unlikely to order annulment where the child has been in the adoptive home for a substantial period, or where the child's likely alternative is placement with another family, or placement in prolonged foster or institutional care. "Adoption is a serious and permanent family institution. A child's legal parenthood cannot be subjected to the fleeting and transitory whims of adult relationships; hence the limited bases on which annulment may be granted." *Adoption of J.S.S.*, 2 A.3d 281, 284 (Me. 2010).

NOTE AND QUESTIONS

Re-homing and its potential for child exploitation and sex trafficking. Until relative recently, "re-homing" usually referred to an owner's decision to give away a dog, cat, or other pet to a friend or stranger. Unwilling or unable to care for the animal, the owner would find the recipient by prior acquaintance, word-of-mouth, or media solicitation. No government authority would monitor the transfer, of course.

In 2013, a five-part Reuters investigation focused public attention on another, and potentially sinister, manifestation of re-homing—adoptive parents who each year give away hundreds of their unwanted adopted children, usually to total strangers, and often by impersonal public solicitation on an Internet chat room or message board. Money sometimes changes hands. The unregulated custody transfers of children to strangers are typically completed with nothing more than a handwritten note or notarized power of attorney, without the official vetting, oversight, and best interests scrutiny that define the adoption process. Megan Twohey, Reuters, *The Child Exchange* (Sept. 9, 2013).

Most re-homings occur with children or adolescents who were adopted internationally, but re-homings of domestic adoptees have also been reported. The Reuters investigation described frustrated adoptive parents who find themselves unprepared to cope with their adoptee's physical, mental, or emotional disabilities that the foreign agency or other intermediary failed to disclose or perhaps did not know about. Some adoptive parents find themselves unable to access or afford expensive mental or physical health treatment for the adoptee. To a stressed adoptive parent who feels ill-equipped to navigate legal processes, unregulated transfer seems like a surer and less burdensome escape than navigating formal annulment or re-adoption.

Re-homings do not constitute adoptions, which can be accomplished only by court order designed to protect the best interests of the prospective adoptee. Because state and federal authorities do not track completed adoptions, however, re-homings may evade attention by the courts or child welfare authorities, who may not know what has happened to the child.

"Children advertised and sold on the Internet are prime targets for trafficking due to the ease of transfer and lack of documentation. Namely, underground sex trafficking operations take full advantage of securing legal rights to vulnerable, unwanted children." Cynthia Hawkins DeBose & Alicia Renee Tarrant, *Sex Trafficking and Adoption Re-Homing: America's 21st Century Salacious Secret*, 7 Wake Forest J. Law & Policy 487, 517 (2017).

Recipients of re-homed child adoptees have reportedly included physical, sexual, and emotional abusers; pedophiles; mentally unbalanced adults; sex traffickers; and others who trawl the Internet for advertisements but whom a court would not find fit to adopt a child *See* Jessica Dixon Weaver, *The Changing Tides of Adoption: Why Marriage, Race, and Family Identity Still Matter*, 71 SMU L. Rev. 159, 168–69 (2018).

A 2016 study found that most U.S. adults had never heard of re-homing of adopted children, but that when they learn they believe the process smacks of child exploitation that should be unlawful. Donaldson Adoption Inst., *Adoption Perceptions Study* 38–39 (2016). Less than half the states, however, have enacted legislation to counter adoptive re-homing, usually by criminalizing advertising or unregulated transfers of available children. *See Steps Have Been Taken to Address Unregulated Custody Transfers of Adopted Children* 30–31 (U.S. Gov't Accountability Office Sept. 2015). Enforcement efforts have reportedly been sporadic, though general criminal child abuse, neglect, and abandonment statutes also remain available. A bill recently introduced in Congress would amend the Child Abuse Prevention and Treatment Act of 1974 (CAPTA) to define unregulated child transfers as acts of child abuse. *When Families Un-Adopt a Child*, Jenn Morson, The Atlantic, Nov. 16, 2018. Aside from trafficking, what dangers does unregulated transfer of custody pose for the re-homed child?

Recognizing the magnitude of re-homing's dangers, a committee of the Uniform Law Commission has drafted a model Unregulated Transfers of Adopted Children Act. https://www.uniformlaws.org/HigherLogic/System/DownloadDocumentFile.ashx?DocumentFileKey=63c8ebc8-22ec-b1ac-0162-e2438a4fa482&forceDialog=0 (Apr. 2019).

B. THE RISE AND DECLINE OF CLOSED ADOPTION

1. Closed Adoption

"Closed adoption"—the practice of sealing adoption records to help ensure confidentiality and complete severance of the legal and social relationship between adoptees and their biological parents—is a relatively recent development. Early adoption statutes from the mid-nineteenth century were not concerned with sealed records:

> Adoption evolved over the next century, becoming more bureaucratic and professionalized. * * * The purpose of these early [20th century] confidentiality restrictions was *not* to prevent those involved in the adoption from having access to information, but to keep the public from viewing these files to determine whether a child was born outside of marriage.

> * * *

> Similarly, during the 1930s and 1940s, when states began issuing new birth certificates to adopted children, the states' goals were to improve the collection of children's vital statistics and reduce the stigma of illegitimacy, not to prevent adopted children from gaining access to their original birth certificates. * * *

> A number of social and professional pressures fueled the shift from confidentiality to secrecy during the post-World War II era.

Adoption agencies used the promise of secrecy as a way to distinguish themselves from less respectable adoption sources. Social workers argued that secrecy would help insure the integrity of the adoptive family by preventing disgruntled biological parents from later attempting to reclaim their children. In addition, social workers believed that the secrecy of records would help biological mothers "recover" from their "indiscretion" and continue with their lives as though they had never had a child.

The changing demographic composition of birth parents also contributed to the rise of secrecy. Prior to World War II, a majority of the birth mothers who surrendered children for adoption were either married or divorced, and often relinquished children only after struggling to support them financially. In the postwar era, birth mothers were younger and predominantly single; the vast majority of their children were born outside of marriage and were relinquished within days of their birth. These changing demographics were accompanied by a shift in attitudes toward unwed mothers. Before World War II, out-of-wedlock pregnancy was often explained as the product of inherent and immutable biological and moral deficiencies. Children born under such circumstances were biologically suspect and women who gave birth outside of marriage were permanently marked as outcast mothers. In the post-World War II era, this biological explanation was replaced with a psychological paradigm that asserted that illegitimacy reflected an emotional rather than a biological disorder, and that such a "maladjusted" female could be "rehabilitated" and reintegrated into society. Key to this rehabilitation was the immediate relinquishment of the child and the permanent severing of ties between the biological mother and the adoptive family. * * *

Secrecy was thus seen as critical to the successful rehabilitation of unwed (white) mothers and to their reentry into the marriage market, as well as to the child's successful integration into her adoptive family. Secrecy also served the interests of childless couples, who sought adoption in unprecedented numbers during an era of celebratory pronatalism, which viewed parenthood as a patriotic necessity and a prerequisite to marital success. Adoption protected these couples from the shame of infertility and created families for them that were seemingly indistinguishable from their biological counterparts. By the mid-1960s, these factors had combined to transmute traditional confidentiality requirements into a regime of sealed records and secrecy * * *

Naomi Cahn & Jana Singer, *Adoption, Identity, and the Constitution: The Case for Opening Closed Records*, 2 U. Pa. J. Const. L. 150, 154–56 (1999).

Adoption confidentiality is now under challenge from two sources: open adoption, in which the adoption is set up to ensure some contact between the biological and adoptive families; and adoptees' efforts to secure access to their original birth certificates.

2. Open Adoption

"Open adoption has now become the norm in practice." Annette Ruth Appell, *Reflections on the Movement Toward a More Child-Centered Adoption*, 32 W. New Eng. L. Rev. 1, 4 (2010). In an open adoption, the child has the opportunity for continuing post-decree contact with the biological parents, siblings, or other relatives. "Post-adoption contact varies considerably in its form (e.g., face-to-face, telephone, emails, texting, and/or social media), frequency (e.g., weekly, monthly, yearly, every few years), consistency (regularly schedules versus erratic contact, relationship quality, and those family members involved in the contact process)." David Brodzinsky & Abbie Goldberg, *Practice Guidelines Supporting Open Adoption In Families Headed by Lesbian and Gay Male Parents* 5 (Donaldson Adoption Inst. 2016). What circumstances help account for the contemporary trend toward open adoption?

The next decision concerns a child who was born in 1997, knew her mother's identity, and had a pre-adoption relationship with her. The decision discusses the courts' authority to order an open adoption in the absence of an agreement between the biological parents and the adoptive parents, and perhaps over the adoptive parents' objection.

ADOPTION OF ILONA
Supreme Judicial Court of Massachusetts, 2011.
944 N.E.2d 115.

GANTS, J.

The Department of Children and Families (department) filed a petition * * * alleging that Ilona was a child in need of care and protection. After five days of trial, a judge in the Juvenile Court found that Ilona's mother and father were "currently unfit, unable and unavailable to further the welfare and best interest of [Ilona]" and that their unfitness was "likely to continue into the indefinite future to a near certitude." The judge concluded that Ilona was a child in need of care and protection, and dispensed with the need for her parents' consent to adoption, guardianship, custody, or other disposition of the child * * *. The judge ordered that Ilona be committed to the custody of the department, and found that Ilona's best interest would be served by the department's plan of adoption, which proposed that Ilona be adopted by her current foster parents. The judge also found that a significant attachment existed between Ilona and her mother and that continued contact between them was in Ilona's best interest, but declined to enter an order as to the frequency or extent of contact between them, concluding that these decisions were "best left to the informed decision making" of Ilona's preadoptive parents.

The mother makes two arguments on appeal. * * * Second, she claims that the judge abused his discretion in declining to order visitation with Ilona after finding that continued contact between them was in Ilona's best interest.

* * * We agree with the Appeals Court that the judge did not err in terminating the mother's parental rights, but do not agree that, in the circumstances of this case, he abused his discretion in declining to order visitation with the mother and leaving decisions about visitation to the sound judgment of the preadoptive parents. Therefore, we affirm the judgment of the Juvenile Court.

* * *

Discussion. * * *

2. *Visitation order.* The judge found that a significant attachment existed between Ilona and her mother, and that continued contact is currently in Ilona's best interest. The judge noted the preadoptive mother's willingness to allow visitation between Ilona and her biological mother, but he did not enter an order requiring visitation, leaving the extent and frequency of contact between them to the "informed decision making" of the preadoptive parents. * * * We * * * affirm the decision of the trial judge.

We have repeatedly recognized the equitable authority of a judge to order visitation between a child and a parent whose parental rights have been terminated, where such visitation is in the child's best interest. * * *

In determining whether to exercise the authority to order visitation, a judge must ask two questions: First, is visitation in the child's best interest? Second, in cases where a family is ready to adopt the child, is an *order* of visitation necessary to protect the child's best interest, or may decisions regarding visitation be left to the judgment of the adoptive family?

As to the first question, a judge should consider, among other factors, whether there is "a significant, existing bond with the biological parent" whose rights have been terminated. A judge may also take into account whether a preadoptive family has been identified and, if so, whether the child "has formed strong, nurturing bonds" with that family.

Where visitation is in the best interest of the child, a judge must then decide whether an order of visitation is warranted. We have recognized that even where the child's custodian is supportive of visitation with the terminated parent, an order of visitation provides clarity and security to a child who may be worried about the loss of a relationship with the biological parent. However, we have also recognized that, while a judge cannot order visitation unless it is in the child's best interest, the best interest of the child does not by itself answer the question whether an order of visitation should enter. *Blixt v. Blixt,* 437 Mass. 649, 657–658, 774 N.E.2d 1052 (2002), citing *Troxel v. Granville,* 530 U.S. 57, 68, 69 (2000) (plurality opinion).

Adoptive parents have the same protected interest in their relationship with the adoptive child as biological parents, and are entitled to the same presumption they will act in the best interest of the child in making decisions regarding the child, including decisions about visitation. Therefore, once a preadoptive family has been identified, a judge must balance the benefit to the child of an order of visitation that will provide assurance that the child will be able to maintain contact with a biological parent, with the intrusion that an order imposes on the rights of the adoptive parents, who are entitled to the presumption that they will act in their child's best interest. A judge should issue an order of visitation only if such an order, on balance, is necessary to protect the child's best interest.[15]

* * *

Here * * * the judge concluded that there was a significant bond between the child and biological parent and that continued contact between them was in the child's best interests. * * * [T]he judge also found that Ilona had a "very warm and nurturing" preadoptive mother, and that Ilona was thriving under her care. In addition, the judge found that the preadoptive mother was supportive of continued contact between Ilona and her mother, and would continue to allow such contact unless it began to harm Ilona. There is no reason to question the presumption that Ilona's preadoptive parents will act in her best interest in evaluating—now and in the future—whether continued contact with her mother is in Ilona's best interest; nor is there any compelling reason requiring that a visitation order be entered in order to protect the best interests of the child. The judge therefore did not abuse his discretion in leaving the issue of visitation to the sound judgment of loving adoptive parents who will be in the best position to gauge whether such visits continue to serve Ilona's best interest, rather than issuing a specific visitation order setting forth the frequency and extent of such visits. * * *

Decree affirmed.

---

[15] Even without an order of visitation, a judge may encourage the prospective adoptive parents and biological parents to enter into an agreement for postadoption visitation or communication, which must be approved by the judge issuing the adoption decree.

NOTES AND QUESTIONS

1. *Questions about* Adoption of Ilona. (a) Did the court properly accommodate the interests of the biological mother, the adoptive parents, and Ilona? (b) What should the court do if Ilona's adoptive parents soon decide to prohibit all visitation between the girl and her biological mother? (c) What factors should a court consider when it decides whether to order visitation in the absence of a private agreement among the biological parent and adoptive parents?

2. *Statutory authorization.* Several states have statutes that authorize courts to order visitation between the adopted child and specified persons—usually the biological parents, grandparents, siblings, or other close relatives—when visitation would be in the best interests of the child. *See, e.g.,* Fla. Stat. § 63.0427 (2018). A few state statutes expressly grant separated siblings standing to petition for visitation with one another. *See, e.g.,* Mass. Gen. Laws, ch. 119, § 26B(b) (2018). Some state statutes expressly preclude visitation orders following adoption. *See, e.g.,* Tenn. Code Ann. § 36–1–121(f) (2018).

Courts have disagreed about whether, in the absence of statutory authorization, courts may exercise equitable authority to order visitation with siblings, biological parents, or other third parties. Some decisions have authorized courts to exercise the sort of equitable authority that *Adoption of Ilona* authorized. Decisions such as *In re Adoption of C.H.*, 554 N.W.2d 737 (Minn. 1996), however, preclude courts from exercising equitable authority to enter post-adoption visitation orders because the adoption act terminates all parental rights and obligations between the adoptee and persons other than the adoptive parents.

Whether based on statute or equitable authority, court orders for post-adoption visitation grounded in the best interests of the child but opposed by the adoptive parents face careful constitutional scrutiny after *Troxel v. Granville*, 530 U.S. 57 (2000), the third-party visitation decision presented in Chapter 13. Why might openness in appropriate cases serve the best interests of the child? What interests might be served by precluding courts, as a matter of law, from ordering openness?

3. *"Contact" agreements.* Some state statutes authorize courts to order specific performance of "contact" agreements, made between the biological and adoptive parents, provided that the court finds that the agreement is in the best interests of the child. States without such statutes disagree about specific enforcement. In *S.M. v. M.P.*, 79 N.E.3d 1050 (Mass. App. Ct. 2017), for example, the court enforced a written visitation agreement between the biological parents and the adoptive parents in accordance with its terms. On the other hand, *Birth Mother v. Adoptive Parents*, 59 P.3d 1233 (Nev. 2002), refused to enforce an agreement giving the biological parent post-adoption visitation rights because the adoption decree granted no such rights; a biological parent had no rights to the child except rights recited in the decree.

3. Adoptees' Rights to "Learn Their Roots"

When the court decrees an adoption in a closed regime, the child is issued an amended birth certificate naming the adoptive parents as the birth parents. The original birth certificate and all other court records are sealed and, in many states, may be released only on court order for good cause. In the absence of the severe emotional or medical necessity that might establish good cause, the biological parents may not learn the identity or whereabouts of the child or adoptive parents, and the adoptive parents and the child may not learn the identities or whereabouts of the biological parents. An adoptee who seeks to learn his or her heritage may learn only what the adoptive parents reveal, and they may not know very much themselves.

The good-cause requirement permits disclosure of identifying information (that is, information which includes the biological parents' names, birth dates, places of birth, and last known addresses) only where the adoptee shows an urgent need for medical, genetic, or other important reasons. Even without such a showing, most states mandate or allow disclosure to adoptive families of an adopted child's health and genetic information. Some states also grant adoptees, when they reach majority, the right to nonidentifying information concerning their biological parents (that is, information about the parents' physical description, ages at the time of adoption, race, nationality, religious background, and talents and hobbies, without revealing the parents' identities).

Confidentiality statutes lose their force when the court orders an open adoption, or specifically enforces a private agreement for such an arrangement. Confidentiality may also be impossible where the adoption is otherwise concluded informally before the parties seek the decree, or where the child has had a pre-adoption relationship with the biological parents or other relatives.

In the absence of privately negotiated, practical, or court-mandated openness, confidentiality statutes impede or thwart the efforts of many adoptees to locate their biological parents. The adoption act's mandate that the child assume a new identity and a new life, however, cannot extinguish the desire of many adoptees for disclosure. Advocacy and support groups help adoptees lobby for legislation easing confidentiality standards and assist adoptees' efforts to locate their birth families. Internet and social media searches sometimes facilitate location efforts.

Children adopted from orphanages overseas, sometimes after surreptitious abandonment by their biological parents, may have been subject to no recordkeeping in their native lands; an abandoned child might not even have a birth certificate or other proof of exact date of birth. "Birth parents from some countries do not want to be traced, for example due to a strong culture of shame." Donaldson Adoption Inst., *Attitudes and*

Perceptions Among Adoption Professionals: Qualitative Research Rep. 15 (2016).

NOTES AND QUESTIONS

1. *Questions about sealed records.* (a) Are the interests of the biological parents, adoptive parents, and the state sufficiently strong today to thwart an adoptee's request for disclosure of identifying information? Do the interests favoring confidentiality lose some force when adoptees seek disclosure of their sealed adoption records after they reach adulthood? (b) Does the state deny adoptees personal autonomy when it legislates an adoption process and denies them information concerning their heritage for the rest of their lives? Or does the state do enough when it assures release of nonidentifying information needed for medical or other important reasons? (c) How might closed adoptions disserve the interests of biological parents?

2. *Emotional or medical need.* "Adoption is an increasingly significant aspect of identity for adopted people as they age, and remains so even when they are adults." Hollee McGinnis, *Beyond Culture Camp: Promoting Healthy Identity Formation in Adoption* 4 (Donaldson Adoption Inst. 2009). Judicial refusal to breach confidentiality continues, however.

In *In re R.D.*, 876 N.W.2d 786 (Iowa 2016), for example, the court denied the application of a 51-year-old woman who, adopted as newborn, sought disclosure of her biological parents' identities. The biological parents had not been given notice of the application proceeding and had not consented to unsealing the adoption records.

Adoptee R.D. presented competent medical evidence that lifelong non-disclosure of her heritage remains a root cause of her depression, anxiety, and alcohol abuse, and that unsealing the adoption records might assist her recovery. The court held that she had failed to overcome the state's non-disclosure statute, which permits unsealing where "opening is shown to be necessary to save the life of or prevent irreparable physical or mental harm to an adopted person or the person's offspring." *Id.* at 790.

The state supreme court held (1) that in weighing the interests of adoptees, adoptive parents, biological parents, and other family members, Iowa's non-disclosure statute strikes a balance "heavily in favor of keeping adoption records sealed," *id.* at 791; (2) that sealing "helps promote the formation of the adoptive family" and "protects the biological parents' right to privacy," *id.* at 796; and (3) that disclosure's "predicted therapeutic benefit" to R.D. did not overcome the statute's non-disclosure mandate because her adoption records contain no medical information and because she "can offer no assurances that her problems will resolve" with disclosure, *id.* at 798.

The state supreme court concluded that any recalibration of the adoption act's heavily pro-confidentiality balance rests with the legislature and not with the courts. *Id.* at 799.

3.   *Disclosure legislation.* Many states have enacted registry statutes, which provide for release of identifying information where the biological parents, the adoptive parents, and the adoptee all register their desire for release. Passive registry statutes allow parties to register their desires, and active registry statutes authorize state authorities to seek out the other parties when one party expresses a desire for disclosure. *See, e.g.*, Colo. Rev. Stat. § 25–2–113.5 (2018) (passive); Or. Rev. Stat. § 109.503 (2018) (active).

An increasing number of states grant adoptees, when they reach adulthood, a right to their original birth certificates, *e.g.*, Alaska Stat. § 18.50.500 (2018); 23 Pa. C.S.A. § 2937 (2018), or a right to the court records of their adoption proceeding, *e.g.*, 9 S.D. Cod. Laws § 25–6–15 (2018). If you were a state legislator, how would you vote on a bill that would grant these rights?

CHAPTER 7

CIVIL AND CRIMINAL REMEDIES FOR FAMILY INJURY

■ ■ ■

This Chapter consists of two sections. Section 1 examines civil and criminal "public law" responses to family injury caused by domestic violence. Section 2 examines "private law" tort remedies for violence and various other injuries to family members and their relationships.

1. DOMESTIC VIOLENCE

A. INTRODUCTION

1. Prevalence and Practice

As a clinical or behavioral matter, domestic violence is "a pattern of assaultive and/or coercive behaviors, including physical, sexual, and psychological attacks, as well as economic coercion, that adults or adolescents use against their intimate partners." U.S. Dep't of Health & Hum. Servs., Children's Bureau, *Definitions of Domestic Violence* (2017). The perpetrator may be a spouse or nonmarital partner, a boyfriend or girlfriend, or another family member. The immediate victim is usually a woman. The violence may be a felony or a misdemeanor. Victims are sometimes identified as survivors, a term that recognizes their efforts to overcome the abuse and protect themselves.

Domestic violence (sometimes called intimate partner violence, or IPV) does not happen only somewhere else; it remains "a devastating social problem that impacts every segment of the population." U.S. Dep't of Health and Human Servs., Children's Bureau, *Domestic Violence and the Child Welfare System* (2014). Cases affected by domestic violence find their way onto a typical family lawyer's calendar. "[A] surprising number of divorces, probably at least 50%, include allegations of intimate partner violence. In custody-litigating families, research shows that two-thirds to three-fourths of cases may involve such allegations." Nancy Ver Steegh et al., *Look Before You Leap: Court System Triage of Family Law Cases Involving Intimate Partner Violence*, 95 Marq. L. Rev. 955, 966–67 (2012).

This Section 1 begins by profiling the prevalence of domestic violence, and then turns to civil and criminal strategies to prevent and counter it.

Later chapters discuss domestic violence in fault-based divorce, property distribution, custody, and visitation. Children and the Law courses typically cover domestic violence that implicates child abuse and child neglect.

As you review the materials in this Section and elsewhere in this book, consider the relationship among domestic violence and various other aspects of family law. For example, under traditional divorce law, domestic violence constituted the fault ground of cruelty. In no-fault divorce, domestic violence now appears not only in contested divorces and custody proceedings, but also in separate actions such as criminal prosecutions, tort suits, and applications for civil protection orders.

2.   Historical Background

Well into the nineteenth century, most domestic violence went unremedied and unpunished because a husband held the common law right to physically chastise, or reasonably "correct," his wife on the rationale that he was responsible for her actions. In *State v. Black*, 60 N.C. 266 (N.C. 1864), for example, the court dismissed assault charges against a husband who pulled his wife along the floor by her hair. The "husband is responsible for the acts of his wife, and he is required to govern his household," the court began. *Id.* at 268. The law permitted the husband to use "such a degree of force as is necessary to control an unruly temper and make [his wife] behave herself * * * unless some permanent injury be inflicted, or there be an excess of violence, or such a degree of cruelty as shows that it is inflicted to gratify his own bad passions." *Id.*

Black explained that the law's refusal to intervene against domestic violence stemmed partly from the premise that authorities should not "invade the domestic forum or go behind the curtain" of family privacy. *Id.* at 267. Addressing the common law's hands-off approach about a century and a half later, Justice Sandra Day O'Connor said this: "In the words of the English poet Alfred, Lord Tennyson, a wife stood in legal relation to her spouse as something just 'better than his dog, a little dearer than his horse.'" Sandra Day O'Connor, The Majesty of the Law 156 (2003).

In 1871, Alabama became one of the first states to disavow the husband's "privilege, ancient though it be, to beat [his wife] with a stick, to pull her hair, choke her, spit in her face or kick her about the floor, or to inflict upon her like indignities." *Fulgham v. State*, 46 Ala. 143, 146–47 (1871). By the end of the nineteenth century, courts had generally repudiated a husband's chastisement privilege, but domestic violence continued without court intervention except sometimes in extreme cases, buttressed by notions of family privacy expressed in the adage that "a man's home is his castle."

For most of the twentieth century, "privacy and the sanctity of the home were ideas that stood in the way of treating an assault on an intimate partner as a crime." Margaret Talbot, *Matters of Privacy*, The New Yorker, Oct. 6, 2014. Recall from Chapter 3 that in *Planned Parenthood of Southeastern Pa. v. Casey*, 505 U.S. 833 (1992), the Court repudiated the common law's patriarchal model of marriage and husbands' domination over their wives. The Court reiterated the trial court's extensive findings about pervasive domestic violence, with a focus on women as victims.

Casey came as fundamental changes in civil and criminal law and practice, and in societal norms, have made domestic violence more visible. The nation has moved from virtually overlooking this violence to acknowledging that it remains a moral and legal concern that imposes serious physical and emotional consequences on survivors and other family members.

Every state now authorizes courts to issue civil protection restraining orders against perpetrators, and most states make domestic violence a significant factor in child custody and visitation decisions. Policies requiring law enforcement to arrest alleged batterers are increasingly common, and prosecutors are increasingly likely to prosecute. Family lawyers and battered women's advocates have shown greater understanding of IPV's harmful effects on immediate victims and others, including children in the household.

Most recently, the #MeToo movement has seen growing numbers of women come forward to accuse public officials and other prominent men of unwanted sexual and other physical imposition. Some accusations (including ones against a member of the President's inner circle) have concerned men's physical and sexual assaults on their wives or intimate partners. *See, e.g.,* Maggie Haberman & Katie Rogers, *Rob Porter, White House Aide, Resigns After Accusations of Abuse,* N.Y. Times, Feb. 7, 2018.

B. DOMESTIC VIOLENCE: A CONTEMPORARY NATIONAL PROFILE

Domestic violence is "the most common tort committed in our country." Joann Sahl, *Can We Forgive Those Who Batter?: Proposing an End To the Collateral Consequences of Civil Domestic Violence Cases,* 100 Marq. L. Rev. 527, 528 (2016). Criminal statistics paint an equally somber portrait. According to the U.S. Department of Justice National Crime Victimization Survey (NCVS), domestic violence accounted for 21% of all violent crimes from 2003 to 2012. Intimate partner violence (15%) accounted for a greater percentage of all violent victimizations than violence committed by immediate family members (4%) or other relatives (2%). On average, 967,710 violent nonfatal victimizations were committed annually by intimates. Jennifer L. Truman & Rachel E. Morgan, *Nonfatal Domestic Violence, 2003–2012*, at 1, 7 (U.S. DOJ 2014).

Women were victims in approximately 76% of the domestic violence crimes reported by the NCVS, and men were victims in approximately 24%. *Id.* at 1. Indeed, from 2001 to 2012 the number of American women murdered by current or former male partners was nearly double the number of American troops killed in the Iraq and Afghanistan wars. *See* Alanna Vagianos, *30 Shocking Domestic Violence Statistics That Remind Us It's an Epidemic,* Huffington Post, Dec. 6, 2017. The National Association of Social Workers calls domestic violence an "egregious disregard of the human rights and dignity of women." NASW, *Legislation, Policies Needed To Prevent and End Culture of Sexual Harassment, Violence* (2017).

In a 2018 analysis of 47 major American cities in the prior decade, the *Washington Post* found that 46% of female homicide victims were killed by an intimate partner. Katie Zezima et al., *Domestic Slayings: Brutal and Foreseeable,* Wash. Post, Dec. 9, 2018. "Killings of intimate partners often are especially brutal, involving close encounters such as stabbings, strangulation and beatings." *Id.*

During the nine years that the NCVS studied, only about 55% of domestic violence incidents were reported to police. Truman & Morgan, *supra* at 9. A survivor sometimes spurns reporting because, for example, she fears that authorities will not believe her or provide effective protection, that the perpetrator will escalate the violence if police intervene, that she will be forced to testify in court, or that she cannot leave the perpetrator, often because he is her primary source of financial support.

Race may also play a role in chronic underreporting. "The criminal justice system's racial bias has discouraged many battered women of color and made them reluctant to call the police for help. Overall, a history of judicial unresponsiveness and racial bias has generated a deep-seated general distrust of the justice system by people of color. This sentiment is exacerbated by the history of hostility" by police. Phyliss Craig-Taylor, *Lifting the Veil: The Intersectionality of Ethics, Culture, and Gender Bias in Domestic Violence Cases,* 32 Rutgers L. Rec. 31, 46 (2008).

Empirical demographic research further profiles the toll exacted by domestic violence. For example:

(a) Nearly three women are killed each day by their intimate partners, such as a spouse, boyfriend, or girlfriend. Mary Emily O'Hara, *Domestic Violence: Nearly Three U.S. Women Killed Every Day by Intimate Partners* (NBC News, Apr. 11, 2017). For each woman killed, nine women are critically injured. U.S. DOJ, *Identifying and Preventing Gender Bias in Law Enforcement*

Response to Sexual Assault and Domestic Violence 6 (DOJ website visited Mar. 23, 2019).

(b) In at least 30% of intimate partner victimizations, the abuser also physically assaults infants and other children in the household. Jonathan D. Thackaray et al., *Intimate Partner Violence: The Role of the Pediatrician*, 125 Pediatrics 1094, 1095 (2010, reaffirmed 2014). Aside from direct physical assault, "[a] child may become the victim of abuse by simply being held in a caregiver's arms while he or she is battered. Older children may be harmed while mediating a crisis or defending the abused caregiver." *Id.* Family pets frequently also become targets of domestic abusers. Daniel M. Lindberg et al., *Prevalence of Abusive Injuries in Siblings and Household Contacts of Physically Abused Children*, 130 Pediatrics 193, 194 (2012).

(c) Women of childbearing age face the highest risk of intimate partner violence, with a prevalence during pregnancy ranging from 3.9% to 8.3%. Phyllis Sharps et al., *Engaging and Retaining Abused Women in Perinatal Home Visitation Programs*, 132 Pediatrics S134, S135 (2013). "Abuse during pregnancy has been associated with several poor health outcomes for the infant, including preterm labor, low birth weight, intracranial injury, and neonatal death." Thackaray, *supra* at 1095.

(d) "Women with disabilities have a 40 percent greater risk of intimate partner violence, especially severe violence, than women without disabilities." Am. Psychol. Ass'n, *Intimate Partner Violence: Facts & Resources* (2018).

(e) Nearly one-third of homeless families with children suffer domestic violence. Pew Charitable Trusts, *Homeless Will Now Be Asked: Are You Fleeing Domestic Violence?* (Jan. 19, 2018).

(f) Physical or emotional violence against elderly victims may be accompanied by "economic abuse in the form of financial exploitation, including theft and fraud. Abuse in later life may be perpetrated by a current or former spouse or intimate partner, as well as by family members, including adult children or grandchildren." U.S. DOJ, *Supporting Domestic Violence Survivors of All Ages and Recognizing Abuse In Later Life* (2017).

NOTES AND QUESTIONS

1. *The perils of leaving.* As women face actual or threatened domestic victimization, the question is sometimes asked, "Why doesn't she just leave the abusive household?" At least two explanations present themselves.

First, domestic violence typically entails a pattern of coercive control by the abuser, who may become increasingly possessive in an effort to retain power over the victim. This power dynamic helps explain why domestic violence survivors may face increased risks of violence, including murder, if they attempt to escape the abusive relationship. *E.g.*, Aviva Orenstein, *Sex, Threats, and Absent Victims: The Lessons of* Regina v. Bedingfield *for Modern Confrontation and Domestic Violence Cases*, 79 Fordham L. Rev. 115, 145 (2010). The Justice Department reports that divorced or separated persons face particularly high rates of intimate partner violence. *See* Shannan Catalano, Bureau of Justice Stats., *Intimate Partner Violence, 1993–2010*, at 5 (2012).

Second, domestic violence survivors who escape an abusive relationship need to find a safe place. They sometimes cannot support themselves and may become homeless, particularly if they are also poor. The batterer may be the survivor's source of support and the father of her children.

2.   *Domestic violence and the workplace.* "Domestic, dating, sexual and stalking violence are workplace issues that do not stay at home when victims and perpetrators go to work." ABA Comm'n on Domestic & Sexual Violence, *Model Workplace DSV Policy*, https://www.americanbar.org/groups/domestic_violence/policyandlegislation/model-workplace-dsv-policy.html (visited Mar. 23, 2019). Indeed, "victimization rates in the workplace were higher than those in the general populace because DSV [domestic and sexual violence] victims are 'overrepresented in the workplace.' " *Id.*

Predictable hours and the known location of employment enable many domestic abusers to find their victims at work. The Centers for Disease Control and Prevention estimates that 9.1% of women and 4.8% of men have missed at least one day of work or school because of intimate partner violence. Matthew J. Breiding et al., Mortality and Morbidity Weekly Rep., *Prevalence and Characteristics of Sexual Violence, Stalking, and Intimate Partner Violence Victimization—National Intimate Partner and Sexual Violence Survey, United States, 2011*, at 12 (CDC 2014).

Domestic violence victims miss more than eight million days of work each year, which is comparable to more than 32,000 full-time jobs. The average female domestic violence victim loses almost four weeks of work each year because of incapacitating or humiliating injuries, a partner who will not let her leave the home, or her use of working hours to begin leaving the abuser. "[I]t is common for victims to lose their jobs due to absences, workplace disruptions, performance problems—or simple prejudice against victims." Deborah A. Widiss, *Domestic Violence and the Workplace: The Explosion of State Legislation and the Need for a Comprehensive Strategy*, 35 Fla. St. L. Rev. 669, 677 (2008).

3.   *Mandatory reporting.* States require health care professionals to report to law enforcement some injuries that appear to have resulted from a criminal act. In a few states, mandatory reporting laws apply specifically to injuries that apparently result from domestic violence. Dania Bardavid et al., *Domestic Violence*, Geo. J. of Gender & L. 211, 233 (2016).

In 2016, Illinois enacted legislation that does not make cosmetologists (hairstylists) mandatory reporters, but requires them to take one hour of training to recognize signs of domestic violence and sexual assault. 225 ILCS 410/3-7 (2018). Trainers provide materials that cosmetologists can give clients who they suspect have been assaulted. The new Illinois law recognizes "the unique relationship between hairdressers and their customers." Christine Hauser, *A New Front Against Domestic Abuse: The Hairstylist's Chair*, N.Y. Times, Dec. 16, 2016.

4. *Stalking and technology.* The Centers for Disease Control and Prevention estimates that 15.8% of women and 5.3% of men during their lifetimes have been victims of stalking, a virulent form of emotional domestic violence. "[C]ommonly experienced stalking tactics were: unwanted phone calls, voice messages, and text messages from the perpetrator: perpetrators showing up or approaching them in places, such as home, school, or work; and being watched, followed, or spied on." Sharon G. Smith et al., *The National Intimate Partner and Sexual Violence Survey, 2010–2012 State Rep.* 2 (CDC 2017).

Cyberstalking is growing more prevalent. According to a National Public Radio survey, 85% of domestic violence shelters work directly "with victims whose abusers tracked them using GPS [Global Positioning System]. Seventy-five percent say they're working with victims whose abusers eavesdropped on their conversation remotely—using hidden mobile apps. And nearly half * * * have a policy against using Facebook on premises, because they are concerned a stalker can pinpoint location." Aarti Shahani, *Smartphones Are Used to Stalk, Control Domestic Abuse Victims* (NPR Sept. 15, 2014).

The *New York Times* reports that more than 200 telephone apps and services enable domestic cyberstalkers to track their victims. Many of these innovations are marketed as benign ways to keep track of children, locate friends, or find lost phones; some devices also advertise their potential for suspicious users to monitor the whereabouts and activities of spouses or partners. Jennifer Valentino-DeVries, *Hundreds of Apps Can Empower Their Stalkers to Track Their Victims*, N.Y. Times, May 19, 2018. The *Times* notes that "stalking is a top warning sign for attempted homicide in domestic violence cases." *Id.*

The *Times* also reports use of smart home technology for emotional domestic abuse, often by men who have left the household against their wives or partners who remain. "Internet-connected locks, speakers, thermostats, lights and cameras * * * are now * * * being used as a means for harassment, monitoring revenge and control. * * * Abusers—using apps on their smartphones, which are connected to the internet-enabled devices—would remotely control everyday devices in the home, sometimes to watch and listen, other times to scare or show power." Nellie Bowles, *Thermostats, Locks and Lights: Digital Tools of Domestic Abuse*, N.Y. Times, June 23, 2018.

Civil protection orders and criminal dispositions typically include "no contact" provisions, which prohibit the perpetrator from knowing face-to-face, telephone, or mail communication with the victim. These provisions now often also prohibit direct digital communication by the Internet or social media, but the meaning of "no contact" is growing more complicated. Ashley Fetters, *Why It's Hard to Protect Domestic-Violence Survivors Online*, The Atlantic, July 11, 2018. For example, does the subject engage in prohibited contact with the victim when he sends an Internet or social media message to a third person, allegedly with knowledge or expectation that the message will reach the victim? *Id.*

A 2014 national survey of victim service providers found that the "third person" is often the immediate victim's child. "[A]busers, who are forbidden from contacting the survivor because of a protection order but have visitation or communication rights with the child, will use the children's technology to try to contact the survivor." Nat'l Network to End Domestic Violence, *A Glimpse From the Field: How Abusers Are Misusing Technology* (2014). The abuser may achieve his aim by spying or eavesdropping on the children, by "asking the child to share information about the survivor or using the child's cellphone to try to contact the survivor," by "gather[ing] information about the survivor through social networks their children are a part of," or by "planting devices on the child's belongings." *Id.*

On the other side of the coin, emerging technology may offer protection rather than encourage intimidation. For example, by court order in a growing number of states, subjects of civil protection orders, or of petitions for these orders, must wear GPS devices to enable authorities to monitor their whereabouts. *See, e.g., Keeping Abusers Away: Done Right, GPS Tracking Can Help Protect Victims*, Pittsburgh Post-Gazette, Dec. 23, 2017.

C. CIVIL PROTECTION ORDERS

Civil protection orders (CPOs), available by statute in every state, are court orders that bar a person who has committed acts of domestic violence from having further harmful contact with a victim. "Protection orders are now the most widely used legal remedy against domestic violence, with more survivors utilizing this civil justice system remedy than seeking tort remedies or having involvement with the criminal justice system." Jane K. Stoever, *Enjoining Abuse: The Case for Indefinite Domestic Violence Protection Orders*, 67 Vand. L. Rev. 1015, 1019 (2014).

CPO statutes generally permit victims to petition the court for injunctive relief, including orders that prohibit the abuser from continuing to assault, threaten, harass, or physically abuse them or others in the household. The court may also order the abuser to stay away from victims' homes, workplaces, or other commonly visited areas, such as the children's schools. CPOs sound in prevention insofar as they regulate the batterer's future behavior, whereas criminal statutes are reactive insofar as they operate only after the victim has been injured or killed.

1.　Seeking a Civil Protection Order

Procedures for obtaining a CPO vary from state to state, but most states allow victims first to seek a temporary *ex parte* order, which the court may issue without the batterer's appearance. The Florida statute appearing below guarantees that in larger communities, a local judge will be available 24 hours a day, seven days a week, to issue these orders.

Ex parte orders provide emergency injunctive relief restraining the batterer from inflicting further violence on the victim, but they remain effective for only a short period. The court may not issue a longer-term, "permanent order" for cause until the batterer has had notice and an opportunity to be heard. Depending on the state, a permanent order may last from several weeks to a year or longer.

These Florida statutes illustrate a representative legislative formula for seeking protection against domestic violence:

Definitions

FLORIDA STATUTES
(2018).

§ 741.28.

(2)　"Domestic violence" means any assault, aggravated assault, battery, aggravated battery, sexual assault, sexual battery, stalking, aggravated stalking, kidnapping, false imprisonment, or any criminal offense resulting in physical injury or death of one family or household member by another family or household member.

(3)　"Family or household member" means spouses, former spouses, persons related by blood or marriage, persons who are presently residing together as if a family or who have resided together in the past as if a family, and persons who are parents of a child in common regardless of whether they have been married. With the exception of persons who have a child in common, the family or household members must be currently residing or have in the past resided together in the same single dwelling unit. * * *

The Court's Injunctive Powers and Duties

FLORIDA STATUTES
(2018).

§ 741.30.

(1)　There is created a cause of action for an injunction for protection against domestic violence.

(a) Any person described in paragraph (e), who is either the victim of domestic violence as defined in s. 741.28 or has reasonable cause to believe he or she is in imminent danger of becoming the victim of any act of domestic violence, has standing in the circuit court to file a sworn petition for an injunction for protection against domestic violence.

* * *

(d) A person's right to petition for an injunction shall not be affected by such person having left a residence or household to avoid domestic violence.

(e) This cause of action for an injunction may be sought by family or household members. No person shall be precluded from seeking injunctive relief pursuant to this chapter solely on the basis that such person is not a spouse.

* * *

(j) The court is prohibited from issuing mutual orders of protection. This does not preclude the court from issuing separate injunctions for protection against domestic violence where each party has complied with the provisions of this section. Compliance with the provisions of this section cannot be waived.

(k) * * * [A] petition for an injunction for protection against domestic violence may be filed in the circuit where the petitioner currently or temporarily resides, where the respondent resides, or where the domestic violence occurred. There is no minimum requirement of residency to petition for an injunction for protection.

* * *

(4) Upon the filing of the petition, the court shall set a hearing to be held at the earliest possible time. The respondent shall be personally served with a copy of the petition, financial affidavit, Uniform Child Custody Jurisdiction and Enforcement Act affidavit, if any, notice of hearing, and temporary injunction, if any, prior to the hearing.

(5)(a)   If it appears to the court that an immediate and present danger of domestic violence exists, the court may grant a temporary injunction ex parte, pending a full hearing, and may grant such relief as the court deems proper, including an injunction:

> 1. Restraining the respondent from committing any acts of domestic violence.

> 2. Awarding to the petitioner the temporary exclusive use and possession of the dwelling that the parties share or excluding the respondent from the residence of the petitioner.

3. * * * [P]roviding the petitioner a temporary parenting plan, including a time-sharing schedule, which may award the petitioner up to 100 percent of the time-sharing. * * *

(b) * * * [I]n a hearing ex parte for the purpose of obtaining such ex parte temporary injunction, no evidence other than verified pleadings or affidavits shall be used as evidence, unless the respondent appears at the hearing or has received reasonable notice of the hearing. A denial of a petition for an ex parte injunction shall be by written order noting the legal grounds for denial. * * *

(c) Any such ex parte temporary injunction shall be effective for a fixed period not to exceed 15 days. A full hearing, as provided by this section, shall be set for a date no later than the date when the temporary injunction ceases to be effective. * * *

(6)(a) Upon notice and hearing, when it appears to the court that the petitioner is either the victim of domestic violence as defined by § 741.28 or has reasonable cause to believe he or she is in imminent danger of becoming a victim of domestic violence, the court may grant such relief as the court deems proper, including an injunction:

1. Restraining the respondent from committing any acts of domestic violence.

2. Awarding to the petitioner the exclusive use and possession of the dwelling that the parties share or excluding the respondent from the residence of the petitioner.

3. * * * [P]roviding the petitioner with 100 percent of the time-sharing in a temporary parenting plan that remains in effect until the order expires. * * *

4. * * * [E]stablishing temporary support for a minor child or children or the petitioner. * * *

5. Ordering the respondent to participate in treatment, intervention, or counseling services to be paid for by the respondent. * * *

6. Referring a petitioner to a certified domestic violence center. * * *

7. Ordering such other relief as the court deems necessary for the protection of a victim of domestic violence, including injunctions or directives to law enforcement agencies, as provided in this section.

(b) In determining whether a petitioner has reasonable cause to believe he or she is in imminent danger of becoming a victim of domestic violence, the court shall consider and evaluate all relevant factors alleged in the petition, including, but not limited to:

1. The history between the petitioner and the respondent, including threats, harassment, stalking, and physical abuse.

2.   Whether the respondent has attempted to harm the petitioner or family members or individuals closely associated with the petitioner.

3.   Whether the respondent has threatened to conceal, kidnap, or harm the petitioner's child or children.

4.   Whether the respondent has intentionally injured or killed a family pet.

5.   Whether the respondent has used, or has threatened to use, against the petitioner any weapons such as guns or knives.

6.   Whether the respondent has physically restrained the petitioner from leaving the home or calling law enforcement.

7.   Whether the respondent has a criminal history involving violence or the threat of violence.

8.   The existence of a verifiable order of protection issued previously or from another jurisdiction.

9.   Whether the respondent has destroyed personal property, including, but not limited to, telephones or other communications equipment, clothing, or other items belonging to the petitioner.

10.   Whether the respondent engaged in any other behavior or conduct that leads the petitioner to have reasonable cause to believe that he or she is in imminent danger of becoming a victim of domestic violence.

* * *

(g)   A final judgment on injunction for protection against domestic violence entered pursuant to this section must, on its face, indicate that it is * * * a first degree misdemeanor, for the respondent to have in his or her care, custody, possession, or control any firearm or ammunition.

* * *

(9)(a)   The court may enforce a violation of an injunction for protection against domestic violence through a civil or criminal contempt proceeding, or the state attorney may prosecute it as a criminal violation * * *. The court may enforce the respondent's compliance with the injunction through any appropriate civil and criminal remedies, including, but not limited to, a monetary assessment or a fine. * * *

24-Hour Availability for Temporary Relief

FLORIDA STATUTES
(2018).

§ 26.20.

[A]t least one * * * judge[ ] shall be available as nearly as possible at all times to hold and conduct hearings in chambers. In each circuit, there must be at least one judge available on Saturdays, Sundays, holidays, and after hours on weekdays to hear motions for a temporary injunction ex parte in domestic violence cases. * * *

NOTES AND QUESTIONS

1.   *Questions about Florida's statutes.* Who is eligible to seek remedies? Against which "family" members may remedies be sought? What remedies may a court grant? What procedures are required for an *ex parte* or a permanent civil protection order? What evidentiary burdens must petitioners satisfy? Do the statutes cover stalking? Do they cover dating violence? Should states make civil protection orders available for financial harms that do not involve physical violence or direct threats, such as refusing to provide access to a telephone, or money for groceries or other necessaries?

2.   *Timing.* Fla. Stat. § 741.30, quoted above, grants standing to "[a]ny person * * * who is * * * the victim of domestic violence." But what if the alleged violent acts occurred years earlier?

In *Thompson v. Schrimsher*, 906 N.W.2d 495 (Minn. 2018), the court upheld the issuance in 2015 of a civil protection order that arose from acts that the cohabitant petitioner alleged occurred in 2011 and 2012. The court chose a victim-protective interpretation of the operative statute: "[T]he plain language of the [Minnesota Domestic Abuse] Act imposes no temporal requirement on when the 'domestic abuse' occurred. * * * [O]nce 'domestic abuse' has been established, the court may examine all of the relevant circumstances proven to determine whether to grant or deny the petition * * *. Relevant circumstances may include, but are not limited to, the timing, frequency, and severity of any alleged instances of 'domestic abuse,' along with the likelihood of further abuse." *Id.* at 500.

PROBLEM 7-1

Susan Brown had been dating Jack Thompson for three years. The couple maintained separate residences in the same Florida city, although they had overnight visits at least three times a week. One day, Jack and Susan had an argument that resulted in Jack hitting Susan so hard that she suffered a black eye. According to § 741.30 of the Florida Statutes, could Susan obtain a civil protection order against Jack? As Susan's lawyer, what arguments would you make that the statute protects her? What arguments would you expect Jack to make in response?

PROBLEM 7-2

Mary Walsh and her brother Tom were in an intense fight. Tom became enraged and hit Mary. They had not resided in the same house for more than 40 years. Because this was not the first time that Tom became violent with Mary, she filed for a civil protection order in Florida. According to the Florida domestic violence statute, § 741.30, may a court grant Mary this protection order? If you were Mary's lawyer, what arguments would you make? What arguments would you expect Tom to make in response?

PROBLEM 7-3

Katherine Johnson, a Florida resident, seeks a civil protection order against her former partner, Ann Smith. Ann has repeatedly beaten Katherine over the past three years of their relationship. The parties previously lived in a house together, but Katherine recently moved out in an attempt to escape the violence. Can Katherine obtain a civil protection order against her partner under Fla. Stat. § 741.30?

2.   Issuing a Civil Protection Order

In *Schultz v. Schultz*, 2010 WL 3075758 * 1–3 (Ohio Ct. App.), a straightforward case, the court issued a permanent civil protective order on proof of serious physical abuse by the husband against his wife:

> * * * Thomas Schultz ("Husband") chased, smacked, and choked his Wife, Christine Schultz ("Wife"), after she took his cell phone. * * *
>
> [Wife testified] that "[m]y husband was furious, chased me through the house, through the dining room, living room, and down the hallway * * *, came and attacked me from behind trying to get the cell phone out of my hand and in the process choked me to where I could not breathe and was cutting off my air supply." * * *
>
> Wife was required to establish by a preponderance of the evidence either that Husband attempted to cause her physical harm or that she was in imminent fear of serious physical harm.* * * [T]he uncontroverted testimony of Wife established that Husband attempted to cause her harm by chasing her, striking her, and choking her, and that based upon this incident, she was in imminent fear of serious physical harm. * * * [T]he facts establish the offense of domestic violence by a preponderance of the evidence. * * *

NOTE AND QUESTIONS

Christine Schultz's entitlement to a permanent civil protection order depended on proof by a preponderance of the evidence, the typical civil standard of persuasion. (a) What are the advantages of this standard in domestic violence cases? (b) What could be some objections to the preponderance standard? (c) What impediments to proof can arise in a domestic violence case?

———

The predicate for the *Schultz* permanent civil protection order was serious physical violence, but the next decision demonstrates that civil protection statutes can reach further than physical force.

CAVANAUGH V. CAVANAUGH

Supreme Court of Rhode Island, 2014.
92 A.3d 200.

JUSTICE ROBINSON, for the Court.

The defendant, Brian Cavanaugh, has appealed from an order * * * restraining and enjoining him from contacting his former wife, Rosanna Cavanaugh (the plaintiff). * * * [W]e affirm the order of the Family Court.

I

Facts and Travel

On August 10, 2012, plaintiff filed a complaint in Family Court seeking protection from abuse * * *. [P]laintiff alleged that she "suffered abuse when the defendant" "[p]laced [her] in fear of imminent physical harm" and engaged in "Stalking, Cyberstalking, [and/or] Harassing." In support of her complaint, plaintiff filed an affidavit stating that she was in fear of defendant because of his "persistent threatening, swearing, and menacing behavior during pick-up/drop-off times [when they would exchange their child, over whom they shared physical custody] and phone calls." She asked the court to enjoin defendant "from contacting, assaulting, molesting, or otherwise interfering with [her] * * *." An *ex parte* "Temporary Order [for] Protection from Abuse" was entered that same day. The Family Court specified, *inter alia,* in the order that defendant may contact plaintiff to facilitate visitation and that the exchange of their child * * * should occur at either the North Smithfield, Rhode Island or Franklin, Massachusetts police stations.

A

The Hearing on Plaintiff's Complaint for Protection from Abuse

* * *

1.   The Testimony of Plaintiff

[P]laintiff testified that she and defendant had formerly been married but that they had divorced in 2011 [and] that there was one child born of that marriage. The plaintiff testified with respect to multiple occasions in the past when defendant had "yelled," "screamed," and sworn at her and had placed her "in fear of bodily harm;" she added that she was "very scared" because that type of conduct on the part of defendant—which she alleged occurred "all the time"—had been "escalat[ing]."

It was plaintiff's testimony that, in August of 2012, her relationship with defendant worsened due to her having filed a motion to modify their child's visitation schedule * * *. The plaintiff then proceeded to testify with respect to three specific phone calls made by defendant to her after the dismissal of that motion. The plaintiff testified that, on the day her motion was dismissed, she received a phone call from defendant, who, in a "gruff, seething kind of tone of voice," said to her: "[A]re, you going to keep f* * * with me now?" The plaintiff then testified that, sometime after that, defendant had called her to "gloat," stating: "Don't 'F' with me and my lawyers." She further testified that, on August 10, 2012, when she was en route to meet defendant so that she could pick up their son pursuant to a coparenting agreement, defendant called her on the phone and said: "So, you're going to stop talking, you know, s* * * about me. Do you understand?" She stated that, because she became "really * * * scared" as a result of that phone call, she called the police in Franklin; she added that an officer then escorted her to the place where she would pick up the child. The plaintiff explained that, following that incident, she filed the complaint for protection from abuse. When asked whether there were any other incidents that placed her "in fear of [defendant] or in fear of bodily harm," she replied in the affirmative. She testified that, during the divorce proceedings, defendant threatened to "throw [her] cats in the pound" and "trashed" her piano; she added that, in May of 2012, defendant "threw something at [her]."

2.   The Testimony of Defendant

The defendant * * * acknowledged that there had been arguments between plaintiff and him before and after their divorce was finalized and that he had resorted to vulgarity during those arguments. He admitted that, following the dismissal of plaintiff's motion to modify the visitation schedule, he had called plaintiff to "gloat[ ]" and that he had used the "F" word during that phone call. He also testified that, during the August 10 phone call testified to by plaintiff, he told her to "stop making up lies about

[him]." It was his testimony that, after that call, plaintiff called the police and that an officer had been present the next time the parties exchanged their son. The defendant acknowledged that his swearing at plaintiff in the midst of a phone call constituted "harassment," but he asserted that she had been "harassing [him] as well."

* * *

III

Analysis

* * * In our judgment, defendant's conduct was clearly the type of conduct that the General Assembly has mandated can be the predicate for the issuance of a protective order. Section 15–15–3(a) expressly authorizes issuance of a protective order on behalf of a "person suffering from domestic abuse." The term "[d]omestic abuse" is defined, with a laudable degree of specificity, in § 15–15–1(2). Among the acts specified in a later subsection of the statute as constituting "domestic abuse" is "[s]talking." That subsection reads in its entirety as follows:

> " 'Stalking' means harassing another person or willfully, maliciously and repeatedly following another person with the intent to place that person in reasonable fear of bodily injury[.]"

It is significant that the just-quoted statutory definition is worded in the disjunctive. Accordingly, for present purposes, it suffices to focus on the first five words of that definition: "Stalking' means harassing another person." In turn, the term "harassing" is statutorily defined as follows:

> " 'Harassing' means following a knowing and willful course of conduct directed at a specific person with the intent to seriously alarm, annoy, or bother the person, and which serves no legitimate purpose. The course of conduct must be such as would cause a reasonable person to suffer substantial emotional distress, or be in fear of bodily injury[.]" Section 15–15–1(8).

In the present action, defendant's conduct fell within the purview of "domestic abuse" because he was "harassing" (and thus "stalking") plaintiff within the meaning of the statute. The plaintiff testified with respect to defendant's repeated use of vulgar language towards her and his threatening demeanor and tone; and she stated in both her complaint and at the hearing before the magistrate that defendant had placed her "in fear of physical harm." The defendant admitted to such conduct, and it is worth noting that he also acknowledged that his swearing at plaintiff in the midst of a phone call constituted "harassment." It is clear to us (1) that defendant was engaging in "a knowing and willful course of conduct" directed at plaintiff, with the intent to "seriously alarm, annoy, or bother" her and (2) that such conduct would cause a reasonable person to "be in fear of bodily injury."

* * * It is apparent * * * from the clear and unambiguous language of the statute that actual physical harm or threats thereof are not required for a finding that, in a given case, "domestic abuse" * * * is present.

* * *

NOTES AND QUESTIONS

1.   *Questions about* Cavanaugh. (a) Did Brian Cavanaugh "cross the line" into threat and vulgarity? (b) On a motion for a civil protection order, should the court give the complainant the benefit of the doubt when obvious confrontation appears and the parties must cooperate because they are co-parenting? (c) As a lawyer for the party who will not have primary physical child custody, what advice would you give your client during dissolution proceedings about what to do or say (or what not to do or say) afterwards, when your legal representation has ended? (d) Before entry of the divorce decree, what precautions might the Cavanaughs or the court have taken to avoid confrontations between ex-spouses during periodic post-divorce transfers of their child for visitation?

2.   *First Amendment speech considerations.* In *Virginia v. Black*, 538 U.S. 343 (2003), the Court held that the First Amendment does not protect expression that constitutes "true threats." The Court provided this definition:

> "True threats" encompass those statements where the speaker means to communicate a serious expression of an intent to commit an act of unlawful violence to a particular individual or group of individuals. The speaker need not actually intend to carry out the threat. Rather, a prohibition on true threats protects individuals from the fear of violence and from the disruption that fear engenders, in addition to protecting people from the possibility that the threatened violence will occur. Intimidation in the constitutionally proscribable sense of the word is a type of true threat, where a speaker directs a threat to a person or group of persons with the intent of placing the victim in fear of bodily harm or death.

Id. at 359–60.

In *Elonis v. United States*, 135 S. Ct. 2001 (2015), however, the Court, 8–1, reversed the former husband's criminal convictions under 18 U.S.C. § 875(c), which proscribes transmitting in interstate commerce "any communication containing any threat * * * to injure the person of another." The Court based reversal on an erroneous jury instruction.

In 2010, after nearly seven years of marriage, Anthony Elonis's wife secured a civil protection order against him. The husband posted responses on Facebook with such tirades as these: "There's one way to love you but a thousand ways to kill you. I'm not going to rest until your body is a mess, soaked in blood and dying from all the little cuts. * * * So hurry up and die, bitch, so I can forgive you." On one of these responses, he belittled the trial court's protection order: "Fold up your [order] and put it in your pocket. Is it thick enough to stop a bullet?" *United States v. Elonis*, 730 F.3d 321, 324–25 (3d Cir. 2013).

The Supreme Court reversed Elonis's convictions for threatening not only his wife, but also patrons and co-workers at his place of employment, law enforcement officers, and an unidentified kindergarten class. The Court did not directly analyze Elonis's First Amendment claims, but focused instead on federal criminal common law.

The Court held that the trial court's instructions permitted the jury to convict if it found only that defendant Elonis communicated what a reasonable person would understand as a threat. The Court held that conviction under § 875(c) also requires a finding that the defendant himself was aware of the communication's threatening nature.

Elonis thus found that the tainted jury instruction had permitted conviction on a finding that the defendant was negligent. The majority declined to decide whether conviction could be sustained by a finding that the defendant acted with reckless disregard for whether a reasonable person would regard his statements as threats, or whether an even stronger showing was required.

Professor Catherine J. Ross wrote that the Supreme Court decision marks "a victory for free speech":

> First, the opinion implicitly reiterates the Court's unwavering position that the emergence of new forms of communication does not require reconsideration of longstanding approaches to free speech or the crafting of special doctrine for online expression. * * *

> Second, the rejection of a negligence standard in criminal prosecutions involving true threats indisputably makes it harder to convict speakers using the true threat doctrine, which is appropriate. As a matter of constitutional law, conviction for issuing a true threat ought to be very difficult to achieve. * * *

> The Court correctly resisted any temptation to premise legal doctrine on the extremely unattractive facts of this case * * *. Instead, the Court's statutory interpretation served the goals of the Speech Clause as well by focusing on risks to the person the Chief Justice['s majority opinion] frames as the "innocent actor." The innocent actor is the one who really was joking (with friends he thought understood his innocent state of mind) but who the state nonetheless punishes for making true threats. * * *

> The essence of the government's argument that it need not show more than that a speaker communicated a set of words was: "trust us." Trust us to exercise our discretion carefully, trust us not to indict and prosecute without good cause. Trust in the government to do the right thing is at odds with the very notion of enforceable civil liberties and rule of law.* * *

At the same time, Professor Ross believes that a properly charged jury could reasonably have concluded that Anthony Elonis had the requisite intent to threaten his former wife. Catherine J. Ross, *Elonis v. United States: True Threat to Free Speech Averted,* Geo. Wash. L. Rev. Docket (Oct. Term 2014).

On remand, the Third Circuit found harmless error and reinstated Elonis' conviction: "The record contains overwhelming evidence demonstrating beyond a reasonable doubt that Elonis knew the threatening nature of his communications, and therefore would have been convicted absent the error." *United States v. Elonis,* 841 F.3d 589, 598 (3d Cir. 2016).

In *Childs v. Ballou,* 148 A.3d 291, 297 (Me. 2016), the court held that as a general matter, the First Amendment does not "prevent a court from restraining 'threatening or abusive communications to persons who have demonstrated a need for protection from an immediate and present danger of domestic abuse.' "

3.   Assessing the Effectiveness of Civil Protection Orders

As the next article discusses, studies show that most battered women are satisfied with entry of a civil protection order, and that they generally feel safer with an order.

SALLY GOLDFARB,
RECONCEIVING CIVIL PROTECTION ORDERS FOR
DOMESTIC VIOLENCE: CAN LAW HELP END THE
ABUSE WITHOUT ENDING THE RELATIONSHIP?
29 Cardozo L. Rev. 1487, 1508–16 (2008).

* * * In many respects, a civil protection order may be more advantageous to the victim than criminal prosecution of the abuser. Many women do not want to have their partners arrested and sent to jail; they view the types of relief offered in a protection order as more likely to benefit themselves and their children. Women of color may be especially hesitant to expose their partners to the criminal justice system, which has historically discriminated against members of minority groups. For immigrants, an additional disincentive for becoming involved with the criminal justice system is the fact that a criminal conviction can lead to deportation.

* * *

1.   Rates of Victim Satisfaction

At their best, civil protection orders can help accomplish many goals, including stopping the violence, protecting the abused woman as well as children and other family members, holding the offender accountable, providing financial support for the victim and her children, and conveying to the offender and the general public that domestic violence will not be tolerated. Empirical studies have consistently shown a high level of satisfaction among women who have obtained protection orders. For example, in a study conducted in three jurisdictions by the National Center for State Courts, over eighty-five percent of women who had obtained protection orders six months earlier felt their lives had improved since getting the order, and over eighty percent felt safer. Similarly, a Wisconsin study found a victim satisfaction rate of eight-six percent, with half of the women reporting that they were very satisfied; ninety-four percent felt that their decision to obtain a protection order was a good one. * * *

2. Rates of Compliance by Batterers

* * * Some studies report significantly reduced rates of violence and/or relatively high rates of compliance following issuance of a protection order. A study based on interviews with battered women in Seattle found a decrease of seventy percent in the occurrence of physical violence in a nine-month period among women who received protection orders in comparison to those who did not receive them. In addition to the reduction in physical violence, this study also showed that women with orders were less likely than those without orders to experience all other forms of abuse except unwanted calls. Similarly, a Texas study showed that women who applied for protection orders reported a significant reduction in average levels of violence during the year following their application, and those who actually received the order reported less violence than qualified applicants who did not receive an order. * * *

* * *

3. Characteristics Affecting Compliance With Protection Orders

Empirical research indicates that characteristics of the batterer and the relationship can affect rates of compliance. Batterers are not all the same; some of them are more likely than others to violate an order. According to [one] study, abusers with records of criminal activity re-abused their victims more than those without criminal records; the probability of re-abuse increased for those with more recent and more extensive criminal records. Other studies reached comparable results. These findings are consistent with the theory that obedience to the law is reduced among members of society who have the least to lose from the social consequences of criminal sanctions. A similar pattern emerged in studies of the effects of arresting batterers, which found that arrest had a stronger deterrent effect among men who were married and employed than among those who were unmarried, unemployed and lived in poor, high-crime neighborhoods. Currently, a high percentage of batterers who are the subjects of protection orders have prior criminal records and other characteristics indicating a heightened risk of recidivism. A protection order alone is relatively unlikely to deter these offenders from further abuse. Paradoxically, the abusers who are most likely to be deterred by protection orders—namely, "middle- or upper-class abusers who do not have prior [criminal] records"—are apparently underrepresented in protection order proceedings.

* * *

6.   Enforcement: The "Achilles' Heel" of Protection Orders

Even though obtaining a protection order may be valuable in and of itself, the fact remains that to achieve their full potential, orders must be properly enforced. Depending on the facts and the law of the jurisdiction, a violation of a protection order may be a misdemeanor or felony, civil or criminal contempt of court, or both. A violation may subject the offender to mandatory arrest. In order to ensure adequate enforcement, effective policies governing protection order violations must be adopted and followed by police, prosecutors, and judges. Currently, enforcement of protection orders is inconsistent. Even where laws requiring strict enforcement have been enacted, they are too often ignored. In fact, poor enforcement may be largely responsible for the results of studies showing high rates of non-compliance with protection orders. * * *

NOTES AND QUESTIONS

1.   *Effectiveness of civil protection orders.* In all states and the District of Columbia, statutes criminalize violations of civil protection orders. Most states treat violations as misdemeanors, and the rest treat violations as felonies. Most states also provide for criminal contempt charges against persons who violate these orders. According to Professor Goldfarb, what factors contribute to a civil protection order's effectiveness?

2.   *Helping the petitioner.* For a civil protection order to be effective, the victim must have a copy with her and must be willing to call police if her abuser attempts to violate it. If you represented a woman who has secured a civil protection order, what would you advise her to do to enforce it? What plans should she make to use the order to its full extent, and how can she use it to protect herself?

4.   Enforcing Civil Protection Orders

As Professor Goldfarb notes, enforcing civil protection orders can present imposing challenges for domestic violence victims. Advocates for battered women warn that filing for an order "can lead to fatal violence because involving the legal system often is a flash point." Katie Zezima et al., *Domestic Slayings: Brutal and Foreseeable*, Wash. Post, Dec. 9, 2018. In a five-city analysis in 2018, the *Washington Post* found that 36% of the men implicated in a domestic killing in the prior decade "had a previous restraining order against them or had been convicted of domestic abuse or a violent crime, including murder." *Id.*

Castle Rock chronicled some of these challenges in an estranged wife's damages action under 42 U.S.C. § 1983 that alleged violation of a Fourteenth Amendment due process property right. Beyond the determinative constitutional issue, the case's tragic facts demonstrate that neither the immediate victim nor other family members can assume a batterer's compliance with a civil protection order, or predict police discretion whether or how to enforce the order.

CASTLE ROCK V. GONZALES

Supreme Court of the United States, 2005.
545 U.S. 748.

JUSTICE SCALIA delivered the opinion of the Court.

We decide in this case whether an individual who has obtained a state-law restraining order has a constitutionally protected property interest in having the police enforce the restraining order when they have probable cause to believe it has been violated.

I

* * * Respondent alleges that petitioner, the town of Castle Rock, Colorado, violated the Due Process Clause of the Fourteenth Amendment to the United States Constitution when its police officers, acting pursuant to official policy or custom, failed to respond properly to her repeated reports that her estranged husband was violating the terms of a restraining order.

The restraining order had been issued by a state trial court several weeks earlier in conjunction with respondent's divorce proceedings. The original form order, issued on May 21, 1999, and served on respondent's husband on June 4, 1999, commanded him not to "molest or disturb the peace of [respondent] or of any child," and to remain at least 100 yards from the family home at all times. * * * The preprinted text on the back of the form included the following **"WARNING"**:

> **"A KNOWING VIOLATION OF A RESTRAINING ORDER IS A CRIME. . . .** A VIOLATION WILL ALSO CONSTITUTE CONTEMPT OF COURT. **YOU MAY BE ARRESTED** WITHOUT NOTICE IF A LAW ENFORCEMENT OFFICER HAS PROBABLE CAUSE TO BELIEVE THAT YOU HAVE KNOWINGLY VIOLATED THIS ORDER."

The preprinted text on the back of the form also included a **"NOTICE TO LAW ENFORCEMENT OFFICIALS,"** which read in part:

> "YOU SHALL USE EVERY REASONABLE MEANS TO ENFORCE THIS RESTRAINING ORDER. YOU SHALL ARREST, OR, IF AN ARREST WOULD BE IMPRACTICAL UNDER THE CIRCUMSTANCES, SEEK A WARRANT FOR

THE ARREST OF THE RESTRAINED PERSON WHEN YOU HAVE INFORMATION AMOUNTING TO PROBABLE CAUSE THAT THE RESTRAINED PERSON HAS VIOLATED OR ATTEMPTED TO VIOLATE ANY PROVISION OF THIS ORDER AND THE RESTRAINED PERSON HAS BEEN PROPERLY SERVED WITH A COPY OF THIS ORDER OR HAS RECEIVED ACTUAL NOTICE OF THE EXISTENCE OF THIS ORDER."

* * *

According to the complaint, at about 5 or 5:30 p.m. on Tuesday, June 22, 1999, respondent's husband took the three daughters while they were playing outside the family home. No advance arrangements had been made for him to see the daughters that evening. When respondent noticed the children were missing, she suspected her husband had taken them. At about 7:30 p.m., she called the Castle Rock Police Department, which dispatched two officers. The complaint continues: "When [the officers] arrived . . . she showed them a copy of the TRO and requested that it be enforced and the three children be returned to her immediately. [The officers] stated that there was nothing they could do about the TRO and suggested that [respondent] call the Police Department again if the three children did not return home by 10:00 p.m."

At approximately 8:30 p.m., respondent talked to her husband on his cellular telephone. He told her "he had the three children [at an] amusement park in Denver." She called the police again and asked them to "have someone check for" her husband or his vehicle at the amusement park and "put out an [all points bulletin]" for her husband, but the officer with whom she spoke "refused to do so," again telling her to "wait until 10:00 p.m. and see if" her husband returned the girls.

At approximately 10:10 p.m., respondent called the police and said her children were still missing, but she was now told to wait until midnight. She called at midnight and told the dispatcher her children were still missing. She went to her husband's apartment and, finding nobody there, called the police at 12:10 a.m.; she was told to wait for an officer to arrive. When none came, she went to the police station at 12:50 a.m. and submitted an incident report. The officer who took the report "made no reasonable effort to enforce the TRO or locate the three children. Instead, he went to dinner."

At approximately 3:20 a.m., respondent's husband arrived at the police station and opened fire with a semiautomatic handgun he had purchased earlier that evening. Police shot back, killing him. Inside the cab of his pickup truck, they found the bodies of all three daughters, whom he had already murdered.

On the basis of the foregoing factual allegations, respondent brought an action under 42 U.S.C. § 1983, claiming that the town violated the Due Process Clause because its police department had "an official policy or custom of failing to respond properly to complaints of restraining order violations" and "tolerate[d] the non-enforcement of restraining orders by its police officers." The complaint also alleged that the town's actions "were taken either willfully, recklessly or with such gross negligence as to indicate wanton disregard and deliberate indifference to" respondent's civil rights.

* * *

II

The Fourteenth Amendment to the United States Constitution provides that a State shall not "deprive any person of life, liberty, or property, without due process of law." In 42 U.S.C. § 1983, Congress has created a federal cause of action for "the deprivation of any rights, privileges, or immunities secured by the Constitution and laws." Respondent claims the benefit of this provision on the ground that she had a property interest in police enforcement of the restraining order against her husband; and that the town deprived her of this property without due process by having a policy that tolerated nonenforcement of restraining orders.

* * * [W]e left a similar question unanswered in *DeShaney v. Winnebago County Dep't of Soc. Servs.* (1989), another case with "undeniably tragic" facts: Local child-protection officials had failed to protect a young boy from beatings by his father that left him severely brain damaged. We held that the so-called "substantive" component of the Due Process Clause does not "require[e] the State to protect the life, liberty, and property of its citizens against invasion by private actors." We noted, however, that the petitioner had not properly preserved the argument that—and we thus "decline[d] to consider" whether—state "child protection statutes gave [him] an 'entitlement' to receive protective services in accordance with the terms of the statute, an entitlement which would enjoy due process protection."

The procedural component of the Due Process Clause does not protect everything that might be described as a "benefit": "To have a property interest in a benefit, a person clearly must have more than an abstract need or desire" and "more than a unilateral expectation of it. He must, instead, have a legitimate claim of entitlement to it." *Bd. of Regents of State Colleges v. Roth*, 408 U.S. 564, 577 (1972). Such entitlements are " 'of course, . . . not created by the Constitution. Rather, they are created and their dimensions are defined by existing rules or understandings that stem from an independent source such as state law.' " * * *

* * *

B

The critical language in the restraining order came not from any part of the order itself (which was signed by the state-court trial judge and directed to the restrained party, respondent's husband), but from the preprinted notice to law-enforcement personnel that appeared on the back of the order. That notice effectively restated the statutory provision describing "peace officers' duties" related to the crime of violation of a restraining order. At the time of the conduct at issue in this case, that provision read as follows:

"(a) Whenever a restraining order is issued, the protected person shall be provided with a copy of such order. *A peace officer shall use every reasonable means to enforce a restraining order.*

"(b) *A peace officer shall arrest, or, if an arrest would be impractical under the circumstances, seek a warrant for the arrest of a restrained person* when the peace officer has information amounting to probable cause that:

"(I) The restrained person has violated or attempted to violate any provision of a restraining order; and

"(II) The restrained person has been properly served with a copy of the restraining order or the restrained person has received actual notice of the existence and substance of such order.

"(c) In making the probable cause determination described in paragraph (b) of this subsection (3), a peace officer shall assume that the information received from the registry is accurate. *A peace officer shall enforce a valid restraining order whether or not there is a record of the restraining order in the registry.*" Colo. Rev. Stat. § 18–6–803.5(3) (1999) (emphases added).

We do not believe that these provisions of Colorado law truly made enforcement of restraining orders *mandatory*. A well established tradition of police discretion has long coexisted with apparently mandatory arrest statutes.

* * *

The deep-rooted nature of law-enforcement discretion, even in the presence of seemingly mandatory legislative commands, is illustrated by *Chicago v. Morales*, 527 U.S. 41 (1999), which involved an ordinance that said a police officer " 'shall order' " persons to disperse in certain circumstances. This Court rejected out of hand the possibility that "the mandatory language of the ordinance ... afford[ed] the police *no* discretion." It is, the Court proclaimed, simply "common sense that *all* police officers must use some discretion in deciding when and where to enforce city ordinances." (emphasis added).

Against that backdrop, a true mandate of police action would require some stronger indication from the Colorado Legislature than "shall use every reasonable means to enforce a restraining order" (or even "shall arrest . . . or . . . seek a warrant"). Colo. Rev. Stat. § 18–6–803.5(3)(a)–(b). * * * It is hard to imagine that a Colorado peace officer would not have some discretion to determine that—despite probable cause to believe a restraining order has been violated—the circumstances of the violation or the competing duties of that officer or his agency counsel decisively against enforcement in a particular instance. The practical necessity for discretion is particularly apparent in a case such as this one, where the suspected violator is not actually present and his whereabouts are unknown.

The dissent correctly points out that, in the specific context of domestic violence, mandatory-arrest statutes have been found in some States to be more mandatory than traditional mandatory-arrest statutes. * * * Even in the domestic-violence context, however, it is unclear how the mandatory-arrest paradigm applies to cases in which the offender is not present to be arrested. As the dissent explains, much of the impetus for mandatory-arrest statutes and policies derived from the idea that it is better for police officers to arrest the aggressor in a domestic-violence incident than to attempt to mediate the dispute or merely to ask the offender to leave the scene. Those other options are only available, of course, when the offender is present at the scene.

*　*　*

Even if the statute could be said to have made enforcement of restraining orders "mandatory" because of the domestic-violence context of the underlying statute, that would not necessarily mean that state law gave *respondent* an entitlement to *enforcement* of the mandate. Making the actions of government employees obligatory can serve various legitimate ends other than the conferral of a benefit on a specific class of people. The serving of public rather than private ends is the normal course of the criminal law because criminal acts, "besides the injury [they do] to individuals, . . . strike at the very being of society; which cannot possibly subsist, where actions of this sort are suffered to escape with impunity." This principle underlies, for example, a Colorado district attorney's discretion to prosecute a domestic assault, even though the victim withdraws her charge.

*　*　*

III

We conclude, therefore, that respondent did not, for purposes of the Due Process Clause, have a property interest in police enforcement of the restraining order against her husband. * * *

In light of today's decision and that in *DeShaney*, the benefit that a third party may receive from having someone else arrested for a crime generally does not trigger protections under the Due Process Clause, neither in its procedural nor in its "substantive" manifestations. * * * Although the framers of the Fourteenth Amendment and the Civil Rights Act of 1871 (the original source of § 1983), did not create a system by which police departments are generally held financially accountable for crimes that better policing might have prevented, the people of Colorado are free to craft such a system under state law.

The judgment of the Court of Appeals is *Reversed*.

JUSTICE SOUTER, with whom JUSTICE BREYER joins, concurring.

I agree with the Court that Jessica Gonzales has shown no violation of an interest protected by the Fourteenth Amendment's Due Process Clause, and I join the Court's opinion. The Court emphasizes the traditional public focus of law enforcement as reason to doubt that these particular legal requirements to provide police services, however unconditional their form, presuppose enforceable individual rights to a certain level of police protection. The Court also notes that the terms of the Colorado statute involved here recognize and preserve the traditional discretion afforded law enforcement officers. Gonzales's claim of a property right thus runs up against police discretion in the face of an individual demand to enforce, and discretion to ignore an individual instruction not to enforce (because, say, of a domestic reconciliation); no one would argue that the beneficiary of a Colorado order like the one here would be authorized to control a court's contempt power or order the police to refrain from arresting. * * *

JUSTICE STEVENS, with whom JUSTICE GINSBURG joins, dissenting.

* * *

III

Three flaws in the Court's rather superficial analysis of the merits highlight the unwisdom of its decision to answer the state-law question *de novo*. First, the Court places undue weight on the various statutes throughout the country that seemingly mandate police enforcement but are generally understood to preserve police discretion. As a result, the Court gives short shrift to the unique case of "mandatory arrest" statutes in the domestic violence context; States passed a wave of these statutes in the 1980's and 1990's with the unmistakable goal of eliminating police discretion in this area. Second, the Court's formalistic analysis fails to take seriously the fact that the Colorado statute at issue in this case was enacted for the benefit of the narrow class of persons who are beneficiaries of domestic restraining orders, and that the order at issue in this case was specifically intended to provide protection to respondent and her children. * * * Finally, the Court is simply wrong to assert that a citizen's interest in the government's commitment to provide police enforcement in certain defined circumstances does not resemble any "traditional conception of property"; in fact, a citizen's property interest in such a commitment is just as concrete and worthy of protection as her interest in any other important service the government or a private firm has undertaken to provide.

In 1994, the Colorado General Assembly passed omnibus legislation targeting domestic violence. The part of the legislation at issue in this case mandates enforcement of a domestic restraining order upon probable cause of a violation, § 18–6–803.5(3), while another part directs that police officers "shall, without undue delay, arrest" a suspect upon "probable cause to believe that a crime or offense of domestic violence has been committed," § 18–6–803.6(1). In adopting this legislation, the Colorado General Assembly joined a nationwide movement of States that took aim at the crisis of police underenforcement in the domestic violence sphere by implementing "mandatory arrest" statutes. The crisis of underenforcement had various causes, not least of which was the perception by police departments and police officers that domestic violence was a private, "family" matter and that arrest was to be used as a last resort. In response to these realities, and emboldened by a well-known 1984 experiment by the Minneapolis police department, "many states enacted mandatory arrest statutes under which a police officer must arrest an abuser when the officer has probable cause to believe that a domestic assault has occurred or that a protection order has been violated." The purpose of these statutes was precisely to "counter police resistance to arrests in domestic violence cases by removing or restricting police officer discretion; mandatory arrest policies would increase police response and reduce batterer recidivism."

Thus, when Colorado passed its statute in 1994, it joined the ranks of 15 States that mandated arrest for domestic violence offenses and 19 States that mandated arrest for domestic restraining order violations.

Given the specific purpose of these statutes, there can be no doubt that the Colorado Legislature used the term "shall" advisedly in its domestic restraining order statute. While "shall" is probably best read to mean "may" in other Colorado statutes that seemingly mandate enforcement, cf. Colo. Rev. Stat. § 31–4–112 (2004) (police "*shall suppress* all riots, disturbances or breaches of the peace, *shall apprehend* all disorderly persons in the city . . ." (emphasis added)), it is clear that the elimination of police discretion was integral to Colorado and its fellow States' solution to the problem of underenforcement in domestic violence cases. Since the text of Colorado's statute perfectly captures this legislative purpose, it is hard to imagine what the Court has in mind when it insists on "some stronger indication from the Colorado Legislature."

* * *

Because the statute's guarantee of police enforcement is triggered by, and operates only in reference to, a judge's granting of a restraining order in favor of an identified " 'protected person,' " there is simply no room to suggest that such a person has received merely an " 'incidental' " or " 'indirect' " benefit. * * * Not only does the Court's doubt about whether Colorado's statute created an entitlement in a protected person fail to take seriously the purpose and nature of restraining orders, but it fails to account for the decisions by other state courts, that recognize that such statutes and restraining orders create individual rights to police action.

IV

* * *

Police enforcement of a restraining order is a government service that is no less concrete and no less valuable than other government services, such as education. The relative novelty of recognizing this type of property interest is explained by the relative novelty of the domestic violence statutes creating a mandatory arrest duty; before this innovation, the unfettered discretion that characterized police enforcement defeated any citizen's "legitimate claim of entitlement" to this service. Novel or not, respondent's claim finds strong support in the principles that underlie our due process jurisprudence. In this case, Colorado law *guaranteed* the provision of a certain service, in certain defined circumstances, to a certain class of beneficiaries, and respondent reasonably relied on that guarantee. * * *

NOTES AND QUESTIONS

1.   *Questions about* Castle Rock. (a) Why does the majority find that Ms. Gonzales had no entitlement to enforcement of the order? (b) Have states such as Colorado done enough by enacting statutes that provide for mandatory arrest of batterers?

2.   *Domestic violence and firearms.* The Supreme Court recognizes that "[f]irearms and domestic strife are a potentially deadly combination." *United States v. Hayes,* 555 U.S. 415, 427 (2009). From 1980 through 2008, more than two-thirds of the murders of spouses or ex-spouses involved use of a firearm. Alexia Cooper & Erica L. Smith, Bureau of Justice Stats., *Homicide Trends in the U.S., 1980–2008,* at 20 (2011). The National Law Enforcement Officers Memorial Fund reports that from 2010 to 2016, "domestic dispute calls had the highest percentage—29 percent—of calls for service that resulted in officer deaths," commonly from perpetrators' use of firearms. Meghan Keneally, ABC

News, *Gun Laws Intended To Protect Domestic Violence Victims Also a Boon For Cops* (Apr. 7, 2018).

Federal law prohibits many batterers from possessing firearms. Title VI of the Violence Against Women Act of 1994 (VAWA), Pub. L. No. 103–322, 108 Stat. 1902 (codified as amended in scattered sections of 8, 16, 18, 28 & 42 U.S.C.), is an amendment to the Gun Control Act of 1968. The Title makes it a federal crime for a person (1) to possess a firearm or ammunition while the person is subject to a qualifying court order restraining him from harassing, stalking, or threatening an intimate partner, or (2) to commit acts that would place the partner in reasonable fear of bodily injury. 18 U.S.C. § 922(g)(8) (2018). To qualify, the protection order (1) must also state that the person presents a credible threat to the victim's physical safety, or it must prohibit the person from using force that would reasonably be expected to cause injury to the victim, and (2) must have been issued following a hearing at which the person had notice and opportunity to be heard. *Id.* The provision does not bar a person from possessing a firearm following an *ex parte* temporary protection pending a restraining order hearing.

In 1996, Congress again amended the Gun Control Act of 1968 to prohibit possession of firearms by anyone convicted of "a misdemeanor crime of domestic violence." 18 U.S.C. § 922(g)(9) (2018). This provision (the so-called Lautenberg Amendment) applies regardless of whether a civil protection order underlies the conviction. The Gun Control Act already prohibited gun ownership by anyone convicted of a crime punishable by imprisonment of longer than a year, but many domestic violence perpetrators are convicted of only misdemeanors.

In *United States v. Castleman*, 572 U.S. 157 (2014), the Court upheld the defendant's indictment under 18 U.S.C. § 922(g)(9) (2018). *Castleman* rejected the defendant's contention that his prior state conviction for "intentionally or knowingly caus[ing] bodily injury to" his child's mother did not qualify as a "misdemeanor crime of domestic violence" because it did not involve "the use or attempted use of physical force." Writing for the Court, Justice Sonia Sotomayor stated that even though the term "violence" ordinarily connotes substantial force, the term "domestic violence" may also include such conduct as pushing, grabbing, shoving, hair pulling and "a squeeze of the arm that causes a bruise." 572 U.S. at 165.

In *Voisine v. United States*, 136 S. Ct. 2272 (2016), the Court upheld application of § 922(g)(9) to persons convicted of reckless acts of domestic violence. The Court held that "[a] person who assaults another recklessly 'use[s]' force, no less than one who carries out that same action knowingly and intelligently." *Id.* at 2280.

Federal courts of appeals have rejected claims that § 922(g)(9) violates the Second Amendment right to bear arms. *Stimmel v. Sessions*, 879 F.3d 198, 201, 203 (6th Cir. 2018) (citing decisions).

3.   *Domestic violence and mass shootings.* After a spate of mass shootings by lone men, Jane Mayer wrote that "what perpetrators of terrorist attacks turn out to often have in common more than any particular religion or ideology, are histories of domestic violence." Jane Mayer, *The Link Between Domestic Violence and Mass Shootings*, The New Yorker, June 16, 2017 (quoting Rebecca Traister in *New York* magazine).

The *New York Times* concurs. "In nine of the 10 deadliest mass shootings in modern American history, the gunmen had records of threatening, stalking or physically abusing loved ones." Editorial Board, *The Terrors of Hearth and Home*, N.Y. Times, Dec. 19, 2017.

A NOTE ON BATTERED WOMAN'S SYNDROME

Battered Woman's Syndrome (BWS) has become a well-recognized term to describe what is commonly characterized as a three-phase cycle of an abusive relationship: (1) a tension-building phase, when the batterer commits relatively minor abusive acts and the victim attempts to placate the batterer to prevent further violence; (2) an acute-battering phase, when the batterer escalates violence and may severely beat the victim; and (3) a loving-contrition phase, when the batterer becomes remorseful, pleads for forgiveness, and typically promises that he will never again abuse the victim. Lenore E. Walker, The Battered Woman 55–70 (1979).

The BWS cycle theory often figures in cases in which victims are accused of striking back against their abusers. If a victim's resort to violence is not contemporaneous with fending off an abusive attack, traditional legal principles made a self-defense claim tenuous by insisting on an objective standard of reasonableness. In *State v. Norman*, 378 S.E.2d 8 (N.C. 1989), for example, the court refused to allow a jury instruction on self-defense for a battered woman who had killed her husband. The court held that the state's self-defense doctrine required proof that the defendant felt an imminent threat, and that "a defendant's subjective belief of what might be 'inevitable' at some indefinite point in the future does not equate to what she believes to be 'imminent.' " *Id.* at 14.

BWS evidence can effectively explain why battered women believe that they are in imminent danger and must use deadly force against their batterers. To understand how domestic violence affects the victim, the syndrome emphasizes the importance of past threats and the severity of the anticipated future harm. The goal is to explain to courts and juries why the defendant reasonably believed that she needed to engage in self-defense, and why retreat was not possible. Unlike the court in *Norman*, most courts today allow expert testimony about BWS in domestic violence-related homicide cases. *See* Leigh Goodmark, *When Is a Battered Woman Not a Battered Woman? When She Fights Back*, 20 Yale J. L. & Feminism 75, 84 (2008).

Professor Elizabeth M. Schneider argues that by accepting expert BWS testimony, courts acknowledge "first, that women act in self-defense under different circumstances and in different ways than men; second, that the law of self-defense incorporates sex bias; and third, that sex-based stereotypes of women generally, and battered or raped women specifically, interfere with jurors' determinations of their claims." Elizabeth M. Schneider, Battered Women & Feminist Lawmaking 132 (2000).

Many states that allow expert BWS testimony have developed gender-neutral terms for the syndrome, such as "Battering and Its Effects" or "Battered Spouse Syndrome." Some of these states recognize the gender-neutral term by statute, and some by case law. For example, Nevada allows admission in criminal proceedings of "evidence of domestic violence and expert testimony concerning the effect of domestic violence, including, without limitation, the effect of physical, emotional or mental abuse, on the beliefs, behavior and perception of the alleged victim of the domestic violence." Nev. Rev. Stat. § 48.061 (2018). BWS has helped explain victims' behavior to courts, but it has been criticized for "reinforc[ing] images of battered women as helpless, meek, and unreliable agents." Laurie S. Kohn, *The Justice System and Domestic Violence: Engaging the Case but Divorcing the Victim*, 32 N.Y.U. Rev. L. & Soc. Change 191, 208 (2008).

Consider why courts would admit BWS evidence. Why might courts be hostile to BWS? What special challenges would confront lawyers who represent clients who assert BWS? How could BWS affect the attorney-client relationship? How might BWS affect the case? What stereotypes about battered women does BWS challenge, and which ones does it reinforce?

D. THE CRIMINAL JUSTICE RESPONSE

1. Arrest

Police departments receive more calls reporting domestic violence than any other category of crime, and responses to these calls can account for up to one-third of police time. Historically, however, police departments have been reluctant to intervene by arresting batterers. For example, a 1984 study found that the typical police response to these calls was only to talk to the batterer. In 1985, a similar study reported that even where the victim suffered serious injury, 50% of the police officers interviewed did not arrest the batterer. Catherine Popham Durant, *Note, When to Arrest: What Influences Police Determination to Arrest When There Is a Report of Domestic Violence?*, 12 S. Cal. Rev. L. & Women's Stud. 301, 305–06 (2003). Reacting to pressure from battered women's advocates and from civil lawsuits that successfully challenged police policies and conduct, several jurisdictions by the 1980s began enacting legislation requiring changes in arrest policies for domestic violence.

One of the earliest civil lawsuits challenging a police domestic violence policy was *Thurman v. City of Torrington*, 595 F. Supp. 1521 (D. Conn. 1984). For eight months, the city police department ignored Ms. Thurman's repeated requests for protection from her husband's threats against her and her child. Once a police officer watched as her husband twice kicked her in the head and did not arrest the husband until he approached her while she was lying on a stretcher.

The jury awarded Ms. Thurman approximately $2.3 million damages for the police department's failure to respond to her repeated requests for protection. The case established that "police policy of treating women and children abused by male relatives or friends differently from persons assaulted by strangers constituted sex discrimination under the Equal Protection Clause." Emily J. Sack, *Battered Women and the State: The Struggle for the Future of Domestic Violence Policy*, 2004 Wis. L. Rev. 1657, 1668.

The movement for increased domestic violence enforcement was supported in 1984 by the "Minneapolis Experiment," which *Castle Rock* mentioned briefly. A comprehensive study conducted by the Minneapolis Police Department evaluated the effectiveness of various types of police responses to domestic violence. Police were randomly assigned to deal with domestic violence offenders in one of three ways: by arresting the offender, by mediating the dispute, or by requiring the offender to vacate the house for eight hours. To compare the relative success of the three police responses, the researchers measured the frequency and seriousness of domestic violence in the six months after police intervention.

The Minneapolis Experiment showed that arresting the batterer had a significantly greater impact on reducing future domestic violence incidents than did the other two police responses. The U.S. Attorney General then recommended that police departments make arrest their response in domestic violence cases. Lawrence W. Sherman, *The Influence of Criminology on Criminal Law: Evaluating Arrests for Misdemeanor Domestic Violence*, 83 J. Crim. L. & Criminology 1, 2, 16–20 (1992).

The Minneapolis study was replicated in five other cities. The results of these five studies qualified the initial findings in two ways. First, arrests for misdemeanor domestic assault varied in their effectiveness in different cities; and second, arrest affected abusers' recidivism rates differently, based on such factors as whether the arrested person was employed. If the abuser was employed, arrest proved a more effective deterrent than if he was not. *Id.* at 25–30.

As the Justices intimated in *Castle Rock*, states have adopted various policies on the arrest question. Some states have implemented policies of either "mandatory" arrest (which requires an arrest if the police have probable cause to believe that an offense has occurred), or "preferred" arrest (which favors arrest if police have probable cause to believe that an offense has occurred). The data show that either policy results in higher arrest rates. David Hirschel et al., *Domestic Violence and Mandatory Arrest Laws: To What Extent Do They Influence Police Arrest Decisions?*, 98 J.

Crim. L. & Criminology 255, 265, 296 (2007). All states permit warrantless arrests on probable cause to believe that a misdemeanor domestic violence offense has occurred, and "most states have enacted preferential or mandatory arrest statutes." Kimberly D. Bailey, *Lost in Translation: Domestic Violence, "The Personal Is Political," and the Criminal Justice System*, 100 J. Crim. L. & Criminology 1255, 1268 (2010).

Is mandatory arrest a good policy for the victim and the community? Are mandatory arrest statutes really mandatory if, as *Castle Rock* held, "[a] well established tradition of police discretion has long coexisted with apparently mandatory arrest statutes"?

2. Prosecution

As state legislatures enacted mandatory arrest laws, battered women's advocates addressed prosecutors' practices. Depending on the jurisdiction, prosecutors had been dismissing between 50% and 80% of domestic violence cases, sometimes at the victim's request. As domestic violence arrests increased, however, many prosecutors began adopting "no-drop" policies. Tamara L. Kuennen, *Private Relationships and Public Problems: Applying Principles of Relational Contract Theory to Domestic Violence*, 2010 B.Y.U. L. Rev. 515, 525–26. A no-drop policy means that the prosecutor, not the victim, decides whether to proceed with a criminal domestic violence case.

Hard no-drop jurisdictions require prosecutors to pursue domestic violence cases regardless of the victims' wishes and may also require victims to testify, under subpoena if necessary. Soft no-drop jurisdictions encourage victims to participate but permit prosecutors to drop cases based on the extent of the victim's participation. "Most jurisdictions with no-drop policies * * * do not force victims to participate in the prosecution. Instead, when possible, prosecutors use the out-of-court statements of victims made in police statements or during 911 calls in lieu of their live testimony in what are called 'victimless' or 'evidence-based' prosecutions." Bailey, *supra* at 1269. Should victims be required to participate in prosecuting their batterer? Should the focus be on what is best for society or on what is best for the individual victim, or is there no conflict?

Many prosecutors also follow a "vertical prosecution" approach, which assigns one prosecutor to handle a case from beginning to end. This approach can promote continuity by ensuring that information is not lost if a file is transferred between prosecutors, and that the victim deals with only one primary person.

Some states also seek to enhance the effectiveness of prosecution by mandating specialization within prosecutors' offices. For example, the Florida Statutes provide: "Each state attorney shall develop special units or assign prosecutors to specialize in the prosecution of domestic violence cases * * *. These prosecutors, specializing in domestic violence cases, and their support staff shall receive training in domestic violence issues." Fla. Stat. § 741.2901(1) (2018).

"Over the past 15 years, more than 200 specialized domestic violence courts have been established in the United States." Olivia Carville, *New York Leads Path To Curtailing Domestic Abuse*, Toronto Star, Mar. 22, 2015, at A4. Most of these "problem solving" courts create an interdisciplinary system of handling domestic violence cases. For example, in New York City and Washington, D.C. courts have combined the court docket's criminal and civil aspects. These programs often provide for coordinating police, prosecutors, counselors, and courts. Another improvement is provision of additional and specialized training to court personnel who handle domestic violence cases. *See* Anat Maytal, *Specialized Domestic Violence Courts: Are They Worth the Trouble in Massachusetts?*, 18 B.U. Pub. Int. J. 187 (2008).

NOTES AND QUESTIONS

1. *No-contact orders.* As discussed above, courts in criminal prosecutions often issue orders that bar the domestic violence defendant from knowing contact with the victim. Adherence to these orders is often a condition of pre-trial release or of sentencing. Criminal no-contact orders can prohibit the defendant from returning to the home, or from being in the victim's presence elsewhere, such as where the victim works.

For example, Rhode Island's statute states: "Because of the likelihood of repeated violence directed at those who have been victims of domestic violence in the past, when a person is charged with or arrested for a crime involving domestic violence, * * * [the court] shall issue a no-contact order prohibiting the person charged or arrested from having contact with the victim." R.I. Gen. Laws § 12–29–4(a)(1) (2018). Criminal no-contact orders are common, but unlike Rhode Island, most other states do not require issuance in every case.

Not all battered women wish to end their relationship with their batterer. These men can be their partners, their providers, the fathers of their children, or their sources of security. Women may also view leaving a relationship, especially a marriage, as a disgrace or a sign of personal failure. Many women may wish to see their partner punished, but may also wish the relationship to continue with the violence stopped. Some stay-away or no-contact orders prohibit violence, but permit continued contact between the parties.

2. *Shaming.* Should shaming—punishments "designed to publicly humiliate, denigrate, or embarrass perpetrators or other criminal wrongdoers"—hold a potential place in the arsenal of criminal law responses to domestic violence? A. Rachel Camp, *Pursuing Accountability for Perpetrators of Intimate Partner Violence: The Peril (and Utility?) of Shame*, 98 B.U. L. Rev. 1677 (2018). Professor Camp reports that "[j]udges have sentenced perpetrators of Intimate Partner Violence ('IPV') to hold signs reading, 'This is

the face of domestic abuse,' among other publicly humiliating sentences." *Id.* She cautions that "[e]ven if stigmatizing perpetrators to achieve accountability has some legitimate purpose, any benefit is outweighed by the fact that shaming perpetrators undermines the goals of violence reduction and survivor safety. Internalized shame can led to externalized violence, thereby increasing, rather than decreasing, a survivor's risk of harm." *Id.*

3. *Batterer intervention programs.* Batterer intervention programs seek to stem domestic violence by changing the perpetrator's behavior and attitudes. The programs are often court-mandated and usually defer a batterer's trial, conviction, or sentencing pending participation in the treatment program.

Batterer intervention programs are generally based on three distinct approaches to domestic violence: (1) the psychotherapeutic approach focuses on the abuser and holds that life experiences influence some people to commit violence; (2) the family systems approach regards violence as symptomatic of a dysfunctional family and assigns responsibility to both partners; and (3) the feminist approach focuses on the batterer's cultural conditioning concerning male dominance. Amanda Dekki, *Note, Punishment or Rehabilitation? The Case for State-Mandated Guidelines for Batterer Intervention Programs in Domestic Violence Cases,* 18 St. John's J. Legal Comment. 549, 566–68 & nn.66–68 (2004). The feminist approach has been praised for not treating victims as complicit participants, but has been criticized for emphasizing socio-cultural factors rather than individual characteristics. *Id.* at 567–68 & n.68.

Many batterer intervention programs are based on a model developed by the Domestic Abuse Intervention Project of Duluth, Minnesota. The programs typically involve classes designed to teach batterers various means of interaction. Often, classes are taught by one female counselor and one male counselor who model healthy behavior in intimate relationships. In addition, the programs contemplate court-designated probation officers who monitor and report on the batterers' program compliance. If the batterer successfully completes the program, charges are generally dismissed. Counselors also familiarize victims with the program's goals and methods, and inform victims about their abuser's progress. *Id.* at 571–72.

Research shows that batterer intervention programs may help some men change their behavior, but the programs' effectiveness in preventing recidivism remains unclear. Lucy Salcido Carter, Doing the Work and Measuring the Progress 5–6 (2010). Some studies have found significant reductions—more than 50%—in the physical abuse perpetrated by batterers after they participate in these programs, with long-term programs more effective than short-term ones. Dekki, *supra* at 573–74. Critics argue, however, that these programs lull victims into believing that the batterer has been cured, which may not be true in particular cases. On the other hand, because victims often return to their batterers even without a treatment program, abuser attendance provides some victims at least some protection. *Id.* at 575–76.

E. OTHER DOMESTIC VIOLENCE ISSUES

1. Gender Inequality

The vast majority of domestic violence victims are women, but the National Crime Victim Survey estimates that a little more than one-fifth of victims are men. To secure the justice system's protection, a male victim may face different challenges than a female victim would face. Gender stereotypes may lead a man to avoid reporting his victimization at all, for fear of being perceived as weak. Authorities may not believe his allegations, and some jurisdictions may have no services for male victims.

In *Woods v. Horton*, 84 Cal. Rptr. 3d 332 (Ct. App. 2008), the court held that programs which assisted only female domestic violence victims practiced gender discrimination unlawful under the state constitution's equal protection clause. Do you agree with the court that the genders are similarly situated with regard to domestic violence?

2. LGBT Inequality

"Women and lesbian, gay, bisexual, and transgender (LGBT) people have been disproportionately affected by crimes of sexual assault and domestic violence, and underenforcement of such offenses can constitute a gender bias on the part of law enforcement agencies." U.S. DOJ, *Identifying and Preventing Gender Bias in Law Enforcement Response to Sexual Assault and Domestic Violence: A Roundtable* Discussion 1 (2016). The National Coalition of Anti-Violence Programs (NCAVP) received 1,976 reports of LGBT intimate partner violence in 2015, a 29.6% increase from 2011. NCAVP, *Lesbian, Gay, Bisexual, Transgender, Queer, and HIV-Affected Intimate Violence in 2015*, at 8 (2016).

When Congress reauthorized the Violence Against Women Act in 2013, the lawmakers added language that expressly covers LGBT victims, language that had not previously appeared in the Act. Most state civil protection order statutes are written in gender-neutral language and thus remain available to LGBT victims. For example, Colorado protects victims with whom the batterer "is living or has lived in the same domicile," or with whom the batterer is "involved or has been involved in an intimate relationship." Colo. Rev. Stat. § 13–14–101(2) (2018). Statutes in some states (including Hawaii, Illinois, Kentucky, New Jersey, Ohio and Pennsylvania) expressly make protection available to same-sex domestic violence victims.

Statutes in a few states, however, expressly exclude individuals in same-sex relationships from the class of persons who can obtain civil protection orders. April Paredes et al., *Domestic Violence*, 19 Geo. J. Gender & L. 265, 273–74 (2018). In *Doe v. State*, 808 S.E.2d 807 (S.C. 2017), the court held that South Carolina's statutory exclusion of unmarried, cohabiting, or formerly cohabiting same-sex couples, violates the Fourteenth Amendment Equal Protection Clause.

LGBT victims suffer similar forms of domestic violence as other victims, but they may also face distinct hurdles to reporting, such as threats of "outing" or of comparable efforts to impose social stigma. When LGBT victims do report, they may experience additional barriers, including a lack of services that focus on non-heterosexual abuse or, for men, shelters that admit only women. *See* Satoko Harada, *Comment: Additional Barriers to Breaking the Silence: Issues to Consider When Representing a Victim of Same-Sex Domestic Violence*, 41 U. Balt. L.F. 150, 157–58 (2011).

3. Alternative Dispute Resolution

As Chapter 15 discusses, courts often encourage or require mediation before parties may proceed in filed divorce cases and other domestic disputes. Several states mandate family mediation, but with exceptions when one party claims prior physical or emotional abuse. Some jurisdictions permit the parties to decide whether mediation is appropriate in light of alleged domestic violence, and others require that the court decide.

Chapter 15 discusses commentators' disagreement about whether the law should mandate—or even permit—mediation in domestic disputes when one party alleges domestic violence.

4. Restorative Justice

As the mediation debate continues, a potentially effective alternative in some domestic violence cases may be restorative justice, an approach that is rooted in criminal law. Restorative justice approaches are less punitive than typical criminal sanctions, and more flexible than remedies ordinarily available in the civil justice system.

In restorative justice, "all the parties with a stake in a particular offence come together to resolve collectively how to deal with the aftermath of the offence and its implications for the future." John Braithwaite, Restorative Justice & Responsive Regulation 11 (2002). Restorative justice features "direct engagement between the perpetrator and victim, the informality of the intervention, and the interagency and community collaboration the conferences involve. * * * Restorative justice programs allow survivors to step out of their roles as passive victims and into an active role in achieving justice, safety, and closure." Laurie S. Kohn, *What's So Funny About Peace, Love, and Understanding? Restorative Justice as a New Paradigm for Domestic Violence Intervention*, 40 Seton Hall L. Rev. 517, 565, 566–67 (2010).

5. Marital Rape

This Chapter's opening paragraphs describe the husband's common law right, recognized during our nation's early decades, to chastise his wife with physical force. Husbands' rights over their wives' personhood, however, extended beyond chastisement. Beginning in the eighteenth century, the common law marital rape exemption provided that even when a man used force, he was legally incapable of raping his wife.

Various explanations have been offered for the husband's affirmative defense to spousal rape charges. English common law, and American common law later, defined rape as unlawful sexual intercourse with a female without her consent. It has been suggested that the marital rape exemption derived from this definition because intercourse between husband and wife is not unlawful. Some commentators have also theorized that the exemption originated from the conception that marriage established each spouse's consent to intercourse with the other. Other commentators say that marital immunity derived from the conception that a wife was her husband's possession, or that marriage was a unity in the name of the husband, who could not rape himself. *See* Sir Matthew Hale, The History of the Pleas of the Crown (1736) ("the husband cannot be guilty of a rape committed by himself upon his lawful wife, for by their mutual matrimonial consent and contract the wife hath given up herself in this kind to her husband, which she cannot retract").

Only in the past three or four decades have states reconsidered the common law marital rape exemption. In 1984, the New York Court of Appeals abolished the exemption in that state. *See People v. Liberta*, 474 N.E.2d 567 (N.Y. 1984). Mr. Liberta and his wife were legally separated and not cohabiting, and he was subject to a civil protection order. The Court of Appeals held that the spousal rape exemption violated the Fourteenth Amendment Equal Protection Clause because the state had no rational basis for distinguishing between marital and nonmarital rape.

After *Liberta*, many other states began abolishing this spousal exemption by decision or statute. Fourteen states have completely abolished it, but 35 states and the District of Columbia retain some form of immunity. John F. Decker & Peter G. Baroni, *"No" Still Means "Yes": The Failure of the "Non-Consent" Reform Movement in American Rape and Sexual Assault Law*, 101 J. Crim. L. & Criminology 1081, 1155–56 (2011) (discussing how most state sexual assault statutes still differentiate sexual activity between spouses from that between non-married individuals). Twenty-six states still provide lesser victim protection, including lesser penalties for the rapist and imposition of a limited reporting time. Lynn Hecht Schafran, *Risk Assessment and Intimate Partner Sexual Abuse: The Hidden Dimension of Domestic Violence*, 93 Judicature 161 (2010) (arguing that diluted sexual assault laws reflect cultural loyalty to the notion that spousal rape is less harmful than rape by strangers).

6. The Violence Against Women Act

In 1994, Congress enacted the Violence Against Women Act (VAWA), the first federal law to directly combat domestic violence. VAWA's regulation of batterers' possession of firearms is discussed above. The Act also helps states, Native American tribes, and local governments develop and strengthen law enforcement, prosecutorial, and judicial strategies to combat violent crimes against women. Pub. L. No. 103–322, 108 Stat. 1902 (codified as amended in scattered sections of 8, 16, 18, 28 & 42 U.S.C.). Since the Act's passage, several billion dollars have supported efforts by victims' advocates, social service professionals, and prosecutors on behalf of domestic violence victims.

VAWA's goals include enhancing the justice system's protection for battered women, and expanding collaboration and cooperation between battered women's support services and the criminal and civil justice systems. The Act has provided funds for many services inside and outside these systems, including police, prosecutors, battered women service providers, and state domestic violence coalitions.

For example, Title II of VAWA, as amended in 2000, provides legal assistance, shelter services, and transitional housing assistance for domestic violence victims and their children. Pub. L. No. 106–386, 1201–1300, 114 Stat. 1491, 1504–09 (2000) (codified as amended in scattered sections of 42 U.S.C.). Title II also authorizes a national domestic violence hotline and federal counselors for victims, and provides funding "[t]o develop policies, educational programs, and training in police departments to improve tracking of cases involving domestic violence and dating violence." 42 U.S.C. § 3796hh(b)(2) (2018). The legislation requires that states grant full faith and credit to civil protection orders issued in another state. 18 U.S.C. § 2265 (2018).

Congress reauthorized VAWA in 2005 and again in 2013. As of this writing (March 25, 2019), however, Congress has let VAWA lapse without reauthorization, which was due for consideration in 2018. On March 13, 2019, the House Judiciary Committee voted along party lines to approve reauthorization, but the *New York Times* predicts that "partisan sparring, particularly over provisions that would require prisons to house transgender people based on the gender they identify with, will continue. That promises to make a once broadly bipartisan law, first passed in the years after the Anita Hill hearings in 1991, rancorous." Emily Cochrane, *Transgender and Gun Rights Are Sticking Points for Violence Against Women Act*, N.Y. Times, Mar. 13, 2019).

NOTES AND QUESTIONS

1. *VAWA's scope.* In *United States v. Morrison*, 529 U.S. 598 (2000), the Court struck down a VAWA provision that created a federal civil damages remedy for gender-motivated crimes of violence, domestic or otherwise. *Morrison* held that Congress exceeded its Commerce Clause power because gender-motivated violence was not an economic activity. The Court also held that the provision exceeded Congress' Fourteenth Amendment enforcement power because the Amendment does not authorize Congress to create a cause of action against private actors.

Morrison overturned only VAWA's private federal civil damages remedy. VAWA also contains criminal provisions that make it a federal felony (1) to travel across state lines "with intent to kill, injure, harass, or intimidate a spouse or intimate partner" and, in the course of travel, "commit[ ] or attempt[ ] to commit a crime of violence"; or (2) to cause a spouse or intimate partner to cross a state line by "force, coercion, duress, or fraud" that results in the person's committing or attempting to commit a crime of violence. 18 U.S.C. § 2261(a)(1)–(2) (2018). Lower courts have upheld these criminal provisions because they regulate channels of interstate commerce. *See, e.g., United States v. Larsen*, 615 F.3d 780, 785–86 (7th Cir. 2010).

"In a VAWA case, the Court must order restitution to pay the victim the full amount of loss. These losses include costs for medical or psychological care, physical therapy, transportation, temporary housing, child care expenses, loss of income, attorney's fees, costs incurred in obtaining a civil protection order, and any other losses suffered by the victim as a result of the offense." U.S. DOJ, *Federal Domestic Violence Laws* (2017).

2. *Battered immigrant women.* Since early 2017, the domestic political climate marked by federal initiatives against undocumented immigration has led to a decrease in domestic violence reports by Hispanic women in the United States. The Houston, Texas police chief explains: "Undocumented immigrants and even lawful immigrants are afraid to report crime. * * * They're seeing the headlines from across the country, where immigration agents are showing up at courthouses, trying to deport people." Cora Engelbrecht, *Fewer Immigrants Are Reporting Domestic Abuse. Police Blame Fear of Deportation*, N.Y. Times, June 3, 2018.

As enacted in 1994, VAWA provided that an immigrant woman could apply for legal residency without her batterer's support provided that she met specified conditions. VAWA provisions, enacted in 2000 and 2005, have attempted to ameliorate some barriers and to limit an abuser's ability to interfere with a victim's citizenship application. *See* Kerry Abrams, *Immigration Law and the Regulation of Marriage*, 91 Minn. L. Rev. 1625, 1695–96 (2007). For example, VAWA now protects a victim "who demonstrates a connection between the legal termination of the marriage within the past 2 years and battering or extreme cruelty by the United States citizen spouse." 8 U.S.C. § 1154(a)(1)(A)(iii)(II)(aa)(CC) (2018).

Under section 360 of the Illegal Immigration Reform and Immigrant Responsibility Act of 1996, domestic violence, stalking, sexual violence, child abuse, and violation of a civil protection order are offenses for which an alien perpetrator in the United States risks deportation. 8 U.S.C. § 1227(a)(2)(E) (2018).

3. *Asylum.* In 2018, the Justice Department announced actions that are expected to close the nation's doors to most foreign nationals who seek asylum from domestic violence in their country of origin.

Under federal law, an asylum applicant must show that "race, religion, nationality, membership in a particular social group, or political opinion was or will be at least one central reason for" persecution. 8 U.S.C. § 1158(b)(1)(B)(i) (2018). For a woman fleeing domestic violence in her country of origin, the key statutory condition is whether she can establish "membership in a particular social group."

Former Attorney General Jeff Sessions ruled that "[a]n applicant seeking to establish persecution based on violent conduct by a private actor must show more than the government's difficulty controlling private behavior. The applicant must show that the government condoned the private actions or demonstrated an inability to protect the victims." U.S. DOJ, Office of the Attorney General, *Matter of A-B-, Respondent* (June 11, 2018).

The former Attorney General forecasted that "there may be exceptional circumstances" in which the statutory test can be met. *Id.* The *New York Times* forecasts, however, that the ruling makes it "all but impossible for asylum seekers to gain entry into the United States by citing fears of domestic abuse * * *, [and] could have a broad effect on the flow of migrants from Central America." Katy Benner & Caitlin Dickerson, *Sessions Says Domestic and Gang Violence Are Not Grounds for Asylum*, N.Y. Times, June 11, 2018.

7. Impact on Children

Domestic violence can destroy entire families. As we saw early in this Chapter, at least 30% of intimate partner victimizations concern abusers who also physically abuse children in the household. Jonathan D. Thackaray et al., *Intimate Partner Violence: The Role of the Pediatrician*, 125 Pediatrics 1094, 1095 (2010).

Children Who Witness Domestic Violence

Direct physical domestic abuse against children does not end the story. Each year, an estimated ten million children witness intimate partner violence committed against a parent. Amy Lewis Gilbert et al., *Child Exposure to Parental Violence and Psychological Distress Associated With Delayed Milestones*, 132 Pediatrics 1577, 1578 (2015). Child witnesses may suffer profound adverse effects, including post-traumatic stress disorder, depression, and other emotional and behavioral problems that can diminish school performance and future well-being. Female child witnesses are more likely to be abused as adults, and male child witnesses are more likely to become abusers as adults. *See, e.g.,* Naomi Cahn, *Child Witnessing of Domestic Violence,* in Handbook of Children, Culture, and Violence 3 (Nancy E. Dowd, Dorothy G. Singer & Robin Fretwell Wilson eds., 2006). A 2018 study found an association between maternal depressive symptoms from IPV and adverse child nutritional and developmental outcomes. *See* Hind H. Neamah et al., *Intimate Partner Violence, Depression, and Child Growth and Development,* 142 Pediatrics e20173457 (July 2018).

Some states specifically criminalize "domestic violence in the presence of a child," *e.g.,* Idaho Code § 18–918(7)(b) (2018), or provide enhanced sentences for such violence where children witness the assault, *e.g.,* Or. Rev. Stat. § 163.160(3) (2018) (class A misdemeanor assault becomes a class C felony when it is "committed in the immediate presence of, or is witnessed by, the [defendant's] or the victim's minor child or stepchild or a minor child residing within the household of the [defendant] or the victim").

The Child Protective System

When domestic violence plagues a household, that violence may be only the proverbial tip of the iceberg. Below the surface may be underlying causes and manifestations of general family dysfunction, including child abuse or neglect that triggers the civil child protective system. The system may serve children and families directly, or it may refer them to other agencies. The system may proceed concurrently with criminal or civil proceedings that target adult abuse. Criminal child abuse or neglect prosecutions are generally reserved for the most serious cases.

The state child protective agency may order supervision of the home, or the agency may remove a maltreated child from the home on an emergency or longer term basis with the juvenile or family court's approval. The court may place the maltreated child in foster care, and also may require parents or other family members to participate in mandated services, which may include counseling and treatment that address issues relating to safety and domestic violence. *See, e.g.,* Douglas E. Abrams et al., Children and the Law: Doctrine, Policy, and Practice ch.4–5 (6th ed. 2017).

Intimate partner violence poignantly overlaps with child protection when a battered women is charged with failing to protect her children from maltreatment inflicted by her batterer. A parent who does not intervene to protect a child can be adjudicated for neglect, even though the parent did not commit acts of abuse. "Failure to protect" usually arises where the state assumes jurisdiction over both the abuser and the non-protecting parent.

When the abuse is severe, the court may remove the child from the parent's custody, and may even terminate parental rights. In *In re J.K.,* 38 S.W.3d 495 (Mo. Ct. App. 2001), for example, the court affirmed termination of the mother's parental rights to her two children. The panel rejected the mother's contention that the state could not terminate her parental rights because she herself was a battered woman and thus could not willfully or intentionally neglect her children.

Recall this Chapter's earlier discussion about why battered women may find it difficult, or even nearly impossible, to leave their batterer without inviting greater risk of harm to themselves and their children. If a battered woman does not remove herself and her children from the batterer, should she be held responsible for failing to protect the children, perhaps in a termination of parental rights proceeding? Or should the state remove the batterer and provide services to domestic violence victims rather than remove the children?

Child Custody and Visitation

As Chapters 12 and 13 explore, domestic violence can have significant implications for court decisions about child custody and visitation in dissolution cases. Parents are presumed fit to raise their children, but states have also developed various presumptions concerning batterers. In most states, proof of violence between the adults is rarely a sufficient basis for completely denying the noncustodial parent visitation absent extraordinary circumstances. But because of the potential for violence inherent in visitation with adjudicated batterers, or in transferring children between parents, courts may mandate supervised visitation or impose other conditions. Even without explicit legislative directive, courts hearing testimony on a custodial parent's fear of further violence may restrict visitation to ensure family members' safety.

8.　Prevention

In 2014, the Centers for Disease Control and Prevention reaffirmed its call for early positive intervention as part of an ongoing national initiative to counter domestic violence. "Because a substantial proportion of sexual violence, stalking, and intimate partner violence is experienced at a young age, primary prevention of these forms of violence must begin early." Matthew J. Breiding et al., Mortality and Morbidity Weekly Rep., *Prevalence and Characteristics of Sexual Violence, Stalking, and Intimate Partner Violence Victimization—National Intimate Partner and Sexual Violence Survey, United States, 2011* (CDC 2014).

The CDC explains that prevention efforts depend on "strategies that address known risk factors for perpetration and [that change] social norms and behaviors." These strategies include "the promotion of healthy relationship behaviors * * *, with the goal of helping adolescents develop these positive behaviors before their first relationships." The agency concludes that "early promotion of healthy relationships while behaviors are still relatively modifiable makes it more likely that young persons can avoid violence in their relationships." *Id.*

Much of this Chapter has concerned the civil and criminal justice systems' reactions to acts of domestic violence that have already occurred. What role should prevention efforts play in initiatives to counter this violence? How would you measure the success or failure of prevention efforts? What barriers might complicate prevention efforts?

2. TORT LAW

Section 1 has explored civil and criminal "public law" responses to family injury caused by domestic violence. In recent decades, historic immunities have yielded to contemporary approaches that favor public intervention and personal accountability.

Section 2 now examines "private law" remedies for violence and various other injuries to family members and their relationships. Somewhat more haltingly, tort law has seen similar transformations from historic immunities to contemporary opportunities for recovery.

Historically, the common law barred most tort actions within the family. If a husband battered his wife or injured his children by negligently driving the family automobile, for example, intra-family immunities precluded tort relief. Courts, however, entertained various tort actions brought against third parties for injuries to family-type relationships— including so-called "heart balm" actions for breach of promise to marry or for similar harms.

Today, the tort landscape is almost reversed. The law has dismantled common law immunities to permit a wide range of tort litigation between family members. At the same time, many courts and legislatures have abolished traditional heart balm torts against third parties, on the ground that granting relief for such intimate conduct is misguided or futile. Practical barriers to tort recovery, such as exclusions in insurance coverage, continue to deter some suits. But the law now generally permits spouses, and often parents and children, to sue one another for negligence, battery, infliction of emotional distress, and other torts.

Abrogation of intra-family tort immunity has produced new dilemmas. Similar to the criminal law, tort law continues to balance impulses to curb harmful conduct with respect for pluralism and family privacy. Courts and legislatures have opened the door to private tort remedies, but have also determined that the law should sometimes judge conduct between family members by more relaxed standards than conduct between persons outside the family. For example, what constitutes actionable "outrage" between strangers may not trigger liability between family members, and the usual reasonableness standard that governs negligence liability may not apply to defendant parents' childrearing judgments.

Even if workable standards of family misconduct can be discerned, debate remains about whether expansion of intra-family tort litigation comports with policies that underlie no-fault divorce. As Chapter 8 discusses, divorce reform beginning in the 1970s sought to suppress judicial inquiries into marital fault as incompetent, uncomfortable, counterproductive, or wasteful. Allowing tort recovery for marital misbehavior may permit similar disquieting inquiries in a separate action, or perhaps even in the divorce action if a party joins one or more tort claims.

Finally, growing diversity in family life has forced courts and legislatures to decide whether to extend family tort rules to nontraditional relationships. Many states' domestic violence laws protect adults and children in nonmarital households, but courts have been more reluctant to expand common law or statutory tort liability to injuries alleged in cohabitation and other nonmarital relationships.

This Chapter's remaining pages survey these and other issues. First, the Chapter describes the law's contemporary retreat from common law intra-family tort immunities and identifies the limited immunities that remain in some states. The Chapter then turns to the contemporary availability of tort recovery within the family. Next, we examine the contemporary availability of tort recovery against third parties for injuries to family-type relationships; this examination explores developments in the law concerning so-called "heart balm" recovery (where liability is shrinking), and loss of consortium (where new calls seek to expand liability to reach nontraditional family relationships).

A. THE CONTEMPORARY RETREAT FROM INTRA-FAMILY TORT IMMUNITIES

The common law traditionally barred one spouse from suing the other in tort. Interspousal immunity was rooted in the English common law conception, introduced in Chapter 3, that husbands and wives were a single legal entity. The notion of a wife suing her husband seemed preposterous because the law required the wife to rely on her husband to sue on her behalf, and because the husband controlled the wife's property. Not until the latter years of the nineteenth century did Married Women's Property Acts largely destroy these rationales for interspousal tort immunity by partially recognizing wives' independent legal identity and control over their property. Interspousal tort immunity nonetheless survived for many decades, based on new policy concerns such as tort litigation's impact on family harmony and judicial resources, and the specter of collusive lawsuits designed to defraud insurance companies.

In addition to interspousal tort immunity, many states recognized tort immunity that shielded parents from liability for negligent or intentional injuries that they inflicted on their children. The historical roots of parent-child immunity are more recent, dating from court decisions in the late 1800s. Beyond arguments grounded in family harmony, parent-child immunity was justified by the law's respect for parents' authority and by reluctance to second-guess childrearing judgments.

In recent decades, courts have grown skeptical about the rationales for interspousal and parent-child tort immunities and have incrementally restricted their scope. A few early decisions, dating back as far as 1917, began eroding common law immunities by allowing recovery for injuries from domestic violence. *See Prosser v. Prosser*, 102 S.E. 787 (S.C. 1920); *Johnson v. Johnson*, 77 So. 335 (Ala. 1917).

Additional cracks in immunity doctrines followed in family members' personal injury actions against a spouse or parent for negligently driving an automobile that had an accident. Courts reasoned that allowing such actions posed relatively little threat to family harmony because recovery would almost certainly come from an insurance company rather than from a loved one's own pocket. *See, e.g., Transamerica Ins. Co. v. Royle*, 656 P.2d 820, 823–24 (Mont. 1983); Carl Tobias, *Interspousal Tort Immunity in America*, 23 Ga. L. Rev. 359 (1989). Courts proceeded to extend tort liability to other claims of negligent or intentional injury.

Interspousal tort immunity has now been all but extinguished. Parent-child immunity has proved more resilient, but many states have scaled it back significantly.

1.   Interspousal Tort Immunity

In the following case, the husband during divorce proceedings filed a separate malicious prosecution action against his wife. He alleged that she had falsely accused him of stalking and harassing her, resulting in his being incarcerated five times.

Maryland decisions had abolished interspousal immunity in actions alleging negligence and intentional torts involving "outrage," but not in actions alleging other intentional torts. *Bozman* surveyed the interspousal immunity defense's background, and Maryland joined the vast majority of other states that have abolished the defense.

BOZMAN V. BOZMAN
Maryland Court of Appeals, 2003.
830 A.2d 450.

BELL, CHIEF JUDGE.

* * *

III.

The doctrine of interspousal immunity in tort cases is a rule of law existing in the common law of Maryland. In *Boblitz* [*v. Boblitz*, 462 A.2d 506, 507 (Md. 1983) (abrogating interspousal immunity in negligence suits)], we noted that it is a rule of "ancient origin" and created "exclusively from judicial decisions." * * *

* * * A more complete statement of the rationale was provided in *Lusby* [*v. Lusby*, 390 A.2d 77, 78–79 (Md. 1978) (abrogating immunity in suits alleging intentional torts involving "outrage")]:

* * *

"By marriage, the husband and wife are one person in the law. * * *. [Blackstone] adds * * *, 'If the wife be injured in her person or her property, she can bring no action for redress without her husband's concurrence, and in his name, as well as her own: neither can she be sued without making the husband a defendant.'"

* * * The *Boblitz* Court, too, commented on the effect of the doctrine on women:

"Application of the words interspousal immunity to this ancient rule of law borders on mockery. It would more aptly be called a 'rule in derogation of married women.' Under it the person or property of a woman upon marriage came under the 'protection and influence' of her husband—for good or ill. She became subservient to his will and fitted with a distasteful yoke of servitude and compelled obeisance that was galling at best and crushing at worst."

Our laws pertaining to the rights of married women were completely revised in 1898, with the enactment of the Married Women's Act. [Among other things, the Act recognized the separate legal identity of married women and their independent authority to bring lawsuits. Nevertheless, this Court] * * * concluded that the Maryland Act "g[a]ve the wife a remedy, by her suit alone, for actionable wrongs which could not theretofore be thus independently redressed," and did not "create, as between husband and wife, personal causes of action which did not exist before the act." [*Furstenburg v. Furstenburg*, 136 A. 534, 536 (Md. 1927).]

That the Court uniformly applied the doctrine, without exception, did not mean that it did not recognize its flaws. * * * [In 1932, the Court described the "fiction of identity" between husband and wife as a "technical and artificial" rationale for interspousal immunity.] The Court in *Gregg* [*v. Gregg*, 87 A.2d 581, 583 (Md. 1952)], labeled the domestic tranquility rationale for the interspousal immunity doctrine "as artificial as" the unity of husband and wife rationale. * * *

* * *

The first breach of the interspousal immunity doctrine in Maryland occurred with our decision in *Lusby* [1978]. There, the wife brought a tort action against her husband for damages. As reported by the Court,

"She alleged that while she was operating her motor vehicle on a public highway the husband 'pulled alongside of [her] in his pick-up truck and pointed a highpowered rifle at her.' She attempted to flee by increasing the speed of her car. [However, her husband and two unknown accomplices in a separate vehicle forced her car off the road, sexually assaulted her, and threatened to kill her if she reported the attack.]"

* * *

The *Lusby* Court concluded:

"We can conceive of no sound public policy in the latter half of the 20th-century which would prevent one spouse from recovering from another for the outrageous conduct here alleged. There certainly can be no domestic tranquility to be preserved in the face of allegations such as we have before us[.]"

* * *

Merely five years after *Lusby,* we were asked "to reexamine the interspousal immunity rule . . . and to declare that rule to be no longer viable in tort cases involving personal injury to a spouse resulting from the negligence of the other spouse." *Boblitz,* 462 A.2d at 506. In that case, a wife sued her husband for injuries she sustained almost a year before the marriage, as a result, she alleged, of his negligence in the operation of an automobile. * * * [Abrogating interspousal immunity for negligence in *Boblitz,* we] explained:

"We share the view now held by the vast majority of American States that the interspousal immunity rule is unsound in the circumstances of modern life in such cases as the subject. It is a vestige of the past. * * *"

* * *

[After canvassing decisions from other states, most of which had abrogated spousal immunity wholly or in part, *Boblitz* identified six primary reasons cited in favor of retaining the interspousal immunity doctrine:]

"1. The unity of husband and wife;

"2. Interspousal tort actions will destroy the harmony of the marital relationship;

"3. Retention of the doctrine will prevent collusive and fraudulent claims;

"4. Retention of the doctrine will guard against an increase in trivial claims;

"5. Divorce and criminal courts furnish adequate redress;

"6. Change is solely within the purview of the Legislature."

* * *

[*Boblitz* examined these reasons:]

"As to (1), the Court stated that the very purpose of Married Women's Acts was to abolish this concept of law; as to (2) the Court expressed the belief that an action in tort for negligence would be less likely to disturb family harmony than permitted causes of action for breach of contract or conversion that typically involve intentional wrongdoing; as to (3), the Court * * * [stated] that 'it seems unjust to deny the claims of the many because of the potentiality for fraud by the few'; and as to (4), the Court declared that the suggested avoidance of trivial claims is subject to the same analytical weakness as the argument regarding collusion. * * *"

* * * [T]he Court [stated that] * * *

"* * * no court in this day and age subscribes seriously to the view that the abrogation of marital immunity for tortious injury is 'unnecessary' because redress for the wrong can be obtained through other means. * * * The criminal law may vindicate society's interest in punishing a wrongdoer but it cannot compensate an injured spouse for her or his suffering and damages. Divorce or separation provide escape from tortious abuse but can hardly be equated with a civil right to redress and compensation for personal injuries."

Finally, as to the sixth rationale for retaining the doctrine, namely, that it is a job for the Legislature, the Court [stated] * * *:

* * *

"* * * [I]in matters of torts involving the marital relationship we cannot 'stubbornly, hollowly and anachronistically' stay bound by the 'shackles' of the 'formalism' of the common law. * * *"

* * * [Nevertheless, *Boblitz* stopped short of abrogating the interspousal immunity doctrine altogether and limited its ruling to negligence actions.] The question to be answered, therefore, * * * is whether those torts * * * that fall in the gap created by *Lusby* and *Boblitz* should be subject to the immunity defense or whether, on the contrary, the time has come to bridge that gap. * * *

* * * By our count, * * * no less than forty-six States have abrogated the doctrine, either fully or partially, leaving only four States still retaining it.

* * *

The respondent argues that alternative remedies, already provided by the courts, are adequate for "garden-variety intentional torts between spouses" * * *. In particular, the respondent emphasizes that Maryland is a marital property State, in which equity, rather than title controls property distribution. She also notes that the statutory scheme provides for the consideration of eleven factors when the equities and rights of the parties are being adjusted, and asserts that tortious conduct may be considered in granting alimony or making a monetary award. In addition, the respondent points to the domestic violence provisions of the Family Law Article, noting that they permit * * * the court to order custody, exclusive use and possession of the family home, spousal support, etc., for up to one year. Finally, the respondent states that the aggrieved spouse has the benefit of the criminal law; he or she may charge the offender and seek restitution for any medical treatment required.

This argument has been rejected * * *. [W]hile divorce dissolves the marriage, thereby preventing future tortious abuse, that is not the same as civil redress or compensation for personal injuries and * * * the criminal law's vindication of society's interest in punishing wrongdoers does not compensate a spouse for injuries and suffering. The "remedies" the respondent proffers are, in the same sense, not compensation for tort damages.

* * *

The overwhelming weight of authority supports the petitioner's argument that the interspousal immunity doctrine should be abrogated. Joining the many of our sister States that have already done so, we abrogate the interspousal immunity rule, a vestige of the past, whose time has come and gone, as to all cases alleging an intentional tort. * * *

NOTES AND QUESTIONS

1.   *Policy concerns about interspousal tort immunity.* *Bozman* demonstrates that in recent years, rejection of interspousal tort immunity has been nearly universal. This immunity survives in limited form in only a few states. *See, e.g., Hand v. Hand,* 99 N.E.3d 181, 184–85 (Ill. App. Ct. 2018) (in wife's negligence suit against her husband driver arising from a motor vehicle accident, court observed that Indiana recognizes interspousal tort immunity in such suits but that Illinois does not).

2.   *Insurance concerns.* Assuming that tort recovery will be paid by the spouses' homeowner or automobile insurance policy, might fear of manufactured claims remain valid? Even if the injury is entirely genuine, should courts be concerned that a judgment paid by an insurance company will inure partly to the tortfeasor's benefit where the couple remains married?

3.   *Marital unity concerns.* In the few states that retain interspousal tort immunity, does any justification for judicial application of that immunity remain after a divorce action has commenced?

2.   Parent-Child Tort Immunity

"The doctrine of parental immunity bars an unemancipated child from suing his or her parents for personal injuries. 'The primary focus of the parental immunity doctrine * * * is the protection of the relationship between the parent and the child.'" *Vincent Delmedico PPA v. Panda Properties, LLC,* 2017 WL 410608865 (Conn. Super. Ct. Aug. 7, 2017). Parent-child tort immunity was grounded not in English common law, but in common law decision making by U.S. courts. As you read *Herzfeld,* consider which opinion you would join if you heard the appeal as a member of the state supreme court. Does *Herzfeld* properly calibrate the interests of parents and their children?

HERZFELD V. HERZFELD

Supreme Court of Florida, 2001.
781 So.2d 1070.

ANSTEAD, J.

* * * At issue in this case is whether the public policies served by the parental immunity doctrine continue to support its valid application to claims of sexual abuse by a parent against a child. * * *

* * * The facts underlying the alleged abuse by the parent against the child are summarized [by the intermediate appellate court] as follows:

The plaintiff [minor child] was placed in the defendant's care as a foster child in 1988. The defendant adopted the plaintiff three years later when the plaintiff was sixteen years old. [Almost six years later, the son alleged that his father had sexually abused him and sought recovery for several intentional tort.] * * *

* * * [T]he [intermediate appellate court] * * * held that because family harmony is already destroyed in sexual abuse cases, "the parental immunity doctrine does not bar the action by the minor child against his parent for damages arising from sexual abuse." * * * We approve * * * the decision of the [intermediate appellate court].

FAMILY MEMBERS' IMMUNITY

* * * Commentators trace the [parent-child immunity] rule's origin to an opinion of the Mississippi Supreme Court decided in 1891. The case involved a young married woman * * * who sued her mother for wrongfully confining her to an insane asylum when she was a minor. In reviewing the young woman's claim, the court noted that "so long as the parent is under obligation to care for, guide, and control, and the child is under reciprocal obligation to aid and comfort and obey, no such action as this can be maintained." The court explained its rationale:

> The peace of society, and of the families composing society, and a sound public policy, designed to subserve the repose of families and the best interests of society, forbid to the minor child a right to appear in court in the assertion of a claim to civil redress for personal injuries suffered at the hands of the parent. The state, through its criminal laws, will give the minor child protection from parental violence and wrong-doing, and this is all the child can be heard to demand.

* * *

In [1903], the Tennessee Supreme Court reasoned that allowing a minor's suit would interfere with public policy supporting discretionary parental control and discipline. * * *

RECENT TRENDS

Although the majority of states in this country initially adopted the parental immunity doctrine in varying degrees, many have now either abrogated the doctrine completely or have established significant exceptions to its application [such as allowing negligence claims covered by liability insurance or specified intentional tort claims]. * * *

Abrogation of the parental immunity doctrine in accident cases has been largely based on the prevalence of liability insurance. Importantly, the courts have emphasized that the domestic harmony policy concern is diminished under these circumstances because the injured child's dispute is actually with the financially responsible insurance carrier rather than with the parents. The courts have also noted that allowing recovery against an insurance fund would not impact family assets. Similarly, claims that fraud would increase in such cases have been rejected either outright as no greater than concerns about fraud in any litigation, or as insufficiently demonstrated.

* * *

INTENTIONAL SEXUAL TORTS

After carefully evaluating the policies behind the parental immunity doctrine, the national trends, and our own prior case law, we conclude that * * * the policies relied upon to support the doctrine are insufficient to continue application of the doctrine to bar intentional sexual tort claims by a child against a parent. * * * [T]he fear of disrupting the fabric and nucleus of families by allowing actions based upon intentional sexual abuse simply appears to be without merit. If indeed the principal reason for the parental immunity doctrine is to preserve family harmony, then it appears that the immunity can have no justification in such cases of intentional and malicious sexual abuse, for in those cases the inescapable conclusion is that the family fabric has already been tragically disrupted by the serious misconduct alleged. * * * [T]he mere additional stress of a lawsuit in such circumstances is an insufficient reason by itself to bar a claim for that misconduct.

Further, while we have genuine concerns that some may abuse the judicial system through false claims in domestic relations cases as well as tort cases, we believe the protections available in the judicial process are adequate to address the issue of false or fraudulent claims in this context as well as others. We find the depletion of family resources argument unpersuasive as well. As was noted by the court below, it is apparent that the depletion of family resources by itself cannot justify the parental immunity theory, since "any time a person is sued for actions not covered by liability insurance, his or her family's resources are threatened."

* * *

Accordingly, because we find that the policies behind the parental immunity doctrine are insufficient to justify barring a minor from recovering for intentional sexual abuse perpetrated by a parent, we approve the opinion and decision below * * *.

It is so ordered.

[A concurring opinion is omitted.]

WELLS, C.J., dissents with an opinion.

* * *

I am concerned that this decision will be used to foster litigation involving children in stances in which the real battle is between the two parents. Although I certainly agree with dealing harshly with parents who abuse their children—sexually, physically, mentally, or emotionally—I find a great deal of wisdom in Judge Cobb's opinion in *Richards* [*v. Richards*, Fla. Dist. Ct. App. (1992)]:

> Recovery against a parent by an individual child for an intentional tort, where insurance is not available, decreases the assets available for the support of other family members who may also be in need of assistance. Moreover, the majority of any punitive damage recovery by the child/plaintiff would pass to the state, further depleting family assets.

> * * * [O]pening the doors to tort actions for damages by children against parents would avail an unscrupulous parent of the opportunity to manipulate a minor child and the legal system by bringing frivolous actions against the other parent. The criminal court, rather than the civil court, is better equipped to process charges such as those leveled in the instant case. As succinctly pointed out in the appellee's brief:

>> The benefits to be gained by a child's intentional tort action against a parent do not justify abrogating the parent/child immunity doctrine. If a parent abuses a minor child, the parent is already obligated by law to provide the minor child with all necessary care, including medical and psychological care. The law also recognizes the child's right to enforce this obligation. It is not necessary that the child be given the right to sue a parent for intentional tort for the obligation to be enforced. The parent's obligation to provide for the child also continues beyond the age of majority if the child is unable to provide for himself or herself as a result of a physical or psychological disability. * * *

>> If the parent/child immunity doctrine is to be abrogated to allow a child to bring an intentional tort action against a parent, it should be done by statute. The legislative setting is better equipped to solve such a complex social issue as that presented by this case. In a legislative setting the whole spectrum of compelling interests can be considered, and a broad solution can be crafted. In the judicial setting, the complex social issue of sexual abuse comes before the court upon a set of facts by a single case. * * *

NOTES AND QUESTIONS

1. *Insurance. Herzfeld* reports that "[a]brogation of the parental immunity doctrine in accident cases has been largely based on the prevalence of liability insurance."

In *Ouradnik v. Ouradnik*, 912 N.W.2d 674 (Minn. 2018), the court permitted the adult son to sue his father for negligence that allegedly caused the son to suffer serious injuries, and to incur significant medical bills, when the son fell from a deer stand while he hunted on the father's 40-acre property. The son's lawyer candidly stated the lawsuit's purpose: "Insurance." John Reinan, *Minnesota Supreme Court Rules that Son Can Sue Dad Over Deer Hunting Accident*, Minneapolis Star-Tribune, June 8, 2018.

The *Star-Tribune* reported that father and son "get along just great," and that the father asked to be sued because Minnesota law requires injured parties to sue the person who injured them rather than to sue directly only the person's insurer. *Id.*

2. *Tort actions by parents against their children.* Should parent-child immunity bar parents from suing their children for tortious injuries? The scenario is not presented often, but "[t]he principle that a parent may not prosecute a tort action against his or her unemancipated minor child is a recognized corollary to parental immunity." *Bentley v. Bentley*, 172 S.W.3d 375, 377 (Ky. 2005). Some courts, however, have abolished children's tort immunity in step with abrogation of parents' immunity. *See, e.g., id.* at 377–78 (abolishing parent-child immunity except for claims arising from "commonplace incidents in family life").

3. *Claim-specific tort immunity. Herzfeld* abrogated parent-child immunity for intentional torts that arise from sexual abuse, but the court expressly declined to extend abrogation to other tort claims against parents. 781 So.2d at 1079 n.17. An earlier Florida decision, *Ard v. Ard*, 414 So.2d 1066 (Fla. 1982), had abrogated parent-child immunity only for negligence claims covered by an insurance policy. Does reshaping parent-child immunity in this piecemeal way make sense? Is it appropriate to allow a tort remedy for sexual abuse while denying one for other forms of physical or emotional abuse? As *Herzfeld's* dissent suggests, would the legislature be a better forum than the courts for determining the contours of abrogation?

4. *Claims of negligent parental supervision. Herzfeld* notes that one rationale for parent-child immunity is that tort liability for childrearing decisions "would interfere with public policy supporting discretionary parental control and discipline."

The U.S. Supreme Court has held that Fourteenth Amendment substantive due process entitles parents' childrearing decisions to heightened protection from judicial oversight. *See, e.g., Troxel v. Granville*, 530 U.S. 57, 65–66 (2000), a principal decision in Chapter 13. The Washington Supreme Court explains that "the primary objective of the modern parental immunity doctrine is to avoid undue judicial interference with the exercise of parental discipline and parental discretion. * * * Parents have a right to raise their children without undue state interference." *Smelser v. Paul*, 398 P.3d 1086, 1089 (Wash. 2017).

To avoid excessive intrusion into parental discretion, some states retain qualified immunity against negligence actions arising from a parent's childrearing judgment. Other states refuse to recognize parental immunity, and instead apply a reasonable-parent standard that measures whether a parent's conduct "comported with that of a reasonable and prudent parent in a similar situation." *Broadbent v. Broadbent*, 907 P.2d 43, 50 (Ariz. 1995). Should the law authorize judges or juries to reach their own judgments about "reasonable" parenting through tort law? If public policy favors barring children's tort suits against their parents for negligent parenting, should public policy bar similar negligence actions brought against parents by a person outside the family, such as a neighbor who is allegedly injured by the child?

B. INTRA-FAMILY TORTS

Where immunity does not bar suit, most tort actions between family members involve straightforward negligence claims, such as ones that arise from driving the family car. As *Herzfeld* suggests, a primary reason for abrogating immunity was that insurers would likely pay any covered judgments.

Insurers responded to abrogation by modifying their insurance policies to exclude liability for intra-family torts, but some courts have held these "family exclusion clauses" to be partially or wholly unenforceable as contrary to public policy. *See, e.g., American Standard Ins. Co. v. Hargrave*, 34 S.W.3d 88 (Mo. 2000). In some states, family exclusion clauses are void in automobile insurance coverage but are otherwise enforceable. *See, e.g., State Farm Mut. Auto. Ins. Co. v. Marley*, 151 S.W.3d 33 (Ky. 2004). As a result, the practical feasibility of intra-family tort recovery today often depends more on public policies that mandate insurance coverage than on remnants of common law immunity.

Notwithstanding the retreat from interspousal and parent-child immunities, many courts measure allegations of tortious conduct within the family by standards different than standards that measure strangers' conduct. Thus, in a real sense, abrogation of immunities has simply reconstructed family privacy concerns from a categorical barrier to tort liability into a more case-by-case (or perhaps tort-by-tort) search for the proper balance.

When the claim relates to driving a car, for example, spousal relationship may have no bearing on the negligence determination. *E.g., Ellis v. Estate of Ellis*, 169 P.3d 441 (Utah 2007) (husband negligently lost control of car on honeymoon trip, killing himself and seriously injuring his wife). But what if the negligence claim rests on something more "domestic," such as the way the family home was maintained? *See, e.g., Nelson v. Nelson*, 50 P.3d 139 (Mont. 2002) (wife may sue husband for negligently exposing her to pesticides on the family ranch). Should the fact that the litigants are married or otherwise related affect determination of the wrongfulness of their conduct, and if so how?

Some matters remain relatively uncontroversial. Few would disagree, for example, that a husband who savagely beats his wife should be liable for battery. *See Cater v. Cater*, 846 S.W.2d 173 (Ark. 1993) (upholding award of compensatory and punitive damages for assault, battery, and outrage). In suits between spouses, courts have applied the usual definition of battery—an intentional harmful or offensive bodily contact—without modification. *E.g., Plath v. Plath*, 428 N.W.2d 392 (Minn. 1988) (finding that husband's act of pushing his wife away, causing her to fall and break her hip, constituted an intentional offensive touching, and thus a battery).

Despite the analytical suitability of traditional battery law, relatively few domestic violence victims actually pursue tort claims. Professor Jennifer B. Wriggins "reviewed thousands of cases on Westlaw in the summer of 2003 and found only thirty-four tort cases dealing with domestic violence." Jennifer B. Wriggins, *Toward a Feminist Revision of Torts*, 13 Am. U. J. Gender Soc. Pol'y & L. 139, 155 (2005). What factors might explain such a low "pursuit rate" for domestic violence injuries?

Withdrawal of interspousal tort immunity roughly coincided with recognition in many states of a new tort, intentional infliction of emotional distress (IIED). Some courts have permitted married persons to sue one another under the tort; other courts have resisted tort law's encroachment on marital relations, particularly in divorce actions in which a party may use tort claims for bargaining advantage. What differences characterize the courts' approaches in the following two decisions?

RICHARDSON V. RICHARDSON
Supreme Court of South Dakota, 2017.
906 N.W.2d 369.

KERN, JUSTICE (on reassignment).

Sally Richardson alleged that her husband Michael forced her to work as a prostitute during the course of their marriage. Sally also alleged that Michael emotionally, physically, and sexually abused her, causing both humiliation and serious health problems. Sally divorced Michael on the grounds of irreconcilable differences, reserving by stipulation the right to bring other nonproperty causes of action against him. Following the divorce, Sally brought suit against Michael, alleging intentional infliction of emotional distress (IIED). The court, bound by our precedent in *Pickering v. Pickering* (S.D. 1989), dismissed Sally's suit for failing to state a claim upon which relief can be granted. We take this opportunity to overrule *Pickering* and reverse and remand the court's order dismissing Sally's suit.

* * *

Analysis and Decision

* * *

In *Pickering*, a woman became pregnant during an extramarital affair. When she exhibited signs of pregnancy, she fooled her husband into believing he fathered the child. The husband eventually learned of the deception and filed for divorce. The husband also sued his estranged wife and her paramour for their deceitful conduct, alleging a variety of causes of action, including IIED. * * * [T]his Court [held] that "the tort of [IIED] should be unavailable as a matter of *public policy* when it is predicated on conduct which leads to the dissolution of a marriage." (emphasis added). While the facts of Sally's case may be distinguishable from the facts in *Pickering*, *Pickering's* broad holding makes no exception for a case such as hers.

Distilled to its core, this case comes down to a single question: Should we uphold the judicially created rule in *Pickering*? We think not. * * *

* * *

* * * [I]n effect, *Pickering* arbitrarily precluded tort relief for conduct that occurred during a marriage that later served as grounds for divorce. The rule operates to obstruct justice and contravene the Legislature's determination that married persons have a substantive right to sue for redress and protection from harm.

* * *

[T]he reasoning [*Pickering*] devoted to IIED is sparse. Indeed, the cupboard is bare when it comes to justifications for *Pickering's* IIED holding * * *.

[T]here is no explanation of why the tort of IIED should be unavailable when it is predicated on conduct that led to the dissolution of a marriage. Moreover, while *Pickering* deemed a cause of action for IIED unnecessary because an alternative remedy existed in "the form of an action against the paramour for alienation of affections," there are at least two problems with this justification. First, the existence of multiple applicable causes of action does not justify a rule eliminating a cause of action. In other contexts, our law does not needlessly winnow down the victim's potential remedies when a tortfeasor commits multiple torts against the victim. Second, this justification is unpersuasive under the facts of this case: Sally has no alternate remedy because her husband was her abuser.

The *Pickering* majority also considered the justification of interfamilial warfare, albeit in the context of the plaintiff's other action for fraud and deceit. The majority stated that these too "should be barred as a matter of public policy" because "the subject matter of this action is not one in which it is appropriate for the courts to intervene[.]" The majority stated that '[a]llowing [the plaintiff] to maintain his cause of action may cause his daughter significant harm. The innocent party, who is now three years old should not be subjected to this type of interfamilial warfare. * * *

* * * [I]t appears that the Court in *Pickering* was concerned with the fact that a three-year-old child would be subjected to the turbulence resulting from her parents' lawsuit. But if this justification is sufficient to deny a harmed spouse his or her remedy, why does the Legislature permit litigation between people with children at all? The familial difficulties that a child would face if her parents were on opposite sides of an IIED action are similar to the difficulties faced in any other suit not barred by public policy and in any divorce or custody proceeding. Further, Sally and Michael have no children. Thus, if familial tranquility is the goal of the *Pickering* rule, it is overbroad and unattainable.

Likewise, the *Pickering* rule does not promote marital harmony. Public policy favors the bedrock institution of marriage and seeks to nourish and foster the marital relationship. The specific holding in *Pickering* is that "the tort of [IIED] should be unavailable as a matter of public policy when it is predicated on conduct which leads to the dissolution of a marriage." But this means that the tort of IIED is available when the marriage does not dissolve. In other words, a person being abused by their spouse may sue for IIED, but only if they stay married to their abuser.

Moreover, for conduct to be actionable under IIED, "it must be so extreme in degree as to go beyond all possible bounds of decency, and be regarded as atrocious, and utterly intolerable in a civilized community." Thus, a spouse seeking to retain the full scope of his or her rights must endure unendurable conduct. * * * Indeed, where such conduct has occurred, there is little marital harmony left to preserve.

In failing to avert familial and marital discord, the *Pickering* rule also diminishes justice because the remaining remedies available through other causes of action may prove inadequate. For example, the torts of battery and assault are available to a harmed spouse under *Pickering*. But intense domestic harm may be inflicted in ways other than physical assault or the threat thereof. "The tort of intentional infliction of emotional distress 'is especially appropriate for a continuing pattern of domestic abuse.'" For example, Sally may be able to bring individual claims of battery and assault against Michael, but she will not be able to seek a remedy, including the possibility of punitive damages, for his outrageous conduct towards her. As the Wyoming Supreme Court recognized, "[e]motional distress is as real and tormenting as physical pain, and psychological well-being deserves as much legal protection as physical well-being."

The *Pickering* rule therefore fails to address the harm remedied by a claim of IIED.

The *Pickering* rule also creates an artificial barrier to tort recovery. * * * [T]he right to sue for IIED should not depend on when an ex-spouse filed for divorce.

The only remaining justification for the *Pickering* rule is to prevent an IIED claim from being filed simultaneously with or after every divorce action and avoid a floodgate of litigation. * * * The assertion, however, that there could be an IIED suit for every argument, whether over "the family dog, who takes out the garbage, who forgot to pay the bill, or who is spending too much money," ignores the high hurdles a plaintiff must clear in order to prove an IIED claim.

"Proof under [IIED] must exceed a rigorous benchmark." A prima facie case for IIED requires a showing of "(1) extreme and outrageous conduct by the defendant; (2) that the defendant intended to cause severe emotional distress; (3) there must be a causal connection between the wrongful conduct and the emotional distress; (4) and severe emotional distress must result." "The law intercedes only when the distress is so severe that no reasonable person should be expected to endure it." Forgetting to take out the garbage and other garden-variety frictions will not rise to this level.

* * * Further, courts are equipped to "sanction attorneys who regularly bring or assist in bringing meritless tort claims in unison with divorce actions * * *." The trial courts of this state are highly competent and routinely apply the appropriate burden of proof to dismiss frivolous claims. * * *

* * *

Numerous states permit IIED suits between current or former spouses for conduct that occurred during marriage. * * * Many courts consider claims for IIED against third parties with whom a spouse committed adultery to be, in effect, actions for alienation of affections or criminal conversion. These courts dismiss such IIED claims primarily because their state's legislature abolished the torts of alienation of affections or criminal conversion via statute. These cases, however, do not support a *Pickering*-type bar on IIED suits between spouses. First, the South Dakota Legislature has not abolished the tort of alienation of affections, although we have abrogated the tort of criminal conversion. Thus, our law permits recovery against a paramour for engaging in adultery to the harm of a plaintiff spouse. Second, these torts are not remedies against a spouse, current or former, but are meant to provide a recovery for the wrongful conduct of a tortfeasor outside of the marriage relationship. Although these cases disapprove of IIED suits for conduct occurring in marriage, they are inapposite to assessing whether Sally has a remedy against Michael.

* * *

SEVERSON, JUSTICE (concurring in result) [omitted].

* * *

HAKKILA V. HAKKILA

Court of Appeals of New Mexico, 1991.
812 P.2d 1320.

HARTZ, JUDGE.

In response to the petition of E. Arnold Hakkila (husband) for dissolution of marriage, Peggy J. Hakkila (wife) counter-petitioned for damages arising from alleged intentional infliction of emotional distress. Husband appeals from the judgment entered against him on the tort claim * * *. We reverse the damage award * * *.

I.   Facts

Husband and wife were married on October 29, 1975. Each had been married before. They permanently separated in February 1985. Husband filed his petition for dissolution of marriage the following month. * * *

The district court found that "[wife's] emotional and mental health, especially since the parties' separation, has been shown to have been characterized by acute depression and one psychotic episode." * * * Apparently all the experts agreed that wife was temporarily emotionally disabled at the time of the hearing.

Finding No. 22 summarized husband's intentional misconduct:

* * * [Husband] on occasions throughout the marriage and continuing until the separation[:]

a.   assaulted and battered [wife],

b.   insulted [wife] in the presence of guests, friends, relatives, and foreign dignitaries,

c.   screamed at [wife] at home and in the presence of others,

d.   on one occasion locked [wife] out of the residence over night in the dead of winter while she had nothing on but a robe,

e.   made repeated demeaning remarks regarding [wife's] sexuality,

f.   continuously stated to [wife] that she was crazy, insane, and incompetent,

g.   refused to allow [wife] to pursue schooling and hobbies,

h.   refused to participate in normal marital relationship with [wife] which ultimately resulted in only having sexual relations with [wife] on four occasions in the last three years of the marriage, [and]

i.   blamed his sexual inadequacies upon [wife].

* * *

* * * [Evidence in the record shows, among other acts,] several incidents of assault and battery. In late 1984 when wife was pushing her finger in husband's chest, he grabbed her wrist and twisted it severely. In 1981 during an argument in their home husband grabbed wife and threw her face down across the room, into a pot full of dirt. In 1978 when wife was putting groceries in the camper, husband slammed part of the camper shell down on her head and the trunk lid on her hands.

* * *

II.   Should We Recognize the Tort of Intentional Infliction of Emotional Distress in the Marital Context?

* * * [In other contexts, New Mexico law has allowed recovery for intentional infliction of emotional distress.] Wife contends that we must recognize the tort when committed by one spouse against the other because New Mexico has abandoned immunity for interspousal torts. Yet the abolition of immunity does not mean that the existence of the marriage must be ignored in determining the scope of liability. * * *

* * * [T]he family relationship can be an important consideration in analyzing intrafamilial torts, both negligent and intentional.

* * *

Considerations that justify limiting liability for intentional infliction of emotional distress to only outrageous conduct also suggest a very limited scope for the tort in the marital context.

Conduct intentionally or recklessly causing emotional distress to one's spouse is prevalent in our society. This is unfortunate but perhaps not surprising, given the length and intensity of the marital relationship. Yet even when the conduct of feuding spouses is not particularly unusual, high emotions can readily cause an offended spouse to view the other's misconduct as "extreme and outrageous." Thus, if the tort of outrage is construed loosely or broadly, claims of outrage may be tacked on in typical marital disputes, taxing judicial resources.

In addition, a spouse's most distressing conduct is likely to be privileged. Partners who are pledged to live together for a lifetime have a right to criticize each other's behavior. * * * "You look awful" or even "I don't love you" can be very wounding, but these statements cannot justify liability.

Not only should intramarital activity ordinarily not be the basis for tort liability, it should also be protected against disclosure in tort litigation. * * * Any litigation of a claim is certain to require exposure of the intimacies of married life. This feature of the tort distinguishes it from intramarital torts already recognized in New Mexico. For example, a suit by one spouse against another arising out of an automobile accident poses no such risk. Nor does one ordinarily think of exposure of an incident of battery as implicating legitimate privacy interests. In contrast, in this case the judge found that it was extreme and outrageous conduct for husband to refuse sexual relations with wife. Should we really use this tort as a basis for inquiry into a matter of such intimacy? In determining the scope of the tort of outrage in the marital context, it is necessary to consider the privacy interests of the accused spouse.

* * *

A cautious approach to the tort of intramarital outrage also finds support in the public policy of New Mexico to avoid inquiry into what went wrong in a marriage. New Mexico was the first state to provide for no-fault divorce on the ground of incompatibility. New Mexico apportions community property without regard to fault, and grants alimony without consideration of punishment to either spouse.

* * *

Consequently, in determining when the tort of outrage should be recognized in the marital setting, the threshold of outrageousness should be set high enough—or the circumstances in which the tort is recognized should be described precisely enough, *e.g.*, child snatching—that the social good from recognizing the tort will not be outweighed by unseemly and invasive litigation of meritless claims.

* * *

III. Did Wife Prove Outrage?

We now move to the specifics of the case before us. * * * The merits of wife's claim can be disposed of summarily. Husband's insults and outbursts fail to meet the legal standard of outrageousness. He was privileged to refrain from intercourse. There was no evidence that the other conduct caused severe emotional distress, as opposed to transient pain or discomfort.

Indeed, this case illustrates the risk of opening the door too wide to claims of this nature. Despite the claim's lack of merit, husband was subjected to a six-day trial, to say nothing of discovery and other preparation, surveying the rights and wrongs of a ten-year marriage. Motions for summary judgment should be viewed sympathetically in similar cases. If the potential harms from this kind of litigation are too frequently realized, it may be necessary to reconsider husband's suggestion that the tort of outrage be denied in the interspousal context.

DONNELLY, JUDGE (specially concurring).

* * * Husband argues on appeal that public policy considerations should preclude a spouse from initiating a cause of action for intentional infliction of emotional distress predicated upon conduct arising during the marriage of the parties and from raising the tort claim in the divorce proceeding.

* * * [I]n *Simmons v. Simmons*, 773 P.2d 602 (Colo. Ct. App. 1988), the Colorado Court of Appeals observed that considerations of fault or misconduct are inappropriate in proceedings for dissolution of marriage, noting that divorce actions are primarily equitable in nature.

* * * Because emotional distress, and at times severe emotional distress, is a concomitant factor accompanying the dissolution of many marriages, litigation of a tort claim for intentional infliction of emotional distress at the same time the court is hearing an action for dissolution of marriage improperly injects issues of fault into no-fault divorce proceedings and is destructive of efforts of the trial court to mediate custody and property disputes or to achieve an equitable resolution of the issues between the parties. * * * The better procedure for the trial judge to follow where a tort claim for outrage is joined with an action for dissolution of marriage is to bifurcate the tort claim from the trial of the divorce proceedings so that the tort claim may be tried separately.

NOTES AND QUESTIONS

1. *Measuring outrage in marriage.* Similar to most courts that permit spouses to sue for IIED, *Richardson* adopts the tort's standard elements without modification for the marital context. The tort requires "conduct * * * so outrageous in character, and so extreme in degree, as to go beyond all possible bounds of decency, and to be regarded as atrocious, and utterly intolerable in a civilized community." Restatement (2d) of Torts § 46, cmt. d (1965).

What standard for outrage for tort recovery against a spouse does *Hakkila* suggest? Is the standard too high? Or, as *Richardson* intimates, does sound judicial application of the usual IIED elements separate meritorious suits from the non-meritorious? Should the marriage's length matter? *Hakkila* suggests that the law should anticipate and privilege some hurtful conduct that might be actionable between strangers. On the other hand, does the marital relationship's intimacy and emotional vulnerability support judging deliberate cruelties *more* harshly?

2. *Compatibility with no-fault divorce.* As Chapter 8 explains, all states now allow some form of divorce without allegation or proof of wrongdoing, though most states also permit divorce on traditional fault grounds. In many

states, courts may not consider marital fault in alimony or property distribution. No state permits consideration of marital fault in determining child support, and marital fault may be considered in custody and visitation decisions only where the misconduct affects the best interests of the child.

Professor Robert G. Spector suggests that the unavailability of divorce as a forum for fault claims has helped fuel interest in interspousal tort litigation. Robert G. Spector, *Marital Torts: The Current Legal Landscape*, 33 Fam. L.Q. 745, 746 (1999). A leading rationale for the shift to no-fault divorce, however, was that judicial assignment of blame for marriage failure is often futile or socially destructive. Does this policy rationale suggest the need to limit the sorts of tort claims that spouses may allege against one another?

Professor Pamela Laufer-Ukeles argues that divorce law's ineptitude in assessing fault should not preclude using tort law. "The transfer of fault litigation from divorce to torts, while often criticized as simply transferring the acrimony from one forum to another, has distinct theoretical and practical advantages, which can preserve what seems inescapably relevant in fault divorce while benefiting from the advantages of no-fault divorce." Pamela Laufer-Ukeles, *Reconstructing Fault: The Case for Spousal Torts*, 79 U. Cin. L. Rev. 207, 211 (2011).

3. *The double-recovery problem.* In states that permit consideration of marital fault in alimony or marital property awards, a tort judgment might duplicate recovery that the party receives in the divorce proceeding.

In *Ross v. Ross*, 2004 WL 792317 (Tex. Ct. App. 2004), for example, the wife divorced her husband for cruelty and requested a disproportionate share of the marital assets based partly on the husband's "fault in the breakup of the marriage." In the same action, the wife sought tort damages for the husband's intentional infliction of emotional distress, claiming that he had engaged in a long pattern of physically and emotionally abusive behavior. The trial court awarded her 60% of the marital assets plus $150,000 in tort damages, more than erasing the husband's share of the property distribution.

Ross stated that when "a tort action is tried with the divorce, the court must avoid awarding a double recovery." *Id.* at * 2. Avoidance, however, can sometimes be difficult. The court of appeals sustained both awards on the ground that that the trial court could have based the wife's disproportionate property award on factors other than the husband's cruelty during the marriage, such as his greater earning capacity. *Id.* at * 12.

4. *Procedural difficulties and questions.* The *Richardson* and *Hakkila* concurrences suggest that the availability of interspousal tort remedies can raise complex procedural questions, including ones concerning preclusion when the tort suit is brought separately from the divorce proceeding. In *Chen v. Fischer*, 810 N.Y.S.2d 96, 98–99 (N.Y. 2005), the court raised another such question when joinder of the tort claim in the divorce proceeding itself is permitted: "[P]ersonal injury tort actions and divorce actions do not constitute a convenient trial unit":

They seek different types of relief and require different types of proof. Moreover, a personal injury action is usually tried by a jury, in contrast to a matrimonial action, which is typically decided by a judge when the issue of fault is not contested. Further, personal injury attorneys are compensated by contingency fee, whereas matrimonial attorneys are prohibited from entering into fee arrangements that are contingent upon the granting of a divorce or a particular property settlement or distributive award.

* * * To require joinder of interspousal personal injury claims with the matrimonial action would complicate and prolong the divorce proceeding. This would be contrary to the goal of expediting these proceedings and minimizing the emotional damage to the parties and their families. Delaying resolution of vital matters such as child support and custody or the distribution of assets to await the outcome of a personal injury action could result in extreme hardship and injustice to the families involved, especially for victims of domestic violence.

C. TORT RECOVERY AGAINST THIRD PARTIES

Even when interspousal tort immunity reigned, the law recognized several family-related tort causes of action against defendants who were outside the intact family. For example, aspirants to marriage—persons not yet shielded by that immunity—could sue for "breach of promise to marry," or for a host of other "heart balm" torts (so-called because damages were meant to soothe the wounded heart after a failed relationship).

Plaintiffs could also recover for various injuries to family relationships occasioned by negligent or intentional injury to a loved one. At one time, these causes of action were gender-specific and patently patriarchal. Loss of consortium claims, for example, were available only to husbands because only wives were obligated to provide services during the marriage. Criminal conversation, alienation of affections, and seduction claims protected only the interests of husbands and fathers in the chastity of their wives and daughters.

Together with contemporary understandings of the Equal Protection Clause, changed social attitudes made these gender distinctions untenable. Most states now provide gender equality, either by extending a cause of action to each spouse or parent, or by abolishing one or more of the causes altogether.

Beyond gender discrimination, most states have reconsidered whether permitting legal redress for wounded hearts reflects sound policy at all. The trend is now against breach-of-promise-to-marry recovery for emotional injury, but most states still permit recovery for loss of consortium—and some have expanded liability to cover additional family relationships. The number of states recognizing criminal conversation, alienation of affections, and seduction claims has fallen dramatically in recent years.

This Section begins by discussing the law's growing hostility to heart balm torts, and then turns to the law's continuing allowance for loss of consortium claims. As you read these materials, consider whether the two lines of doctrine create tension with one another.

1. Heart Balm Torts

At common law, a host of torts protected interests in family relations against intentional disruption by outsiders. A jilted party could recover for breach of promise to marry. A plaintiff whose spouse had an affair could sue the paramour for alienation of affections. Other actions provided tort recovery directly for wrongful sexual intercourse: Criminal conversation created liability for having intercourse with the plaintiff's spouse. Seduction provided a parent, and in some states the seducer's target, recovery for deceitful courting.

By case law or statute in recent decades, most states have abolished one or more of these amatory torts. *See, e.g., Coulson v. Snyder*, 390 P.3d 1139 (Alaska 2017) (abolishing alienation of affections); Wyo. Stat. Ann. § 1–23–101 (2018): "The rights of action to recover money as damage for the alienation of affections, criminal conversation, seduction or breach of contract to marry are abolished. No act done in this state shall give rise, either in or out of this state, to any of the rights of action abolished. No contract to marry made in this state shall give rise, either in or out of this state, to any right of action for the breach thereof."

Where the common law torts persist, courts now construe them narrowly or limit available remedies. The following two decisions provide historical background and demonstrate that plaintiffs today still turn to the courts, sometimes by attempting to cast their complaints against persons outside the family as alleging recognized causes of action.

BROWN V. STRUM

U.S. District Court for the District of Connecticut, 2004.
350 F. Supp. 2d 346.

ARTERTON, DISTRICT JUDGE.

Plaintiff Cleveland Brown brings a personal injury lawsuit against Adam Strum, alleging fraud and intentional infliction of emotional distress after the termination of their two-month romantic relationship. * * * Defendant now moves to dismiss the complaint for failure to state a claim upon which relief may be granted * * *. For the reasons that follow, Defendant's Motion to Dismiss is GRANTED.

I.   Factual Background

The following facts are alleged in the complaint. Brown and Strum were members of an online dating service known as Match.Com. On September 17, 2002, Strum read the plaintiff's online profile and emailed her through the Match.Com service. Brown viewed Strum's online profile, which indicated that Strum was divorced, and then answered his email. On September 24, 2002, the parties spoke over the phone, and Strum again, in answer to a question from Brown, represented that he was divorced and looking to remarry and have more children.

Over the next few weeks, Brown and Strum met in person several times. * * * The parties also spoke on the telephone "almost daily" during this time. On the weekend of October 4, 2002, Strum and Brown went to Puerto Rico together. They saw each other several times over the next few weeks, and "engaged in sexual relations on most occasions."

Brown alleges that throughout this time, Strum "kept reinforcing [her] belief that he was divorced and interested in marrying her." * * *

* * *

III. Discussion

Plaintiff argues that Defendant's conduct amounts to fraud because he induced her to enter a romantic relationship and to engage in sexual relations upon the false representation that he was unmarried. She further alleges that the defendant's conduct amounted to intentional infliction of emotional distress because he knew that she was particularly vulnerable and took advantage of her sensitivities. The defendant counters that plaintiff's complaint is no more than an attempt to circumvent statutes in Connecticut and New York that eliminated so-called "heart balm" causes of action, including seduction, breach of promise to marry, criminal conversation, and alienation of affections.

* * *

B.   Common Law "Heart Balm" Actions

At common law, a plaintiff could bring a variety of damages actions arising in the context of romantic relationships. These included causes of action for alienation of affections, criminal conversation, seduction, and breach of promise to marry. Only a spouse could bring an action for alienation of affections or criminal conversation; the former tort action provided redress against a third party who won the love of the plaintiff's spouse, while the latter involved sexual intercourse with the plaintiff's spouse. Because no spousal relationship is alleged, these two tort actions are inapplicable here.

* * * In Connecticut, a woman could not maintain a cause of action for her own seduction, absent an allegation of forcible rape. Thus Brown's

action could not have been maintained on her own behalf as a seduction claim in Connecticut. New York common law, however, allowed a woman to maintain an action for seduction on her own behalf.

Under both Connecticut and New York common law, there existed a tort action for breach of a promise to marry. This action could be maintained by an unmarried plaintiff who received and relied on the defendant's promise to marry him/her, which the defendant broke. Commonly, such tort actions were brought when a fiancé "enter[ed] into and [broke] off a sexual relationship by means of allegedly false promises" to marry the plaintiff.

Both Connecticut and New York have statutorily abolished the cause of action for breach of promise to marry. New York also abolished its common law cause of action for seduction, and even criminalized the filing of any lawsuit alleging any abolished heart balm claim.

The Connecticut Supreme Court explained its legislature's reasoning in barring heart balm actions as follows:

> . . . [T]he Act was designed to do away with excessive claims for damages, claims coercive by their very nature and, all too frequently, fraudulent in character; the purpose was to prevent the recovery of damages based upon contused feelings, sentimental bruises, blighted affections, wounded pride, mental anguish and social humiliation; for impairment of health, for expenditures made in anticipation of the wedding, for the deprivation of other opportunities to marry and for the loss of the pecuniary and social advantages which the marriage offered.

The New York legislature was motivated by similar concerns * * *.

C.   Emotional Distress and Fraud

Courts of both states have held that a plaintiff may not circumvent the statutory prohibition on heart balm actions by recharacterizing them as emotional distress or fraud claims. To determine whether a plaintiff has a bona fide claim or is simply using an emotional distress claim to evade the anti-heart balm statute, courts look to the underlying factual allegations of the complaint. * * *

The Connecticut Supreme Court has also made clear that an action for fraud may not be maintained as a method of circumventing [the statute abolishing breach of promise to marry claims. A fraud action relating to a promise to marry only may be maintained in Connecticut for "restitution of specific property or money transferred in reliance on various false and fraudulent representations, apart from any promise to marry, as to their intended use." Thus, a plaintiff was permitted to maintain an action where he sued to recover money spent renovating the defendant's house in reliance on defendant's promise that she would marry him and allow him to move in with her. However, the Supreme Court carefully distinguished an action to regain property from one "to recover for the breach [of a promise to marry] itself."

* * *

Plaintiff Brown has not made any equivalent allegations in the instant case triggering any exception. * * *

* * *

"The conduct described in the complaint is dishonorable, but this court is powerless to provide plaintiff the relief she seeks." Plaintiff may not circumvent clear statutory directives by reframing her claims as fraud or infliction of emotional distress.

NOTE

1.   *Breach of promise to marry.* As *Brown* reports, a few states continue to recognize a general action for breach of promise to marry. What policies support (or reject) this continued recognition?

2.   *Breach of promise to divorce?* In *Norton v. McOsker,* 407 F.3d 501 (1st Cir. 2005), the "other woman" in a 23-year adulterous relationship sued her lover for breaching an alleged promise to "divorce his wife, marry [the plaintiff] and take care of her for the rest of her life." Applying Rhode Island law in the diversity action, the First Circuit held that legal enforcement of a promise to divorce would be contrary to public policy. The court of appeals, however, then analyzed whether the plaintiff might vindicate her expectation of lifetime support from the husband under promissory estoppel. The panel ultimately denied relief on the grounds that any promise made by the husband was too vague, and that the plaintiff's claimed reliance was unreasonable. *Id.* at 506–08.

What public policy might be offended by compensating a broken promise to divorce? If it is a policy against destabilizing marriage, would enforcing a promise of financial support to an extramarital lover pose any less threat? Is a policy against destabilizing marriage forceful in a nation whose annual divorce rate under no-fault regimes remains high despite recent declines?

3.   *Legislative action. Brown* is an unusual federal court foray into family tort law based on the parties' diversity of citizenship. Citing the Rhode Island legislature's desire to preclude recovery for mere " 'contused feelings [and] sentimental bruises,' " the court bars intentional infliction of emotional distress claims that arise from intimate misconduct in dating. In contrast, *Richardson* refused to bar IIED claims between spouses, noting that the usual IIED "outrageous conduct" standard sets the bar sufficiently high to avoid imposing liability unless the defendant's conduct is "so extreme in degree as to go beyond all possible bounds of decency."

Consider whether *Brown* could similarly have screened out insubstantial injury claims by applying the standard IIED elements (called "rigorous" in *Richardson*). The contrasting outcomes in *Brown* and *Richardson* arguably turn the traditional common law rule on its head: recovery for intimate injury is allowed *within* marriage, but denied *outside* marriage. In evaluating *Brown's* outcome, consider the following decision.

HELSEL V. NOELLSCH

Supreme Court of Missouri, 2003.
107 S.W.3d 231.

RICHARD B. TEITELMAN, JUDGE.

Katherine and David Helsel divorced in January 2001. In March 2001, [Katherine] Helsel filed suit against Sivi Noellsch for alienation of affection, alleging that Noellsch intentionally interfered with the marriage and caused it to fail.[1] A jury returned a verdict in favor of Helsel. * * * Because alienation of affection is premised upon antiquated concepts, faulty assumptions, and is inconsistent with precedent, the tort is abolished in Missouri. The judgment is reversed.

I.   History of the Tort

In order to ensure pure bloodlines and discourage adultery, the early Germanic tribes provided that men were entitled to payment from the wife's lover so that the husband could purchase a new spouse. As successors to the Germanic tradition, the Anglo-Saxons also provided a cause of action for men to recover for another's interference with the marital relationship. The basis for this cause of action was that wives were viewed as valuable servants to their husband. Later, early English common law established two causes of action, enticement and seduction, which are the precursors to the modern day torts of alienation of affection and criminal conversation. The purpose underlying both causes of action was to vindicate the husband's property rights in his wife.

Beginning with New York in 1864, almost every state in this country eventually established a cause of action for alienation of affection in which men, but not women, could vindicate their rights in the marital relationship. In the late nineteenth and early twentieth centuries, most states, including Missouri, acted to equalize the legal status of wives by allowing them to sue in their own names. Therefore, the original justification for the tort, that husbands had a property right in their wives, was undermined. Nonetheless, the tort persisted, but with a new rationale. Modern courts came to justify suits for alienation of affection as a means of preserving marriage and the family.

---

[1] In Missouri, a claim of alienation of affection requires proof that 1) the defendant engaged in wrongful conduct; 2) the plaintiff lost the affections or consortium of his or her spouse; and, 3) there was a causal connection between the defendant's conduct and the plaintiff's loss.

II. Abolition

There are many persuasive reasons for abolishing the tort of alienation of affection. * * *

* * *

Even though the original property concepts remain inextricably bound to the tort, some still argue that suits for alienation of affection must be retained as a useful means of preserving marriages and protecting families. While these are laudable goals, it is unlikely that suits for alienation of affection actually serve this purpose. To the contrary, the opposite is likely true.

First, suits for alienation of affection are almost exclusively brought after the marriage is either legally dissolved or irretrievably broken. Revenge, not reconciliation, is often the primary motive.

Second, by filing suit, the plaintiff is publicly acknowledging the intimate details that led to the breakdown of the marriage. The necessarily adversarial positions taken in litigation over intensely personal and private matters does not serve as a useful means of preserving the marriage.

* * *

In *Thomas v. Siddiqui*, [869 S.W.2d 740 (Mo. 1994),] this Court abolished the closely related common-law tort of criminal conversation. The only difference between alienation of affection and criminal conversation is that criminal conversation requires proof of an adulterous sexual relationship. However, this difference in the elements of the torts does not provide a good basis [for] distinguishing alienation of affection from criminal conversation because both torts simply represent different ways of interfering with the same relational interests. Moreover, in reality, criminal conversation and alienation of affection are typically alleged concurrently as the conduct at issue almost always involves adultery. If a spouse cannot recover because of an adulterous affair under a criminal conversation theory, a spouse should likewise be barred from recovery by simply attaching the moniker of "alienation of affection" to the petition. Consistency demands that the tort of alienation of affection be abolished as was the tort of criminal conversation.

III. Conclusion

When the reason for a rule of law disappears, so too should the rule. * * * The tort of alienation of affection is abolished in Missouri.[3]

---

[3] This holding brings Missouri in line with the overwhelming majority of jurisdictions that have already abolished alienation of affection. ["Alienation of affection is still a viable tort claim in five states: Mississippi, Hawaii, North Carolina, South Dakota, and Utah." H. Hunter Bruton,

DUANE BENTON, JUDGE, dissenting.

The common law consistently compensates for interference with the marriage relation—"loss of consortium." Loss of consortium is the second of three elements in an alienation of affection claim. * * *

In tort cases where a spouse is injured, the other spouse often has a separate claim for loss of consortium. * * * In alienation of affection—an intentional tort—a defendant's intentional conduct causes the loss. It is inconsistent that the law compensates for negligent conduct causing a loss of consortium, but (after this opinion) does not compensate for intentional conduct causing the same loss.

* * *

The first reason the majority advances is the "antiquated property concepts" that originally justified alienation of affection. The original justification for loss of consortium was to compensate (only) a husband for his losses from an injury to his wife. If the origin of a cause of action is decisive, consistency dictates abolishing loss of consortium claims.

The majority's second reason is "faulty assumptions." The majority expresses concern that suits for alienation of affection are brought after a marriage is dissolved or broken. This does not justify abolishing the tort, because claims for loss of consortium may be brought after the marriage relation ends.

The majority intends to prevent public acknowledgment of the "intimate details" of the marriage and its breakdown. Again, this concern applies equally to loss of consortium claims.

> The most common explanation for allowing recovery for loss of consortium by a spouse . . . is the impairment or destruction of the sexual life of a married couple by a tort-feasor as an element of damage in the spouse's consortium action. . . . [But] there are other elements, such as love, affection, care and companionship. . . .

The third reason advanced to abolish alienation of affection is "consistency" with abolition of the tort of criminal conversation nine years ago in *Thomas v. Siddiqui*, 869 S.W.2d 740 (Mo. banc 1994). To the contrary, a rationale for abolishing criminal conversation was that the tort of alienation of affection would still compensate for interference with the marriage relation.

The *Thomas* case recognized that—contrary to the majority's assertion—there is a difference between the torts. Criminal conversation had only two elements: 1) an actual marriage, and 2) defendant had sexual

The Questionable Constitutionality of Curtailing Cuckolding: Alienation-of-Affection and Criminal Conversation Torts, 65 Duke L.J. 755, 760 (2016)—eds.]

intercourse with plaintiff's spouse. The only defense to criminal conversation was consent by the plaintiff. Damages were presumed.

Alienation of affection has three elements: 1) defendant's wrongful conduct; 2) plaintiff's loss of consortium; and, 3) a causal connection between defendant's conduct and plaintiff's loss. There are various defenses to alienation of affection, including causation, and the lack of wrongful conduct. Damages must be proved.

* * *

Because I would leave further action to the General Assembly, I dissent.

NOTES AND QUESTIONS

1.   *Reframing amatory tort claims.* As *Brown* and *Helsel* illustrate, most states have barred tort recovery for soured romance, even when plaintiffs try to frame their claims in other terms, such as fraud or breach of fiduciary duty. As Judge Benton's dissent points out, however, the traditional torts linger in some form in a few states, sometimes recast as intentional infliction of emotional distress or another cause of action.

2.   *Adultery torts.* In recent years, some voices have suggested that courts and legislatures have gone too far by eliminating liability for interference with marital relations. Given the courts' acknowledgment of society's powerful interests in marriage stability (recited in *Richardson* and *Helsel* above), should tort law remain available to deter adultery?

Consider *Malecek v. Williams*, 804 S.E.2d 592 (N.C. Ct. App. 2017), which upheld the facial constitutionality of the common law alienation of affections and criminal conversation torts. The court acknowledged that the torts "were born out of misogyny and in modern times are often used as tools for enterprising divorce lawyers seeking leverage over the other side." *Id.* at 594. But the court concluded that "the State's interest in preserving these torts is strong. * * * [They] deter conduct that causes personal injury; they protect promises made during the marriage; and they help preserve the institution of marriage, which provides innumerable benefits to our society." *Id.* at 596.

3.   *A contemporary role for the seduction tort?* What about tort protection for sexual misconduct outside of marriage? Some states continue to recognize a "tort of 'seduction of a person under the age of legal consent,'" although contemporary case law rarely applies the tort. *Donaldson v. Dep't of Real Estate*, 36 Cal. Rptr. 3d 577, 589 (Ct. App. 2005); Wash. Rev. Code Ann. § 4.24.020 (2018) ("A father or mother[ ] may maintain an action as plaintiff for the seduction of a child."). But is there any place for a contemporary seduction tort involving consenting adults? A few states have yet to abolish the tort. *E.g.*, *Schroeder v. Winyard*, 873 N.E.2d 35, 40 (Ill. App. Ct. 2007) (allowing husband to sue wife's paramour for alienation of affections and acknowledging

continued existence of tort of seduction). How would you distinguish such decisions from *Lawrence v. Texas*, a principal decision in Chapter 1?

PROBLEM 7-4

During Brian and Marva's 14-year marriage, Marva gave birth to two children. Unbeknownst to Brian, the biological father to both children was actually George, with whom Marva had been carrying on an affair for almost the entire marriage. Marva and George had secretly determined that George was the children's biological father, and Brian never suspected that Marva had been unfaithful. Brian was present for the births of both children and was always a devoted and caring father to them.

Marva periodically took the children to visit George and kept the visits secret from Brian. She ultimately cut off the visits when the children, then aged seven and nine, began asking difficult questions about George's identity and the reason for the secretive visits. George then filed an action to establish his paternity and visitation rights, at which point Brian learned the truth of Marva's affair and the children's parentage.

Brian has now sued George for fraud and intentional infliction of emotional distress for knowingly allowing Brian to develop a loving and bonded relationship with the children over many years without disclosing the truth of his parentage. The state in which the parties live has previously enacted statutes abolishing alienation of affections and criminal conversation actions. George has moved to dismiss the lawsuit on the grounds that the claims are barred by the heart balm statute, and that recognizing a duty to disclose paternity under these circumstances would be against public policy. How should the trial court rule on George's motion? What if George and Marva had merely suspected George's paternity of the children without ever having taken steps to confirm it?

2. Loss of Consortium

Loss of consortium actions seek to compensate family members for impairment of their intimate relationship with a tortiously injured loved one. Spouses may recover for the loss of the services, companionship, or society of a spouse who is wrongfully injured or killed. Many courts recognize a similar claim for damage to the intimate relationship between parents and their children. For example, a motorist who negligently collides with another driver may be held liable not only to the injured driver for physical injuries directly caused, but also to the driver's spouse or children for any impairment of their relationship with their injured loved one.

"The compensable elements of a claim of loss of consortium of a spouse include loss of love and affection, loss of companionship, loss of material services, loss of support, loss of aid and assistance, and loss of felicity. The elements of the child's claim are the same except for any component of sexual relations." *Peters v. Williams*, 917 So.2d 702, 712 (La. Ct. App. 2005) (wife and daughter could recover against defendant who negligently injured the husband-father in a traffic accident).

Some states permit recovery for spousal loss of consortium, but do not permit similar claims by parents or children. *See, e.g., Riley v. Keenan*, 967 A.2d 868, 877 (N.J. Super. Ct. App. Div. 2009) (children's claims). A parent may recover for "loss of services of a child upon a proper showing of the value of lost services," but may not recover damages for emotional injuries occasioned by lost love and companionship. *See Santoro v. Donnelly*, 340 F. Supp. 2d 464, 492–93 (S.D.N.Y. 2004).

At the other end of the spectrum, a few states allow loss-of-consortium claims to the parents of even an adult child. *See, e.g., Adams v. United States*, 669 F. Supp. 2d 1203, 1207 (D. Mont. 2009) (recovery allowed where parents and adult child had "an extraordinarily close and interdependent relationship"); or to grandparents for a grandchild's injury or death, *Fernandez v. Walgreen Hastings Co.*, 968 P.2d 774, 784 (N.M. 1998) (grandparent may recover where she was "a family caretaker and provider of parental affection to the deceased" minor grandchild).

NOTES AND QUESTIONS

1. *Relationship to heart balm torts.* Is Judge Benton, dissenting in *Helsel*, correct that it is inconsistent to allow recovery for loss of consortium but to deny recovery for alienation of affections and other heart balm torts?

2. *Loss of consortium in nontraditional families.* Increasingly in recent years, plaintiffs have sought loss of consortium recovery in the absence of a formal, legally recognized family relationship. This issue is discussed in Chapter 4 ("Other Incidents of Nonmarital Cohabitation").

3. *Wrongful birth.* Parents may ordinarily recover for their minor child's wrongful death. Where a child is killed through tortious misconduct, "the surviving parent, or parents, may recover for loss of affection and companionship that would have been derived from such child during its minority, in addition to all other elements of the damage usually recoverable in a wrongful death action." Ky. Rev. Stat. § 411.135 (2018).

The question whether parents may recover for the "wrongful birth" of a child with disabilities has proved more controversial. "[In] * * * a wrongful life suit, * * * a disabled child brings suit against her parents' physician—for example, if the parents chose to conceive and give birth to a child as a result of the physician's negligent prenatal counseling. Nearly every state prohibits wrongful life suits on the basis that a child cannot claim to be injured by having been born. Most also prohibit wrongful birth suits, which are similar claims brought by the parents of the disabled child. * * * 'We instinctively recoil from the notion that parents may suffer a compensable injury on the birth of a child.'" Nadia N. Sawicki, *A New Life for Wrongful Living*, 58 N.Y.L. Sch. L. Rev. 279, 289 (2013/2014).

CHAPTER 8

DIVORCE

■ ■ ■

The preceding chapters have focused primarily upon legal regulation of marriage and ongoing family life, or upon attempts to establish families through marriage, cohabitation, or parenthood. This Chapter commences an extended and regrettably necessary study of the laws of family dissolution. Domestic relations cases constitute about one-third of the civil dockets of the state courts, so divorce is necessarily an important focus of state judicial systems, and of family law practice.

Chapter 2 introduced the idea that the state is a third party to every marriage. This Chapter examines the application of that idea to the law of exiting marriage through divorce.[a] Chapters 9 through 13 will explore the major ramifications of that exit, including property distribution, alimony, child support, custody, and visitation. As with other major areas of family law, a crucial question to ask about the evolution of divorce law is: "From what to what?" Divorce law reflects significant transformation, evident not only in evolving understandings of fault-based grounds but also in the "no-fault" revolution. Divorce law continues to develop, as evidenced by discussions of what role the state might play in reducing the prevalence of divorce and whether the divorce process itself should be reformed to mitigate its effects on children and post-divorce parenting. Debates about such reforms inevitably implicate questions about the relationship between law and culture.

1. INTRODUCTION

Public discussions of divorce often paint a bleak picture of an out-of-control divorce rate, or even of a divorce epidemic in the United States. A frequently repeated statistic is that half of all marriages will end in divorce—a prediction that persists even as the risk of divorce has declined. Claire Cain Miller, *The Divorce Surge is Over, But the Myth Lives On*, N.Y. Times, Dec. 2, 2014, at A3. The high divorce rate is often attributed to the

---

[a] *Editors' Note:* Chapter 2 discussed another way a marriage may end, annulment, which applies when there is an impediment to marriage, a defect dating back to the inception of a marriage, rendering the marriage void or voidable. By contrast to a divorce, an annulment is premised on the idea that a valid marriage never came into being. This chapter discusses civil, not religious, divorce. Chapter 16 explains (at **pages 1099–1102**) how, in the context of civil divorce actions, family law courts are called upon to enforce terms of marital contracts that are entered into in connection with religious marriages.

"no-fault revolution" that began in 1969. As with most popular accounts, the doomsday portrait of American marriage is partly true and partly false.

As one report explains: "The American divorce rate today is about twice that of 1960, but has declined since hitting its highest point in [U.S.] history in the early 1980s." Elizabeth Marquardt et al., State of Our Unions: Marriage in America 2012 67, National Marriage Project (2012). One factor in the rapid rise of divorce in the 1970s and early 1980s was the widespread adoption of "no-fault" divorce laws in the 1970s. After that surge, the divorce rate leveled out and has been edging downward, suggesting a "slight increase in marital stability." *Id.* at 69; Rose M. Kreider & Renee Ellis, Number, Timing, and Duration of Marriages and Divorces: 2009 (U.S. Census Bureau, May 2011). In each succeeding decade since the 1970s, couples entering into first marriages have had a lower likelihood of divorce than couples doing so in the prior decade. Betsey Stevenson & Justin Wolfers, *Marriage and Divorce: Changes and Their Driving Forces*, 21 J. Econ. Persp. 27 (2007).

Between 2008 and 2016, for example, the divorce rate dropped 18%. Philip N. Cohen, *The Coming Divorce Decline* (Nov. 14, 2018), https://osf. io/preprints/socarxiv/h2sk6/. In 2017, a Gallup Poll found both that (1) "the national divorce rate has fallen to its lowest point in decades" and that (2) "73% of U.S. adults say divorce is 'morally acceptable,' a new high by one percentage point." Andrew Dugan, *U.S. Divorce Rate Dips, but Moral Acceptability Hits New High*, Gallup (July 7, 2017).[b] The poll found that, "historically, unmarried adults, excluding widows, have been highly accepting of divorce even if they themselves were not divorced," while married individuals were "once more reticent than others to say divorce is morally acceptable." But "[i]n 2015–2017, for the first time, married adults were about as likely as unmarried adults to say divorce is morally acceptable." *Id.* "[V]ery religious Americans" remain the "most morally opposed to divorce," but the poll found that "for the first time, a majority of this group (51%) calls divorce morally acceptable." *Id.* The Gallup Poll speculated that the falling divorce rate and the rising acceptance of divorce may be parts of a societal shift in which "both marriage and divorce are no

---

[b]   *Editors' Note:* This poll data requires careful scrutiny to understand its import because there are different ways to measure the divorce rate. Gallup measures the divorce rate by the number of divorces per 1000 people (using data from the Centers for Disease Control and Prevention). One problem with assessing trends in this "rate" is that, as the rate of marriage declines, the number of married people in the overall population declines, which also affects the number of divorces. Another survey, which found that the divorce rate dropped three years in a row and reached its lowest point in "nearly 40 years," measured the rate of divorces "per 1000 married women age 15 or older." Abigail Abrams, *Divorce Rate in U.S. Drops to Nearly 40-Year Low*, Time (Dec. 4, 2016). Using that measure, the 2015 divorce rate was 16.9 divorces per 1000 married women in 2015, down from "a peak of almost 23" per 1000 in 1980. *Id.* If one compared that divorce rate with the rate of marriages per every 1000 unmarried women age 15 or older— 32.2 marriages in 2015—then it might seem that the divorce rate was 50%.

longer viewed in moral terms, but rather seen as legal or formal processes."
Id. Do you agree?

Some observers predict a continuing decline in the divorce rate, a trend
that is "all the more remarkable," given the more permissive attitudes
toward divorce and the increased prevalence of cohabitation. Cohen, *The
Coming Divorce Decline, supra,* at 6. What accounts for the decline? One
factor, sociologist Philip N. Cohen concludes, is generational differences:
younger women have lower divorce rates than older women. Further, "the
risk profile for newly marriage couples has shifted toward more protective
characteristics" that make divorce less likely. *Id.* at 5. "Over the last
decade, newly married women have become more likely to be in their first
marriages, more likely to have BA degrees or higher education, less likely
to be under 25, and less likely to have [their] own children in the
households." *Id.* at 5. Further, couples who "persist through cohabitation
and enter marital unions at high levels of economic interdependence"
experience "greater [marital] stability." These trends, Cohen concludes,
point toward a system in which "marriage is rarer, and more stable, than
it was in the past," but is also "an increasingly central component of
structure of social inequality." *Id.* at 6.

This demographic data highlights some of the factors associated with
whether a marriage is likely to end in divorce, such as age at first marriage,
educational level, and whether it is a first or subsequent marriage. For
example, age at marriage has been a "consistent" predictor of "marital
failure": marriages entered into during one's teens or early 20s are
significantly more likely to fail than marriages entered into later. Vivian
Hamilton, *Age of Marital Capacity,* 92 B.U. L. Rev. 1817, 1844–45 (2012).
In addition, risk of divorce is correlated with such factors as spouses'
income, religious affiliation, race, ethnicity, and family history of divorce.
State of Our Unions, *supra,* at 72. One study, for example, suggests that
the risk of marriage failure is 30% lower for couples with an annual income
over $50,000 than for those making less than $25,000. *Id.* at 74; *see also*
Olga Khazan, *The Divorce-Proof Marriage,* Atlantic (Oct. 14, 2014) (divorce
rate is cut in half for couples with more than $125,000 combined income).
Marriages are also the "most susceptible to divorce in the early years," with
eight years as the median duration of first marriages ending in divorce.
Kreider & Ellis, Number, Timing, and Duration of Marriages and Divorces,
supra, at 13, 15–16.

Nonetheless, despite the decreasing divorce rate, "the prevalence of
divorce in the United States remains higher than in most European
countries." *Id.* at 5. Sociologist Andrew J. Cherlin coined the term
"marriage-go-round" to capture that, in the United States, there is both
"more marriage but also more divorce," as well as "more movement into
and out of marriages and cohabiting relationships" than in other Western
countries, leading to more household transitions for children. Andrew J.

Cherlin, The Marriage-Go-Round: The State of Marriage and the Family in America Today 19–24 (2009). In 2017, there were 800,000 divorces in the U.S., compared with over 2.2 million marriages. CDC/NCHS, Provisional Number of Marriages and Marriage Rate, 2000–2017, https://www.cdc.gov/nchs/data/dvs/national-marriage-divorce-rates-00-17.pdf. The annual revenue the wedding industry generates continues to rise, reaching $72 billion in 2016. Sarah Schmidt, *Blog: The Wedding Industry in 2017 and Beyond*, Market Research.Com (May 16, 2017). A 2018 survey found that the average cost of a wedding in the U.S. was $33,391 (excluding the honeymoon). Maggie Seaver, *The National Average Cost of a Wedding is $33,931*, The Knot (2018).

Divorce ranks high among inventories of life's most stressful events and often involves many negative emotions. *See* Robert E. Emery, Renegotiating Family Relationships: Divorce, Child Custody, and Mediation 215 (1994). Even "amicable" divorces entail economic and relationship adjustments; studies find, however, that children whose parents undergo "high conflict" divorces, with "ongoing legal battles, an inability * * * to coordinate childrearing practices after the divorce, hostile family environments, and children witnessing overt verbal and physical aggression," experience worse outcomes than children whose parents "minimized conflict during divorce." Clare Huntington, Failure to Flourish: How Family Law Undermines Family Relationships 33 (2014). (The effects of divorce on children are described in greater detail in Chapters 12 and 13.) As this Chapter and later chapters explain, to the extent that some of divorce's painful effects stem from the divorce process itself, one focus of family law reform has been to improve that process, such as by shifting from adversarial to more problem-solving and collaborative processes, matters discussed in Chapter 15.

There are some notable gender differences relevant to divorce. For example, available studies indicate that women initiate most divorces. *See* Margaret F. Brinig, Family, Law, and Community: Supporting the Covenant 81 (2010) (noting that "the proportion of wife-filed cases" was "about 60% for most of the nineteenth century" and "more than 70% in some states" immediately after introduction of no-fault divorce; and that, "[t]oday, with some variation among states," women file for divorce in "slightly above two-thirds" of cases); E. Mavis Hetherington & John Kelly, For Better or For Worse: Divorce Reconsidered 8 (2002) (noting that in a comprehensive study of 1,400 families, "two out of every three marriages ended because the wife walked out").

This gender disparity might seem surprising given that women are more likely to bear the brunt of divorce's economic dislocation and are less likely to remarry. Yet, studies also show that men and women tend to experience and benefit from marriage differently. As Professor Brinig summarizes: "[M]en 'profit' in many ways from marriage, regardless of quality, while women 'profit' in terms of health, longevity, and mental health only when the marriage goes well." Brinig, *supra,* at 74. For men, marriage also generally brings greater earning capacity.

Health disparities also exist. Married adults generally are less likely to be in poor health than widowed, divorced, or cohabiting adults, but "the health effects of marriage vary by marital quality, especially for women," for whom "marital quality, not simply marital status, is strongly correlated to better health outcomes." W. Bradford Wilcox et al., Why Marriage Matters: Thirty Conclusions From the Social Sciences 31 (Institute for American Values and National Marriage Project, 3d ed. 2011). The negative effect of "poor marital quality" on health grows with age, so that "remaining in a long-term low-quality marriage may actually be worse for one's overall health than getting divorced." *Id.* at 32.

Moreover, "divorced women in large numbers reveal that * * * they are happier than while they were married," and "report relief and certainty that they were right in leaving their marriages," while noncustodial fathers "tended to be more depressed." Brinig, *supra,* at 83. Brinig offers this analysis of the impact of the gender differential in marital benefit on when a spouse files for divorce:

> [D]ivorce contains costs in the form of attorneys' fees, harm to children, financial losses, and even today the loss of the comfort of being married. As a result, the divorce event (or process) provides a hurdle that "channels" people to remain married even though the union is marginal at best. The marriages that eventuate in divorce, therefore, belong to those couples in which at least one individual believes life is better after divorce in spite of these costs. This one individual tends to be a woman who files with the expectation that she will receive custody (who at least does not suffer the additional cost of losing her children and the status that comes with them).

Id. at 84.

As more same-sex couples marry and divorce, their experiences will provide new information about this calculus of whether to remain in or leave a marriage. Brinig's analysis, in any event, suggests the importance of considering the impact upon divorce decisions of legal rules governing other areas of law relevant to family dissolution, such as child custody. *See* June Carbone and Naomi Cahn, Marriage Markets: How Inequality is Remaking the American Family 117, 197 (2014) (arguing that the growing presumption in favor of "[s]hared custody has * * * become a divorce deterrent for women" and has reduced men's risk—during divorce—of "loss of access to the children in whom they have invested time, resources, love, and affection").

2. DIVORCE IN HISTORICAL CONTEXT

Divorce is a current topic of debate, but is also an ancient institution. For example, under Athenian law, a husband or wife needed only to file a notice with a magistrate to end all marital ties. Sarah B. Pomeroy, Goddesses, Whores, Wives, and Slaves: Women in Classical Antiquity 64–65 (1975). The divorce process was also relatively easy in early Egypt. Either the wife or husband could initiate a divorce, but only women were required to show cause, typically physical cruelty. Barbara Watterson, Women in Ancient Egypt 70–72 (1991). Divorce was permitted under Roman law and, in early modern Europe, under both Anglo-Saxon and Germanic law.

By the thirteenth century, the Roman Catholic Church had developed a theology of marriage as a sacrament and an indissoluble union, and canon law reflected this model of marriage. Marriages could be annulled due to specified impediments, but "divorce in the modern sense was not permitted at canon law." John Witte, Jr., From Sacrament to Contract: Marriage, Religion, and Law in the Western Tradition 32–36 (1997). Because of the Church's legal and political power in the Western world from 1200 to 1500, "the church's canon law of marriage was the supreme law of marriage in much of the West." *Id.* Divorce was prohibited because the "public marriage law of Catholic countries" (such as France, Spain, Italy, and Portugal) reflected the sacramental model of marriage. *Id.* at 41.

Beginning in the sixteenth century, the Reformation brought new interest in Protestant Europe in making divorce more accessible. The Protestant reformers favored the availability of divorce, and political leaders translated these new Protestant ideas into "new civil marriage statutes." *Id.* at 43. Protestant notions of the proper boundaries of divorce, however, shaped these new laws:

> Protestant reformers considered that the dissolution of marriage was not to be seen 'as a remedy for marriage breakdown as such but as punishment for matrimonial crime and as a relief for the victim of the crime.' Therefore the petitioner had to be demonstrably innocent and many divorce laws only permitted remarriage for the innocent spouse. The guilty spouse had to be severely punished 'if not by death, then by banishment or imprisonment or fine.' * * * The introduction of divorce into the Reformed countries was therefore by no means a recognition of the individual's liberty to escape from an unhappy marriage. Divorce, irrespective of the competent authority (state or ecclesiastical), was strictly regulated and extremely difficult to obtain.

Masha Antokolskaia, *Convergence and Divergence of Divorce Laws in Europe,* 18 Child and Fam. L. Q. 307, 309–10 (2006).

Even this limited allowance of divorce, however, was too liberal for England. Before 1857, the ecclesiastical courts, which followed canon law, had exclusive jurisdiction over marriage. These courts were empowered to grant legal separation ("divorce *a mensa et thoro*") or annulment where a religious impediment had already rendered the attempted marriage defective, but could not grant absolute divorce. Professor Homer H. Clark, Jr. provides this summary of divorce practice in the ecclesiastical courts:

> (a) True divorce in the modern sense of the term could never be granted for any reason. (b) Divorce a mensa et thoro, or limited divorce, without a right of remarriage, could be granted for adultery or cruelty. (c) Annulments[,] sometimes confusingly referred to as divorces *a vinculo*, were granted freely for impediments existing at the time of the marriage. The impediments most commonly relied upon were affinity, consanguinity, and prior informal marriage, and since the Church held very remote degrees of relationship to be objectionable, annulments on these grounds became useful devices for evading the prohibition on divorce.

Homer H. Clark, Jr., The Law of Domestic Relations in the United States § 12.1, at 406 (2d ed. 1988). The ecclesiastical courts' power ended in 1857 when Parliament established the Court of Divorce and Matrimonial Causes, which had jurisdiction to grant absolute divorces and related relief by judicial decree.

Divorce was more freely available in America and was a matter for the civil courts from the earliest days of the colonies. Though the United States rejected the use of religious courts, the nation accepted in broad outline the religiously-grounded premises of *fault-based* divorce. Under this system, divorce was available only to an innocent party victimized by the spouse's serious misconduct. A party who was unable to prove the spouse's serious misconduct was barred from obtaining a divorce; likewise, a party whose own misconduct offset the spouse's could be barred from obtaining a divorce. Such rules made sense from a perspective that viewed divorce as a mechanism for punishing moral wrongs rather than for redressing family conflict. But the rules could be cruel to those whose family conflicts led them into court.

A fitting illustration is provided by an 1890 California case, in which a Los Angeles woman sought a divorce after her husband defied a premarital pledge to give up excessive drinking and verbally abused her when he was drunk. *See Waldron v. Waldron*, 24 P. 649 (Cal. 1890). The trial court granted the wife a divorce, but the California Supreme Court reversed because, in effect, she had not suffered enough. The husband's "defamatory, obscene, and profane language" was "wholly unjustified, inexcusable, and unmanly," the court agreed, but did not justify divorce absent proof that the behavior had resulted in bodily harm to the wife. *Id.* at 653. The state supreme court explained:

> The grave remedy of divorce is disproportioned to the petty marital wrongs and annoyances whose injurious effect upon the body or health cannot be shown * * *. Many of such wrongs and annoyances, productive of more or less unhappiness, must be borne, if they cannot be justly remedied or avoided by the parties themselves.

Id. at 651. The court's parting advice to the unhappy wife was to avoid nagging her husband about his misbehavior, and to try to melt his heart through "uniform kindness" instead. *Id.* at 653.

Until the advent of no-fault divorce provided more systematic relief, litigants and judges managed to make traditional fault-based divorce somewhat more tolerable through a series of innovations and artifices. First, judges and legislators over time added more malleable offenses— "mental cruelty," for example—to the list of traditional fault grounds, making it easier for litigants to claim misconduct. Second, judges regularly looked the other way when litigants gamed the system by colluding to manufacture artificial fault grounds or bury legitimate defenses. And, finally, resourceful litigants could often circumvent legal barriers to divorce in one state by temporarily migrating to another jurisdiction with shorter residency requirements and looser conceptions of fault. There was, in effect, a "flourishing business of divorce tourism," and Nevada, which reduced the residency requirement to six weeks, emerged among the states as the winner. Joanna L. Grossman & Lawrence M. Friedman, Inside the Castle: Law and the Family in 20th Century America 168–169 (2011). " 'Going to Reno' became almost synonymous with divorce." *Id.* at 169. Indeed, the 1939 film *The Women* (remade in 2008), humorously portrayed the dynamics among several society women from Manhattan waiting out the residency requirement at a dude ranch outside Reno. The fault-based divorce system was not a source of pride for anyone, but common artifices made the system tolerable until no-fault divorce arrived in the 1970s.

3. CONTEMPORARY GROUNDS FOR DIVORCE

American divorce law was transformed within a little more than a decade, starting in 1969. Dissatisfaction with the traditional fault-based divorce system had been building for decades. Many observers had come to see the system, with its attendant prying, perjury and collusion, as corrupt, inhumane, and "rotting from within." Lawrence M. Friedman, *A Dead Language: Divorce Law and Practice Before No-Fault*, 86 Va. L. Rev. 1497, 1498 (2000). In 1969, California Governor Ronald Reagan signed into law the nation's first "no-fault" divorce statute. In 1970, a draft of the Uniform Marriage and Divorce Act (UMDA) recommended no-fault divorce, and the idea spread rapidly across the country. *See* Herma Hill Kay, *"Making Marriage and Divorce Safe for Women" Revisited*, 32 Hofstra L. Rev. 71, 74–75 (2003).

By the mid-1980s, nearly every state had adopted some form of the no-fault system for divorce. The last hold-out was New York: until 2010, the only alternative to a fault-based divorce was a divorce based on the parties living separate and apart for one or more years after entering into a written separation agreement. N.Y. Dom. Rel. Law § 170(6) (2008) (repealed). In 2010, after years of debate, the New York legislature added the no-fault ground of "irretrievable breakdown." N.Y. Dom. Rel. Law § 170(7) (2019). No-fault divorce laws vary in the language they use to describe the new grounds, but they share a simple and important premise. Instead of seeking to blame one spouse for victimizing the other, no-fault laws look simply to marital breakdown. Depending on the legislative directive, if a court finds that a marriage has suffered an "irretrievable breakdown," that the spouses have stopped cohabitating for a statutorily set time, or that the spouses have "irreconcilable differences," the court may dissolve the marriage, without assigning a specific cause for the collapse or blame between the parties. The court must also find "no reasonable prospect of reconciliation," and, depending on the state statute, may order a "conciliation conference" or counseling.

In California, proponents of no-fault reform envisioned this new judicial role as therapeutic: the judge could determine which marriages were dead and should end and which marriages, perhaps with the help of social workers and mental health professionals, could be saved. That vision of judges promoting reconciliation, however, failed to materialize; instead, studies in California and Iowa—the first two states to adopt no-fault divorce—found that no judge had denied a petition for divorce. *See* J. Herbie DiFonzo, Beneath the Fault Line: The Popular and Legal Culture of Divorce in Twentieth-Century America 167–72 (1997).

Arrival of no-fault divorce reshaped divorce practice everywhere in the United States, but it did not altogether supplant the traditional fault-based system of divorce. In fact, most states simply added no-fault as an alternative route to divorce, while retaining the fault-based system. As a result, even decades after the "so-called no-fault divorce 'revolution,' only a small minority of states [and the District of Columbia] are 'true' no-fault jurisdictions." Peter Nash Swisher, *Marriage and Some Troubling Issues with No-Fault Divorce*, 17 Regent U.L. Rev. 243, 258 (2004–05); *see also* Linda D. Elrod & Robert G. Spector, *A Review of the Year 2017 in Family Law: Immigration Issues Impact Families*, 51 Fam. L.Q. 501, 560–68 (Chart 4) (2018) (listing 15 states plus the District of Columbia as having no-fault as sole ground; in another state, Missouri, petitioner must prove one of five fault grounds only if the other party denies the marriage is irretrievably broken). In 2016, Illinois joined the ranks of exclusively "no fault" jurisdictions. 750 Ill. Comp. Stat. 5/401 (2019).

No-fault divorce dispenses with the need to prove fault, but often requires the spouses to live separately for a specified period before a divorce may be granted. And, regardless of whether divorce is sought on fault or no-fault grounds, most states require that divorce petitioners establish their residency for a specified minimum period in the state where they petition for divorce. As Chapter 17 explains, such residency (or domicile) provides a state court with the personal jurisdiction over one or both of the parties that is necessary to grant a divorce. The time periods for establishing residency vary from jurisdiction to jurisdiction, from as short as six weeks (in Idaho and Nevada) to as long as one year (in several states, including Iowa and Massachusetts). In Kentucky, for example, where no-fault is the sole ground for divorce, a party may obtain a divorce with a petition claiming state residency of at least 180 days and 60 days of living separate and apart from the other spouse. The no-fault divorce laws of some states, such as New Mexico and Oregon, do not require couples to live separate and apart but do impose a residency requirement. *See* Elrod & Spector, *A Review of the Year 2017 in Family Law, supra*, at 560–68 (Chart 4).

The required period that spouses must live separate and apart before they can divorce varies from state to state. *Id.* In addition, it often varies depending on whether both spouses, or only one, desire divorce. For example, in the District of Columbia, a voluntary separation by the parties requires six months of living apart prior to filing for divorce, while an involuntary separation requires a full year's separation before the court is authorized to grant a divorce. D.C. Code § 16–904(a) (2019). In 2015, Connecticut amended its divorce law to add a simplified divorce process, "nonadversial dissolution of marriage," which allows eligible parties to move to waive the 90-day waiting period that would otherwise apply, and to obtain a divorce in 35 days or less. Conn. Pub. Acts No 15–7 (now Conn. Gen. Stat. § 46b–44a (2019)). (Eligibility factors are discussed later in this chapter.)

Before marriage was uniformly available to same-sex couples, married couples validly married in one state but residing in a state that did not recognize their marriage as valid because of a state Defense of Marriage Act ("DOMA") often encountered difficulty dissolving their marriage. Courts in the state of residence often concluded that they could not issue a divorce because the underlying marriage was void. *See* Mary Patricia Byrn & Morgan L. Holcomb, *Wedlocked,* 67 U. Miami 1 (2012) (collecting decisions). Same-sex married couples should no longer face that obstacle, since, in *Obergefell v. Hodges*, 135 S. Ct. 2584, 2607–08 (2015) (a principal case in Chapter 2), the Supreme Court struck down such DOMAs and held that "there is no lawful basis for a State to refuse to recognize or recognize a lawful same-sex marriage performed in another State on the ground of its same-sex character." As discussed in Chapter 4, however, couples seeking to dissolve out-of-state civil unions or domestic partnerships may face challenges in some states.

Why would a spouse ever seek a fault-based divorce when no-fault divorce is available? First, obtaining a divorce is sometimes faster under the fault system. No-fault divorce typically requires a waiting period during which the parties live apart, but proof of a fault ground ordinarily permits immediate divorce, subject only to the pace of the court docket. Second, litigating fault can have financial implications in states that permit consideration of marital fault in shaping property and alimony awards. And, finally, some spouses genuinely desire a forum in which they can win formal acknowledgment of their sense of injury and force their spouse to incur a measure of public accountability.

Thus, many divorcing couples continue to use fault-based divorce law today. Further, parties seeking to divorce sometimes assert both fault and no-fault grounds, requiring the court to determine whether to grant a fault-based or no-fault divorce. Some critics of no-fault divorce, moreover, have called recently for revitalizing fault principles in divorce. Accordingly, understanding modern divorce law requires careful attention to both fault and no-fault grounds. The next Section of this Chapter surveys the contemporary law of fault-based divorce. The following Section then describes prevailing no-fault laws, Section 6 assesses recent calls to counter the so-called "no-fault revolution" by making divorce, once again, harder to obtain or by otherwise slowing down the process to encourage reconciliation. Section 7 explains legal separation.

4. FAULT-BASED DIVORCE

Originally, the fault grounds for obtaining a divorce were very few. Adultery was universally recognized as a ground—until 1967, it was the only ground for divorce in New York—and many states added desertion. Some states went further and allowed divorce for physical cruelty. Beyond these basic grounds, states varied considerably, with southern states generally the most restrictive. Over time, additional and often more contestable fault grounds were added, including mental cruelty and "indignities."

The defenses allowed against divorce actions underscored that the ultimate aim of divorce law in this earlier period was, like early tort law, to vindicate the innocent and punish the guilty. The material in this Section briefly surveys the most common fault grounds and defenses. The recent dates of these decisions demonstrate that fault grounds survive in robust form, and continue to evolve, in many states where legislative compromise prevented wholehearted embrace of no-fault divorce.

A. FAULT GROUNDS

1. Physical Cruelty

Cruelty as a ground for divorce traces its roots directly to the English ecclesiastical courts, where it was recognized as a ground for divorce *a mensa et thoro,* that is, legal separation. In its original form, "cruelty" required acts of bodily harm, or threats of bodily harm, substantial enough to be deemed reasonably intolerable. *See, e.g., Waldron, supra,* 24 P. at 650. Reflecting the traditional view, one court explained that "not every occurrence of actual violence constitutes a ground for divorce. It is only actual violence, or threats inducing the reasonable apprehension of violence, of a degree attended with danger to life or health that is a ground for divorce." *Boldon v. Boldon,* 354 So.2d 275, 275–76 (Ala. Ct. Civ. App. 1978). As the decision below indicates, judicial conceptions of just what level of abuse should be considered "tolerable" have changed significantly in recent years.

[handwritten: Takeaway: where domestic violence has been inflicted + threats have been made, courts should not hesitate to grant a fault-based divorce based on cruelty and excessively vicious conduct (especially facts indicate that it's repeated)]

DAS V. DAS

Court of Special Appeals of Maryland, 2000.
754 A.2d 441.

THIEME, JUDGE.

* * *

The parties were married on August 13, 1978, in New Delhi, India. Two children were born of the marriage: Radha, on October 7, 1983, and Jaya, on October 3, 1985.

The parties separated in January 1998, following entry of a domestic violence protective order granted to Wife by the District Court of Montgomery County. The order granted the Wife custody of the children, who are minors. * * * *[handwritten: facts]*

[Thereafter, the Husband fled the country, first to Japan and ultimately to India, taking Radha with him. A default judgment was entered against the Husband in the subsequent divorce action, granting the Wife a divorce on grounds of cruelty and excessively vicious conduct and awarding the Wife custody of both children. Through counsel in the United States, the Husband appealed.]

* * *

IV.

The Divorce

* * * Husband asks if the trial court erred or abused its discretion in granting Wife an absolute divorce. He argues that the facts alleged by Wife *[handwritten: Husband's argument]* at the August 11 hearing do not support grounds for divorce based on either cruelty or excessively vicious conduct because they * * * fail to reach the level of egregiousness described in some of our older cases. * * * We disagree.

Whether the events that bring a divorce complainant to court constitute cruelty or excessively vicious conduct has never been the stuff of which bright line rules are made, and even now our standards are shifting. Only recently, in 1998, did the legislature make cruelty and excessively vicious conduct grounds for absolute divorce in Maryland. Before that time, cruelty of treatment gave grounds for limited divorce only, a rule that originated in English ecclesiastical courts. Because divorce itself was disfavored by the church, the rule existed only to protect the victim-party from further and more serious physical harm. "The cruelty which entitles the injured party to a divorce . . . consists in that sort of conduct which endangers the life or health of the complainant, and renders cohabitation unsafe." *Harris v. Harris,* 161 Eng. Rep. 697 (1813). Maryland adopted this English rule, as the Court of Appeals explained in *Scheinin v. Scheinin,* 89 A.2d 609 ([Md.] 1952) ("In 1851 Chancellor Johnson announced in the High Court of Chancery that the words 'cruelty of treatment' as contained in the Maryland divorce statute would be given the same interpretation as given to them by the English Ecclesiastical Courts.") (citations omitted). The English rule, as articulated in *Scheinin* and older cases, was for many years our gold standard, setting the parameters for what constituted cruelty:

> Ordinarily a single act of violence slight in character does not constitute cruelty of treatment as a cause for divorce. But it is now accepted in Maryland, as well as generally throughout the country, that a single act may be sufficient to constitute the basis for a divorce on the ground of cruelty, if it indicates an intention to do serious bodily harm or is of such a character as to threaten serious danger in the future.

Id. [at 612.]

The Court in *Scheinin,* however, went on to point out that the original definition of "cruelty" had grown more broad, to encompass mental as well as physical abuse:

> It is now accepted that cruelty as a cause for divorce includes any conduct on the part of the husband or wife which is calculated to seriously impair the health or permanently destroy the happiness of the other. Thus any misconduct of a husband that endangers, or creates a reasonable apprehension that it will endanger, the wife's safety or health to a degree rendering it physically or mentally impracticable for her to properly discharge the marital duties constitutes cruelty within the meaning of the divorce statute.

Also outdated

Id. Even under this more modern definition, the cases for limited divorce on grounds of cruelty and excessively vicious conduct—there are no reported cases for absolute divorce on these grounds—show remarkable tolerance for abusive behavior. "[A] divorce cannot be granted on the ground of cruelty of treatment merely because the parties have lived together unhappily as a result of unruly tempers and marital wranglings. . . . [M]arital neglect, rudeness of manner, and the use of profane and abusive language do not constitute cruelty." *Id.*; *see also Harrison v. Harrison*, 164 A.2d 901 (Md. 1960) (where husband struck wife and gave her a black eye, a "single act of violence complained of by appellee does not measure up to what the law of this State requires for a showing of cruelty . . . [or justify] the wife's living apart from her husband"); *Bonwit v. Bonwit*, 181 A. 237 (Md. 1935) (husband's "violent outbursts of temper, accompanied in some instances by . . . slapping" wife did not constitute cruelty); *McKane v. McKane*, 137 A. 288 (Md. 1927) (husband's "spells," caused by drinking, during which he called wife vile names, implied unchastity on her part, cursed her, pouted, and refused to eat did not constitute cruelty). On the other hand, the Court of Appeals upheld a limited divorce on grounds of cruelty where it appeared that one party had been in significant peril, *e.g.*, incidents of drunken rage and physical abuse that required the wife to seek police intervention and seek refuge with relatives. *See Hilbert v. Hilbert*, 177 A. 914 (Md. 1935).

Key from law.

In reviewing these oft-cited cases on cruelty and excessively vicious conduct, we note that most are quite old and give victims little relief from their aggressive partners by modern standards. In part, we believe, the courts' reluctance to grant relief stems from the fact that cruelty and excessively vicious conduct were grounds for limited and not for absolute divorce, and Maryland courts have historically disfavored divorce from bed and board. *See, e.g., Bonwit*, [181 A. at 239] ("[T]he policy of the law of this state looks with disfavor upon divorces *a mensa et thoro.* . . . 'It is not the function of the courts . . . to arbitrate family quarrels, but to determine upon the evidence whether either of the parties has been guilty of such conduct as would make a continuance of the marital relation inconsistent with the health, self-respect, and reasonable comfort of the other.' "). Disapproval of limited divorce likely colored past analysis in the cases where cruelty or excessively vicious conduct was alleged.

In more recent years, however, a greater awareness and intolerance of domestic violence has shifted our public policy toward allowing the dissolution of marriages with a violence element. In the courts, we have responded to this trend by permitting absolute divorce on grounds of constructive desertion, a doctrine far friendlier to victims of violence in terms of the quality of proof required to grant freedom from the shackles of an abusive spouse. Likewise, the General Assembly responded in 1980 by enacting the domestic violence statute, which grants Maryland courts the power to issue civil protective orders and offers various forms of relief to victims. In 1998, as part of its continuing modernization of our family law, the legislature acknowledged that persons subject to domestic abuse should be entitled to seek absolute divorce immediately without a waiting period prior to the filing of a complaint. It thus expanded the grounds for absolute divorce to include cruelty and excessively vicious conduct.

In the courts, we are now left holding a stack of cases—all "good law"— dating from the 1920's that no longer square with our modern understanding of appropriate family interaction. Verbal and physical abuse may have been tolerated in another era, and our predecessors at bar may have placed the continuity of the marital bond above the well-being of individual participants, but our values are different today. * * *

Against this background, we turn to the instant case. Husband claims that his conduct toward Wife never "endangered her life, person, or health, or would have otherwise caused her to feel apprehension of bodily suffering," and, to be sure, during her brief time on the witness stand on August 11, Wife did not account for the particulars of specific violent incidents. Nevertheless, from Wife's direct testimony and in the pleadings, the court below learned that the history of violence between Husband and Wife justified entry of a one-year protective order in January 1998, after a particularly violent incident that was "one in several cases of domestic violence." Wife went on to testify that the parties' marriage was an arranged marriage, which "in our culture . . . the way it is conducted is basically subservience." She spoke of ongoing cruelty, including "making me stay up all night in order to listen to him, isolating me from my friends and from my family, and not allowing contact as much as possible. . . . [H]itting, pinching, pulling hair, etc." Wife testified in some detail how Husband's controlling behavior harmed her previously close relationship with her family. She told the court how she has continuing health problems, including cardiac arrhythmia brought on by the "stress of the marriage and the tensions at home." Wife also spoke with fear of Husband's taunting questions about what she might do when the protective order expired. Although Wife's testimony did not track Husband's mistreatment of her in minute detail, it is clear from that testimony and the very existence of a protective order that Husband's conduct far exceeded mere "sallies of passion, harshness, [and] rudeness," *Short*, [135 A. at 176], and in fact threatened Wife's physical and emotional well-being. "[W]here violence has been inflicted and threats have been made," as in the instant case, "a Court of Equity should not hesitate to grant relief, especially where the facts indicate a probability that violence might be repeated." *Timanus v. Timanus*, 10 A.2d 322[, 325 (Md.] 1940).

* * *

Judgment Affirmed.

1. *Absolute versus limited divorce.* Why might the Maryland courts have been more reluctant to find adequate grounds for a divorce *a mensa et thoro* than to permit an absolute divorce? Are the courts not also forced to "arbitrate family quarrels" in deciding whether to grant an absolute divorce? What accounts for the *Das* court's decision to adopt a broader definition of "cruelty"? Do you think that the availability of no-fault divorce provides a reason for courts to relax traditional understandings of fault grounds?

2. *Changing attitudes toward family violence. Das* recites several decisions reflecting the "old" tolerance of domestic violence. Many older decisions show an even more shocking tolerance. In *DeMott v. DeMott*, 92 S.E.2d 342, 345 (Va. 1956), for example, the court found insufficient evidence of cruelty in an attack by a husband in which he "grabbed [his wife], threw her against the wall, and threatened her with a knife."

Moreover, as legal historian William Nelson has observed, a double standard existed: "[C]ases held that one or two isolated acts of violence by a husband against his wife did not amount to cruel and inhuman treatment," yet "the courts were clear that a single violent act by a wife against her husband amounted to wrongdoing on her part." William E. Nelson, *Patriarchy or Equality: Family Values or Individuality,* 70 St. John's L. Rev. 435, 517 (1996).

Notwithstanding changing attitudes concerning both violence and gender, some recent decisions continue to reflect a surprising tolerance. In *S.K. v. I.K.*, 2010 WL 1371943 (N.Y. Sup. Ct. 2010), the court held that testimony that a wife had initiated "at least forty instances of violence" against her husband, including an incident in which she lunged at him with a Samurai sword, was insufficient to show "cruel and inhuman treatment" because "no one sustained any physical injuries, [and] neither party was seen at a hospital or by any doctor." *Id.* at *5, *8–*9.

2. Mental Cruelty

As *Das* indicates, many jurisdictions eventually enlarged or supplemented the original divorce ground of physical cruelty to include mental cruelty. The addition of mental cruelty was an important step toward liberalizing divorce law. Even with common statutory modifiers such as "extreme and repeated," the concept of psychological mistreatment was sufficiently vague and malleable to permit broad application. *See* DiFonzo, Beneath the Fault Line, *supra,* at 51–55, 61. Called "indignities" in some states, mental cruelty requires a showing of "habitual, continuous, permanent and plain manifestation of settled hate, alienation, and estrangement on the part of one spouse, sufficient to render the condition of the other intolerable." *Lundy v. Lundy*, 445 S.W.3d 518, 520 (Ark. Ct. App. 2014). To make such a showing, "[m]ere uncongeniality and quarrelsomeness, without more, are not enough." *Id.*

The conduct supporting a cruelty charge may include physical and mental elements. For example, In *Evans v. Evans*, 610 S.E.2d 264, 269 (N.C. Ct. App. 2005), the court found evidence of sufficiently intolerable "indignities" where a wife, in addition to slapping her husband 15 to 20 times for four or five years and allowing the home to fall into a slovenly condition while he was away, sent sexually explicit emails to another man, carried condoms in her purse, and disappeared for several days at a time.

A Mississippi appellate court recently upheld a grant of divorce for "habitual cruelty" based on the "cumulative effect of the [husband's] degrading sexual behavior, cursing and yelling, habitual gambling, jealousy, [and] stalking" of his wife at her place of employment, which led her to fear him and experience a "decline" in health. *Harmon v. Harmon*, 141 So. 3d 37, 42 (Miss. Ct. App. 2014). Applying the statutory criteria, the court concluded that the conduct "made the marriage revolting" to the wife, "destroying the basis for the marriage." *Id.* In a subsequent decision, a Mississippi appellate court upheld a grant of divorce to the wife for "habitual cruel and inhuman treatment" because she contracted herpes from her husband, who knew that his first wife had herpes and that he might have it (he was never tested), but never told his new wife "until she told him that she had contracted the disease." *Farris v. Farris*, 202 So.3d 223 (Miss. Ct. App. 2016).

Some courts hold that the quantum and gravity of "cruelty" required to justify divorce is higher in a long marriage than in a shorter one. *See, e.g.*, *S.K.*, 2010 WL 1371943, at *8. Is such variability sensible? Should the definition of "cruelty" vary also depending upon the individual sensitivities of the couple at issue?

As discussed in Chapter 7, with the erosion of interspousal tort immunity, conduct that may establish cruelty may also support a tort claim, such as intentional infliction of emotional distress. If a jurisdiction no longer allows fault-based grounds, a tort claim may be the only legal remedy available to a spouse.

3. "Spousal Domestic Abuse" as Cruelty   *& how cruelty is defined here*

Das concluded that acts of domestic violence by one spouse against the other met the statutory ground of "cruelty." Some state statutes explicitly include domestic violence in their definitions of cruelty. In 2017, the Mississippi legislature expanded the statutory definition of "habitual cruel and inhuman treatment" to include "spousal domestic abuse." Such abuse "may be established through the reliable testimony of a single credible witness, who may be the injured party," and "includes, but is not limited to" the following:

> That the injured party's spouse attempted to cause, or purposely, knowingly or recklessly caused bodily injury to the injured party,

or that the injured party's spouse attempted by physical menace to put the injured party in fear of imminent serious bodily harm; or,

That the injured party's spouse engaged in a pattern of behavior against the injured party of threats or intimidation, emotional or verbal abuse, forced isolation, sexual extortion or sexual abuse, or stalking or aggravated stalking * * * if the pattern of behavior rises above the level of unkindness or rudeness or incompatibility or want of affection.

Miss. Code Ann. § 93–5–1 (2019). One state legislator commented on the significance of this amendment: "Many victims of domestic violence are too embarrassed, ashamed or afraid to pursue divorce. Specifically including domestic violence as grounds for divorce makes clear that domestic abuse is unacceptable and there is a way out of a toxic relationship." Geoff Pender, *Mississippi Passes Domestic Abuse Divorce Reform*, The Clarion-Ledger (Mar. 28, 2017) (quoting Sen. Sally Doty).

4. Adultery

Adultery is the oldest of all fault grounds for divorce. At one time, adultery was also a crime in almost all the states. It is still a crime in nearly half the states, although rarely prosecuted. Peter Nicolas, *The Lavender Letter: Applying the Law of Adultery to Same-Sex Couples and Same-Sex Conduct*, 63 Fla. L. Rev. 97, 100 (2011) (counting 24 states and territories with "statutes on the books making it a crime to commit adultery"); Ethan Bronner, *Adultery, An Ancient Crime that Remains on Many Books*, N.Y. Times (Nov. 14, 2012). Despite Justice Scalia's prediction, in his dissent, that *Lawrence v. Texas* (2003) (Chapter 1) "effectively decrees the end of all moral legislation," including criminal laws against adultery, most courts have upheld such state laws in the face of post-*Lawrence* constitutional challenges. *See, e.g., Beecham v. Henderson County, Tenn.*, 422 F.3d 372 (6th Cir. 2005); Nicolas, *The Lavender Letter, supra*, at 100–01 (citing decisions). As Chapter 7 discusses, at common law, spouses could also bring various tort claims ("heart balm" or "amatory" torts) against a third party who alienated the affections of their spouse or engaged in sexual relations with them; in recent decades, most states have abolished or repealed these amatory torts.

Nonetheless, some state legislatures have repealed their criminal adultery laws. In 2018, Massachusetts did so in the Negating Archaic Statutes Targeting Young Women Act (known as the "NASTY Women Act"). Mass. Gen. Laws ch. 272, § 18–21 (2019). Should other states follow Massachusetts's lead, or should they continue to treat adultery as a crime? Are there legitimate grounds for prohibiting adultery other than moral disapproval? *See, e.g.,* Deborah Rhode, Adultery: Infidelity and the Law

(2016) (arguing that "adultery should not be a basis for criminal or civil liability, employment decisions, or custody or alimony awards").

The meaning of adultery has varied over time and place. Historically, some colonies followed the English common law, which itself followed the Bible, in defining "adultery" only as an act of sexual intercourse between a married woman with someone not her husband. Nicolas, *The Lavender Letter, supra,* at 105–08. On this view, the "heinousness" of adultery lay not in "the alienation of the wife's affections" or "loss of her company," but in its "tendency to adulterate the issue of an innocent husband," by "exposing [him] to maintain another man's children, and having them succeed to his inheritance." *State v. Lash,* 16 N.J.L. 380, 387 (N.J. Sup. Ct. 1838) (ruling that a married man did not commit crime of adultery with a single woman).

Other colonies adopted the broader, "gender-neutral" definition (taken in ecclesiastical law) that adultery was any act of sexual intercourse by a married person—husband or wife—with someone not his or her spouse. Nicolas, *The Lavender Letter, supra,* at 107. While some jurisdictions treated the third party as guilty only of "fornication"—rather than adultery—if he or she were unmarried, others treated them as also guilty of adultery. *Id.* at 108.

Today, the divorce law of most states defines adultery broadly to include all forms of sexual contact between persons of any gender—not just intercourse. *See* N.Y. Dom. Rel. Law § 170(4) (2019) (defining adultery as "commission of an act of sexual intercourse, oral sexual conduct or anal sexual conduct"); *Brown v. Brown,* 665 S.E.2d 174, 178 (S.C. Ct. App. 2008) (defining adultery to include all forms of "sexual intimacy," including kissing and fondling). *But see In re Blanchflower,* 834 A.2d 1010, 1011–12 (N.H. 2003) (ruling that same-sex liaison does not count as "adultery" for divorce purposes). On this broader view, "adultery exists when one spouse rejects the other by entering into a personal intimate sexual relationship with any other person, irrespective of the specific sexual acts performed, the marital status, or the gender of the third party." *S.B. v. S.J.B.,* 609 A.2d 124, 127 (N.J. Super. Ct. 1992). This emphasis on pursuing sexual intimacy outside of marriage raises questions (discussed below) about whether the definition of adultery should expand as technology makes new forms of sexual intimacy possible.

Given the broad definition of adultery, spouses wishing to rely on adultery as a ground for divorce more often encounter evidentiary, rather than definitional, challenges. Because of the nature of the offense, direct proof is usually in short supply. Accordingly, divorce law has long permitted proof of adultery to be made through circumstantial evidence. Nonetheless, even "[s]trongly suspicious circumstances" are often found insufficient, particularly if a jurisdiction requires proof by clear and convincing evidence. *See, e.g., Kidd v. Kidd*, 2014 WL 2586346 at *3 (Va. Ct. App. 2014) (summarizing Virginia precedents). Many jurisdictions require that the evidence effectively exclude any possible innocent explanation. *Id.; see also Spence v. Spence*, 930 So.2d 415, 419 (Miss. Ct. App. 2006) ("the evidence must be logical, tend to prove the facts charged, and be inconsistent with a reasonable theory of innocence"). The following case, involving mutual allegations of adultery, illustrates the variety of forms of circumstantial evidence on which parties might rely.

> ## MICK-SKAGGS V. SKAGGS
> Court of Appeals of South Carolina, 2014.
> 766 S.E.2d 870.

[handwritten margin note: & Takeaway: To obtain a divorce based on adultery, a spouse must demonstrate the other spouse's inclination and opportunity to commit adultery by a clear preponderance of evidence that is sufficiently definite to identify the time and place of the adultery and the circumstances under which the adultery was committed.]

WILLIAMS, J.

On appeal, Coleen Mick-Skaggs (Wife) claims the family court erred in (1) denying Wife's request for a divorce on the grounds of William Skaggs' (Husband) adultery; (2) denying her request for alimony when Husband failed to prove she committed adultery; [and] (3) improperly admitting certain photographs into evidence * * * We affirm.

FACTS/PROCEDURAL HISTORY

Husband and Wife married on February 9, 1991. After approximately eighteen years of marriage, the parties separated in October 2009. Wife then filed for divorce in December 2009 on the grounds of Husband's adultery. Husband timely answered and counterclaimed, accusing Wife of adultery. Husband subsequently amended his pleadings to request a divorce based on one year's continuous separation. At the time of the parties' divorce, Wife was forty-seven years old and Husband was forty-nine years old. *[handwritten: they each accused the other of adultery]*

Prior to the final hearing, the family court issued a temporary order requiring Husband to maintain health insurance for Wife and to pay Wife $1,500 in alimony per month. By the date of the final hearing, the parties reached an agreement on the equitable division of marital property and the division of marital debt. The primary issues to be decided at the final hearing were adultery and alimony. * * *

To support his adultery claim, Husband introduced certain text messages sent from Wife's phone. Husband read the following text, which Wife asserted was sent by one of her friends from her phone as a joke. It read:

> I'm at Aynor Bar now. . . . I'm dancing with about half a dozen and French kissing them all down to the floor, and they don't kiss like small-mouth brim. They actually know how to kiss. LOL. Got a couple off-duty P.D. officers here, too. Gonna let me (sic) strip search my ass if they want to. . . . I love being single and free.

Leaving for Texas for cutting horse congress, and I'm gonna have so much fun roping me a cowboy who knows what a real man is all about. 6–2, thirty-five years old. . . .

Husband also called William Russo, a co-worker and friend of Husband, to support his allegations of Wife's adultery. Russo stated that on the night of Wife's birthday, he arrived at the Cattle Company bar around midnight. Upon walking into the bar, he claimed he saw Wife with a couple and another male. Upon Husband's request, Russo stated he stayed outside the bar for approximately an hour and a half until the bar closed at 1:30 a.m. At that time, Russo observed Wife exit the bar with the same male. Russo stated, "At one point, she had her head in his lap asleep or whatever and, you know, there was certainly some hanging on each other while they were on the front porch. Some affection."

Russo testified Wife eventually took a cab home, and the male followed the cab in his separate vehicle. Russo observed the male enter Wife's home. Russo stated he waited outside Wife's house for approximately twenty-five or thirty minutes, and the male did not leave while Russo was there. Husband corroborated Russo's testimony and stated that on the morning after Wife's birthday, he drove by Wife's home at 5:30 a.m., and an unoccupied car was still parked outside Wife's home.

At the conclusion of Russo's testimony, Husband sought to introduce into evidence several photographs taken by Russo that evening. Wife's counsel objected to the pictures on the grounds they were poor quality and unfairly depicted the scene. The family court admitted the photographs over Wife's objection, ruling, "I think it's admissible, I honestly can't tell what it is, you know. He says what it is, and I'm not—I'll overrule the objection. [Russo] took the picture. That's what it—it is what it is."

Mary Katherine Fisher, who boards horses at the parties' barn, corroborated Russo's testimony. She testified she observed Wife kissing the same male outside the Cattle Company bar on the night of Wife's birthday. In an effort to discredit Fisher's testimony, Wife cross-examined Fisher, who admitted to filing two actions against Wife, which were ultimately dismissed, prior to the final hearing.

Husband testified regarding the allegations of his adultery made by Wife. Husband denied cheating on Wife, claiming Wife accused him of having an affair with at least seventeen different women. However, when questioned by Wife's counsel, Husband acknowledged he had feelings for another woman, Destiny Athey, and even stated, "Yeah, the lady I had an affair with. . . ."

In response to Husband's allegations of adultery, Wife recounted the night of her birthday. Wife testified she went to Applebee's Neighborhood Bar and Grill with some friends for dinner and then went to the Cattle Company bar for drinks. She confirmed she "started off with red wine . . .

had a couple of beers, and then when [her] other friends got there, they bought [her] a couple of shots." Wife claimed that at the end of the night, she called a cab and went home by herself. She denied the male at the bar stayed at her home that evening.

In support of Wife's allegations against Husband, Wife called Katherine Bujarski, another person who boards horses at Husband and Wife's barn, to testify. Bujarski stated she observed Husband and Debbie Scott (Scott) sitting together at a horse show within the last year. Bujarski testified Husband was rubbing Scott's lower back underneath her shirt. Tamara Tindal, a private investigator, also testified at the final hearing regarding her observations of Husband and Scott. Tindal was hired by a third party, Larry Scott, to conduct surveillance on his wife. Tindal stated she observed Scott and Husband alone on at least five occasions at Husband's barn within the two weeks prior to trial. All of these occurrences were in the evening, with two of these meetings occurring from 11:30 p.m. until 12:59 a.m. and 12:05 a.m. until 12:40 a.m. Tindal stated Husband and Scott were inside the barn[1] during her surveillance, so she did not know whether Husband committed adultery during those times.

[handwritten margin note: More evidence that the husband cheated]

At the conclusion of all the testimony, the family court approved the parties' settlement agreement. The court granted the parties a divorce based on one year's continuous separation and stated,

> I'm doing it on these grounds because as I see the evidence, we have evidence of adultery, at least inclination and opportunity on both sides of the case . . . which means that we have, as I see it, uncorroborated evidence of adultery on both sides. For a divorce to be granted on the grounds of adultery, as I understand the law, it needs to be corroborated.

In denying Wife's claim to alimony, the court held, "I don't think adultery as a bar to alimony had to be corroborated as does adultery as a ground for divorce." The court then recounted Russo's testimony and found it to be credible proof that Wife committed adultery and should be barred from receiving alimony. * * *

* * *

ISSUES ON APPEAL

1. Did the family court err in denying Wife's request for a divorce on the grounds of Husband's adultery?

2. Did the family court err in finding Wife committed adultery, and thus, in barring Wife from receiving alimony?[c]

---

[1] Wife's daughter confirmed that Husband's living quarters were inside the barn.

[c] *Editors' Note:* The wife also unsuccessfully appealed the trial court's admission into evidence of certain photographs introduced by the husband.

* * *

LAW/ANALYSIS

1. Grounds for Divorce

Wife claims the family court erred in granting the parties a no-fault divorce because she presented sufficient evidence that Husband committed adultery. We agree Wife presented sufficient evidence to establish Husband's adultery, but we find the family court acted within its discretion in awarding the parties a no-fault divorce. *[handwritten: ← court has the discretion to award a no-fault divorce]*

In its final order, the family court held Husband and Wife were entitled to a divorce on the ground of one year's continuous separation. Neither party claims the one year's separation was an improper ground for divorce on appeal; rather, Wife argues the family court should have granted her a divorce based on Husband's adultery. Although Husband and Wife presented evidence at trial that each spouse engaged in extramarital conduct during the course of their marriage, the family court heard this evidence and chose to instead grant the parties a no-fault divorce. Aware of our de novo review, we find the family court was in the best position to assess the parties' and witnesses' testimony as well as the evidence presented in determining which ground for divorce was most appropriate under the circumstances. *See* * * * *Lucas v. Lucas,* 302 S.E.2d 863, 864 (1983) (finding it was within the family court's discretion to deny a divorce on one ground and grant it on another ground).

Further, because the granting of a divorce to Wife on the ground of adultery would not have dissolved the marriage any more completely, we need not alter the family court's decision on this issue. * * *

2. Wife's entitlement to alimony

Next, Wife contends the family court erred in denying her request for alimony because Husband did not sufficiently demonstrate she committed adultery. We disagree.

In support of its decision to deny Wife alimony, the family court cited to the testimony of Wife, Russo, and Fisher as evidence of Wife's adultery. The family court then held, "The uncorroborated testimony of adultery is sufficient to bar [Wife] from receiving alimony, although insufficient to grant a divorce on the grounds of adultery." Although we agree with the family court's denial of alimony to Wife, we disagree with the family court's statement of the law. Further, we find there is sufficient corroborating testimony.

Corroboration is typically required in divorce actions, but this rule may be relaxed when it is evident that collusion does not exist. * * * In this instance, there was no collusion between the parties as evidenced by the contested nature of the divorce. *See McLaughlin,* 136 S.E.2d at 540 (acknowledging some states' adoption of a rule that permits courts to grant a divorce based on the plaintiff's uncorroborated testimony in contested cases and stating that only slight corroboration is necessary in certain contested cases in our state).

Based on our review of the record, we find Husband presented sufficient corroborating testimony. * * * Although we decline to modify the grounds for divorce, we concur with the family court's conclusion that Husband presented a clear preponderance of evidence of Wife's adultery to bar Wife from receiving alimony. We find that based upon the testimony of Russo, Husband, and others that Wife committed adultery on the night of her birthday. While Wife would only admit she went to the bar and consumed a substantial amount of alcohol that evening, several witnesses observed Wife being affectionate with a man throughout the course of that evening. The evidence shows this same man followed Wife home in the early morning hours, and after being invited inside by Wife, entered Wife's house. We also find Wife's subsequent text messages are circumstantial evidence that indicate a continued disposition to commit adultery. *See Perry v. Perry,* 390 S.E.2d 480, 481–82 (Ct. App. 1990) (finding circumstantial evidence over an extended period of time indicating wife's infidelity was sufficient to prove wife was disposed to commit adultery because the adultery could be inferred from the circumstances). We hold the foregoing testimony shows inclination and opportunity and is "sufficiently definite to identify the time and place of offense and the circumstances under which it was committed." *See Loftis v. Loftis,* 325 S.E.2d 73, 74 (Ct. App. 1985).

Accordingly, we affirm the family court's decision to deny Wife alimony. We also affirm the family court's order as it pertains to reimbursement for temporary alimony. * * *

CONCLUSION

[W]e affirm the family court's order finding Husband and Wife are entitled to a divorce on the ground of one year's continuous separation. We also affirm the family court's decision to deny Wife's request for alimony, * * * and its ruling on each party's entitlement to attorney's fees. Accordingly, the family court's decision is

AFFIRMED.

NOTES AND QUESTIONS

1. *The elements of adultery.* The South Carolina court, like courts in other jurisdictions, requires the elements of (1) inclination and (2) opportunity. In this case, both spouses alleged adultery against each other. How did each attempt to provide evidence of the other's adultery?

2. *Heightened proof requirements.* In South Carolina, "[p]roof of adultery as a ground for divorce must be 'clear and positive and the infidelity must be established by a clear preponderance of the evidence.'" *Brown, supra,* 665 S.E.2d at 178. Many jurisdictions insist upon heightened proof of adultery, such as by "clear and convincing evidence." *See, e.g., Kidd, supra,* 2014 WL 2586346, at *3 ("even 'strongly suspicious circumstances' are insufficient"); *Marcotte v. Marcotte,* 886 So.2d 671, 679 (La. Ct. App. 2004). Is there a good reason to require a higher standard of proof to establish adultery than to establish that someone is guilty of "cruelty" or "indignities"?

3. *Circumstantial evidence of adultery.* Although courts often demand clear and convincing proof of adultery, parties may rely on circumstantial evidence showing "an adulterous inclination and a reasonable opportunity to satisfy that inclination." In *Curtis v. Curtis,* for example, the court sustained a finding of adultery based upon evidence that the husband had lived intermittently in the home of another woman in another city, including photographs taken by a private investigator showing the husband stringing Christmas lights at the woman's home and the husband's own testimony that he spent Christmas in the home. 796 So.2d 1044 (Miss. Ct. App. 2001). Although the investigator observed no expressions of affection or intimacy between the husband and the other woman—the husband insisted that he was merely renting a separate bedroom in the house while separated from his wife—the court held that the evidence reasonably supported an inference of adultery. *Id.* at 1049–51; *see also Slight v. Slight,* 2009 WL 3173907, at *1 (N.C. Ct. App. 2009) (finding adultery based on evidence of "salacious emails sent between [wife] and her ex-husband that indicated the two were having an affair" and wife's admission that "she had created a dating profile on the website 'Date a Millionaire'"); *Popham v. Popham,* 607 S.E.2d 575, 576 (Ga. 2005) (wife permitted to introduce evidence of husband's prescription for Viagra). In *Brown,* for example, the reviewing court disagreed with the family court that wife and third party's "continued and secretive meetings in various parking lots" failed to "provide sufficient evidence to establish an opportunity to commit adultery;" it further ruled that the wife's and third party's testimony established inclination, since both admitted to activities that were "sexual in nature," such as kissing and intimate touching). 665 S.E.2d at 179.

By contrast, in *Fore v. Fore,* 109 So. 3d 137 (Miss. Ct. App. 2013), the reviewing court upheld the chancellor's conclusion (after a five-day trial that produced "a transcript well in excess of 800 pages," including reports by private investigators) that neither spouse had proved the other's adultery by clear and convincing evidence. Rather, each "became lonely and frustrated after their separation" and "developed what was claimed by both to be purely platonic relationships with members of the opposite sex." The "possibility" existed that each had an "adulterous inclination," but the "evidence of opportunity" to act on such inclination was "insufficient" and certainly not "clear and convincing." *Id.* at 141. Because the parties sued one another solely on the ground of adultery, the court denied the divorce, leaving them married to each other.

4. *Post-separation adultery. Curtis,* mentioned in the preceding note, rested its finding of adultery on conduct that commenced *after* the spouses were separated and planning divorce. Courts granting divorces based on post-separation adultery point out that spouses remain married until a final divorce decree is entered, and that infidelity while separated may destroy any prospect for reconciliation. *See Curtis,* 796 So.2d at 1051; *Barnett v. Barnett,* 908 So.2d 833, 836–37 (Miss. Ct. App. 2005). Some courts, however, have been more reluctant to grant divorce based on post-separation adultery, at least where alternative grounds exist. *See Smith v. Smith,* 964 So.2d 663 (Ala. Ct. Civ. App. 2005). As discussed below, however, post-separation adultery may be relevant to defenses such as recrimination. *See, e.g., In re Ross & Ross,* 146 A.3d 1232 (N.H. 2016).

5. *The relationship between "fault" and "no-fault."* In *Mick-Skaggs,* the parties sued based on fault and no-fault grounds, and the judge chose to grant the parties a no-fault divorce. Other jurisdictions similarly affirm that, where "dual or multiple grounds for divorce exist," the trial court holds "sound discretion" to "select the grounds" upon which to grant a divorce. *See Willson v. Willson,* 2013 WL 1729567 (Va. Ct. App. 2013) (rejecting wife's argument that trial court abused discretion by granting her divorce on ground of living separate and apart rather than on cruelty and constructive desertion). Where parties allege fault and no-fault grounds, why might a court favor granting a divorce on no-fault grounds? How can the court grant a divorce on a no-fault basis, rather than for fault, but then consider fault in denying the wife alimony, as the court did in *Mick-Skaggs?* We will learn more about the continuing relevance of fault in many states, even in a no-fault regime, when we examine property distribution (in Chapter 9) and alimony (in Chapter 10).

6. *Virtual infidelity and online activity: adultery or "adulter-ish"?* If contemporary law views the harm of adultery as rejection of one's spouse combined with "out-of-marriage intimacy" (*S.B.,* 609 A.2d at 127), need that intimacy take physical form? Professor Brenda Cossman observes that evolving social understandings appear to embrace "an ever-expanding definition of infidelity," including "virtual" and other "non-sexual encounters." Brenda Cossman, *The New Politics of Adultery,* 15 Colum. J. Gender & L. 274, 274–77 (2006). It may be an exaggeration to label the Internet "the biggest threat marriage has ever faced," but research suggests that "the rise in online infidelity has kept marriage counselors busy and has been blamed for many divorces." Sandi S. Varnado, *Avatars, Scarlet "A's," and Adultery in the Technological Age,* 55 Ariz. L. Rev. 371, 375 (2013); *cf.* Andrew Feldstein, *Is Cyber Sex Grounds for Divorce?,* HuffPost Living (Canada) (Jan. 5, 2012) (arguing that while "virtual infidelity" does not meet legal definition of "intimate sexual activity" under Canada's Divorce Act, it can still have "very real" and "devastating" consequences and "will become an increasingly important issue in many divorces in the future").

In 2012, a wife sued for divorce based on adultery because her husband was engaged in an "emotional affair" online with a woman in another state. *Beckwith v. Beckwith,* 2013 WL 4726691 (W. Va. 2013). West Virginia's highest court ruled that "sexual intercourse is necessary to establish adultery," and that no authority supported the wife's argument that "an 'emotional affair' should be considered grounds for divorce." *Id.* at *2.

Should the legal definition of adultery expand to include sexually explicit online or cellphone communication between a married person and another person or persons? *See, e.g.*, Kwame Anthony Appiah, *The Ethicist: My Wife Found My Sexy Phone Pics and Won't Let It Go*, N.Y. Times (Oct. 18, 2017) (describing a married man's exchange of sexual pictures with another woman as "a liaison that, if not adulterous, was certainly adulter-ish"). Is "online infidelity" a form of "betrayal" of the emotional and sexual exclusivity of marriage that should constitute grounds for divorce? *See* Varnado, *Avatars, Scarlet "A's," and Adultery, supra*, at 409–15 (arguing that some instances of online infidelity should qualify as adultery). Or are there sound policy reasons not to expand the definition of adultery to include online activity? Of course, if a spouse actually travels to meet an online partner in person, courts may find adultery without much difficulty. *See Bower v. Bower*, 758 So.2d 405, 408 (Miss. 2000) (upholding finding of adultery where wife, among other acts, traveled to another city and spent the weekend at a motel with a man she met on the Internet).

7. *Detecting virtual and actual infidelity.* If you were representing a client in a divorce action who complained of their spouse's online activity, how would this shape your representation? What if your client instead admitted to cyberaffairs and asked whether they would have any impact on the divorce proceeding? For a spouse seeking to monitor covertly another spouse's Internet use, a startling range of "spyware" technologies is available. For a discussion both of the ethical implications for lawyers posed by this spyware and of how forensic analysis of computers may be an element in a divorce, *see* Sharon Nelson and John Simek, *Adultery in the Electronic Era: Spyware, Avatars, and Cybersex*, Wyo. Law. 20 (Dec. 2008). Some efforts to monitor a spouse's electronic communications, for example, may violate state eavesdropping laws. *See, e.g.*, 720 Ill. Comp. Stat. 5/14–1 (2019). Do spouses have any reasonable expectation of privacy concerning their online activity?

8. *Adultery, infidelity, and "consensual non-monagamy."* Is sexual fidelity, or monogamy, a necessary marital ideal or "essential" of marriage? For example, a 2018 poll found that 88% of Americans believed that it was "morally wrong" for a married person to have an affair. Gallup News Service, *Gallup Poll Social Series: Values and Beliefs* (May 10, 2018). *But see Is Monogamy Over?*, Time, Sept. 21, 2015, at 64–65 (gathering a range of views). What is the state's interest in supporting monogamy?

What if a married couple does not view sexual monogamy as an essential of their marriage? Professor Edward Stein argues that "consensual non-monogamy" (engaging in extra-marital sex with a spouse's consent) is "importantly different" from infidelity (where one's spouse does not know about the extra-marital sexual activity); he further argues that, "in a pluralist society like ours, the law should not favor monogamy over consensual non-monogamy the way it currently does," and that adultery law should be reformed. Edward Stein, *Adultery, Infidelity, and Consensual Non-Monogamy* (unpublished paper, Nov. 2018). Do you agree with Stein?

PROBLEM 8-1

You are a family law attorney and a potential new client, Chester, tells you that he wants to file for divorce from his spouse, Terry, for adultery. He offers the following details. Several months ago, Terry became increasingly secretive, distant, and argumentative. She began leaving the house without telling Chester where she was going, and would stay out until 3 or 4 a.m. two or three nights a week. When she was at home, she spent more and more time in a separate room from Chester and their daughter, Morgan, and was constantly talking on her phone or texting. Terry has stopped sharing a bedroom with Chester and has refused to have any sexually intimate contact with him, as well.

A month ago, Chester received a text-message alert around midnight that $180 had been withdrawn from their joint checking account at a local casino. This is about the amount it costs to rent a room at the casino's hotel. Chester arranged for his mother to watch Morgan and drove to the casino, where he found Terry's car in the parking lot. At 8 a.m. the next morning, he observed Terry come out of the casino with a man, Marcus, whom he recognized as a former customer of Terry's when she worked at a local department store. Marcus carried two overnight bags, one of which Chester recognized as Terry's because of its distinct orange color. They got in her car and Marcus drove until he got out at his own home.

Chester has a video of this. When he asked Terry about the casino incident, she claimed that she did not stay in one of the casino hotel rooms, but spent the entire $180 gambling. She allowed Marcus to drive her home because she was tired after gambling all night. A few weeks ago, Chester's mother, who lives near Chester and Terry's home, recognized Marcus's car driving away from the marital home one morning when Chester was not there. Chester also has two recent photos of Terry and Marcus sitting and talking together at a club. When he showed Terry the pictures, she said that she and Marcus met at the club every Thursday evening, but denied "doing anything wrong" with him.

Assuming that the law concerning adultery is similar in your jurisdiction to that of South Carolina's, what would you advise Chester concerning whether a suit for divorce based on adultery is likely to be successful? What other information would you want before offering your advice?

5. Desertion

One of the most widely accepted divorce grounds, desertion is typically defined as the willful abandonment of cohabitation for a sufficient period of time, usually lasting at least one year. *See, e.g.*, 23 Pa. Cons. Stat. Ann. § 3301 (West 2019) ("willful and malicious desertion, and absence from the habitation of the injured and innocent spouse, without a reasonable cause, for the period of one or more years"). The other requisite element is the offending spouse's intent to abandon. Desertion claims have raised a tangle of questions, not all of them clearly resolved. For instance, can a spouse abandon marital cohabitation without actually leaving the marital home? Most jurisdictions say no, but some have allowed desertion premised on the spouses living separately under the same roof and ceasing sexual relations. Which approach better serves sound policy considerations?

The concept of "constructive desertion" presents further complications. Like the concept of "constructive eviction" in landlord-tenant law, a party who has left the marriage may be permitted to show that their spouse drove them to leave by making life within the marital home reasonably intolerable. As you might expect, however, just what conduct will meet that test is not always clear. Although "nagging, rudeness, and abusive language, standing alone, will generally not justify one spouse in leaving the other, * * * the camel's back may nonetheless be broken" by a habitual pattern of abusive conduct or demands for " 'abnormal' sexual relations." *Lemley v. Lemley*, 649 A.2d 1119, 1127–28 (Md. Ct. App. 1994).

The concepts of "constructive desertion" and "cruelty" may overlap when both are premised on acts of violence or other mistreatment, but "constructive desertion" may be established with a smaller quantum of proof. *See Das, supra,* 754 A.2d at 460 n.24. In *C.P. v. G.P.*, 800 N.Y.S.2d 343 (Sup. Ct. 2005), the court concluded that a husband's refusal for the last twelve years of a 33-year marriage to share a meal with his wife, attend family funerals, events, or holidays, engage in any but the briefest exchange of words, or sleep with his wife did not constitute cruelty, but did state a case of "constructive abandonment." *See also Ricketts v. Ricketts*, 903 A.2d 857 (Md. 2006) (holding that husband could establish cause for legal separation (or "limited divorce") based on constructive desertion if he could prove that his wife "forced him" out of the marital bedroom and ceased having marital relations, while still living in the same home).

B. FAULT-BASED BARS AND DEFENSES

Traditional divorce law matched the array of fault grounds with an array of special bars and defenses capable of defeating the action for divorce. Like the fault grounds themselves, these defenses were borrowed from English ecclesiastical court practice. In keeping with the premise that the court should award a fault-based divorce only to an innocent party wronged by a blameworthy spouse, the bars and defenses each seek to determine whether the party seeking a divorce is guilty of some misconduct that should preclude relief.

1. Recrimination

Recrimination is an affirmative defense predicated on the claim that both spouses were guilty of offsetting faults. As Professor Clark sums it up, "[r]ecrimination is the outrageous legal principle which ordains that when both spouses have grounds for divorce, neither may have a decree." Clark, The Law of Domestic Relations, *supra,* at § 13.11, 527. Denial of relief was nominally consistent with traditional equitable doctrines, which deny relief to those with "unclean hands," and resulted in the rather strange policy of keeping two wrongdoers locked together in the unbreakable bonds of matrimony.

Recrimination came into even greater use as divorce law expanded fault grounds to include grounds such as mental cruelty. With this expansion, it became easier for the respondent to assemble plausible "cross-claims" of fault. Because of recrimination's somewhat bizarre implications, courts have long disfavored the defense. Many jurisdictions have repealed it altogether; others have limited its application to specific claims (namely, adultery), or to cases in which the respondent and petitioner allegedly committed conduct establishing the same fault ground. Even when the defense is available on the books, courts often seem reluctant to apply it in specific cases. *See, e.g., Jenkins v. Jenkins,* 55 So. 3d 1094, 1097 (Miss. Ct. App. 2010) (holding that the lower court did not err in rejecting the husband's recrimination defense to wife's petition for divorce based on his habitual cruel and inhuman treatment; because evidence was "scant" of adulterous acts by the wife before separation or that such acts caused the separation).

In *In re Ross & Ross,* 146 A.3d 1232 (N.H. 2016), however, the court indicated that the recrimination defense remains alive and well in New Hampshire. The petitioner wife had filed for divorce on grounds both of fault and irreconcilable differences, and the respondent husband cross-petitioned on fault-based grounds (for wife's alleged adultery) and on grounds of irreconcilable differences. "Approximately eleven months after the petitioner filed for divorce, the respondent began a sexual relationship with another woman. The petitioner filed a motion to dismiss, alleging recrimination by the respondent." *Id.* at 1233. Over the husband's objection, the trial court granted the wife's motion and entered a final decree of divorce on the ground of "irreconcilable differences." *Id.*

On appeal, the husband argued that because his "infidelity" occurred eleven months after the parties separated, it "could not be used as a basis for the defense of recrimination." Thus, the trial court erred in dismissing his fault-based ground. *Id.* The wife countered that there was no error, because the husband "was not an 'innocent party' within the meaning" of New Hampshire's statute, which provided that "[a] divorce from the bonds of matrimony shall be decreed in favor of the *innocent party* for any of" the causes enumerated, including "adultery of either party." *Id.* at 1234. The New Hampshire Supreme Court agreed:

> "[I]nnocent" means "free from guilt," and * * *a spouse who is guilty of an offense against the other spouse, which would be grounds for divorce, cannot himself obtain" a divorce. "In other words, recrimination is a defense against a spouse who is not innocent."

Id. The court also rejected the husband's argument that the trial court erred because conduct that took place *after* separation could not trigger recrimination:

> Generally, although the misconduct of the plaintiff occurs after the commencement of his or her suit, it is as fully effective to bar the right to a [fault-based] divorce therein as if it had occurred previous to the commencement of the suit." * * * [The] * * * plain language of [the statute], which states that a divorce "shall be decreed in favor of the innocent party"* * * necessarily requires that one be an "innocent party" at the time of the decree [and] makes no exception for fault-based grounds that arise prior to the final decree, regardless of whether they arise before or after the filing of the divorce petition. * * * Here, it is undisputed that the respondent was still married when he began a sexual relationship with a woman who was not his wife.

Id. The court also rejected the husband's argument that "the defense of recrimination is unavailable to the [wife] because his adultery did not cause the breakdown of the marriage":

> [R]ecrimination does not turn upon which party's conduct caused the marital breakdown. Rather, the "right to set up one matrimonial offense in bar of another is an application of the equitable rule that one who invokes the aid of a court must come into it with a clear conscience and clean hands." Causation is not an element of the defense of recrimination.

Id. at 1234–1235. The husband asserted "that '[i]t is not reasonable to suggest, in these times of protracted discovery and litigation, that a party to a divorce must remain celibate for the duration of the proceedings' to obtain a fault-based divorce." The court countered that he should direct such an argument to the legislature. *Id.*

NOTES AND QUESTIONS

1. *Should timing matter?* If you were a New Hampshire state legislator, would you clarify whether and how recrimination should apply to post-separation conduct of the sort at issue in *Ross*?

2.   *Why fault or "no fault" matters.* Why did it matter to the respondent husband in *Ross* whether the divorce was granted on fault or no-fault grounds? The husband argued that the trial court should have awarded him more than half the marital estate, based on his cross-petition for a fault-based divorce. Instead, because the trial court granted the divorce for irreconcilable differences, fault would not be considered on the questions of property division or alimony. *Ross*, 146 A. 3d at 1235. Chapters 9 and 10 explore further whether and how fault is relevant to such economic matters at divorce.

2.   Provocation

The provocation defense is available to a respondent who claims that their own faulty conduct was reasonably provoked by the petitioner's. The petitioner's provoking conduct need not be so serious that it qualifies as a freestanding fault ground, but it must be serious enough to make the respondent's faulty reaction proportionate to the provocation.

3.   Connivance

Like the entrapment defense in criminal law, connivance bars relief where the party seeking the divorce is found to have participated in manufacturing the fault upon which divorce is sought. The typical scenario is where one spouse engineers the other's adultery by arranging and encouraging a tryst with a third person. *See, e.g., Hollis v. Hollis*, 427 S.E.2d 233 (Va. Ct. App. 1993).

4.   Condonation

The condonation defense alleges that the respondent has already forgiven the fault ground raised and thus cannot be invoked to dissolve the marriage. The rationale is that if the victim of the wrong has already generously wiped the slate clean, the victim should not be permitted to go back on their word—unless the wrongdoing spouse "revived" the prior wrong by committing another bad act. "Condonation" may be either express, as where the wronged spouse gives verbal dispensation, or implied, as where the wronged spouse signals forgiveness by resuming normal marital relations.

IN RE MARRIAGE OF HIGHTOWER
Appellate Court of Illinois, 2005.
830 N.E.2d 862.

JUSTICE GROMETER delivered the opinion of the court.

* * *

Petitioner first asserts that the trial court erred in denying her April 10, 2003, petition for dissolution of marriage on the ground of adultery. * * * In this case, it is undisputed that respondent was unfaithful to petitioner during the parties' marriage. However, respondent raised the affirmative defense of condonation.

"Condonation, in the law of divorce[,] is the forgiveness of an antecedent matrimonial offense on condition that it shall not be repeated and that the offender shall thereafter treat the forgiving party with conjugal kindness." *Quagliano v. Quagliano*, 236 N.E.2d 748 (Ill. App. Ct. 1968). Condonation is a question of intent and is to be shown by words and deeds that reflect full, free, and voluntary forgiveness. The burden is on the party raising the affirmative defense of condonation to prove by a preponderance of the evidence that the wronged party intended to forgive the matrimonial offenses of his or her spouse. Whether an injured spouse intended to forgive the marital offense is a question of fact which turns on appraising the credibility of the witnesses and weighing their testimony. * * *

In determining whether a party intended to forgive his or her spouse's behavior, courts look to a combination of factors, including an expression of forgiveness, the fact of cohabitation, the length of time the parties cohabited after the injured spouse learned of the matrimonial offense, whether the cohabitation was the result of necessity, and whether the parties continued to have sexual relations. In this case, petitioner admitted that she learned of petitioner's infidelity between 1995 and 1997 while the parties were undergoing counseling. Respondent testified that petitioner forgave him for his conduct. The parties continued to live together for several years following respondent's admission, and there was no evidence that this living arrangement was continued out of necessity. Moreover, respondent testified that he and petitioner shared the same room, shared domestic duties, and continued sexual relations until petitioner filed for divorce in May 2001. Based on this evidence, we conclude that the trial court's finding on the issue of condonation is not against the manifest weight of the evidence.

* * *

NOTES AND QUESTIONS

1. *Revival of fault following condonation.* Generally, "[c]ondonation is conditioned on the offending spouse's continued good behavior." *Brewer v. Brewer*, 919 So.2d 135, 139 (Miss. Ct. App. 2005). Thus, prior fault, even if initially forgiven, may be "revived" as a ground for divorce if the errant spouse reoffends. In *Brewer*, for example, the court held that a wife's prior adultery was not condoned, despite her husband's resumption of marital relations with knowledge of her affair, because she committed additional acts of adultery during a later separation. *Cf. Kidd, supra,* 2014 WL 2586346 at *5 (ruling that "the husband condoned any adultery committed by the wife when he reconciled with her" on two occasions, each time after learning of her extramarital sexual conduct, and did not prove that she committed any further adultery preceding

their final separation). Although *Brewer* involved repeated acts of adultery, the misconduct reviving prior fault need not itself qualify as a new fault ground for divorce; lesser offenses will suffice as long as they " 'amount to more than slight acts of coldness, unkindness, or mere quarrelling, and [are] . . . so pronounced as to raise a reasonable probability that if the marriage relation is continued a new cause for divorce will arise.' " *Tigert v. Tigert,* 595 P.2d 815, 819–20 (Okla. Ct. App. 1979).

2. *The condonation defense's effect on marital reconciliation.* "The rationale behind allowing the [condonation] defense is that reconciliations will be encouraged and society's interest in the continuation of marital relationships furthered by allowing the errant spouse some protection under the law." *Tigert, supra,* 595 P.2d at 820. Do you agree that condonation will promote reconciliation? Might the condonation defense discourage reconciliation by treating forgiveness as a legal waiver?

3. *Effect of condonation on economic orders at divorce.* If a jurisdiction considers fault in making equitable distribution of property or awarding spousal support (topics taken up in Chapters 9 and 10), condonation may also be relevant. In *Kidd, supra,* 2014 WL 2586346 at *1, the court held that the trial court did not abuse its discretion when it concluded that the wife's alleged adultery did not affect the equitable distribution award because of the husband's condonation of "any adultery shown to have occurred."

5. Collusion

Collusion exists when the spouses conspire to manufacture grounds for a divorce. Fault-based divorce, of course, did not allow divorces founded on the parties' mere consent. If parties sought to circumvent that rule by offering evidence of a phony fault ground, or by agreeing to suppress truthful evidence of an available defense, their collusion (if discovered) would bar a divorce.

This rule posed a potential challenge for spouses who were negotiating the terms of their divorce. If one agreed, for example, not to defend in exchange for some promise relating to property or alimony—the normal stuff of settlement negotiations—their agreement might be considered collusion. Other defenses might be forfeited if not asserted by the defending spouse, but collusion is a bar to fault-based divorce, which the court may raise on its own because collusion implicates the court's subject matter jurisdiction.

The bar against collusive divorce existed within a legal system that, by universal understanding, was rife with collusion. *See* Friedman, *A Dead Language, supra,* at 1504–07. From interests of both efficiency and humanity, judges did not generally police the collusion bar aggressively and often cooperated by entering default judgments in uncontested divorces. As Professor DiFonzo writes, "[t]he Michigan divorce judge who opened morning hearings in uncontested cases by intoning 'Let the perjury begin,' understood the strictly symbolic character of the courtroom rituals." DiFonzo, Beneath the Fault Line, *supra*, at 90. Nevertheless, the collusion bar remained at the ready and sometimes denied relief. *See* Friedman, *A Dead Language, supra*, at 1507. Notably, decades later, when the New York legislature debated adding "no-fault" divorce, some supporters observed that New York's restrictive divorce law induced some couples to testify falsely to fault grounds to speed up the divorce process. Nicholas Confessore, *N.Y. Moves Closer to No-Fault Divorce,* N.Y. Times (June 15, 2010).

PROBLEM 8-2

In April, 2019, three years into their marriage, Rachael confronted her husband, Tom, with suspicions that he was having an affair with a co-worker, Phoebe. Tom admitted having dinner and drinks with Phoebe after work on four or five occasions, and socializing with Phoebe on two weekends when Rachael was away on business trips. He insisted, however, that he was only trying to give Phoebe emotional support while she was separating from her husband.

Tom denied having an affair but promised to stop socializing with Phoebe in the future, and Rachael relented. Tom and Rachael enjoyed relative marital harmony for the next four months, until one afternoon in August when Rachael happened to spot Tom's car leaving the parking lot of a local motel. Driving closer, Rachael saw that Tom was driving and Phoebe was in the passenger seat. Furious, Rachael pulled her car alongside Tom's. When Tom sped up to avoid her, Rachael chased them and ultimately rammed Tom's rear bumper twice before her own car spun into a ditch. No one was injured in the incident, but Tom and Phoebe were greatly frightened and alarmed. Later that day, Tom moved out of the marital home and has not returned. Tom has admitted that he and Phoebe rented a room in the motel during their lunch hour, but he insists they did so only to have a private, quiet place to talk about issues relating to Phoebe's impending divorce. He and Phoebe both deny having a sexual relationship.

What advice would you give Rachael about her prospects for obtaining an immediate divorce? What advice would you give Tom if he wished to file for divorce? If the parties were both amenable, could they simply stipulate to the necessary grounds?

5. NO-FAULT DIVORCE

As mentioned in Section 3, dissatisfaction with the corruption and hardships of traditional fault-based divorce led to enactment of no-fault divorce in California in 1969 and to its rapid acceptance in other states over the next 15 years. As the materials in this Section explain, no-fault divorce in most jurisdictions requires a judicial finding that the marriage is "irretrievably broken" and satisfaction of a waiting period while living "separate and apart." In most states, no-fault divorce is an alternative to fault-based divorce; in 15 states and the District of Columbia, however, divorce may be obtained only on no-fault grounds. *See* Elrod & Spector, *A Review of the Year in Family Law, supra,* at 662–65 (Chart 4) (explaining that in a sixteenth state, Missouri, if one party denies that a marriage is "irretrievably broken," traditional fault grounds such as adultery and abandonment become relevant to establishing marital breakdown).

The statutory excerpts that follow illustrate two typical no-fault regimes, the first in a jurisdiction that recognizes only no-fault grounds for divorce and the second in a jurisdiction that simply added no-fault grounds to supplement the pre-existing fault-based regime. As you examine no-fault divorce statutes and their application by courts, consider how the idea that the state is a third party to every marriage and divorce applies in a no-fault regime.

A. EXCLUSIVE NO-FAULT REGIMES

The approach recommended by the UMDA in 1970 makes "irretrievable breakdown" of the marriage the exclusive ground for divorce. The UMDA approach is implemented in the statutory excerpt below, adopted by Kentucky in 1972. The approach, however, remains the minority rule nationwide. As you read the excerpt, consider how the stated purposes of the exclusive no-fault statute differ from the underlying objectives of traditional fault-based divorce.

Chapter 403 of the Kentucky Revised Statutes
Dissolution of Marriage (2019)

403.110 Purpose of chapter

This chapter shall be liberally construed and applied to promote its underlying purposes, which are to:

(1) Strengthen and preserve the integrity of marriage and safeguard family relationships;

(2) Promote the amicable settlement of disputes that have arisen between parties to a marriage;

(3) Mitigate the potential harm to the spouses and their children caused by the process of legal dissolution of marriage;

(4) Make reasonable provision for spouse and minor children during and after litigation; and

(5) Make the law of legal dissolution of marriage effective for dealing with the realities of matrimonial experience by making irretrievable breakdown of the marriage relationship the sole basis for its dissolution.

403.140 Marriage—Court may enter decree of dissolution or separation

(1) The Circuit Court shall enter a decree of dissolution of marriage if:

[the petitioner satisfies the jurisdiction and conciliation requirements of the statute and]:

* * *

(c) The court finds that the marriage is irretrievably broken * * *.

* * *

403.170 Marriage; irretrievable breakdown

(1) If both of the parties by petition or otherwise have stated under oath or affirmation that the marriage is irretrievably broken, or one of the parties has so stated and the other has not denied it, the court, after hearing, shall make a finding whether the marriage is irretrievably broken. No decree shall be entered until the parties have lived apart for 60 days. Living apart shall include living under the same roof without sexual cohabitation. The court may order a conciliation conference as a part of the hearing.

(2) If one of the parties has denied under oath or affirmation that the marriage is irretrievably broken, the court shall consider all relevant factors, including the circumstances that gave rise to filing the petition and the prospect of reconciliation, and shall:

(a) Make a finding whether the marriage is irretrievably broken; or

(b) Continue the matter for further hearing not fewer than 30 nor more than 60 days later, or as soon thereafter as the matter may be reached on the court's calendar, and may suggest to the parties that they seek counseling.

The court, at the request of either party shall, or on its own motion may, order a conciliation conference. At the adjourned hearing the court shall make a finding whether the marriage is irretrievably broken.

(3) A finding of irretrievable breakdown is a determination that there is no reasonable prospect of reconciliation.

Ky. Rev. Stat. Ann. §§ 403.110, 403.140, 403.170 (2019).

B. MIXED FAULT/NO-FAULT REGIMES

Most jurisdictions have added no-fault provisions to their existing fault laws. In these jurisdictions, illustrated by the Pennsylvania statute below, a party seeking a divorce may elect whether to proceed on fault or no-fault grounds.

Title 23, Section 3301 of the Pennsylvania Consolidated Statutes

§ 3301. Grounds for divorce

(a) Fault.—The court may grant a divorce to the innocent and injured spouse whenever it is judged that the other spouse has:

(1) Committed willful and malicious desertion, and absence from the habitation of the injured and innocent spouse, without a reasonable cause, for the period of one or more years.

(2) Committed adultery.

(3) By cruel and barbarous treatment, endangered the life or health of the injured and innocent spouse.

(4) Knowingly entered into a bigamous marriage while a former marriage is still subsisting.

(5) Been sentenced to imprisonment for a term of two or more years upon conviction of having committed a crime.

(6) Offered such indignities to the innocent and injured spouse as to render that spouse's condition intolerable and life burdensome.

(b) Institutionalization.—The court may grant a divorce from a spouse upon the ground that insanity or serious mental disorder has resulted in confinement in a mental institution for at least 18 months immediately before the commencement of an action under this part and where there is no reasonable prospect that the spouse will be discharged from inpatient care during the 18 months subsequent to the commencement of the action. * * *

(c) Mutual consent.—

(1) The court may grant a divorce where it is alleged that the marriage is irretrievably broken and 90 days have elapsed from the date of commencement of an action under this part and an affidavit has been filed by each of the parties evidencing that each of the parties consents to the divorce.

(2) The consent of a party shall be presumed where that party has been convicted of committing a personal injury crime against the other party.

(d) Irretrievable breakdown.—

(1) The court may grant a divorce where a complaint has been filed alleging that the marriage is irretrievably broken and an

affidavit has been filed alleging that the parties have lived separate and apart for a period of at least one year and that the marriage is irretrievably broken and the defendant either:

(i) Does not deny the allegations set forth in the affidavit.

(ii) Denies one or more of the allegations set forth in the affidavit but, after notice and hearing, the court determines that the parties have lived separate and apart for a period of at least one year and that the marriage is irretrievably broken.

(2) If a hearing has been held pursuant to paragraph (1)(ii) and the court determines that there is a reasonable prospect of reconciliation, then the court shall continue the matter for a period not less than 90 days nor more than 120 days unless the parties agree to a period in excess of 120 days. During this period, the court shall require counseling as provided in section 3302 (relating to counseling). If the parties have not reconciled at the expiration of the time period and one party states under oath that the marriage is irretrievably broken, the court shall determine whether the marriage is irretrievably broken. If the court determines that the marriage is irretrievably broken, the court shall grant the divorce. Otherwise, the court shall deny the divorce.

(e) No hearing required in certain cases.—If grounds for divorce alleged in the complaint or counterclaim are established under subsection (c) or (d), the court shall grant a divorce without requiring a hearing on any other grounds.

23 Pa. Cons. Stat. Ann. § 3301 (West 2019).

C. LIVING SEPARATE AND APART

In its original form, the UMDA did not require any separation period and allowed divorce solely on a finding that the marriage was "irretrievably broken." After a few years, the UMDA was revised to permit no-fault divorce only where "the court finds that the marriage is irretrievably broken, if the finding is supported by evidence that (i) the parties have lived separate and apart for a period of more than 180 days next preceding the commencement of the proceeding, or (ii) there is serious marital discord adversely affecting the attitude of one or both of the parties toward the marriage." UMDA, § 302(a)(2), 9A U.L.A. 200.

Some states have embraced the UMDA's approach without modification, permitting divorce without any waiting period on a showing of "serious marital discord." But most states, including Kentucky and Pennsylvania, have added a mandatory separation period to their no-fault laws. Kentucky requires a relatively short wait of 60 days. *See* Ky. Rev. Stat. Ann. § 403.170(1) (quoted above). Pennsylvania used to mandate a two-year separation period, but, in 2016, the legislature reduced the period to one year. Where both spouses consent to the divorce, the period is 90 days. Note that a party's consent is "presumed" if the party "has been convicted of committing a personal injury crime against the other party." (*See* Pennsylvania's statute, quoted above.) What purpose is served by requiring the parties to endure a separation period before granting a divorce? Why shorten the wait when both spouses agree? Are the purposes different for couples with minor dependent children than for other couples?

No matter what length a state prescribes for the required separation, disputes may arise over whether the parties have genuinely lived "separate and apart" for the requisite period. Some disputes involve whether the parties may live "separately" within the same dwelling; other disputes concern disagreement about the date on which their separation began. The following decision presents both questions. As you read it, consider whether the purposes of the statutory separation period were satisfied by the manner in which these spouses lived "separate and apart."

FREY V. FREY
Superior Court of Pennsylvania, 2003.
821 A.2d 623.

STEVENS, J.

This is an appeal from the May 10, 2002 order entered in the Court of Common Pleas of Fayette County issuing a final decree in divorce * * *.

[Wife "oppos[ed] the entry of a divorce decree on the grounds that the parties had not lived separate and apart for at least two years and the marriage was not irretrievably broken."[d] The trial court accepted Husband's contention that the parties' separation commenced on August 6, 1999, and granted a no-fault divorce.]

* * *

* * * On direct examination, Husband testified that he filed a complaint in divorce on August 6, 1999, and when he filed the complaint, he and Wife were living in the same residence with their daughter. Husband testified that, prior to this time, he occasionally ate meals with Wife and his daughter, but he and Wife had not slept together in the same bed since March 23, 1998. * * * Husband indicated that he refused to move because he had no other house, he had built the house, his daughter lived in the house, and his lumber company was located next to the house. * * *

---

[d] *Editors' Note:* At the time of this case, 23 Pa. Cons. Stat. Ann. § 3301 required parties to lives separate and apart for two years. As mentioned above, in 2016, the legislature reduced it to one year.

Husband admitted that, following the filing of the divorce complaint, he, Wife, and their daughter went on vacations to Walt Disney World and Myrtle Beach. However, Husband testified that he and Wife did not sleep together while on vacation, and the sole purpose for the trips was to benefit their daughter. * * *

On cross-examination, Husband admitted that in December 1999, Wife attended the lumber company's Christmas party, and on December 31, 1999, he and Wife hosted a party at their house. Husband testified that he stayed at home on New Year's Eve so that he could be with his daughter. Husband further admitted that he and Wife saw a marriage counselor in March and August of 2000, and during the summer of 2000, Husband coached his daughter's t-ball team, with Wife being present. Husband also took Wife and their daughter to a concert at the local fair during the summer of 2000 because he had been given the tickets as a gift, and they went again in September 2001. * * * Husband testified that in May 2001, he, Wife, and their daughter went to Monroeville, Pennsylvania for a weekend of shopping. Husband indicated that he did this solely for his daughter because he had promised that he would take her. * * *

* * *

Wife testified that she believes the parties separated in October 2001 because that is when she and Husband first met with attorneys and Wife came to realize that the parties would not reconcile. Wife testified that from 1999 to October 2001, she, Husband, and their daughter attended school activities and holidays, went to the movies and dinner, and went on vacations together. Wife admitted that Husband generally eats with his mother, but she indicated that she washed all of his clothes, with the exception of his shirts. Wife testified that from 1999 to 2001 she and Husband had sexual intercourse on a regular basis, and the last time they had sexual intercourse was the weekend of October 28, 2001. * * *

* * *

Wife first contends that the trial court erred in concluding that the parties' date of separation was August 6, 1999, and not October 2001, and, therefore, the statutory period for a no-fault divorce was not met. * * *

* * * Subsection 3301(d)(1) provides that the court may grant a no-fault divorce where a complaint has been filed alleging that the marriage is irretrievably broken and an affidavit has been filed alleging that the parties have lived separate and apart for a period of at least two years. When considering a challenge to the trial court's determination of the date of separation, we have applied the following standard:

> The Divorce Code defines "separate and apart" as follows: "Complete cessation of any and all cohabitation, whether living in the same residence or not." 23 Pa. [Cons. Stat. Ann.] § 3103. In

Thomas v. Thomas, 483 A.2d 945 (Pa. Super. Ct. 1984), this [C]ourt held that "cohabitation" means "the mutual assumption of those rights and duties attendant to the relationship of husband and wife." Thus, the gravamen of the phrase "separate and apart" becomes the existence of separate lives not separate roofs. * * *

Wellner v. Wellner, 699 A.2d 1278, 1281 (Pa. Super. Ct. 1997) (citations and quotations omitted). * * *

Applying the foregoing, we conclude that the trial court did not err when it determined the date of separation to be August 6, 1999, as the date is supported by sufficient, credible evidence. For example, Husband testified that, as of August 6, 1999 to the time of the hearing, he did not sleep in the same room as Wife, and, in fact, he used the marital residence for sleeping purposes only. Husband testified that he remained in the house for reasons other than those relating to Wife. As for the eating of meals, Husband testified that, after August 6, 1999, he usually ate meals at his mother's house and that, when he did eat at the marital residence, it was with his daughter only. Husband testified that Wife washes his work jeans sometimes, but he takes all of his shirts to his mother and he sometimes washes his own jeans. With regard to vacations and other outings, Husband admitted that he went on vacations and other outings with Wife and his daughter after August 6, 1999; however, Husband specifically testified that such activities were for the benefit of his daughter only and Wife was aware of this fact. Husband did not engage in sexual intercourse or sleep in the same bed as Wife during the vacations, and as Husband testified, he and Wife gave the appearance that everything was fine for the sake of their daughter. Based on the aforementioned, we conclude that the evidence supported the August 6, 1999 separation date.

We specifically disagree with Wife's contention that the fact she attended the lumber company's 1999 Christmas party, the parties sought counseling twice in 2000, and the parties had dinner together in October 2001 requires a finding that the date of separation should be after August 6, 1999. This Court has held that isolated attempts at reconciliation do not begin running anew the marital relationship. Moreover, the fact Wife's testimony differed from Husband's in many respects is not determinative in this case. Husband testified that, after August 6, 1999, he and Wife did not have sexual relations[;] however, Wife testified that they regularly had sexual relations. Apparently finding neither spouse to be totally forthcoming, the trial court concluded that occasional sexual relations occurred between Husband and Wife following August 6, 1999.[4] The trial

---

[4] We note that the trial court properly found that occasional sexual contact between Husband and Wife after August 6, 1999 did not require a conclusion that the parties were cohabiting.

court was free to make its credibility determination, and we will not disturb this determination on appeal.

In sum, the evidence in this case reveals that Husband and Wife led separate lives, even though the parties generally slept under the same roof, and their activities together were knowingly performed solely for the benefit of their daughter. Husband should not be penalized for attempting to make life for his daughter more pleasurable and his isolated, unsuccessful attempts at reconciliation. We believe that "cohabitation" contemplates more of a martial relationship than what occurred in this case after August 6, 1999. As such, we conclude that the trial court did not err in this regard.

* * *

Affirmed.

NOTES AND QUESTIONS

1. *Sharing the same dwelling.* Most states agree that parties to a no-fault divorce should be required to satisfy a period of separation, but states disagree on precisely what it means for two spouses to live "separate and apart." Some states agree with *Frey* that parties may satisfy the requisite separation period while living in the same house, so long as they are effectively living separate lives. *See, e.g.*, Ky. Rev. Stat. Ann. § 403.170(1) (West 2019) (quoted above); *In re Marriage of A.J.H.*, 2002 WL 31454020, at *1 n.1 (Del. Fam. Ct. 2002). But other jurisdictions require the parties to live in separate dwellings. *See, e.g.*, *Viator v. Miller*, 900 So.2d 1135, 1138 n.1 (La. Ct. App. 2005); *In re Marriage of Norviel*, 126 Cal. Rptr.2d 148 (Cal. Ct. App. 2002). What concerns might affect the choice between these two positions?

2. *Intention to end the marriage.* Even where the parties indisputably live "apart," they may not be considered "separated" unless their removal is accompanied by subjective intention to dissolve their marriage. "The separation must be 'coupled with an intention on the part of at least one of the parties to live separate and apart permanently, and [this] intention must be shown to have been present at the beginning' of the separation period." *Pearson v. Vanlowe*, 2005 WL 524597, at *4 (Va. Ct. App. 2005). Thus, if the parties are separated by one spouse's military duty or incarceration, the absence will not count as "living separate and apart" unless at least one party makes clear an intent never to resume cohabitation. *See Sinha v. Sinha*, 526 A.2d 765, 767–68 (Pa. 1987).

3. *Factors in determining the parties' intention to separate.* As *Frey* illustrates, "[d]etermination of whether and when the parties have 'lived separate and apart without cohabitation' is a fact-based inquiry, requiring examination of all the circumstances before the court." *Bchara v. Bchara*, 563 S.E.2d 398, 402 (Va. Ct. App. 2002). Particularly where the parties claim to have lived separately while sharing the same home, the outcome often turns on careful attention to their interaction, such as whether they "continued to

attend social outings together, or continued to act jointly in financial matters." *In re Marriage of Shaughnessy*, 2004 WL 1759260, at *3 (Cal. Ct. App. 2004).

Bchara found that the parties satisfied Virginia's one-year separation period. After discovering a videotape of her husband having sex with another woman, the wife moved all of his possessions out of the master bedroom and into a guest bedroom. In addition:

> Wife testified in deposition that she stopped depositing money into their joint account after discovering the videotape. She also stopped going to church with husband and stopped attending his family's functions after the discovery. She admitted buying groceries, doing laundry, and cooking food that husband ate. She also accepted flowers from husband, given to her in their son's name on Mother's Day of 2000.

563 S.E.2d at 402. These circumstances demonstrated the wife's intention to live "separate and apart" from her husband. "Continuing to share food and keep a clean house are not behaviors that, as a matter of law, require a finding that the parties were living together." *Id.*

By contrast, in *Catalano v. Catalano*, 68 Va. Cir. 80 (Va. Cir. Ct. 2005), the wife moved into a guest bedroom after discovering that her husband had divided a shared bank account. The spouses ceased all intimate relations but "agreed that they would stay together for the sake of the kids until the end of the school year," and continued to share some activities together as a family:

> Although Mr. Catalano expressed to coworkers and some family members that he was separated from his wife, he continued to host and attend family gatherings with his wife, as well as to attend various church services and numerous and varied other social functions with her until he moved out of the marital home. In short, the parties continued to hold themselves out as a couple. The parties continued to take some meals together, and the family went out to dinner once a week. Throughout the period, Ms. Catalano continued to do the cooking and shopping for the family, cleaning of the dishes, house and laundry. Mr. Catalano continued to support financially the family activities.

Id. at 81–82. *Catalano* concluded that, "although the parties slept in separate bedrooms, they did not live physically separate and apart, without cohabitation, while they remained under one roof," and, therefore, were not eligible, under Virginia's statute, for a divorce based on one year of separation. *Id.* at 82. If you represented a party who wished a no-fault divorce based on living separate and apart, what steps would you suggest the client take to make clear the intent and the fact of separation?

4.   *Effect of reconciliation attempts on the separation period.* If separated spouses reconcile and resume cohabiting, their reconciliation may reset the clock on their separation period for a later divorce. As in *Frey*, however, courts distinguish between brief overtures toward reconciliation (which will not

terminate the separation period) and intentional resumption of the marital relationship (which will). For example, in *Pearson* (mentioned in Note 1), the trial court awarded the wife a divorce based on the parties living "separate and apart without cohabitation" for one year, beginning in October 1999. On appeal, the husband argued that the trial court erred because of "the wife's hope for reconciliation, and the parties' 'dating' relationship and sexual contact during the separation period." *Pearson, supra*, 2005 WL 524597, at *3. Notably, the couple had a prior physical separation: in October 1997, the husband moved out of their home and told the wife there was "no chance of reconciliation." *Id.* at *1. In May 1999, however, they began living together again until early October 1999, when the husband again moved out of the house due to conflicts over the wife's adult daughter. On October 12, 1999, the wife wrote the husband a letter stating that she considered the marriage over and asked him for a separation agreement. In her pleadings, the wife indicated that she intended the separation to be permanent unless "husband met her conditions for reconciliation," which he failed to do. *Id.*

The trial court held that their separation began in mid-October 1999, and continued uninterrupted for the required one-year statutory period. The court reached this conclusion even though the parties began "a dating relationship" six months into their separation, including a resumption of "occasional" sexual relations for a few months, and an exchange of some "affectionate correspondence." *See id.* at *2. The court found that the "wife's references to marriage counseling and reconciliation were attempts to improve communications with husband, indicating her intent 'to ease the hardship of getting out of the marriage on everybody,' and 'not an intent to resume the marriage.'" *Id.*

The *Pearson* appellate court agreed that, from mid-October 1999, the wife's "intent" was "to permanently end the marriage" unless husband met certain conditions; there was "no evidence" they intended to resume permanent cohabitation or marital life. *Id.* at *4. "'Mere casual cohabitation between the parties, after the separation, unaccompanied by resumption of normal married life * * * is not sufficient to show a reconciliation or an agreement to live and cohabit together again on a permanent basis as husband and wife.'" *Id.* at *4 (internal citation omitted). Why might courts decline to treat reconciliation attempts as terminating a separation? In *Pearson*, should the parties' initial separation between 1997 and 1999 have provided a sufficient basis for a no-fault divorce in October 1999? Why or why not?

5. *Effect of "sexting" on living apart*. If resuming sexual relations can interrupt the separation period, then what about "phone sex"? In *Bergeris v. Bergeris*, 90 A.3d 553, 553 (Md. Ct. Spec. App. 2014), the wife challenged her husband's request for divorce based on a 12-month separation on the ground that she "continued to have sexual relations" with him during that period by way of "sexually explicit or provocative telephone conversations and text messages." The wife prevailed at trial because her husband conceded the contact, and the court stated that "without cohabitation means without sexual relations," not "without sexual intercourse," and thus, "phone sex comes within

the broader definition of sexual relations that is broader than sexual intercourse." *Id.* at 555. The reviewing court reversed, ruling that "occasional instances of telephonic or electronic communication talking about sex, unaccompanied by intimate physical sexual contact, do not rise to the level of cohabitation." *Id.* at 559.

6. *The role of separation agreements.* Parties often negotiate formal agreements at the time of their separation. These agreements can prove highly useful for several purposes. First, parties may use an agreement to make unambiguous their intention to live "separate and apart." For example, *Catalano* found no intent to separate, partly because the wife "specifically rejected the idea of entering into a proposed property settlement agreement to establish a date of separation." *Catalano, supra,* 68 Va. Cir. at 82.

Beyond establishing no-fault grounds for divorce, separation agreements commonly play a dominant role in determining the financial and other consequences of dissolution. As Chapter 16 discusses in detail, parties may specify how their property is to be divided at divorce, the terms of any spousal support, and custody arrangements for their children, and courts will normally defer, often incorporating the parties' agreement as part of the divorce decree. In some states, parties may enforce the terms of a separation agreement to divide their property even before the divorce, allowing for an earlier severance of economic entanglements. *See, e.g., Grider v. Grider,* 968 S.W.2d 653, 654–55 (Ark. Ct. App. 1998).

D. IRRETRIEVABLE BREAKDOWN

"Irretrievable breakdown of the marriage" has been defined to mean that "either or both of the spouses are unable or unwilling to cohabit and there are no prospects for reconciliation." *Caffyn v. Caffyn,* 806 N.E.2d 415, 419 n.6 (Mass. 2004). What if one spouse wants to end the marriage but the other is convinced that their conflicts can be overcome or resolved through counseling or other intervention? Do you agree with the way the following court resolved this dilemma?

RICHTER V. RICHTER
Court of Appeals of Minnesota, 2001.
625 N.W.2d 490.

SHUMAKER, JUDGE.

* * *

The parties married in 1983 and wife petitioned to dissolve the marriage in September 1999. Husband opposed wife's attempts to dissolve the marriage. * * * On April 25, husband, pro se, moved to dismiss the proceeding, alleging, among other things, that (a) there was no irretrievable breakdown of the marriage; (b) marriage is a contract; and (c) the statutes allowing dissolution of a marriage infringed on the constitutional right to contract. * * *

[The district court denied the husband's motion to dismiss and a later motion for a continuance. The husband then declined to participate in the hearing on the divorce petition and the court granted the wife's request for divorce after hearing her testimony.]

* * *

Minnesota allows marriages to be dissolved if there has been an "irretrievable breakdown of the marriage relationship." Minn. Stat. § 518.06, subd. 1 (2000). While husband denies challenging the constitutionality of * * * Minnesota's dissolution statute, he argues that to be constitutional, the statute cannot be construed to allow "divorce on demand" because that would interfere with his right to contract. *See* U.S. Const. art. I, § 10 (prohibiting laws "impairing the obligation of contracts"); Minn. Const. art. I, § 11 (same). * * * Such an argument assumes that the Minnesota dissolution statutes allow "divorce on demand" and that marriage is a contract. Both assumptions are incorrect.

I.

In Minnesota, if there is a dispute about whether a marriage is irretrievably broken, "the court shall consider all relevant factors" and find whether the marriage is irretrievably broken. Minn. Stat. § 518.13, subd. 2 (2000). "Irretrievable breakdown" occurs when "there is no reasonable prospect of reconciliation." *Id.* To find irretrievable breakdown of a marriage in a case where the existence of such a breakdown is contested,

> [t]he finding [of irretrievable breakdown] must be supported by evidence that (i) the parties have lived separate and apart for a period of not less than 180 days immediately preceding the commencement of the proceeding, or (ii) there is serious marital discord adversely affecting the attitude of one or both of the parties.

Id. Here, the parties had been separated, but not for 180 days, before wife petitioned to dissolve the marriage. The district court, however, believed wife's testimony about the state of the parties' marriage and found an irretrievable breakdown of the marriage. A party's testimony is a sufficient basis for a finding of irretrievable breakdown of a marriage. *See Hagerty v. Hagerty*, 281 N.W.2d 386, 388 (Minn. 1979) (stating irretrievable breakdown "can also be shown by evidence of only one party's belief that it is the existing state, particularly where the parties have been living apart"); *Hollander v. Hollander*, 359 N.W.2d 55, 56–57 (Minn. App. 1984) (affirming finding of irretrievable breakdown [and] noting that, among other things, it was supported by wife's testimony). A statute that requires proof of "no reasonable prospect of reconciliation" and "serious marital discord adversely affecting the attitude of one or both of the parties" before a marriage can be dissolved does not allow "divorce on demand." Moreover, husband's withdrawal from the courtroom means he neither entered evidence contrary to wife's assertions on this point nor cross-examined her regarding the state of the marriage. Thus, the only evidence regarding the state of the parties' marriage was wife's uncontradicted testimony.

II.

Marriage, "so far as its validity in law is concerned," is a contract. Minn. Stat. § 517.01 (2000). That marriage is a contract for determining its *validity* does *not* mean marriage is a contract in the usual sense of that term. * * *

Any doubt * * * was eliminated in *Maynard v. Hill,* 125 U.S. 190 (1888). There, a husband moved away from his wife and to the Oregon Territory. Once there, he, without the knowledge or consent of his wife, procured a divorce. Later, he died. In the resulting litigation involving his estate, the validity of the divorce was questioned. The Supreme Court stated:

> * * * Assuming that the prohibition of the federal constitution against the impairment of contracts by state legislation applies equally, as would seem to be the opinion of the supreme court of the territory, to legislation by territorial legislatures, *we are clear that marriage is not a contract within the meaning of the prohibition.* As was said by Chief Justice Marshall in the *Dartmouth College Case* * * *: "The provision of the constitution never has been understood to embrace other contracts than those which respect property or some object of value, and confer rights which may be asserted in a court of justice. It never has been understood to restrict the general right of the legislature to legislate on the subject of divorces."

Maynard, 125 U.S. at 210 (emphasis added).

* * *

The Minnesota dissolution statutes do not allow "divorce on demand," marriage is not a contract for purposes of the Contract Clauses of the United States and Minnesota Constitutions, and husband has not shown that the district court abused its discretion in denying his request for a continuance [or committed clear error in finding that the marriage was irretrievably broken]. Therefore, we affirm the district court.

Affirmed.

NOTES AND QUESTIONS

1. *Unilateral divorce.* Even where both parties seek to divorce, no-fault statutes generally require a judicial determination that the marriage is, in fact, "irretrievably broken." In *Dubose v. Dubose*, 132 So. 3d 17 (Ala. Civ. Ct. App. 2013), the court reversed the trial court's order granting divorce because the order was based only on the parties stipulation to the divorce and not on any evidence indicating that the parties were incompatible or that there had been an irretrievable breakdown of the marriage. The appellate court explained that no fault divorce law did not eliminate the traditional prohibition of "consensual divorces," and that to obtain a divorce on the ground of incompatibility, there must be proof of such incompatibility. *Id.* at 20.

As to what constitutes such proof, courts have widely considered that one partner's resolute wish to leave the marriage conclusively establishes breakdown. Should irretrievable breakdown mean something different where both spouses wish to divorce than where one spouse opposes the divorce? *Richter* upheld the trial court's finding of irretrievable breakdown partly based on the husband's failure to cross-examine his wife concerning the state of their marriage, but could any cross-examination have convinced the court that the marriage was sound? Does the *Richter* court convincingly demonstrate that the Minnesota law (taken from the current UMDA) does not provide for "divorce on demand"? On this point, two family law historians observe that, in adopting no-fault, "many reformers wanted to legitimate consensual divorce—divorce by agreement" of husband and wife, but "it was unilateral divorce, a much more radical change, that actually occurred." While the statutes, read literally, did not permit "divorce on demand," they "came to mean simply this: if either party wanted out, and for any reason, the marriage was over." Grossman & Friedman, Inside the Castle, *supra,* at 176–77.

Until 2010, couples not divorcing on fault grounds in New York had to mutually consent to a separation agreement and live separate and apart for a year before they could divorce. In 2010, after years of debate, New York finally abandoned this mutual consent requirement and added "irretrievable breakdown" as a unilateral no-fault ground. *See* Lauren Guidice, Note, *New York and Divorce: Finding Fault in a No-Fault System*, 19 J.L. & Pol'y 787 (2011). Supporters hailed the legislation for liberating couples from unhappy marriages, but critics warned that it would deprive some dependent spouses of a vital bargaining chip to encourage reconciliation or ensure fair monetary terms on divorce. Do you agree with the criticism that unilateral no-fault shifts the balance of power from the spouse who wants to stay in and preserve the marriage to the spouse who wants to end the marriage?

2. *Repair and reconciliation.* What powers do courts have under no-fault statutes to encourage reconciliation or to deny divorce? Does the state have a legitimate interest in trying to save marriages? If not, why demand that parties plead and prove irretrievable breakdown and that a court make a finding about prospects for reconciliation? If it does, then why not order reasonable efforts to repair a marriage? In *Hagerty v. Hagerty*, 281 N.W.2d 386

(Minn. 1979), mentioned in *Richter*, the court rebuffed a wife's suggestion that her marriage could be saved if the court would only order her husband to seek treatment for his alcoholism. Should the court have ordered the treatment?

Should the public interest in whether parties divorce depend on whether they have minor dependent children? Forty-six states have parent education programs. Many of these states mandate attendance as a result of state statutes; other states have county or district-wide mandates, or judicial rules or orders. Susan L. Pollet and Melissa Lombreglia, *A Nationwide Survey of Mandatory Parent Education*, 46 Fam. Ct. Rev. 375 (2008). An aim of these programs is to prevent or reduce negative child outcomes by educating parents about the harmful effects on children of parental conflict connected with the divorce process and to help to prepare parents for cooperative, post-divorce parenting. *Id.* at 376; *see also* Peter Salem et al., *Taking Stock of Parent Education in the Family Courts: Envisioning a Public Health Approach*, 51 Fam. Ct. Rev. 131 (2013). Chapter 13 will elaborate on legal issues arising in post-dissolution co-parenting and other strategies to minimize conflict.

If states are willing to require participation in educational programs as part of the divorce process, why not require treatment for the underlying causes of marital discord in order to avoid divorce? Should courts try to do more to preserve marriages when there are minor children, at least if the marriage is not high conflict or dangerous? As discussed in Section 6 below, some commentators propose that courts and legislators should do more to promote marriage repair and to help couples explore reconciliation.

3. *Withholding divorce.* In exceptional cases, courts sometimes decline to find an "irretrievable breakdown." Consider *In re Estate of Carlisle*, 653 N.W.2d 368, 368–69 (Iowa 2002):

> Francis and Dorothy Carlisle had been married for sixty-five years when, in 1998, Dorothy fell and broke her hip. She wanted to install a bathroom on the first floor of their home to accommodate her resulting disability. Francis refused because it would be too expensive to cut into the limestone walls of their home. Dorothy moved in with her daughter. On August 16, 1999, she filed a petition for legal separation and maintenance. Francis answered and counterclaimed for a decree of dissolution. Francis acknowledged that his wife "has been a wonderful lady and this action should never have happened." Nevertheless, he wanted a dissolution because he did not want Dorothy to request more property from him.

> On May 23, 2000, the district court entered a decree of separate maintenance. The court's opinion stated that, "There has *not* been a breakdown in the marital relationship to the extent that the legitimate objects of matrimony have been destroyed."

Id. Are the facts of *Carlisle* really distinguishable from those of *Richter*? What "legitimate objects of matrimony" might remain in the Carlisle marriage?

4. *Consent divorce and "nonadversarial dissolution of marriage."* Under many no-fault divorce laws (including the Pennsylvania' excerpted statute excerpted, *supra*, at 528–529), divorce is made easier where both parties consent, by shortening the required separation or waiting period. A court still must make a finding of irretrievable breakdown or irreconcilable differences.

Some states have gone even further in allowing divorce on mutual consent. Effective October 1, 2015, Connecticut added a new "action for a nonadversarial dissolution of marriage" to be commenced by "the filing of a joint petition in the judicial district in which one of the parties resides." As mentioned earlier in the chapter, the parties may obtain a divorce in thirty-five days or less, compared with the regular process, which includes at least a 90-day waiting period. State of Connecticut Judicial Branch, *Nonadversarial Law Takes Effect Oct. 1, 2015.* To use this procedure, the parties must meet twelve eligibility factors, including that "(1) the marriage has broken down irretrievably; (2) the duration of the marriage does not exceed nine years; (3) neither party to the action is pregnant; (4) no children were born to or adopted by the parties prior to, or during the marriage; (5) neither party has an interest or title in real property; (6) the total combined fair market value of all property owned by either party, less any amount owed on such property, is less than eighty thousand dollars; (7) neither party has a defined benefit pension plan;" and (11) that "a restraining order . . .between the parties is not in effect." Conn. Gen. Stat. § 46b–44a (2019).

The new Connecticut legislation further provides that both parties must provide financial affidavits with the joint petition and a certification attesting, under oath, that: (1) they agree to proceed by consent, (2) neither "is acting under duress or coercion," and (3) each is "waiving any right to a trial, alimony, spousal support or an appeal." *Id.* The judge may grant a divorce "on the papers" alone, so that the parties do not need to come to court.

What do laws like Connecticut's suggest about the state's role as a third party in every marriage and divorce? Is there any reason not to extend this new "non-adversarial divorce" process to other spouses seeking to divorce who do not meet the eligibility factors, as long as they are not in disagreement? *See Editorial: New Connecticut Divorce Law Offers Benefits to Few,* New Haven Register (Oct. 7, 2015).

5. *California summary dissolution.* California law permits some married couples with relatively few entanglements to obtain a divorce through a summary legal process. To qualify for summary dissolution, the couple must both desire a divorce, have been married no more than five years, have no children and only modest financial assets (and no real estate), waive any claim to spousal support, and agree on the disposition of community property. Couples who qualify can then file a joint petition for dissolution, which a court will grant in due course following a six-month waiting period. *See* Cal. Fam. Code §§ 2400–2406 (2019).

6. *Other constitutional attacks on no-fault divorce.* For many spouses who married at a time when divorce was available only for fault, the

introduction of no-fault divorce came as a shock and effectively stripped them of the ability to deny a divorce to a wrongdoing spouse. As in *Richter*, many spouses resisted application of no-fault laws on constitutional grounds. These efforts uniformly failed. *See, e.g., In re Marriage of Walton*, 104 Cal. Rptr. 472 (Cal. Ct. App. 1972) (rejecting due process and Contract Clause arguments); *Gluck v. Gluck*, 435 A.2d 35 (Conn. 1980) (rejecting claim of unconstitutional vagueness); *Buchholz v. Buchholz*, 248 N.W.2d 21 (Neb. 1976) (rejecting equal protection and due process arguments).

In a more recent challenge, Shawn Hall Lecuona, who opposed her husband Mark Leucona's petition for divorce on the no-fault ground of "insupportability," argued that *Obergefell v. Hodges,* 135 S. Ct. 2584 (2015) (Chapter 2) should restrict her husband's "unilateral invocation of Texas's no-fault divorce law." *Lecuona v. Lecuona*, 2018 WL 2994587 (Tex. Ct. App., June 15, 2018). She argued that *Obergefell* struck down state bans on same-sex marriage as violating the fundamental right to marry, a right inherent in "the liberty of the person." She argued that because she opposed divorce on religious grounds, Texas's law unconstitutionally infringed her protected interests. The Court of Appeals of Texas disagreed, calling it a "novel and significant expansion of *Obergefell*":

> We cannot agree that *Obergefell*, whose analysis is rooted in the Supreme Court's view of personal liberty, either directly or by implication recognizes what would effectively be an affirmative constitutional right of one spouse to compel an unwilling other spouse to remain married, in derogation of both the other spouse's liberty and state divorce laws.

Id. at *1.

PROBLEM 8-3

Ruth and Kenneth separated after ten years of marriage in March 2017 because of disputes over debts and spending. They sold the marital home, divided the proceeds, and moved into separate residences until April 2019. During that month, the parties discussed a possible reconciliation; and in May of the same year, Kenneth moved into Ruth's residence. During the next two months, Ruth and Kenneth shared the same bedroom and resumed sexual relations, shared household chores, opened a joint checking account, and had a social life as husband and wife.

The parties' attempt at reconciliation failed in July 2019. Kenneth moved out and immediately filed for divorce. In his petition, he asserted that the marriage had suffered an "irretrievable breakdown" and that the parties had lived "separate and apart" for two years, as required by the state's no-fault divorce law. Ruth contests the divorce on the grounds that their differences over money could be bridged through financial counseling and that they have not satisfied the state's separation period for no-fault divorce. What advice would you give Ruth about her prospects for resisting divorce? Would your advice be any different as a family law practitioner in Minnesota (where the wife sued for divorce in *Richter*) rather than Pennsylvania (where the Freys lived)?

6. QUESTIONING NO-FAULT DIVORCE

No-fault divorce won remarkably rapid and widespread acceptance in U.S. law after its introduction in 1969. Grossman & Friedman, Inside the Castle, *supra,* at 177 ("It was as if a dam had broken"). No-fault divorce remains controversial, however, and since its introduction, has faced a wide range of criticisms, including that it has reduced commitment within marriage, increased the divorce rate, reduced the economic security of women and children, condoned misconduct within marriage, and encouraged hasty entry into marriage by ensuring easy exit. The controversy has not faded in the five decades since its arrival. For example, in 2002, in justifying governmental efforts to strengthen marriage and reduce divorce, former Oklahoma Governor Frank Keating quipped: "It's easier to get out of a marriage contract with children than it is to get out of a Tupperware contract." *Frontline #2106: Let's Get Married* (PBS, Nov. 14, 2002); *see also* DiFonzo, Beneath the Fault Line, *supra.* In 2011, , interest in divorce reform once again seemed resurgent, when three Republican presidential candidates signed a pledge ("The Marriage Vow") supporting "extended 'second chance' or 'cooling-off' periods for those seeking a 'quickie divorce.'" Scott Keyes, *Conservatives Aren't Just Fighting Same-Sex Marriage. They're Also Trying to Stop Divorce*, Wash. Post (Apr. 14, 2014); *see* The Family Leader, The Marriage Vow: A Declaration of Dependence upon Marriage and Family (2011).

A. DEBATES ABOUT LAW, CULTURE, AND THE DIVORCE RATE

The debate over no fault divorce implicates the question of the relationship between law and culture. In the late 1990s and early 2000s, some critics of the "divorce revolution" proposed a "marriage movement" to shore up a "marriage culture." *See* The Marriage Movement: A Statement of Principles (2000). However, even participants in that movement have disagreed about the causal relationship between law and culture in terms of ways to "curb the American appetite for divorce." *See End No-Fault Divorce?,* 75 First Things 24, 27 (1997) (quoting Barbara Dafoe Whitehead).

In a classic debate about whether to end no fault divorce, Maggie Gallagher (also a founder of the National Organization for Marriage, which opposed legalizing same-sex marriage) argued for ending no-fault because: "while there are many social and economic factors conspiring to weaken our marriages, no-fault divorce laws have pushed us over the edge from being a society in which the majority of marriages succeed to one in which (according to demographers' estimates) a majority of new marriages will fail. When divorce is made quicker and nonjudgmental, more marriages fail." *Id.* at 27.

In response, Barbara Dafoe Whitehead argued that "[t]he divorce revolution was a cultural rather than legal phenomenon. It grew out of a historic transformation in ideas and practices regarding sex, marriage, and parenthood." Further, making a fault requirement the sole avenue for getting a divorce "would do more harm than good." Not only does "the fault barrier come[ ] too late in the divorcing process," but "[s]ome marriages will be preserved that probably should end, including those that involve physical violence and abuse." *Id.* 27–28. Whitehead instead wrote favorably about an emerging "marriage-saving movement" by marriage therapists and others focused on "helping couples acquire better communication and conflict-resolution skills," which would lead to "lower levels of marital dissatisfaction and breakup." *Id.* at 29–30.

As these competing views indicate, the precise cause-and-effect relationship between no-fault divorce law and the rise in the divorce rate has been hotly debated. "In almost every state, divorce rates started to rise before the legal changes occurred." Stephane Mechoulan, *Divorce Laws and the Structure of the American Family*, 35 J. Legal Stud. 143 (2006). It is difficult to "disentangle the causation process," and to sort out whether the new no-fault laws accelerated, even if they not create, the upward surge in divorce rates, or whether the new laws "merely involve[d] an upgrading of the legal texts, and adjustment to the common practice of courts and new attitudes regarding marriages." *Id.*

In considering the reasons for the initial rise in the divorce rate, some scholars conclude "it is likely that part of the explanation lies in the transition in family life and gender roles occurring throughout the 1960s and 1970s," adding that "[c]ouples marrying after the 1970s were better calibrated about how their family lie would play out and were better matched for a life together based upon modern gender roles." Betsey Stevenson and Justin Wolfers, *Trends in Marital Stability, in* Research Handbook on the Economics of Family Law 107 (Lloyd R. Cohen and Joshua D. Wright eds., 2011). Even if no-fault divorce has increased the number of divorces, does that provide a sufficient reason to curtail no-fault?

Sociologist Andrew Cherlin argues that people in the United States "partner, unpartner, and repartner faster than do people in any other Western nation" because most Americans draw on two cultural frameworks that are in tension with each other. Cherlin, The Marriage-Go-Round, *supra*, at 15. The "cultural model of marriage" maintains that (1) "marriage is the best way to live one's family life;" (2) "a marriage should be a permanent, loving relationship;" (3) "a marriage should be a sexually exclusive partnership;" and (4) "divorce should be a last resort." *Id.* at 26. By contrast, the "cultural model of individualism" emphasizes that (1) "one's primary obligation is to oneself rather than to one's partner and children"; (2) "individuals must make choices over the life course about the kinds of intimate lives they wish to lead;" (3) "a variety of living arrangements are acceptable;" and (4) "people who are personally dissatisfied with marriages and other intimate partnership are justified in ending them." *Id.* at 31.

Do you find Cherlin's analysis of culture helpful for making sense of current attitudes and patterns concerning marriage and divorce? Consider, for example, the Gallup Poll findings (discussed earlier in this Chapter) that "the national divorce rate has fallen to its lowest point in decades," even as a record percentage of adults (73%) say that divorce is "morally acceptable." *U.S. Divorce Rate Dips, supra.* How might Cherlin analyze the demographic data discussed in Section 1, supra, about different risk factors for divorce?

B. DEBATES ABOUT LEGAL REFORM OF NO-FAULT DIVORCE LAW

Over the decades, various social commentators, legal scholars, and state lawmakers have called for divorce reform, including repealing no-fault divorce. *See* Lynn D. Wardle, *Divorce Reform at the Turn of the Millennium: Certainties and Possibilities*, 33 Fam. L.Q. 783, 784 (1999) (diagnosing a "significant, widespread, and growing social movement to reform unilateral no-fault divorce laws"). Nonetheless, one comprehensive review of legislative reform since 1990 found only a "limited amount of divorce reform legislation passed," and "limited legislative momentum" for tackling such reform. Alan J. Hawkins, *A Proposal for a Feasible, First-Step, Legislative Agenda for Divorce Reform*, 26 BYU J. Pub. L. 215, 216 (2012).

Some critics of no-fault divorce have urged attention to shoring up marital commitment at the point of marriage itself as a way of reducing— or at least slowing down—divorce rates. For example, as an attempt to "lessen the problems of divorce by strengthening the institution of marriage," three states (Louisiana, Arkansas, and Arizona) offer "covenant marriage" as an option that allows prospective spouses to agree to a more restrictive set of rules for dissolution. Katherine Shaw Spaht, *Covenant Marriage Laws: A Model for Compromise, in* Marriage and Divorce in a Multicultural Context 120–21 (Joel A. Nichols, ed., 2012).

The architect of Louisiana's covenant marriage law, Katherine Shaw Spaht, explains that the term "covenant" as linked to "marriage" carries both the idea of a "special form of contract with specific formalities and greater binding force," and the religious idea of "an unbreakable and perpetual agreement between the Creator and mankind." *Id.* at 120. Covenant marriage generally contains "three unique components": (1) a requirement of mandatory premarital counseling, which "stresses the seriousness of marriage and the expectation that the couple's marriage will be lifelong"; (2) a "declaration of intent" that marriage is a life-time covenant between husband and wife and that if problems arise during the marriage, the couple will "make reasonable efforts to preserve the marriage if marital difficulties arise" and seek marital counseling; and (3) limited fault-based grounds for seeking divorce or legal separation and a longer separation period. *Id.*

In Louisiana, for example, dissolution of a covenant marriage requires proof of specific fault grounds (from a narrow list of serious offenses) or satisfaction of an extended separation period (two years or, if there are minor children, three and a half years). La. Rev. Stat. § 9:272 to 9:276 (2019); *see also* Ark. Code Ann. § 9–11–801 to 9–11–811 (2019) (fault-based grounds for divorce limited to adultery, commission of a felony or "infamous crime," or physical or sexual abuse of a spouse of child of either spouse; divorce based on legal separation requires two years, or, if there are minor children, two and a half years if there are minor children; one year if separation was granted for abuse of child of either spouse); Ariz. Rev. Stat. § 25–901 to 25–906 (2019) (listing grounds).

Professors John Witte, Jr. and Joel Nichols suggest that giving couples a choice between forms of marriage and requiring pre-marital counseling for covenant marriage may help "inaptly matched couples" discover their incompatible expectations about marriage before marrying: "If one engaged party wants a [standard] marriage and the other a covenant marriage, the disparity in prospective commitment should, for many couples, be too plain to ignore." John Witte Jr. & Joel A. Nichols, *More Than a Mere Contract: Marriage as Contract and Covenant in Law and Theology*, 5 U. St. Thomas L.J. 595, 598 (2008). Do you agree?

So far, an "exceedingly small" number of newly married couples—2% to 3%—have opted for covenant marriage in the three states where it is available. Spaht, *Covenant Marriage Laws*, *supra*, at 125; Katherine Shaw Spaht, *Covenant Marriage Seven Years Later: Its As Yet Unfulfilled Promise*, 65 La. L. Rev. 605 (2005). Periodically, legislators in other states have proposed covenant marriage laws, but no new laws have been enacted.

One study concluded that covenant marriage seems to produce stronger and happier marriages than "standard form" marriage. *See* Margaret F. Brinig & Steven L. Nock, *What Does Covenant Mean for Relationships?*, 18 Notre Dame J. L. Ethics & Pub. Pol'y 137, 159–60 (2004) (discussing unpublished study by Steven L. Nock, Laura Sanchez, Julia C. Wilson & James D. Wright, *Intimate Equity: The Early Years of Covenant and Standard Marriages*). After controlling for some of the variables that might steer some couples toward covenant marriage (such as political ideology, religious background, education, and income), the study found that couples who opted for covenant marriage reported more marital satisfaction and stability and experienced faster income growth after two years of marriage than their counterparts who opted for standard marriages. *See id.* at 158–60.

A subsequent study compared standard couples and covenant couples and found gender differences in both couples, with wives' satisfaction declining in both groups "at a more pronounced rate, compared with husbands." Alfred DeMaris et al., *Developmental Patterns in Marital Satisfactions: Another Look at Covenant Marriage,* 74 J. Marr. & Fam. 989, 1000–01 (2012). The study also found, for covenant husbands, "a significant positive effect of covenant status on marital satisfaction level," which might be due to the premarital counseling requirement, which "most likely sensitizes men to behaviors that need either to be cultivated or suppressed in order to render their marriages viable." *Id.*

Given the limited use of covenant marriage in the three states where it is available, is it likely to have any significant impact on the divorce rate? Given that covenant marriage gives couples seeking to marry another option, is there any reason for legislators to oppose it? If covenant marriage helps to produce stronger and more satisfying marital bonds than standard marriage, should state laws aggressively encourage (or even require) couples to choose covenant marriage?

Other divorce reform proposals focus particularly on preventing or slowing down divorce when couples have minor children. Family law scholars have asked whether the law should do more to keep parents together in light of social science findings that, while children whose parents' marriage had a high level of discord benefit from divorce, "in cases where the level of discord was low, children's well-being suffered when their parents divorced and these negative effects seemed to follow them into adulthood." Solangel Maldonado, *Facilitating Forgiveness and Reconciliation in "Good Enough" Marriages,* 13 Pepp. Disp. Res. L. J. 105, 106 (2013) (discussing Paul R. Amato, *Children of Divorce in the 1990s: An Update of the Amato and Keith (1991) Meta-Analysis,* 15 J. Fam. Psych. 335 (2001)).

The following excerpted report offers one recent proposal on how to reduce the divorce rate and do more to save marriages. William J. Doherty is a professor of family social science and marriage therapist, and Leah Ward Sears is the former chief justice of the Georgia Supreme Court. Some commentary on their proposal follows.

WILLIAM J. DOHERTY & LEAH WARD SEARS, SECOND CHANCES: A PROPOSAL TO REDUCE UNNECESSARY DIVORCE

(Institute for American Values, 2011).

No one advocates for keeping destructive marriages together. Divorce is a necessary safety valve in some cases. But in recent years scholars have gained a deeper understanding of the problems felt by couples who divorce, as well as the impact of divorce on children. * * *

There is a popular assumption among professionals and the public that divorce happens only after a long process of misery and conflict drives the spouses to end the marriage. * * * This scenario turns out to be inaccurate for many couples confronting divorce. [M]ost couples who divorce actually look quite similar to most couples who do not divorce. [They] report *average happiness and low levels of conflict* in their marriages in the years prior to the divorce. It is the minority of divorcing couples who, during their marriages, experienced high conflict, alienation, and sometimes abuse.

* * * Professor [Paul] Amato and sociologist Alan Booth offer this promising conclusion: "Our results suggest that divorces with the greatest potential to harm children *occur in marriages that have the greatest potential for reconciliation.*" (emphasis added).[e]

* * * More than half of U.S. divorces today appear to take place in low-conflict homes in which the best outcome for children would probably be a continuation of the marriage. * * *

For the past forty years, law and judicial policy on divorce have been crafted with the assumption that once couples file for divorce, the marriage is over and the only realistic goal is a fair, constructive divorce. Conversations with judges and divorce attorneys about the topic of marital reconciliation are often met with some version of the following: "It's not our job to be marriage counselors, and by the time people get to us they want help with getting a divorce, not with saving their marriage."

It was not always this way. In the 1960s, many family court professionals saw their first goal as helping couples reconcile if possible, and then, if this was not possible, helping them have a constructive divorce. * * * The assumption * * * was that many couples filing for divorce could be helped

---

e   *Editors' Note:* The authors cite to several studies by Paul Amato, including Alan Booth & Paul R. Amato, *Parental Predivorce Relations and Offspring Postdivorce Well-Being*, 63 J. Marr and Fam. 197 (2001); Paul R. Amato & Bryndl Holmann-Marriott, *A Comparison of High-and Low-Distress Marriages that End in Divorce*, 69 J. Marr and Fam. 621 (2007). The authors also cite to a study of marital happiness, finding that one-third of couples who "had ever reported low marital happiness later on experienced a turnaround." Jared R. Anderson, Mark J. Van Ryzin, & William J. Doherty, *Developmental Trajectories of Marital happiness in Continuously Married Individuals: A Group Modeling Approach*, 24 J. Fam. Psych. 586 (2010).

to reconcile by teams of legal and mental health professionals. Even if they were not successful, it was worth the effort by the courts.

This "reconciliation first" approach was short-lived. * * * Marital reconciliation was quietly dropped from the Association of Family and Conciliation Court's organization's mission statement as court professionals turned their full attention to "helping couples end their marriages with a greater sense of dignity and self-worth and with less trauma to themselves and their children." By the 1980s and 1990s, mediation and other forms of collaborative practice replaced marriage counseling in professionals' work with divorcing couples. No one denied the possibility that marital reconciliation could occur as a result of a good, collaborative divorce process, but restoring the marital relationship was no longer an intentional focus of divorce practice in the United States.

However, neither the early enthusiasm for reconciliation services nor the later abandonment of these services was informed by actual research on divorcing couples. *[N]o studies asked divorcing people if they would be interested in exploring marital reconciliation with professional help.*

Intrigued by this knowledge gap, an author of this report, William Doherty * * * [and] his colleagues * * * set out to identify how many parents in the divorce process believe that restoring their marriage is still possible and if they might be interested in services to help them reconcile. A sample of 2,484 divorcing parents completed surveys following their currently required parenting classes.[f] About one in four individual-parents indicated some belief (responding "yes" or "maybe") that their marriage could still be saved, and in about one in nine couples both partners did. As for interest in reconciliation services, about three in ten individual parents indicated potential interest. Among couples, about one in three had one partner interested but not the other, and in over 10 percent of couples both partners indicated some degree of interest in reconciliation services. * * * The fact that a significant minority of individuals and couples surveyed even well into the divorce process expressed interest in learning more about reconciliation suggests that the proportion of couples open to reconciliation might be even higher at the outset * * *—before the process itself has caused additional strife.

The research findings presented in this report clearly suggest that today's very high U.S. divorce rate is not only costly to taxpayers, it is not only *harmful* to children, it is also, to a degree that we are only now understanding, *preventable.*

---

[f]   *Editors' Note:* The study is William J. Doherty, Brian J. Willoughby, & Bruce Peterson, *Interest in Marital Reconciliation Among Divorcing Parents,* 49 Fam. Ct. Rev. 313 (2012).

Recommendations

[The authors detail several recommendations for "giving married couples a second chance when it comes to their marriage," including the following.]

Extend the Waiting Period for Divorce

Across America there is considerable variation in the period that states require couples to wait before they can finalize their divorce * * * ranging from no wait at all to two years. We recommend that states adopt a waiting period of at least one year from the date of filing for divorce * * *. * * * We offer [several] reasons why [states should do so].

1. *Law carries meaning about what we value as a society.* Many states have a waiting period between obtaining a marriage license and the marriage ceremony. The reasoning is that marriage is a serious decision and marrying impulsively should be discouraged. We believe that family stability and the well-being of children are high enough public values that states should require a "cooling off" period before a divorce is granted. This period should be long enough for both spouses to consider options for reconciliation and to be certain that divorce is the best way to solve their marital problems.

2. *People making a decision to divorce are often at one of the most intense emotional periods of their lives.* Those seeking to divorce may be feeling betrayed by something their spouse did. They may be in the throes of a new romantic relationship, reacting to a health or job crisis, or in the midst of depression. People in "hot states" of emotion are prone to make costly decisions based on systematic errors, particularly in the areas of life with which they do not have a lot of experience, such as deciding to divorce. Behavioral economists tell us that such people are prone to overestimate the short-term benefits of taking action and underestimate the likelihood that they will feel better in the future if they hang on. * * *

Research supports the idea that some couples rush to divorce. * * *

3. *The law moves couples more rapidly towards divorce than perhaps they had intended or faster than both spouses want.* Very short waiting periods, combined with little or no help for exiting the divorce superhighway, leaves little possibility for either spouse to consider reconciliation. In some cases, spouses who do not necessarily want a divorce (at least not yet) visit a lawyer mainly to get the other spouse's attention. [B]efore they know it they can become caught up in legal and relationship turbulence, propelled towards a divorce they may later regret.

Even if one spouse is determined not to reconcile, there are strong reasons to think that the pace of the divorce should follow the spouse who is less interested in getting the divorce. * * * [F]our out of five marriages end[] unilaterally. Such divorces begin at one spouse's insistence—most often the wife's. Pushing a reluctant spouse, often a husband, to move too quickly through a painful dissolution can increase conflict and litigation at the time of the divorce, and can exacerbate post-divorce conflicts over hot-button issues such as children and money. Anecdotally, we have heard judges say that spouses who feel forced to divorce immediately are the most difficult people to deal with in the courts, both during the divorce process and later in re-litigation.

Overall, a waiting period can allow the spouse who is considering initiating a divorce time to think it over more carefully, as well as give the other spouse time to adjust to what is happening, not feel pushed, and perhaps become a constructive part of a process he or she does not want-even if it turns out that reconciliation is not a viable option for the couple.

4.   Today, waiting periods to finalize divorce vary considerably among the states, and no other Western nation has waiting periods as short as America has.

In Western Europe, three-year waiting periods, which can be shortened by mutual consent, are common. * * *

The impact of waiting periods on divorce rates is challenging to study scientifically. In the U.S., states differ in social and economic factors associated with divorce and spouses * * * can move across state lines to seek a divorce. [W]hile the scientific case for waiting periods cannot be considered definitive, a strong defense can be made that they seem to work to diminish divorce rates.

* * *

6.   [W]aiting periods can be waived in the case of domestic violence.

Domestic violence situations present special concern that can be handled with a waiver of the divorce finalization waiting period in those cases in which there is a threat to a spouse or the children. * * * Further, children on average are at greater risk of suffering physical or sexual abuse in post-divorce families when cohabiting boyfriends and stepfathers enter their lives. Overall children on average have more to gain than to lose from a divorce finalization waiting period when it might reduce the risk of experiencing multiple family transitions and adults coming in and out of their lives that too often follow in the wake of divorce.

7.   The public generally supports making divorces involving children somewhat harder to get.

Polling consistently shows that most Americans favor more speed bumps on the road to divorce for couples with children. * * * [B]oth liberals and conservatives have expressed support for a waiting period combined with other ways to help couples contemplating divorce. * * *

Provide Education about the Reconciliation Option

When people think about how to save marriages, they often think of marriage counseling. [T]here are already thousands of therapists who do marriage counseling in every state in the nation, [so] some might ask why we propose to require something called "reconciliation education." * * * [T]here is reason to believe that the quality of marriage counseling services available in many communities is inadequate to serve as the main resource for couples at high risk for divorce. * * * [M]arriage counseling alone, as currently practiced * * *, cannot be viewed as a powerful enough resource to help at-risk couples who may wish to avoid divorce. * * *

Fortunately, we already have resources in many states that can be built upon to help couples in crisis. In recent decades, forty-six states across the U.S. have implemented some form of required parenting classes for divorcing couples with minor children. * * * The goal of these classes is to reduce conflict between divorcing parents and to teach positive co-parenting strategies to use during and after the divorce. * * *

[E]ven though parenting classes are usually required, most parents do not take them until well into their divorce proceedings. In addition, these classes currently do not offer a reconciliation module for parents who might be interested in learning more about and exploring that option.

We recommend that existing state statutes on mandatory courses for divorcing parents be modified to specify that the following content on reconciliation be included:

- Questions to help individual spouses reflect on their potential interest in reconciliation

- Research on reconciliation interests among divorcing couples

- The potential benefits of avoiding divorce for children and adults

- Resources to assist with reconciliation

- Information on when the risk of domestic violence should rule out working on reconciliation at this time

We further recommend that states require completion of a four-hour parent education course *before* either spouse files for divorce [and], before the court accepts any legal paperwork. [B]oth parties would have to take a course, either online or in a classroom, that would teach communication and conflict management skills related to co-parenting and offer information and encouragement on marital reconciliation. * * *

This proposal represents an important coming together of divorce educators and marriage advocates. Divorce educators have long been frustrated by the fact that parents often delay taking co-parenting classes until after they have made many avoidable co-parenting mistakes that have hurt themselves and their children. Our proposal appeals to divorce educators because it reaches all couples at the outset of the divorce process—before the effects of the process itself lead to poor co-parenting practices. [T]he proposal appeals to marriage advocates because it reaches couples at a time when reconciliation may be most possible.

Whether couples ultimately decide to proceed with their divorce or to reconcile, these classes will help them to learn more about possible parenting strategies. The classes will also teach parents what the research says about marriage, divorce, and children, and how to access resources in their communities if they need further support. * * *

Some might respond that our proposal is nice in theory—but how exactly are already budget-crunched states supposed to expand classes for all parents considering divorce? * * * We suggest that the key to making mandatory pre-filing education feasible is the recent availability of high-quality, evidence-based online education for parents going through divorce. * * *

NOTES AND QUESTIONS

1.   *The relationship between law and culture.* Do you think that "culture" affects the rate of divorce? Commitment to marriage? What role can or should law play to strengthen marriage? How does cultural change come about? What kind of messages do you think fault and no-fault divorce laws send? Whitehead refers to the potential of marriage education as part of a "marriage-saving movement" led by marriage therapists and other professionals In Chapter 2, we saw that some states have offered couples a shorter waiting period for a marriage license and a lowered or waived license fee it they take an approved marriage education or marriage counseling program. Do you support such legal incentives?

2.   *No-fault divorce and the interests of women.* Much of the debate over no-fault divorce centers on its impact on women. As Professor Margaret Brinig observes, "the standard view is that the increases in divorce rates brought about by no-fault were the result of husbands unilaterally absconding with disproportionate shares of marital property." Brinig, Family, Law, and Community, *supra*, at 83. However, as discussed earlier in this Chapter, women file for divorce more often than men do, despite the financial and social hardships faced after divorce and despite "the evidence that divorce harms many children." *Id.* "[M]en do somewhat better financially than their former wives, at least without taking into account tax consequences," but "[b]oth men and women seem to suffer financially from loss of economies of scale relative to couples that stay together." Margaret F. Brinig, *Empirical Work in Family Law*, 2002 U. Ill. L. Rev. 1083, 1099–1100; *see also* Margaret F. Brinig & Douglas W. Allen, *"These Boots Are Made for Walking": Why Most Divorce Filers Are Women*, 2 Am. L. & Econ. Rev. 126 (2000); Hetherington & Kelly, For Better or For Worse, *supra*, at 48–49.

Some critics have contended that unilateral no-fault divorce has aggravated the financial blow of divorce to women by eliminating any need for husbands to bargain for wives' consent. *See, e.g.*, Allen Parkman, No-Fault Divorce: What Went Wrong? 1–6, 44–46, 76–87 (1992). Other scholars have disagreed. Comparing divorces in New York (where no-fault divorce was available only by mutual consent until 2010) with other jurisdictions, Professor Marsha Garrison found no clear economic advantage for New York wives. *See* Marsha Garrison, *The Economics of Divorce: Changing Rules, Changing Results, in* Divorce Reform at the Crossroads 75, 90 (Stephen D. Sugarman & Herma Hill Kay, eds., 1990). Accordingly, she found it "unlikely that the adoption of no-fault grounds for divorce has played the dominant role in producing reduced awards to divorced wives." *Id.* at 100. In addition, given that wives initiate most divorces, creating new barriers to divorce may frustrate more women than men. Research also suggests that the adoption of no-fault divorce correlated with a decline in domestic violence and spousal murder rates. Betsey Stevenson & Justin Wolfers, *Bargaining in the Shadow of Law: Divorce Laws and Family Distress*, Quarterly J. Econ. 267 (Feb. 2006).

3. *No-fault divorce and the interests of children.* To the extent that no-fault divorce is linked to a higher incidence of divorce, some critics have charged that no-fault has harmed children. These critics appeal to child well-being as a reason to make divorce more difficult to obtain. A premise of the Doherty and Sears proposal, for example, is that many children would benefit from a lower divorce rate and that many divorces may be preventable. As Chapter 12 will discuss, the issue of the impact of divorce upon children is complicated. The evidence about the long-term impact of divorce on children is mixed because several factors influence that impact, including the level of discord of conflict their parents had prior to divorce, the level of conflict in the legal process itself, and whether parents can provide children with the relationships they need after divorce. *See* Huntington, Failure to Flourish, *supra*, at 32–34 (2014) (summarizing the research).

In one influential study, prominent divorce researcher, E. Mavis Hetherington found that, while many children have initial adjustment problems, the vast majority function normally by several years later. Hetherington & Kelly, For Better or For Worse, *supra*. Reviewing that book, political scientist William A. Galston took issue with the comparatively positive way that Hetherington framed her findings:

> [Hetherington's] work shows that 20 to 25 percent of young people from divorced families have experienced serious problems, compared to only 10 percent from non-divorced families. In a *New York Times* interview, she acknowledged that this two-fold increase in risk is larger than the association between smoking and cancer.

> In this context, the framing and presentation of her findings is nothing short of astonishing. The crucial chapter is, "Mostly Happy: Children of Divorce as Young Adults." The crucial finding is as follows: "The big headline in my data is that *80 percent of children*

from divorced homes eventually are able to adapt to their new life and become reasonably well adjusted." * * *

But what of it? A thought-experiment, if you will: Imagine a new smoking study entitled "Mostly Healthy," which emphasized that the overwhelming majority of smokers do not contract cancer and *enjoy reasonably full and healthy lives*. It would be true, statistically, but beside the point. Why does Hetherington think divorce presents a different case? * * *

William A. Galston, *What About the Children?*, Blueprint Mag. (Democratic Leadership Council, Washington, D.C.), May 21, 2002 (emphasis in original). Galston has long proposed a two-track approach to divorce, mandating " 'braking' mechanisms that require parents contemplating divorce to pause for reflection." William A. Galston, Liberal Purposes 286 (1991); William Galston, *Braking Divorce for the Sake of Children*, Am. Enterprise (May-June 1996), at 36. What role do you think evidence about child outcomes should play in shaping divorce law?

4. *Should the law do more to encourage reconciliation and prevent divorce?* As Doherty and Sears note, most states now have mandatory programs to educate divorcing parents about how to help their children cope with dissolution. Do you agree with Doherty and Sears that a useful extension of that education would be to include information on reconciliation? For example, Utah requires all parties with minor children to take a mandatory "divorce orientation course"—within 60 days after filing a petition for divorce—that is "neutral" and "unbiased" and includes "options available as alternatives to divorce" and "resources available to improve or strengthen the marriage." Utah Code Ann. § 30–3.11.4 (2019). Would you support this type of a law? If so, do you think that requiring that education *before* filing for divorce is justifiable?

The authors rely on the findings of social scientist Paul R. Amato and his colleagues that, while children whose parents had high levels of discord during marriage benefited from divorce, children of parents in "good enough" marriages, with low-levels of conflict, experienced negative effects on well-being and would do better if their parents stayed together. *See, e.g.,* Paul R. Amato, *Good Enough Marriages: Parental Discord, Divorce, and Children's Long Term Well-Being,* 9 Va. J. Soc. Pol'y & L. 71 (2001). Law professor Solangel Maldonado similarly relies on Amato's work in proposing that "the law should attempt to 'gently' discourage low-discord couples from divorcing by (1) informing them of the long-term negative effects that their divorce may have on children, and (2) providing them the resources they need to 'save' their marriage if they so desire." Maldonado, *Facilitating Forgiveness, supra,* at 109. Professor Maldonado, however, does not advocate mandatory counseling and argues that, at present, states with waiting periods fail to provide couples with appropriate resources for saving their marriage or facilitating reconciliation. *Id.* at 109–110.

Should family law move closer to no-fault's original, therapeutic ideal, which contemplated that while couples in dead marriages should be allowed to end them, family courts and the helping professions should help to preserve marriages that could be preserved? Should parents be encouraged to stay together for the sake of their children? Or, is "the time for reconciliation" likely over by the time the couple initiates divorce, so that "the real focus should be on the future relationship of the couple as co-parents"? Huntington, Failure to Flourish, *supra*, at 118.

5. *Mandatory or longer waiting periods.* One commentator on the Doherty and Sears proposal has argued that the proposed mandatory one-year waiting period when a divorcing couple has children is "a terrible idea," and leaves readers "with the impression that divorce is available on demand," while, in fact, in most states, couples seeking a no-fault divorce have to live separate and apart for at least six months and often for longer. Alexandra Harwin, *A Mandatory One-Year Waiting Period for Divorcing Parents Is a Terrible Idea,* Slate (Oct. 26, 2011). Harwin argues, that, "[a]t best, this would leave families in prolonged limbo, preventing them from getting on with their lives." And "[a]t worst, the long wait after filing could encourage the 90 percent of couples unlikely to reconcile to run into court as quickly as possible"—a result "hardly conducive to reconciliation." *Id.* For a more positive assessment, *see* Maggie Gallagher, *A Modest Proposal to Reduce Unnecessary Divorce,* Public Discourse (Oct. 27, 2011) (calling the Doherty-Sears proposal a "brilliant piece of work" and worth pursuing for the sake of children). Would children necessarily benefit from longer separation periods? Does the state have any interest in slowing down the divorce process when a couple has no minor children? For an overview of some recent legislative efforts to lengthen waiting periods, *see* Keyes, *Conservatives Aren't Just Fighting Same-Sex Marriage, supra.*

6. *Reducing conflict through a problem-solving model.* As discussed in Chapter 1, one significant shift in family law practice in the last several decades is from an adversarial model to a nonadversarial, problem-solving model. In the divorce context, one example is taking a more holistic, multidisciplinary approach so that parents undergoing the divorce process work with a team of legal, mental health, and social work professionals to help parents address the legal and psychological aspects of dissolution and to "provide families with resources to ratchet back the level of conflict." G.M. Filisko, *Paradigm Shift: Model Program Brings Holistic Solutions to Divorce,* A.B.A.J. (Feb. 2015).

PROBLEM 8-4

A state senator seeks your advice about whether to support any of four divorce-reform bills pending before the state legislature:

(1) The first bill would allow "summary nonadversarial divorce" to any couple without children who agreed on all financial and property issues relating to their dissolution. Such couples would be automatically granted a

divorce upon the filing of a joint petition and a written agreement setting out the terms of their property distribution and any support obligations.

(2) The second bill would continue to allow couples without children to obtain a no-fault divorce upon satisfaction of a six-month separation period, but would permit divorce between couples with minor, dependent children only if a court determined that divorce would be in the children's "best interests." The bill would also provide for the appointment of independent counsel to represent the children in the proceeding.

(3) The third bill would enact the Doherty-Sears "second chances" proposal excerpted above, requiring (except where domestic violence is alleged) (a) that parents with minor children complete a mandatory marriage dissolution education program with content on reconciliation before filing for divorce and (b) that a court grant a divorce only after a one-year waiting period from the time of filing.

(4) The fourth bill would adopt a version of "covenant marriage," so that couples seeking to marry would be asked to choose between a standard-form marriage (with the usual no-fault grounds for divorce) and a covenant marriage, in which divorce would be possible only upon proof of traditional fault grounds or the satisfaction of a five-year separation period.

In addition to providing your views on these proposals, the senator has invited you to suggest any reform ideas of your own. The senator also asks you how the fact that, in the majority of divorce cases brought in your state, one or both of the parties does not have an attorney and instead is self-represented (*pro se*) might bear on evaluating these proposals or your own ideas for reform.

7. LEGAL SEPARATION

The English ecclesiastical courts did not allow absolute divorce, but they did permit spouses to effect a formal legal separation through divorce *a mensa et thoro*, or divorce from bed and board. In U.S. law, this remedy, sometimes called "limited divorce," was carried over and offered as an alternative to divorce. In some states today, divorce from bed and board has been supplanted by, or exists alongside, the action for "separate maintenance." Both actions are essentially similar in that they seek to formalize marital property and support rights where a married couple intends to remain married while living separate and apart. There are, however, some significant distinctions between them.

Das v. Das (which you read earlier in the chapter) discussed Maryland's evolving approach to whether cruelty was a basis only for limited, rather than absolute, divorce. The following Maryland statutes exemplify the current similarities and distinctions between the grounds and requirements for an absolute divorce and legal separation:

Section 7–103 of the Maryland Code

Absolute divorce

(a) Grounds for absolute divorce.—The court may decree an absolute divorce on the following grounds:

    (1) adultery;

    (2) desertion, if:

        (i) the desertion has continued for 12 months without interruption before the filing of the application for divorce;

        (ii) the desertion is deliberate and final; and

        (iii) there is no reasonable expectation of reconciliation;

    (3) conviction of a felony or misdemeanor in any state or in any court of the United States if before the filing of the application for divorce the defendant has:

        (i) been sentenced to serve at least 3 years or an indeterminate sentence in a penal institution; and

        (ii) served 12 months of the sentence;

    (4) 12-month separation, when the parties have lived separate and apart without cohabitation for 12 months without interruption before the filing of the application for divorce;

    (5) insanity * * *;

    (6) cruelty of treatment toward the complaining party or a minor child of the complaining party, if there is no reasonable expectation of reconciliation; or

    (7) excessively vicious conduct toward the complaining party or a minor child of the complaining party, if there is no reasonable expectation of reconciliation; or

    (8) mutual consent, if:

        (i) the parties execute and submit to the court a written settlement agreement signed by both parties that resolves all issues relating to:

    1. alimony

    2. the distribution of property, * * *; and

    3. the care, custody, access, and support of minor or dependent children. * * *

        (iv) after reviewing the settlement agreement, the court is satisfied that any terms of the agreement relating to minor or dependent children are in the best interests of those children.

* * *

Md. Code Ann., Fam. Law § 7–103(a) (2019).

Section 7–102 of the Maryland Code

Limited divorce

(a) Grounds for limited divorce.—The court may decree a limited divorce on the following grounds:

(1) cruelty of treatment of the complaining party or of a minor child of the complaining party;

(2) excessively vicious conduct to the complaining party or to a minor child of the complaining party;

(3) desertion; or

(4) separation, if the parties are living separate and apart without cohabitation; * * *

(b) the court may decree a divorce under this section for a limited time or for an indefinite time.

(c) The court that granted a decree of limited divorce may revoke the decree at any time on the joint application of the parties.

(d) If an absolute divorce is prayed and the evidence is sufficient to entitle the parties to a limited divorce, but not to an absolute divorce, the court may decree a limited divorce.

Id. § 7–102(a)–(d).

———

A divorce from bed and board generally requires proof of a ground that would justify absolute divorce. In some states, the grounds are somewhat narrower than for absolute divorce. *See, e.g.,* N.C. Gen. Stat. § 50–7 (2019) (listing only fault grounds); Va. Code Ann. § 20–95 (2019) (requiring proof of "cruelty, reasonable apprehension of bodily hurt, willful desertion or abandonment"). In other states, the grounds are somewhat broader. *See, e.g.,* R.I. Gen. Laws § 15–5–9 (2019) (stating that divorce from bed and board "may be granted for any of the causes for which by law a divorce from the bond of marriage may be decreed, *and for other causes which may seem to require a divorce from bed and board*") (emphasis added). Once an adequate ground is shown, the court may enter a decree dividing the couple's property and ordering payment of support while the couple lives apart.

An order of separate maintenance, by contrast, is available in some states without proof of a traditional divorce ground, simply on a showing that the parties intend to live separate and apart. A separate maintenance decree can fix the parties' support obligations and specify which party shall occupy the marital home or hold other marital property, but the decree typically does not—and, in some states, cannot—actually divide legal ownership of marital property. *See Grider, supra,* 968 S.W.2d at 655. Accordingly, marital property rights may continue to accrue after entry of an order of separate maintenance, whereas these rights ordinarily do not continue in cases of divorce from bed and board. *See In re Estate of Carlisle,* 653 N.W.2d 368 (Iowa 2002) (wife qualified as a "surviving spouse" entitled to an elective share of her husband's estate, notwithstanding prior entry of decree of separate maintenance).

In recent years, statutes in some states have simplified matters by eliminating the need to draw such distinctions. These statutes authorize courts to enter a decree of "legal separation" for separating spouses on terms basically identical to those possible for no-fault divorce. *See, e.g.,* Ala. Code § 30–2–40 (2019); Alaska Stat. § 25.24.410 (2019); Ariz. Rev. Stat. § 25–313 (2019). Even here, however, state laws continue to vary on whether a divorce ground or the spouses' mutual consent is required.

Why might spouses, who otherwise have grounds for divorce, desire a legal separation instead? Legal separation may be the best option for those who still hope for reconciliation, who have religious or other objections to divorce, or who wish to retain the legal or other benefits of marriage without actually sharing life together as a married couple. In *D.L.J. v. B.R.J.,* 887 So.2d 242 (Ala. Ct. Civ. App. 2003), for example, a wife who had been diagnosed with brain cancer substituted a petition for legal separation for her earlier request for divorce so that she could maintain health insurance through her husband. Can you think of circumstances in which you would advise a client to seek a legal separation rather than a divorce?

CHAPTER 9

DIVISION OF MARITAL PROPERTY
AT DISSOLUTION

■ ■ ■

Marriage has traditionally provided a bright line for determining who is entitled to share property with a significant other if and when it comes time to break up. This Chapter discusses the disposition of marital property when a marriage dissolves. Chapter 10 will cover alimony.

The division of marital property and alimony are frequently considered together by textbooks as well as courts, but they have different rationales and raise distinctive problems. Division of marital property is premised on the principle that marriage is a partnership that must be unwound fully and fairly when it terminates. Because marriage is a collaboration, contemporary law assumes that both parties have earned their respective shares of the marital assets, a concept that will be discussed more fully below. In contrast, continuing maintenance payments respond to the need of a former spouse "who is unable to support him or herself through appropriate employment * * *." *Schenk v. Schenk*, 880 A.2d 633, 640 n.7 (Pa. Super. Ct. 2005). As you learned in Chapter 4, a minority of jurisdictions apply some of these principles to cohabitants and domestic partnerships.

Reliance on property distribution is favored because decisions regarding distribution, unlike alimony, are final and eliminate the need for continuing interaction between former spouses. Once an order governing the distribution of marital property has been entered and the property distributed, the distribution is final and may not be modified. Subsequent changes in the value of the property do not give rise to a claim for modification in any jurisdiction. J. Thomas Oldham, Divorce, Separation and the Distribution of Property § 13.03[14] (2017). Any other policy would lead to chaos and continued entanglement. The sole exception arises where a party to a divorce subsequently discovers extrinsic fraud. *Id.*

News coverage of celebrity divorces suggests that divorce battles always rage over how to split up the riches. *See Rich People Problems: Developer Allegedly Shrinks Estranged Wife's Apartment In 432 Park for Revenge*, Gothamist (Sept. 27, 2017).

In reality, however, most families facing divorce have few, if any, valuable assets. Families with a typical net worth will not normally be inclined to litigate the division of assets, nor can they easily afford to do so.

The most recent studies draw from reports by the Federal Reserve and the Census Bureau that report 2013 figures. In 2013 the median net worth of white households was $144,200. Pew Research Ctr., On Views of Race and Inequality, Blacks and Whites Are Worlds Apart (June 27, 2016).

A 2017 study of data collected by the Federal Reserve showed that the bottom one-fifth of households headed by a person aged 65–74 averaged $4,100 in net wealth, and only 22% percent owned their home—with "ownership" meaning a remaining mortgage averaging 97% of the home's current value. David Rosnick & Dean Baker, Ctr. for Econ. & Policy Research, *The Wealth of Households: An Analysis of the 2016 Survey of Consumer Finances* 24 (2017).

The most recent available data show that in 2016 an estimated 10.4% of all American homeowners owed more on their homes than their homes were worth, down from a peak of 13.1% at the end of 2015. Svenja Gudell, *Q4 2016 Negative Equity Report: Improvement Continues, But at a Much Slower Rate*, Zillow Real Estate Res. (Mar. 7, 2017).

While older couples have often accumulated more assets than their younger counterparts, most Americans do not have enough saved for retirement, even if they remain together with their long-term spouse or partner. The median level of "retirement savings in IRAs and 401(k)-type plans among workers ages 55–64 is $15,000." Schwartz Ctr. for Econ. Policy Analysis The New Sch., *Near Retirees at All Incomes Are Almost 1/3 Short of Target Retirement Savings,* The New School SCEPA (Sept. 19, 2017). In 2017, "[l]ow-, middle-, and high-income near retirees are almost one-third short of savings they need to maintain their standard of living in retirement." *Id.*

The economic picture is even bleaker for persons of color. The median net worth of Hispanic and Black households in 2013 was $14,000 and $11,200 respectively. Pew, *supra, Race and Inequality*. About one-quarter of all Hispanic and Black households had no assets other than a vehicle in 2009; only six percent of white households had no assets. *Race in America: Tracking 50 Years of Demographic Trends,* Pew Research Ctr. (Aug. 22, 2013). Another study focusing on racial disparities excluded assets like cars that could not easily be converted to cash and found an even more dire picture. Dedrick Asante-Muhammad et al., *The Road to Zero Wealth: How the Racial Divide Is Hollowing Out the Middle Class,* Prosperity Now (2017). It reported that White households in the middle quintile "own nearly eight times as much wealth ($86,100) as middle-income Black earners ($11,000) and ten times as much wealth as middle-income Latino earners ($8,600). *Id.* at 5. Projecting forward based on current data, the authors forecast an accelerating wealth gap that they expected would leave median Black households with zero wealth in 2053, while the wealth of White households continues to grow. *Id.*

Although most people—regardless of race or ethnicity—do not have substantial assets to divide upon divorce, it is essential for lawyers to understand the default rules that govern marriage and property. Knowing the rules may help many individuals avoid unpleasant surprises. In the following Sections, you will learn about the types of property regimes that various states impose during marriage and at dissolution, what counts as property, how to decide whether property belongs to the marriage or to the individual spouse, what principles govern the division of the property that is subject to distribution at divorce, the valuation and distribution of property and enforcement of court orders respecting property distribution, and how marital financial obligations may persist even after divorce and into one party's bankruptcy.

Remember that the default rules are just that: rules that apply unless the couple opts out of them by executing a private agreement. Such private agreements, including prenuptial agreements executed before marriage, post-marital agreements executed during marriage, and separation agreements executed when a marriage dissolves, will be covered in detail in Chapter 16. You will, however, see examples of such agreements in this Chapter, and should think about what individuals need to do during the marriage to render such agreements effective in the event they end up litigating the terms of their divorce.

1. PROPERTY REGIMES DURING MARRIAGE AND AT DIVORCE

State residency determines the regime that governs marital property during the marriage and property disposition at divorce. Most states apply different rules to property ownership during marriage and at dissolution.

The first part of this Section introduces the two basic property regimes that apply during marriage: title theory and community property. The next part will describe the regimes that govern division of property at divorce. Some community property regimes continue to apply community property principles at divorce. However, all states that use a title regime during marriage currently require that marital property be subjected to "equitable distribution" in the event that the marriage dissolves.

A. TITLE THEORY

The title theory, or "separate property," system emerged from British and American common law. Under this approach, the spouse who holds title to each asset retains ownership of it. As discussed in Chapter 3, under the common law theory of coverture, husbands owned all property acquired during marriage. Even after the mid-nineteenth century—when many states enacted married women's property statutes that allowed married women to retain separate property during the marriage and at divorce—courts in title states "continued to adhere to the common law rules based on title when confronted with the task of dividing marital property upon divorce. The allocation of marital property to the party who held title thereto tended to reward the spouse directly responsible for its acquisition, while overlooking the contribution of the homemaking spouse." *White v. White*, 324 S.E.2d 829, 831 (N.C. 1985).

The common law title system for divorce "at times resulted in unjust distributions, especially [in] cases of a traditional family where most property was titled in the husband * * *." *Ferguson v. Ferguson*, 639 So.2d 921, 926 (Miss. 1994). Although most states continue to apply the title system during the course of a marriage, in 1994 Mississippi became the last state to abandon the title system for dividing marital assets when a marriage dissolves. *Id.* at 926–27. All remaining title theory states limit its application to the life of the marriage. In these separate property states, the person who holds the title to property has no legal obligation to consult with his or her spouse regarding the use or disposition of the property during the marriage.

As you may recall from your Property course, three forms of title may be used to record shared ownership of real property: joint tenancy, tenancy by the entirety, and tenancy in common. In joint tenancy, each tenant is the owner of the whole estate and of an undivided part of the estate. After the death of one joint tenant, the surviving tenant or tenants continue as owners of the whole estate. As applied to spouses, the surviving spouse becomes the owner of the whole without any need for probate or estate taxes. The form of tenancy by the entirety is reserved for married couples, as it requires "unity of person." As with joint tenancy, the surviving tenant receives ownership of the entire estate. The major difference between joint tenancy and tenancy by the entirety is that a tenancy by the entirety is protected from partition except by mutual consent or operation of law. A third form of joint ownership is tenancy in common, in which each tenant has an equal right to possession, but no right of survivorship. This form of ownership is generally not recommended for married couples because a spouse could bequeath his or her share to a third party. The forms of title summarized here only apply if the spouses share ownership of real property. Remember that under the title system, primary wage earners often held title to many forms of property in their own names. As you will see later in this Chapter, the form of title may have continuing relevance at divorce.

B. COMMUNITY PROPERTY

Community property systems developed from Spanish and French law, initially imported from Mexico to California before it became a U.S. territory, and to Louisiana under the influence of French-based civil law. *See Spreckels v. Spreckels*, 48 P. 228, 230 (Cal. 1897); *Bender v. Pfaff*, 282 U.S. 127 (1930). Eight states are traditional community property states today.[a] Under the community property regime, each spouse has a present, vested one-half interest in all property acquired during the marriage unless the property falls within the definition of separate property, discussed below. At divorce, three community property states require division of all community property into equal shares.[b]

During the marriage, community property is distinguished from "separate property." Separate property usually includes property acquired by either spouse before the marriage, or during the marriage by gift, bequest or devise. Community property regimes sometimes refer to the marriage itself as a community or "partnership." *Bender*, 282 U.S. at 131. Therefore, during the marriage, neither spouse may dispose of community property without the consent of the other spouse. This was not always the case. Consistent with theories of coverture discussed in Chapter 3, husbands in California "had exclusive management and control of the spouses' community property prior to 1975" when the legislature amended the code "to give the wife joint management and control of community property * * *." *Ashodian v. Ashodian*, 157 Cal. Rptr. 555, 558 (Ct. App. 1979).

C. PROPERTY REGIMES GOVERNING DISSOLUTION

At one time, it mattered a great deal whether or not a couple lived in a community property state. Before reforms designed to accomplish equitable distribution of marital property became effective in the last decades of the twentieth century in title states, the primary wage earner (almost always the husband) normally held title to most or all of the family's property, and at divorce the title holder was considered the sole owner of the property titled in his name. This meant that any property awarded at divorce to the non-title-holding spouse was seen as a distribution from her husband's property not as a share of property she already owned in partnership with her husband. Because the wife did not have a "right" to a share of the property as a co-owner, she often received

---

[a]   *Editors' Note:* Arizona, California, Idaho, Louisiana, Nevada, New Mexico, Texas and Washington. Wisconsin is a community property state during marriage and a "kitchen sink" regime at divorce. (The term is explained on pages 568–569). *See Gerczak v. Estate of Gerczak*, 702 N.W.2d 72 (Wis. Ct. App. 2005); *Wierman v. Wierman*, 387 N.W.2d 744 (Wis. 1986).

[b]   *Editors' Note:* California, Louisiana and New Mexico. ALI, Principles of the Law of Family Dissolution: Analysis and Recommendations 22 n.31 (2002). Many community property states require an equitable rather than an equal division of property at divorce. J. Thomas Oldham, Divorce, Separation and the Distribution of Property, *supra*, § 3.03.5 (2017).

very little at divorce. As you will see later in this Chapter, contributions to the family's well-being that did not generate monetary compensation were ignored under the common law title system.

Under contemporary law, the differences between property regimes are more significant during a marriage than at dissolution. Today, the two regimes that govern property distribution at divorce—title theory and community property—lead to virtually indistinguishable results. Moreover, most community property states require equitable rather than equal division of assets at divorce.

"Equitable distribution reflects the idea that marriage is a partnership enterprise to which both spouses make valuable contributions," entitling each spouse to a fair share of the property acquired during the marriage, regardless of how it is titled. *White, supra*, 324 S.E.2d at 832. In this respect, title theory jurisdictions (also known as separate property or common law regimes) resemble community property jurisdictions. Today, most states and the District of Columbia are equitable distribution jurisdictions at divorce, but apply title theory during the course of the marriage. In other words, spouses in those states may own property in their own names during a marriage, regardless of when or how they obtained it.

Although specific provisions and nuances may vary by jurisdiction, the overall approach at divorce is similar in each separate property state. Most jurisdictions provide some guidance to trial courts through a list of relevant factors to be considered. The factors tend to illustrate "two basic but conflicting principles: Property should be allocated in proportion to the spousal contributions to its acquisition, and property should be allocated according to relative spousal need." ALI, Principles of the Law of Family Dissolution: Analysis and Recommendations § 4.09 cmt. a (2002). As in community property regimes, the division requires a court to determine whether each asset is marital or separate. Like community property states, title theory states generally characterize property acquired before marriage, or through gift or inheritance bestowed upon only one spouse, as separate.

During divorce, the process of dividing the property that the couple shares by virtue of being married generally requires three steps: (1) identifying and characterizing each asset as marital or separate; (2) valuing each asset that is marital; and (3) distributing all divisible assets equitably or equally, or, in the alternative, ordering a monetary award from one spouse to another to adjust their financial positions in accordance with the court's decision. In most jurisdictions, whether they apply common law or community property rules, courts may divide only marital property at divorce. A minority of states (discussed below) authorize courts to divide all property owned by the couple or by either member, regardless of when or how it was acquired. In those jurisdictions, courts do not need to characterize the property, they only need to identify all of the property available for distribution.

Each of the four approaches to marital and separate property presented below shares a common principle: the labor and contributions of either spouse during marriage creates a body of mutual assets. The approaches differ in their views of what constitutes a contribution, what constitutes compensation for labor, and whether and to what extent assets acquired without the contribution of either spouse are divisible if and when the marriage dissolves.

1. A Sample Title Theory Regime

Title 23, Section 3501 of the Pennsylvania Consolidated Statutes

(a) General rule—As used in this chapter, "marital property" means all property acquired by either party during the marriage and the increase in value of any nonmarital property acquired pursuant to paragraphs (1) and (3) * * *. However, marital property does not include:

(1) Property acquired prior to marriage or property acquired in exchange for property acquired prior to the marriage.

(2) Property excluded by valid agreement of the parties entered into before, during or after the marriage,

(3) Property acquired by gift, except between spouses, bequest, devise or descent or property acquired in exchange for such property.

(4) Property acquired after final separation until the date of divorce, except for property acquired in exchange for marital assets.

(5) Property which a party has sold, granted, conveyed or otherwise disposed of in good faith and for value prior to the date of final separation.

(6) Veterans' benefits exempt from attachment, levy or seizure pursuant to the act of September 2, 1958 (Public Law 85–857, 72 Stat. 1229), as amended, except for those benefits received by a veteran where the veteran has waived a portion of his military retirement pay in order to receive veterans' compensation.

(7) Property to the extent to which the property has been mortgaged or otherwise encumbered in good faith for value prior to the date of final separation.

(8) Any payment received as a result of an award or settlement for any cause of action or claim which accrued prior to the marriage or after the date of final separation regardless of when the payment was received.

* * *

(b) Presumption—All real or personal property acquired by either party during the marriage is presumed to be marital property regardless of whether title is held individually or by the parties in some form of co-ownership such as joint tenancy, tenancy in common or tenancy by the entirety. The presumption of marital property is overcome by a showing that the property was acquired by a method listed in subsection (a).

23 Pa. Stat. and Cons. Stat. Ann. § 3501 (West 2010).

2. A Sample Community Property Regime

Article 1, Section 21 of the California Constitution

Property owned before marriage or acquired during marriage by gift, will, or inheritance is separate property.

Cal. Const. art. 1, § 21.

Section 760 of the California Family Code

Except as otherwise provided by statute, all property, real or personal, wherever situated, acquired by a married person during the marriage while domiciled in this state is community property.

Cal. Fam. Code § 760 (West 2004).

Section 770 of the California Family Code

§ 770. (a)   Separate property of a married person includes all of the following:

(1) All property owned by the person before marriage.

(2) All property acquired by the person after marriage by gift, bequest, devise, or descent.

(3) The rents, issues, and profits of the property described in this section.

(b) A married person may, without the consent of the person's spouse, convey the person's separate property.

Id. § 770.

3. Hotchpot, or "Kitchen Sink," Jurisdictions

Eleven states follow some variation of the model set forth in the Uniform Marriage and Divorce Act, which permits a court to consider and "divide all property owned by either or both spouses, regardless of how or when it was acquired." Oldham, *Divorce, Separation and the Distribution of Property, supra,* § 3.03[2].ᶜ This approach is sometimes called the "all-property" method. The alternative terms "hotchpot" and "kitchen sink" capture the idea—all assets belonging to either spouse separately or to both spouses jointly are thrown into the pot and are up for grabs. The hotchpot approach eliminates legal disputes over the characterization of assets as marital or separate (what goes in the pot), but may exacerbate disputes over how to distribute the assets equitably. Proponents of the hotchpot approach argue that it makes equity easier to achieve after a long marriage in which the spouses have very different resources at their disposal. ALI, Principles of the Law of Family Dissolution: Analysis and Recommendations § 4.03 cmt. a (2002). The Connecticut statute provides a simple example.

Section 46b–81 of the Connecticut General Statutes

Assignment of property and transfer of title.

> (a)   At the time of entering a decree * * * dissolving a marriage * * *, the * * * court may assign to either spouse all or any part of the estate of the other spouse. * * *

Conn. Gen. Stat. § 46b–81 (West, Westlaw current through the 2018 Feb. Reg. Sess.).

4.   Proposal for Reform: The ALI Principles

AMERICAN LAW INSTITUTE,
PRINCIPLES OF THE LAW OF FAMILY DISSOLUTION:
ANALYSIS AND RECOMMENDATIONS
(2002).

§ 4.03   Definition of Marital and Separate Property

(1) Property acquired during marriage is marital property, except as otherwise expressly provided * * *.

(2) Inheritances, including bequests and devises, and gifts from third parties, are the separate property of the acquiring spouse even if acquired during marriage.

ᶜ   *Editors' Note:* For our purposes, the states include Connecticut, Hawaii, Indiana, Kansas, Massachusetts, Montana, New Hampshire, North Dakota, Oregon, South Dakota, Vermont and Wyoming. Oldham, Divorce, Separation and the Distribution of Property, *supra,* § 3.03 (2). However, the classification of a state as a kitchen sink jurisdiction or a separate property regime is not always clear from the statute or the common law. Oldham says: "The distinction between some "kitchen sink" and "marital property" states * * * is made somewhat fuzzy" when courts choose which property is divisible. *Id.* Indeed experts differ in their classification of a regimes. The authors of another leading treatise lists three all-property states in addition to Oldham's eleven: Nebraska, Oregon, and Utah. 3 Family Law and Practice § 37.04(3)(a) notes 6, 8, 9, LexisNexis (Arnold H. Rutkin ed., database updated Nov. 2018).

(3) Property received in exchange for separate property is separate property even if acquired during the marriage.

* * *

§ 4.06   Property Acquired in Exchange for Marital or Separate Property

* * *

(3) Property acquired on credit before marriage is presumed to be the separate property of the acquiring spouse, except that the acquired property is marital property to the extent the principal balance of the loan is reduced with payments made from marital property.

* * *

§ 4.08   Deferred or Contingent Earnings and Wage Substitutes

(1) Property earned by labor performed during marriage is marital property whether received before, during, or after the marriage. * * *

* * *

NOTES AND QUESTIONS

1.   *Compare the approaches.* In what respects does the ALI proposal resemble each of the other regimes? What does it add that is completely new? As you read the cases presented in this Chapter, consider which regime governs each case, and whether the results would have been different if the parties had appeared in a jurisdiction that used another approach to dividing marital property.

2.   *"Personal" property.* Property we commonly think of as "personal"—such as clothing and art—is marital property if purchased with marital funds, and therefore is subject to division. Personal property should not be confused with "separate" property, which belongs solely to one spouse. Gifts received from a spouse may or may not be considered separate property, depending on such factors as the source of the funds used to acquire the gift and the donor's intent. Is a valuable diamond cocktail ring a husband purchased with marital funds for the couple's anniversary the wife's "separate" property for purposes of valuing the couple's total marital assets? Or is the ring merely "personal," but marital and thus subject to division? Would it matter whether the husband told his wife at the time he gave her the ring, "I know it is a big indulgence, but we can always sell it if we hit hard times," or, alternatively, "now, no matter what the future holds for us, you will always be provided for"?

2. CHARACTERIZATION AND TREATMENT OF SEPARATE ASSETS

As the statutes presented earlier in this Chapter make clear, in both community property and common law property jurisdictions, it is crucial to determine whether each asset is marital or separate property. Characterization is a threshold issue because outside of kitchen sink jurisdictions the courts must assign all separate property to the individual to whom it belongs. The court must characterize each asset independently as separate or marital because the balance of factors may tilt differently depending on the history of the particular asset. The court then divides marital assets between the parties, either equitably or equally, depending on the jurisdiction. In equitable distribution jurisdictions, knowing the value of the separate property assigned to each spouse may affect the court's assessment of how to divide the marital assets in a fair manner. The question of what constitutes an equitable result will be discussed in greater detail later in this Chapter.

The legal regimes in most or all jurisdictions show a preference for finding that property whose characterization is unclear should be labeled as marital. In New York, a title theory jurisdiction, the highest court explained that "marital property should be 'construed broadly in order to give effect to the "economic partnership" concept of the marriage relationship.' By contrast, separate property—denoted as an exception to marital property—should be construed 'narrowly.' " *Fields v. Fields*, 931 N.E.2d 1039, 1041 (N.Y. 2010); *M.G. v. D.G.*, 2016 WL 5927268 (N.Y. Sup. Ct. Oct. 6, 2016).

An asset's initial character as either separate or marital may change over the course of a marriage. At one extreme, a spouse may expressly make a gift of her separate property to the marital union. Assets may also change character by more subtle means, as described more fully below. A spouse who seeks to show that property that appears to be separate should be treated as marital bears the burden to show that its characterization has shifted so that the separate property comes within the applicable statute's definition of marital property. *Keyt v. Keyt*, 244 S.W.3d 321, 328 (Tenn. 2007). The Supreme Court of Tennessee has described how a spouse's separate property may become marital property by either "commingling" or "transmutation":

> [s]eparate property becomes marital property [by commingling] if inextricably mingled with marital property or with the separate property of the other spouse. If the separate property continues to be segregated or can be traced into its product, commingling does not occur * * * [Transmutation] occurs when separate property is treated in such a way as to give evidence of an intention that it become marital property * * * [T]hese doctrines create[] a rebuttable presumption of a gift to the marital estate.

Langschmidt v. Langschmidt, 81 S.W.3d 741, 747 (Tenn. 2002).

The highest court in the District of Columbia reviewed cases from other jurisdictions to provide a more concrete explanation of both terms.

Araya v. Keleta, 65 A.3d 40, 55 (D.C. 2013) (discussing *Price v. Price*, 355 S.E.2d 905, 911–912 (Va. Ct. App. 1987). The court drew from a Virginia divorce case, which involved a dispute over a diamond ring. During their marriage, the couple had created the ring by combining stones from a ring the wife owned before the marriage with stones from a ring purchased with marital property. The resulting ring was marital property, the opinion explained, because: "[w]hen separate property is combined or commingled with marital property. . . the separate property loses its character as separate property and the 'new' property created [through "transmutation"] is marital." Although the commingling of the separate and marital rings could be undone, and the stones were traceable, the creation of the new ring resulted in transmutation. Rationales for finding transmutation, the D.C. court explained, include "family use," or sufficient blending to cause property that had belonged to one spouse to lose its separate character. *Id.* at 55.

A. CHARACTERIZATION OF ASSETS

The following decision, from a common law jurisdiction, demonstrates how the characterization of property can change, or be "transmuted," during a marriage. The case also illustrates that though the characterization of property may appear simple at first glance, it often turns out to be complex upon closer examination of the facts. Among the issues you will want to consider while reading the case are the potential for title to remain important at divorce, and the evidentiary issues that arise when a court tries to determine the intentions of spouses and their relatives after the fact. You will recall that the statutory regime governing division of property at dissolution is a default rule. In this case, the spouses executed a valid prenuptial agreement that listed their separate assets before they entered the marriage. The agreement specified their intention not to create marital property. As you read the case, consider how the issues that appear to have been governed by the couple's agreement might have come out in the absence of the prenuptial agreement, and think about how the court treated the agreement.

NACK V. EDWARDS NACK
Virginia Court of Appeals, 2007.
2007 WL 2592902.

HUMPHREYS, J.

Steven Douglas Nack ("husband") appeals from a final divorce decree entered August 11, 2006. Husband argues that the trial court erred by classifying: (1) a Legg Mason investment portfolio; (2) a 1987 Mercedes-Benz; and (3) a 1993 Lexus, buffalo, and assorted farm equipment as marital property.[1] * * * For the following reasons, we reverse the trial court regarding the classification of the Mercedes-Benz and the Lexus, and affirm the trial court regarding the investment portfolio, buffalo, and farm equipment. * * *

ANALYSIS

Husband contends that the trial court erred by failing to retrace the separate funds that husband contributed to the Legg Mason account, and by classifying the two automobiles, buffalo, and farm equipment as marital property.

* * *

A. Legg Mason

Husband first argues that the trial court erred in failing to retrace the separate funds he contributed to the joint Legg Mason account. * * * We disagree.

Code § 20–107.3(A)(2)(i) defines marital property as "all property titled in the names of both parties, whether as joint tenants, tenants by the entirety or otherwise, except as provided by [Code § 20–107.3(A)(3)]," which recognizes the concept of part marital and part separate, or "hybrid" property. *See Rahbaran v. Rahbaran*, 494 S.E.2d 135, 140 (1997). Code § 20–107.3(A)(3) "presupposes that separate property has not been segregated but, rather, combined with marital property." *Id.* at 141. When such assets are combined by the contribution of one to another, resulting in the loss of identity of the contributed property, the classification of the contributed property shall be transmuted to the category of property receiving the contribution. However, to the extent the contributed property is retraceable by a preponderance of the evidence and was not a gift, such contributed property shall retain its original classification.

"In order to trace the separate portion of hybrid property, a party must prove that the claimed separate portion is identifiably derived from a separate asset. Whether a transmuted asset can be traced back to a separate property interest is determined by the circumstances of each case[.]" *Asgari v. Asgari*, 533 S.E.2d 643, 648 (2000). However, "if a party 'chooses to commingle marital and non-marital funds to the point that direct tracing is impossible,' the claimed separate property loses its separate status." *Rahbaran*, 494 S.E.2d at 141 (quoting *Melrod v. Melrod*, 574 A.2d 1, 5 (Md. Ct. Spec. App. 1990)). "Even if a party can prove that some part of an asset is separate, if the court cannot determine the separate amount, the 'unknown amount contributed from the separate source

---

[1]   The farm equipment included a John Deere tractor, a Kawasaki mule farm utility vehicle, water jugs, a palpation cage, and a "buffalo squeeze chute."

transmutes by commingling and becomes marital property.' " *Id.* at 141 (quoting Brett R. Turner, *Equitable Distribution of Property* 268 (1994)).

Here, husband deposited his separate assets from White City[d] and his Fidelity account into the parties' joint checking account, thereby commingling separate and marital assets.[3] The parties continuously deposited and withdrew unspecified sums of marital funds from the account. Husband provided no account balances, deposit slips, cancelled checks, or any other documentation that would have enabled the court to retrace his separate assets.[4] Thus, in late 1997 and early 1998, when husband and wife withdrew funds from their joint checking account to acquire their joint Cornerstone account, which later became the [jointly titled] Legg Mason account, "the identity of husband's separate funds had been lost in countless unspecified transactions involving marital funds, resulting in the irreversible transmutation of separate into marital property."

* * *. Because the Legg Mason accounts were jointly titled, husband was unable to prove that his White City and Fidelity funds regained any separate identity in the Legg Mason accounts, and thus the trial court was unable to retrace these funds as husband's separate assets. The trial court, therefore, did not abuse its discretion by classifying the Legg Mason portfolio as marital property, and we affirm the trial court on this issue.

B.   The 1987 Mercedes and the 1993 Lexus

Husband next argues that the trial court erred in classifying the 1987 Mercedes as marital property, because it was his separate property prior to the marriage, remained titled in his name, and was not a gift [to his wife or to the marital estate]. He also argues that the Lexus is his separate property pursuant to the prenuptial agreement. We agree with husband that both automobiles remain his separate property.

---

[d]   *Editors' Note:* "White City" refers to money the husband received from the sale of stock in White City Electric company which he owned before the marriage and sold during the marriage.

[3]   The dissent notes that "[h]usband insists that the parties maintained separate finances and that the accounts at both First Virginia and Cornerstone were his accounts, set up as joint accounts purely for convenience." This assertion is of no moment, because wife testified to the contrary at trial, the trial court implicitly accepted wife's testimony over husband's, and our standard of review compels us to view the facts in the light most favorable to wife as the party who prevailed below. *Black v. Powers*, 628 S.E.2d 546, 549 (Va. Ct. App. 2006).

[4]   In reasoning that the Cornerstone account "included part marital, part separate and part hybrid property," the dissent notes two checks to husband from his parents totaling $10,464.73, deposited into the joint checking account on the same day as the first payment to Cornerstone, and submitted into evidence by wife. In citing these checks as evidence by which the trial court could have retraced a portion of husband's assets, the dissent ignores wife's testimony that these checks represented gifts "put into [their] joint account [and] used for anything." Thus, viewing the evidence most favorably to wife, these checks represent joint gifts made from husband's parents to both husband and wife as a couple, and therefore the checks from husband's parents to husband are not evidence from which the trial court could retrace husband's separate assets. Furthermore, wife testified that these checks were not deposited into the joint account specifically to fund the Cornerstone account.

Property acquired by either party before the marriage is presumed to remain separate property. As stated above, however, [the] Code * * * provides:

> When marital property and separate property are commingled by contributing one category of property to another, resulting in the loss of identity of the contributed property, the classification of the contributed property shall be transmuted to the category of property receiving the contribution. However, to the extent the contributed property is retraceable by a preponderance of the evidence and was not a gift, such contributed property shall retain its original classification.

1.   The Mercedes

In this case, the commissioner recommended the classification of the Mercedes as marital property. In her report, the commissioner noted that around 1999 or 2000, wife began to drive the 1987 Mercedes SL, a vehicle that had previously "sat in the garage for 10 or 12 years and 'rotted.' From that point on, [wife] was the primary driver of the Mercedes SL until the parties' separation. Joint funds were used to . . . pay for the upkeep and maintenance of the . . . Mercedes." The classification of the Mercedes as marital property solely on this basis was an abuse of discretion by the trial court, and we reverse that decision.

Here, wife made payments for upkeep and maintenance of the Mercedes, thereby contributing marital property to husband's separate property. Wife's payments therefore transmuted to separate property, the category of property receiving the contribution, and the burden then falls upon wife to retrace her payments. Under this statute, wife's payments for the upkeep of the Mercedes make the Mercedes hybrid property at best. However, the prenuptial agreement * * * provides that the Mercedes, listed in the prenuptial agreement as husband's separate property acquired prior to the marriage, remain separate property in any event, regardless of wife's financial contributions towards the vehicle's upkeep. Thus, the Mercedes remains husband's separate property, and the trial court erred in classifying the Mercedes as marital property. Accordingly, we reverse the trial court's classification of the Mercedes.

2.   The Lexus

Husband next argues that the Lexus is titled in his name and, thus, remains his separate property under the agreement.

"The owner of an automobile is the party who has legal title to it." *McDuffie v. Commonwealth of Virginia*, 638 S.E.2d 139, 141 (2006); *see also* Code § 46.2–100. * * *

Husband had sole legal title to the Lexus. Husband is thus the vehicle's owner, and as a result, the Lexus is his separate property.

Pursuant to the prenuptial agreement, wife forfeited any interest she may have had in the Lexus by virtue of her financial contributions towards the vehicle. The Lexus remains husband's separate property, and the trial court abused its discretion in classifying it as marital property. Thus, we reverse the judgment of the trial court in this regard as well.

C.   The Buffalo and Farm Equipment

Husband's final contention on appeal is that the trial court erred in classifying the buffalo and assorted farm equipment as marital, because the prenuptial agreement prohibited the creation of marital property. We affirm the trial court's classification of the buffalo and farm equipment as marital property.

"Property acquired during the marriage is presumptively marital, unless shown to be separate property." *Robinson v. Robinson*, 621 S.E.2d 147, 152 (Va. Ct. App. 2005); Code § 20–107.3(A)(2)(iii). Husband concedes that the parties used their joint checking account to purchase all of these items during the marriage. However, as noted above, husband argues that the parties' joint First Virginia checking account was only for convenience and that the parties intended to keep their money separate. Thus, husband reasons that the joint checking account was his "de facto" separate account. Accordingly, husband concludes that the buffalo and farm equipment were all purchased from separate funds and, therefore, remain his separate property under the relinquishment of claims section of the prenuptial agreement. However, the only evidence husband presented that the First Virginia account was, in fact, intended to be his separate property was his own testimony. As stated above, wife disputed the testimony, and the chancellor implicitly rejected husband's testimony. In fact, wife testified that she deposited a portion of her paycheck into the First Virginia account, and offered into evidence several checks from husband's parents made to her as gifts of their estate that were deposited into the account.

Viewing the evidence in the light most favorable to wife, we reject husband's assertion that the First Virginia account was comprised solely of husband's separate property. Because husband and wife purchased the farm equipment and buffalo with marital property, and because husband did not meet his burden of retracing his separate funds from these purchases, we affirm the trial court's classification of this property as marital.

* * *

CONCLUSION

For the reasons stated therein, we affirm the trial court's classification of the Legg Mason account, buffalo, and farm equipment as marital property, and reverse the trial court's classification of the Mercedes and

Lexus as marital property. * * * We remand the case for further proceedings consistent with this opinion.

Affirmed in part, reversed in part, and remanded.

* * *

HALEY, J., concurring, in part, and dissenting, in part.

I respectfully dissent only as to the majority's conclusion regarding the Legg Mason account.

The parties entered into a prenuptial agreement on September 4, 1992. Attached to that agreement was a schedule of their respective separate property. Husband's separate property included stock in White City Electric Company (White City Electric) and an account at Fidelity Investments (Fidelity). The majority concludes that husband failed to trace this separate property into Legg Mason. I disagree.

The Legg Mason account at issue was funded in February 1999, by transfer from husband and wife's joint investment account with Cornerstone Capital Management (Cornerstone). The source of funds in the Cornerstone account, therefore, is critical to our evaluation of this cause. In 1997, husband received a distribution in the amount of $273,146 for his ownership of White City Electric stock, listed as husband's separate property in the prenuptial agreement. Husband deposited the White City Electric distribution in a joint checking account at First Virginia Bank. In addition to his salary and other income, the First Virginia Bank also included money received from husband's Fidelity account (listed as his separate property in the prenuptial agreement) and money given by husband's parents to both parties as tax-free gifts from their estate.[8]

On September 7, 1997, husband and wife * * * open[ed] a joint account [at Cornerstone], for the purpose of funding their retirement 10 to 15 years later. To finance the Cornerstone account, husband and wife wrote three checks. First, * * * wife wrote a check to Cornerstone in the amount of $20,000, drawn on the parties' joint checking account at First Virginia.[9]

---

[8] Both husband and his father argue that the gifts were intended to be for husband. Nevertheless, husband's parents wrote several checks to wife for the purpose of passing their estate tax-free to the parties. * * * [Editors' Note: Each individual is allowed to make an unlimited number of annual gifts without incurring tax consequences. People who anticipate that their estates will be subject to taxation after they die often use this provision of the Internal Revenue Code to transfer assets to their children while they are alive. The Code, however, limits the amount of each annual tax-free gift to a particular individual. In 2019 the limit is set at $15,000 for each gift. The wealthy can double the amount of the annual transfer by writing checks to their children and to the spouses of their children. The intent of the donor in transferring funds to those spouses commonly becomes an issue at divorce.]

[9] Wife offered evidence, in the form of a check register, to show that the parties deposited $20,038.73 into their First Virginia account to cover the first check written to Cornerstone on September 26, 1997. The checks deposited include: 1) $9,500 to husband from his mother; 2) $9,500 to wife from husband's parents; 3) $73 to husband and wife from the Commonwealth of Virginia Department of Taxation; and, 4) $964.73 to husband from his parents.

[Later] wife wrote a second check from that account in the amount of $77,500. Shortly thereafter, husband wrote a check to Cornerstone from the same First Virginia account in the amount of $155,000.

* * *. Because the Legg Mason account was financed with both separate and marital assets, the statutory guidelines for classification of commingled property necessarily apply. Code § 20–107.3(A) provides, in pertinent part:

(3) The court shall classify property as part marital property and part separate property as follows:

* * *

(d) When marital property and separate property are commingled by contributing one category of property to another, resulting in the loss of identity of the contributed property, the classification of the contributed property shall be transmuted to the category of property receiving the contribution. However, to the extent the contributed property is retraceable by a preponderance of the evidence and was not a gift, such contributed property shall retain its original classification.

(e) When marital property and separate property are commingled into newly acquired property resulting in the loss of identity of the contributing properties, the commingled property shall be deemed transmuted to marital property. However, to the extent the contributed property is retraceable by a preponderance of the evidence and was not a gift, the contributed property shall retain its original classification.

[H]usband may retain his separate property if he can show the property "is retraceable by a preponderance of the evidence and was not a gift" [to his spouse or to the marital estate].* * *.

In *Rahbaran v. Rahbaran*, 494 S.E.2d 135, 141 (1997), this Court held:

In order to trace the separate portion of hybrid property, a party must prove that the claimed separate portion is identifiably derived from a separate asset. This process involves two steps: a party must (1) establish the identity of a portion of hybrid property and (2) directly trace that portion to a separate asset.

"When a party satisfies this test, and by a preponderance of the evidence traces his or her separate contributions to commingled property, the code states that the contributed separate property *shall* retain its original classification." Husband can prevail, therefore, by sufficiently tracing the source of the Legg Mason funds to his separate property.

The Legg Mason account was initiated by a transfer of funds from the parties' joint account at Cornerstone. Therefore, we must look to the source of the Cornerstone funds to determine whether husband's separate property financed the Legg Mason account.

[Judge Haley then provides a detailed analysis of how the White City funds and funds from the husband's Fidelity account made their way to the Cornerstone account, and then to Legg Mason, to show that the funds are traceable to the husband's separate property. The dissent notes that the wife corroborated this history of how the funds moved from one account to another. The dissent continues:]

* * * In the parties' prenuptial agreement, the Fidelity account was listed as husband's separate property. However, * * * husband testified that, since the parties were married, "roughly $20,000" of wife's money (gifts received from husband's parents) had been deposited into the Fidelity account.

[O]n the same day that wife wrote a $20,000 check to Cornerstone, a deposit was made to the parties' joint account at First Virginia in the amount of $20,038.73, ostensibly to cover the check to Cornerstone. That deposit included a check from husband's parents to wife for $9,500. * * *

The evidence overwhelmingly suggests, therefore, that the Cornerstone account included part marital, part separate, and part hybrid property. * * * [T]he total equity contributed to the Cornerstone account by the parties equaled $252,500. Of this amount, however, husband withdrew $55,000 to purchase an annuity in his name. [The majority held that the annuity retained its separate character]. Therefore, the total contributed equity that was later transferred to the Legg Mason account equaled the difference, $197,500. At least a portion of that balance necessarily came from husband's separate property.

* * *

* * * I would hold that husband traced those contributions of separate property into Legg Mason, that Legg Mason was part wife's separate property, part husband's separate property, and part marital property, and thus remand to the trial court to apportion the same. * * *

NOTES AND QUESTIONS

1. *Impact of mischaracterization.* If a court mischaracterizes marital property as separate or vice versa, and the mischaracterized property has more than de minimus impact on distribution, the mistake is a reversible abuse of discretion because it prevents a "just" division of the marital assets. *Graves v. Tomlinson*, 329 S.W.3d 128, 153 (Tex. App. 2010).

2. *The level of proof required.* After one party has shown evidence of transmutation or commingling, the spouse who argues that marital property is really separate property bears the burden of proof to provide evidence demonstrating an intent to keep the property separate, or evidence tracing the

contested property back to separate property. The evidentiary standard varies depending on the jurisdiction. Texas, for example, requires clear and convincing evidence to "overcome the community property presumption." *Graves, supra*, 329 S.W.3d at 140 n.1. In most jurisdictions adding a spouse's name to the title to separate property creates a strong presumption that the spouses own the property together. In Arkansas, for example, adding a spouse's name to the title to separate property creates a strong presumption that the spouses own the property together, which "can be overcome only by clear and convincing evidence that a spouse did not intend a gift." *Adams v. Adams*, 432 S.W.3d 49, 59 (Ark. Ct. App. 2014).

3. *The date of acquisition.* In *Isbell v. Willoughby*, 2005 WL 1744468 (Cal. Ct. App. July 26, 2005), the wife appealed the trial court's holding that the couple's beagle was the husband's separate "property." The court analyzed the problem by asking when the beagle was acquired. The husband had purchased the beagle in May 1994, shortly before the couple moved in together and more than a year before they married. The beagle was, and remained, separate property, even though the parties shared the dog during the marriage, and the husband had left the dog in the wife's care after executing the separation agreement while he was away completing job training. (In *Isbell* the beagle is treated like any other property. In Chapter 12 you will read about recent developments in conflicts over who gets to keep an animal companion).

To what extent did the timing of the acquisition of the Legg Mason account, the buffalo and the farm equipment influence the *Nack* court's characterization of these properties as marital? What other factors did the court weigh in each instance? Was the majority correct in finding the creation of marital property notwithstanding the apparent intent of the prenuptial agreement, when neither party challenged its validity or enforceability? What policy considerations may have been in play?

4. *Tracing.* As *Nack* demonstrates, when a divorcing party claims that commingled property remains separate, one crucial inquiry is whether the separate property is traceable. "The commingling of separate property with other property of any type does not destroy the identity of the property as separate property, except when the separate property is not traceable." Ohio Rev. Code Ann. § 3105.171(A)(6)(b) (Westlaw 2011). "When non-marital property is exchanged for property acquired following the marriage, the party claiming some non-marital component must 'trace' the non-marital asset onto the disputed asset. Tracing involves the process of tracking property's ownership * * * from the time of its origins to the present." *Epperson v. Epperson*, 2011 WL 918549, at *5 (Ky. Ct. App. Mar. 18, 2011). The "mere commingling of funds does not automatically make them marital" if they are not "so commingled as to be untraceable." *Myers v. Myers*, 705 S.E.2d 86, 92 (S.C. Ct. App. 2011).

It is often possible to trace even liquid assets, such as cash, back to separate property. Do you think that the majority or the dissent in *Nack* was more convincing in its treatment of the Legg Mason account? Why?

In some jurisdictions, such as Florida, however, courts reject efforts to trace the source of commingled funds. *Dravis v. Dravis*, 170 So.3d 849, 852 (Fla. Dist. Ct. App. 2015), *applying Pfrengle v. Pfrengle*, 976 So.2d 1134, 1136 (Fla. Dist. Ct. App. 2008) ("Money is fungible, and once commingled it loses its separate character" as do all funds in the commingled account).

The length of time the assets are commingled may matter. In *In re Marriage of Wojcik*, 838 N.E.2d 282 (Ill. App. Ct. 2005), each spouse argued that a means of transport was separate property. Paul Wojcik argued that his motorcycle, purchased with funds inherited from his father after the funds had been deposited in the parties' joint checking account for several months, was his separate property. His wife Karen, in turn, argued that a Mercury Sable she purchased with money her brother had given her as a gift (after she deposited the funds in the couple's checking account for one day) was her separate property. The court distinguished the two sets of transactions, holding that Karen's car was her separate property, but that Paul's motorcycle was a marital asset subject to distribution. In dividing up the marital property, however, the court distributed the motorcycle to Paul.

5. *Does title still matter?* The *Nack* court states that the title to the Lexus is dispositive—showing that the car was the husband's separate property. Similarly, the court recognized the annuity titled in the husband's name as his separate property because it was purchased with traceable funds. Just a year earlier, however, the same court had found the lack of donative intent overcame joint title in property purchased with separate funds. *Lesesne v. Zablocki*, 2007 WL 49651 (Va. Ct. App. Jan. 9, 2007). In Mississippi, the form of title does not create any presumption that property is either marital or separate. *Rhodes v. Rhodes*, 52 So.3d 430, 437 (Miss. Ct. App. 2011). Other jurisdictions have attempted to bolster predictability by using "a more bright-line approach that classified real property as marital if it were held in joint ownership during the marriage," ignoring intent and motivation. *Hedges v. Pitcher*, 942 A.2d 1217, 1221 (Me. 2008).

6. *What constitutes a gift?* The husband in *Nack* denied that he intended to make a gift of any of his property to the marital estate. In most jurisdictions, the doctrines of commingling and transmutation share the underlying rationale that merging separate property into joint property creates a presumption of donative intent. The fact that property can be traced back to separate property does not prevent its re-characterization where donative intent or retitling renders it divisible. *Steinmann v. Steinmann*, 749 N.W.2d 145 (Wis. 2008). "Donative intent is presumed where property is transferred, or transmuted, from non-divisible property to joint tenancy subject to division." *Id.* at 155. Similarly, in *Kruse v. Kruse*, 242 P.3d 1011 (Wyo. 2010), the court found that a husband negated the prenuptial agreement that listed the home as his separate property but he transmuted the home into a marital asset subject to division in the divorce proceedings when he changed the title from the marital home he had owned before the marriage to joint ownership.

Nack also involves an undeveloped dispute over whether the gifts the wife received from her in-laws were her separate property. Donative intent has three elements: "(1) the intention on the part of the donor to make the gift; (2) delivery or transfer of the gift; and (3) acceptance of the gift by the donee." *Sfreddo v. Sfreddo*, 720 S.E.2d 145, 150 (Va. Ct. App. 2012). Courts may consider whether the donor intended one spouse "to be the sole recipient" or intended the gift or inheritance to be shared by the spouses. *See, e.g., In re Marriage of McDermott*, 827 N.W.2d 671, 679 (Iowa 2013). How did the *Nack* court treat the checks the wife received from her in-laws? In-laws may be able to protect gifts intended for their children from their children's spouses by executing clear documents indicating intent, accompanied by acknowledgements and or quitclaims executed by those spouses—but only if the spouses sign voluntarily after full disclosure of the character and value of the property. *In the Matter of Bolster*, 146 Wash. App. 1042 (Ct. App. 2008).

7.   *How to avoid commingling.* Before her marriage, Jean Johnson found land she wanted to purchase, but she did not close the deal until a month after her wedding. The mortgage, note, and title on the property were all in her birth name as were her signatures on those documents. Jean made the down payment with a check from her mother's mutual funds, and made the monthly mortgage payments either from joint accounts she shared with her son from an earlier marriage or with her mother, or from proceeds from the sale of her mother's house. Finally, Jean paid the taxes on the property from a separate account she maintained in her own name. The court rebuffed the husband's claim that the property was marital because it was acquired during the marriage. *Johnson v. Johnson*, 979 So.2d 350 (Fla. Dist. Ct. App. 2008). *See also Maher v. Maher*, 2016 WL 4536283 (Tex. App. Aug. 30, 2016) (wife established that gifts from her parents were separate property by producing evidence of the receipt of the funds and the separate accounts into which she deposited them). In contrast, in *Patel v. Patel* separate property was transmuted when husband "conducted hundreds of inter-account transactions" among accounts in his name and joint accounts with his wife, his father and his daughter. *Patel v. Patel*, 2006 WL 2594179 (Va. Ct. App. Sept. 12, 2006).

8.   *Contributions and reimbursement.* As the rule cited in *Nack* indicates, transmutation can work in either direction—from separate to marital or marital to separate. In *Nack*, the majority notes that the wife contributed marital property to the upkeep and maintenance of the husband's Mercedes, thus transmuting marital property to separate property, or "at best" hybrid property, that is, part separate and part marital. What would the characterization of the Mercedes and the Lexus have been in the absence of the prenuptial agreement?

Where the spouse who contributed property to a marital acquisition can document the contribution, he or she may be entitled to reimbursement. For example, if one spouse contributes separate funds to the down payment for a house, and can trace those funds, then reimbursement is appropriate. *Noble v. Noble*, 911 N.Y.S.2d 252 (App. Div. 2010) (affirming reimbursement of a

$200,000 down payment for the family home that wife received from her mother although the funds were deposited in a joint account for six weeks).

Contribution may also take the form of uncompensated labor, for example, either improving the value of a tangible asset or contributing uncompensated labor to the other spouse's business or profession, as when a doctor's wife acts as his office manager or bookkeeper. Contributions of homemakers will be discussed below.

9.   *Premarital agreements.* A court may use a premarital agreement to trace the parties' assets and determine whether they are marital or separate. In *Charlson v. Charlson*, 892 N.W. 2d 903 (S.D. 2017), the court did just that. Angela, the wife, wanted to protect her assets before marrying Donald. In the PreMarital Agreement ("PMA"), Angela listed three Taco John's restaurants, a home, an investment account, and two vehicles. Donald listed "0 assets." Eventually, the parties filed for divorce. When Donald argued that Angela's assets were marital property, the court rejected his argument, because "Donald 'isolated[d] one sentence in Paragraph 7 of the PMA to support his claim' and ignored the contract language that comingling of separate property shall not change separate property to marital property." *Id.* at *3. The South Dakota Supreme Court affirmed, stating that "the terms of the PMA specifically speak to the parties' intent to protect separate property regardless of any act by either spouse." *Id.* at *6. Furthermore, the court held that "[t]he PMA accounts for commingling and the circuit court did not err when it interpreted the PMA to allow for tracing." *Id.* at *7.

10.   *The family home.* Disagreements sometimes center on the characterization of the family home, especially where one party acquired the home before marriage but marital funds and labor subsequently contributed to the mortgage and upkeep. Special rules may govern the treatment of the marital home. Statutes and common law often create a rebuttable presumption that a marital residence purchased after the marriage is marital property. *See, e.g., Fields v. Fields*, 931 N.E.2d 1039, 1043 (N.Y. 2010) (marital residence); *Rhodes v. Rhodes*, 52 So.3d 430 (Miss. Ct. App. 2011) (discussing the "family use" doctrine for homes as well as furnishings).

Where the divorcing couple has minor children, courts often try to award the family home to the parent who receives physical custody where it is economically feasible to do so regardless of whether the marital home was characterized as marital or separate property. The current doctrine urges parents and courts to avoid abrupt changes to the child's environment. Sandra Morgan Little, 1 Child Custody and Visitation Law and Practice § 10.09, LexisNexis (database updated Oct. 2018). This was not always the case. In her pivotal work on the impoverishment of women and children following divorce, Lenore Weitzman argued that California's community property regime often meant that the home had to be sold in order to divide the marital assets; sale of the marital home forced custodial mothers and their children to move to smaller residences in less desirable neighborhoods that were in different school districts. These dislocations exacerbated the child's sense of loss following divorce. Lenore J. Weitzman, The Divorce Revolution: The Unexpected Social and Economic Consequences for Women and Children in America 31, 369 (1985).

The law in Maryland exemplifies the contemporary approach. The preamble to the 1978 Maryland marital property statute instructs courts to pay *"particular and favorable attention"* to the needs of minor children when adjusting the property interests of their parents in a dissolution proceeding. *Maness v. Sawyer*, 950 A.2d 830, 838 (Md. Ct. Spec. App. 2008). According to the court, the legislature further instructed the courts to award the family home to the parent who receives primary residential custody of the children so that the children may " 'live in an environment and community which is familiar to them.' " *Id.* For that reason, the court may even specify that when it is time for the custodial parent to move out of the family home, the move must be delayed until the after the end of the school year. *Id.* at 835. The Maryland court notes that this approach is not only what the law requires, it is "the right thing to do." *Id.* While the law has been modified since 1978, "the best interests of any child" remains the first factor for a court to consider when awarding the family home in a divorce, regardless of how the home is titled. MD. Code Ann., Fam. Law § 8–208 (LexisNexis 2012). *See also Coristine v. Coristine*, 53 So. 3d 1204 (Fla. Dist. Ct. App. 2011) ("As a general rule, a trial court should award the primary residential parent exclusive use and possession of the marital residence until the youngest child reaches majority * * *").

Creative arrangements allowing for delay in the sale of the family home until a triggering event, such as the year the youngest child enters or graduates from college, are common. The goal of preserving the child's residence generally favors custodial parents (not necessarily the mother) receiving the family home. *Schmidt v. Schmidt*, 660 N.W.2d 196 (N.D. 2003) (affirming award of custody to the father, where the family lived on a farm that had been in his family for generations, near extended family with whom the children had a close bond).

B. APPRECIATION OF SEPARATE PROPERTY DURING THE MARRIAGE

Most states distinguish between ownership of separate property and ownership of any appreciation in the value of the separate property during the marriage.

This issue is considered in the next decision, involving a stockyard in which the husband and his brother were partners before and during the marriage.

MIDDENDORF V. MIDDENDORF

Supreme Court of Ohio, 1998.
696 N.E.2d 575.

LUNDBERG STRATTON, JUSTICE.

In this case, we examine the legal standards for determining when appreciation in separate property becomes marital property for purposes of the division of property in a domestic relations case under R.C. § 3105.171. Max asserts that in order for a court to determine that an increase in separate property is marital property, the court must find that *both* spouses have expended significant marital funds or labor directly contributing to the increase or that the non-owning spouse must contribute substantial work to improvement and maintenance of the separate property. We disagree.

* * * R.C. 3105.171(A)(3)(a), as amended, states:

" 'Marital property' means * * * all of the following:" * * *

"(iii) * * * all income and appreciation on separate property, due to the labor, monetary, or in-kind contribution of *either or both of the spouses* that occurred during the marriage." 144 Ohio Laws, Part I, 1754–1755 (emphasis added).

R.C. 3105.171(A)(6)(a) states:

" 'Separate property' means all real and personal property and any interest in real or personal property that is found by the court to be any of the following:

* * *

"(iii) Passive income and appreciation acquired from separate property by one spouse during the marriage."

Finally, R.C. 3105.171(A)(4) states:

" 'Passive income' means income acquired other than as a result of the labor, monetary, or in-kind contribution of either spouse."

* * *

The plain language of R.C. 3105.171(A)(3)(a)(iii) unambiguously mandates that when *either* spouse makes a labor, money, or in-kind contribution that *causes* an increase in the value of separate property, that increase in value is deemed marital property.

* * * Accordingly, the appellate court did not err in affirming the trial court's interpretation of R.C. 3105.171, that an increase in the value of separate property due to *either* spouse's efforts is marital property.

We must now determine if there was sufficient evidence to support the trial court's determination that there was an increase in the value of the stockyard during Max and Pat's marriage and that the increase was *due to* the labor, money, or in-kind contributions made by Max. If the evidence indicates that the appreciation of the separate property is *not due* to the input of Max's (or Pat's) labor, money, or in-kind contributions, the increase in the value of the stockyard is passive appreciation and remains separate property.

A trial court has broad discretion in making divisions of property in domestic cases. A trial court's decision will be upheld absent an abuse of discretion. "Abuse of discretion" is more than an error of law or judgment; it implies that the court acted in an unreasonable, arbitrary, or unconscionable fashion. If there is some competent, credible evidence to support the trial court's decision, there is no abuse of discretion. Therefore, if there is some competent, credible evidence that there was an increase in the value of the stockyard during the marriage and that the increase in the valuation was due to labor, money, or in-kind contributions of either Max or Pat, or both, the increase in valuation is classified as marital property and subject to division.

On remand from the court of appeals, the magistrate hired Philip Brandt as an independent expert to value the stockyard. Brandt testified that the value of the stockyard when the Middendorfs were married was $201,389 and the value in December 1992, the stipulated date for purposes of determining value, was $309,930. Thus, the increase was $108,541. Both the magistrate and the court rejected the defense expert's testimony and found the court-appointed expert more credible. This testimony provided credible evidence of an increase in the value of the stockyard during the Middendorfs' marriage.

The second issue upon which we must determine if credible evidence has been submitted is whether this increase in value of the stockyard was *due to* labor, monetary, or in-kind contribution by Max.

The stockyard business primarily involves buying hogs from farmers and then reselling them to the slaughterhouse. As a sideline, the stockyard would contract with farmers to feed the hogs until the hogs reached a marketable size, whereupon they would be sold to a meatpacking company. * * *

Max argues that there is no evidence that the increase in the stockyard's value was due to his funds or labor. Max asserts that the increase was due solely to passive appreciation from "market changes." However, Max's position fails to take into account all of the other factors contributing to the increase.

Passive forces such as market conditions may influence the profitability of a business. However, it is the employees and their labor input that make a company productive. In today's business environment, executives and managers figure heavily in the success or failure of a company, and in the attendant risks (*e.g.*, termination, demotion) and rewards (*e.g.*, bonuses, stock options) that go with the respective position. These individuals are the persons responsible for making pivotal decisions that result in the success or failure of the company. There is no reason that these factors should not likewise be relevant in determining a spouse's input into the success of a business.

[M]onitoring market prices in order to make timely purchases and sales, deciding the numbers of hogs purchased, and deciding whether to contract with farmers to care for hogs are a few of the calculated decisions made by the stockyard management that also affect profitability. Thus, no matter how high hog prices went, the business would not operate, let alone increase in value, without the necessary ingredients of labor and leadership from the owners and management. Making these calculated decisions was part of Max's responsibilities as a livestock buyer and co-owner of the stockyard. Max testified that he spent long hours working there * * *.

* * * The trial court found that "the increase in value of Middendorf Stockyard Company was the direct result of the pivotal role which [Max] played in the management of the company during the course of the marriage." The appeals court found that [ ] Max "played a vital role in the management of the Stockyards. * * *." * * *

Although we note that Pat contributed substantial efforts to the family relationship that freed Max of the responsibilities of the home and children and enabled him to devote more time to the business, we need not reach the issue of the value of her contributions. Because Max's efforts contributed to the appreciation of the Middendorf Stockyards, the requirements of R.C. 3105.171(A)(3)(a)(iii) are met, as the statute requires the contribution of only one spouse. Thus, we find some competent, credible evidence that Max's interest in the stockyard increased in value by $108,541, during Max and Pat's marriage, due to Max's labor. Therefore, the trial court did not abuse its discretion in finding that the $108,541 appreciation of the stockyard was a marital asset to be divided between Max and Pat. Accordingly, we affirm the judgment of the court of appeals.

NOTES AND QUESTIONS

1. *More on* Middendorf. The Middendorfs married in 1986 and divorced in 1993. During the marriage, Max's three children from a prior marriage lived in the couple's home. No children were born to the marriage. Before the marriage, Pat worked as an interior designer. She gave decorating advice on the improvements to the marital residence, which had been Max's home prior to the marriage. Because her advice was professional in nature, Pat received a share of the appreciation on the marital residence. The house was located on,

and adjacent to, farmland that came from Max's family. In an earlier proceeding, an appellate court reversed the award of a portion of the appreciation of the land to the wife, holding that the crop land appreciated over time without any contribution from either party. *Middendorf v. Middendorf*, 1996 WL 740968 (Ohio Ct. App. Dec. 17, 1996).

2.   *How do other states treat the appreciation in value of a separate asset?* Many states in addition to Ohio treat appreciation in the value of a separate asset during a marriage as nonmarital unless either spouse puts resources or effort into the appreciation. *E.g., Henton v. Henton*, 2014 WL 5470187, at *4– 5 (Ky. Ct. App. Oct. 3, 2014). In other jurisdictions, at one extreme the California code provides that all income and profit from separate property remains separate. Cal. Fam. Code § 770(a)(3) (2004). Other states, however, treat the appreciation of a separate asset as marital, regardless of whether either of the spouses contributed to the appreciation. *See, e.g.*, Or. Rev. Stat. Ann. § 107.105(1)(f) West 2016); 23 Pa. Stat. and Cons. Stat. Ann. § 3501(a)(1) (West 2010).

3.   *Brokerage accounts.* In *David v. David*, 767 S.E.2d 241 (Va. Ct. App. 2015), the husband had the burden of proving that an increase in the value of his brokerage account was attributable to something other than his personal efforts to maximize the value. The wife testified that the husband devoted significant time researching emerging companies and stocks, while the husband testified that he seldom made trades on the account and he invested for the long term. During the marriage, the value of the account increased from $234,783 to $551,521. The wife argued that the increase in the value of the account be considered marital property because of the husband's efforts. The court agreed that the increase of $316,521 was marital property, and awarded the wife half.

4.   *When does marriage end for purposes of property distribution?* Marital property accumulates only during the marriage. All jurisdictions agree that a marriage begins on the day the legal ceremony takes place. Jurisdictions differ, however, about when the marriage ends for purposes of continuing to acquire marital property. Two separate but related issues arise: First, at what point does property acquired by one spouse cease to be counted as marital? Second, at what point should marital property be valued for purposes of distribution? Some jurisdictions regard as separate all property (and increases in value) acquired after the date of legal separation. *See, e.g.*, Cal. Fam. Code § 771 (West 2004 & Supp. 2018); Wash Rev. Code Ann. § 26.09.080 (West 2016). Others continue to count as marital all property acquired until the date on which one party files for divorce, the trial is held, or the divorce is granted. *See, e.g.*, N.Y. Dom. Rel. Law § 236B(1)(c) (McKinney Supp. 2018) (counting as marital property accumulated until the execution of a separation agreement or commencement of the action for divorce); *Fitzwater v. Fitzwater*, 151 S.W. 3d 135 (Mo. Ct. App. 2004) (the date for determining and valuing marital assets is the date of trial); Ark. Code Ann. § 9–12–315(b)(3) (West Supp. 2018) (property acquired after separation but before absolute divorce is considered marital property).

Which approach seems most equitable? Which approach seems more amenable to manipulation by a sophisticated spouse?

5.   *Non-monetary contributions that do not add value.* What if a woman works very hard to improve the value of a house her husband owned before the marriage, but the appraiser concludes that the improvements did not significantly enhance its value because a prospective buyer might "raze the house and build a new one on the site?" *See Quinn v. Quinn,* 689 N.W.2d 605, 612 (Neb. Ct. App. 2004). What if a declining real estate market means that despite the improvements, the house is worth less than when she moved in?

3.   THE CONTRIBUTIONS OF HOMEMAKERS

The *Middendorf* court noted that it did not have to evaluate the extent to which Pat's contribution as a homemaker freed Max to run the stockyards, because the statute required that only one of them contributed to the increase in the value of the business. Under the common law title system courts regularly failed to accord credit to homemakers for their contributions. As Mississippi's highest court explained in announcing that it would no longer apply the title system: "to allow a system of property division to ignore non-financial contributions is to create a likelihood of unjust division of property." *Ferguson v. Ferguson,* 639 So.2d 921, 926 (Miss. 1994). Under the separate property system "a traditional housewife and mother," the court explained, was often left "with nothing but a claim for alimony, which often proved unenforceable. In a family where both spouses worked, but the husband's resources were devoted to investments while the wife's earnings were devoted to paying the family expenses or vice versa, the same unfair results ensued. The flaw of the separate property system, however, is not merely that it will occasionally ignore the financial contributions of the non-title-holding spouse. The system [was] also unable to take account of a spouse's non-financial contribution. In the case of many traditional housewives such non-financial contributions are often considerable." *Id.*

Today, equitable distribution of all marital assets in title jurisdictions is the primary acknowledgement of homemaker contributions to the marital estate. The homemaker spouse is entitled to a fair share of the assets, the argument goes, because she contributed to the accumulation of those assets even if she did not earn a wage. Contribution is not limited by gender. *Gillespie v. Gillespie,* 106 So. 3d 869 (Miss. Ct. App. 2013) (a husband who stayed home to raise the couple's child had made a sufficient contribution to be entitled to half of the wife's retirement account).

Assigning a dollar value to the contributions of homemakers proves more difficult. Courts often struggle to calculate the value of a homemaker's services:

* * * This value can be determined using at least three different calculations: the cost of replacing a homemaker's services with market labor; the lost opportunity costs borne by the homemaker by virtue of devoting her time to homemaking instead of market labor; and econometric models based on economic theory and statistical analysis. While the lost opportunity cost model is popular * * *, it also has been criticized by feminists for its focus on the costs borne by homemakers and failure to account for the benefits primary wage earners enjoy as a result of gendered divisions of domestic labor. Specifically, primary homemakers make it possible for primary wage earners to achieve "ideal-worker" status * * * largely unhindered by child care or other domestic responsibilities.

Martha M. Ertman, *Commercializing Marriage: A Proposal for Valuing Women's Work Through Premarital Security Agreements*, 77 Tex. L. Rev. 17, 21–22 (1998).

Estimates of a homemaker's value by economists and other experts vary wildly. One study calculated the market value of a mother's services based on job titles including "chauffeurs, cooks, psychologists, money managers and more" at over $113,000 a year for a full time "stay-at-home mom" and over $67,000 a year for a part timer who also has a "9-to-5 job." Mandi Woodruff, *Here's How Much It Would Cost to Replace Your Mom*, Business Insider, May 8, 2013 (citing a study by Salary.com). The salary estimate included substantial overtime pay since the survey of 6,000 mothers revealed that full-time mothers worked about 94 hours each week. *Id.* The part-time mothers also earned hypothetical overtime: they worked an average of 58 hours a week as moms. *Id.* By 2017 Salary.com estimated the median annual salary for a stay-at-home mother who works an average of 96 hours each week at $162,581 based on the time spent on each task and the market pay for workers performing those jobs. *Mother's Job Continues to Increase in Complexity and Paycheck Increases in Value*, Salary.com (May 13, 2017).

Other studies, as well as insurance companies, place the economic value of homemakers much lower when homemakers die or are incapacitated. In the real world, families do not replace all of the functions a homemaker performs with paid labor, and the employees they hire are paid on average between $10 and $15 an hour. Liz Pulliam Weston, *What's a Homemaker Worth? The Shocking Truth*, MSN Money, May 4, 2003, *available at* http://moneycentral.msn.com/content/CollegeandFamily/P468 00.asp (citing an economist). For this reason, the lifetime economic value assigned to a woman homemaker who dies at age 30 is around $300,000 as compared to a 30-year-old worker making just under $20 an hour, currently valued at over $1 million. *Id.* This low value is reflected in statutes that govern the insurance industry. *See, e.g.,* Minn. Stat. Ann. § 65B.44 (West

Supp. 2018) (benefits for loss of full-time homemaker "shall be subject to a maximum of $200 per week" in Minnesota).

Courts, in contrast, increasingly recognize the complex interaction of the spousal roles. The modern approach to determining "a spouse's contribution which justifies equitable distribution" is to look "not only at cash contributions and assistance in the spouse's workplace or business, but also to domestic work in the home such as caring for children, cooking meals, cleaning house, and washing and ironing clothes. 'The persistent attempts made to put a monetary value on a homemaker's contributions are likely to undervalue the magnitude of such contributions.' The spouse who is accumulating the monetary assets will have more time to accumulate more assets if someone is taking care of all of the domestic responsibilities." *Haney v. Haney*, 907 So.2d 948, 955 (Miss. 2005).

Homemakers of every social class still run the risk that their contributions to the family and to their spouses' careers will not receive adequate recognition in the form of property distribution in the event the marriage dissolves. They also assume significant opportunity costs, including declining future employment prospects and loss of retirement savings and other benefits that may leave them disadvantaged after divorce. *See* Pamela Laufer-Ukeles, *Selective Recognition of Gender Difference in the Law: Revaluing the Caretaker Role*, 31 Harv. J. L. & Gender 1 (2008).

QUESTIONS

1.   *Economic value of homemaker services.* Does it matter what economic value is assigned to a homemaker's services if he or she receives an equitable share of marital assets at divorce? In other words, is equitable distribution a sufficient compensation for full-time homemaking? Should a homemaker be compensated for the opportunity costs of giving up or interrupting a career? If so, should homemakers be compensated differently depending on the nature of the job they gave up?

2.   *The role of broader social forces.* When spouses decide that one of them should be a full-time homemaker, is their choice of which spouse should stay at home truly a joint personal plan or is the choice largely predetermined by larger societal expectations and the preferences of employers?

3.   *Should familial caretaking be compensated?* Professor Martha Fineman has argued that caretaking is a societal function that should be compensated by society. Martha Fineman, The Autonomy Myth: A Theory of Dependency (2005). What are the pros and cons of a government payment to an adult who takes care of dependent children or adults at home? Would such a payment be likely to affect the distribution of responsibilities in families or the economic repercussions of family dissolution?

PROBLEM 9-1

Gordon and Ellen married in 2012 and separated two years later. No children were born of the marriage. Neither party was employed during the marriage. Their sole source of income was approximately $50,000 a month, after taxes, which Gordon received as a beneficiary of a family trust valued at nearly $60 million. Gordon is one of several beneficiaries, does not control the trust, and cannot invade the principal.

During the marriage, the couple established joint checking and savings accounts. The trust payments were electronically deposited into the joint checking account every month, and used to pay virtually all of their expenses. They used the funds, among other things, to make a down payment and mortgage payments on a home known as "Bleak House" in which they held joint title. They also purchased two late model luxury cars, furnished their home, and added a swimming pool and basketball court. At the date of separation, the checking account contained nearly $70,000.

Ellen took primary responsibility for paying the bills, and urged her husband to curb his spendthrift ways. Each month Ellen took responsibility for transferring funds to the joint savings account, which contained $244,000 when they separated. She also took care of the home and cooking. Gordon did the grocery shopping and maintained the exterior of their home.

You are the trial judge in an equitable distribution jurisdiction, and are hearing Ellen's petition for divorce. Ellen argues that all of the parties' assets should be equitably distributed because Gordon's use of his trust fund indicated his desire to make a gift to her. Gordon argues that it was simply more convenient to have joint accounts and joint titles, and that no intent to transfer ownership should be inferred. Ellen also argues that the savings account would never have been funded absent her efforts.

What assets are subject to distribution? Why? How would you distribute the assets? Would the result differ in a "kitchen sink" jurisdiction?

4. THE NEW PROPERTY AND ITS COMMON FORMS

Traditionally, parties to a divorce claimed only tangible property, following Blackstone's definition of property ownership as the "definite right of use, control and disposition which one may lawfully exercise over particular things or objects." William Blackstone, quoted in Oldham, Divorce . . . the Distribution of Property, *supra*, § 5.02. Today, according to Professor J. Thomas Oldham:

> There is great confusion in family law regarding the appropriate analysis for determining the existence of property. * * *
>
> The confusion * * * stems from the dramatic changes that have occurred in the types of rights that are valuable.

* * *

[A]n increasing number of the valuable rights held by middle class individuals relate to things other than tangible property. For example, a person's career * * * [is] quite valuable to that person. * * * Other examples [include] * * * certain fringe benefits relating to a job, such as seniority rights, stock options, pension rights, union membership, and paid vacation and sick leave time.

These rights are all valuable, but does that mean they are all 'property' which should be valued and divided at divorce? Few state divorce statutes define what property means in this context. * * *

Many divorce courts have been reluctant to expand the scope of 'property' to include intangible rights. * * *

* * *

[Some] states have developed a broader concept of what constitutes divisible property. * * * For example, courts have concluded that increased earning capacity, a possible future inheritance, a contingent trust interest, a professional degree, a professional license, and professional goodwill all are divisible property. * * *

Other states have accepted a broader definition of property by statute. For example, the West Virginia statute provides that "marital property" includes "every valuable right and interest, corporeal or incorporeal, tangible or intangible." *Id.*

Valuation of nontraditional forms of property may prove particularly complicated, especially when the value of the property received in compensation for work performed during the marriage may not become clear until sometime in the future. Stock options are a classic example. Because the resolution of all issues related to distribution is final and not subject to modification after the divorce is granted, the parties and the court must engage in a delicate balancing act to neither overstate nor understate the future potential of such holdings in a manner that would be unjust to either party.

Spouses make claims on many forms of "new property," and jurisdictions differ on the treatment of some of them. At divorce many couples and courts divide property that the law once uniformly deemed separate, including pension rights, stock options, and business goodwill. The rest of this Section explores some of the most significant forms of new property.

A. INTELLECTUAL PROPERTY

Federal law has long recognized and protected property rights in intellectual work. U.S. Const. art. I § 8. Intellectual property falls into three main categories: patents granted under 35 U.S.C. § 1 et seq. (2012 & Supp. V 2017); copyrights granted under 17 U.S.C. § 101 et seq. (2012 & Supp. V 2017); and royalty rights created by contract, as well as undeveloped or incipient rights that may arise before any of the preceding instruments are perfected. Intellectual property—like real property—can be transferred directly or through licensing, and a lively marketplace exists for it. It so closely resembles tangible property that it has been easy for courts to find it divisible at divorce. Brett R. Turner, *Division of Intellectual Property Interests Upon Divorce*, 12 Divorce Litig. 17, 22 (2000).

The handful of state appellate courts that have expressly addressed the question of whether intellectual property is divisible at divorce have held that rights in intellectual property are marital if they meet the conditions attaching to the creation of marital property in general (*e.g.,* was work performed during the marriage, were marital assets invested in promoting or developing the property, etc.). *Teller v. Teller*, 53 P.3d 240 (Haw. 2002); *In re Monslow*, 912 P. 2d 735 (Kan. 1996). Since 1935 numerous lower courts have awarded shares in intellectual property at divorce without analyzing whether it is divisible. *Lorraine v. Lorraine*, 48 P.2d 48 (Cal. Dist. Ct. App. 1935) (patent). Thus, it may be conceptually misleading to lump intellectual property rights with "new" property as some commentators do.

On the other hand, the division of intellectual property raises some of the same issues as the division of more inchoate forms of property, including: how to assess its present and future value; whether to divide the asset itself (*i.e.,* ownership of the patent or copyright) where the law permits, attribute a present value to it or allocate shares of any future income derived from it without dividing the property itself; what happens when the post-divorce actions of one spouse will determine whether the property vests and how much it is ultimately worth; and the complexities that arise when property is created gradually, over a long period of time, before, during and after a marriage. These issues are discussed below as they play out when various forms of intangible property are considered in the context of distributing property at divorce.

B. PROFESSIONAL LICENSES, PROFESSIONAL DEGREES AND FUTURE EARNING CAPACITY

In 1985, New York became the first (and only) state in the nation to treat a professional license as a marital asset, awarding a share of a license to practice medicine to the spouse who had supported the doctor through school where the couple divorced as soon as he received his license—a regime that remained in place for more than thirty years. *O'Brien v. O'Brien*, 489 N.E. 2d 712 (N.Y. 1985). In *Holterman v. Holterman*, 814 N.E. 2d 765 (N.Y. 2004), the highest court in New York reaffirmed the *O'Brien* doctrine, holding that the non-license-holding spouse was entitled to a share of the projected worth of the professional license even when she had enjoyed the enhanced income it produced during the marriage. *See also Mula v. Mula*, 16 N.Y.S. 2d 868 (App. Div. 2015) (finding that the wife was entitled to 50% of the husband's CPA practice and license). No other state ever fully followed New York's *O'Brien/Holterman* approach in the arena of professional education and licenses.

In 2015 the New York legislature expressly repudiated the *O'Brien* approach which had been widely criticized. Act of Sept. 25, 2015, ch. 269, 2015 N. Y. Law 831. The 2015 statute instructs courts that they "shall not consider enhanced earning capacity arising from a license, degree, celebrity goodwill, or career enhancement" in defining and dividing marital property. But the statute leaves courts some discretion in crafting an equitable division: "the court shall consider the direct or indirect contributions to the development during the marriage of the enhanced earning capacity of the other spouse." *Id.* As you will see, this approach resembles the law in many other jurisdictions.

Valuing what social scientists call "human capital," which includes the combination of education, opportunity and enhanced earning potential, is increasingly important as courts around the country use other theories to reach similar results. For example, the California statute expressly provides that professional education, training and earning capacity are separate property but allows reimbursement of community funds used to support that education. The California code further instructs trial courts to consider whether the standard of living of the marital estate has already benefited from one spouse's professional training. Cal. Fam. Code § 2641 (West 2004).

Pennsylvania courts use the concept of "equitable reimbursement" to compensate "a spouse for his or her contribution to the marriage where the marital assets are insufficient to do so," often through monthly installment payments that are distinguishable from alimony. *See, e.g., Schenk v. Schenk*, 880 A.2d 633, 640 (Pa. Super. Ct. 2005). The concept is appropriately applied where one spouse supports the other through graduate training that enhances earning capacity and the couple separates before jointly reaping the benefits of the degree. *Id.*

In the District of Columbia, the factors listed for the court to consider in crafting an equitable distribution of marital assets include: "the opportunity of each party for future acquisition of assets and income," and "each party's contribution to the education of the other party which enhanced the other party's earning ability." D.C. Code § 16–910 (b)(6)–(8)

(2017). Consideration of enhanced earning capacity includes an assessment of professional training and reputation.

Courts have found that educational debt can be marital property. In *Polacheck v. Polacheck*, 5 N.E.3d 1088 (Ohio Ct. App. 2013), the court found that the wife's economic circumstances warranted weighing equitable considerations, and that the wife's $40,000 student loan debt was not solely her responsibility.

C. PENSION PLANS AND RETIREMENT ACCOUNTS

Next to the marital home, a pension plan is generally a couple's most valuable asset. Every jurisdiction treats an employer-sponsored retirement plan as a marital asset. *See, e.g., Coggin v. Coggin*, 837 So.2d 772, 775 (Miss. Ct. App. 2003). According to data collected by the federal Bureau of Labor Statistics, in 2017 only 66% of all private sector workers had access to an employer-sponsored retirement savings or defined benefit pension plan, and only 50% of eligible workers participated. Pension Rights Center, *How Many American Workers Participate in Workplace Retirement Plans?* (Jan. 18, 2018). Those who work for state and local governments are far more likely to have access to a retirement plan and to participate in it. *Id.*

Most traditional pension plans raise complex valuation issues because their future value is normally not easy to predict from their present value. For example, the pension may or may not have vested or matured at the date of dissolution. "Vesting" means that the employee is entitled to retain plan benefits even if employment is terminated. Pension plans "mature" when the employee reaches retirement age and can reap the benefits. Even if a plan has neither vested nor matured, it is subject to valuation and distribution. Sometimes pension plans decline in value due to market fluctuation over time. *See Grecian v. Grecian*, 97 P.3d 468 (Idaho Ct. App. 2004) (holding that where the divorce decree awarded wife 50% of the value of the husband's 401K plan on the date of divorce, husband bore the entire loss when the account declined in value). Some retirement plans are "defined benefit" pension plans, in which the monthly benefits payable to an employee at retirement are generally based on a formula that reflects factors including the length of the employee's service and his or her salary level. Whether the retirement plan is a "defined contribution" plan, based on individual contributions (like a 401(k) plan), or is a defined benefit plan, the ultimate value of the retirement package may change based on choices the employed spouse makes after divorce. Workers today are far less likely to have a defined benefit pension plan than they were in the past, and the lower their income, the less likely they are to have such retirement coverage. David Rosnick & Dean Baker, Ctr. for Econ. & Policy Research, *The Wealth of Households: An Analysis of the 2016 Survey of Consumer Finances* 1, 16 (2017).

Federal law protects the claims of former spouses to the proportion of the private pension awarded to them under the divorce decree. The Employment Retirement Income Security Act of 1974 ("ERISA"), 29 U.S.C. §§ 1001–1461 (2012 & Supp. V 2017), regulates most private employer-sponsored retirement plans. ERISA permits state courts to divide pension benefits along with other marital assets at divorce and facilitates enforcement by creating qualified domestic relations orders ("QDRO"s), which recognize the rights of a person other than the plan beneficiary, often called an "alternate payee," to receive benefits under the plan "if and when the benefits are actually received." *Sampson v. Sampson*, 816 N.E.2d 999, 1005 n.12 (Mass. App. Ct. 2004).

A QDRO authorizes the pension administrator either to segregate a portion of the participant's account into a separate account exclusively for the former spouse or to pay a percentage or lump-sum portion of the benefits directly to the recipient former spouse; without a court-approved QDRO, the administrator cannot divide the participant's interest. It is the responsibility of the attorney for the party who receives a share of a spouse's pension plan to prepare the appropriate documents, obtain an order from the trial court, and submit the order to the plan administrator. The failure to submit properly prepared and executed QDROs first to the court and then to the plan administrator creates frequent segregation, distribution and enforcement problems. *E.g., Butler v. Butler*, 768 S.E. 2d 332 (N.C. Ct. App. 2015) (failure of the wife's attorney to file the QDRO with the plan administrator precludes recovery from her former husband who received the full amount of his pension during the first two years of his retirement; the wife may consider a malpractice action against her attorney).

Federal retirement benefits are treated under separate legislation, but also allow assignment of a proportion of the benefit pursuant to a divorce decree. *See, e.g.*, 5 U.S.C. § 8445 (2012) (providing rights to former spouses under the Federal Employees' Retirement System); 10 U.S.C. § 1408 (2012 & Supp. V 2017) (military retirement pensions); 45 U.S.C. § 231(a) (2012) (amending the Railroad Retirement Act). In *Howell v. Howell*, a veteran waived a share of his retirement pay in order to receive "nontaxable disability benefits" from the Federal Government. 137 S. Ct. 1400, 1402 (2017). The Supreme Court of Arizona had affirmed the lower court's decision to "treat[ ] as community property and award[ ] to a veteran's spouse upon divorce a portion of the veteran's total retirement pay" in compliance with 10 U.S.C. § 1408(c)(1). *Id.* at 1404. However, the state Supreme Court found that indemnification was inappropriate because it gave the divorced spouse a "vested interest" in the veteran's waiver. *Id.* at 1405.

Reviewing *Howell*, the U.S. Supreme Court addressed the question of whether the state of Arizona could increase the amount the veteran's former spouse would receive each month from the veteran's retirement pay "in order to indemnify the divorced spouse for the loss caused by the veteran's waiver." *Id.*

In 2017 the Supreme Court weighed in on indemnification of former spouses of military personnel in 2017. The Court held that a state court cannot protect a former spouse's share of a military retirement pension where the veteran waives a portion of his retirement pay after the divorce in order to receive instead service-related disability payments which are exempt from income tax. *Howell, supra* at 1402. The Court reversed the Arizona decision that awarded the wife a higher proportion of the veteran's retirement pay in order to indemnify her from the loss of income caused by his election to take lower retirement benefits after the divorce was final.

Federal law also governs access to a spouse's social security benefits after divorce. Social Security benefits may not be assigned after a short marriage. 42 U.S.C. § 407(a) (2012). Courts are divided as to whether a spouse's expectations of Social Security benefits may be taken into account when crafting an equitable distribution. *See In re Marriage of Crook,* 813 N.E.2d 198, 202, 205 (Ill. 2004) (summarizing the split and holding that Social Security benefits may not be used to offset unequal marital distribution because "[c]alling a duck a horse does not change the fact that it is still a duck"); *Dunmore v. Dunmore,* 420 P.3d 1187 (Alaska 2018) (noting that state courts remain divided and adopting the majority approach that Social Security benefits are not speculative where one spouse is already receiving benefits—the benefits may be considered as one of the factors in crafting an equitable distribution).

However, when a marriage that has lasted more than ten years is dissolved, the spouse who earns less may receive up to 50% of the Social Security benefits accrued during the marriage by the higher earning spouse. Beginning two years after the divorce is final, the divorced recipient of a share of Social Security benefits may apply for benefits once both spouses have turned 62 (whether or not the spouse who earned the benefits has elected to begin taking payments) unless he or she has remarried or is the primary insured under a Social Security account in his or her own name that is equal to or larger than the full amount payable to the former spouse under the account. 20 C.F.R. § 404.331 (2018).

D. STOCK OPTIONS

Stock options (an employee's right to purchase shares of the employer's stock in the future at a price designated today) are an important part of many compensation packages. *See* Tracy A. Thomas, *The New Marital Property of Employee Stock Options,* 35 Fam. L.Q. 497 (2001) (stock options are "[o]ne of the most valuable assets in a dissolution case today"). Stock options are marital property to the extent that they constitute deferred compensation for work performed during the marriage. *Schuman v. Schuman*, 717 S.E.2d 410, 411 (Va. 2011).

Like pension plans, the present value of stock options that have not yet matured is hard to estimate and calls for expert calculations. *E.g., In re Marriage of Farmer*, 259 P.3d 256, 263 (Wash. 2011) (en banc).

A stock option is a mere expectancy, because if the stock price declines, the employee may decide not to exercise his or her option to purchase the stock. Nonetheless, several valuation methods are possible, including calculation of a present value, deferred distribution, or transfer of the options themselves if the employer permits such transfer. Florida courts, for example, use the same method to value stock options that they apply to unvested pensions—a method known as the coverture fraction: " 'the numerator is the amount of time the employee was married while participating in the plan, and the denominator is the total time the employee has in the plan.' " *Fritz v. Fritz*, 161 So.2d 425, 428 (Fla. Dist. Ct. App. 2014).

E. BUSINESS GOODWILL AND OTHER SMALL BUSINESS ISSUES

Small businesses may depend primarily on the principals' abilities, and therefore may be worth far more than their book value. This gap between book value and actual value is known as "goodwill."

Business goodwill is generally regarded as a divisible marital asset, and distinguished from personal goodwill. A precise definition of goodwill is elusive at best. An appellate court in Oregon described "goodwill" as "a concept of chameleon capability." *Slater & Slater*, 245 P.3d 676 (Or. Ct. App. 2010). It then turned to the distinction between personal goodwill and the goodwill inherent in a business:

> The semantic and analytic confusion is especially marked—both in our case law and *in the case law of our sister states—when it comes to assessing the goodwill of a professional practice* or a closely held business or corporation, specifically in determining whether a principal owner's individual skills and qualities are properly included in that valuation. * * * Nevertheless, aside from some slippage at the margins, our cases, like those of the majority of courts that have considered the issue * * * have generally distinguished between the intangible income-producing assets of business—that is, its "goodwill"—from the value that inheres to the personal traits of that business's employees or owners. Indeed, the import of those decisions is that "personal goodwill" is not, in fact, "goodwill" for purposes of valuation in the marital dissolution context. * * * [O]ur cases demonstrate that, for purposes of valuation in this context, cognizable "goodwill" refers to the value

of a business "over and above the value of its assets" irrespective of the owner's or professional's continued "personal services[.]" * * * Accordingly, where a business has no value above and beyond its assets absent "the owner personally promis[ing] his [or her] services to accompany the sale of the business," * * * there is no goodwill.

Id. at 681–82. The court concluded that personal goodwill is indistinguishable from future earning capacity and thus is not marital property. Enterprise goodwill is marital property in most jurisdictions but may be very difficult to value if no sale of the business is contemplated. *Id.* If the business is sold and the sale includes a noncompetition agreement, the value of that agreement remains the separate property of the principal. *Id.* at 683.

The Supreme Court of Wisconsin takes a minority position, holding that courts do not need to distinguish between personal and business goodwill when dividing assets at divorce. *McReath v. McReath*, 800 N.W.2d 399 (Wis. 2011). The court explained that personal goodwill resembles other income-producing assets subject to division. *Id.*

Owners of small businesses frequently use the businesses to acquire property for personal use, creating additional valuation problems. For example, in *Gohl v. Gohl,* 700 N.W.2d 625 (Neb. Ct. App. 2005), the couple owned Golight, a small business which had recently won a patent infringement suit against Wal-Mart. Because Wal-Mart was appealing that decision at the time of the divorce hearing, the ultimate value of Golight hinged on the still-unknown outcome of the litigation. After the couple separated, Golight provided the husband with a car and housing. The husband was also a partner in a second business, Gohl Brothers, engaged in farming and oil leases. Gohl Brothers owned the marital home. Gohl Brothers obviously was not a party to the divorce litigation, and thus was beyond the court's jurisdiction. The court awarded the marital home to the wife and ordered the husband to convince the partnership to deliver the marital home to the wife or to pay her an additional sum equal to the value of the home. The partnership ultimately "consent[ed]" to transfer the home to the wife. *Id.* at 628–30.

Adding to the complexity, Golight owned a bed-and-breakfast property known as Waterfjord House valued at $700,000, which had produced an income of only $16,000 in its most profitable year. After the separation, the husband spent hundreds of thousands of dollars of Golight funds renovating Waterfjord House. Describing Waterfjord House as "a voracious consumer of Golight's capital," an appellate court remanded for consideration of "whether the expenditures in the Waterfjord House were merely a sham to obscure the financial status of Golight by artificially and unreasonably inflating its debt load, and thereby obscuring its profitability and valuation." *Id.* at 637.

F. PERSONAL INJURY: DISABILITY PENSIONS AND TORT RECOVERIES

Whether recoveries for personal injuries are considered marital property depends on how the compensation is characterized. To the extent that the award is for pain and suffering, it is the personal property of the individual who suffered the injury. *Williams v. Williams*, 129 So.3d 233, 238–39 (Miss. Ct. App. 2013). However, an award for economic losses becomes marital property.

Awards and compensation for loss of consortium are generally found to be the separate property of the uninjured spouse. In *Conrad v. Conrad*, 612 S.E.2d 772 (W. Va. 2005), the court analyzed various approaches to disability insurance benefits. Many states, it found, consider the benefits marital, absent a statute to the contrary. Other states regard private disability benefits as marital if the policy premiums were purchased with marital funds or the benefits were obtained as compensation for past services as part of employment benefits. Still other jurisdictions regard all disability payments as separate property because the payments are intended to replace future earnings. *Conrad* declined to adopt a *per se* rule, but held that treatment should be based on evidence of the parties' intent and other case-by-case factual determinations. *Id.* at 776–77 (following *Metz v. Metz*, 61 P.3d 383 (Wyo. 2003)).

NOTES AND QUESTIONS

1. *Accrued vacation time.* Unused, accrued vacation time may be difficult to value at divorce because the employer will compensate the employee for the unused time at the salary the employee earns when he or she ultimately leaves the employer. The timing and the salary are unknown at divorce. Using the approach toward the new property discussed above, a California appellate court held that it was reversible error for a family court to refuse to award a spouse half of her husband's accrued vacation time. The husband was old enough to retire, and if he had done so the exact value of the unused vacation time would have been known. *In re Marriage of Moore*, 171 Cal. Rptr. 3d 762, 767 (Ct. App. 2014). What if he had not been eligible to retire?

2. *Compensation for wrongful imprisonment.* If a man is exonerated based on DNA evidence after serving a lengthy prison sentence, should his wife be entitled to a share of the damages he receives from the state on his release? A man who served 25 years for crimes he did not commit remained married during his first ten years in prison, until his wife divorced him. After he was released and received compensation from the state, his ex-wife sought and received over $100,000 of his award based on the argument that he would have earned wages in at least that amount had he not been in prison. An appellate

reversed the award to the wife, holding that the damages the husband received were calculated based on the number of years he served without any consideration of forgone earnings but rather to compensate him for the personal harm he had suffered. *Phillips v. Tucker*, 442 S.W.3d 543 (Tex. App. 2014). What form of new property did the court appear to base its analysis on? Would (or should) it make any difference if the wife had not divorced him, raised their two children while he was in jail, and he left her after receiving the damages award?

3. *Lotteries.* Lotteries, bingo and other games leading to awards of cash have been around for a long time, but raise questions resembling those that surround newer kinds of property interests. Lottery winnings arise in a surprising number of cases, given the odds against winning a substantial sum. *See* ALI, Principles of the Law of Family Dissolution: Analysis and Recommendations § 4.03 (2002). Lottery winnings are subject to division at divorce even if the award is made over many decades. It is settled law that "the proceeds of a winning lottery ticket acquired by a spouse during the marriage constitute marital property," subject to equitable distribution. *Questel v. Questel*, 960 N.Y.S.2d 860, 863 (Sup. Ct. 2013).

However, courts may engage in the same sort of analysis that applies to other kinds of property. For example, they may examine whether the ticket was purchased with marital or separate funds, whether the proceeds were acquired actively or passively, and what would be "equitable." *See, e.g., Noel v. Noel*, 884 So.2d 615 (La. Ct. App. 2004). One Indiana case involved a man who won the lottery after purchasing a scratch off ticket with earned (*i.e.*, marital) funds. Because he had long lived separately from his wife, the winner resisted sharing his windfall with her. The Indiana Court of Appeals affirmed the trial court's decision to award the wife a share of the $2 million winnings. But, because the couple had been living separately with completely separate assets and finances for the last six years of their marriage, the court also affirmed the decision that the wife was only entitled to $50,000, a mere 2.5% of the husband's bounty. *In re Marriage of Perez*, 7 N.E.3d 1009, 1011 (Ind. Ct. App. 2014).

4. *Bonus payments.* The wife signed a Transaction Bonus Agreement ("TBA") with her long-time employer. The TBA ensured she would receive a bonus at closing if she succeeded in selling the company. *King v. Howard*, 158 A.3d 878 (Del. 2017). She sold the company and was paid the bonus prior to the divorce. *Id.* at *1. The Supreme Court of Delaware found that the bonus was subject to equitable distribution because it was earned during the marriage and received after separation but before the divorce.

5. *Indian Health Services.* National origin may play into whether or not health insurance is characterized as marital property or separate property. For example, Indian Health Services insurance has been characterized as separate property when the Alaska Supreme Court took into consideration the identity of an Alaskan native whose spouse was not a member of a tribe. *Horning v. Horning*, 389 P.3d 61 (Alaska 2017).

PROBLEM 9-2

Frozen embryos are another emerging form of new property. The state in which this case arises has a statute that expressly provides that pre-embryos (eggs that have been fertilized but not yet implanted in a uterus) are not "persons."

A couple in the process of divorcing cannot reach an agreement about what to do with pre-embryos they created during the marriage in order to have additional children later on. During the marriage they had three children born through IVF who are all thriving.

The written agreement the spouses signed when creating the embryos did not provide for treatment of the preembyos in the event of divorce. Now, the wife wants to keep the embryos so that she can have more children. The husband wants the embryos distributed to him; he plans to have them discarded because he does not want more children or the financial responsibilities that would accompany fatherhood even after divorce.

This is a case of first impression in your jurisdiction, where you are the clerk to the judge who has been assigned the divorce case. The first question is whether the pre-embryos are marital property, and if so, do they have a special character within the treatment of property?

Your research also reveals that other jurisdictions have adopted three approaches to the frozen embryo question in divorces:

1.   The contract approach which looks to prior agreements between the parties to determine their intent;

2.   The balancing of interests approach which evaluates the parties' competing interests in claiming the pre-embryos; and

3.   The emerging mutual consent approach, which effectively gives one of the parties veto power over use of the pre-embryos.

What are the arguments for and against each of these approaches, and for the preliminary issue of whether to treat the pre-embryos like any other marital property? What will you advise the judge to do?

5. VALUATION, DISTRIBUTION AND ENFORCEMENT

In addition to identifying property and characterizing it, the court must assign each piece of property a value, apportion the divisible property in accordance with the state law (equitably or equally), and issue an order that will accomplish the distribution the court has determined to be appropriate. Distribution may involve a literal divvying up of tangible and intangible assets, or it may take the form of one spouse buying the other out through an "equalization payment," in which one spouse keeps some or all of the non-fungible assets and transfers cash to the other in an amount that represents the recipient's share.

You have already encountered disputes over valuation in *Middendorf*, where the parties disagreed about the value of the stockyard as well as about what caused it to increase in value, and in the discussion of the special problems that may arise in valuing certain kinds of property interests that will be perfected in the future. Valuation raises a number of interrelated issues.

Start with one that sounds simple: what should the date of valuation be? It is crucial to distinguish the date of valuation from how long accumulation continues to be treated as marital. The dates for purposes of accumulating marital property and valuation may be different. In other words, a state (or a judge, if the dates are left to judicial discretion) may treat all property acquired after the legal separation as separate, but may value the marital estate as of the date of the divorce decree.

States vary in the timing of valuation. Some use the date of separation, others the date of trial, and still others the date on which the decree issues, or even the date of the final decree in the event of remand. Oldham, *supra*, § 13.03[6]. At least one state uses the date of filing of the divorce complaint or commencement of the marital litigation. *Teeter v. Teeter*, 759 S.E.2d 144, 150 (S.C. Ct. App. 2014). Some states, like Indiana, leave the date of valuation up to the discretion of the court. *Granzow v. Granzow*, 855 N.E.2d 680, 685 (Ind. Ct. App. 2006) (any date between filing divorce petition and end of trial); *Wagner v. Wagner*, 136 So. 3d 718, 719–20 (Fla. Dist. Ct. App. 2014); *In re Marriage of Schmidt*, 329 P.3d 570, 575 (Mont. 2014) (equity in apportioning property is more important than "designating the moment" for valuing it).

Due to appreciation and fluctuation, the date on which marital property is valued may prove quite significant and equitable considerations may enter into the decision. For example, in *McCulloch v. McCulloch*, 69 A.3d 810 (R.I. 2013), the appellate court reversed the trial court's decision to enforce the value the parties had assigned to the husband's company when they executed a stipulation. The appellate court ruled that the judge should have honored the husband's request that the value of his company be reassessed following a dramatic economic downturn that was not in his control and that occurred after the agreement was executed but before the divorce decree issued.

All of these issues can prove complicated, and rarely more so than when the couple's major asset consists of shares in a closely-held corporation. A 'closely held' company has a limited number of shareholders who are active in managing the company, and whose eligibility to own shares is generally set forth in an agreement that also controls other aspects of how the corporation is governed.

Many small businesses are formed as corporations in order to receive tax advantages and protect the owners from personal liability in the event of lawsuits. State and federal statutes permit businesses to take a restricted corporate form, whether as a closely-held corporation that controls who can purchase shares, or as a limited liability corporation (a hybrid form with some of the characteristics of a partnership) or similar arrangements. These corporate forms were not designed as a defensive tool in anticipation of divorce litigation, but the ownership of closely-held corporations—another form of property unknown to Blackstone—comes up frequently in family law.

When an owner of shares in a closely-held corporation divorces, his or her spouse frequently claims a right to a portion of the company's value even though the corporation may bar outsiders, including spouses and former spouses of shareholders, from owning stock in the company. It is not unusual for the shareholder to be employed by the corporation, and for the other shareholders to include members of the shareholder's extended family. Because the ownership of shares in closely-held corporations is usually restricted, it can be hard to determine the market value of the shares, especially when one party's shares amount to a minority (or non-controlling) interest in the corporation, or are non-voting shares which entitle the owner to a portion of any profits that are distributed, but do not give the shareholder an official right to participate in corporate decisions.

Recurrent questions that arise in divorce proceedings include whether the shareholding spouse has voting shares, or a controlling interest, that would allow the spouse to force the corporate to liquidate a portion of its assets to fund distribution of marital wealth, and whether the shareholder can force the corporation to distribute available cash. Another common issue arises from the fact that owners of close corporations have many ways of subsidizing their lifestyle without taking large salaries, and often choose to leave profits in the corporation rather than taking the profits out of the business.

Because one goal of property distribution is to disentangle the divorcing spouses from each other, transferring ownership of shares in a family business from one spouse to the other is frowned on even when the corporate by-laws would permit it. All of these issues, as well as questions about valuation and enforcement, arise in the following case from Indiana. Neither of the parties challenged the characterization of the property at issue as marital and neither challenged the court's decision to divide their net worth equally.

Indiana is a common law, equitable distribution state with a rebuttable presumption that equal division of marital property at dissolution is "just and reasonable." Ind. Code Ann. § 31–15–7–5 (West 2018).

CRIDER V. CRIDER

Court of Appeals of Indiana. 2014.
15 N.E.3d 1042.

BARNES, JUDGE.

Jeff Crider appeals various parts of the trial court's decree dissolving his marriage to Christina Crider, as well as several post-judgment orders. Several business entities in which Jeff has an interest also have intervened in this case. We affirm in part, reverse in part, and remand.

Issues

The restated issues before us are:

I. whether the trial court properly ordered Jeff to pay any attorney fees Christina might incur in enforcing a monetary judgment;

II. whether the trial court properly ordered Jeff to make a cash equalization payment to Christina of $4,752,066 plus 8% statutory post-judgment interest;

III. whether the trial court properly valued a closely-held business in which Jeff held stock;

* * *

V. whether the trial court properly excluded from the marital estate purported loans Jeff's father made to him;

* * *

VII. whether the trial court properly granted Christina a security interest in Jeff's stock and membership interests in several closely-held family businesses and ordered that one-half of those stock and membership interests be transferred to Christina if Jeff failed to pay the cash equalization payment within 180 days of the dissolution decree;

* * *

IX. whether the trial court properly ordered attachment of future loan proceeds Jeff may receive in order to satisfy the equalization judgment;

* * *

Facts

Jeff and Christina were married in 1992. They had two children during their marriage, one of whom is now emancipated. [At Jeff's request, Christina became a "stay-at-home" parent.] In May 2009, Christina filed [a] divorce petition.

Jeff is involved in a large number of business entities with his father, Robert, and his brother, Steve. The primary family business is Crider & Crider, Inc. ("CO"), which is engaged in road and other construction work primarily in the Bloomington area. Jeff, Robert, and Steve are the only shareholders of this closely-held * * * corporation. Jeff owns approximately 42.25% of the stock, Steve 42.25%, and Robert the remaining 15.5%. Two of the other family businesses are Logan Land Development, LLC, ("Logan") and North Park, LLC. Both entities own property in a planned unit development ("PUD") site in Bloomington called North Park. Jeff's interest in these entities is 33%. Other business entities at issue here, along with Jeff's interest therein, are: [seven limited liability corporations (LLCs) in which Jeff owns interests ranging from 24% to 50%]. We will refer to the Crider businesses together as the "Crider Entities." None of the Crider Entities were joined in the dissolution action; after a final dissolution decree was entered, they were granted permission to intervene in the case.

In 1993, Robert, Jeff, and Steve signed a stock transfer restriction agreement with respect to their holdings in CCI. The agreement prohibited any shareholder from encumbering any of their shares without prior written consent from the other shareholders, unless certain narrow exceptions inapplicable here were met. * * *

The LLCs also had restrictions on the transfer of membership interests written into their operating agreements. * * *.

* * *

Jeff's finances are complicated. There can be no doubt, however, that he earns considerably more per year than the $72,000 in salary that he received from CCI and that Jeff often characterizes as his only income.

* * *

* * * The last time Jeff provided a personal financial statement was in 2007, before Christina filed for divorce, and it estimated his personal net worth at more than $11,000,000. * * *

* * * The Criders' lifestyle also reflected a high level of income. The marital home sold for nearly $1.5 million during the pendency of the divorce, the couple owned a condominium in Hilton Head, South Carolina, they had floor tickets to Indiana University basketball games, and they took private flights for vacations. * * *

* * *

The trial court conducted a dissolution hearing over the course of eleven days and received extensive evidence and testimony from both parties. In part, there was widely divergent testimony from various experts regarding the proper valuation of CCI and Jeff's interest in it.

* * * The parties * * * presented varying evidence regarding the value of the heavy machinery and equipment that CCI owned. Christina's accounting expert utilized an appraisal that valued the machinery and

equipment at $20.1 million, using * * * methodology that valued all the machinery and equipment CCI owned in 2009. Jeff's accounting expert, by contrast, utilized different appraisals, based on sales of comparable equipment and machinery at auction, with a resulting value range between $9,599,575 and $10.2 million. Ultimately, Christina's expert placed a total value on CCI of $15.6 million, with the value of Jeff's interest being $4,321,000.

* * *

Christina's and Jeff's experts also differed as to the proper valuation of [other companies].

On June 26, 2013, the trial court entered a final dissolution decree, accompanied by extensive findings of fact and conclusions thereon. With respect to the valuation of CCI, the trial court largely accepted the methodology and conclusions of Christina's expert, except with respect to the valuation of the company's heavy equipment and machinery. * * *. However, the trial court also noted that Jeff's experts failed to appraise all the equipment and machinery CCI owned in 2009, which it had chosen as the marital estate's proper valuation date. The trial court assigned a value of $11 million to the equipment and machinery. * * *. The trial court found CCI to have a total value of $10,150,746, and Jeff's 42.5% interest in the company to be worth $2,810,506, after discounts for non-marketability and the fact that many of Jeff's shares were non-voting.

* * *

The trial court also excluded the purported loans from Robert to Jeff as marital liabilities. It did include the note payable by Robert to Jeff as a marital asset, as Jeff agreed it should be. The trial court also excluded the $1,649,994.48 loan from Jeff to CCI as a marital asset.

Ultimately, the trial court found that the total value of Jeff's business and real estate interests in 2009 was over $11 million, which was offset by little marital debt. The trial court evenly split the marital estate, which resulted in Christina and Jeff each being entitled to $5,510,930 in assets. However, because Christina received few liquid assets, the trial court required Jeff to make an equalization payment to Christina of $4,752,066. It also reduced that required payment to a judgment and ordered that it bear statutory interest, unless Jeff paid it in full within ninety days.

In order to secure payment of the judgment, the trial court ordered as follows:

Christy shall be given a security lien on all of Jeff's shares and ownership interests in Crider & Crider and the Crider Entities (and of any successor to or affiliate thereof). Jeff shall pledge his shares and ownership interests in these businesses to secure Christy's judgment.

[In the event that Jeff did not pay the judgment in full within 180 days, the court awarded Christy "ownership and control of one half of Jeff's shares in Crider & Crider and the Crider Entities." She would continue to retain ownership and control until Jeff paid the judgment and accumulated interest in full.

"Jeff did not pay the equalization judgment to Christina" within the 180 days. When Cristina initiated a proceeding to collect the judgment, the court granted the Crider Entities permission to intervene.]

On January 10, 2014, the trial court [granted Christina's enforcement motion, awarding her temporary ownership and control of half of Jeff's shares that had been pledged to guarantee the equalization payment. The court further ordered the companies not to distribute to Jeff any amounts that he would have received based on those shares, but to forward such payments instead to Christina.]

Analysis

* * *

I. Attorney Fees

The first issue we address is whether the trial court erred in ordering Jeff to pay any attorney fees Christina might incur in attempting to collect the equalization judgment. Ind. Code § 31–15–10–1(a) provides that a trial court in a dissolution proceeding "periodically may order a party to pay a reasonable amount . . . for attorney's fees . . ., including amounts for legal services provided and costs incurred before the commencement of the proceedings or after entry of judgment." "We review a trial court's decision on attorney fees in connection with a dissolution decree for an abuse of discretion." *Troyer v. Troyer,* 987 N.E.2d 1130, 1142 (Ind. Ct. App. 2013). When deciding whether to award attorney fees to a party in a divorce, trial courts must consider the relative resources of the parties, their economic condition, the ability of the parties to engage in gainful employment and earn adequate income, and other factors that bear on the reasonableness of the award. The legislative purpose * * * is to ensure that a party in a dissolution proceeding is able to retain representation when he or she would otherwise be unable to afford an attorney. *Id.* at 1143. "When one party is in a superior position to pay fees over the other party, an award of attorney fees is proper." *Id.*

* * * This court * * * has held that trial courts enjoy "broad discretion in awarding attorney fees, *including prospective awards. . . .*" * * *

[U]ntil th[e] judgment is paid, Christina is in an extremely disadvantageous economic position as compared to Jeff * * *. And, the prospective award of attorney fees only extends to such time as Christina collects the judgment and is made roughly economically equal with Jeff; it does not continue indefinitely. [T]he precise amount of such fees must be reasonable, must be supported by evidence from Christina as to such reasonableness, and is subject to challenge by Jeff as to their reasonableness. In other words, Christina (and her attorneys) are not entitled to a "blank check" with respect to attorney fees. * * *.

II. Post-Judgment Interest

[W]hether to award post-judgment interest falls within a trial court's discretion "in the course of fashioning a just and reasonable division of property." * * *

* * *

Jeff argues in part that it was excessive to award statutory post-judgment interest because it amounts to approximately $1,041 per day, which exceeds the income the trial court imputed to him post-dissolution ($200,000 annually) by over $500 every day. This argument is misleading, because the imputed income of $200,000 annually was based upon Jeff's payment of the equalization judgment through liquidation of some of his assets. Those same assets and business interests have been generating annual income to Jeff of up to $900,000 or more and have given him a personal net worth of approximately $11 million. Until Jeff in fact pays that judgment, at which time the accrual of post-judgment interest will end, that accrual of interest is not unreasonable in relation to Jeff's income and net worth.

Jeff also contends * * * that it is unfair to award post-judgment interest because it is difficult or impossible for him to pay the sizable equalization judgment, because he was awarded very few liquid assets in the dissolution decree, as opposed to his interests in the various Crider Entities. He, moreover, seems to claim he cannot liquidate those interests because he does not possess a controlling interest in any of the various Crider Entities that made up the vast majority of his net worth. The question, however, is * * * whether he controls his own interests in them. He clearly does so. Simply put, Jeff might have to drastically alter the nature and scope of his business interests in order to pay the judgment. He may have to encumber, sell off, or liquidate some of those interests. If he truly, absolutely is unable to do so, then Christina is entitled to receive the benefits of those interests until she receives her fair share of the marital estate.

Although the judgment here is undeniably large, * * * Jeff is not entitled to stand idly by and continue his own personal status quo while Christina does not receive the judgment to which she is entitled. * * * The trial court did not abuse its discretion * * *

III. Valuation of CCI

We now turn our attention to the trial court's valuation of CCI. "We review a trial court's decision in ascertaining the value of property in a dissolution action for an abuse of discretion." Generally, there is no abuse of discretion if a trial court's chosen valuation is within the range of values supported by the evidence. *Id.* * * *

* * *

B.   Equipment and Machinery

Jeff also contends the trial court erred in placing a value of $11 million on CCI's in-stock heavy equipment and machinery when valuing CCI as a whole. Again, Jeff's two appraisers valued the inventory at either $9,559,575 or $10.2 million, while Christina's valued it at $20.1 million. Jeff essentially contends that because none of the three expert appraisals came up with a value of $11 million for the equipment and machinery, the trial court erroneously picked a number out of thin air that is not supported by any evidence. We disagree * * *.

As a general rule, a trial court does not abuse its discretion in valuing property in a dissolution so long as its chosen valuation is within the range of values supported by the evidence. * * *.

Here, * * * the trial court's findings are adequate to explain how it arrived at the $11 million figure. The trial court noted with respect to the three different valuations of the equipment, "Each of the reports presented by the parties has its flaws." * * * However, the trial court also found that Jeff's appraisers had failed to value all of the equipment that CCI actually owned in 2009, which the trial court concluded was the relevant date for valuing CCI; * * *. Because of this discrepancy, the trial court valued the equipment at $11 million in 2009, taking into account the equipment not counted by Jeff's appraisers * * *.

* * *

V.   Loans from Jeff's Father

Jeff next argues that the trial court erred in not including several purported loans made to Jeff by his father, Robert, as liabilities reducing the total amount of the marital estate. * * * Jeff [also] contends the trial court erred in not including a loan [of over $2 million] Jeff purportedly made [in 2008] to CCI as an asset within the marital estate. [CCI rewrote the promissory notes to reflect a lower amount as an outstanding debt to Jeff, even though it had never] made any payments to Jeff on the loan.

Marital property includes both assets and liabilities. [The court expressed puzzlement at Jeff's desire to treat his loan to CCI as a marital asset. If the "purported loan from Jeff to CCI were to be included in the marital estate as an asset," Jeff would owe Christina an additional $800,000.]

As for loans Robert purportedly made to Jeff, the essence of Jeff's argument is that because the loans were evidenced by promissory notes, the trial court was required to include them in the marital estate as liabilities. Prior cases have clearly held, however, that courts are not required to accept one party's characterization of funds received from a third party as a debt as opposed to an outright gift. *See Macher v. Macher,* 746 N.E.2d 120, 124 (Ind. Ct. App. 2001) (holding that funds advanced by husband's parents as down payment for purchase of marital residence was a gift and not a loan, where there was no promissory note or other documentation, no payments were made to parents for several years, and no payments were requested). When deciding whether the exchange of money is either a gift or a loan, courts will consider factors such as an expectation or agreement regarding repayment or the accrual and payment of interest.

* * *

Here, Robert purportedly [made three loans to Jeff between 2001 and 2007, totaling over $2 million]. Jeff never made any payments on any of these purported loans, despite the due dates as indicated in all three promissory notes having passed. There is no evidence that Robert ever requested any payments. * * * Jeff * * * admits * * * that these purported loans "were an estate planning device" * * * and part of an overall plan to reduce the size of Robert's estate. [A] reasonable corollary to such an admission is that [Robert] simply intended to give this money away to Jeff with no expectation of repayment. And a reasonable corollary to *that* conclusion is that the purported loans are not liabilities of Jeff's. Also, with respect to the 2007 notes, the trial court found them to be consistent with other financial dealings that may have been calculated to reduce Jeff's apparent net worth and income in the final years of the marriage after Christina's first attempts to end it, such as CCI's drastically reduced distributions to shareholders and Jeff's failure to provide personal financial statements to lending institutions after 2007.

* * * Quintessentially, it was a factual matter for the trial court to decide the actual intent of Jeff and Robert with respect to the various loans they exchanged amongst themselves. We cannot say it abused its discretion in excluding the three purported loans from Robert to Jeff as actual marital liabilities * * *.

* * *

VII. Ownership and Control of CCI
and other Crider Entities

Next, we address the complex and sensitive issue of the trial court's use of security liens against Jeff's various interests in the Crider Entities as a means of enforcing the equalization judgment. * * *

As a preliminary issue, the Crider Entities claim they were deprived of due process because they were not served with notice of the divorce proceedings before the trial court impacted their businesses by granting Christina a security interest in Jeff's interests therein in the dissolution decree. We find nothing improper here. Typically, the only proper parties to a marital dissolution proceeding are the spouses. [T]he original dissolution decree here * * * granted Christina a security interest against Jeff's ownership interests in the Crider Entities. We acknowledge and agree that the Crider Entities were entitled to notice and an opportunity to be heard with respect to any enforcement or foreclosure of Christina's security interests [which they received by intervening in and participating in the collection proceedings and this appeal.]

[A] trial court entering a dissolution decree with an equalization judgment "may provide for the security, bond, or other guarantee that is satisfactory to the court to secure the division of property." It is abundantly clear that the trial court was permitted to grant Christina a security interest against Jeff's CCI stock and his membership interests in the LLCs, and that such liens could be foreclosed to pay the equalization judgment. * * *

* * *

Ownership interests in closely-held businesses present special challenges when it comes to equitably dividing a marital estate. As a general rule, "[t]he creation of joint control or ownership of assets in divorced persons should be avoided unless there are insufficient assets to otherwise divide the property." 24 Am. Jur. 2d Divorce & Separation § 535 (2014). Additionally, "[w]here the marital property includes stock in a close corporation, an award to one spouse of such stock, subject to an obligation to pay the other spouse an appropriate sum, constitutes an equitable division, serving to disengage the parties' financial affairs and to reduce the likelihood of interference with one another or with the operations of the company." *Id.* Courts generally recognize that the success of a closely-held business "is usually dependent upon the business skills of the principal shareholder, and that a division of the shares could effectively destroy his or her incentive or ability to operate the business, thereby jeopardizing the continued operation of the corporate business and the stockholders' interests." Thus, continued entanglement by two spouses in a closely-held business after divorce generally should be avoided, unless it is impossible to do so because of the absence of other liquid assets in the marital estate to equitably divide the property.

Here, much of Jeff's sizable net worth was tied up in his stock and membership interests in the Crider Entities. There were not enough liquid assets to simply award Christina her fair share of the marital estate and entirely avoid some continued entanglement between Jeff and Christina in those businesses. The granting of security interests against Jeff's stock and membership interests to guarantee payment of the equalization judgment—with the implication that such interests could be foreclosed if the judgment was not paid—was appropriate. To the extent Jeff and the Crider Entities suggest that any kind of transfer of Jeff's stock and membership interests is absolutely forbidden, they practically write those stock and interests out of the marital estate. That is improper, and Jeff does not argue that the stock and membership interests are not marital property. Otherwise, Jeff could perpetually refuse to pay the equalization judgment, and Christina would have very limited recourse for collecting it.

Our supreme court in *F.B.I. Farms* [*v. Moore*, 798 N.E.2d 440 (Ind. 2003)] stated, very clearly, that a stock transfer restriction agreement simply cannot apply to some involuntary transfers and expressly held, "In a dissolution, the interests of the spouse require permitting transfer over the stated intent of the parties." [*Id.*] at 449. [A] corporation's articles and bylaws, including stock transfer restriction agreements, constitute a contract between the shareholders themselves and between the corporation and the shareholders. *See id.* at 445. It is not a contract with the world at large. * * * A business's internal bylaws or operating agreement cannot act as a magic shield that protects it from innocent third-party creditors.

The trial court's order, however, could have done more to avoid continued entanglement between Jeff and Christina in the family businesses. The order * * * purported to automatically give Christina full "ownership and control" of one-half of those stock and interests * * * until the judgment was paid in full. This broad, undefined language regarding "ownership and control" has the potential to cause grave mischief by allowing Christina to insert herself into the management of the Crider Entities, where she never had any such role. We believe there were better solutions available to the trial court than to complicate the nature of the closely-held Crider Entities in this fashion.

We first address Jeff's stock in CCI * * *. [T]he trial court could have significantly minimized the impact of granting Christina an interest in one-half of Jeff's shares in the company upon his failure to pay the judgment. * * * Jeff owns a total of 109 shares of CCI. Of that number, seventy-nine are *non-voting* shares. Christina could be given an equitable interest only in 55.5 shares of Jeff's non-voting CCI stock. Thus, Christina would be entitled to receive distributions from CCI without being allowed to participate in management of the company, * * *

Alternatively, *F.B.I. Farms* sets out a very clear roadmap for what to do when stock in a closely-held corporation subject to a stock transfer restriction agreement is used as security to guarantee the payment of a dissolution decree's property equalization judgment, and that payment is not made. Any sale of such stock to satisfy a judgment must be accomplished through the well-settled procedures for execution of a lien through a sheriff's sale, which is what occurred in *F.B.I. Farms.* * * *. CCI would be entitled to notice of and participation in such proceedings. Also, CCI and its shareholders would be entitled to insist upon compliance with those parts of the stock transfer restriction agreement that give first CCI, and then the shareholders if CCI declines, the right to purchase the stock before any other sale could take place. * * *. And, if an outside third party does purchase the stock with knowledge of the stock transfer restriction agreement, that third party would be bound by the agreement in the future * * *. * * *

[T]he trial court's automatic granting of "ownership *and control*" of [Jeff's LLC] interests upon Jeff's failure to pay the equalization judgment violates statutory law regarding LLCs. [T]he statutory definition of an "interest" in an LLC "means the member's economic rights in the limited liability company, including the member's share of the profits and losses of the limited liability company and the right to receive distributions from the limited liability company." Additionally, Indiana Code Section 23–18–6–3 provides that if an interest in an LLC is assigned, the assignee is entitled to receive "only the distributions to which the assignor would be entitled," and that assignment of an interest "does not of itself dissolve the limited liability company or entitle the assignee to participate in the management and affairs of the limited liability company or to become or exercise any rights of a member . . ." * * *

Here, the trial court exceeded statutory authority by purporting to grant Christina "control" of one-half of Jeff's LLC membership interests. * * *. [The members of the LLCs have the option to purchase the membership interests outright themselves rather than allowing their involuntary assignment to Christina. The scope of any * * * order can only permit Christina to receive distributions from the LLCs; she is not allowed to participate in the management of those businesses * * *. * * *

In sum, the trial court was fully empowered to grant Christina a security interest in Jeff's business holdings * * *. But it went too far in automatically transferring "ownership and control" of those holdings to Christina [when Jeff failed to meet the deadline for making the equalization payment] within 180 days; we reverse the dissolution decree to that extent. * * *

* * *

Conclusion

We cannot say the trial court erred in ordering Jeff to pay to Christina an equalization judgment of $4,752,066, plus interest accruing after ninety days, and to pay any attorney fees Christina incurs in collecting the judgment. We also find no clear error in the trial court's valuation[ ] of CCI, * * * and in its decisions to exclude purported loans made by Robert to Jeff from liabilities of the marital estate; * * * Although the trial court did not err in granting Christina security interests in Jeff's CCI stock and his LLC membership interests, we find error in its decision to automatically vest "ownership and control" in those stock and membership interests upon Jeff's failure to pay the equalization judgment within 180 days.

* * *

BAKER, J., and CRONE, J., concur.

NOTES AND QUESTIONS

1.   *Attorney's fees—who pays?* As *Crider* illustrates, courts hearing divorce cases have broad equitable powers to order that one party pay the other spouse's attorney's fees. The trial court decision will not be reversed except for abuse of discretion, but the court must determine whether the fees requested are reasonable. Many states provide for awards of attorney's fees by statute in limited circumstances. *E.g.,* Tex. Fam. Code Ann. § 106.002 (West 2014); Fla. Stat. Ann. § 61.16 (West 2012). These awards are predominantly made to ensure that each party has access to comparable counsel. *See, e.g., Schecter v. Schecter,* 109 So.3d 833, 837 (Fla. Dist. Ct. App. 2013).

In practice, at separation many affluent couples negotiate an agreement that the party with greater access to assets will pay the other party's attorney's fees. The other party's lawyer may accept or continue the representation, and accept such payment, only where the lawyer "determines that there will be no interference with the lawyer's independent professional judgment and there is informed consent from the client." Model Rules of Prof'l Conduct, r. 1.8(f) cmt 11 (Am. Bar Ass'n 2002); *see also* Model Rules of Prof'l Conduct, r. 5.4(c) (Am. Bar Ass'n 2002) ("A lawyer shall not permit a person who * * * pays the lawyer to render legal services for another to direct or regulate the lawyer's professional judgment in rendering such legal services.").

2.   *How else might Christina Crider have financed her enforcement efforts?* A relatively recent industry treats divorce as an investment opportunity. Firms like Balance Point Divorce Funding finance the non-breadwinner spouse's divorce costs, ranging from legal fees to living expenses, in exchange for a share of the proceeds. Binyamin Appelbaum, *Taking Sides in a Divorce, Chasing Profit,* N.Y. Times, Dec. 4, 2010, at A1; *see* Bibeane Metsch-Garcia, *Eliminating Financiers from the Equation: A Call for Court Mandated Fee Shifting in Divorces,* 113 Mich. L. Rev. 1271, 1274 (2015) (arguing that "third party divorce funding is not an appropriate or equitable option"). What image of women and of attorneys do these businesses convey? What do you think of divorce as an investment opportunity?

3.   *Are shares in closely-held corporations separate or marital property?* Jeff never argued that his shares in the family businesses were not marital property, but other minority shareholders in family businesses have convinced courts that they are powerless to control the accumulated but undistributed profits in such corporations. *In re Marriage of Joynt,* 874 N.E.2d 916 (Ill. App. Ct. 2007) (husband, who owned one-third of the shares, was employed as the

company's president, and would inherit a controlling interest when his father died). In *Joynt*, the court deemed it significant that the husband received a salary within industry norms, which had supported the family. How might the analysis differ if the husband had received a much lower salary than another company might have paid him for similar work? There are a variety of tax and estate planning incentives for shareholder-employees to take relatively modest salaries, as Jeff did. How might that decision disadvantage a spouse at divorce?

4. *Methods of valuation.* Normally, judges rely on appraisals and other expert opinions if the parties are unwilling to stipulate the value of an asset that cannot easily be measured, as you saw in *Crider* and earlier in *Middendorf* where the value of the stockyard was disputed. Experts, in turn, rely on a number of methodologies in valuing assets, and some individual experts themselves offer competing models and results for the judge's consideration. In *Crider*, the trial court heard conflicting testimony on the value of several businesses. In a part of the appellate opinion you did not read, the court noted some of the different methodologies Cristina and Jeff's experts had used. The judge may accept any of the recognized methods of appraisal. Some experts offer the judges more than one approach, even if they yield different valuations. *See, e.g., Collins v. Collins*, 104 P.3d 1059, 1063 (Mont. 2004) (affirming the decision below where the wife's expert "testified to three different methods used when valuing a business" and the court chose one of them). As one appellate court summarized the broad discretion accorded to the trial court: "When the opinions of valuation experts diverge, a judge may 'accept one reasonable opinion and reject the other' * * * The judge may also 'reject expert opinion altogether and arrive at a valuation on other evidence.'" *Adams v. Adams*, 945 N.E.2d 844, 864 (Mass. 2011) (findings will not be overturned unless "clearly erroneous"). The trial court's decision on valuation will be sustained as long as "it is supported by competent, credible evidence and is not * * * arbitrary, unreasonable, or unconscionable." *Chattree v. Chattree*, 8 N.E.3d 390, 403 (Ohio Ct. App. 2014).

Despite the enormous leeway accorded to trial courts with respect to valuation, a manifest error is subject to reversal. Where a husband gave his wife's Rolex (her separate property) to his paramour to sell, yielding $5,000, but a recent appraisal had estimated the value of the watch at over $27,000, the trial court erred by treating the watch as marital property and treating the $5,000 the paramour gave the husband as reflecting the market value of the instrument. *Thomas v. Thomas*, 974 N.E.2d 679, 686 (Ohio Ct. App. 2012).

In *Caveney v. Caveney*, 960 N.E.2d 331 (Mass. App. Ct. 2012), the court held it was reversible error to apply a discount to the value of the wife's shares in a closely-held corporation on the ground that the shares were not a liquid asset, and that she was only a minority shareholder. The court explained that where no sale was imminent, or even contemplated, a marketability discount unfairly reduced the value of the shares in the absence of "extraordinary circumstances." *Id.* at 340 (quoting *Bernier v. Bernier*, 873 N.E.2d 216 (Mass. 2007)). *Bernier* had explained, "Close corporations by their nature have less value to outsiders, but at the same time their value may be even greater to other share-holders who want to keep their business in the form of a close corporation." *Bernier*, 873 N.E.2d at 232 (quoting *Brown v. Brown*, 792 A.2d 463, 487 (N.J. Super. Ct. App. Div. 2002)). Assuming this reasoning is correct, would Jeff Crider have likely been able to negotiate a fair price if he offered to sell his shares to his brother or father?

5. *Treatment of personal and corporate loans.* The *Crider* court comments that marital property includes liabilities as well as assets. The final section of this Chapter will examine the treatment of debt. At this point, consider a narrower question: what were the purposes of the loans from Jeff's father to him, and the loans that Jeff claims he made to CCI? In a portion of the opinion you did not read, the court commented, there "is some robbing Peter to pay Paul here, as a loan from Jeff to CCI would seem to be an outstanding liability of CCI that would affect its net worth and, therefore, Jeff's total net worth as a CCI shareholder." *Crider*, 15 N.E.3d at 1074, n.6.

If the court had accepted Jeff's arguments about each set of loans, how would that have affected the size of the equalization payment? How did the court analyze the loan transactions Jeff alleged had occurred? Was the trial court's skepticism justified? What do the loans reveal about the special character of closely-held corporations?

6. *Structure of distribution and guarantees.* When marital property is illiquid, or it would be disadvantageous to sell assets on the date of the divorce degree due to market conditions or potential tax liabilities, distribution of property awards can be delayed and even take place over many years. Indeed, "courts have broad equitable authority to grant relief and fashion appropriate remedies in dissolution proceedings." *Farmer v. Farmer*, 259 P.3d 256, 266 (Wash. 2011) (en banc). Jeff Crider, who claimed to be cash poor, was given 180 days to organize his finances in order to transfer Christina's share of the property to her.

When distribution is to be paid in installments, or where there is reason to suspect that the former spouse will prove recalcitrant, courts have the equitable power in marital cases to order obligors to guarantee satisfaction of their obligations and to craft solutions tailored to the couple's situation. When people have fewer assets than the Criders, courts often require a party to maintain life insurance naming the former spouse as the beneficiary until the obligation is paid off, or place a lien on a piece of real property.

The means of securing Jeff's obligation was a central issue in *Crider*. The appellate court held that Christian could not be given "ownership and control" of half of Jeff's shares in the Crider Entities, but could be designated the recipient of all distributions made to the holder of those shares. What is the basis of that distinction, and what practical difference does it make? Why did the trial court use the shares for securitization of the divorce judgment?

7. *Attorney's obligation to secure payment.* In *Winters v. Patel*, 154 F. App'x 299 (3d Cir. 2005), the Third Circuit affirmed a jury verdict finding that an attorney committed malpractice when he failed to take the necessary steps

to secure a former husband's obligations to his ex-wife, the attorney's client. The parties had agreed, and the court had ordered, that the husband would transfer $143,000 in marital assets to his wife after the divorce in four installments. The parties' agreement contemplated that the husband's retirement plan would secure the obligation, and that the husband would maintain a life insurance policy for the benefit of his ex-wife until he had completed the payments. The wife's attorney never perfected either of the guarantees. When the former husband, who had remarried, died unexpectedly without having completed his payments, his current wife successfully claimed both his life insurance benefits and the proceeds of his pension plan. A jury ordered the former wife's attorney to pay her nearly $300,000 in compensatory damages, including attorney's fees for the malpractice action.

8.   *Are Christina and other former spouses adequately protected?* In a footnote to *Crider*, the court commented that it was relying on the good faith of the Crider family to make payments to Cristina while she held her security interest in the shares: "We are cognizant of the potential danger here in the management of the Crider Entities—Robert, Steve, and Jeff—deciding to make no or little distributions to Christina. One would hope such would not be the case, but that they would rather seek to make fair distributions to her, and the sooner such distributions are made in an amount sufficient to pay off the equalization judgment, the sooner she is disentangled from the Crider Entities." *Crider*, 15 N.E.3d at 1074, n.17. Do the Crider Entities have to distribute profits? Can they raise the salaries of the shareholders who work for the companies to compensate for a decision not to distribute profits? If they do, does Christina have any recourse?

In *Caveney*, the husband similarly failed to comply with portions of the divorce decree, including orders that he pay his wife's attorney's fees of $175,000, an equalization payment of over $260,000 and transfer half of his retirement account to her. *Caveney, supra*, 960 N.E.2d at 343. After the judge found that the husband "had the present ability to pay" the equalization amount, she found him guilty of contempt and ordered that he be jailed for ninety days or until he purged himself of contempt by paying his former wife. The husband elected to serve the ninety days. *Id.*

6. WHAT DISTRIBUTION IS EQUITABLE?

During the era when only fault-based grounds justified divorce, fault was also the key to distributing assets and awarding alimony. That is no longer the case. When the Uniform Law Commission was established in 1892, it identified the law of marriage and divorce as one of two areas clearly appropriate for development of uniform laws. However, the ULC did not issue a report on marriage and divorce until 1970. When it did so, it advocated reform of the entire conceptual culture from fault to no-fault, and urged that states make all of the ancillary changes such rethinking required. To that end, the committee that drafted the Uniform Marriage and Divorce Act (UMDA) concluded that the "distribution of property upon the termination of a marriage should be treated, as nearly as possible, like the distribution of assets incidental to the dissolution of a partnership." UMDA prefatory note, 9A U.L.A. (1973). As you have observed in your readings for this course, the UMDA is the basis for much contemporary family law. The UMDA expressly states that one of its purposes is to "make reasonable provision for spouse and minor children during and after litigation." *Id.* at § 102(5); 9A U.L.A. (1998).

By statute or common law, each state provides a list of factors for trial courts to consider when dividing property at divorce. The factors are not assigned weight, and some factors may conflict with others in particular cases. For example, a court may be required to evaluate each spouse's need for post-marital support as well as each spouse's contribution to the marital estate. One spouse may have great need for support, but may not have made any contribution to the marital estate. Which factor is more important? One expert has concluded that legislatures intentionally enact "vague and ambiguous" property division statutes "because it is impossible to set forth one definite set of property division principles that should be applied to all marriages." Oldham, *supra*, § 13.02[1].

The theory behind the award of maintenance differs from the partnership notion that supports equitable distribution of property, but courts are generally instructed to consider the relationship between property distribution and the need for continuing maintenance. *See, e.g.*, Vt. Stat. Ann. tit. 15, § 751(b) (2010). "The two forms of relief are simply separate but closely intertwined ways of getting to the same result." *Ware v. Ware*, 748 A.2d 1031, 1048 (Md. Ct. Spec. App. 2000). "All awards to a spouse must be considered together to decide if they are equitable and fair." *Coggin v. Coggin*, 837 So.2d 772, 775 (Miss. Ct. App. 2003).

A. AN EQUITABLE DISTRIBUTION STATUTE

As discussed in the beginning of this Chapter, approaches to distribution include "equal" division under a few community property regimes, and "equitable distribution" in others as well as in most common law states. Some equitable distribution states require a fair and equitable distribution, while others mandate equal division or instruct courts to begin with a rebuttable presumption that property should be distributed equally.

Pennsylvania's equitable distribution statute, which follows, is representative.

Title 23, Section 3502 of the Pennsylvania Consolidated Statutes

(a) General rule.—Upon the request of either party in an action for divorce or annulment, the court shall equitably divide, distribute or assign, in kind or otherwise, the marital property between the parties without regard to marital misconduct in such percentages and in such manner as the court deems just, after considering all relevant factors. The court may consider each marital asset or group of assets independently and apply a different percentage to each marital asset or group of assets. Factors which are relevant to the equitable division of marital property include the following:

(1)   The length of the marriage.

(2)   Any prior marriage of either party.

(3)   The age, health, station, amount and sources of income, vocational skills, employability, estate, liabilities and needs of each of the parties.

(4)   The contribution by one party to the education, training or increased earning power of the other party.

(5)   The opportunity of each party for future acquisitions of capital assets and income.

(6)   The sources of income of both parties, including, but not limited to, medical, retirement, insurance or other benefits.

(7)   The contribution or dissipation of each party in the acquisition, preservation, depreciation or appreciation of the marital property, including the contribution of a party as homemaker.

(8)   The value of the property set apart to each party.

(9)   The standard of living of the parties established during the marriage.

(10) The economic circumstances of each party, including Federal, State and local tax ramifications, at the time the division of property is to become effective.

(10.1)   The Federal, State and local tax ramifications associated with each asset to be divided, distributed or assigned, which ramifications needs not be immediate or and certain.

(10.2)   The expense of sale, transfer or liquidation associated with a particular asset, which expense need not be immediate and certain.

(11) Whether the party will be serving as the custodian of any dependent minor children.

23 Pa. Stat. & Cons. Stat. Ann. § 3502(a) (West 2010).

NOTE

Tax implications. Sections 10 through 10.2 of the Pennsylvania statute instruct judges to consider the tax implications of property distribution. Since the statute aims to achieve equity between the two spouses, it contemplates that divorcing parties (and judges) will take tax consequences into account when structuring the division of assets. Distribution of assets does not appear as a transfer on either spouse's tax return, because the property already belongs to both of them. The sole exception is that where assets must be sold to affect the division of marital property, the proceeds of the sale may be subject to capital gains tax, or may even be treated as income if the couple has not owned the property long enough to treat the increase in value as a capital gain. Divorces finalized before the end of 2018 in which the higher earner makes maintenance payments to the lower earner may deduct those payments from the obligor's income for tax purposes, and attribute them as income to the recipient who is likely to be in a lower tax bracket. That accommodation was eliminated in the 2017 revisions to the tax code.

B. UNEVEN DIVISION OF ASSETS

The following opinion considers whether an uneven division of marital assets is equitable. Massachusetts is a common law, kitchen sink jurisdiction that requires the court to reach an equitable result in distributing property. In reading the opinion below, consider how much discretion the trial court has in crafting an equitable distribution, the extent to which the court considered whether property was marital notwithstanding the kitchen sink statute, and what factors seem to have influenced the trial court in dividing the assets. The case also continues our discussion of the new property because it involves the meaning and value of a Nobel Prize in physics.

KETTERLE V. KETTERLE
Appeals Court of Massachusetts, 2004.
814 N.E.2d 385.

KAFKER, J.

Central to this dispute about the division of marital assets is the husband's 2001 Nobel Prize for Physics.[1] The judge found that winning the Nobel Prize identified the husband as a superstar in the scientific and academic universe, and she projected his having substantial ability to acquire future income and assets. Relying heavily on this factor, she assigned the wife a greater percentage of the existing marital assets.

The husband has appealed, claiming (1) the wife received a disproportionate share of the assets, (2) the $83,000 the judge assigned to the husband out of the 2001 Nobel Prize proceeds, which was his share

---

[1]   The husband won the Nobel Prize for Physics for his work on Bose-Einstein condensates. "Bose-Einstein condensation has been described as making atoms behave like the photons in a laser beam," rather than move about in their normal state, where they "flit around randomly." 2001 Nobel Prizes, MIT Technology Review, March, 2002, at 15. The condensates have near and long-term applications: "One technological application that promises to bear fruit in the near term is using the condensates to create super-accurate atomic clocks or to make ultra-precise measurements of forces like rotation and gravity. Even further down the road are possible applications in quantum computing and nanotechnology." *Ibid.*

after taxes and his gift to his mentor of one-half of the prize money,[2] was illusory, and (3) the judge prematurely assigned to him the cost of his three children's college education.

We conclude that (1) the judge did not abuse her discretion in her overall division of assets, including her consideration of the Nobel Prize's impact on his ability to acquire future income and assets, (2) the judge's crediting of the husband with $83,000 in Nobel Prize proceeds was not clearly erroneous, and (3) the judge did not err in ordering the husband to pay the imminent college costs of the oldest child, but did err in ordering the husband to pay the future college costs of the two younger children.

Facts. The plaintiff, Gabriele Ketterle (wife) and the defendant, Wolfgang Ketterle (husband), were married on September 20, 1985, in Germany. This seventeen-year marriage was the first for both parties. They had three children, born March 6, 1986, October 25, 1988, and September 28, 1992.

[T]he husband was a tenured full professor at the Massachusetts Institute of Technology (MIT), whose total wages from MIT were $179,160.98 in 2001. His health was also excellent. The wife worked part-time as a teacher's aide earning $7,317.98 in 2001. Although her physical health was fine, her mental health was "fragile." In August, 2001, she was committed for a time to McLean Hospital because of a suicide attempt and severe depression. She continued to be maintained on three kinds of antidepressants.

The judge found "much to admire in the conduct of both [parties] as spouses and as parents." The husband's brilliance and hard work made the family financially secure. "The wife's total commitment to child rearing and tending to the home permitted the husband to pursue his career," which involved "very long hours at his laboratory." The wife also came to the United States from Germany to enhance her husband's career despite her "lack of fluency in English and . . . familiarity with . . . American culture."

The judge identified five basic marital assets: the former marital home in Brookline (equity of $578,000), the husband's new home (equity of $70,000), the after-tax proceeds from the Nobel Prize (this totaled either $83,000 or $166,000 depending on whether the mentor's share is included or excluded), the husband's retirement/pension funds (approximately $183,000[3]), and the wife's bank account ($54,000).

---

[2] In about 1990, the husband and his mentor, David Pritchard, started working together at the Massachusetts Institute of Technology (MIT) on Bose-Einstein condensation. In 1993, in order to keep the husband at MIT, Pritchard took the "extraordinary" step of turning the entire project—"equipment, students and grants"—over to the husband. 2001 Nobel Prizes, MIT Technology Review, March, 2002, at 15.

[3] The husband's retirement assets consist of a 401k account and a defined benefit pension plan. At the time of the divorce, there was $109,401.92 in the 401k plan, in which MIT matched the husband's contribution dollar for dollar. The husband's interest in the defined benefit plan was

The judge awarded the marital home to the wife, and the retirement/pension funds and the after-tax Nobel Prize proceeds to the husband.[4] The judge also permitted the husband to give away one-half of his Nobel Prize money to his mentor as she was "fully persuaded that the husband's motivation is admirable and honorable, and in . . . keeping with the lofty, humanitarian, and generous values embodied by the rich history and tradition of the Nobel Prize." The judge made this ruling, however, "hand-in-glove" with her ruling that the wife not be required, as the husband requested, to refinance the marital home to provide him with cash that would permit him to take, as he argued, "his half." She also rejected his contention that he was "cash-poor."

According to the judge's calculations, she gave the wife either sixty-eight percent or sixty-two percent of the assets, depending on how the mentor's share of the award is considered. In explaining her division of assets, the judge relied "heavily" upon the statutory factor of the "ability of the parties to acquire future income and assets." The judge concluded that the husband's ability is excellent, as he retains a retirement asset in which his employer "matches his future contributions dollar for dollar," and his "receipt of the Nobel [P]rize opens wide new horizons for his income potential." The wife's future prospects were found to be "paltry and stagnant by comparison." The judge found that the wife had "no likelihood of acquiring significant future assets or increasing her earned income."

The parties were given joint legal custody of the three children with, as the parties agreed, the oldest and youngest children residing primarily with the wife and the middle child residing with the husband. The husband was ordered to pay monthly child support of $2,500 to the wife and monthly alimony of $2,000.

* * *

Discussion. The husband objects to the "disproportionate" division of marital assets. Nevertheless, "an equitable, rather than an equal, division of property is the ultimate goal of [the relevant statute on alimony and assignment of property]." *Williams v. Massa*, [728 N.E.2d 932, 939] ([Mass.] 2000). As provided by statute, the trial judge has "broad discretion to 'assign to either the husband or the wife all or any part of the estate of the other,' after consideration of the factors enumerated in the statute. . . . A division of marital property which is supported by findings as to the

---

$73,649.89 at the time of the divorce. The projected worth of the defined benefit plan by the year 2023, when the husband becomes 65 years old, was $684,409.

4   The judge carved out for purposes of division the equity in the husband's new home and the wife's bank account, treating them as essentially a wash. This was because the parties earlier had equally divided a joint bank account, each taking $97,000. The husband used his share mostly to purchase and furnish his new home and the wife saved most of her share in her bank account.

required factors will not be disturbed on appeal unless 'plainly wrong and excessive.'" *Passemato v. Passemato*, [691 N.E.2d 549, 553] ([Mass.] 1998).

There is no question that the judge here expressly considered all the appropriate factors. She also exercised her discretion to give more weight to some factors than others, particularly the ability to acquire future income and assets.[7] The husband contends that the judge's heavy reliance on this factor was misplaced because the judge erroneously found (1) that the husband's future income and assets would be enhanced as a result of his receipt of the Nobel Prize; and (2) the wife would be unable to increase her earning capacity.

The judge's findings on the wife's inability to acquire future income and assets are well-supported, given the wife's limited vocational skills and mental illness. In regard to the husband, the judge emphasized not only the Nobel Prize but also the husband's lucrative retirement plan. There is no dispute regarding the valuation of the retirement plan. We also discern no error in the judge's determination that the Nobel Prize, in combination with the husband's brilliance, work ethic, good health, and relative youth (he was forty-four years old at the time of the trial), will provide him with significant future income and assets given the extraordinary nature of his scientific breakthrough, its worldwide recognition, and its projected near and long-term technological applications. The husband's and wife's ability to acquire future income and assets are therefore strikingly different and justify the judge's heavy reliance on this factor. *See* Kindregan & Inker, Family Law and Practice § 40:18, at 45 (3d ed. 2002) ("If the evidence demonstrates that one party has little or no ability to produce income and little prospect of obtaining assets by other means [such as inheritance], and the other party has a history of producing income, then a strong case exists for property assignment and/or alimony in favor of the party with minimal economic prospects").

The husband also contends that the judge created a seventy-six—twenty-four split of assets, not the sixty-eight—thirty-two split that she intended. He argues that there were only two assets: the house and the retirement plan, because all of the Nobel Prize money was offset by his liabilities. We conclude, however, that the judge's crediting him with $83,000 out of the Nobel Prize proceeds was not clearly erroneous, as the prize proceeds have remained under his exclusive control since their receipt, and even when the taxes and the mentor's share are subtracted, $83,000 remains.

The husband was also awarded the right to give $83,000 of the Nobel Prize proceeds to his mentor. The judge correctly treated this commitment

---

[7] The husband's argument that the judge did not properly consider the husband's contribution to the marriage is without support in the record. She just weighed his contribution differently than he did.

as a professional or moral obligation and not a legal debt. Although the wife has not appealed, and therefore this issue is waived, the $83,000 promised to the mentor should have been included in the marital estate. * * * In sum, the husband has no basis for arguing that he was shortchanged $83,000.

* * *

Conclusion. [T]he judgment is affirmed. [The concurring opinion by LENK, J. is omitted.]

NOTES AND QUESTIONS

1. *How uneven may the division be and still be "equitable"?* In *Wade v. Wade*, 878 A.2d 303 (Vt. 2005), the court upheld an order awarding 90% of the marital assets to the wife as equitable. The court found that the trial judge had not abused his discretion because the family lived in a house the wife had purchased before the marriage and had used gifts from the wife's mother and the wife, who ran a nursery school, used her earnings to pay the mortgage and household expenses; the husband, who chose to work only sporadically, did not serve as a homemaker and ran up substantial credit card debt for his personal expenses. The court rejected the husband's argument that he was entitled to more property or to alimony because the marriage lasted 12 years, he lacked a college degree, and he needed more money to provide "a proper home" for their 14-year-old daughter when she spent the night with him under the parenting agreement. *See also Many Fox King v. King*, 2017 WL 5010783 (Vt. Oct. 27, 2017) (upholding award of marital home—amounting to 87% of the marital assets—to the husband, whose family provided much of the funding and who did much of the construction himself).

It may be an abuse of discretion to award one party an amount that exceeds the total marital assets while awarding the other party remaining debts. *Smith v. Smith*, 938 N.E.2d 857, 861 (Ind. Ct. App. 2010) (absent a finding of dissipation of assets, the trial court erred in awarding the wife $11,440.50 while awarding the husband debts amounting to $4,977.50).

2. *When will an appellate court find a distribution inequitable?* "[A] disproportionate division must be supported by some reasonable basis." *Smith v. Smith*, 143 S.W.3d 206, 214 (Tex. App. 2004). Because distributions will be reversed only for abuse of discretion, the single most important cause of reversal is the trial court's failure to state that it has examined and applied the relevant factors, or to state reasons for disproportionate divisions. *See, e.g., Gohl v. Gohl*, 700 N.W.2d 625, 638 (Neb. Ct. App. 2005) (discussed on page 600 *supra*) (remanding a case involving complex issues in which the trial court set "arbitrary time limitations" for presentation of evidence creating an "incomplete and inadequate" record).

Appellate courts will, however, sometimes overturn a trial court's disproportionate division of marital assets. In *Lee v. Lee*, 91 So.3d 63 (Ala. Civ. App. 2012), the appellate court reversed an award that gave the wife in a marriage which had lasted more than 30 years assets totaling roughly $68,000 (including the marital home and her individual credit card debt) while awarding the husband what appeared to be negative $13,527, an amount that included all of the marital debt. The husband was also awarded his construction company, tools and two trucks, but no value had been assigned to those assets, nor was it clear whether the trial court had treated the business as marital property. Reversing the award as an abuse of discretion, the appellate court emphasized that neither party had engaged in misconduct related to the marriage, and that the husband's diagnosis with rheumatoid arthritis had diminished his future earning capacity. Did the trial or the appellate court reach the correct result?

3.   *The "prodigious earner."* The equities are particularly controversial where the marital estate is so substantial that the lower-earning spouse can maintain his or her accustomed life style without receiving an "equal" share. In such circumstances, many courts award the phenomenally successful earner, or so-called "prodigious spouse," a disproportionate share of the marital assets. Debra DiMaggio, *The "Prodigious Spouse": Equitable Distribution and Wealthy Wage Earner*, 91 Ill. B.J. 460 (2003). High earners, who have accumulated high-asset marital estates, argue that they should be compensated for the demanding nature of their jobs outside the home. *Id.*

While we have already considered the contributions of homemakers, the wives of very successful executives often make the distinct argument that they make special contributions as "corporate wives" who, in addition to managing the usual domestic duties, contribute to their husband's careers by extensive work-related entertainment and travel. *Wendt v. Wendt*, 757 A.2d 1225, 1230 (Conn. App. Ct. 2000). They demand a fair share of the resulting wealth and lifestyle. *Id.* Lorna Wendt, who successfully appealed from a trial court's award of 10% of the marital property accumulated during her marriage to a successful CEO, asserts: "My case was never about the money. It was about someone implying I was a ten percent participant in my partnership. In reality, I always gave 100 percent, putting my career on hold to raise the children, manage the household and support him in his business endeavors." Equality in Marriage Institute, Lorna Wendt, http://www.equalityinmarriage.org/lorna.html (archived page).

For marital estates valued in the multiple millions or more, one critical factor in determining whether the award is equitable is whether it provides the dependent spouse sufficient assets to generate income that will support substantially the same lifestyle as prevailed during the marriage, but in cases involving prodigious wealth, there is enough money to support the lifestyle many times over. No state directs the court to look at the size of the marital estate, or to differentiate between a marital estate valued at $3 million and one valued at $100 million. David N. Hofstein et al., *Equitable Distribution Involving Large Marital Estates*, 26 J. Am. Acad. of Matrimonial Law 311 (2014). A share of the assets that exceeds what is needed to maintain the life style of the homemaker spouse may be regarded as exceeding the value of that spouse's contribution. *Id.* at 325. Courts may examine whether the spouse who was unemployed (or earned significantly less income) acted as a "corporate spouse," who directly contributed to the prodigious earner's acquisition of assets. *Id.* at 326–28.

In 2014 an Oklahoma court ordered Harold Hamm, who was at that time the 24th richest man in the country, to pay nearly one billion dollars to his ex-wife in addition to the "roughly $25 million" he had paid her while the divorce was pending. Other than the amounts involved, the order looked like those you have read about in this Chapter. Mrs. Hamm, who once worked as a lawyer for Hamm's company, does not appear to have been employed during the couple's marriage, which lasted from 1988 to 2012, when the divorce petition was filed. She did not claim to have been a corporate wife. For his part, Hamm denied that the exponential rise in his net worth during the marriage was attributable to his "skill and prowess," a view that conflicted with the company's SEC filings over the years and that the judge rejected. The court ordered Hamm to make an initial payment to his ex-wife of $320 million dollars, and then to pay the property distribution out in monthly payments of seven million dollars, secured by shares of stock in Hamm's oil company. The couple also haggled over homes, airport hangars, home furnishings and two horses, as well as "certain family pictures, a few books, guns, * * *, geode in quartz display, and his hand tools." Hamm received all of these except for the geode in quartz display, denied "without explanation." According to reports, Hamm retains multiple billions of dollars even after the divorce. David Segal, *An Oklahoma Oilman's Billion-Dollar Divorce*, N.Y. Times, Nov.11, 2014, at B1.

While England used to award wives of wealthy husbands only one-third of the total capital assets and aimed to bring dependent spouses up to a "reasonable requirement" of support, in 2000 the House of Lords held that "equality of division" should be the usual yardstick against which to measure judicial discretion. *White v. White*, [2001] 1 AC 596. It is alleged that this change has made London the "divorce capital" of the world for the very wealthy who may own homes there as well as in other countries where the courts are less generous in divvying up assets at divorce than they are in England or the U.S. Courts in Great Britain have made several record-breaking awards in contested divorces. *E.g.*, Jenny Anderson, *British Hedge Fund Titan Is Ordered to Pay Ex-Wife $531 Million*, N.Y. Times, Nov. 28, 2014, at B1.

4.   *Fault-related factors.* The Pennsylvania statute, reproduced above, specifically bars consideration of marital misconduct in establishing distribution awards, but a significant number of states—including pure no-fault jurisdictions—allow the court to consider contributions to marital breakdown as a factor in equitable distribution. The Territory of Guam expressly requires that "where there is a finding of adultery or extreme cruelty the innocent spouse is entitled to a greater share of the community property" and the trial court has "wide latitude in apportionment" so long as the innocent spouse receives a greater share. *Sablan v. Sablan*, 2017 Guam 3 ¶ 102. *Compare Maher v. Maher*, 2016 WL 4536283 (Tex. Ct. App. 2016) (while the trial court has discretion to award a larger share of the property to one spouse as a penalty for the other spouse's adultery, the court is not required to do so). *See* Oldham, *supra*, § 13.02[1][a] (listing jurisdictions).

Federal law generally provides that "domestic support obligations" (defined as, among other things, "debts owed to or recoverable by * * * a spouse, former spouse * * * in the nature of alimony * * * or * * * established * * * by reason of * * * a separation agreement, divorce decree, or property settlement agreement") "shall not be dischargeable in bankruptcy." 11 U.S.C. §§ 101(14A), 523(a)(5) (2012). This language applies to all bankruptcy filings under Chapter 7 of the 2005 Bankruptcy Act, and to what are known as "hardship" cases under Chapter 13: in both instances no divorce-related obligations are dischargeable in bankruptcy. They must be paid. However, the statute imposes a means test and other obstacles to filing under Chapter 7, and forces "better-off households" to file under Chapter 13, the terms of which are generally less favorable to petitioners.[e] Donald P. Morgan et al., *Subprime Foreclosures and the 2005 Bankruptcy Reform*, FRBNY Economic Policy Review 1 (2011).

If the bankrupt party files under Chapter 13, distinctions based on the function of post-dissolution payments from the person declaring bankruptcy to his or her former spouse may prove significant: only domestic support obligations are automatically nondischargeable. A federal bankruptcy court may therefore need to determine if payments have been correctly characterized as domestic support (maintenance or child support) and remain binding or alternatively are owed pursuant to property distribution, in which case they may be discharged in bankruptcy. Note that these issues arise in a federal bankruptcy court, not a state court, and apply federal bankruptcy law, not state law governing the dissolution of marriages.

The following case illustrates the way that federal bankruptcy courts analyze the characterization of divorce-related payments in bankruptcy cases.

IN RE PHEGLEY

United States Bankruptcy Appellate Panel for the Eighth Circuit, 2011.
443 B.R. 154.

SALADINO, BANKRUPTCY JUDGE.

John Phegley appeals the bankruptcy court's memorandum and order dated August 3, 2010, and the judgment pursuant thereto * * * which determined that Mr. Phegley's debts for monthly maintenance payments and attorney's fees pursuant to a state court marriage dissolution proceeding are excepted from discharge pursuant to 11 U.S.C. § 523(a)(5). For the reasons stated below, we affirm.

BACKGROUND

John J. Phegley ("John") and Sheri L. Phegley ("Sheri") were married on May 9, 1998, and lived in Missouri. On June 3, 2009, the Circuit Court of Jackson County Missouri entered a Judgment and Decree of Dissolution of Marriage ("Decree") that dissolved the marriage of John and Sheri. The Decree provided, *inter alia,* that the parties were awarded joint physical and legal custody of the two minor children of the marriage. John was ordered to pay child support to Sheri in the amount of $325.00 per month.

The Decree further provided that John shall pay to Sheri:

[T]he sum of one thousand two hundred fifty and 00/100 dollars ($1,250.00) per month as and for contractual maintenance for a period of forty-eight (48) months beginning on the 1st day of July, 2009 and continuing on the 1st day of each month until the final payment is due at which time [John's] maintenance obligation shall terminate; provided, however, that such maintenance may earlier terminate upon [Sheri's] remarriage or the death of either party.

In addition, John and Sheri were each awarded certain specified items of marital property and John was ordered to pay Sheri $32,371.98 as equalization of property. Finally, the Decree provided that John "shall pay a portion of [Sheri's] attorney's fees in the amount of nine thousand one hundred seventy-eight and 69/100 dollars ($9,178.69). . . ."

On September 2, 2009, John filed a Chapter 13 bankruptcy petition. Subsequently, Sheri filed a complaint to determine dischargeability of indebtedness pursuant to 11 U.S.C. § 523. * * * Sheri contended that the attorney's fees of $9,178.69 and the monthly maintenance payments of $1,250.00 are nondischargeable as domestic support obligations pursuant to U.S.C. § 523(a)(5). John asserts that the debts are not domestic support obligations, but instead are a division of marital property and should not be excepted from discharge.

The bankruptcy court found that the maintenance payments and attorney's fees awarded in the Decree are nondischargeable as domestic support obligations * * *. John appeals.

STANDARD OF REVIEW

The determination of whether an award arising out of marital dissolution proceedings was intended to serve as an award for alimony, maintenance, or support, or whether it was intended to serve as a property settlement is a question of fact to be decided by the bankruptcy court. *Williams v. Williams (In re Williams),* 703 F.2d 1055, 1056 (8th Cir.1983). We review the bankruptcy court's findings of fact for clear error and its conclusions of law de novo.

DISCUSSION

In its opinion, the bankruptcy court correctly identified the general legal principles applicable to this matter as follows:

Pursuant to 11 U.S.C. § 101(14A), the term "domestic support obligation" means:

[A] debt that accrues before, on, or after the date of the order for relief in a case under this title, including interest that accrues on that debt as provided under applicable nonbankruptcy law notwithstanding any other provision of this title, that is—

(A) owed to or recoverable by—

(i) a spouse, former spouse, or child of the debtor or such child's parent, legal guardian, or responsible relative; or

. . .

(B) in the nature of alimony, maintenance, or support (including assistance provided by a governmental unit) of such spouse, former spouse, or child of the debtor or such child's parent, without regard to whether such debt is expressly so designated;

(C) established or subject to establishment before, on, or after the date of the order for relief in a case under this title, by reason of applicable provisions of—

(i) a separation agreement, divorce decree, or property settlement agreement;

. . .

(D) not assigned to a nongovernmental entity, unless that obligation is assigned voluntarily by the spouse, former spouse, child of the debtor, or such child's parent, legal guardian, or responsible relative for the purpose of collecting the debt.

This definition was enacted by the Bankruptcy Abuse Prevention and Consumer Protection Act of 2005 ("BAPCPA") and has an impact throughout the Bankruptcy Code on issues of discharge, the automatic stay, priorities, exemptions, the means test, and the calculation of disposable income in a Chapter 13 case. For purposes of the case at hand, discharge is at issue. Domestic support obligations are not discharged in Chapter 13 cases. * * * Further, domestic support obligations are priority claims pursuant to 11 U.S.C. § 507(a)(1)(A). * * *. [W]hether the debt is in the nature of alimony, maintenance, or support as required under § 101(14A)(B) is the issue of this adversary proceeding.

[handwritten annotation: Court's Holding]

* * * When deciding whether a debt should be characterized as one for support or property settlement, the crucial question is the function the award was intended to serve.

Whether a particular debt is a support obligation or part of a property settlement is a question of federal bankruptcy law, not state law. *See Williams*, 703 F.2d at 1056. A divorce decree's characterization of an award as maintenance or alimony does not bind a bankruptcy court but is however a starting point for the determination of the award's intended function. The burden of proof * * * is on the party asserting that the debt is nondischargeable.

Factors considered by the courts in making this determination include: the language and substance of the agreement in the context of surrounding circumstances, using extrinsic evidence if necessary; the relative financial conditions of the parties at the time of the divorce; the respective employment histories and prospects for financial support; the fact that one party or another receives the marital property; the periodic nature of the payments; and whether it would be difficult for the former spouse and children to subsist without the payments.

Exceptions from discharge for spousal and child support deserve a liberal construction, and the policy underlying § 523 favors the enforcement of familial obligations over a fresh start for the debtor, even if the support obligation is owed directly to a third party.

After correctly describing the * * * legal standards, the bankruptcy court then proceeded to apply those standards to the facts of this case. First, in determining that the monthly maintenance payments awarded by the Decree did constitute domestic support obligations excepted from discharge pursuant to § 523(a)(5), the bankruptcy court noted that the Decree specifically held that the monthly maintenance payments were necessary so that Sheri could continue her education and pursue her teaching certificate and that she could not presently earn sufficient income to support herself. In addition, the Decree provided that the monthly maintenance payments would terminate upon death or remarriage. Those factors are indicative of domestic support obligations. As the bankruptcy court found, the state court "clearly took into account the parties' income and expenses, their employment at the time of dissolution and ability to obtain a job, [Sheri's] continuing schooling and whether [Sheri] could support herself without monthly maintenance payments during the time period that she was continuing her education." Those findings are clearly supported by the record and are not clearly erroneous.

John's primary argument on appeal is that the Decree granted the "maintenance" payments to Sheri only because John was awarded the marital asset referred to as "renewal premiums." As a former insurance agent, John was entitled to receive additional income if and when any insurance policies he had previously sold were renewed by the insured and the premiums are paid. Thus, the renewal premium income is contingent upon the policies being renewed, and John was awarded all of the rights to that potential income. His theory appears to be that the state court judge only awarded the "maintenance" payments as a way of dividing the contingent renewal premium income. However, * * * that position simply is not supported by the record.

* * *

The bankruptcy court's determination that the function and purpose of the maintenance payments were to provide support to Sheri is amply supported by the record and will not be overturned.

The bankruptcy court also found that the attorney fee award was in the nature of support. The disparities in the parties' education, training, employment history, and earning capacity all led the bankruptcy court to find that the attorney fee award was made to balance those disparities and was, therefore, intended as support. The record supports the bankruptcy court's finding.

Accordingly, we affirm the decision of the bankruptcy court.

NOTES

1.   *Attorneys' fees as a form of maintenance. Phegley* treats the former husband's obligation to pay a portion of the wife's attorneys' fees as nondischargeable support. In doing so, the court relies on *Williams*, which expressly held:

> undertakings by one spouse to pay the other's debts, including a debt to a lawyer for fees, can be "support" for bankruptcy purposes. So can periodic payments required to be made to a former spouse, even if the decree labels these payments "property settlement." Whether in any given case such obligations are in fact "support" and therefore not dischargeable in bankruptcy, is a question of fact to be decided by the Bankruptcy Court as trier of fact in light of all the facts and circumstances relevant to the intention of the parties.

Williams v. Williams, 703 F.2d 1055, 1057–58 (8th Cir. 1983).

In a case resembling *Phegley*, but perhaps more extreme, a bankruptcy court held the former husband's obligation to pay part of his ex-wife's attorney's fees were "in the nature of support" in light of her "dire circumstances" and the fact that "she'd likely be homeless without [his] support." *In re Waldorf*, 2018 WL 4998117 (Bank. E.D. Pa. Oct. 15, 2018). The husband had argued unsuccessfully that the trial court had awarded the attorney's fees to the wife "to punish him for his bad behavior," not to support his wife.

2. *To what extent may bankruptcy courts consider the equities in determining the nature of post-divorce payments?* Bankruptcy courts have long had considerable discretion to try to structure an equitable result. For example, in *In re Duffy*, 331 B.R. 137 (S.D.N.Y. 2005), *aff'd*, 344 B.R. 237 (S.D.N.Y 2006), Dr. Duffy agreed to a court-ordered settlement under which he would pay his ex-wife $2,000 a month for ten years as compensation for her interest in his medical practice established during the marriage. After Dr. Duffy had paid $165,000 of his $240,000 obligation, he suffered extreme mental health disorders, including depression and obsessive compulsive disorder, which contributed to the loss of his medical license. He was alternately unemployed and working at very low-level jobs when the family court threatened to jail him for contempt because he was so far in arrears on his alimony and child support payments. The federal bankruptcy court held that the payments the family court had designated as alimony had been so labeled to make them deductible from Dr. Duffy's then-high income, and were in fact disguised equitable distribution payments. The court discharged him from further payments. The equities were clearly on Dr. Duffy's side, as his wife had left him for another man whom she subsequently married and was quite comfortable.

3. *More marital debt than property.* In the common bankruptcy case associated with divorce, marital debt considerably outweighs marital and separate assets combined. A case from Tennessee, offers a representative fact situation. *Mason v. Mason*, 2010 WL 5541056, at *6 (Tenn. Ct. App. Dec. 28, 2010). The husband, who was assigned responsibility for the monthly payments toward the marital credit card debt under Chapter 13 bankruptcy proceedings, was unable to work for nine months following triple bypass surgery and other illnesses. He was also paying alimony and child support. To keep costs down, the husband was living with his mother and relied on others for rides to and from work.

When a married couple is in arrears on mortgage payments and foreclosure proceedings have been initiated but not resolved, it may be impossible for the family court to accurately value the home or the debt on the home. There is often nothing to divide and, when neither party has significant potential for future earnings, no prospect that either will be able to pay off their outstanding debts much less pay the other anything in the future.

In one such case, where the court anticipated that the foreclosure process "will likely result in a bankruptcy proceeding on behalf of one or both of the parties" and that each would remain "jointly liable on any debt that may result from the deficiency" in their mortgage payments, the divorce decree did not distribute either the home or the debt on the home. The court further anticipated the interaction between its distribution order and the inchoate bankruptcy proceedings by expressly ordering that the divorce decree did not include any "domestic support obligation" that could not be discharged by a federal bankruptcy court. *Bargmann v. Bargmann*, 2011 WL 1026095, at *2 (Tenn. Ct. App. Mar. 22, 2011). This outcome aimed to give the bankruptcy court the discretion it needed to structure a workable bankruptcy plan for each spouse following the divorce.

4. *The interaction between ongoing proceedings for divorce and bankruptcy.* As one federal bankruptcy court explained, "[C]omplications often arise regarding the division of property between divorcing spouses when one spouse has filed for bankruptcy" but the divorce has not yet been finalized. *In re Sauro*, 2008 WL 2237036, at *2 (Bankr. D.N.J. May 30, 2008). "The interplay of bankruptcy law and state family law presents complicated issues for both the federal and state courts * * *. As these areas have become increasingly intertwined" the tension between the federal requirement to give the debtor a fresh start and the state court's exclusive jurisdiction over dissolution has mounted. *Id.* In *Sauro*, the bankruptcy trustee for the debtor wife, with the husband's consent, sold the marital residence held by the couple as tenants in the entirety, and used half of the proceeds to satisfy the wife's creditors. The trustee kept the remaining proceeds of the sale in trust as part of the bankruptcy proceeding. The bankruptcy court ordered the trustee to distribute the husband's share of the proceeds from the sale of the home to him immediately, holding that neither the trustee nor the creditors have any right to the non-debtor's money. The court further held that if the state court distributed any portion of the husband's proceeds to the wife as part of equitable distribution, such funds would remain outside the reach of the bankruptcy court because more than 180 days had passed since the wife filed for bankruptcy and in accordance with federal law any funds received by the debtor after that time are not part of the bankrupt estate. Courts remain alert to the possibility that post-separation transfers between spouses may be intended to protect assets after one spouse has filed for bankruptcy, which would constitute fraud.

Obligations under a divorce decree to pay third party creditors (like the attorney in *Phegley*) are debts "in the course of a divorce or separation" that are not dischargeable in bankruptcy under the 2005 Bankruptcy Act. What happens under the state court divorce decree when the federal bankruptcy court discharges the obligation to the third-party creditor? The Kentucky Supreme Court confronted this question in 2011. *Howard v. Howard*, 336 S.W. 3d 433 (Ky. 2011). Under a settlement agreement incorporated into the divorce decree, the husband in *Howard* was obligated to pay the couple's joint debt on a Dodge Durango (which had already been repossessed by the time they divorced). About a year after the divorce, when the husband filed for bankruptcy, creditors pursued the wife for the outstanding car loan. The federal bankruptcy court discharged the husband's obligation to the creditor for the Durango. The wife brought a contempt motion against the husband in state family court for his failure to pay the debt. The state court determined that the divorce decree created "two distinct obligations": the underlying marital debt to a third party and a separate obligation to the wife that formed part of the division of marital debts and assets. The obligation to the wife could not be discharged under federal law. The state's highest court ruled that the family court could enforce the husband's obligation to the wife with every means at its disposal, including holding him in contempt. *Id.* at 445.

5.   *Does the ability to shelter separate assets after divorce encourage marital break-up?* Some commentators have voiced concern that "strategic divorce" may be used to shelter the non-debtor spouse's separate property from obligations that existed during the marriage in community property jurisdictions, or may even result in creditors seeking to intervene in divorce litigation to protect their own interests in both community property and kitchen sink jurisdictions. *See* James R. Ratner, *Creditor and Debtor Windfalls from Divorce,* 3 Est. Plan. & Community Prop. L.J. 211 (2011). Where courts suspect that couples have agreed to allocate debt in a manner designed to defeat creditors' claims, they will reject proposed settlement agreements. For example, the Supreme Court of Washington voided a settlement agreement executed in anticipation of a tort judgment and effective three months before marital dissolution that assigned more than 90% of marital assets to the non-tortfeasor spouse. Since the marital community was liable for the tort, the court held the settlement agreement to be a fraudulent transfer. *Clayton v. Wilson,* 227 P.3d 278 (Wash. 2010).

8.   HAVE WE ACHIEVED EQUITY?

Despite high expectations, equitable distribution has not resolved the economic hardships that divorce imposes. Commentators have identified a number of concerns about the remaining inequities of equitable distribution. Before you read further, you might want to think about the goals of the current approach to property distribution at dissolution, whether the system appears to be achieving its goals, and whether it has the correct goals.

Although the proportion of married women who are full time homemakers has declined, Professor Mary Ziegler reports the existence of "a firm consensus that divorce hurts homemakers * * *. Although family court practices have become somewhat more just over the past twenty years, women still tend to suffer a substantial decrease in standard of living after divorce. Estimates of the decrease range from 15 to 27%. * * * Most scholars agree that 'divorce under the new divorce laws has been economically devastating for many women and children.'" Mary Ziegler, *An Incomplete Revolution: Feminists And The Legacy Of Marital-Property Reform,* 19 Mich. J. Gender & L. 259, 264 (2013).

Some urge that a partnership theory of marriage does not serve all spouses equally well. Laura Rosenbury argues that the homemaking wives of wealthy men are the primary beneficiaries of the dominant contemporary approach, while "women who both work outside of the home and do the bulk of the care work within the home" won't be rewarded for their uncompensated labor because it will be seen as "wifely sacrifice" instead of contribution. *Laura A. Rosenbury, Two Ways to End a Marriage: Divorce or Death*, 2005 Utah L. Rev. 1227, 1274–75, 1282–84, 1289 (2005).

Some commentators urge that all states adopt equal division of marital assets. Knowing that property will be split 50/50 would eliminate the need to assess each individual's contribution. These authors urge that equal division will encourage the parties to a marriage to engage in sharing behavior during the marriage, and to be less individualistic when making choices about behavior and finances. *E.g.,* Carolyn J. Franz & Hanoch Dagan, *Properties of Marriage*, 104 Colum. L. Rev. 75 (2004).

Consider the following proposals for reform:

1.   Property "acquired during a relationship between the spouses that immediately preceded their marriage, and which was a domestic-partner relationship * * * as defined [in another section]," should be "treated as if it were acquired during the marriage." ALI, Principles of Family Dissolution, § 4.03(6).

2.   Separate property should be gradually re-characterized as marital in marriages of long duration. *Id.* at § 4.12.

3.   Care work should have the same status as work outside the home, and future earning power and income streams should be taken into account when dividing assets. Alicia Brokars Kelly, *Actualizing Intimate Partnership Theory*, 50 Fam. Ct. Rev. 258 (2012).

QUESTIONS

1.   Which of the three existing approaches to property distribution do you think seems most fair: equitable distribution, equal division or all-property (kitchen sink)? What are the strengths and weaknesses of each?

2.   Evaluate the proposals for change set forth above. What problems is each proposal responding to? Will the proposal effectively address those problems? If you were in the state legislature, which of the proposals would you pursue, and why?

3.   Can one set of reforms effectively address the issues that confront different families? Can a "one size fits all" approach to property distribution achieve equity in every case or does the solution depend on the nature and longevity of the marriage?

4.   Should the rules at dissolution be structured in the hope of affecting how people behave within their marriages, or simply try to achieve fairness when marriages fall apart? What impact are each of the proposals above likely to have, if any, on whether people choose to marry? What incentives and disincentives to marriage do they offer?

5.   Does your knowledge about what spouses are entitled to receive when a marriage dissolves change your view of whether cohabitants should be

entitled to share in any wealth that either of them have accrued while living together? If so, how and why?

6.   Do any of the proposals set forth above address the special challenges that face households in the lowest quintile? Can you think of any legal changes that would help those families at dissolution?

CHAPTER 10

ALIMONY

■ ■ ■

1. OVERVIEW

Post-divorce financial arrangements between spouses typically address both property division and alimony. As you saw in Chapter 9, property division concerns assets and debts the parties acquire during the marriage, and alimony (also called maintenance or spousal support) concerns ongoing payments by one spouse to the other after the marriage ends. Although alimony and property division serve different purposes, courts often consider the two forms of post-divorce inter-adult financial allocations together.

Because of traditional assumptions about roles within marriage, alimony was historically available only to the wife, and it was meant to provide her with the support she would have continued to receive had she remained married. Alimony also served as a form of supplemental compensation to the wife because, under a title-based property distribution system, the husband received almost all of the couple's marital property. Even so, during the era of fault divorce, alimony was often available only to the "innocent" spouse based on the other spouse's breach of the marital obligation. In reality, however, the "guilty" spouse often held the power to manipulate the terms of the divorce because of the need to prove cause to secure a divorce: the dependent spouse, who often had the greater desire for divorce (and thus the greater need for proof), was forced to negotiate and agree to the financially secure spouse's terms. Moreover, courts awarded alimony only infrequently. Indeed, alimony was granted in fewer than 10% of all divorces at the turn of the twentieth century, and during the 1970s and early eighties, even as no-fault divorce swept through the states, approximately 15% of divorced women reported that courts had awarded them alimony. Cynthia Starnes, The Marriage Buyout: The Troubled Trajectory of U.S. Alimony Law 44–45 (2014).

Traditional justifications for alimony are no longer adequate in light of the growth of no-fault divorce and equitable distribution of marital property, the increasing equality of women, and other changes in the family.

A. THE HISTORY OF ALIMONY

The current status of alimony derives from its complex past.

1. Changing Views of Alimony

The following article reviews the history of alimony and efforts to develop a rationale for this form of ongoing, post-dissolution support. It is a helpful guide to the evolving expectations about what spouses owe one another or should be able to expect post-divorce and what can be expected of them with respect to economic self-sufficiency.

MARY KAY KISTHARDT,
RE-THINKING ALIMONY: THE AAML'S CONSIDERATIONS
FOR CALCULATING ALIMONY, SPOUSAL
SUPPORT OR MAINTENANCE

21 J. Am. Acad. Matrim. Law. 61, 62, 65–73 (2008).

* * *

The initial rationale for alimony or support had its origins in the English common law system. Historically there were two remedies from the bonds of marriage. Although an absolute divorce was theoretically possible, it required an act of Parliament and was therefore hardly ever used. More commonly a plea was made for a separation from bed and board (mensa et thoro). This action available from the ecclesiastical courts constituted a legal separation, as absolute divorce was prohibited under canon law. A husband who secured such a divorce retained the right to control his wife's property and the corresponding duty to support his wife. Even after Parliament authorized the courts to grant absolute divorces, the concept of alimony remained. The initial rationale appeared be premised on the fact that women gave up their property rights at marriage and after the marriage ended they were without the means to support themselves. The original award of alimony was similar to the wife's claim of dower, and courts used the traditional one-third of the property standard so instead of one-third of the estate at the husband's death she would receive one-third of the income of her husband at the time of the divorce. The concept of alimony came across the Atlantic with the founding of the colonies but seemingly without a corresponding rationale.

The introduction of the Married Women's Property Acts [which states began to adopt during the first half of the nineteenth century] changed the ability of women to retain property, but alimony remained. It appears that at least one rationale was based on contract theories because, for many courts, the role of fault played a significant role. Alimony then became damages for breach of the marital contract reflected in the fact that in most states it was only available to the innocent and injured spouse. The measure of damages often approximated the standard of living the wife would have enjoyed but for her husband's breach. Alternatively it represented compensatory damages for tortious conduct.

B. The Beginning of the "Modern Era"

In the 1970's the economic picture of spouses at divorce began to change. Many states adopted principles of equitable distribution allowing for property acquired during the marriage to be divided between the spouses regardless of how it was titled. This allowed economically dependent spouses to retain assets that were previously unavailable to them. Property division was used to address the inequities. These statutes resulted in decreasing spousal support awards.

In addition, women, who were historically the economically dependent spouses, joined the workforce in increasing numbers. * * * However, the practical reality of women's financial dependency remained in many marriages.

With the advent of no-fault divorce, alimony also lost its punitive rationale. The Uniform Marriage and Divorce Act (UMDA) changed the character of these awards to one that was almost exclusively needs based and at the same time gave spousal support a new name: maintenance. Maintenance was only available to the spouse who had an inability to meet his or her reasonable needs through appropriate employment. The marital standard of living was only one of six factors relied upon in making awards under the UMDA, where the focus was now on "self-support" even if it was at a substantially lower level than existed during the marriage. In addition, when awards were made they were generally only for a short term, sufficient to allow the dependent spouse to become "self-supporting." This spousal support reform often left wives, who were frequently the financially dependent spouses in long-term marriages, without permanent support.

Maintenance was sometimes awarded for "rehabilitative" purposes such as providing income for the time it takes the recipient to acquire skills or education necessary to become self-supporting. Short-term transitional awards were used to make a spouse economically self sufficient as soon as possible.

C. 1990's Reforms

In response to the denial of long-term awards for those most in need of them, the "second wave" of reform took place in the 1990's and expanded the factors justifying an award beyond "need." This new legislation encouraged courts to base awards more on the unique facts of a case and less on broad assumptions about need and the obligation to become self-supporting in spite of the loss of earning capacity that often occurs in long term marriages. * * *

NOTES AND QUESTIONS

1. *What now?* Professor Kisthardt offers a succinct summary of the status of contemporary alimony. As an additional set of reforms, states have begun to make "alimony predictable, if not understandable," along two different tracks: 1) establishing guidelines for alimony awards; and 2) limiting permanent alimony to longer-lasting marriages. Laura W. Morgan, *Spousal Support in Practice; An Update*, 51 Fam. L.Q. 39, 40 (2017). These trends are discussed later in the Chapter.

2. *Predictability*. With alimony, tension surfaces between a "clean break" model of marital dissolution and that of an ongoing financial relationship between former spouses. What policies do you think justify such an ongoing relationship today? As you review the other materials in the Chapter, consider what rationale provides the most compelling basis for requiring that one former spouse continue to transfer money to the other after the marriage has ended.

2. Alimony and Gender

For most of our history, many state alimony statutes explicitly excluded men as potential recipients. This gender-based regime changed entirely with *Orr v. Orr*, 440 U.S. 268 (1979). In *Orr*, a case which involved a wife who earned more than her husband, the Supreme Court struck down Alabama's alimony statute, which explicitly provided that courts could order only husbands to pay. The Court stated:

> Appellant [husband] views the Alabama alimony statutes as effectively announcing the State's preference for an allocation of family responsibilities under which the wife plays a dependent role, and as seeking for their objective the reinforcement of that model among the State's citizens. We agree, as he urges, that prior cases settle that this purpose cannot sustain the statutes. * * * If the statute is to survive constitutional attack, therefore, it must be validated on some other basis.

> The opinion of the Alabama Court of Civil Appeals suggests other purposes that the statute may serve. Its opinion states that the Alabama statutes were "designed" for "the wife of a broken marriage who needs financial assistance." This may be read as asserting either of two legislative objectives. One is a legislative purpose to provide help for needy spouses, using sex as a proxy for need. The other is a goal of compensating women for past discrimination during marriage, which assertedly has left them unprepared to fend for themselves in the working world following divorce. We concede, of course, that assisting needy spouses is a legitimate and important governmental objective. We have also recognized "[r]eduction of the disparity in economic condition between men and women caused by the long history of

discrimination against women . . . as . . . an important governmental objective." *Califano v. Webster*, 430 U.S. [313, 317 (1977)]. * * *

But in this case, even if sex were a reliable proxy for need, and even if the institution of marriage did discriminate against women, these factors still would "not adequately justify the salient features of" Alabama's statutory scheme, *Craig v. Boren*, [429 U.S. at 202–03]. Under the statute, individualized hearings at which the parties' relative financial circumstances are considered *already* occur. There is no reason, therefore, to use sex as a proxy for need. Needy males could be helped along with needy females with little if any additional burden on the State. * * *

Moreover, use of a gender classification actually produces perverse results in this case. As compared to a gender-neutral law placing alimony obligations on the spouse able to pay, the present Alabama statutes give an advantage only to the financially secure wife whose husband is in need. Although such a wife might have to pay alimony under a gender-neutral statute, the present statutes exempt her from that obligation.

Today, all states have gender-neutral alimony statutes that permit either spouse to receive an award. An increasing number of husbands are outearned by their spouses. The law in practice, however, does not always reflect the law on the books. Under 2% of all alimony awards are received by men. U.S. Census, Personal Income in 2016 Tbl. PINC-08 (2017) (4,000 of 243,000 alimony recipients in 2017 were male). Almost half of divorce lawyers report having seen an increase in the number of women who pay alimony. AAML, *Big Increase of Women Paying Alimony and Child Support* (2018). Of course, even when a spouse can support one household independently, it may prove difficult or impossible to fund two households.

Alimony may help equalize some disparate impacts of divorce. In 1985, Lenore Weitzman created great awareness of this issue with her book, The Divorce Revolution: The Unexpected Social and Economic Consequences for Women and Children in America (1985). Weitzman's study of California divorces suggested that the economic effects of divorce had significantly different impacts on men and women. She found that men experienced a 42% gain in their standards of living after divorce, but that women experienced a 73% decrease in their standards of living. *Id.* at 323. These statistics do not, Professor Weitzman explained, necessarily reflect changes in salaries; instead, they are based on the increase in expenses relative to income for female-headed households with children, and on the decrease in expenses for male-headed households without children. *Id.* at 340–42.

Scholars have questioned the accuracy of Weitzman's data and the magnitude of the differences between men and women's standards of living post-divorce, but subsequent studies confirm her general conclusion. *See* J. Herbie Difonzo & Ruth C. Stern, *The Winding Road From Form to Function: A Brief History of Contemporary Marriage*, 21 J. Am. Acad. Matrim. Law. 1 (2008). Indeed, the Census Bureau found that, during the first year after divorce, 23% of women, compared to 15% of men, received public assistance, and that recently divorced women were twice as likely as recently divorced men to be in poverty (22% v. 11%). Diana B Elliott & Tavia Simmons, Marital Events of Americans: 2009 10 (2011). Following divorce, women's household income fell by 41 percent, on average; men's fell as well, but only by half as much, Stacy Rapacon, *Why Women Should Rethink Their Finances After Divorce*, U.S. News, Aug. 14, 2017. Though perhaps not quite as attention grabbing as Weitzman's 1985 finding of 73%, these numbers still show the diverging financial impact of divorce.

Because alimony awards involve ongoing transfers of money, they are available to only a small percentage of divorcing couples, usually relatively affluent ones. As a result, use of alimony is subject to some criticism because of its lack of relevance to: "women of limited economic means and women of color, who are less likely to ever be married and who, if married, are unlikely to be married to a man with the kind of job that would make a generous alimony award a promising path to economic independence." Laura T. Kessler, *Getting Class*, 56 Buff. L. Rev. 915, 923–24 (2008).

NOTE AND QUESTION

Do you agree with Professor Kessler that the availability of alimony is flawed because it is primarily limited to affluent, and white, couples? *See* Keith L. Shoji, *Review: Alimony: Race, Privilege, and Dependency in the Search for Theory*, 20 J. Contemp. Legal Issues 115 (2011–2012). In 2016, of the 243,000 people who received alimony, only approximately 12,000 were black. 2016 Person Income Table of Contents.

B. THE UNIFORM MARRIAGE AND DIVORCE ACT

As Professor Kisthardt notes, the 1970 Uniform Marriage and Divorce Act (UMDA) established a standard for alimony or maintenance awards that focused on spousal need, rather than fault. Once a spouse established need, the Act directed the court to consider several factors in deciding on the award's amount and length.

UNIFORM MARRIAGE AND DIVORCE ACT
9A U.L.A. 446 (1998).

§ 308.   Maintenance

(a) In a proceeding for dissolution of marriage, legal separation, or maintenance * * * the court may grant a maintenance order for either spouse only if it finds that the spouse seeking maintenance:

(1)   lacks sufficient property to provide for his reasonable needs; and

(2)   is unable to support himself through appropriate employment or is the custodian of a child whose condition or circumstances make it appropriate that the custodian not be required to seek employment outside the home.

(b)   The maintenance order shall be in amounts and for periods of time the court deems just, without regard to marital misconduct, and after considering all relevant factors, including:

(1)   the financial resources of the party seeking maintenance, including marital property apportioned to him, his ability to meet his needs independently, and to the extent to which a provision for support of a child living with the party includes a sum for that party as custodian;

(2)   the time necessary to acquire sufficient education or training to enable the party seeking maintenance to find appropriate employment;

(3)   the standard of living during the marriage;

(4)   the duration of the marriage;

(5)   the age and the physical and emotional condition of the spouse seeking maintenance; and

(6)   the ability of the spouse from whom maintenance is sought to meet his needs while meeting those of the spouse seeking maintenance.

NOTES AND QUESTIONS

1.   *Interpreting the Uniform Marriage and Divorce Act*. In evaluating the UMDA and the other approaches to alimony discussed in this Chapter, consider the impact of the various policies on the recipient spouse. What assumptions do the statutes make about the appropriateness of an alimony award?

2.   *Rate of alimony awards*. Despite the extensive discussion of alimony indicated by the initial material in this Chapter, very few spouses actually receive it today.

Spousal support practices also vary widely based on state. According to a survey of family law attorneys, in states such as Indiana, Louisiana, and Texas, alimony awards are rare and limited to instances of severe hardship. In California, a spousal support award is very likely if the spouses' incomes at divorce are significantly different. Other states show variation based on different parts of each state as well as different judges. J. Thomas Oldham, *A Survey of Lawyers' Observations About the Principles Governing the Award of Spousal Support*, 51 Fam. L.Q. 1, 6–8 (2017).

2. JUSTIFICATIONS FOR ALIMONY

This Section considers the rationale for alimony awards, while the next Section examines how courts apply various rationales when they make alimony awards. As you will see, courts refer to the public policy goals as they decide on alimony awards. Accordingly, understanding the different rationales for awarding alimony will help you understand the laws themselves as well as courts' application of those laws.

Justifications for alimony have evolved over the years in concert with laws concerning the availability of divorce and the scope of property distribution. As a result of the development of the no-fault divorce system, the old gender-based rationale based on "innocence" or "guilt" no longer provided a principled basis for alimony awards.

Regardless of the form that alimony takes, the fundamental policy issue today is why one spouse must support the other once a marriage has ended and any marital property has been distributed equitably.

A. RATIONALES FOR ALIMONY AWARDS

As you learned at the beginning of the Chapter, alimony awards lack consistency from state to state. Some inconsistencies may result from difficulties in identifying a justification for such ongoing support payments in a world of no-fault divorce, where marriages may be of limited duration, and where both spouses increasingly contribute financially to the household during the marriage. Courts, legislatures and commentators have identified various rationales for alimony, but each justification raises its own set of issues. Alimony might be awarded based on theories of providing compensation, addressing needs, rewarding contractual expectations, or dissolving a partnership. As you review these justifications, consider how they relate to, and overlap with, the types of alimony discussed in this Chapter. The next excerpt provides a summary of potential contemporary rationales for awarding alimony.

CYNTHIA STARNES,
THE MARRIAGE BUYOUT: THE TROUBLED
TRAJECTORY OF U.S. ALIMONY LAW
128–129, 132–142 (2014).

* * *

The Search for a Contemporary Rationale

In extreme cases, the pragmatic justification for alimony is simple enough: alimony protects the state from the job of supporting a divorced spouse who without alimony would be thrust into poverty. But need alone does not explain why an ex-spouse rather than one's children, siblings, parents, or community should be responsible for meeting need. Moreover, trial courts are given broad discretion to define "need" and state self-interest does not explain cases in which need is defined in ways that have little to do with avoiding poverty. Nor can pragmatism alone answer the many questions surrounding an alimony award—How much? How long? On what grounds modification or termination?

The law's inability to articulate a justification for alimony is more than an abstract concern. The broad discretion vested in judges to determine alimony eligibility, duration and value, together with the absence of a theory to guide decision-making, have produced an alimony regime marked by unpredictability, uncertainty, and confusion. Some legal actors have responded to the dysfunction of current alimony law by endorsing alimony guidelines, but the lack of consensus on an underlying theory of alimony confounds efforts to identify a mathematical formula for generating the numbers that populate these guidelines. If guideline numbers are predictable, they are not necessarily equitable or consistent across jurisdictions. The absence of an underlying theory also leaves alimony vulnerable to myth, misconception, and hype—all of which characterize a new, energized anti-alimony reform movement that has reignited sentiments popular 40 years ago. Alimony is at a crossroads. If it is to survive it must have a rationale.

But first a threshold point. If alimony has no rationale consistent with contemporary understandings of marriage, maybe it shouldn't survive. Indeed, some have argued that alimony is an outdated remedy, a relic of coverture that has outlived its time. The problem with this response is that alimony is often the only available tool for addressing inequities in the spouse's financial positioning at divorce. As we have seen, most divorcing couples have minimal property. If marital roles have disparately affected the spouses' individual earning capacity—a common scenario in the many homes in which one spouse serves as primary caregiver—divorce will set one partner free to enjoy most of the long-term benefits of marital teamwork while the other bears most of the costs. * * *

Most reform theorists focus primarily on one of three interests: (1) a claimant's contributions to the other spouse (contribution theory); (2) a claimant's expected gain (gain theory); and (3) a claimant's loss (loss theory). These foci are familiar to any student of contracts, for they suggest the three classic contract interests of restitution, expectation, and reliance. * * *

To be sure, marriage is more than an ordinary contract. But in addition to "the mores," it is also a contract. And, as we shall see, contract principles and rules can be very useful. Yet contemporary commentators often assume contract is an inappropriate metaphor for marriage. * * *

The first objection is that contract is too crass a model for an institution as venerable as marriage. A contract model, the reasoning goes, promotes an alienated, cynical view of marriage that debases its intimate nature. . .

Secondly, the availability of no-fault divorce has led some to assume that marriage has become an at-will relationship, which makes a contract metaphor inapt. * * *

Even scholars who resist a contract metaphor often focus their alimony theories on protection of an interest familiar to the law of contract. These theories can be loosely categorized as (1) contribution theory, (2) expectation theory, and (3) reliance theory.

A. Contribution Theory

Contribution theory is the most modest effort to explain alimony. Based on principles of restitution, contribution theory aims to protect a promisee's "interest in having restored to him any benefit that he has conferred on the other party." As Joan Krauskopf explains: "The basic requirements are that one person has received a benefit at the expense of another, and that as between them it would be unjust for the recipient to retain the benefit without compensation to the other person." By way of analogy, an alimony theory based on restitution measures the contributions a claimant made to her spouse and then asks whether justice requires that she be reimbursed. * * *

B. Gain Theory

Gain theory offers a more generous compensation rationale for the divorcing spouse who finances her mate's education or training. * * *

Gain theory offers straightforward and workable quantification models. In its most radical form, a gain-based formula might require lifetime income sharing. * * * Gain theorists have much in common. Their focus is on the collaboration, teamwork, and partnership between spouses who join together to produce mutual benefits the couple expects to share—income and a home with children. If the parties divorce, the couple continues to share children, but without a divorce court's intervention, the primary wage-earner will take all the human capital benefits of the marital division of labor. As an equal stakeholder in the marriage, the primary caregiver is entitled to an equal share of the financial fruits of marriage. * * *

Gain theory is generally not interested in relative spousal contributions. The assumption is that spouses are equals—a default rule drawn from visions of contemporary marriage. Equality of status does not depend on the type or size of each spouses' contribution. As equals, spouses are entitled to share equally in the returns on joint investments, and in what has become a collective pool of human capital—no matter who brought home the bigger paycheck, no matter who cooked dinner more often or better. * * *

C. Loss Theory

Loss theorists focus on the reliance costs of participating in a "failed" marriage. Compensation thus aims to put an injured party "in as good a position as he would have been in had the contract not been made." In the family setting, Margaret Brinig and June Carbone describe two types of reliance: (1) "a lost opportunity to marry someone else," and (2) "sacrifices in career development." * * *

The most detailed version of loss theory comes from the American Law Institute. In a "principal conceptual innovation," the *ALI Principles* cast alimony as "compensation for loss rather than relief of need." * * * The ALI gives alimony a new name—compensatory spousal payments—and claims that its recharacterization transforms an alimony petition from a "plea for help" to a "claim of entitlement."

NOTES AND QUESTIONS

1.   *Rational rationales.* What are the different rationales for alimony awards identified in this reading? Which do you find most compelling? Why? Or do you think alimony lacks a rational basis altogether?

2.   *Self-sufficiency.* Does a spouse deserve support based simply on an inability to achieve self-sufficiency after divorce? Should an alimony award depend on whether a specified level of difference exists between the respective incomes of the two spouses?

B. THE ALI APPROACH: COMPENSATION FOR LOSS

As you have seen, the American Law Institute Principles of the Law of Family Dissolution use the concept of "compensatory payments" to support the spouse who has incurred a loss in earning capacity during the marriage based on bearing greater caretaking responsibilities for the family. ALI Principles of the Law of Family Dissolution: Analysis and

Recommendations § 5.03 (2002). The primary justification for these payments is to provide a just allocation of the financial losses resulting from divorce. To determine which spouse needs support, the Principles abolish any mention of fault and instead focus on the difference in the spouses' financial standing.

AMERICAN LAW INSTITUTE, PRINCIPLES OF THE LAW OF FAMILY DISSOLUTION: ANALYSIS AND RECOMMENDATIONS
(2002).

§ 5.04   Compensation for Loss of Marital Living Standard

(1)   A person married to someone with significantly greater wealth or earning capacity is entitled at dissolution to compensation for a portion of the loss in the standard of living he or she would otherwise experience, when the marriage was of sufficient duration that equity requires that some portion of the loss be treated as the spouses' joint responsibility.

(2)   Entitlement to an award under this section should be determined by a rule of statewide application under which a presumption of entitlement arises in marriages of specified duration and spousal-income disparity.

* * *

§ 5.05   Compensation for Primary Caretaker's Residual Loss in Earning Capacity

(1)   A spouse should be entitled at dissolution to compensation for the earning-capacity loss arising from his or her disproportionate share during marriage of the care of the marital children, or of the children of either spouse.

(2)   Entitlement to an award under this section should be determined by a rule of statewide application under which a presumption of entitlement arises at the dissolution of a marriage in which

(a)   there are or have been marital children, or children of either spouse;

(b)   while under the age of majority the children have lived with the claimant (or with both spouses, when the claim is against the stepparent of the children), for a minimum period specified in the rule; and

(c)   the claimant's earning capacity at dissolution is substantially less than that of the other spouse.

(3)   A presumption of entitlement governs in the absence of a determination by the trial court that the claimant did not provide

substantially more than half of the total care that both spouses together provided for the children.

NOTES AND QUESTIONS

1.   *Justifying compensation for loss.* In critiquing the Uniform Marriage and Divorce Act's reliance on need, and in justifying a standard based on compensation for loss, the Principles explain:

> A spouse frequently seems in need at the conclusion of a marriage because its dissolution imposes a particularly severe loss on him or her. The intuition that the former spouse has an obligation to meet that need arises from the perception that the need results from the unfair allocation of the financial losses arising from the marital failure. * * *

Principles, § 5.02 cmt. a.

Is this explanation persuasive? Do reasons other than unfair allocation of losses arising from the marriage's failure justify why an ex-spouse might have a continuing obligation to support the other? Should the Principles be based on return on investment rather than compensation for loss?

2.   *Fault.* Like the laws in many jurisdictions, the Principles eschew consideration of fault, the traditional basis for alimony awards. Should fault of any kind have a role in alimony?

3.   *Criticism.* Some scholars have critiqued the Principles' approach to alimony for failing to provide adequate compensation for caregiving. E.g., Merle H. Weiner, *Caregiver Payments and the Obligation to Give Care or Share*, 58 Vill. L. Rev. 135, 164–68 (2014). For example, what protections are available—or should be—for a spouse who has provided much of the caretaking but has an equal earning capacity?

PROBLEM 10-1

You are a member of the ALI task force responsible for reevaluating the ALI approach. What revisions will you suggest? Consider, for example, whether the terms "equity" and "substantial injustice" in § 5.04 need clarification.

3. HOW SHOULD COURTS AWARD ALIMONY?

Courts must consider numerous factors in deciding alimony claims during divorce proceedings, as discussed below. If a court determines that an alimony award is appropriate, then the court must then decide its form and amount. This Section examines the various types of alimony and the means for awarding it. As you read about the different means of making awards, think about how they relate to the justifications discussed in the previous Section.

A. DEFINING ALIMONY AWARDS

Alimony payments can generally be classified according to their duration. Alimony may be temporary (alimony *pendente lite)*, involving payments only while the parties are litigating to determine their respective rights and obligations arising out of the marriage. The goal of alimony *pendente lite* is to provide the dependent spouse a means of support during the divorce proceedings. Courts generally award temporary alimony based on the dependent spouse's reasonable need and the other spouse's ability to pay.

Final awards may take various forms depending on the reason for the award. Consider which of the justifications for alimony awards might support each different form that an alimony award might take.

1. Rehabilitative alimony—Support is provided for a definite period while the recipient seeks to become "self supporting." The period varies, depending on the type of "rehabilitation" the recipient needs, such as updating existing skills or acquiring new ones. For example, Florida's statute specifies that rehabilitative alimony can be awarded for "1. The redevelopment of previous skills or credentials; or 2. The acquisition of education, training, or work experience necessary to develop appropriate employment skills or credentials," but it requires "a specific and defined rehabilitative plan which shall be included as a part of any order awarding rehabilitative alimony." Fla. Stat. Ann. § 61.08(6) (2018).

2. Reimbursement alimony—With this type of alimony, the spouse whose financial contributions during the marriage directly enhanced the other spouse's earning capacity is awarded compensation. New Jersey provides that reimbursement alimony is available where "one party supported the other through an advanced education, anticipating participation in the fruits of the earning capacity generated by that education." N.J. Stat. Ann. § 2A:34–23(e) (2017). In contrast to most other forms of alimony awards, reimbursement alimony is typically not modifiable based on changed circumstances. *Id.* Reimbursement alimony is designed to compensate one spouse for enhancing the other's earning capacity, typically through support for graduate or professional school. Based on the acknowledgement that both spouses worked toward attaining the degree, the law recognizes that both should be entitled to claim some of the benefits.

Determining when to award reimbursement alimony and the appropriate amount may be difficult. For example, Oregon considers several factors, including the "extent to which the marital estate has already benefited from the contribution" in deciding on the amount of "compensatory spousal support." Or. Rev. Stat. Ann. § 107.105 (2018).

3. Bridge-the-gap (or limited-duration) alimony—This type of alimony "is appropriate in a short-term marriage where one of the spouses needs a short period to place themselves in an economically independent position.

Marshal S. Willick, *A Universal Approach to Alimony: How Alimony Should Be Calculated and Why*, 27 J. Am. Acad. Matrim. Law. 153, 166 (2015). New Mexico courts, for example, may award "transitional spousal support to supplement the income of the receiving spouse for a limited period of time; provided that the period shall be clearly stated in the court's final order." N.M. Stat. Ann. § 40–4–7(B)(1)(b) (2018).

4. Permanent, indefinite or periodic alimony—The spouse receives support for an undefined duration, awarded in periodic installments, to take effect from the final order of dissolution until either party's death or the recipient's remarriage. Courts award this type of payment, for example, after determining that the dependent spouse, because of age, illness or disability, "cannot reasonably be expected" to become self-supporting, or the resulting differences in the parties' respective standards of living would be "unconscionably disparate." Md. Code Ann., Fam. Law § 11–106(c) (2018). An award of permanent alimony is the exception, not the rule.

5. "Lump-sum" alimony—This form of alimony is a single payment. In nonlitigious divorces, a lump sum alimony payment is often an attractive option, permitting immediate financial settlement. Courts commonly make lump-sum awards only when periodic payments cannot be implemented for some specific reason, such as where the payor has a substance abuse problem or is a habitual spendthrift. Other courts make a rehabilitative lump-sum award when rehabilitation expenses are all due immediately (e.g., tuition for a final year of schooling), or when periodic rehabilitative support cannot be awarded for some other reason. Lump-sum alimony is generally awarded in one payment, though some courts have allowed for installment payments when necessary.

PROBLEM 10-2

If you were a state legislator reviewing alimony statutes, which model would you choose? Would you implement guidelines or presumptions? If so, on what would they be based? If you were a judge, which approach would you prefer? A litigant?

PROBLEM 10-3

The Oregon alimony statute recognizes three different kinds of awards. "Transitional spousal support" is designed to facilitate the recipient's training for employment; "[s]pousal maintenance is 'a contribution by one spouse to the support of the other for either a specified or an indefinite period' "; and "compensatory spousal support" offers reimbursement when one party has significantly contributed to the other party's acquisition of skills. *In re Marriage of Harris*, 244 P.3d 801, 805–06 (Or. 2010). You are a law clerk to an Oregon Supreme Court judge considering the following case. The husband entered dental school in 1992, and his wife dropped out of college shortly thereafter, working to support them and their child. The trial court rejected her claim for compensatory support, deciding that the wife made a " 'typical contribution for a spouse at the age and place in their lives where the parties were when they got married, and Wife's contribution during the marriage was also a typical and expected contribution.' " *Id.* at 805. The appellate court upheld the trial court's decision because, among other reasons, the parties had accumulated almost $1.5 million in marital property and had lived a comfortable lifestyle for the ten years prior to the divorce. *Id.* at 813. The judge for whom you are clerking would like to find that the extensive property should not preclude a compensatory spousal award. In light of the *Holterman* case (briefly discussed in Chapter 9), and the different justifications for alimony discussed earlier in the Chapter, what theories support the judge's decision? How will you explain your judge's rejection of the lower courts' analyses? How should the judge consider one spouse's contribution to the other's acquisition of skills?

B. DETERMINING ALIMONY AWARDS

As an example of one state's approach to alimony and its articulation of the various forms of alimony, the New Jersey statute includes a list of nonexclusive factors for the court to consider. Note that no single factor determinative, and with judges retaining significant discretion. It also carefully sets out the different forms of alimony that can be awarded. The statute applies to divorce proceedings as well as to civil union dissolution proceedings.

N.J. STAT. ANN. § 2A:34–23 (2018)

§ 2A:34–23. Alimony, maintenance

* * *

b. In all actions brought for divorce, dissolution of a civil union, divorce from bed and board, legal separation from a partner in a civil union couple or nullity the court may award one or more of the following types of alimony: open durational alimony; rehabilitative alimony; limited duration alimony or reimbursement alimony to either party. In so doing the court shall consider, but not be limited to, the following factors:

(1) The actual need and ability of the parties to pay;

(2) The duration of the marriage or civil union;

(3) The age, physical and emotional health of the parties;

(4) The standard of living established in the marriage or civil union and the likelihood that each party can maintain a reasonably comparable standard of living, with neither party having a greater entitlement to that standard of living than the other;

(5) The earning capacities, educational levels, vocational skills, and employability of the parties;

(6) The length of absence from the job market of the party seeking maintenance;

(7) The parental responsibilities for the children;

(8) The time and expense necessary to acquire sufficient education or training to enable the party seeking maintenance to find appropriate employment, the availability of the training and employment, and the opportunity for future acquisitions of capital assets and income;

(9) The history of the financial or non-financial contributions to the marriage or civil union by each party including contributions to the care and education of the children and interruption of personal careers or educational opportunities;

(10) The equitable distribution of property ordered and any payouts on equitable distribution, directly or indirectly, out of current income, to the extent this consideration is reasonable, just and fair;

(11) The income available to either party through investment of any assets held by that party;

(12) The tax treatment and consequences to both parties of any alimony award, including the designation of all or a portion of the payment as a non-taxable payment;

(13) The nature, amount, and length of pendente lite support paid, if any; and

(14) Any other factors which the court may deem relevant.

* * *

d.   Rehabilitative alimony shall be awarded based upon a plan in which the payee shows the scope of rehabilitation, the steps to be taken, and the time frame, including a period of employment during which rehabilitation will occur. An award of rehabilitative alimony may be modified based either upon changed circumstances, or upon the nonoccurrence of circumstances that the court found would occur at the time of the rehabilitative award.

This section is not intended to preclude a court from modifying permanent alimony awards based upon the law.

e. Reimbursement alimony may be awarded under circumstances in which one party supported the other through an advanced education, anticipating participation in the fruits of the earning capacity generated by that education. * * *

NOTES AND QUESTIONS

1. *Forms.* Unlike New Jersey, many states have not adopted statutes that explicitly explain the types of alimony that might be awarded. Is the New Jersey approach a good model, or is it an excessive limit on the court's discretion? Must a New Jersey court consider each of the listed factors?

2. *Which factors?* In most states, a statutory list of factors helps guide alimony decisions. Almost all jurisdictions consider standard of living as a factor in calculating the amount of alimony to award, and most states consider status as a custodial parent. More than half of the states include marital fault as a factor, in at least some situations. *Charts*, 51 Fam. L.Q. 543, 544–46 (2018). California requires the court to consider any evidence of domestic violence, including child abuse, and a domestic violence conviction results in a rebuttable presumption that alimony should be terminated or denied. Cal. Fam. Code Sec. 4320(i), 4325 (2018). Are there other factors that should be included in alimony statutes?

1. Evaluating Factors

The next case shows a court considering how to use its discretion to make an appropriate alimony award. Consider which of the various rationales for alimony explain the court's award.

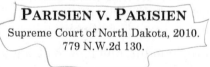

PARISIEN V. PARISIEN
Supreme Court of North Dakota, 2010.
779 N.W.2d 130.

SANDSTROM, JUSTICE.

Ronald Parisien appeals from a divorce judgment, arguing the district court erroneously awarded Jill Parisien permanent spousal support. We affirm.

I

Ronald and Jill Parisien were married in 1975. They have four living adult children. Jill Parisien sued for divorce in September 2008 on the grounds of adultery, extreme cruelty, willful neglect, conviction of felony, and irreconcilable differences. The case was tried in December 2008, and the district court issued a memorandum opinion and judgment granting the divorce the same month. The district court found the marriage "failed due to the personal, marital and financial misconduct of Ronald."

At the time of the divorce, Jill Parisien was 50 years old, earning $24,000 annually, and Ronald Parisien was 52 years old, with an income of $63,350 in 2008. Their primary assets consisted of seventy acres of land Jill Parisien had inherited from her family during the marriage, a home Ronald and Jill Parisien had built on that land, and Ronald Parisien's retirement account, which was worth $47,030. The district court awarded Jill Parisien property worth $110,050, less debt of $21,990, including the house and seventy acres of land she had inherited from her family. Ronald Parisien was awarded property worth $64,330, less debt of $19,695, including his retirement account.

The district court said an award of permanent spousal support was more appropriate than a temporary rehabilitative spousal support award, because of Jill Parisien's age, health difficulties, and earning capacity. The court found Jill Parisien, who was 50 years old at the time of the divorce, had reached her maximum earning capacity at $24,000 a year, and to exceed that level of earnings, she would need to further her education, which at this stage of her life would not necessarily be rewarded. The district court awarded Jill Parisien $1,500 per month in spousal support for two years, and $1,250 per month in spousal support thereafter. Spousal support would terminate upon her death, her remarriage or cohabitation for more than sixty days, or her attainment of age sixty-five. * * *

II

Ronald Parisien argues the district court erred in awarding Jill Parisien spousal support.

A district court may award spousal support to a party in a divorce action for any period of time. N.D.C.C. § 14–05–24.1. Spousal support determinations are findings of fact and will not be set aside unless clearly erroneous. A finding of fact is clearly erroneous if it induced by an erroneous view of the law, if there is no evidence to support it, or if this Court is left with a definite and firm conviction a mistake has been made. In awarding spousal support, the district court must consider the relevant factors of [previous cases'] guidelines. Factors to consider under [previous cases'] guidelines include:

& key factors to consider

> the respective ages of the parties, their earning ability, the duration of the marriage and conduct of the parties during the marriage, their station in life, the circumstances and necessities of each, their health and physical condition, their financial circumstances as shown by the property owned at the time, its value at the time, its income-producing capacity, if any, whether accumulated before or after the marriage, and such other matters as may be material.

The needs of the spouse seeking support and the supporting spouse's needs and ability to pay must also be considered * * *.

There are two types of spousal support. While permanent spousal support is appropriate to provide traditional maintenance for a spouse who is incapable of rehabilitation, rehabilitative spousal support is awarded to provide a spouse time and resources to acquire an education, training, work skills, or experience that will enable the spouse to become self-supporting. Rehabilitative spousal support is preferred, but permanent spousal support may be required to maintain a spouse who cannot be adequately retrained to independent economic status.

A

Ronald Parisien contends the district court did not properly consider his ability to pay spousal support. Spousal support awards must be made in consideration of the needs of the spouse seeking support and of the supporting spouse's needs and ability to pay.

Ronald Parisien argues the district court's finding of the parties' income disparity is far greater than it is in reality. He is employed as a building construction technology instructor at Turtle Mountain Community College, a nine-month position for which he receives $52,225 per year. The district court also found he is regularly employed during the summer months and earned $11,125 at Turtle Mountain Community College during the summer of 2008, thus making his total gross income $63,350 for the year 2008. Ronald Parisien argues the district court adopted the highest possible figure based upon the testimony presented. * * *

Additionally, he contends the district court adopted the lowest possible figure in determining Jill Parisien's gross income. He contends Jill Parisien has the capacity to work more than forty hours a week. At trial, Jill Parisien testified she makes $12 an hour and works forty hours per week. While she previously worked two jobs, she terminated the second job on medical advice. There is ample evidence to support the district court's finding that Ronald Parisien's total gross income is $63,350 per year and Jill Parisien's total gross income is $24,000 per year. The district court's finding of the parties' income levels is not clear error. Ronald Parisien agreed at trial that his actual total gross income for 2008 was $63,350. His stated monthly expenses totaled $2,389.

Ronald Parisien argues the district court did not balance "the burdens created by the separation when it is impossible to maintain two households at the predivorce standard of living." Although a more explicit analysis would be desirable, we believe the district court sufficiently analyzed property distribution and spousal support under the [previous cases'] guidelines and considered Jill Parisien's needs and Ronald Parisien's needs and ability to pay spousal support.

B

Ronald Parisien also contends the district court failed to consider the already lopsided property distribution before making an award of spousal support.

At the time of trial, the district court found Jill Parisien had reached her maximum earning capacity at $24,000 a year, and to exceed that level she would need to further her education, which "at this stage of her life" would not "necessarily be rewarded." * * * The court also found this factor weighed in favor of spousal support. While the thirty-three year marriage was long-term—a factor which normally would result in an equal division of property and debts—the district court found Ronald Parisien's misconduct and Jill Parisien's efforts to support the family during his incarceration had to be recognized. The district court found that while there was no suggestion of misconduct by Jill Parisien, Ronald Parisien had participated in a long-term affair and engaged in criminal activities, causing the end of the marriage and economic harm to Jill Parisien. The district court found Ronald Parisien is in good health (other than having high blood pressure), while Jill Parisien has diabetes, which is a matter of concern to her healthcare provider. The district court found the parties do not have any income-producing property and must live off their respective earnings. * * *

* * * The district court focused on Ronald Parisien's greater earning capacity; his marital, financial, and criminal misconduct; Jill Parisien's necessities to maintain her home; Jill Parisien's health; and the origin of the marital property. It explained that substantial repairs on the family home are necessary to render it habitable on a long-term basis. Thus, although Jill Parisien received a greater share of the property distribution, it was not clearly erroneous for the district court to award her spousal support as well.

NOTES AND QUESTIONS

1. *Two is more expensive than one.* The North Dakota spousal support statute simply requires the court to "[t]ak[e] into consideration the circumstances of the parties," and cases have developed guidelines to structure decision making. N.D. Cent. Code § 14–05–24.1 (2018). Which factors were most significant to the court? What was the impact of Jill Parisien's age on the alimony award and its form? Ronald Parisien's arguments are common in alimony actions. Which, if any, did you find most persuasive?

2. *Fault.* Even with no-fault divorce, the traditional rationale for alimony may retain some validity. The UMDA removed fault from the guidelines for determining entitlement to alimony, but some states retain fault-based alimony. For example, a South Carolina court must consider, among other factors, "marital misconduct or fault" where the misconduct has

"contributed to the breakup of the marriage." S.C. Code Ann. § 20–3–130(C)(10)(2018). (This issue was important in the *Mick-Skaggs* case discussed in Chapter 8). As discussed earlier many states allow courts to consider marital fault as one factor in establishing the award. Victims of domestic violence may also be particularly sympathetic candidates for fault-based awards.

Considering fault in the alimony determination, however, can produce problems. First, a determination of fault may require the type of "dirty laundry" fact-finding that no-fault divorce was designed, in part, to prevent. Second, in some states (such as South Dakota), the court is required to determine "relative fault." Such a determination may be quite complex, because both parties often share responsibility for the breakdown of the marriage. *See, e.g., Lovejoy v. Lovejoy*, 782 N.W.2d 669, 672 (S.D. 2010) ("In deciding whether alimony is warranted, the court should consider . . . [among other things] the relative fault in the termination of the marriage"). Finally, to the extent that fault-based alimony "rewards" innocence, it may diminish the importance of other factors that may be significant to alimony, such as the spouses' reasonable expectations or needs. Can you think of other problems with an alimony calculus that permits consideration of fault?

3.   *The relationship between property distribution and alimony.* In *McKee v. McKee*, 664 S.E.2d 505 (Va. Ct. App. 2008), the husband transferred his interest in the marital home to the wife, who agreed to become responsible for all remaining mortgage payments. The court of appeals upheld the trial court's consideration of the wife's mortgage payments when determining the amount of spousal support.

2.   Income Equalization

Post-divorce disparity of income is another factor courts may consider in alimony determinations. When an economically dominant spouse and an economically dependent spouse separate, one foreseeable consequence is that the dependent spouse's standard of living will fall. The following decision sets forth some of the considerations involved in determining whether the award should take the form of income equalization.

YOUNG V. YOUNG
Supreme Judicial Court of Massachusetts, 2017.
478 Mass. 1.

The Probate and Family Court judge in this divorce action made two rulings that are the primary subjects of this appeal. First, the judge found that, where the husband's income from his employment was "on an upward trajectory," the wife may only maintain a standard of living "consistent with the marital lifestyle (which was **one** where the parties['] needs expanded in accordance with the increasingly available income)" by an award of general term alimony that increases commensurate with the increase in the husband's income. Second, the judge found that, because of "the complex nature of [the husband's] compensation over and above his base salary and bonus," and because of "the constantly shifting nature of [the husband's] compensation," "it is reasonable and fair in the circumstances" to award alimony to the wife in the amount of thirty-three per cent of the husband's gross income, rather than a fixed amount.

We conclude that, where the supporting spouse (here, the husband) has the ability to pay, the need for support of the recipient spouse (here, the wife) under general term alimony is the amount required to enable her to maintain the standard of living she had at the time of the separation leading to the divorce, not the amount required to enable her to maintain the standard of living she would have had in the future if the couple had not divorced. We also conclude that, although there might be circumstances where it is reasonable and fair to award a percentage of the supporting spouse's income as general term alimony to the recipient spouse, those circumstances are not present in this case. We therefore remand the case to the Probate and Family Court with instructions to reevaluate the alimony judgment in light of our opinion and enter a new judgment accordingly.

Background. Derek L. Young (husband) and Joy G. Young (wife) had been married for nearly twenty-four years when the husband filed a complaint for divorce in the Probate and Family Court in January, 2013. The wife filed a complaint for divorce **one** week later, and the two actions were effectively treated as **one**. In October, 2013, the judge ordered the husband to pay temporary alimony in the amount of $48,950 per month. After a four-day trial, the judge made voluminous findings of fact and issued an amended judgment of divorce on September 25, 2015. The judge found that the husband works as a "high level executive" with a financial institution who receives substantial compensation in various forms. Apart from his annual base salary (which was $350,000 in 2014) and an annual bonus (which was $1.6 million in 2013), he receives compensation through at least seven different compensation programs or share plans, including several types of stock options, a special bonus program, investor entity units, and opportunities to purchase shares of common stock at a discount. The compensation programs vary in how consistently they produce income and in the amount of income they produce. Some investment assets that are earned are liquid and immediately transferrable, and some may not be transferred or converted to cash until sometime in the future. The amount earned, above and beyond the base salary and annual bonus, through these compensation programs is both considerable and variable. The husband's gross income from 2008 through 2012 was approximately $1.53 million in 2008, $2.07 million in 2009, $3.81 million in 2010, $7.96 million in 2011, and $7.76 million in 2012.

The judge found that the parties agreed early in their marriage that the husband would work and the wife would "be a stay-at-home parent and not be employed outside the home." As a result, the wife has not worked outside the home since 1992, and the judge found that she "has no ability to be employed at a level to allow her to maintain a lifestyle post divorce similar to that maintained during the marriage without alimony."

The husband's substantial compensation package allowed the parties to enjoy "an affluent, upper-class station in life and marital lifestyle during their marriage." The couple's expenses increased as the husband's income increased during the course of his employment. Before the separation, the parties were living in a lavish, eight-bedroom home, driving luxury vehicles, and regularly dining out three to four times a week at expensive restaurants. They had purchased a summer home in Nantucket, were spending "tens of thousands of dollars on articles of clothing and handbags" from designer stores, and regularly enjoyed expensive vacations.

The judge found that, after the parties separated, the wife maintained a level of spending similar to what she spent during the marriage. According to the wife's [updated] September 10, 2014, financial statement, the wife's weekly expenses had increased to $12,575.77 (or $653,940 per year). * * * The judge did not make a finding regarding her actual weekly or annual expenses or needs.

The wife sought alimony in the amount of $713,781.49 per year. After considering the husband's ability to pay, the wife's needs, and the other factors required by G. L. c. 208, § 34, the judge did not set a fixed amount of general term alimony but instead ordered the husband to pay the wife each year alimony in the amount of thirty-three per cent of his annual gross income.4 * * * The judge reasoned, "Because the parties lived with the expectation and reality that [the husband's] bonus level is on an upward trajectory, and given the fact that their needs historically followed this upward trajectory, * * * it is reasonable and fair in the circumstances to use a percentage for the future alimony particularly given the constantly shifting nature of [the husband's] compensation." The judge appointed a special master to oversee compliance with the judgment and to assist in resolving disputes that might arise.

The husband appealed, and we transferred the case to this court on our own motion.

Discussion.

[T]he Alimony Reform Act of 2011, establishes presumptive parameters [for an award]: the amount of general term alimony "should generally not exceed the recipient's need or [thirty] to [thirty-five] per cent of the difference between the parties' gross incomes established at the time of the order being issued." G. L. c. 208, § 53 (b).

A judge must consider and weigh all the relevant factors, but where the supporting spouse has the ability to pay, "the recipient spouse's need for support is generally the amount needed to allow that spouse to maintain the lifestyle he or she enjoyed prior to termination of the marriage." Two of the statutory factors in § 53 (a) are "marital lifestyle" and the "ability of each party to maintain the marital lifestyle." Both focus on the spouses' lifestyle during the marriage. Thus, both the act and the case law interpret "need" in terms of the marital lifestyle the parties enjoyed during the marriage, as established by the judge at the time of the order being issued, in this case, the judgment of divorce.

Where, as so often happens, the couple's collective income is inadequate to allow both spouses to maintain the lifestyle they enjoyed during the marriage after their household is divided in two through divorce, "the recipient spouse 'does not have an absolute right to live a lifestyle to which he or she has been accustomed in a marriage to the detriment of the provider spouse.'" *Pierce*, 455 Mass. at 296, 916 N.E.2d 330, quoting *Heins*, 422 Mass. at 484, 664 N.E.2d 10. Instead, "[t]he judge must consider all the statutory factors and reach a fair balance of sacrifice between the former spouses when financial resources are inadequate to maintain the marital standard of living." Pierce, supra. The act presumptively provides that the "fair balance of sacrifice" means that the supporting spouse generally should not be required to pay more than thirty-five percent of the difference between the parties' gross incomes. G. L. c. 208, § 53 (b).

Here, given the husband's substantial ability to pay, the determination of alimony rested solely on the wife's needs, that is, the amount necessary to allow her to maintain the lifestyle she enjoyed prior to the termination of the marriage. Where, as here, the husband's income grew considerably over the years and the marital lifestyle grew with it, the wife's need for alimony reflects the need to enjoy the more expensive lifestyle she had grown accustomed to before the marriage ended. The judge here appropriately recognized that "the parties' needs expanded in accordance with the increasingly available income" during the marriage, but the judge erred in determining that the wife's need for support is to continue to expand after the divorce commensurate with the anticipated "upward trajectory" of the husband's income. * * * Even if the parties enjoyed an upwardly mobile lifestyle for the duration of their marriage, nothing in the language of the statute or our case law suggests that the recipient spouse is entitled, by way of alimony, to enjoy a lifestyle beyond what he or she experienced during the marriage. * * *

NOTES AND QUESTION

1.   *Should the wife have received more?* Professor Merle Weiner explains that "alimony should reflect the gain that the claimant would have obtained had she remained married" and that it:

makes a lot of sense for parents who were in a marital or marital-like relationship and are seeking a remedy at the end of that relationship. The remedy is appropriate because the parties' marriage involved an implicit agreement that both would contribute to maximize the couple's collective well-being and both would share in the bounty, including the couple's economic prosperity.

Merle H. Weiner, *Caregiver Payments and the Obligation to Give Care or Share*, 59 Vill. L. Rev. 135, 204–05 (2014).

Wages may constitute the primary source of income. Should it matter whether one spouse serves as the primary caretaker and relinquishes job opportunities, providing support for the other spouse's employment?

2. *The "partnership" justification*. Partnership theory, which views marriage as analogous to a partnership, with an agreement to share profits, assets and debt, could provide a basis for income equalization.

> The question [of] how courts should reflect the notion of economic partnership and compensate spouses for specialization of labor in marital property division [might be solved by recognizing that] contributing spouses should have a property right to a portion of the earning spouse's income not just during marriage but also for a certain number of years post-divorce in order to equalize their financial situations.

Allison Anna Tait, *Divorce Equality*, 90 Wash. L. Rev. 1245, 1285–86, 1290 (2015).

Do you think the partnership analogy is useful?

3. *Imputation of income and self-support*. What assumptions should courts make about the ability of a homemaking spouse to become self-sufficient? In *Reynolds v. Reynolds*, 216 Md. App. 205 (Md. Ct. Spec. App. 2014), both spouses had attended Yale Law School and had significant earning potential upon graduation in the early 1980s; however, the wife left the workforce in 1990 upon giving birth to twins and experiencing multiple medical complications, while the husband worked in private practice, making as much as $800,000 per year. At the time of divorce, the wife was 56 years old and had been a homemaker for over two decades. The trial court awarded alimony based on what it viewed as the "unconscionable dispar[ity]" between the income of the husband and wife (a difference of over $700,000 annually), and the court of appeals affirmed, noting that "this was not a case where Wife was likely to progress in her career to a point where she would be self-supporting on a scale sufficient to meet her needs or bridge th[e] income and lifestyle gap" between her married life and her life after divorce. *Id.* at 222.

PROBLEM 10-4

You are a trial court judge assigned to the family law docket. The following four cases are part of your current calendar. Your jurisdiction provides for award of alimony in an amount "based on the judge's discretion, considering the circumstances of the parties." How will you decide these four cases, each of which concerns the first marriage for both spouses? Will you award alimony in all four? If you would, what type, how much and for how long? If not, then why not?

a.   Sally and Bob married in 2015 after both had finished college. They moved to a different city so Bob could work as a manager at a large corporation. Sally took an entry level position as a sales clerk, expecting to leave the workforce in the next few years to start a family. However, Sally did not become pregnant and after four years of marriage, the couple sought a divorce based on irreconcilable differences.

b.   Susan and Bernice married in 2015 after both had finished college. They moved to a different city so Bernice could work as a manager at a large corporation. Susan took an entry level position as a sales clerk, expecting to leave the workforce in the next few years to start a family. Susan became pregnant after three years of marriage, and quit work when she neared the end of her pregnancy. Within the first year after the birth of their child, the couple decided to divorce.

c.   Jim and Nancy marry in 2009, when both are in their late 20s. Jim has built up a solid career as a car salesman, and Nancy spent her years after college working in secretarial positions. After they marry, Nancy returns to law school and, within the next five years, obtains a position at a law firm, substantially exceeding Jim's salary in the car business. After ten years of marriage, the couple divorces.

d.   Sam and Jill marry in 1994. While married, Jill returns to graduate school to receive a Ph.D., and Sam returns to law school for a J.D. Initially, Sam works as a government lawyer and Jill works as a college professor. After several years, though, the couple has five children, and Jill decides to teach part-time until the children reach high school. The couple divorces after 25 years of marriage, with two children still in elementary school

e.   The Utah alimony statute explicitly provides that: "The court may, under appropriate circumstances, attempt to equalize the parties' respective standards of living." Utah Code Ann. § 30–3–5.(8)(f) (2018). Consider whether this would have changed your analysis in problems a–d above.

3.   Establishing Alimony Guidelines

As discussed earlier, given the various and differing factors that courts consider in alimony determinations and the trial judge's broad discretion, awards vary widely from state to state, family court to family court, and even from trial judge to trial judge. In response to this unpredictability and inconsistency, a growing number of states and local court systems have promulgated formulas to help courts determine the amount and duration of alimony awards. The goal of these guidelines is to facilitate a more consistent and predictable framework for assessing the appropriate amount of an alimony award rather than relying on the judge's discretion to apply a series of factors specified by statute or previous cases, and this may provide guidance for divorce settlements. *See* Morgan, *supra*, at 41 n.8. And, as you saw earlier in the Chapter, the American Law Institute's Principles of Family Dissolution advocate guidelines. Some states provide guidelines only as to duration; for example, Alabama has a strong preference for rehabilitative alimony to be awarded for five years or less, but if periodic alimony is ordered, it should not "exceed the length of the marriage [ ] with the exception that if a party is married for 20 years or longer, there shall be no time limit" as to duration. Al. St. Sec. 30–2–57 (2018).

The Massachusetts statute, portions of which are set out below and later in the Chapter, seeks to limit judicial discretion and establish predictability. As you read the statute, think about whether there are other possible consequences of the guideline approach.

MASS. GEN. L. CH. 208 (2018)

§ 49.   * * *

(b) Except upon a written finding by the court that deviation beyond the time limits of this section are required in the interests of justice, if the length of the marriage is 20 years or less, general term alimony shall terminate no later than a date certain under the following durational limits:

(1) If the length of the marriage is 5 years or less, general term alimony shall continue for not longer than one-half the number of months of the marriage.

(2) If the length of the marriage is 10 years or less, but more than 5 years, general term alimony shall continue for not longer than 60 per cent of the number of months of the marriage.

(3) If the length of the marriage is 15 years or less, but more than 10 years, general term alimony shall continue for not longer than 70 per cent of the number of months of the marriage.

(4) If the length of the marriage is 20 years or less, but more than 15 years, general term alimony shall continue for not longer than 80 per cent of the number of months of the marriage.

(c) The court may order alimony for an indefinite length of time for marriages for which the length of the marriage was longer than 20 years.

* * *

§ 53.   Determination of form, amount and duration of alimony; maximum amount; income calculation; deviations; concurrent child support orders

* * *

(b) Except for reimbursement alimony or circumstances warranting deviation for other forms of alimony, the amount of alimony should generally not exceed the recipient's need or 30 to 35 per cent of the difference between the parties' gross incomes established at the time of the order being issued.

* * *

(f)   In determining the incomes of parties with respect to the issue of alimony, the court may attribute income to a party who is unemployed or underemployed.

(g)   If a court orders alimony concurrent with or subsequent to a child support order, the combined duration of alimony and child support shall not exceed the longer of: (i) the alimony or child support duration available at the time of divorce; or (ii) rehabilitative alimony beginning upon the termination of child support.

NOTES AND QUESTIONS

1.   *Cabining discretion: guidelines v. factors.* Do guidelines provide models for consistent awards? Do alimony guidelines or factors better account for the variations in roles, responsibilities and earning capacities within different marriages? Consider whether a one-size-fits all approach is appropriate. Why?

2.   *Different approaches.* Massachusetts sets out guidelines not just for duration of alimony but also for amount. Other states have developed their own approaches to alimony guidelines, ranging from mathematical formulas to limits based on length of marriage or amount of obligor's income or the type of alimony. For example, in Indiana, the law prevents the court from awarding divorcing spouses more than three years of rehabilitative support. Ind. Code Ann. § 31–15–7–2(3) (2018). In Maine, courts apply rebuttable presumptions that general support "may not be awarded if the parties were married for less than 10 years * * * [and] that general support may not be awarded for a term exceeding ½ the length of the marriage if the parties were married for at least 10 years but not more than 20 years as of the date of the filing of the action for divorce." The presumptions do not apply to other forms of alimony, such as reimbursement or pendente lite. Me. Rev. Stat. Ann. tit. 19–A, § 951–A(2)(A)(1) (2018). Texas has a similar approach to awards in shorter marriage, although alimony will be awarded when, for example, the obligee spouse is disabled. Support may not exceed the lesser of $5,000 or 20% of the obligor's average gross monthly income. *See* Tex. Fam. Code Ann. §§ 8.051–.055 (2018). By contrast, a New Jersey court noted that, in adopting the statute excerpted

above, its "Legislature declined to adopt a formulaic approach to the calculation of alimony." *Waldbaum v. Waldbaum*, 2017 WL 6577410, at *12 (N.J. Super. Ct. App. Div. Dec. 26, 2017)(unpublished opinion)

4. ENFORCEMENT OF ALIMONY AWARDS

Once the court awards alimony, issues remain concerning enforcement of the ongoing alimony obligation. Divorced spouses sometimes pay early installments, but then fail to continue payment. State statutes may authorize enforcement through various means, such as "attachment, garnishment, execution or contempt." *E.g.,* N.M. Stat. Ann. § 40–4–19 (2018).

A. JUDICIAL ENFORCEMENT

To enforce an alimony award, the recipient spouse may need to bring another lawsuit. Courts can retain jurisdiction over divorce decrees, which then become enforceable through civil and criminal contempt proceedings. (Issues concerning the relationship between a court decree and a separation agreement are discussed in Chapter 16.)

In *Wooters v. Wooters,* 911 N.E.2d 234, 236 (Mass. App. Ct. 2009), the parties were divorced in 1994, and the husband, an attorney, was required to pay one-third of his "gross annual employment income" as alimony. In 2006, he exercised some of the stock options he had received through his employment, but failed to include them as part of the income subject to the alimony obligation. The trial court found the husband in civil contempt and ordered him to pay the alimony in arrears. Finding that the husband had not met the standard for contempt, which was "clear and undoubted disobedience of a clear and unequivocal command," the appellate court reversed the contempt finding, although the husband was still required to pay his arrears. *Id.* at 239.

Some state statutes treat failure to pay court-ordered alimony an as contempt of court subject to imprisonment or other sanction. In Louisiana, for example, contempt arising from nonpayment of court-ordered spousal support is punishable by up to three months in jail as well as a $500 fine. La. Rev. Stat. Ann. § 13:4611(1)(d)(i) (2019).

B. PRIVATE ENFORCEMENT METHODS

As alternatives to a judicial enforcement action, other creative means exit for securing the payment of alimony. The marital settlement agreement may provide for enforcement through a lien, for example. *E.g., Pipitone v. Pipitone*, 23 So. 3d 131, 134 (Fla. Dist. Ct. App. 2009). A settlement agreement providing for alimony may retain its status as a contract, and thus be enforceable through breach of contract claims. 24A Am. Jur. 2d *Divorce and Separation* § 1067 (2018).

Two additional useful methods involve establishing a separate trust for alimony awards, or requiring the payor spouse to obtain life insurance. In *Haber v. Haber,* 2013 WL 6122596 (N.J. Super. Ct. Nov. 22, 2013)(unpublished opinion), the family court ordered that $250,000 be held in trust by the husband to secure his support payments.

As noted in Chapter 9, life insurance may similarly ensure protection of the payee spouse's interest or help recover any unpaid alimony obligations. While spousal support typically terminates upon the death of the obligor, the parties may agree otherwise. *See, e.g.,* Me. Rev. Stat. Ann. tit. 19–A, § 951–A(7) (2018) ("The court may also order the obligated party to maintain life insurance or to otherwise provide security for the payment of spousal support in the event the obligation may survive the obligated party's death"). However, states may specify that a payor spouse can be required to obtain life insurance only when special circumstances demonstrate need for this precaution. In *Levy v. Levy,* 900 So.2d 737 (Fla. Dist. Ct. App. 2005), for example, the court denied the former wife's request for an order that her husband purchase life insurance to secure her permanent alimony award. The court held that the wife had failed to produce " 'evidence of the payor's insurability, the cost of the proposed insurance, and the payor's ability to afford the insurance.' " *Id.* at 745. In *Waldorf v. Waldorf,* the court remanded for a determination of the appropriate amount of life insurance required to secure the husband's obligations. 2014 WL 2515732 (N.J. Sup. Ct. June 5, 2014)(unpublished opinion).

C. ENFORCEMENT FOR MILITARY PERSONNEL

The Uniformed Services Former Spouses Protection Act allows state courts to distribute a military service member's retirement pay to former spouses, under the Defense Department's enforcement authority. A portion can be paid directly to a former spouse to fulfill a court's alimony award. The Act applies only if the parties have been married for at least ten years, and if the payor spouse performed at least ten years of military service during the marriage. Pursuant to the Act as well as consumer protection laws, the spouse is entitled to no more than a certain percentage of the payor's disposable retirement pay. Not all former spouses will automatically receive a portion of the retirement benefits. Former spouses cannot collect for past due payments, but the Act provides an important procedure for guaranteeing collection of future alimony. 10 U.S.C. § 1408 (2018); Defense Financing and Accounting Service, *Legal Overview* (2013), *How to Apply* (2018).

But where alimony proceedings involve a spouse who is currently serving in the military, as you saw in Chapter 9, the Servicemembers Civil Relief Act, 50 U.S.C.A. § 3901 *et seq.* (2018), may make it difficult for the other spouse to enforce an alimony award because it authorizes the temporary suspension of civil proceedings against servicemembers while they are on active duty.

D. ATTACHMENT OF WAGES

Courts may also enforce an alimony award by attaching a portion of the payor's earnings, just as it can attach wages for past due child support payments. *E.g.*, Fla. Stat. Ann. § 61.12 (2018). This attachment removes a portion of the payor's earnings from his or her paycheck. The payor's employer receives a notice of wage attachment, instructing the employer to pay a portion of the payor's salary to a levying officer. If the employer fails to comply, it will be liable for contempt and may be forced to repay the withheld balance.

5. MODIFICATION AND TERMINATION OF ALIMONY

Unless an alimony order prevents modification, the obligor or obligee spouse may normally petition the court to increase or decrease alimony due to an unexpected and substantial change in circumstance concerning the financial situation of either spouse.

In deciding whether to modify an alimony award, courts generally have considerable discretion in the absence of a written spousal agreement that precludes modification. Statutes may require a court to examine both spouses' changed financial circumstances. Courts typically consider several factors, including the effects of modification on the other party, the length of the marriage itself, each party's current health, the purpose of the alimony originally awarded, the foreseeability of the change, and other relevant factors. Courts also evaluate whether the changes are self-induced, or whether they are based on factors beyond the control of the payor or payee. *See* Mark R. Soboslai, *Three Steps to Modification: Responding to a Change in Circumstances*, 25-SPG Fam. Advoc. 35 (2003). Note that, as you saw in Chapter 9, bankruptcy does not provide grounds for modification, pursuant to federal law.

An order may specify the conditions on which it can be terminated, and state statutes establish standards for termination. Parties must comply with state law concerning modification or termination, which typically prevents retroactive changes prior to the filing of a motion to modify. *See, e.g.*, Minn. Stat. § 518A.39 Subd. 2 (e) (2018). Even if the parties agree to retroactive modification, courts can invalidate the agreement if it permits retroactivity prior to the service of notice of a modification motion. *Leifur v. Leifur*, 820 N.W.2d 40, 43 (Minn. Ct. App. 2012).

A. MODIFICATION

Courts recognize the need for modification, but they also make clear that changes in financial situation or physical health do not, by themselves, create a right to modification. Indeed, what constitutes a change may itself be unclear. Nevada's statute resolves such disputes by explicitly stating that a change in the obligor's gross income of 20 percent or more constitutes changed circumstances that require a review of whether modification is appropriate. Nev. Rev. Stat. Sec. 125.150(12) (2018).

MARTINDALE V. MARTINDALE
Tennessee Court of Appeals, Aug. 22, 2005.
2005 WL 94366.[a]

HOLLY M. KIRBY, J.

This is a post-divorce alimony case. The parties were divorced in 1995 and the mother was awarded rehabilitative alimony for seven years. In 2003, the trial court extended the rehabilitative alimony until the youngest of the parties' four children graduated from high school. The extension of alimony was based on the demands of being the primary residential parent for the parties' four young sons, two of whom were found to have learning disabilities. The father appealed the extension of rehabilitative alimony. We affirm.

Plaintiff/Appellant Michael Lynn Martindale, M.D., ("Father") and Defendant/Appellee Margo Miller Martindale ("Mother") were divorced on March 31, 1995. At the time of the divorce, the parties had four minor children: Michael Rand Martindale, born September 11, 1988, Miles Thomas Martindale, born February 8, 1990, Austin Edward Martindale, born December 12, 1991, and Miller Christian Martindale, born April 24, 1993. Mother worked teaching school while Father was in medical school. When the parties' first child was born, Mother became a full-time homemaker. Father's medical practice was with Jackson Clinic.

At the time of the divorce, the parties entered into a Marital Dissolution Agreement ("MDA"), which was incorporated into the final divorce decree. Under the final decree, Mother was awarded sole physical and legal custody of the children * * *.

Under the final decree, Father agreed to pay wife $5,000.00 per month as rehabilitative alimony. The alimony was to continue until two and one-half years after the youngest child entered the first grade. This resulted in monthly alimony payments to Mother for seven years, scheduled to end on February 15, 2002.

---

[a] Unpublished opinion.

On February 8, 2002, prior to the termination of the alimony payments, Mother filed a Motion * * * to Modify Final Order. In this petition, Mother sought * * * to continue the rehabilitative alimony, and to award alimony *in futuro*.

A hearing on the issues was held on April 24, 2002. Both parties testified extensively regarding child support, alimony, and financial issues. Father testified that when the parties divorced, he made approximately $292,000, and that since 1997 he had made in excess of $400,000 per year. Mother worked at a medical clinic for $15.00 per hour. She worked part-time so that she could be available for the children's activities after school, and to assist their two learning-disabled sons with their school work. * * *

At the end of the hearing, the trial court found that Mother ha[d] not been able to rehabilitate herself as contemplated in the MDA * * * due to the demands of being custodian and primary care parent for four young sons, whose demands on her times and energy [have] increased every year. And the Court finds this will probably continue to [be] so.

The trial court also noted that the learning problems of two of the sons could not have been contemplated when the parties entered into the MDA. As a result, the trial court continued the $5,000 monthly rehabilitative alimony until the youngest child graduates from high school. * * * [Father appealed.]

Modification of an alimony award is factually driven, calling for a careful balance of many factors. The trial court is given wide latitude, and its decision will not be disturbed unless it is "not supported by the evidence or is contrary to the public policies reflected in the applicable statutes." *Bogan v. Bogan*, 60 S.W.3d 721, 727 (Tenn. 2001). * * *

Father asserts that the evidence showed that Mother had rehabilitated herself, and therefore the trial court erred in extending Mother's rehabilitative alimony. The record shows that Mother became recertified to teach school, and that Mother was employed part-time in a medical clinic. However, Mother also offered substantial testimony on the amount of time needed to care for the four children, due to their extensive extracurricular activities and the learning disabilities of two of the children. Mother testified that the children's demands on her time prevent her from working a forty-hour work week. Based on this testimony, the trial court found that Mother was not fully rehabilitated and would be unable to fully rehabilitate herself until the children graduate from high school. After a full review of the record, we cannot say that the evidence preponderates against this finding.

Father further asserts that the evidence did not show that Mother's alleged inability to rehabilitate herself was due to unforeseen circumstances. Father argues that an award of alimony can only be modified "upon a showing of a substantial and material change" as provided in Tennessee Code Annotated § 36–5–101. Father argues that there has been no material change in circumstances and that Mother's current situation is exactly what the parties contemplated when the MDA was signed. The trial court, however, found that the learning disabilities of the parties' two sons could not have been contemplated when the parties signed the MDA, and that it adversely impacted Mother's ability to work full-time and to rehabilitate herself. From our review of the record, the evidence does not preponderate against this finding.

Finally, Father asserts that if Mother is not rehabilitated, it is because she did not make a reasonable attempt to rehabilitate herself. Father argues that Mother knew that she had seven years of rehabilitative alimony but did not use this time [to] further her education or prepare for a new career. After hearing the evidence, the trial court found that Mother "has not been able to rehabilitate herself as contemplated in the MDA . . . due to the demands of being custodian and primary care parent for four young sons." Again, the evidence in the record does not preponderate against this finding.

Mother argues on appeal that the award of rehabilitative alimony should be converted to alimony *in futuro*, and that the trial court erred in refusing to do so. She notes that she will be 51 years old when the younger child graduates from high school, and contends that, in view of the disparity in income between the parties, rehabilitation is not possible. The trial court found that Mother could not be fully rehabilitated until the youngest son graduates from high school. The trial court did not find that Mother cannot be rehabilitated, and declined to convert the award to alimony *in futuro* at that time. After reviewing the record, we cannot find that the trial court erred in declining Mother's request.* * *

NOTES AND QUESTIONS

1.   *Meeting the standard.* Tennessee requires a substantial and material change in circumstances to justify modifying an alimony award. *Bogan*, 60 S.W.3d at 727. Did the court apply this standard appropriately? Are there additional facts that the court might have considered? How should courts consider one parent's provision of care to children? As part of its alimony reform system, Massachusetts limits rehabilitative alimony to no longer than 5 years, although that can be extended if there are "compelling circumstances" where unforeseen events prevent the recipient from being self-supporting at the end of the term "with due consideration to the length of the marriage." Mass. Gen. Laws Ann. 208 § 50 (2018). Was that standard met in *Martindale*?

2.   *Legitimate changes in the payor's income.* When Lee and Kimberly Herring divorced in 2008, he was required to pay $1,000 per month in spousal support. Subsequently, he was convicted of numerous sexual offenses involving the parties' daughter (these actions had been a major contribution to the divorce), and incarcerated. Pursuant to the Vermont statute, alimony can be

terminated based " 'upon a showing of a real, substantial, and unanticipated change of circumstances,' " but the trial court found that the incarceration was not an unanticipated change in circumstances. *Herring v. Herring*, 24 A.3d 574, 576 (Vt. 2011). The Vermont Supreme Court reversed, noting that alimony modification is generally not available when a spouse voluntarily terminates employment without good cause. Nonetheless, "the incarceration was involuntary although the conduct that resulted in the incarceration may have been voluntary." *Id.* at 578. Not all courts find that incarceration is a sufficient basis. *See, e.g.,* In *Malcolm v. Malcolm*, 2018 WL 1182898, at *5 (Md. Ct. Spec. App. Mar. 7, 2018), the Court found that incarceration constituted "a material change in circumstances that justified the award of alimony" because incarceration decreased the payor's expenses. Should the nature of the offense (such as whether it involved a family member) affect whether incarceration meets the standard?

A Utah court found that the husband's entitlement to Social Security benefits constituted a material change of circumstances. *Young v. Young*, 201 P.3d 301, 308 (Utah 2009). What other actions by the payor should constitute a basis for modification?

Involuntary changes can, of course, constitute the requisite basis for modification. An Indiana court found that the husband's "unemployment at the time of the hearing and drastic reduction in income was a result of factors beyond his control, namely, his own chronic illness." *Banks v. Banks*, 980 N.E.2d 423, 428 (Ind. Ct. App. 2012), transfer denied, 985 N.E.2d 738 (Ind. 2013).

3.   *Legitimate changes in the payee's income.* A Mississippi court refused to modify a husband's spousal support obligation when his wife, a stay-at-home mother during the marriage, returned to work. The court found that, even with her work income, the wife's standard of living did not exceed her husband's, and that her net income was much less than her husband's. *Dix v. Dix*, 941 So.2d 913, 917–18 (Miss. Ct. App. 2006). A Utah case found that the wife's sale of property she received through property distribution that resulted in an additional $45,000 income each year did not constitute an unforeseeable change in circumstances warranting a decrease. *MacDonald v. MacDonald*, 430 P.3d 612 (Utah 2018). A husband was successful in modifying his temporary alimony obligation after his wife won the lottery. As the court found, a "substantial change in circumstances occurred when Defendant became the winner." *Questel v. Questel*, 960 N.Y.S.2d 860, 864 (Sup. Ct. 2013). A decrease in rent caused by a divorced woman's cohabitation with her boyfriend—even though she was now paying him rent—could constitute the requisite "change of circumstances so as to alter the financial needs of the alimony recipient." *Murphy v. Murphy*, 181 Conn. App. 716, 722 (2018).

PROBLEM 10-5

You are Ms. Martindale's attorney. In light of the court's rejection of her request to order her permanent alimony and because she will be 51 when her youngest graduates from high school, what advice would you give her about what to do in the next seven years to prepare for that time? Would you advise her to consider "outsourcing" some care?

PROBLEM 10-6

If you were drafting an alimony provision for a divorce agreement, which factors would you deem acceptable as bases for modification? How would those factors differ if you were representing the payor or the recipient? Would your agreement recite any situations in which alimony should not be modifiable?

B. TERMINATION

Historically, most states provided that alimony ended upon either party's death or upon the recipient's remarriage. Many states retain these grounds but have also added that alimony will end upon the recipient's cohabitation, unless a court order or an agreement between the parties provides otherwise. *See, e.g.*, Utah Code Ann. § 30–3–5(9)–(10) (2018). In Tennessee, the recipient's death or remarriage terminates alimony, while cohabitation raises a rebuttable presumption that the alimony should be modified or terminated. Tenn. Code § 36–5–121 (2018).

States have begun to consider other grounds for termination and to enact bans on permanent alimony. Consider the benefits and drawbacks of such an approach based on portions of the Massachusetts statute set out below.

MASS. GEN. L. CH. 208, § 49 (2018)

(d)   General term alimony shall be suspended, reduced or terminated upon the cohabitation of the recipient spouse when the payor shows that the recipient spouse has maintained a common household, as defined in this subsection, with another person for a continuous period of at least 3 months.

(1)   Persons are deemed to maintain a common household when they share a primary residence together with or without others. In determining whether the recipient is maintaining a common household, the court may consider any of the following factors:

(i)   oral or written statements or representations made to third parties regarding the relationship of the persons;

(ii)   the economic interdependence of the couple or economic dependence of 1 person on the other;

(iii) the persons engaging in conduct and collaborative roles in furtherance of their life together;

(iv) the benefit in the life of either or both of the persons from their relationship;

(v) the community reputation of the persons as a couple; or

(vi) other relevant and material factors.

(2) An alimony obligation suspended, reduced or terminated under this subsection may be reinstated upon termination of the recipient's common household relationship; but, if reinstated, it shall not extend beyond the termination date of the original order.

(e) Unless the payor and recipient agree otherwise, general term alimony may be modified in duration or amount upon a material change of circumstances warranting modification. Modification may be permanent, indefinite or for a finite duration, as may be appropriate. Nothing in this section shall be construed to permit alimony reinstatement after the recipient's remarriage, except by the parties' express written agreement.

(f) Once issued, general term alimony orders shall terminate upon the payor attaining the full retirement age. The payor's ability to work beyond the full retirement age shall not be a reason to extend alimony, provided that:

(1) When the court enters an initial alimony judgment, the court may set a different alimony termination date for good cause shown; provided, however, that in granting deviation, the court shall enter written findings of the reasons for deviation.

(2) The court may grant a recipient an extension of an existing alimony order for good cause shown; provided, however, that in granting an extension, the court shall enter written findings of:

(i) a material change of circumstance that occurred after entry of the alimony judgment; and

(ii) reasons for the extension that are supported by clear and convincing evidence.

NOTES AND QUESTIONS

1. *Cohabitation with whom?* Some statutes specifically state that modification is available only for cohabitation with a member of the opposite sex. *See, e.g.*, Ala. Code § 30–2–55 (2018). In Oklahoma, "voluntary cohabitation of a former spouse with a member of the opposite sex shall be a ground to modify provisions of a final judgment or order for alimony as support." Okla. St. Ann. tit. 43, § 134(C) (2017). Connecticut has adopted a different approach, allowing modification of an alimony award where the recipient "is living with another person under circumstances which the court finds should result in the modification, suspension, reduction or termination of alimony because the living arrangements cause such a change of circumstances

as to alter the financial needs of that party." Conn. Gen. Stat. § 46b–86(b) (2018). In Utah, the paying spouse must "establish that the former spouse *is* cohabiting at the time the paying spouse files the motion to terminate alimony," and showing that the former spouse had previously cohabitated with someone else is not sufficient. *Scott v. Scott*, 2017 UT 66, ¶ 33 (emphasis added). As a later court explained, its state's supreme court held, "in a Seussian burst of anapestic tetrameter, that " 'is should mean is and not was or has been.' " *O'Hearon v. Hansen*, 409 P.3d 85, 91 (Utah 2017).

2.   *What is cohabitation? What is marriage?* The Massachusetts statute specifies the meaning of cohabitation, but determining whether cohabitation has occurred is not always straightforward. In a South Carolina case, the wife sought to end her payments of alimony because of her husband's cohabitation. The husband claimed that the governing statute required co-residence for at least ninety "consecutive days," and his girlfriend "lived" with her son several days each week. Although the lower court found that any break in the ninety-day co-residential period did not necessarily overcome the wife's claim, the South Carolina Supreme Court reversed. It held that "[i]f the statute merely required the supported spouse to 'reside with' his paramour, then termination of [the] alimony obligation would be proper. However, the statute mandates cohabitation for ninety *consecutive* days." *McKinney v. Pedery*, 776 S.E.2d 566, 572 (S.C. 2015).

Questions of proof can be complex. For example, Illinois allows for termination of alimony upon the recipient's remarriage or cohabitation "with another person on a resident, continuing conjugal basis." 750 Ill. Comp. Stat. Ann. 5/510(c) (2018). An Illinois court permitted the obligor to introduce Facebook Status posts to show how his wife presented her new relationship. *In re Marriage of Miller*, 40 N.E.3d 206 (Ill. App. 2015). Ultimately, however, the court found that an "intimate dating relationship" did not satisfy the statute and reinstated the husband's alimony award of approximately $100,000 per year.

Should a civil union or domestic partnership terminate the obligation to pay alimony under a statute specifying termination upon marriage? (Chapter 8 discusses the revival of alimony following an annulment.)

3.   *Agreeing to end alimony.* As with most other financial issues upon divorce, the parties can agree when alimony will end. For example, in *In re Marriage of Wolf*, 258 P.3d 995 (Mont. 2011), the spouses entered into a dissolution agreement which specifically provided that alimony would not terminate upon the husband-payor's death, but that it would terminate upon the wife's death or cohabitation with anyone for longer than six months. How can alimony continue beyond the payor's death?

4.   *Why terminate alimony?* Why should cohabitation or remarriage have any impact on an alimony award? Professor Cynthia Starnes found "no satisfactory answer to the question of why an alimony recipient should pay a price for choosing to live with a lover." Cynthia Lee Starnes, *I'll Be Watching You: Alimony and the Cohabitation Rule*, 50 Fam. L.Q. 261, 262 (2016).

Instead, the strong intuition supporting the rule remains rooted "in archaic principles of coverture, which cast a wife not as a marital partner, but rather as a man's burden, dependent on her husband for protection and survival until the next man comes along to relieve him of the task." Cynthia Lee Starnes, One More Time: Alimony, Intuition, and the Remarriage-Termination Rule, 81 Ind. L.J. 971, 999 (2006). Do you agree? Is there a better justification for the rule? *See* Albertina Antognini, *Against Nonmarital Exceptionalism*, 51 U.C. Davis L. Rev. 1891, 1903 (2018).

PROBLEM 10-7

In Oregon, remarriage and cohabitation are analyzed in the same manner as any other change in circumstances, and they do not, by themselves, constitute bases for termination. Leon sues to terminate his alimony obligation to pay $3,500/month to his ex-wife indefinitely after she marries a lawyer whose monthly income is more than $7,000/month. You are the judge tasked with deciding whether Leon's circumstances have changed substantially so as to warrant termination of alimony. What is your holding? *See In re Marriage of Lenhart*, 162 P.3d 292 (Or. Ct. App. 2007) (determining that the ex-wife's circumstances had not changed substantially; even if half of her new husband's income were attributed to her, this was inadequate to satisfy the legal standard to justify changing the alimony award).

6. TAX CONSEQUENCES OF ALIMONY

Unlike property distribution, which has no tax consequences unless property is sold, alimony traditionally had tax implications and will continue to do so for many former spouses. For divorces finalized prior to January 1, 2019, alimony could be deducted from the payor's gross income (presumably taxed at a higher rate than the recipient's), and taxed to the recipient under federal law, although the parties could agree otherwise. Parties who divorced prior to 2019 may continue to avail themselves of this tax advantage so long as their alimony payments remain in place.

Alimony is defined to include any payment in cash if:

(i) such payment is received by (or on behalf of) a spouse under a divorce or separation instrument [ ]

(ii) in the case of an individual legally separated from the individual's spouse under a decree of divorce or of separate maintenance, the payee spouse and the payor spouse are not members of the same household at the time such payment is made, and

(iii) there is no liability to make any such payment for any period after the death of the payee spouse and there is no liability to make any payment (in cash or property) as a substitute for such payments after the death of the payee spouse.

26 U.S.C. § 152(d)(5)(B) (Supp. V 2018).

Because of the tax deduction for the higher earner, prior to 2019, many couples negotiated agreements providing that the lower earner would accept less property in exchange for higher alimony payments. The federal government put in place a number of restrictions to try to ensure that maintenance payments were what they claimed to be.

The 2017 tax law eliminates the alimony deduction for payors moving forward and allows recipients to receive the transfer without paying income tax on it. Since the recipient usually makes less money—and is thus in a lower tax bracket—it now costs more to the payor to give the recipient the same amount in alimony. The net result may be more money in taxes, and less to the recipient, which may make divorce settlements more difficult to reach.

Here's an example:

if W is taxed at a 10% marginal rate, and H is taxed at a 30% marginal rate, $100 earnings by H will be subject to $30 in tax, leaving him $70 to pay as alimony. Under prior law, the alimony would have been deductible to H, leaving him $100 to pay to W, who would have to pay $10 tax on that amount, leaving her $90 to spend.

Linda Sugin, *The Social Meaning of the Tax Cuts and Jobs Act*, 128 Yale L.J. Forum 403, 412 (2018).

NOTES AND QUESTIONS

1.   *Theory of alimony.* According to Professor Patricia Cain, the previous tax treatment of alimony suggests an "underlying principle * * * that the now-divided family will only be taxed once on the income that is used to support its prior members. This principle is consistent with the notion that the spousal unit is a single economic unit for federal tax purposes." Patricia Cain, *Taxing Families Fairly*, 48 Santa Clara L. Rev 805, 828 (2008). By contrast, transfers between former nonmarital partners have never been entitled to the same favorable treatment. *Id.* at 830. Does this seem equitable? Even today, transfers between nonmarital partners that are higher than the annual gift tax exclusion ($15,000 in 2019) are subject to a gift tax; if such transfers were made as part of any alimony payment, then there would be no gift tax consequences.

2.   *Lying on your tax form.* There is evidence of a substantial gap between the payments reported and those actually made. While almost 600,000 taxpayers claimed they paid more than $12 billion in alimony in 2015, fewer than 415,000 filers reported receiving spousal support, and the total amount they reported receiving was only $10 billion—a substantial discrepancy from the amount payors claimed to have transferred to former

spouses. Tyler Hardcastle & Margaret Ryznar, *Reconsidering the Tax Treatment of Alimony*, 162 Tax Notes 299–300 (2019).

Why might payors have reported an alimony payment? Why might payees not have done so? Consider the changed incentives beginning Jan. 1, 2019.

PROBLEM 10-8

Jen and Len are in the process of negotiating a separation agreement. Assume that Jen's tax bracket is 35% (all income is taxed at 35%), while Len's is 20%. Jen agrees to pay Len $65,000 a year in alimony.

What is the actual cost to Jen of paying that $65,000—that is, how much of Jen's taxable income would be used to produce the alimony transfer? *See* George D. Karibjanian, Richard S. Franklin, & Lester B Law, *Alimony, Prenuptial Agreements, and Trusts Under the 2017 Tax Act—Part 1*, 44 Fam. L. Rep. 1246 (2018).

CHAPTER 11

CHILD SUPPORT

■ ■ ■

1. THE CONTEMPORARY LANDSCAPE AND FUTURE CHALLENGES

Child support—payments for children who do not live with both of their parents—presents some of the thorniest questions in family law, with passions that can run deep. Approximately "30% of the adult population either has paid child support or has been the person to whom someone else was ordered to pay it. Such data suggest that more Americans have been subject to child support orders, as obligor or obligee, than to any other kind of civil judgment." Ira Mark Ellman & Tara O'Toole Ellman, *The Theory of Child Support*, 45 Harv. J. on Legis. 107, 108 (2008).

This Chapter explores the nature of the child support obligation, and how support awards are established, maintained, modified, and enforced. The child support obligation is an important manifestation of "federal family law" because since the 1970s, the federal government has closely regulated the obligation's establishment, maintenance, modification, and enforcement in tandem with the states.

The Chapter also explores dilemmas that confront low-income noncustodial obligor parents, who owe a bulk of unpaid child support. Recent years have seen the emergence of public initiatives designed to encourage child support payment by poor noncustodial parents, who (contrary to what some policymakers and politicians say) may be "dead broke" rather than "deadbeat."

The Chapter's final pages explore how, in recent years, the federal government has promoted "Responsible Fatherhood" by focusing on, among other things, the effects of fathers' absence on the financial and emotional support of many children. The nationwide focus pinpoints an evident paradox: "Although fathers have undertaken increased child-care responsibility over the last four decades, the prevalence of father-absence has been simultaneously increasing." Laurie S. Kohn, *Engaging Men as Fathers: The Courts, the Law, and Father-Absence in Low-Income Families*, 35 Cardozo L. Rev. 511, 516 (2013) (a principal article excerpted near the end of this Chapter).

A. THE CONTEMPORARY CHILD SUPPORT LANDSCAPE: AN OVERVIEW

The right to support is held by both children of divorce and nonmarital children. Counting marital and nonmarital children, "[a]pproximately one-third of all children in the United States live apart from a parent, and half of all children will experience parental separation during their childhood." Kye Lippold, *Estimating the Nonresident Parent Population in National Surveys* (Urban Inst. 2017). Unless parental rights are terminated, both legally recognized parents retain a support obligation until the child reaches majority and sometimes longer. Two family law scholars note that "child support has replaced spousal support as the most significant continuing financial tie between most separating couples." June Carbone & Naomi Cahn, *Marriage, Parentage, and Child Support*, 45 Fam. L.Q. 219, 229 (2011).

The percentage of marriages ending in divorce is lower for couples married in the 1990s or later than the percentage for couples who married in the 1970s and 1980s. Even today, however, approximately one third of marriages will end in divorce. Claire Cain Miller, *The Divorce Surge Is Over, But the Myth Lives On*, N.Y. Times, Dec. 2, 2014, at A3.

The median age at first divorce is relatively young, about 30.0 years for men and 30.1 years for women. U.S. Census Bureau, Rose M. Kreider & Renee Ellis, *Current Population Reports, Number, Timing, and Duration of Marriages and Divorces: 2009*, at 17 (2011). Young divorcing couples typically have one or more minor dependent children, and divorces each year involve more than one million children, who find themselves living temporarily or permanently in single-parent households. George J. Cohen & Carol C. Weitzman, *Helping Children and Families Deal With Divorce and Separation*, 138 Pediatrics e20163020 (Dec. 2016).

Divorce statistics tell only part of the story. In 2016, 42.4% of births in the United States were to unmarried women aged 15–44, a sizeable number but a 2% decline from 2015 and the lowest level since 2007. *See* Joyce A. Martin et al., *Births: Final Data for 2016*, 67 Nat'l Vital Stats. Reps. 6 (U.S. Dep't of Health and Hum. Servs. 2018). Many of these women will raise their children without marrying the other biological parent.

Almost 83% of custodial parents in single-parent households are mothers. Carmen Solomon-Fears, *Child Support: An Overview of Census Bureau Data on Recipients* 2 (Cong. Res. Serv. 2016). The numbers reach across American society. "Once largely limited to poor women and minorities, motherhood without marriage has settled deeply into middle America." Jason DeParle & Sabrina Tavernise, *For Women Under 30, Most Births Occur Outside Marriage*, N.Y. Times, Feb. 17, 2012. "One group still largely resists the trend: college graduates, who overwhelmingly marry before having children." *Id.*

At the same time, "[t]he percentage of children living with one parent who live with just their father saw an increase from 12.5 percent in 2007 to 16.1 percent in 2017." U.S. Census Bureau, *More Children Live With Just Their Fathers Than a Decade Ago*, Rel. No. CB17-187 (Nov. 2017).

B. THE CHALLENGES OF POVERTY: AN OVERVIEW

For marital and nonmarital children alike, receipt of child support can be critical to the standard of living in the custodial parent's household. This article introduces the scope of the personal and social challenges that continue to mark efforts to enhance rates of payment by low-income child support obligors.

ELAINE SORENSEN,
CHILD SUPPORT PLAYS AN INCREASINGLY IMPORTANT ROLE FOR POOR CUSTODIAL FAMILIES

http://www.urban.org/UploadedPDF/412272–child-
support-plays-important-role.pdf. (2010).

The child support program has become a critical public program for children, serving 17 million children, representing nearly one in four children in the United States Among social welfare programs, only the Medicaid program serves more children. It is also an important source of income for poor families, lifting a million people from poverty in 2008.

* * * Unlike other social welfare programs, child support is a private transfer, paid by the noncustodial parent and usually transferred to the custodial family through the child support enforcement program. The child support enforcement program is operated at the state and local level and regulated by the federal government.

In 2008, 625,000 children would have been poor if they had not received child support, increasing child poverty by 4.4 percent. Most of these children (477,000) would have lived in deep poverty (below 50 percent of the federal poverty level) as a result of losing their child support income. In addition to benefiting children, 413,000 adults would have been poor if their families had not received child support. Just like the children, most of these adults (275,000) would have lived in deep poverty. Without child support income, these families would need an additional $4.4 billion to escape poverty. * * *

Congress enacted welfare reform in 1996, replacing an open-ended entitlement with a time-limited benefit that has strict work requirements, called Temporary Assistance for Needy Families (TANF). At the same time, it also greatly expanded the authority of the child support enforcement program. The intent of these reforms was to increase the role of work and child support so that poor families did not need to rely on cash assistance. Ten years later, the data show that this has indeed occurred. Since 1996, the relative importance of child support and earnings has increased while cash assistance for poor and deeply poor custodial families makes up a substantially smaller part of family income.

Among poor custodial families, the average percent of family income that comes from child support has doubled in the past ten years from 5 to 10 percent. The average percentage of family income from earnings has also increased from 50 to 57 percent. At the same time, poor custodial families have become less dependent on public assistance. * * *

Poor custodial families who received child support also experienced gains in child support. * * * Child support represents, on average, 40 percent of their family income, up from 29 percent in 1997. Earnings have also increased for these families, going from an average 39 to 43 percent of family income between 1997 and 2007. In contrast, the average percent of family income from TANF dropped from 15 to 3 percent.

These trends are even more apparent among deeply poor custodial families (families with income below 50 percent of the federal poverty level). For these families, the average percent of family income that comes from TANF dropped from 30 to 17 percent between 1997 and 2007, while the average percent of family income from child support tripled, increasing from 5 to 15 percent. Earnings, on the other hand, have remained unchanged during this period for deeply poor custodial families, representing an average 43 percent of family income. * * *

Among deeply poor custodial families who received child support, the average amount received was $2,702, up 32 percent in real terms from 10 years earlier. Given this large increase in child support, it is not surprising to see that the average percent of family income from child support has increased from 38 to 63 percent between 1997 and 2007. Earnings have also increased for these families during this time. In sharp contrast, they experienced a dramatic decline in family income from TANF, falling from an average 26 to 4 percent.

Part of the reason poor and deeply poor families are receiving more child support is because they are less likely to be on TANF. While on TANF, the government tends to keep most, if not all, child support collected on recipients' behalf to recoup the cost of providing welfare. Now that these families are less likely to be on TANF, they are receiving more of their child support. In addition, the child support program has become more effective at collecting child support, which appears to be benefiting poor and deeply poor custodial families.

NOTES

1.   *The need continues*. The crucial effects of child support receipt on poor and deeply poor custodial households, reported by Sorensen, remain:

Over the past two decades, child support has become an increasingly important source of income for the lowest income families. In 2013, child support represented, on average, 41 percent of poor custodial families' income if they received it, up from 29 percent in 1997. The benefit was even more pronounced among deeply poor custodial families (those who live below 50 percent of the federal poverty level) if they received it. For these families, the average percentage of family income from child support was 65 percent, up from 38 percent in 1997. * * *

Among all poor custodial families, the average percent of family income that comes from child support has doubled since 1997, from 5 percent to 10 percent. At the same time, poor custodial families receive less cash public assistance. In 2013, these families received an average of 7 percent of their family income from TANF, down from 21 percent in 1997. Today, child support represents a larger share of family income than TANF for all poor custodial families. * * *

These trends are even more apparent among deeply poor custodial families. * * * For all deeply poor families, the average percent of family income that comes from TANF dropped from 30 percent to 13 percent between 1997 and 2013, while the average percent of family income from child support nearly tripled, increasing from 5 percent to 13 percent. Today the average percent of family income that comes from public cash assistance and child support is the same for all deeply poor families. * * *.

U.S. Dep't of Health & Human Servs., Office of Child Support Enforcement, *The Child Support Program is a Good Investment* 6–7 (Dec. 2016).

2.   *Assignment and pass-through.* A custodial parent who receives public assistance must sign over to the government the right to collect any child support. When it collects support from the obligor, the government may reimburse itself for the payments it has made to the custodial parent before turning over any of the child support funds to her. States, however, may elect to pass through modest amounts of child support to the intended recipients (the custodial parent and children) before reimbursing the federal government. To the extent that states choose pass-through, child support becomes an even more important safety net for poor and extremely poor families. Linda Giannarelli et al., *Reducing Child Poverty in the U.S.* 35 (Urban Inst. 2015).

"Despite strong evidence that policies under which an obligor's support is passed through to the residential parent without a reduction in public benefits increase children's support without reducing parental workforce participation or producing large public costs, about half of the states retain all support payments they collect from obligors whose children receive public assistance." Margaret F. Brinig & Marsha Garrison, *Getting Blood From Stones: Results and Policy Implications of an Empirical Investigation of Child Support Practice In St. Joseph County, Indiana Paternity Actions*, 56 Fam. Ct. Rev. 521, 523–24 (2018).

2. THE NATURE OF THE CHILD SUPPORT OBLIGATION

For marital and nonmarital children alike, the right to parental child support is grounded in biology. Unless parental rights are terminated, a biological parent must support the child regardless of whether he or she was ever married to the other parent, whether the two parents were together only once to conceive the child, or whether they ever maintained a household together. *Hermesmann* demonstrates the strength of both the biological obligation and the child's right.

A. THE SOURCE OF THE OBLIGATION

STATE EX REL. HERMESMANN V. SEYER

Supreme Court of Kansas, 1993.
847 P.2d 1273.

HOLMES, C. J.

Colleen Hermesmann routinely provided care for Shane Seyer as a baby sitter or day care provider during 1987 and 1988. The two began a sexual relationship at a time when Colleen was 16 years old and Shane was only 12. The relationship continued over a period of several months and the parties engaged in sexual intercourse on an average of a couple of times a week. As a result, a daughter, Melanie, was born to Colleen on May 30, 1989. At the time of the conception of the child, Shane was 13 years old and Colleen was 17. Colleen applied for and received financial assistance through the Aid to Families with Dependent Children program (ADC) from SRS [the Kansas Department of Social and Rehabilitation Services—eds.].

On January 15, 1991, the district attorney's office of Shawnee County filed a petition requesting that Colleen Hermesmann be adjudicated as a juvenile offender for engaging in the act of sexual intercourse with a child under the age of 16, Shanandoah (Shane) Seyer, to whom she was not married * * *. Thereafter, Colleen Hermesmann entered into a plea agreement with the district attorney's office, wherein she agreed to stipulate to the lesser offense of contributing to a child's misconduct. On September 11, 1991, the juvenile court accepted the stipulation, and adjudicated Colleen Hermesmann to be a juvenile offender.

On March 8, 1991, SRS filed a petition on behalf of Colleen Hermesmann, alleging that Shane Seyer was the father of Colleen's minor daughter, Melanie. The petition also alleged that SRS had provided benefits through the ADC program to Colleen on behalf of the child and that Colleen had assigned support rights due herself and her child to SRS. The petition requested that the court determine paternity and order Shane to reimburse SRS for all assistance expended by SRS on Melanie's behalf.

* * *

The court found that the issue of Shane's consent was irrelevant and ordered Shane to pay child support of $50 per month. The court also granted SRS a joint and several judgment against Shane and Colleen in the amount of $7,068, for assistance provided by the ADC program on behalf of Melanie through February 1992. The judgment included medical and other birthing expenses as well as assistance paid after Melanie's birth.

* * *

Shane asserts as his first issue that, because he was a minor under the age of 16 at the time of conception, he was legally incapable of consenting to sexual intercourse and therefore cannot be held legally responsible for the birth of his child.

* * *

Shane does not contest that he is the biological father of the child. As a father, he has a common-law duty, as well as a statutory duty, to support his minor child. This duty applies equally to parents of children born out of wedlock.

* * * We conclude that the issue of consent to sexual activity under the criminal statutes is irrelevant in a civil action to determine paternity and for support of the minor child of such activity. * * *

For Shane's next issue, he asserts that it is not sound public policy for a court to order a youth to pay child support for a child conceived during the crime of indecent liberties with a child when the victim was unable to consent to the sexual intercourse.

* * *

This State's interest in requiring minor parents to support their children overrides the State's competing interest in protecting juveniles from improvident acts, even when such acts may include criminal activity on the part of the other parent. Considering the three persons directly involved, Shane, Colleen, and Melanie, the interests of Melanie are superior, as a matter of public policy, to those of either or both of her parents. This minor child, the only truly innocent party, is entitled to support from both her parents regardless of their ages.

As his third issue, Shane asserts that the district court erred in finding he and Colleen were jointly and severally liable for the child support. He argues that, as Colleen was the perpetrator of the crime of statutory rape, she alone should be held responsible for the consequences of the act.

* * *

Nowhere does the law in this state suggest that the mother's "wrongdoing" can operate as a setoff or bar to a father's liability for child support. Under the facts as presented to this court, the district court properly held that Shane owes a duty of support to Melanie and properly ordered that Shane and Colleen were jointly and severally liable for the monies previously paid by SRS.

* * *

NOTES AND QUESTIONS

1. *Questions about* Hermesmann. (a) Does *Hermesmann* suggest reasons why no state permits consideration of parental misconduct when the court establishes or modifies a child support award? (b) What advice would *Hermesmann* lead you to impart to teenagers? (c) As a practical matter, how do you think Shane Seyer or a similarly situated teen would meet the child support obligation?

2. *The child support obligation's strength.* Courts call the parent's child support obligation "absolute," *A.J.M.M. v. J.R.M.*, 2016 WL 4954144 (Pa. Super. Ct. Sept. 15, 2016), and "paramount," *Christensen v. Christensen*, 400 P.3d 1219, 1230 (Utah Ct. App. 2017). Thirteen-year-old Shane Seyer was a sex-crime victim. Statutes seek to protect child victims from sexual abuse, one of the strongest child-protective policies known to the law. The Kansas Supreme Court acknowledged this policy's strength, but—like other courts that have decided the question—held that the policy yields to children's right to receive financial support from their biological parents. Are minor males and minor females similarly situated in the context of statutory rape, or should the outcome in *Seyer* have been different if a minor female were the victim?

Hermesmann concerned a child conceived during "statutory rape" (that is, nonforcible sexual activity with a victim under the age of consent) perpetrated by another juvenile. Courts have likewise uniformly imposed child support obligations on minors who conceive children with adult perpetrators, who the law might assume would have a stronger influence over less experienced juveniles. For example, *In re Paternity of K.B.*, 104 P.3d 1132 (Okla. Ct. Civ. App. 2004), concerned a child conceived by a 15-year-old boy and a 19-year-old woman. Citing *Hermesmann*, *K.B.* held that the "public policy mandating parental support of children outweighs any policy of protecting minors from the consequences of their willing participation in sexual misconduct with adults." *Id.* at 1135.

Should the law impose similar strict child support liability on the minor or adult victim of a *forcible* rape? *See* Chapter 5, which treats the Uniform Parentage Act § 614.

3. *Trickery.* Where one parent tricks the other into conceiving the child, such as by lying about using birth control, the tricked parent must nonetheless pay child support. In *N.E. v. Hedges*, 391 F.3d 832, 834 (6th Cir. 2004), for example, the court imposed a support obligation on a biological father who

alleged that the child's mother fraudulently claimed that her birth control pills would prevent pregnancy. She then left the state and married another man. The father might have had a civil fraud claim against the mother, but parents allegedly defrauded into conception have found such actions difficult to win.

4.   *The commencement of the child support obligation.* The biological parent's child support obligation begins at the marital or nonmarital child's birth, even if the parent did not know about the birth, or if paternity was not established until later. *E.g., Loosvelt v. Brown,* 760 S.E.2d 351, 356 (N.C. Ct. App. 2014).

Where a court does not enter an initial support order until the child is older, however, this rule does not necessarily guarantee an order retroactive to the date of the child's birth. If the court enters the support order when the parties divorce, the order dates from separation or divorce because "[i]n an intact family, the law assumes that parents will provide for the children as well as they can." *Kiken v. Kiken,* 694 A.2d 557, 560 (N.J. 1997). The assumption, grounded in constitutional rights of family privacy and autonomy, prevails during an intact marriage as long as the parents provide at least a minimal level of support sufficient to defeat a neglect petition in the juvenile or family court. *See, e.g., In re A.P.,* 770 N.W.2d 403, 412 (Mich. Ct. App. 2009). If the child was born outside marriage but the parents lived together for some period after the child's birth, the law may similarly presume that both parents supported the child while they lived together in the nonmarital household. *See, e.g., Motie v. Motie,* 132 So.3d 1210, 1214–15 (Fla. Dist. Ct. App. 2014).

Where unmarried parents have not lived together since the child's birth, courts may enter an order retroactive to the date of birth, even where the mother has concealed the nonmarital child from the father for several years. *See, e.g., In re State ex rel. Reitenour,* 807 A.2d 1259 (N.H. 2002) (14-year-old child). The award will typically come with accumulated interest, which can complicate and perhaps thwart enforcement efforts by imposing sometimes insurmountable burdens on a financially distressed obligor. "The primary factor that has caused arrears to grow so dramatically has been the assessment of interest on a routine basis." Elaine Sorensen et al., *Assessing Child Support Arrears in Nine Large States and the Nation,* Part D (Urban Inst. 2007).

Because the sudden burden occasioned by a retroactive order dating from the child's birth may make full or even partial payment less likely, some states have restricted the reach of retroactivity. Michigan and Texas, for example, have eliminated the policy of setting support orders retroactive to the child's birth in paternity cases. Texas courts may look back four years from the date of filing, and Michigan courts may look back to the date of filing unless the obligor's avoidance has been willful. *Id.* at 10.

Some courts have rejected retroactivity by applying such equitable grounds as waiver, estoppel, or laches arising from the custodial parent's unreasonable delay in seeking child support. Some courts leave the door slightly ajar. "[L]aches and estoppel are not favored defenses in the context of child support," *Tovsland v. Reub,* 686 N.W.2d 392, 402 (S.D. 2004), and should be applied "only under the rarest of circumstances," *Dep't of Revenue ex rel. Thorman v. Holley*, 86 So.3d 1199, 1203 (Fla. Dist. Ct. App. 2012) (laches). The same can be said about waiver. Why the rejection, disfavor, and rarity?

The laches defense may play a role, however, where its application would *benefit* the child because the obligor belatedly seeks reimbursement for child support overpayments previously made. In *Bohlen v. Heller*, 2015 WL 6087621 *1–2 (Iowa Ct. App. Oct. 14, 2015), for example, the court held that laches barred the father from recovering child support that he had paid for nearly six years after the court terminated his parental rights; income withholding continued from the father's paychecks because he "was not paying proper attention." The court reasoned that "[m]uch of the money had already been spent." *Id.*

5. *Emancipation.* Emancipation is the process by which a minor attains rights and obligations of adulthood before (or sometimes after) reaching the general age of majority. A judicial order of emancipation typically ends the obligation to pay future child support unless the parent has agreed to pay post-emancipation support. *See, e.g., Ricci v. Ricci*, 154 A.3d 215, 230 (N.J. Super. Ct. App. Div. 2017). Emancipation, however, typically does not relieve the obligation to pay arrears (support payments that came due before the court entered the emancipation order). *See, e.g., McKinney v. Hamp*, ___ So.3d ___, 2018 WL 793995 (Miss. Feb. 8, 2018).

The grounds for emancipation differ from state to state. A discrete event, such as the minor's marriage or entry into active military service, may produce emancipation as a matter of law. On a case-by-case basis, the court may also order emancipation in the best interests of the child.

Courts generally order best-interests emancipation only where the child near the age of majority can fend for himself emotionally and financially. *See, e.g., Edmonds v. Edmonds*, 935 So.2d 980 (Miss. 2006) (divorced father must continue to support his 14-year-old son, who was convicted as an adult of murder and was sentenced to life imprisonment; continued support would help pay for the boy's appeal and would provide him minimal expenses in prison). The importance of best-interests emancipation has diminished since the early 1970s, when most states lowered the general age of majority from 21 to 18.

6. *Can a "hateful" minor forfeit a right to support?* In extraordinary cases, alienation from a noncustodial parent may present a ground for terminating support before the child reaches majority. In *Copeland v. Copeland*, 235 So.3d 91 (Miss. 2017), for example, the court order granted the divorced non-custodial father's motion to terminate his support obligation to his two children, ages 17 and 13. At least the younger child was below the age ordinarily considered for best-interests emancipation, and *Copeland* made no determination that the children could fend for themselves.

The *Copeland* trial court found that the two children, "through emails and text messages, as well as in-court testimony, have referenced their hatred and their unwillingness to have a relationship with their natural father. They have sent vicious, venomous, and hateful emails and texts directed especially to him over and over and over again expressing their distaste, lack of love, and, in fact, their hatred for him to the point that they wish that he, in fact, were dead, or under certain circumstances, that they would kill him." *Id.* at 96. The state supreme court held that "the children's clear and extreme conduct forfeited their right to support from their father." *Id.* at 97.

Do you think that this holding about forfeiting the right to support should apply if the custodial parent encouraged the children's conduct?

B. THE SUPPORT OBLIGATIONS OF PERSONS OTHER THAN BIOLOGICAL PARENTS

In *Troxel v. Granville,* 530 U.S. 57, 63 (2000), a principal decision in Chapter 13, Justice Sandra Day O'Connor's plurality opinion noted that "[t]he demographic changes of the past century make it difficult to speak of an average American family. The composition of families varies greatly from household to household." In some circumstances, persons other than the biological parents may hold or share a child support obligation.

a.   *Stepparents.* A stepparent is usually defined as a person who is married to one of the child's biological parents, but who has not adopted the child. As family configurations have changed, the term is now being used also to define some households that are formed by cohabitation rather than marriage. See Rose M. Kreider & Daphne A, Lofquist, U.S. Census Bureau, *Adopted Children and Stepchildren: 2010,* at 19 (2014).

Adoption is possible only where a court has terminated the parental rights of the child's other biological parent by consent or in a contested proceeding. In the absence of an adoption, the noncustodial biological parent remains obligated to support the child.

The metes and bounds of the stepparent support obligation vitally affect today's youth because an estimated one-third of children will live in a stepfamily before reaching adulthood. *See* J. Herbie DiFonzo & Ruth C. Stern, *Rights of Parenthood and Parentage in Nontraditional Families,* 51 Fam. Ct. Rev. 104, 109 (2013).

From a sense of moral obligation, most wage-earning stepparents probably contribute directly to a stepchild's daily support while they are married to the custodial parent and living with the child, without concern for (or perhaps even knowledge of) what the law requires. Indirect support also characterizes step households. "The stepparent contributing to his blended family's rent or electric bill is necessarily contributing to the cost of housing his stepchildren. * * * Even for items that are in principle consumed separately, such as groceries, considerable vigilance would be needed to ensure a stepchild realized no benefit, and it is hard to imagine a marriage could survive the tension created by one spouse's aggressive efforts to avoid conferring any benefits on the other spouse's children." Ira

Mark Ellman & Sanford L. Braver, *Child Support and the Custodial Mother's Move or Remarriage* 5 (July 22, 2014) (presented at the 2014 Conf. on Empirical Legal Studies held at Berkeley).

Moral or social obligation aside, the common law imposes no legal duty on a stepparent to support a stepchild merely because of marriage to the child's biological parent. Some states, however, have statutes that require stepparents to support stepchildren who live in their households, though the support obligation is usually more limited than the obligation the law imposes on biological or adoptive parents. The stepparent's obligation may be only secondary, or may be imposed only where the stepchild would otherwise be a public charge. *See, e.g.,* Ky. Rev. Stat. § 205.310 (2018). The stepparent may be able to recover from the noncustodial parent the amounts provided in support. *See, e.g.,* Mo. Rev. Stat. § 453.400 (2018). Even where termination might be harsh on the dependent child, the support obligation may terminate when the stepparent and biological parent dissolve their relationship or when the biological parent dies.

The *in loco parentis* or estoppel doctrines may impose support obligations on stepparents in circumstances discussed next, and courts have also enforced stepparents' agreements to support their stepchildren even where support is not otherwise required by law. *See, e.g., Thacker v. Thacker,* 311 S.W.3d 402, 407 (Mo. Ct. App. 2010).

b.   *Persons* in loco parentis *and parents by estoppel.* Under the *in loco parentis* ("in the place of the parent") doctrine, a person who assumes parental obligations is treated as a parent for some purposes. *See, e.g.,* Margaret M. Mahoney, *Stepparents as Third Parties in Relation to Their Stepchildren,* 40 Fam. L.Q. 81, 100 (2006). In child support cases, courts determine whether the person intentionally assumed parental obligations, including the child support obligation. *See, e.g., A.S. v. I.S.,* 130 A.3d 763, 764–65, 770 (Pa. 2015) (stepfather was obligated to pay child support because he "insisted upon and became a full parent in every sense of that concept"; during the divorce proceedings, he "aggressively litigated for shared legal and physical custody * * *, including the filing of an action to prevent his former spouse from relocating with" her biological children).

Because *in loco parentis* relationships can be terminated at will, a stepparent or other adult in the household typically can avoid continued financial responsibility when the marriage ends by simply declaring that the relationship no longer exists. *See, e.g., In re B.S.M.,* 251 P.3d 511 (Colo. Ct. App. 2010). The *in loco parentis* doctrine thus tends to be relevant only to prior support, and to third-party claims.

Promissory estoppel or equitable estoppel may also impose a support obligation on persons who promise support, treat the child as their own, or discourage contact between the noncustodial biological parent and the child. Because courts reserve estoppel and other equitable doctrines for particularly compelling cases, however, sympathetic facts do not always produce a support order. *See, e.g., In re Glaude*, 855 A.2d 494, 495 (N.H. 2004) (refusing to apply equitable estoppel against the stepfather who received physical custody of his stepson when he and the biological mother divorced, and who supported the boy for nine years until the biological mother resumed custody).

Should state legislatures impose support obligations on all residential stepparents, or should courts apply the *in loco parentis* or estoppel doctrines on a case-by-case basis? Which approach is more child-protective? Which approach better reflects the settled expectations of most adults in stepfamilies? Why might a court be reluctant to impose a continuing support obligation on stepparents merely for nurturing stepchildren who live in their households?

c.   *Adoptive parents.* Adoption, the focus of Chapter 6, is "the legal equivalent of biological parenthood." *Smith v. OFFER*, 431 U.S. 816, 844 n.51 (1977). Where a court terminates a biological parent's parental rights as a prelude to adoption, the biological parent generally must continue paying child support until the court enters the adoption decree. *E.g., Greene County Dep't of Soc. Servs. v. Ward*, 870 N.E.2d 1132, 1133 (N.Y. 2007). The decree terminates the biological parent's future obligation to support the child, and the adoptive parents assume that obligation.

d.   *Grandparents.* About 6% of children today live in households maintained by their grandparents, double the percentage of 1970. Shawn Fremstad & Melissa Boteach, *Valuing All Our Families* 7 (Center for Am. Progress 2015). About 13% of grandparents (mostly grandmothers) are the primary caregivers for one or more of their grandchildren. Jessica Dixon Weaver, *Grandma in the White House: Legal Support for Intergenerational Caregiving*, 43 Seton Hall L. Rev. 1, 7 (2013).

These grandparents care for the children in one or more recurrent circumstances. One or both parents may be incapacitated by drug addiction or another condition or disability. *Id.* at 4–8, 12. The opioid epidemic has swelled the numbers of grandparent caregivers, much as the crack cocaine epidemic swelled the numbers in the 1980s and 1990s. Teresa Wiltz, *Why More Grandparents Are Raising Children* (Pew Charitable Trusts 2016). Often these grandparent caregivers do not have economic and social resources sufficient for care. *Id.*

Aside from parental incapacitation, a single parent who remains in the workforce may need an adult to supervise the children at home during working hours; the children may need supervision when both of their parents work outside the home; the parents may face homelessness for mortgage foreclosure or similar family emergency; or the parents may be unable to afford (or may not wish to deplete the family budget by paying for) day care by a non-relative.

Many of these grandparent caregivers doubtlessly provide much, or sometimes all, the financial support for raising the children. At common law, however, a grandparent has no legal obligation to support a grandchild merely because of the grandparent-grandchild relationship. *See, e.g., In re Carlson*, 545 B.R. 229, 234–35 (Bankr. N.D. Ill. 2016). In most states, a legally enforceable support obligation may arise only where the grandparent is the child's legal guardian or custodian, where the *in loco parentis* or the estoppel doctrine imposes the obligation, or where the grandparent has agreed to provide support.

More than a dozen states impose a statutory support obligation on grandparents whose unemancipated minor children become parents. The statutory obligation usually continues until the unemancipated minor child/parent reaches majority. *See, e.g.*, Mo. Rev. Stat. § 210.847.1 (2018). In California, by contrast, "[a] parent does not have the duty to support a child of the parent's child." Cal. Fam. Code § 3930 (2018). Which approach represents sounder public policy?

e. *Children's support for their parents.* Moved by a sense of moral obligation, adult children often informally provide their elderly parents financial support. Adult children have a legal obligation to provide that support, however, in only about 30 states where a "filial responsibility" statute imposes the obligation.

As growing numbers of Baby Boomers reach their retirement years, these statutes have attracted renewed attention because medical advances have produced longer life expectancies, which in turn have increased the prospect that older adults will suffer diminished capacity, illness, and perhaps prolonged disability. The divorce rate has also left growing numbers of the elderly without spousal support, and Social Security and other public support programs have not always kept pace with costs of living and health care.

Some financial planners and health care professionals forecast more aggressive resort to filial responsibility statutes by nursing homes and other health care providers seeking payment for goods and services. *See, e.g.*, Greg Iacurci, *Children On the Hook for Long-Term Care: Growing Enforcement of Filial Laws Could Be a "Sleeping Giant,"* Investment News, June 6, 2016.

At the present time, however, the impact of filial responsibility statutes may be more theoretical than real. Katherine C. Pearson, *Filial Support Laws in the Modern Era: Domestic and International Comparison of Enforcement Practices for Laws Requiring Adult Children to Support Indigent Parents*, 20 Elder L.J. 269 (2013). These statutes typically impose much lower obligations than parents' obligations to support their children. Many destitute parents have children in difficult financial straits themselves, and children are charged with an obligation to support a parent only where the children have sufficient means after providing for their own spouse and children.

Parents may enforce filial responsibility statutes in private support actions, but such actions are rare, perhaps because of parents' reluctance to burden their children. Aside from the prospect of civil enforcement by government agencies or private creditors, some states impose criminal liability on children for nonsupport of their elderly parents, though prosecutions are scarce. In several states, civil and criminal filial responsibility laws on the books for decades have apparently never been invoked.

In states without a filial responsibility statute, what might a private provider of goods or services do to help insure that the recipient's child will be legally obligated to pay all or part of the bills?

PROBLEM 11-1

You are a newly elected member of the state House of Representatives, and you have just been assigned to the Children, Youth, and Families Committee. The committee is considering whether to report this bill favorably to the full House:

> Sec. 1.   A stepparent shall support his or her stepchild to the same extent that a biological or adoptive parent is required to support his or her child so long as the stepchild is living in the same home as the stepparent. However, nothing in this section shall be construed as abrogating or in any way diminishing the duty a parent otherwise would have to provide child support, and no court shall consider the income of a stepparent, or the amount actually provided for a stepchild by a stepparent, in determining the amount of child support to be paid by a biological or adoptive parent.

> Sec. 2.   A biological or adoptive parent shall be liable to a stepparent for the sum of money expended by a stepparent for the support of a stepchild when that sum of money was expended because of the neglect or refusal of the biological or adoptive parent to pay any part of or all of the court-ordered amount of support.

> Sec. 3.   This statute shall not abrogate or diminish the common law right that a stepparent may possess to recover from a biological or adoptive parent the expense of providing necessaries for a stepchild in the absence of a court order for child support determining the amount of support to be paid by a biological or adoptive parent.

* * *

How would you vote? If you favor the bill's concept, would you recommend any changes to it during committee deliberations?

PROBLEM 11-2

You are an influential state senator. This bill has cleared committee and will soon be debated by the full senate:

> In any action to determine child support needs and obligations for a child whose alleged father is less than 18 years old, the parents of the alleged father and the parents of the mother, if the mother is also less than 18 years old, shall be made joint parties and may be jointly liable for the support ordered by the court to the child until both the father and the mother reach the age of 18 years.

How would you vote on this bill? What amendments, if any, would you suggest? As you prepare for floor debate, what policy considerations weigh in favor of, or against, the bill? If you were informed that a fit parent controls a grandparent's right to visit their grandchildren, would this information affect your thinking? *See Troxel v. Granville*, 530 U.S. 57 (2000), a principal case in Chapter 13.

PROBLEM 11-3

You are a state legislator who will soon vote on a bill that would require children to support their elderly parents. What policy considerations would you weigh in deciding how to vote? If you favor such a bill, what should be the standard of support?

C. POST-MAJORITY SUPPORT OBLIGATIONS

In most circumstances, a parent's support obligation terminates when the child reaches the general age of majority, which most states lowered from 21 to 18 in the early 1970s. The lower age creates new dilemmas for parents and their children. At 21, most young people have completed high school; many have nearly completed college or other post-secondary training; and many have entered, or will soon enter, an occupation or trade. But at 18, a young person might not have completed high school and may face the most costly period of life, arising from financing higher education.

Many young adults face substantial housing costs, burdensome post-secondary education debts, and an uncertain job market in difficult economic times. In these circumstances, parents may informally support their children or provide housing even after the legal support obligation ends.

"Despite the prevailing American ideology of individualism and the assumption that adults should be self-sufficient, it is the norm rather than the exception for young adults to receive financial support from their parents." Sally F. Goldfarb, *Who Pays For the "Boomerang Generation"?: A Legal Perspective On Financial Support For Young Adults*, 37 Harv. J. of Law & Gender 45, 47 (2014). In a 2018 survey, Merrill Lynch found that 79% of parents continue providing financial support to their adult children, particularly during the early years of the child's adulthood. Parental support may range from payments for expensive obligations such as higher education and weddings, to payments for groceries, cell phones, and the like. Merrill Lynch, *The Financial Journey of Modern Parenting: Joy, Complexity and Sacrifice* 3, 20 (2018). In the aggregate, the payments equal twice the amounts that parents devote to their own retirement savings. *Id.*

In 2016, the U.S. Census Bureau reported that about one-third of 18–34-year-olds live in their parents' home, more than the number of persons in this age group who live with a spouse. *See* BBC, *A Third of US Millennials Still Live At Home, Census Report Finds*, http://www.bbc.com/news/world-us-canada-39660656 (Apr. 20, 2017). The percentage is apparently the highest in U.S. history. Chris Kirkham, *Percentage of Young Americans Living With Parents Rises to 75-Year High*, Wall St. J., Dec. 21, 2016.

Legally enforceable post-majority support obligations present a different matter. Despite the federalization of parental support obligations, parents' obligations to children who are over the general age of majority remain matters for state-by-state response. In some states but not others, the law compels parents to provide post-majority support in some circumstances, either to help their child achieve economic self-sufficiency or because the child can never become self-supporting. The two circumstances are support through some period of post-secondary education, and support for an adult child who has a physical or mental disability that was diagnosed before the child reached majority. In some states, the support obligation also extends to children whose disability happened after majority.

1. Support During Post-Secondary Education

The common law imposed no obligation on parents to support their children's pursuit of post-secondary education past majority. Any such obligation would have been out of place for much of our nation's early history, when children were not even required to attend elementary and secondary school, and when college and university education was available to only a select few. In *Middlebury College v. Chandler*, 16 Vt. 683, 683 (1844), for example, the court held that the father was not obligated to pay for his son's college education because the evidence did not show "wealth, or station in society, or that [the son] exhibited peculiar indications of genius or talent, which would suggest the fitness and expediency of a college education for him, more than for the generality of youth in community."

In recent years, however, growing numbers of 18–24-year-olds have sought post-secondary education, which is widely seen as important to career entry and lifelong advancement. At the same time, the cost of higher education has outpaced inflation almost every year for at least the past three decades or so, threatening to place advanced study beyond the reach of many high school graduates without incurring sizeable debt non-dischargeable in bankruptcy, and without some financial support from their parents.

In response to these developments, about a third of the states have statutes or case law that requires divorced, never married, or separated parents to support their children's pursuit of higher education past the age of 18. The statutes take various approaches. "Three states permit a child to collect higher-education support to the age of twenty-three, one state permits support to the age of twenty-two, and five states and the District of Columbia permit support to the age of twenty-one. Some states with and without age limitations also limit support to achieve an undergraduate degree only. * * * The majority of states * * * will enforce higher-education support only when parents have agreed in a contract or in the divorce decree." Monica Hof Wallace, *A Federal Referendum: Extending Child Support for Higher Education*, 58 U. Kan. L. Rev. 665, 680–81 (2010).

Courts have rejected equal protection challenges to post-majority educational support laws that do not apply to parents who are living in intact families. *See, e.g., In re Marriage of Kohring*, 999 S.W.2d 228 (Mo. 1999), which held that the state has a rational basis for enhancing higher education opportunities for children whose parents do not live together.

In an empirical study published in 2017, Professor Leslie Joan Harris found that post-majority education laws indeed result in higher proportions of children of single-parent households obtaining post-secondary education and graduating from college. She concludes that these laws "appear to address one of the great disadvantages to children of not growing up in home with both their legal parents, that they generally have lower levels of academic achievement and are much less likely to go to college than their counterparts living with both legal parents." Leslie Joan Harris, *Child Support For Post-Secondary Education: Empirical and Historical Perspectives*, 29 J. Am. Acad. Matrim. Law. 299, 300 (2017). A persisting objection to these laws is that they "apply only to divorced or never-married and separated parents; parents whose marriages are intact are exempt." *Id.* at 300–01.

Among the states that authorize courts to impose educational support obligations past majority, some states (including New York, in *Pamela T.* below) specify that the court may base its order directly on the costs of tuition, books, and other expenses. Other states' courts reach the same result in the absence of statutory specification. The general approach is to impose the obligation on only the noncustodial parent, perhaps on the rationale that the custodial parent will be more likely to provide support voluntarily. *See, e.g.,* William V. Fabricius et al., *Divorced Parents'*

Financial Support of Their Children's College Expenses, 41 Fam. Ct. Rev. 224, 224–25 (2003).

This trial court divorce decision, affirmed in a brief intermediate appellate court opinion, places post-secondary educational support in context.

PAMELA T. v. MARC B.

Supreme Court of New York, 2011.
930 N.Y.S.2d 857, *aff'd*, 942 N.Y.S.2d 516 (App. Div. 2012).

MATTHEW F. COOPER, J.

The college application process can be an extremely stressful experience in a young person's life. Not only is there the prospect of living away from home, often for the very first time, and concerns about making new friends and adjusting to a new environment, but there are difficult decisions to be made as to where to apply and then, if accepted, the crucial choice as to which college or university to actually attend. Unfortunately, for the child of a high-conflict divorce, the anxiety surrounding the process is made that much more intense by the child's awareness that his or her choice of a college will provide yet another opportunity for parental strife. In many cases the strife will center on how much the parent who is obligated to pay child support will have to contribute towards the cost of the child's college education. And in New York, the battle is often over what is known as the [State University of New York or] "SUNY cap."

This divorce is by every definition high-conflict, and it is one where money has always been a major issue. The parties, both of whom are attorneys, have regularly returned to court since the entry of the judgment of divorce in 2008 to litigate an endless succession of post-judgment motions. This motion, their sixteenth, results from what one would normally assume to be a cause for celebration: the acceptance of their elder child, who has struggled with a learning disability, to Syracuse University and his decision to attend that institution of higher learning. Instead, the parties are before the court because the defendant-father insists that he should be able to invoke the SUNY cap and not be made to pay any more than he would have had to pay if the child had opted to attend a state-funded public school in the State University of New York (SUNY) system, like the State University of New York at Binghamton (SUNY Binghamton), as opposed to a non-state funded private school, like Syracuse.

* * * [T]he SUNY cap—to the extent that it stands for the proposition that before a parent can be compelled to contribute towards the cost of a private college there must be a showing that a child cannot receive an adequate education at a state college—is a doctrine that in many cases is harmful to the children of divorced parents, acts to discriminate against them, and is largely unworkable.

Background

The parties were divorced on December 23, 2008. They have two sons, one who is 18 and one who is 16. The judgment of divorce incorporated a custody agreement and a stipulation of settlement [which made no decision about payment of the children's college tuition and expenses—eds.]

* * *

[The elder son] graduated in 2011 from Beacon High School, a selective public high school in Manhattan. He was accepted at Syracuse University, SUNY Binghamton and SUNY Buffalo, along with a number of other schools. Syracuse, which awarded him $3,000 in financial aid, costs approximately $53,000 a year to attend as an undergraduate, while SUNY Binghamton and SUNY Buffalo cost only about $18,000 a year. Although the child visited Binghamton and gave serious consideration to going there, he ultimately decided to attend Syracuse. He is now a freshman there studying computer engineering and computer graphics.

* * *

The parties are both practicing attorneys in New York City. Plaintiff works for the Metropolitan Transit Authority Inspector General's Office and defendant is self-employed as a solo practitioner. Plaintiff's 2010 federal income tax return reports an adjusted gross income of $109,896. Defendant's 2010 federal income tax return reports an adjusted gross income of $105,135. Both parties have savings and retirement accounts, largely as a result of inheritances. Plaintiff's net worth statement shows she has assets of approximately $1,230,000. Defendant's net worth statement shows he has approximately $580,000. Both plaintiff and defendant went to private undergraduate colleges and law schools * * *.

The Parties' Contentions

Plaintiff * * * requests that defendant be directed to pay one-half of the following expenses for both children: all college related tuition, fees, housing, and meal costs, and all college preparation costs including tutors, entrance exam study courses, and application fees.

In opposing plaintiff's motion, defendant does not oppose an order directing him to contribute to his older child's college education, but he asks the court to apply the SUNY cap and limit his responsibility to a percentage of the costs of a state university education rather than to a percentage of a private college education. Defendant's position in this regard is based on his claim that he is unable to meet the financial demands of paying for private college and on his belief that his son can receive as good an education at SUNY Binghamton as he can at Syracuse. * * *

Analysis

I.   College Expenses for the Elder Child

Prior to September 1989, a court, "absent unusual circumstances or a voluntary agreement," was without the authority to order a parent to pay college expenses. As society changed and a college education became more a necessity than a luxury, the law changed as well. The enactment of Domestic Relations Law (DRL) section 240 (1–b)(c)(7) reflected the legislature's realization of the important role that college played in the lives of our young people and it conferred upon the courts of this state the authority to "direct a parent to contribute to a child's private college education, even in the absence of special circumstances or a voluntary agreement." The statute provides that when a court exercises its discretion to direct such a contribution from a parent, it is to do so "having regard for the circumstances of the case and the parties, the best interests of the child, and the requirements of justice." DRL § 240 (1–b)(c)(7). Case law [sets] forth specific factors that are to be considered in determining whether to award college expenses. These factors include the educational background of the parents and their financial ability to provide the necessary funds, the child's academic ability and endeavors, and the type of college that would be most suitable for the child.

* * *

One thing that DRL § 240 (1–b)(c)(7) does not provide for is a SUNY cap. The SUNY cap is a concept that has been judicially created * * *. [The] cases * * * provide little in the way of instruction as to when a SUNY cap might be properly applied over the objection of the parent who is seeking an award for college expenses.

* * *

One of the circumstances under which the SUNY cap is to be applied is where the parties have entered a binding stipulation or separation agreement specifically providing for such a limitation on the amount a parent is to contribute towards a child's college education, irrespective of whether the child attends a public or a private college. Another situation * * * is where an agreement specifically requires both parties to consent to decisions concerning college and one party withholds consent on the basis of the cost of a particular college. * * *

[Defendant argues] * * * that the SUNY cap should be applied where the proponent of private education fails to establish that the private college in question provides a superior education to that of a state college.

* * *

What defendant wants * * * is for plaintiff to be required to prove that Syracuse is a better school than SUNY Binghamton in order for him to be required to pay Syracuse's higher expenses. If this were to happen, the court would be placed in the position of being a kind of judicial college evaluator. For a number of reasons, this is something that this court cannot and will not do. While courts have occasionally been called upon to evaluate the difference between a public and private school education, this has almost always been within the context of private elementary and high school. To extend this evaluative process to the arena of individual state and private colleges, which is in effect what defendant is advocating, would require a court to take on a role as a "college rating entity" * * *

Even if the court were willing to enter the college ratings arena, there are no judicially manageable standards to use in a post-judgment divorce proceeding for determining the quality of education a student will receive at Syracuse University as compared to SUNY Binghamton, or for that matter as compared to any of the approximately four-thousand other colleges and universities in the United States. One can only imagine weeks of testimony with regard to each school on such things as the SAT scores of the incoming freshman class, the credentials of each faculty member, the success rate of the school's alumni, the quality of campus facilities, the size of the classes and the amount of individual attention a student can expect to receive, and the overall level of satisfaction or dissatisfaction that the student body experiences. And then in order to have persuasive witnesses with the requisite personal knowledge, there is the prospect of the parties calling the admissions director, dean, provost, department chairs, librarian, alumni director, and even students from the particular college that each side is championing as the finer bastion of academic excellence. Under these circumstances, it is difficult to conceive of a workable procedure—let alone a methodology—for a court to make a finding that one college is "better" than another.

It might be fair then to ask why a court just can't "go to the books," as it were, and make its determination based simply on the rankings assigned to a school by the various college guides. After all, colleges live and die by these rankings, and families of college applicants often come to regard the college guides as veritable bibles. The problem with the guides, however, * * * is that ranking colleges is "an act of real audacity" given the complexity of the matter. * * * [P]opular college ranking entities typically employ methodologies based on evaluators' prejudices that use ineffective proxies for quality, producing rankings systems that essentially measure institutional wealth. Consequently, the guides are of limited evidentiary value, not only because they constitute inadmissible hearsay, but because of the highly subjective nature of their conclusions.

The real issue is what college or university is the best for the individual child in question in the ways that matter most to that particular child. Unquestionably, the selection of a college for a child goes far beyond the statistical and the quantifiable, and is instead a very personal, very subjective decision. It is a decision that should be made not by a court but by the child, ideally with the help and support of both parents.

Here, the child chose to attend Syracuse University instead of SUNY Binghamton because he evidently felt that it would be the better school for him. * * *

This is by no means to imply that the educational experience that one can obtain at a New York State public college is somehow inferior to that offered by a private college. It is not. * * * But there is one thing the SUNY system should not be. Contrary to what proponents of a wide and liberal application of the SUNY cap might urge, the SUNY system should not be the assumed destination of the children of divorce.

In this case, it has been shown that there is ample reason to support the child's choice of Syracuse, irrespective of whether it is ranked lower, higher or the same as SUNY Binghamton or any other SUNY school. Provided that the funds are available to finance the child's education, the fact that Syracuse is a private school and costs more than a public school is not a reason to interfere with the child going to the school *he* chose and *he* wants to attend. This is particularly so in light of the fact that both his parents went to private colleges. * * *

[T]he court must now consider one remaining crucial factor. That factor is defendant's ability to pay. It is defendant's position that * * * he lacks the means to do so. Consequently, he contends that he should have to pay no more than $9,000 a year towards his son's education, an amount that is roughly 50% of the present annual cost of a SUNY school.

The court rejects defendant's contention as to his inability to pay a significant share of the child's actual educational expenses now being incurred at Syracuse. * * *

* * * Here, defendant has the income and the assets—as well as the ability to keep producing substantial income through his law practice—to make a significant contribution to his sons's college education. Although defendant's contribution should be less than plaintiff's, based on the difference between their net assets, and in particular what each of them presently has available for eventual retirement, that contribution should not be subject to some artificial construct like the SUNY cap. Rather, it should be based, as with all other child support obligations, on the respective finances of the parties. On this basis, the court concludes that defendant shall be obligated to contribute 40% of the total cost of the elder child attending Syracuse University, with those costs to include tuition, room and board, fees and books. The contribution shall begin with the 2011–2012 school year.

[The court dismissed as premature the motion concerning the college tuition and expenses of the younger son, who would not graduate from high school for a year and a half.]

NOTES AND QUESTIONS

1. *Questions about* Pamela T. (a) When the *Pamela T.* parties divorced, what measures might they have taken to help avoid the necessity for bringing and defending this motion concerning post-secondary education support? (b) Do you agree with the court that the motion about the younger son was premature? What might the court have done now to help avoid the need for the parties to return to court yet again when that child applies to college? (c) Should a divorced obligor parent have the same influence on the child's choice of a college or university as a parent would have in an intact family? (d) Why should the law obligate divorced, never-married, or separated parents to pay post-majority support for their children's higher education, when many or most parents from intact households do not pay for their children's higher education? *See, e.g.,* CNN, Blake Ellis, *Fewer Parents Helping to Pay For College* (June 26, 2014).

2. *Weighing the interests.* Resolution of cases such as *Pamela T.* may turn on the facts. In *In re Paternity of Pickett*, 44 N.E.3d 756 (Ind. Ct. App. 2015), for example, the court based the divorced father's child support obligation, not on his daughter's expenses at the private university that she chose to attend (Butler University), but on the lower in-state expenses charged by a state institution (Ball State University) to which she had also been accepted.

Pickett held that the child support order must balance "the advantages of the more expensive college in relation to the needs and abilities of the child with the increased hardship of the parent." *Id.* at 765. Ball State's expenses were about half of Butler's, and the father earned only about $39,000 a year.

2. Support for Adult Children with Disabilities

"Depending on what definition is used, between six and eighteen percent of children in the United States live with a disability. Advances in treatment of newborns with low birth weight and other serious medical conditions have dramatically increased the number of families that include a child with a disability. * * * About a quarter of children in households with incomes below the poverty line have disabilities such as vision impairments, hearing impairments, or learning disabilities. That translates into 15.8 to 19.9 million children. By comparison, about a fifth of non-poor children have such disabilities, or 11.9 to 13.6 million children." Karen Syma Czapanskiy, *Chalimony: Seeking Equity Between Parents of Children With Disabilities and Chronic Illnesses*, 34 N.Y.U. Rev. L. & Soc. Change 253, 256 (2010).

A sense of moral obligation may lead parents to provide post-majority support to their child who has a physical or mental disability. States disagree, however, about whether to impose a continuing legal duty to support adult children with disabilities who cannot otherwise support themselves. "Nine [states] recognize no such duty. Twenty-four recognize such a duty only if the child becomes disabled prior to majority or emancipation. The remaining eighteen, plus the District of Columbia, impose a duty of support regardless of when disability occurs." Sande L. Buhai, *Parental Support of Adult Children with Disabilities*, 91 Minn. L. Rev. 710, 775 (2007); Erica Fumagalli, *A Survey of Child Support For Adults With Impairments*, 29 J. Am. Acad. of Matrim. Law. 433, 447 (2017) (presenting state-by-state table). In states that recognize a legal duty, the duty applies to parents of marital and nonmarital children alike, irrespective of whether or when the parents' relationship has ended. *See, e.g., State ex rel. Moore v. McCampbell*, 2010 WL 2079701 (Iowa Ct. App. May 26, 2010).

The next decision concerns the legal obligation to provide support for an adult child whose disability manifested itself during minority.

HASTINGS V. HASTINGS

Third District Court of Appeal of Florida, 2003.
841 So.2d 484.

FLETCHER, JUDGE.

In 1953 Jean Audrey Hastings, n/k/a Jean Audrey Shepard [mother] and Lawrence Vaeth Hastings [father] divorced. The father was ordered to pay child support until their son reached the age of 21.[1] In 2001 the father filed a declaratory action, seeking to have determined whether he has an obligation to pay support for his 50-year-old son, who has an autism-related, chronic condition (Asperger's syndrome) for which he began receiving treatment at age 8.[2] The mother and the son counter-petitioned for the establishment of support for the son under Section 743.07(2), Florida Statutes, a savings clause enacted when the disability of nonage was removed for persons 18 years of age and over. Section 743.07(2) reads in pertinent part:

> This section shall not prohibit any court of competent jurisdiction from requiring support for a dependent person beyond the age of 18 years when such dependency is because of a mental or physical incapacity which began prior to such person reaching majority . . .

---

[1]   The age of majority at that time.

[2]   The mother supported the parties' dependent son by herself from the time the son was 21 until recently when she became unable to continue doing so.

By this enactment the legislature did not create a right or a cause of action, but "saved" any common law right or cause of action from extinction by section 743.07(1).

The trial court granted summary judgment for the father, apparently concluding that after the passage of many years it is now too late for the support action to be brought. We disagree.

"* * * [T]here is no doubt that the son has a common law right of support from his parents. * * *

In summary, the right to support belongs to the mentally or physically disabled adult child whose disability began prior to her or his majority, and the duty of support lies with both parents, throughout their lives. Thus the issue of support is not totally resolved in divorce actions wherein the mother and father allocate (or have allocated for them) the support payments for their dependent child as such a dependent person can bring an action in accordance with the rule establishing appropriate parties in actions involving legal incompetents. * * *

Reversed and remanded for further proceedings consistent herewith.

QUESTIONS

Disabilities and support. Where state law obligates parents to support their disabled child past majority, the obligation may last for the lifetimes of the parent or child, as it likely will in *Hastings*. What policy considerations underlie imposition of the continuing obligation? What policy considerations argue against imposition?

3. THE FEDERALIZATION OF CHILD SUPPORT

Child support is a prominent example, not only of how the federal government participates in regulating various family rights and responsibilities, but also of how welfare law and family law intersect. In effect, child support is an example of federal family law. Surprising as it may seem today, the significant federal role in child support establishment, maintenance, modification, and enforcement began only relatively recently.

For most of the nation's history, child support was the province of the states and their courts. Women and children were often the ultimate losers:

"State judges systematically underestimated the costs of raising children; overestimated the ability of custodial parents, usually mothers, to maximize income while providing child care; and bent over backwards to accommodate the family and career needs of non-custodial parents. State trial court discretion, combined with the absence of any clear theory or objective for child support awards, resulted in child support orders that were pathetically low by any standard."

Sylvia Law, *Access to Justice: The Social Responsibility of Lawyers: Families and Federalism*, Wash. U. J.L. & Pol'y 175, 186–88 (2000).

Responding to disarray and inconsistency in the states, Congress in 1988 mandated that states adopt child support guidelines, whose prescribed amount in a particular case would govern unless a court expressly stated reasons for deviation. Family Support Act of 1988, Pub. L. No. 100–485, 102 Stat. 2343 (1988). Because Congress did not mandate any particular guideline method, states have created their own methods by statute, administrative regulation, or court rule. The guidelines, which are based on the child's needs and the parent's ability to pay, apply both to initial entry of the support amount and to orders modifying that amount. This Section discusses the kinds of guidelines that states have adopted and explores their operation.

State child support guidelines follow one of three general models: the "Income Shares Model" (which 38 states and the District of Columbia use), the "Percentage of the Obligor's Income" model (which nine states use), and the "Melson formula" (which three states use). Charles J. Meyer et al., *Child Support Determinations in High Income Families—A Survey of the Fifty States*, 28 J. Am. Acad. of Matrim. Law. 473, 485–87 (2016).

Under the Income Shares model, the parents' income is combined and each parent is responsible for a prorated share. The Percentage of the Obligor's Income model considers only the obligor's income, whether the mother or the father. Both models stem from the premise that marital and nonmarital children should continue to receive the same amount of support that they would have received if the parents had not divorced or dissolved their relationship. Jane C. Venohr, *Child Support Guidelines and Guidelines Reviews: State Differences and Common Issues*, 47 Fam. L.Q. 327, 329, 331 (2013).

The Melson Formula is named after Delaware Family Court Judge Elwood F. Melson, Jr., who created the formula for use in his court. The formula "first considers the basic needs of the child and each parent. Basic needs amounts relate to the poverty level or a similar subsistence amount. If the obligated parent's income is more than sufficient to cover his or her prorated share of the child's basic needs and the parent's own basic needs, an additional percentage of the obligated parent's remaining income is assigned to child support. This last step allows the child to share in the standard of living afforded by the obligated parent." *Id.* at 331–32.

The child support guidelines demonstrate that diminished family privacy is an inevitable consequence of divorce. "While a family is intact, the parents' choice of employment, child care, and standard of living are left to the parties, as long as the child's basic needs are met. Upon divorce, however, courts are plunged into the divorced parents' personal lives to ensure that the interests of minor children are protected." *Chen v. Warner*, 695 N.W.2d 758, 769 (Wis. 2005).

4. THE OPERATION OF STATE CHILD SUPPORT GUIDELINES

As often happens, the devil is in the details because state guidelines are marked by both similarities and important differences. "State guidelines vary with respect to the income basis for the determination of support; the estimates of spending on children upon which the guidelines are based; the treatment of child care costs; the treatment of medical insurance and out-of-pocket expenditures for medical care; provisions for other children to whom the parent owes a duty of support; adjustments for parenting time; and provisions for adjusting support when the obligor is low-income." Jo Michelle Beld & Len Biernat, *Federal Intent for State Child Support Guidelines: Income Shares, Cost Shares, and the Realities of Shared Parenting*, 37 Fam. L.Q. 165, 166 (2003).

A. WHAT IS "INCOME"?

1. The Guidelines Definition

All guidelines require determination of parental "income." To protect and provide for children, the guidelines define "income" broadly to include a wide array of sources, including some sources that the Internal Revenue Service does not define as income for federal tax purposes. *See, e.g., Carmer v. Carmer*, 45 N.E.3d 512, 517 (Ind. Ct. App. 2015) (monthly structured annuity payments from a personal injury settlement).

KENTUCKY REVISED STATUTES
(2018).

§ 403.212.

(2) For the purposes of the child support guidelines:

(a) "Income" means actual gross income of the parent if employed to full capacity or potential income if unemployed or underemployed.

(b) "Gross income" includes income from any source, except as excluded in this subsection, and includes but is not limited to income from salaries, wages, retirement and pension funds, commissions, bonuses, dividends, severance pay, pensions, interest, trust income, annuities, capital gains, Social Security benefits, workers' compensation benefits, unemployment insurance benefits, disability insurance benefits, Supplemental Security Income (SSI), gifts, prizes, and alimony or maintenance received. Specifically excluded are benefits received from means-tested public assistance programs, including but not limited to public assistance as defined under Title IV-A of the Federal Social Security Act, and food stamps.

(c) For income from self-employment, rent, royalties, proprietorship of a business, or joint ownership of a partnership or closely held corporation, "gross income" means gross receipts minus ordinary and necessary expenses required for self-employment or business operation. * * * Expense reimbursement or in-kind payments received by a parent in the course of employment, self-employment, or operation of a business or personal use of business property or payments of expenses by a business, shall be counted as income if they are significant and reduce personal living expenses such as a company or business car, free housing, reimbursed meals, or club dues.

(d) If a parent is voluntarily unemployed or underemployed, child support shall be calculated based on a determination of potential income, except that a determination of potential income shall not be made for a parent who is physically or mentally incapacitated or is caring for a very young child, age three (3) or younger, for whom the parents owe a joint legal responsibility. Potential income shall be determined based upon employment potential and probable earnings level based on the obligor's or obligee's recent work history, occupational qualifications, and prevailing job opportunities and earnings levels in the community. A court may find a parent to be voluntarily unemployed or underemployed without finding that the parent intended to avoid or reduce the child support obligation.

(e) "Imputed child support obligation" means the amount of child support the parent would be required to pay from application of the child support guidelines.

QUESTIONS

The contours of "income." Under Ky. Rev. Stat. § 403.212, would a parent's income include his or her receipt of any or all of the following: lottery winnings; recovery in a personal injury suit; in-kind payments (for example, a car or housing provided by the employer); an inheritance; an *inter vivos* gift; or commissions, overtime pay, or severance pay?

2. Imputing Income to an Unemployed or Underemployed Parent

When an obligor parent appears to be voluntarily unemployed or voluntarily underemployed, imputing income to the parent can be an issue on an initial child support order or on a motion to modify an existing order. Imputing income on modification motions is treated below in Section 5.C.

"Most states have adopted the dual obligation principle under which child support is the responsibility of both parents, allocated in proportion to their incomes. The labor force participation of both parents is therefore determinative of their respective child support obligations. If one parent is not participating in the labor force to the fullest extent possible, the other parent's share of the total parental support will be higher. One remedy for this arguably unfair allocation of support is the imputation of income to the parent who is earning too little. In most states, such imputation is permissible when a parent's labor force participation should produce more income, based on the parent's education and experience. When income is imputed, allocation of the child support obligation is based on the parent's potential income, rather than her actual income." Karen Syma Czapanskiy, *supra* at 274.

Imputation decisions reflect conflicting values. Child support obligors should retain the opportunity to make reasonable career choices and other lifestyle decisions, even where the decision results in loss of income, at least temporarily; but dissolution does not end the parents' obligations to support their children. *Hawkins v. Hawkins*, 742 S.E.2d 677, 684 (S.C. Ct. App. 2013).

Where imputation is raised on an initial order or later on a modification motion, the court must decide whether the obligor acted in good faith, or whether the obligor's voluntary unemployment or underemployment resulted from efforts to "shirk" obligations to the child, or from other wrongdoing. "Shirking is an employment decision to reduce or forgo income that is both voluntary and unreasonable under the circumstances." *In re Paternity of J.R.B.*, 2013 WL 12182230 * 1 (Wis. Ct. App. Apr. 30, 2013).

The determination of how much income to impute turns on findings concerning the obligor parent's earning capacity. " 'Earning capacity is composed of (1) the ability to work, including such factors as age, occupation, skills, education, health, background, work experience and qualifications; (2) the willingness to work exemplified through good faith efforts, due diligence and meaningful attempts to secure employment; and (3) an opportunity to work which means an employer who is willing to hire.' " *Mendoza v. Ramos*, 105 Cal. Rptr.3d 853, 857 (Ct. App. 2010).

Before imputing income for unemployment or underemployment, the court may issue a seek-work order directing the obligor to attempt to find employment within a specified period, file regular reports showing at least a specified minimum number of attempts, and list the employers to which the obligor applied. *See, e.g.*, Mont. Code Ann. § 40–5–291 (2018). Violating a seek-work order can expose the obligor to citation for civil contempt.

PROBLEM 11-4

When Mike and Julie Brown divorced, the court awarded the 46-year-old wife $200 monthly in rehabilitative alimony for two years. She had a high school education and, during the couple's 13-year marriage, was a homemaker who cared for the two children. The husband was an engineer earning more than $63,000 annually, plus stock options and other fringe benefits. During the two-year rehabilitative period, Julie became a full-time student pursuing a nursing degree. In calculating her child support obligation, should the court impute income to her during that two-year period? Would a seek-work order be appropriate?

PROBLEM 11-5

When John and Jean Smith of Lexington, Kentucky divorced after a ten-year marriage, John received primary physical custody of their two children. Eight years earlier, Jean earned an annual salary of $33,000 in her last full-time job, which she left so that she could stay home and raise the children. Since then, she has earned a masters degree in electrical engineering, but has not reentered the work force.

In the divorce proceeding, the trial court imputed an annual income of $66,000 after taking judicial notice of the U.S. Department of Labor's Bureau of Labor Statistics Report, which placed the national median annual earnings for electrical engineers at $64,910.00. Applying the Kentucky statute quoted above, did the trial court decide correctly? Does the statute's imputation provision properly weigh the interests of both parents and the two children?

B. DEVIATING FROM THE GUIDELINES AMOUNT

The parent's income is applied to the guidelines schedule, which recites a support amount for each child the obligor parent must support. Federal regulations require that states review their guidelines at least once every four years to help assure that the prescribed amounts keep pace with the costs of parenting children.

By congressional mandate, states apply a rebuttable presumption that the guidelines amount is the correct amount of child support payable. The mandate permits the court to deviate from (or to "adjust" or "vary") the guidelines amount, either upward or downward. The court may deviate, however, only on a written or specific finding on the record that the guidelines amount would be unjust or inappropriate in a particular case, as determined under criteria established by the state. Because federal regulations intend deviation to be the exception rather than the rule, only a compelling showing rebuts the presumption. The guidelines amount prevails in 85% or more of child support cases. Sanford L. Braver et al., *Public Intuitions About Fair Child Support Allocations: Converging Evidence for a "Fair Shares" Rule*, 20 Psychol. Pub. Pol'y & L. 146 (2014).

KENTUCKY REVISED STATUTES
(2018).

§ 403.211.

(3) A written finding or specific finding on the record that the application of the guidelines would be unjust or inappropriate in a particular case shall be sufficient to rebut the presumption and allow for an appropriate adjustment of the guideline award if based upon one (1) or more of the following criteria:

(a) A child's extraordinary medical or dental needs;

(b) A child's extraordinary educational, job training, or special needs;

(c) Either parent's own extraordinary needs, such as medical expenses;

(d) The independent financial resources, if any, of the child or children;

(e) Combined monthly adjusted parental gross income in excess of the Kentucky child support guidelines;

(f) The parents of the child, having demonstrated knowledge of the amount of child support established by the Kentucky child support guidelines, have agreed to child support different from the guideline amount. However, no such agreement shall be the basis of any deviation if public assistance is being paid on behalf of a child under the provisions of Part D of Title IV of the Federal Social Security Act; and

(g) Any similar factor of an extraordinary nature specifically identified by the court which would make application of the guidelines inappropriate.

(4) "Extraordinary" as used in this section shall be determined by the court in its discretion.

NOTES AND QUESTIONS

1. *"Parenting time."* Initially states calibrated their child support guidelines on the model that traditionally prevailed in most divided households—one parent with sole physical custody of the children, and the other parent with reasonable visitation or else little contact with the child. The schedule presumed a custodial parent who had direct ongoing expenses while the child was living under her roof, and a noncustodial parent who would contribute support payments. "Visitation" normally reflected the expectation that the child would live with the noncustodial parent for no more than a modest period each year. Courts could consider unusual custody arrangements as grounds for deviating from the presumed guidelines amount in exceptional cases.

As you will learn in Chapters 12 and 13, more and more divided families since the early 1980s have been marked by custody and visitation arrangements ("parenting plans") that depart from the traditional model. States have wrestled with contentions that the guidelines unfairly burden noncustodial parents (typically fathers) whose children live with them for periods longer than the modest periods that mark traditional visitation. These parents, it is claimed, are victims of "double-dipping" because they may shoulder greater direct support costs during these longer periods while also remaining obligated to pay support under guidelines that calculate support based on circumstances that traditionally marked divided families.

Today "[t]he majority of states, mostly through statutory guidelines but at times through case law, consider the amount of time a child spends with each parent as a relevant factor in determining child support. States vary in the ways they account for parenting time; yet, the general principle is that the more time a parent spends with a child the less he or she will be required to pay in child support." Gaia Bernstein & Zvi Triger, *Over-Parenting*, 44 U.C. Davis L. Rev. 1221, 1245–46 (2011).

State guidelines differ concerning the minimum amount of shared-parenting time that will trigger entitlement to an adjustment of child support owed. In Nebraska, for example:

> [A]n adjustment in child support may be made at the discretion of the court when visitation or parenting time substantially exceeds alternating weekends and holidays and 28 days or more in any 90-day period. During visitation or parenting time periods of 28 days or more in any 90-day period, support payments may be reduced by up to 80 percent. The amount of any reduction for extended parenting time shall be specified in the court's order and shall be presumed to apply to the months designated in the order.

Neb. Ct. R. § 4–210 (2018).

Formulas that reduce support payments for the time the child spends with the noncustodial parent may introduce new inequities, however, because that parent's direct expenses do not necessarily reduce the custodial parent's expenses, such as housing and utility costs. Professor Marygold S. Melli notes other potential problems with reliance on formulas:

> First, it rewards nonresidential parents disproportionately for spending small amounts of extra time with their children. * * * Second, if ordinary visitation has already been factored in and the basic child support award has already been discounted for the expenditures by the nonresidential parent on ordinary visitation, a formula based on a strict proportional time with the child doubles the discounts for ordinary visitation.

Marygold S. Melli, *Guideline Review: Child Support and Time Sharing by Parents*, 33 Fam. L. Q. 219, 228 (1999).

2. *The child's resources.* Some state guidelines permit or require the court to consider the child's financial resources in determining the parent's basic support obligation. *See, e.g.,* Mo. Rev. Stat. § 452.340.1(1) (2018). How might the court consider these resources in other states (such as Kentucky, whose statutes defining parental income and permissible deviation are quoted above) in which the child's financial resources do not directly affect the determination?

Where the child is a trust beneficiary, the question whether the income reduces the parent's obligation or justifies a downward deviation may depend on the child's needs, the settlor's intent expressed in the trust, or the child's ability to access the funds. *See, e.g., Cutts v. Trippe,* 57 A.3d 1006, 1011 (Md. Ct. Spec. App. 2012).

The child's resources may also include Social Security, which provides more benefits to children than any other government social program. Most Americans are familiar with Social Security as a retirement insurance program. Social Security, however, is also a family insurance program that provides income support to disabled workers and their families, and to survivors of workers who die. In 2017, the Social Security Administration distributed benefits each month to about 4.2 million children because one or both of their parents had died, retired, or become disabled. Nearly one million children also benefit from Social Security because the child has a specified disability such as Down syndrome. *See* Social Sec. Admin., *Benefits for Children,* https://www.ssa.gov/pubs/EN-05-10085.pdf (2018).

In some states, the child's Social Security benefits remain his or her property and do not diminish the parental support obligation. In other states, the parent is entitled to a credit in the amount of the benefits received for any reason. In still other states, Social Security benefits paid because of the parent's disability or retirement may, in the court's discretion, diminish the support obligation after considering the child's needs.

3. *Parental agreement.* As a general matter, a parent may agree to pay child support in an amount higher than the presumed guidelines amount even if no court has ordered such a deviation. *See, e.g., Gore v. Grant,* 349 P.3d 779, 785 (Utah Ct. App. 2015). Such agreements remain subject to court approval, but the law views them as "legitimate incidents of parental authority and control * * * entitled to serious consideration by a court." *Pursley v. Pursley,* 144 S.W.3d 820, 825 (Ky. 2004).

A parent's purported agreement to pay only an amount lower than the guidelines amount generally meets court disapproval because the child support right is held by the child, and not by either parent. In *Perkinson v. Perkinson,* 989 N.E.2d 758 (Ind. 2013), for example, the court refused to enforce the husband's agreement to waive parenting plan rights in return for the wife's agreement that he pay no support for their child. The court found the agreement "repugnant and contrary to public policy," and instructed lawyers generally to "refuse to be a part of such discussion and [to] advise their clients that any such discussion is unacceptable." *Id.* at 760. Under what sorts of circumstances might a court approve an agreement that a parent pay only support below the guidelines amount?

These issues are discussed further in Chapter 16 on privatizing the ramifications of marriage and divorce.

C. THE GUIDELINES' OUTER LIMITS

1. Low-Income Obligors

Federal law specifies that state child support guidelines apply to all parents, including parents in poverty. 45 C.F.R. § 302.56 (2018). States vary, however, in their approaches to the support obligations of low-income obligors whose poverty is not caused by voluntary unemployment or voluntary underemployment. "Most states base their guidelines on economic data that reflect average child-rearing expenditures, but reduce these amounts for very low-income parents." Jane C. Venohr, *Child Support Guidelines and Guidelines Reviews: State Differences and Common Issues*, 47 Fam. L.Q. 327, 329–30 (2013).

Some state guidelines specify that means-tested public assistance benefits do not constitute income; a child support award of $0 would be warranted where the parent has no non-benefit income. Some states leave indigent parents' support obligations to judicial discretion, without stating any presumed or absolute amount that the parent must pay. Other states create a presumption that a poor noncustodial parent must pay the lowest support amount recited on the guidelines schedule; the presumption may be rebutted where the amount would be unjust or inappropriate, though the state may also limit the amount of arrears that may accumulate against a poor parent. *See, e.g.,* N.Y. Fam. Ct. Act § 413(1)(g) (2018) (not more than $500).

Still other states mandate an irrebuttable minimum support amount, regardless of the payor's income; the irrebuttable minimum may be quite low, but downward deviation is unavailable. *See, e.g.,* Ky. Rev. Stat. Ann. § 403.212(4), (6) (2018) ($60 per month). Where a noncustodial parent's monthly child support obligation is reduced to a relatively minuscule amount (say, $50) or even to zero, does the reduction sufficiently consider the circumstances of the custodial parent (who may be in similar financial straits) and the child? What purposes are served, or perhaps disserved, by mandating payment of minuscule amounts?

In its mandate legislation, Congress intended "to ensure that [the state guidelines'] application results in the determination of appropriate child support award amounts." 42 U.S.C. § 667(a) (2018). With poor obligors, however, a gulf may separate intent from application. Poor noncustodial fathers may be destined to fall into arrears because they did not appear in the proceeding that established the initial order, or because they appeared without a lawyer to negotiate realistic obligations with the state's experienced representatives. *See* Karin Martinson & Demetra Nightingale, *Ten Key Findings From Responsible Fatherhood Initiatives* 7 (Urban Inst. 2008). Or the initial child support order may be based on imputed income in an amount that a person could earn locally from a minimum-wage job during a 40-hour workweek, even though underemployed obligors may receive less than the minimum wage or may work less than full-time each week. As arrears mount, "[p]oor fathers often face child support orders that are set at levels they cannot pay; their orders are rarely modified during periods of unemployment, and they accrue unrealistic levels of debt. This may motivate fathers to lose contact with their families and evade the child support system." *Id.* at 3.

Child support enforcement may be frustrated when the initial order sets an amount that the poor obligor, with little or no income, cannot pay without impoverishing himself. Section 6 below explores enforcement challenges and proposals to improve payment rates by enhancing the earning capacities of poor obligors.

2. High-Income Obligors

Most state guidelines maintain schedules that determine child support obligations for parents with annual incomes between $0 and about $70,000 to $180,000 or more. Judges must frequently establish support obligations for parents such as Mr. Ciampa, whose incomes are "off the schedule" at the high end.

CIAMPA V. CIAMPA

Court of Appeals of Kentucky, 2013.
415 S.W.3d 97.

CLAYTON, JUDGE:

* * *

FACTS

Peter R. Ciampa and Cynthia L. Ciampa (hereinafter "Cindy") were married in 1988. Three daughters were born of the marriage. In November 2005, they separated and filed for dissolution of the marriage. A decree of dissolution was granted on December 4, 2006. * * *

This issue on appeal is child support. The pertinent history of child support begins with the * * * property settlement agreement. Therein, Peter agreed to provide Cindy with $6,000 per month in child support for their three daughters. Next, in June 2010, when the parties' oldest daughter turned 18, Cindy made a motion, which among other things, included a request for modification of child support. The family court held a hearing on the various issues including child support. * * * [T]he family court made extensive findings regarding reasonable living expenses for the remaining two minor children and ordered that Peter's monthly child support payment remain at $6,000 per month.

Next, in June 2012, Peter moved for a modification of child support because the second daughter would turn eighteen in July 2012, and he would only be responsible for child support for one child. * * * [T]he family court entered findings of fact and an order modifying child support on October 17, 2012. This order reduced the child support monthly payment from $6,000 to $5,800.

Thereafter, Peter made a motion to alter, amend, or vacate, or in the alternative, make more specific findings. * * * [T]he family court made additional findings but denied the request to reduce the amount of its original, monthly child support. Peter now appeals from this order.

* * *

ANALYSIS

Child Support

The child support guidelines set out in Kentucky Revised Statutes (KRS) 403.212 serve as a rebuttable presumption for the establishment or modification of the amount of child support. Nevertheless, family courts may deviate from the guidelines when they make specific findings that application of the guidelines would not be just or appropriate. Specifically, the family court may use its judicial discretion to set child support outside the guidelines in circumstances where combined adjusted parental gross income exceeds the uppermost level of the guidelines.

In the case at hand, Peter is self-employed as an oral surgeon. According to his 2011 tax return, he earned $728,046 in taxable income and $89,627 in tax-exempt income, which combined provided him with a total annual income of $817,673. Cindy does not work outside the home. She provided a 2011 tax return that showed that she had taxable income of $32,681 and tax-exempt income of $19,723, which provides her a total annual income of $52,404.

Consequently, according to the parties' tax returns, their combined income is more than $870,000, which is indisputably outside the income guidelines of the child support charts. The uppermost annual income level listed in the child support guidelines is $180,000. Thus, pursuant to the statutory instructions, the family court "may use its judicial discretion in determining child support in circumstances where combined adjusted parental gross income exceeds the uppermost levels of the guideline table."

Setting child support outside the guidelines

* * * [T]he family court * * * noted the child's reasonable needs were $6,617 per month despite the fact that Cindy submitted proffered expenses

totally [sic] $9,312.27. Notably, in the family court's second set of findings, the family court determined that some of the requested expenses for the child were not reasonable. Therefore, the family court did not include these expenses when it calculated the amount of the monthly child support.

Peter's arguments challenging the child support

Peter proffers several arguments to undermine the credibility of the family court's decision. We, however, are not persuaded by these arguments. His major concerns are the family court's inclusion of a *future* expense, that is, the purchase of a car when the minor child turns 16; the admissibility of certain evidence provided by Cindy to the family court substantiating the expenses of the child; and, the family court's handling of housing and other expenses as reasonable needs of the child. Further, Peter questions whether the intent of the statute is met when the family court ordered only a three per cent reduction in the child support amount and the child support is for one rather than two children.

With reference to the prorated amount for the purchase of a car, we see no reason to second-guess the family court judge. * * * [N]othing prevents Peter from making a motion to be reimbursed for the car expense if Cindy does not purchase the car for the child.

Next, Peter maintains that the expenses submitted by Cindy were not adequately substantiated * * *. * * * [T]he family court deemed that the expenses were substantiated. Moreover, his counsel had adequate opportunity to challenge them.

We now address Peter's contention that the family court erred when it included housing and other expenses in its calculus of reasonable needs of the child. Peter's arguments are based primarily on the fact that the amounts were not significantly reduced from 2010 when child support had previously been set. * * *

It is the task of the family court to determine the reasonable portion of housing expenses to allocate for a child when establishing child support. Moreover, reasonable household expenses resulting from a child living in the home are certainly part of the child support equation. Here, Peter has not challenged that the family court has authority to appropriately deviate from the child support guidelines when it provides written findings of fact to support the amount ordered. Having decided that the family court had evidence to support the child support amount that it eventually ordered, we ascertain no abuse of discretion in regard to the amount of household expenses allocated to the child.

* * *

In response to Peter's argument that the intent of the statute is not met when only a three per cent reduction in the child support amount is ordered and the child support is for one rather than two children, we make several observations. First, [the statute] does not express any intentionality but merely lists the amount of child support to be paid when parties' income is not outside the guidelines.

Moreover, parents not only have a universal and moral duty to support and maintain their minor children, but they also have a statutory duty. And child support is a statutory duty intended to benefit the children not the parents. The legal obligation to support children remains until the children are emancipated.

In light of the statutory and moral imperatives for child support, it is the duty of the family court to consider the minutiae and details necessary to fashion a reasonable child support order. It is not the province of an appellate court to delve into these details. Here, the family court made a thorough and conscientious record of the rationale behind the decision, including that the parents' resources were outside the purview of the child support guidelines. For that reason, we hold that the family court's decision regarding the amount of the child support was not unreasonable because it was based on the child's expenses and the parents' resources.

* * * *Downing v. Downing,* 45 S.W.3d 449 (Ky. App. 2001) * * * imposes limitations on the trial court when setting child support in cases where the parties' gross income exceeds the child support guidelines and the parties have not agreed to child support. Peter cites the statement from *Downing* that "[b]eyond a certain point, additional child support serves no purpose but to provide extravagance and unwarranted transfer of wealth[,]" and argues that this is the case here.

But the *Downing* Court explained that "any decision to set child support above the guidelines must be based primarily on the child's needs." It supported the view that children should continue to live at the standard of living to which they had grown accustomed prior to the parents' divorce. And the *Downing* Court further reasoned that the needs of the children should be based on the parents' financial ability to meet those needs.

In essence, our Court in *Downing* disabused any mathematical calculation extrapolated from the guidelines * * *.

In its order, the family court found that Cindy submitted expenses in the amount of $9,312.27. The family court, however, determined that the reasonable needs of the child were $6,617 per month and disallowed certain expenses as unreasonable. The disallowed expenses were those related to the child's owning a horse, the purchase of new furniture and redecorating the child's bedroom, employment of a nutritionist and personal trainer for the child, and $100 of the money allotted for the purchase of a car.

Here, the family court considered the reasonable day-to-day needs of the parties' child, the parties' ability to pay, and decided on an appropriate child support amount. * * *

* * * [N]othing leads us to believe that the findings and orders are arbitrary, unreasonable, unfair, or unsupported by sound legal principles.

CONCLUSION

The family court carefully reviewed the parties' income, lifestyle, and the child's expenses. And it provided written findings to support its order. Legally, the family court has met the statutory and case law requirements for a deviation from the child support guidelines when the parties' income is over the threshold of the child support guidelines. There is no abuse of discretion, and we affirm the decision * * *.

MAZE, JUDGE, concurring:

I agree with the result reached by the majority, but on slightly different grounds. As the majority correctly notes, Peter agreed to pay $6000 per month for the support of his three daughters. At the time he executed this agreement, he was aware that this amount was in excess of the amount required under Kentucky's Child Support Guidelines. It is well-established that parties may agree to support in excess of the Guidelines. Such agreements are an enforceable contract between the parties, and it is not the place of the courts to disturb it absent some showing of fraud, undue influence, overreaching or manifest unfairness. Peter does not make any such showing.

The difficulty in this case arises because the agreement provides for support in the amount of $6000 for all three children, but does not include provisions for modification of upon emancipation of one or more, but not all of the children. However, [the statute] provides that provisions for support shall be terminated by emancipation of the child "[u]nless otherwise agreed in writing or expressly provided in the decree. . . ." In this case, the trial court properly considered the emancipation of the two older daughters as a basis for modification of the agreement's provisions regarding child support.

Nevertheless, the trial court heard evidence and made extensive findings regarding the reasonable needs of the remaining daughter. As the majority correctly holds, the trial court has the authority to deviate from the child support guidelines when it provides written findings of facts to support the amount ordered. Although I might quibble with some of these expenses, I agree with the majority that the trial court's findings are supported by substantial evidence and were not an abuse of its discretion. With the exception of the allowance for purchasing a car, the trial court noted that the claimed expenses were consistent with the standard of living established for the child during and after the marriage.

NOTES AND QUESTIONS

1. *Questions about* Ciampa. (a) The court of appeals majority noted that "the parties in this case have been before the family court often." When parties retain counsel to pursue multiple post-dissolution motions spanning months or years, what effects might the parents' disputes have on their children? (b) What factors did the trial court weigh in determining the appropriateness and amount of a child support award based on Mr. Ciampa's off-the-schedule income?

2. *Determining the child's "reasonable needs." Ciampa* makes much of the child's "reasonable needs," one factor that (together with the parent's ability to pay) is central under the child support guidelines. In the ordinary case, the guidelines themselves address the needs question by assigning a presumptive support amount based on parental income and permitted adjustments. But how does the court determine the child's needs when (as in *Ciampa*) some amount of the income of one or both parents is off the schedule at the high end and the court has discretion about how much support to assign from that amount?

One might say, as Blackstone did, that needs (as opposed to "wants") consist of only the bare essentials of life—modest food, clothing, and shelter. William Blackstone, 1 Commentaries on the Laws of England *447. Courts determining child support awards, however, hold that a child's needs depend on the parents' station in life, and thus that a child of wealthy parents "is entitled to, and therefore 'needs' something more than the bare necessities of life." *In re Marriage of Cryer*, 131 Cal. Rptr.3d 424, 433 (Ct. App. 2011). Child support guidelines also express this flexible understanding of needs. *See, e.g., Massachusetts Child Support Guidelines* (2018) (child support should "meet the child's survival needs in the first instance, but to the extent either parent enjoys a higher standard of living, [should] entitle the child to enjoy that higher standard").

3. *Tensions between child support and spousal maintenance.* Mr. Ciampa alleged that his ex-wife's expenses were "not adequately substantiated." Obligors often complain that their ex-spouses spend child support payments on themselves as disguised alimony, and not on the child. Should it matter that a larger support payment from the noncustodial parent will inevitably benefit not only the child but also the custodial parent? Can such incidental benefit to the custodial parent be avoided?

Child support is a right held by the child, but the obligor parent pays installments to the custodial parent, either directly or through the court. Courts sometimes liken custodial parents to constructive trustees or fiduciaries who hold support payments for the child's use and benefit, *e.g., Perkinson v. Perkinson*, 989 N.E.2d 758, 762 (Ind. 2013), but the custodial parent generally controls discretionary spending.

Many states have statutes that authorize the court to order the custodial parent to account for the spending, and the court may hold the custodial parent responsible for spending as the child's fiduciary in an extraordinary case. *See, e.g.,* Mo. Rev. Stat. § 452.342 (2018). Courts have generally not been receptive, however, to obligors' accusations that the custodial parent spends some or all of the money on herself and not on the child.

4. *Formulas for high-income obligors.* States differ in their treatment of the portion of an obligor's income that is off the schedule at the high end. Which of the following approaches did *Ciampa* apply?

a. Some states "extrapolate" the guidelines upward, *e.g., Smith v. Stewart,* 684 A.2d 265 (Vt. 1996). For the portion of off-the-schedule income, the parent pays the percentage assigned to the highest level of income stated on the schedule; the overall support amount is subject to deviation based on the child's needs and the parent's ability to pay.

b. Some states presume that the guidelines' highest award amount is the proper amount in high-income-obligor cases, but permit courts to deviate from that amount based on the parties' standard of living and the child's needs. The court denied upward deviation in *State v. Hall,* 418 N.W.2d 187 (Minn. Ct. App. 1988), which affirmed a $1000 monthly child support award entered against entertainer Daryl Hall in favor of his son. Hall and the mother had never been married to each other, had never lived together, and had only one sexual encounter. Hall's net income was about $1.4 million a year, or $116,000 per month. The mother's monthly income consisted of about $437 in public assistance payments and an average of $120 in food stamps.

The $1000 monthly award entered against Hall was the presumptive guideline amount for payors earning $4000 or more per month, the highest income amount on the schedule at that time. The schedule thus stopped at a relatively low maximum amount and vested discretion in the trial court to deviate in appropriate cases.

c. Some states apply common law standards, to the off-the-schedule portion, such as those codified in Section 309 of the Uniform Marriage and Divorce Act, which consider generally the child's needs and the parent's ability to pay. The guidelines create no formula or presumption for that portion.

Which approach do you favor, and why?

5. *Absence of a joint household.* When a parent's obligation for high-end off-the-schedule income is calculated for the initial order or on a motion to modify the child support amount, does it matter that the parents never maintained a household together (as was the case in *State v. Hall,* discussed above)?

In *Smith v. Freeman,* 814 A.2d 65 (Md. Ct. Spec. App. 2002), the custodial mother moved for upward modification of support for the five-year-old nonmarital child of a professional football player who earned about $1.2 million a year when the parties signed their initial support agreement, and about $3.2 million a year by the time the mother filed her modification motion. The trial court denied the motion on the ground that the child had not grown accustomed to her father's wealth because the unmarried parents never resided in a single household. The intermediate appellate court vacated the judgment:

> Regardless of whether a child is born out-of-wedlock or to parents whose marriage ended in divorce, every child is entitled to a level of support commensurate with the parents' economic position. A system that rewards those children whose parents were once married to each other, or who had at least lived together, would contravene the objective of the Guidelines "to achieve equity and consistency in child support awards."

Id. at 84.

6. *Income fluctuation.* In some cases involving income that is off-the-guidelines schedule at the high end, the obligor parent's income fluctuates from year to year. Where annual income fluctuates significantly without wrongdoing by the parent, many states' guidelines permit entry of a support order based on an average of the parent's recent annual income, usually for the immediately prior two to five years. *See, e.g., Anderson v. Anderson*, 323 P.3d 895, 899 (Mont. 2014) (three years). What purpose do these income-averaging provisions seek to serve?

5. MODIFICATION OF CHILD SUPPORT ORDERS

Because a child support order defines only the parent's present obligation, the order is modifiable until the obligation ends. *See, e.g., Fetherkile v. Fetherkile*, 907 N.W.2d 275, 291 (Neb. 2018). The order may remain in force for nearly two decades or more, unless a parent seeks modification based on changes in the child's needs, the parent's ability to pay, or both. A parent may seek downward modification of the amount he or she must pay, or upward modification of the amount the other parent must pay. Parents' agreements purporting to prohibit modification of support orders are unenforceable as contrary to the public policy of protecting the child's right to payment. *See, e.g., Matter of Marriage of Sheil*, 398 P.3d 425, 427 (Or. Ct. App. 2017).

A. THE "CHANGE OF CIRCUMSTANCES" STANDARD

UNIFORM MARRIAGE AND DIVORCE ACT
(2018).

§ 316(a).

* * * [T]he provisions of any decree respecting maintenance or [child] support may be modified * * * only upon a showing of changed circumstances so substantial and continuing as to make the terms unconscionable.

IOWA CODE

(2018).

§ 598.21C.1.

* * * [T]he court may subsequently modify child * * * support orders when there is a substantial change of circumstances. In determining whether there is a substantial change in circumstances, the court shall consider the following:

    a.   Changes in the employment, earning capacity, income, or resources of a party.

    b.   Receipt by a party of an inheritance, pension, or other gift.

    c.   Changes in the medical expenses of a party.

    d.   Changes in the number or needs of dependents of a party.

    e.   Changes in the physical, mental, or emotional health of a party.

    f.   Changes in the residence of a party.

    g.   Remarriage of a party.

    h.   Possible support of a party by another person.

    i.   Changes in the physical, emotional, or educational needs of a child whose support is governed by the order.

* * *

    l.   Other factors the court determines to be relevant in an individual case.

NOTES

    1.   *Initial questions.* In what way is the UMDA standard more difficult to establish than Iowa's? What policies underlie a high threshold for modifying outstanding child support orders? How strict should the "substantial change of circumstances" standard be?

    2.   *The Bradley Amendment's effect on the modification standard.* In 1986, Congress enacted the Bradley Amendment, which requires states to maintain laws that (1) provide that each unpaid, court-ordered child support installment constitutes a vested right of the child when due, (2) prohibit retroactive modification of past-due child support installments, (3) consider a past-due child support installment as a final judgment, and (4) extend full faith and credit to enforcement of judgments for past-due child support. Why do you think Congress concluded that the Bradley Amendment was necessary?

    By treating each past-due unpaid child support installment as a vested right of the child entitled to full faith and credit, the Bradley Amendment could hurt a good-faith obligor who delays or avoids seeking downward modification by court order, and who instead reaches an informal arrangement with the custodial parent. Parents without legal representation, who may be unaware of the Amendment and without means to move for modification, are particularly likely to opt for informality (often with the recipient's tacit approval or acquiescence). The Amendment means, however, that after a lengthy period of informal adjustment, the full support bill is already past due (in most states, with interest at the statutory rate) when the custodial parent seeks enforcement.

The Bradley Amendment can also work hardship on noncustodial parents who make nonconforming child support payments—sums spent informally on the children for gifts, clothes, and the like—in addition to (or instead of) making support payments in the manner or amount prescribed in the child support order. Informal support does not excuse payments mandated by the order, and does not create entitlement to a credit for these payments.

States have blunted the Bradley Amendment's effect on some good-faith obligors by enacting statutes or guidelines provisions that, as a matter of law, abate the child support obligation during extended periods when the child resides with the obligor. *See, e.g.,* Mo. Rev. Stat. § 453.340.2 (2018). Despite these abatement provisions, what advice would you give an obligor who anticipates making nonconforming payments or agreeing to an extended change of the child's residency?

B. APPLYING THE "CHANGE OF CIRCUMSTANCES" STANDARD

Statutes such as Iowa Code § 598.21C.1 (quoted above) establish multi-factor tests that leave much to judicial discretion. In a decision that affirmed upward modification, *Nelson* delivers firm lessons about heeding the legislative judgments reflected in the child support guidelines.

IN RE MARRIAGE OF NELSON
Supreme Court of Iowa, 1997.
570 N.W.2d 103.

HARRIS, JUSTICE.

Respondent-appellant Scott J. Nelson appeals from a district court ruling modifying and increasing his child support obligations for two children from $425 per month to $695 per month. * * *

Jane and Scott, married in 1984, are parents to two children: Reann, born May 30, 1983, and Jessica, born July 12, 1985. Their marriage was dissolved in September 1989. At that time, Scott was a law student. The parties agreed his completion of law school would be a substantial change in circumstances justifying a review of child support. The original decree ordered Scott to pay $137.50 per month per child in child support. In March 1993, Jane filed a modification action requesting an increase in Scott's child support payments. Jane had remarried. The district court increased

Scott's child support payments for both children to a total of $425 per month.

On August 30, 1995, Jane filed a second modification action seeking an increase in child support payments. At trial, Jane offered evidence Scott's income had increased from $15,000 per year in 1991 to $38,524 in 1994. Jane testified her second husband is a farmer, but that she worked part-time at the Manning hospital earning $5.20 per hour as a cook. She has two children from her second marriage. Scott argued that excluding the bonus he received in 1994 his net annual income increased only $408 from what he earned in 1993. He also argued Jane and her new husband's net worth had increased $70,000 since 1992 while his had stayed the same. The district court found Scott's income had increased and accordingly increased his child support obligations to $695 per month.

* * *

When justice clearly demands it, the guidelines provide for a modicum of flexibility. Special circumstances can call for an adjustment up or down when necessary to do justice between the parties. Any request for variation should however be viewed with great caution. It must be remembered that impetus for the guidelines came from the federal and state legislatures and the amounts were fixed only after exhaustive study of suggestions invited from all known public and private interests. The guidelines must therefore be respected as carefully considered social determinations.

Scott nevertheless contends the special circumstances of this case qualify for a deviation from the guidelines and that the trial court's failure to adjust his obligation downward was error. He claims the modification order, which requires him to pay $695 per month, leaves him seven percent of his net income to cover his own living expenses, therefore impoverishing him and causing an undue financial burden. He argues his law school loan payments—totaling $417 per month—constitute a special circumstance.
* * *

Scott submitted a financial affidavit in November 1995. He listed his net income at $1950 and his total monthly expenses at $2150. Scott's expenses were calculated using the prior child support payments of $425, but did not list the $181 he pays in health insurance to his children. Considering the 1995 modification, Scott's monthly expenses equal $2358 with only $1846 in monthly net income. He does make car payments of $358 a month for a vehicle he needs in his work. He lives modestly and it would be very difficult to decrease his expenses.

There is nothing startling or even unusual about Scott's bleak financial position. It is typical of the financial dilemmas routinely presented in domestic court disputes. With very rare exceptions, involving persons of affluence, child support payments are more than the obligor can readily afford—and much less than reasonably needed for the child or children involved. The guidelines were drafted with full appreciation of this dismal reality and specify the priorities to be considered in fixing support orders. In yielding to the guidelines, we are not insensitive to the difficult financial bind in which Scott is placed. But yield we must.

Retirement of indebtedness is expressly made a lower priority than the needs of children. In common with many persons obliged to pay child support payments, Scott faces most of all a burdensome indebtedness. In Scott's case two obligations—for student loans ($417.34 per month) and car payments ($358.60 per month)—represent $775.94 of the $2150.94 he lists as monthly expenses. It was obviously reasonable—and perhaps to the children's eventual benefit—for Scott to complete his legal education. Jane subscribed to the plan by agreeing to reduced support while he finished his studies, though she did not agree to reduced support during all the years it takes to retire the student loans. For a ten-year period this would amount to more than half of the usual child support period. Notwithstanding Scott's financial bind, the guidelines clearly and expressly render the reduction of debt a priority status inferior to the needs of his children. The guidelines presuppose that debts can be refinanced, but that childhood cannot be postponed.

[The court affirmed the upward modification order.]

NOTES AND QUESTIONS

1.   Nelson: *what does justice demand?* What "considered social determinations" do Iowa's child support guidelines reflect? Do you agree with how the state supreme court applies them?

2.   *The parent's remarriage or obligations to a new relationship.* After entry of a child support order, an obligor may incur support obligations to one or more children of a new marital or nonmarital relationship. Courts disagree about whether, and if so how, a parent's obligations to children of the new relationship may affect the support entitlement of children of the earlier one.

"First in time, first in right" decisions create a preference for the first family's children. In *Mandel v. Mandel*, 906 N.E.2d 1016, 1023 n.11 (Mass. App. Ct. 2009), for example, the court specified that a child support obligor "enters into a second marriage conscious of his obligations to his former wife and children 'so that the second marriage with its attendant obligations affords him no relief.'"

Other decisions, however, hold that the state's child support guidelines permit apportionment of payments among children of multiple relationships. In *T.S.R. v. State ex rel. Dep't of Family Services*, 406 P.3d 729 (Wyo. 2017), for example, the court affirmed a trial court order that granted the father downward modification of his child support obligation to the nonmarital daughter he fathered with his girlfriend in 2004. The basis of the modification motion was that in 2008, the father had a child with another woman whom he married shortly thereafter. *T.S.R.* held that the trial court did not abuse its discretion by finding that the amount of the support order for the first child was subject to deviation downward from the guidelines' presumptive amount as "unjust or inappropriate" because the father now had support obligations to two children rather than one.

Which approach—*Mandel's* or *T.S.R.'s*—better comports with the realities that characterize many contemporary families? Should it matter whether the obligor's new spouse or partner has an income higher (or lower) than the obligor's?

3. *Health or special medical needs.* The obligor parent's health or special medical needs may support downward modification of a child support order. *See, e.g., Shamieka B. v. Lishomwa H.*, 938 N.Y.S.2d 65 (App. Div. 2012) (obligor father's chemotherapy treatments, which resulted in debilitating symptoms, were a substantial change of circumstances that warranted downward modification); *but see Aranova v. Aranov*, 909 N.Y.S.2d 125 (App. Div. 2010) (denying downward modification motion of father who alleged that he was disabled and unable to work from a mental health condition; he was receiving Social Security disability benefits, was working for a period during his alleged disability, and failed to set aside money from a legal settlement to support his children).

The child's health or other special medical needs may support upward modification of the support award. In *Miller v. Jacobsen*, 714 N.W.2d 69 (S.D. 2006), for example, the court increased the father's support obligation for his 15-year-old son, who was born with cerebral palsy and a seizure disorder and needed a specially equipped van and professional caregivers as he grew older.

4. *The parent's lost or changed employment.* In an era marked by corporate and business layoffs and employment insecurity, child support obligors may lose employment for reasons beyond their control. The court may grant downward modification of support obligations, at least temporarily, while the obligor seeks reemployment. *See, e.g., Garza v. Garza*, 846 N.W.2d 626 (Neb. 2014) (father, laid off without fault, was attempting unsuccessfully to find new employment, and had lost eligibility for state and federal unemployment compensation).

The court may also grant downward modification where it finds that the parent changed employment and accepted lower compensation in a good-faith effort for self-improvement. *See, e.g., Lucante v. Lucante*, 2010 WL 4570211 (N.J. Super. Ct. App. Div. Aug. 26, 2010) (noncustodial father accepted a promotion at a lower initial salary, but with opportunities for advancement and higher future salary that would benefit the children).

The court may deny downward modification, however, where the obligor parent's criminal behavior or other wrongdoing leads to unemployment. In *Hays v. Hays*, 2016 WL 304538 * 3 (Neb. Ct. App. Jan. 26, 2016), for example, the court denied the mother's downward modification motion because she lost her nursing position and nursing license for drug use, which she knew was unlawful and contrary to her employer's policies.

5. *Other recurring grounds for modification.* Various other changed circumstances frequently underlie motions for modification of child support orders. Resolution depends on the court's fact-specific inquiry based on the guidelines' definition of "income" and application of the standard for modification.

a. *Lottery winnings.* In *In re Marriage of Bohn*, 8 P.3d 539 (Colo. Ct. App. 2000), the 1996 divorce decree ordered the father to pay $352 per month in child support, based on his $2,472 monthly gross income. In 1998, the father won $1.2 million gross in the state lottery. After taxes were withheld, he received a one-time lump sum payment of $816,000. The trial court held that the entire $1.2 million was gross income for the 1998 calendar year, and thus that the father's monthly gross income for that year was $104,743.17. The court ordered him to pay child support of $4,208 per month for that year. Because the child support statute specified application of gross monthly income, *Bohn* rejected the father's contention that his modified child support amount for 1998 should be based on his net lottery winnings because he would never have access to the portion withheld for taxes.

b. *Personal injury and other tort recoveries.* In *In re Jerome*, 843 A.2d 325 (N.H. 2004), the court held that the noncustodial mother's $560,000 annuity, received to settle a personal injury claim, constituted "income" under New Hampshire's child support guidelines, which define "income" to include "all income from any source" and specifically include "annuities." The court rejected the mother's contention that the annuity was designed to make her whole and not to compensate for lost income. The state supreme court affirmed upward modification of her child support obligation.

In *In re Marriage of Fortner*, 52 N.E.3d 682 (Ill. App. Ct. 2016), the court held that proceeds the obligor received from a wrongful death settlement did not constitute "income" to him, but increased his financial resources and thus warranted modifying upward the child support amount he would pay that year.

c. *In-kind compensation.* In *Morrow v. Becker*, 3 N.E.3d 144 (Ohio 2013), the court held that the husband's income included the annual values of a company car, car insurance, and cellular telephone provided by his employer. "If his employer did not provide a car, Morrow would have had to purchase or lease one on his own, using his own funds." *Id.* at 147.

d. *Inheritances.* Where a parent inherits property after entry of a support order, the inheritance may be a basis for upward modification of the initial child support award. Even where the guidelines definition of "income" does not list "inheritances," the definition usually recites "gifts." Courts "discern no appreciable difference between one who receives property by an *inter vivos* gift and one who receives the same or similar property by testamentary transfer." *Gardner v. Yrttima*, 743 N.E.2d 353, 358 (Ind. Ct. App. 2001).

e.   Inter vivos *gifts*. In *In re Fulton*, 910 A.2d 1180 (N.H. 2006), the ex-husband sought downward modification of his child support obligation because his unemployed ex-wife's family was regularly providing her money, which he and the court characterized as gifts. The child support guidelines' definition of "income," however, did not specifically include "gifts." *Fulton* denied modification on the ground that gifts did not constitute income within that definition. Some courts hold, however, that even where a gift to a payor does not constitute income, the gift might nonetheless provide a ground for upward deviation from the presumed guideline amount. *E.g., Suzanne D. v. Stephen W.*, 65 A.3d 965, 970, 973 (Pa. Super. Ct. 2013) (ordering upward deviation of biological father's obligation because regular, substantial monetary gifts from his father would likely continue, and because the biological father's income was significantly greater than the mother's).

f.   *Commissions, overtime pay, and other remuneration from employment.* In *Markey v. Carney*, 705 N.W.2d 13, 19–20 (Iowa 2005), the court held that a child support obligor's commissions and overtime pay constitute income, unless the amounts are uncertain or speculative. Bonuses and lump-sum severance payments received from an employer may similarly constitute income. *See, e.g., Ornelas v. Ornelas*, 978 N.E.2d 946, 954 (Ohio Ct. App. 2012) (bonuses); *Walker v. Walker*, 868 A.2d 887, 889 (Me. 2005) (lump sum severance pay).

6.   *Avoiding rancor.* By including cost of living adjustments (COLAs) in the initial order, parties may avoid future modification motions based on inflationary erosion of the value of periodic child support over time. Courts are receptive to applying COLA provisions as written, but may retain authority to approve any adjustments to ensure consistency with statutory and guidelines criteria. *See, e.g., King v. Gerstenschlager*, 2012 WL 3491479 (N.J. Super. Ct. App. Div. Aug. 16, 2012).

States have also enacted "rules of thumb" that establish entitlement to modification when the existing child support amount varies by more than a specified percentage or dollar amount above or below the amount that would be due currently under the guidelines. *See, e.g.,* Iowa Code § 598.21C(2)(a) (2018) (10% or more).

Parents, who may agree on initial support amounts, may also agree later on modification. The restrictions on the parents' power to agree initially also apply to modification agreements. Parents may agree to modification to a greater amount than the child support guidelines establish, but ordinarily may not agree to modification to a lesser amount. *See, e.g., In re Marriage of Swart*, 2017 WL 1053873 * 5 (Minn. Ct. App. Mar. 20, 2017).

PROBLEM 11-6

As a state legislator, would you vote to enact Section 3.19(1) of the ALI Principles of the Law of Family Dissolution, which provides:

A child-support award should be subject to review at least once every three years in order to reassess the child-support award in light of the parents' current economic circumstances. The review should include reapplication of the child-support formula * * *. The periodic review * * * should be automatic, without a petition by either parent. The review should be performed by an agency designated by the court or legislature.

ALI, Principles of the Law of Family Dissolution: Analysis and Recommendations § 3.19(1) (2002).

C. IMPUTING INCOME ON MODIFICATION

As discussed above, a court deciding whether to impute income in an initial order or on a modification motion must consider whether the obligor acted in good faith, or whether the obligor's diminished income resulted from voluntary efforts to "shirk" obligations to the child, or from other wrongdoing. The court may find shirking where the unemployed or underemployed parent voluntarily fails to earn to his or her full capacity to avoid paying child support, or where the parent unreasonably makes a voluntary decision that results in significantly lower income. *See, e.g., Edwin K. v. Bonnie W.*, 805 S.E.2d 416, 421 (W. Va. 2017) (on motion for upward modification, court imputed income to the obligor father who left "gainful and lucrative employment with health benefits in the local job market to pursue self-employment in a field [plumbing] in which he had been previously unsuccessful, and which was not providing ample income to support the business itself, much less its owner and his child").

As you read *Pollard*, consider whether the mother shirked her responsibilities to the two children of her first marriage.

IN RE MARRIAGE OF POLLARD
Court of Appeals of Washington, 2000.
991 P.2d 1201.

SCHULTHEIS, J.

A parent may not avoid a child support obligation by voluntarily remaining unemployed or underemployed. Joan Pollard Brookins's petition for modification of a child support order was granted, decreasing the amount she paid to her ex-husband, Martin Pollard, for support of the couple's two children. Mr. Pollard appeals, contending the trial court erred in failing to impute income to Ms. Brookins, who quit working full time to care for the two children of her new marriage. We reverse and remand for recalculation of child support.

The Pollards were divorced in Washington in October 1989. The support order entered at that time provided that Ms. Pollard would pay

Mr. Pollard, as custodial parent, $217 per month for the couple's two children, born in 1983 and 1984.

In January 1997, Ms. Pollard, now Ms. Brookins, petitioned in Lincoln County for modification of the child support order, claiming change in income. Both Mr. Pollard and Ms. Brookins had been in active military service while married. After remarriage and the birth of two additional children, Ms. Brookins had left military service and now worked part time for the military while working full time as a mother and homemaker. She lived in Norfolk, Virginia. Mr. Pollard had also remarried and moved from the state, and was now living in Astoria, Oregon. He, too, had left the military and was attempting to find full-time work in the private sector.

Affidavits from the parties indicate that during 1997 Mr. Pollard earned approximately $31,000 as an electrician. During the last year of her full-time military employment, Ms. Brookins earned approximately $22,150. By January 1998, Ms. Brookins was a full-time mother and homemaker, making approximately $323 per month in her part-time work for the military. She requested reduction of her support obligation to $58 per month ($29 per child), effective from the date she filed the petition in January 1997.

In April 1998, the trial court modified the support order, reducing Ms. Brookins's obligation to $85 per month ($42.50 per child), with a starting date of February 1, 1997. * * * In the findings and conclusions entered on the modification, the court indicated the original order had been modified because Ms. Brookins's income had been substantially reduced. The court concluded that "[t]he mother is not voluntarily underemployed with an intent to avoid child support but is working as a mother in the home full time raising children." * * *

Modification of Child Support

Mr. Pollard argues on appeal that the trial court erred in failing to impute income to Ms. Brookins, a career woman who voluntarily quit working full time to work part time and care for the two children of her new marriage.

* * * In setting child support, the trial court must take into consideration all factors bearing upon the needs of the children and the parents' ability to pay. Overall, the child support order should meet each child's basic needs and should provide any "additional child support commensurate with the parents' income, resources, and standard of living." To facilitate these goals, the Legislature directs that the child support obligation should be "equitably apportioned between the parents."

In proceedings to modify child support, the trial court applies the uniform child support schedule, basing the support obligation on the combined monthly incomes of both parents. Voluntary unemployment or underemployment will not allow a parent to avoid his or her financial obligation to the children who are the subjects of the support order. When assessing the income and resources of each household, the court must impute income to a parent when that parent is voluntarily unemployed or voluntarily underemployed. The court determines whether to impute income by evaluating the parent's work history, education, health, age and any other relevant factor. If the court decides the parent is "gainfully employed on a full-time basis," but also underemployed, the court makes a further determination whether the parent is purposely underemployed to reduce his or her support obligation.

In this case, the trial court found that Ms. Brookins was "working as a mother in the home full time raising children" and refused to impute income because it found that she was "not voluntarily underemployed with an intent to avoid child support[.]" This finding is open to two interpretations. One, the court may have meant that Ms. Brookins was a full-time worker, voluntarily underemployed, but not with an intent to avoid child support. Pursuant to RCW 26.19.071(6), however, an underemployed parent may not escape imputation of income unless he or she is *gainfully* employed on a full-time basis and is not underemployed to reduce the support obligation. Because Ms. Brookins's full-time work as a mother and homemaker is not "gainful," she does not come within this provision of RCW 26.19.71(6).

Two, the court may have meant that Ms. Brookins was *not* voluntarily underemployed. The facts do not support this interpretation. Clearly Ms. Brookins's choice to leave the military and her former salary of over $22,000 per year (based on a 1995 W-2 form) was voluntary, motivated by her desire to raise the two young children of her new family. * * * While laudable, these actions cannot adversely affect her obligation to the two older children she had with Mr. Pollard. * * * "[B]y choosing not to allow a parent to escape child support obligations because of the existence of a new family we are recognizing the needs of children to the love, support, and sacrifice of both parents." If the shoe were on the other foot, and a noncustodial father sought to reduce his child support obligation because he chose to stay home with his children from a new marriage, most courts would impute income to such a voluntarily unemployed or underemployed parent. * * * The mother should be held to a like standard. * * *.

Under either interpretation of the findings, the trial court abused its discretion in finding that Ms. Brookins was not voluntarily underemployed and in failing to impute income to her. Accordingly, we reverse the order of child support modification for abuse of discretion. Remand is necessary to recalculate child support.

NOTES AND QUESTIONS

1. *Questions about* Pollard. (a) In common parlance, are homemaking and child care "gainful" activities akin to employment for wages or salary? (b) When a court decides whether to impute income, should it consider homemaking and child care to be gainful employment? (c) Does the approach taken in this case unfairly lock a divorced parent into pre-divorce roles? Compare the commentary in Chapter 12 about using the primary caregiver or approximation rule to allocate parenting time.

2. *Some recurring examples.* On motions to modify child support orders, courts have considered imputing income to obligors in a variety of circumstances. In each case below, consider why the court did, or did not, impute income:

a. *Further education.* In *Kelly v. Hougham*, 504 N.W.2d 440 (Wis. Ct. App. 1993), the court declined to impute income to an ex-husband who left a well-paying job to return to school. The court found that the husband acted reasonably because he delayed returning to school until his former wife finished law school and secured a well-paying job, continued to work part-time at a reasonable wage while attending school, and expected that further schooling would substantially increase his income and thus benefit the children before too long.

In *Marriage of Braatz*, 2010 WL 772882 (Minn. Ct. App. Mar. 9, 2010), however, the court imputed income to the father, who voluntarily retired from the Air Force a few months after his divorce and began working toward a bachelor's degree in operations management by taking online courses. He remained unemployed while taking the courses and made no inquiries about potential job prospects, and the court found that he could have pursued the degree while remaining in the military, without losing income.

b. *Relocation.* In *Abouhalkah v. Sharps*, 795 N.E.2d 488 (Ind. Ct. App. 2003), the court declined to impute income to a father whose earnings fell after he left his previous employer, which was moving the father's department from Indiana to Minnesota. The court found that the father in Indiana left the employer not to avoid paying child support, but to avoid relocating out-of-state a few hundred miles away from his children.

In *In re Marriage of McKenzie*, 709 N.W.2d 528 (Iowa 2006), however, the ex-husband's annual income fell from $45,260 (with a company that had employed him for 22 years) to $21,199 when he relocated from Iowa to South Carolina to be with his girlfriend. The trial court imputed income to him at the higher figure because his obligation to his child outweighed his "desire for self-fulfillment." *Id.* at 534.

c. *Early retirement.* In *Smedley v. Lowman*, 2 A.3d 1226 (Pa. Super. Ct. 2010), the court imputed income to a father who, after more than 30 years of service, retired in good health at age 52 from a city police department that had not been pressuring him to retire. His fully vested annual pension of $25,000 represented only about half of his former salary, but he expressed no interest in seeking part-time employment to supplement the pension.

In *Denomme v. Denomme,* 2014 WL 1345089 (Conn. Super. Ct. Mar. 12, 2014), however, the court modified downward the child support obligation of the husband who voluntarily retired from the Navy after serving more than 22 years. He testified that he retired because of the combat wounds he witnessed in the Afghanistan war, the mental strain of numerous deployments, and the risk that further deployments could lead to a mental breakdown.

d.   *The new spouse's income.* In *Miller v. Clough,* 165 P.3d 594, 599–601 (Alaska 2007), the issue was whether the income of the ex-wife's wealthy new husband should be considered in calculating her child support obligation. Because the imputation statute directed the court to consider only the obligor's "work history, qualifications, and job opportunities," the court held that imputed income could not be based on a later spouse's financial circumstances.

As the trial court considered the relative financial circumstances of the divorced parties in *In re Marriage of Nelson* above, should the court have considered the income of the custodial ex-wife's new husband, the children's stepfather with whom they were living?

e.   *Parental fault.* In *Rutland v. Rutland,* 121 So.3d 776, 777 (La. Ct. App. 2013), the court imputed income to the noncustodial father who had been fired from two positions, including one with the parish sheriff's office for sleeping on the job.

PROBLEM 11-7

John and Mary Jones married in 2004 and divorced in 2016, when their two children were eleven and eight years old. At the time of the divorce, John was a staff psychologist at a local community hospital. Two years later, he sought new employment after the hospital notified him that the terms of his employment and salary would change dramatically. He became a psychologist in a nearby public school system at a salary of $44,000, about $20,000 less than his former hospital salary. John receives his salary from the school district in twelve monthly installments, but he has a nine-month contract, with duties during the district's three-month summer recess. John pays about $1000 per month in child support for the two children.

You are the trial judge hearing John's motion to reduce his child support obligation on the ground that he has had a substantial and involuntary decrease in his salary. Mary moves to increase John's support obligation by imputing income to him for the summer recess. How would you rule on Mary's motion? Would your answer be different if John has primary physical custody of the children for much of the summer? What if John had no school district duties, and no primary custody of his children, during the summer recess?

PROBLEM 11-8

When David and Cindy Smith were divorced, Cindy received physical custody of the couple's only child. The court ordered David, a machinist and shop steward earning $19.50 an hour at a local tractor assembly plant, to pay $120 per week in child support. Earlier this week, David moved for downward modification of the child support amount on the ground that he is no longer able to pursue his regular occupation because his union went out on strike against the employer three days earlier. David has belonged to the union for 20 years, and he supports the strike. In his motion papers, David asserted that the strike's purpose is "to protect our jobs, our families' future." He denied taking part in the strike to avoid paying child support to his former wife.

If you were David's lawyer, what arguments would you make to support the motion? If you were Cindy's lawyer, what arguments would you make in opposition? If you were the judge hearing the modification motion, what factors would you consider in deciding whether to grant the motion? If you were inclined to grant the motion, would you grant permanent downward modification?

6. CHILD SUPPORT ENFORCEMENT

"The life of the law is in its enforcement." Roscoe Pound, *Mechanical Jurisprudence*, 8 Colum. L. Rev. 605, 619 (1908). In the child support context, Dean Pound's dictum counsels that the efficacy of state child support guidelines depends on public and private enforcement because words and schedules alone protect no one, and the guidelines do not apply themselves.

Before the 1980's, the lack of effective state child support enforcement mechanisms produced what two scholars have called "in practice * * * a voluntary system." Ira Mark Ellman & Sanford L. Braver, *Child Support and the Custodial Mother's Move or Remarriage* 2 (July 22, 2014) (presented at the 2014 Conf. on Empirical Legal Studies held at Berkeley).

The enforcement picture has improved, but much remains to be accomplished. On the one hand, "[a]bout 7 in 10 custodial parents (69.3 percent) who were supposed to receive child support in 2015 received some payments." On the other, "less than half (43.5 percent) of custodial parents who were supposed to receive child support received full child support payments." U.S. Census Bur., Timothy Grall, *Current Population Reps., Custodial Mothers and Fathers and Their Child Support: 2015*, at 1 (2018).

A. CIVIL ENFORCEMENT

Most child support orders today may be established or modified by an administrative agency or by a court. This development arises from increased federal involvement in child support enforcement, the history of which the following article traces.

MONICA HOF WALLACE,
CHILD SUPPORT SAVINGS ACCOUNTS: AN INNOVATIVE
APPROACH TO CHILD SUPPORT ENFORCEMENT
85 N.C. L. Rev. 1155, 1158–64 (2007).

Historically, only state governments were tasked with enforcement of child support orders. The federal government became involved in child support enforcement in the latter half of the twentieth century. At that point, the social landscape of the country had begun to change, and steadily rising divorce rates, coupled with an escalating number of children born to single mothers, placed a new strain on the funds of the Nation's public assistance program.

In these early stages of federal involvement, the government focused on collecting support owed to a single group of the Nation's children—those living in families receiving assistance under national welfare programs. A large motivating force behind the federal government's entrance into the field was purely economic—an attempt to cut federal welfare spending by transferring the financial burden of supporting welfare children back to the children's delinquent parents.

In the mid-1970s, the focus of the federal government's involvement in child support enforcement shifted to include the needs of children and families not receiving public assistance. This new wave of federal involvement began with the Social Services Amendments of 1974, which created Title IV-D of the Social Security Act. Title IV-D gave rise to a new federal initiative, the Child Support Enforcement and Paternity Establishment Program. This novel program evidenced a congressional push to prevent families not receiving government benefits from entering the welfare system by helping them obtain child support and establish paternity for children born outside of marriage.

Title IV-D also created an Assistant Secretary of Child Support, who reports to the Secretary of the Department of Health and Human Services, and directed the Assistant Secretary to administer, oversee, and assist in the implementation of the states' child support enforcement programs. The Social Services Amendments of 1974 placed responsibility for the enforcement of all child support obligations (to welfare and nonwelfare children) at both the federal and state levels. Primarily, the federal role was to oversee and evaluate state and local agencies implementing the federal laws.

The federal government continued its involvement in the arena of child support enforcement law with the passage of additional legislation in the years following the Social Services Amendments of 1974. In 1981, Title IV-D was amended by the Omnibus Budget Reconciliation Act, which authorized both state and federal government to withhold portions of funds due to delinquent obligors and reroute those funds to the child. For instance, it authorized the Internal Revenue Service to withhold portions of the federal income tax refunds of noncustodial parents who owed child support. It also required that states withhold portions of unemployment benefit payments to parents owing support in order to fulfill their delinquent obligation.

Next, Congress passed the Child Support Enforcement Amendments of 1984. These amendments equalized many services between welfare and nonassisted families and improved interstate enforcement of child support orders. Most importantly, the 1984 amendments required each state to use improved enforcement techniques, such as (1) mandatory income withholding; (2) expedited processes for establishing and enforcing support orders; (3) state income tax refund interceptions; (4) liens against real and personal property, and security or bonds to assure compliance with support obligations; and (5) reports of support delinquency information to consumer reporting agencies.

These amendments produced a nationwide mandate to make existing enforcement techniques more effective by supplementing ordinary wage withholding procedures with new initiatives such as allowing states to withhold portions of their state income tax refunds. Most importantly, these amendments allowed states to use child support enforcement techniques that proved to be more effective against delinquent parents without traditional wage-earning jobs. By moving away from simple income withholding, these newer enforcement techniques, such as the ability to report nonpaying parents to credit bureaus, coupled with the strengthening of traditional mechanisms like real and personal property liens, made nonpaying parents feel the effects of their irresponsibility in more aspects of their everyday lives.

The Family Support Act ("FSA") of 1988 was yet another federal initiative in the area of child support enforcement. The FSA focused on immediate wage withholding and locating absent parents. The FSA also required that each state have an operational automated national child support enforcement system.

The most recent major federal child support enforcement initiative was contained in the Personal Responsibility and Work Opportunity Reconciliation Act of 1996 ("PRWORA"). PRWORA required states' child support enforcement systems to comply with both new and existing federal standards before that state became eligible to receive federal dollars for Temporary Assistance to Needy Families ("TANF"). The legislation also required states to institute tougher enforcement techniques, such as additional income withholding, seizure of assets, and withholding and suspension of licenses. PRWORA also established a National Directory of New Hires aimed at cracking down on delinquent parents across state lines.

PRWORA augmented many of the federal enforcement initiatives that had come about in previous legislative actions and mandated that all states implement new enforcement tactics. One of the nontraditional enforcement techniques that the Act required state systems to support was the revocation or denial of a nonpaying parent's licenses. Another nontraditional enforcement technique highlighted by PRWORA is the denial or revocation of a passport to a parent owing more than $5,000 of child support. These two strategies took aim not at delinquent parents' wallets but at their personal preferences, individual mobility, and daily life activities.

In 1998, Congress passed * * * [t]he Child Support Performance and Incentive Act [which] provides new incentive payments to states that comply with federal guidelines and alternative penalty reductions to states whose compliance plans would otherwise be disapproved, but are making a good faith effort to correct their deficiencies.

* * *

Today, there is increasing legislative resolve at both federal and state levels to improve the collection of child support payments. The Office of Child Support Enforcement ("OCSE") has implemented innovative guidelines for states to follow in their child support collection efforts. And, although each state administers its own child support enforcement program, the federal government plays a major role in each program's oversight, implementation, and monitoring.

The Child Support Enforcement Program "has changed from one that recoups welfare costs to one which serves a mostly non-welfare clientele." Federal involvement in child support enforcement has come a long way from its initial economically motivated entrance into this area of law. In approximately fifty years, federal legislation has become the overarching force behind states' child support enforcement efforts, regardless of the family's financial situation. * * *

NOTES AND QUESTIONS

1. *The Child Support Enforcement program (CSE).* As part of the CSE program that Congress created in the Social Services Amendments of 1974, each participating state maintains an agency (the so-called "IV-D agency") that enforces and administers child support in the state, including collection efforts where the obligor or obligee, or both, live in the state. Among other things, the IV-D agency helps custodial parents locate noncustodial parents; establish paternity where necessary; and establish, enforce, and modify child support obligations.

As Professor Wallace's excerpt details, Congress has expanded the IV-D program over time. When Congress mandated the IV-D agencies in 1974 in an effort to ease strains on public assistance budgets, the lawmakers specified that the agencies would serve only parents on public assistance, who were required to cooperate with the agencies' collection efforts as a condition of receiving that assistance unless good cause for non-cooperation were shown. In 1984, Congress extended IV-D agency services to other custodial parents, who would pay a nominal fee.

Today the CSE program "is estimated to handle at least 50% of all child support cases; the remaining cases are handled by private attorneys, collection agencies, or through mutual agreements between the parents." Carmen Solomon-Fears, *Child Support: An Overview of Census Bureau Data on Recipients* 1 (Cong. Res. Serv. 2016). In 2013, the CSE program collected $28.0 billion in child support payments and served 15.6 million cases. *Id.*

2. *Demographics.* The 2010 Census showed these characteristics of custodial families who use the IV-D program's services. (Custodial families are ones in which one or more children live with a parent and the other parent lives outside the household.):

- Over 60 percent of custodial families participate in the IV-D program;

- Approximately half of the families in the IV-D program had incomes below 150 percent of the poverty threshold;

- Nearly 90 percent of custodial parents in the IV-D program are female, their average age is 36 years old, and over half have just one child in the IV-D program;

- Almost half of the custodial parents in the IV-D program are non-Hispanic white, another 27 percent are non-Hispanic black, and 20 percent are Hispanic;

- Thirteen percent of custodial parents in the IV-D program lived in a different state than the noncustodial parent and another 2 percent lived in a different country;

- According to custodial parents, 64 percent of noncustodial parents in the IV-D program spent time with their youngest nonresident child in the past year; and

- Custodial parents who are poor, never married, under the age of 30, and have limited education are much more likely to receive IV-D services than other custodial parents.

Kye Lippold & Elaine Sorensen, *Characteristics of Families Served by the Child Support (IV-D) Program; 2010 Census Survey Results* 4 (Urban Inst. 2013).

3. *Custodial mothers' decisions not to seek child support awards.* The CSE program's availability to all custodial parents is grounded in the policy premise that regardless of the family's economic circumstances, payment of child support normally has positive impact on children and their families. *See, e.g.,* U.S. Dep't of Health & Human Servs., Office of Child Support

Enforcement, *The Child Support Program is a Good Investment* 9 (Dec. 2016) ("A large body of research shows that child support has positive benefits on the cognitive and educational outcomes of children.* * * Research also shows that receiving child support reduces the risk of child maltreatment.").

Some custodial mothers, however, choose not to seek child support payments. Federal law requires custodial mothers receiving public assistance to cooperate in good faith with the state in paternity determination and collection efforts unless "good cause" for noncooperation is established. PRWORA leaves it to individual states to define good cause, but most states have embraced the prior federal agency definition, which stated that good cause existed when the parents' relationship was marked by domestic violence, or when the child was conceived by rape or incest.

Forgoing child support is an option for custodial mothers who are not on public assistance. Aside from a history of domestic violence in the relationship or household, why might a custodial mother choose not to seek child support payments from the child's father?

4. *Civil contempt.* Where an obligor parent can pay court-ordered support but refuses to do so, the court may hold the parent in civil contempt and jail him until he complies. *See, e.g., McCullough v. McCullough*, 910 N.W.2d 515 (Neb. 2018) (upholding civil contempt finding). The state may presume that the obligor can pay court-ordered child support, placing the burden on him to rebut the presumption. The obligor must be released if he satisfies the burden. *See, e.g., Ceballos v. Castillo*, 926 N.Y.S.2d 142 (App. Div. 2011).

"Civil contempt proceedings in child support cases constitute one part of a highly complex system designed to assure a noncustodial parent's regular payment of funds typically necessary for the support of his children." *Turner v. Rogers*, 564 U.S. 431, 443 (2011). The federal government has cautioned that "routine use of contempt for non-payment of child support is likely to be an ineffective strategy," but that "coercive enforcement remedies, such as contempt, have a role to play." *Id.* at 444.

Turner held that the South Carolina trial court had violated the civil contemnor's due process liberty interest by ordering him incarcerated without sufficiently determining his ability to pay court-ordered child support. A comprehensive 2013 study, however, found that that South Carolina's courts were still not adequately assessing low-income obligors' financial circumstances in civil contempt proceedings arising from inability to pay. "Close to 70% of indigent (or unemployed) obligors were held in contempt and received jail sentences in both 2010 and 2013." Elizabeth G. Patterson, *Turner in the Trenches: A Study of How Turner v. Rogers Affected Child Support Contempt Proceedings*, 25 Geo. J. on Poverty L. and Policy 75, 111–12 (2017).

5. *Privatizing child support collection.* PRWORA authorizes states to privatize child support collection "through contracts with charitable, religious, or private organizations." 42 U.S.C. § 604(a) (2018). Several states have

privatized some or all child support collection efforts, statewide or locally, by contracting with private firms to supplement or replace services otherwise provided by public IV-D agencies. Depending on the jurisdiction, the private firms may collect past-due support, and may also perform other functions such as processing payments, establishing paternity and support orders, and locating parents.

When state efforts to locate obligors and collect child support have failed, some custodial parents have engaged private, for-profit collection agencies, which the media sometimes call "bounty hunters." These private collection agencies sometimes charge parents as much as one-third of any amounts recovered.

6. *Child support and bankruptcy.* The Bankruptcy Abuse and Prevention and Consumer Protection Act of 2005, Pub. L. No. 109–8, 119 Stat. 23 (2005), included provisions designed to help insure that obligors filing for bankruptcy continue paying child support, and that child support obligations receive high priority in bankruptcy:

> One of these provisions clarifies that proceedings to establish or modify a domestic support obligation (e.g., child support) owed to a governmental unit (e.g., state CSE agencies) are exempt from the automatic stay. An automatic stay bars creditors from taking measures to collect a debt pending resolution of the bankruptcy proceeding. Another provision allows for the continued operation of wage withholding for domestic support obligations (e.g., child support). Further, the Bankruptcy Reform Act, for example, requires that noncustodial parents filing for Chapter 13 bankruptcy [under which filers submit a repayment plan to the court agreeing to pay part or all of their debts over time, usually three to five years] must be current on their child support obligations to confirm a repayment plan. In addition, the Bankruptcy Reform Act provides child support with the first priority for payment of unsecured claims, up from a seventh-level priority under previous Bankruptcy Code provisions.

U.S. Gov't Accountability Office, *Bankruptcy and Child Support Enforcement: Improved Information Sharing Possible without Routine Data Matching* 10–11 (2008).

B. CRIMINAL ENFORCEMENT

Most child support enforcement is done through the civil process, but state and federal criminal law also plays a role. Most criminal child support enforcement arises under state laws that authorize imprisonment for willful nonpayment of amounts that the obligor can pay based on actual or imputed income.

"In some states, a judge will base child support orders on the amount he or she *believes* a father can pay, not on his actual income." Eleanor Pratt, *Child Support Enforcement Can Hurt Black, Low-Income, Noncustodial*

Fathers and Their Kids 2 (Urban Inst. 2016) (emphasis in original). A later conviction for non-payment, sometimes based on expectations that were unrealistic at the outset, can worsen matters for incarcerated parents and their families. "As the poor fathers face insurmountable child-support policies and Dickensian child-support tribunals, the criminal justice system further beats them down and attacks them from multiple directions. The inability of impoverished fathers to pay unrealistic child-support obligations is increasingly criminalized; many fathers are jailed because they are poor and have failed to pay. * * * Once incarcerated, the fathers may lose their jobs." Daniel L. Hatcher, *Forgotten Fathers,* 93 B.U. L. Rev. 897, 911–12 (2013); Frances Robles & Shaila Dewan, *Skip Child Support. Go to Jail. Repeat,* N.Y. Times, Apr. 19, 2015.

Incarceration for willful failure to pay court ordered child support does not offend state constitutional provisions prohibiting imprisonment for debt because child support is not a debt, but rather an obligation that parents owe to their children and society. *See, e.g., In re Braden,* 483 S.W.3d 659, 664 (Tex. Ct. App. 2015).

The Child Support Recovery Act of 1992 (CSRA), 18 U.S.C. § 228 (2018), makes it a federal crime (1) to willfully fail to pay support to a child who resides in another state, where the obligation has remained unpaid for more than a year or exceeds $5,000, or (2) to travel in interstate or foreign commerce with intent to evade a support obligation. The statute provides greater punishment for second or later offenses, or where the obligation has remained unpaid for longer than two years or exceeds $10,000. The Deadbeat Parents Punishment Act of 1998 amended the CSRA to increase the punishments and create a rebuttable presumption that the parent in arrears had the ability to pay the obligations due. The presumption shifts to that parent the burden of proving inability to pay. *Id.*

The CSRA's terms covered an estimated four million noncustodial parents who were behind in support payments to their children who lived in other states. For sheer numbers, however, this volume of prosecutions has not happened. U.S. Attorneys prosecute fewer than 60,000 persons a year for all federal crimes, and the Federal Bureau of Investigation (which has primary investigatory jurisdiction over the CSRA) handles only about 10,000 cases of all types annually. The Justice Department has confined CSRA prosecutions to a modest number of cases that charge obligors who owe substantial amounts, including cases with international jurisdictional overtones. *See* U.S. Dep't of Justice, *Prosecutive Guidelines and Procedures for the Child Support Recovery Act of 1992* (updated Mar. 8, 2017).

PROBLEM 11-9

You are the newly elected county prosecutor, and you have been invited to appear at a public forum on child support enforcement. The other panelists will include child advocates, representatives from fathers' rights groups, social workers, and academics. You have been asked to speak about the factors a prosecutor should consider in deciding whether to indict a parent for willful nonsupport, or whether to leave support enforcement to civil authorities. You understand that the decision whether to indict, convict, and imprison a parent in arrears presents complex issues for prosecutors and courts. What will you say at the forum?

C. CHALLENGES TO CIVIL AND CRIMINAL ENFORCEMENT

As laws with such names as the Deadbeat Parents Punishment Act (mentioned above) indicate, "[t]he universal perception that all parents who fail to pay support are 'deadbeat dads' remains a powerful cultural narrative and tough enforcement against parents that fail to pay is resonant with the body politic." Ann Cammett, *Deadbeats, Deadbrokes, and Prisoners*, 18 Geo. J. on Poverty L. & Pol'y 127, 130 (2011). Professor Cammett observes: "This narrative driving child support enforcement has become progressively more punitive without allowing for meaningful political and policy discourse that distinguishes deadbeats from 'deadbrokes'—those who simply don't have the ability to pay." *Id.*

"[T]he vast majority of unpaid child support is owed by the very poor." Frances Robles & Shaila Dewan, *supra*. Indeed, "[i]n 2015, it is estimated that 254,000 noncustodial parents fell into poverty as a result of paying child support, making it harder for them to meet their own basic human needs." U.S. Dep't of Health & Human Servs., Office of Child Support Enforcement, *The Child Support Program is a Good Investment* 11 (Dec. 2016).

"While child support enforcement efforts have increased collections for many mothers, largely from fathers who have stable jobs and can afford to pay, they have not worked well for poor fathers and mothers. Poor fathers often face child support orders that are set at levels they cannot pay; their orders are rarely modified during periods of unemployment, and they can accrue unrealistic levels of debt. This may motivate fathers to lose contact with their families and evade the child support system." Carmen Solomon-Fears, *Child Support: An Overview of Census Bureau Data on Recipients* 3 (Cong. Res. Serv. 2013).

"Studies have estimated that low-income, noncustodial fathers are disproportionately black, and * * * that black men are more likely to be poor, face labor market discrimination, and have limited social networks to help them stay employed and able to pay their child support orders." Eleanor Pratt, *Child Support Enforcement Can Hurt Black, Low-Income, Noncustodial Fathers and Their Kids* 2 (Urban Inst. 2016). It is "relatively common" for many of these cash-strapped fathers to provide "in-kind support—meaning non-cash goods purchased by the father (e.g., diapers, clothing, food, and gifts) or services (e.g., as child care) that the father pays for directly." Jennifer B. Kane et al., *How Much In-Kind Support Do Low-Income Nonresident Fathers Provide? A Mixed-Method Analysis*, 77 J. Marriage & Fam. 591, 591 (2015).

With so much unpaid child support owed by absent fathers who are mired in poverty, commentators and national leaders have focused attention on "Responsible Fatherhood." The focus grew out of child support enforcement efforts and recognition that some fathers were "deadbroke," rather than "deadbeat." The concept also rests on a premise that fathers can make important non-economic contributions to their children's upbringing. As Professor Linda C. McClain explains, the concept dominated congressional debates about reauthorizing the TANF program, a part of PRWORA (discussed in Professor Wallace's excerpt above):

> During the TANF reauthorization debates, lawmakers focused intensely on promoting "healthy marriage" and "responsible fatherhood." Lawmakers argued that welfare reform had been a success in moving mothers "from welfare to work," but less successful in achieving its family-formation goals, such as reinforcing the concept that marriage is the proper setting in which to have children and that the two-parent, mother-father marital family is both the best guarantor of child wellbeing and a potent anti-poverty device. Lawmakers pondered: How could public policy make men more "marriageable"? Might relationship and marriage education help? Training in parenthood skills? Household financial management? * * * [W]hat about investment in men's human capital, such as through education and job training? All of these solutions were features in the various "responsible fatherhood" initiatives proposed over the years and in the ultimate legislation, the Deficit Reduction Act of 2005 (DRA), which authorized grants to governmental and nongovernmental groups to promote healthy marriage and responsible fatherhood. Even prior to the DRA, the Department of Health and Human Services' Administration for Children and Families had launched a "Healthy Marriage Initiative." The DRA also established the Healthy Marriage and Responsible Fatherhood Program and funded the still-ongoing National Healthy Marriage Resource Center and National Responsible Fatherhood Clearinghouse websites.

> * * *

> One important feature of [the] debates [concerning reauthorization of PRWORA and TANF] was the concern that the intense focus on moving mothers from welfare to work * * * was leaving poor men behind. What should "personal responsibility"

mean as applied to men, not only to women? Certainly, Congress interpreted fathers' personal responsibility to entail financial support, and it called for getting tough on "deadbeat dads" by expanding efforts to establish paternity and collect child support. But what if dads faced economic and other structural barriers that made taking "personal responsibility" difficult? Did the government have any obligation to help? The Clinton Administration spoke about the problems of "dead-broke" dads * * * [R]esponsible-fatherhood initiatives * * * also included noneconomic aspects of parenthood in defining "responsible fatherhood," such as active involvement by a father in his child's life. * * * President [Barack Obama] promoted responsible fatherhood as "every father taking responsibility for his child's intellectual, emotional, and financial well-being." For example responsible-fatherhood campaigns launched under the Obama Administration promote active parenting, urging men to "take time to be a dad today."

Linda C. McClain, *Family: The Other Marriage Equality Problem* (panel), 93 B.U. L. Rev. 921, 938–40 (2013).

As of 2018, the Department of Health and Human Services continues to sponsor the National Responsible Fatherhood Clearinghouse, with its Obama-era "take time to be a dad today" slogan and the stated purpose of strengthening and supporting fathers and families. https://www. fatherhood.gov/ (visited Mar. 26, 2019). *See, e.g.*, M. Robin Dion et al., *Responsible Fatherhood Programs in the Parents and Children Together (PACT) Evaluation*, 53 Fam. Ct. Rev. 292 (Apr. 2015).

Efforts to translate responsibility into financial and emotional support from low-income fathers, however, face daunting challenges that sometimes stem from household dynamics. Two leading researchers conclude that initially "most men at the bottom * * * are actually eager to claim fatherhood and to engage in at least some aspects of the role." Kathryn Edin & Timothy J. Nelson, Doing the Best I Can: Fatherhood in the Inner City 224 (2013). Many of the relationships they form with their children, however, ultimately fall short of meeting the child's parenting and financial needs and the custodial mother's expectations. "[T]he tasks these men actually end up performing in their children's lives are more like those of a favorite uncle," providing consumer items and visiting sporadically. *Id.* at 225. Edin and Nelson found that such fathers face obstacles that keep them from meeting their own ideals of fatherhood, which include their own behavioral shortcomings, their under- or unemployment, the mother's gatekeeping role in deciding whether the father sees the child, and the child's indifference or hostility to a paternal relationship. *Id.* at 208.

The next article addresses some of the obstacles, explaining that achieving the policy goals of "responsible fatherhood" adherents may demand a more nuanced approach than policymakers, lawmakers, and courts have generally embraced. The article describes the absent-father issue, and discusses overarching challenges created by the intricate relationships between custody and support in families in which payment of child support can have the greatest impact. The article urges a coordinated response that implicates the legal system and includes alternative dispute resolution, Chapter 15's focus.

LAURIE S. KOHN,
ENGAGING MEN AS FATHERS: THE COURTS, THE LAW, AND FATHER-ABSENCE IN LOW-INCOME FAMILIES
35 Cardozo L. Rev. 511, 512–57 (2013).

Father-absence is an ever-increasing trend in our country. Exacerbated by poverty, father-absence leaves a disproportionately high percentage of low-income children living with their mothers and enjoying little to no paternal contact. Many sociological, cultural, and economic factors contribute to the likelihood of father-absence and drive fathers away from their children even before they have forged any relationship at all. As such, father-absence is commonly considered to be a non-legal problem. However, the cohort of fathers who become absent only after interactions with the custody and child support systems challenges that characterization and raises questions about the potential relationship between fathers' involvement with the legal system and their subsequent absence.

Engaged fathers can disappear from the lives of their children after custody proceedings or after the imposition or enforcement of child support obligations. Even fathers who litigate aggressively for custody or visitation may retreat from the lives of their children in the aftermath of court proceedings. Mothers who affirmatively support these father-child relationships are left without a meaningful remedy in the face of father-absence. Motions to enforce visitation orders to coerce fathers to spend time with their children rarely prevail in court, nor are they likely to achieve positive father-child engagement. Likewise, though judges are far more likely to entertain contempt actions in the child support system, enforcement seeks child support collection but not healthy father-child involvement. As such, father-absence among this cohort of court-involved families largely evades a litigation remedy to encourage and enhance the paternal relationship.

* * *

* * * [S]tudies indicate that involved nonresident fathers can be critical to child well-being. Engaged nonresident fathers can play an important role in supporting child development, ensuring academic success, and fostering self-esteem in children. Further, studies illustrate a correlation between negative outcomes for children, such as early sexual activity and delinquency, and father-absence. * * * If fathers enter the legal system with the intention of maintaining relationships with their children, the system is failing children if the fathers' system interaction unintentionally extinguishes that intention. Finally, when custodial mothers seek support from the court to maintain or increase father-presence in the context of a custody or child support action, the court system has an obligation to the well-being of children to minimize its role in impeding that goal.

* * *

I.   TRENDS IN FATHER-ABSENCE

* * * In one large-scale study of the general population of families with nonresident fathers, mothers reported that 34% of the fathers had no contact with the child's household at all. The statistics related to fragile families, in which the parents never marry, paint an even bleaker picture. The Fragile Families Report of 2010 reported that one year after birth, roughly 40% of nonresident fathers did not visit with their children on a regular basis, defined as at least one time a month. As the children grow, fathers in fragile families become less engaged. By the time children turn five years old, nearly 50% of fathers fail to see their children on a regular basis. * * *

Demographics are relevant to father-absence as well. Father-absence is less likely in families with mothers who are college graduates. Further, employed fathers are more likely to have regular contact with their children. Other studies have echoed the finding that fathers at higher socioeconomic levels maintain more consistent contact with their children than their counterparts at lower socioeconomic levels.

Although precise data reflecting the number of fathers who obtain some kind of custody or visitation order and then disappear from the lives of their children are hard to extrapolate, studies suggest that it is a significant cohort. One study of families with custody orders found that 32% of nonresident fathers had not spent any time with their children in the past year. A study of divorced parents, a group likely to have custody orders in place as part of a divorce action, found that two years after divorce, only one-quarter of noncustodial fathers visited with their children once a week or more. The study reported that between 18% and 25% of those children no longer had any contact with their fathers three years following divorce.

In contrast, * * * multiple studies illustrate that many low-income fathers want to be involved but that economic disadvantages hamper their ability to remain engaged.

* * *

II. BARRIERS TO PATERNAL ENGAGEMENT

The concept of the absent father conjures up images of men who procreate without regard to consequences and disappear without remorse. Popular culture typically paints the picture of this iconic absent father as a young, low-income African American man. * * *

In fact, by most accounts, African American men are less likely than Caucasian or Hispanic men to be absent fathers. * * * [R]esearch indicates that the concept of fatherhood and the ideal of being an engaged father are important to the vast majority of men. * * * Studies of low-income fathers noted the emotional distress fathers displayed when discussing their absence from the lives of their children.

* * * [C]ommon barriers * * * impede the father-child relationship and result in paternal absence * * *. [A]lthough a number of these impediments seem, at first blush, unrelated to the legal system, interactions with the legal system as currently configured often exacerbate the barriers that the legal system is well positioned to alleviate.

A. *Relational Barriers to Paternal Engagement*

* * * The relationship between separated parents is self-evidently prone to inherent conflict. First, co-parenting demands parental interaction. Especially when the children are young, interactions between a nonresident parent and his children are often mediated by and intertwined with the custodial parent from a logistical and emotional perspective. Second, after the dissolution of the relationship between the parents, the interaction between parents is often fraught with an emotional complexity and a struggle for control that almost inevitably affects the children. Third, fathers point to conflict produced by new maternal romantic relationships. New romantic partners introduced into a family dynamic that is already fragile can result in increased tension, resentment on the part of the nonresident father, and the deployment of tighter control by mothers. Finally, the court process itself can enhance conflict.

Apart from overt conflict, lack of support from custodial mothers also hinders fathers' engagement. Fathers report feeling inhibited from engaging with their children when mothers fail to support their involvement either explicitly or implicitly. Many fathers complain that mothers act as "gatekeepers," regulating and influencing the relationship between children and their nonresident fathers, taking advantage of their disproportionate access to the children, and often leaving fathers feeling undermined and helpless. * * *

B. *Structural Barriers to Father-Presence*

* * * A father with limited resources may not have access to transportation to facilitate frequent visitation, or may be forced to use unreliable transportation that may make him late for visits or that may not be safe or practicable to use to transport children. * * *

* * * Barriers posed by work can manifest themselves in various ways in the lives of low-income men. For this cohort, the barriers tend to be more prominent than they are for men at higher income levels since these fathers usually occupy positions with less flexibility, autonomy, and security. * * * Many fathers who work hourly jobs tend to work in the evening and weekends, during the most convenient hours to visit with school-aged children. * * *

Finally, a father who lacks resources may not have an appropriate home to which to bring his children for visitation. This may be particularly true of fathers who have been living with their children prior to involvement with the legal system. After the dissolution of a family relationship, for example, low-income fathers can struggle to find permanent housing, often sleeping in shelters or at friends' homes. Such residences may be unsafe or inappropriate for children; additionally, fathers may feel ashamed of their impermanence and want to hide this reality from their children until they have more respectable housing. * * *

C. *Role Barriers to Paternal Engagement*

For fathers who have lived with their children prior to court involvement or child support enforcement, the legal action may involve the dissolution of the family relationship. When a family dissolves, predetermined roles and the family structure are thrown into chaos. For these fathers, role barriers may be a salient impediment to paternal engagement. * * *

1. Role Ambiguity

When the court adjudicates custody, court orders seek to render explicit the new structure of parenting relationships. However, court orders have their limits. Most court orders merely award joint or sole physical and/or legal custody and set a visitation or parenting schedule. Court orders generally stop there in terms of allocating responsibility within the new family structure. * * * With very few exceptions, court orders refrain from divvying up specific parenting responsibilities, and very few separated parents are able to proactively identify and negotiate such issues on their own. * * *

Low-income fathers report being unsure of what mothers expect of them. * * * Of course, role ambiguity in turn breeds conflict between parents, which, as discussed above, may be the most significant inhibitor for fathers.

2.   Dissatisfaction with the New Role

Once the father is no longer part of the original family structure, * * * [e]ngagement with his children is no longer casual, unpremeditated, and spontaneous. Instead, it derives either from a court-ordered schedule or an agreement with the mother, and its time parameters are usually circumscribed. The very nature of this interaction profoundly shifts, and though it may absolve a father of some of the more tedious parenting tasks, it can also transform the relationship into a more superficial one. * * *

Fathers also report that the limited nature of non-primary physical custody or visitation causes them emotional pain that can lead them to reject the visitation altogether. * * *

Finally, a father's discomfort with his new role may stem from feelings of inadequacy in the role of sole care-giving parent. Despite changes in family law and changes in women's employment opportunities, child-rearing remains extremely gender-differentiated. In a home with both a mother and father, the mother ordinarily undertakes a disproportionate share of child-care responsibilities in relation to the father. Consequently, when a father is offered time alone with a child, possibly to even include overnight visitation, he may perceive himself to be incompetent to undertake the task because of inexperience. * * *

D.   *Social Norm Barriers to Paternal Engagement*

* * * Social norms that create expectations that mothers will nurture and fathers will merely provide for their children can dissuade a father from taking advantage of his visitation and custody rights. Gender roles operating in the family have traditionally cast women as nurturers and men as breadwinners. * * *

[S]ocial norms influence judicial handling of family law cases, resulting in decisions that may perpetuate role differentiation and fail to support paternal caretaking. * * *

III.   THE LEGAL SYSTEM'S ROLE IN ENTRENCHING AND REDUCING BARRIERS

* * * [T]he legal system can play a role in reducing barriers to fathers and in facilitating paternal relationships, especially for this group of low-income court-involved fathers. For the fathers who have previously shared a home with their children, the court system's involvement occurs at a critical moment of family instability—the time when new family norms take root and there is a high potential for fracture. For many of these fathers, this time also introduces them to the child support system and its requirements. Because the legal system can engage fathers at this critical moment, its role as an inhibitor or facilitator to positive paternal engagement could be influential in arresting the trend of increasing father-absence.

* * *

A.   *Child Support and Father-Absence*

* * * In the past fifteen years, government programs to collect child support and to establish parentage, as mandated by both federal legislation and local statutes, have become increasingly aggressive. In addition to establishing criminal penalties for failure to pay child support, some jurisdictions have also conditioned the receipt of public benefits on a mother's cooperation with establishing parentage. While renewed efforts at child support enforcement have been successful on several fronts, current enforcement programs can be more problematic than effective in the population of low-income fathers with little ability to pay in terms of both collection and paternal engagement. * * *

Though the child support order for an unemployed father might be as low as fifty dollars per month, such an obligation might still be impossible to meet. Research suggests that the majority of low-income fathers' failure to meet their obligations is not because of their unwillingness to support their children, but because they do not earn enough to satisfy their obligations. When a parent fails to comply with his support obligation, the court can impose job search requirements, require regular enforcement hearings, and ultimately impose sanctions, including criminal contempt. For these fathers, the continual pressure from the government to obtain a job, meet obligations, compensate for arrears, or face sanctions, contempt, or criminal penalties and their collateral consequences can have a significant deterrent effect on paternal engagement. * * *

1.   Assignment of Child Support to the Government as Reimbursement for Government Benefits

Under federal and state child support law, current and former recipients of Temporary Assistance to Needy Families (TANF) must assign their rights to child support to the government as reimbursement for benefits. The family retains a claim to support monies that exceed the total amount of cash assistance the family has received. * * *

Welfare cost recovery negatively affects paternal engagement in several ways. First, noncustodial fathers are denied the opportunity to directly benefit their families, often rendering fathers resentful of the government and their families and incentivized to disappear to avoid burdensome and seemingly senseless payments. * * *

Second, family conflict is specifically kindled, rather than tamped, by assignment rules. The mother may not receive any direct support from the father, even if he is meeting his obligations. Further, she is likely to understand that each month that the noncustodial parent fails to meet his obligation corresponds to a future month of payment being withheld even after she leaves TANF. Noncustodial fathers, likewise, are driven to resent custodial mothers for relying on government support and creating a debt to the state for which the fathers are obligated.

Third, assignment deprives parents of the right to negotiate their own child support arrangements, impeding the ability of a family to effectively meet the needs of the children, and eliminating what is often a powerful bargaining tool for mothers. * * *

Finally, assignment drives custodial families further into poverty, putting strain on parental relations and negatively affecting paternal engagement. With TANF payments so low in every state that an average family's income on TANF does not reach 50% of the poverty line and amounts to less than $300 per month in fourteen states, many mothers are greatly in need of child support payments to make ends meet. * * * [Professor Kohn discusses pass-through, which Section 1 of this Chapter discussed.]

* * *

2.   The Ban on In-Kind Support Payments

* * * Child support guidelines currently specify that the payor parent derives no credit for in-kind or informal payments. Informal payments, constituting mere gifts, cannot defray current or past child support obligations. The ban on in-kind payments reflects child support law's unwavering commitment to enforcing monetary obligations against noncustodial parents. While this goal is laudable in seeking to maximize support for children, this inflexible principle can fortify impediments by stoking parental conflict, incentivizing fathers to flee or enter the underground economy, and reinforcing the message that paternal non-monetary contributions are irrelevant. In the end, it likely deprives children of available support.

* * *

Easing the blanket ban on informal and in-kind payments would likely increase support payments by low-income fathers. Fathers express an interest in being able to contribute money when they can and to compensate with other contributions when necessary. * * * Indeed, in-kind payments may be more prevalent than formal child support payments. * * *

Mothers express an interest in informal and in-kind payments because many realize they are more likely to receive such support from struggling low-income fathers and because they are able to bargain with noncustodial fathers as necessary to meet their needs. In-kind payments provide a way for noncustodial fathers to contribute when they are financially unable to meet their formal obligations. When fathers are able to meet their formal obligations, research suggests that in-kind payments do not lower formal child support payments.

Eliminating the ban would likely encourage parental contact and positive father involvement. Generally, research indicates that the formal nature and the amount of child support are far less important to children's well-being than the act of supporting a child. Since low-income fathers are more likely to pay child support in a less formal manner, support for informal payments enhances the likelihood that children will reap the benefits of paternal support. * * * Moreover, the legal preference for wage withholding and automated payments of child support requires formal child support to transfer without contact between the payor and family; whereas in-kind payments generally depend on contact.

Of course, the informality of this arrangement poses risks for the family. For custodial parents, payments might be unreliable and the obligation unenforceable. Further, a mother risks making herself vulnerable to manipulation by the noncustodial parent. Particularly when the family has experienced domestic violence, the potential for coercion is significant. For noncustodial parents, the informality of the agreement creates opportunities for enforcement actions with little opportunity to defend themselves. As such, fathers, too, might end up vulnerable to manipulation. Further, the family, in general, might be hurt by this arrangement for it might increase parental conflict.

Finally, and not insignificantly, the government would lose the opportunity to track payments and enforce obligations, which it does to assure noncustodial parents fulfill their obligations to their children who otherwise might depend solely on government benefits. It is, of course, also possible that noncustodial parents would contribute less in-kind or informally than they would be obligated to pay in the formal system.

* * *

B. Court System Responses to Father Engagement

* * *

1. Procedural Responses

* * * Adversarial justice may be particularly poorly suited to family law matters due to the complex and dynamic nature of the problems and solutions and because of the long-term intimate relationship between the parties. When parents separate, mother and father are bound to experience friction. However, when the parties come to court to have their separation overseen and adjudicated by a judge, the court is in a position to minimize or exacerbate that conflict. * * *.

a. Alternative Dispute Resolution

[M]ediation services traditionally have been aimed at cases on the divorce docket rather than the custody docket, which includes never-married parents litigating custody and child support. Through the mediation, parties seek to resolve disputes without resorting to an adversarial conflict. * * *

Collaborative law has gained popularity over the last decade and is designed to reduce conflict and promote cooperation between parties. Its use in family law cases has increased as parents have become more aware of the effects of conflict and court battles on children. * * * Under the uniform collaborative law guidelines, parties and attorneys are encouraged to abandon puffery, obfuscation, and misrepresentation in favor of disclosure and honesty. * * *

A final dispute resolution approach, restorative justice, has been gaining in acceptance in the United States over the last several decades, primarily in the criminal justice arena, and focuses on addressing harms caused by legally actionable behavior by engaging the victims and offenders themselves, as well as the community. By addressing the underlying needs of the parties, restorative justice proponents seek to work outside or alongside the traditional criminal and civil justice system to achieve broader and more flexible resolutions. * * *

Alternative dispute resolution mechanisms hold the potential to reduce some salient barriers to father-presence. A uniform focus across all three programs on non-adversarial resolution serves the important goal of reducing conflict between separating parents. Because researchers and fathers alike have noted that parental conflict creates a significant impediment to the father-child relationship, a program that reduces the conflict at the critical moment of separation might well ease this barrier. In addition, because these resolution techniques occur outside the courtroom in private settings, parties are less likely to leave humiliated by the revelation of private facts or allegations.

* * *

Alternative dispute resolution is inappropriate for some cases, and should not be mandated in these instances. Any informal case resolution may disadvantage women because women may be less comfortable asserting themselves or exerting power in an informal setting. However, allowing parties to opt in to mediation can relieve some of this challenge; as can providing the opportunity for shuttle negotiations in the context of mediation in which the parties are never simultaneously in the room with the mediator. Inherent coercion, however, can still infect the decision to opt into an informal procedure and the procedure itself.

In addition, all three alternative dispute mechanisms have been deemed inappropriate for cases involving domestic violence because of the frequency of power and control dynamics at play. While some scholars now argue that informal case resolutions can be handled in a way that does not disadvantage a domestic violence victim or put her at risk, it is clear that, at a minimum, safeguards such as effective screening and intervention for danger and coercion must be implemented.

All three procedures can also be cost-limiting or even cost-prohibitive. * * *

However, models for making alternative dispute resolution techniques available at little or no cost to low-income individuals have been increasing nationwide. * * *

Despite their limitations, each of these procedures has already displayed some promise of delivering on their goals. * * *

b. Problem-Solving Courts

* * * Problem-solving courts are distinguishable from traditional courts in that they involve collaboration between the court, social services, and litigants. Further, judges take a proactive role in solving underlying family problems on the path to resolving legal issues.

Custody, divorce, and child support cases lend themselves well to a problem-solving approach. These cases generally involve complex parental relationships, long-term risks of conflict between parents, logistical challenges of sharing child custody, a range of possible barriers to low-income parents, and the particular challenges of child support enforcement for financially-strapped fathers. A problem-solving model could address a range of barriers identified as impediments to engaged fatherhood. Problem-solving courts seek to reduce conflict and focus instead on effective resolution. Further, problem-solving courts proactively address barriers and engage litigants and concerned parties in brainstorming successful solutions. * * * Partnerships with resource providers could provide fathers with the support they need to meet their obligations and simultaneously engage positively and consistently with their children.

* * *

Problem-solving courts also have their limitations. Problem-solving courts necessitate extensive court involvement. Multiple court hearings, court oversight, and mandatory referrals are necessary to allow the court to play the constructive role expected of problem-solving courts. For low-income litigants, who often experience extensive government intrusion related to public benefits, such involvement may be unwanted and may interfere too severely with a litigant's work obligations. * * *

* * *

c. Post-Resolution Status Hearings

* * * Short of a wholesale transformation into a problem-solving court, a traditional domestic relations court could reap some of the problem-solving benefits by implementing regular post-resolution status hearings.

At such hearings, the parties would be expected to report on compliance, assess their satisfaction with the parenting plan, and raise any perceived challenges to effective co-parenting that have become clear after several months of living with a court order. Such status hearings would offer the judge the opportunity to resolve conflicts and adjust any orders with the consent of the parties.

* * *

Of course, such status hearings may, in high conflict cases, only aggravate the conflict and encourage ongoing litigation. However, after the first status hearing, the judge could have the discretion to cease future hearings or refer the parties for other services. * * *

2. Programmatic Responses

[Professor Kohn discusses (1) court-based parent education programs, which are designed to inform both parents about the ways to minimize the impact of parental separation," (2) parenting coordinators, "who can intervene during the adjudicatory or post-adjudicatory phase of a custody case, address the day-to-day issues high-conflict families experience in enacting their parenting plans, and (3) visitation and access centers, which can "provide a monitored, appropriate venue for short visits."]

NOTES AND QUESTIONS

1. *Questions about father-absence.* (a) What kinds of barriers does Professor Kohn identify to noncustodial fathers' engagement with their children? (b) Which of her proposals do you think would help increase fathers' economic and non-economic contributions to their children's lives? (c) What constructive roles can alternative dispute resolution play in encouraging these contributions?

2. *The federal presumption.* In the Deadbeat Parents Punishment Act of 1998 (discussed in Section 6.B.above), should Congress have created a rebuttable presumption that a parent, prosecuted for nonpayment under the Child Support Recovery Act, can pay the obligations due?

3. *Parental incarceration.* Nationwide imprisonment rates pose daunting challenges to efforts to collect child support arrears. "Nearly 3 million US children under the age of 18 have a parent in jail or prison." Bryce Peterson, *Children of Incarcerated Parents Framework Document* (Urban Inst. 2015). "The U.S. penal population of 2.2 million adults is the largest in the world. * * * Those who are incarcerated in U.S. prisons come largely from the most disadvantaged segments of the population." Nat'l Res. Council, *The Growth of Incarceration in the United States: Exploring Causes and Consequences* 2, 6 (2014).

Incarceration does not extinguish the inmate's child support obligation unless the court terminates his or her parental rights. Many states prohibit downward modification during imprisonment on the ground that "an individual's actions that lead to incarceration are voluntary" within the meaning of the guidelines that permit imputing income for unemployment or underemployment. *Wilkerson v. Wilkerson*, 220 So.3d 480, 483 (Fla. Dist. Ct. App. 2017).

On the other hand, some states require inmates to pay support only in amounts they are capable of paying. "A court may only impute income * * * that the parent can earn while incarcerated. But the court may require an incarcerated parent to pay child support in excess of his or her earning capacity if the parent has access to other assets." *King v. King*, 66 A.3d 593, 597 (Me. 2013).

Should the state prohibit modification of child support obligations while the parent is in prison? Consider this commentary:

ANN CAMMETT, DEADBEATS, DEADBROKES, AND PRISONERS
18 Geo. J. Poverty L. & Pol'y 127, 129–31 (2011).

* * * In the case of incarcerated parents, * * * aggressive enforcement and uncollectible debt can manifest in unintended consequences that hamper the larger goal of ongoing parental support.

Prisoners are also parents, and in many states they amass huge child support arrears during a period of incarceration. Such a debt does not relate to real income since prisoners earn little or no money, the debt will likely never be collected, and the support arrearage will not ultimately redound to the benefit of their children. This dynamic has been further complicated by an important element of the support model that we have embraced in the United States: absolute enforcement against all nonresident parents who have fallen behind in child support, regardless of their circumstances. A wide range of very serious sanctions, such as onerous salary garnishment, driver's license suspension, re-incarceration, and many others can be triggered against parents when they are released. Moreover, pursuant to federal law—specifically the Bradley Amendment— debt from child support arrears cannot be modified or discharged by a court once it is accrued. These automatic penalties are counterproductive, as they make it more difficult for formerly incarcerated parents to pay ongoing support as they attempt to successfully reintegrate into society and resume contact with their children. Rather, automatic child support enforcement creates perverse incentives that alienate parents from the formal economy and drive them underground—and away from their families. Such a paradigm cannot be in the best interests of their children and runs counter to the goals of the child support program.

* * * [I]n the case of prisoners, state courts often conflate blame for criminal conduct with one's actual ability to earn money while

incarcerated, using debt accumulation and obligation as a proxy for further punishment. Yet, debt accrued during incarceration does not typically represent a resource from which children will eventually benefit. A financial obligation on the books, unmoored to real earning capacity, may remain unpaid forever because it does not represent real income or future earnings. It is quite simply an uncollectible debt that does not benefit children, the state, or society. * * *

NOTE

Civil rights lawyer and advocate Michelle Alexander argues that "[m]ass incarceration in the United States has emerged as a stunningly comprehensive and well-disguised system of racialized social control that functions in a manner strikingly similar to Jim Crow." Michelle Alexander, The New Jim Crow 4 (2010). "Recent estimates suggest that by age 17, 24.2 percent of non-Hispanic black children and 10.7 percent of Hispanic children—but only 3.9 percent of non-Hispanic white children—will experience parental incarceration." Kristin Turney & Rebecca Goodsell, *Parental Incarceration and Children's Wellbeing*, 28 The Future of Children 147, 149 (Spring 2018).

"About half of all inmates have at least one child," *id.* at 148, and racially disparate incarceration rates help skew child support enforcement. "Some ex-offenders are thrown back in prison because they have been unable—with no place to live, and no decent job—to pay back thousands of dollars of * * * child support." Michelle Alexander, *supra* at 151.

PROBLEM 11-10

You have practiced family law for more than a decade and are a leading member of the state bar association's family law committee. You have agreed to speak at a bar-sponsored continuing legal education program next month, "Child Support Enforcement: Yesterday, Today, and Tomorrow." Other family lawyers will address the history of state and federal child support enforcement efforts, and will provide an overview and critique of present efforts. You will present recommendations for improving rates of child support payment by avoiding accumulation of arrears, particularly among obligors who are unemployed or otherwise report little or no income. What will you recommend?

CHAPTER 12

CHILD CUSTODY

■ ■ ■

1. INTRODUCTION

Child custody decisions are among the most divisive for parents, the most difficult for judges, and the most critical for the children themselves. Most parents agree about initial custody and visitation arrangements, but many others litigate the issues, both at the time of divorce and afterwards. The stakes are high—and emotions run high too. Even when parents who are dissolving their relationship reach a private agreement concerning child custody and visitation, the agreement does not become effective until a court approves it. This Chapter considers how courts make initial child custody decisions when the parents cannot reach an agreement. Chapter 13 will look at some custody and visitation issues that are commonly the subjects of prolonged, repeated litigation after the parents' relationship dissolves.

The most recent census data show that as of 2016 the majority of children in the United States (76%) lived with two married parents, though this family form has been declining for some time. U.S. Census Bureau, Current Population Survey, 2016 Annual Social and Economic Supplement. Over 40% of all children born each year are born to unmarried parents. Brady E. Hamilton et al., National Center for Health Statistics, *Births: Preliminary Data for 2014, National Vital Statistics Reports Vol. 64 No. 12* (2015). The combination of a high divorce rate and high percentages of children born outside of marriage means that a substantial portion of children in the U.S. will be the subject of custody decisions at some point during childhood.

Some unmarried parents are "single," but many are cohabiting. (See the discussion of cohabitation in Chapter 4). Indeed, nearly one-quarter of all births today are to cohabiting parents. W. Bradford Wilcox & Andrew J. Cherlin, Center on Children and Families at Brookings, *The Marginalization of Marriage in Middle America* 2 (2011). The children of cohabitants are even more likely to become the subject of custody decisions at some point than children born to married parents because cohabitation in the U.S. "remains largely a short term relationship, even when children are involved." *Id.* Experts predict that "65 percent of children born to cohabiting parents will see their parents part by age 12, compared to just 24 percent of children born to married parents." *Id.* When the informal arrangements unmarried couples tend to make respecting the care of their children break down, many of them end up in court. And courts are also called upon to decide custody disputes over children born after their parents had what the judge describes as a brief relationship.

Twenty-four percent of all children in the U.S. lived with only one parent in 2016. U.S. Census Bureau (2016), *supra*. Over 80% of those children lived with their mothers, a proportion that has remained steady since 1994. *Id*. at 4. The proportion of households headed by a single mother more than doubled, growing from 12% to 26% between 1980 and 2009. *Id*. The rise in the proportion of children who live primarily with a father is equally striking: in 1960, just over one percent of single-parent households were headed by a single father, compared to 18 to 24% of single-parent households in 2013. Gretchen Livingston, *The Rise of Single Fathers,* Pew Research Social & Demographic Trends (July 2, 2013); Timothy Greil, U.S. Census Bureau, *Custodial Mothers and Fathers and Their Child Support: 2011* 4 (2013). Fathers who have primary custody are far more likely to have been married to their children's mother than to have cohabited with her. Greil, *supra*, at 1, 4. Seven percent of children live with both of their parents in homes where the parents are cohabiting but unmarried. Gretchen Livingstone, *About one-third of U.S. children are living with an unmarried parent* (Pew Research Center 2018) at 2. Some children who live with only one of their biological parents nonetheless live in a household with two adults, whether married or unmarried. Almost 1.6 million U.S. children live with a parent who is cohabiting with a new partner who is not the child's biological parent. Jonathan Vespa et al., U.S. Census Bureau, *America's Families and Living Arrangements: 2012 (*2012) at 16; Gretchen Livingstone, *The Changing Profile of Unmarried Parents* (Pew Research Center 2018) (35% of unmarried parents are living with a partner) at 2.

All children are likely to suffer some degree of dislocation and trauma if the household in which they live dissolves regardless of whether their parents are married or cohabit, or whether the adult who lives with or is married to their parent and helps care for them is a biological stranger. In second half of the twentieth century, social science studies predicted catastrophic effects for children of divorce, but a large body of empirical research has since provided a more balanced, albeit complex, understanding of the impact of divorce on children.

A review of the more than one thousand studies of childhood adjustment over the last 50 years summarized the consensus in 2012: "the most important factors that promote healthy development and adjustment" include:

    a.   The quality of infants', children's, or adolescents' relationships with their parents or parent figures;

b. The quality of the relationships between the parents and other significant adults (conflict between them is associated with maladjustment while harmonious relationships between the adults support healthy adjustment); and

c. The availability of adequate economic, social, and physical resources

Michael E. Lamb, *Mothers, Fathers, Families, and Circumstances: Factors Affecting Children's Development*, 16 Applied Developmental Sci. 98, 99 (2012). Risk factors related to all three adjustment indicators may be present while the parents live together as cohabitants or in a marriage, and issues related to all three may be triggered when parents split up. *Id.* at 103.

The long-term effects of family dissolution on an individual child correlate with the child's individual resilience and support systems. While "the vast majority of children and adolescents who spend their childhoods living apart from one of their parents are well adjusted," empirical studies show that children who grow up in a single parent household are "more likely to have adjustment difficulties than children" who grew up "in two-parent families." *Id.* at 102. As indicated above, the most important variables in children's long-term adjustment following their parents' break up are whether the children continue to have positive relationships with both parents, whether there are sufficient economic and social resources to ensure stability, and the level of conflict between the parents before, during and after the breakup—particularly if the children are aware of (or drawn into) the acrimony. *Id.* at 103.

Long-term, unresolved conflicts, many of which are litigated and re-litigated, as you will see in Chapter 13, are widely considered to be among the most harmful aspect of family breakup for children. Susan W. Savard, *Through the Eyes of a Child: Impact and Measures to Protect Children in High-Conflict Family Law Litigation*, 84 Fla. B.J. 57 (2010). A 2013 survey of empirical data collected over the last three decades, however, suggests that a more refined approach is needed. The author suggests that it is important to distinguish prolonged parental conflict following dissolution from protracted litigation and to look at both protective factors (*e.g.*, warm and effective parenting) and risk factors (*e.g.*, loss of relationship with one parent, cohabiting by the residential parent). Joan B. Kelly, *Risk and Protective Factors Associated with Child and Adolescent Adjustment Following Separation and Divorce: Social Science Applications*, in Kathryn F. Kuehnle & Leslie M. Drozd, Parenting Plan Evaluations: Applied Research for the Family Court 49–84 (2013). Family law practitioners often encourage their clients to reduce stress on their children by pursuing conciliatory methods of resolving their custody and visitation disputes, and many parents are able to do so. (Alternatives to litigation, including mediation and collaborative divorce, are presented in Chapter 15).

This Chapter primarily examines the standards courts apply and the factors courts consider when, as a last resort, they are called upon to impose custody and visitation decisions on a family. As with decisions about how to divide a family's material assets, discussed in Chapter 9, private bargaining takes place in the shadow of the participants' predictions about the resolution the courts would likely impose.

By definition, all of the judicial decisions presented in this Chapter were necessary because parents could not agree about how to allocate caretaking and decisionmaking authority for their children.

The first Section of this Chapter explains the contemporary understanding of the constitutional rights of fit parents to the care, custody, and nurture of their children. The Chapter continues with a review of presumptions that once determined the outcome of custody disputes between parents—an evolution from rigid rules based on gender to standards that guide judges when they are forced to choose between two loving and fit parents. The Chapter then examines in detail the "best interests of the child" standard that governs child custody decisions today in most jurisdictions, the factors that courts often weigh in determining the child's best interests in custody disputes, and ways of learning what the children themselves want. Finally, you will learn about contemporary views of shared parenting time, commonly known as "joint custody"; the new terminology emphasizes that both adults continue to parent their children.

2. CONSTITUTIONAL CONSIDERATIONS

Chapter 1 introduced *Meyer* and *Pierce*, the Supreme Court decisions that established a parent's Fourteenth Amendment substantive due process liberty interest in the care, custody and nurture of his or her children. These decisions presumed a model of married parents who agreed about major family decisions. Custody disputes are grounded in constitutional law emanating from the *Meyer-Pierce* line of decisions, but parental discord can strain the classic model. Other complex issues arise when a custody dispute pits a biological parent against a nonparent. A custody dispute between a child's father and maternal grandparents gave rise to the following custody decision that examines the evolution of the parental rights doctrine.

MCDERMOTT V. DOUGHERTY

Court of Appeals of Maryland, 2005.
869 A.2d 751.

CATHELL, J.

This appeal arises as an outgrowth of the lengthy and unfortunately acrimonious dispute over custody of Patrick Michael McDermott * * *, the minor son of petitioner Charles David McDermott * * *, between Mr. McDermott and respondents, Hugh and Marjorie Dougherty, the child's maternal grandparents * * *.[1]

* * * The circuit court issued its decision on September 8, 2003, awarding the maternal grandparents sole legal and physical custody of the child based upon that court's finding that Ms. Dougherty was "unfit," and, *although not finding Mr. McDermott an "unfit"* parent, the court found that his employment in the merchant marine, requiring him to spend months-long intervals at sea, constituted "exceptional circumstances" as that term was defined in *Ross v. Hoffman*, 372 A.2d 582, 593 (Md. 1977), and the "best interest of the child" and need for a stable living situation thus warranted that custody be placed with the Doughertys. * * *

[The intermediate court affirmed the lower court's decision.]

* * *

We hold that in disputed custody cases where private third parties are attempting to gain custody of children from their natural parents, the trial court must first find that both natural parents are unfit to have custody of their children or that extraordinary circumstances exist which are significantly detrimental to the child remaining in the custody of the parent or parents, before a trial court should consider the "best interests of the child" standard as a means of deciding the dispute.

We further hold that under circumstances in which there is no finding of parental unfitness, the requirements of a parent's employment, such that he is required to be away at sea, or otherwise appropriately absent from the State for a period of time, and for which time he or she made appropriate arrangements for the care of the child, do not constitute "extraordinary or exceptional circumstances" to support the awarding of custody to a third party.

Accordingly, we shall reverse and direct the lower courts to grant custody of Patrick to petitioner. Although we find the declaration, announced by the plurality opinion in *Troxel* [*v. Granville*], affirming "the fundamental right of parents to make decisions concerning the care, custody, and control of their children," 530 U.S. 57, 66 (2000), to be

---

[1] There has also been litigation between petitioner and Laura A. Dougherty * * *, the child's natural mother and petitioner's former wife. The conflicts between them are not at issue in the present case.

instructive, our determination also rests upon the potential for absurd results that might result from a holding that denies custody to a fit and willing parent on the basis that the means by which he or she supports himself or herself and his or her family calls for his or her periodic absence from the State although having arranged suitable and safe alternative care for the child, or based upon the fact that the child, in a particular case, might be "better raised" by grandparents. * * *

I.   Facts

By the time of the current dispute there had been a lengthy series of events in the dispute over the custody of Patrick Michael McDermott, born April 30, 1995, to Charles David McDermott and Laura A. Dougherty, who were married on November 26, 1994 * * *. [T]he spouses separated shortly after Patrick's birth. * * *.

[Ms. Dougherty, who had a history of alcohol abuse, was incarcerated after her fourth conviction for drunk driving. Just before beginning her jail term in 2002, Ms. Dougherty, who had residential custody of Patrick, signed a power of attorney entrusting Patrick to the care of her parents. At about the same time, McDermott filed for a modification of custody under which he would share custody with the child's maternal grandparents. Just before filing his petition, McDermott signed on for six months of employment at sea.

While McDermott was at sea, his relationship with his former wife's parents deteriorated. In February 2002, the Doughertys filed for third-party custody of Patrick by *ex parte* order, requesting McDermott's parents share joint legal custody with them. At an *ex parte* hearing, the court ordered temporary joint legal custody to the Doughertys and McDermott's parents, with residential custody to the Doughertys. When McDermott returned from sea, the Doughertys allowed Patrick to return to his father "to mollify the child's sustained entreaties and crying that he wanted to be with his father." McDermott filed a petition seeking permanent legal and physical custody of Patrick; his parents supported the petition, but the Doughertys filed an opposition.

In December 2002, McDermott retained an attorney, and went to sea again in early 2003 "in order to 'make the money to pay' " the attorney who was handling his custody case. During a two-week break in March 2003, McDermott returned to Maryland to see his son.

The court ultimately found the mother, Ms. Dougherty, to be unfit to have custody of Patrick.

The merits trial on McDermott's custody petition and the Dougherty's' opposition took place in July 2003. The maternal grandparents argued that by this time they had provided a stable home for Patrick for four years. The parties continued to jostle for custody while the ruling remained pending.

In September 2003, the trial court granted sole legal and physical custody to the Doughertys. McDermott appealed.]

II. Discussion

A. *Fundamental Constitutional Parental Right to Raise One's Children*

One of the earlie[st] United States Supreme Court cases in respect to parental rights, and one that has been described in subsequent cases as seminal, is the case of *Meyer v. Nebraska,* 262 U.S. 390 (1923) * * *. It is important primarily for its language, which stressed the importance of family in our society. * * *

* * *

One of the early cases citing to *Meyer* was *Pierce v. Society of Sisters of the Holy Names of Jesus and Mary,* 268 U.S. 510, 530 (1925) * * *. The Court [relied on *Meyer* for the proposition that: "The child is not the mere creature of the state; those who nurture him and direct his destiny have the right, coupled with the high duty, to recognize and prepare him for additional obligations."]

* * *

In the 1970's the United States Supreme Court wrestled with a series of cases that, although not always directly concerning custody issues, continued to recognize the importance of the rights of parents.

In *Stanley v. Illinois,* 405 U.S. 645, 651–58 (1972) * * * [t]he Court said:

* * *

"The private interest here, that of a man in the children he has sired and raised, undeniably warrants deference and, absent a powerful countervailing interest, protection. It is plain that the interest of a parent in the companionship, care, custody, and management of his or her children 'come[s] to this Court with a momentum for respect lacking when appeal is made to liberties which derive merely from shifting economic arrangements.'

"The Court has frequently emphasized the importance of family. The rights to conceive and raise one's children have been deemed 'essential,' *Meyer v. Nebraska,* [262 U.S. at 399], 'basic civil rights of man,' *Skinner v. Oklahoma,* 316 U.S. 535, 541 (1942), and '[r]ights far more precious . . . than property rights,' *May v. Anderson,* 345 U.S. 528, 533 (1953). 'It is cardinal with us that the custody, care and nurture of the child reside first in the parents, whose primary function and freedom include preparation for obligations the state can neither supply nor hinder.' *Prince v.*

Massachusetts, 321 U.S. 158, 166 (1944). The integrity of the family unit has found protection in the Due Process Clause of the Fourteenth Amendment, the Equal Protection Clause of the Fourteenth Amendment, and the Ninth Amendment, *Griswold v. Connecticut*, 381 U.S. 479, 496 (1965) (Goldberg, J., concurring).

* * *

In the exclusionary zoning case of *Moore v. City of East Cleveland*, 431 U.S. 494, 499–508 (1977) [*Ed.'s note*: Chapter 1 of this book] * * *, the Court noted:

> "* * * 'This Court has long recognized that freedom of personal choice in matters of marriage and family life is one of the liberties protected by the Due Process Clause of the Fourteenth Amendment.' A host of cases, tracing their lineage to *Meyer* . . . have consistently acknowledged a 'private realm of family life which the state cannot enter.' Of course, the family is not beyond regulation. But when the government intrudes on choices concerning family living arrangements, this Court must examine carefully the importance of the governmental interests advanced and the extent to which they are served by the challenged regulation.["]

* * *

Quilloin v. Walcott, 434 U.S. 246 (1978), was a factually unusual case, and is one of, if not the only, case in which the Supreme Court upheld the sole use of the "best interests" standard in regard to the third party placement of children, although at the same time it opined that *if a parent were fit* it would generally be constitutionally prohibited to take custody from that parent on the basis of the "best interest of the child."

* * *

> "We have little doubt that the Due Process Clause would be offended '[i]f a State were to attempt to force the breakup of a natural family, over the objections of the parents and their children, *without some showing of unfitness and for the sole reason that to do so was thought to be in the children's best interest.*' But this is not a case in which the unwed father at any time had, or sought, actual or legal custody of his child. * * * ["]

[*Id.*] at 254–55 (emphasis added).

* * *

In *M.L.B. v. S.L.J.*, 519 U.S. 102, 116 (1996) [*Ed.'s note*: an appeal by a biological mother whose parental rights had been terminated to free her child for a step-parent adoption], the Court reversed a Mississippi case which had upheld a state statute that required certain fees to be paid before an appeal could be taken. * * * The Court found for the mother. Justice Ginsburg writing for the Court stated that:

> "Choices about marriage, family life, and the upbringing of children are among associational rights this Court has ranked as 'of basic importance in our society,' rights sheltered by the Fourteenth Amendment against the State's unwarranted usurpation, disregard, or disrespect. * * *

* * *

> "[T]he Court was unanimously of the view that 'the interest of parents in their relationship with their children is sufficiently fundamental to come within the finite class of liberty interests protected by the Fourteenth Amendment.' It was also the Court's unanimous view that '[f]ew consequences of judicial action are so grave as the severance of natural family ties.' "

In the recent case of *Troxel v. Granville*, [530 U.S. 57 (2000)][a] the Court reaffirmed its principles, in a challenge to a third party visitation statute in the state of Washington. * * *

In *Troxel*, a mother desired to limit her children's visitation with the parents of their deceased father, a man to whom she had never been married. The paternal grandparents invoked a Washington statute that permitted any person to petition the superior court for visitation rights of any child at any time, and gave discretion to the court to grant visitation when in the best interest of the children, without regard to any change in circumstances. * * * In criticizing the trial court's "slender findings" in support of its visitation order, the United States Supreme Court faulted the statute's failure to accord sufficient deference to the parent's interests * * *. In addition, *Troxel* observed that the trial court did not order non-parental visitation based upon "any special factors [*i.e.,* exceptional circumstances] that might justify the State's interference with [the mother's] fundamental right to make decisions concerning the rearing of her [children]." [*Id.*] at 68 (alterations added).

* * *

[T]he *Troxel* decision affirmed the Washington Supreme Court's invalidation of a state statute because the Due Process Clause does not permit a State to "infringe on the fundamental right of parents to make child rearing decisions simply because a state judge believes a 'better' decision could be made." * * * *Troxel* * * * recognizes the parent's fundamental right to direct his or her children's care, custody and control,

---

[a]   *Editors' Note: Troxel* is included in Chapter 13.

and it impliedly rejects the substitution of a judge's opinion that a particular child would be better raised in a situation a trial judge prefers.[13]

* * *

The circumstances of the case *sub judice* illuminate a complexity in the "best interests of the child" standard that governs, *inter alia,* custody disputes between parents. In a situation in which both parents seek custody, each parent proceeds in possession, so to speak, of a constitutionally-protected fundamental parental right. Neither parent has a superior claim to the exercise of this right to provide "care, custody, and control" of the children. *See* Md. Code [Ann. Fam. Law] § 5–203(d)(2) [2004].[14] Effectively, then, each fit parent's constitutional right neutralizes the other parent's constitutional right, leaving, generally, the best interests of the child as the *sole standard* to apply to these types of custody decisions. Thus, in evaluating each parent's request for custody, the parents commence as presumptive equals and a trial court undertakes a balancing of each parent's relative merits to serve as the primary custodial parent; the child's best interests tips the scale in favor of an award of custody to one parent or the other.

Where the dispute is between a fit parent and a private third party, however, both parties do not begin on equal footing in respect to rights to "care, custody, and control" of the children. The parent is asserting a fundamental constitutional right. The third party is not. A private third party has no fundamental constitutional right to raise the children of others. Generally, absent a constitutional statute, the non-governmental third party has no rights, constitutional or otherwise, to raise someone else's child.

B. Best Interests of the Child in the Absence of Parental Unfitness and Extraordinary or Exceptional Circumstances

The arguments and outcome of the instant case in no way alter the "best interests of the child" standard that governs courts' assessments of disputes *between fit parents* involving visitation or custody. We have frequently and repeatedly emphasized that in situations where it applies, it is the central consideration. So critical is the best interests standard that it has garnered superlative language in the many cases in which the concept appears: This Court labeled it "of transcendent importance" in

---

[13] Every child might be "better" in a different situation in the opinion of one judge or another. The "best interest" standard is not a rule to be used to take children away from fit parents and give them to third parties because a judge believes the child will be better off with richer, better educated, more stable, third parties. If that were so, no parent would be safe from having his or her children given to others to raise. The phrase "best interests of the child" is not synonymous with "with whomever the child would be better off." Children are born into different circumstances. They are dealt different hands. The vast majority of them cope. Some from humble origins and upbringing even end up on state supreme courts. It is simply the way life is.

[14] Md. Code [Ann., Fam. Law] § 5–203(d)(2) [2004] states, "Neither parent is presumed to have any right to custody that is superior to the right of the other parent."

Dietrich v. Anderson, 43 A.2d 186, 191 (Md. 1945), as the "ultimate test" in *Fanning v. Warfield*, 248 A.2d 890, 894 (Md. 1969), and as the "controlling factor" in *In re Adoption/Guardianship No. 10941*, 642 A.2d 201, 208 (Md. 1994). Although the child's well-being remains the focus of a court's analysis in disputes between fit parents, "[t]he best interests standard does not ignore the interests of the parents and their importance to the child. We recognize that in almost all cases, it is in the best interests of the child to have reasonable maximum opportunity to develop a close and loving relationship with each parent." *Boswell v. Boswell*, 721 A.2d 662, 669 (Md. 1998).

C. Standards for Custody Determination

When considering the application of the "best interests of the child" standard it is essential to frame the different situations in which it is attempted to be applied. First, and certainly the most important application of the standard, is in disputes between fit natural parents, each of whom has equal constitutional rights to parent. In those cases the dispute can be resolved best if not solely, by an application of the "best interests of the child" standard. This situation most often arises in marriage dissolution issues between natural parents and it is necessary to resolve the matters of custody and visitation between two constitutionally equally qualified parents. * * *

The second most frequent situation in which that standard has been applied is, we believe, in the various types of state proceedings in which the states are injecting themselves into the parenting situation in the exercise of their generally recognized power to protect the child. * * *

[This case involves a third category], generically referred to as "third-party" custody disputes, *i.e.*, persons other than natural parents or the State attempting, directly or indirectly, to gain or maintain custody or visitation in respect to the children of natural parents. * * *

Even within the third party subset of custody actions there are further differences. Some states have conceptualized the idea of * * * third parties who have, in effect, become parents and thus, the case is considered according to the standards that apply between natural parents. This further reduces the number of pure third party cases. * * * In still other pure third party cases, in respect to the standard to be used, all parties seeking custody of children are designated as third parties. In that situation there are no constitutional rights involved (although in some cases constitutional claims are made using terms such as "psychological parent" and the like) and the "best interest" standard is generally applied. * * *

* * *

D. Holding

The best interests of the child standard is, axiomatically, of a different nature than a parent's fundamental constitutional right. Moreover, the best interests of the child standard in third party cases is not simply an adding of the "pluses" offered by one party over another. Were that so, any third party who offered a better neighborhood, better schooling, more financial capability, or more stability would consistently prevail in obtaining custody in spite of a fit natural parent's constitutional right to parent. Our case law does not allow for such a result that would dilute a parent's constitutional right to rear his or her child based merely upon such considerations. Quite simply, the non-constitutional best interests of the child standard, absent extraordinary (*i.e.*, exceptional) circumstances, does not override a parent's fundamental constitutional right to raise his or her child when the case is between a fit parent, to whom the fundamental parental right is inherent, and a third party who does not possess such constitutionally-protected parental rights. In cases *between fit natural parents* who both have the fundamental constitutional rights to parent, the best interests of the child will be the "ultimate, determinative factor." In respect to third party custody disputes, we shall adopt for Maryland, if we have not already done so, the majority position. In the balancing of court-created or statutorily-created "standards," such as "the best interest of the child" test, with fundamental constitutional rights, in private custody actions involving private third parties where the parents are fit, absent extraordinary (*i.e.*, exceptional) circumstances, the constitutional right is the ultimate determinative factor; and only if the parents are unfit or extraordinary circumstances exist is the "best interest of the child" test to be considered * * *.

E. Factors for a Finding of "Exceptional Circumstances"

* * *

* * *We stated in *Ross v. Hoffman*:

"The factors which emerge from our prior decisions which may be of probative value in determining the existence of exceptional circumstances include the [1] length of time the child has been away from the biological parent, [2] the age of the child when care was assumed by the third party, [3] the possible emotional effect on the child of a change of custody, [4] the period of time which elapsed before the parent sought to reclaim the child, [5] the nature and strength of the ties between the child and the third party custodian, [6] the intensity and genuineness of the parent's desire to have the child, [7] the stability and certainty as to the child's future in the custody of the parent."

[372 A.2d 582, 593 (1977)] (alterations added). * * *

The circuit court examined each of the *Hoffman* guidelines in turn, and, in its opinion, found Mr. McDermott's relationship with Patrick to be wanting, particularly in relation to his absences from the child's life while at sea. The circuit court presented the following summary in its September 2003 memorandum opinion, which stated, in relevant part:

* * *

6. *The intensity and genuineness of the parent's desire to have the child.* It is clear from Mr. McDermott's testimony that he feels that Patrick's interests are served by being in his custody, that his care and custody would be superior to any other family member, and that he has a genuine interest in raising Patrick. However, the court is unable to agree with the totality of Mr. McDermott's self-assessment. It has appeared at various time[s] during these proceedings that Mr. McDermott's interest in having custody of Patrick was not strictly limited to his desire to care for Patrick, but also his desire to control Ms. Dougherty, and that he has used Patrick as a pawn in the ongoing engagement between Ms. Dougherty and himself. * * *

7. *The stability and certainty as to the child's future in the custody of the parent.* Mr. McDermott was initially awarded custody in this case. For the most part, custody was changed first to Ms. Dougherty and then to the Doughertys because of Mr. McDermott's lengthy periods of absence from the State due to his employment as a merchant seaman. It would appear that Mr. McDermott's periodic absences and relinquishment of custody [have] had adverse effects on Patrick. For example, shortly after Ms. Dougherty's arrest and subsequent incarceration in early 2002, Mr. McDermott signed onto ship going to Africa and not expected to return until summer 2002. . . . It is self-evident that a revolving door of custodians would not be in Patrick's best interest, now or in the future."

We conclude that the circuit court inappropriately found that the absences inherent in Mr. McDermott's job requirements constituted "exceptional circumstances."

First, we note that, although the [circuit court] expressed some reservation as to Mr. McDermott's ability to provide a "consistent and stable environment for his child," it failed to find Mr. McDermott to be an unfit parent and it is presumed that fit parents act in the best interests of their children. * * *

Mr. McDermott's parental fitness having been established, or more precisely, not adjudged to be lacking, the inquiry, according to *Hoffman*, shifts to examining whether any "exceptional circumstances" exist that might overcome the presumption favoring a fit parent's rearing of his child * * *. It is in this latter phase of the inquiry that the circuit court erred by inappropriately equating "exceptional circumstances" with the absences occasioned by Mr. McDermott's merchant marine work. By finding that the dictates of Mr. McDermott's employment voided his right to be a custodial parent, the circuit court overlooked its own lack of a finding of unfitness and failed to accord petitioner with the presumptive benefits of a natural parent, especially a fit natural parent.

[T]his Court [has previously] explained the requisite showing to overcome the presumption that a child's best interests are served by the child's remaining in the custody of the parent:

> "Where parents claim the custody of a child, there is a *prima facie* presumption that the welfare will be best subserved in the care and custody of its parents rather than in the custody of others, and the burden is then cast upon the parties opposing them to show the contrary." * * *[44]

F.　Father's Employment in the Merchant Marine

Mr. McDermott is a graduate of the United States Merchant Marine Academy and a licensed ship Captain in the Merchant Marine. Many of his previous jobs have involved maritime work. Prior to his marriage he worked aboard ships but upon his marriage he ceased ocean-going and worked primarily in the Port of Baltimore. Following his divorce from Ms. Dougherty, petitioner accepted periodic jobs which took him to sea for several months at a time. Such is the nature of much maritime work, and the attendant required time commitments also are not uncommon in other lines of work including military deployments, ground transportation of goods, natural gas and oil production, offshore commercial fishing, sport fishing, etc.

Mr. McDermott's job duties do not involve work that is illegal, untoward, or otherwise injurious. Nor is there evidence in this case of any illegal conduct on his part. * * * This Court recognizes Maryland's tradition as a maritime State * * * and going to sea is but one of many occupations which require the worker to depart the State and absent himself or herself for months at a time. We would be loathe to reach a holding that jeopardizes a fit parent's right to custody of his child, by the change of custody to third parties, simply because the source of what is his livelihood and his means to support himself and his family takes him from the State for months' long periods of time.

---

[44] * * * Our courts over the years have found "exceptional circumstances" in awarding custody even to third parties, generally upon a parent's prolonged, non-work-related absence and the child's having been in the consistent care of a third party for a period of years. * * * *In the present case, the father's absences have not been computed in years' long periods, nor is there evidence that the child has failed to maintain bonds with him.* * * *

* * *

The absences inherent to Mr. McDermott's merchant marine work are not unlike those required of military personnel or others in occupations mandating periods of service away from one's home. Custody issues should be determined on a case-by-case basis. * * *

* * *

Although the Doughertys did not maintain Patrick in their home and raise the child from infancy, the relative regularity of their contribution as well as the positive contribution of all grandparents must be acknowledged. Nevertheless, their efforts on Patrick's behalf under the circumstances of this case cannot overcome the fundamental constitutional right of a fit parent to exercise care and custody of his child and the circuit court, clearly impressed with the grandparents' care, cannot invoke absences occasioned by the parent's proper employment in support of placing the child with the grandparents due to "exceptional circumstances."

* * *

III. Conclusion

In this case there is no doubt that Patrick loves his father and Mr. McDermott loves his son. Petitioner has maintained his relationship with his son since the child's birth, even when the child was not domiciled with him. The results of myriad examinations, reports and testimony were insufficient to convince the circuit court that Mr. McDermott was an unfit parent, and clearly, Mr. McDermott's vigorous use of the family courts provides insight on his desire to have custody of Patrick. Courts cannot preempt the established and constitutionally-protected fundamental rights of a parent, who is not "unfit," simply because that parent's job takes him from the State for extended periods of time or merely because a child might be better off, in a particular judge's view, living elsewhere. The circuit court erred in invoking the dictates of Mr. McDermott's work as a merchant marine, insofar as the requirements of the job caused him to be absent from the state for several months-long periods of time, and arriving at the conclusion that application of the guidelines for "exceptional circumstances" warranted placing Patrick in the custody of his maternal grandparents.

We reverse the judgment of the Court of Special Appeals and remand to that court with instructions to reverse the decision of the circuit court. The case is ordered remanded to the circuit court in order for it to address the issue of counsel fees. All costs to be paid by respondents.[49]

---

[49] * * * The Court has gone to great lengths to affirm that the present opinion is limited to the context of attempts by pure third parties to gain custody over the children of others. * * *

Judgment of the court of special appeals reversed. Case remanded to that court * * *.

WILNER, J. concurs.

I concur in the judgment because it is clear to me that, under the standards that this Court has consistently applied since *Ross v. Hoffman*, 372 A.2d 582 (1977), the trial court erred in granting custody of Patrick to the Doughertys. [I]t is not clear to me what the Court has really done in its 113-page slip opinion, other than to sow uncertainty and confusion in an area that demands clear and accessible guidelines.

In *Ross*, this Court, synthesizing earlier decisions, laid out a very clear standard for resolving custody disputes between a parent and a non-parent. We said:

> "* * * When the dispute is between a biological parent and a third party, it is presumed that the child's best interest is subserved by custody in the parent. That presumption is overcome and such custody will be denied if (a) the parent is unfit to have custody, or (b) if there are such exceptional circumstances as [to] make such custody detrimental to the best interest of the child."

Id. at 587.

We recognized in *Ross* that parents "have the natural right to the custody of their children," but regarded the strong presumption in favor of such custody as sufficient to protect that right. We made clear that "the ordinary entitlement of parents to the custody of their minor children" was not absolute and that it "would not be enforced inexorably, contrary to the best interest of the child, on the theory of an absolute legal right."

* * *

Only two years ago, in *Shurupoff v. Vockroth*, * * * we consciously and clearly confirmed what we said and held in *Ross*: "The court must always, necessarily, inquire into what is in the child's best interest, *for that is the ultimate, determinative factor*." [814 A.2d 543, 557 (2003)] (emphasis added). * * *

The Court today, in a 113-page slip opinion suggests, with its right hand, that the best interest of the child standard no longer applies in disputes between a parent and a non-parent—that the parent's Constitutional right to custody is predominant—but, with its left hand, seems to indicate that that is not the case at all, and that, in the end, courts must act in the child's best interest. Why the Court chooses to take such an unnecessarily convoluted path is a mystery to me.

* * *

In the end, even under the Court's new approach, the trial court will have to apply the best interest standard. The Court agrees that a parent's Constitutional right to raise his/her children is not absolute. It agrees that custody may be denied to a parent if the evidence shows that the parent is unfit, and it even continues to bless the alternative basis for denying parental custody—exceptional circumstances *which would made* [sic] *parental custody detrimental to the child's best interest.* That will necessarily require the court to examine and be governed by what is in the child's best interest. So why go through 113 pages of convolution to say, in the end, what has already been said, confirmed, and reconfirmed in a few clear simple paragraphs?

NOTES AND QUESTIONS

1.   *Patrick McDermott.* Patrick McDermott was ten years old when the case reached the Court of Appeals, Maryland's highest court. Does the court give any indication that the trial court ever asked the boy what custodial arrangement he preferred? Should it have done so? What do you think the result in *McDermott* would have been if the father testified that he planned to take Patrick with him for months while he was aboard ship, thereby causing the boy to miss school? Who would likely have received custody if Patrick's mother had been a fit custodian? Why?

2.   *The risks of asking for help.* A custodial parent may find it impossible to provide adequately for a child for some period of time for many reasons, including illness, financial instability, or military service. Under *Meyer* and *Pierce*, parents have a presumptive right to custody of their children, but they may forfeit this right through their actions, no matter how fit they may be in other respects. Decisions turn on the facts. For example, a parent may relinquish the parental presumption of custody if he leaves his children in the temporary custody of a third party for too long or if a court construes his behavior as desertion. *Vaughn v. Davis*, 36 So.3d 1261 (Miss. 2010). How long is too long?

Parents in distress may choose to place their children temporarily with a relative or friend on the condition that they will regain custody once their problems have been resolved. If the temporary custodian bonds with the child, or comes to view the parent as unfit, however, the custodian may turn around and seek a judicial determination of custody, as the grandparents did in *McDermott*.

Courts consider many factors in determining whether a parent may regain custody of a child once relinquished for temporary informal care. In New York, for example, the factors include how long "the children has lived with the nonparent, the quality of that relationship and the length of time the biological parent allowed such custody to continue without trying to assume the primary parental role." *Heather U. v. Janice V.*, 57 N.Y.S.3d 762, 765 (3d Dep't 2017).

3. *Distinguishing the nature of child custody disputes. McDermott* distinguishes among at least three kinds of child custody disputes: (1) disputes between two legal parents, (2) disputes between one or two parents on the one hand, and a third party on the other (the situation in *McDermott* itself), and (3) disputes in which the state challenges parental custody based on alleged abuse or neglect. What difference do these distinctions make in determining the standards the court applies and the strength of the parents' constitutional rights?

In what appears to be a case of first impression, the Supreme Court of Alaska rejected constitutional claims that an indigent parent should have a right to appointed counsel in a custody dispute between parents in which the other parent had retained counsel. *Dennis O. v. Stephanie O.*, 393 P.3d 401 (Alaska 2017). Pointing to the distinctions among the categories of custody disputes, the court reasoned that private custody disputes "do not threaten termination of parental rights." It distinguished three categories of custody cases in which Alaska is required to provide representation to indigent parents: (1) where the other parent in a private custody dispute is represented by a state agency; (2) in an action brought by the state to terminate parental rights; and (3) in nonconsensual adoption proceedings that could lead to termination of parental rights. The court held that the liberty interest at stake in a dispute between two parents did not reach "the magnitude" of the risk of termination of parental rights, that the risk of error was reduced by the various support systems in place for pro se litigants, and that the government had numerous countervailing interests, included avoiding the high cost of providing counsel and the risk that appointing counsel would encourage and prolong litigation. (Applying the factors set forth in *Matthews v. Eldridge*, 424 U.S. 319 (1976) for use in challenges to state actions that deprive citizens of liberty interests). While rejecting a categorical right to counsel where one party in a custody dispute was unrepresented and the other had a lawyer, the court entertained the possibility that some individuals could show that they would be prejudiced unless the court appointed counsel for them (e.g., a person with disabilities or a parent unable to attend the hearing).

4. *Is child custody a zero-sum game?* Is it possible to weigh each parent's constitutional interest in his or her child equally, and at the same time make each child's best interests paramount to the custody decision? What are the obstacles to balancing each of these concerns with the others?

5. *What are "exceptional circumstances"? McDermott* states the majority rule, which protects the rights of fit parents to custody of their children in contests against third parties. Absent allegations of neglect or abuse, courts rarely find "exceptional circumstances" sufficient to deny custody to a biological or adoptive parent. *Burak v. Burak*, 168 A.3d 883 (Md. 2017) (surveying cases and reversing award of custody to grandparent/intervenors in custody dispute between biological parents). In *Burak v. Burak* a Maryland appellate court listed factors for determining whether a parent is "unfit" in the context of a third party suit for custody based on exceptional circumstances,

including neglect, abandonment and detrimental impact on the child and held that the listed factors are "not the exclusive criteria."

In one of the rare decisions to recognize exceptional circumstances a New York court found that exceptional circumstances warranted awarding custody to the boyfriend of a recently deceased custodial mother instead of the relatively uninvolved father. The boyfriend—who had fathered the two half-siblings who resided with the boy and his mother—had "fostered a close relationship" with the boy over several years, and the siblings were close. The father's visitation rights continued. *Pettaway v. Savage*, 928 N.Y.S.2d 869, 870 (N.Y. App. Div. 2011).

In 2015 another New York court upheld an award of custody to a grandmother, where a four-year-old boy with severe developmental delays requiring special education had lived with his grandmother most of his life, the grandmother was a special education teacher, both parents had substance abuse problems, the mother was incarcerated, and the father, who was on parole, downplayed the boy's learning issues and was unlikely to engage the mother or grandmother in the child's care. *Curless v. McLarney*, 4 N.Y.S.3d 666 (App. Div.2015).

What other circumstances do you think courts should consider as "exceptional"?

6. *Competing policy grounds.* A number of competing policy considerations are at stake in a case like *McDermott*. Society may generally want to encourage parents to rely on extended family in times of crisis without jeopardizing their parental rights. Therefore, it may be disconcerting that the grandparents refused to return Patrick when asked, and thus accomplished their goal of entrenching him even further in their household while the litigation progressed. How should the courts weigh such concerns against the needs of a particular child whose fate is being determined in a custody dispute? Should a third party ever be able to defeat a fit legal parent's custody claim?

7. *Special protections for parents on active military duty.* Some courts are less solicitous of the sacrifices made by members of the nation's armed services than the *McDermott* court. Lacking a legislative definition of "temporary" relinquishment of custody, the highest court in Alaska reached a different conclusion than the *McDermott* court. Affirming a grant of physical custody to the mother, the Alaska Supreme Court concluded that a father's deployment, which resulted in his absence for a third of each year, was more than "temporary." *Rosenblum v. Perales*, 303 P.3d 500, 506 (Alaska 2013) (holding that "regular deployments of up to four months of every year for the indefinite future are not 'temporary' because they are not 'continuing for a limited time'; it is also reasonable to conclude that the disruption this schedule would cause to [the child] is more than a 'temporary disruption' "). Is military service overseas unique? How might such cases be distinguishable from *McDermott*?

The Service Members Civil Relief Act (SCRA), first adopted in 1940, provides that civil actions that "may adversely affect" service members on active duty shall be temporarily suspended. 50 App. U.S.C.A. § 3902 (Supp. V 2017). The Act protects military personnel so that they will not be disadvantaged while serving their country. Although the highest concentration of cases involving military personnel concern "paternity, divorce and post-divorce" issues, neither the 1940 Act, amendments to it, nor a comprehensive redrafting in 2003 addressed family law issues specifically. Kristen M.H. Coyne et al., *The SCRA and Family Law: More Than Just Stays and Delays*, 43 Fam. L.Q. 315, 315–16 (2009). Aware that deployment can lead to temporary or permanent loss of custody, in 2008 Congress clarified that the procedural protections of the SCRA (including appointment of counsel and the right to suspension of the hearing) apply to child custody disputes. *Id.* at 323. Such stays, however, become discretionary after the person has been deployed for more than 90 days, and observers report that judges commonly decline to extend the stay because the child's need for a decision seems more important. Uniform Law Commission, Deployed Parent Custody and Visitation Act Summary (2014).

Every state and the District of Columbia has enacted a statute designed to address the custody issues that arise when one parent is deployed, but the statutes vary greatly in what they cover and how they resolve the issues. As a result, the Uniform Law Commissioners (ULC) promulgated a Uniform Deployed Parents Custody and Visitation Act in 2013 which provides that parents can make private arrangements to cover the period of deployment, requires expedited hearings for parents who cannot negotiate temporary terms, and establishes a procedure for ending temporary custody upon the deployed parent's return if the parents require court intervention. As of 2018, at least ten states had enacted the Uniform Deployed Parents Custody and Visitation Act; several other states had introduced or enacted similar legislation supporting the custody rights of deployed parents. National Conference of State Legislatures, *Military Parent Custody and Visitation* (April 18, 2017). http://www.ncsl.org/research/military-and-veterans-affaris/military-parent-custody-and-visitation.aspx.

Substantive questions remain open in many jurisdictions, however, including whether a custodial parent may assign a third party to take care of her child while she is on active duty without facing a challenge from the child's other parent, and whether a temporary order granting custody to the parent who does not normally have custody should—or will—necessarily be rescinded when the service member returns from active duty. Should the sacrifices made by service members outweigh changes in the child's emotional attachments that may have taken place while the service member was overseas? Should the rights of the two parents continue to stand in equipoise after one of them has served her country in battle?

3. EVOLUTION OF STANDARDS GOVERNING CHILD CUSTODY

During the colonial period and the early republic, American jurisdictions followed English common law, which gave fathers absolute control of their children according to the doctrine of *pater familias*, a concept rooted in Roman law, which made the father "master" of the family, with authority over its members. Judges sometimes deviated from the rule, but their primary task was to determine whether a specific situation required deviation. By the 1820s, however, pressure from women's groups led courts to shift their focus and consider whether mothers should be treated equally, or even receive preferential treatment. *See* Michael Grossberg, Governing the Hearth: Law and the Family in Nineteenth Century America 244–47 (1985). By the middle of the twentieth century, as divorce rates began to rise, mothers became the sole or primary custodians in the vast majority of cases. More recently, fathers have demanded to be on equal footing with mothers in custody disputes, and acceptance of shared parenting has become widespread.

This Section discusses the four major standards that have been applied to child custody decisions: (1) the largely defunct tender years doctrine that relied expressly on gender; (2) the best interests of the child; and (3) the psychological parent doctrine; and (4) the ALI's approximation standard, designed to "approximate" the share of parenting that existed before separation, related to the developing view that courts don't need to choose one parent over the other as a sole custodian.

A. THE TENDER YEARS DOCTRINE

When fathers no longer automatically received custody, and courts began to hear disputes between mothers and fathers a number of presumptions developed to guide decisions. By the late nineteenth century, one rule, that emerged as a new orthodoxy was that children of "tender years"—that is, infants and very young children—should be placed with their mother, unless she was unfit to care for them.

The doctrine expressly rested on gender stereotyping. During the first few years of life, it was thought, children of either sex belonged with their mothers. After that, girls belonged with mothers, boys with fathers. Beginning in the 1970s and accelerating during the 1980s, state courts held that the tender years doctrine violated emerging constitutional law concerning gender equality (which you read about in Chapter 3). *See* Lynne Marie Kohm, *Tracing the Foundation of the Best Interests of the Child Standard in American Jurisprudence*, 10 J.L. & Fam. Stud. 337 (2008).

In 1973, New York's highest court held that the doctrine was inconsistent with recent statutory amendments providing that "there shall be no *prima facie* right to the custody of the child in either parent," and that the doctrine did not serve the modern determinative statutory standard—the best interests of the child. *Watts v. Watts*, 350 N.Y.S.2d 285, 287 (Fam. Ct. 1973). *Watts* held that a persistent preference for mothers—revealed in the facts of the case before it, and in data showing that "in well over ninety percent of the cases adjudicated, the mother is awarded custody"—violated fathers' rights to equal treatment under the law. *Id*. at 286. The court concluded that the tender years presumption was "based on outdated social stereotypes rather than rational and up-to-date consideration of the welfare of the children involved." *Id*. at 287. On remand, the family court awarded custody to the father. *Watts'* constitutional underpinnings came from *Frontiero v. Richardson*, 411 U.S. 677 (1973), and other decisions on gender discrimination discussed in Chapter 3 of this book.

Today, all 50 states have rejected the tender years doctrine. Julie E. Artis, *Judging the Best Interests of the Child: Judges' Accounts of the Tender Years Doctrine*, 38 Law & Soc'y Rev. 769, 774 (2004). However, some theorists, judges, and lawyers continue to believe that mothers are more important than fathers in the early stages of child development. Some trial courts expressly continue to apply the tender years doctrine and may be reversed for doing so. *See Johnson v. Adair*, 884 So.2d 1169, 1171 (Fla. Dist. Ct. App. 2004) (holding that the trial court's grant of custody to mother "based on the [tender] age of the child" was contrary to statutes designed "to override the court's persistence in applying this doctrine").

The doctrine survives in modified form in a distinct minority of jurisdictions. In Mississippi the tender years doctrine continues to serve as one of many factors in child custody determinations. *McCarty v. McCarty*, 52 So. 3d 1221, 1228 (Miss. Ct. App. 2011) (treating the tender years doctrine as a presumption that can be rebutted by other factors, but observing that it does not apply to seven-year-olds and is weaker for male children than for girls of tender years).

B. THE BEST INTERESTS OF THE CHILD

By the beginning of the nineteenth century, the presumption favoring fathers began to yield to the rights of mothers and some courts began to balance the rights of both parents. Initially, courts were likely to find the father's presumptive rights rebutted only where they found him egregiously immoral—where, for example, they found evidence of adultery, alcoholism or spousal abuse. By the 1830s and 1840s, some states had enacted legislation that authorized courts to determine child custody on a case-by-case basis, placing the mother and father on an equal footing because " 'the happiness and welfare of the child are to determine its care and custody.' " Michael Grossberg, *Governing the Hearth*, *supra*, at 241 (quoting a Massachusetts statute enacted in the 1840s). This approach came to be known as "the best interests of the child."

Courts and legislatures have long used the term "best interests of the child" to describe the standard that should govern child custody decisions. Most of the cases you will read in this Chapter examine aspects of the best interests approach and the factors that come into play in the best interests analysis. As you read, bear in mind that many observers have asked whether the best interests approach is a standard or a euphemism for unfettered judicial discretion.

Although the best interests standard abandoned the express presumptions about gender that were the basis of the tender years doctrine, gender norms continued to play a role in many discussions of best interests. The persistence of gender norms is seen, for example, in some judicial opinions about parental disputes regarding children's names.

The choice of name is an important decision that reflects many aspects of identity. Traditionally, children of married parents received their father's surname, and some children of unmarried parents did too. Today, in most jurisdictions, both married and unmarried parents may elect to give their child either parent's surname or a hyphenated name, and in some jurisdictions, any surname they choose.

But courts may be called upon to determine a child's name when unmarried parents cannot agree, or married parents divorce and one of them petitions to change the child's name. In these circumstances, most jurisdictions expressly apply the best interests of the child analysis to the choice of name. *Emma v. Evans*, 71 A.3d 862 (N.J. 2013). The adoption of this standard for naming disputes—as for custody decisions—was intended to end gendered and "paternalistic preferences" associated with tradition and reflecting considerations resembling those at play in the tender years doctrine. *Id.* at 868. *See also In re H.S.B.*, 401 S.W.3d 77 (Tex. App. 2011*)*. And, because mothers are so much more likely than fathers to have primary custody of children, in 2013 New Jersey's highest court announced that principles of gender equality required it to abandon an older approach that had presumed the custodial parent's choice of surname should govern—in this instance putting fathers on an equal footing with mothers. *Emma v. Evans*, 71 A.3d at 876. In the context of a dispute over changing a name that both parents agreed to when the child was born, the best interest approach requires consideration of the child's own interests, including potential anxiety, embarrassment, and confusion stemming either from having a different name than the custodial parent and siblings, or from changing a name the child has had for many years. *Id.*

A minority of jurisdictions continue to honor tradition. In 2013 West Virginia's highest court overturned an order providing a hyphenated surname name composed of both parents' surnames to a nonmarital child. *In re Name Change of Jenna A. J.*, 744 S.E.2d 269 (W. Va. 2013). The court held that the mother had not presented clear and convincing evidence that the change would be in the child's best interests as West Virginia requires when depriving a child of the father's surname. A dissenting justice rebuked the court, saying "our precedents are outmoded and completely unmoored from what should be the focus in these cases: the best interests of the child, taking into account the realities of the child's living circumstances." *Id.* at 274 (Workman, J., dissenting).

C. THE PSYCHOLOGICAL PARENT AND THE ROLE OF EXPERTS

The principle that the psychological parent should have physical custody of the child has played an important role in child custody decisions since the 1970s. The primary caretaker (the person who performs the bulk of the day-to-day child care) will usually also be the psychological parent— the adult who the child regards as an emotional anchor. This approach stems from an effort to apply psychoanalytic principles and expertise in child development to the legal issues surrounding child custody. The "psychological parent" concept was developed by Joseph Goldstein, Anna Freud and Albert Solnit, three child psychoanalysts, one of whom (Goldstein) was also a lawyer. More than a thousand child custody decisions have cited their writings.

Goldstein, Freud and Solnit—along with many other scholars and practitioners—criticized the "best interests of the child" standard for failing to provide sufficient guidance to courts, failing to achieve certainty of outcome, and failing to ensure that the child's needs remained in the forefront of the decisionmaking process. They drew on the psychological literature of "attachment theory," which emerged from studies of young children separated from their parents during the World War II bombing of England. Family law scholar Lee Teitelbaum discussed the importance of child psychology to best interests decisions in the United States: "Judicial acceptance of the importance of continuity in child-raising, most famously (although not originally) set out in Goldstein, Freud, and Solnit's *Beyond the Best Interests of the Child*, has powerfully affected custodial practices in this country and abroad. * * * The weight given to continuity is found * * * in the widespread use of a presumption favoring custody in the parent who was the primary care giver before divorce." Lee E. Teitelbaum, *Rays of Light: Other Disciplines and Family Law*, 1 J.L. & Fam. Stud. 1, 2 (1999).

Goldstein, Freud and Solnit placed the child's needs and perceptions at the heart of the custody decisions. Their work on custody emphasized four foundational principles:

    1.   The psychological parent model, which they acknowledged was difficult to define;

    2.   The child's need for continuity of "relationships, surrounding and environmental influence";

3.   Emphasis on the child's sense of time, characterized by urgency and the need for quick resolution of legal disputes; and

4.   Because of the limits of law as a predictor of future behavior and development, replacing the "best interests" standard with "the least detrimental alternative"—the "specific placement and procedure for placement which maximizes, in accord with the child's sense of time and on the basis of short-term predictions given the limitations of knowledge, his or her opportunity for being wanted and for maintaining on a continuous basis a relationship with at least one adult who is * * * his psychological parent."

Joseph Goldstein, Anna Freud & Albert J. Solnit, Beyond the Best Interests of the Child 53 (1973).

Attachment theory studies show how early interactions between children and parents affect the child's long-term sense of security and well-being. At the time Goldstein, Freud and Solnit wrote, attachment theory focused almost entirely on bonds between mothers and young children, largely ignoring both relationships between children and fathers and the adjustments that occur as children mature. Social changes in family structure, and fathers' increasingly visible claims in the context of custody disputes, have led to criticisms of the model Goldstein et al. developed for evaluating custody battles, but the basic principles set forth above remain influential. (Their work remains much more uniformly accepted in the context of the child welfare and foster care systems, where they cautioned against excessive intervention in families and argued that state intervention could itself be harmful.)

An increased focus on the child's needs and perceptions—whether to identify a psychological parent or evaluate best interests—led to increased reliance on testimony from experts in fields such as psychology, psychiatry, and social work. In the events leading up to *McDermott v. Dougherty*, for example, the trial court heard testimony from experts during the divorce proceedings regarding both parents' fitness. You will see many references to similar expert testimony as you read the cases in this Chapter and the next one.

Anna Freud (Sigmund Freud's daughter and a leading scholar of attachment theory) applied these principles in discussing the Iowa Supreme Court's 1966 decision in *Painter v. Bannister*—a case that resembled *McDermott. Painter v. Bannister,* 140 N.W.2d 152 (Iowa 1966). *Painter* involved a custody dispute between grandparents and their son-in-law who had asked his in-laws to temporarily take care of the couple's five-year-old son, Mark, after his wife died in a car accident. When the father sought Mark's return, the grandparents refused to turn the boy over to his father, who then sought a writ of habeas corpus.

The trial court in *Painter* heard expert testimony from "an eminent child psychologist" who had known the grandparents for a long time, and who interviewed Mark and his grandparents, but never met the father. *Id.* at 156–57. Although the expert testified that he thought the grandparents would provide a more stable home and that the grandfather functioned as a "father figure" to Mark, the trial judge ordered that Mark return to his father. *Id.* at 157.

The state Supreme Court reversed, and ordered that Mark stay with his grandparents, in whose home he had remained during the appeals process. The Supreme Court proclaimed its reliance on the psychologist's expert testimony. It denied that it was influenced by the "highly contrasting backgrounds" and homes of the parties: the grandparents and all of their children graduated from college, and they offered Mark "a stable, dependable, conventional, middle-class, middlewest" upbringing, while the father, who held a G.E.D., had a sporadic employment history, and a "Bohemian approach . . . to life." *Id.* at 154.

Dr. Freud used the *Painter* facts to highlight the differences between legal and clinical approaches to child custody decisions following divorce, discussing what she would have done had she been asked to consult on the case. She explained that a clinical resolution of custody differs from a court's imposition of a legal solution on the parties to a child custody dispute and argued for a very different kind of expert consultation than the one the court received in *Painter*. Unlike courts, she wrote, psychoanalysts "are in the lucky position not to have to pronounce judgment. [Psychoanalysts] merely formulate advice." Psychoanalysts and other trained mental health professionals often take a very different view than courts about what facts are significant and even about what the facts signify. Anna Freud, *Painter v. Bannister: Postscript by a Psychoanalyst*, in 7 Writings of Anna Freud 247–55 (1967).

Dr. Freud explained that unlike the trial judge, she would "discount the importance of the 'biological father' ":

> The 'blood-ties' between parent and child as well as the alleged paternal and maternal 'instincts' are biological concepts which, only too often, prove vague and unreliable when transferred to the field of psychology. Psychologically speaking, the child's 'father' is the adult man to whom the child attaches a particular, psychologically distinctive set of feelings. When this type of emotional tie is disrupted, the child's feelings suffer. When such separations occur during phases of development in which the child is particularly vulnerable, the whole foundation of his personality may be shaken. The presence of or the reunion with a biological father to whom no such ties exist will not recompense the child for the loss which he has suffered. Conversely, the biological father's

or mother's unselfish love for their child is by no means to be taken for granted. It happens often enough that biological parents fail in their duty to the child, while other adults who are less closely related to him, i.e., who have no 'instinctive' basis for their feeling, successfully take over the parental role.

Id.

Equally important, psychoanalysts are less impressed than some courts with "benefits such as a 'stable, dependable background' with educational and professional opportunities," which weighed heavily in the *Painter* court's decision to leave Mark with his grandparents. Important as such external advantages are, [psychoanalysts] have seen too often that they can be wasted unless they are accompanied by the internal emotional constellations which enable the children to profit from them. Children are known to thrive in socially and financially unstable situations if they are firmly attached to their parents, and to come to grief under the best social conditions when such emotional security is missing." *Id.*

Dr. Freud explained that she could not anticipate what opinion she would give if she had the opportunity to interview all of the family members. "We shall advise that Mark had better stay with his grandparents provided that the following facts be ascertained: that the transfer of his attachment from the parents to the grandparents is fairly complete and promises to be permanent during his childhood; that, given this attachment, a further change is not advisable; and that the grandparents, on their part, cherish Mark for his own sake, not only as a replacement for the daughter who was killed, nor as a pawn in the battle with their son-in-law." On the other hand, if the interviews revealed that "Mr. Painter still retains his place as 'father' in Mark's mind and that in spite of separation and new experiences the child's feelings and fantasies continue to revolve around him; that anger about the 'desertion' (and perhaps blame for his mother's death) have not succeeded in turning this relationship into a predominantly hostile one; that the father cherishes Mark for his own sake * * *" she would recommend that the court return Mark to his father's care. *Id.*

A high-quality child custody consultation is extremely intensive. Freud and her co-authors never offered an opinion in a custody evaluation unless they (or a member of their team) had interviewed each of the potential custodial figures alone, each of them with the child or children, and the child without the adults. The best practices for court-ordered custody evaluations still call for interviews with each parent alone, and each parent together with the child or children. The evaluator should also initially see the siblings together and then, if warranted, separately. Even young children can be interviewed alone if the interviewer relies on correct techniques, such as using dollhouses and dolls, or drawing a family portrait. Stephen P. Herman, *Child Custody Evaluations and the Need for Standards of Care and Peer Review*, 1 J. Center for Child. & Cts. 139, 142 (1999). "Collateral interviews" may also be conducted with other family members, and with other people who know the family well, including teachers. *Id.* at 141. With the parents' permission, the clinician can examine school and other records pertaining to the child. Finally, the evaluator must write a clear, accessible and comprehensive report to the court explaining the reasoning behind each conclusion. *Id.* at 144.

The psychological parent and best interests approaches to custody frequently require lawyers and judges to consider a range of issues beyond their legal expertise, much as might happen in complex products liability or antitrust cases. Several issues arise about the use of experts in child custody cases, including the conditions of the expert's appointment, the best methods for evaluating the child's needs and relationships, and the weight the court should accord to the expert's opinion. *See* Janet M. Bowermaster, *Legal Presumptions and the Role of Mental Health Professionals in Child Custody Proceedings*, 40 Duq. L. Rev. 265 (2002).

A leader in forensic child psychiatry has stated "it is an egregious error for a clinician to be selected by one party, to perform a one-sided evaluation, or to offer an opinion based on interviews with only one of the parties." He cautions that "mental health professionals performing child custody evaluations should do so only if they have been court appointed or agreed to by all sides." Herman, *supra,* at 141. Today, the literature on expert witnesses generally "assumes the evaluator is a court-appointed neutral with access to both parties and all of the involved children." Milfred D. & Jonathan W. Gould, *Science, Mental Health Consultants, and Attorney-Expert Relationships in Child Custody*, 48 Fam. L.Q. 1, 4 (2014).

The properly-trained expert is able to assess the interactions among the family members in the light of "the theoretical literature and empirical research on families, child development, parenting and divorce" which they "must reliably apply . . . to the facts of the case." Robert A. Simon & Philip M. Stahl, *Analysis in Child-Custody-Evaluation Reports: A Crucial Component*, 48 Fam. L.Q. 35, 36 (2014). Unfortunately, all experts are not equally well-trained, adept or neutral. They need to keep up with the empirical literature, ground recommendations in facts, and be prepared to defend their reports in what one scholar calls an "increasingly demanding forensic setting." Kelly,*supra* at 49. A New York court lambasted a psychologist who agreed to serve as both the child's therapist and the mother's paid expert witness after several therapists refused to perform both roles, and then delivered what the judge labeled "result-oriented" testimony. John Caher, *Judge Finds Mother 'Cannot Be Trusted' With Custody of Son*, N.Y.L.J., Nov. 12, 2014 at 1, 6.

Still, some scholars argue that the family courts are not demanding enough, and too quickly yield to the temptation to defer to the expert's recommendation. Elizabeth Scott & Robert E. Emery, *Gender Politics and Child Custody: The Puzzling Persistence of the Best-Interests Standard*, 77 Law & Contemp. Probs. 69, 93–95 (2014).

NOTES AND QUESTIONS

1. *Guidelines for conducting custody evaluations.* Several professional guidelines apply to psychiatrists and psychologists who conduct child custody evaluations, which involve specialized skills. Most experts urge that the principles of confidentiality and protecting the patient from harm caution against a treating therapist serving as a forensic consultant about the patient, but other experts have argued that the treating therapist knows more about the family than a consultant who has just arrived on the scene. *Compare* Herman, *supra,* at 145, *with* Jean Koh Peters, Representing Children in Child Protective Proceedings: Ethical and Practical Dimensions 592–94 (3d ed. 2007).

Even if best practices are followed, do any risks accompany a decision to involve the children in their parents' custody dispute by evaluating them? How should lawyers discuss these risks with their clients?

2. *Primary caretaker factors—West Virginia.* West Virginia expressly adopted the primary caretaker approach in *Garska v. McCoy*, 278 S.E.2d 357 (W. Va. 1981), which reversed an order that had granted custody to a parent who had visited the child only briefly on a few occasions. *Garska* defined a primary caretaker (presumably entitled to custody) as the "parent who, until the initiation of divorce proceedings, has been primarily responsible for the caring and nurturing of the child." *Id.* at 358. Although West Virginia has since abandoned the primary caretaker approach as being dispositive, the concrete factors set out in *Garska* to guide lower courts remain helpful. The state's highest court offered this nonexclusive list of caring and nurturing duties that would help determine which parent had been the child's "primary caretaker":

(1) preparing and planning of meals;

(2) bathing, grooming, and dressing;

(3) purchasing, cleaning, and care of clothes;

(4) medical care * * *;

(5) arranging for social interaction among peers * * *;

(6) arranging * * * babysitting, daycare, etc.;

(7) putting child to bed at night * * *;

(8) disciplining * * *;

(9) educating, i.e. religious, cultural, social, etc.; and

(10) teaching elementary skills, i.e., reading, writing and arithmetic.

Id. at 363.

Garska also noted that parents might use custody improperly "as a coercive weapon" in divorce proceedings, that determining the relative fitness of two equally suited parents can be a near-impossible judicial task, and that the law needs a clear standard that couples can rely upon when negotiating a settlement. Effective in 2000, West Virginia adopted the pertinent custody provisions of the then-draft ALI Principles of Family Dissolution, discussed below at page 808. The current statute continues to scrutinize each parent's history as a caretaker, but favors shared parenting responsibilities rather than designating one parent as the primary caretaker. *See* W. Va. Code Ann. § 48–1–210 (LexisNexis 2015).

3.   *How to identify the primary caretaker.* The question of which parent is the primary caretaker is frequently litigated. If one parent is a homemaker and the other works for wages outside the home, is remunerative work outside the home a form of caretaking? In families with such arrangements, does the primary caretaker presumption resurrect the overtly gender-based tender years presumption by favoring the homemaker, usually the woman? Does the primary caretaker presumption work best when the parents' individual relationships with the children are so clearly different that no presumption is needed?

4.   *Current approaches to the primary caretaker presumption.* No state today expressly follows a primary caretaker presumption, but several states consider primary caretaking as a factor in child custody determinations. *See, e.g.,* Michigan Child Custody Act of 1970, Mich. Comp. Laws Ann. § 722.23 (West Supp. 2018) (*infra* at page 804).

The highest court in North Dakota, which had earlier concisely explained that parent-child ties are "not about which parent fixes the most meals or washes the most clothes [but] about bonding," in 2012 reiterated that although the state's custody statute did not use the term "primary caretaker," the concept " 'inheres in the statutory factors' and deserves recognition." *Schmidt v. Schmidt,* 660 N.W.2d 196, 200 (N.D. 2003); *Deyle v. Deyle,* 825 N.W.2d 245, 254 (N.D. 2012). The statute's enumerated factors, "if properly construed," the court held, "go to the overriding importance of the stability, continuity, and permanence embodied in a primary caretaker's relationship with the children." *Id.* Stability and continuity are key elements in determining psychological parenthood.

5.   *Stasis or dynamism?* Professor Teitelbaum warned of the dangers of regarding past as prologue in human relationships:

> Divorced mothers commonly must find new or increased employment; fathers usually have greater financial resources, and remarriage by the father may make available care in the home. Likely his new wife would remain at home to care for her stepchild. Although these circumstances seem relevant on their face to custodial decisions,

none—perhaps for policy as well as practical reasons has been explored. * * *

Lee E. Teitelbaum, *Rays of Light: Other Disciplines and Family Law*, 1 J.L. & Fam. Stud. 1, 10 (1999).

6.   *Only one psychological parent?* Professor Jean Koh Peters concludes that:

> [The] Goldstein, Freud, and Solnit psychological parenting model has captured the discourse and in many ways deepened lawyers' basic understanding of child developmental needs. The model has exhorted children's lawyers to treat time as precious and to put their client's interests first.

Jean Koh Peters, *supra*, 613–14.

She and others, however, have criticized Goldstein, Freud and Solnit for insisting that each child only has one "psychological parent." Goldstein et al. argued that the psychological parent should have sole decisionmaking power, including authority to protect children from any relationships to which the parent objected, including visits by the other parent. They also insisted that the child does not need an independent voice in custody hearings because the primary caretaker adequately represents the child's interests. Those views have been largely discredited, as you will see later in this Chapter.

PROBLEM 12-1

You are a law professor serving on a drafting committee for an interdisciplinary national panel charged with resolving the question:

> Where the best interests of the child clearly point to one outcome in a custody case, and the rights of the parent or parents point toward a different solution, how should judges resolve the conflict?

The committee hears conflicting testimony. Mental health professionals urge that "when a child's best interests conflict with fairness for the interested adults, the child's best interests shall be paramount." Albert J. Solnit et al., When Home Is No Haven: Child Placement Issues 12 (1992). A sitting appellate judge testifies that "while psychiatric considerations may very well be important, they must not be made determinative * * * because often times 'psychiatry and the law are not co-extensive.' " *T.B. v. L.R.M.*, 874 A.2d 34, 38 (Pa. Super. Ct. 2005).

You are asked to summarize the considerations that lawyers must weigh in determining the answer to the question the committee is charged with answering. Based on what you have read so far in this Chapter, what would you say?

D. CONTEMPORARY INTERPRETATIONS OF THE BEST INTERESTS OF THE CHILD

Commentators have proposed a number of alternatives designed to impose more structure on child custody decisions. Two leading approaches are presented by the Uniform Marriage and Divorce Act's definition of "best interest of the child," and by the American Law Institute's Principles of the Law of Family Dissolution. How much guidance would these provisions offer judges and parents trying to resolve a custody dispute? The UMDA, the state statutes and the ALI Principles that are set out below are designed to guide judges in choosing between two parents, both of whom seek custody.

1. Uniform Marriage and Divorce Act (1998)

§ 402.   Best Interest of Child

The court shall determine custody in accordance with the best interest of the child. The court shall consider all relevant factors including:

(1) the wishes of the child's parent or parents as to his custody;

(2) the wishes of the child as to his custodian;

(3) the interaction and interrelationship of the child with his parent or parents, his siblings, and any other person who may significantly affect the child's best interest;

(4) the child's adjustment to his home, school, and community; and

(5) the mental and physical health of all individuals involved.

The court shall not consider conduct of a proposed custodian that does not affect his relationship to the child.

9A U.L.A. 282 (1998).

2. Statutory Definitions of "Best Interests"

State statutes governing divorce give varying meanings to the term "best interests of the child." The following statutes demonstrate some of the different approaches state legislatures have enacted to guide judicial determinations of child custody.

MICHIGAN CHILD CUSTODY ACT

Sec. 3.   As used in this act, the "best interests of the child" means the sum total of the following factors to be considered, evaluated, and determined by the court:

(a) The love, affection, and other emotional ties existing between the parties involved and the child.

(b) The capacity and disposition of the parties involved to give the child love, affection, and guidance and to continue the education and raising of the child in his or her religion or creed, if any.

(c) The capacity and disposition of the parties involved to provide the child with food, clothing, medical care or other remedial care recognized and permitted under the laws of this state in place of medical care, and other material needs.

(d) The length of time the child has lived in a stable, satisfactory environment, and the desirability of maintaining continuity.

(e) The permanence, as a family unit, of the existing or proposed custodial home or homes.

(f) The moral fitness of the parties involved.

(g) The mental and physical health of the parties involved.

(h) The home, school, and community record of the child.

(i) The reasonable preference of the child, if the court considers the child to be of sufficient age to express preference.

(j) The willingness and ability of each of the parties to facilitate and encourage a close and continuing parent-child relationship between the child and the other parent or the child and the parents. A court may not consider negatively for the purposes of this factor any reasonable action taken by a parent to protect a child or that parent from sexual assault or domestic violence by the child's other parent.

(k) Domestic violence, regardless of whether the violence was directed against or witnessed by the child.

(*l*) Any other factor considered by the court to be relevant to a particular child custody dispute.

Mich. Comp. Laws Ann. § 722.23 (West Supp. 2018).

Section 3011 of the California Family Code

Factors considered in determining best interest of child

In making a determination of the best interest of the child * * * the court shall, among any other factors it finds relevant, * * * consider all of the following:

(a) The health, safety, and welfare of the child.

(b) (1) Any history of abuse by one parent or any other person seeking custody against any of the following:

> (A) A child to whom he or she is related by blood or affinity or with whom he or she has had a caretaking relationship, no matter how temporary.

(B) The other parent.

(C) A parent, current spouse, or cohabitant, of the parent or person seeking custody, or a person with whom the parent or person seeking custody has a dating or engagement relationship.

(2) As a prerequisite to considering allegations of abuse, the court may require independent corroboration, including, but not limited to, written reports by law enforcement agencies, child protective services * * * courts, medical facilities, or * * * organizations providing services to victims of sexual assault or domestic violence. * * *

(c) The nature and amount of contact with both parents * * *.

(d) The habitual or continual illegal use of controlled substances, the habitual or continual abuse of alcohol, or the habitual or continual abuse of prescribed controlled substances by either parent. Before considering these allegations, the court may first require independent corroboration [from the same kinds of sources set forth in § b (2) above].

(e) (1) Where allegations about a parent pursuant to subdivision (b) or (d) have been brought to the attention of the court in the current proceeding, and the court makes an order for sole or joint custody to that parent, the court shall state its reasons in writing or on the record. In these circumstances, the court shall ensure that any order regarding custody or visitation is specific as to time, day, place, and manner of transfer of the child * * *.

(2) The provisions of this subdivision shall not apply if the parties stipulate in writing or on the record regarding custody or visitation.

Cal. Fam. Code § 3011 (West, Westlaw through ch. 1016 of 2018 Reg. Sess.).

NOTES AND QUESTIONS

1. *The totality of the circumstances.* The vast majority of states have specified factors for courts to consider in assessing child custody claims, but some states expressly rely on a "totality of the circumstances" test for determining the best interests of the child, acknowledging that while "principles certainly provide guidance, child custody disputes, by their very nature, must be analyzed on a case-by-case basis." *John A. v. Bridget M.*, 791 N.Y.S.2d 421, 429 (N.Y. App. Div. 2005) (Sullivan, J., concurring); ("It is always necessary to consider the totality of the circumstances when determining custody") (Saxe, J., concurring). *Id.* at 431. Thus, New York courts hold that no one factor can be determinative, no matter how significant that factor may seem. *Margaret M.C. v. William J.C.*, 972 N.Y.S.2d 396 (Sup. Ct. 2012).

Would the Michigan and California formulations necessarily produce different outcomes than the sparser UMDA formulation quoted above on page 804?

2. *Abuse of controlled substances or alcohol.* The California statute expressly includes either parent's abuse of controlled substances or alcohol as a factor to weigh in the best interests inquiry. Substance abuse problems regularly arise in child custody cases, both in contests between parents and when the child welfare system alleges child abuse or neglect. How should courts treat the medical use of marijuana, which was legal in some thirty U.S. jurisdictions in 2018? National Conference of State Legislators, State Medical Marijuana Laws (April 27, 2018)). http://www.ncsl.org/research/health/state-medical-marijuana-laws.aspx.

Case law is just beginning to emerge, but Maine's highest court has held that it did not violate a parent's rights under the state's medical marijuana act to award custody to the mother where the father used "large amounts of marijuana" to treat his medical condition, had "a great deal of marijuana, in many forms, all over the home" and had exposed the child to marijuana use. Moreover, the trial court found that the father's ability to care for the child while high was impaired. His eyes were bloodshot and his thinking "appeared slow." The state Supreme Court held that language in the statute barring denial of custody based on legal use of medical marijuana did not foreclose examining whether the parent's ability to care for the child was impaired or negatively affected by the search for and use of drugs, or whether the parent stored drugs in places that were accessible to the child. *Daggett v. Sternick*, 109 A.3d 1137 (Me. 2015) (interpreting the Maine Medical Use of Marijuana Act, which was repealed in 2018, effective 2019).

Professor Catherine J. Ross says that it would be "misguided to ignore the pernicious effects that parental substance abuse may have on children, regardless of the precise substance of choice. Substance abuse can alter judgment, diminish impulse control, and stimulate aggression. At the core of the problem, substance abuse may make it impossible for a parent to perceive—much less respond to—a child's needs." Catherine J. Ross, *The Tyranny of Time: Vulnerable Children, "Bad" Mothers, and Statutory Deadlines in Parental Termination Proceedings*, 11 Va. J. Soc. Pol'y & L. 176, 210–11 (2004). The rise in the number of children actually or virtually abandoned by parents addicted to opioids and methamphetamines illustrates the problem. Julia Lurie, *Children of the Opioid Epidemic Are Flooding Foster Homes*, Mother Jones (July/August 2017). A rising number of children also die or are hospitalized after consuming an adult's opioids. Julie Turkowitz, *'Pills are Everywhere': Opioid Crisis and Its Youngest Victims*, N.Y. Times, Sept. 21, 2017, at A15. Which approach illustrated by the statutes set forth above should states adopt to protect children when the custody dispute is between two parents, one of whom is a substance abuser?

3. *Illegal substances and child custody.* The Americans with Disabilities Act of 1990 ("ADA") recognizes substance abuse as a disability for individuals

who have stopped using illegal drugs, but the Act does not apply to custody disputes. *See In re Marriage of Czapranski v. Czapranski*, 63 P.3d 499 (Mont. 2003) (upholding lower court's finding of sufficient evidence to support terminating joint custody because of mother's history of chemical dependence, need for inpatient care, and associated instability and risk to the child).

PROBLEM 12-2

In an effort to avoid custody determinations grounded in gender-based factors, your state's legislature recently amended the divorce act to provide that "no preference may be given to either parent in the awarding of custody because of that parent's gender, or because of the age or gender of the child." You are a trial court judge with a heavy divorce docket. This week you will hear two cases in which both parents have mounted strong claims for custody. The first case involves a four-month-old infant whom the mother is nursing. The second case involves a 14-year-old boy, whose father will present expert testimony that teenage boys thrive best when they live in a household with a strong father figure. What effect, if any, will the new statute likely have on your decision making?

3. The ALI Principles

The ALI has proposed an approach that aims to "approximate" family patterns before dissolution. It expressly contemplates shared parenting time.

AMERICAN LAW INSTITUTE, PRINCIPLES OF THE LAW OF FAMILY DISSOLUTION: ANALYSIS AND RECOMMENDATIONS
(2002).

§ 2.08 Allocation of Custodial Responsibility

(1) Unless otherwise resolved by agreement of the parents * * *, the court should allocate custodial responsibility so that the proportion of custodial time the child spends with each parent approximates the proportion of time each parent spent performing caretaking functions for the child prior to the parents' separation or, if the parents never lived together, before the filing of the action, except to the extent required under § 2.11[b] or necessary to achieve one or more of the following objectives:

> (a) to permit the child to have a relationship with each parent which, in the case of a legal parent or a parent by estoppel who has performed a reasonable share of parenting functions, should be no less than a

---

[b] Section 2.11 concerns parenting plans, which are detailed written descriptions of each parents' rights and responsibilities. You will learn about parenting plans later in this Chapter.

presumptive amount of custodial time set by a uniform rule of statewide application;

(b)   to accommodate the firm and reasonable preferences of a child who has reached a specific age, set by a uniform rule of statewide application;

(c)   to keep siblings together when the court finds that doing so is necessary to their welfare;

(d)   to protect the child's welfare when the presumptive allocation under this section would harm the child because of a gross disparity in the quality of the emotional attachment between each parent and the child or in each parent's demonstrated ability or availability to meet the child's needs;

(e)   to take into account any prior agreement, other than one under § 2.06,[c] that would be appropriate to consider in light of the circumstances as a whole, including the reasonable expectations of the parties, the extent to which they could have reasonably anticipated the events that occurred and their significance, and the interests of the child;

to avoid an allocation of custodial responsibility that would be extremely impractical or that would interfere substantially with the child's need for stability in light of economic, physical, or other circumstances, including the distance between the parents' residences, the cost and difficulty of transporting the child, each parent's and the child's daily schedules, and the ability of the parents to cooperate in the arrangement;

(f)   to apply the Principles set forth in § 2.17(4) [governing relocation by the custodial parent when] one parent relocates or proposes to relocate at a distance that will impair the ability of a parent to exercise the presumptive amount of custodial responsibility under this section;

(g)   to avoid substantial and almost certain harm to the child.

(2)   In determining the proportion of caretaking functions each parent previously performed for the child under Paragraph (1), the court should not consider the division of functions arising from temporary arrangements after the parents' separation, whether those arrangements are consensual or by court order. The court may take into account information relating to the temporary arrangements in determining other issues under this section.

---

[c]   Section 2.06 provides that "[t]he court should order provisions of a parenting plan agreed to by the parents, unless the agreement (a) is not knowing or voluntary, or (b) would be harmful to the child."

(3) If the court is unable to allocate custodial responsibility under Paragraph (1) because there is no history of past performance of caretaking functions, as in the case of a newborn, or because the history does not establish a sufficiently clear pattern of caretaking, the court should allocate custodial responsibility based on the child's best interests, taking into account the factors and considerations that are set forth in this Chapter, preserving to the extent possible this section's priority on the share of past caretaking functions each parent performed.

(4) In determining how to schedule the custodial time allocated to each parent, the court should take account of economic, physical, and other practical circumstances, such as those listed in Paragraph (1)(f).

NOTES AND QUESTIONS

1. *Origins of the ALI's approximation standard.* Professor Elizabeth S. Scott first advocated what she called an "approximation" standard for allocating child custody based partly on the positive correlation between past caretaking roles and the parents' preferences. Elizabeth S. Scott, *Pluralism, Parental Preference, and Child Custody*, 80 Calif. L. Rev. 615 (1992). Professor Scott argued that a rule that seeks to replicate past parental roles within the particular family would best account for the range of family norms in contemporary society. She hoped that the approximation standard would ameliorate the destructive effects of bargaining at divorce by promoting continuity and stability for children and encouraging cooperative rather than adversarial resolution of custody. She also predicted that this approach would encourage both parents to invest in parenting before and after divorce.

Professor Katharine T. Bartlett, who served as the reporter for the custody section of the ALI Principles, relied heavily on Professor Scott's work. Katharine T. Bartlett, *Preference, Presumption, Predisposition, and Common Sense: From Traditional Custody Doctrines to the American Law Institute's Family Dissolution Project*, 36 Fam. L.Q. 11 (2002). Professor Bartlett believes that "[t]he role of presumptions and preferences in refining rather than eliminating the best-interests standard is important to a greater general understanding of custody conflict." *Id.* at 16. She argues that the Principles introduce greater predictability to custody disputes by bringing specificity to those generalized presumptions. *Id.* at 24; *see also* Elizabeth Barker Brandt, *Concerns at the Margins of Supervised Access to Children*, 9 J.L. & Fam. Stud. 201 (2007).

2. *Criticisms of the ALI's approximation standard.* Ironically, a principal criticism of the ALI approximation standard is that it fails to achieve gender equality because so many families continue to follow traditional gender roles. Critics worry about whether the ALI's approach to custody is fair to fathers, because so many mothers still serve as primary caretakers while the parents live together.

Professor Andrew Schepard, for example, has expressed concern that the approximation standard would most likely allocate more of a child's post-dissolution time to the mother because "mothers do most of the pre-divorce work of caring for children." He argues, "men will likely perceive the approximation presumption as gender-biased and an incentive for women to file for divorce." He acknowledges that the ALI proposal rewards parents who spend more of their time caring for children, but argues that "[a] custody award to a parent * * * should not be a form of indirect compensation for time expended on child rearing." Instead, custody should be determined according to what a child needs, rather than what a parent deserves. Andrew I. Schepard, Children, Courts, and Custody: Interdisciplinary Models for Divorcing Families 167–69 (2004).

The approximation standard may also fail to recognize the dynamic nature of marital relationships. Professor Schepard, echoing Professor Teitelbaum's critique of the primary caretaker approach (*supra*, pages 796 and 803), criticizes the static quality of the approximation approach. Schepard argues that because the ALI standard is based on past performance, it "does not take into account the probability of post-divorce change in parenting roles. It is difficult to say with any degree of confidence that pre-divorce or separation caretaking arrangements in a particular family will remain stable after divorce or after separation. Many parents take new jobs and new partners after divorce. Some reduce their work loads to spend more time with their children." *Id.* at 169. He concludes that the law should grant parents the flexibility to redefine their relationship to work, to their children, and to each other after divorce rather than rigidly continuing pre-divorce patterns. *Id.* As with many other aspects of divorce, parents may negotiate post-dissolution divisions of labor that recognize their shifting priorities.

In 2014, Professor Bartlett defended the ALI standards against these and other criticisms. Katherine T. Bartlett, *Prioritizing Past Caretaking in Child-Custody Decisions*, 77 Law & Contemp. Probs. 29 (2014) (answering, among others, Michael R. Clisham & Robin Fretwell Wilson, *American Law Institute's* Principles of the Law of Family Dissolution, *Eight Years After Adoption: Guiding Principles or Obligatory Footnote?*, 42 Fam. L.Q. 573, 576, 596 (2008)). She argues that although courts and legislatures have not expressly adopted past caretaking as a decisive factor in custody decisions, a qualitative analysis of custody decisions reveals that courts rely on the history of caretaking as part of the best interests analysis in initial custody determinations, petitions to modify custody, and custody disputes involving third-party caretakers. Bartlett, *Prioritizing Past Caretaking, supra,* at 38.

Bartlett urges that past caretaking should be prioritized in state law in order to reduce pervasive indeterminacy in custody decisions. She believes that the ALI standards are easier for courts to adjudicate than other approaches to custody because the standards require historical fact-finding rather than "speculations about the future." *Id.* at 32. Bartlett notes that one court might view information about a caretaking parent as a negative, while another court in the same state might view it as a positive. She cites the example of a parent's decision to live with his or her own parents which one court viewed as directing more resources to the child, while another court viewed a similar decision as symptomatic of irresponsibility. *Id.* at 39. Ultimately, Bartlett posits that wider adoption of the ALI's approximation standard would result in more consistent and child-centered custody decisions—only the time spent caring for the child would count, making a court's value judgments largely irrelevant. *Id.* at 10.

What differences do you see between the primary caretaker and the approximation standards?

4. FACTORS IN DETERMINING BEST INTERESTS

Depending on the jurisdiction, a court may apply the best interests balancing test, a contemporary statute that does not impose a presumption, or the totality-of-the-circumstances common law approach. Regardless of the specific approach, child custody cases by their very nature are intensely fact specific. The decisions in this Section illustrate how courts weigh various factors in determining "best interests" under statutes or common law; the decisions also illustrate the lingering impact of some considerations that the law has formally discarded. You will see that several factors may come into play in the same case, and other factors may be lurking behind the opinion without receiving explicit scrutiny.

A. HOME ENVIRONMENT, HEALTH ISSUES AND GENDER ROLES

The Mississippi Supreme Court has observed that while the common law factors that its state courts apply in custody disputes "are extremely helpful in navigating what is usually a labyrinth of interests and emotions, they are certainly not the equivalent of a mathematical formula. Determining custody of a child is not an exact science." *Lee v. Lee*, 798 So.2d 1284, 1288 (Miss. 2001). As you read the next opinion, consider how much guidance the common law factors applicable in Mississippi provide for the courts and whether the case would have been likely to come out the same way if the roles of the mother and father had been reversed.

BLEVINS V. BARDWELL
Supreme Court of Mississippi, 2001.
784 So.2d 166.

PITTMAN, CHIEF JUSTICE, for the Court:

Adam L. Blevins appeals a chancery court judgment awarding the permanent paramount care, custody and control of his daughter Darby Colleen Blevins to her mother Dawn Elizabeth Bardwell (Funsch).

[handwritten margin note: Takeaway: The primary consideration in all child custody cases is the best interest and welfare of the child]

Facts and Proceedings Below

Adam Blevins and Dawn Bardwell (now Funsch) met in June of 1996 while both were stationed at Keesler Air Force base in Biloxi, Mississippi. After a period of friendship, they became romantically involved. This brief relationship temporarily ended just a few weeks before Dawn married her "high school sweetheart," Jason Singleton, that August. About a month later Dawn began treatment for stress and depression at the Keesler Mental Health Clinic. Despite Dawn's marriage, Adam and Dawn renewed their romance. While still married to Jason, Dawn discovered that she was pregnant and received an honorable discharge from the Air Force. She then moved in with Adam in January of 1997. From that time forward Adam and Dawn lived together and proclaimed themselves a couple.

Darby Colleen Blevins was born July 19, 1997. Over the following two weeks a DNA parentage test was administered; Dawn's divorce from Jason was finalized; and it was conclusively proven that Adam was Darby's biological father. Adam and Dawn continued to co-habitate unmarried and care for their daughter, with Dawn being the primary care giver. During this time Adam worked full time, and Dawn held a part time job. Both admitted in testimony that it was their intention to marry at some point in the future.

Eventually Dawn decided to reenlist in the Air Force. Because the Air Force prohibits custodial single parents from enlisting, Dawn executed a "Order Approving Custody of Child" granting custody of Darby to Adam. At the time both believed they would marry at the conclusion of Dawn's technical training, or alternatively, once Dawn gained "permanent party" status, she would regain custody of Darby without jeopardizing her position in the Air Force. Adam and Dawn agree that they intended the change of custody to be a temporary arrangement.

Dawn left for technical training in July of 1998. Adam served as the primary care giver for Darby over the next 9 months. After Dawn came home on leave in September of 1998, relations became strained between the couple. By the end of her five-day leave Dawn and Adam had ended their relationship. Before leaving for her new assignment at Lackland Air Force Base in San Antonio, Texas, Dawn expressed her desire to take Darby with her since Dawn had successfully attained "permanent party" status. Adam refused to allow Dawn to take Darby citing his custody rights per the "Order Approving Custody of Child." Dawn and Adam have not lived together since.

A month after her arrival at Lackland Air Force Base, Dawn filed her Complaint in the Chancery Court of the Second Judicial District of Harrison County, Mississippi, for Change in Custody and Other Relief in the hope of regaining custody of Darby. While working at Lackland, Dawn met Anthony Funsch, whom she later married prior to the custody hearing.

[margin note: Dawn's complaint]

Dawn claims that in the months leading up to the custody hearing, while Darby was still in her father's custody, Adam was uncooperative in allowing visitation and promoting a close relationship between Dawn and Darby. Dawn also asserts that, on occasion, the chancery court was forced to implement visitation on behalf of Dawn, although there is nothing in the record to support this assertion. Prior to the court hearing in April of 1999 Adam and Darby moved to Melbourne, Kentucky, so that Adam could be with his father who was suffering from a number of serious illnesses.

[margin note: lower court's opinion]

After a four-day hearing, the chancellor issued the court's Memorandum Opinion and Judgment providing the following: 1) the prior order which awarded custody to Adam was a temporary, non-final adjudication of custody; 2) joint legal custody of Darby was awarded to both parties; 3) paramount care, custody and control of Darby was awarded to Dawn; 4) visitation was awarded to Adam, and 5) Adam was ordered to pay child support. From this judgment Adam appeals the award of paramount care, custody and control of Darby to Dawn.

Discussion

I. DID THE TRIAL COURT CORRECTLY DETERMINE THAT THE CUSTODY AGREEMENT WAS TEMPORARY?

* * *

At the time of their agreement regarding Darby's custody, Dawn and Adam intended to marry sometime after Dawn completed her training in the Air Force. Ultimately, they did not marry, and there was a need for the hearing below to determine permanent custody. It is undisputed that both parties voluntarily stipulated that the custody agreement made before Dawn's reentry into the Air Force was temporary in nature. Because single mothers with custody of children are not allowed to reenlist, the chancellor duly noted the pressure on Dawn to agree to the custody order so that she could return to the Air Force.

[margin note: explanation of the temp. change in child custody agreement]

On its face, the "Order Approving Custody of Child" granting custody of Darby to Adam contains no language to indicate that it is anything but an order for permanent custody.[1] This Court gives great deference to the sanctity of orders made by chancellors and the belief that orders should be followed as they are written. *We are able to revisit this order because both parties agree that it was intended to be temporary.*

* * *

---

[1]   It is often said that no child custody order is permanent. Technically, this is correct because custody is always subject to modification in the best interest of the child. The terms "permanent" and "temporary" are used here because they are the terms chosen by the chancellor to distinguish between the chancery court award of custody arising out of the custody arrangement which Adam and Dawn temporarily entered into for the sole purpose of enabling Dawn to reenlist in the Air Force and a regular chancery court award of custody that is intended to continue indefinitely, until modified by order of the court.

[O]f greatest importance as this is a child custody matter, we must defer to the polestar consideration in every child custody case, the best interests of the child.

Because of our determination that the custody order was, in fact, temporary, the chancellor was free to make a *de novo* original award of custody based on the factors in *Albright v. Albright*, 437 So.2d 1003, 1005 (Miss. 1983). The chancellor did make such an analysis in awarding custody to Dawn and on every single factor where the chancellor favored one parent over the other, the chancellor concluded that custody with Dawn was favorable.

* * *

Thus, there should be no reversal of the chancellor's finding that Dawn should have custody. Accordingly, the chancellor's decision should be affirmed.

II.   DID THE TRIAL COURT PROPERLY APPLY THE *ALBRIGHT* FACTORS TO THE EVIDENCE PRESENTED AT TRIAL?

This Court has stated that child custody matters are within the chancellor's discretion, and this Court will not reverse absent a finding that the chancellor was manifestly wrong, clearly erroneous, or applied an erroneous legal standard. * * * *Albright* clearly states that the primary consideration in all child custody cases is "the best interest and welfare of the child". *Id.* at 1005. *Albright* sets forth a number of factors which should be considered by a chancellor in a child custody case:

> We reaffirm the rule that the polestar consideration in child custody cases is the best interest and welfare of the child. The age of the child is subordinated to that rule and is but one factor to be considered. Age should carry no greater weight than other factors to be considered, such as: health, and sex of the child; a determination of the parent that has had the continuity of care prior to the separation; which has the best parenting skills and which has the willingness and capacity to provide primary child care; the employment of the parent and responsibilities of employment; physical and mental health and age of parents; emotional ties of parent and child; moral fitness of parents; the home, school and community record of the child; the preference of the child at the age sufficient to express a preference by law; stability of home environment and employment of each parent, and other factors relevant to the parent-child relationship.

Id.

Adam claims that the Chancellor erred in the application of the following factors: A) age, B) health of parties, C) future religious example, D) home environment, and E) willingness and ability to provide primary care. Dawn contends that the Chancellor properly considered the *Albright* factors before rendering her decision.

* * *

B) Health of Parents *& Adam's key argument*

Adam claims that the Chancellor erred in giving an edge in health to Dawn because Adam smokes. and, in addition, that Dawn's medical records were not properly considered when the Chancellor assessed the health of the parents. The records in question are from October, 1996, when Dawn received counseling from a military psychologist. The evaluations of the psychologist included statements that she suffered from an "adjustment disorder with depressed mood" and a provisional "schizoid personality disorder." These evaluations also mentioned the risk of potential suicide and that Dawn might be harmful to others. Dawn admitted at the trial that these records were accurate. Adam argues that the chancellor's conclusion is not a true reflection of the evidence that was presented before the court and that her conclusion was not supported by substantial evidence * * *.

Dawn addresses the health of the parents issue by pointing out that the Chancellor actually addressed physical and mental health in two separate subparagraphs (g and h of the court's opinion). In the first subparagraph, (g), the chancellor states:

> Adam smokes, Dawn does not so the mother has somewhat of an edge in health.

In subparagraph (h) the chancellor stated:

> Much was attempted to be made of Dawn's medical records. The Court agrees with the testimony of the recruiting officer, there was nothing negative in her file. This is also proven by the fact that the Air Force took her back. If anything, the Court would hold Adam's failure to sign his medical waiver against him. His attorney's explanation that they hadn't presented them with one is unconvincing. This issue of medical waivers was fully discussed with the Court, when Dawn delivered hers, Adam certainly had the opportunity to deliver a signed waiver.

Dawn believes that the chancellor properly reviewed the medical records in question when coming to her decision regarding Dawn's mental health. Dawn relies on statements made by the Chancellor that show the records were properly considered. After Dawn's counsel objected to their admission into evidence, the chancellor stated,

> * * * I am going to look at these medical records knowing that they obtain hearsay, knowing that she has said under oath that she has never committed suicide, never attempted to commit suicide. That her diagnosis was stress-related to an adjustment [to the]

military. She has testified that she has absolutely no mental
health problems now and I know what her testimony has been and
I've noted all the objections for the record.

The Chancellor further states:

> * * * the reason I am letting the medical records in is I think * * *
> one of the factors in *Albright* is mental health. And I feel like I
> need to look at the record to make an informed decision.

Dawn contends that the Chancellor was free to give these medical
records whatever weight she deemed proper and points out that the
medical records being reviewed predated Darby's birth by almost a year.
She also argues that if these medical records were so damaging then the
Air Force would not have allowed her to reenlist. Testimony of Dawn's air
force recruiter confirms that the records that he is required to review when
she explored reenlisting did not contain any negative or derogatory
information. Testimony does not clearly indicate whether the medical
records in question were part of what the Air Force recruiter considered in
Dawn's allowance to reenlist, but the recruiter did state that the military
records he reviewed would contain any information that the Air Force
considered "negative or derogatory."

[handwritten margin note: DAWN defends prior mental health issues]

* * *

The record clearly indicates that the Chancellor properly considered
the mental and physical health of both parents and that her decision was
based on the factors as outlined in *Albright*. Because of this, and the fact
that Adam failed to request specific findings of fact and conclusions of law,
this Court is hard pressed to find that the Chancellor's decision is
manifestly wrong, clearly erroneous, or the result of the application of an
erroneous legal standard. This Court has stated that child custody matters
are solely within the Chancellor's discretion and we find that there was no
abuse of this discretion in the Chancellor's determination of the health of
the parents.

[handwritten margin note: Court: this is solely within the chancellor's discretion]

* * *

D) Home Environment *[handwritten: Another Adam argument]*

Adam argues that the Chancellor incorrectly focused on Adam's infirm
father in making her determination regarding home environment and
ignored many of the surrounding facts and circumstances that could have
resulted in a different conclusion. Adam offers that a comparison of both
homes reveals that Adam's was favorable over Dawn's at the time of the
hearing. Adam was living in a house located on seven acres in Kentucky
while Dawn was in a one bedroom apartment. Adam's mother, aunt,
grandmother and grandfather were all within twenty minutes of him while
Dawn's parents were three hours from her.

key

Adam's father is an HIV positive hemophiliac and suffers from cancer. Adam's father also smokes three to four packs of cigarettes a day. The Chancellor considered these factors and stated * * *:

> The Court would like to make it perfectly clear that it is not penalizing Adam because he moved to take care of his critically ill father, it is commendable. Nor is the Court reacting to an irrational fear or prejudice of persons who are HIV positive. The Court does however, question if the home of a critically ill patient, regardless of the illness, is the best environment in which to raise a toddler. It also is not assuring to hear that the paternal grandfather smokes three to four packs of cigarettes a day, even if it is true he does not smoke when Darby is home. The atmosphere of the home would still have to be tainted with smoke. The Court finds the stability of the home environment should favor Dawn.

key ruling

This Court does not see that the Chancellor abused her discretion in considering home environment in order to determine who received custody of Darby. It also cannot be said that the Chancellor's decision regarding home environment is manifestly wrong, clearly erroneous, or the result of the application of an erroneous legal standard.

* * *

Conclusion

Based on the foregoing analysis, we affirm the judgment of the Harrison County Chancery Court.

AFFIRMED.

NOTES AND QUESTIONS

1. *Custody disputes concerning nonmarital children.* At one time, most states heard custody disputes concerning marital and nonmarital children in different courts and under different statutes. By the end of the twentieth century, however, all custody cases were heard in the same courts and decided under the same statutes regardless of the parents' marital status. *See, e.g., Wyatt v. White*, 626 So.2d 816 (La. Ct. App. 1993).

Unmarried parents like Dawn and Adam often fail to obtain a court order formalizing their custody arrangements. In some jurisdictions, the lack of a court order exposes the custodial parent to the risk of losing custody if the informal structure falls apart and the noncustodial parent petitions for custody. The court may treat the petition as an initial custody hearing and give no preference to the parent who has cared for the child since birth or even for many years. *Purser v. Owens*, 722 S.E.2d 225 (S.C. Ct. App. 2011). Other courts, noting the children's need for continuity, may find the children's best interests served by awarding permanent physical custody to the residential parent even where one or both parents intended the initial arrangement to be temporary.

2.   *Continuity.* Do the trial and appellate court decisions in *Blevins v. Bardwell* weigh continuity of care for Darby? Under the various standards and balancing tests you read about in the beginning of this Chapter, what outcome would be best for Darby? What concerns do you think the courts were balancing against concerns about continuity?

Faced with the risk of "temporary" agreements becoming permanent, a divorcing or unmarried parent may understandably be reluctant to give the other parent custody even temporarily while awaiting a judicial resolution. Acrimonious custody battles may begin well before the parents ever enter a courtroom. Unfortunately, this early race to create continuity of residence may quickly intensify an already hostile relationship, exposing children to prolonged periods of discord and upheaval that outlast the custody decree.

3.   *What impact does parental gender have?* Do you think the outcome in *Blevins* would have been different if Adam, who cared for his daughter and his ailing father while the child's mother pursued her career and her new relationship, had been a woman? Dawn, the mother in *Blevins*, was fortunate that the court did not hold either her military career or her series of romantic partners against her. The impact of an unconventional lifestyle will be discussed later in this Chapter.

Gender role reversals may prove problematic for mothers in custody disputes. Olga Jacobsen, for example, held a graduate degree in environmental engineering and worked full-time. Her husband Jarrod, who had once earned nearly twice as much as Olga, declined to look for another job after he was laid off in 2009. He began to stay home with the couple's young child. Olga's workday ended at 2:45, and she took care of the couple's son starting at 3:30. Olga signed the boy up for all the activities to which his father took him, scheduled doctor's appointments, provided health insurance, and organized all of the boy's play dates. The father, in turn, "exposed the child to violent video games, movies, and music with questionable lyrics," causing the court to issue an order to prevent exposure to these materials. During the divorce proceedings the judge also ordered Jarrod to find a job within 18 months. Nonetheless, the trial court considered the father the primary caretaker, and awarded him custody, as well as the family home. The appellate court reversed. *Jacobsen v. Jacobsen*, 2013 WL 1400618 at *12 (Tenn. Ct. App. Apr. 5, 2013).

4.   *Smoking by parents.* Although some courts have considered the dangers of secondhand smoke for decades, the publication of a major study by scholars at Harvard in 2006 appears to have increased the level of judicial scrutiny of parental smoking. *Pierce v. Pierce*, 860 N.E.2d 1087, 1093 (Ohio Ct. App. 2006) (holding that the trial court did not err in naming the father the residential parent where, all other factors being equal, the mother smoked and father did not); *In re Drake L.*, 2010 WL 2787829 (Tenn. Ct. App. July 13, 2010) (mother's smoking in the home with the child present "is certainly a relevant

factor" supporting transfer of custody to the non-smoking father, even though the child does not have a respiratory illness).

Courts have long held that a parent's smoking may be a legitimate reason to limit visitation, especially where a child was particularly vulnerable due to asthma or another health condition. *See, e.g., Badeaux v. Badeaux*, 541 So.2d 301, 302–03 (La. Ct. App. 1989). By 2011, a trial court in Tennessee—a tobacco-growing region—on its own initiative barred both parents from smoking "in the car or in the house" when their daughter was with them even though she did not appear especially vulnerable to smoke. *Bargmann v. Bargmann*, 2011 WL 1026095 at *2 (Tenn. Ct. App. Mar. 22, 2011).

5.   *Care of elderly parents.* How should the court view Adam's decision to care for his dying father? Consider that some of the court's concerns about the appropriateness of Adam's home focused on the grandfather's smoking, his HIV status, and the fact that he was dying of cancer. Are any of these considerations appropriate? Are they distinguishable from one another? Would it matter if the source of the grandfather's HIV infection were not traceable to blood transfusions he received as a hemophiliac? Should the trial court have focused more clearly on the "commendable" aspects of Adam's commitment to taking care of his father? As a matter of social policy, what behavior should the law encourage for people in Adam's position? Note that Adam is exceptional in that he not only took care of his daughter, but also took care of his dying father, a role far more commonly performed by women. Does this ruling promote the most desirable social goals?

6.   *Parents with disabilities.* In *Blevins v. Bardwell*, the issue of Dawn's mental health status was before the court but the evidence that she suffered from serious depression was not convincing. If the court had been convinced that she suffered from depression that was not being treated successfully, what would the next step in the court's analysis have been?

The Americans with Disabilities Act of 1990 (ADA), a federal statute, prohibits discrimination against persons with disabilities in many areas, including employment, public transportation, public accommodations, housing, and education, but (as you read earlier) the act does not apply to child custody cases. In custody cases, the court may consider a parent's physical and mental health when determining the best interests of the child.

In a landmark decision—*In re Marriage of Carney*—the trial court awarded custody to the father after the mother relinquished custody of their two sons. 598 P.2d 36 (Cal. 1979). The mother had virtually no contact with the children until five years later, when the father became a quadriplegic after a Jeep accident that occurred while he was serving in the military reserve. The trial court then granted the mother physical custody of the two children and permitted her to remove them from their father's California home to her New York home. The California Supreme Court reversed on the ground that the trial court had "premised its ruling on outdated stereotypes of both the parental role and the ability of the handicapped to fill that role." *Id.* at 37. The state supreme court discussed the "common knowledge that many persons with physical handicaps have demonstrated their ability to adequately support and control their children and to give them the benefits of stability and security through love and attention," and the public policy of integrating disabled persons "into the responsibilities and satisfactions of family life, cornerstone of our social system." *Id*. at 44–45.

Carney held that it was impermissible for a court to rely on a parent's disability "as *prima facie* evidence of the person's unfitness as a parent or of probable detriment to the child":

> [R]ather, in all cases the court must view the handicapped [sic] person as an individual and the family as a whole. To achieve this, the court should inquire into the person's actual and potential physical capabilities, learn how he or she has adapted to the disability and manages its problems, consider how the other members of the household have adjusted thereto, and take into account the special contributions the person may make to the family despite—or even because of—the handicap. Weighing these and all relevant factors together, the court should then carefully determine whether the parent's condition will in fact have a substantial and lasting adverse effect on the best interests of the child.

Id. at 42.

Several states have enacted legislation incorporating the principle established in *Carney*. For example, in 2013 Oregon prohibited courts from considering a parent's disability when determining custody or visitation unless the court finds that the limitations stemming from the disability would likely endanger the health, welfare, or safety of the child. Or. Rev. Stat. Ann. § 107.137 (West 2016).

B. ALLEGATIONS OF IMMORALITY

The Michigan statute (set out on page 804) and other state statutes continue to list parental morality as a factor for the courts to consider in custody disputes. *See* Fla. Stat. Ann. § 61.13(3)(f) (West Supp. 2019). It is also one of the *Albright* factors summarized in *Blevins v. Bardwell, supra,* page 812 that guide custody decisions in Mississippi. And the "moral fitness of each party, as it affects the welfare of the child" is one of the statutory factors set out in Louisiana, whose courts considered a dispute over custody and visitation in the following case.

There was a time when an adulterous parent had little chance of obtaining custody, but in the last few decades, with the decline of fault-based divorce, parental morality has become less important in determining custody—at least as an expressly acknowledged factor.

As you read the opinion set out below, consider what role the father's alleged sexual proclivities played in the decision to award the mother sole custody despite a statutory preference for joint custody, whether it was necessary for the court to consider the father's moral fitness, and what impact, if any, the father's behavior had on the child who was four years old when the case reached the appellate court.

KAPTEIN V. KAPTEIN
Court of Appeal of Louisiana, 2017.
221 So.3d 231.

BROUSSARD, JUSTICE.

In this custody dispute, appellant/defendant, Jesse Kaptein, appeals a trial court's decision that awarded sole custody of C.E.K.[d] to appellee/plaintiff, Heather Kaptein, continued the suspension of FaceTime visitation, and determined that reasonable visitation with him was not in the best interest of the child. For the reasons that follow, we hereby affirm the trial court's judgment that awarded sole custody of C.E.K. to Ms. Kaptein, but reverse that part of the judgment regarding the suspension of FaceTime visitation with Mr. Kaptein.

FACTS AND PROCEDURAL HISTORY

The parties' daughter, C.E.K., was born on February 25, 2013. On April 30, 2014, Ms. Kaptein filed a petition for divorce and requested sole custody of C.E.K. After a hearing, on May 19, 2015, the trial court awarded Ms. Kaptein interim sole custody, while Mr. Kaptein was awarded interim supervised visitation with C.E.K. each month from the first Saturday until the second Sunday for a minimum time period of two (2) hours to a maximum of eight (8) hours each day, and FaceTime visits. Mr. Kaptein was also ordered to pay Ms. Kaptein interim spousal support of $15,000 per month and child support of $5,000 per month. In her reasons for judgment, the judge stated as follows:

> The Court finds Mr. Kaptein's lifestyle and travel are not stable. Mr. Kaptein admitted to engaging in multiple extra-marital affairs, with not one, but multiple women in several different countries. He also admitted to paying the travel expenses for such women, so he could not only have sex with them, but have unprotected sex with them, thereby jeopardizing his health, and that of his wife, Mrs. Kaptein. Mr. Kaptein's testimony and admitted indiscretions demonstrate a reckless disregard for his personal safety, which calls into question the safety of the minor child. Adultery alone does not demonstrate a lack of moral fitness on behalf of Mr. Kaptein, but his precarious nature, including the frequency, location, and disregard for safety—exhibited by unprotected sex with women in different countries—does. Mr.

---

[d]   *Editors' Note:* The opinion sporadically puts brackets around C.E.K.'s middle initial. In the interests of clarity and uniformity we have omitted those brackets where they appear in the printed opinion.

Kaptein does not have a stable home, he does not live or work in the United States, nor will he be in this country for an extended period of time. Although Mr. Kaptein's accomplishments as a businessman are commendable, his choices to pursue a career and a scandalous lifestyle away from his family, weigh against him. Therefore, this Court finds it in the best interest of the minor child to award interim sole custody to Mrs. Kaptein.

* * *

[Ms. Kaptein filed two motions for contempt alleging that Mr. Kaptein had failed to make child support and interim maintenance payments and arrearages as ordered]

After a hearing held on January 26, 2016 on Ms. Kaptein's [motions], the trial court signed a written judgment on February 4, 2016, that (1) granted Ms. Kaptein's [motion] for contempt and found that as of the date of the hearing, Mr. Kaptein owed $78,000.00 in past due support * * * and (4) suspended Mr. Kaptein's rights to visitation through FaceTime pending further orders from the trial court. [T]he trial court set the final custody hearing on July 1, 2016.

* * *

[After the July 1] hearing on Ms. Kaptein's motion for sole custody * * * the trial court granted Ms. Kaptein sole custody, maintained its previous order suspending Mr. Kaptein's FaceTime visitation, and held that "reasonable visitation with Mr. Kaptein is not in the best interest of the child." In its reasons for judgment, the trial court stated:

In any determination of child custody, the paramount consideration is the best interest of the child. * * * The Court finds Ms. Kaptein met her burden in showing by clear and convincing evidence that sole custody is in the best interest of the child.

(1) The love, affection, and other emotional ties between each party and the child.

Ms. Kaptein has strong emotional ties with C.E.K. Contrarily, no evidence was presented to show that the child has strong ties to Mr. Kaptein. Mr. Kaptein has failed to demonstrate a willingness to be a part of C.E.K.'s life. Ms. Kaptein testified, on cross-examination, that C.E.K. has never asked the whereabouts of her father. This factor weighs strongly in favor of Ms. Kaptein.

(2) The capacity and disposition of each party to give the child love, affection, and spiritual guidance and to continue the education and rearing of the child.

Mr. Kaptein has shown little interest in providing C.E.K. with love and guidance. He has not seen C.E.K. for over half of her life because he has resided in a different country. Mr. Kaptein has previously testified he is an atheist. Ms. Kaptein has been the sole caretaker of C.E.K. and testified she takes C.E.K. to church * * * No evidence, aside from Mr. Kaptein's alleged desire to lift the FaceTime visitation suspension, was presented to show Mr. Kaptein is interested in seeing or rearing his child.

* * *

Ms. Kaptein has [provided] stability for the minor child.

(6)   The moral fitness of each party, insofar as it affects the welfare of the child.

* * * Mr. Kaptein has a sexual obsession that adversely affects his ability and his fitness to raise C.E.K. Mr. Kaptein is more interested in traveling and engaging in lavish sex parties than he is in being a father. Ms. Kaptein testified that during their marriage, Mr. Kaptein lied to her, had sex with various women from different countries, and at this point she does not know him anymore. On cross-examination, Ms. Kaptein testified that C.E.K. is not aware of Mr. Kaptein's sexual habits. Nevertheless, the Court finds that Mr. Kaptein's lifestyle, his lack of credibility, his failure to comply with court orders and failure to take interest in seeing his child during these formative years of her life, demonstrate that his moral fitness would be a detriment to the child.

* * *

(10) The willingness and ability of each party to facilitate and encourage a close and continuing relationship between the child and the other party.

Ms. Kaptein testified she does not think Mr. Kaptein is fit to co-parent C.E.K. because of his risqué lifestyle. She stated she would be willing to co-parent with Mr. Kaptein once he has completed the recommendations made by [the court-appointed psychologist].

* * *

(12) The responsibility for the care and rearing of the child previously exercised by each party.

Ms. Kaptein has taken responsibility for 100% of the care and rearing of the minor child. Mr. Kaptein has not visited with C.E.K. since September of 2015.

Pursuant to *La. C.C. art. 136*, a parent not granted custody or joint custody of a child is entitled to reasonable visitation rights unless the court finds, after a hearing, that visitation would not be in the best interest of the child. *La. C.C. art. 136.* The Court finds that due to Mr. Kaptein's failure to comply with visitation, his promiscuous lifestyle, and his departure from the child's life, reasonable visitation does not serve the best interest of the minor child.

* * *

Mr. Kaptein now appeals this final judgment, assigning the following assignments of error: (1) the trial court erred in awarding sole custody to Ms. Kaptein; (2) the trial court erred in ruling that reasonable visitation with him is not in the best interest of C.E.K., and in continuing the suspension of FaceTime visitation with C.E.K. * * *.

DISCUSSION

The trial court shall award custody in accordance with the best interest of the child. *La. C.C.* art. 131. In determining the best interest of the child, "[e]ach case must be viewed in light of the child's age, the situation of the parents, and any other factor relevant to the particular case." If there is no [parental] agreement, or if the agreement is not in the best interest of the child, then the trial court shall award joint custody unless custody in one parent is shown by clear and convincing evidence to be in the best interest of the child. As stated by the Louisiana Supreme Court, "[i]t is the child's emotional, physical, material and social well-being and health that are the court's very purpose in child custody cases; the court must protect the child from the real possibility that the parents are engaged in a bitter, vengeful, and highly emotional conflict." *Hodges v. Hodges,* 181 So. 3d 700, 702 (La. 2015).

The first issue * * * is whether the trial judge erred in awarding Ms. Kaptein sole custody of C.E.K. * * *

* * *

[T]he trial court determined from clear and convincing evidence that the best interest of C.E.K., now 4 years old, was served by the award of sole custody to her mother. Although Mr. Kaptein alleges that there was no evidence presented at the custody trial that showed joint custody would be harmful to C.E.K., we find that the trial record reflects a reasonable factual basis for the trial judge's award of sole custody to Ms. Kaptein. Specifically, * * * the fact that Mr. Kaptein had not seen C.E.K. for ten months preceding the custody trial, has not paid the court ordered child support as previously ordered, has consistently failed to provide his contact information to the court, as well as his attorneys throughout the custody proceedings, and has failed to appear for the interim and final custody hearings. After a review of the record, we agree with the trial court that Mr. Kaptein failed to demonstrate a willingness to be a part of C.E.K.'s life when he lives in a different country and thus was not able to see C.E.K. for over half of her life. Under the particular facts of this case, we find no legal error in the trial court's determination that sole custody with Ms. Kaptein is in the best interest of C.E.K.

facetime issue ✱

The second issue to address is whether the trial court erred in ruling that reasonable visitation with Mr. Kaptein is not in the best interest of C.E.K., and continued the suspension of FaceTime visitation with C.E.K.[e] Mr. Kaptein argues on appeal that the trial court suspended his FaceTime visitation on February 4, 2016, as a punitive measure after finding him in contempt of court for not paying, in full, the court's orders relating to child support and interim spousal support. Mr. Kaptein alleges in his appellate brief that the trial court's July 1, 2016 judgment "seems more [of] a punishment for his sex life and his inability to pay $20,000 per month than an appropriate ruling based on the best interests of the child—because no matter how bad a husband Mr. Kaptein [he] was, it simply cannot be said that the child's interests are best served by cutting her off completely from her father." Conversely, Ms. Kaptein argues that it is not in C.E.K.'s best interest to have a digital relationship with Mr. Kaptein and that the trial court properly suspended the FaceTime visitation.

La. C.C. art. 136 provides that "[a] parent not granted custody or joint custody of a child is entitled to reasonable visitation rights unless the court finds, after a hearing, that visitation would not be in the best interest of the child." As with custody, the paramount criterion for determining a noncustodial parent's right to visitation is the best interest of the child.

High burden to prohibit visitation ✱

Louisiana courts have consistently held that denial of visitation rights to a parent is an *extreme measure* warranted only by "*conclusive evidence* that visitation would *seriously endanger* the child's physical, mental, moral, or emotional health." Further, the question of visitation is always open to change when the conditions warrant it. *Becnel v. Becnel*, 732 So.2d 589, 592–93 (La. Ct. App. 1999). When there have been restrictions placed on a noncustodial parent's visitation rights, those restrictions should be lifted when it is shown to be in the child's best interest. *Id.*

[The record shows] that Mr. Kaptein and C.E.K. were enjoying their FaceTime visitation up until [the court] suspended Mr. Kaptein's rights to such visitation after finding him in contempt of court. * * * Ms. Kaptein testified that * * * C.E.K. was unaware of Mr. Kaptein's sexual behavior and/or relationships, and that she had no complaints concerning previous FaceTime visits with Mr. Kaptein or his behavior during those visits with C.E.K. The record is void of any conclusive evidence that FaceTime visitation with Mr. Kaptein poses any risk to C.E.K. or that it is detrimental to the child. In fact, Dr. Bauer [who performed a court-ordered "mental health" evaluation] stated * * * that C.E.K. "should continue to have the opportunity to communicate with her father through Facetime or

---

[e]   *Editors' Note:* Visitation rights and restrictions on visitation are discussed in Chapter 13.

Skype on a regular basis" and that as C.E.K. "gets older and becomes more cognizant and aware of the process, the time can be extended and she can become more independent in conversations with her father and his family." For these reasons, we reverse the trial court's ruling, which continued the suspension of FaceTime visitation, as well as its finding that reasonable visitation is not in the best interest of the child, and we hereby reinstate Mr. Kaptein's rights to FaceTime visitation with C.E.K. as previously ordered.

* * *

For these reasons, we hereby reverse that part of the judgment suspending Face Time visitation and affirm the trial court in all other respects.

AFFIRMED IN PART; REVERSED IN PART

NOTES AND QUESTIONS

1. *Morality as a statutory factor in assessing best interests and the "nexus" test.* The Louisiana statute applied in *Kaptein* provides that courts should consider each parent's "moral fitness, insofar as it affects the welfare of the child." Did the trial court consider how the father's behavior affected his daughter? How much weight did the trial court give to the comparative morals of the mother and the father?

Under the contemporary approach in order to establish that a parent's immoral behavior warrants denial of custody, the other parent must demonstrate a nexus between that behavior and harm to the child. This focus on the relationship between parental misconduct and the child's best interest reflects a movement away from punishing the morally guilty parent and instead focusing on the child's needs. The vast majority of jurisdictions "at least purport" to use the nexus test today. Courtney G. Joslin et al., Lesbian, Gay, Bisexual and Transgender Family Law § 1.8 Westlaw (database updated Aug. 2018); Linda D. Elrod, Child Custody Practice and Procedure § 4:24 Westlaw (database updated March 2018) ("[M]arital misconduct must be shown to have a present adverse impact on the child to be relevant"). Appellate courts in South Carolina have explained that while "a parent's morality" is "a proper consideration in custody disputes," the inquiry "is limited in its force and effect to the relevance it has, either directly or indirectly, on the welfare of the child. Thus, conduct that is immoral must also be shown to be detrimental to the welfare of a child before it is of legal significance in a custody dispute." *Blalock v. Blalock*, 2011 WL 11735801 at *1 (S.C. Ct. App. Nov. 28, 2011).

The appellate court in *Kaptein* did not criticize the trial judge for relying so heavily on the father's immorality even in the absence of any showing the what the judge termed the father's "pleasure habits" and "sexual addiction" had any impact on the child. At age four she was completely unaware of his behavior. Was the court concerned that as she grew older she would become aware and that such knowledge might adversely affect her? Would that have been a legitimate consideration?

Arguably, the facts in *Kaptein* were so dramatic that it was unnecessary for the court to consider the father's morality, because he could be said to have effectively abdicated his paternal role. He did not exercise his visitation rights, refused to comply with support orders for his child, and would not even provide an address to the court or his own counsel. If Mr. Kaptein had been an unmarried father, would a court have been likely to accord him paternal rights? It is hard to imagine what a joint custody order would have looked like in *Kaptein*, or how it could have been carried out.

2.   *Postscript to* Kaptein. During the pendency of the litigation that resulted in the opinion set forth above, the mother also successfully petitioned the juvenile court to terminate the father's parental rights. The appellate court reversed, in a decision issued about six months after the opinion you read. *State ex rel. C.E.K.*, 234 So.3d 1059 (La. Ct. App. 2017). It held that the mother's allegation that the father had abandoned the child failed on the merits because although he had not paid the full child support amounts ordered by the court, he had made "regular" and "significant contributions" to the child's support, showing no intention to "permanently avoid parental responsibility," and his failure to communicate with the child was attributable to the trial court's order barring FaceTime communication while the father was living abroad, not to the father's independent choices.

3.   *Adultery still matters.* Where parental immorality is one of a number of factors that the judge is directed to consider in determining custody, adultery may continue to carry significant weight. It may do so even where the statute is silent. For example, a parent's poor judgment, reflected in her conduct (before the divorce decree was issued) in "openly sharing a bed" with her boyfriend while her two sons aged seven and ten were spending the night in the same hotel room, supported a decision to award custody to the father. *P.C. v. K.C.*, 2011 WL 2586384 (N.Y. Sup. Ct. June 27, 2011) (mother put her own needs before her sons').

A Mississippi appellate court upheld an award of joint custody to the parents of an eight-year-old boy who had lived his entire life with his mother, based in part on the mother's moral history: she had "began cohabiting with her first husband, Harry, two months after meeting him and had begun dating and living with her current husband, Daniel, while still married to, but separated from, Harry," behavior the trial court deemed "promiscuous." *Roberts v. Eads*, 235 So.3d 1425, 1430 (Miss. Ct. App. 2017). The child was born while the parents were cohabiting, but they never married. The trial court noted approvingly that the father had been "in a stable marriage for over six years," while the mother, now expecting a child with her current husband, 'had been in multiple relationships and marriages." *Id.* at 1430.

4.   *The argument that infidelity frequently harms children.* Professor Lynn Wardle argues that the contemporary refusal to admit or consider evidence of parental fault in custody hearings "tragically turns a blind eye to

the significant harms that parental infidelity generally causes for children." Lynn D. Wardle, *Parental Infidelity and the "No-Harm" Rule in Custody Litigation*, 52 Cath. U. L. Rev. 81, 81 (2002). He notes that courts have found harm where the parent's adultery has been outrageous rather than discreet, the infidelities have been numerous, the adultery "has been obsessive to the point of neglecting the child," or the child has witnessed adulterous acts. *Id.* at 89. Under what circumstances, if any, do you think infidelity should influence a custody decision?

5. *Sexual orientation and gender identity.* The gender of a parent's new partner or partners may or may not make a difference to the court's evaluation of harm to the child depending on both the jurisdiction and the judge.

For many years, in many jurisdictions, LGBT parents were considered morally unfit per se where the other parent was a heterosexual. As recently as 2007, at least half the states and the District of Columbia took the view that a parent's sexual orientation could be a factor in the best interests analysis but could not determine the outcome of a custody dispute absent a showing of harm to the children. Ada Orakwusi, *Child Custody, Visitation and Termination of Parental Rights*, 8 Geo. J. Gender & L. 619, 634–35 (2007).

These views have undergone rapid—though not universal— transformation. For example, in 2012 an appellate court in Kentucky expressly held that because the enumerated best interest factors allowed consideration of a parent's "misconduct" but did not mention sexual orientation it was reversible error for a judge to award custody to the father based on the mother's sexual orientation in the absence of a showing that the children were harmed by it or that it interfered with their relationship with their mother. *Maxwell v. Maxwell*, 382 S.W.3d 892 (Ky. Ct. App. 2012). The court also held that "being a member of a same-sex partnership alone does not meet the criterion for sexual misconduct." *Id.* at 898.

In contrast, an Arizona court found that a father's process of transitioning from Zachary to Zoe had an adverse effect on his young children. The trial court found that the children were confused that " 'the person they know as "Daddy" now dresses and presents herself as a woman and wishes to be called "Mommy." Father is certainly free to be who he or she wishes to be [b]ut the consequences of and confusion caused by his choices in the lives of 4 and 2 year old children cannot be ignored.' " *Tipsword v. Tipsword*, 2013 WL 1320444 at *2 (Ariz. Ct. App. Apr. 2, 2013) (quoting and affirming the trial court order granting custody to the mother, but reversing conditions imposed on father that he should present as a man during visits).

In 2015 the Supreme Court recognized the right of persons in same-sex intimate relationships to marry. *Obergefell v. Hodges*, 135 S. Ct. 2584 (2015), It also condemned discrimination against lesbians and gays through references to "unjustified inequality within our most fundamental institutions that once went unnoticed and unchallenged." *Id.* at 2590.

But *Obergefell* did not address discrimination against LGBT persons outside denial of the right to marry. In the absence of laws that prohibit discrimination on the basis of sexual orientation or gender identity, LGBT parents who share children with a heterosexual parent may remain at risk of losing custody battles. It remains to be seen whether litigation against other forms of discrimination (e.g., in employment, housing or custody determinations) will be needed, or what the outcome of such litigation would be. In the context of custody disputes, at least one state court has noted that it awaits the legislature's instructions as to "what changes to the law are necessary and/or appropriate in custody proceedings involving same-sex relationships" in light of *Obergefell*. *In re C.A.C.*, 231 So.3d 58 (La. Ct. of App. 2017) (applying general custody principles to affirm a joint custody order for the child of a biological mother and her lesbian former life partner).

6. *Judicially-imposed conditions on custodial parents*. Courts regularly impose conditions on both custodial and noncustodial parents, but such orders may be an abuse of discretion if there is no threat of harm to the children or, in some jurisdictions, if the other parent did not request the condition. The *Kaptein* appellate court reversed the portion of the decree that denied the father FaceTime with his daughter, but did not reverse the finding that in-person visits would not be in the child's best interests. It held that the father was entitled to "reasonable visitation," accomplished for the time being online, and that such visits were in the child's best interests. Was there any indication that in-person visits would "seriously endanger" the child as required by the statute before such visits could be denied?

In an interim order issued in 2015 when the child was two years old, the *Kaptein* trial court accepted the recommendations of the custody evaluator and ordered the father to " 'participate in an assessment and treatment regarding his sexual behaviors and relationship issues, including a comprehensive sexual addiction evaluation.' " The father failed to obey this order, as he failed to obey the financial orders. *State ex rel. C.E.K.*, 234 So. 3d 1059 (La. Ct. App. 2017). Was the order warranted on the facts?

In *Bargmann v. Bargmann*, 2011 WL 1026095 at *6 (Tenn. Ct. App. Mar. 22, 2011) the Tennessee Court of Appeals reversed the trial court's order barring the noncustodial mother's boyfriend from spending the night with her when the child visited. The mother was cohabiting with her boyfriend, who stayed in a hotel during the girl's overnight visits. The trial judge opined that nonmarital relations were "[u]psetting because it's amoral but, more than that, because it set a pattern for the girl to follow." *Id.* at *5. The appellate court reversed because there was no evidence that the child's welfare was being jeopardized; it declined to allow "the trial court's personal notions of moral rectitude" to substitute for proof of harm to the child. *Id.* at *6.

In 2001, a South Dakota family court imposed several conditions on a mother who had allegedly engaged in misconduct including an adulterous relationship in which one encounter occurred in her home after the couple shared a bottle of wine while the child was sleeping in another room, and protracted internet use which her husband termed an "addiction," and which included "highly erotic" conversations with men she encountered in chatrooms. *Zepeda v. Zepeda*, 632 N.W.2d 48, 51–2 (S.D. 2001). During the trial, the judge conditioned the mother's temporary custody on her compliance with the following express conditions: she could not " 'have any men in her apartment or in her presence while the child [was] present"; she could not consume any alcohol (although there was no evidence she abused alcohol); and she could not use the Internet "unless required by her employment." *Id*. at 52. Ultimately, the judge concluded that the mother's " 'appalling' " conduct had no harmful impact on the couple's son, and awarded the mother primary physical custody. *Id*. at 53 (affirming custody award to the mother as not clearly erroneous, though a "close" call, but expressly stating the panel did "not condone [the mother's] misconduct").

In Arkansas a longstanding common law policy had prompted courts to restrict parents' extramarital cohabitation in the presence of the children in order to promote a "stable environment." *Moix v. Moix*, 430 S.W.3d 680, 686 (Ark. 2013). "[I]n more recent cases," however, the state's highest court appears to have relaxed this standard, in favor of an evidence-based analysis of "concrete proof of likely harm to the children." *Id*. at 686 (holding that the "public policy against romantic cohabitation" does not always override the best interest of the children analysis and reversing an order preventing the father's long-term domestic partner from being present during the child's overnight visits). *Accord Bamberg v. Bamberg*, 435 S.W.3d 6, 9 (Ark. Ct. App. 2014) (overturning cohabitation restriction on the mother where her same-sex paramour played a critical role in helping her care for a "severely disabled" child who was "unable to understand the implications of overnight guests").

7.   *Online communications*. While *Kaptein* involves behavior in the real world, online communications play an increasingly important role in family law disputes where parties point to online communications as evidence of immorality and lack of fidelity. Despite widespread popular belief and media reports that Internet use can be blamed in one way or another for one in five divorces or is a factor in roughly 80% of marital breakups, the assertions remain anecdotal and no reliable evidence substantiates them. Carl Bialik, *Irreconcilable Claim: Facebook Causes 1 in 5 Divorces*, Wall St. J., Mar. 12, 2011, at A2 (discussing lack of evidence).

In 2014 the Supreme Court of Mississippi, sitting en banc, overturned an award of custody to the father because the trial court erroneously gave undue weight to the mother's immoral online behavior. *Borden v. State*, 122 So.3d 818 (Miss. Ct. App. 2014) (*en banc*). The mother was alleged to have reconnected with two male high school classmates on Facebook prior to the couple's separation. She was photographed at a bar with both of them, and met one of them at his hotel room where they were interrupted by the man's wife. The mother admitted to "inappropriate" Facebook communications with one of the men, captured in 75 pages of transcripts of online communications introduced at trial, which the judges described as "quite explicit." Nonetheless, the trial court ruled that the evidence was not sufficient to support divorce on the ground of adultery. But the judge found the mother's behavior justified award of custody to the father under three *Albright* factors: moral fitness, parenting skills, and stable home environment. The trial judge had condemned the wife: " 'She should have been at home taking care of those children . . . instead of out partying . . . and meeting with another man at a motel . . .' * * * 'She should have 'stayed off the internet and stayed off of her contact [sic] with her two boyfriends . . .' " *Id.* at ¶ 9. The state's Supreme Court held this was reversible error because the court had imputed a parenting deficit based on the mother's moral failings, without showing a connection between her alleged immorality and her parenting. "Determinations of child custody are not . . . an opportunity to punish a parent for his or her marital misconduct." *Id.* at ¶ 6.

Online communication raises a number of issues that the law has yet to resolve. It arguably facilitates "meeting" prospective lovers and reconnecting with former flames. But are online communications or underlying flaws in the marriage to blame? The novel emergence of relationships confined to the virtual world raises numerous intriguing questions about the meaning of betrayal that courts have not yet resolved, as discussed in Chapter 8. Does virtual infidelity (online sexual banter, or sex with an avatar) without physical contact in the real-world amount to adultery? Can a preoccupation with online communications—no matter how tame—amount to a form of abandonment, as some have alleged?

8.   *Can a nexus be found where the parent's sexual behavior is limited to the virtual, on-line world? What conditions can a court impose?* After a husband discontinued sexual liaisons with prostitutes and assured the court that he had abandoned the use of sexual sites on the Internet since receiving psychological counseling, the court concluded that it was "highly unlikely" that he would "expose his son to his sexual interests." Nonetheless, to protect the son during his visits to his father's home, the court imposed conditions including: if the father obtains a home computer he must purchase and install equipment that blocks him from opening adult content and only the Guardian ad Litem ("GAL") shall have access to the password; the father may not reveal his home address to anyone on an adult Internet site; no unrelated adults are allowed in the father's home while the son is there unless they are the parents of a child who is having a play date with the son; and both parents and the son were to continue psychotherapy until released by their respective therapists or by court order because such treatment would serve the child's best interests. *Gorman v. Gorman,* 2008 WL 344612 at *7, 11 (Conn. Super. Ct. Jan. 24, 2008).

A court in Iowa was forced to balance the custody claims of a father who accessed pornography on the Internet against the claims of a mother who met a man online and corresponded with him for a year before inviting him to the family home while her husband was away and then travelling with him for a month. The court awarded physical custody to the father. *In re the Marriage of Eldred,* 2010 WL 5342966 (Iowa Ct. App. Dec. 22, 2010).

C. RACE

Some factors that courts commonly weighed in custody disputes at one time implicate constitutional concerns that go beyond the individual parties before the court. As you read the following case, consider whether race is unique.

PALMORE V. SIDOTI
Supreme Court of the United States, 1984.
466 U.S. 429.

CHIEF JUSTICE BURGER delivered the opinion of the Court.

* * *

I

When petitioner Linda Sidoti Palmore and respondent Anthony J. Sidoti, both Caucasians, were divorced in May 1980 in Florida, the mother was awarded custody of their 3-year-old daughter.

In September 1981 the father sought custody of the child by filing a petition to modify the prior judgment because of changed conditions. The change was that the child's mother was then cohabiting with a Negro, Clarence Palmore, Jr., whom she married two months later. Additionally, the father made several allegations of instances in which the mother had not properly cared for the child.

After hearing testimony from both parties and considering a court counselor's investigative report, the court noted that the father had made allegations about the child's care, but the court made no findings with respect to these allegations. On the contrary, the court made a finding that "there is no issue as to either party's devotion to the child, adequacy of housing facilities, or respectability of the new spouse of either parent."

The court then addressed the recommendations of the court counselor, who had made an earlier report "in [another] case coming out of this circuit also involving the social consequences of an interracial marriage. *Niles v. Niles,* 299 So.2d 162 [(Fla. Dist. Ct. App. 1974)]." From this vague reference to that earlier case, the court turned to the present case and noted the counselor's recommendation for a change in custody because "[t]he wife [petitioner] has chosen for herself, and for her child, a life-style unacceptable to the father *and to society.* . . . The child . . . is, or at school age will be, subject to environmental pressures not of choice."

The court then concluded that the best interests of the child would be served by awarding custody to the father. The court's rationale is * * * [that]:

"The father's evident resentment of the mother's choice of a black partner is not sufficient to wrest custody from the mother. It is of some significance, however, that the mother did see fit to bring a man into her home and carry on a sexual relationship with him without being married to him. Such action tended to place gratification of her own desires ahead of her concern for the child's future welfare. *This Court feels that despite the strides that have been made in bettering relations between the races in this country, it is inevitable that Melanie will, if allowed to remain in her present situation and attains school age and thus more vulnerable to peer pressures, suffer from the social stigmatization that is sure to come.*"

The Second District Court of Appeal affirmed without opinion, thus denying the Florida Supreme Court jurisdiction to review the case. We granted certiorari, and we reverse.

II

The judgment of a state court determining or reviewing a child custody decision is not ordinarily a likely candidate for review by this Court. However, the court's opinion, after stating that the "father's evident resentment of the mother's choice of a black partner is not sufficient" to deprive her of custody, then turns to what it regarded as the damaging impact on the child from remaining in a racially mixed household. This raises important federal concerns arising from the Constitution's commitment to eradicating discrimination based on race.

The Florida court did not focus directly on the parental qualifications of the natural mother or her present husband, or indeed on the father's qualifications to have custody of the child. The court found that "there is no issue as to either party's devotion to the child, adequacy of housing facilities, or respectability of the new spouse of either parent." This, taken with the absence of any negative finding as to the quality of the care provided by the mother, constitutes a rejection of any claim of petitioner's unfitness to continue the custody of her child.

The court correctly stated that the child's welfare was the controlling factor. But that court was entirely candid and made no effort to place its holding on any ground other than race. Taking the court's findings and rationale at face value, it is clear that the outcome would have been different had petitioner married a Caucasian male of similar respectability.

A core purpose of the Fourteenth Amendment was to do away with all governmentally imposed discrimination based on race. *See Strauder v. West Virginia*, 100 U.S. 303, 307–08, 310 (1880). Classifying persons according to their race is more likely to reflect racial prejudice than legitimate public concerns; the race, not the person, dictates the category. *See Personnel Administrator of Mass. v. Feeney*, 442 U.S. 256, 272 (1979).

Such classifications are subject to the most exacting scrutiny; to pass constitutional muster, they must be justified by a compelling governmental interest and must be "necessary . . . to the accomplishment" of their legitimate purpose, *McLaughlin v. Florida,* 379 U.S. 184, 196 (1964);. *See Loving v. Virginia,* 388 U.S. 1, 11 (1967).

The State, of course, has a duty of the highest order to protect the interests of minor children, particularly those of tender years. In common with most states, Florida law mandates that custody determinations be made in the best interests of the children involved. The goal of granting custody based on the best interests of the child is indisputably a substantial governmental interest for purposes of the Equal Protection Clause.

It would ignore reality to suggest that racial and ethnic prejudices do not exist or that all manifestations of those prejudices have been eliminated. There is a risk that a child living with a stepparent of a different race may be subject to a variety of pressures and stresses not present if the child were living with parents of the same racial or ethnic origin.

The question, however, is whether the reality of private biases and the possible injury they might inflict are permissible considerations for removal of an infant child from the custody of its natural mother. We have little difficulty concluding that they are not. The Constitution cannot control such prejudices but neither can it tolerate them. Private biases may be outside the reach of the law, but the law cannot, directly or indirectly, give them effect. "Public officials sworn to uphold the Constitution may not avoid a constitutional duty by bowing to the hypothetical effects of private racial prejudice that they assume to be both widely and deeply held." *Palmer v. Thompson,* 403 U.S. 217, 260–61 (1971) (WHITE, J., dissenting).

This is by no means the first time that acknowledged racial prejudice has been invoked to justify racial classifications. In *Buchanan v. Warley,* 245 U.S. 60 (1917), for example, this Court invalidated a Kentucky law forbidding Negroes to buy homes in white neighborhoods.

> "It is urged that this proposed segregation will promote the public peace by preventing race conflicts. Desirable as this is, and important as is the preservation of the public peace, this aim cannot be accomplished by laws or ordinances which deny rights created or protected by the Federal Constitution."

Id. at 81. Whatever problems racially mixed households may pose for children in 1984 can no more support a denial of constitutional rights than could the stresses that residential integration was thought to entail in 1917. The effects of racial prejudice, however real, cannot justify a racial classification removing an infant child from the custody of its natural mother found to be an appropriate person to have such custody.

The judgment of the District Court of Appeal is reversed.

It is so ordered.

NOTES AND QUESTIONS

1. *Epilogue: Melanie's father retained custody.* Professor Randall Kennedy has commented that "there often exists a gap between formal rights declared on paper and the actual enjoyment of those rights":

> * * * This gap was vividly illustrated by the frustration faced by Linda Sidoti Palmore after her victory [in the Supreme Court]. Even though the Supreme Court had ruled in her favor, she did not regain custody of her daughter. During the pendency of the case, Anthony Sidoti had moved Melanie and his new wife to a new home in Texas. After losing in the federal Supreme Court, he appealed for help to various state courts, which responded affirmatively. First, a Texas court issued a restraining order that barred Linda Palmore from taking custody of Melanie. Then, Judge Buck, in Florida [the judge who had issued the initial order removing Melanie from her mother's custody], granted Anthony Sidoti's request to transfer the case to judicial authorities in Texas. * * * The Florida court also rejected the argument that allowing Sidoti to retain custody of his child amounted to defiance of the Supreme Court's ruling. The Supreme Court, it noted, had not expressly ordered that custody of Melanie be awarded to Mrs. Palmore * * *. * * *

Randall Kennedy, Interracial Intimacies: Sex, Marriage, Identity and Adoption 384–85 (2003).

2. *The passage of time as a factor in determining best interests.* As suggested by the *Palmore* outcome, the emphasis on stability and continuity as critical aspects of the best interests evaluation often means that "possession is nine-tenths of the law."

Melanie was three years old when her father sought to remove her from her mother's custody. By the time the Supreme Court ruled on the case she was eight. When the Florida District Court of Appeals rejected Linda Palmore's appeal from the trial court's order transferring jurisdiction to Texas, it explained:

> * * * Under all the circumstances we cannot say that at this time it has been established to be in Melanie's best interests that she be ordered returned to her mother and that the trial court erred in not so ordering.

> The eight-year-old child appears to have had substantial upheavals of her life, and we find no compelling reason at this point to add a further upheaval. The record indicates that Melanie lived with both her parents until they separated when she was about two and one-half years old. She then lived with her mother for about two years

until her father was awarded custody. After only two months with her father, Melanie was returned to her mother by court order. She stayed with her mother for about eight months, and then was ordered to her father's custody, where she has remained for about two and one-half years except for a ten-day visit with her mother in August 1984. We cannot disagree that it appears to be in the best interests of Melanie that she continue in the status quo at least for the time being until the custody issue is finally resolved.

Palmore v. Sidoti, 472 So.2d 843, 846–47 (Fla. Dist. Ct. App. 1985).

Was *Palmore* simply an "easy case" for the unanimous Supreme Court because the trial judge was entirely candid about what he was doing? Did the outcome after remand serve society's interest in racial harmony by allowing Melanie to live with a parent who objected to her having an African-American stepfather?

3.   *Race as a persistent factor in custody disputes.* In 2010 a New Jersey appellate court reversed a family court order awarding residential custody to the black mother of a bi-racial child on the ground that the trial judge had, among other things, violated the custodial rights of the white father "in relying upon issues of race * * *." *Areyan v. Areyan*, 2010 WL 1753257 at *5 (N.J. Super. Ct. App. Div. Apr. 18, 2010). The mother's expert witness had based a number of conclusions on the child's race and opined that the child would be better off in her mother's school district because it had a large number of nonwhite students, and the trial judge had implicitly relied on the "improper factor" of "the child's biracial status." *Id.* at *6. *See* Solangel Moldonado, *Bias in the Family: Race, Ethnicity, and Culture in Custody Disputes*, 55 Fam. Ct. Rev. 213 (2017) (examining the persistence of implicit bias in custody disputes).

4.   *Transformed demographics.* The increase in interracial marriages and cohabitation is likely to diminish the lingering role of race in custody decisions. For example, 17% of all new marriages in the United States in 2015 were interracial or interethnic including marriages between Hispanics and non-Hispanic whites). Kristen Bialik, *Key facts about race and marriage, 50 years after* Loving *v.* Virginia, Pew Research Center (2017). Interracial relationships are even more common among cohabitants, whether they are same-sex or opposite sex couples. Vespa et al., *America's Families, supra,* at 17.

It comes as no surprise given these figures that the number of interracial children is also growing. The 2010 Census revealed that the proportion of people who identified themselves as multiracial had increased dramatically since 2000, the first year in which the Census Bureau allowed respondents to choose more than one racial identification. Susan Saulny, *Census Data Presents Rise in Multiracial Population of Youths*, N.Y. Times, Mar. 25, 2010, at A3. Fourteen percent of children under the age of one are multiracial or multiethnic, nearly triple the proportion in 1980. Bialik, *supra*. That said, parents and children in biracial and multiracial families may still encounter many questions, rude and racist comments, and other negative reactions from strangers. *See* Susan Saulny, *In Strangers' Glances at Family, Tensions Linger,* N.Y. Times, Oct. 13, 2011, at A1, A12. Or they may not be perceived by third parties to be a family.

D. SIBLINGS AND RELIGION

As you have seen, courts making custody decisions often confront several difficult issues at once in responding to the tangled realities of family life. This is especially apparent in the following case.

ARTHUR V. ARTHUR

Court of Appeals of Ohio, 1998.
720 N.E.2d 176.

WILLIAM B. HOFFMAN, JUDGE.

Plaintiff-appellant/cross-appellee Cindy A. Arthur (hereinafter "wife") appeals the October 16, 1997 Judgment Entry/Decree of Divorce of the Fairfield County Court of Common Pleas, Domestic Relations Division, granting her a divorce from defendant-appellee/cross-appellant Michael J. Arthur (hereinafter "husband") and approving a shared parenting plan for the couple's four minor children. Husband appeals that decree as well as the March 31, 1998 Judgment Entry finding him in contempt of court.

Statement of the Facts and Case

Husband and wife were married in Vincennes, Indiana on August 15, 1981. Four children were born as issue of the marriage: Megan Jo * * *, Eric M. * * *, Jacob M. * * *, and Mary K. * * *.

Upon her graduation from high school in 1978, wife worked in a department store in the Vincennes, Indiana area. Following a brief marriage to another individual, wife met husband, who was working part-time in the same department store while attending Vincennes University. In 1983, husband completed an associates degree in computer science. While husband attended school, wife supported the couple. After wife gave birth to their first child, Megan, in 1983, the couple decided wife would remain at home full-time.

In 1987, husband accepted a job offer in the Columbus, Ohio area. Around the same time, wife began regularly watching the television ministry of the World Harvest Church (hereinafter "the Church"), which originates from Columbus. After the family moved to Ohio, they attended the Church. In November, 1987, husband accepted a position with the Church as the Director of Computer Operations.

The Church became the focal point of the family. Their lives centered around the Church, including worship, friendships, and activities. The children attended the World Harvest Christian Academy ("the Academy"), a church affiliated school. The children's contacts outside the Church were limited.

In 1994, husband left his position with the Church to accept a position with Cap Gemini America, Inc. Prior to leaving his employment with the Church, husband began to disassociate himself from the institution and its members.

In December, 1995 husband informed wife he desired a divorce. On or about December 24, 1995, husband moved out of the marital residence. On January 12, 1996, wife filed a complaint for divorce. * * *

[On] March 26, 1996, the trial court entered temporary orders for a shared parenting arrangement. Pursuant to the temporary orders, wife was designated the residential parent and legal custodian of the four children for school purposes. Husband was granted possession of the children on weekends and for short weeknight visits, subject to timely notice. Throughout the proceedings, husband and wife contested the issues of custody and the children's enrollment at the Academy.

The matter proceeded to trial. At trial, Dr. John Mason, the court appointed psychologist, reiterated the concerns he voiced in his report to the trial court regarding the children's attendance at the Academy, which, he opined, shielded them from the real world. Mason testified, while in wife's custody, the children's outside contacts were limited to church members. Due to the lack of cooperation between husband and wife, Mason recommended shared parenting in order to avoid the development of parental-alienation syndrome.

Mason met with the three oldest children on several occasions. During the initial visit, the children expressed a desire to stay with wife and continue their education at the Academy. Although the children expressed little interest in living with husband, they indicated their desire to visit him on a regular basis. When the children originally expressed these desires, they had not been visiting husband because * * * [he was cohabiting with another woman]. After visits with husband commenced, the three children told Mason they wanted to live with husband. The children reiterated this position over the course of their visits with Mason.

Mason testified that sports are paramount in the boys' lives. With husband, the boys became involved in organized, competitive sports leagues. When Megan originally saw Mason, she stated she considered living with husband because she did not want to attend Bible College for two years before she started regular college. During her last meeting with Mason, Megan told him wife informed her she could make the decision regarding her attendance at Bible College.

Regarding the children's continued enrollment at the Academy, Mason expressed his concerns regarding the cloistering aspect of the school and the limited social contact the children had outside of the Church environment. The testimony revealed that the Academy has below average class sizes, problems with staffing, teachers who lacked practical experience, and a lack of curriculum. The extra curricular activities available to the children were limited and included only noncompetitive activities. A substantial portion of the school day was devoted to bible studies. All of the text books used at the school had a religious emphasis.

* * *

After hearing all the evidence, the trial court entered findings of fact and conclusions of law on August 12, 1997. On October 16, 1997, the trial court filed the Judgment Entry/Decree of Divorce. Pursuant to the divorce decree, wife was named the residential parent for school purposes of Megan and Mary, and husband was named the residential parent for school purposes of Jacob and Eric.

* * *

I

In her first assignment, wife maintains that the trial court abused its discretion in separating the four children by ordering a shared parenting plan.

The standard of review of an appellate court of a trial court's determination in a custody proceeding is abuse of discretion. * * * We must look to the totality of the circumstances in the case *sub judice* and determine whether the trial court acted unreasonably, arbitrarily, or unconscionably.

During a divorce proceeding, a trial court is required to allocate the parental rights and responsibilities for the care of the minor children pursuant to [the applicable statute]. The trial court has two options when allocating parental rights and responsibilities. The court may either designate one parent as the residential parent and legal custodian who bears the primary rights and responsibilities for the care of the children, or may issue a shared-parenting order requiring the parents to share all or some of the aspects of the physical and legal care of the children.

Despite the trial court's classification of the custody order as a shared-parenting plan and wife's attack on the same basis, the practical effect is a split custody order. Generally, this Court would not encourage a trial court to resolve a custody dispute in such a manner, however; under the facts of the case *sub judice*, we do not find the trial court abused its discretion in ordering split custody.

The testimony at trial revealed that the children, particularly the boys, had interests outside the activities available at the Church and the Academy. By designating husband as the residential parent of Eric and

Jacob, the court gave the boys an opportunity to engage in organized sports, activities which were extremely important to them.

Although the trial court's custody determination results in a separation of the children, the record reveals that the order establishes an extensive visitation schedule for wife with the boys, for husband with the girls, and for the children together. Pursuant to the order, the children are together one hundred eighty-five whole days during the year, and seventy-two partial days during the year, resulting in only one hundred eight days of separation.

In support of her position, wife contends the trial court improperly considered her religious affiliation when the court determined she should not be designated the residential parent for all the children. Wife relies on *Pater v. Pater*, 588 N.E.2d 794 [(Ohio 1992)], in which the Ohio Supreme Court held:

> A parent may not be denied custody on the basis of his or her religious practices unless there is probative evidence that those practices will adversely effect the mental or physical health of the child. Evidence that the child will not be permitted to participate in certain social or patriotic activities is not sufficient to prove possible harm.

[*Id.* at 800.]

A review of the trial court's findings of fact and conclusions of law belies wife's argument that the trial court improperly considered wife's religious affiliation. In its findings of fact, the trial court stated its concerns about the education the children were receiving at the Academy, including the below average class sizes, the problems with teacher staffing, the lack of teacher experience, the lack of curriculum, and the sheltered life style. The trial court did not indicate any concerns regarding the religious philosophy of the Church. Rather, the trial court's concerns centered around the quality of education the children were receiving. The testimony regarding the Worthington Public School System revealed the public school the children would attend offered gifted programs and a wide curriculum.

We agree with *Pater*, that a parent may not be denied custody on the basis of his or her religious practices unless such practices adversely affect the mental or physical well-being of the child. We find that the trial court in the instant action did not deny wife custody of all the children based upon her affiliation with the Church. Rather, the trial court merely raised concerns about the education the children were receiving at a school that happens to be church affiliated.

Wife's first assignment of error is overruled.

* * *

NOTES AND QUESTIONS

1. *Should siblings always stay together after their parents split up?* Most jurisdictions acknowledge the strong connection that frequently exists among siblings and express a preference for keeping siblings together. *See, e.g., Alverson v. Alverson*, 28 So. 3d 784 (Ala. Civ. App. 2009) (decision to separate siblings should be based on a "compelling" reason). The ALI Principles propose that in allocating custody, one objective should be "to keep siblings together where the court finds that doing so is necessary to their welfare." ALI, *supra*, § 2.08(c) (2002). Some family court judges estimate that siblings are only separated in about 5% of all divorced or separated families, and that a decision to separate siblings usually originates with the parents. David M. Shumaker et al., *The Forgotten Bonds: The Assessment and Contemplation of Sibling Attachment in Divorce and Parental Separation*, 49 Fam. Ct. Rev. 46, 50 (2011).

2. *When is it appropriate to separate siblings?* The preference for keeping siblings together is consistent with the emphasis on maintaining continuity in children's lives and preserving family bonds. Because "courts should be cautious about dividing custody of children," it is not an abuse of discretion to make a collective custody decision respecting the group of siblings instead of analyzing the best interests of each child individually. *Schlieve v. Schlieve*, 846 N.W.2d 733, 740 (N.D. 2014).

Appellate courts, however, permit separation where the siblings have different needs. *See, e.g., Duhn v. Johnson*, 779 N.W.2d 79 (Iowa Ct. App. 2009) (finding the general presumption against separating siblings, including half-siblings, is not ironclad); *Stephanie W. v. Maxwell V.*, 274 P.3d 1185, 1192 (Alaska 2012) (not an abuse of discretion to separate a child from his half-siblings where the bond is "not of overwhelming importance to [him] or to his well-being" and other best interests factors support the designation of custodial parent). Other exceptions to the general rule against split custody can be found when (1) the siblings have never lived together or have been separated for a substantial amount of time; (2) the siblings express a strong preference to live with different parents; (3) the siblings do not get along well with one another; or (4) a significant age difference separates the siblings. ALI, *supra*, § 2.08 cmt. g. In determining whether to separate siblings, courts also consider the parents' respective capacities to care for their children and the parents' moral, mental or physical qualifications. *See, e.g.*, Jay M. Zitter, Annotation, *Child Custody: Separating Children by Custody Awards to Different Parents—Post-1975 Cases*, 67 A.L.R. 4th 354 (1989 & Supp. 2018).

Unique issues arise in custodial disputes involving half- and step-siblings. Courts have "traditionally applied the policy of keeping siblings together in custody decisions only to children of the same marriage." *In re D.R.L.M.*, 84 S.W.3d 281, 303 (Tex. Ct. App. 2002). Accordingly, courts have ordered split custody more frequently for half-siblings than for siblings who share both biological parents. 24A Am. Jur. 2d *Divorce and Separation* § 860 (2018). Where the bond between the half-siblings is strong, however, courts increasingly prefer to keep them together. *Id.*; *In re the Marriage of Flibotte*,

2009 WL 5126114 (Iowa Ct. App. Dec. 30, 2009) (awarding custody to the father in whose home the children had bonded with a half-sister and step-sister).

Separation of siblings is also a serious issue in adoption (addressed in Chapter 17) and foster care. Separation in these settings offers potentially useful analogies for custody cases. Based on improved understanding of the importance of sibling bonding, a number of states have enacted statutes that protect the visitation rights of siblings in the child welfare system even after the parents' rights have been terminated and one or more (but not all) siblings adopted. *See In re D.C. and D.C.*, 4 A.3d 1004, 1013 n.5 (N.J. 2010) (collecting statutes). These statutes are premised on the reciprocal rights of siblings to maintain the sibling relationship. Should sibling relationships receive more formal protections in private custody disputes?

3. *Religion as an element of best interests.* In some jurisdictions, spiritual or religious well-being is one of the statutory "best interests" factors for courts to consider. Some trial courts continue to consider a parent's piety or religious practices as a factor in determining best interests. For example, in a portion of the *Blevins v. Bardwell* opinion not reproduced in this casebook, the court held that it was not an abuse of discretion to consider each parent's likely "future religious example," and to determine that the mother was much more committed to her child's religious training. 784 So.2d 166, 176 (Miss. 2001).

As a condition of a divorce decree, an Indiana trial court in 2005 ordered a couple practicing Wiccan, a form of paganism, not to expose their child to the non-mainstream religion's beliefs and rituals. *Jones v. Jones*, 832 N.E.2d 1057, 1061 (Ind. Ct. App. 2005). The appellate court held the decision to be an abuse of discretion and ordered that the limitation on "parental authority to determine the religious training" of the child be stricken from the decree. *Id.* But in 2008 an Arkansas court upheld a decision awarding custody of a two-year-old to the father he had never lived with, based in large part on the mother's participation in what the trial court judge called the Wiccan "cult," even though no evidence was presented of a connection between the mother's religious beliefs and the child's well-being. *Hicks v. Cook*, 288 S.W.3d 244, 248–49 (Ark. Ct. App. 2008).

4. *Conflicting parental beliefs and First Amendment rights.* The First Amendment's religion clauses may limit the court's capacity to use religious practices and beliefs as a basis for choosing one parent over the other in a custody dispute. And yet, in *Pietrzak* v. *Schroeder*, 759 N.W.2d 734, 744–45 (S.D. 2009) the court found the lower court had not abused its discretion when, awarding residential custody to the father, the judge observed that the father had been a life-long Roman Catholic while the mother had recently changed denominations and become a more fervent believer. The South Dakota Supreme Court noted that "religion is a legitimate factor" though courts do not need to "weigh the number of years" each parent has practiced his or her faith as the trial judge did from the bench. *Id.* at 742 The Supreme Court ignored the trial judge's discourse on Proverbs 3:5 (reversing on other grounds).

The Supreme Court of Kansas considered the impact of religious differences between parents in *Harrison v. Tauheed*, 256 P.3d 851 (Kan. 2011). The court concluded that it would be a mistake for a trial court either to base a custody decision on religious belief or to completely ignore religious beliefs and practices. Adopting the majority view, the court held that the correct approach is to:

> differentiate between religious beliefs on the one hand and religiously motivated actions or conduct with implications for the child's welfare on the other. Disapproval of mere *belief or nonbelief* cannot be a consideration in a custody determination * * *. Yet consideration of religiously motivated *behavior* with an impact on a child's welfare cannot be ignored.

Id. at 853.

In a custody dispute between unmarried parents, where the mother's religious beliefs led her to believe that the body can heal itself and caused her to refuse to vaccinate the child, the court awarded the father (who accepted medical care) responsibility for making all medical decisions. *Winters v. Brown*, 51 So. 3d 656 (Fla. Dist. Ct. App. 2011).

Nonetheless, most jurisdictions hold that each parent has a right to expose the child to the religious practices he or she observes, absent a clear showing of harm to the child. *Schlieve v. Schlieve*, 846 N.W.2d at 743–44 (reversible error to impose religious obligations during parenting time—"this is for the parents alone to decide."). In the classic case of *Abbo v. Briskin*, 660 So.2d 1157 (Fla. Dist. Ct. App. 1995), a man and a woman of different faiths met and fell in love. When their daughter was four-and-a-half years old, they divorced. The principal dispute at trial was the child's religion. The appellate court held that the courts may not decide "in favor of a specific religion over the objection of the other parent. As with married parents who share diverse religious beliefs, the question of a child's religion must be left to the parents even if they clash. A child's religion is no proper business of judges." *Id.* at 1159.

New York courts expressly decline to enforce any provisions in "custody agreements that provide for a specific religious upbringing" unless the agreement serves the best interests of the children. *Weisberger v. Weisberger*, 60 N.Y. S.3d 265 (App. Div. 2017) (reversing transfer of custody to the father where mother who had always been the primary caretaker had come out as a lesbian, breached an agreement to raise the children as ultra-orthodox Jews (Hasidim), disparaged the father's religious beliefs, and allowed the children to dress immodestly and to violate dietary laws and Sabbath observance).

In one frequently cited case, the judge explained why religious questions come up in custody disputes:

> * * * In intact families, parents are left to decide their children's 'best interests' on an *ad hoc* basis. Significantly, "a marital couple is not an independent entity with a mind and heart of its own, but an association of two individuals with a separate intellectual and

emotional makeup." One parent may be a Republican the other a Democrat, one may be a Capitalist the other a Communist, or one may be a Christian and the other a Jew. Parents in healthy marriages may disagree about important matters; and, despite serious, even irreconcilable, differences on important matters, the government could certainly not step in, choose sides, and impose an orthodox uniformity in such matters to protect judicially or bureaucratically determined "best interests" of the children of such parents. Rather, intervention is permitted only upon a showing of a substantial risk of harm to the child in absence of intervention, and that the intervention proposed is the least intrusive means adequate to prevent the harm.

Zummo v. Zummo, 574 A.2d 1130, 1139–40 (Pa. Super. Ct. 1990) (quoting *Eisenstadt v. Baird*, 405 U.S. 438, 453 (1972)). In the next chapter you will see how disputes over the children's religious training often continue after the parents' relationship terminates.

5. *Preserving choice for the child.* Where divorcing devout Hindu parents disagreed about whether to perform the Hindu ritual of Chudakarana on their three-year-old daughter, the trial court reserved performance of the ceremony "until the child is of sufficient age to make that determination herself, absent a written agreement between the parties." *Sagar v. Sagar*, 781 N.E.2d 54, 56 (Mass. App. Ct. 2003). Chudakarana is a ritual in which mantras are recited while a priest removes hair from five parts of the child's head, and the child's head is then shaved and an auspicious mark is placed on the child's forehead. The court concluded that since the parents had competing free exercise claims, it was unclear whether the ceremony was integral to the Hindu faith. The father seemed motivated at least in part by a wish to control family members, and he conceded that atonement could be made by later performance.

E. A NOTE ON "CUSTODY" OF ANIMAL COMPANIONS, COMMONLY KNOWN AS PETS

The law governing who gets to keep a beloved dog, cat, fish, or even an aardvark or other less common companion, after a household breaks up is changing. Historically, courts took a strict property approach—treating pets as personal property. For instance, applying the traditional approach in 2012, a Texas court ruled that ownership of a Shih Tzu lay with the wife because she purchased the dog. *Oldenburg v. Oldenburg*, 2012 WL 858645, 1 (Tex. App. Mar. 15, 2012). The court did not weigh the fact that the husband was the dog's primary caretaker: he took the dog to work with him every day. Instead, the court regarded this history as irrelevant under the strict property approach because the wife had purchased the dog. *See Desanctis v. Pritchard*, 803 A.2d 230 (Pa. Super. Ct. 2002) (holding that despite the status owners bestow on their pets, Pennsylvania law considers dogs to be personal property); *see also* Cal. Penal. Code § 491 (West 2010) (declaring dogs personal property and stating that their value is to be ascertained in the same manner as the value of other property).

Recently, however, more progressive courts, with New York courts in the lead, have carved out newer ways of deciding animal custody cases— notably, the "best for all" and "best interest of the pet" approach.

Travis v. Murray, 977 N.Y.S.2d 621 (Sup. Ct. 2013) led the way to the "best for all concerned" standard in 2013 with a detailed analysis of how courts should analyze custody claims concerning animals. *Travis* involved two divorcing women fighting over their miniature dachshund, Joey. The court recognized that "dogs play an ever more important role in our emotional lives" (citing John Homans, *The Rise of Dog Identity Politics*, New York Magazine, Feb. 1, 2010 at 20). Rather than treat Joey as chattel, the court conducted a hearing during which each spouse had an opportunity to show not only why she would benefit from having Joey in her life, but also why Joey had a better chance of living, prospering, loving, and being loved in her care. *Travis* noted it would be helpful to consider who bore the major responsibility before the break-up for meeting Joey's needs, including feeding, walking, grooming, taking him to the veterinarian, and who spent more time with Joey on a regular basis, a standard that looks a lot like the best interests or psychological parent analysis in disputes over child custody. The *Travis* court proposed, and applied, the "best for all concerned" standard, which it distinguished from a "best interests" analysis on the basis, among other things, that it would be "unworkable and unwarranted" to bring the full panoply of resources used in child custody cases (experts, extensive testimony and interviews with the subjects of the dispute) to bear on "gauging a dog's happiness." *Id.* at 459. *Travis* further held that custody of an animal should not be shared, and should not be open to modification, because courts do not have the resources to devote to cases about animal companions. *See Hennet v. Allan*, 981 N.Y.S.2d 293, 297 (Sup. Ct. 2014) (applying *Travis* to dog shared by former cohabitants because "pets are more than just 'personal property' when it comes to disputes between owners," they are "a 'special category of property'" to which property releases do not attach; a *Travis* hearing is required).

In *Hament v. Baker*, 97 A.3d 461 (Vt. 2014), the court recognized that although pets are property, pets are also living beings that form emotional attachments with their owners running in both directions. The *Hament* court considered several factors as part of the "best for all standard," including the animal's welfare and the emotional connection between the animal and each spouse. As in *Travis*, the *Hament* court found it had no authority to impose an enforceable visitation order for the dog, and no legislative authority to supervise shared care of a companion animal. *Id.* at 465 (divorcing couple may agree to visitation, but ultimately the dog is property, the division is final, and the family court—though it appropriately weighed "the dog's welfare and its emotional connection between the animal and each spouse"—may neither modify the distribution nor enforce a visitation schedule).

In addition to the best for all standard, some courts apply the "best interest of the pet" standard. This approach looks to (i) which party has been the primary caretaker of the pet; (ii) the stability of the home environment of each party; and (iii) the quality of the preexisting relationship between each party and the pet. *See* Christopher G. Rhodes, *Who Gets the Dog When the Marriage Gets 'Ruff': Complications Arising from the Classification of Family Pets As Traditional Property*, 9 Est. Plan. & Community Prop. L.J. 293, 314 (2017).

Most recently, a few state legislatures have weighed in. A California statute that became effective in 2019 provides that pets will no longer be treated solely as property in divorce proceedings. Instead, either party to the divorce may petition for "sole or joint ownership of a community property pet animal taking into consideration the care of the pet." Assemb. B. 2274, 2017–2018 Leg., Reg. Sess. (Cal. 2018).

F. DOMESTIC VIOLENCE

Both the medical and legal professions have weighed in on the relationship between domestic violence and child custody: professionals in both fields agree that perpetrators of domestic violence should not receive custody of their children. In 1998, the American Psychological Association ("APA") reported that "an abusive man is more likely than a nonviolent father to seek sole physical custody of his children and may be just as likely (or even more likely) to be awarded custody as the mother." Am. Psychological Ass'n, Report of the American Psychological Association Presidential Task Force on Violence and the Family, Issues and Dilemmas in Family Violence, Issue 5 (1998), http://www.apa.org/pi/pii/familyvio/issue5.html. An APA Presidential Task Force also found that courts often minimize the harmful impact to a child who witnesses violence between parents. According to the APA, some courts ignore the advice of psychologists that "it may be better for children's development to restrict the father's access to them and avoid continued danger to both mothers and the children." *Id.*

In 2000, the American Bar Association recommended that states address the safety of adult and child domestic violence victims during visitation and visitation exchanges. ABA policy calls on attorneys to seek protective orders for clients who are victims of domestic violence. Linda D. Elrod & Robert G. Spector, *A Review of the Year in Family Law: Redefining Families, Reforming Custody Jurisdiction, and Refining Support Issues*, 34 Fam. L.Q. 607 (2001).

In the following opinion, a Massachusetts appellate court considers what behaviors amount to domestic violence, how to protect a custodial parent from an abusive former spouse, and how to balance every biological parent's visitation rights with the need to protect victims of domestic violence.

SCHECHTER V. SCHECHTER

Appeals Court of Massachusetts, 2015.
37 N.E.3d 632.

AGNES, J.

These are consolidated appeals by the defendant Yan Schechter (the father) from a judgment of divorce * * * and an abuse prevention order. One child, a son who is still a minor (the child), was born of the marriage. The judgment awarded sole legal and physical custody of the child to the plaintiff Karina Schechter (the mother). The father's appeal presents [several] issues [including] the custody determination and the validity of a judgment provision suspending the father's visitation rights for one year, along with a corresponding * * * order precluding any contact between the father and child during that period. * * *

Background. The consolidated trial in these cases occurred over eighteen days in 2010 and 2011, and included testimony from thirty-eight witnesses, and 132 exhibits. The conscientious judge made 330 findings of fact, as well as detailed rulings of law. We first summarize the judge's findings, setting forth other facts later in connection with the specific legal issues we address.

The father is a Ukrainian immigrant whose family initially lived in Israel and then moved to Boston in 1988 when he was nearly sixteen. The father and his family have lived in Boston for the past twenty years. The mother emigrated from Uzbekistan and eventually moved to Boston in 1999 at age twenty to pursue educational opportunities. The father graduated from Brandeis University and had early success in a small business and as a computer consultant. Throughout their relationship, there were numerous instances of emotional and economic abuse,[5] as well

---

[5] In relationships in which there is domestic violence, the victim is often economically dependent on the perpetrator. *See* Note, *Domestic Violence and Custody Litigation: The Need for Statutory Reform*, 13 Hofstra L. Rev. 407, 426 (1985), cited in *Opinion of the Justices*, 427 Mass. 1201, 1209, 691 N.E.2d 911 (1998). Experts in the field of domestic violence describe economic or financial abuse as an element of the perpetrator's coercive control of the victim. *See E.C.* v. *RCM of Washington, Inc.*, 92 A.3d 305, 319 (D.C. 2014); *State* v. *Newell*, 710 N.W.2d 6, 27 (Iowa 2006). "The CDC [Centers for Disease Control and Prevention] defines coercive control as a form of psychological aggression that includes 'behaviors that are intended to monitor, control, or threaten an intimate partner.' . . . [O]ne type of coercive control behavior includes economic abuse, defined as 'behaviors that control a woman's ability to acquire, use, and maintain economic resources.'" Kim, *Credit Cards: Weapons for Domestic Violence*, 22 Duke J. Gender L. & Policy 281, 285 (2015) (citations omitted). Economic abuse has also been defined as "[m]aking or attempting to make a person financially dependent, e.g., maintaining total control over financial resources, withholding

as physical abuse and the threat of physical abuse, by the father against the mother.

The father and the mother began dating in the summer of 2001 while they were both living in New York City. That fall, they both relocated to Boston, where the mother began her final year of college while continuing to work as a dental hygienist. The father became involved in the residential real estate business and again met with success. Initially, the couple lived with the father's parents and then moved in with friends of the father. From the inception, it was evident that the father's family did not support the relationship. In December, 2001, the parties found out that the mother was pregnant. The father proposed marriage and the mother accepted. The father's family did not respond well to the engagement, and urged him to obtain a prenuptial agreement. The mother experienced a miscarriage in early 2002. The couple agreed to conceive another child. The mother learned that she was pregnant again in May of 2002. Meanwhile, the couple found a condominium unit they both liked in Brighton and the father purchased it in the name of his real estate company.

During that same month, the mother graduated from college and started preparing for the Dental Admission Test (DAT). The couple decided it was best for the mother not to work and to focus on studying for her DAT. In spite of this agreement, the father continually criticized the mother for avoiding work and implied that she was exaggerating her morning sickness. He made disparaging comments to her suggesting that she was worthless, and did little to assist her with household chores.

emotional abuse against mom

1. *Marriage.* On December 18, 2002, days before their marriage, the parties signed a prenuptial agreement that the father had been discussing with lawyers since December of 2001. The father had real estate assets in the greater Boston area estimated to be worth over seven million dollars. They were married on December 22, 2002.

The father's emotional abuse of the mother was constant and continued during their marriage, as documented in the judge's findings of fact in great detail. The mother gave birth in February of 2003. During this time, the mother chose to pursue a degree as a dentist. By April of 2008, the stock market had suffered a serious downturn and the father had a

---

access to money, forbidding attendance at school or employment." Johnson, *Redefining Harm, Reimagining Remedies, and Reclaiming Domestic Violence Law*, 42 U.C. Davis L. Rev. 1107, 1120 (2009). *See* Conner, *Financial Freedom: Women, Money, and Domestic Abuse*, 20 Wm. & Mary J. of Women & L. 339, 358 (2014). In this case, the judge found that the father had the mother's car towed and was on the scene for the removal of the car, and then told the mother that everything belonged to him, that she would only get the clothes that she brought to the United States, and that she could only take public transit until she earned enough to buy a car. At other times, he cancelled and later restored her credit cards when they fought. After one particular fight the mother went to the grocery store to find all of her credit cards cancelled, and the father did not restore them until the parties made up. At another time he also took and cut the mother's credit cards in half in front of her.

breakdown, becoming extremely anxious over his real estate business. He was hospitalized and constructively incapacitated.

By September of 2008, the mother returned to school and the father became frustrated that the mother did not spend more of her free time with him. He did not approve of the mother's friendships with particular female friends. By the time the mother prepared to graduate from dental school, the father told the mother that he wanted her to stay home and care for the household. The mother started work as a dentist in the practice where she had previously been employed as a dental assistant for ten years. * * *

2.   *Separation.* On May 30, 2009, the father and the mother separated. Soon after the father left their home, he telephoned the mother and said that he intended to get a divorce and needed to speak with her that night after the child went to bed. She agreed to talk. The mother and child then went to visit a friend. As the mother was leaving to return home, she found that her car was being towed and saw the father emerge from the tow truck's passenger seat. He got into his own car and drove away, staring at her intently with an angry look as he passed. Afraid to go home, the mother and child spent the night at the friend's house. The father, by his own account, grew furious. He expected that the mother would get a ride home so that he could kiss the child good night and have a discussion with her about the marriage. He failed to understand the natural response to the intimidation of having one's car towed.

While at the family home waiting for the mother, the father gathered up several pairs of her shoes, some boots, and a purse and put them in the oven. He turned the oven on and left. He stated that "[i]t seemed like the most harmless way to piss her off." The father's father went to the home to shut the oven off.

The parties did not live together after the father moved out of the home. The father attempted to get key access to the building adjacent to and overlooking the marital home, but his request was not granted.

3.   *Legal proceedings.* On June 8, 2009, the mother filed a complaint for divorce. On September 14, 2009, she filed a separate complaint in which she sought protection from abuse under G. L. c. 209A. In support of the protective order issued by the court, the judge cited an instance in which the father threatened, "I'm coming with an axe to chop you up," after the mother would not agree to let the child have a sleepover. On another occasion months later, when the mother picked up the child from a supervised visit with the father, the supervisor witnessed as the father pulled up behind the mother's car, "revved" his engine, swerved his car back and forth, then accelerated around her car, completely crossing the double line in the street, and raced away.

     * * *

4.   *Guardian ad litem report.* As part of the proceedings, a psychologist was appointed as guardian ad litem (GAL) on behalf of the child to evaluate the issues of custody and parenting time, and later the issue of removal. The GAL issued an extensive report dated April 15, 2010 (and supplemented that September), that detailed his observations and interactions with family members. The report concluded that the father dominates both the mother and the child with his words and actions. The father appeared to have agendas concerning information he wanted to discuss or disclose and rewarded the child when he cooperated. On the other hand, the GAL observed that "[the mother] allows [the child] to be himself and have his own thoughts and feelings, and to express them without fear or reservation." The GAL cited a number of parenting decisions that reflected poor judgment on the father's part. The GAL pointed out that there was extensive "mudslinging" by the father against the mother, while the mother focused only on trying to do what is best for the child.[9]

Discussion. 1.   *Standard of review.* The judge's factual findings must be left undisturbed absent a showing that they are plainly wrong or clearly erroneous. This deferential standard applies to our review of cases involving custody and visitation. However, in reviewing the ultimate determination on custody and visitation, we consider whether there was an abuse of discretion in how the judge accounted for the child's best interests.

2.   *Parenting issues.* a. *Custody and visitation.* i. *The terms of the judgment.* The judgment ordered that the mother have sole legal and physical custody of the child and that "[t]here shall be a one year cessation of any contact between [the child] and his father." * * * In exercising discretion, the judge is authorized "to consider the widest range of permissible evidence."

The father maintains that "the minimal findings here do not support any plausible contention that the best interests of the child standard was properly applied here." This is a gross mischaracterization of the basis for the judge's rulings. The judge dealt with the parties for more than two years and had numerous opportunities to observe their interactions, as well as to assess witness accounts of how they treated each other and interacted with their child. The judge also had the benefit of the comprehensive and detailed GAL report * * *. The judge documented numerous instances of the father's abusive and degrading conduct toward the mother before and during the marriage, including several instances in which the father threatened to kill or do great bodily harm to the mother. In making a decision about legal or physical custody, a judge "shall consider whether or

---

[9]   Unsatisfied with the GAL interviews, the father provided a recording of his own interview with the child that was "clearly staged." During a supervised dinner on March 7, 2010, the father took the child into the bathroom and told him his mother was at fault for what was going on in the family.

not the child's present or past living conditions adversely affect his physical, mental, moral or emotional health." Furthermore, in such cases the judge "shall consider evidence of past or present abuse toward a parent or child as a factor contrary to the best interest of the child."[10] Where there is a finding of "a pattern or serious incident of abuse," the judge must employ a rebuttable presumption that sole or shared custody with the abusive parent is not in the child's best interests.[11] Here, the rebuttable presumption applied. The [order of protection] that issued as to the mother, discussed in more detail *infra*, rested on a finding that the father placed the mother in fear of imminent serious physical harm. (The father does not challenge this aspect of the [protective] order.) In the circumstances, this amounted to a finding of a "serious incident of abuse" * * * which triggered the presumption.

We recognize that "parents have a fundamental interest in their relationships with their children that is constitutionally protected." However, the strong expression of public policy by our Legislature that a child's welfare must be the paramount concern when a judge determines custody, means that a judge is authorized not only to order sole legal and physical custody with one parent when it serves the best interests of the child, but also that a judge is authorized to impose conditions and restrictions on and to suspend any visitation by the other parent when it is determined that visitation would not be in the best interests of the child.[f] In cases such as this, our duty as a reviewing court is to ensure that the record reflects that all relevant factors have been considered by the judge, and that the decision is based on a fair weighing of the factors.

In this case, the judge made findings that the father was domineering in his relations with the mother and child. The judge credited the GAL's observation that the father repeatedly made negative comments and

---

[10] *General Laws c. 208, § 31A*, defines "abuse" as follows: "the occurrence of one or more of the following acts between a parent and the other parent or between a parent and child: (a) attempting to cause or causing bodily injury; or (b) placing another in reasonable fear of imminent bodily injury."

[11] The statute specifies, "[a] probate and family court's finding, by a preponderance of the evidence, that a pattern or serious incident of abuse has occurred shall create a rebuttable presumption that it is not in the best interests of the child to be placed in sole custody, shared legal custody or shared physical custody with the abusive parent. Such presumption may be rebutted by a preponderance of the evidence that such custody award is in the best interests of the child." *G. L. c. 208, § 31A.* (We note that this same rebuttable presumption governs temporary custody determinations in abuse prevention proceedings in the Probate and Family Court. *G. L. c. 209A, § 3[d].*) The section defines "serious incident of abuse" as "the occurrence of one or more of the following acts between a parent and the other parent or between a parent and child: (a) attempting to cause or causing serious bodily injury; (b) placing another in reasonable fear of imminent serious bodily injury; or (c) causing another to engage involuntarily in sexual relations by force, threat or duress." *G. L. c. 208, § 31A.* Finally, the statute directs, "[i]f the court finds that a pattern or serious incident of abuse has occurred and issues a temporary or permanent custody order, the court shall within 90 days enter written findings of fact as to the effects of the abuse on the child, which findings demonstrate that such order is in the furtherance of the child's best interests and provides for the safety and well-being of the child." *Ibid.* * * *

[f] *Editors' Note:* Visitation rights and restrictions on visitation are discussed in Chapter 13.

disparaging references to the mother in the child's presence, "and spent considerable time and impassioned energy impugning [the mother's] moral character." The judge also documented the father's lack of insight into the destructive nature of his behaviors, his tendency to blame others for everything, and his lack of impulse control. As the judge correctly noted, "[a] determination of whether a parent is able to separate his or her needs and interests from those of the minor children and whether a parent's actions will compromise the minor children's relationship with the other parent are relevant factors in determining custody." Finally, the judge explained why neither unsupervised nor supervised visitation between the father and the child was feasible.[12]

The judge's decision to suspend visitation for one year is also supported by his extensive findings that over the course of their relationship, the father had engaged in physical, emotional, and financial abuse of the mother, and, in his interactions with the child, had damaged the mother's relationship with the child.[13] Children who experience domestic violence, whether as direct witnesses or indirectly as members of the household in which violence occurs, "suffer deep and profound harms."[14] * * * The findings are amply supported by the evidence * * *

ii. *The G. L. c. 209A order.* The original abuse prevention order was an emergency order issued ex parte on September 13, 2009, as a result of an episode over whether the father could have an overnight visitation with their child at the home of the child's friend. (There was an order in effect at the time that required written consent by both parties for the father to have an overnight visit.) Several days later, the court conducted an extension hearing at which it heard from the mother and the father as well as their attorneys. The judge credited the mother's account of the events, which involved threatening behavior and impulsive misconduct directed toward her by the father in the presence of the child.[15] The judge extended

---

[12] The judge added that "[a]llowing unsupervised contact between [the father] and [the child] would be a capitulation to a manipulative parental alienator. Continuing to allow supervised contact between [the father] and [the child] is a recipe for continued misery. No list of rules prohibiting certain behaviors could ever encompass all the ways [the father] will find to harass, intimidate, berate, and manipulate all those involved. The hard reality is that it is in [the child's] best interest to place a moratorium on any communication or contact between him and his father."

[13] The judge found that * * * the father's behavior is not transitorily connected to the divorce action; it is symptomatic of a more permanent condition. Many of the behaviors described predate any contemplation of divorce by the parties. They also predate the financial crisis of 2008 when the father was under great stress. The father cannot have unsupervised visits because he will cause [the child] serious emotional harm and destroy [the child's] relationship with the mother * * * [The child] needs for his mother to have the opportunity to safely rebuild her strength and that outweighs, for the near future, the child's need to continue the relationship with his father wherein the father uses manipulation to twist [the child's] thoughts and confuse him. If the mother is not safe, secure, and protected, [the child] will have two dysfunctional parents." * * *

[14] "Very disruptive symptoms related to trauma can be exhibited by children even when they have not been personally subjected to direct physical or sexual abuse." Guidelines for Judicial Practice: Abuse Prevention Proceedings § 12.02, Commentary (Admin. Office of Trial Ct. 2011).

[15] The judge found that the father sought the mother's consent for the overnight via a telephonic text message. After consulting with the parenting coordinator, the mother telephoned

the abuse prevention order for one year, and later extended it again on several occasions prior to the consolidated trial.

The order was made a permanent abuse prevention order on * * * the same day the divorce judgment entered. The judge's endorsement [indicated that the order preventing contact between the father and the child] "may be reviewed after one year." * * *

The father does not challenge the substance of the c. 209A order insofar as it bars him from abusing or contacting the mother. * * *

The father challenge[s] the judge's decision to incorporate the one-year suspension of visitation into the permanent abuse prevention order under c. 209A. The argument is that, in order to include a no contact with a child provision in an abuse prevention order[,] there must be evidence of and a judicial finding that the child was suffering from "abuse".[17] It is true that the statute requires a person seeking an abuse prevention order, such as the mother in this case, to demonstrate that she was suffering from "abuse," * * *, in order to obtain any relief * * * "Abuse" under G. L. c. 209A, § 1, requires a judicial determination that the plaintiff is in danger of imminent *and* serious physical or sexual harm [quoting the statutory definition set out in the footnotes to the opinion].

However, * * * a judge is not also required to find that the defendant has committed a separate act or acts of abuse against the parties' child to order that the defendant have no contact with that child. * * *. As the statute also expressly provides, "a finding by [the Probate and Family Court] by a preponderance of the evidence that a pattern or serious incident of abuse, toward a parent *or* child has occurred shall create a rebuttable presumption that it is not in the best interests of the child to be placed in sole custody, shared legal custody or shared physical custody with the abusive parent" (emphasis supplied). Additionally, in abuse prevention proceedings, "[i]f ordering visitation to the abusive parent, the court shall provide for the safety and well-being of the child and the safety of the abused parent." That an act of serious abuse or a pattern of abuse committed by one parent against another parent may support the issuance of a c. 209A order on behalf of the abused parent as well as an order

---

the child's friend's home and asked to speak to the child. The father took the telephone from the child and told the mother the child wanted to sleep over and then hung up. The judge found that "[the father] then called back screaming in a rage. Seeing [the mother] shaking and hearing [the father's] voice yelling, [a family friend who was with the mother] took the phone himself in time to hear [the father] threaten to kill [the mother] with an ax[e]. [The family friend] heard [the father] say in Russian, 'I'm coming with an axe to chop you up.'" The judge also found that although the child is not fluent in Russian, he heard and understood enough of the conversation to be "aware that his father was very mad and intended to 'kick his mother's butt.'"

[17] [After repeating the statutory definition provided in the statute and set out in footnote 11, the opinion continues:] There is only one finding by the judge here that addresses the father's use of force against the child. The judge found that on one occasion the father slapped the child on the back of his neck for misbehaving while in the custody of the babysitter. Without more, we cannot say that this was an act of abuse within the meaning of G. L. c. 209A, § 1.

prohibiting the abuser from having contact with the child * * * reflects the critical understanding * * * that children who experience domestic violence "suffer deep and profound harms."

[T]he judge's well documented findings of fact showed that there was at least one "serious incident of abuse" by the father against the mother—i.e., placing her in reasonable fear of imminent serious bodily injury—* * * that the child witnessed the father's abusive behavior toward the mother; and that any contact between the father and the child within a period of at least one year would damage the mother's relationship with the child and be harmful to the child. These findings not only justified the provisions of the c. 209A order directly ensuring the safety of the mother, but also supplied the basis for the provisions of the final order regarding child custody, contact, and visitation [which is subject to modification in the future].

* * *

Conclusion. For the reasons set forth above, the judge's detailed findings of fact support his award of physical and legal custody to the mother and his conclusion that a suspension of visitation between the father and the child for a period of one year was in the best interests of the child. [T]he order is affirmed. * * *

So ordered.

NOTES AND QUESTIONS

1.   *How courts treat evidence of domestic violence.* All 50 states and the District of Columbia require courts to consider domestic violence committed by one parent against the other when ruling on a visitation or custody dispute between the parents. https://www.americanbar.org/content/dam/aba/administrative/domestic_violence1/Charts/2014%20Joint%20Custody%20Chart.authcheckdam.pdf.

Beyond that, states adopt different stances. New York, Indiana and some other states only require the court to *consider* domestic violence by either parent as one of the enumerated factors it takes into account when it assesses the child's best interests. N.Y. Dom. Rel. § 240 (McKinney Supp. 2018); Ind. Code Ann. § 31–14–13–2 (West 2018). As of 2018, however, evidence of domestic violence created a rebuttable presumption against awarding custody to the abusive parent in 20 jurisdictions. 129 Am. Jur. Proof of Facts 3d 217 (Updated April 2018) (collecting statutes); *e.g.*, Mass. Ann. Laws ch. 208 § 31A (LexisNexis 2011). That does not, however, preclude a parent who has committed domestic violence from receiving custody if the presumption is rebutted. Which approach makes better sense?

Some states, like Tennessee, remove judicial discretion in cases involving domestic violence. The Tennessee statute mandates that parenting time shall be limited for parents who have engaged in "[p]hysical or sexual abuse or a pattern of emotional abuse of the parent [or] child;" it is reversible error for a judge to award primary residential custody to the abuser. Tenn. Code Ann. § 36–6–406 (2017), *Jacobsen v. Jacobsen*, 2013 WL 1400618 at *4, 6 (Tenn. Ct. App. Apr. 5, 2013) (reversing assignment of residential custody to father who punched a hole in the wall and threw a metal faucet at mother in front of child, smashed a shower door so the glass shattered and cut mother, and displayed other anger management problems).

Still other states expressly direct courts to take domestic violence into account when establishing visitation rights, or as a defense to an allegation that the victim abandoned the children by fleeing the home. In Rhode Island, for example, where the court has made a finding of domestic violence it must "consider as primary the safety and well-being of the child and of the parent who is the victim of domestic or family violence." R.I. Gen. Laws § 15–5–16 (g)(2) (2017).

However, these statutes are no panacea. Many or most of the statutes fail to define what acts rise to the level of domestic violence or the level of proof required to show that such violence occurred. *Schechter* appears to take a broad view of what constitutes domestic violence, including within its scope "coercive control," psychological aggression, and "economic abuse." Some cases involve physical violence of a sort not apparent in *Schechter* but, as *Schechter* makes clear, incidents such as punching, threatening with a weapon and the like are not required in every jurisdiction for the court to conclude domestic violence has occurred. *C.G. v. E.G.*, 2016 WL 3921510 (N.J. Super. Ct. Ch. Div. June 30, 2016) (interpreting statutory revisions enacted in 2015 that "emphasized the reality" that domestic violence is not limited to "only physical abuse."). Even where the record shows physical attacks and threats of bodily harm, abusers sometimes are awarded custody. *See, Wissink v. Wissink*, 301 A.D.2d 36 (2002) (court erred in awarding custody of teenager to father who had, among other things, threatened the mother with a knife while the girl sat on her lap without first ordering comprehensive psychological evaluations).

The approach taken in *Schechter*—emphasizing the risks to a child who observes domestic violence between his or her parents—is unfortunately not the norm. Very few statutes require any inquiry into whether the child witnessed or was aware of the violence, much less whether it had an adverse impact on the child (as witnessing or being aware of violence presumptively does). Leslie Joan Harris, *Failure to Protect from Exposure to Domestic Violence in Private Custody Contests*, 44 Fam. L. Q. 169, 176 (2010). That defect is especially problematic when it results in the victim of domestic violence losing custody on the ground that the victim failed to protect the child from exposure to the violence perpetuated by the abuser. *Id.* at 176–80.

2.   *More about the Schechters.* Perhaps the most pervasive myth about domestic violence is that "domestic violence happens in low-income families, or people with substance abuse problems, or only to people who grew in a violent family." Domestic Violence Action Center, *Common Myths About Domestic Violence* (https://domesticviolenceactioncenter.org/common-myths/) (last

available: March 26, 2018). Note that the Schechters were well educated and affluent. Their case demonstrates that no stratum of society, even the wealthy, is immune to domestic violence, as is clear from tabloid stories about celebrities like Billy Murray, Charlie Sheen, and Chris Brown abusing their partners. This is why Susan Weitzman founded The Weitzman Center, a nonprofit aimed at raising awareness about "upscale abuse." Dr Weitzman, the author of *Not to People Like Us: Hidden Abuse in Upscale Marriages,* argues that higher income individuals suffer behind what she calls "a veil of silence." They believe domestic abuse is only happening to them—partly because "[n]o one can hear you scream on a 3-acre lot." *Domestic Violence in Affluent Marriages,* Domestic Shelters (Mar. 9, 2016), https://www.domesticshelters.org/domestic-violence-articles-information/domestic-violence-in-affluent-marriages#.WuZBsK2ZN mB.

In footnote 5 the *Schechter* opinion discusses the ways in which domestic abusers frequently use financial control to restrict their partner's independence, a situation you saw in the *McGuire* case in Chapter 3. In a portion of *Schechter* you did not read, the court upheld the lower court's ruling that the Schechters' prenuptial agreement was void because, among other things, it was "unfair and unreasonable at the time it was executed." (Premarital agreements will be discussed in Chapter 16). When the couple married, there was "an enormous disparity" in their assets: he was worth seven and a half million dollars, while she had assets of $2,500. Among other things, the prenuptial agreement provided that the husband held all of the equity in the marital home as of the date of the marriage, and in the event of divorce the wife would only receive half of any increase in that value. The court observed that under the agreement the wife might leave the marriage without any share of marital assets at all: "[I]f the equity in the home did not go up, the wife would receive no assets. If the husband chose to encumber the home to the maximum extent possible, the wife would receive no assets." *Schechter v. Schechter,* 88 Mass. App. Ct. 239, 259, 37 N.E.3d 632, 649 (2015). Or, the husband could have sold the home and rented instead. All of this was part of a pattern of control.

3.   *Obstacles to achieving statutory intent.* Numerous studies have shown that "courts often award custody, joint custody, and unsupervised visitation to abusers," perhaps in part because "many evaluators," like many judges, "know nothing about domestic violence and insist that it does not harm children." Lynn Hecht Schafran, *Domestic Violence, Developing Brains, and the Lifespan: New Knowledge from Neuroscience,* 53 Judges J. 32, 35 (2014). Some children form close attachments to abusers—both those who abuse them and those who abuse their other parent. Absent compelling support, GALs and judges err when they defer to those children's preferences about who they want to live with. *See Wissink v. Wissink,* 749 N.Y.S.2d 550 (App. Div. 2002) (remanding for fuller evaluation and hearings a case in which the father received custody even though he had attacked the mother on more than one occasion and in the daughter's presence, even enlisting the daughter's assistance, and once held a knife to the mother's throat while the daughter sat on her lap).

Courts are sometimes so reluctant to completely deprive a parent of access to his or her child, that judges impose joint custody even in the face of domestic abuse. This can happen even in states whose statutes clearly intend to deprive perpetrators of domestic violence of custody. For example, despite the provisions of the California statute set out at page 805, trial judges in California can look to Cal. Fam. Code § 3044 to allow a father who has committed domestic violence against a mother to rebut the presumption against awarding him physical or legal custody by finding that a preponderance of the evidence establishes that it is in the child's best interest for the abusive parent to receive joint or sole custody. *See Celia S. v. Hugo H.*, 207 Cal. Rptr. 3d 756 (Ct. App. 2016), as modified (Sept. 23, 2016) (reversing a joint custody award to a father who spit at and punched the mother, and pulled her hair).

4.   *The neuroscience of exposure to domestic violence.* The article cited by the court in Note 3 by Lynn Hecht Shafran, a leader in judicial training on issues involving gender bias, summarized studies that show how exposure to violence in the household triggers the "fight or flight" stress reaction in children. Repeated episodes of this reaction, research has demonstrated, causes " 'the biologic embedment of stress,' " which can cause "long-term behavioral, health, and social problems" that were hidden from view until recent advances in neuroscience enabled scientists to study the impact of witnessing domestic violence on neuroendocrine systems and the neural networks they regulate. Shafran, *Domestic Violence, supra,* at 32 (summarizing article appearing in the New England Journal of Medicine). Shafran urged judges to re-conceptualize the harms done to children: "What if, instead of saying that children exposed to domestic violence are 'at risk,' we said children exposed to domestic violence are 'at risk of brain damage?' " *Id.* at 35.

5.   *Unwarranted accusations of domestic violence as litigation strategy?* While some courts have erred in not taking allegations of domestic violence against adults or children seriously enough, this risk should not completely overshadow the competing risk that before or after divorce adults will falsely accuse each other of abusing children in order to gain the upper hand in a custody battle. For example, during and after divorce proceedings a West Virginia mother reported her husband to the state child welfare authorities three times for abusing the youngest of their four children who were living with him. The state engaged in two full investigations, against which the husband who had custody had to defend himself. The youngest child entered foster care during one of the investigations. The family court ultimately ordered the mother to reimburse the father for the costs of defending himself, granted him full custody of all of the children and terminated the mother's parental rights on the ground that her baseless allegations had emotionally harmed the children. *In re John T.*, 695 S.E.2d 868 (W. Va. 2010) (affirming decision). *See also, e.g., In re A.M.R.*, 101 N.E.3d 1194, 1195 (Ohio Ct. App. 2017) (mother sought to end shared custody after father allegedly made "fraudulent allegations of abuse" against her to the county's child welfare office); *Eisenlohr*

v. Eisenlohr, 2011 WL 1566201 (Conn. Super. Ct. Apr. 1, 2011) (holding that the mother manipulated the child in order to prevail in a custody dispute, bribing her to support the mother's repeated baseless reports of abuse to the child welfare agency, and modifying the custody order to give sole custody to the father, and ordering mother not to file any additional false reports of abuse or face sanctions); *Bloch v. Bloch*, 2010 WL 3447897 at *1, 6 (Mich. Ct. App. Sept. 2, 2010) (after the trial court held in the divorce litigation that the mother had filed or caused to be filed several false allegations of physical and sexual abuse of the child against the father, and awarded custody to the father, the father is entitled under Michigan law to bring a separate tort action against the mother for malicious prosecution or defamation); *Malenko v. Handrahan*, 979 A.2d 1269, 1273 (Me. 2009) (affirming the trial court's conclusion at the divorce trial that the father had not engaged in domestic violence against the mother, noting the court's express findings about the mother's demeanor, lack of candor, and tendency "to perceive events differently than others"); *Handrahan v. Malenko*, 12 A.3d 79 (Me. 2011) (respecting the same family, upholding trial court decision that after divorce the mother had not shown that father had abused the child by a preponderance of the evidence).

6.   *Friendly parent provisions versus accusations of alienation or violence.* "Friendly parent" provisions, which require courts "to consider which parent is more likely to encourage close contact with the other parent" are widely used, as you saw in the statutes set forth earlier in this Chapter. The friendly parent concept played a role in the *Schechter* decision because the father constantly denigrated the mother, while the mother hoped the father would become a better parent, adding to the list of factors that favored awarding custody to the mother.

It is difficult for courts to balance legitimate concerns about a child's safety against the principle that the custodial parent should strive to include the other parent in the child's life. As a policy matter, Alaska's highest court has ruled that "it is common sense that in a custody proceeding, good faith allegations by one parent against the other parent regarding behavior relevant to the custody decision and the child's best interests should not be held against the reporting parent" when the trial court examines who would best promote the child's relationship with the other parent. *Stephanie W. v. Maxwell V.*, 319 P.3d 219, 229 (Alaska 2014) (mother's unsubstantiated initial allegation that father sexually abused the child may have been made in good faith, but the court was entitled to weigh her subsequent allegation that the father was manufacturing methamphetamine at home, which had "almost no support," in evaluating whether she would foster a relationship with the father).

Friendly parent provisions pose special problems where an abuser is able to present an attractive image to the court and promises to make the child available to the victim. When a victim who wants sole custody seeks to limit visits, or needs to conceal her address from an abuser, the court may regard her as less than a friendly parent. Janet R. Johnston & Nancy Ver Steegh, *Historical Trends in Family Court Response to Intimate Partner Violence: Perspectives of Critics and Proponents of Current Practices*, 51 Fam. Ct. Rev.

63, 64–65 (2013). As a result, mothers' advocates have pressed for categorical bars on awarding custody to individuals who abuse their adult partners or their children—with substantial success as Note 1 explained.

Fathers' advocates in turn have responded to what they see as a wave of false domestic violence allegations with their own theory that custodial parents (primarily mothers) actively seek to sabotage the non-residential parent's relationship with the child. One father's rights group—the National Parents Organization—filed an amicus curiae brief supporting the father in *Schechter*.

In its most extreme form the accusation that custodial parents sabotage the non-custodial parent's relationship with their children is labeled "parental alienation syndrome" ("PAS"). No scientific evidence supports the theory, as experts repeatedly admonish: "Despite having been introduced 30 years ago, there remains no credible scientific evidence supporting parental alienation syndrome * * * The concept has not gained general acceptance in the scientific field, and there remains no test, no data, or any experiment to support claims made concerning PAS. Because of this lack of scientific credibility, many organizations—scientific, medical, and legal—continue to reject its use and acceptance." Rebecca M. Thomas & James T. Richardson, *Parental Alienation Syndrome 30 Years on and Still Junk Science*, Judges' J., Summer 2015, at 22. Nonetheless, the medical-sounding term continues to crop up in many custody hearings—both judges and forensic evaluators rely on it, even though several appellate courts have expressly rejected its use as evidence. Joan Meier and Sean Dickson, *Mapping Gender: Shedding Empirical Light on Family Courts' Treatment of Cases Involving Abuse and Alienation*, 35 Law & Ineq. 311 (2017); Elizabeth S. Scott & Richard E. Emery, *Gender Politics and Child Custody: The Puzzling Persistence of the Best-Interests Standard*, 70 Law & Contemp. Probs. 70, 96–100 (2014). At the extreme, allegations of alienation may result in the child being removed from the parent to whom the child is most attached, especially when fathers accuse mothers of alienation. Meier & Dickson, *supra* at 325.

Although PAS is unsubstantiated, the custodial parent's attitude matters. One of the most critical determinants of whether non-residential fathers continue to be actively engaged with their children is whether the mother encourages paternal involvement. Kathryn Edin & Timothy J. Nelson, Doing the Best I Can: Fatherhood and the Inner City (2013); Laurie S. Kohn, *Engaging Men as Fathers: The Courts, the Law, and Father-Absence in Low-Income Families*, 35 Cardozo L. Rev. 511, 521–23 (2013); Marsha Kline Pruett & J, Herbie DiFonzo, *Closing the Gap: Research, Policy, Practice, and Shared Parenting*, 52 Fam. Ct. Rev. 152, 162 (2014).

7. *What happens after one parent kills the other?* In 2005 a teenager won a pathbreaking legal battle to be adopted after his father killed his mother.

A teen who won a groundbreaking legal battle last summer to "divorce" his killer father walked out of court Thursday with new adoptive parents. "I don't think I'll ever be over it," Patrick Holland said of his mother's 1998 slaying by his father, "but it's a step forward. It's about the biggest step you can take at one time."

Patrick, 15, was adopted by Ron and Rita Lazisky; the pair have been his guardians and were close friends of the teen's mother. The Laziskys, of Sandown, N.H., have cared for Patrick since shortly after Daniel Holland fatally shot Liz Holland at the family's Quincy, Mass. home. Then 8, Patrick found his mother's body the following morning. Daniel Holland is serving life in prison without parole.

Patrick was one of the first children to initiate a parental-rights termination proceeding against one parent for killing the other. He argued Daniel Holland forfeited any right to be his father the night he shot Liz Holland eight times.

Katharine Webster, Associated Press, *Adoption Final for Teen Who "Divorced" Killer Dad*, Charleston Daily Mail, March 25, 2005, at P3C.

Some jurisdictions have since enacted statutes that bar the award of custody or visitation to a parent who has been convicted of murdering the other parent, the custodian or a sibling of any child who is the subject of the custody proceeding. N.Y. Dom. Rel. Law § 240 (1–c)(a) (McKinney Supp. 2018); *see also* Ariz. Rev. Stat. Ann. § 25–403.05 (2017) (presumption that a parent convicted of murdering the other parent is not an appropriate custodian may be rebutted by a finding that "there is no significant risk to the child" and the person convicted was the victim of domestic violence at the hands of the murdered parent). In 2014, a Tennessee appellate court expressly held that it was in the best interests of a child whose father had murdered his mother in front of him and was serving a life sentence in prison to terminate the father's parental rights and give custody of the child to his maternal uncle and his wife, who had been caring for the boy since his mother's death in 2007. *In re Jacob B.*, 2014 BL 6682472 (Tenn. Ct. App. Nov. 25, 2014). Presumably, these facts would also satisfy the extraordinary circumstances standard for assigning custody to a third party.

8.   *Abuse and Child Protection Services.* What happens to a child when neither parent is a fit parent? In the absence of stable parents, courts may consider granting custody to other appropriate adults in the family, the most common being grandparents rather than committing the child to the custody of the state through the child welfare system. *See Randallson v. Green*, 203 So. 3d 1190 (Miss. Ct. App. 2016) (grandparents were granted full legal and physical custody of granddaughter after evidence was presented that mother misused her prescription-drugs, threatened suicide, and that there was domestic violence, and further evidence of the deplorable condition of parents' home, including animal urine and feces, animal vomit, fleas, rats, boxes, filth, and their generally inability to maintain the condition of the home). However, not every child has grandparents to rely on and so children who have witnessed or suffered abused may enter foster care. *See Matter of E.B.*, 2017 WL 1737922 (Ohio Ct. App. May 4, 2017) (allowing siblings to be separated and placed in different foster homes). *See also Care & Prot. of Polly*, 2017 WL 3400656 (Mass.

App. Ct. Aug. 9, 2017) (finding that mother's prolonged pattern of allowing domestic violence in the home and in front of the children, and then repeatedly lying about it to the police and the department warranted placing the children in the custody of the state's protective services agency).

G. THE CHILD'S PREFERENCE

Most states require courts to consider a sufficiently mature child's custody preference, but leave questions about maturity and the weight of the mature child's preference to judicial discretion. UMDA § 402, 9A U.L.A. 282 (1998); *see, e.g.*, Cal. Fam. Code § 3042(a) (West Supp. 2018); Fla. Stat. Ann. § 61.13(3)(i) (West Supp. 2019); *see also* ALI, Principles of the Law of Family Dissolution: Analysis and Recommendations § 2.08 Reporter's Notes to cmt. f (2002). In all states, the younger the child, the less likely that his or her opinion will be solicited, much less taken seriously.

In 2016 the highest court in the District of Columbia held that it was reversible error for a court to fail to determine the custody preferences of the children who were 14, 9, and 7 when the court considered their mother's petition for modification of the custody arrangements. *Dugama v. Ayatew*, 145 A.3d 517 (D.C. 2016). The Court of Appeals held that the trial judge must receive "evidence relating to the children's wishes," and expressly noted that all of the children—including the seven year old—were "old enough to be capable of expressing an opinion." *Id.* at 521. The court remanded the case, leaving the decision about the best way to elicit the siblings' views to the trial judge's discretion. *Id.* at 522. A few states require deference to the wishes of children over a specified age (generally 12 to 14 years old). *See D.A. v. R.C.*, 105 A.3d 1103 (N.J. Super. Ct. App. Div. 2014) (finding trial court was required to take the preferences of a 14-year-old into consideration).

Longitudinal research indicates that teenagers who are more satisfied with their relationship with their primary residential parent were less likely to engage in delinquent behaviors. Such research, child custody expert Joan Kelly concludes, indicates the importance of directly obtaining and giving weight to adolescent views of each pre-separation parent-child relationship and to seek children's input about their future living arrangements. Joan B. Kelly, *Risk and Protective Factors Associated with Child and Adolescent Adjustment Following Separation and Divorce: Social Science Applications*, in Kathryn F. Kuehnle & Leslie M. Drozd, Parenting Plan Evaluations: Applied Research for the Family Court 49, 53–54 (2013).

Hearing a child's views is not the same as deferring to them. In Mississippi, for example, the applicable statute provides that the court "may consider" the preference of a child older than 12 and shall "explain in detail" why the child's wishes "were or were not honored." Miss. Code Ann. § 93–11–65(1)(a)(West Supp. 2017). Mississippi accorded more weight to children's views in an earlier iteration of the Code, which until 2006 gave children over the age of 12 the "privilege" of choosing between fit parents so long as their choice corresponded with what the court perceived to be in their best interest. Miss. Code Ann. § 93–11–65(1)(a)(West Supp. 2017) (change discussed in *Phillips v. Phillips*, 45 So. 3d 684, 694 (Miss. Ct. App. 2010) (the child's preference was never "outcome determinative")). Wyoming follows a similar approach. In *DeMers v. Nicks*, 366 P.3d 977 (Wyo. 2016), the supreme court of Wyoming found that the trial court acted within its discretion when it held that it was in best interest of the minor son for his father to have primary custody, notwithstanding the son's stated preference to live with his mother, as the court was not persuaded that the son was mature enough to decide what was in his best interests, the son indicated he would be comfortable with either parent, and stated that he did not want to make the custody decision. Honoring the child's wishes when possible is part of the totality of the circumstances approach used in New York. *Margaret M.C. v. William J.C.*, 972 N.Y.S.2d 396, 399 (Sup. Ct. 2012).

Part 1 of this Section examines the ways in which courts elicit children's views, the roles assigned to adults who are charged with representing a child's interests before a court, and the expectations, rules and uncertainties that surround the work of guardians ad litem ("GALs") in different jurisdictions. It then turns to due process concerns that arise when a court receives evidence of the children's views by means that do not satisfy the norms of evidence. Part 2 focuses on the current debate over "best interests" lawyering for children and what is actually happening in state courts.

1.   How Does the Child Speak?

The issue of how the child's wishes should be communicated to the court is the subject of much debate. If the court does hear from the child, it is important that the child (and the parents) understand that the judge alone is responsible for the ultimate outcome. This information is seen as relieving the child of the burden of being "responsible" for choosing, and also reflects the reality that where the child's wishes are considered, they remain only one factor and are not dispositive. *Hammeren v. Hammeren*, 823 N.W.2d 482, 488 (N.D. 2012); *Mullendore v. Mullendore*, 288 P.3d 948, 954 (Okla. Civ. App. 2012).

Courts have traditionally used two primary methods of ascertaining a child's preferences. First, the child may speak directly to the judge, either by testifying in open court or through an *in camera* interview in which the child is usually promised confidentiality. Second, the child may speak by delegation through an appointed representative.

Oregon's statutory scheme, for example, provides that a court may elicit the child's views in custody actions in three ways: (i) by appointing counsel for the child; (ii) retaining an expert witness to interview the child; or (iii) hearing directly from the child through testimony or in conference. The statute specifies that if the judge hears directly from the child, the court "may exclude from the conference the parents and other persons if the court finds that such action would be likely to be in the best interests of the child * * *. However, the court shall permit an attorney for each party to attend the conference and question the child, and the conference shall be reported." Or. Rev. Stat. Ann. § 107.425(2), (6)–(7) (West Supp. 2018).

It is well settled that children may testify under oath in open court. The Federal Rules of Evidence, adopted in whole or in part by many states, allow a child to testify under oath in any matter. To satisfy the requirement that witnesses testify on oath or affirmation, courts generally make a threshold inquiry into whether the child understands the difference between truth and falsehood. Roughly two-thirds of the states also require a preliminary inquiry into the competency of child witnesses below a specified age. Such hearings frequently emphasize the child's ability to understand questions and communicate responses to them, as well as the child's awareness of the duty to tell the truth. *See* Lucy S. McGough, Child Witnesses: Fragile Voices in the American Legal System, 97–99 (1994). It is widely believed, however, that the stress of testifying under oath should be avoided, especially for younger children. Further, testimony in open court may be less reliable than informal communication where children are concerned. When children testify, their statements may be affected by their parents' presence in the courtroom.

In the 21st century the use of *in camera* interviews to learn the children's wishes concerning their custody, long considered the method of inquiry that best protects children's emotional interests, has given rise to a host of challenges based on the due process rights of the parents who are the parties to custody disputes. In *Couch v. Couch*, 146 S.W.3d 923 (Ky. 2004), the court addressed these issues:

> In an action concerning custody or visitation, any procedure whereby the trial court prohibits disclosure of the transcript of a child's interview to the parties raises significant due process questions. The parties are entitled to know what evidence is used or relied upon by the trial court, and have the right generally to present rebutting evidence or to cross-examine, unless such right is waived. If a trial court accepts and acts upon statements made by the child during the *in camera* interview, it is manifestly unfair not to record and disclose the contents of the interview in order to provide an opportunity for rebuttal.

Id. at 925. *Couch* upheld the trial court's discretion to conduct *in camera* interviews without the parties and counsel, but held that a record must be made so that the parties have the opportunity to determine and contradict the accuracy of child's statements and facts. *Id.* Alaska's highest court also confirmed in 2012 that judges have the discretion to hear children's views *in camera*, at least so long as sufficient evidence from other sources supports their decisions. *Helen S.K. v. Samuel M. K.*, 288 P.3d 463, 475 (Alaska 2012) (no violation of noncustodial mother's rights where the *in camera* interviews were recorded and the judge summarized them for the parties).

Similarly, the Wyoming Supreme Court has held that where one parent withholds consent to an *in camera* interview of the child whose custody is at issue, the parties or the court "should fashion a procedure that protects the parents' rights while minimizing the stress and trauma to the child." *Holiday v. Holiday*, 247 P.3d 29, 33 (Wyo. 2011). The court may conduct an *in camera* interview with the parties' attorneys present, create a record through recording or by using a court reporter, have the child testify in open court, retain a neutral expert to interview the child, or fashion "another suitable procedure" for eliciting the child's views. *Id.* at 33. The court emphasized the importance of hearing the views of a child who is old enough "to understand the effects of expressing a preference," provided that the trial court understands the risks that the child may be influenced by a parent or prove less reliable than adult witnesses in other respects. *Id.* at 33. The court reversed the trial court's custody ruling because the judge had failed to elicit the views of the oldest child, age 11, and remanded so the child's views would be heard.

Creating a record of an *in camera* interview facilitates appellate review in addition to protecting the parents' procedural rights. Some state courts have held that the due process rights of parents are preserved by allowing appellate courts to review the record without making it available to the parent. *Myers v. Myers*, 867 N.E.2d 848 (Ohio Ct. App. 2007). This approach allows the child to speak honestly and the trial judge to preserve confidences. *In re T.M.M.*, 102 N.E.3d 558 (Ohio Ct. App. 2017) (in camera interviews are confidential); *In re A.M.R.*, 101 N.E.3d 1194 (Ohio App. 8 Dist. 2017) (transcripts of in camera interviews prepared for appellate review shall not be made available to the parents, but because the child's attorney may be present an attorney for a child who was unable to attend the interview due to health problems is entitled to review the transcript).

The highest court in the District of Columbia, announcing a rule that courts may use *in camera* interviews of children in custody cases where open testimony would prove harmful to the children, found harmless error in the failure to make a record of an interview. *McN. v. R.J.H., Sr.*, 979 A.2d 1195, 1202–04 (D.C. 2009). It upheld a custody determination where a judge excluded parents and their attorneys from an interview with two children aged 10 and 14, and failed to record the conversation, but "provided a detailed narration of the substance of the interviews" to the parties in open court in time for the parties' attorneys to respond during closing statements. *Id.* The court reasoned that part of protecting the child's best interests was protecting the child from "the harmful effects of in-court testimony. * * * Eliciting [the child's] choice between parents is often emotionally wrenching, and announcing that choice in open court could add significantly to the child's emotional toll." *Id.* at 1199. The court held that moving forward *in camera* interviews in the District must be recorded so that the parties may respond to the factual allegations made during the interviews and so that a full record is available for meaningful appellate review. *Id.*

A second method of eliciting the child's preferences is through appointment of a guardian ad litem. Judges often appoint GALs in order to learn more about the child and/or the child's views. In most states, children are not entitled to have a GAL appointed for them in private custody disputes unless abuse or neglect is alleged. All courts, however, have the equitable power to appoint GALs at their discretion. The same GAL is normally appointed to represent all siblings in the family, even though it is possible that the siblings may not all agree about what they want. The court may order one or both parents to pay the GAL.

A GAL may be either a lawyer or a layperson. Some GALs are Court Appointed Special Advocates (CASAs), laypersons who receive special training to serve as GALs. The proper role when the GAL is in fact an attorney is hotly debated, as discussed below.

The parameters of the GAL's job may vary greatly depending on the judge and the jurisdiction. GALs may perform diverse roles, including fact-gatherer, advocate for the child's best interests, advocate for the child's views, or some combination of roles. Appointment of a GAL is no guarantee that the court will hear the child's views. Depending on the jurisdiction and the terms of the GAL's appointment, the GAL may or may not convey the child's own views to the court or may convey them in a dismissive manner. A GAL may, for example, communicate the child's views to the court while simultaneously serving as a quasi-special master who investigates the circumstances and formulates his or her own quite different opinion about the child's best interests. *Auclair v. Auclair*, 730 A.2d 1260 (Md. Ct. Spec. App. 1999).

The Supreme Court of South Carolina has expressly held that a GAL in a private custody dispute "functions as a representative of the court, appointed to assist the court in making its determination of custody by advocating for the best interest of the children and providing the court with an objective view." *Patel v. Patel*, 555 S.E.2d 386, 389 (S.C. 2001). *Patel* also set baseline standards for GALs, beginning with the responsibility to:

> conduct an *independent, balanced, and impartial* investigation to determine the facts relevant to the situation of the child and the family, which should include: reviewing relevant documents;

meeting with and observing the child in the home setting and considering the child's wishes, if appropriate; and interviewing parents, caregivers, and others with knowledge relevant to the case * * *.

Id. at 390 (emphasis by the court).

Other jurisdictions have underscored that the court must ultimately make its own determinations. *E.g., Carr v. Buenger*, 113 Haw. 452 (Ct. App. 2014) (error to allow GAL to craft the parenting plan, though harmless in the instant case); *Engel v. Engel*, 71 A.3d 1124 (Vt. 2012) (error to delegate decisions about visits and supervision to the children's treatment team, collecting cases from other jurisdictions).

When a GAL offers evidence directly, additional procedural due process concerns are triggered. The GAL frequently transmits hearsay to the court in written reports, or may offer opinions without qualifying as an expert witness. The Supreme Court of Illinois has held that when a GAL functions as both fact-finder and an advocate for the child's preference, and where the court relies on the GAL's written report in its findings of fact, the parent holds the right to cross-examine the GAL as a witness. *In re Marriage of Bates*, 819 N.E.2d 714 (Ill. 2004). In Ohio, a GAL may rely on and transmit to the court the out-of-court statements of persons she interviewed without violating the rule against hearsay if the parties have an opportunity to cross-examine the GAL. *Bates-Brown v. Brown*, 2007 WL 2822596 (Ohio Ct. App. Sept. 28, 2007).

Formal testimony by an attorney who is serving as a GAL is especially fraught with difficulties. The lawyer GAL who formally testifies as a sworn witness would appear to violate Model Rule 3.7 of the ABA Model Rules of Professional Conduct, which states that a "lawyer shall not act as an advocate at a trial in which the lawyer is likely to be a necessary witness * * *." Even if the lawyer GAL does not necessarily advocate for the position preferred by the child, the GAL arguably advocates for a position, namely, the GAL's own conclusion about the best interests of the child. The comments to the Model Rules focus on possible confusion or prejudice in the jurors' minds, but no exception appears for bench trials, the format in which courts decide child custody cases. Moreover, the GAL's formal testimony about the child's wishes is likely to be challenged as hearsay, *e.g., In re Marriage of Bates*, 819 N.E.2d 714 (Ill. 2004), although it may meet an exception, similar to the exception in the Federal Rules of Evidence with respect to the speaker's present state of mind or then-existing mental or emotional condition. *See* Fed. R. Evid. 803(1)–(3).

2. Contemporary Debates About the Role of Attorneys for Children in Custody Disputes

Some of the problems discussed above could be alleviated by using the attorney model of representation for children in custody disputes and allowing the attorney to present evidence through witnesses and documents. The Oregon statute provides that if the children request an attorney in a custody case, the court "shall appoint counsel for the child or children." Or. Rev. Stat. Ann. § 107.425(6) (West Supp. 2018). Wyoming and other jurisdictions also provide that the judge may learn the child's view by appointing a lawyer for the child but, like Oregon, do not specify what the attorney's role should be.

Professor Catherine J. Ross has argued that where children have attorneys, the attorneys should ensure that the children's voices are heard:

> Where children are concerned * * * courts and commentators too frequently collapse the roles of attorneys and guardians *ad litem*. The differences in these roles should be stark. Attorneys are bound by professional standards that require them to pursue the wishes and objectives of the child where the child is capable of making considered decisions in his [or her] own interest. The guardian *ad litem*, in contrast, presents an independent voice in the litigation and is charged with protecting the child's best interest [as the guardian understands it] rather than the child's viewpoint.

Catherine J. Ross, *From Vulnerability to Voice: Appointing Counsel for Children in Civil Litigation*, 64 Fordham L. Rev. 1571, 1615 (1996). Professor Ross argues that the attorney's advocacy of the child's preference is only one factor in the judge's decision, which the judge will properly weigh against the other views presented.

While most courts do not share this viewpoint, some do. For example, an appellate court in Ohio reversed a custody award where the attorney GAL's unsworn testimony urged the court to grant custody to one parent, while the ten-year-old child told the judge *in camera* and in a letter submitted to the court that she wanted to live with the other parent. The appellate court reversed because the court below failed to appoint a separate attorney to advocate for the child's preference. *In re Butler*, 2006 WL 2533010 (Ohio Ct. App. Sept. 5, 2006) (dependency action involving the mother, but not the father who sought custody).

Some observers worry about allowing an attorney to advocate for the child's viewpoint when the attorney perceives that viewpoint to be wrongheaded. The bases for this concern include role identification with parents, distrust of children, and a sense that children are inherently less "rational" than adults, and do not always accurately identify their own best interests, much less act on them. Attorneys, however, may not be competent to substitute their own judgment for that of their clients. They may lack specialized training or expertise in assessing the variety of emotionally-charged issues likely to come into play in litigation involving a child's life choices.

The following article reviews some of the most important contemporary debates surrounding the role of lawyers for children in private custody disputes. At the outset you will see that authoritative professional groups with which you are already familiar (the ABA and the ULC) have taken competing positions on the role of lawyers who represent children.

BARBARA A. ATWOOD,
REPRESENTING CHILDREN WHO CAN'T OR WON'T DIRECT
COUNSEL: BEST INTERESTS LAWYERING
OR NO LAWYER AT ALL?

53 Ariz. L. Rev. 381, 381–84, 386–92, 395, 397–98, 401–02, 408–10, 412 (2011).

INTRODUCTION

Over the past two decades, children's rights scholars and child advocacy groups have argued with increasing force that children's lawyers should function as traditional, client-directed attorneys and that lawyers overstep their professional role—with the potential to do serious harm—when they engage in discretionary best interests representation. Whether grounded in an insistence on lawyers' professional boundaries or in a vision of child-client empowerment, the end goal has been the same: to confine lawyers to their core role as advocates of clients' wishes.

Until recently, the strongest push for client-directed lawyering had come primarily from those who represent children in juvenile court, either in delinquency or in child welfare proceedings, and it was driven by a robust children's rights perspective. In 2009, however, the American Academy of Matrimonial Lawyers (AAML) released its revised standards for representation of children in custody proceedings[5] and recommended that family courts should appoint lawyers for children for only one purpose: "to advocate for the outcome desired by the child." The AAML Standards are * * * driven * * * by the goal of maintaining strict professional constraints on attorneys. * * *

* * *

[M]any children at the time of custody proceedings are of an age when capacity to direct counsel is at least in question. * * * Nevertheless, the

---

[5] *See* Am. Acad. Of Matrimonial Lawyers, *Representing Children: Standards for Attorneys for Children in Custody or Visitation Proceedings with Commentary*, 22 J. Am. Acad. Matrimonial Law 227 (2009) [hereinafter *AAML 2009 Standards*].

appointment of counsel for children may produce several practical benefits. Children's attorneys can enhance the court's understanding of the child's perspective, facilitate the introduction of evidence, sharpen the presentation of factual and legal issues, promote dispute resolution, and protect the child from the harms of litigation itself. * * *

* * *

The child who is unable or unwilling to direct counsel poses a unique puzzle for legal ethics: unlike the incapacitated adult, the child's sense of identity is often inchoate but evolving, so the risk of paternalistic, value-laden lawyering is real. [T]his Article tries to find common ground among various groups to highlight the practical need for, and benefits of, best interests lawyering.

I.   What Legislators and Judges Want

The movement to redefine children's lawyers as client directed and to eliminate best interests representation has gained strength in the twenty-first century but has yet to produce a corresponding transformation in the law on the ground. Debates continue about the value of appointing attorneys for children and about the role such representatives should play, once appointed. * * * Affording children the right to have their views taken seriously can affirm a child's sense of dignity and self-worth and, concomitantly, enhance the decision maker's understanding of the dispute. Nevertheless, the governing legal framework within the United States in most states has stopped short of recognizing a child's right of participation or of requiring lawyers to advocate children's wishes. This Part briefly summarizes the positions advanced by professional groups and then turns to the quite different world of codified law, court opinions, and judicial attitudes.

A.   Competing Professional Guideline

The American Bar Association has taken inconsistent positions on the role of children's lawyers. In 1995 the ABA took a firm but not absolute stance favoring client-directed lawyering for children in abuse and neglect proceedings.[28] While permitting the lawyer to advocate the child's "legal interests" if the child cannot or does not express a position, the ABA Abuse and Neglect Standards generally require a lawyer to maintain a traditional lawyer-client relationship with a child who is capable of directing counsel. Under the Standards, the attorney "owes the same duties of undivided loyalty, confidentiality, and competent representation to the child as is due an adult client." In reports or * * * as agents of the court [:] * * * "a lawyer

---

[28] Proposed Standards of Practice for Lawyers Who Represent Children in Abuse and Neglect Cases * * * (1995), *reprinted in* 29 Fam. L.Q. 375 (1995) [hereinafter ABA ABUSE AND NEGLECT STANDARDS].

should always remain a lawyer whether representing a child or a child's best interests."

The Uniform Law Commission (ULC) entered the fray in 2006 with the Uniform Representation of Children in Abuse, Neglect, and Custody Proceedings Act, for which this Author was the Reporter. The ULC attempted * * * to provide concrete guidance for the discretionary appointment of children's lawyers in family law cases; to differentiate the role of a lawyer from the nonlawyer guardian ad litem model; and to provide clear child-centered performance standards for children's lawyers. In implementing the last objective, the ULC proposed two categories of children's lawyers: the traditional child's attorney, and the "best interests attorney," defined as "an attorney who provides legal representation for a child to protect the child's best interests without being bound by the child's directives or objectives." [T]he ULC's * * * endorsement of best interests representation as one alternative for children's attorneys [led to a] contentious debate * * * within the ABA * * * and the ULC ultimately withdrew the Act from consideration by the ABA House of Delegates [but promulgated it without ABA approval].

* * *

Professor [Martin] Guggenheim has described with evident dismay the entrenched view among New York family judges that children's lawyers * * * should be free to advocate a position that will serve their clients' interests, whether or not the position is articulated by the child. * * * Professor Guggenheim decried the lack of ethical constraints on the lawyers' advocacy. As he sees it, judges want children's lawyers to tell them what to do because it makes their jobs easier.

* * * Professor Guggenheim sees grave danger in best interests advocacy: "* * * children's lawyers * * * conclude what is best for their clients based on invisible factors that have more to tell us about the values and beliefs of the lawyers than about what is good for the children." * * *

B. State Law Receptivity

[T]he laws of most states * * * to permit children's lawyers to engage in best interests representation. * * * States vary in their approach to child representation in family court, with the majority authorizing the discretionary appointment of a legal representative—whether denominated an attorney or a guardian ad litem—to represent the child's best interests. Importantly, some states authorize the appointment of either a traditional attorney or a best interests representative, or both, at the court's discretion.

[I]n a few states attorneys exercise the core responsibility to decide whether they should represent a child's best interests or a child's directives. In this model, the judge appoints an attorney for a child and, after interviewing the child client, the lawyer determines whether the child is capable of directing the representation.

* * *

C. The Arizona Experience

* * * Since 2006, Arizona judges have been operating under a regime very similar to that proposed by the Uniform Law Commission—a framework in which judges not only decide whether to appoint a representative for a child but also choose the role for that representative. * * * Rule 10 [of the provisions governing family court] authorizes the appointment of representatives and permits judges to select from three categories: "best interests attorney," "child's attorney," and "court-appointed advisor."

Rule 10 and its commentary draw a sharp distinction between attorneys—whether child's attorney or best interests attorney—and the court-appointed advisor. * * * While the Rule does not define the role of child's attorney or best interests attorney, the drafters drew on the existing standards developed by other professional groups. * * * [For example, by expressly barring the best interests attorney from testifying or submitting a written report into evidence].

* * *

The family court judges [in Arizona] acknowledged that due to cost, appointments occur in only a small percentage of custody cases. * * * [T]he judges generally viewed the appointment of children's lawyers as very helpful * * *. * * * Significantly, a majority of the family court judges preferred the best interests attorney as the norm * * *, with some judges reporting that they rarely if ever appoint a traditional child's attorney in a custody dispute. Two clear rationales emerged for this preference: the desire for the child's representative to be able to participate as an attorney in the litigation, and the desire for a broader presentation of evidence than would be offered if the lawyer's advocacy were limited to the child's expressed wishes.

According to several judges, the appointment of a lawyer rather than a nonlawyer has distinct advantages. * * * As one judge put it, "I want a lawyer, someone who can present evidence, file motions, cross-examine witnesses. That's essential." * * * Another judge * * * [appoints lawyers because they] can recognize and identify legal issues that may arise in the course of the case.

* * *

* * * [E]thical tensions can arise for the traditional child's attorney if a mature child expresses a desire that conflicts with the lawyer's position on the child's best interests.* * *

[T]he appointment of a child's attorney can pose two distinct risks. One danger is that the attorney, in looking to the child for direction, will push the child into expressing a preference in the custody dispute, thus exacerbating the risk of intense loyalty conflicts for the child. * * * In contrast, * * * through witness testimony and evidentiary presentations, the best interests attorney can bring the child's voice into the litigation in a manner that respects the child's desire to remain neutral vis-à-vis his or her parents.

A second and related risk * * * is that children are not fixed beings with settled goals but are constantly evolving toward adulthood. A child's expressed preferences may shift over time, sometimes sharply, and are subject to influence—if not manipulation—by parents and others close to the child.

* * *

[P]olicy arguments for client-directed lawyering that rest on the desire to enhance children's autonomy need to take account of advances in scientific understanding of brain maturation.

Over the last decade, research has shown that cognitive and emotional maturation in children and adolescents is a protracted process of longer duration than was previously known and that the parts of the brain responsible for decisionmaking and impulse control are particularly slow to develop.

* * *

Neural immaturity of children and adolescents does not mean that children's viewpoints should be disregarded. The child's own sense of dignity may be intertwined with the decisionmaker's willingness to listen to the child's story. Moreover, a decisionmaker's understanding of the issues will be enhanced through knowledge of the child's perspective. Neural immaturity, nevertheless, * * * means that the child's preferences may be short-lived and the result of variable psychosocial conditions. [T]he desires that the child expresses on day one may be replaced by quite different goals with a different emotional resonance the following week. Legal representation of a child—an individual who is in a state of becoming—is challenging precisely because of the fluid nature of children's identities.

[T]ests for capacity that are tailored to the adult client would likely exclude a majority of children. Some scholars take the position that every child can communicate his or her views in some fashion and that the competence that is critical is the *lawyer's* competence to read the child's signals, whether conveyed through actual words, body language, or even eye movements.

* * *

[I]f a lawyer is appointed for a child in a contentious custody battle, and that child is unable to formulate and express considered goals for the representation, * * * three camps would take markedly different positions as to the representation: the first group would have the lawyer represent the child's wishes, whether gleaned through careful observation and interaction or formulated as a substituted judgment based on what the child might have expressed were the child able; the second group would not appoint counsel at all; and the third group would have the lawyer engage outright in representation of the child's interests. The laws of most states endorse the third approach.

* * *

NOTES AND QUESTIONS

1. *How should a judge decide?* If you were the family court judge and listened to the child express a wish to be in the physical custody of one parent rather than the other, what factors might help you determine how much weight to give to that expressed wish?

2. *An international perspective: the United Nations Convention on the Rights of the Child.* Every nation in the world, with the exception of the United States and South Sudan (which gained independence in 2011) has ratified the United Nations Convention on the Rights of the Child, promulgated in 1989. Somalia, the latest country to ratify the Convention, did so in January 2015. The Convention recognizes that a child has separate interests from his or her parents in every legal proceeding and requires that all decisions affecting children be resolved based on the "best interests of the child." Arts. 12 and 3. Because the child's voice is often absent from hearings that will determine his or her home until majority, the failure to grant children representation in child custody cases, and the fact that the child's preference is only one in a long list of factors, would appear to violate Article 12, were it binding in the United States. *See* Mary Ann Mason, *The U.S. and the International Children's Rights Crusade: Leader or Laggard?*, 38 J. Soc. Hist. 955 (2005). How do you think ratification by the United States would have altered the outcome of custody decisions you have read so far in which the children's preference played a role? Do you think the United States should adopt the Convention's approach to this issue? Why or why not?

3. *Comparing competing standards.* Which approach to the representation of children in custody disputes do you find most persuasive? Why? In an ordinary civil proceeding, would adults and corporate entities necessarily be satisfied if they were denied the right to a lawyer based on the court's appointment of a representative to argue for their best interests and the court's assurance that it too would watch out for those interests?

4. *Can parents block the appointment of a GAL?* In *In re the Marriage of Metzger*, 169 Cal. Rptr. 3d 382 (Ct. App. 2014), where the trial on child custody issues lasted nearly a year, the judge appointed a best interests GAL in

accordance with the California statute. The GAL he chose was an attorney who had a master's degree in forensic psychology. One of the contested issues was whether the child had autism, as the mother insisted. The father objected to the appointment on three grounds: (i) appointment of a GAL violated the father's parental rights including the right to speak for his child and to control who she associates with; (ii) the court's order that the parents split the $100,000 cost of the GAL's services deprived him of property without a hearing and impeded his ability to determine his child's best interests because the father preferred to put the money in his daughter's college fund; and (iii) the court could not order him to make the child available to meet with the GAL. The appellate court ruled against the father on all grounds. It expressly held that the state has a compelling interest in protecting a child's best interests in a custody hearing. This justifies appointment of a GAL who has access to the child where custody is hotly contested, the court needs access to materials not otherwise available to it, knowledgeable counsel is available, and the best interest of the child appears to require independent representation. *Id.* at 385–86. The court advised that "counsel cannot adequately represent the child's interests without meeting with the child in order to interview and observe her." *Id.* at 388. Finally, the court reminded the father that he could present his own alternative view of his daughter's best interests to the judge. *Id.* at 386.

5. *May children who are the subjects of custody disputes be parties to their parents' divorce litigation?* The Federal Rules of Civil Procedure require courts to allow parties to intervene if they have an interest in the subject matter of the action and a decision in the action "may as a practical matter impair or impede the movant's ability to protect its interest, unless existing parties adequately represent that interest." Fed. R. Civ. P. 24. Petitioners may intervene in federal litigation with the court's permission if a statute authorizes them to do so or if they have "a claim or defense that shares with the main action a common question of law or fact." *Id.* Do you think the children whose best interests are considered in private custody litigation meet the ordinary civil standard for intervention as of right or permissive intervention?

Every state court that has considered this question has strongly rebuffed the children's claims that they needed to appear as party-intervenors to ensure that their views received adequate consideration. In Maryland, three of the four siblings wanted the court to fire the GAL who disagreed with them, to appoint an attorney who would represent their views, and to intervene as parties. They lost on all counts. *Auclair v. Auclair*, 730 A.2d 1260 (Md Ct. Spec. App. 1999). Similarly, in Maine, the court held that minor children are not entitled to intervene in their parents' custody dispute. *Miller v. Miller*, 677 A.2d 64 (Me. 1996), Trial courts in Maine hold statutory authority to appoint a GAL for children in custody disputes. The *Miller* court noted, however, that no statute entitles children to an additional representative to advocate for their views. Appellate courts in both *Auclair* and *Miller* concluded that even though children have an interest in the outcome of their parents' custody litigation, denial of intervention did not violate the children's rights because the trial court and the GAL were obligated to act in their best interests and to consider their preferences for custody. *Miller* also concluded that the state had a substantial interest in not including children as parties represented by counsel, because intervention would complicate the proceedings and "result in a substantial additional financial burden on both the parties and [the] court system." *Id.* at 70; *see also In re Stapleford,* 931 A.2d 1199 (N.H. 2007).

6. *How long do a GAL or attorney's duties to the court and the child last?* The generally applicable rules governing attorneys indicate that the attorney continues to serve until the matter is completely resolved—that is, through any appeals. One Texas court, however, has ruled that where an attorney is appointed to "assist the [trial] court in protecting a child's best interests rather than to provide legal services to the child," that attorney lacks standing to file an appellate brief because the trial court is not a party to the appeal. *O'Connor v. O'Connor,* 245 S.W.3d 511, 515 (Tex. App. 2007).

In some jurisdictions the appointment can continue until the child reaches the age of majority. *Metzger, supra,* 169 Cal. Rptr. 3d at 388.

PROBLEM 12-3

You have recently been appointed to represent a ten-year-old girl in a bitter custody dispute between her parents. During your career as a lawyer, you have never represented a minor before, and the judge has not given you any instructions. You ask the other attorneys in your office what your role should be, and the advice they give you is all over the place. What should you do?

5. SHARED PARENTING: GENDER WARS OR A STEP FORWARD?

Widespread support for joint custody (also known as "shared parenting time") developed during the last quarter of the twentieth century and into the twenty-first, inspired primarily by a desire to bring gender and emotional equality to child custody decisions. The move toward shared parenting emerged from changes in gender roles and parental involvement prior to dissolution, alliances of fathers who seek an active role in their children's lives, an appreciation of the harm the adversary process may do to the parents' ability to cooperate with each other in raising their children, and increased attention to negative impact of parental hostility on the children themselves.

"Joint *legal* custody" confers on both parents shared decision-making about important issues. The Georgia Code, for example, states: joint legal custody "means both parents have equal rights and responsibilities for major decisions concerning the child, including the child's education, health care, extracurricular activities, and religious training." Ga. Code Ann. § 19–9–6(5) (2018).

"Joint *physical* custody" generally confers on both parents shared day-to-day decision making and responsibility for their children. Although the term is often thought to mean the right to have the children divide their time roughly equally between both homes, it covers a spectrum of arrangements, ranging from what is normally considered "liberal visitation" to equal parenting time.

Even where one parent receives sole physical and legal custody, today the other parent normally retains a protected interest in the child. As one court explained the structure of its decree: "Both parties should understand that the granting of sole legal and physical custody of the minor child to one parent *does not terminate the parental rights of the other party*. The custodial parent will still have, under the orders to be issued as part of this decision, an absolute obligation to not only keep the other parent informed about all issues regarding [the child], but also to make reasonable efforts to consult with the other parent prior to making major decisions." *Case v. Jones*, 2011 WL 1565813 at *2 (Conn. Super. Ct. Mar. 28, 2011). Consultation, however, is not the same as shared decision-making.

But the division of parental rights is seldom so stark. Fit parents generally share legal custody, and often share day-to-day parenting, although one parent may be designated as the primary residential parent.

In jurisdictions that give a preference to joint custody, courts begin their child custody determinations with a presumption that both parents love their children and that the child will benefit from having a continuing custodial relationship with both parents. When the court orders joint custody, neither parent is considered better than the other.

Some of the earliest support for joint custody reflected an appreciation of the limitations of the adversary process as a means for discovering which adult was the "best" parent. In 1975 Professor Robert Mnookin highlighted the limitations of the adjudicative process as a vehicle for identifying the preferred custodial parent, and argued that "[w]e would more frankly acknowledge both our ignorance and the presumed equality of the natural parents were we to flip a coin." Robert H. Mnookin, *Child-Custody Adjudication: Judicial Functions in the Face of Indeterminacy*, 39 Law & Contemp. Probs. 226, 289 (1975). Mnookin himself acknowledged that the idea of using a coin toss to determine child custody appears "callous" or even "repulsive" to most observers. He argued, however, that our response to a custody lottery "may reflect an intuitive appreciation of the importance of the educational, participatory, and symbolic values of adjudication as a mode of dispute settlement." *Id.* at 291.

Differences in statutory, judicial and common understandings of what constitutes joint physical (also known as "residential") custody have led to profound variations in assessments of how many jurisdictions permit, favor, or presume joint custody. As Professor Herbie DiFonzo summed it up:

> The applicability, appropriateness, and even the definition of joint custody are in a state of fluctuation. The term itself is often used rather loosely and confusingly in both popular journals and professional publications, including statutes and judicial opinions throughout the United States, the United Kingdom, Australia, Canada, and New Zealand. As the Maryland Court of Appeals once complained, "[t]he inability of courts and commentators to agree on what is meant by the term 'joint custody' makes difficult the task of distilling principles and guidelines from a rapidly growing body of literature and case law. What one writer sees as an amorphous concept another sees as a structured legal arrangement.

J. Herbie DiFonzo, *From the Rule of One to Shared Parenting: Custody Presumptions in Law and Policy*, 52 Fam. Ct. Rev. 213, 216 (2014).

Despite definitional issues, it seems fair to say that all states allow joint custody. Some give it preference, some permit it only where both parents seek it, and others permit courts to impose joint custody even against the wishes of one or both parties. *Id.* at 216–18. *But see* Katherine T. Bartlett, *Prioritizing Past Caretaking in Child-Custody*, 77 Law & Contemp. Probs. 29, 30–32 (2014) (reporting a retreat from presumptions favoring joint custody).

In the last decade, a number of jurisdictions have tried to clarify that joint physical custody does not always mean equal time with the children. The Nevada Supreme Court, for example, expressly adopted Missouri's statutory definition of joint physical custody as meaning that custody is "shared by the parents in such a way to ensure the child or children of frequent associations and a continuing relationship with both parents." *Rivero v. Rivero*, 216 P.3d 213, 223 (Nev. 2009) (collecting similar definitions from other jurisdictions).

A. FEMINISTS, FATHERS' RIGHTS AND PUBLIC POLICY

Gender neutral standards for resolving child custody disputes emerged in the 1970s in the wake of several trends you have read about in earlier chapters: the rising divorce rate that began to manifest itself in the 1960s, new constitutional doctrines about equal protection and gender that inspired men to fight for custody, and social changes that sent women into the work force in growing numbers and undermined the assumption that mothers were normally primary caretakers. The idea of joint custody originated with fathers who asserted their right to parent even after divorce. In 1979, California enacted the first joint custody statute in the nation—one that imposed a presumption in favor of shared parenting—and by 1991 more than 40 states had adopted statutes providing for joint custody as either the preferred policy or as an option. Joan B. Kelly, *The Determination of Child Custody*, 4 Future Child. 1121, 122–23 (1994), While fathers' rights groups promoted shared parenting, some feminists resisted the trend which they felt gave too little credit to the labor women performed during marriage and kept formerly-married adults entangled in each other's lives. *Id.* at 123; Jana B. Singer, *Dispute Resolution and the Postdivorce Family: Implications of a Paradigm Shift*, 47 Fam. Ct. Rev. 363, 366 (2009).

Changing gender roles within the family, discussed in Chapter 3, have led to a very different vision of fathering than obtained in the 1950s and '60s. Fathers, on average, spend more time with their children than their fathers or grandfathers did, but most fathers still spend less time than mothers taking care of children. While the gap between mothers and fathers in time spent on child care has narrowed, mothers still spend more than twice as many hours a week on child care as their husbands or partners. Gretchen Livingston & Kim Parker, Pew Research Ctr., *A Tale of Two Fathers: More Are Active, But More Are Absent* 3 (2011). The amount of time fathers who live in the same household as their children spend in caretaking more than doubled between 1985 and 2000—from an average of 3 hours to 6.5 hours each week. *Id.* Fathers report talking with their child about the child's day, helping the child with homework, sharing meals and taking the child to or from activities, as well as bathing, feeding and reading to younger children. *Id.* at 14, 16. These more actively engaged fathers are more prone to seek—and get—shared parenting arrangements than earlier generations of fathers.

Even more striking, the number of stay-at-home dads who have primary responsibility for the household's children has nearly doubled since 1989—roughly two million men reported that they were the primary caretakers in 2012. Gretchen Livingston, Pew Research Ctr., *Growing Number of Dads at Home with the Kids: Biggest increase among those caring for family* 5 (2014). Roughly one-quarter report that they are home primarily to care for the children, while another one-quarter report that they are home primarily because they are unemployed. *Id.* at 5–6.

When parents separate, a non-residential parent is entitled to visitation (which the ALI calls "parenting time"), discussed in the next chapter. A classic empirical study of families at three junctures following divorce confirmed the common wisdom that the typical father who does not have primary residential custody maintains contact with the children through one or two overnight visits bi-weekly, and some daytime visits. Robert H. Mnookin & Eleanor Maccoby, *Facing the Dilemmas of Child Custody*, 10 Va. J. Soc. Pol'y & L. 54, 57 (2002). That continues to be considered the norm for "liberal visitation," and may also be considered joint physical custody depending on the jurisdiction and the labels attached. Some jurisdictions specify a minimum number of overnights in each house per year to qualify as shared residential custody, at least for purposes of calculating child support obligations. *E.g.*, D.C. Code § 16–916–01 (Supp. 2018) (a parent whose child resides with him or her 35% of the year—the equivalent of "liberal visitation"—or more is presumed to have "shared physical custody").

More recent data, however, suggests that this image of liberal visitation may be idealized. A national study conducted from 2006 to 2010 revealed that over one-quarter of fathers who do not live with their children had not seen their children in more than one year. Livingston & Parker, *supra*, at 4. Many fathers who are not residential custodians keep in touch primarily through telephone and email, but nearly one-third of fathers who do not live with their children communicate with them less than once a month. *Id.*

Accumulating social science data demonstrates "the benefits of more involvement of fathers with their children" after family breakup. The social science literature is less clear, however, about "what 'more involvement' means in actual time spent with children. [T]he pattern that has prevailed for decades 'of contact four days per month, sometimes with a brief midweek visit, has contributed to the demonstrated deterioration in closeness to [non-residential] father-child relationships over time, and sadness, longing, and a sense of deprivation among children.' " Joan B. Kelly, *Risk and Protective Factors Associated with Child and Adolescent Adjustment Following Separation and Divorce: Social Science Applications*, in Kathryn F. Kuehnle & Leslie M. Drozd, Parenting Plan Evaluations: Applied Research for the Family Court 68 (2013).

Organized fathers' rights groups have advocated for reductions in child support obligations when parents share residential custody, in addition to seeking joint custody as a matter of course. Shared custody may restrict the autonomy of the primary residential parent, who is still most often a woman. Elizabeth S. Scott & Robert E. Emery, *Gender Politics and Child Custody: The Puzzling Persistence of the Best-Interests Standard*, 77 Law & Contemp. Probs. 69 (2014). In response, some feminist scholars have argued that mothers are disadvantaged in custody fights because courts respond favorably to engaged fathers, though the most recent studies supporting that claim are nearly 15 years old. *Id.* at 80.

In 2014, Elizabeth Scott and Robert Emery summarized several decades of legislative and policy battles over shared custody as a "deadlock" in the gender wars: "The primary front in this war has been a protracted battle over joint custody. Fathers' groups have lobbied hard for statutes favoring joint physical custody, but they have been opposed vigorously by women's advocates" who prefer the best interests standard with its focus on who has done more caretaking thus far in the child's life. *Id.* at 71, 76 n. 38, 100.

B. REEVALUATING SHARED PHYSICAL CUSTODY: IOWA

Over the last forty years, legislative reforms, popular referenda, and common law have tinkered with the rules governing joint custody. California, which once led the way by establishing a presumption in favor of joint custody in all cases, currently presumes that a joint custody award is in the best interest of the child only when both parents have agreed to share custody. Cal. Fam. Code § 3080 (West 2014). Other states too have recalibrated their approaches to joint custody, but the statutory changes do not all point in one direction. Maine, for example, encourages judges to award joint physical custody even if only one parent requests it, unless the judge can explain why the arrangement would not be in the best interests of the child. Me. Rev. Stat. Ann. tit. 19–A, § 1653 (Westlaw through 2017 Reg, Sess. and 2d Spec. Sess.). In contrast, the Minnesota legislature clarified in 2014 that there is no presumption in that state for or against joint custody (except where there is a history of domestic violence); the statute instructs judges on how to navigate a joint custody arrangement when faced with parents who disagree. Minn. Stat. Ann. § 518.17 (West Supp. 2018).

In Iowa, where the courts had long disfavored joint physical custody, the legislature amended the family law code effective in 2005 to provide that, so long as it is reasonable and in the best interest of the child, courts should make the custody award that will "assure the child the opportunity for the maximum continuing physical and emotional contact with both parents * * *." Iowa Code § 598.41 (West Supp. 2018). In 2007, the Supreme Court of Iowa used a case involving a challenge to an award of joint physical custody to survey the scholarship on the benefits and risks of joint physical custody. It concluded: "The current social science research cited by advocates of joint custody or joint physical care, * * * is not definitive on many key questions. * * * While it seems clear that children often benefit from a continuing relationship with both parents after divorce, the research has not established the amount of contact necessary to maintain a "close relationship." *In re the Marriage of Hansen, 733 N.W. 2d 683, 695 (Iowa 2007).*

The court declined to formulate a general approach to joint custody, opining: "the joint physical care issue must be examined in each case on the unique facts * * *. Any consideration of joint physical care, however, must still be based on * * * the best interest of the child. Physical care issues are not to be resolved based upon perceived fairness to the *spouses*, but primarily upon what is best for the *child*." *Id.*

Nonetheless, the court articulated the factors that Iowa courts should consider "when determining if joint physical care is in the best interests of the child." As summarized in a subsequent opinion, *Hansen* instructs judges, first, "where there are two suitable parents" to consider "stability and continuity of care giving, which 'tend[s] to favor a spouse who, prior to divorce, was primarily responsible for physical care.' A second factor is the ability of the parents to communicate and show mutual respect. The third factor is the degree of conflict between the parents, because joint physical care requires 'substantial and regular interaction between the parents.' " *Hansen* noted that when one parent objects to shared custody "the likelihood of its success is reduced," but in Iowa that is not a bar to a joint custody order. The fourth and final "factor is the degree to which the parties agree about their approach to daily matters concerning the children. While these four factors are significant to determining the appropriateness of joint physical care," the court underscored, "they are not exclusive, and we must consider 'the total setting presented by each unique case.' " *In re Marriage of West*, 2013 WL 988880 at *2 (Iowa Ct. App. Mar. 13, 2013) (unpublished table decision) (quoting *Hansen, supra*, at 695).

In the following opinion, an Iowa appellate court applies these principles to a father's challenge to the award of joint physical custody where neither party filed a motion seeking it. As you read, consider how the *Hansen* factors apply and whether the court is being fully transparent about its reasoning.

IN RE THE MARRIAGE OF CERWICK

Court of Appeals of Iowa, 2013.
834 N.W.2d 872 (unpublished table decision), 2013 WL 2370722.

MULLINS, J.

Justin Cerwick appeals from a divorce decree awarding joint physical care of three children to him and his former wife, Machelle Cerwick. Justin argues the issue of joint physical care was not properly before the district court because neither party requested it. He further contends that even if the issue of joint physical care were properly before the court, the court erred in awarding joint physical care and should have awarded him physical care. * * *

I.   Background Facts and Proceedings

We are called upon to determine whether the district court erred in granting Justin and Machelle joint physical care of their three children— J.C. (born in 2005), N.C. (born in 2007), and S.C. (born in 2010) * * *. At the time of their divorce in 2012, Justin was thirty years old and Machelle was twenty-eight years old.

When Justin and Machelle met, both were high school graduates and in good health. Justin and Machelle worked together at the same company and were soon engaged to be married. Approximately eight months after the engagement Machelle learned she was pregnant with her first child, J.C. Around the same time she learned of her pregnancy, both Machelle and Justin were laid off. Machelle subsequently obtained a job at a local hospital while Justin began work at a facility manufacturing gypsum board.

After their second child was born in 2007, Machelle returned to school to pursue an associate's degree in radiology technology. While she was in school, Justin supported the family financially and Machelle served as the children's primary caregiver. Machelle graduated in 2010. Although Machelle was unable to obtain a job in her desired field, she eventually secured employment at an animal food production company. Machelle worked from 3:00 p.m. to 11:00 p.m. for twelve days and then had two days off.

In 2010, Justin was fired from his job. He and Machelle agreed that he would return to school to pursue an associate's degree as a diesel mechanic. While he was in school, Justin was not employed and served as the children's primary caregiver.

[T]he couple's relationship began to deteriorate. Machelle asserted that they fought all the time and it was unhealthy for the children. While there was no evidence of physical abuse, Justin did punch a hole in the wall of their family home.

In early 2011, the parties separated. Machelle left the marital home; Justin remained in the marital home with the children. Initially, Machelle lived with her father in his home. She then moved into a two-bedroom apartment of her own.

After marital counseling failed, Justin filed for divorce in April 2011. Machelle recommended alternating care of the children on a daily basis during the week and switching care every other weekend. This arrangement was unsuccessful and led to police intervention on several occasions. Justin moved for physical care. Machelle responded with a motion for temporary joint physical care, which Justin resisted.

In June 2011, the district court held a hearing on Machelle's motion for temporary joint physical care. The district court found that "[w]hile both parties are capable of caring for the children, current circumstances render Machelle's proposed shared care arrangement undesirable. The children would be constantly changing homes and schedules, often daily. Moreover, Machelle's living accommodations militate against having children for extended periods." The court then placed temporary physical care of the children with Justin.

In August 2011, the court awarded Justin temporary support in the amount of $900.00 per month. The same day * * * Justin learned Machelle quit her job. After quitting her job Machelle enrolled in a premed program at a local community college. Machelle subsequently expressed her desire to finish a two-year pre-med program, transfer to a four-year university, and then attend medical school in pursuit of becoming a doctor. After enrolling in school, Machelle moved to modify child support and visitation.

In September 2011, the district court held a hearing on Machelle's motion to modify child support and visitation. The district court found

> [Machelle's] decision to quit a $38,000 per year job during the pendency of this action to return to school to pursue a course of study that is not reasonably calculated to increase her employability in the foreseeable future, where the parties have three young children and a negative net worth, and Justin earns less than $25,000 per year, to be selfish and irresponsible.

The court also found that "communication and cooperation between the parties appears to have further deteriorated since the June hearing, essentially precluding shared care. The court then expanded visitation slightly, reduced child support to $450 per month, and otherwise overruled Machelle's motion.

In February 2012, the district court held a trial on the dissolution of marriage petition. The court found

> [T]he case . . . was highly contentions and filled with acrimony and incrimination. Little evidence was received that was not intended to cast a negative light on the opposing party and virtually no evidence was presented that would assist this court in finding a working resolution of the gritty issues presented. The parties were focused on "attacking" and "tearing down" one another in the presentation of their respective cases.

Both parties requested physical care. Neither party requested joint physical care. Machelle did, however, submit three different child support worksheets—one if the court were to award physical care to her, one if the court were to award physical care to Justin, and one if the court were to award joint physical care. The court awarded Justin and Machelle joint physical care * * * and ordered minimal child support. * * *

Justin appeals the court's joint physical care order.

II. Standard & Scope of Review

We review cases tried in equity de novo. *See In re Marriage of Hansen*, 733 N.W.2d 683, 690 (Iowa 2007). We give deference to the district court's findings * * *.

* * *

III. Analysis

Justin contends the district court erred in awarding joint physical care because neither he nor Machelle requested [it. A] brief historical examination of relevant legislative action [will be] helpful. In 1997, the Iowa legislature defined the term "joint physical care" for the first time but did not explain its substantive application. [In] 2004, the legislature amended Iowa Code section 598.41(5) to read, in part: "If joint legal custody is awarded to both parents, the court may award joint physical care to both joint custodial parents upon the request of either parent." 2004 Iowa Acts 1169 (now codified at Iowa Code § 598.41(5)(a) (2013)); *see also Hansen,* 733 N.W.2d at 691–92.

We do not require the parties to use magic words to request joint physical care. *In re Marriage of Fennelly and Breckenfelder,* 737 N.W.2d 97, 102 (Iowa 2007). Nor are our courts "interested in creating a trap for the unwary with respect to something so paramount." *Id.* Our statute makes clear, however, that the district court may consider joint physical care *upon the request of either party. See* Iowa Code § 598.41(5)(a) (2011); * * * The legislature could have provided that the district court may consider joint physical care whenever the best interest of the children so required—rather than upon the request of either parent. * * * It did not do so. *See id.*

In this case, neither party requested joint physical care. Both parties essentially conceded joint physical care was not appropriate. The record is replete with evidence supporting the district court's finding that this case was "highly contentious and filled with acrimony"—including several unfounded child abuse allegations and police intervention. Thus, we find the issue of joint physical care not properly before the district court and not in the children's best interest. *See * * * In re Marriage of Hynick,* 727 N.W.2d 575, 580 (Iowa 2007) (finding the parties' lack of mutual respect and inability to communicate made joint physical care inappropriate).

As we find the district court erred in ordering joint physical care, we must determine which caregiver should be awarded physical care. * * *

The transition from the parties' separation to divorce has been highly contentious—particularly with respect to the issue of physical care. * * * In attempting to share physical care after separation, each party lobbed criminal allegations of physical abuse against the other and contacted the Department of Human Services and the local police on several occasions. Justin alleges that Machelle's parenting style is irresponsible. He argues she improperly clothed the children and is responsible for the children's frequent tardiness and absence from school. Machelle, on the other hand, attacks Justin's parental style as overly controlling and physically and verbally abusive.

Justin has been the primary caregiver since the parties separated in February 2011. * * *. The principles of continuity, stability, and approximation favor placing physical care with Justin. *See Hansen,* 733 N.W.2d at 700. [W]e find Justin's home environment most likely to bring the children to physical, mental, and social maturity. * * *

[W]e modify the district court decision awarding joint physical care and find awarding Justin physical care is in the children's best interest. Iowa * * * requires the parent awarded physical care to support the other caregiver's relationship with the children. We expect Justin to * * * foster the children's relationship with their mother through liberal visitation and mutual respect. Justin's physical care shall not affect Machelle's rights and responsibilities as a joint legal custodian of the child. *See* Iowa Code § 598.41(5)(b) (2014).

IV. Conclusion

We find the issue of joint physical care was not properly before the district court as neither party requested such an arrangement * * *. Given Justin's status as the primary caregiver since the parties separated, we find that the concepts of continuity, stability, and approximation favor placing physical care with Justin as the environment most likely to foster the children's physical, mental, and social maturity. Thus, we affirm the district court's divorce decree but modify to award Justin physical care. We direct the district court to award Machelle liberal visitation and remand to set forth an appropriate visitation schedule * * *.

AFFIRMED AS MODIFIED AND REMANDED.

NOTES AND QUESTIONS

1. *Propriety of awarding joint custody.* Many courts have held (and experts generally agree) that the most important criteria for an award of joint custody are the parties' agreement and their ability to cooperate in reaching shared decisions in matters affecting the children's welfare. *Hansen, supra,* at 698 (reversing award of joint custody in light of extensive parental conflict and clash of parenting styles); *Stibich v. Stibich,* 491 S.W.3d 475, 479 (Ark. Ct. App. 2016) (award of joint legal custody is reversible error where the parents fought "about even the most insignificant matters" and were unwilling to "agree on *anything*"). Conversely, a court may find that an award of joint legal custody and frequent overnight visits is appropriate even over one parent's objection where the parties "conduct themselves with civility," are able to compromise, and "set aside personal feelings for the sake of the child." *Victoria H. v. Tetsuhito A.,* 974 N.Y.S.2d 56, 56 (App. Div. 2013). How do you think a judge is able to distinguish between these two situations?

2. *Cerwick.* Was the court's assertion that Machelle had not sought joint physical custody accurate? How would the factors set forth in *Hansen* have applied to the facts in *Cerwick* if the court had used them? Were the trial

court's criticisms of Machelle's behavior warranted in light of what you read in Chapters 10 and 11 about the treatment of parental decisions to pursue further education to increase long term earning capacity?

3. *Specific arrangements.* The trial court in *Cerwick* voiced concern about the children's frequent moves between homes under Machelle's temporary plan. Similarly, the Iowa Supreme Court looked askance at a trial court's order that joint custody be accomplished by moving the children every six months. *Hansen, supra,* at 701. Other courts have also emphasized the importance of minimizing disruption and instability and ensuring that school-age children are in living arrangements that promote educational continuity.

It is not always possible for parents who share residential custody to facilitate stability as children move between homes. Responding to the burdens imposed by the growth of such arrangements, in 2013 New Hampshire modified the state code to relieve school districts of the obligation to provide transportation for the children of divorced parents who share custody beyond one designated school district. N.H. Rev. Stat. Ann. § 193:12(II)(a)(2)(b) (2018).

4. *Income tax consequences.* The parent with whom the child resides is allowed to claim the child as a dependent when he or she files federal income taxes unless the divorce decree or a written declaration expressly assigns the tax deduction or any applicable tax credits to the noncustodial parent. 26 U.S.C.A. § 152(e) (2012). When parents share custody, the court's order must assign the deduction and any tax credits, and the final judgment must be fully executed before that assignment becomes effective. *Hendricks v. C.I.R.*, 108 T.C.M. (CCH) 317 (T.C. 2014) (divorce decree permissibly awarded each parent the right to claim two of the four children as dependents for income tax purposes every other year). Although it is common to think of the assignment of the dependent allowance as benefitting high income taxpayers, in *Hendricks* the I.R.S. had originally ruled that the father could not receive the Earned Income Tax Credit he sought (a federal subsidy based on the number of children in the home, described in Chapter 3). *Id.*

5. *"Custody blackmail."* In a classic 1984 article, Chief Justice Richard Neely of the West Virginia Supreme Court of Appeals, formerly a practicing domestic relations lawyer, explained how a party may use "custody blackmail" to abuse joint custody claims during divorce negotiations:

> Divorce decrees are typically drafted for the parties after compromises reached through private negotiation. These compromises are then approved by a judge, who generally gives them only the most perfunctory sort of review. The result is that parties (usually husbands) are free to use whatever leverage is available to obtain a favorable settlement. In practice, this tends to mean that husbands will threaten custody fights, with all of the accompanying traumas and uncertainties * * * as a means of intimidating wives into accepting less child support and alimony than is sufficient to allow the mother to live and raise the children appropriately as a single

parent. Because women are usually unwilling to accept even a minor risk of losing custody, such techniques are generally successful.

Richard Neely, *The Primary Caretaker Parent Rule: Child Custody and the Dynamics of Greed*, 3 Yale L. & Pol'y Rev. 168, 177 (1984).

If Chief Justice Neely is correct, how would a statute favoring joint custody likely affect divorce negotiations?

6. *Criticisms of joint custody.* A number of scholars have noted that the burdens that post-divorce co-parenting imposes on adults—burdens increasingly imposed by the state through shared legal custody whether or not residential custody is shared—are "highly gendered," Jana B. Singer, *Dispute Resolution and the Postdivorce Family: Implications of a Paradigm Shift*, 47 Fam. Ct. Rev. 363, 366 (2009). Professor Jana Singer argued that the primary residential parent (still most commonly the mother) is "doubly disadvantaged," "by the dissolution of the couple's economic partnership and then by the decision-making restrictions that accompany judicially-mandated postdivorce co-parenting." *Id.* at 366.

Where one parent bears primary day-to-day responsibility for the child, is it fair to make him share all decisions with a legal co-parent who may live far away and rarely visit or speak to the child? Is joint physical custody as feasible for those with limited financial resources as it is for the affluent? What extra financial costs might be imposed by shared caretaking?

7. *Domestic violence and joint custody.* Earlier in this Chapter you read about domestic violence as a factor in custody decisions. What special considerations arise when joint custody is awarded in a case where one parent has abused the other? In *Cerwick*, both parties made allegations of physical abuse that the court considered unsubstantiated. What additional details would you like to know? What evidence would you ask for?

In 2014, Rhode Island's highest court expressly affirmed a family court order that awarded shared physical custody despite the husband's verbal harassment and threats that had led the judge to issue a restraining order that survived the divorce decree. The restraining order provided an exception so that the father could telephone to arrange for exchanging the child, with drop off and pick up to take place at police stations near the parents' respective homes. *Cavanaugh v. Cavanaugh*, 92 A.3d 200 (R.I. 2014).

Meanwhile, in Arizona, the legislature amended the state code effective in 2014 expressly to respond to the problem of judges who award shared legal custody in families with a history of domestic violence. The statute provides:

A. [J]oint legal decision-making shall not be awarded if the court makes a finding of the existence of significant domestic violence [as defined in another statute] or if the court finds by a preponderance of the evidence that there has been a significant history of domestic violence.

B.   The court shall consider evidence of domestic violence as being contrary to the best interests of the child. The court shall consider the safety and well-being of the child and of the victim of the act of domestic violence to be of primary importance. * * *

* * *

D.   [T]here is a rebuttable presumption that an award of sole or joint legal decision-making to the parent who committed the act of domestic violence is contrary to the child's best interests. This presumption does not apply if both parents have committed an act of domestic violence. * * *

Ariz. Rev. Stat. Ann. § 25–403.03 (2017).

Should records of domestic violence by both parties cancel each other out? What evidence might be sufficient to overcome the statutory presumption against awarding shared legal custody to a parent with a history of domestic violence?

PROBLEM 12-4

Joe and Haley met at a bar and had a very brief relationship that resulted in the birth of a child Haley named Brittney. Paternity tests established the Joe was the Brittney's father. Joe and Haley informally agreed to raise Brittney together. Brittney resided with Joe and his wife (whom he married during Haley's pregnancy) during the work week, and with Haley on the weekends. When Brittney was one year old Joe's wife gave birth to a baby boy. Brittney was very excited to have a baby brother.

Haley moved numerous times during the first few years of Brittney's life, often sharing apartments with roommates whom she did not know well. Joe did not consider Haley's living situation appropriate for a small child, and repeatedly threatened to go to court to seek custody, There were other issues too. Joe's family attended a Methodist church every Sunday. Haley was a lapsed Roman Catholic, who scoffed at churchgoing.

When Brittney was four, and Haley had just signed a lease on a one-bedroom apartment of her own with a special space for Brittney, Joe received an attractive job offer in another city about two hours away from where he and Haley currently lived. He wanted to move and to take Brittney with him and the rest of his family.

Joe filed a petition for an initial custody order, asking the court to award him shared legal custody and sole residential custody with liberal visits between Haley and Brittney. Haley objected. She seeks an order for shared legal and physical custody. Assume, for reasons that will be discussed in the next chapter, that if the court orders shared custody and makes Joe the residential parent Joe cannot accept the new job and relocate without the court's permission.

You are Joe's attorney. What arguments would you make in support of his petition? What do you expect Haley to argue? How do you expect the court to rule on this initial custody matter? Should it make a difference that Joe and Haley were never married to each other and indeed barely knew each other before Brittney was conceived and born?

C. PROMOTING CO-PARENTING

It may be that "shared parenting after separation or divorce is one of the most hotly debated issues in family law today," as a 2014 study group reported, but, even so, legal professionals, court reformers and academics have coalesced around the importance of reducing parental conflict and helping parents to work together to raise their children with as little disagreement and animosity as possible. Marsha Kline Pruitt & J. Herbie DiFonzo, *Closing the Gap: Research, Policy, Practice, and Shared Parenting*, 52 Fam. Ct. Rev. 152, 153 (2014) (Final Report of the AFCC Think Tank). This trend is not limited to the United States. It is visible in Canada, England, Australia and New Zealand as well. In these societies, it has become common to say that marriage may be temporary, but parenting is forever. "[P]rotecting the co[-]parenting relationship," a recent article posits, "is an important public-policy goal for both married families and for families in which parents live apart, a goal that might trump well-intentioned efforts by the court to intervene to protect children's best interests." Kimberly C. Emery & Robert E. Emery, *Who Knows What Is Best for Children? Honoring Agreements and Contracts Between Parents Who Live Apart*, 77 Law & Contemp. Probs. 151, 153–54 (2014).

The Florida legislature expressly incorporated this view when it revised the state's custody statute in 2010: "It is the public policy of this state that each minor child has frequent and continuing contact with both parents after the parents separate or the marriage is dissolved, and to encourage parents to share the rights and responsibilities, and joys, of childrearing." Fla. Stat. Ann. § 61.13(2)(c)(1) (West Supp. 2019). To accomplish this policy goal, commentators have recommended changes both at the time of divorce and with respect to the structure of parental interaction in the future.

First, at the time of separation, commentators argue, parents should be encouraged to devise their own parenting arrangements, and if they can't reach agreement on their own, they should turn to mediation or collaborative divorce methods (see Chapter 15) rather than litigation. Litigation, they contend, exacerbates conflict—particularly in child custody disputes where the core issue is who is a "better" parent and the dispute focuses on each parent's arguable flaws. California has required parents to enter mediation before scheduling a custody hearing since 1981. Emery & Emery, *Honoring Agreements, supra,* at 154–162.

Second, looking forward, parents should prepare to work together amicably by attending parenting education classes (offered either by the family court or private providers, in person or online). Courts may require parents to attend. Peter Salem et al., *Taking Stock of Parenting Education in the Family Courts: Envisioning a Public Health Approach*, 51 Fam. Ct. Rev. 131 (2013). Parenting classes may also be imposed after shared parenting proves problematic as you will see in the next chapter.

Parenting plans—which set forth the detailed particulars of hours, holidays, responsibilities etc. for shared custody or visitation—are increasingly mandated by state law, and most states provide a model plan which parents can modify before they present it to the court for approval. Linda Elrod, Child Custody Prac. & Proc. § 4: 7 (March 2018 update) (most jurisdictions require parents to submit a parenting plan in at least some kinds of custody cases). The ALI, and some jurisdictions, expressly require the judge to accept the provisions of the parenting plan that both parents have agreed on, and most judges do that even where the statute does not limit their discretion. Emery & Emery, *Honoring Agreements, supra,* at 167. When parents cannot agree on a plan, some state statutes provide that the court will substitute a standard plan generated for the state or judicial jurisdiction. *E.g.,* Ariz. Rev. Stat. Ann. § 25–403.02.D (2017).

Parents engaged in negotiating parenting plans are well advised to consider how the child's needs may evolve over time (a one-year-old child may not be able to handle as many transitions between homes for overnight visits as a twelve-year-old preteenager, while teenagers may have their own plans and voice their own strong preferences). Indeed, many court systems and professional organizations provide specific guidance on designing age-appropriate parenting plans. *See* Association of Family and Conciliation Courts (Mass. Chapter), *Planning for Shared Parenting: A Guide for Parents Living Apart* (2005). The ideal parenting agreement anticipates that the needs of the children and adults may evolve and provides mechanisms for adjustments without recourse to litigation if the parents cannot agree to modifications. For example, the parenting plan can require that disagreements be resolved through mediation, an evaluation, or by hiring a parenting coordinator (usually a social worker or mental health professional appointed to help parents in high conflict divorces).

Several states, including Florida, have recently revised their custody statutes to incorporate the contemporary disposition toward shared parenting—starting with the normative importance of terminology. Proposals for reform are pending in others.

The following excerpt sets out revisions to the Arizona Statutes that became effective on January 1, 2013. As you read, think about the reasoning behind the new sections, and whether you agree with the policy choices the legislature made. The statute maintains the best interests of the child as the standard for custody decisions, and provides factors for the court to consider in determining best interests. The factors are to be used in assigning "legal decision-making and parenting time," using the new terminology the statute adopts. The term "visitation" is reserved for "a schedule of time that occurs with a child by someone other than a legal parent." Ariz. Rev. Stat. Ann.§§ 25–401 (2017).

ARIZONA REVISED STATUTES ANNOTATED

Sole and joint legal decision-making and parenting time

A.   In awarding legal decision-making, the court may order sole legal decision-making or joint legal decision-making.

B.   In determining the level of decision-making that is in the child's best interests, the court shall consider the [best interests factors enumerated elsewhere in the code] and all of the following:

    1.   The agreement or lack of an agreement by the parents regarding joint legal decision-making.

    2.   Whether a parent's lack of an agreement is unreasonable or is influenced by an issue not related to the child's best interests.

    3.   The past, present and future abilities of the parents to cooperate in decision-making about the child to the extent required by the order of joint legal decision-making.

    4.   Whether the joint legal decision-making arrangement is logistically possible.

C.   An order for sole legal decision-making does not allow the parent designated as sole legal decision-maker to alter unilaterally a court-ordered parenting time plan.

D.   A parent who is not granted sole or joint legal decision-making is entitled to reasonable parenting time to ensure that the minor child has substantial, frequent, meaningful and continuing contact with the parent unless the court finds, after a hearing, that parenting time would endanger the child's physical, mental, moral or emotional health.

Parenting plans

A.   If the child's parents cannot agree on a plan for legal decision-making or parenting time, each parent must submit a proposed parenting plan.

B.   Consistent with the child's best interests * * *, the court shall adopt a parenting plan that provides for both parents to share legal decision-making regarding their child and that maximizes their respective parenting time. The court shall not prefer a parent's proposed plan because of the parent's or child's gender.

C.   Parenting plans shall include at least the following:

1. A designation of the legal decision-making as joint or sole * * *.

2. Each parent's rights and responsibilities for the personal care of the child and for decisions in areas such as education, health care and religious training.

3. A practical schedule of parenting time for the child, including holidays and school vacations.

4. A procedure for the exchanges of the child, including location and responsibility for transportation.

5. A procedure by which proposed changes, disputes and alleged breaches may be mediated or resolved, which may include the use of conciliation services or private counseling.

6. A procedure for periodic review of the plan's terms by the parents.

7. A procedure for communicating with each other about the child, including methods and frequency.

8. A statement that each party has read, understands and will abide by the notification requirements * * *.

D. If the parents are unable to agree on any element to be included in a parenting plan, the court shall determine that element. The court may determine other factors that are necessary to promote and protect the emotional and physical health of the child.

E. Shared legal decision-making does not necessarily mean equal parenting time.

Ariz. Rev. Stat. Ann. § 25–403 (2017).

NOTES AND QUESTIONS

1. *Interpreting the statute.* Does the Arizona statute favor or disfavor shared parenting, or is it neutral? What concerns about joint custody is it trying to anticipate or address? How does the statute treat a parenting plan presented by both parents? How much discretion does the judge have if the parents cannot agree on all of the details of the parenting plan?

2. In 2014 the Tennessee legislature amended the code provisions respecting the best interests of the child to emphasize, among other things, the importance of parents being able to collaborate in caring for their children. The code provides that in addition to the familiar factors implicated in best interests (e.g., stability, continuity and emotional attachment) the court should look at whether one parent has ever denied the other access to the child in violation of a court order or refused to attend a "court ordered parent education seminar." It also requires consideration of "the character and behavior of any other person who resides in or frequents the home of a parent and such person's interactions with the child," and the "reasonable preference of the child of

twelve (12) years or older," with the option of taking the opinions of younger children into account. Tenn. Code Ann. § 36–6–106 (2017).

PROBLEM 12-5

If you were a member of the state legislature, would you have voted for or against the Arizona statute set out above? Why? Would you have proposed any amendments and, if so, to what effect and why? Would you support an amendment specifying a minimum percentage of parenting time that each parent must receive? If so, should that be closer to 20% or 40% and why? Would you place any limitations on that provision?

CHAPTER 13

VISITATION AND POST-DISSOLUTION CUSTODY DISPUTES

■ ■ ■

After reading Chapter 12, you may agree with a Connecticut trial judge who observed that a parent "can no more win" a bitter custody dispute "than win an earthquake." *Davidson v. Davidson*, 2008 WL 1799679, at *1 (Conn. Super. Ct. Apr. 2, 2008). These disputes, she said, have "no 'winner'" but only "tragic victims"—the children. *Id.* Consider these statements as you examine the law that governs disputes over custody and visitation that continue to fester after the court's initial decree has determined the parties' rights and obligations.

This Chapter covers a range of issues that can involve parents in ongoing, acrimonious litigation after the initial custody decision. Only a small proportion of custody cases continue to be litigated after the court issues its initial decree, but judges commonly feel inundated with post-divorce litigation concerning enforcement of visitation rights, disagreements about childrearing, and requests to modify custodial arrangements or the terms of parenting agreements.

Because of the importance, relative frequency, and difficulty of these seemingly endless disputes, this casebook devotes a separate chapter to post-dissolution disputes about custody and visitation. These complex, often intractable issues are gaining increasing attention: indeed, four cases excerpted or discussed in this Chapter reached the Supreme Court in just fourteen years—between 2000 and 2014. As you will see, many factors considered in the initial custody decision (discussed in Chapter 12) continue to fuel conflict between parents after dissolution: religion, educational choices, the other parent's sexual behavior and morality, and so forth.

As with other terms at the core of dissolution, modern terms such as "parenting time" and "time sharing" are increasingly used in statutes instead of traditional terms like "visitation." However, because many statutes and reported opinions continue to use the language of "custody" and "visitation," and to avoid confusion, we use "visitation" throughout the Chapter except where quoted material uses a different term.

The Chapter opens by considering the impact on children of unabated acrimony between parents who share custody. Section 2 turns to visitation, including the noncustodial parent's rights to visitation; under what circumstances that right may be restricted; the rights of third parties, such as grandparents, to seek visitation; and the status and claims of de facto parents (adults who are not a child's legal parent but have functioned as a parent with the legal parent's consent) who seek custody or visitation.

Many of the cases in the Chapter involve petitions for modification of an earlier child custody ruling. Section 3 explores the standard for modification and the common problem of relocation by the custodial parent. Finally, Section 4 examines the legal remedies available when a parent absconds with children in violation of custody and visitation orders, either within the United States or across international boundaries, by looking at parental kidnapping and the Hague Convention.

1. DISPUTES ABOUT MAJOR CHILDREARING DECISIONS

Perpetual disputes about custody, visitation and childrearing reflect a myriad of issues that often survive dissolution of the parents' relationship. These issues include each parent's conviction that he or she is the better parent who understands what is best for the child. The custodial parent (or both parents where physical custody is shared) often perceives that he or she is being forced to prolong a terminated relationship with the other parent; the noncustodial parent in turn may resent that his or her interest in the child has been severely diminished because the child now "belongs" to the custodial parent. Because struggles for control frequently lie at the heart of troubled marriages, hostility toward a former spouse (or lover) may be a defense mechanism against confronting the severity and finality of the lost relationship. Finally, custody disputes offer an opportunity to prolong control over a former partner.

A. COLLAPSE OF JOINT PARENTING

The following case provides an excellent, if extreme, example of the extent of animosity between some parents following divorce. The gulf dividing the parents at divorce frequently generates post-divorce disputes over religious upbringing, relocation, educational choices, and access to the children's daily activities—all of which were in play in the dispute that led to the opinion set forth below.

NICITA V. KITTREDGE

Superior Court of Connecticut, 2004.
2004 WL 2284292.

PRESTLEY, J.

* * *

This highly contentious case involves the filing of numerous post-judgment motions by both parents with respect to their two young children, Alec and Madison. After numerous days of hearing, testimony from many witnesses, including at least two experts and exhibits entered, this court makes the following findings.

Findings

The parties' marriage was dissolved on June 6, 2001 by agreement. [T]he parties agreed to joint legal custody of the minor children, primary residence with the defendant * * * [the mother, who] would be responsible for all day-to-day decisions regarding the children's care. The agreement noted that major decisions, as defined in the agreement, "shall be considered and discussed in depth by and agreed to by both parties to the greatest extent possible." Those major decisions were defined in the judgment. In entering this agreement, the parties recognized that their powers would not be exercised "for the purpose of frustrating, denying, or controlling in any manner the lifestyle of the other parent." Finally, the parties agreed that they would "exert their best efforts to work cooperatively in developing future plans consistent with the best interests of the children and in amicably resolving such disputes as may arise."

To suggest that the above provisions have been largely ignored would be an understatement. The court file is replete with no less than seventy-five motions having been filed by both parties, during the pendency of the dissolution action, within weeks of the date of dissolution, and over the past three years. Many of these motions were resolved by agreement or after hearing only to have new motions filed within a short period of time. Additional motions have been filed since the hearing closed and as recently as last week * * *.

At least two and possibly three Guardians *Ad Litem* have been appointed to represent the children. The first withdrew because of alleged threats of litigation made by the defendant's family members. At one point an attorney was appointed to represent the GAL. There have been allegations made by the plaintiff of threats made against him by the defendant's attorneys.

This case has a long and tortured history of events that led up to the demise of the marriage and has continued since the dissolution. [T]he stepfather * * * moved into the marital home within weeks of the plaintiff moving out. The children's religious upbringing has been the source of numerous motions and perhaps the most contentious topic of dispute between the parties.

The defendant is remarried and lives in Burlington, Connecticut with her husband and the two children. The plaintiff continues to reside in Farmington, Connecticut but works in the state of New York, has a girlfriend there and spends the majority of his time with his children there visiting his family, his girlfriend and her children as well.

* * *

Custody and Parenting Schedule

There have been a few modifications to the parenting plan since the date of dissolution. There is at present, no primary residential designation. The current custody and visitation arrangement allows for a traditional schedule but specifically also includes parenting time by the plaintiff every other weekend from Friday until Monday, mid-week access from Wednesday to Thursday and an additional 10 days access throughout the year. The plaintiff has also had access to the children on alternating Mondays overnight. The children are at the plaintiff's home a minimum of twelve nights per month. April vacation and Christmas vacation weeks and Easter Sunday are reserved to the plaintiff as are two non-consecutive weeks in the summertime. The children are happy with the current schedule.

There was ample evidence offered throughout the course of the protracted hearings that compel this court to conclude that both parties have taken actions that have undermined the other parent and have been detrimental to the children. They are hypercritical of one another on an unrelenting basis. The defendant has consistently taken unilateral action over the objection of or without seeking input from the plaintiff. The plaintiff is consistent in rigidly resisting any attempt or position offered by the defendant when she does seek his input.

[T]hese issues have been recurring and have been the subject of motions in the past. While the number of examples of inappropriate conduct by the parties is too numerous to list, the following are a sample:

Religion

The parties were married by both a priest and a rabbi. During the course of their marriage, they celebrated both Christmas and Chanukah. When Alec was born, they had a Jewish baby naming ceremony but there was no Bris ceremony. It is clear to the court that the parties, individually and collectively, had not committed to raising their children as either Jewish or Christian by the date of the dissolution.

At some point after the dissolution, the defendant made the unilateral decision that the children would be raised in the Jewish faith. The plaintiff, who is Catholic, was upset about this unilateral decision for the reason that he did not agree to it. This issue became the subject of a series of motions with the plaintiff ultimately agreeing that the children would be raised in the Jewish faith. Alec was then signed up to attend Hebrew school, which takes place every Sunday morning during the school year from 3rd grade until he is 9 or 10 years old when the program becomes more intense in preparation for being Bas or Bar Mitzvah'd. [The father] has refused to allow Alec to attend Hebrew school on his weekend time with his children. He has also begun to take the children to church on his weekends with them and has affirmatively given them mixed messages about their religion.

Relocation

At some point, the defendant made the unilateral decision that she and her new husband would move from Farmington, Connecticut where the plaintiff resides and the children attended school to Burlington, Connecticut and a new school district. She listed her house for sale without informing the plaintiff and he only learned of the impending move from a neighbor. Again, this unilateral decision resulted in a flurry of motions with the end result being that the plaintiff agreed to allow the children to make this move.

Therapy

Alec began having stomach problems with vomiting, quite possibly in response to the tension created by the animosity between the parties. There were discussions with his teacher and the school social worker about starting him in therapy. The defendant unilaterally began to bring Alec to a therapist without consulting the plaintiff, which in this case, the court finds was appropriate. The plaintiff did not take any action to oppose this in court but then the defendant changed the therapist, purportedly because the therapist was recommending that the children spend more time with the plaintiff. She did this without consulting the plaintiff and apparently gave short shrift to the fact that the new therapist was "out-of-network" and therefore not covered by the plaintiff's insurance. She then demanded that the plaintiff share in the expense of the out-of-network therapist.

* * *

Other Examples

* * *

In the course of signing up her children for activities, the defendant listed her current husband as "the father" on activities registration forms and her husband and her brother as emergency contacts as well. Nowhere was the plaintiff listed as the parent or as an emergency contact. As a consequence, on at least one occasion, the children's day camp administrators refused to send the plaintiff forms or information about their program.

The defendant unilaterally committed the children to activities on a regular basis and then would inform the plaintiff. Some of these activities impacted on the plaintiff's parenting schedule with the children. This was, in part, due to the plaintiff's unwillingness to respond to requests by the defendant for activity input in a timely fashion. This was especially true when the defendant needed to make a decision about summer day camp in order to secure a spot for each of the children. Despite her repeated attempts to get feedback from the plaintiff, he refused to select his summer vacation time until the very last moment as specified in the original judgment but well beyond the date needed to secure the children a place.

* * *

On at least one occasion, the plaintiff requested medication from the defendant for Alec's asthma, the defendant indicated that she was too busy and the stepfather replied "you'll get what she gives you."

The plaintiff does not want the stepfather at Alec's ball games and there have been several unpleasant encounters. * * *

Both the stepfather and the plaintiff's girlfriend seem to be entirely appropriate and very loving to the children. It is indeed unfortunate that these four individuals cannot be actively involved with the children without such involvement becoming unpleasant, confrontational and uncomfortable for the children.

The Children

The children are beautiful, bright and articulate. Currently, Alec is in karate and baseball. Madison is in Daisy Scouts, soccer, dance and piano. The children also attend summer day camp at Camp Chase and Winding Trails. Since the decision was made to allow the children to be raised in the Jewish faith, they now identify themselves as Jews.

The children are happy to see the plaintiff and enjoy the time that they spend with him in New York, with his fiancée and her children, with the plaintiff's extended family, and at his home. Unfortunately, Alec is intensely aware of the tension, animosity, and belligerence that exists between his parents and he is very uncomfortable when he is in the presence of both his stepfather and his father. In fact, he indicated to the GAL that he must ask the parent he is with to speak to his other parent when they run into them. There is much that the children are not revealing to either parent about their feelings vis-à-vis the current untenable situation. Alec believes that there is a list of topics that he cannot discuss with either parent. All of this has manifested in Alec having physical symptoms of illness, necessitating therapy for this third grader.

Alec is told by the defendant that he is Jewish and by the plaintiff that he is Catholic and Jewish. He is very confused about his religious identity.

There is no question in the court's mind that each of these parties, individually, love these children and take excellent care of them when they are in their respective homes. * * * Individually, both the defendant and the plaintiff are very good parents.

Collectively, however, the parties' co-parenting of these children is a disaster. Their positions are so intractable that neither party is capable of compromise. * * * Mediation and the Peace Program[a] do not seem to have assisted the parties in resolving differences. * * *

[T]he original orders in the judgment of dissolution must be modified in order to minimize contact between the parties and to minimize any opportunities the parties may have to continue to battle each other, all to the detriment of Alec and Madison.

Orders

1. The joint custody order shall remain in place. Except in the event of an emergency, all major decisions making shall be mutually agreed upon by the parties. Those decisions include but are not limited to non-routine medical treatment and relocation.

2. The defendant shall be primarily responsible for making the day-to-day decisions for the children including the scheduling of their activities. The defendant shall request input from the plaintiff before scheduling but may schedule the children in no more than two activities per child per season without the plaintiff's agreement. The defendant shall make her best efforts not to schedule activities that interfere with the plaintiff's parenting time. The plaintiff will make his best efforts to take the children to their activities on his parenting time. All information regarding the children's activities shall be provided to the plaintiff in a timely fashion.

3. This court is cognizant of the plaintiff's ties to the state of New York, the children's need to spend time with his extended family, and his need to parent autonomously. While continuity for the children would certainly be in their best interests, the plaintiff will have to decide whether to take the children to those activities that impact on his weekends with them. * * * The plaintiff shall not schedule the children for any activities with any substantial time commitment without the agreement of the defendant.

4. The defendant shall be authorized to make all decisions involving routine doctor's and dentist's appointments including the selection of those

---

[a] *Editors' Note:* Family courts in most counties offer a PEACE program which courts can encourage or order divorcing and never-married parents to attend. The programs are designed to minimize parental conflict, teach parenting skills, and help parents learn how to establish and abide by parenting schedules with smooth transitions.

professionals so long as she seeks the plaintiff's input and bears the added expense of any out-of-network providers.

5. The defendant shall provide the plaintiff's parent contact information on each and every application in the appropriate place for each and every activity and school that the children are engaged with. The plaintiff will have independent access to all of his children's activity providers regardless of whether he is paying the bill or not.

6. Both parties are encouraged to participate in their children's education. The defendant shall be authorized to make the final day-to-day educational decisions for the children after seeking the plaintiff's input. The children are permitted to attend private school locally as long as the defendant bears the cost of this extraordinary expense.

7. The plaintiff shall be permitted and encouraged to participate in the children's therapy as recommended by their therapist. Any out-of-network therapy expenses, including sessions involving participation by the plaintiff, above and beyond those in-network expenses that the plaintiff would have otherwise been responsible for under his insurance plan, shall be borne by the defendant.

8. Other than in a true emergency situation, there shall be no telephone contact by either parent to the other's home. The children may enjoy unlimited telephone contact with the nonresidential parent as they wish. Those conversations shall take place with the children afforded some privacy. The parents will communicate only by email and in a civil, non-sarcastic manner.

9. Each parent shall provide the other parent with all necessary medications for the child during his time at the other parent's home.

10. [The parents shall inform each other about their respective vacation plans by a set date.]

11. The children shall continue to be formally raised in the Jewish faith as agreed upon by the parties. While it is hoped that [plaintiff] at some point will participate in the Bar or Bas Mitzvah [sic] events in the children's lives, he shall not be required to bring the children to Hebrew school on his weekends with them. * * * Any Hebrew School tutoring costs resulting from the defendant's decision to raise the children in the Jewish faith, the joint custodial arrangement and the plaintiff's reluctance to be involved in the children's religious education, shall be borne by the defendant.

12. This court would have no problem with the plaintiff exposing the children to his religion if it was confident that the children would not be pressured to take part in rituals that might confuse them. Unfortunately, this issue has become yet another forum for contention and a source of strife between the parties. Therefore, the children shall not attend church

with the plaintiff except for those holidays which have a secular component to them such as Easter Sunday and Christmas, and any other celebrations such as baptism, funerals and weddings. They shall not take part in any sacrament events such as receiving communion or ashes nor shall they be encouraged to engage in any Christian rituals such as kneeling and making the sign of the cross.

13. The current parenting schedule shall be maintained with the formal inclusion of the alternating Monday overnights with the plaintiff. * * * Barring a *bona fide* emergency, pick up by the plaintiff shall be by 7:00 p.m. with 30 minutes of leeway to account for the plaintiff's commute. Drop-off by the plaintiff shall be at the defendant's home at 7:15 a.m. All pickups and drop-offs shall be at the defendant's residence curbside unless otherwise agreed upon.

14. The plaintiff shall have the first opportunity to coach his children's teams. There is nothing to preclude the stepfather's involvement as well but it is hoped that the stepfather will take into account the feelings of the children and the extraordinary sensitivities in this case in deciding his level of involvement.

15. Neither party shall speak in a derogatory fashion about the other party, the party's religion or the party's significant other.

* * *

NOTES AND QUESTIONS

1. *Is continued joint custody appropriate when parents express extreme animosity toward each other?* As you read in Chapter 12, joint custody is appropriate only when it is in the child's best interests and the parents can cooperate. Even when the parents agree about custody and visitation arrangements, the court may modify provisions of a marital settlement agreement relating to care, custody and education based on its *parens patriae* authority to decide in the child's best interests. *E.g.*, Md. Code Ann., Fam. Law § 8–103 (LexisNexis 2012).

For example, the co-parenting counselor in *In re Paternity of A.S.*, 948 N.E.2d 380, 388 (Ind. Ct. App. 2011) recommended that the two parents "communicate in writing to reduce hostility." Where the breakdown in communication is egregious, joint custody may no longer serve the child's best interest and the court may assign custody to one parent. *Id.* at 383 (the parents' relationship was so acrimonious that they were unable to agree on when the child should wear a coat or have her hair cut).

Such problems are so pervasive among parents who share custody that a divorced father started a website to help parents who do not live together to coordinate their children's schedules, pickup times and so forth without having to speak to each other; registered families may use tools such as a color-coded calendar that makes clear when the child is with each parent and what commitments the child has each day. www.ourfamilywizard.com. Similar sites have sprung up, some of which offer parenting advice as well. The most recent—coParenter—is an app initiated by a family court judge who thought it would help reduce repeated judicial intervention where the problems could be easily resolved. The app relied on academic research, was pilot tested in the judge's Riverside county, California family court, and offers parents access to digital mediation. Lydia Dishman, *Exclusive: This app helps divorced parents stop fighting and save money*, Fast Company, Jan. 17, 2019.

2. *Parenting plans.* The judge's order in *Nicita* amounted to a very detailed parenting plan. In light of all the circumstances, do you think that the judge in *Nicita* crafted a solution that is likely to prove workable? Which, if any, of the court's orders in *Nicita* are enforceable? How can the court enforce them?

How far can a court go in holding accountable a parent who willfully disobeys the parenting plan and court orders and succeeds in depriving the other parent of parenting time? Can the court hold the offending parent in contempt? In 2016 a Missouri appellate court affirmed a trial court order holding the mother in civil contempt for completely frustrating the father's visitation in a contentious custody dispute that had resulted in numerous court appearances over the years. *D.R.P. v. M.P.P.*, 484 S.W.3d 822 (Mo. Ct. App. 2016). The court affirmed an order committing the mother to a correctional facility "until she purged herself of the contempt." *Id.* at 826. The mother, the court noted, "holds the keys to the jail upon her compliance with the trial court's judgment." *Id.* at 829. Would the judge in *Nicita* be justified in holding the mother in contempt and threatening to jail her?

3. *What do Alec and Madison seek?* Have the children in *Nicita* managed to communicate their views? If so, how? What outcome do you think they seek?

4. *Practical limits on a court's powers.* In a third-party visitation case, the Connecticut Supreme Court discussed the arsenal of weapons at the disposal of a frustrated family court confronting uncooperative custodial parents. *DiGiovanna v. St. George*, 12 A.3d 900 (Conn. 2011). Referring to a mother who appeared to lack the "capacity" not to harm her child if the court ordered visitation with her former live-in boyfriend (who was not the child's father), the state's highest court commented: "the court may not have concluded that it *lacked* authority to compel the defendant's compliance, but, rather, that it would have been *futile* to employ" the tools at its disposal, including citing her for contempt, ordering counseling etc. *Id.* at 911. "Policy considerations," however, mandate that the court use every available means to enforce its orders. To do otherwise, the state's Supreme Court concluded, "would create a powerful incentive in every visitation contest for a parent to threaten to create a hostile environment if visitation is ordered and to communicate an unwillingness to act otherwise." *Id.*

5. *Disagreements about educational decisions.* In *Nicita*, the mother apparently was considering enrolling the children in private schools. Why did

the court specify that the children must attend "local" schools? Why did the court specify who should pay for the children's schooling?

Disputes often arise when children have special educational needs because of learning disabilities or severe disciplinary problems. Parents of these children may resort to the courts after failing to agree on the appropriate educational setting. In *Case v. Jones,* 2011 WL 1565813 at *2–3 (Conn. Super. Ct. Mar. 28, 2011) the court granted sole legal and physical custody of the child to the father, based, in part, on the fact that the child had special needs and required a stable home and school environment, which the court concluded the only the father could provide.

In other instances, the parents simply have different approaches. In *In re Kurowski,* 20 A.3d 306 (N.H. 2011), after the parents divorced, the mother home schooled the couple's daughter, primarily for religious reasons— providing another example of how disputes over education and religion are often intertwined. The father, who shared legal and physical custody, objected. A compromise in which the mother homeschooled the girl but allowed her to take several classes at a public school broke down. The trial court then ordered the mother to send the girl to public school. The state's highest court upheld the decision. Although the parents have equal constitutional rights as co-parents, the court reasoned, "[b]ecause the parties could not reach a joint decision * * *, the trial court was left to decide the dispute, guided by the best interests standard. * * *." *Id.* at 316. The trial court found the girl was "bored" and "lonely" at home. *Id.* The court also deemed it significant that the mother's religious influence, untempered by any alternative views, had interfered with the girl's relationship with her father who she feared was going to hell.

6.   *Medical information and medications.* The dispute over medical bills and treatment in *Nicita* is fairly common among non-cooperating divorced and estranged parents. While many disputes focus on the failure to provide prescribed medications, disputes may also involve overuse of doctors. *E.g., Topolski v. Topolski,* 844 N.W.2d 875 (N.D. 2014) (neglect of dental health, skin rash, etc.); *In re Izabella M.,* 2013 WL 453067 (Conn. Super. Ct. Jan. 8, 2013) (allegations that mother engaged in Munchausen's Syndrome by Proxy and falsified child's medical history, leading to involvement of child welfare officials while the child resided with father).

Where a parent fails or refuses to share medical information or medications with the other parent who has visitation or custodial rights, would failure or refusal ever cross the line so that prosecution for child endangerment would be appropriate? What would be an appropriate penalty? Is it possible to promote continuity of care and achieve justice between feuding parents in such a situation?

7.   *How long does parental acrimony last?* Parental conflicts over their children can last well into the child's adulthood. In 2005, the divorced parents of 28-year-old Staff Sergeant Jason Hendrix, who was killed in the Iraq war, fought over whether to bury him in the maternal or paternal family plot. The father won, based on the 1993 decree that awarded him custody and on the

Army's internal rules for deciding such conflicts. The funeral was delayed for more than a month pending judicial resolution of the custody dispute. Matthew B. Stannard, *Burial-Rights Fight: Court Sides With Father In Clash Over Where Soldier Will Be Laid To Rest*, S.F. Chron., Mar. 24, 2005, at A1. The legal dispute continued even after Sgt. Hendrix was interred next to his paternal grandfather. Ken McLaughlin, *Battle Continues Over Soldier's Body*, Contra Costa Times (Walnut Creek, Cal.), Nov. 4, 2005, at Q4.

So too, after Scott Patrick Wilson, who had just graduated from college, died in a car accident in Florida his parents fought for several years over his ashes. The father wanted the ashes sent to Georgia, but offered to split them with the mother. She, in turn, argued the ashes should stay in Florida, that it was "disgusting" to contemplate dividing them, and said the idea violated her religious beliefs. The court appointed a third party to determine the final resting place. Jacqui Goddard, *Sex, murder and adoption: The wild trial of the polo king*, Daily Beast (Oct. 28, 2014).

8.   *Court-affiliated parent education programs.* Prior to the decision you read, the parents in *Nicita* had participated in a court-affiliated program that teaches parents about how divorce impacts children and how to co-parent after divorce. As you read in Chapter 12, every state offers some form of parent education in conjunction with divorce. The programs vary in scope and intensity, as well as in whether participation is mandatory or voluntary.

9.   *Parenting coordinators.* Courts in many jurisdictions appoint parenting coordinators in high conflict divorce cases. Parenting coordinators are mental health or legal professionals who have training in mediation. They bring a child-centered focus to resolution of conflicts about childrearing decisions and the day-to-day details of the parenting plan and often have enforcement powers. Sometimes the court delegates certain decision-making authority to a parenting coordinator, or the parents agree to abide by the coordinator's decisions. *See Jordan v. Jordan*, 14 A.3d 1136 (D.C. 2011) (upholding appointment of a parenting coordinator and delegation of some decisions to the coordinator, as comparable to the use of special masters in court cases).

Statutes and court rules have increasingly authorized the appointment of parenting coordinators. Linda D. Elrod, Child Custody Practice and Procedure § 15:1, Westlaw (database update Mar. 2018). In Florida, for example, the court rules provide that the court can appoint a parenting coordinator whenever the best interests of the child support the decision. *In re Amendments to the Florida Family Law Rules of Procedure*, 27 So.3d 650 (Fla. 2010). The Kansas statute provides for appointment of a "case manager" to resolve "any contested issue of child custody or parenting time" where, among other things, dispute resolution has "been tried and failed," or "repetitive conflict" has occurred, evidenced by, for example, the filing of two or more unsuccessful motions pertaining to custody arrangements within a six-month period. Kan. Stat. Ann. § 23–3508 (West, Westlaw current through laws in effect on or before July 1, 2018).

In other jurisdictions courts rely on their general equitable powers to make such appointments. *Jordan, supra,* 14 A.3d at 1153, 1153 n.14. Parents are generally ordered to pay the parenting coordinator. The District of Columbia provides parenting coordinators for low-income couples. *Id.* at 1154.

The judge, however, is ultimately responsible for decisions and orders. It may be an abuse of discretion to delegate certain decisions to a parenting coordinator, or to give a parenting coordinator authority to impose a resolution over one parent's objections. *Bower v. Bournay-Bower,* 15 N.E.3d 745 (Mass. 2014).

B. TIE-BREAKING ARRANGEMENTS

Courts are justifiably reluctant to serve as continuing arbiters when parents who share custody cannot resolve their disputes about major decisions or values. But if the alternative is to give one parent more weight in decision-making, what does it mean to be a legal custodian with a minority vote? The Supreme Court considered the ramifications of awarding tie-breaking powers to one parent in *Elk Grove Unified School District v. Newdow,* 542 U.S. 1 (2004). Michael Newdow, a doctor, licensed attorney, and self-proclaimed atheist, shared custody of his daughter with her mother with whom he had only a brief relationship before the child was conceived and born. Newdow sought a declaratory judgment that the words "under God" in the Pledge of Allegiance recited daily at his daughter's elementary school violated the Establishment Clause, as well as his right as an atheist and a parent to inculcate his beliefs in his daughter. The child's mother, a practicing Christian, disagreed with Newdow's desire to challenge the use of "under God" in the pledge recited in public schools, and asserted that the child also believed in God. When the parents could not resolve their differences, the family court gave the mother "what amounts to a tie-breaking vote" about the daughter's education after consulting with Newdow. *Id.* at 14 n.6 (Stevens, J.) Newdow represented himself throughout the litigation, including at oral argument before the Supreme Court.

The Ninth Circuit held that Newdow had standing "as a parent to challenge a practice that interferes with his right to direct the religious education of his daughter." *Newdow v. U.S. Congress,* 292 F.3d 597, 602 (9th Cir. 2002) (*Newdow I*), and ruled in his favor. The Supreme Court granted certiorari to consider whether Newdow had standing as a noncustodial parent to challenge the school district's policy. As the litigation progressed, however, the family court in California restored Newdow's joint custody status, and the mother conceded that the two parents had always shared physical custody. *Newdow,* 542 U.S. at 22 n.1 (Rehnquist, C.J., *concurring*). The Supreme Court focused on whether Newdow's parental status allowed him to litigate on his daughter's behalf over her mother's objections. The majority never reached the constitutional question regarding the content of the Pledge of Allegiance because it held that Newdow lacked standing in light of the mother's tie-breaking vote.

Writing for the majority, Justice Stevens explained:

Newdow contends that despite [the mother's] final authority, he retains "an unrestricted right to inculcate in his daughter—free from governmental interference—the atheistic beliefs he finds persuasive." The difficulty with that argument is that Newdow's rights, as in many cases touching upon family relations, cannot be viewed in isolation. This case concerns not merely Newdow's interest in inculcating his child with his views on religion, but also the rights of the child's mother as a parent generally and under the Superior Court orders specifically. And most important, it implicates the interests of a young child who finds herself at the center of a highly public debate over her custody, the propriety of a widespread national ritual, and the meaning of our Constitution.

The interests of the affected persons in this case are in many respects antagonistic. Of course, legal disharmony in family relations is not uncommon, and in many instances that disharmony poses no bar to federal-court adjudication of proper federal questions. What makes this case different is that Newdow's standing derives entirely from his relationship with his daughter, but he lacks the right to litigate as her next friend. [T]he interests of this parent and this child are not parallel and, indeed, are potentially in conflict.

Newdow's parental status is defined by California's domestic relations law. Our custom on questions of state law ordinarily is to defer to the interpretation of the Court of Appeals for the Circuit in which the State is located. In this case, the Court of Appeals, which possesses greater familiarity with California law, concluded that state law vests in Newdow a cognizable right to influence his daughter's religious upbringing. * * * Animated by a conception of "family privacy" * * * the state cases create a zone of private authority within which each parent, whether custodial or noncustodial, remains free to impart to the child his or her religious perspective.

* * * The California cases simply do not [address whether] 'Newdow has a right to dictate to others what they may and may not say to his child respecting religion' nor do they address whether a parent has standing to reach outside the private parent-child sphere to restrain the acts of a third party. Newdow lacks standing to pursue his claim in federal court.

Id. at 15–17.

Writing separately, Chief Justice Rehnquist chastised the majority for substituting its interpretation of California law for that of the Court of Appeals. The Ninth Circuit had held that under California law the mother's " 'veto power' does not override [Newdow's] right to challenge the Pledge ceremony." *Id.* at 23–24 (Rehnquist, C.J., *concurring*).

Agreeing that Newdow "cannot name his daughter as a party to a lawsuit against [the mother's] wishes, the Chief Justice saw the crux of Newdow's claim differently: Newdow, he wrote, "does not seek to tell just anyone what he or she may say to his daughter * * * [he] asserts that the School District's Pledge ceremony infringes his right under California law to expose his daughter to his religious views. [T]he daughter *is not the source* of respondent's standing; instead it is their relationship that provides respondent his standing, which is clear once respondent's interest is properly described." *Id.* at 24.

NOTES AND QUESTIONS

1.   *What does it mean for a parent to share legal custody after* Newdow? Because *Newdow* held that the father lacked standing to maintain the suit, the Court did not reach the merits. Many commentators feared that the decision would undermine the status of parents who have legal custody but not physical custody of their children, or even of parents who hold joint custody but less than equal "voting rights" in disputes. State courts, however, do not appear to have applied the doctrine more broadly in family law disputes. In practical terms, what does it mean for a parent to hold joint legal or physical custody if the other parent holds a tie-breaking vote? Does the procedural right to have one's views considered by the ultimate decision maker adequately preserve the other parent's rights to the "care, custody, and nurture" of the children?

If parents are unable to reach decisions jointly, should a court determine which parent bears primary responsibility for the breakdown in shared decision-making before denying either parent an equal role in making decisions? Other alternative tiebreakers, such as methods of alternative dispute resolution, including post-divorce arbitration, are discussed in Chapter 15.

2.   *The relationship between the parents' free exercise rights and the Establishment Clause in parental disputes over religious training.* As the notes following *Arthur* in the previous chapter indicated, the Free Exercise Clause confers on parents both the individual right to practice their religion and the right to instill their religious beliefs in their children. In *Greene v. Greene*, 701 S.E.2d 911 (Ga. Ct. App. 2010), the Christian father and the Jewish mother agreed to share legal custody with the mother becoming the sole physical custodian. Their agreement, incorporated in the court's order, gave the wife the "tie-breaking" vote in all decisions, except those involving school or extracurricular activities. *Id.* at 913. The father initially agreed the child would be raised as a Jew, but he began to take the child to church, prayed with her, read the Bible to her, and allowed his mother to teach her about Jesus Christ,

telling the child "that she was Jewish on the outside and Christian on the inside." *Id*. The appellate court upheld a contempt judgment against the father for violating the custody order, and explained: "even in the absence of an agreement, the custodial parent has the authority to determine religious training, and * * * '[o]nce custody has been awarded, courts should be loath to interfere with the religious training sanctioned by the custodian, since no end of difficulties would arise if judges sought to prescribe or proscribe the selection of a religious faith made by a custodial parent.' " *Id*. at 914 (quoting *Appelbaum v. Hames*, 284 S.E.2d 58, 60 (Ga. Ct. App. 1981)).

As you read in Chapter 12, where a parent's own religious beliefs evolve over time, lower courts have held that the Free Exercise Clause may bar judges from enforcing parental agreements about their children's religious upbringing. *Weisberger v. Weisberger*, 60 N.Y.S.3d 265 (App. Div. 2017) (clauses in settlement agreement requiring specific religious upbringing will not be enforced unless in the best interests of the children).

Courts in some jurisdictions emphasize that each legal parent retains a constitutional right to educate the child in the parent's own religion absent a clear showing that doing so would substantially harm the child. *Finnerty v. Clutter*, 917 N.E.2d 154, 157 (Ind. Ct. App. 2009) (noncustodial father is not required to take the children to church during his parenting time, or to reschedule his visits so that the mother could take the children to church).

In addition, some courts have held that the Establishment Clause bars courts from examining the appropriateness of any religious practice or belief. The general principle is that a court may not consider "a parent's religious beliefs and practices" in determining or modifying custody "unless there is a showing" that those beliefs or practices are causing "actual harm to the health or welfare of the child." *Harrison v. Tauheed*, 235 P.3d 547, 549 (Kan. Ct. App. 2010). Nonetheless, a court may intervene where religious practices or disputes affect the best interests of the child. *Holder v. Holder*, 872 N.E.2d 1239, 1242–44 (Ohio Ct. App. 2007). As one Pennsylvania court summarized the doctrine:

> The vast majority of courts addressing th[e] issue [of the deleterious effects, if any, of exposing children to a competing religion after grounding them in the tenets of an earlier religion] have concluded that each parent must be free to provide religious exposure and instruction, as that parent sees fit, during any and all periods of legal custody or visitation without restrictions, unless the challenged beliefs or conduct of the parent are demonstrated to present a substantial threat of present or future, physical or emotional harm to the child in absence of the proposed restriction.

Hicks v. Hicks, 868 A.2d 1245, 1249 (Pa. Super. Ct. 2005) (quoting trial court opinion).

2. VISITATION

Visitation is often thought of as a form of temporary custody. When one parent receives sole physical custody, the other parent normally receives liberal visitation with the child. Visitation is best conceptualized as temporary custody for a discrete period of time, regardless of whether the noncustodial parent shares legal custody with the custodial parent. This Section discusses noncustodial parents' rights to have access to their children, and the extent to which grandparents and others may seek court intervention when parents frustrate visitation with them.

A. THE FIT NONCUSTODIAL PARENT'S RIGHT TO VISITATION

Generally, all fit noncustodial parents are entitled to visitation, on the premise that it serves children's interests by promoting healthy child development. Parents have a right to visitation with their children unless visitation would be detrimental to the best interests of the child.

The Uniform Marriage and Divorce Act (UMDA) provides:

§ 407.   Visitation

(a) A parent not granted custody of a child is entitled to reasonable visitation rights unless the court finds, after a hearing, that visitation would endanger seriously the child's physical, mental, moral or emotional health.

(b) The court may modify an order granting or denying visitation rights whenever the modification would serve the best interests of the child; but the court shall not restrict a parent's visitation rights unless it finds that the visitation would endanger seriously the child's physical, mental, moral or emotional health.

9A U.L.A. 398 (1998). Note that the UMDA standard for denying visitation is much more difficult to satisfy than the "best interests" standard, which gives judges discretion to choose between parents for purposes of custody.

Consistent with its reform agenda, the American Law Institute abandoned the concept of visitation, which it regards as a form of "custodial responsibility." The ALI drafters noted in 2002 that several states had already "moved away from the terminology of custody and visitation to alternative language more accommodating of a continuum of residential arrangements." ALI, Principles of the Law of Family Dissolution: Analysis and Recommendations § 2.03 cmts. e–f (2002) (citing Florida, Maine, Michigan, Montana, Ohio, Texas, Vermont, Washington and Wisconsin). Such alternative language includes "residential provisions," "parental rights and responsibilities," and "parental contact" or "parental time."

PROBLEM 13-1

You are a family court judge. Last year when you entered the divorce judgment for the Smiths, who have two children, ages 9 and 12, you gave the parents joint custody, but made the mother the primary residential parent. Because the father had a history of abusing alcohol and illegal substances, including DUI convictions, the custody order specified that the father "shall not have any alcohol or illegal substances in his possession while the children are in his care in this State." The mother later moved to another state, but the children spend school vacations with the father in your jurisdiction.

While the children were visiting him last month, the father was arrested for driving while intoxicated and possession of marijuana. He pled guilty. The mother has moved to find the father in contempt of the custody order and seeks to discontinue visitation in this state. She is willing to allow the father to see the children if he travels to her home.

The father argues that he did not violate the order because the children were staying overnight at his mother's house when he was arrested.

Applying the UMDA, how would you resolve the following issues:

(1) Is the phrase "in his care" limited to times when the children are in the father's immediate presence?

(2) Should the court cite the father for contempt, and if so, what would be an appropriate penalty?

(3) Do the father's actions justify limiting or eliminating his visitation rights?

B. DENIAL OF VISITATION

Custodial parents and child development experts lament that the relationships between noncustodial parents and children are often so attenuated that parents and children become strangers for all practical purposes. But the fault cannot be attributed exclusively to the noncustodial parent whose visits and calls decline over time. Custodial parents frequently frustrate visitation with the noncustodial parent. Courts may find it difficult to sort out whether the custodial parent thwarts visits, or whether older children themselves are disinclined to pursue the relationship. As you read the following decision, consider whether an effective and equitable remedy exists even where the court concludes that the custodial parent has engineered a breakdown in the relationship between the noncustodial parent and the children. Note that the remedy the court grants at the request of the noncustodial parent in the following case is extremely uncommon.

USACK V. USACK

Supreme Court of New York, Appellate Division, 2005.
793 N.Y.S. 2d 223.

SPAIN, J.

* * *

The parties were married for 20 years and had three children, a son born in 1983 and daughters born in 1986 and 1988. Plaintiff [husband] commenced this action for divorce in early 2002 and defendant moved out of the marital residence later that year and cross-claimed for divorce. After a nonjury trial, Supreme Court, among other things, awarded plaintiff a divorce upon the parties' stipulation, distributed their property, and granted plaintiff custody of the daughters and exclusive ownership and possession of the marital residence. The court ordered defendant to pay child support and a portion of the uninsured medical expenses for all three children.

Supreme Court [the trial court] issued a detailed written decision containing extensive findings of fact which accurately portrays the tragedy often visited upon children—even teenage children—who have been manipulated into parental estrangement. The court denied defendant's request that she be relieved, permanently or temporarily, of her child support obligations. That request was based upon, among other grounds, plaintiff's near complete frustration of any relationship, communication or contact between defendant and her children since December 2001, when plaintiff first learned of and told the children about defendant's relationship with another man. The court found that "plaintiff and [the] children have rejected every effort of defendant to demonstrate her continued devotion to her offspring with a vehemence which is remarkable for its undiminished intensity over a protracted period which still continues." The court also concluded that plaintiff had "encouraged" the children's "unbridled enmity" toward and "total exclus[ion]" of their mother through "a course of conduct calculated to inflict the most grievous emotional injury upon her." The court ultimately determined that there was insufficient circumstantial or professional evidence to attribute the children's uniform attitudes and behavior to plaintiff.

Defendant now appeals, contending that her child support obligation should have been suspended due to plaintiff's deliberate actions in alienating their children from her, a conclusion we find inescapable on this record and from Supreme Court's findings of fact, which we adopt.

A parent, of course, has a statutory duty to support a child until the age of 21 [in New York]. However, "where it can be established by the noncustodial parent that the custodial parent has unjustifiably frustrated the noncustodial parent's right of reasonable access, child support payments may be suspended." *Smith v. Bombard*, [741 N.Y.S.2d 336, 338 (2002)].

* * * The Law Guardian expressed to Supreme Court the children's wishes to remain with their father and control their own contact with their mother.[1] Plaintiff testified that while the marriage began to experience difficulties in early 2001, the family was "perfectly happy" and defendant enjoyed a close relationship with the children and was very involved in all of their activities until he revealed defendant's affair to them in December 2001. He claimed that, after that discovery, they unilaterally chose to completely ostracize defendant and reject all of her repeated efforts to communicate, to attend their sporting activities or to have any meaningful contact or relationship with her, although she continued to live in the family home. This ostracism and estrangement of defendant from the family continued for nine months, unabated, until September 2002, when defendant finally moved out, and it continued until the time of the trial. Plaintiff, whose credibility Supreme Court found to be "seriously impaired," denied actively discouraging or preventing the children's relationship with defendant. He did not address many of the specific incidents to which defendant thereafter testified, and failed to demonstrate any meaningful efforts on his part to facilitate the children's continued relationship with their mother.

The testimony of defendant, credited by Supreme Court and much of it unrefuted, detailed plaintiff's callous and insensitive conduct toward defendant prior to December 2001, which the court recognized as the probable inducement for defendant's affair. She also described plaintiff's relentless actions—following the discovery of her affair—in excluding defendant from the family entirely, vehemently rejecting any efforts on her part to have a meaningful relationship with her children or to continue any parental role and involvement. Her testimony established that plaintiff, among other things, often yelled at her to leave, disparaged her, locked her out, and told the children that defendant did not want to be—and was no longer—part of their family because she had chosen someone else. Plaintiff also used his immediate family members to care for the children and shield them from interaction with defendant at home in his absence and he did nothing to dissuade the children's public humiliation of defendant.

By his example, his actions and his inaction, plaintiff orchestrated and encouraged the estrangement of defendant from the children. He exploited their unhappiness toward her over the affair and the break-up of the family and manipulated their loyalty to him—and the exclusion of defendant—to

---

[1]   [I]t is not proper for a Law Guardian to make a "report" to a court. Here, the Law Guardian submitted—at Supreme Court's direction—a report containing her own unsworn observations regarding the parties, recounting personal interactions or opinions about them, all of which, we note, could have been explored and elicited by calling witnesses and upon cross-examination of the parties and other witnesses.

punish her for her rejection of him. As Supreme Court noted in reducing defendant's child support arrears, the treatment of defendant was "needlessly vindictive" and, we find, a clear violation of plaintiff's responsibility "to assure meaningful contact between the children and the other parent". *Raybin v. Raybin*, [613 N.Y.S.2d 726, 729 (1994)]. Indeed, plaintiff utterly failed in his duty to rise above his anger at defendant to affirmatively encourage the children to have contact and a relationship with their mother. Instead, he chose * * * to deprive them of the undeniable benefit and right of having two loving, supportive parents; he also denied defendant her right to a normal relationship with them. Most importantly, plaintiff never—at any time—suggested that defendant had been other than a dedicated, eager, involved, loving, willing and hard working mother who genuinely pursued a continued role in the lives of her children. Clearly, defendant's decision to engage in and pursue an extramarital affair while continuing to reside with plaintiff and the children resulted in turmoil in the children's lives. However, plaintiff did not demonstrate that defendant exposed the children to anything related to that affair * * *.

Thus, we find that defendant amply met her burden of demonstrating that plaintiff deliberately frustrated her relationship and visitation with the children. While alteration of defendant's child support obligations may be an imperfect remedy with which to address plaintiff's harmful, unfair conduct, there is no proof that suspending defendant's obligations temporarily would result in the children becoming public charges. Accordingly, defendant's support obligations are suspended pending further court order upon a showing that plaintiff has made good faith efforts to actively encourage and restore defendant's relationship with the children, and defendant's visitation with the children.

* * *

NOTES AND QUESTIONS

1. Usack *represents an exception to the general rule. Usack* noted that suspending child support was an "imperfect remedy." The decision conflicts with settled law in most jurisdictions: denial of visitation is no defense to an action for failure to pay support. It has long been established that the obligation to pay child support is generally distinct from the question of access to the child for visitation: "a substantial majority of the courts have held that while refusal to pay child support is reprehensible, a [noncustodial parent's] visitation rights cannot be conditioned upon compliance with a support order." *Sampson v. Johnson*, 846 A.2d 278, 287 (D.C. 2004). *See also R.B.O. v. Jefferson County Dep't of Human Res.*, 70 So.3d 1286 (Ala. Civ. App. 2011). What is the reasoning behind the general rule that support obligations survive despite denial of visitation? Most courts assume that "support payments are necessary for the child's welfare, and that terminating or suspending the obligation to make them would therefore be harmful to children." Ira Mark

Ellman, *Should Visitation Denial Affect the Obligation to Pay Support?*, 36 Ariz. St. L.J. 661, 664 (2004).

This is also true in New York, but *Usack* is distinguishable because the mother sought to have her child support obligation *suspended* until she had access to the children. New York's statute expressly authorizes a court to suspend maintenance payments where the recipient has "wrongfully interfered" with the obligor's visitation rights. N.Y. Dom. Rel. Law § 241 (McKinney 2010). That section of the statute does not mention child support. As *Usack* demonstrates, however, the courts have read the statute more broadly. While courts rarely impose this remedy, *Usack* does not stand alone in New York. *Rodman v. Friedman*, 978 N.Y.S.2d 127 (App. Div. 2013). Does the distinction between withholding child support and withholding maintenance make sense? Do you believe the *Usack* decision was in the best interests of the children?

Noncustodial parents who resist payment of child support sometimes complain that (1) the children do not benefit from the payments, which they believe are used to subsidize the custodial parent's standard of living, or that (2) the noncustodial parent has no control over the custodial parent's choices about how to spend the money on the children's behalf. To reduce friction between parents that might contribute to a breakdown of support payments and/or visitation, some states authorize courts to order the custodial parent to provide periodic accountings showing how the child support money is spent. *See, e.g.,* Mo. Ann. Stat. § 452.342 (West 2003).

In 2014 Congress recognized that more liberal visitation was likely to result in better compliance with child support obligation. It adopted a "sense of the Congress" resolution urging that when courts establish child support orders they should also order "[i]ncreased parental access and visitation" as a means to promote "more engaged" non-residential parents and "improved child support collections." The sense of the Congress is nothing more than a sentiment—it carries no funding and has no enforcement mechanism. Preventing Sex Trafficking and Strengthening Families Act, Pub. L. No. 113–183, § 303, 128 Stat. 1919, 1946 (2014).

2.   *Other forms of interference.* Some custodial parents interfere with visitation by disrupting or entirely blocking telephone or Internet communication between the child and the noncustodial parent. *See In re Marriage of Almquist*, 704 N.E.2d 68, 72 (Ill. App. Ct. 1998) (imposing criminal contempt on mother, whose loud playing of audiotapes during phone conversations constituted obnoxious interference).

Communication by electronic devices in addition to in-person visits are commonplace today, but just over a decade ago were not taken for granted. In 2004, Utah became the first state to enact a law expressly authorizing courts to order virtual visitation. Utah Code Ann. § 30–3–35(2)(p) (LexisNexis Supp. 2018). For an example of a virtual visitation information website, see http://www.internetvisitation.org.

3. *The wronged noncustodial parent.* Like the mother in *Usack,* many noncustodial parents feel that they have been wrongly denied visitation by the custodial parent, and that they should not have to pay child support if their relationship with the child is frustrated. Should it matter whether the custodial parent is interfering with visits, or whether the child independently decides to discontinue visitation? How would a court determine which is true? How important is the child's age to such a determination? What effect do you think the court's decision will have on the relationships between the Usack children and each of their parents? Did the court have other remedies at its disposal, either at the time of the divorce decree or when it rendered the decision you read?

4. *Remedies and enforcement.* Noncustodial parents who believe that the custodial parent is interfering with their visitation rights may seek a variety of remedies in addition to reduction or tolling of child support obligations. The range of potential remedies includes modification of the visitation order or parenting agreement to provide a more detailed schedule and conditions for visitation, additional "make-up" visitation, contempt proceedings, and, in particularly egregious cases, civil damages for intentional infliction of emotional distress. *See, e.g., In re Marriage of Myers,* 99 P.3d 398, 401 (Wash. Ct. App. 2004) ("A parent who refuses to perform the duties imposed by a parenting plan is *per se* acting in bad faith."); *Dobies v. Brefka,* 921 N.Y.S.2d 349 (App. Div. 2011) (terminating father's child support obligation for the older child who refused to see him and sentencing the custodial mother to 60 days in jail for willful violation of court orders).

What are the relative advantages and disadvantages of each of these remedies?

5. *Parental discretion during visits.* You have seen that some courts impose stringent conditions designed to promote consistency during visits. Other courts, however, have held that unless the child's best interests require the court to impose conditions to enforce the primary custodian's decisions, the court should resist invitations to reduce the noncustodial parent "to little more than a babysitting function." *Miller v. Smith,* 989 A.2d 537, 539 (Vt. 2009) (affirming refusal to order the father to take the child to gymnastics lessons during visits). To hold otherwise would create a "nightmare" for parents and courts, in which parties would return " 'with an endless string of disputes over * * * sports, music lessons, gymnastics classes and friends' birthday parties.' " *Id.* at 539. Under this view, each parent generally gets to make decisions about how to spend his or her parenting time.

6. *Supervised visitation.* Where courts expressly find that a child might be harmed during unsupervised visitation with a noncustodial parent, they may order visitation supervised by a third party. Courts may find the child at risk of harm where, for example, evidence supports a finding of physical or sexual abuse, or where the noncustodial parent suffers from mental illness or has a substance abuse problem. *See Dufresne v. Dufresne,* 992 So.2d 579 (La. Ct. App. 2008); *Ex parte Thompson,* 51 So.3d 265 (Ala. 2010).

However, courts may not impose conditions on visits absent "substantial evidence" that the best interests of the child require such conditions, focusing on a link between parental behavior and the child's well-being. *Green v. Parks*, 338 P.3d 312 (Alaska 2014) (reversing restrictions on the father's consumption of alcohol during visits and for eight hours before visits where there was no evidence of alcohol abuse and the court did not make specific findings). *See also Kraft v. Kraft*, 2011 WL 4572911 (Del. Oct. 4, 2011) (father's alleged sex addiction, including use of prostitutes and association with sex offenders he met at a therapeutic support group, did not justify restrictions on visits "in the absence of a link between the alleged addition and any danger" to the child).

Supervised visits may occur in a variety of settings, including a designated visitation center run by a private or public agency; a therapist's office; a neutral public place such as a fast-food restaurant or park; or a private home, including the home of the noncustodial parent or a relative of the parent. Supervisors may include professionals, such as licensed social workers, or friends or relatives. *See e.g.*, *Cummings v. Ames*, 2005 WL 2621447 (N.J. Super. Ct. App. Div. Oct. 17, 2005) ("The monitor could be the parties' nanny, their 15-year-old eldest daughter (if and only if she was willing to serve in that role), or some other relative or third-party jointly agreed to by the parties."). Supervision by a private agency or professional is extremely expensive. In *Cummings*, the mother spent $7,000 for supervision in just four months, before the court allowed an alternative arrangement. The parties ultimately agreed to use the child's piano teacher as a supervisor every other week.

In *Cummings*, the appellate panel initially suggested that a teenage sibling might be an appropriate supervisor, if willing, but ultimately retracted that suggestion. *Id.* at *5. Why would it be inappropriate to designate one of the parties' older children as a supervisor for visits? Under what conditions, if any, would it be wise to use a relative as a supervisor?

In addition to deciding whether supervision is warranted, and what kind of supervision is needed, the family court must decide how long to continue supervision, whether to reduce the constraints on visits, and when, if ever, to allow unsupervised visitation. In some divorce cases, allegations of abuse result in long-term involvement with the family by the state's child protection agencies; other cases may never reach a public agency if the court concludes the allegations are unsubstantiated. *See Simburger v. Simburger*, 701 N.W.2d 880 (N.D. 2005); *S.B. v. J.P.*, 831 N.E.2d 959 (Mass. App. Ct. 2005).

7. *Domestic violence and visitation.* Sometimes supervised visitation or supervised transfers of the child are impossible or inappropriate because serious domestic violence requires the court to hide the custodial parent's location from the noncustodial parent. Domestic violence victims "face the greatest risk of violence and lethality during the actual separation and in the ensuing years," as the abuser seeks to assert continued control over the victim or force the victim to return. Jane K. Stoever, *Enjoining Abuse: The Case for Indefinite Domestic Violence Protection Orders*, 67 Vand. L. Rev. 1015, 1025 (2014).

C. THIRD-PARTY VISITATION

In Chapter 12, you read about the efforts of grandparents to gain or retain custody of their grandchildren in *McDermott v. Dougherty* and *Painter v. Bannister*. Grandparents and other third parties frequently turn to the courts in an effort to gain or expand visitation over the custodial parent's objections. In *Troxel v. Granville*, 530 U.S. 57 (2000), the Supreme Court reaffirmed the liberty interest of parents in the "care, custody and control of their children" in reviewing the scope of a parent's right to control visitation with third parties. The case involved a mother who limited, but did not cut off, her children's visitation with the parents of their deceased father, a man to whom she had never been married. The plurality opinion authored by Justice O'Connor faulted the statute's failure to accord sufficient deference to the mother's interests, concluding that the Due Process Clause does not permit a State to "infringe on the fundamental right of parents to make child rearing decisions simply because a state judge believes a 'better' decision could be made." *Id.* at 72–73.

The following excerpt provides a glimpse into the widely divergent views of the justices. (You may find it useful to review the summary of the major parental rights cases set forth in *McDermott v. Dougherty* in Chapter 12 and *Moore v. East Cleveland* in Chapter 1—both of which involve grandparents who are active caretakers—before or after reading the following opinions.)

TROXEL V. GRANVILLE
Supreme Court of the United States, 2000.
530 U.S. 57.

JUSTICE O'CONNOR announced the judgment of the Court and delivered an opinion, in which THE CHIEF JUSTICE, JUSTICE GINSBURG, and JUSTICE BREYER join.

Section 26.10.160(3) of the Revised Code of Washington permits "[a]ny person" to petition a superior court for visitation rights "at any time," and authorizes that court to grant such visitation rights whenever "visitation may serve the best interest of the child." Petitioners Jenifer and Gary Troxel petitioned a Washington Superior Court for the right to visit their grandchildren, Isabelle and Natalie Troxel. Respondent Tommie Granville, the mother of Isabelle and Natalie, opposed the petition. The case ultimately reached the Washington Supreme Court, which held that § 26.10.160(3) unconstitutionally interferes with the fundamental right of parents to rear their children.

Tommie Granville and Brad Troxel shared a relationship that ended in June 1991. The two never married, but they had two daughters, Isabelle and Natalie. Jenifer and Gary Troxel are Brad's parents, and thus the paternal grandparents of Isabelle and Natalie. After Tommie and Brad separated in 1991, Brad lived with his parents and regularly brought his daughters to his parents' home for weekend visitation. Brad committed suicide in May 1993. Although the Troxels at first continued to see Isabelle and Natalie on a regular basis after their son's death, Tommie Granville informed the Troxels in October 1993 that she wished to limit their visitation with her daughters to one short visit per month.

In December 1993, the Troxels by fil[ed] a petition to obtain visitation rights with Isabelle and Natalie [pursuant to] Section 2610.160(3) * * *. [T]he Troxels requested two weekends of overnight visitation per month and two weeks of visitation each summer. Granville did not oppose visitation altogether, but instead asked the court to order one day of visitation per month with no overnight stay. In 1995, the Superior Court [ordered] visitation one weekend per month, one week during the summer, and four hours on both of the petitioning grandparents' birthdays.

Granville appealed, during which time she married Kelly Wynn. [T]he Washington Court of Appeals remanded the case to the Superior Court * * *. On remand, the Superior Court found that visitation was in Isabelle and Natalie's best interests:

> "The Petitioners [the Troxels] are part of a large, central, loving family, all located in this area, and the Petitioners can provide opportunities for the children in the areas of cousins and music.

> ". . . The court took into consideration all factors regarding the best interest of the children and considered all the testimony before it. The children would be benefited from spending quality time with the Petitioners, provided that that time is balanced with time with the childrens' [sic] nuclear family. The court finds that the childrens' [sic] best interests are served by spending time with their mother and stepfather's other six children."

Approximately nine months after the Superior Court entered its order on remand, Granville's husband formally adopted Isabelle and Natalie.

The Washington Court of Appeals reversed the lower court's visitation order * * *. * * *

The Washington Supreme Court * * * affirmed. * * * We granted certiorari, and now affirm the judgment.

II

The demographic changes of the past century make it difficult to speak of an average American family. * * * Persons outside the nuclear family are called upon with increasing frequency to assist in the everyday tasks of child rearing. In many cases, grandparents play an important role. For example, in 1998, approximately 4 million children—or 5.6 percent of all children under age 18—lived in the household of their grandparents.

* * * Because grandparents and other relatives undertake duties of a parental nature in many households, States have sought to ensure the welfare of the children therein by protecting the relationships those children form with such third parties. The States' nonparental visitation statutes are further supported by a recognition, which varies from State to State, that children should have the opportunity to benefit from relationships with statutorily specified persons—for example, their grandparents. The extension of statutory rights in this area to persons other than a child's parents, however, comes with an obvious cost. [T]hese statutes can present questions of constitutional import. In this case, we are presented with just such a question. Specifically, we are asked to decide whether § 26.10.160(3), as applied to Tommie Granville and her family, violates the Federal Constitution.

* * *

The liberty interest at issue in this case—the interest of parents in the care, custody, and control of their children—is perhaps the oldest of the fundamental liberty interests recognized by this Court. [Justice O'Connor discusses the cases that recognized the substantive due process rights of parents, beginning with *Meyer v. Nebraska* and *Pierce v. Society of Sisters*, introduced in Chapter 1 of this book and reviewed in *McDermott* v. *Dougherty in* Chapter 12].

* * * In light of * * * this extensive precedent, it cannot now be doubted that the Due Process Clause of the Fourteenth Amendment protects the fundamental right of parents to make decisions concerning the care, custody, and control of their children.

Section 26.10.160(3), as applied to Granville and her family in this case, unconstitutionally infringes on that fundamental parental right. The Washington nonparental visitation statute is breathtakingly broad. According to the statute's text, "*[a]ny person* may petition the court for visitation rights *at any time*," and the court may grant such visitation rights whenever "visitation may serve *the best interest of the child*." That language effectively permits any third party seeking visitation to subject any decision by a parent concerning visitation of the parent's children to state-court review. Once the visitation petition has been filed in court and the matter is placed before a judge, a parent's decision that visitation would not be in the child's best interest is accorded no deference. * * * Instead, the Washington statute places the best-interest determination solely in the hands of the judge. Should the judge disagree with the parent's estimation of the child's best interests, the judge's view necessarily prevails. Thus, in practical effect, in the State of Washington a court can disregard and overturn *any* decision by a fit custodial parent concerning visitation whenever a third party affected by the decision files a visitation petition, based solely on the judge's determination of the child's best interests. * * *

Turning to * * * this case, the record reveals that the Superior Court's order was based on precisely the type of mere disagreement we have just described and nothing more. * * *

[T]he Troxels did not allege, and no court has found, that Granville was an unfit parent. * * * So long as a parent adequately cares for his or her children (*i.e.*, is fit), there will normally be no reason for the State to inject itself into the private realm of the family to * * * question the ability of that parent to make the best decisions concerning the rearing of that parent's children.

[T]he Superior Court judge explained:

> "* * * I think in most situations a commonsensical approach [is that] it is normally in the best interest of the children to spend quality time with the grandparent, unless the grandparent, *[sic]* there are some issues or problems involved wherein * * * their lifestyles are going to impact adversely upon the children. That certainly isn't the case here from what I can tell."

The judge's comments suggest that he presumed the grandparents' request should be granted unless the children would be "impact[ed] adversely." In effect, the judge placed on Granville, the fit custodial parent, the burden of *disproving* that visitation would be in the best interest of her daughters. * * *

The decisional framework employed by the Superior Court directly contravened the traditional presumption that a fit parent will act in the best interest of his or her child. In that respect, the court's presumption failed to provide any protection for Granville's fundamental constitutional right to make decisions concerning the rearing of her own daughters. In an ideal world, parents might always seek to cultivate the bonds between grandparents and their grandchildren. Needless to say, however, our world is far from perfect, and in it the decision whether such an intergenerational relationship would be beneficial in any specific case is for the parent to make in the first instance. And, if a fit parent's decision of the kind at issue here becomes subject to judicial review, the court must accord at least some special weight to the parent's own determination.

Finally, we note that there is no allegation that Granville ever sought to cut off visitation entirely. * * *

[T]he visitation order in this case was an unconstitutional infringement on Granville's fundamental right to make decisions concerning the care, custody, and control of her two daughters. The Washington Superior Court failed to accord the determination of Granville, a fit custodial parent, any material weight. In fact, the Superior Court made only two formal findings in support of its visitation order. First, the Troxels "are part of a large, central, loving family, all located in this area, and the [Troxels] can provide opportunities for the children in the areas of cousins and music." Second, "[t]he children would be benefitted from spending quality time with the [Troxels], provided that that time is balanced with time with the childrens' *[sic]* nuclear family." These slender findings * * * show that this case involves nothing more than a simple disagreement between the Washington Superior Court and Granville concerning her children's best interests. The Superior Court's announced reason for ordering one week of visitation in the summer demonstrates our conclusion well: "I look back on some personal experiences. . . . We always spen[t] as kids a week with one set of grandparents and another set of grandparents, [and] it happened to work out in our family that [it] turned out to be an enjoyable experience. Maybe that can, in this family, if that is how it works out." * * * [T]he Due Process Clause does not permit a State to infringe on the fundamental right of parents to make childrearing decisions simply because a state judge believes a "better" decision could be made. * * * Accordingly, we hold that § 26.10.160(3), as applied in this case, is unconstitutional.

* * * We do not, and need not, define today the precise scope of the parental due process right in the visitation context. * * *

* * *

[The concurring opinion of SOUTER, J. is omitted].

JUSTICE THOMAS, concurring in the judgment.

I write separately to note that neither party has argued that our substantive due process cases were wrongly decided and that the original understanding of the Due Process Clause precludes judicial enforcement of unenumerated rights under that constitutional provision. As a result, I express no view on the merits of this matter, and I understand the plurality as well to leave the resolution of that issue for another day.

* * *

STEVENS, J., dissenting.

* * *

A parent's rights with respect to her child have * * * never been regarded as absolute, but rather are limited by the existence of an actual, developed relationship with a child, and are tied to the presence or absence of some embodiment of family. These limitations have arisen, not simply out of the definition of parenthood itself, but because of this Court's assumption that a parent's interests in a child must be balanced against the State's long-recognized interests as *parens patriae,* and, critically, the child's own complementary interest in preserving relationships that serve her welfare and protection [citations omitted].

While this Court has not yet had occasion to elucidate the nature of a child's liberty interests in preserving established familial or family-like bonds, [*Michael H.* v. *Gerald D.*,] 491 U.S. [110,] 130 (reserving the question), it seems to me extremely likely that, to the extent parents and families have fundamental liberty interests in preserving such intimate relationships, so, too, do children have these interests, and so, too, must their interests be balanced in the equation. At a minimum, our prior cases recognizing that children are, generally speaking, constitutionally protected actors require that this Court reject any suggestion that when it comes to parental rights, children are so much chattel. See *ante* (opinion of O'CONNOR, J.) (describing States' recognition of "an independent third-party interest in a child"). The constitutional protection against arbitrary state interference with parental rights should not be extended to prevent the States from protecting children against the arbitrary exercise of parental authority that is not in fact motivated by an interest in the welfare of the child.

This is not, of course, to suggest that a child's liberty interest in maintaining contact with a particular individual is to be treated invariably as on a par with that child's parents' contrary interests. Because our substantive due process case law includes a strong presumption that a parent will act in the best interest of her child, it would be necessary, were the state appellate courts actually to confront a challenge to the statute as applied, to consider whether the trial court's assessment of the "best interest of the child" incorporated that presumption. * * *

JUSTICE SCALIA, dissenting.

* * *

* * * The sheer diversity of today's opinions persuades me that the theory of unenumerated parental rights * * * has small claim to *stare decisis* protection. A legal principle that can be thought to produce such diverse outcomes in the relatively simple case before us here is not a legal principle that has induced substantial reliance. While I would not now overrule those earlier cases (that has not been urged), neither would I extend the theory upon which they rested to this new context.

* * *

For these reasons, I would reverse the judgment below.

JUSTICE KENNEDY, dissenting.

* * *

I would remand the case to the state court for further proceedings. * * *

The State Supreme Court sought to give content to the parent's right by announcing a categorical rule that third parties who seek visitation must always prove the denial of visitation would harm the child. * * *

While it might be argued as an abstract matter that in some sense the child is always harmed if his or her best interests are not considered, the law of domestic relations, as it has evolved to this point, treats as distinct the two standards, one harm to the child and the other the best interests of the child. * * *

* * *

My principal concern is that the holding seems to proceed from the assumption that the parent or parents who resist visitation have always been the child's primary caregivers and that the third parties who seek visitation have no legitimate and established relationship with the child. That idea, in turn, appears influenced by the concept that the conventional nuclear family ought to establish the visitation standard for every domestic relations case. As we all know, this is simply not the structure or prevailing condition in many households. * * *

Cases are sure to arise—perhaps a substantial number of cases—in which a third party, by acting in a caregiving role over a significant period of time, has developed a relationship with a child which is not necessarily subject to absolute parental veto. Some pre-existing relationships, then, serve to identify persons who have a strong attachment to the child with the concomitant motivation to act in a responsible way to ensure the child's welfare. * * *

* * *

Since 1965 all 50 States have enacted a third-party visitation statute of some sort. Each of these statutes, save one, permits a court order to issue in certain cases if visitation is found to be in the best interests of the child. * * * Many States limit the identity of permissible petitioners by restricting visitation petitions to grandparents, or by requiring petitioners to show a substantial relationship with a child, or both. * * *

[A] domestic relations proceeding in and of itself can constitute state intervention that is so disruptive of the parent-child relationship that the constitutional right of a custodial parent to make certain basic determinations for the child's welfare becomes implicated. * * * If a single parent who is struggling to raise a child is faced with visitation demands from a third party, the attorney's fees alone might destroy her hopes and plans for the child's future. * * *

It should suffice in this case to reverse the holding of the State Supreme Court that the application of the best interests of the child standard is always unconstitutional in third-party visitation cases. * * *

NOTES AND QUESTIONS

1. *Later developments.* When the Supreme Court decided *Troxel* in 2000, all 50 states had some form of grandparent visitation statute and the Court declined to hold that such statutes violate due process "as a *per se* matter." *Troxel,* 530 U.S. at 73. State statutes regarding third-party visitation, often perceived as creating rights for grandparents, in fact generally only give grandparents and others standing in court to seek visitation rather than creating substantive rights. Jeff Atkinson, *Shifts in the Law Regarding the Rights of Third Parties to Seek Visitation and Custody of Children,* 47 Fam. L. Q. 1 (2013). Contemporary statutes vary widely in language and effect. *Id.*

State courts and legislatures have attempted to craft solutions that comport with *Troxel's* requirements, insofar as a plurality opinion can be clearly interpreted. In Connecticut, for example, courts must balance the parental "interest in the care, custody and control" of children against the risk that children will suffer " 'from real and substantial emotional harm' " if deprived of relationships with third parties who meet certain statutory criteria. *DiGiovanna v. St. George,* 12 A.3d 900, 911 (Conn. 2011).

For many years after *Troxel* was decided the Washington legislature considered but failed to enact bills recognizing third party visitation claims. Kenneth W. Weber, 20 Washington Practice Series, Family and Property Law § 33.21 (2014). In 2018 Washington enacted an act granting "relatives, including but not limited to grandparents" the right to seek visitation by petitioning the courts, restoring the number of states with such statutes to 50, the pre-*Troxel* count. Act of Mar. 22, 2018, ch. 183, 2018 Wash. Sess. Laws 955.

2. *The rights of grandparents to visit with grandchildren after their own child's death.* As in *Troxel,* many grandparent visitation cases arise after one parent dies and the surviving parent limits or denies visitation by the deceased parent's own parents. In *Harrold v. Collier* Ohio's highest court unanimously upheld a statute aimed specifically at this contingency. Brittany Collier, the child of an unmarried mother, lived with her mother and her maternal grandparents for the first two years of her life. After Brittany's mother died of cancer, her maternal grandparents received temporary custody. But two years later, her biological father received custody and denied visitation to the maternal grandparents, leading to protracted litigation. Brittany did not move into her father's home until she was five. 836 N.E.2d 1165, 1169 (Ohio 2005).

Collier upheld a statute that expressly protects the visitation rights of grandparents of a child whose unmarried parent is deceased if a court finds visitation to be in the best interests of the child. *Id.* at 1169. The statute also extends to the deceased parent's other relatives. The court rejected the father's challenge to the statute under *Troxel,* but held that Ohio courts must "afford special weight to the wishes of parents of minor children when considering petitions for nonparental visitation." *Id.* at 1168. It explained, however, that "nothing in *Troxel* suggests that a parent's wishes should be placed before a child's best interests." *Id.* at 1172. Do you agree with *Collier's* interpretation of *Troxel*?

3. *May living parents deny their own parents visitation with their children?* This is an all-too-common form of dispute, and the answer depends on the statutory scheme in the jurisdiction. In Ohio, for example, the relatives of a deceased parent may petition the court for the right to visit the surviving child, as discussed in the previous note. After the mother of two young children died, the father's relationship with both sets of grandparents deteriorated and the number of visits declined. When the maternal grandparents petitioned for increased visitation under the Ohio statute, the paternal grandmother (the father's own mother) also filed a claim for visitation based on her status as a "relative" of the deceased mother, that is, as her mother-in-law. *In re R.V.*, 941 N.E.2d 1216 (Ohio Ct. App. 2010). Over strong dissents, the court joined several other jurisdictions in holding that "relatives" include those created by affinity as well as consanguinity. *Id.* at 1218–19. If the children's mother had lived, however, neither set of grandparents would have had a cause of action in Ohio to pursue visitation rights over the objection of the children's parents.

One Louisiana court held that a grandmother could pursue and receive visitation rights under the code's "extraordinary circumstances" provision allowing reasonable visitation that serves the best interest of the child. *Broussard-Scher v. Legendre*, 60 So. 3d 1290 (La. Ct. App. 2011). The court found that *Troxel* posed no impediment in light of uncontroverted expert testimony at trial that the parents' refusal to allow visits was contrary to the child's best interests. *Id.* at 1298.

After *Troxel*, New Jersey's highest court construed the state's statute to require that grandparents who seek visitation over the objection of a parent must show that the child would suffer harm absent visitation in order to justify the infringement on the parent's rights that a visitation order would entail. *Moriarty v. Bradt*, 827 A.2d 203 (2003). In New Hampshire the statute provides that a court may order "reasonable visitation privileges" to grandparents if the court concludes that doing so is in the child's best interests. N.H. Rev. Stat. Ann. § 461–A:6 (V) (Supp. 2018). However, the court must consider whether such visits would interfere with the parent's authority over the child or with the parental relationship. *In re Rupa*, 13 A.3d 307, 313 (N.H. 2010).

4. *Meddlesome grandparents.* Delaware's highest court reversed an order awarding grandparents visits with their three grandchildren over the parents' objections because the grandparents "were never satisfied" with the number or length of visits, were "vicious," and disparaged the parents on social media and in person. *Grant v. Grant*, 178 A.3d 1051 (Del. 2017) (grandparents failed to meet their statutory burden to show by clear and convincing evidence that the parents' objections to visits were "unreasonable").

5. *Do separated siblings have a right to visit each other?* Where a child lives with a parent who has no right to visit the child's sibling, the child usually has no standing to seek visitation. In a few states, like New Jersey, the third-party visitation statute places siblings on the same footing with grandparents in seeking visitation rights. N.J. Stat. Ann. 9:2–7.1 (West 2013). Washington

State's relative visitation statute includes step-siblings. Wash. Rev. Code Ann. § 26.11.010(2)(a) (West, Westlaw through 2018 Reg. Sess.).

A number of state appellate courts have concluded that siblings who seek visitation are third parties who lack standing unless the state's visitation statute expressly includes them. *In re M.B.B. v. E.R.W.*, 100 P.3d 415, 420 (Wyo. 2004) (no common law right for a sibling to seek visitation).

The highest court in Maryland held that a teenage girl, who had been removed from her father's home due to his abuse, was a third party when she sought visits with her younger half-siblings who remained in the family home: "A sibling, whether full, half * * * remains a third party," even if she entered in the foster care system through no fault of her own. *In re Victoria C.*, 88 A.3d 749, 764 (Md. 2014). Nonetheless, the court remanded the matter to the trial court which had ordered Victoria's father and stepmother to allow her to see her siblings, for an inquiry into: whether jurisdiction could be found to enter a visitation order; whether exceptional circumstances such as those discussed in *McDermott v. Dougherty*, 869 A.2d 751 (Md. 2005) (which you read in the last chapter) existed; and whether denial of visitation would adversely affect her younger brother. *Id.* at 765. The appellate court held that the impact of losing contact with her siblings on Victoria herself was not a proper subject of judicial inquiry due to her third-party status—the focus of inquiry must be on the child who the third party wishes to visit. *But see In re Victoria C.*, 88 A.3d at 766–77 (Adkins, J., dissenting) (some jurisdictions consider sibling visitation to be a constitutional right).

Other close relatives in the direct ancestral line may also lack standing if the statute does not expressly name them. In 2014 a Mississippi court held that great-grandparents were not entitled to seek visitation because they were not included as "grandparents" under the state code. *Lott v. Alexander*, 134 So. 3d 369 (Miss. Ct. App. 2014). In contrast, the Supreme Court of Nebraska affirmed an order granting unsupervised visitation to a cousin of the mother's who had raised the child virtually without interruption since birth after the court denied the cousin custody in light of the parental preference doctrine. *Windham v. Griffin*, 887 N.W.2d 710 (Neb. 2016).

6. *May grandparents seek custody after* Troxel? The Idaho Supreme Court expressly upheld a state statute that gave grandparents with whom a child resided in "a stable relationship" the same standing as a natural parent in custody disputes. *Hernandez v. Hernandez*, 265 P.3d 495 (Idaho 2011). The court reasoned that *Troxel* had "limited" precedential value because there was no majority consensus about why the breathtakingly broad Washington statute violated the mother's rights as applied. Further, the Idaho court noted, "it is hard to imagine" how children would come to reside with their grandparents in a stable relationship without the consent or at least the acquiescence of the children's parents. *Id.* at *500.

Turning to the facts in *Hernandez*, the court held that the lower court correctly applied Idaho's grandparent caretaker statute when it modified an earlier order giving custody to the mother, and instead awarded the father and the custodial maternal grandmother a form of shared residential custody. The mother, to whom the trial court had awarded custody, left the children with their grandmother in 2001, and the children remained in their grandmother's care until 2008. In 2008 the mother asked the court to transfer custody to the father, who had not seen the children for six years and had paid only sporadic child support, without informing the court that the children had been living with their grandmother. The grandmother then petitioned for custody. The state's highest court affirmed the order below, which gave the father sole legal custody and physical custody for most of the year, and awarded the grandmother six weeks of residential custody during summer vacations. Do you think this was the right result? Did the grandmother receive shared custody, as the court framed it, or an intensive form of visitation? If the Idaho statute had applied to *McDermott* do you think the results would have been different?

Grandparents and other third parties who serve as full-time caretakers for children at the parents' request, or with the parents' consent, or due to parental incapacity (such as addiction to opioids and other illegal drugs), may transition from third party status to legal parenthood through statutory provisions and equitable doctrines explored in the next Section.

D. VISITATION AND CUSTODY RIGHTS OF DE FACTO PARENTS

Adults and children may develop strong ties in the absence of formal legal parenthood. Grandparents and other relatives may be a child's primary caretaker for a significant period, but other adults commonly live in the same household with children and function as a parent. For example, when unmarried couples raise one partner's children together, the children often regard both adults as their parents; in many states, however, only one adult has a legal claim to parenthood after the couple breaks up. In jurisdictions that recognize equitable claims to parenthood based on the role a third party has played in the child's life, a biological or legal "stranger"—that is, an adult who is not the child's biological, adoptive, or presumed biological parent based on marriage, and yet functions as a parent—may have standing to request that a court order visitation or even to petition for legal or physical custody. Courts may find a basis for an equitable parenting claim in the common law, the best interests of the child standard, or in the express provisions of state statutes. *See* Pamela Laufer-Ukeles & Ayelet Blecher-Prigat, *Between Function and Form: Towards a Differentiated Model of Functional Parenthood*, 20 Geo. Mason L. Rev. 419, 423–24 (2013).

As indicated in the notes following *Troxel*, the constitutional right of legal parents to decide which adults spend time with their children bears directly on the claims of all third parties, including not only grandparents and other relatives but also unmarried partners of a legal parent.

A key, and perhaps confusing, difference between the grandparents who sought visitation in *Troxel* and the former partner or other claimant to equitable parenting status who seeks visitation is that the former partner initially must convince the court that he or she is not a third party at all, but a parent who deserves legal recognition.

Equitable parenting doctrine may distinguish between two entwined concepts, the right to custody and the right to visitation. One Pennsylvania court referred to a biological parent's unrelated same-sex partner as "certainly fit to exercise partial custody of the child for the purpose of visitation." *T.B. v. L.R.M.*, 874 A.2d 34, 37 (Pa. Super. Ct. 2005). Biological parents have argued that if their former partners receive recognition as de facto parents, any rights flowing from that status should be limited to visitation. Sometimes, particularly when the children are very young, the passage of time has weakened emotional ties with the parent who has been denied visitation while litigation proceeds, undermining the de facto parent's arguments for custody. The right to visitation, however, is not diminished by lack of contact in most jurisdictions. *V.C. v. M.J.B.*, 748 A.2d 539 (N.J. 2000).

Although recognition of a functional parenthood claim can occur during an initial custody hearing, many unmarried couples do not go to court when they split up, as you saw in *Blevins v. Bardwell*, which you read in Chapter 12. Indeed, virtually all reported cases about the right of a parent's former partner to visit a child reach the courts only after an initial informal agreement to allow visits falls apart and the legal parent prohibits further contact between the former partner and the child. The former partner usually must convince the court that she is not a third party at all, but an equitable or de facto parent who deserves legal recognition and the protections that run with parenthood. As you will see, the availability of equitable parenthood status depends on where the parties live: states may give third parties the same rights as any other parent, slightly diminished rights, or no rights.

1. Who Qualifies as an Equitable or De Facto Parent

States vary in the labels they assign to third parties who claim parenthood, and there are technical distinctions as well. The terms include: (i) "parent by estoppel," "equitable parent" or "in loco parentis"; (ii) de facto parent; or (iii) functional parent. Many courts use these terms interchangeably, although in some states, the terms may each provide a distinct set of rights. These relationships generally render the formalities of legal adoption unnecessary.

Legal parents have constitutionally-based rights to the care and custody of their children. However, the American Law Institute's *Principles of the Law of Family Dissolution: Analysis and Recommendations*, the Uniform Parentage Act, most recently revised in

2017, and a new statute promulgated by the Uniform Law Commissioners in 2018 all urge states to recognize the role of a nonparent who has lived with the child and, by agreement with the legal parent, helped raise the child and taken on "full parental responsibilities." ALI, Principles § 2.03(b) (2002).

a. Statutory Approaches

i. The ALI Principles

The ALI Principles, issued in 2002 and never revised, are a product of their time in the way they link parenthood to biology and reflect gendered definitions of classic family roles, as seen in Section 203 (1)(b) of the ALI's definition of parenthood by estoppel:

(b) A parent by estoppel is an individual who, though not a legal parent,

(i) is obligated to pay child support; or

(ii) lived with the child for at least two years and

    (A) over that period had a reasonable, good faith belief that he was the child's biological father * * * and fully accepted parental responsibilities consistent with that belief, and

    (B) if some time thereafter that belief no longer existed, continued to make reasonable, good-faith efforts to accept responsibilities as the child's father.

The rest of the definition is consistent with other contemporary approaches set out in the following pages:

(iii) [the parent has] lived with the child since birth, holding out and accepting full and permanent responsibilities as a parent, as part of a prior co-parenting agreement with the child's legal parent * * * to raise the child together each with full parental rights and responsibilities [and] the court finds that recognition of the individual as a parent is in the child's best interests; or

(iv) lived with the child for at least two years, holding out and accepting full and permanent responsibilities as a parent, pursuant to an agreement with the child's parent * * *, when the court finds that recognition of the individual as a parent is in the child's best interests.

ALI Principles § 2.03(1)(b) (2002).

The ALI distinguishes a de facto parent from a parent by estoppel. Section 2.03 of the ALI Principles defines a de facto parent as follows:

(c)   A *de facto parent* is an individual other than a legal parent or a parent by estoppel who, for a significant period of time not less than two years,

(i)   lived with the child and,

(ii) for reasons primarily other than financial compensation, and with the agreement of the legal parent to form a parent-child relationship, or as a result of a complete failure or inability of any legal parent to perform caretaking functions,

(A)   regularly performed a majority of the caretaking functions for the child, or

(B)   regularly performed a share of caretaking functions at least as great as that of the parent with whom the child primarily lived.

ALI, Principles § 2.03(1)(c) (2002).

Establishing de facto parenthood, however, does not put the de facto parent on the same legal footing as the other parent under the ALI approach. The ALI gives priority to legal parents and parents by estoppel in custody disputes, unless the legal parent has failed to perform "a reasonable share of parenting functions" or assigning custody to the legal parent would "cause harm to the child." ALI Principles § 2.18(1).

ii.   The Uniform Parentage Act

The most recent iteration of the UPA, adopted in 2017, expressly aims to remove all presumptions based on biology or gender. Unif. Parentage Act § 204 cmt (amended 2017), 9B U.L.A. 139 (Supp. 2018). Previously many of the disputes in which de facto parenthood arose involved same sex couples, but now that marriages between individuals of the same sex are legal in every jurisdiction, the UPA and courts expressly contemplate a wider variety of facts that will trigger equitable parenthood claims, as well as cases in which more than two people may claim to have acted as parents. *Id.* The 2017 UPA provisions on equitable parenthood expressly drew on reforms and trends in the states. UPA (2017) § 609 cmt. As of late 2018 the new UPA has been adopted in California, Vermont and Washington.

The 2017 UPA sets forth the following terms for gaining standing to claim de facto parenthood, and for prevailing in that claim.

SECTION 204. PRESUMPTION OF PARENTAGE.

(a) An individual is presumed to be a parent of a child if:

* * *

(2) the individual resided in the same household with the child for the first two years of the life of the child, including any period of temporary absence, and openly held out the child as the individual's child.

* * *

SECTION 609. ADJUDICATING CLAIM OF DE FACTO PARENTAGE OF CHILD.

* * *

(b) An individual who claims to be a de facto parent of a child must commence a proceeding to establish parentage of a child under this section:

(1) before the child attains 18 years of age; and

(2) while the child is alive.

* * *

(d) In a proceeding to adjudicate parentage of an individual who claims to be a de facto parent of the child, if there is only one other individual who is a parent or has a claim to parentage of the child, the court shall adjudicate the individual who claims to be a de facto parent to be a parent of the child if the individual demonstrates by clear-and-convincing evidence that:

(1) the individual resided with the child as a regular member of the child's household for a significant period;

(2) the individual engaged in consistent caretaking of the child;

(3) the individual undertook full and permanent responsibilities of a parent of the child without expectation of financial compensation;

(4) the individual held out the child as the individual's child;

(5) the individual established a bonded and dependent relationship with the child which is parental in nature;

(6) another parent of the child fostered or supported the bonded and dependent relationship required under paragraph (5); and

(7) continuing the relationship between the individual and the child is in the best interest of the child.

iii. Uniform Nonparent Custody and Visitation Act

In 2018 the Uniform Law Commissioners approved a Uniform Nonparent Custody and Visitation Act designed to clarify the visitation rights of nonparents who have played a significant role in a child's life while living with the child's legal parent even if those adults do not qualify as de facto or equitable parents. The Act would create custody and visitation rights for nonparents who have served as "consistent caretakers" for a child without compensation and for other nonparents in circumstances where denial of "custody or visitation would result in harm to the child." Consistent with *Troxel*, the Act is premised on a rebuttable presumption that the parent's decision is in the child's best interest. The Act would protect relationships between children and adults including, but not limited to, former live-in partners and stepparents.

NOTES AND QUESTIONS

1.   *Does the legal regime matter?* What differences, if any, exist between the ALI approach and the UPA?

2.   *How many?* How do each of the approaches—ALI, UPA, and the 2018 Uniform Act—deal with the possibility that the legal parent has a series of serious relationships during the child's minority creating multiple third parties who might want to claim equitable parenting status?

3.   *Why give biological parents preference?* The courts in many states generally presume that biological parents have a unique substantive due process claim to the care of their children that the Constitution protects, and you have read many of the Supreme Court cases that discuss the parental liberty interest in offspring. *See Hawkins v. Grese*, 809 S.E.2d 441, 447 (Va. Ct. App. 2018) ("biological parentage is a unique relationship predating any legal arrangement"; recognition of other kinds of parents varies from state to state and lacks a constitutional dimension). But Professor Douglas NeJaime argues that limiting the liberty interest in parenting to biological parents "is neither required by our constitutional tradition nor consistent with contemporary constitutional" jurisprudence, and is inconsistent as well "with the pluralistic forms of family that society features and that law, including constitutional law, increasingly protects." Douglas NeJaime, *The Constitution of Parenthood* (Jan. 20, 2019 draft). NeJaime emphasizes the functional approach to parenthood reflected in the statutory approaches you have just read.

b.   Common Law Approaches

While some jurisdictions expressly provide for de facto parenthood through statute, a growing number of jurisdictions have developed de facto parenthood through case law. Courts in several states have adopted a four-part test for finding de facto parenthood enunciated by the Supreme Court of Wisconsin in a case involving a same-sex couple. This common law approach bears a close resemblance to the statutory approaches you have just read. The adult who petitions a court for recognition as a de facto parent "must prove four elements":

(1) that the biological or adoptive parent consented to, and fostered, the petitioner's formation and establishment of a parent-like relationship with the child;

(2) that the petitioner and the child lived together in the same household;

(3) that the petitioner assumed obligations of parenthood by taking significant responsibility for the child's care, education and development, including contributing towards the child's support, without expectation of financial compensation; and

(4) that the petitioner has been in a parental role for a length of time sufficient to have established with the child a bonded, dependent relationship parental in nature.

In re Custody of H.S.H-K., 533 N.W.2d 419, 421 (Wis. 1995). The test may be used for opposite sex couples as well as same sex couples, and for couples who never married as well as those who have divorced.

Note the first element carefully: the legal parent must have "consented to, and fostered" the functional parent relationship. This is intended to protect the legal parent's constitutional rights—the liberty interest in parenthood recognized in a series of Supreme Court rulings.

States have grappled with the legal status of former stepparents who seek visitation or, less frequently, custody. Traditionally, stepparents did not have independent visitation rights but such rights may be created by statute or common law. However, by 2009 roughly one-third of the states had statutes under which stepparents could seek visitation. Ayelet Blecher-Prigat, *Rethinking Visitation: From a Parental to a Relational Right*, 16 Duke J. Gender L. & Pol'y 1, 8 (2009). Other states reach the same result as a matter of common law.

Stepparents in some jurisdictions have no right to seek visitation; any rights they possess may be limited by statute or rest in the trial court's discretion. In Mississippi, for example, a stepparent has no right to visitation over the objection of a fit biological parent even where a biological father asserts claims against a residential stepfather after the mother dies in childbirth. *Neely v. Welch*, 194 So.3d 149, 156, 160 (Miss. Ct. App. 2015) (to overcome deference to the biological parent's decisions or custodial rights, the stepparent must show by clear and convincing evidence that the biological parent abandoned or deserted the child, is "so immoral as to be detrimental to the child," or is unfit to have custody; same standards apply for court-ordered visitation). *See also* Appellee's Reply Brief, *In re the Parenting of C.T.C.*, 2014 WL 4162469 (Mont. Aug. 13, 2014) (stepmother who raised child from infancy until the father's death must show clear and convincing evidence that visits are in the girl's best interests to overcome objections of the fit mother with whom the girl currently lives).

Washington's highest court grappled with whether a former stepparent—divorced from the child's legal parent—should be able to assert a claim for recognition as a de facto parent under the four-part Wisconsin test for *de facto* parentage that Washington had adopted as a matter of common law. *In the Matter of the Custody of B.M.H.*, 315 P.3d 470, 479 (Wash. 2013) (en banc).

The child at the center of the dispute had only one surviving parent, the mother; the biological father had died while the mother was pregnant. Mr. Holt, the stepfather, now divorced from the mother and seeking third party visitation rights, was the biological and custodial father of the mother's older child. The stepfather had been involved in the younger child's life since before the child was born, having helped the mother through her pregnancy after her fiancé, the biological father, died. The stepfather was present at the child's birth. After the child's birth, mother and stepfather married and divorced.

The en banc court held that the stepfather could seek de facto parenthood status in order to pursue court-ordered visitation and "nonparental" custody. *Id.* The court explained:

> Because there is no statutory avenue for Mr. Holt to petition for parentage, the de facto parentage doctrine fills this gap and provides for meaningful adjudication of whether Mr. Holt has undertaken a permanent role as B.M.H.'s parent. The de facto parentage test protects Ms. Holt's constitutional rights by requiring that she consented to the parent-child relationship.

* * *

> * * * De facto parentage is a flexible equitable remedy that complements legislative enactments where parent-child relationships arise in ways that are not contemplated in the statutory scheme. * * * The de facto parentage doctrine incorporates constitutionally required deference to parents by requiring that the biological or legal parent consent to and foster the parentlike relationship. Once a petitioner has made the threshold showing that the natural or legal parent consented to and fostered the parent-like relationship, the State is no longer "interfering on behalf of a third party in an insular family unit but is enforcing the rights and obligations of parenthood that attach to de facto parents." Under the test, attaining de facto parent status is "no easy task."

* * *

> * * * The de facto parentage doctrine properly balances [Mr. Holt's] interests in an adjudication of parentage against the deference we give biological parents * * *.

Id. at 478, 480.

A dissenting judge worried, however, that the "de facto parent test is too easily met in the stepparent-child setting. Facts that lend themselves to an inference of consent to a parent-child relationship are indistinguishable from facts that show the parent wants the marriage to prevail and a family unit to be formed. When the marriage ends, the inference is no longer justifiable." *Id.* at 480 (Madsen, C.J., *concurring/dissenting*). When the Washington legislature enacted a relative visitation statute four years later, it appeared to side with the majority—"spouses" of any blood relative may petition for visitation "even after the marriage is terminated." Wash. Rev. Code Ann. § 26.11.010(2)(a)(iv) (West, Westlaw through 2018 Reg. Sess.).

NOTES AND QUESTIONS

1. *Other states.* The Pennsylvania Supreme Court has held that regardless of the nature of the biological parent's relationship with an individual who seeks recognition as a de facto parent, a de facto parenting relationship is created where "the child has established strong psychological bonds" with a nonbiological parent figure who "has lived with the child and provided care, nurture and affection, assuming in the child's eye a stature like that of a parent." *T.B. v. L.R.M.*, 786 A.2d 913, 917 (Pa. 2001). By contrast, the Wyoming Supreme Court refused to adopt the doctrines of parenthood by estoppel or de facto parenthood, deeming such law reform the province of the legislature, rather than the judiciary, and identifying problems with allocating rights between the biological parent and other parental figures. *L.P. v. L.F.*, 338 P.3d 908 (Wyo. 2014). For a discussion of state approaches to the establishment and rights of de facto parenthood, *see* Courtney G. Joslin, *Leaving No (Nonmarital) Child Behind*, 48 Fam. L.Q. 495 (2014).

2. *How far do equitable rights go?* Some jurisdictions limit equitable parenting claims. In Michigan, for example, equitable parenthood doctrines only apply in the context of marriage. *See Harmon v. Davis*, 800 N.W.2d 63 (Mich. 2011) (Kelley, J., *dissenting*); *Sheardown v. Guastella*, 324 Mich. App. 251 (Ct. App.2018) (no equitable parenting claims for unmarried partners).

Still other states do not recognize equitable parenting claims at all. *E.g.*, *Hawkins* v. *Grese*, 809 S.E. 2d 441, 448 (Va. Ct. App. 2018) (anticipating that such claims would open a "Pandora's box of unintended consequences").

3. *Can a neighbor become a psychological parent with standing?* In *V.C. v. M.J.B.*, 748 A.2d 539 (N.J. 2000), in a case involving an unmarried same sex couple the New Jersey Supreme Court "gave standing, in certain circumstances, to third parties who previously had no right to seek custody or visitation at all, and the holding was not intended to apply only to domestic partners or step-parents." *P.B. v. T.H.*, 851 A.2d 780, 786 (N.J. Super. Ct. App. Div. 2004). *P.B.* involved two children the state had removed from their substance-abusing mother and placed with their aunt, a single mother

expecting her second child. When the aunt became overwhelmed, P.B., a neighbor, volunteered to care for the two children, who eventually moved into P.B.'s home. Later, when a custody dispute arose, P.B. claimed that she had been the psychological parent of the younger child, an infant. The trial court held that P.B. was indeed the psychological parent. The appellate court concluded that P.B. had standing to seek custody of the child and remanded the case for determination of whether P.B. met the requirements for finding that a third party is a psychological parent.

4. *Third-party caretakers.* Some jurisdictions, exemplified by Colorado, have expressly created legal rights for de facto parents by statute when the child lives with a third party instead of either legal parent. Colo. Rev. Stat. Ann. § 14–10–123(1)(b) (West, Westlaw through 2d Reg. Sess. Of the 71st Gen. Assemb. 2014). Interpreting the state's "parenting responsibility" statute, Colorado appellate courts have held that if a parent voluntarily permitted the nonparent to assume responsibility for the physical care of the child, including some decisionmaking authority, the nonparent has standing to seek custody. *In re E.S.*, 264 P.3d 623, 625 (Colo. App. 2011) (a woman who raised a child on and off for years with her own children with the father's consent and with "temporary guardianship" has standing to challenge the father for primary parenting responsibility and is no "mere babysitter"). *E.S.* made clear that before a court could award primary custody to a nonparent over a parent who had not been found unfit, the court must find by clear and convincing evidence that giving a third party primary parenting responsibilities is in the child's best interests. *Id.*

One commentator has argued that people who are compensated for full-time childcare should be eligible for recognition as de facto parents. Pamela Laufer-Ukeles, *Money, Caregiving, and Kinship: Should Paid Caregivers Be Allowed to Obtain De facto Parental Status?*, 74 Mo. L. Rev 25 (2009) (including paid caregivers along with foster parents and others). The UPA expressly repudiated this approach in 2017.

PROBLEM 13-2

You are a state legislator considering what policy your state should adopt with respect to third-party claims to parenthood. What are the competing social policy goals? How should the state balance the goal of encouraging the partners of legal parents to play active roles in the lives of the children in the household with the perceived risk that helping raise a child may impose ongoing responsibilities after the relationship ends? Should any proposed statute require that the legal parent's intent be stated formally, perhaps in writing or in front of witnesses, when the third party's relationship with the child begins, or within some set period of time after the parties move in together (assuming that they share a household), or a number of years prior to the litigation?

PROBLEM 13-3

When she married Sam, Mother had a young daughter—Julie—from an earlier marriage that ended in divorce. Sam was an engaged stepfather, and when Mother tragically died in a motorcycle accident, Sam continued to care for and raise Julie. Sam remarried, and his new wife enthusiastically became a caretaker for Julie too. They provided 100% of the financial support for Julie, took her to school, helped with homework, cared for her when she was sick and arranged and took her to all of her extracurricular activities. About a year after Sam remarried, Julie's biological father, who had not been in contact for since Sam married Julie's mother, appeared and demanded custody of his daughter. Sam had no choice by to comply, as he did not think he had any legal rights to custody.

Julie's biological father took her to live in another state, expressly to frustrate visits between Julie, her stepfather and her stepfather's wife. Sam and his wife petitioned for and received "parenting/visitation time" with Julie under the state's third-party visitation statute. The statute requires third parties seeking visitation to show by clear and convincing evidence: (a) that the child's biological parent (a) "engaged in conduct that is contrary to the child-parent relationship;" (b) that a "parent-child relationship" exists between the petitioner and the child; and (c) that continuation of the relationship would serve the child's best interests. What outcome?

Assuming that the jurisdiction recognizes de facto parenting status, should Sam have filed a petition to be recognized as a parent to Julie rather than asked for visitation as a third party? What, if any, difference would it have made to the legal requirements? What would the likely outcome have been? What difference might it have made to the disposition?

What claims could Sam's current wife make?

3. MODIFICATION OF CUSTODY OR VISITATION ORDERS

Many of the materials you read earlier in this Chapter concerned modification of custody or visitation orders. This Section focuses on the legal standards that govern modification. First, you will read about the generally applicable grounds for modification. You will then explore one of the most common reasons that a parent petitions for modification—the relocation of the parent who has primary physical custody. As you will see, relocation cases have generated their own subset of legal standards for modification.

A. THE STANDARD

Because of the state's *parens patriae* interest in the welfare of children, courts retain jurisdiction over custody and visitation matters until the child reaches the age of majority. A trial court may modify child custody orders, including consent decrees, but will not do so lightly because modification disrupts whatever stability the child has achieved since the original decree. To modify a custody arrangement, a trial court in most states must find (i) that circumstances have changed substantially since the original decree was entered; and (ii) that the change in custody will serve the best interests of the child. *See, e.g.*, N.D. Cent. Code § 14–09–6.6 (2017). To avoid re-litigation of issues aired in the initial custody determination, most jurisdictions also require that the change of circumstances have occurred after the initial decree, and that it could not have been foreseeable by the parties at the time of the initial decree. *Id.* A handful of jurisdictions, including Georgia, Kansas and New Hampshire, allow modification based on the child's best interests without any showing of changed circumstances. *E.g.*, Ga. Code Ann. § 19–9–3(b) (2018); *In re Choy*, 919 A.2d 801 (N.H. 2007) (holding that legislation enacted in 2000 eliminated the changed circumstances requirement for modifying a custody decree).

Many state statutes also prevent courts from modifying custody decrees until a specified period has elapsed since the initial decree or any prior decree, often two years. *See* ALI, Principles § 2.15 Reporter's Notes to cmt. a (2002); Ga. Code Ann. § 19–9–3(b) (2018).

The North Dakota statute set forth below provides a clear example of all of these principles.

§ 14–09–06.6. Limitations on post judgment modifications of primary residential responsibility

1.   Unless agreed to in writing by the parties, or if included in the parenting plan, no motion for an order to modify primary residential responsibility may be made earlier than two years after the date of entry of an order establishing primary residential responsibility, except in accordance with subsection 3.

2.   Unless agreed to in writing by the parties, or if included in the parenting plan, if a motion for modification has been disposed of upon its merits, no subsequent motion may be filed within two years of disposition of the prior motion, except in accordance with subsection 5.

3.   The time limitation in subsections 1 and 2 does not apply if the court finds:

    a.   The persistent and willful denial or interference with parenting time;

    b.   The child's present environment may endanger the child's physical or emotional health or impair the child's emotional development; or

    c.   The primary residential responsibility for the child has changed to the other parent for longer than six months.

    4.   * * * The court shall consider [a motion for modification of primary residential responsibility] without oral argument or evidentiary hearing and shall deny the motion unless the court finds the moving party has established a prima facie case justifying a modification. The court shall set a date for an evidentiary hearing only if a prima facie case is established.

* * *

    6.   The court may modify the primary residential responsibility after the two-year period following the date of entry of an order establishing primary residential responsibility if the court finds:

    a.   On the basis of facts that have arisen since the prior order or which were unknown to the court at the time of the prior order, a material change has occurred in the circumstances of the child or the parties; and

    b.   The modification is necessary to serve the best interests of the child.

    7.   The court may modify a prior order concerning primary residential responsibility at any time if the court finds a stipulated agreement by the parties to modify the order is in the best interests of the child.

    8.   Upon a motion to modify primary residential responsibility under this section, the burden of proof is on the moving party.

N.D. Cent. Code 14–09–06.06 (2017).

B. SUBSTANTIAL CHANGE OF CIRCUMSTANCES

The following decision from Alaska's highest court explores what constitutes a substantial change of circumstances.

KRISTEN L. V. BENJAMIN W.

Supreme Court of Alaska, 2014.
2014 WL 2716842.

MEMORANDUM OPINION AND JUDGMENT

INTRODUCTION

[T]here is only one issue to decide—did the superior court err in concluding there had been a substantial change of circumstances affecting the parties' two children warranting consideration of the children's best interests for a possible custody modification? Because we see no such error, we affirm the superior court's custody modification.

BACKGROUND

Kristen and Benjamin divorced in early 2012. Under the terms of their custody agreement, they shared legal custody of their two sons, one born in 2003 and one in 2005. Kristen, who lives in Anchorage, was to have primary physical custody of the children; Benjamin, who is in the Air Force and lives in California, was to have weekly Skype contact and the children were to travel to California for Christmas and summer visitations.

Kristen and Benjamin were aware before the divorce that their younger child engaged in feminine behaviors, including wearing girl's clothing and nail polish. Both parties apparently assumed the child was going through a "phase," although they had differing views—Benjamin was more accepting of the child's behavior than Kristen, as reflected in a 2011 letter from Kristen's attorney to Benjamin's attorney:

> My client is very concerned about [the younger child]. Apparently your client and his various family find it amusing to dress [the younger child] in girls' clothing, to paint his fingernails, to give him princess dolls and other girly items including placing make-up upon his face. This is not cute, or amusing. It is causing difficulties with the child interacting with other children at school. No doubt, it is not in his best interest. It is requested that this behavior be immediately terminated.

In June 2013 the children arrived in California for their summer visitation with Benjamin. Benjamin noticed bruises on the younger child, including a large one on the child's back. When asked what caused the bruises, the child hid his face in a pillow and was unresponsive. The child later said that Kristen and her husband caused the bruises. * * *

Benjamin reported the child's statements to police * * *, and he took both children to see a professional counselor in late June. Benjamin showed the counselor pictures of the bruises, advised her of the younger child's feminine phase, and expressed concern about possible physical and emotional abuse of the children in Kristen's household.

Both children reported to the counselor that bruises on the younger child's arm were the result of Kristen's gripping him tightly and that the large bruise on the younger child's back was the result of Kristen's throwing him into his bedroom onto a toy. The younger child also told the counselor that "she should have been born a girl and that she was born into the wrong body." Both children told the counselor that Kristen did not support the younger child's gender expression—the older child said that Kristen told him "gays are sick and it's sick for [the younger child] to play with girl toys." After meeting twice with the children, the counselor filed a mandatory report with California's Child Protection Services (CPS) due to her concern that Kristen had abused them.

In mid-July 2013 Benjamin filed a motion to modify custody based on his concerns about physical and emotional abuse of the children while with Kristen. [T]he superior court ordered an evidentiary hearing to determine whether there had been a substantial change of circumstances affecting the children, and, if so, whether the best interests of the children warranted a change in custody.

After the hearing, the superior court concluded that there had been a substantial change of circumstances affecting the children because of Kristen's "domestic violence and inability to deal with her child's transgender issue." The court determined that a custody change was warranted under two different analyses, one involving the statutory presumption arising from domestic violence and one involving consideration of statutory "best interests" factors for awarding custody. Under each analysis the superior court came to the same conclusion: sole legal and primary physical custody of the children should be with Benjamin, with Kristen having limited unsupervised visitation in California and potential unsupervised visitation in Alaska after complying with a number of conditions.

Kristen appeals the custody modification, but her argument is limited to challenging the superior court's factual findings underlying the conclusion that there had been a substantial change of circumstances affecting the children that warranted consideration of a custody modification. * * *

CUSTODY MODIFICATION FRAMEWORK

Alaska Statute 25.20.110(a) provides that "[a]n award of custody of a child or visitation with the child may be modified if the court determines that a change in circumstances requires the modification of the award and the modification is in the best interests of the child." The party moving for custody modification has the burden to establish that a substantial change has occurred. "The required change in circumstance must be significant or substantial, and must be demonstrated relative to the facts and circumstances that existed at the time of the prior custody order that the party seeks to modify." Once the court has found such a change, the court "must then determine whether modification of the arrangement is in the best interests of the child."

The superior court's findings of fact underlying a determination of a substantial change of circumstances are reviewed for clear error. Assuming there has been a substantial change of circumstances, the superior court's custody decision is reviewed for abuse of discretion * * *.

DISCUSSION

Substantial Change of Circumstances

The superior court concluded that there had been a substantial change of circumstances affecting the children because of Kristen's "domestic violence and inability to deal with her child's transgender issue." Because domestic violence involving a child constitutes a significant change of circumstances affecting the child as a matter of law, we consider this aspect of the superior court's determination first; if we affirm it, then we do not need to consider the other aspect of the superior court's determination.

The superior court heard testimony from four sources: (1) Benjamin and his new wife; (2) the children's counselor; (3) a number of people who supported Kristen; and (4) Kristen and her new husband. We outline that testimony and the superior court's credibility findings as follows.

Benjamin and his new wife testified about finding bruises on the younger child, and Benjamin presented photographs at trial purportedly showing bruises on the child's legs, arms, and back. Benjamin and his wife also testified about the younger child's gender expression, the children's interactions with the counselor, and the CPS investigation. The superior court found they testified credibly that they did not cause the younger child's bruises. The court also noted the photographs * * * showed five different bruises "not of the type that would be caused by mere horseplay."

The children's counselor provided expert testimony about children and gender issues. She testified that the younger child identified as female and that, based on her discussions with the children, Kristen was unsupportive of this. She stated that the children told her they were often physically abused by their mother and stepfather. The counselor stated the older child said he is afraid of his mother and he tries to keep her from getting angry. She testified that the younger child told her the largest bruise was caused when Kristen "literally threw" the child, who landed on a toy, and that she believed this statement. The court found the counselor's testimony credible and said she was not a "hired gun." * * *. Lastly, the court noted that the counselor's testimony about the children's statements was admissible under two hearsay exceptions, the medical treatment exception and the catchall exception, and that the statements were "trustworthy and the information is worthy of belief."

Kristen [called nine witnesses, each of whom] testified that Kristen was a good mother and that they did not believe she was abusive. * * *

Kristen and her new husband testified that the younger child is feminine and often dresses in various costumes. They testified that neither of them is homophobic and that Kristen's negative reaction to her child dressing as a girl was because she was afraid it would cause bullying. They also testified that they do not abuse the children and that they did not cause the bruises. [T]he court was not persuaded by her or her witnesses' testimony—the court found that Kristen "perpetrated multiple instances of domestic violence . . . in the privacy of her home" and "created a façade in public such that her parade of witnesses all testify that she's the greatest mother ever."

On appeal * * * the crux of Kristen's argument is that the superior court improperly weighed the evidence and should not have given any significant weight to the counselor's testimony. But "the trial court, not this court, performs the function of judging the credibility of witnesses and weighing conflicting evidence." The superior court made specific findings of fact about the credibility of the witnesses and weighed their testimony accordingly * * *. Therefore, * * * the superior court did not err in determining that there had been a substantial change of circumstances warranting consideration of a custody modification.

Because the superior court came to the same custody decision under the best interests analysis as it did using the statutory presumption arising from domestic violence, we do not need to consider whether [it] correctly applied the domestic violence presumption.

* * *

Because we affirm the superior court's finding that Kristen committed domestic violence against the children, we do not need to address the court's other finding underlying its change of circumstances determination.

* * *

CONCLUSION

We AFFIRM the superior court's custody modification decision.

NOTES AND QUESTIONS

1. *The unexplored question in* Kristen L. v. Benjamin W.: *was the mother's attitude toward her son's sexual identity a "substantial" change in circumstance warranting modification of custody?* It is estimated that approximately 0.6 percent of the adult population of the United States identify as transgender. *Doe v. Boyertown Area Sch. Dist.,* 897 F. 3d 518, 522 (3d Cir. 2018). Transgender youth are at higher risk than their peers of attempting suicide and may display other symptoms of distress including anxiety and depression. *Id.* at 523.

When a family is intact, or parents agree on how to respond to a child's emerging sexual identity, there is normally no role for state intervention unless the parents seek treatment that violates state law. As of the beginning of 2019 fifteen states and the District of Columbia forbid licensed health care professionals from using certain aversion therapy techniques (commonly referred to as "conversion therapy") alleged in the face of scientific evidence to the contrary to "cure" minors of homosexuality. Michael Gold, *A Ban on*

'Conversion Therapy' Is Passed After Years of Effort, N.Y. Times, Jan 22, 2019 A17 (New York becomes latest state to ban conversion therapy). In custody disputes, however, the court must determine which parent better serves the child's best interests, and may look at each parent's reaction to a child's sexual identity.

If the mother in *Kristen L. v. Benjamin W.* had not physically attacked her son, but had belittled him, put him in counseling to change his gender identity, and otherwise failed to offer him emotional support, would that pattern of behavior have sufficed to warrant modifying custody?

Since most states require that new information have emerged since the last custody order to satisfy the threshold requirement of a substantial change, what difference would it make if the son had always seemed a bit "effeminate" (as was alleged in *Kristen L.*) and the mother's views about traditional gender and gender roles were also known to the father before the divorce?

Very few cases to date have addressed custody disagreements respecting transgender youth. Jaime B. Margolis, *Two Divorced Parents, One Transgender Child, Many Voices*, 15 Whittier J. Child & Fam. Advoc. 125, 125 (2016) (arguing that mental health experts do and should inform judicial decisions). However, gender dysphoria was at the heart of a 2018 appellate opinion about a custody dispute in Arizona. The issues included when the child's interest in a "female" identity first emerged, whether the mother was encouraging that interest, and numerous conditions the trial court placed on the mother, including an order not to discuss gender preference with the children or respond to their questions about the subject. *Paul E. v. Courtney F.*, 418 P.3d 413 (Ariz. Ct. App. 2018) (reversing numerous orders but leaving in place an assignment of sole decisionmaking authority to the father who opposed supporting the child's pursuit of a female identity). In an unreported dispute, an Ohio family court awarded legal and residential custody of a transgender 17-year-old to his grandparents who supported the use of hormone treatments that would be covered by their health insurance, and respected his change of name in contrast to the parents who opposed the transition, triggering suicidal urges in the teenager. *Transgender identity, in their words*, CNN (Feb. 16, 2018).

2. *Focus on the primary residential parent.* In most jurisdictions the focus is on the changed circumstances of the custodial parent, not on improvements in the noncustodial parent's circumstances that might have supported that parent's initial custody claim. For example, a noncustodial parent's improved mental health will not ordinarily lead to a change of custody. Deterioration of the custodial parent's circumstances, however, is a material change. *State v. Neustel*, 790 N.W.2d 476 (N.D. 2010) (finding a material change where in the five years since the mother received primary residential custody she had been involved in "long-term relationships" with five different men who moved in and out of the home, causing "disorder" in the children's lives, moved several times and "concentrat[ed] more on her own needs than on those of" the daughter whose father sought a transfer of custody). A material

"change of circumstances" often turns out to be a conglomeration of changes, adding up to a different calculation of the child's best interests. ALI Principles § 2.15 cmt. c.

When a custodial parent willfully denies visitation ordered by the court, that behavior in itself constitutes a change of circumstances that may warrant modification of the custody order. *Miller-Jenkins v. Miller-Jenkins*, 12 A.3d 768 (Vt. 2010) (award of sole legal and physical custody to former same-sex partner after biological mother repeatedly violated visitation orders, where transfer of custody served child's best interests).

3. *Applying the North Dakota statute.* In *Topolski v. Topolski*, 844 N.W.2d 875 (N.D. 2014), the state's highest court considered a challenge to the application of the modification statute set forth on pages 940–941. The Topalskis divorced in March, 2010 when their only child was two years old. Their separation agreement, incorporated in the divorce judgment, provided that Jean, the mother, would have primary residential responsibility. In December of 2012, Thomas successfully petitioned for modification, alleging dental and medical neglect (some of the child's teeth had turned black and dental decay was causing ear aches), failure to treat a serious skin ailment and delay in keeping follow-up doctor's appointments, failure to alert Thomas that the boy had been in a serious car accident and other lapses in communication, smoking in the car with the boy present, and the boy's lack of progress in kindergarten which was not attributable to any learning disabilities. Thomas was also worried about Jean's home environment in which methamphetamine was used and manufactured by one of the three serious boyfriends she had been involved with since the divorce. Various state and private social service agencies had become involved with Jean's household. Despite all of these developments, Jean appealed the transfer of custody to Thomas. The court clarified that the best interests analysis at modification required consideration of the factors set out in the custody statute, and found that the trial court had implicitly referred to the statute in modifying the Topalskis' custody decree. Jean in turn alleged that the trial judge had failed to consider Thomas's pre-divorce conduct. The court ruled that Jean correctly stated North Dakota common law: where a court has not made findings at the time of divorce because it accepts the parties' stipulation regarding custody, consideration of pre-divorce conduct is not only appropriate but required at a modification hearing. However, it went on to hold that the trial court was aware of Thomas's earlier criminal convictions, but chose not to weigh them, or not to weigh them heavily—an appropriate exercise of discretion given that the convictions were not recent and did not seem likely to affect the child's well-being.

4. *New revelations about pre-existing facts.* What if the mother in *Kristen L.* had abused the child prior to the divorce, but the father either consented to the boy living with her or failed to inform the family court about the facts? Would the father now be able to raise the mother's pre-divorce behavior in support of his petition for modification? The highest court in Hawaii broke with the prevalent approach when it held that the best interests of the child trumps the changed circumstances requirement for modification of

custody arrangements. The case involved a mother who did not disclose domestic violence at the time of her divorce, when she consented to the father having residential custody, but decided to reveal that she had been the victim of domestic violence when the father planned to move with the child from Hawaii to the mainland. *Tumaneng v. Tumaneng*, 382 P. 3d 280 (Haw. 2016) (reversible error for the trial court to decline to hear evidence respecting domestic violence predating the divorce decree).

5. *A lesser standard to modify joint custody?* Some jurisdictions engage in a less stringent inquiry for modifying joint physical custody. ALI, Principles § 2.15 cmt. a. In Alabama, for example, the courts view an initial award of joint physical custody as the equivalent of "no prior custody determination," so that it is appropriate to engage in a best interests determination ab initio in subsequent modification proceedings. *Knight v. Knight*, 53 So.3d 942, 953 (Ala. Civ. App. 2010); *cf. Neustel, supra*, 790 N.W.2d at 480 (it is reversible error to treat a modification of primary physical custody "as an initial determination; a change of custody must be 'considered against the backdrop of the stability' " of the current arrangement).

In considering petitions to modify joint residential custody, courts may find that the parents' inability to cooperate constitutes a material change of circumstance, or that the children's need for consistency is a changed circumstance when they are old enough to enroll in school. Where both parents request that joint custody be terminated, and evidence of parental strife exists, "the antithesis of the concept of joint custody" is in play, and the trial court's refusal to grant custody to only one parent is reversible error. *Doah-Uyen Thi Le v. Thang Q. Nguyen*, 241 P.3d 647, 653 (Okla. Civ. App. 2010) (parents disagreed about the choice of school, sports and church and allegedly failed to exchange critical information about, for instance, the mother's loss of employment and health insurance for herself and the children, and the father's decision to enroll the children in a different school).

6. *Informal adjustments to custody arrangements.* Anecdotal evidence and court histories suggest that many parents reach informal agreements to modify custody and visitation arrangements as time passes. Because such informal arrangements may later lead to disputes, it is advisable to reduce the new terms to writing, and to have the arrangements approved by the court with jurisdiction over custody matters. *See Hurtt v. Hurtt*, 216 S.W.3d 604, 610 (Ark. Ct. App. 2005) ("The parties cannot modify the divorce decree without permission from the court. Absent a subsequent modification, the language in the divorce decree controls"). The North Dakota statute set out at pages 940–941 recognizes that such de facto modifications are common, and allows the court to issue an order giving effect to the parents' agreement when the arrangement has lasted for at least six months, even if the two-year time period for modification has not run.

PROBLEM 13-4

When Tina and Joe divorced in 2012, they agreed to joint legal and physical custody of their sons, who were then eight and ten years old. Joe had been married before. Joe's first wife, Kelli, spent over a decade in psychiatric hospitals after shooting and killing the two young children she and Joe had together. A court had found her not guilty by reason of insanity. In 2014 the state released Kelli after psychiatrists concluded that she no longer posed a risk to anyone. Shortly after her release, Kelli and Joe began seeing each other and resumed their intimate relationship. In 2017 they remarried.

Tina had not known that Kelli was involved with Joe or that she was present when the boys were in Joe's home until the boys told her about their father's marriage. She went to court in 2018, seeking sole physical custody and an order providing for supervised visitation with Joe. Joe opposes any change, arguing that the boys already have an established relationship with their stepmother, that she was never convicted of a crime, and that she now poses no risk.

What test should the judge apply, what factors should the judge consider, and how should the judge rule?

C. RELOCATION

American mobility has reached "record lows" according to the most recent census data: between 2015 and 2016 roughly ten percent of Americans relocated, just slightly less than the percentage of Finns or Danes who moved. Richard Florida, *American Mobility Has Declined,* CityLab (Feb. 2, 2017). Historically, however, Americans have often moved long distances, and, according to census data, separated or divorced people are far more likely to move than their married counterparts and families with children are more likely to move than those in adult-only households. Peter J. Mateyka, U.S. Census Bureau, Desire to Move and Residential Mobility: 2010–2011 at 2, 7–8 (2015). One or both parents commonly relocate after their relationship has ended. Parents frequently move to pursue educational or career opportunities, to establish a home with a new spouse or partner, or to be closer to a support network of family members or friends.

Disputes arising from a custodial parent's proposed relocation frequently lead the other parent to petition for modification of custody on the ground that the move constitutes a material change in circumstances and that the proposed move would undermine the petitioner's visitation rights and relationship with the child. *[margin note: material change in circumstances bc of the relocation?]*

The ALI Principles issued in 2002 presume that a parent's relocation does not constitute a substantial change in circumstances permitting modification of custodial arrangements unless the "relocation significantly impairs either parent's ability to exercise responsibilities the parent has

[handwritten margin note: BUT: presumption that a parent's relocation does NOT constitute a substantial change in circumstances unless it impairs either parent's ability to exercise responsibilities]

been exercising or attempting to exercise under the parenting plan." ALI, Principles § 2.17(1). Of course, if one parent moves a long distance, the move may easily "significantly impair" the arrangements of parents with joint physical custody or generous visitation patterns. The ALI Principles expressly provide that the court should allow the parent who exercises "the clear majority of custodial responsibility" to relocate (after giving notice to the other parent) "for a valid purpose, in good faith" to a location that promotes the purpose. *Id.* The ALI lists generally valid reasons for moving, including the most common purposes generally accepted by courts, such as to be near extended family, to pursue career or educational opportunities, or to join a new spouse or significant other who lives elsewhere. *Id.*

Those remain the most common reasons that parents assert for proposed moves. Professor Theresa Glennon reviewed all decisions available on Westlaw involving relocation over a five-year period ending June 1, 2006. Her findings confirmed that the reasons for relocating cited by the ALI were the reasons given in the bulk of cases, 90% of which involved mothers with custody. Theresa Glennon, *Still Partners? Examining the Consequences of Post-Dissolution Parenting*, 41 Fam. L. Q. 105 (2007).

Professor Glennon raised some concerns about the ways in which custody, and the judicial doctrine that has governed relocation cases in many jurisdictions, continue to entangle parents long after they separate:

> Parents who divorce or separate are strongly encouraged to co-parent their children. * * *.

> The co-parenting approach * * * falls into sharp conflict with the economic clean break model, under which divorced persons and cohabitants who part ways are entirely separate individuals, unencumbered by ongoing legal or financial relationships, free to build new lives and make a fresh start. * * *

> Relocation disputes provide a context in which the tension between these two models is most acute.

                              * * *

> Relocation disputes * * * usually develop after dissolution when the parent who has sole custody or is the majority-time residential parent, usually the mother, seeks to move away from the other parent. * * * State approaches to these disputes vary widely, and the outcome of any dispute is far from certain.

                              * * *

> Relocation disputes have spawned their own doctrine. [M]ost states have developed a doctrinal approach that is specific to relocation disputes. Many states now require the parent who

seeks to change the child's principal residence to provide notice to the other parent. * * *

Glennon, *supra*, at 107, 118, 119. In 2007 Glennon concluded, "broad categories fail to capture the diversity of state approaches to relocation." *Id.* at 120.

In just over a decade since Glennon wrote, the pendulum has swung from presumptions favoring the custodial parent's freedom to relocate, and some subsequent presumptions that emphasized the non-custodial parent's right to preserve an existing relationship with the child toward decision-making on a case-by-case basis that emphasizes the child's best interests. The law is catching up with a frequently quoted opinion from New York's highest court, which observed: "[l]ike Humpty Dumpty, a family, once broken by divorce, cannot be put back together in precisely the same way." The court held that "each relocation request must be considered on its own merits * * * with predominant emphasis being placed on what outcome is most likely to serve the best interests of the child." *Tropea v. Tropea*, 665 N.E.2d 145, 150–51 (N.Y. 1996).

In many states, the most recent cases and statutory revisions make the best interests of the child test and the facts surrounding each family's circumstances the express touchstone for relocation cases. *Bisbing v. Bisbing*, 166 A.3d 1155, 1167, 1167 n. 4 (N.J. 2017) ("Today, the majority of states, either by statute or case law, impose a best interests test when considering a relocation application filed by a parent with primary custody or custody for the majority of the child's time; some have recently abandoned a presumption in favor "of permitting a primary custodian to relocate") (collecting cases). A minority of states continue to favor allowing a primary custodian to relocate, though they may express that position as a rebuttable presumption. *Id.* (collecting cases and statutes). In some states, best interests analysis only comes into play after the parent opposing relocation convinces the court that there is a good reason to block the proposed move.

In the following opinion, the highest court in Tennessee recounts the state's struggles to articulate the best standard for handling relocation cases, and reassesses the common law interpreting the applicable statute. As you read, consider how and to what extent Tennessee incorporates best interest analysis in relocation cases.

Takeaway: some jurisdictions allow parents with primary custody to relocate with the child unless the other parent shows that the move is vindictive, poses harm to the child, or serves no reasonable purpose.

ARAGON V. ARAGON

Supreme Court of Tennessee, 2017.
513 S.W.3d 447.

OPINION

HOLLY KIRBY, J.

FACTUAL AND PROCEDURAL BACKGROUND

Facts= dad sought to move to AZ for a new job

In this post-divorce litigation, we * * * address the standard for determining what constitutes a "reasonable purpose" for a parent's relocation with the parties' child under Tennessee's parental relocation statute, Tennessee Code Annotated § 36–6–108. In this case, the father spent the majority of the residential parenting time with the parties' child. He sought to move with the child to Arizona because he had secured an advantageous job in an area where he and the child would live near his parents and his extended family and have their support, and where he and the child would live near some of the mother's extended family as well. The trial court held that the father did not have a reasonable purpose for the relocation. In a divided opinion, the Court of Appeals affirmed. The dissent in the Court of Appeals questioned the interpretation of the term "reasonable purpose" used by the majority, which originated in a prior Court of Appeals decision, *Webster v. Webster*, 2006 WL 3008019 (Tenn. Ct. App. Oct. 24, 2006), that construed the term "reasonable purpose" to mean one that is significant or substantial when weighed against the loss to the parent opposing the relocation. We overrule *Webster* insofar as it misconstrued the meaning of the term "reasonable purpose" as used in Tennessee's parental relocation statute. Accordingly, we reverse the trial court and the Court of Appeals and remand the case to the trial court for further proceedings consistent with this Opinion.

Petitioner/Appellee Cassidy Lynne Aragon ("Mother") and Respondent/Appellant Reynaldo Manuel Aragon ("Father") were married in 2006. In June 2007, one child was born of the marriage, daughter A.C.A. ("Daughter"). About a year later, the parties separated. * * * In 2010, the trial court entered the final divorce decree. The parties' divorce decree incorporated an agreed parenting plan that did not designate a primary residential parent. * * * The parenting plan explained: "The parties anticipate that their child-sharing arrangement with the children will fluctuate radically based upon antic[ip]ated future work schedules of wife, the husband's school schedule and travel costs back and forth to have visitation with the children, in conjunction with issues relative to a step-child of this relationship." For this reason, they decided to deviate from the Child Support Guidelines and impose "no direct obligation to exchange support."

After the divorce, Father lived in Clarksville, Tennessee, where he pursued an associate's degree in nursing. Mother maintained a residence in Hermitage, Tennessee, about an hour from Clarksville. However, during the parties' separation and after the divorce, Mother spent significant time working overseas as a contractor in human intelligence/targeting analysis.

Due to Mother's work abroad, it is uncontroverted that, after the divorce, Father spent substantially more residential parenting time with their daughter than did Mother. Father also served as the primary caregiver for Mother's older daughter from a previous relationship; both girls were raised together.

In her contracting work, Mother made between $8,000 and $15,000 per month. She also received $560 per month in child support for her older child from that child's father. At times, Mother sent Father financial support * * *. Mother * * * also claimed that she often also forwarded to Father the child support she received for her older child, because Father was caring for both children. * * *.

Prior to Father's anticipated May 2012 graduation from nursing school, Father sought and was offered a nursing job at the Tucson Medical Center in Tucson, Arizona. In March 2012, Father notified Mother that he intended to relocate to Tucson with their child. * * * The parties could not agree on Father's relocation to Tucson, so * * * Father filed a petition in the trial court asking the trial court to modify the parenting plan and permit Father to relocate to Tucson with Daughter. The petition asserted that the relocation to Tucson was for a reasonable purpose and was in Daughter's best interest. Father claimed * * * that his anticipated employment in Tucson offered him "the opportunity for greater income over his current options in the state of Tennessee." Father [stated he] "has an extensive family support system in the Tucson, Arizona area including his parents and several aunts, uncles and cousins" and that the relocation could "provide many opportunities for the minor child to interact with the Father's family that are otherwise unavailable in Tennessee." * * *

[Mother contested] Father's petition to relocate with their child. She asserted that the relocation would cause hardship for her in exercising her residential parenting with Daughter. She claimed that Father's proposed relocation would serve "no purpose," was not in the child's best interest, and would "separate the child from her extended family [including] her half-sister with whom she has a close sister-like relationship."

Pending trial, the parties entered into an agreed [temporary] order permitting Father to relocate to Arizona with Daughter and establishing a temporary parenting schedule. * * *.

Trial Court Proceedings

* * *

* * * Father said that he wanted to relocate because he believed that the overall life he could provide Daughter in Arizona would be better than

what he could provide her in Clarksville. He sought stability and the opportunity for her to develop relationships with extended family.

Father * * * secured a job as a registered nurse on the neurology floor at Tucson Medical Center, the same hospital where his mother had worked for thirty years. * * * Father emphasized that, while neither he nor Mother have family in the Clarksville area, both of them have family in and around Tucson. Relocating to Arizona would allow him to "foster those relationships" and provide a support network for him and the parties' child.

Father * * * claimed that Mother "would bounce back and forth between several contracts, either quitting them, doing layoffs, or being fired from them." * * *

* * * Most of the time while he was in nursing school, Father spent his time studying and caring for the children and did not work outside the home. While he attended nursing school, Father relied on a combination of Mother's financial support, student loans, and credit cards for income.

Mother testified [that d]uring the marriage, after both Mother and Father spent several months unemployed, she secured a job in Iraq, with the goal of earning enough money for her and Father to both get further schooling. After their divorce, * * * Mother claimed they agreed that, if Father enrolled in and completed nursing school, "he'd be able to go anywhere and work anywhere . . . and [Mother] could pursue [her] degree as well." * * *. Mother said it was her understanding that, once Father graduated from nursing school, both parties would live in middle Tennessee and equally share residential parenting time; she claimed that Father "said that would be the best situation because it's close to me, the girls could be in a great * * * school system, I already have a house there, and we could just do the 50/50."

While working outside of the United States, Mother obtained her bachelor's degree in eighteen months. * * *. Mother felt at the time that the "sacrifice" of her being abroad while Father took care of the children and went to school would be "worth it, because both of us would be educated," able to "support ourselves and [the] children and split them 50/50." * * *

At the time of trial, Mother was "confident" that she would be offered a job as a research analyst in a criminal justice position in Nashville, but she did not yet actually have a job. She had received several job offers in Washington, D.C., but had not yet made a decision. Mother was considering attending Belmont University College of Law in Nashville, relocating to New Hampshire to attend the University of New Hampshire, or relocating to Fayetteville, North Carolina, to be closer to her older daughter's father. Mother noted that her then-boyfriend was scheduled to be stationed in Fayetteville.

* * *

[Both paternal grandparents testified that they] would be available for some childcare for Daughter, including staying at Father's home overnight while Father was working. * * *.

* * *

[T]he trial court issued a temporary order [which] held that Father's proposed relocation was not reasonable. It designat[ed] Mother as the primary residential parent, with alternate residential parenting time for Father during the summer and extended school holidays.

On January 7, 2013, the trial court issued a[n] opinion * * * that there was "no proof" that Father had better career opportunities in Tucson than in Tennessee because Father had not pursued nursing jobs in Tennessee. It specifically credited Mother's testimony that she gave up her equal residential parenting to work abroad with the understanding that Father would get his nursing education and eventually obtain nursing employment in middle Tennessee. After getting the benefit of this agreement, the trial court found, Father decided to move to Tucson with the parties' daughter. The trial court conceded that Father "posits a rational basis for his move," but it nevertheless held that the proposed relocation was "not reasonable under all the circumstances."

[In August, the court modified the parenting plan. The order designated the mother as the primary custodian, giving the mother 285 days and the father 80 days of parenting time.] Father appealed.

Appellate Proceedings

[This was the second appeal. In the first, the court remanded the case for further proceedings because the trial court had not considered the child's best interests, as required by the applicable statute, after concluding that the father's proposed move served no "reasonable purpose." On remand, the trial court "took no additional proof," reiterated its earlier holding that the move served no reasonable purpose and held that the child's best interest favored awarding primary residential custody to the Mother. That order is the subject of this appeal].

In [this] appeal, Father again argued that the trial court erred in holding that his requested relocation did not have a reasonable purpose and in holding that it was in Daughter's best interest to designate Mother as the primary residential parent. In a split opinion, the majority of the Court of Appeals affirmed.

* * *

[T]he majority stated: "[T]he 'reasonable purpose' of relocating must be 'substantial when weighed against the gravity of the loss of the non-custodial parent's ability to participate fully in their children's lives . . . .' (quoting [a case] quoting *Webster v. Webster*, 2006 WL 3008019, at *14

(Tenn. Ct. App. 2006)). Under this standard, the majority concluded that the evidence did not preponderate against the trial court's holding on reasonable purpose. It affirmed the trial court's holding on best interest, [denial of] permission for Father to relocate with Daughter and designat[ation] of Mother as the primary residential parent.

The dissent * * * viewed the description of "reasonable purpose" recited by the majority as incongruent with the natural and ordinary meaning of the term "reasonable purpose" as used in the Parental Relocation Statute. *Id.* at *9 (McBrayer, J., dissenting). * * *

Father sought permission to appeal to this Court, which we granted.

ANALYSIS

"One of the most common post-divorce flashpoints occurs when the primary residential parent decides to move with her child or children to another city or state." [With one limited exception], this Court has not addressed Tennessee's Parental Relocation Statute, Tennessee Code Annotated section 36–6–108, since its enactment. We do so now.

Overview

For many years prior to the enactment of the Parental Relocation Statute, under Tennessee caselaw, custodial parents had virtually unfettered authority to move their children away from non-custodial parents, regardless of reason. As time went on, the value of having both parents involved in child-rearing became more broadly recognized. Tennessee courts began to hold that a non-custodial parent could prevent relocation of his child under some circumstances, provided the non-custodial parent could prove that the move was not in the best interest of the child. However, because there was no statute governing the issue, trial court decisions varied widely.

* * *

Not surprisingly, [the absence of statutory guidance cases listing factors for the lower courts to consider] only spawned further uncertainty. [T]he Court took up the issue again in *Aaby v. Strange*, 924 S.W.2d 623, 629 (Tenn. 1996), *clarified on reh'g* (June 24, 1996), the decision that provided the framework for the current statute. * * *

* * *

After reviewing the caselaw on relocation, the *Aaby* Court reaffirmed the goals * * * were to "(1) limit[ ] judicial intervention in post-divorce family decision-making, and (2) mak[e] disputes easier of resolution if they must be litigated." The Court observed that "the interests of the custodial parent and the interests of the child are basically interrelated, even if they are not always precisely the same." It then overruled prior caselaw and adopted a standard that made it quite difficult for a noncustodial parent to defeat the custodial parent's petition to relocate with the parties' child: the petition would be denied only if the non-custodial parent could prove that the custodial parent's motives were vindictive or that the move posed a specific, serious threat of harm to the child. Finding no such proof, the *Aaby* Court held in favor of the mother, permitting relocation.

* * *

In 1998, * * * Tennessee's legislature considered competing approaches to parental relocation and ultimately adopted * * * the Parental Relocation Statute at issue in this case.

The Parental Relocation Statute sets out a comprehensive framework for disputes involving the relocation of a primary residential parent [beginning with a requirement that a parent who wishes to relocate with a child or children provide notice to the other parent].

Regardless of the proportion of residential parenting time the non-relocating parent spends with the subject child, if he opposes the proposed relocation with the child, he [has thirty days to] file "a petition in opposition to removal of the child" If the parents "are actually spending substantially equal intervals of time with the child," then there is "[n]o presumption in favor of or against the request to relocate with the child." The court then determines whether to permit the requested relocation "based upon the best interests of the child." *"best interests of the child" for relocation standard*

* * *

[W]here the parents are not spending substantially equal periods of time with their child, [the statute provides that] the parent seeking to relocate must notify the other parent of the intent to relocate and state his or her reasons for the proposed relocation. The burden then falls to the parent opposing the move to file a petition and prove one of the [three] enumerated grounds [for blocking the move: "the parent's motive for relocating with the child is vindictive[;] the relocation poses a threat of specific and serious harm to the child[; or * * * the proposed relocation 'does not have a reasonable purpose."] If this burden of proof is carried, the trial court may consider the best interest of the child and decide whether to permit the relocation. If this burden of proof is not carried, the trial court is obliged to grant permission for the relocation.

※ opposing parent must prove 1 of there 3 things

* * * In this case, even though the parenting plan awarded the parties equal residential parenting time with their child, the trial court found that Father spent substantially more residential parenting time with Daughter, and Mother has not appealed this finding. Consequently, it is uncontroverted that that the statutory provisions applicable to this appeal are those that govern parental relocation petitions where the parties do not spend equal intervals of time with the subject child.

※ dad spends way more time with the child than MOM

Application of Statute

We now consider how the trial court's analysis squares with the analytical framework set forth in the Parental Relocation Statute.

[T]he trial court * * * denied Father permission to relocate on the ground that his proposed relocation was not for a reasonable purpose. [It] credited Mother's testimony that she had sacrificed her parenting time with her daughters in order to secure work to support the family and allow both parents, first Father and then Mother, to further their education. It credited Mother's testimony that the parties had an understanding that, once Father completed his nursing education, they would both settle in middle Tennessee and essentially split their parenting time equally. * * *.

* * *

* * * Having found that Father's proposed relocation was not for a reasonable purpose, the trial court went on to consider the child's best interest and ultimately designated Mother as the primary residential parent.

We consider first whether the trial court's analysis comports with the allocation of the burden of proof set forth in the Parental Relocation Statute. * * *

As discussed above, where the parents are not spending substantially equal time with their child, [the Statute] includes a legislatively mandated presumption in favor of permitting the parent spending the most residential parenting time with the child to relocate with the child. *See* Tenn. Code Ann. § 36–6–108(d) (providing that the relocating parent "shall" be permitted to do so unless the court finds one of the enumerated grounds [for denying permission]). The petitioner—the parent opposing relocation—bears the burden of proving grounds for denying permission to relocate. This allocation of the burden of proof has been recognized repeatedly by our Court of Appeals.

[I]n support of its holding that the proposed move had no reasonable purpose, the trial court commented that there was "no proof in this case that Mr. Aragon has better job opportunities, greater salary opportunities or career advancement opportunities in the Tucson area" and "no proof whatsoever with regard to Mr. Aragon's comparable job opportunities in the Middle Tennessee or Southern Kentucky area because he has not . . . pursued such opportunities." These comments appear to place the burden of proof on Father to show a reasonable purpose for the move, rather than placing the burden of proof where the statute requires, on Mother as the parent opposing the relocation.

* * * Father argues next that the trial court ascribed an overly expansive meaning to the term "reasonable purpose" as used in [the statute].

[T]he passage quoted by the majority on the Court of Appeals below and criticized by the dissent, [relied on] *Webster v. Webster*, 2006 WL 3008019, at *14 (Tenn. Ct. App. Oct. 24, 2006). In *Webster*, the Court of Appeals reviewed the development of Tennessee's Parental Relocation Statute [and] explained that section 36–6–108 carries a strong presumption in favor of the relocating parent, mandating a grant of permission to relocate unless the parent opposing relocation proves at least one of the three enumerated grounds.

The *Webster* court interpreted the phrase "reasonable purpose" in light of the fact that the legislature drew from both the *Aaby* majority and the *Aaby* dissent in fashioning the statute:

> [The *Aaby* dissent] emphasized the seriousness of the loss, to the child as well as the non-custodial parent, of the opportunity for the non-custodial parent to participate in the child's activities, such as soccer games and recitals, even if the activities do not fall within the non-custodial parent's designated "parenting time" [;] advocated requiring the parent who proposes to relocate to establish "some reason" for the move[; and urged] an approach that would "not destroy the efforts" of non-custodial parents "to participate more fully in their children's lives. . . ."

* * *

Interpreting the statutory term "reasonable purpose" against this background, *Webster* concluded * * *: "In context, it is clear that the 'reasonable purpose' of the proposed relocation must be a significant purpose, substantial when weighed against the gravity of the loss of the non-custodial parent's ability 'to participate fully in their children's lives in a more meaningful way.' " *Id.* at *14 (quoting *Aaby*, 924 S.W.2d at 631 (White, J., dissenting)).

* * *

Because the term "reasonable purpose" is not defined in the Parental Relocation Statute and its meaning is not necessarily plain, we consider the legislative history.

* * *

[L]egislative discussion of the relocation bill indicated that the intent was to ensure that children would have "the security of being with that parent that the judge thought or the parties thought was the right parent to have the child most of the time." The legislators acknowledged how hotly disputed relocation cases are and emphasized the need to reduce litigation; otherwise, one legislator commented, "Lawyers are going to win; kids are going to lose." He added: "[I]f the child has been with one parent, and there's nothing but the move going on, and there's a reasonable reason for the move, then we think that parent ought to be able to move." * * *

* * *

[T]he *Webster* court's view of the term "reasonable purpose" encourages trial courts to consider evidence that has little to do with the proposed purpose of the move and more to do with the perceived overall fairness of the primary residential parent's decision to relocate or whether the move is in the child's best interest. * * * The rigid structure of section 36–6–108—in which best interest is reached *only* if and when the parent opposing the move proves one of the grounds—suggests that the "reasonable purpose" ground is not intended to be a guise under which the trial court may determine whether the parent's decision to relocate is wise or fair or in the child's best interest.

Accordingly, we overrule *Webster v. Webster* insofar as it interpreted the term "reasonable purpose" * * * to mean "a significant purpose, substantial when weighed against the gravity of the loss of the noncustodial parent's ability to participate fully in their children's lives in a more meaningful way." The term "reasonable purpose" should be given its ordinary meaning.

* * * Mother put on virtually no evidence showing that Father's purpose for the proposed relocation was not a reasonable one. Under the natural and ordinary meaning of the term "reasonable purpose" * * *, we must conclude that Father stated a reasonable purpose for relocating to Arizona with Daughter and Mother did not carry her burden of establishing a ground for denying Father permission to relocate. On this basis, we reverse the holding of the trial court and the Court of Appeals that Father had no reasonable purpose for the proposed relocation.

* * *

CONCLUSION

* * * Under the natural and ordinary meaning of the term "reasonable purpose" * * *, we hold that Father stated a reasonable purpose for relocating to Arizona with the parties' child and Mother did not carry her burden of establishing a ground for denying Father permission to relocate with the child. [W]e reverse the holding of the trial court and the Court of Appeals that Father had no reasonable purpose for the proposed relocation. * * * On remand, the trial court is authorized to fashion an appropriate transitional parenting plan that results, within a reasonable time, in designating Father as primary residential parent and permitting him to live in Arizona with Daughter.

NOTES AND QUESTIONS

1.   *Different standards for shared and primary residential custody.* The mother in *Aragon* conceded that the parties had not shared parenting of their daughter despite an agreement according them shared parenting; the father testified that he had the children 80% of the time. Therefore, *Aragon* was treated as a case involving a primary residential custodian—the father—who the lower courts nonetheless denied the right to relocate with his child.

Like many states, Tennessee uses a different analysis in considering petitions involving relocation where parents share custody from the one they use when one parent has been designated the primary residential custodian. What are the distinctions in Tennessee, and what impact are those distinctions likely to have on the outcome in any given case?

While there are sound social policy reasons for distinguishing shared custody arrangements when it comes to relocation requests, risks and complexities also arise when legal regimes distinguish between relocation cases based on whether one parent has been designated the primary residential custodian. First, as you saw in Chapter 12, there are multiple definitions of shared parenting. What does the statute or common law mean to include when formulating standards to govern relocation cases? Second, when the distinction imposes different policy preferences or presumptions, "tethering the relocation standard to one party's status as the parent of primary residence * * * may generate unnecessary disputes regarding that designation," resulting in additional litigation. *Bishbing*, 166 A.3d at 1169 (reversing earlier case law distinguishing between cases involving shared custody and a primary residential parent, and holding that best interests governs both sets of relocation cases). Another risk is that parents negotiating parenting agreements and custody arrangements may insist on a shared parenting designation they don't really desire, with a view toward the risk that the other parent may seek to relocate at a later date. Courts may respond by looking at how the parents actually shared responsibilities. *See Cooper v. Kalkwarf*, 532 S.W.3d 58, 67 (Ark. 2017) (announcing that standards applicable to a parent with primary residential custody—favoring that parent's right to move—will only be applied in relocation cases when "the parent seeking to relocate is not just labelled the "primary" custodian in the divorce decree *but also spends significantly more time with the child* than the other parent.").

2.   *Best interests in relocation cases.* If the court does undertake a best interest analysis in a relocation case involving a primary residential parent the contemporary view no longer allows it to conclude, as the *Aaby* court did 1996, that "the interests of the custodial parent and the interests of the child are basically interrelated, even if they are not always precisely the same." If the *Aragon* court had concluded that the parents shared custody, the court's decision about whether the father could relocate with the daughter would have rested entirely on a best interest analysis. How do you think the father's relocation request would fare under a best interest analysis?

3. *Substantial change in circumstances.* One could argue that any time a custodial parent moves a long distance from another parent who is engaged with the child or children, that constitutes a substantial change in circumstances that could affect a child's best interests. However, in 2012, the highest court in Wyoming held that while a custodial parent's decision to relocate did not always constitute a significant change of circumstances warranting consideration of a petition to modify custody, relocation could satisfy that threshold requirement in particular cases depending on the facts. *Arnott v. Arnott,* 293 P.3d 440 (Wyo. 2012).

Why have states developed a separate legal regime for so-called move-away cases? First, as the discussion of the legislative history in Tennessee suggests, to avoid congestion in the courts. Where states require notice to the noncustodial parent, courts do not normally need to get involved unless the noncustodial parent objects to the move. Second, to impose legislative or judicially-crafted preferences in such cases, designed to promote more uniform treatment of proposed moves. Such preferences can be designed to favor the decisions made by parents who have primary custody, can instead favor preserving the relationship between a non-custodial parent and the child, or can be neutral. Third, as shared parenting became more widespread, states recognized that allowing one of the parents to move 100 miles or more would undermine the shared parenting arrangement, and might call for a different analysis or set of priorities.

Would the outcome in *Aragon* likely have been different from the ultimate outcome if the state's highest court ruled under the traditional approach to modification of custody orders?

4. *The constitutional right to interstate travel.* A number of appellate courts have considered—and rejected—claims by parents who hold primary residential custody that denying them the right to move infringes their constitutional right to travel. Courts have uniformly pointed out that the parent remains free to move to another state, to be treated appropriately by that state, and even to become a citizen of that state. An adverse decision by a family court merely means that the custodial parent cannot take a child or children along: the parent gets to choose whether to move or to maintain residential custody. *Bisbing v. Bisbing,* 166 A.3d 1155, 1170–71(N.J. 2017); *In re Marriage of Ciesluk* 113 P.3d 135, 143 (Colo. 2005); *Baxendale v. Raich,* 878 N.E.2d 1252, 1259 (Ind. 2008) ("the child's interests are powerful countervailing considerations that cannot be swept aside as irrelevant * * *. In addition, * * * the nonrelocating parent's interest in parenting is itself of constitutional dimension."); *Light v. D'Amato,* 105 A.3d 447 (Me. 2014) (an order providing that custody would revert to the father if the mother moved to Italy as she planned did not violate mother's right to travel).

5. *Continuing advantage for primary custodian and burdens of proof.* Some states continue to favor allowing the parent who spends the most time with the child to relocate, at least where the relocation minimally intrudes on the other parent's parenting time, but also impose a best interests analysis.

For example, in 2018, Wisconsin revised its relocation statute to provide that where a proposed relocation "only minimally changes or affects the current * * * schedule," the court "shall" approve a proposed relocation. Wis. Stat. Ann. § 767.481(4)(West, Westlaw through 2017–2018 Biennial Sess.). If, however, the relocation will significantly affect the parenting schedule, and both parents have exercised their "physical placement" time, "the court shall decide all contested relocation motions * * * for modification of legal custody or physical placement in the best interest of the child" by applying the factors set out in the statute that governs child custody decisions generally. *Id.* Florida's statute provides that if one parent objects to relocation, the custodial parent who wishes to relocate bears the initial burden "to prove by a preponderance of the evidence that relocation is in the best interest of the child." If that burden is met, "the burden shifts to the nonrelocating parent * * * to show by a preponderance of the evidence that the proposed relocation is not in the best interest of the child." Fla. Stat. Ann. § 61.13001(8) (West Supp. 2019) (listing factors the court must consider in determining whether to allow relocation by the primary residential parent). What does the Tennessee regime require, and how did the trial court run afoul of it in *Aragon*?

6.   *The Aragons.* The mother in *Aragon* was not at all certain where she planned to live after the litigation ended. Should the court have been concerned about her proposed moves and comparative residential instability? Do you think the outcome below might have been different if the parents' genders were reversed? Did the trial court err in considering the agreement the mother testified the parents had made about what would happen when she returned home: that it would be her turn to get her career off the ground and then they would share custody in Tennessee? Would that agreement have been an appropriate consideration in a dispute over how to divide property or whether maintenance was warranted? Is there an analytical distinction?

Note that the father had already accepted and started his job in Arizona when the temporary order issued. He was free to relocate—just not to bring his child. It was arguably too late for him to "choose" between his job and his child, which is how the courts generally formulate the dilemma when they deny a custodial parent permission to move. Note too that the two girls—step-siblings who had been raised together by the father—would be separated if the father kept custody of his biological child. How important do you think that might have been to the trial court's decision? Should it play a role in the best interests determination? Should the father have petitioned for custody of his step-daughter and, if so, what could he have argued?

7.   *Bad faith.* The ALI, statutes and common law standards refer to moves undertaken in good faith. If a court suspects that the move is motivated wholly or partly by desire to frustrate the other parents' access to the child, the court will normally refuse to allow the move, either by barring the move, or by modifying custody if the current custodian moves. *See, e.g.*, La. Rev. Stat. Ann. § 9:355.14(A)(5) (2018) (courts must consider the relocating parent's efforts to "promote or thwart the relationship" between the child and the other parent). In *Galarza v. Galarza*, 231 P.3d 694 (Okla. Civ. App. 2009), the court affirmed

an order terminating joint legal custody, transferring residential custody to the father and awarding him sole legal custody. The trial court had found that the mother, who sought to relocate, knew before the initial decree that her future husband had accepted a job in another state but failed to disclose this fact when negotiating the custody agreement which the court subsequently approved. Denying the mother permission to relocate, the appellate judge opined, "if this is not bad faith, I don't know what is." *Id.* at 697.

8.   *Should the noncustodial parent have unrestricted freedom to relocate?* Any limitations on mobility apply only to custodial parents. What argument could be made that it is in the child's best interest for a parent with visitation rights to remain nearby? Would a policy that required parents to remain near each other during a child's minority have an impact on the diminution of many relationships between children and noncustodial parents? Professor Merle H. Weiner argues that proposed relocation by noncustodial parents should be subject to trial court review, as it currently is in only a handful of jurisdictions. Merle H. Weiner, *Inertia and Inequality: Reconceptualizing Disputes Over Parental Relocation*, 40 U.C. Davis L. Rev. 1747 (2007). If either parent relocates far away, who should bear the increased costs of visitation, such as airfare?

Just as courts have uniformly rejected constitutional claims by primary residential parents based on the right to travel, they have rejected equal protection claims by primary custodians. *Fredman v. Fredman* 960 So.2d 52, 60 (Fla. Dist. Ct. App. 2007) (custodial and noncustodial parents are not similarly situated because when a noncustodial parent moves his or her choice does not affect the other parent's relationship with the child or children).

9.   *Are settlement agreements restricting relocation enforceable?* As part of their divorce, the parties in *Helton v. Helton*, 2004 WL 63478 (Tenn. Ct. App. Jan. 13, 2004), executed a marital dissolution agreement that contained the wife's promise "not to move the child from Davidson or adjoining counties without husband's written permission." According to the agreement, the wife also acknowledged that "it [was] in the manifest best interest of [the child] that he remain and be raised in Metro-Davidson County or contiguous counties near his father." *Id.* The mother later remarried, and her new husband accepted a job offer in Mississippi. The mother informed the father that she intended to relocate to Mississippi with the child to join her husband. Citing the marital dissolution agreement, the father moved to prevent relocation of the child. The court held that the father was not entitled to enforce the marital dissolution agreement:

> A provision in a divorce decree for the care, custody and control of minor children 'shall remain within the control of the court and be subject to such changes or modifications as the exigencies of the case may require.' Tenn. Code Ann. § 36–6–101(a). Our courts have accordingly held that when a marital dissolution agreement with regard to custody is incorporated into a final decree, it is considered to have merged into that decree. Such agreements thereby lose their

contractual nature and remain subject to the court's continuing jurisdiction, so that they may be modified as circumstances change. The parties cannot bargain away the court's continuing jurisdiction over the care of the child and cannot irrevocably agree to the best interests of the child without regard to future developments or changes of circumstances.

Id. at *5.

In contrast, an appellate court in Connecticut held that it was not an abuse of discretion for the trial court to consider the parties' agreement (incorporated in the divorce decree) that the mother who had primary residential custody would not move more than "32.5 driving miles" away from the marital home when the mother filed her second post-judgment motion for permission to relocate to Boston where her new husband worked. The father received the marital home as part of the divorce and remained in it to provide stability for the couple's son during weekend visits. The trial court "accurately pointed out that [mother and the man she married shortly after divorcing] married with the knowledge that these restrictions were in place." The trial court held that the mother had not proven a legitimate reason for relocation, and that the move was not in the child's best interests. *Regan v. Regan*, 68 A.3d 172, 179 (Conn. App. Ct. 2013).

In 2017, New Jersey's highest court held that where a settlement agreement incorporated into a judicial decree restricted the primary residential parent's discretion to move with the child to another state over the other parent's objection, the noncustodial father bore the burden of showing changed circumstances in his motion to block the mother's move with the children to facilitate her new husband's medical career. *Brisbing*, 166 A.3d 1155, 1171–72 (the importance of the existing frequent and meaningful interaction with both parents should form part of the best interests analysis on remand; the father was "extensively involved" in his children's lives, even caring for them before school several mornings a week in the mother's home after she left for work). In *Brisbing*, the courts rejected the father's challenge to the settlement agreement based on what he called the mother's "bad faith" during negotiations in failing to disclose the seriousness of her relationship with the man who would become her next husband. *Id.* at 1158–59. Implicit in the father's argument was the idea that had he known, he would have insisted on shared residential custody, placing his legal rights on firmer ground under the then-applicable law in the event that the mother sought to relocate. *Id.*

10. *Court-imposed restrictions on relocation at the time of the initial custody decree.* In *Spahmer v. Gullette*, 113 P.3d 158 (Colo. 2005), the court held that the trial court abused its discretion when it ordered the single mother of an 11-month-old girl, Jordan, to remain in the home state of the child's father as part of the initial allocation of parental rights. *Id.* at 159–60. The parties' relationship lasted 13 months, ending just after Jordan was born. Shortly after their breakup, the father consented to the mother's plan to spend Christmas with Jordan and the mother's family in Arizona. He subsequently

became concerned that the mother was planning to remove Jordan from Colorado permanently, and filed an action to allocate parental rights and responsibilities. Because the trial court's temporary orders provided that the mother must obtain the permission of either the father or the court to remove Jordan from Colorado, the mother moved for permission to relocate permanently with Jordan to Arizona. In its subsequent orders allocating parental responsibilities, the trial court ordered the mother to remain in the Denver-Boulder metropolitan area because "Jordan was born here and has spent the entire eleven months of her life to date here. Jordan is to remain a Colorado girl." *Id.* at 160.

Finding on appeal that the trial court had abused its discretion, the state Supreme Court concluded: "in an initial determination to allocate parental responsibilities, a court has no statutory authority to order a parent to live in a specific location. Rather, the court must accept the location in which each party intends to live, and allocate parental responsibilities accordingly in the best interests of the child." *Id.* at 161.

D. INTERNATIONAL RELOCATION

International relocation of children is increasingly common. It presents unique jurisdictional and enforcement problems for child custody orders. *In re Marriage of Condon*, 73 Cal.Rptr. 2d 33, 46 (Ct. App. 1998), remains the best summary of the special problems posed by international relocation cases:

> First, the cultural problem. In some cases, to move a child from this country to another is to subject him or her to cultural conditions and practices far different from those experienced by American citizens or to deprive the child of important protections and advantages not available in the other country. To pose an extreme example, who could dispute a proposed relocation of a female child to a country practicing genital mutilation represents a "changed condition" requiring an inquiry whether this move is in the "best interests" of that child? Similarly, how about a move to a country where females were not offered the opportunity for higher education or the freedom to pursue careers? Or a move of any preteen or teenager to a country where the language is one unfamiliar to that child. Or, consider a proposed relocation of any child to a nation governed by a dictator or any nation which denies its citizens the freedoms and rights guaranteed in the United States and other democracies.

> Second, the distance problem. Except for Mexico or Canada, foreign relocation cases in this state inevitably involve a move to a different continent—typically 8,000 miles or further and 8 or more time zones away from California. With those great distances come problems of expense, jet lag, and the like. For a person of

average income or below, an order relocating his or her child to a faraway foreign country is ordinarily tantamount to an order terminating that parent's custody and visitation rights.

Third, and most difficult, is the jurisdictional problem. California court orders governing child custody lack any enforceability in many foreign jurisdictions and lack guaranteed enforceability even in those which subscribe to the Hague Convention on the Civil Aspects of International Child Abduction [the "Hague convention"].[b] Thus, the California courts cannot guarantee any custody and visitation arrangements they order for the non-moving parent will be honored.

* * *

Id. at 42.

The court proceeded to explain these three problems in practical terms:

[E]xcept for those of considerable means, any relocation to another continent is likely to represent a *de facto* termination of the non-moving parent's rights to visitation and the child's rights to maintain a relationship with that parent. Thus, when a relocation would have this practical effect, before allowing the move-away a trial court should require the moving parent to satisfy the burden of showing the termination of those rights would be in the best interests of the child. If the moving parent cannot satisfy this burden, perhaps he or she could tender an arrangement where the moving parent finances the other parent's visitation or the child spends alternate years in the two countries, or some other plan which accommodates the valuable relationship between the non-moving parent and the child.

Finally, before permitting any relocation which purports to maintain custody and visitation rights in the non-moving parent, the trial court should take steps to insure its orders to that effect will remain enforceable throughout the minority of the affected children. Unless the law of the country where the children are to move guarantees enforceability of custody and visitation orders issued by American courts, and there may be no such country, the court will be required to use its ingenuity to ensure the moving parent adheres to its orders and does not seek to invalidate or modify them in a foreign court.

---

[b] *Editors' Note:* The Hague Convention, discussed later in this Chapter, provides that signatory nations will return children who were "wrongfully removed" from the country where they live with a parent who has residential custody will be returned to the country which is the child's habitual residence with the custodial parent.

Id. at 43.

Condon upheld the trial court's discretion to permit the mother to relocate with her two sons to Australia, with the father having physical custody of the children in California for 12 weeks each year during school vacation, and in Australia for up to 15 days per month. The court of appeal ordered the trial court to amend its order permitting relocation to include the mother's stipulation to the continuing jurisdiction of the California courts and appropriate sanctions to enforce that stipulation.

NOTES AND QUESTIONS

1. *Good faith and the best interests of the child in international relocation.* As we explained earlier in this chapter, U.S. citizens have the right to migrate, resettle, find a new job and start a new life. But just as with relocation within the United States, when one parent wishes to relocate abroad, the relocating parent must prove the move is being made in good faith or absence of malice by showing that "the move with the child is for a sensible reason and is not a scheme devised simply to frustrate the other parent's right to maintain contact with the child." The Honorable Connie Peterson, *Relocation of Children by the Custodial Parent*, 65 Am. Jur. Trials 127, § 47 (database updated 2018). The most common good faith reasons for international relocation overlap with those given for domestic moves: employment or educational opportunities for the custodial parent or the custodial parent's new spouse. *Id.*

And, as with relocation within the U.S., parents who wish to take their children with them to a new location are expected to seek the court's permission if the other parent does not consent. In *J.M. v. G.H.*, 175 Cal. Rptr. 3d 371 (Ct. App. 2014), the court allowed the mother to relocate from the U.S. to her native Israel with her son, Joey, even though the father contested the move. Despite the mother's past dishonesty, sense of ownership over her child, smoking, and driving on a suspended license, the court found that Joey had not been affected the mother's bad actions and was bright, well-adjusted and happy. The court found the mother was not moving to Israel in bad faith: her job prospects were better in Israel, her visa in the U.S. was expiring, and she would no longer be dependent on the father in Israel. *Id.* at 374. Further, although Joey was bonded to both parents, "his connection to [his mother] was stronger," he was familiar with Israel, spoke the language, and had family there, so moving with his mother to Israel would be less detrimental to him than giving his father primary custody. *Id.* at 376. Additionally, the father could afford trips to Israel to visit his son or to bring his son to the United States. *Id.* at 376.

Conversely, a Connecticut appellate court found a mother's motion to relocate to France with her 12-year-old son was not for a legitimate purpose because she could not legally work in France. *Tow v. Tow*, 64 A.3d 128, 132–33 (Conn. Ct. App. 2013). The mother, who wanted to marry a man who lived in France, claimed the move was "an incredible cultural opportunity" because of a speed-skating coach for the son. However, the court found that Connecticut offered speed skating opportunities, and moving would irreparably harm the child by diminishing his contact with his father. *Id.* at 133.

2.   *Income and social class inequities? Condon* acknowledges the financial burden of maintaining contact between a noncustodial parent and a child who lives on another continent, and observes that allowing the move of the custodial parent and child might be the equivalent of terminating one parent's rights. An alternative to that outcome would be for the court to deny permission to move, as the Supreme Court of Rhode Island did in 2018. A custodial mother, an Australian citizen, wanted to return home with her four children. She was receiving food stamps, got by with help from friends and church members, and her home was in foreclosure. In Australia, she would be entitled to a virtually-free college education, already had a good job offer and could live rent free with her family; because she was not a U.S. citizen she did not even qualify for educational loans in Rhode Island where she was unemployed. Noting the expense of sending the children to see their fisherman father several times a year as the mother proposed, the state's highest court agreed with the trial judge that neither parent could afford the plane fare, and the parents "utter loathing" for each other threatened to undermine compliance with the plan. *Ainsworth v. Ainsworth*, 186 A.3d 1074 (R.I. 2018). It appears from the decision that the mother would have no choice but to remain in Rhode Island.

4.   PARENTS WHO KIDNAP THEIR OWN CHILDREN

When high conflict over custody and visitation persists, some parents take matters into their own hands by absconding with the children.

A.   HOW WIDESPREAD A PROBLEM IS KIDNAPPING OF CHILDREN BY THEIR PARENTS?

Precise figures are unavailable because data are not uniformly collected throughout the United States. The most recent estimates (which are unfortunately more than a decade old) indicate that the highest proportion of missing children are runaways; the next largest group missing for more than a few hours are children abducted by parents or relatives, usually in the context of a custody dispute. J. Robert Flores, U.S. Dep't of Justice, NCJ 196465, National Estimates of Missing Children: An Overview 6 (2002). Where the risk of abduction is apparent, supervised visitation and travel restrictions are warranted. *Katare v. Katare,* 283 P.3d 546 (Wash. 2012). You will learn about federal laws aimed at parental abductions in Chapter 17.

Abduction of children by their parents is illegal in every U.S. jurisdiction, even where statutes are silent about whether kidnapping laws apply to parents. Only the peculiarities of the language in the state statue account for the outcome in the case described below.

B. CASE NOTE: *STATE OF NEW JERSEY V. FROLAND*

The scheme with which the state charged the defendants in *State v. Froland*, 874 A.2d 568 (N.J. Super. Ct. App. Div. 2005), *aff'd in part, rev'd in part*, 936 A.2d 947 (N.J. 2008), was elaborate. John Kindt and his former wife shared legal custody of their two children, ages nine and ten. Pursuant to the parenting agreement, the mother dropped the children off at their father's house on December 27, 2000, with an understanding that he would return them to her two days later. Due to a snowstorm, they agreed to delay the children's return until December 30. When the mother called the father's home on December 29, she discovered the phone had been disconnected and, checking up, found his house deserted. She filed a missing persons report with the police.

When the police searched the father's home they discovered three computers with their hard drives stripped and correspondence with boat sales establishments in New Jersey and South Carolina. Further investigation revealed that the father and stepmother, Stacey Froland Kindt, using an alias, had purchased a boat. The Kindts also obtained copies of the birth certificates and medical records for three children (the father's two children and the stepmother's 19-year-old nephew who lived with them), and obtained passports for all five stating that they intended to visit New Zealand. The father and stepmother also wrote to their respective parents, explaining that they were taking the children and "intended to flee to a jurisdiction friendly to their position—that Kindt, as the children's father, should have more say in their upbringing." The stepmother withdrew over $50,000 from a bank account.

On December 29, Kindt and his wife abandoned the family minivan at Newark airport to throw the police off-track. The family then took a train from New Jersey to North Carolina where Kindt cancelled the boat contract in New Jersey and purchased a boat in North Carolina using a pseudonym. On January 20, 2001, the group set sail from North Carolina. As luck would have it, the Coast Guard picked them up when their boat became disabled. The police arrested Kindt, Froland, and her teenage nephew who had been helping them.

A police search of the boat uncovered a to-do list for the abduction, a global positioning system, charts for North Carolina, Florida and the Bahamas, and books including "Hide Your Assets and Disappear" and "How to be Invisible." A letter from the stepmother to her mother set up a "safe" messaging system and explained, "[we] believe very strongly (and the Bible supports us) that the father is the head of the household. He is held personally accountable to God for how his children turn out and is therefore responsible for all instruction, reproof, guidance, and discipline."

The state charged Kindt, Froland, and Froland's nephew with various counts of kidnapping, interference with custody, conspiracy, and contempt of court. At trial, Kindt argued that he could not be convicted of kidnapping his own children. Following an interlocutory appeal, the jury convicted him of all counts except kidnapping. He was sentenced to seven years in custody, and confined to a halfway house pending appeal. Froland was found guilty of first degree kidnapping as well as several other charges. She served sixteen months of a seven-year sentence while her appeal was pending. On appeal she argued that the plain language of the New Jersey statute indicated that a parent cannot be found guilty of kidnapping his own children, and that "she in turn cannot be guilty of kidnapping because she acted with a parent's permission." The Supreme Court of New Jersey agreed.

The New Jersey kidnapping statute provides that the removal of a minor without the consent of a parent, or with the use of "force, threat or deception" is unlawful. The state did not present evidence that Kindt and Froland used "force, threat or deception," although it could have, and probably should have, done so. This left the question of parental consent. The court reasoned that if the legislature had intended to limit the term "parent" to parents with sole custody in the context of the kidnapping statute, it should have done so expressly. Applying the rule of lenity to the criminal kidnapping statute, the court nonetheless found that Froland was not "immune from punishment" as her "behavior falls squarely within the strictures of the interference with custody statute."

The New Jersey Supreme Court chastised the Appellate Division for treating "kidnapping and interference with custody as overlapping criminal provisions" when "in fact, the statutes were * * * designed to address entirely distinct conduct." The court found that New Jersey intended to follow the approach set out in the ALI's Model Penal Code, which sought to limit kidnapping charges against parents to situations involving "force, threat or deception." The drafters expressly "posited the irrelevancy of custody arrangements" since the use of force, threat or deception rendered a noncustodial parent vulnerable to kidnapping charges, while enactment of a statute criminalizing interference with custody would cover the remaining ground and protect "the rights of 'the child's other parent.' " Moreover, the court pointed out that the interference with custody statute carries serious penalties, and contemplates imprisonment for a first offense.

NOTES AND QUESTIONS

1. *What is the difference between kidnapping and civil interference with parental custody?* Kidnapping is a criminal offense, prosecuted by the state. Most states will hold a parent criminally liable for absconding with a child in order to unlawfully deprive the other parent of access to the child. *See State v. Adler*, 2011 WL 1743783 (Minn. Ct. App. May 9, 2011) (upholding a jury verdict against mother who deprived father of his custodial rights by kidnapping the children).

As you saw in the discussion of *Froland*, the Model Penal Code endorses criminalizing interference with custody, but it is important to distinguish such criminal statutes from civil actions with the same title. Intentional interference with a custodial relationship was a common law tort, pursued as a civil action to compensate the parent who was wrongfully deprived of his or her custodial relationship with the child. The tort originated in English common law, and the ALI has included the cause of action since the first Restatement of Torts (1938). *See* Restatement (Second) of Torts § 700 (ALI 1977). Succinctly stated, the " 'elements of the cause of action include that the plaintiff had superior custody rights to the child and that the defendant intentionally interfered with those rights.' " *Stewart v. Walker*, 5 So.3d 746, 748 (Fla. Dist. Ct. App. 2009), quoting *Stone v. Wall*, 734 So.2d 1038, 1042 (Fla. 1999). The tort embraces inducements and offers of shelter to adolescents who run away, as well as actions that constitute or resemble kidnapping. The remedy may include reimbursement for the costs of locating and pursuing the child as well as punitive damages. In *Kalifa v. Shannon*, 945 A.2d 1244 (Md. 2008), the court found punitive damages could be awarded where the mother intentionally interfered with the father's custodial and visitation rights by fleeing to Egypt with the couple's two young children.

A majority of the courts that have considered the question—courts in at least 20 states and the District of Columbia—have recognized claims for the tort of intentional interference with a custodial relationship. The highest courts of four states, however, have expressly declined to recognize the tort. *Hopper v. Swinnerton*, 317 P.3d 698, 705 (Idaho 2013); *Hoblyn v. Johnson*, 55 P.3d 1219, 1225 (Wyo. 2002); *Zaharias v. Gammill*, 844 P.2d 137, 140 (Okla.1992); and *Larson v. Dunn*, 460 N.W.2d 39, 46 (Minn. 1990).

Some states limit the scope of the tort so that parents can only sue third parties for tortious interference, but cannot sue each other. Responding to certified questions about state law from a federal court, the highest court in Virginia announced, as a matter of first impression, that the state recognized tortious interference with parental rights as a civil cause of action. It adopted the elements essential to the tort from a West Virginia case: the complainant must have a right to maintain a parental relationship with the child; a person who is not the other parent intentionally interfered with the parental relationship; that intentional interference "caused harm" to the complaining parent's parental or custodial relationship with the child; and "damages resulted." The harm includes loss of companionship, which is compensable by money damages. *Wyatt v. McDermott*, 725 S.E.2d 553, 559, 562 (Va. 2012) (*citing Kessel v. Leavitt*, 511 S.E.2d 720 (W. Va. 1998)). In *Wyatt*, the unmarried father of a newborn child who the mother placed for adoption immediately after birth without his knowledge was permitted to sue the mother's attorney for tortious interference. The father alleged that the attorney instructed the mother to hide her plans from the father and not to disclose his address on the birth certificate as required by law.

Affirmative defenses to the tort have traditionally been available. These include the defendant's reasonable, good faith belief that removing the child was proper, and that the defendant acted to prevent physical harm to the child. *See, e.g., Brown v. Brown*, 800 So.2d 359 (Fla. Dist. Ct. App. 2001) (the defendants, the child's stepmother and aunt, may argue the affirmative defenses where they sheltered a boy who ran away from a residential treatment facility in which his mother had placed him, after the boy told the defendants that the institution drugged him and kept him locked up, and that if forced to return he would run away to live on the streets). Similar defenses are available in criminal proceedings for interference with custody. *See* Ariz. Rev. Stat. Ann. § 13–1302(c) (2010); Ohio Rev. Code. Ann. § 2919.23(c) (West 2006).

2.   *What punishment is appropriate for kidnapping by parents?* Do you agree or disagree with the *Froland* court's reading of the kidnapping statute as applied to a father and stepmother? What are the arguments for and against sending a parent who kidnaps his or her child to prison?

3.   *Does it matter how long the child has been with the kidnapper?* Some noncustodial parents may kidnap their children with the hope that, after many years, courts would allow them to continue as the custodial parent because the children have been with them for so long. Since preserving continuity in such cases would only encourage child abductions, the social policy of discouraging abductions normally trumps the best-interests emphasis on continuity of care.

C. TREATMENT OF INTERNATIONAL CHILD ABDUCTION UNDER THE HAGUE CONVENTION

The United States ratified and implemented the Hague Convention on the Civil Aspects of International Child Abduction in 1988. International Child Abduction Remedies Act (ICARA), currently found at 22 U.S.C. §§ 9001–9011 (Supp. V 2017). Of the 98 countries that have signed the Convention, only 77 have mutual agreements with the United States that provide full enforcement. Dep't of State, Annual Report on Int'l Child Abduction i, 4 (2018). In 2017, the most recent year for which figures are available, there were 215 abducted or wrongfully retained children returned to the United States. *Id.* at 6. Of these, only 55 were returned from non-Convention countries. One hundred ninety-seven cases reported to the Department of State were "resolved" without the return of the child to the United States. Of these cases, 138 came from Convention countries, and another 59 were from non-Convention countries. *Id.* Among states with mutual agreements with the United States, Mexico had the highest number of reported abduction cases, with 95 new abduction cases involving 138 children reported in 2017. *Id.* at 81.

The Supreme Court summarized the Convention's purposes in *Abbott v. Abbott*, 560 U.S. 1 (2010), the first controversy involving the treaty to reach the Court:

> * * * The Convention was adopted in 1980 in response to the problem of international child abductions during domestic disputes. The Convention seeks "to secure the prompt return of children wrongfully removed to or retained in any Contracting State," and "to ensure that rights of custody and of access under the law of one Contracting State are effectively respected in the other Contracting States." Art. 1, Treaty Doc., at 7.
>
> * * *
>
> The Convention's central operating feature is the return remedy. When a child under the age of 16 has been wrongfully removed or retained, the country to which the child has been brought must "order the return of the child forthwith," unless certain exceptions apply. See, *e.g.*, Arts. 4, 12, *ibid.* A removal is "wrongful" where the child was removed in violation of "rights of custody." The Convention defines "rights of custody" to "include rights relating to the care of the person of the child and, in particular, the right to determine the child's place of residence." Art. 5(a), *id.*, at 7. A return remedy does not alter the pre-abduction allocation of custody rights but leaves custodial decisions to the courts of the country of habitual residence. Art. 19, *id.*, at 11. * * *

Id. at 6.

* * *

———

The following excerpt from the Convention sets out its central premises and procedures.

CONVENTION ON THE CIVIL ASPECTS OF INTERNATIONAL CHILD ABDUCTION, 1980

T.I.A.S. No. 11,670, 1343 U.N.T.S. 89, 98–99, 100–101.

Chapter I—Scope of the Convention

* * *

Article 3

The removal or the retention of a child is to be considered wrongful where:

a)   it is in breach of rights of custody attributed to a person, an institution or any other body, either jointly or alone, under the law of the State in which the child was habitually resident immediately before the removal or retention; and

b)   at the time of removal or retention those rights were actually exercised, either jointly or alone, or would have been so exercised but for the removal or retention.

The rights of custody mentioned in sub-paragraph *a* above, may arise in particular by operation of law or by reason of a judicial or administrative decision, or by reason of an agreement having legal effect under the law of that State.

Article 4

The Convention shall apply to any child who was habitually resident in a Contracting State immediately before any breach of custody or access rights. The Convention shall cease to apply when the child attains the age of 16 years.

* * *

Article 8

Any person, institution or other body claiming that a child has been removed or retained in breach of custody rights may apply either to the Central Authority of the child's habitual residence or to the Central Authority of any other Contracting State for assistance in securing the return of the child. * * *

* * *

Article 12

Where a child has been wrongfully removed or retained in terms of Article 3 and, at the date of the commencement of the proceedings before the judicial or administrative authority of the Contracting State where the child is, a period of less than one year has elapsed from the date of the wrongful removal or retention, the authority concerned shall order the return of the child forthwith.

The judicial or administrative authority, even where the proceedings have been commenced after the expiration of the period of one year referred to in the preceding paragraph, shall also order the return of the child, unless it is demonstrated that the child is now settled in its new environment.

* * *

Article 13

Notwithstanding the provisions of the preceding Article, the judicial or administrative authority of the requested State is not bound to order the return of the child if the person, institution or other body which opposes its return establishes that:

> a)   the person, institution or other body having the care of the person of the child was not actually exercising the custody rights at the time of removal or retention, or had consented to or subsequently acquiesced in the removal or retention; or

> b)   there is a grave risk that his or her return would expose the child to physical or psychological harm or otherwise place the child in an intolerable situation.

The judicial or administrative authority may also refuse to order the return of the child if it finds that the child objects to being returned and has attained an age and degree of maturity at which it is appropriate to take account of its views.

* * *

———

The following opinion explains how the Convention is supposed to function in international disputes between parents where the child has been taken from one country to another.

CUELLAR V. JOYCE

U.S. Court of Appeals for the Ninth Circuit, 2010.
596 F.3d 505.

KOZINSKI, C. J.:

Petitioner seeks the return of her daughter to Panama under the Hague Convention on the Civil Aspects of International Child Abduction. The father opposes return; he claims that the mother is neglectful and very poor, that the child has grown used to living in America and that the child's medical needs cannot be addressed in Panama.

I

Richard Joyce built a sailboat and sailed it to Panama, where he met Leyda Cuellar. He's a college professor; she was an exotic dancer. They married in Panama, where she eventually gave birth to a baby girl whom we call K.C. Leyda lives in Neuva Livia, a neighborhood that Richard describes as "slum-like," "beyond the end of the road" and "very dangerous," although Leyda points out that Richard never complained when they were dating.

When K.C. was nineteen months old, Richard arranged for Leyda and K.C. to meet him in Australia. At the Sydney airport, Richard separated himself and K.C. from Leyda and flew to the United States, leaving Leyda behind without her passport. Leyda tracked Richard down in Montana, where he currently lives with K.C., and petitioned the district court there for K.C.'s return. The district court denied relief and Leyda appeals.

II

The Hague Convention seeks to deter parents from abducting their children across national borders by limiting the main incentive for international abduction—the forum shopping of custody disputes. *See Mozes v. Mozes*, 239 F.3d 1067, 1070 (9th Cir. 2001). A court that receives a petition under the Hague Convention may not resolve the question of who, as between the parents, is best suited to have custody of the child. *See id.* With a few narrow exceptions, the court must return the abducted child to its country of habitual residence so that the courts of *that* country can determine custody.

This policy of deterrence gives way to concern for the welfare of the child only in extreme cases. Article 13(b) of the treaty provides that return need not be ordered where "there is a grave risk that . . . return would expose the child to physical or psychological harm or otherwise place the child in an intolerable situation." So as not to impair the Convention's general policy, this exception is "narrowly drawn," *Asvesta Petroutsas*, 580 F.3d 1000, 1020 (9th Cir. 2009) (quoting *In re Adan*, 437 F.3d 381, 395 (3d Cir. 2006)), and all facts supporting the exception must be established by clear and convincing evidence. 42 U.S.C. § 11603(e)(2)(A). The exception "is not license for a court in the abducted-to country to speculate on where the child would be happiest." *Gaudin v. Remis*, 415 F.3d 1028, 1035 (9th Cir. 2005) (quoting *Friedrich v. Friedrich*, 78 F.3d 1060, 1068 (6th Cir. 1996)).

The district court found that "K.C. was a habitual resident of Panama and the removal or retention of K.C. did breach the rights of custody attributed to [Leyda]. Additionally, [Leyda] was exercising her custody rights at the time of the removal or retention." The district court also assumed (but did not find) that Leyda did not consent to removal. It nevertheless withheld relief under this grave risk exception. The court cited Leyda's living conditions in Panama, K.C.'s medical needs and K.C.'s psychological attachment to the United States and her father. We review the district court's factual findings for clear error, but determine de novo whether those facts establish a grave risk of harm. *See Mozes*, 239 F.3d at 1073; *Silverman v. Silverman*, 338 F.3d 886, 896 (8th Cir. 2003).

A. Living Conditions. The district court credited Richard's testimony about the home where Leyda lived with K.C.: that the home "has no indoor running water"; that "residents in this area use a nearby creek and outhouse for waste disposal"; and that the home "has no climate control, no refrigeration, and very little furniture." Accepting all this as true * * * it comes nowhere close to establishing a grave risk of harm if K.C. were returned to Panama to live with her mother. Billions of people live in circumstances similar to those described by Richard. If that amounted to a grave risk of harm, parents in more developed countries would have unchecked power to abduct children from countries with a lower standard of living. At the time the Convention was adopted, the State Department took care to emphasize that grave risk doesn't "encompass . . . a home where money is in short supply, or where educational or other opportunities are more limited." 51 Fed. Reg. 10494, 10510 (1986) * * *.

The district court acknowledged that poverty is not a reason to deny relief. However, it expressed * * * "concerns about whether K.C. was properly nourished during the time she lived in Panama." The district court made no finding that K.C. was malnourished or that her diet in Panama had imperiled her health. Nor was there evidence that could have supported such a finding. Richard testified that K.C.'s "diet was poor, so she was kind of small and thin," * * *. This plainly does not amount to clear and convincing evidence of a grave risk of harm, and the district court erred by denying relief on that basis.

The district court also denied relief based on its conclusion that "K.C. suffered a serious head injury that was easily preventable" while in her mother's care. The district court appears to have credited Richard's testimony on this matter, which it recounted as follows:

> K.C. was playing in a wheeled walker on a concrete construction platform which had no guardrails and she fell seven feet off the ground to a concrete platform, landing on her head. K.C. was unconscious from the fall and was taken to a health care facility where an x-ray was taken.

The district court also relied on Richard's testimony that K.C. was sometimes cared for by a sick relative, had frequent ear infections and had unexplained burns behind her earlobes. Based on this testimony, the district court concluded that Leyda was so neglectful that to return K.C. to her custody would be "unsafe."

By drawing this conclusion about Leyda's fitness as a parent, the district court overstepped its mandate and impermissibly addressed the ultimate question of custody. Well-cared-for children do occasionally have accidents, and leaving a child with a sick relative may or may not be neglectful, depending on the circumstances. Richard's feeble showing— even if believed verbatim, as the district court seems to have done—falls far short of clear and convincing evidence of "serious abuse" that is "a great deal more than minimal." *Gaudin,* 415 F.3d at 1035 (citations and internal quotation marks omitted). Indeed, troubling as K.C.'s fall may be, she was subsequently given medical treatment, including an x-ray. It was not the district court's prerogative to determine whether Richard or Leyda was the better parent.

Richard tries to fashion an exception to this rule where the abducting parent believes the legal system in the country of habitual residence is too corrupt to fairly decide the issue of custody. Richard testified:

> I believe that if [K.C.] goes back to Panama, she'll be lost the moment she gets off the plane. Neuva Livia is outside the bounds of what we consider a civilization, and that will just be it. I can't show up down there in some local court in Neuva Livia as the gringo and argue anything. I don't believe I'll ever see her again.

It's unsurprising that Richard thinks he'll get a better shake in the courts of his home country; parents who abduct their children across international boundaries are generally driven by the same hope. But the animating idea behind the Hague Convention is to eliminate "any tactical advantages gained by absconding with a child." *Holder v. Holder,* 392 F.3d 1009, 1013 (9th Cir. 2004). The time to take such considerations into account is before undertaking the volitional acts that lead to conception. Once the child is born, the remote parent must accept the country where the child is habitually resident and its legal system as given. Absent a showing of grave risk, or that one of the Convention's other narrowly-drawn exceptions applies, whatever case the remote parent may have for custody must be made there.

* * *

B.   Medical Concerns. The district court concluded that K.C. exhibits * * * a lack of coordination that may be symptomatic of a number of underlying neurological conditions. The district court based this finding on Richard's testimony regarding a diagnosis by an unidentified physician, testimony by a professor of early childhood education whose primary area of study is "intergenerational patterns of intimacy and autonomy" and a written statement by Richard's sister (a registered nurse) prepared a full year after she examined K.C. * * *. None of this amounted to clear and convincing evidence of a medical condition. The district court clearly erred in finding that it did.

Even if the record did support a conclusion that K.C. exhibits ataxia, there's still no basis to conclude that returning her to Panama would pose a grave risk of harm. * * * Richard testified that he didn't even have an appointment for K.C. to see a doctor. Although Richard testified that Panama lacks the medical services that K.C. needs, nothing he said indicates that he is knowledgeable about the limits of the Panamanian health system. To the contrary, he admitted on cross-examination that he didn't know what care doctors in Panama could provide. The district court's finding that "Panama has doctors but they will not have the specialized treatment and therapy that K.C. needs" is unsupported by the record.

A parent may be able to defeat or delay return by showing that it would disrupt an ongoing course of medical treatment and severely impact the child's health. But the parent would have to provide clear and convincing evidence both of the child's serious medical needs and of the home country's inability to provide the necessary care. That evidence was entirely lacking here.

C. Psychological Harm. The district court also denied relief based on K.C.'s attachment to the United States and her father, and the psychological harm that would result if she were to return to Panama. This was a very serious error. The fact that a child has grown accustomed to her new home is never a valid concern under the grave risk exception, as "it is the *abduction* that causes the pangs of subsequent return." *Friedrich,* 78 F.3d at 1068 * * *. Rather than allowing an abducting parent to profit from the psychological dislocation that he has caused, the Convention attempts to avoid the harm by deterring parents from abducting their children in the first place.

* * * [in original]

There's nothing special about this case; it falls squarely within the heartland of the Hague Convention. Richard has provided absolutely no evidence that should have delayed K.C.'s return to her habitual residence in Panama. Indeed, the delay in this case can only have exacerbated the harm caused by K.C.'s abduction. The Hague Convention does not allow abducting parents to resort to courts in their home country in order to thwart return of the child to its habitual residence. District courts considering Hague Convention cases are cautioned not to allow abducting parents to manipulate judicial process for purpose of delay, as Richard obviously has here.

We reverse the district court's determination that K.C. would suffer a grave risk of harm if returned to Panama. * * *.

Although the parties presented evidence on the question of whether Leyda consented to K.C.'s removal to the United States, the district court assumed, without deciding, that Leyda did not consent. Because a finding of consent would defeat Leyda's petition, we would normally remand for a determination of that issue. In this case, however, a remand would be pointless. The only evidence of consent that Richard presented was the fact that Leyda allowed herself to be separated from Richard and K.C. at the airport in Sydney. This is plainly insufficient. Being victim of a successful abduction can never prove consent. Even ambiguous statements or actions don't suffice; the Convention requires the parent opposing removal to "unequivocally demonstrate that [the petitioning parent] consented to the child's indefinite stay in [America]." *Asvesta*, 580 F.3d at 1019. There's no such evidence here; in fact, Leyda's email to Richard shortly after the abduction, imploring him to "give me back my baby" and stating that "I'm going to die if you don't return her," provides strong evidence to the contrary. A remand for findings as to consent would achieve only unnecessary delay, as the record would not support a finding that Leyda consented.

We order Richard to transfer custody of K.C. to Leyda by 1:00 p.m. MST on the third business day following the issuance of this opinion. Within 10 days of receiving custody, Leyda shall return to Panama with K.C.; Leyda may request a limited extension upon a convincing showing of good cause. The district court shall provide Leyda with all of K.C.'s travel documents and take all steps necessary to ensure that Richard complies with this order, including, if necessary, ordering intervention of the United States Marshals Service.

REVERSED.

NOTES AND QUESTIONS

1.   *Administering the Convention.* The State Department administers both "outgoing" and "incoming" cases under the Convention. With respect to the outgoing cases, involving children whose habitual residence is the United States, the State Department helps the custodial parent or guardian to locate the child and to prepare the application for return. The incoming cases involve children wrongfully brought to the United States from a foreign signatory country. The State Department offers assistance in locating the child and in attempting to secure voluntary return of the child.

2.   *Habitual residence.* Under the Convention, a child is wrongfully removed when removal violates the "custody rights" of another adult under the laws of the country in which the child "habitually resides." Hague Convention, *supra*, art. 4, 5. The Convention does not define "habitual residence." According to the Ninth Circuit, "[d]etermination of 'habitual residence' is 'perhaps the most important inquiry under the Convention.'" *Murphy v. Sloan*, 764 F.3d 1144, 1150 (9th Cir. 2014) (citations omitted). Courts must interpret the meaning of both "habitual residence" and "custody rights." *Id.* art. 16; Linda Silberman, *Interpreting the Hague Abduction Convention: In Search of a Global Jurisprudence*, 38 U.C. Davis L. Rev. 1049, 1055–63 (2005). A child's "habitual residence" is not necessarily the same as the child's "home state"—a

concept used by courts in the United States to determine jurisdiction in various matters related to custody and support (discussed in Chapter 17). "Home state" emphasizes the child's physical presence for the six months before removal. *See, e.g.,* Parental Kidnapping Prevention Act, 28 U.S.C. § 1738A(b)(4) (2012) ("home State means the State in which, immediately preceding the time involved, the child lived with his parents, a parent, or a person acting as parent, for at least six consecutive months"); Uniform Child Custody Jurisdiction and Enforcement Act, Fla. Stat. Ann. § 61.514 (West 2012)) (providing that Florida is the home state if it was "the home state of the child on the date of the commencement of the proceeding, or was the home state of the child within 6 months before the commencement of the proceeding and the child is absent from this state but a parent or person acting as a parent continues to live in this state.").

Federal appellate decisions are not entirely uniform in their definitions of what constitutes a "habitual residence" under the Convention. The Second Circuit has developed a two-part test that involves: (1) a combination of physical presence and acclimation to the location; and (2) the parents' shared intent as demonstrated by both statements and actions. *See, e.g., Gitter v. Gitter*, 396 F.3d 124, 134 (2d Cir. 2005). Although the habitual residence is normally where the child usually lives, the two-part test "is flexible enough to account for the varied circumstances of the individual cases." *Guzzo v. Cristofano*, 719 F.3d 100, 109 (2d Cir. 2013).

The Eighth Circuit takes a slightly different approach: "the first step in determining a child's habitual residence is to discern when the alleged wrongful removal or retention took place, for 'the text of the Convention directs courts to only one point in time in determining habitual residence: the point in time immediately before the removal or retention.'" *Mendoza v. Silva*, 987 F. Supp. 2d 883, 899 (N.D. Iowa 2013) (quoting *Barzilay v. Barzilay*, 600 F.3d 912, 918 (8th Cir. 2010)) (quoting *Silverman v. Silverman*, 338 F.3d 886, 897 (8th Cir. 2003) (en banc)). After determining the date of the alleged wrongful removal or retention, a court then considers the "factors relevant to the determination of habitual residence: 'the settled purpose of the move to the new country from the child's perspective, parental intent regarding the move, the change in geography, the passage of time, and the acclimatization of the child to the new country.'" *Barzilay*, 600 F.3d at 918 (citations omitted). The "settled purpose" element is critical to the determination of habitual residence, and in the Eighth Circuit it must be viewed from the child's perspective. *Id.* at 920 (citations omitted) ("[D]etermination of habitual residence under the Hague Convention is a fact intensive inquiry particularly sensitive to the perspective and circumstances of the child."); *see, e.g., Mendoza, supra*, 987 F. Supp. 2d at 900.

The Fifth Circuit, "like the majority of circuits," has "adopted an approach that begins with the parents' shared intent or settled purpose regarding their child's residence." *Berezowsky v. Ojeda*, 765 F.3d 456, 466 (5th Cir. 2014), *cert. denied*, 135 S. Ct. 1531 (2015). Under this test, the parents must have a shared intent that the child is abandoning one habitual residence and taking up another. *Id. See also Alanis v. Reyes*, 230 F. Supp. 3d 535 (N.D. Miss. 2017) (citing *Berezowsky, supra*, and *Delgado v. Osuma*, 837 F.3d 571 (5th Cir. 2016)). This approach may fail to provide clear guidance to courts when "the persons entitled to fix the child's residence no longer agree on where it has been fixed." *Mozes, supra*, 239 F.3d at 1076. The court in *Mozes* placed situations like these into three categories: First, cases where "both parents and the child translocate together under circumstances suggesting that they intend to make their home in the new country." *Id.* Courts generally find clear intent based on these actions. Second, cases in which "the child's initial translocation from an established habitual residence was clearly intended to be of a specific, delimited period. In these cases, courts have generally refused to find that the changed intentions of one parent led to an alteration in the child's habitual residence." *Id.* Third, and most difficult, "are cases where the petitioning parent had earlier consented to let the child stay abroad for some period of ambiguous duration." *Id.* at 1076–77.

Still other courts consider both the child's perspective and parental intent when deciding habitual residence. *See Karkkainen v. Kovalchuk*, 445 F.3d 280, 292 (3d Cir. 2006) (quoting *Mozes*, 239 F.3d at 1079–80) (noting that both are considered because "the child's knowledge of these [parental] intentions is likely to color its attitude to the contacts it is making"); *Blackledge v. Blackledge*, 2016 WL 4493691 (W.D. Pa. 2016) (*Karkkainen* remains the Third Circuit standard for assessing habitual residence).

3. *Defenses under the Convention*. Once a petitioner has established that the child has been wrongfully removed or retained, the child must be returned to the state of habitual residence unless an affirmative defense applies. The Convention recognizes four affirmative defenses: (1) the child has become well settled in her new environment; (2) the parent filing the petition for return was not actually exercising custody rights at the time of the wrongful removal or the parent had consented or acquiesced to the removal or retention; (3) returning the child would pose a grave risk to the child or otherwise place her in an intolerable situation; and (4) returning the child would violate the fundamental principles of the returning State relating to the protection of human rights and fundamental freedoms. Hague Convention, *supra*, arts. 12, 13, 20. These defenses are meant to be construed narrowly, and judges have broad discretion to reject a defense. *Habrzyk v. Habrzyk*, 775 F. Supp. 2d 1054, 1065 (N.D. Ill. 2011).

The Hague Convention does not apply to minors over the age of 16. Hague Convention, art. 16. Teenagers aged 16 or older may consent to removal or seek to return to their home country, but must do so without the Convention's assistance. Younger children have no right to testify or have the court credit their views. *Kufner v. Kufner*, 519 F.3d 33, 40 (1st Cir. 2008).

The most frequently stated reason for denying a return petition is that doing so would expose the child to a grave risk of harm. Hague Convention, art. 13(b); Hague Conference on Private International Law, *A Statistical Analysis of Applications Made in 2008 Under the Hague Convention of 25*

*October 1980 on the Civil Aspects of International Child Abduction, Part III—
National Reports,* Prel. Doc. No. 8 C, 204 (May 2011) at [hereinafter *Statistical
Analysis*]. Article 13(b) exceptions have been successfully invoked in a variety
of circumstances. *See Ermini v. Vittori,* 738 F.3d 153 (2d Cir. 2014) (autistic
child brought to U.S. to seek therapy not available in Italy faced sufficiently
grave risks of psychological harm if separated from that therapy that denial of
return petition was appropriate); *Acosta v. Acosta,* 725 F.3d 868 (8th Cir. 2013)
("grave risk of harm" satisfied where clear and convincing evidence showed
that Peruvian father had severe anger management problems, had verbally
and physically abused the mother in front of the children and acted violently
toward others in front of them); *Baran v. Beaty,* 526 F.3d 1340, 1346 (11th Cir.
2008) (appellate court affirmed the trial court's refusal to return the child
where the Australian father was violent and a drunk).

In *Kofler v. Kofler,* 2007 WL 2081712, at *11–12 (W.D. Ark. July 18, 2007),
the father lived in a small apartment, there were no bedrooms for any of the
children and not enough room for all three children to visit together, and
petitioner's parents, who live in Switzerland, planned to petition for joint
custody. The court found that return would place the children in an intolerable
situation. Is *Kofler* consistent with *Cuellar*?

Arguments pursuant to Article 20 that fundamental rights will be
jeopardized if the child is returned, however, rarely succeed in blocking return.
Rachel Koehn, *Family Law Frustrations: Addressing Hague Convention Issues
in Federal Courts,* 69 Baylor L. Rev. 636 (2017) (attributing the failure to
recognize a risk of grave harm and other deficits in the application of the Hague
Convention to the federal courts' lack of familiarity with either the Convention
or the general principles of family law). Article 20 might bar the return of a
child if the child would be subject to female genital mutilation in her country
of habitual residence, or if honor crimes were common in her community or
country. *See* Carol S. Bruch, *Religious Law, Secular Practices, and Children's
Human Rights in Child Abduction Cases Under the Hague Child Abduction
Convention,* 33 N.Y.U J. Int'l L. & Pol. 49, 56 (2000).

4.   *The one-year requirement and the "well settled" defense.* Under the
Convention, when a court receives a petition for return within one year of the
child's wrongful removal, the court "shall order the return of the child
forthwith." Hague Convention, Art. 12 at 9. Additionally, "[w]here the
proceedings have been commenced after the expiration of the period of one
year" from the date of the wrongful removal, the court "shall order the return
of the child, unless it is demonstrated that the child is now settled in its new
environment." *Id.*

But what if the abducting parent purposely conceals the child's location,
and a petition for return is not filed within a year? The U.S. Supreme Court
answered this question in *Lozano v. Montoya Alvarez,* where the mother
abducted her daughter from the United Kingdom and took her to New York.
Lozano v. Montoya Alvarez, 572 U.S. 1 (2014). Despite serious efforts, the
father, Lozano, could not locate her for over 16 months. The Court unanimously

held that the Convention is not subject to "equitable tolling," which would pause the running of "a statute of limitations when a litigant has pursued his rights diligently but some extraordinary circumstance prevents him from bringing timely action." *Id.* at 10.

The Court found that the parties to the Convention did not intend equitable tolling to apply to the one-year period for several reasons. First, the one-year period is not considered a statute of limitations because expiration "does not eliminate the remedy the Convention affords the left-behind parent," and the "continued availability of the return remedy after one year preserves the possibility for relief." *Id.* at 11–12. When the return petition is filed more than one year after the abduction, the judge has discretion not to return the child if the child is "now settled" in its new environment. *Id.* at 14–15. Second, equitable tolling, a principle of United States law, has not been adopted by foreign courts and is not applicable to proceedings under treaties between nations. *Id.* at 15.

Some observers fear that *Lozano* will encourage parental abduction, and make it harder to achieve the return of children. However, U.S. courts have found that the pattern of behavior accompanying efforts to conceal the child's location can prevent the stable attachments that allow a child to be "settled in its new environment." Hiding often involves moving from place to place or keeping the child out of community activities or school, making it less likely that a court will consider the child to be "well settled." *In re R.V.B.*, 29 F. Supp. 3d 243 (E.D.N.Y. 2014) (child not well settled where the mother and child—on tourist visas—moved frequently, child changed schools, and mother changed jobs several times); *Bobadilla v. Cordero*, 2014 WL 3869998, at *4 (M.D.N.C. Aug. 6, 2014) (quoting *Lozano, supra*, at 17 for the proposition that "American courts have found * * * that steps taken to promote concealment can also prevent the stable attachments that make a child 'settled.' ").

Expiration of the one-year period does not automatically result in non-return. Instead it opens the door to considering the child's interest in his or her current settlement. *Lozano, supra,* at 17. Concurring in *Lozano*, Justice Alito explained that allowing consideration of the child's perception of being well settled does not prevent courts from taking other factors into consideration, and does not inhibit a judge's discretionary power to order return. *Id.* 19–21.

What do you think? Should bad faith be taken into consideration? What are the policy implications of the ruling in *Lozano*?

5. *Domestic violence and the Hague Convention.* The most recent available data shows that 67% of the absconding parents in Hague Convention proceedings were mothers. Lowe, *Statistical Analysis, supra* at 6. The drafters of the Convention were not contemplating the scenario of mothers fleeing abusive relationships, but allegations that domestic violence led a parent to flee with her children present some of the hardest cases under the Hague Convention. Courts often appear either "unsympathetic to the plea of a female abductor who alleges abuse and refuses to return with the child" or conclude that spousal violence is irrelevant under the Convention. Eran Stroeger,

International Child Abduction and Children's Rights: Two Means to the Same End, 32 Mich. J. Int'l L. 511, 530 (2011); Kevin Wayne Puckett, *Hague Convention on International Child Abduction: Can Domestic Violence Establish the Grave Risk Defense Under Article 13?*, 30 J. Am. Acad. Matrim. Law. 259 (2017).

Three kinds of situations involving domestic violence are commonly seen in Hague Convention cases.

First, cases where the petitioner has abused the children. To constitute a grave risk of harm sufficient to overcome the presumption of a return order, the abuse must be severe and must be proven. *Compare Altamiranda Vale v. Avila*, 538 F.3d 581, 587 (7th Cir. 2008) (one episode of striking with a video game chord insufficient); *with Acosta, supra*, 725 F.3d at 876 ("high risk" that father "would abuse the children in the future" and might even kill them).

Second, cases involving spousal abuse, but no abuse of the children. Courts take different approaches to these cases. *Compare Tabacchi v. Harrison*, 2000 WL 190576, at *13 (N.D. Ill. Feb. 10, 2000) ("Although Tabacchi's behavior toward his wife is unacceptable, to qualify as a grave risk of harm under the convention, the risk must be to the child."), *with Miltiadous v. Tetervak*, 686 F. Supp. 2d 544 (E.D. Pa. 2010) (finding that even though the father never physically abused the children, the father's physical abuse of his wife fulfilled Article 13(b)'s grave risk of harm requirement and the children did not have to be returned to Cyprus).

Third, cases involving spousal abuse witnessed by the children, which some but not all courts treat as creating a risk of grave harm. *Ermini, supra*, 758 F.3d 153, 164 ("Spousal violence . . . can also establish a grave risk of harm to the child, particularly when it occurs in the presence of the child."). *See* Stroeger, *International Child Abduction, supra* at 530 (courts often decline to find that "witnessing domestic violence" creates grounds for denying return).

Should flight from domestic violence constitute a complete bar to the return remedy? If so, what evidentiary standard should be applied when the alleged abuser is not at the hearing but in a different country? Should it matter whether the child was exposed to the domestic violence, or is the fact of spousal abuse sufficient to justify flight?

The answers to these questions, never entirely clear, are currently in limbo in the U.S. In 2018 the U.S. announced that flight from domestic or gang violence would no longer constitute grounds for asylum. U.S. Citizenship and Immigration Servs., PM-602-0162m Guidance for Processing Reasonable Fear, Credible Fear, Asylum and Refugee Claims in Accordance with Matter of A-B- (July 11, 2018). However, the Department of Justice analysis on which that policy rested—*Matter of A-B-*, 27 I & N. Dec. 316 (U.S. Att'y Gen. June 11, 2018)—has been successfully challenged in federal court as this book goes to press. *Grace v. Whittaker*, 2018 WL 6628081 (D. D.C. Dec. 17, 2018) (Sullivan, J.) (granting preliminary injunction abrogating the decision in *A-B-* and the resulting policy). The federal government is expected to appeal.

6. *Violation of visitation rights under the Convention.* Denying access to parents who have a right to visitation but no custodial rights is not considered a violation under the Hague Convention. *Croll v. Croll,* 229 F.3d 133, 137–38 (2d Cir. 2000); *Kufner v. Kufner,* 519 F.3d 33, 39 (1st Cir. 2008); *Vale v. Avila,* 538 F.3d 581, 583 (7th Cir. 2008). Should it be?

In *Abbott,* the Court held that when a parent holds "the authority to consent before the other parent may take the child to another country," that amounts to having a right of custody under the Convention—but only if that is the view of the home country. *Abbott, supra,* 560 U.S. at 1. Should denial of visitation be treated as the equivalent of failure to return a child to the custodial parent under the Convention?

7. *Some parents have no legal rights to their children.* A parent who has no legal rights to his or her children cannot file for return under the Hague Convention. Art. 3. You have seen that in the United States fit parents generally share legal custody and are entitled to visitation. That is not the case in all countries. For example, Japan has historically emphasized a "clean break" after divorce, which typically means "the divorced father must take a life-long break not only from his former wife, but also from his children." Maryl Sattler, *The Problem of Paternal Relocation: Closing the Loophole in the Law of International Child Abduction,* 67 Wash. & Lee L. Rev. 1709, 1711 (2010). Similarly, unmarried fathers in Ireland may encounter obstacles to seeking return because they may not be recognized as legal guardians. *Redmond v. Redmond,* 724 F.3d 729 (7th Cir. 2013). *See* Jennifer O'Brien, Family Law in Ireland: Overview, Practical Law Coutry Q&A 0-567-9207 (2017) (traditionally where parents were not married the mother became the sole legal and custodian of the children; after legislative reforms adopted in 2015, a father who had cohabited with the mother for at least 12 consecutive months, including not less than 3 consecutive months with the child, the father is entitled to be a legal guardian).

8. *What happens if a parent removes a child from the home state before a custody order has issued?* In *Carrascosa v. McGuire,* 520 F.3d 249 (3d Cir. 2008). Here, the parents executed an interim parenting agreement while their divorce was pending. The agreement specified that neither parent could remove their daughter, Victoria, from the United States without the other parent's signed consent. In violation of the agreement, the mother took Victoria to Spain where she sought and received a divorce. A federal warrant was issued for the mother's arrest and, when she returned to the U.S. without Victoria, she was jailed for contempt of court. The mother had already remained in jail for two years when the Third Circuit rejected her petition for *habeas corpus.* Victoria had not seen either parent for several years when the matter reached the Court of Appeals. The court concluded that under the law of the child's home state, New Jersey, both parents had equal custody rights until their parental rights were adjudicated in divorce proceedings. The court reasoned that "the Hague Convention is designed to put all participants in a custody dispute back into the positions they would have been in but for one parent's

wrongful removal of the child." *Id.* at 260. This required Victoria's return to New Jersey, whose courts alone could resolve the original custody dispute.

After numerous hearings in state and federal courts, the New Jersey courts awarded custody of Victoria to her father, while courts in Spain decreed that Victoria could not leave that country until she turns 18. In November 2009, a jury in New Jersey found the mother guilty of eight counts of custodial interference and one count of contempt of court, and in December of that year, a judge sentenced the mother to 14 years in prison. Karen Sudol, *Mother Guilty of Violating Custody: She Refuses to Bring Child Back From Spain*, The Record (Bergen County, NJ), Nov. 13, 2009, at L01; Kibret Markos, *Mom Jailed for Refusing to Return Girl to Her Dad*, The Star-Ledger (Newark, NJ), Dec. 24, 2009, at O23. In 2011, the law firm that had held Victoria's American passport in trust in 2005 was ordered to pay $950,000 to the father and to Victoria, because it had turned over Victoria's passport to the mother allowing her to abscond to Spain with the child. Kibert Markos, *Law Firm Hit with $950,000 Judgment in Passport Case*, The Record (Bergen County, NJ), May 11, 2011, at L02.

PROBLEM 13-5

Imagine that in *New Jersey v. Froland* (discussed earlier in this Chapter) the boat had not broken down and the children had been brought to another country. How would the case be handled if the children were taken to a country that signed the Convention and had a return agreement with the United States? How would you advise the mother if the children were taken to a country that had not signed the Convention?

CHAPTER 14

ETHICS IN CONTEMPORARY FAMILY LAW PRACTICE

■ ■ ■

1. ETHICAL FOUNDATIONS

A. INTRODUCTION

Like lawyers who practice in other fields, family lawyers face vexing ethical questions in their relationships with clients, courts, opponents, and third parties. Questions can arise under the full range of ethical rules. Ethical questions surface throughout this book, but this Chapter complements the required professional responsibility course by treating major ethical questions that frequently influence domestic relations practice.

After discussing family lawyers' primary roles and obligations to their clients, the Chapter discusses (1) many parties' inability to afford legal representation in dissolution and other domestic relations cases; (2) the family lawyer's obligation to maintain client confidences; (3) potential conflicts of interest that often confront family lawyers; (4) the family lawyer's obligations to third parties and opponents; (5) the family lawyer's obligations to the parties' children; and (6) misconduct by family lawyers in their own divorces and in their personal affairs generally. The Chapter concludes by briefly discussing the relationship between ethics and malpractice.

The character of domestic relations practice, discussed in Chapter 1, may create distinct ethical pressures on lawyers. "Attorneys in family law practice, as a group, represent one of the largest areas of practice for disciplinary complaints and malpractice suits." Barbara Glesner Fines, *The Changing Landscape of Disciplinary Risks in Family Law Practice*, 50 Fam. L.Q. 367, 367 (2016).

Because family law intimately concerns personal lives, lawyers may bear the brunt of a client's anger at the process, and the client's frustration with the case's outcome. "That over ninety percent of disciplinary complaints in domestic relations cases are dismissed is one indication that these complaints reflect unrealistic expectations or ongoing conflict in the underlying cases." *Id.* at 368.

B. PROFESSIONAL ROLES AND OBLIGATIONS

Like other lawyers, family lawyers serve their clients in four primary roles. The lawyer is (1) an *advisor* who "provides a client with an informed understanding of the client's legal rights and obligations and explains their practical implications"; (2) an *advocate* who "zealously asserts the client's position under the rules of the adversary system"; (3) a *negotiator* who "seeks a result advantageous to the client but consistent with requirements of honest dealings with others"; and (4) an *evaluator* who "acts by examining a client's legal affairs and reporting about them to the client or to others." Model Rules of Prof'l Conduct, Preamble (2018).

In these various roles, domestic relations lawyers face multiple layers of professional and legal influences. Most prominent is the state's mandatory code of ethics, which regulates all lawyers. Unless otherwise specified, this Chapter cites and applies the 2018 version of the ABA Model Rules of Professional Conduct.

Unofficial sources may also influence the ethics of family lawyers. The American Academy of Matrimonial Lawyers (AAML), for example, has promulgated codes including the aspirational *Bounds of Advocacy, Goals for Family Lawyers*, which is directed at AAML members. These guidelines may urge higher standards than those set by the Model Rules, and may influence non-member family lawyers when state bar associations endorse the guidelines. The American Law Institute has promulgated the Restatement (Third) of the Law Governing Lawyers (2000 & Supp. 2018), which, like other restatements, assembles principles gleaned from official sources such as statutes, decisions, and codes. As Chapter 15 discusses, lawyers serving as mediators or arbitrators in domestic relations cases also feel the influence of ethical constraints relating to that service, including unofficial ethical codes.

The Model Rules recite several basic ethical obligations to clients, including these:

(1) *Competence.*

"A lawyer shall provide competent representation to a client. Competent representation requires the legal knowledge, skill, thoroughness and preparation reasonably necessary for the representation." Model Rule 1.1.

Model Rule 1.1 may impose distinct obligations on domestic relations lawyers now that no-fault divorce has steered dissolution proceedings away from proof of spousal wrongdoing and more toward often-complex property and child-related issues, and now that domestic relations practice frequently concerns families who do not conform to the traditional nuclear family model. Some domestic relations cases raise state and federal legal issues that may lie beyond the lawyer's immediate competence, such as complex tax or bankruptcy matters. Some cases raise issues that require collaboration with professionals from other disciplines such as psychology or social work. Sandra Day O'Connor, *Remarks: The Supreme Court and the Family*, 3 U. Pa. J. Const. L. 573, 573, 576 (2001).

The intricacies and complexities that mark contemporary domestic relations practice suggest that attorneys should remain wary of the assumption that "any lawyer can handle a divorce." Attorneys not competent in family law may take on family law cases "either as a way to generate revenue during periods of economic challenge or in response to the request of their own friends or family members for assistance." Fines, *supra* at 367. The lawyer can face disciplinary proceedings for mishandling such an undertaking.

Demonstrating the professional risks is *In re Disciplinary Proceedings Against Marchan*, 910 N.W.2d 531 (Wis. 2018), which upheld the six-month suspension of a lawyer who mishandled a divorce case for a woman with whom the lawyer was acquainted socially. The lawyer did not have a law office, and met with the client either at the client's home or in parks. Among other things, the court concluded that the lawyer "lacked experience in divorce cases, had a limited legal practice, and used poor judgment in becoming involved in a complicated divorce on behalf of someone she knew socially." *Id.* at 538.

(2) *Diligence.*

"A lawyer shall act with reasonable diligence and promptness in representing a client." Model Rule 1.3. A family lawyer's failure to heed this command can be particularly serious because "[c]lients in contested divorce proceedings, especially involving child custody disputes, need expeditious resolution of the issues in order that they may get on with their lives." *In re Daugherty*, 83 P.3d 789, 793 (Kan. 2004). In *In re Nichols*, 45 So.3d 603 (La. 2010), the court suspended the lawyer who, for more than two years, failed to inform his client that she was required to attend a parenting class before her divorce could be finalized, failed to secure a divorce judgment, and failed to obtain a child custody judgment.

(3) *Informing the client.*

"A lawyer shall explain a matter to the extent reasonably necessary to permit the client to make informed decisions regarding the representation." Model Rule 1.4(b).

Because so many domestic relations clients lack experience with lawyers or litigation, the lawyer often needs to explain the proceeding to the client. An early step is to explain the attorney-client privilege (a matter treated in Section 3 below). Lay clients who do not understand the privilege may resist full and frank discussion by assuming that the court or opponent can later compel the lawyer to reveal sensitive information and communications that the lawyer and client shared with one other.

When the lawyer explains substantive and procedural family law to a lay client, the lawyer must speak in language whose content and tone the client can understand, consistent with the client's attention span at a particular session. Family law clients are often upset before they consult a lawyer, and they "may have an especially hard time absorbing the information if lawyers use legal or dispute resolution terminology instead of plain English." John Lande & Forrest S. Mosten, *Family Lawyering: Past, Present, and Future*, 51 Fam. Ct. Rev. 20, 23 (Jan. 2013).

The AAML recommends that lawyers "advise the client of the emotional and economic impact of divorce and explore the feasibility of reconciliation," including marriage counseling or therapy. AAML, *Bounds of Advocacy, supra* § 1.2. "Although few attorneys are qualified to do psychological counseling, a discussion of the emotional and monetary repercussions of divorce is appropriate." *Id.* cmt.

(4) *Communicating with the client.*

As the lawyer provides ongoing information, the lawyer must also maintain open lines of communication with the client. "Reasonable communication between the lawyer and the client is necessary for the client effectively to participate in the representation." Model Rule 1.4, cmt.1. "The lawyer must keep the client reasonably informed about the matter," and must "promptly comply with a client's reasonable requests for information." Restatement (Third) of the Law Governing Lawyers, *supra* § 20.

Family lawyers need to weigh the emotions, trauma, and tensions frequently felt by divorce and other domestic relations clients who are at low points in their lives. Family lawyers sometimes face client complaints or professional discipline for carelessness that has little or nothing to do with their knowledge of the law. Failure to return telephone calls in a timely fashion, for example, irks clients and overlooks a common courtesy that lawyers should have learned before law school. *See, e.g.*, Debra Cassens Weiss, *These Common Mistakes Can Lead to Lawyer Ethics Complaints*, A.B.A. J. (Feb. 10, 2016).

In *Kentucky Bar Ass'n v. Gallaher*, 539 S.W.3d 29 (Ky. 2018), for example, the court suspended the lawyer for, among other things, failing to appear in family court for the case, failing to perform any services for the client, and failing to respond to the client's telephone calls.

(5) *Fraud.*

Model Rule 8.4(c) provides that a lawyer may not "engage in conduct involving dishonesty, fraud, deceit or misrepresentation." Model Rule 1.0(d) defines "fraud" as "conduct that is fraudulent under the substantive or procedural law of the applicable jurisdiction and has a purpose to deceive."

Other more specific ethical rules concerning fraud may also apply. Model Rule 1.2(d), for example, provides that "[a] lawyer shall not counsel a client to engage, or assist a client, in conduct that the lawyer knows is criminal or fraudulent, but a lawyer may discuss the legal consequences of any proposed course of conduct with a client and may counsel or assist a client to make a good faith effort to determine the validity, scope, meaning or application of the law."

Model Rule 4.1 provides further: "In the course of representing a client a lawyer shall not knowingly: (a) make a false statement of material fact or law to a third person; or (b) fail to disclose a material fact when disclosure is necessary to avoid assisting a criminal or fraudulent act by a client," unless the Rules otherwise prohibit disclosure relating to representation of the client.

Temptation toward committing fraud sometimes lurks in domestic relations cases, particularly if the lawyer succumbs to the emotionalism that may drive the client. In *In re Belding*, 589 S.E.2d 197 (S.C. 2003), for example, the court suspended the husband's lawyer for one year for drafting a fictitious set of divorce documents designed to "shock" the wife into mending the parties' marriage. The documents included a summons and complaint with a fictitious docket number and a fictitious filing stamp from the clerk's office, a fictitious consent order to change venue with the signatures of the family court judge and lawyers forged by the suspended lawyer, and fictitious discovery requests with counsel's signature forged.

NOTE

Candor toward the court. In addition to the lawyer's obligations to the client, Model Rule 3.3(a) provides that a lawyer may not knowingly "make a false statement of fact or law to a tribunal or fail to correct a false statement of material fact or law previously made to the tribunal by the lawyer." The Rule further provides that the lawyer may not "offer evidence that the lawyer knows to be false."

In matrimonial cases, the first provision may be particularly relevant when the lawyer drafts the separation agreement, which the parties generally submit to the court as the basis for the decree. The second provision relates to any document or testimonial evidence entered during the proceeding. In *Kentucky Bar Association v. Rye*, 336 S.W.3d 462 (Ky. 2011), for example, the court publicly reprimanded the lawyer for, among other things, falsely telling the court that he was unaware of the divorce client's relocation outside the state with the parties' child.

A lawyer's lack of candor toward the court may also implicate Model Rule 8.4(c) and (d) ("It is professional misconduct for a lawyer to: * * * engage in conduct involving dishonesty, fraud, deceit or misrepresentation [or] * * * engage in conduct that is prejudicial to the administration of justice.").

PROBLEM 14-1

You are a family lawyer newly admitted to the bar, and you have been consulted by a potential client who runs a small business. You did not take either an accountancy or a business organizations course in law school, nor do you know much about how to value a business. May you still represent the client? What steps might you take? How would you explain these steps to the client?

2. ACCESS TO DOMESTIC RELATIONS COUNSEL

In today's challenging economic times, more and more civil litigants appear *pro se*, usually because they cannot afford to retain counsel but do not qualify for free legal services. The national increase appears greatest in domestic relations cases, which include persons from all walks of life. "[O]n average, eighty percent of all family law cases involve at least one self-represented litigant, while in 50% of the cases, both litigants proceed on their own." Amy G. Applegate & Connie J.A. Beck, *Self-Represented Parties in Mediation: Fifty Years Later It Remains the Elephant In the Room*, 51 Fam. Ct. Rev. 87, 87 (2013). In addition to cost, high rates of self-representation in family law cases may stem partly from concern that lawyers will prolong or complicate the process, or from unwillingness to confide sensitive family matters even to a lawyer.

"[A] two-tiered system of justice has resulted in most jurisdictions. Not only do represented parties benefit from individual counseling, they may also have access to dispute resolution processes and other services not available to self-represented parties." Nancy Ver Steegh et al., *Look Before You Leap: Court System Triage of Family Law Cases Involving Intimate Partner Violence*, 95 Marq. L. Rev. 955, 958–59 (2012). In domestic relations cases as in other fields, cases involving one or more *pro se* litigants also burden the court, whose judges, clerks, and other staff may need to take special measures to compensate for a litigant's lack of legal training.

Nearly all states have responded to the needs of *pro se* family law filers with official court websites and similar resources that provide model petitions, answers, and other basic forms with instructions written in plain English, and often also in various foreign languages. *See, e.g.,* Missouri Courts, *Representing Yourself in a Family Law Case*, https://www.self represent.mo.gov/page.jsp?id=5240 (visited Mar. 26, 2019). Some state courts also provide case managers to help unrepresented parties navigate the family law process. Some parties, particularly ones with few marital assets in uncontested divorce proceedings, engage on-line companies which provide forms that the party or the company itself fills out and files in court without a lawyer. Other family law parties seek guidance from self-help books and Internet websites.

As self-representation rates continue to rise in domestic relations and other areas of law, national and state bar associations have facilitated provision of "unbundled legal services" (or "limited-scope representation"), arrangements in which the lawyer provides the client some, but not all, tasks traditionally associated with full-service representation.

Model Rule 1.2(c) provides: "A lawyer may limit the scope of representation if the limitation is reasonable under the circumstances and the client gives informed consent." In 2013, the ABA adopted a resolution that encourages lawyers "when appropriate, to consider limiting the scope of their representation, including the unbundling of legal services as a means of increasing access to legal services." https://www.americanbar.org/content/dam/aba/administrative/delivery_legal_services/ls_del_unbundling_resolution_108.authcheckdam.pdf (visited Mar. 26, 2019).

"Unbundling is both a growing method of increasing legal access for the underserved and an untapped market for family lawyers." Forrest S. Mosten & Elizabeth Potter Scully, Unbundled Legal Services: A Family Lawyer's Guide xi (2017). As the number of lawyers offering unbundled services grows, the next article discusses ethical concerns that accompany this emerging model of limited representation.

JESSICA K. STEINBERG,
IN PURSUIT OF JUSTICE? CASE OUTCOMES AND THE
DELIVERY OF UNBUNDLED LEGAL SERVICES

18 Geo. J. on Poverty L. & Pol'y 454–56, 458, 461–63, 465–70 (2011).

* * * Hailed as an innovation in the delivery of legal services, "unbundling" is a piecemeal lawyering model in which a lawyer provides assistance with a discrete legal task *only* and does not perform the full range of services expected from traditional legal representation. That is, while attorneys engaged in traditional representation commit to carry out a full "bundle" of acts that take a client through the resolution of his legal problem, the term "unbundled" refers to the disaggregation of those acts, with the attorney and client agreeing that only one, or a few, legal tasks will be undertaken. A recipient of unbundled aid does not typically enjoy the benefits of a lawyer's advocacy before a tribunal or with an adversary. Rather, a limited form of help—an advice session or document preparation, for example—constitutes the entire lawyering relationship, and the recipient goes on to handle all remaining aspects of the litigation *pro se*.

* * *

With its rise in prominence over the past decade, the ethical viability of unbundled legal services has been the subject of much public deliberation. Scholars, lawyers, and other critics have questioned whether the types of activities undertaken as part of the delivery of unbundled aid run afoul of rules of professional conduct and other canons governing law practice. In an example of ethical attack, judges have branded the ghostwriting of documents—a hallmark of the unbundled model—a flagrant violation of a lawyer's duties to the court and opposing parties. Proponents of unbundled services have defended all aspects of the model, decrying an interpretation of ethical canons that erects barriers to the expansion of access to justice for the poor. * * *

II. Unbundled Legal Services and Access to Justice

* * *

B. *Unbundling for the Middle Class Versus the Poor*

Unbundling first came into vogue formally as a way of providing affordable legal services to the middle class—those that might need assistance with one particular aspect of their legal case, but could competently handle the rest of their matter *pro se*. Proponents of unbundling often speak of the model as a way to expand choice and empower litigants of limited means. Whereas traditionally, a litigant had to choose between hiring a cost-prohibitive attorney and handling his own legal matter without any representation or attorney guidance, unbundling provides a third option: a litigant can hire an attorney, at a set price, for a discrete task, within his means, and where he believes it might be most beneficial.

* * * Although no formal distinction has been drawn between the unbundled services paid for by the middle class, and those delivered to the indigent, the theoretical underpinnings of the model are quite different for the two sets of litigants.

For the middle class, unbundling offers the benefits of choice and affordability. It dissolves the all-or-nothing model of lawyering and creates an opportunity to access the expertise of a lawyer only when the client determines that one is needed most. In the low-income context, however, the element of choice is effectively nonexistent. Low-income clients do not "hire" lawyers to assist with a particular portion of a legal matter and do not dictate where the representation begins and ends. Instead, legal services organizations make programmatic determinations about how best to serve their client populations or how to respond to the priorities of funders, and then design unbundled legal aid programs accordingly. These programmatic decisions are undoubtedly made with the intention of doing the most good with the fewest resources and—in the absence of data—are made based on the intuition and expertise of staff. * * *

C. Ethical Critiques and Reform

Ethical critiques have plagued unbundling from the outset. The abridgement of the attorney-client relationship, which is demanded by the provision of limited services, has been denounced as incompatible with the duties of competence, diligence, and zeal. And component parts of unbundled practice—notably, ghostwriting—have been attacked as a violation of the duty of candor to the tribunal and an exploitation of *pro se* leniency. Scholars and practitioners who support unbundling have argued that the model—in all forms—is permitted by current rules and, where that argument is ineffectual, have pursued the updating of ethical norms to permit unfettered unbundling.

Because of unbundling's purported promise to increase access to justice for under-represented populations, the American Bar Association (ABA), as well as local access to justice commissions, have heeded the call to enact ethical reforms in an effort to preserve and promote unbundled legal services. * * *.

1.   Ethical Critique and Debate

a.   The Unbundled Attorney-Client Relationship

* * *

The ethical duties of competence, diligence, and zeal pose challenging issues for a lawyer providing unbundled legal services: Can an attorney satisfy the duty to make a "factual inquiry" by relying solely on the client's representation of facts? Does "thoroughness" require a lawyer to advise a client on legal issues that are outside the scope of the discrete task the lawyer has agreed to undertake? Can a lawyer respond to a client's brief question without a diagnostic interview that might capture additional facts and impact the answer?

Compounding these ethical quandaries is debate over whether, and in what circumstances, an attorney-client relationship forms during the delivery of unbundled legal aid. Some providers contend that the provision of one-time advice, particularly via hotline or in group settings, does not create an attorney-client relationship governed by traditional ethics rules and, though best efforts should be made to deliver advice competently, there exists no formal obligation to comply with a prescribed duty of competence. Others counter that an attorney-client relationship always forms once a client shares confidential information, and that the ethical standards espoused by the Model Rules must be liberally interpreted, or expressly amended, to clarify that competent representation is contextual and can be rendered even when contact between lawyer and client is limited to a brief consultation or telephone advice.

b.   Ghostwriting

In the mid-to-late 1990s, a trio of district court opinions forcefully condemned ghostwriting as unethical, setting off spirited debate about the viability of the practice. The courts focused in particular on the fundamental unfairness ghostwriting poses to the adverse party and whether the failure of the ghostwriting attorney to identify herself induces the court to provide unwarranted leniency to a litigant who is not truly proceeding *pro se.* * * * Some scholars contend that claims regarding *pro se* leniency are greatly inflated and that, in fact, judges liberally construe all pleadings and do not accord any special benefit to the unrepresented. These scholars believe that courts have hastily branded ghostwriting as unfair and unethical, particularly because it is often obvious on the face of the pleading that a lawyer had a hand in preparing it.

* * *

2.   Ethical Reform

The adoption of ethical reforms to permit lawyering short of full representation has been the primary focus of unbundling proponents since the public prominence of the model has grown. * * *

The ABA addressed some, but not all, of the ethical concerns related to curtailment of the attorney-client relationship in its revisions to the Model Rules in 2002. * * * [A]s long as the client agrees to the limited representation, and the attorney acts competently given the services she has agreed to perform, the unbundled relationship is ethically valid. The Model Rules take great pains to make clear that unbundling is permissible; yet, in practice, the new standards are still difficult to apply and require further interpretation. Many of the same questions persist: In a brief advice session, what factual information must a lawyer discern if she is to provide competent assistance? If a diagnostic interview is performed, but facts remain unclear, must a lawyer undertake further investigation before proffering advice and/or ghostwriting assistance? Proponents of unbundling continue to press for additional rules that clarify which forms of unbundled legal aid lawyers can ethically provide.

The states—via adoption of new court rules, amendments to statutes, and opinions issued by ethics commissions—have addressed ghostwriting, with mixed results. * * *

NOTES AND QUESTIONS

1.   *Questions about unbundling.* (a) How would you explain unbundling to a prospective domestic relations client at the first meeting? (b) Does the unbundling of legal services raise concerns about the sound administration of justice? (c) Should states enact legislation or promulgate procedural rules that authorize courts to appoint counsel for parties who cannot afford to retain

counsel in their dissolution? If you believe that the answer is yes, should such authority be plenary, or should it be limited to uncontested dissolutions? To contested dissolutions?

2. *Contingent fees.* At least among lower- and middle-income plaintiffs, the impetus toward unbundling in family law may be fueled by the near-total prohibition on contingent-fee agreements in divorce cases. In the typical contingent-fee arrangement in other fields of law, lawyer and client agree in writing that the lawyer will receive a fixed percentage of the client's recovery from a settlement or judgment (usually about one-third), but nothing if there is no recovery. Lawyer and client sometimes agree instead that the lawyer will be paid by the hour, but with a bonus for a specified favorable result.

Model Rule 1.5(d)(1) prohibits fees "in a domestic relations matter, the payment or amount of which is contingent upon the securing of a divorce or upon the amount of alimony or support, or property settlement in lieu thereof." Agreements for such contingent fees are unenforceable as contrary to public policy. *See, e.g., Medina v. Richard A. Kraslow, P.C.*, 53 N.Y.S.3d 116, 117–18 (App. Div. 2017). Because the Model Rule and its predecessors specify divorce, the Rule has generally not been interpreted to prohibit contingent-fee arrangements in actions between unmarried cohabitants or in paternity proceedings. *See, e.g., Mont. Ethics Op. 990119* (undated). What policy concerns underlie the prohibitions contained in Model Rule 1.5(d)(1)?

Model Rule 1.5 also does not preclude contingent-fee agreements "in connection with the recovery of post-judgment balances due under support, alimony or other financial orders because such contracts do not implicate the same policy concerns" that the general prohibition implicates. Model Rule 1.5, cmt.6. These post-judgment actions are seen as collection proceedings, with the parties' respective rights and obligations already determined by the divorce decree. The contingent fee diverts a portion of recovered funds from the intended recipients, but a successful post-judgment action provides recipients funds they otherwise might not receive.

3. CLIENT CONFIDENCES

"A lawyer shall not reveal information relating to the representation of a client unless the client gives informed consent [or] the disclosure is impliedly authorized in order to carry out the representation." Model Rule 1.6(a). Confidentiality aims to encourage persons to seek legal advice by assuring that lawyer and client can communicate freely and frankly with one another without fear of later compelled disclosure. The assurance is central to the consultations, negotiations, and drafting that characterize the typical domestic relations representation.

The Model Rule reaches both the lawyer's communications with the client and other information concerning the representation. In *In re Skinner*, 758 S.E.2d 788 (Ga. 2014), for example, the court publicly reprimanded the lawyer who, responding to a former divorce client's negative reviews of her on three consumer Internet pages, posted an Internet response that disclosed some personal and confidential information about the client that the lawyer gained during representation.

Model Rule 1.6(b)(1) provides a limited exception to the lawyer's obligation to maintain client confidences: "A lawyer may reveal information relating to the representation of a client to the extent the lawyer reasonably believes necessary * * * to prevent reasonably certain death or substantial bodily harm." Where the lawyer suspects that the client is abusing the children, the lawyer may struggle with impulses to report the abuse to child protective or law enforcement authorities. State child abuse reporting statutes create classes of "mandatory reporters," persons such as educators, medical personnel, and law enforcement agents, who must report reasonably suspected child abuse or face possible criminal sanction for non-reporting. Reporting statutes normally do not list lawyers among mandatory reporters.

The literature amply demonstrates the substantial physical and emotional harm that child abuse can cause victims in the short term and the long term. *See, e.g.*, Douglas E. Abrams et al., Children and the Law: Doctrine, Policy, and Practice ch. 4 (6th ed. 2017). Does the Model Rule, which is grounded in "the overriding value of life and physical integrity," require or permit family lawyers to report physical or sexual abuse that they reasonably suspect their clients are perpetrating? Model Rule 1.6(b)(1), cmt.6. To the extent that the Model Rules would prevent lawyers from reporting, do the Rules serve the best interests of children?

Rates of reported child sexual abuse seem about six times higher in families involved in custody disputes than in the general population, either because rates of abuse are higher in these families, or because custody disputes produce higher rates of emotional distress and anxiety. *See* Andrew I. Schepard, Children, Courts and Custody 97 (2004).

Where the client seeking tactical advantage insists on making allegations that the lawyer believes are baseless, the lawyer may consider withdrawing from the representation because "the client insists upon taking action that the lawyer considers repugnant or with which the lawyer has a fundamental disagreement." Model Rule 1.16(b)(4).

PROBLEM 14-2

You are a leading member of the local family law bar. After an initial conference, you have agreed to represent John Jones in the divorce case that his wife has just filed. When would you explain attorney-client confidentiality to your new client? What would you say?

PROBLEM 14-3

You represent Paula Perkins, your city's mayor, in her divorce proceedings. Because of her official position and the pointed statements she and her estranged husband have made, the impending divorce has attracted considerable media attention. A reporter phones and asks you to comment on reports that the marriage has been marked by the husband's intermittent domestic violence, and that the children have missed several days of school in the last two months. What will you say to the reporter? Would your answer be any different if the husband's lawyer called you and wanted to know whether Mayor Perkins was seeing another man?

4. CONFLICTS OF INTEREST

A. GENERAL STANDARDS

"In representing a client, a lawyer shall exercise independent professional judgment and render candid advice." Model Rule 2.1. Model Rule 1.7(a) prohibits a lawyer from representing a client if the representation involves a "concurrent conflict of interest"—that is, if "the representation of one client will be directly adverse to another client," or if "there is a significant risk that the representation of one or more clients will be materially limited by the lawyer's responsibilities to another client, a former client or a third person or by a personal interest of the lawyer."

Where a concurrent conflict of interest exists, however, Model Rule 1.7(b) permits a lawyer to represent a client if:

(1) the lawyer reasonably believes that the lawyer will be able to provide competent and diligent representation to each affected client;

(2) the representation is not prohibited by law;

(3) the representation does not involve the assertion of a claim by one client against another client represented by the lawyer in the same litigation or other proceeding before a tribunal; and

(4) each affected client gives informed consent, confirmed in writing.

B. DUAL REPRESENTATION

A divorcing couple may ask a lawyer to represent both parties, particularly when the parties appear "amicable" and willing to cooperate with one another. The parties typically say that they seek to save money and reduce adversarial tensions by retaining a shared lawyer, and each party provides informed written consent to dual representation.

For the lawyer, dual representation invites genuine potential for conflict of interest. For example, if the parties' adverse interests arise and cannot be reconciled before entry of the final decree, the lawyer must ordinarily withdraw from representing either party. The result can be additional cost, delay, embarrassment, and recrimination.

In some states, dual representation of divorcing spouses constitutes a *per se* ethical violation because even if the parties give informed written consent, the likelihood of conflict remains too great. In states that determine the propriety of dual representation of divorcing spouses on a case-by-case basis, family lawyers undertaking such representation run a risk because proceedings that seem amicable at the outset may be marked by disagreements before the court enters the final decree.

"There is no getting around the fact that divorce is adversarial," wrote former West Virginia Chief Justice Richard Neely. "In any given family, the hours that children spend with their parents, the future earning capacities of the husband and wife, and all the accumulated property constitute a pie of a given size. Divorce splits up that pie, and a larger slice for one person necessarily means a smaller slice for the other. It is impossible for one lawyer simultaneously to advise each party to a divorce to demand a bigger slice of the pie." Richard Neely, The Divorce Decision: The Legal and Human Consequences of Ending a Marriage 140–41 (1984).

Even in an evidently amicable divorce, does Model Rule 1.7 permit dual representation of divorcing spouses? Is the parties' relationship "directly adverse" within the meaning of Rule 1.7(a)(1)? Is there a "significant risk" that representation of one spouse will be "materially limited by the lawyer's responsibilities" to the other? Is dual representation "consentable" under Model Rule 1.7(b)? Why do some jurisdictions prohibit such representation, even with the parties' informed written consent?

PROBLEM 14-4

Bob and Roberta Ricketts, acquaintances of yours from local school committees, visit your law office together one afternoon to say that they wish to dissolve their marriage after 14 years. They would like you to represent both of them in the divorce proceedings and begin drawing up the papers as soon as possible. They assure you that the divorce is "amicable," that they have talked through the issues, and that they have reached agreement about the property and child-related issues. What questions would you ask Bob and Roberta, and how would you respond to their request? What else would you need to research?

C. DUTIES TO CURRENT CLIENTS

Lawyers sometimes face potential conflicts of interest because one or both parties, perhaps facing personal crisis inherent in dissolution, have grown comfortable with the lawyer through prior personal or professional dealings. The parties may even have come to regard the lawyer as the "family attorney." One party, for example, may seek to retain a lawyer who still represents the other party or both parties in a business venture or other matter unrelated to the dissolution. The other party is a current client of the lawyer.

With narrow exceptions, "[a] lawyer shall not use information relating to representation of a client to the disadvantage of the client unless the client gives informed consent." Model Rule 1.8(b). Such use would violate the duty of loyalty that the lawyer owes to the client.

In one case, the lawyer was representing a husband and wife as co-executors of an estate in which they were beneficiaries of a substantial minority interest in a valuable piece of real estate. The lawyer had obtained no confidential information from the husband individually, and had never represented the husband or wife on any other matter. The state bar association's ethics committee concluded that the lawyer could not represent the wife in divorce proceedings unless the lawyer held the reasonable belief recited in Model Rule 1.7(b) and the husband gave the requisite written consent. "If the divorce proceedings are going to be 'amicable' so that those proceedings will not produce any rancor that might spill over into the estate matter, then perhaps the [reasonable belief] test can be met. The possibility of contention in the divorce proceedings would, by contrast, point in the opposite direction." The ethics committee also concluded that the lawyer could not cure a conflict by withdrawing from representing the husband as co-executor. *See* Mass. Formal & Informal Ops. 2002–1.

D. DUTIES TO FORMER CLIENTS

Model Rule 1.9(a) provides that "[a] lawyer who has formerly represented a client in a matter shall not thereafter represent another person in the same or a substantially related matter in which that person's interests are materially adverse to the interests of the former client unless the former client gives informed consent, confirmed in writing." Even with this informed consent, "[a] lawyer who has formerly represented a client in a matter or whose present or former firm has formerly represented a client in a matter shall not thereafter * * * use information relating to the representation to the disadvantage of the former client except * * * when the information has become generally known * * *." Model Rule 1.9(c)(1).

Two matters are "substantially related" where the lawyer "reasonably could have learned confidential information in the first representation that would be of significance in the second." Information that the lawyer could reasonably have learned is presumed to have been learned. The presumption is generally not rebuttable because rebuttal evidence would require the former client to reveal the confidential information that it seeks to protect. *See* Restatement (Third) of the Law Governing Lawyers § 132A, cmt. d(iii) (2000 & Supp. 2018). The lawyer may be disciplined for using confidential information even if the lawyer does not publicly disclose it.

A party to a dissolution might seek to retain a lawyer who formerly represented one or both parties in a matter concerning, for example, a family-owned business or other family affairs. Even where the former representation has concluded, representing either party in the dissolution proceeding may present a conflict of interest where the other party may have provided significant confidential information. In *Sessa v. Parrotta*, 985 N.Y.S.2d 128 (App. Div. 2014), however, the court declined to disqualify the husband's divorce lawyer, who had previously represented the wife to prepare her will; the court found that the prior representation and the divorce proceeding were not "substantially related." *Id.* at 129.

E. DUTIES TO PROSPECTIVE CLIENTS

Where a person consults with a lawyer concerning the possibility of creating a client-lawyer relationship, the person may be a "prospective client" entitled to protection from conflicts of interest, even if no such relationship is created. Model Rule 1.18 provides that with limited exceptions, the lawyer "shall not use or reveal information learned in the consultation," or "represent a client with interests materially adverse to those of a prospective client in the same or a substantially related matter if the lawyer received information from the prospective client that could be significantly harmful to that person in the matter."

In *In re Marriage of Perry*, 293 P.3d 170 (Mont. 2013), the court denied the wife's motion to disqualify the husband's lawyer even though the wife was a prospective client. Her telephone consultations with the lawyer occurred several years before divorce papers were filed; the information she disclosed was not significantly harmful to her in the divorce case; and the lawyer did not become involved in the divorce case until it had proceeded for three years, by which time substantially more information had been disclosed than the information that the wife claimed to have shared.

Particularly in a small community, why and how might one party try to create a prospective-client relationship without seriously considering retaining the lawyer in an impending divorce or other family law proceeding? What precautions should lawyers take to diminish the possibility of such creation?

F. SEXUAL RELATIONS BETWEEN FAMILY LAWYER AND CLIENT

Sexual relations with clients are not confined to family lawyers, but the issue draws particular attention in domestic relations cases because of the intimate nature of the legal issues, and because some clients remain dependent and emotionally vulnerable throughout the high-stakes proceeding.

In 2003, the American Bar Association added Model Rule 1.8(j): "A lawyer shall not have sexual relations with a client unless a consensual sexual relationship existed between them when the client-lawyer relationship commenced." This *per se* rule, adopted in most states and not limited to family law representation, means that disciplinary action is appropriate even without a showing that that the sexual relationship was unlawful or compromised the client's interests. The dual aims are to preserve lawyers' independent professional judgment and to protect clients. *See, e.g., Disciplinary Counsel v. Benbow,* 106 N.E.3d 57 (Ohio 2018) (lawyer suspended for two years for engaging in sexual activity in a courthouse conference room with a client he represented in a child-visitation matter).

"Sexual relations" violating Model Rule 1.8(j) may arise from messages that the lawyer sends by texting, email, or similar technology, even without physical sexual contact between lawyer and client. For example, in *In re Disciplinary Matter Involving Stanton,* 376 P.3d 693 (Alaska 2016), the court suspended the lawyer for three years. The disciplinary board and the state supreme court found that while the lawyer represented a 23-year-old woman pro bono in a child custody proceeding, he and the client began exchanging texts that "display[ed] lewd content and nude photos." *Id.* at 695. Similarly, in *Disciplinary Counsel v. Bartels,* 87 N.E.3d 155 (Ohio 2016), the court suspended the lawyer for one year for exchanging sexually oriented text messages with the client she was representing in a divorce proceeding.

What policy considerations justify Rule 1.8(j)? Do you find the justifications persuasive?

5. OBLIGATIONS TO THIRD PARTIES AND OPPONENTS

During emotional domestic relations proceedings, the client may ask the lawyer to "try to reason with" the other party, who may or may not be represented by counsel. *Barrett* invites attention to the outer limits of Model Rule 4.3, which concerns a lawyer's communications with an unrepresented person. The Rule is central to domestic relations practice because litigants appearing *pro se* are often inexperienced in legal matters.

BARRETT V. VIRGINIA STATE BAR

Supreme Court of Virginia, 2005.
611 S.E.2d 375.

AGEE, JUSTICE.

This case presents an appeal of right from a ruling of the Virginia State Bar Disciplinary Board ("the Board"). Timothy M. Barrett challenges the Board's order of August 5, 2004, suspending his license to practice law in the Commonwealth for a period of three years * * *.

I.   RULE 4.3(b)

Timothy M. Barrett and Valerie Jill Rhudy were married in 1990. * * *

In the summer of 2001, Barrett and Rhudy separated. She took the couple's six children and moved from the marital home in Virginia Beach to her parents' home in Grayson County.

Rule 4.3(b) provides as follows:

A lawyer shall not give advice to a person who is not represented by a lawyer, other than the advice to secure counsel, if the interests of such person are or have a reasonable possibility of being in conflict with the interest of the client.

The Board found that Barrett violated this rule because it concluded certain statements in two electronic mail ("e-mail") communications he wrote to Rhudy after the separation, but before she retained counsel, constituted legal advice. On July 25, 2001, Barrett sent an e-mail to Rhudy containing the following:

Venue will not be had in Grayson County. Virginia law is clear that venue is in Virginia Beach.

. . . .

Under the doctrine of imputed income, the Court will have to look at your skills and experience and determine their value in the marketplace. . . . You can easily get a job . . . [making] $2,165.00 per month. . . .

In light of the fact that you are living with your parents and have no expenses . . . this income will be more than sufficient to meet your needs. I . . . just make enough to pay my own bills . . . Thus, it is unlikely that you will . . . obtain spousal support from me.

I . . . will file for . . . spousal support to have you help me pay you [sic] fair share of our $200,000+ indebtedness. Since I am barely making it on my income and you have income to spare, you might end up paying me spousal support.

. . .

In light of the fact that . . . I . . . am staying in the maritial [sic] home . . . I believe that I will obtain the children. . . . [Y]ou will have to get a job to pay me my spousal support. . . . The Court will prefer the children staying with a [parent] . . . there is no question that I can set up a home away from home and even continue to home school our kids. Therefore, it is likely that you will lose this fight. And of course, if I have the kids you will be paying me child support. . . .

I am prepared for the fight.

("July e-mail").

Barrett sent Rhudy another e-mail on September 12, 2001, in which he included the following:

I will avail myself of every substantive law and procedural and evidentiary rule in the books for which a good faith claim exists. This means that you, the kids and your attorney will be in Court in Virginia Beach weekly . . . You are looking at attorney's expenses that will greatly exceed $10,000. . . . I will also appeal . . . every negative ruling . . . causing your costs to likely exceed $30,000.00. . . .

You have no case against me for adultery. . . . [The facts] show[ ] that you deserted me. . . . Your e-mails . . . show . . . that you were cruel to me. This means that I will obtain a divorce from you on fault grounds, which means you can say goodbye to spousal support. . . .

I remain in the marrital [sic] home . . . I have all the kids [sic] toys and property, that your parents' home is grossly insufficient for the children, that I can home school the older kids while watching the younger whereas you will have to put the younger in day care to fulfill your duty to financially support the kids, I believe that I will get the kids no problem. . . .

[T]he family debt . . . is subject to equitable distribution, which means you could be socked with half my lawschool [sic] debt, half the credit care [sic] debt, have [sic] my firm debt, etc.

("September e-mail").

The foregoing e-mail passages were interwoven with many requests from Barrett to Rhudy to return home, professing his love for her and the children and exhorting Rhudy for reasons of faith to reunite the family because it was God's will. * * *

In finding that Barrett gave unauthorized legal advice to an unrepresented person in violation of Rule 4.3(b), the Board opined that "Barrett cannot send those two e-mails stating what he did." Barrett contends that Rule 4.3(b) was not meant to bar communications between a husband and wife, and that construing it as such interferes with the sanctity of marriage. He further contends the e-mails only stated his opinions and were not advice to Rhudy.

* * *

Comment [1] to Rule 4.3 of the Virginia Rules of Professional Conduct cautions that "[a]n unrepresented person, particularly one not experienced in dealing with legal matters, might assume that a lawyer is disinterested in loyalties or is a disinterested authority on the law."

* * *

In the case at bar, * * * Barrett expressed only his opinion that he held a superior legal position on certain issues in controversy between himself and Rhudy. His statements may have been intimidating, but he did not purport to give legal advice. Rhudy knew that Barrett was a lawyer and that he had interests opposed to hers. We find that the concern articulated by the Comment to Rule 4.3 is not borne out in this case.

While the Bar argues that there is no "marital" exception to Rule 4.3(b), neither does it ask us to set out a per se rule that all communication by a lawyer, to his or her unrepresented spouse in a divorce proceeding discussing legal issues pertinent to the divorce, is prohibited under Rule 4.3(b). We do not find there is such a per se rule, but it is otherwise unnecessary for us to address that point because upon our independent review of the entire record, we find that there was not sufficient evidence to support the Board's finding that Barrett's e-mail statements to Rhudy were legal advice rather than statements of his opinion of their legal situation. Therefore, we will set aside the Board's finding that Barrett violated Rule 4.3(b).

* * *

JUSTICE KEENAN, with whom CHIEF JUSTICE HASSELL and SENIOR JUSTICE COMPTON join, concurring in part and dissenting in part.

* * *

I would hold that [Barrett's] explanations constituted legal advice intended to influence the conduct of a party who had conflicting legal interests and who was not represented by counsel. Without question, Barrett's conduct would have been a violation of Rule 4.3(b) had he communicated this advice to a pro se litigant whose spouse Barrett was representing. Thus, the majority's conclusion necessarily implies that there is a "spousal exception" to Rule 4.3(b), under which an attorney may attempt to influence his or her spouse's conduct by imparting legal advice in a harassing manner regarding the parties' conflicting legal interests.

Such a conclusion, however, is contrary to the plain language of Rule 4.3(b), which provides no "spousal exception." Moreover, Barrett's use of legal advice as a "sword" in his marital conflict is clearly a type of conduct that Rule 4.3(b) is designed to discourage. It is hard to imagine a situation in which an attorney would be in a stronger position to improperly influence another's conduct by giving legal advice.

NOTES AND QUESTIONS

1.   *Constitutional and policy questions raised in* Barrett. Virginia Rule 4.3(b), quoted in *Barrett*, closely tracks the third and final sentence of ABA Model Rule 4.3. In the two earlier sentences not quoted in *Barrett*, ABA Model Rule 4.3 also provides that the lawyer shall not state or imply that the lawyer is disinterested; and must make reasonable efforts to correct any misunderstanding where the lawyer knows or reasonably should know that the unrepresented person misunderstands the lawyer's role in the matter.

These commands raise interesting constitutional and policy questions where, as in *Barrett*, the unrepresented party is the lawyer's spouse before entry of the divorce decree. (a) If a state disciplines a *pro se* lawyer for communicating with his or her unrepresented spouse about their impending dissolution, does the state interfere unduly (or perhaps even unconstitutionally) with the marital relationship? (b) Would such application of the Model Rules diminish prospects for reconciliation or inhibit the spouses' ability to manage their affairs and raise their children? Or would application help level the playing field between the lawyer spouse and the lay spouse? (c) If Timothy Barrett had been a layperson rather than a lawyer, would he likely have had the legal knowledge to make some of the statements he made in his e-mails? Would a recipient in his wife's position reasonably have given the e-mail statements more credence because they were made by a lawyer rather than a layperson?

2.   *The family lawyer's relations with third parties: improper purpose.* Model Rule 4.4(a) provides: "In representing a client, a lawyer shall not use means that have no substantial purpose other than to embarrass, delay, or burden a third person, or use methods of obtaining evidence that violate the legal rights of such a person." *See, e.g., Kentucky Bar Ass'n v. Glidewell*, 348 S.W.3d 759, 760 (Ky. 2011) (lawyer suspended for three years for filing an unlawful lien against real property awarded to the client's wife in a divorce proceeding, and then refusing to remove the lien). Despite the command of Model Rule 4.4, "divorce lawyers have provoked criticism for client-driven litigation tactics that inflict emotional and financial harm on opposing parties and children." Barbara Ann Atwood, *Representing Children Who Can't or Won't Direct Counsel: Best Interests Lawyering or No Lawyer at All?*, 53 Ariz. L. Rev. 381, 384 (2011).

3.   *May a lawyer represent a domestic relations client against an opponent who is represented by the lawyer's spouse or other immediate family member?* The Model Rules take a case-by-case approach, but emphasize the

informed consent of both clients: "[E]ach client is entitled to know of the existence and implications of the relationship between the lawyers before the lawyer agrees to undertake the representation. Thus, a lawyer related to another lawyer, e.g., as parent, child, sibling or spouse, ordinarily may not represent a client where that lawyer is representing another party, unless each client gives informed consent." Model Rule 1.7, cmt. 11. Should this rule extend to lawyers who are engaged to one another? Who cohabit with one another?

PROBLEM 14-5

You represent Frank Friedman in his divorce proceedings against his wife, Dolores, who you know is proceeding *pro se*. You have scheduled a negotiating session for the parties, which you plan to attend. What should you say to Dolores about your relationship with Frank and her, and when and how should you say it?

6. OBLIGATIONS TO THE PARTIES' CHILDREN

A. OBLIGATIONS WHEN REPRESENTING A PARENT

A significant percentage of dissolution and other family law proceedings involve parents who have one or more minor dependent children. The children are not parties to the proceedings, but the outcome will affect their emotional and perhaps financial well-being.

May a lawyer representing a parent seek an outcome that the lawyer believes would serve the best interests of the children, even where the outcome would be inconsistent with the client-parent's interests? Model Rule 1.2(a) states the essence of the attorney-client relationship: "[A] lawyer shall abide by a client's decisions concerning the objectives of representation."

In *Person v. Behnke*, 611 N.E.2d 1350, 1355 (Ill. App. Ct. 1993), the court expressed the prevailing view: "[L]awyers in a divorce proceeding owe a duty to their clients—the parents—not to the children of their clients." Two commentators, however, advocate a broader view. "As an attorney for a parent, your zealous advocacy must be tailored to the best interest of the entire family, including balancing how your advocacy * * * will affect family relations well into the future. * * * It is important to remember that for you, the case ends with an order from a judge; but for your client and the children, the order is only the beginning." Liisa R. Speaker & Jodi M. Latuszek, *Communicating With Children in Custody Disputes*, 33 Fam. Adv. 44, 47 (No. 2 Fall 2010).

The lawyer's ethical obligation to heed the client's decisions concerning the objectives of representation, imposed by Model Rule 1.2, may disturb a lawyer who senses that the client is inattentive to, or unconcerned about, the child's best interests as the lawyer perceives them. Decisions such as

Person, however, "generally reject the notion that a lawyer for a parent has any duty to a child. Their rationale is that the lawyer would not be able to represent his or her client effectively if required to advocate for another party—the child—with adverse interests." Andrew Schepard, *Kramer vs. Kramer Revisited: A Comment on* The Miller Commission Report *and the Obligation of Divorce Lawyers for Parents to Discuss Alternative Dispute Resolution with Their Clients*, 27 Pace L. Rev. 677, 693 (2007).

What if the lawyer believes that the client does not actually want custody of the children, but seeks custody as a bargaining chip to induce the other parent to accept a lower property settlement or forego alimony? The Model Rules of Professional Conduct do not yield a definitive answer, but Model Rule 2.1 permits a lawyer rendering advice to "refer not only to law but to other considerations such as moral * * * [and] social * * * factors, that may be relevant to the client's situation." Model Rule 3.1 provides further that a lawyer may not assert or controvert an issue in a legal proceeding unless there is a nonfrivolous basis for the position, but the Rule applies only in a legal proceeding.

In accordance with these Rules, a lawyer can advise the client about the hurt that children may suffer from bad-faith custody claims, and about the "immorality of a terroristic threat directed to an area of especial vulnerability." Lewis Becker, *Ethical Concerns in Negotiating Family Law Agreements*, 30 Fam. L.Q. 587, 628–29 (1996). If the client refuses to abandon the bad-faith claim, the lawyer might withdraw from representation under Model Rule 1.16(b)(4) because "the client insists upon taking action that the lawyer considers repugnant or with which the lawyer has a fundamental disagreement." "Moreover, even a lawyer who decides to continue to represent the client should advise the client, unless there is clear state law to the contrary, that some judicial decisions have upheld an attack on the validity of an agreement where the consent of the party attacking the agreement was secured by a threat to contest custody." *Id.*

B. OBLIGATIONS WHEN REPRESENTING A CHILD

"The legal representation of children is a rapidly developing professional field," and "a recognized area of practice." *Uniform Representation of Children in Abuse, Neglect, and Custody Proceedings Act, Prefatory Note*, 42 Fam. L.Q. 5 (2008). Section 310 of the Uniform Marriage and Divorce Act authorizes the court, on either parent's motion or on its own motion, to "appoint an attorney to represent the interests of a minor or dependent child with respect to his support, custody, and visitation." *Id.* cmt.

By statute in many states, courts may appoint a guardian *ad litem* in proceedings for divorce or legal separation, or in other proceedings that raise any of the three children's issues. The court's authority is generally discretionary, though some states mandate appointment of a representative for the child when custody or visitation is contested and one or both parties allege abuse or neglect. *See, e.g.*, Mo. Rev. Stat. § 452.423 (2018). Where the court holds discretionary authority to appoint counsel for the child, what factors should the court consider in deciding whether to make an appointment in a particular case?

The nature of the appointed lawyer's professional obligations to the child remains a matter of spirited debate among scholars and practitioners. The ABA Model Rules of Professional Conduct, the Uniform Law Commission, the American Academy of Matrimonial Lawyers, and leading commentators and child advocacy organizations disagree about whether appointed lawyers must represent the child's wishes, or whether these lawyers may represent the child's best interests. Chapter 12 ("Child Custody") treats this controversy.

7. DOMESTIC MISCONDUCT BY LAWYERS

A. LAWYERS' EMOTIONS AS DOMESTIC RELATIONS PARTIES

As in *Barrett* above, *pro se* lawyers caught up in their own divorce proceedings sometimes face professional sanction because, like some other divorcing spouses, they may let their emotions get the better of them. One writer calls lawyers' self-representation in divorce cases an "ethical minefield." Louis Parley, *Lawyers, Their Divorces, and Legal Ethics*, 30 Fam. L.Q. 661, 676 (1996).

Unless a particular Model Rule clearly suggests otherwise, the rule applies not only to lawyers as they represent clients, but also to lawyers who appear as *pro se* litigants, "whose clients are themselves." *In re Chiofalo*, 909 N.Y.S.2d 36, 39 (App. Div. 2010) (ordering two-year suspension of a lawyer spouse who, arising from his divorce action, "sent a series of hostile, obscene, and derogatory written messages to his wife, her successive lawyers, the children's law guardian, the law clerk for the judge presiding over his matrimonial matter and others."). *See also, e.g., Matter of Schorr*, 86 N.Y.S.3d 75 (App. Div. 2018) (issuing public reprimand of lawyer spouse who made an unauthorized hidden recording of a court conference in his divorce action, in violation of state regulations).

B. DOMESTIC MISCONDUCT BY LAWYERS UNRELATED TO CLIENT REPRESENTATION

"A lawyer, as a member of the legal profession, is * * * an officer of the legal system and a public citizen having special responsibility for the quality of justice." Model Rules, Preamble [1]. Under Model Rule 8.4, disciplinary action may result where a lawyer "commit[s] a criminal act that reflects adversely on the lawyer's honesty, trustworthiness or fitness as a lawyer in other respects"; "engage[s] in conduct involving dishonesty, fraud, deceit or misrepresentation"; or "engage[s] in conduct that is prejudicial to the administration of justice."

Rule 8.4's command extends to lawyers' non-professional conduct. "[O]ffenses committed by an attorney in his capacity as a private individual and not in any professional capacity will nevertheless justify disciplinary proceedings if the misconduct is indicative of moral unfitness for the profession." *State ex rel. Counsel for Discipline v. Wintroub*, 765 N.W.2d 482, 491 (Neb. 2009). In *Statewide Grievance Committee v. Ganim*, 87 A.3d 1078, 1081 (Conn. 2014), for example, the court invoked Rule 8.4 to deny the application for reinstatement to the bar after the lawyer served a lengthy prison sentence for 16 federal felonies that he committed as a city mayor.

The focus here is on family law, however. Under Rule 8.4, lawyers remain subject to discipline for committing acts of domestic misconduct unaccompanied by family law proceedings. For example, in *In re Disciplinary Proceedings Against Gorokhovsky*, 840 N.W.2d 126, 131 (Wis. 2013), the court suspended the lawyer for 60 days for, among other things, misdemeanor convictions on two counts of battery and a single count of disorderly conduct arising from his acts of domestic violence against his wife.

A lawyer's failure to comply with an order to pay child support or alimony may also lead to professional discipline for violating Rule 8.4. *See, e.g., Disciplinary Counsel v. Wrage*, 10 N.E.3d 679 (Ohio 2014) (lawyer suspended for two years for, among other things, willfully failing to pay ordered child support).

8. THE RELATIONSHIP BETWEEN ETHICS AND MALPRACTICE

Mirroring the relatively high rate of ethics complaints filed against family lawyers (mentioned in this Chapter's first paragraphs), family lawyers are also named in about 13% of malpractice claims that clients file each year. Only claims against personal injury plaintiffs' lawyers and real estate lawyers exceed this percentage. *See* Am. Bar Ass'n, *Profile of Legal Malpractice Claims, 2012–2015*, at 11 (2016).

To prevail in a legal malpractice action, the plaintiff must prove "(1) the existence of an attorney-client relationship between the defendant and plaintiff giving rise to a duty; (2) the attorney, by either an act or a failure to act, breached that duty; (3) this breach proximately caused injury to the plaintiff; and (4) the plaintiff sustained actual injury, loss, or damage." *Kraklio v. Simmons*, 909 N.W.2d 427, 434 (Iowa 2018).

The Model Rules state that "[v]iolation of a Rule should not itself give rise to a cause of action against a lawyer nor should it create any presumption in such a case that a legal duty has been breached." Model Rules, Preamble [20]. The Rules' admissibility as proof of liability in malpractice suits, however, differs from state to state. "[O]ne jurisdiction [Michigan] allows the violation of an ethical rule to create a rebuttable presumption of negligence. * * * A second approach, adopted by a larger number of courts, is that ethical rule violations are inadmissible in legal malpractice claims. But overwhelmingly, a third approach is that the violation of an ethical rule alone does not establish a per se private cause of action for legal malpractice but may be used as relevant evidence for the standard of care." *Stender v. Blessum*, 897 N.W.2d 491, 503 (Iowa 2017).

Regardless of the ethical rules' effect on establishing malpractice, malpractice claims against family lawyers may be grounded in ethical lapses, such as ones arising from representing both divorcing spouses, representing one divorcing spouse after having represented the other in previous matters, engaging in sexual relations with a client, or disclosing the client's confidences without authorization. *See* Ronald E. Mallen & Jeffrey M. Smith, Legal Malpractice ch. 28 ("Family law") (2014).

Malpractice claims may also arise from the lawyer's alleged failure to understand and apply the substantive law, such as failure to grasp a property settlement's tax or pension consequences. Most malpractice claims against domestic relations lawyers arise from property settlements, but clients also frequently allege negligence in drafting or negotiating premarital agreements, or in resolving custody and spousal or child support matters. *Id.* § 28.3.

A malpractice action grounded in negligence may lie even where the family lawyer committed no ethical violation. In *Sachs v. Downs Rachlin Martin PLLC*, 179 A.3d 182 (Vt. 2017), for example, the lawyer negligently advised the unwed pregnant client that under state law, a child support award would be retroactive to the child's date of birth. The lawyer advised that by not filing an action for paternity and support until at least a year after the child's birth, the client could increase the chances that the father would not seek legal or physical custody or visitation rights. The court found that the lawyer " 'did no specific research to support her opinion as to the retroactivity of child support,' instead relying on her experience as a family law attorney." *Id.* at 184–85. The client relied on the lawyer's incorrect advice, lost fifteen months of child support, and recovered damages from her lawyer on the malpractice claim.

CHAPTER 15

ALTERNATIVE DISPUTE RESOLUTION

■ ■ ■

Historically, parties seeking dissolution had few alternatives other than adversary proceedings in open court. These proceedings frequently multiplied costs, gave judges considerable control over resolution of intimate family affairs, and heightened antagonisms that frequently attend adversary civil litigation.

Chapters 1 and 8 describe the frequently corrupt nature of domestic relations trials before the early 1970s. Efforts to reduce antagonisms seem especially worthwhile in family law because, unlike civil litigants in many other fields, family members cannot always simply disengage and go their separate ways after the court enters judgment. Disengagement appears most unlikely when the family includes minor dependent children, who will likely face continuing consequences.

Alternative dispute resolution (ADR) methods dominate twenty-first century family law because few dissolutions proceed to full trial. "Over the past three decades, * * * [m]ediation, collaboration, and other non-adversarial processes have replaced a traditional, law-oriented adversarial regime" in family disputes. Jane C. Murphy & Jana B. Singer, *Moving Family Dispute Resolution From the Court System to the Community*, 75 Md. L. Rev. Endnotes 9 (2016).

The decline of family law trials has not occurred in a vacuum because "[a]lternative dispute resolution has become a substantial part of the civil justice system" generally. ABA Model Rules of Prof'l Conduct, Model Rule 2.4, cmt.1 (2018). This Chapter explores four ADR methods that characterize contemporary family law practice: (1) direct negotiation between the parties; (2) mediation, in which one or more private third-party neutrals facilitate the parties' negotiation, without authority to impose a settlement; (3) arbitration, in which the parties agree to submit all or part of their case to one or more private third-party neutrals to render a binding decision largely beyond judicial review; and (4) collaborative law, in which parties seeking a less adversarial divorce agree that both lawyers would be disqualified from further representing their clients if negotiations collapse and the case moves to adversary litigation.

As you proceed through this Chapter, consider the capacity of each of these four ADR methods to serve (or disserve) the interests of parties and children in proceedings that are frequently marked by emotion, power imbalance, and the prospect that some rights and obligations will outlast the immediate resolution.

1. NEGOTIATION

In direct negotiation, disputants seek to resolve their rights and obligations before filing suit, before a final court decision, or perhaps before any proceedings in open court. Across the wide range of American law, upwards of 90% of filed federal and state civil actions are settled or otherwise resolved without trial each year, a figure that also reflects family practice. "Most current estimates of the actual percentage of divorce cases settled by judges and litigation are quite low—usually less than ten percent." Milfred D. Dale, *Don't Forget the Children: Court Protection From Parental Conflict Is In the Best Interests of Children*, 52 Fam. Ct. Rev. 648, 651 (2014).

Family law proceedings have featured negotiation for decades, but most prominently in recent generations. No-fault divorce has "effectively changed the core story about divorce from one about guilt and innocence to one that minimized the importance of fault and instead created a complex forward-looking inquiry. This new regime effectively discouraged parties from seeking judicial resolution of their disputes and encouraged them to resolve their disputes through negotiation or mediation." Ray D. Madoff, *Lurking in the Shadow: The Unseen Hand of Doctrine in Dispute Resolution*, 76 S. Cal. L. Rev. 161, 166 (2002).

The ABA Section of Family Law urges counsel to "[e]xplore settlement possibilities at the earliest reasonable date." *American Bar Association Section of Family Law Civility Standards*, 40 Fam. L.Q. xv, xvi (Winter 2007). "Negotiation is especially important in family law cases. Often, minor children are involved, and bitter conflict can leave emotional scars for the rest of their lives. The parties themselves also can suffer long-term emotional and economic damage." John Lande, *Overcoming Roadblocks To Reaching Settlement In Family Law Cases*, 40 Family Advocate 26, 29 (Winter 2018).

Unlike other civil litigants who often consider settlement only after an interlocutory court decision such as denial of summary judgment makes trial imminent, domestic relations parties typically begin negotiating with little outside pressure, often even before suit is filed. Once the parties retain counsel, the lawyers typically participate in the give-and-take and can serve an educative function. "By sharing their impressions and teaching the client how to appreciate and empathize with the underlying needs and goals of their spouse, lawyers can help their clients to maximize their effectiveness in formulating and presenting their proposals." Forrest S. Mosten, *Unbundled Services To Enhance Peacemaking For Divorcing Families*, 53 Fam. Ct. Rev. 439, 442 (2015).

During early negotiation and beyond, family lawyers today may need to grapple with the parties' heightened personal antagonisms. In a 2017 survey conducted by the American Academy of Matrimonial Lawyers (AAML), 41% of the organization's members said that the current political climate in Washington has "worsened the tone of divorces. In all, 54% of the attorneys cite an increase in the number of contentious divorce cases during the past three years, while 52% find that divorcing spouses are becoming more hostile." AAML, *Divorces Overheating in U.S. Political Climate Finds Survey of Nation's Top Attorneys*, June 26, 2017.

Personal antagonisms may grow even worse. As explained in Chapter 10, in 2018 President Trump signed tax legislation that, beginning with divorces finalized in 2019, ends federal deductions for alimony paid. In an AAML poll of the nation's top family lawyers, nearly two-thirds of respondents said that they expect divorce negotiations to become "more acrimonious" with the new alimony provision. AAML, *New Tax Plan to Make Divorce More Acrimonious Finds Survey of Nation's Top Attorneys*, Feb. 14, 2018. "Battles will ensue since alimony payers will have less of a tax incentive to be generous to their former spouses." Ben Steverman, Bloomberg, *Trump's Tax Law Could Make Divorces More Bitter*, Feb. 15, 2018.

We know that most divorce cases conclude without trial, but instead with the parties' request that the court enter the final decree based on their negotiated agreement. You might wonder about the role that substantive family law—statutes, judicial precedents, and various support guidelines—plays in formulating such agreements. When parties negotiate the terms of their dissolution, rather than have the court decide their rights and obligations, the parties engage in "private ordering." The next article explains the centrality of substantive family law doctrine in private ordering by parties and their lawyers.

ROBERT H. MNOOKIN & LEWIS KORNHAUSER, BARGAINING IN THE SHADOW OF THE LAW: THE CASE OF DIVORCE

88 Yale L.J. 950, 950–51, 959, 968–75 (1979).

* * * We see the primary function of contemporary divorce law not as imposing order from above, but rather as providing a framework within which divorcing couples can themselves determine their postdissolution rights and responsibilities. This process by which parties to a marriage are empowered to create their own legally enforceable commitments is a form of "private ordering."

* * *

"Typically, the parties do not go to court at all, until they have worked matters out and are ready for the rubber stamp." Both in the United States and in England, the overwhelming majority of divorcing couples resolve distributional questions concerning marital property, alimony, child support, and custody without bringing any contested issue to court for adjudication.

* * *

II.   The Elements of a Bargaining Model

* * *

2.   *How Legal Rules Create Bargaining Endowments*

Divorcing parents do not bargain over the division of family wealth and custodial prerogatives in a vacuum; they bargain in the shadow of the law. The legal rules governing alimony, child support, marital property, and custody give each parent certain claims based on what each would get if the case went to trial. In other words, the outcome that the law will impose if no agreement is reached gives each parent certain bargaining chips—an endowment of sorts.

A simplified example may be illustrative. Assume that in disputed custody cases the law flatly provided that all mothers had the right to custody of minor children and that all fathers only had the right to visitation two weeks a month. Absent some contrary agreement acceptable to both parents, a court would order this arrangement. Assume further that the legal rules relating to marital property, alimony, and child support gave the mother some determinate share of the family's economic resources. In negotiations under this regime, neither spouse would ever consent to a division that left him or her worse off than if he or she insisted on going to court. The range of negotiated outcomes would be limited to those that leave both parents as well off as they would be in the absence of a bargain.

If private ordering were allowed, we would not necessarily expect parents to split custody and money the way a judge would if they failed to agree. The father might well negotiate for more child-time and the mother for less. This result might occur either because the father made the mother better off by giving her additional money to compensate her for accepting less child-time, or because the mother found custody burdensome and considered herself better off with less custody. Indeed, she might agree to accept less money, or even to pay the father, if he agreed to relieve her of some child-rearing responsibilities. In all events, because the parents' tastes with regard to the trade-offs between money and child-time may differ, it will often be possible for the parties to negotiate some outcome that makes both better off than they would be if they simply accepted the result a court would impose.

3. *Private Ordering Against a Backdrop of Uncertainty*

Legal rules are generally not as simple or straightforward as is suggested by the last example. Often, the outcome in court is far from certain, with any number of outcomes possible. Indeed, existing legal standards governing custody, alimony, child support, and marital property are all striking for their lack of precision and thus provide a bargaining backdrop clouded by uncertainty. The almost universal judicial standard for resolving custody disputes is the "best interests of the child." Except in situations when one parent poses a substantial threat to the child's well-being, predicting who will get custody under this standard is difficult indeed, especially given the increasing pressure to reject any presumption in favor of maternal custody. Similarly, standards governing alimony and child support are also extraordinarily vague and allow courts broad discretion in disputed cases.

Analyzing the effects of uncertainty on bargaining is an extremely complicated task. It is apparent, however, that the effects in any particular case will depend in part on the attitudes of the two spouses toward risk—what economists call "risk preferences." * * *

Because drawing straws, like flipping a coin, gives each parent a fifty percent chance of receiving full custody, economic theory suggests that for each parent the "expected" outcome is half-custody. We cannot, however, simply assume that each parent will bargain as if receiving half of the child's time were certain. Attitudes toward risk may be defined by asking a parent to compare two alternatives: (1) a certainty of having one-half of the child's time; or (2) a gamble in which the "expected" or average outcome is one-half of the child's time. By definition, a parent who treats these alternatives as equally desirable is risk-neutral. A parent who would accept a certain outcome of less than half-custody in order to avoid the gamble—the chance of losing the coin flip and receiving no custody—is risk-averse. Other parents may be risk preferers: they would rather take the gamble and have a fifty percent chance of winning full custody than accept the certain outcome of split custody.

The reality of custody litigation is more complicated, and the knowledge of the parties much less complete, than in our hypothetical. The parties in the example know the standard for decision and the odds of winning custody in court. But in real situations, the exact odds of various possible outcomes are not known by the parties; often they do not even know what information or criteria the judge will use in deciding.

4. *Transaction Costs*

Costs are involved in resolving the distributional consequences of separation or divorce, and in securing the divorce itself. The transaction costs that the parties must bear may take many forms, some financial and some emotional. The most obvious and tangible involve the expenditure of money. Professional fees—particularly for lawyers—must be paid by one or both parties. In addition, there are filing fees and court costs. More difficult to measure, but also important, are the emotional and psychological costs involved in the dispute-settlement process. Lawsuits generally are emotionally burdensome; the psychological costs imposed by bargaining (and still more by litigation) are particularly acute in divorce.

The magnitude of these transaction costs, both actual and expected, can influence negotiations and the outcome of bargaining. In the dissolution process, one spouse, and that spouse's attorney, can substantially affect the magnitude of the transaction costs that must be borne by the other spouse. As is generally the case, the party better able to bear the transaction costs, whether financial or emotional, will have an advantage in divorce bargaining.

In divorce, transaction costs will generally tend to be (1) higher if there are minor children involved, because of the additional and intensely emotional allocational issues to be determined; (2) an increasing function of the amount of property and income the spouses have, since it is rational to spend more on negotiation when the possible rewards are higher; and (3) higher when there is a broad range of possible outcomes in court.

5.   *Strategic Behavior*

The actual bargain that is struck through negotiations—indeed, whether a bargain is struck at all—depends on the negotiation process. During this process, each party transmits information about his or her own preferences to the other. This information may be accurate or intentionally inaccurate; each party may promise, threaten, or bluff. Parties may intentionally exaggerate their chances of winning in court in the hope of persuading the other side to accept less. Or they may threaten to impose substantial transaction costs—economic or psychological—on the other side. In short, there are a variety of ways in which the parties may engage in strategic behavior during the bargaining process.

Opportunities for strategic behavior exist because the parties often will not know with certainty (1) the other side's true preferences with regard to the allocational outcomes; (2) the other spouse's preference or attitudes towards risk; and (3) what the outcome in court will be, or even what the actual odds in court are. Although parents may know a great deal about each other's preferences for money and children, complete knowledge of the other spouse's attitudes is unlikely.

How do parties and their representatives actually behave during the process? Two alternative models are suggested by the literature: (1) a *Strategic Model*, which would characterize the process as "a relatively norm-free process centered on the transmutation of underlying bargaining strength into agreement by the exercise of power, horse-trading, threat, and bluff"; and (2) a *Norm-Centered Model*, which would characterize the process by elements normally associated with adjudication—the parties and their representatives would invoke rules, cite precedents, and engage in reasoned elaboration. Anecdotal observation suggests that each model captures part of the flavor of the process. The parties and their representatives do make appeals to legal and social norms in negotiation, but they frequently threaten and bluff as well.

C. The Task Facing the Spouses and the Process of Negotiation

The task facing divorcing spouses can be summarized, based on the preceding analysis, as one of attempting through bargaining to divide money and child-rearing responsibilities to reflect personal preferences. Even though the interests of the two parents may substantially conflict, opportunities for making both parents better off through a negotiated agreement will exist to the extent that parental preferences differ.

This analysis suggests why most divorcing couples never require adjudication for dispute settlement. The parties gain substantial advantages when they can reach an agreement concerning the distributional consequences of divorce. They can minimize the transaction costs involved in adjudication. They can avoid its risks and uncertainties, and negotiate an agreement that may better reflect their individual preferences.

Furthermore, divorcing spouses usually have no incentive to take cases to court for their precedential value. Unlike insurance companies, public-interest organizations, and other "repeat players," a divorcing spouse will generally have no expectation that an adjudicated case will create precedent, or that any precedent created will be of personal benefit in future litigation.

Given the advantages of negotiated settlements, why do divorcing spouses ever require courtroom adjudication of their disputes? There are a variety of reasons why some divorce cases will be litigated:

1. *Spite.* One or both parties may be motivated in substantial measure by a desire to punish the other spouse, rather than simply to increase their own net worth.

2. *Distaste for Negotiation.* Even though it costs more, one or both parties may prefer the adjudicative process (with third-party decision) to any process that requires a voluntary agreement with the other spouse. Face-to-face contact may be extremely distasteful, and the parties may not be able to negotiate—even with lawyers acting as intermediaries—because of distrust or distaste.

3. *Calling the Bluff—The Breakdown of Negotiations.* If the parties get heavily engaged in strategic behavior and get carried away with making threats, a courtroom battle may result, despite both parties' preference for a settlement. Negotiations may resemble a game of "chicken"

in which two teenagers set their cars on a collision course to see who turns first. Some crack-ups may result.

4. *Uncertainty and Risk Preferences.* The exact odds for any given outcome in court are unknown, and it has been suggested that litigants typically overestimate their chances of winning. To the extent that one or both of the parties typically overestimate their chances of winning, more cases will be litigated than in a world in which the outcome is uncertain but the odds are known. * * *

5. *No Middle Ground.* If the object of dispute cannot be divided into small enough increments—whether because of the law, the practical circumstances, or the nature of the subject at issue—there may be no middle ground on which to strike a feasible compromise. Optimal bargaining occurs when, in economic terminology, nothing is indivisible.

How do parties negotiating a divorce or other family dissolution matters bargain "in the shadow of the law"? Is the legal backdrop to this bargaining still as "clouded by uncertainty" today as it was in 1979, given such developments as federally-mandated child support guidelines and the trend toward state alimony guidelines? Is private ordering in dissolution actions appropriate? What limits should the law place on the parties' capacity to determine the family's affairs in the shadow of the law? Consider this article, in which one of the earlier article's authors revisited both the promise and the peril of private ordering:

ROBERT H. MNOOKIN,
DIVORCE BARGAINING: THE LIMITS
ON PRIVATE ORDERING

18 U. Mich. J.L.Reform 1015, 1017–21, 1024–26, 1031–33 (1985).

* * *

I.   The Advantages of Private Ordering

* * * The core justification [for private ordering] is rooted in notions of human liberty. The liberal ideal that individuals have fundamental rights, and should freely choose to make of their lives what they wish supports private ordering. * * *

Private ordering is also justified on grounds of efficiency. Ordinarily, the parties themselves are in the best position to evaluate the comparative advantages of alternative arrangements. * * * Through negotiations, opportunities exist for making *both* spouses better off than either would be if a court or some third party simply imposed a result. A consensual solution, by definition, more likely conforms with the preferences of each spouse than would a result imposed by a court. Parental preferences often vary with regard to money and child-rearing responsibilities. Through negotiations, a greater likelihood exists that divorcing spouses can divide money and child-rearing responsibilities to reflect their own individual preferences.

Finally, obvious and substantial savings occur when a couple can resolve the distributional consequences of divorce without resort to formal adjudication. The financial cost of litigation, both private and public, lessens. A negotiated settlement allows the parties to avoid the pain of the formal adversarial proceedings and the risks and uncertainties of litigation, which may involve all-or-nothing consequences. Given the substantial delays that often characterize contested judicial proceedings, agreement often saves time and allows each spouse to proceed with his or her life. In short, against a backdrop of fair standards in the shadow of which a couple bargains, divorcing couples should have very broad powers to make their own arrangements. Additionally, significant limitations are inconsistent with the premises of no-fault divorce. The state should encourage parties to settle the distributional consequences of divorce for themselves. The state should also provide an efficient and fair mechanism for enforcing such agreements and for settling disputes when the parties are unable to agree.

II.   Justifications for Limitations on Private Ordering

A.   Capacity

* * * [T]he general defense of private ordering * * * is premised on the notion that divorce bargaining involves rational, self-interested individuals—that the average adult has the intelligence and experience to make a well-informed judgment concerning the desirability of entering into a particular divorce settlement. Given the tasks facing an individual at the time of divorce, and the characteristics of the relationship between divorcing spouses, there are reasons to fear that this may not always be the case.

Informed bargaining requires a divorcing spouse to assess his or her own preferences concerning alternative arrangements. Radical changes in life circumstances complicate such assessments. Within a short period of time, separation and divorce often subject spouses to the stresses of many changes. "[S]pouses need to adjust to new living arrangements, new jobs, new financial burdens, new patterns of parenting, and new conditions of social and sexual life." It may be particularly difficult for a parent to assess custodial alternatives. The past will supply a very incomplete guide to the future. Preferences may stem from past experiences in which child-rearing tasks were performed in an ongoing two-parent family, and dissolution or divorce inevitably alters this division of responsibilities. Childrearing may have new advantages or disadvantages for the parents' own needs. A parent interested in dating may find the child an intrusion in a way that the child never was during marriage. Because children and parents both change, and changes occur unpredictably, projecting parental preferences for custody into the future presents a formidable task. Nevertheless, most parents have some self-awareness, however imperfect, and no third party (such as a judge) is likely to have better information about a parent's tastes, present or future.

Separation often brings in its wake psychological turmoil and substantial emotional distress that can make deliberative and well-informed judgments unlikely. It can arouse "feelings about the (former) spouse, such as love, hate, bitterness, guilt, anger, envy, concern, and attachment; feelings about the marriage, such as regret, disappointment, bitterness, sadness, and failure; and more general feelings such as failure, depression, euphoria, relief, guilt, lowered self-esteem, and lowered self-confidence." * * * "Emotional roller-coasters are common at this stage, causing many people to feel permanent emotional instability." "[T]his is the worst possible time to make any permanent decisions—especially legal ones. * * *"

Such emotional turmoil may prevent for a time any negotiated settlement. Or it may lead to a settlement that a party later regrets.

* * *

B.   Unequal Bargaining Power

A second possible justification for imposing limits on private ordering lies in a simple idea. In negotiations between two competent adults, if great disparity in bargaining power exists, some bargains may arise that are unconscionably one-sided. The notion of bargaining power has intuitive appeal, but defies easy definition. Moreover, to speak of "unequal" bargaining power implies that one can know when parties have "equal" bargaining power. * * * [I]t is possible to suggest why one divorcing spouse may be seen as having greater ability to bring about an outcome favorable to himself or herself.

First, bargaining is influenced by the partners' respective legal endowments. The legal rules governing marital property, alimony, child support, and custody give each spouse certain claims based on what each would get if the case goes to trial. * * * These endowments themselves can create unequal bargaining power. * * * To the extent that negotiated settlements simply reflect differences in bargaining power based on the legal rules themselves, no justification arises for a claim of unfairness in an individual case. Instead, the state should consider changing the legal endowments.

Second, bargaining is very much influenced by each party's preferences, i.e., how each party subjectively evaluates alternative outcomes. These preferences are not simply matters of taste. A party's economic resources and life circumstances mold them. The parties' relative bargaining power depends on how each spouse subjectively evaluates the outcome a court would impose. * * *

A third element that affects bargaining concerns uncertainty, and the parties' attitudes towards risk. Often the outcome in court is far from certain, and the parties are negotiating against a backdrop clouded by substantial uncertainty. Because the parties may have different risk preferences, this uncertainty can differentially affect the two spouses. If substantial variance exists among the possible court-imposed outcomes, the relatively more risk-averse party is comparatively disadvantaged.

A fourth element that affects bargaining relates to the differential ability to withstand the transaction costs—both emotional and economic— involved in negotiations. A party who has no immediate need for settlement, enjoys negotiations, and has plenty of resources to pay a lawyer, has an obvious advantage over an impatient opponent who hates negotiations, and cannot afford to wait.

A fifth element concerns the bargaining process itself, and strategic behavior. In divorce bargaining, the spouses may not know each other's true preferences. Negotiations often involve attempts by each side to discern the other side's true preferences, while making credible claims about their own preferences and their intentions if a particular proposal is not accepted. "Bargainers bluff, argue for their positions, attempt to deceive or manipulate each other, and make power plays to gain advantage." Some people are more skilled negotiators than others. They are better at manipulating information and managing impressions. They have a more refined sense of tactical action. These differences can create inequalities in negotiations.

* * *

C. Externalities—Third Party Effects

Third party effects provide the last set of reasons that justify limiting private ordering. A legal system that gives divorcing couples freedom to determine for themselves their postdissolution rights and responsibilities may lead to settlements that reflect the spouses' interests. But negotiated agreements can also have important consequences for third parties, and affect social interests that private negotiations fail to consider adequately.

* * * The most important third party effects concern the children, although externalities can exist with respect to other family members as well. At a conceptual level, one can easily see how a negotiated settlement may reflect parental preferences but not the child's desires or needs. * * * For example, a father may threaten a custody fight over the child, not because he wants custody, but because he wants to push his wife into accepting less support, even though this will have a detrimental effect on

the child. A custodial parent, eager to escape an unhappy marriage, may offer to settle for a small amount in order to sever relations soon. A custodial parent may negotiate to eliminate largely the child's contact with the other parent, not because of the child's wants or needs, but because the custodial parent despises his ex-spouse and wants nothing more to do with her.

Concerns about the effects of divorce on children underlie many of the formal limitations on private ordering, e.g., the requirement of court review of private agreements relating to custody and child support; the legal rules prohibiting parents from making nonmodifiable and binding agreements concerning these elements. * * *

With this background in negotiation, consider this Problem, which transitions from explanation to counseling, two staples of what lawyers do.

PROBLEM 15-1

A friend confides to you that she is about to file for divorce but has no experience with lawyers, judges, or the legal system. Because money is tight in her family, she is considering self-representation rather than hiring a lawyer. After practicing family law for more than 15 years, you know that the vast majority of divorce cases are settled without trial, but that negotiated settlement is not always the best path. What advice would you provide your friend concerning (1) whether to proceed *pro se,* and (2) the relative advantages and disadvantages of forgoing trial by reaching a negotiated settlement? To help formulate your advice, what questions would you ask the client? In what ways is domestic relations negotiation typically different from negotiation in business and commercial cases?

2. MEDIATION

Mediation, "the workhorse of family dispute resolution," is negotiation that the parties conduct with one or more private third-party neutrals who facilitate, without authority to impose a settlement. Nancy Ver Steegh, *Family Court Reform and ADR: Shifting Values and Expectations Transform the Divorce Process,* 42 Fam. L.Q. 659, 662 (Fall 2008). Many couples engage private mediators to help them resolve contested issues, and courts often recommend or mandate mediation before the parties proceed.

Chapter 14 has discussed how the inability of many family law parties to afford legal representation has produced rising rates of self-representation and greater resort to unbundled legal services. Parties may also opt for mediation as a perceived cost-saving measure.

A. THE NATURE OF DOMESTIC RELATIONS MEDIATION

Mediating parties agree to present all or part of their dispute to the mediator, who helps them identify priorities, define the legal issues, express emotions, and reach points of agreement. Mediating parties hold considerable latitude to frame issues and concerns, unbound by the rules of evidence or other formalities that shape trials. Unlike arbitrators, mediators have no authority to impose a binding decision. Nor do mediators even have authority to require that the parties reach an agreement.

Mediation differs from direct negotiation, which, whether or not conducted with the parties' lawyers, is done without one or more third-party neutrals. Mediation can be facilitative or evaluative. In facilitative mediation, "the mediator merely relays proposals"; in evaluative mediation, "the mediator offer[s] opinions and suggest[s] solutions to issues." Gregg Herman, *ADR and Family Law*, 14 Disp. Resol. Mag. 37, 37–38 (Spring/Summer 2008).

At the end of each session that results in tentative points of agreement, the mediator generally drafts a memorandum of understanding that identifies these points and sends the memorandum to the parties for their review. When the mediation concludes, the mediator sends the parties any completed terms of agreement. Once the parties execute the agreement, it is enforceable under contract law. *See, e.g., In re Lovell-Osburn*, 448 S.W.3d 616, 620 (Tex. Ct. App. 2014). The agreement is submitted to the court for entry as a binding order, or for incorporation into the decree. Where the parties reach no agreement or reach agreement on only some issues, unsettled issues proceed to other forms of dispute resolution, including perhaps trial.

Because decision making authority rests with the parties, proponents praise mediation as a "consensual" process, rather than an "adjudicative" one such as litigation or arbitration. But does mediation live up to its proponents' praise in divorce, child support, and child custody cases? One research summary provides generally positive, but mixed, results:

> The percentage of mediated family cases producing some form of agreement has been reported to be as low as 46% and as high as 94%. A variety of studies have discovered that the vast majority of mediation participants are satisfied with their experience. Mediation is especially satisfactory to parties when compared to divorce litigation. * * * Although parties that settle their disputes report greater satisfaction than those whose mediations do not produce agreement, satisfaction with mediation is driven by factors beyond its ability to lead to agreement. * * * Participants find satisfaction in mediation because of the process, rather than

the outcome. In particular, parties value the opportunity to tell their story to a neutral party. * * *

Some studies have found that mediation increases compliance [with child support and parenting obligations], while others have found no effect, or only a short-term effect. One study found reduced conflict between disputing parents during the two-year period following a custody mediation. This reduced level of conflict was not found more than two years after the mediation, however the study concluded that the mediation experience may have taught participants to use a "more direct and mutual style" in resolving their conflicts. * * *

[T]he evidence on the benefit to children is inconsistent. * * * [T]he particular circumstances of a family court mediation program, including the amount of time and funding available for each case, and the quality of the mediators available, [may be] important determinants of its long-term success.

* * * Some of the more ambitious claims regarding mediation's benefits—that it reduces inter-parent conflict and that it aids children's long-term adjustment to divorce—are not supported by the evidence. * * *

The empirical evidence on facilitative mediation of custody disputes clearly establishes that it consistently produces settlement and party satisfaction. The evidence also indicates, tentatively, that facilitative mediation can improve inter-parent relationships and compliance with custody agreements, at least in the short term. The intuitively-appealing idea of a natural harmony between facilitative mediation and parenting disputes does seem to have basis in fact. * * *

Noel Semple, *Judicial Settlement-Seeking in Parenting Cases: A Mock Trial*, 2013 J. Disp. Resol. 301, 324–27.

B. ETHICAL AND PRACTICAL CONSIDERATIONS

Whether voluntary or mandated, family mediation can present distinctive ethical and practical issues for mediators and parties alike, including these:

1. Mediators' Qualifications and Ethics

The ranks of family mediators include not only lawyers, but also professionals trained in conflict resolution and such disciplines as child psychology, social work, mental health, marriage counseling, education, or family systems. Clergy, retired judges, and other professionals trained in conflict resolution also sometimes serve as family mediators. Because domestic relations cases often raise both legal and emotional issues, family mediators may work as a team in "co-mediation." Lawyer-mental health professional teams, and male-female teams mediate in some communities.

Minimum qualifications of private family mediators often depend on standards set by the providers themselves, and some commentators have complained that these standards are not uniformly high. By statute or court rule, several states provide minimum qualifications for mediators in mandated programs, which may include a specified number of hours of mediation training. *See, e.g.*, Or. R. Mediator Qualifs., § 1.1 et seq. (2018). Several states require mediators to be certified or licensed. I John A. Fiske & Michael L. Leshin, Mass. Divorce Law Practice Manual 3–39 (3d ed. 2012).

In 2001, the American Bar Association House of Delegates approved the *Model Standards of Practice for Family and Divorce Mediation*, which consist of 13 general principles to guide family law mediators. The Model Standards do not have binding effect, but they may affect the thinking of legislatures, courts, and private professional groups. Model Standard II states: "A family mediator shall be qualified by education and training to undertake the mediation." The Model Standards further indicate that private and court-appointed family mediators should:

1. have knowledge of family law;

2. have knowledge of and training in the impact of family conflict on parents, children and other participants, including knowledge of child development, domestic abuse and child abuse and neglect;

3. have education and training specific to the process of mediation; [and]

4. be able to recognize the impact of culture and diversity.

Model Standards of Practice for Family and Divorce Mediation, Overview and Definitions, Standard II, at iii–iv.

The Model Standards of Conduct for Mediators were prepared by a joint committee of the American Arbitration Association, the ABA Section of Dispute Resolution, and the Association of Conflict Resolution. The Model Standards, applicable in mediations generally, were revised in 2005 and each participating organization has approved them. https://www. americanbar.org/content/dam/aba/migrated/dispute/documents/model_ standards_conduct_april2007.authcheckdam.pdf (visited Mar. 26, 2019).

Professor Abrams explains the "personal factor" that links written ethical standards to their actual application:

Ethical codes are indispensable foundations, but they are just that—foundations. Words on paper do not apply themselves, and judgment calls arise when mediators and arbitrators interpret and apply code provisions in particular circumstances that shape individual cases. Reputation for integrity, dignity, and trust * * * may stem from how a mediator or arbitrator bridges the gap between written words and their actual interpretation and application. A personal compass can make the difference for a mediator or arbitrator even when shortcuts or inattention might not bring a realistic risk of professional discipline or other untoward consequences under the ethical rules.

Douglas E. Abrams, *Professor Roebuck's Lessons for Mediators, Arbitrators, and Historians*, 2016 J. Dispute Resol. 351, 353.

2.   Lawyer-Mediators

Family lawyer-mediators may be trained in tax law, pension law, or other specialties central to the parties' circumstances. When parties seek legal advice from the mediator during the mediation, does the lawyer-mediator risk violating ethics rules concerning dual representation, conflicts of interest, or offering legal advice in a neutral's role?

The ABA Model Rules of Professional Conduct specify that "a lawyer may serve as a third-party neutral, a nonrepresentational role helping the parties to resolve a dispute or other matter." Model Rules of Prof'l Conduct, Preamble [3] (2018). "Service as a third-party neutral may include service as * * * a mediator." Model Rule 2.4(a). To avoid confusion by lay parties, the lawyer serving as a third-party neutral must "inform unrepresented parties that the lawyer is not representing them. When the lawyer knows or reasonably should know that a party does not understand the role of the lawyer-mediator in the matter, the lawyer shall explain the difference between the lawyer's role as a third-party neutral and the lawyer's roles as one who represents a client." Model Rule 2.4(b).

State bar association ethics committees have generally advised lawyer-mediators not to represent a mediating party in the later family law proceeding if the mediation fails to resolve some or all of the issues. Model Rule 1.12(a), however, may work a change in the virtual prohibition articulated by ethics opinions. This Rule now permits parties to waive objections to conflicts involving such representation: "[A] lawyer shall not represent anyone in connection with a matter in which the lawyer participated personally and substantially as a * * * mediator or other third-party neutral, unless all parties to the proceeding give informed consent, confirmed in writing."

3.   Should Parties' Lawyers Attend or Advise?

In civil cases generally, lawyers' presence in mediation has increased in recent years. Jacqueline Nolan-Haley, *Mediation: The "New*

Arbitration," 17 Harv. Negot. L. Rev. 61, 63 (2012). In most family mediations in which a party retains counsel, the lawyer prepares the client for the process, and then either appears at the table or advises the client in the background. Forrest S. Mosten, *Lawyer as Peacemaker: Building a Successful Law Practice Without Ever Going to Court,* 43 Fam. L.Q. 489, 502 (Fall 2009).

At least in the short run, lawyers' participation in family mediation can increase the costs incurred by the parties, who must pay both the mediator and their own lawyer. Some commentators argue, however, that overall costs would probably remain unchanged because settlements would come earlier and would more likely be comprehensive, and because discovery costs may be reduced. *See, e.g.,* Craig A. McEwen et al., *Bring in the Lawyers: Challenging the Dominant Approaches in Divorce Mediation,* 79 Minn. L. Rev. 1317, 1394–95 (1995). One study found that "parents settled their disputes in about half the time when assigned to mediation versus adversary settlement." Robert E. Emery et al., *Divorce Mediation: Research and Reflections,* 43 Fam. Ct. Rev. 22, 27 (2005).

As a family lawyer, would you recommend to your client that you attend or otherwise participate in the client's mediation sessions?

4. Unauthorized Practice of Law (UPL)

The UPL doctrine restricts the practice of law to persons who hold law licenses and have been admitted to the state bar after examination for education and character. *See* Restatement (Third) of the Law Governing Lawyers §§ 2, 4 (2000 & Supp. 2018). For nonlawyer mediators, "it appears universally accepted that providing mediation services is not the practice of law. However, depending on the jurisdiction, certain activities may be deemed to be or become the practice of law, especially when parties are self-represented. These activities include the mediator discussing the law with the self-represented party(ies); drafting the mediation agreement; drafting other documents needed to resolve (or at times, initiate) the family law case; and filing documents for self-represented parties." Amy G. Applegate & Connie J.A. Beck, *Self-Represented Parties in Mediation: Fifty Years Later It Remains the Elephant In the Room,* 51 Fam. Ct. Rev. 87, 96 (Jan. 2013).

5. Mandated ("Court-Annexed") Mediation

In recent years, statutes mandating mediation in divorce cases before the parties proceed to court have spread rapidly. Utah Code Ann. § 30–3–39 (2018), for example, provides:

> (1) There is established a mandatory domestic mediation program to help reduce the time and tensions associated with obtaining a divorce.

(2) If, after the filing of an answer to a complaint of divorce, there are any remaining contested issues, the parties shall participate in good faith in at least one session of mediation. * * *

(4) Unless otherwise ordered by the court or the parties agree upon a different payment arrangement, the cost of mediation shall be divided equally between the parties.

(5) The director of dispute resolution programs for the courts, the court, or the mediator may excuse either party from the requirement to mediate for good cause. * * *

Should courts have authority to mandate mediation as a precondition to judicial resolution? In mandated family mediation, what if one party appears at the mediation session, sits down at the table, declines to speak, and does nothing more? Legislatures and courts have adopted rules requiring good faith participation in mandatory family mediation, but sanctions for lawyers' bad faith participation are relatively rare. Why? If family mediation is beneficial for some parties, why should courts need to mandate it?

Does a mandate that parties mediate their family disputes before proceeding to court deny a party access to the courts? In *Karamanoglu v. Gourlaouen*, 140 A.3d 1249 (Me. 2016), a divorce decree provision mandated that the parties mediate disputes about parental rights and responsibilities before either could initiate court action. The state supreme court held that the provision "materially frustrated" a party's right to free and timely access to the courts. Among other things, the mandate caused pre-filing delay that may affect the best interests of children, and that could deter claims where the parties' relationship has been marked by domestic violence. *Id.* at 1258–59.

6. Should the Parties' Minor Children Participate?

The *ABA Model Standards of Practice for Family and Divorce Mediation* require mediators to "assist participants in determining how to promote the best interests of children." *ABA Model Standards,* Standard VIII (2001). The *Model Standards* continue: "Except in extraordinary circumstances, the children should not participate in the mediation process without the consent of both parents and the children's court-appointed representative." *Id.*

Professionals disagree, however, about whether—and if so, how— minor dependent children should participate in their parents' divorce mediation. Some voices argue that participation can risk "harming children by placing them in the middle of their parents' disputes, pressuring them to choose sides, and relying too much on children's unreliable opinions and sometimes whimsical positions." Stacey Platt, *Set Another Place At the Table: Child Participation In Family Separation Cases*, 17 Cardozo J. of

Conflict Resol. 749, 749 (2016). Other voices counter that participation can help "ensur[e] a just process in which children are provided the opportunity to be heard before decisions are made that will impact them directly and significantly, as children and beyond." *Id.*

Would you advise your client to permit the children to participate? Would you provide the same advice in all cases? What factors might influence your advice in a particular case? What sort of participation would you recommend?

7. Confidentiality

Most states have enacted legislation that seeks to enhance confidentiality in mediation. Sarah R. Cole et al., Mediation: Law, Policy & Practice § 8.1, at 295–96 (2018). The Uniform Mediation Act (UMA) explains that "frank exchange can be achieved only if the participants know that what is said in the mediation will not be used to their detriment through later court proceedings and other adjudicatory processes." UMA prefatory note 1 (2001).

To encourage states to recognize a uniform testimonial privilege nationally, section 4(a) of the UMA states that "[a] mediation communication is privileged * * * and is not subject to discovery or admissible in evidence in a proceeding." The Act defines "mediation communication" broadly to include oral, written and nonverbal statements made while convening a mediation, while selecting a mediator or during the mediation itself. *Id.* § 2(a).

Despite the state legislation and the uniform act, "some information leaks from mediation sessions.* * * Whether the flow of information is a trickle or a flood is determined by the practices of each dispute resolution program, the series of laws that vary among the jurisdictions, and choice of law principles." Cole et al., *supra,* at 297–98.

Several states provide for confidentiality of some or all matters that arise during the mediation. Some states also recognize a testimonial privilege covering some or all statements made to or by a mediator during mediation. Where mediation does not resolve a dispute, the mediator in these states may not testify (voluntarily or by subpoena of a party or the court) about covered matters discussed in mediation, or about recommendations that the mediator made to the parties. *Id.* § 8.12. Confidentiality may be breached, however, when attendees at the mediation session include the child's court-appointed guardian *ad litem*, who may be bound to report to the court matters within the GAL's knowledge that bear on the best interests of the child. For that reason, some commentators argue against the GAL's participation in mediation. *See* Suzanne J. Schmitz, *Guardians ad Litem Do Not Belong in Family Mediations*, 8 Pepp. Disp. Resol. L.J. 221 (2008).

If you were representing a party in family mediation in a state that has enacted section 4(a) of the UMA, what cautionary advice would the section lead you to provide your client before beginning mediation?

PROBLEM 15-2

You are an experienced family lawyer and mediator retained by Jack Richards and Judy King to mediate the terms of their divorce. The couple cannot agree on many things lately, but you would like to encourage them to speak freely and openly about circumstances relating to their property, their future economic prospects, and the needs of their two young children.

1.   If the couple asks you whether each should retain a lawyer before the first mediation session, what would you say? If they begin mediation without having retained counsel, what advice would you provide as the mediation proceeds and concludes?

2.   If the couple asks you during the mediation about the relative strengths or weaknesses of one or more of their claims, would you provide that advice?

3.   What would you tell the couple about whether the statements they make, and documents they produce, would remain confidential if the mediation does not produce final resolution and they proceed to trial? When would you tell them?

4.   If the couple asks you whether their children should participate in the mediation, what would you tell them? What questions might you ask?

5.   What would you recommend if the couple cannot agree about whether their children should participate?

PROBLEM 15-3

Bob and Roberta Ricketts are acquaintances of yours from your college days. They visit your law office together one afternoon to say that they wish to divorce after 14 years. They would like you to represent them in the divorce proceedings and to begin drawing up the papers as soon as possible. Citing ethical concerns, you decline to undertake dual representation. But if Bob and Roberta agree, may you serve as a mediator seeking to resolve the issues that arise in their dissolution proceeding? If you agree to serve, what ground rules would you set for the mediation?

C. GENDER AND CULTURE

Family mediation's consensual process, lauded as a virtue by proponents, has also been condemned as a vice. Critics have asserted that mediation, like direct family negotiation and other ADR methods, may produce subtle pressures to settle. These pressures, critics explain, may deprive an emotionally or financially weaker party and the children of protections afforded by the substantive law that a court would apply in formal adjudication.

More specifically, critics assert that in at least four ways, mediation may perpetuate power imbalances grounded in gender or culture. First, mediation may increase the risk of prejudice when informality displaces the formal rules and other trappings of court adjudication. Second, minorities and women may be more apt than other parties to make concessions. Third, mediator impartiality may be difficult or impossible to achieve in proceedings involving women or minorities. Fourth, non-public mediated settlements may be more likely to turn on private values, than on the public values reflected in statutory and case law that courts apply in formal adjudication. Sharon Press, *Court-Connected Mediation and Minorities: A Report Card*, 39 Cap. U. L. Rev. 819, 825–34 (2011).

It behooves mediators to remain alert for ways that impulses grounded in gender or culture may influence a mediation's process and outcome. Carol Izumi, *Implicit Bias and Prejudice in Mediation*, 70 SMU L. Rev. 681 (2017). A leading negotiation text warns that "[m]aking assumptions about someone based on their group characteristics is insulting, as well as factually risky. It denies that person his or her individuality. * * * Each of us is affected by myriad aspects of our environment and upbringing, our culture and group identity, but in no individually predictable way." Roger Fisher et al., Getting to Yes: Negotiating Agreement Without Giving In 167–68 (2d ed. 1991).

1. Gender

MARGARET F. BRINIG,
DOES MEDIATION SYSTEMATICALLY
DISADVANTAGE WOMEN?
2 Wm. & Mary J. Women & L. 1, 4–5, 6, 33–34 (1995).

* * *

Feminists have raised a number of objections to the use of mediation instead of the adversarial process. Some writers argue that because women, more than men, seek connection through relationships, women might systematically fare worse. Others argue that women might trade custody for money to avoid litigation because, where custody is concerned, women are more risk averse than their husbands. There is also a more generalized fear that husbands will take advantage of their wives' lack of power within the marital relationship.

* * *

* * * [A] divorce mediator must be conscious of power imbalances brought about by the difference in men's and women's earning power and by physical abuse if present in the relationship. Given this awareness, mediation remains a fair, as well as an inexpensive and time-saving, process for marriage dissolution. There is nothing inherent in being a woman that precludes a successful mediation of marital problems.

* * *

From an empirical standpoint, it is unclear whether gender differences impede women's ability to mediate successfully. Women are apparently not more risk averse. They do not trade money for more custodial time because of risk aversion, but just appear to want to be with their children more than their husbands do. Since mothers get more child support as visitation time with fathers increases, fathers are willing to "pay" for time with their children up to a point.

Feminists who claim that women are more altruistic than men also will have difficulty supporting their conclusions according to the data. Women do not give more in terms of percentages or money than men. Women seem to do more volunteer work and a larger share of housework and child care than their husbands. This difference in utilization of "leisure time," or more accurately, non-labor market activity, may not be due to unselfish and caring behavior. Greater time spent with children may occur because women derive more utility from them than their husbands do, other things being equal. Because of the husbands' greater earning potential, it is more efficient for women, with their lower opportunity costs, to work less or more flexible hours. This accommodates not only child care, with its positive value, but also housework, which most women do not actually enjoy.

The difference in earning power and consequently power within the relationship appears to be the real culprit in this story. Men have an easier exit from marriage because their investments are readily transferable. Therefore they can behave opportunistically during the marriage and can have less to lose during mediation at dissolution. Women's threats are not as credible, so they may have to settle for less. They also have a higher marginal utility of income, since their income on average is lower than their husbands'.

Because mediation is swifter, less expensive, and easier on children, it is a good alternative to litigation in many divorce cases. Many women who have tried mediation liked it. However, congested courts cannot justify mandatory mediation in cases where one spouse holds a monopoly on marital power. No one should order mediation when there has been abuse within the family, substance abuse, or systematic hiding of assets.

2. Domestic Violence

Gender issues in mediation may become more complicated where prior domestic violence (explored in Chapter 7) is alleged or established. Many feminists and battered women's advocates have argued that courts should never order mandatory family mediation when a party alleges prior domestic violence. These advocates worry that victims will suffer further victimization because many mediators do not understand the realities of intimate partner violence, including how separation from the batterer may risk further violence. A fearful victim might yield to the batterer's demands at the mediation table. Some victims of prior domestic violence "may not even meet the legal standard of competence to mediate, due to impaired decision-making related to self-interested outcomes. For example, victims might agree to unsafe provisions, such as child visitation arrangements that put the victim and/or the children in possibly dangerous contact with the abuser." John W. Putz et al., *Comparing the Mediation Agreements of Families With and Without a History of Intimate Partner Violence*, 50 Fam. Ct. Rev. 413, 414 (2012).

Heeding these critiques, most state statutes and court rules mandating divorce mediation carry exemptions where a party alleges prior domestic violence. In this circumstance, some states ban mediation altogether; other states allow the survivor to decide whether to mediate, or leave determination to the court's discretion; other states vest in the mediator discretion whether to proceed. Thomas Luchs, *Is Your Client a Good Candidate for Mediation? Screen Early, Screen Often, and Screen For Domestic Violence*, 28 J. Am. Acad. Matrim. Law. 455, 460 (2016).

Domestic violence survivors may wish to mediate their family disputes, particularly if safety measures are taken and other dispute resolution methods seem less appealing. John Lande, *The Revolution in Family Law Dispute Resolution*, 24 J. Am. Acad. Matrimonial Laws. 411, 425 (2012). Professor Nancy Ver Steegh argues that domestic violence victims should retain autonomy to make informed choices about whether to mediate. Nancy Ver Steegh, *Yes, No and Maybe: Informed Decision Making About Divorce Mediation in the Presence of Domestic Violence*, 9 Wm. & Mary J. Women & L. 145, 147 (2003). Proponents of case-by-case determination note that stresses of adversarial litigation may also bring risk of future violence.

3. Culture

The ABA *Model Standards of Practice for Family and Divorce Mediation* call on mediators to "be sensitive to the impact of culture * * * on parenting philosophy and other decisions," and to "continuously strive to understand the impact of culture and diversity on the mediator's practice." *Model Standards of Practice, supra*, Overview and Definitions, Standards VIII & XIII, at viii, xi.

Two perspectives underscore the roles of sensitivity and understanding. First, Professor Cynthia R. Mabry states that after generations of racism, mistrust, biases, and stereotypes, whites and

African Americans have "different views of the world, different family values, different ways of responding to the dispute resolution process and different ways of rearing children." Family mediation must "reflect cultural values of people of color and their divergent social and physical environments." Cynthia R. Mabry, *African Americans "Are Not Carbon Copies" of White Americans—The Role of African American Culture in Mediation of Family Disputes*, 13 Ohio St. J. on Disp. Resol. 405, 421 (1998). "[M]ediators should be educated about cultural practices and issues that affect how African American families operate. * * * More specifically, mediators involved in resolution of family disputes should endeavor to understand dissimilarities between African American and white familial experiences." *Id.* at 423, 459.

For example, Professor Mabry urges mediators to refrain from calling adult African Americans by their first names without permission. "By referring to older persons by their first names, the mediator innocently may be attempting to be friendly and casual. Without permission to be informal, however, African American participants may be offended, harbor unverbalized anger or view the mediator as disrespectful." *Id.* at 432.

Second, two commentators state that in mediation with Hispanic couples, mediators should "gather family history, including migration and socioeconomic standing for several generations, so as to fully understand the meaning of the presenting problems and the most likely range of outcomes. Unless we have a true understanding of the cultural background and worldview of the participants, we will be ineffective in creating outcomes that are culturally consistent and able to withstand the economic and social pressures that will be placed on them." Alison Taylor & Ernest A. Sanchez, *Out of the White Box: Adapting Mediation to the Needs of Hispanic and Other Minorities Within American Society*, 29 Fam. & Concil. Cts. Rev. 114, 119 (1991).

3. ARBITRATION

A. THE NATURE OF DOMESTIC RELATIONS ARBITRATION

1. Introduction

In arbitration, parties agree to submit their dispute to a private decision maker—a single arbitrator or an arbitral panel—whose binding decision, rendered after hearing each side's evidence, remains largely beyond judicial review. The Federal Arbitration Act, 9 U.S.C. §§ 1–16 (2018), mandates that arbitration agreements that the parties reach before or after the dispute arises "shall be valid, irrevocable, and enforceable, save upon such grounds as exist at law or in equity for the revocation of any contract." *Id.* § 2. The saving clause permits courts to invalidate arbitration agreements only "by 'generally applicable contract defenses, such as fraud, duress, or unconscionability.' " *Epic Sys. Corp. v. Lewis*, 138 S. Ct. 1612, 1622 (2018).

Some states have also enacted legislation that specifically authorizes and regulates domestic relations arbitration. *See, e.g.*, N.C. Gen. Stat. §§ 50–41 to –62 (2018).

"Court-annexed" family arbitration, which some state statutes or court rules mandate without the parties' agreement, is essentially a nonbinding settlement and conciliation device designed to encourage parties to resolve their differences short of trial based on clearer perceptions of the merits of their respective positions. Binding family arbitration without the parties' agreement to arbitrate would likely violate constitutional rights of access to the courts. *Cf. Warren v. State Farm Mut. Auto. Ins. Co.*, 899 So.2d 1090, 1095 n.5 (Fla. 2005) (statute that mandated binding commercial arbitration unconstitutionally denied the party's right of access to the courts).

Arbitration may also resolve disputes between parents who, after entry of the divorce decree, remain prone to continued conflict about child custody and visitation. The parties may agree to arbitrate when a post-decree dispute arises, or their separation agreement may contain an arbitration clause covering future disputes. The agreement may provide for an arbitrator named by the parties or one appointed by the court.

2. Procedure and Ethics

Where a party files suit on a claim covered by an arbitration agreement, the court stays or dismisses the judicial proceeding and issues an order compelling arbitration. A court may overturn an arbitral award only where the arbitrator engaged in fraud, corruption, or other serious misconduct (or, in some jurisdictions, also where the arbitrator "manifestly disregarded" the applicable law). *See, e.g., W & J Harlan Farms, Inc. v. Cargill, Inc.*, 2011 WL 1560988 * 1 (S.D. Ind. Apr. 21, 2011).

Only the court may grant a divorce and enter the divorce decree, but parties may agree to arbitrate one or more of the incidents of the divorce, such as property distribution, alimony, or the child-related issues of custody, visitation, or support. The parties may sign an arbitration agreement before they marry (for example, in a premarital agreement), when they separate, or while the divorce action is pending. Some parties contemplating divorce turn immediately to arbitration; other parties agree to arbitrate only matters that they fail to resolve by negotiation; still other parties agree to mediation-arbitration ("med/arb"), which has the mediator or another designated person decide—as an arbitrator—any matters that the parties do not settle in mediation.

Minority group or religious arbitration sometimes surfaces in divorce and other domestic relations matters. "[A]s long as an arbitration is conducted pursuant to a valid agreement, parties of the same religion can have religious authorities resolve their disputes in accordance with religious law, and that resolution can have the binding force of U.S. law." Michael A. Helfand, *Religious Arbitration and the New Multiculturalism: Negotiating Conflicting Legal Orders*, 86 NYU L. Rev. 1231, 1237 (2011). *See, e.g., Zar v. Yaghoobzar*, 76 N.Y.S.3d 625 (App. Div. 2018) (confirming rabbinical court's arbitral award in divorce proceedings).

Professor Helfand, however, notes "growing resistance to the possibility of ceding authority and autonomy to cultural groups" through state court enforcement of arbitral decisions reached pursuant to procedural and substantive religious law. *Id.* at 1232–33. The resistance stems at least partly from concern about importing Islamic law into the American legal system. *Id.* at 1239. Professor Helfand advocates closer application of courts' settled authority to vacate religious arbitral awards that appear "contrary to public policy." *Id.* at 1293.

Arbitration practice will likely remain an important skill for domestic relations lawyers because use of family arbitration appears to be increasing and represented parties rarely appear in arbitration without their lawyer. Lawyers who represent clients in arbitration are governed by ethical standards such as the ABA Model Rules of Professional Conduct. In 2005, the AAML also adopted a Model Family Law Arbitration Act. The AAML urges that lawyers serving as arbitrators comply with all relevant rules applicable to judges, including the ABA Code of Judicial Conduct and the AAML's *Bounds of Advocacy, Goals for Family Lawyers* § 9.2 (2000).

B. DOMESTIC RELATIONS ARBITRATION AND CHILDREN

Agreements to arbitrate one or more of family law's child-related issues (custody, visitation, or support) present special concerns grounded in the state's *parens patriae* authority to protect children. Until the late 1970s, courts applied a judicially created "public policy" exception to the Federal Arbitration Act's mandate. The exception held that agreements to arbitrate various classes of disputes—including disputes arising under the antitrust laws or some federal securities laws—were unenforceable as contrary to public policy. Similarly off-limits were domestic relations disputes concerning one or more of the child-related issues. *See, e.g.,* Stewart E. Sterk, *Enforceability of Agreement to Arbitrate: An Examination of the Public Policy Defense*, 2 Cardozo L. Rev. 481 (1981).

A premise behind the domestic relations public policy exception was that because children were not parties to their parents' arbitration agreement, the privately chosen arbitrator's decision should not bind the publicly constituted court on matters that vitally affect the children's lives. *Id.* at 498. Courts also concluded that the interests of one or both arbitrating parents might diverge from the best interests of their children; where neither parent would be a fit custodian, for example, a court might award third-party custody but the arbitrator, who serves only by the parents' agreement, might have no authority or inclination to do so.

Beginning in the early 1980s, the Supreme Court rejected the public policy exception. *See, e.g., Rodriguez de Quijas v. Shearson/American Express, Inc.*, 490 U.S. 477 (1989). Today, federal courts enforce arbitration agreements under the Federal Arbitration Act unless an exception to enforcement is found in the FAA itself or in another statute. Federal decisions interpreting the FAA do not necessarily bind state courts in the interpretation of state arbitration acts; in domestic relations and other fields, however, most state court decisions have similarly held that only the legislature may create exceptions to arbitrability.

Abandonment of the public policy exception left children potentially vulnerable in family law arbitration because only a few state arbitration or divorce acts expressly address the enforceability of arbitral custody, visitation, or support awards. In the wake of the exception's demise, two questions arise: (1) may parties arbitrate one or more of these child-related issues?, and (2) if they may, how closely may (or must) courts review the arbitral award before entering the divorce decree? The following unanimous decision treats these questions.

FAWZY V. FAWZY

Supreme Court of New Jersey, 2009.
973 A.2d 347.

JUSTICE LONG delivered the opinion of the Court.

At issue in this appeal is whether parties to a matrimonial action may agree to submit questions regarding child custody and parenting time to binding arbitration, and if so, what standard of review will apply. More particularly, we have been asked by a matrimonial litigant to declare arbitration of issues involving children an affront to the exercise of our *parens patriae* jurisdiction. Alternatively, we have been requested to establish a best-interests standard as the basis for judicial intervention into an otherwise binding arbitration award.

We hold that within the constitutionally protected sphere of parental autonomy is the right of parents to choose the forum in which their disputes over child custody and rearing will be resolved, including arbitration. Deference to the parties' choice of forum requires certainty regarding that choice; an agreement to arbitrate must be in writing or otherwise recorded and must clearly establish that the parties are aware of their rights to a judicial determination and have knowingly and voluntarily waived them.

Once arbitrated, the matter is subject to review under the narrow provisions of New Jersey's version of the Uniform Arbitration Act ("Arbitration Act"). The only exception is the case in which a party establishes that the arbitrator's award threatens harm to the child. Best interests is not the standard for judicial review of an arbitration award. Only a threat of harm will justify judicial infringement on the fundamental right of parents to decide how to resolve disputes over their children's upbringing.

A child-custody or parenting-time arbitration should be conducted in accordance with the principles established in the Arbitration Act. However, because the Arbitration Act does not require the recording of testimony or a statement of findings and conclusions by the arbitrator, we depart from it by mandating that a record of all documentary evidence adduced during the arbitration proceedings be kept; that testimony be recorded; and that the arbitrator issue findings of fact and conclusions of law in respect of the award of custody and parenting time. Without that, courts will be in no position to evaluate a challenge to the award.

I.

Plaintiff, Christine Saba Fawzy, and defendant, Samih M. Fawzy, were married on September 28, 1991, and have two children born in 1996 and 1997, respectively. On September 13, 2005, Mrs. Fawzy filed a complaint for divorce. Leonard R. Busch, Esq., was appointed as guardian ad litem for the children.

On January 22, 2007, the day on which the trial on all issues was to take place, the parties apparently notified the judge that they had agreed to arbitrate in place of proceeding to trial. The judge informed Busch * * * that "* * * the parties have agreed to let you arbitrate all issues." * * *

[The parties placed on the record their oral agreement in open court to submit the case to arbitration.] * * * On March 6, 2007, judgment of divorce was entered, including reference to the agreement to arbitrate. The attorneys signed an interim arbitration order on March 14, 2007 which stated that "[t]he parties agreed to enter into Binding Arbitration pursuant to [the Arbitration Act]."

* * * On March 28, 2007, while the arbitration process was in progress, Mr. Fawzy filed an order to show cause seeking to restrain Busch from issuing a custody or parenting-time award, on the grounds that those issues could not, as a matter of law, be arbitrated, and that, in any event, he was rushed and pressured into agreeing to the arbitration.

* * * [At a hearing,] [t]he judge denied the application * * *.

Busch issued a custody and parenting-time award on April 4, 2007, which granted the parties joint legal custody with primary physical custody to Mrs. Fawzy; designated Mrs. Fawzy as the parent of primary residence;

and granted Mr. Fawzy weekday, weekend, vacation, and holiday parenting time. Arbitration continued on the remaining financial issues.

* * * The trial judge * * * entered an amended judgment of divorce on May 14, 2007, which confirmed the [arbitral] award; he also ordered both Mr. and Mrs. Fawzy to comply with its terms.

* * * [T]he Appellate Division * * * held that matrimonial litigants cannot submit custody issues to final, binding, non-appealable arbitration. Thus the Appellate Division reversed the judge's decision and remanded for a plenary hearing on the custody and parenting-time issues.

* * * We * * * now affirm the judgment of the Appellate Division, but not for the reasons it expressed.

* * *

III

* * *

We note that there is no express bar to the arbitration of family law matters in the Arbitration Act. * * *

[T]he * * * majority of our sister states that have addressed the issue have concluded that parents are empowered to submit child-custody and parenting-time issues to arbitration in the exercise of their parental autonomy.

* * *

IV.

* * * [T]he case is really about the intersection between parents' fundamental liberty interest in the care, custody, and control of their children, and the state's interest in the protection of those children [citing *Meyer v. Nebraska*, 262 U.S. 390, 399 (1923); *Pierce v. Society of Sisters*, 268 U.S. 510 (1925), and *Prince v. Massachusetts*, 321 U.S. 158, 166 (1944), which Chapter 1 discusses—eds.]. * * *

Indeed, the primary role of parents in the upbringing of their children is now established beyond debate as an enduring tradition to which we have unflinchingly given voice. * * *

Deference to parental autonomy means that the State does not second-guess parental decision making or interfere with the shared opinion of parents regarding how a child should be raised. Nor does it impose its own notion of a child's best interests on a family. Rather, the State permits to stand unchallenged parental judgments that it might not have made or that could be characterized as unwise. That is because parental autonomy includes the "freedom to decide wrongly."

Nevertheless, "[t]he right of parents to the care and custody of their children is not absolute." * * *

Indeed, the state has an obligation, under the *parens patriae* doctrine, to intervene where it is necessary to prevent harm to a child. * * *

> * * * [T]he only state interest warranting the invocation of the State's *parens patriae* jurisdiction to overcome the presumption in favor of a parent's decision * * * is the avoidance of harm to the child. When no harm threatens a child's welfare, the State lacks a sufficiently compelling justification for the infringement on the fundamental right of parents to raise their children as they see fit. * * *.

V.

The question then becomes whether the right to parental autonomy subsumes the right to submit issues of child custody and parenting time to an arbitrator for disposition. We think it does. As we have said, the entitlement to autonomous family privacy includes the fundamental right of parents to make decisions regarding custody, parenting time, health, education, and other child-welfare issues between themselves, without state interference. That right does not evaporate when an intact marriage breaks down. * * * [W]hen matrimonial litigants reach a settlement on issues regarding child custody, support, and parenting time, as a practical matter the court does not inquire into the merits of the agreement. It is only when the parents cannot agree that the court becomes the default decision maker.

* * *

VI.

* * * [W]here no harm to the child is threatened, there is no justification for the infringement on the parents' choice to be bound by the arbitrator's decision. In the absence of a claim of harm, the parties are limited to the remedies provided in the Arbitration Act. On the contrary, where harm is claimed and a prima facie case advanced, the court must determine the harm issue. If no finding of harm ensues, the award will only be subject to review under the Arbitration Act standard. If there is a finding of harm, the presumption in favor of the parents' choice of arbitration will be overcome and it will fall to the court to decide what is in the child's best interests.

Mere disagreement with the arbitrator's decision obviously will not satisfy the harm standard. The threat of harm is a significantly higher burden than a best-interests analysis. * * *.

In our view, the hybrid model we have adopted at once advances the purposes of arbitration by providing a final, speedy, and inexpensive resolution of the dispute; affords deference to parental decision making by allowing the parents to choose the person who will resolve the matter; and leaves open the availability of court intervention where it is necessary to prevent harm to the child.

VII.

* * *

We * * * direct that when parties in a dissolution proceeding agree to arbitrate their dispute, the general rules governing the conduct of arbitration shall apply. However, in respect of child-custody and parenting-time issues only, a record of all documentary evidence shall be kept; all testimony shall be recorded verbatim; and the arbitrator shall state in writing or otherwise record his or her findings of fact and conclusions of law with a focus on the best-interests standard. It is only upon such a record that an evaluation of the threat of harm can take place without an entirely new trial. Any arbitration award regarding child-custody and parenting-time issues that results from procedures other than those that we have mandated will be subject to vacation upon motion.

* * *

IX.

[The state Supreme Court held that the parents' oral arbitration agreement, made in open court after a colloquy with the trial judge, was insufficient because the record did not disclose that they understood the rights they were relinquishing.] * * *

NOTE AND QUESTIONS

Questions about Fawzy. (a) What is the difference between the harm-to-the-child standard and the best-interests-of-the-child standard? (b) Do *Fawzy's* holding and rationale require courts to strike down any statute that prohibits arbitration of one or more of the child-related issues? (c) Assume that a divorcing couple arbitrates child custody and visitation in a jurisdiction that permits arbitration of these issues. The court enters the divorce decree, which incorporates the arbitral award. Three years later, one parent moves to modify the arbitral award on the ground that circumstances have substantially changed, the general custody modification standard discussed in Chapter 12. May the court entertain the motion? Who decides whether to grant or deny it, an arbitrator or the court?

PROBLEM 15-4

When Bill Smith and Brenda Brown divorced a few years ago, their marital settlement agreement, which was incorporated into the divorce decree, provided for arbitration if they could not agree about whether their two children should attend private school in a future year. The arbitration clause stated:

> By April 1 of each year, the parties shall reach agreement as to whether or not private school is necessary for the children for the next school year. If they cannot agree, they will go to arbitration. If the arbitrator finds a need for private school for the children, Husband will pay 60% of the private school tuition and expenses, and Wife shall pay the remaining 40%.

When the parties failed to agree about private school, Bill moved to compel arbitration. Brenda argues that the parties' arbitration clause is unenforceable under state law, which provides that parties may not arbitrate "any dispute involving child custody, visitation or support." Is the dispute between Bill and Brenda arbitrable?

4. COLLABORATIVE FAMILY LAW

"[C]ollaborative divorce is reshaping divorce practices across the country." Rachel Rebouché, *A Case Against Collaboration*, 76 Md. L. Rev. 547, 550 (2017).

This ADR method had its conception in 1990. In 2001, Texas became the first state to enact legislation recognizing and regulating collaborative law practice in dissolution cases. *See* Tex. Fam. Code § 6.603(e)–(g) (2018, as repealed and replaced in 2011). Several other states have followed with collaborative law legislation or court rules. The practice's prominence led the Uniform Law Commission to approve a Uniform Collaborative Law Act in 2009, and to amend it the following year. Sixteen states and the District of Columbia have enacted legislation or court rules along the lines of the uniform act. https://www.uniformlaws.org/committees/community-home? CommunityKey=fdd1de2f-baea-42d3-bc16-a33d74438eaf (visited Mar. 26, 2019). Several of these states limit collaborative law to family law actions.

Some lawyers report that their domestic relations practices consist largely or entirely of collaborative law, and some law firms train all their domestic relations lawyers in it. Growing numbers of lawyers and law firms list collaborative family law among their specialties, and collaborative practitioners are often organized in local practice groups, which develop standard forms and procedures.

The following two article excerpts describe collaborative law and the caution that should attend its use by family lawyers and their clients.

JOHN LANDE & FORREST S. MOSTEN,
COLLABORATIVE LAWYERS' DUTIES TO SCREEN THE
APPROPRIATENESS OF COLLABORATIVE LAW AND
OBTAIN CLIENTS' INFORMED CONSENT TO
USE COLLABORATIVE LAW

25 Ohio St. J. on Disp. Resol. 347, 349–70, 393–406, 411 (2010).

I.   INTRODUCTION

Collaborative Law (CL) is an impressive dispute resolution process that offers significant benefits for disputants in appropriate cases. In CL, the lawyers and clients sign a "participation agreement" promising to use an interest-based approach to negotiation and fully disclose all relevant information. A key element of the participation agreement is the "disqualification agreement," which provides that both CL lawyers would be disqualified from representing their clients if the case is litigated. The disqualification agreement is intended to motivate parties and lawyers to focus exclusively on interest-based negotiation, because termination of a CL process would require both parties to hire new lawyers if they want legal representation. Although a CL process can be used in many types of cases, virtually all of the cases to date have been in family law matters. * * *

* * *

While CL often provides real benefits, it also poses significant, non-obvious risks in some cases, and lawyers are required to inform participants about the risks of the process and screen cases for appropriateness. Once parties get into a CL process, it is purposely designed to have parties make a commitment to stay in the process. However, if CL does not produce a cost-effective, timely, and satisfying result, the parties may exhaust resources that they might need to resolve the matter. * * * [I]t seems especially important to consider both the benefits and risks of CL and compare CL with other process options carefully before starting CL, given the exit barrier of the disqualification agreement in the CL process. * * * Although CL lawyers have an obligation to assess the appropriateness of CL (as well as other dispute resolution processes that might be appropriate in a case) and provide relevant information, there is no uniquely "right" answer about which process is best in each case. Ultimately, parties must choose for themselves. * * *

* * *

II.   COLLABORATIVE LAW MATERIALS REGARDING APPROPRIATENESS AND INFORMED CONSENT TO USE COLLABORATIVE LAW

[In this section's review of commentary by leading CL writers, the article discusses factors that lawyers and clients should weigh when they determine the appropriateness of CL in light of specific potential risks and possible alternatives—eds.]

A. *Discussion of Appropriateness and Informed Consent in Collaborative Law in Collaborative Law Books*

* * *

* * * Shields et al. write that at the initial meeting with a client, CL lawyers should present CL "as one option for the client to consider, along with mediation and the traditional legal approach including litigation. The purpose of this discussion is to screen for appropriateness for CFL [Collaborative Family Law—eds.], and to help the client make an informed choice as to the most appropriate dispute resolution process for her."[29] * * *

Several authors emphasize that CL lawyers should not press clients to use CL. * * *

[T]hese are factors to consider in assessing appropriateness [of using CL] * * *.

1. *Personal Motivation and Suitability*

* * * In general, these factors involve a desire by all parties to listen to each other, take responsibility, cooperate respectfully in the process, share all relevant information, and take reasonable positions. * * *

* * *

Shields et al. write that CL is not appropriate if "one party is not willing to participate in a cooperative, problem-solving way" or is not willing to "disclose sensitive information." * * *

* * *

Tesler indicates that the following factors are useful "guidelines" in screening clients: "commitment to avoid litigation;" expression of "genuine respect for and trust in one another;" "commitment to positive co-parenting;" lack of "need to blame others for all the problems they are facing;" "willingness to accept personal responsibility for their part in the situation;" and not having "great difficulty [in] managing their emotions." * * *[48]

* * *

2. *Trustworthiness*

* * * Abney writes that parties must be willing to disclose all relevant information and that "[w]hen collaborative lawyers have their initial

---

[29] Richard W. Shields et al., Collaborative Family Law: Another Way to Resolve Family Disputes 41 (2003).

[48] Pauline H. Tesler, Collaborative Law: Achieving Effective Resolution in Divorce Without Litigation 99 (2d ed. 2008).

consultation with prospective clients, and the lawyers get an uncomfortable feeling about the parties' intentions or ability to be honest, the attorneys would do well to decline representation of those parties."[52]
* * *

* * *

3.   *Domestic Violence*

* * *

Cameron * * * says that in determining whether a case is appropriate for a Collaborative process, people should consider whether the timing is appropriate, whether the abused spouse may "push for settlement, *any* settlement" to end the conflict, and whether the spouse can participate safely.[62] She argues that "Collaborative practice has some process components that make it more suitable than mediation for resolving matters when there has been abuse—each spouse has his or her own advocate, which can go some distance toward leveling power imbalances."
* * *

* * *

* * * Victims of abuse should "make sure that [they are] not put in an unsafe environment where [they] may feel physically or emotionally threatened. If [they] are truly afraid of physical harm from [their] spouse, the Collaborative process can't work; [they] may need to seek legal protection and more traditional proceedings."[67]

Abney also argues that CL may be particularly helpful in some cases involving domestic violence. She states that a "prudent person would not recommend" CL in "disputes involving serious physical assault, [or] sexual abuse" as these situations "could be difficult and sometimes impossible for the collaborative process. . . . While these situations are extremely stressful and communication between the parties is difficult, there are still some advantages in the collaborative process for parties in these kinds of circumstances that are not available in litigation." * * *

4.   *Fear or Intimidation*

* * * Webb and Ousky write that "[e]ven without a history of abuse, you may still feel intimidated by your spouse as a result of other dynamics in your relationship." To assess this factor, they advise potential parties to consider whether there is a "marked imbalance of power . . ., climate of

---

[52]   Sherrie R. Abney, Avoiding Litigation: A Guide to Civil Collaborative Law 73 (2006).

[62]   Nancy J. Cameron, Collaborative Practice: Deepening the Dialogue 156 (2004) (emphasis in original).

[67]   Stuart G. Webb & Ronald D. Ousky, The Collaborative Way to Divorce: The Revolutionary Method That Results in Less Stress, Lower Costs, and Happier Kids-Without Going to Court 46 (2006).

distrust . . ., blaming and name-calling, . . . [or if] one or the other of the parties want to control everything." * * *

* * *

5. *Mental Illness*

* * * Cameron identifies several mental health issues that may require cases be "screened out of the collaborative process," including cases involving: a party who has a "history of mental health problems;" is currently "on medication or on disability for mental health reasons;" has been diagnosed with a personality disorder (or a professional has suggested that there may be a personality disorder); has been "hospitaliz[ed] for mental illness;" or who has "attempted or threatened to commit suicide."

* * *

6. *Substance Abuse*

* * * Webb and Ousky write that "success with Collaborative process ultimately will depend on [the parties'] willingness to get help [they] need" if one of them has "any addictions, such as alcoholism, drug addiction, or compulsive gambling," or codependency issues resulting from living with someone with an addiction. * * *

7. *Suitability of Lawyers*

* * * Shields et al. state that, "[T]he CFL process cannot be followed unless both lawyers are qualified to conduct the process. The lawyer should refuse to enter into a Participation Agreement with another lawyer who has not been trained in CFL." * * *

> CFL lawyers chosen by the parties must also assess whether they have the capacity to collaborate together. They may have a poor track record of working together and there may be a low level of trust between them. * * *

* * *

8. *Risks of Disqualification* * * *

C. *Practical Challenges in Screening for Appropriateness of Collaborative Law*

* * * The process of providing sufficient information to clients and screening clients is complicated for several reasons. First, some of the challenging dynamics, especially in family law cases, are not immediately apparent and parties may be reluctant to share relevant information, especially at the outset. Second, the appropriateness of CL in challenging cases may depend on the availability, potential utility, and explanation of additional professional services, as well as the parties' willingness to use them. Third, appropriateness of CL normally should be assessed relative

to other process options. In some cases CL may not be ideal, but parties may prefer it to the available alternatives. Conversely, in some cases CL may not necessarily be inappropriate but parties may prefer other options. * * *

* * *

When lawyers and parties consider what dispute resolution process to use, the choice is normally based on a comparison of other plausible alternatives. In some cases, the parties might be satisfied by several different processes. In difficult cases, there may be no ideal process and parties choose what they hope to be the least harmful process. For example, in cases involving a substantial history of domestic violence, there are problems with traditional litigation, mediation, Cooperative Practice, and CL. Thus, in considering the choice of process, competent lawyers help clients weigh the advantages and disadvantages of the alternatives considering the facts of each case as part of the normal process of client intake, orientation, interviewing, and counseling.

Different dispute resolution processes are likely to entail different amounts of time and money, which may be a significant consideration for many parties in comparing processes. * * * Although one may make generalizations about the amount of time and expense incurred in using different processes, assessments vary in particular cases and may depend on various factors, such as degree of conflict, preferences of other side about dispute resolution processes, reaction of each side to the others' process proposals, the amount of professional services used, and effectiveness of negotiation efforts, among others. Although investing more time and money may produce a better process and result, some parties may not be able to afford or want to invest as much as might be required for optimal results. * * *

* * *

III. ETHICAL RULES AND LEGAL STANDARDS RELEVANT TO SCREENING FOR APPROPRIATENESS AND OBTAINING INFORMED CONSENT

Under the Model Rules of Professional Conduct, CL lawyers have a duty to screen potential CL cases for appropriateness and obtain clients' informed consent to use CL. * * *

A. *Requirement of Reasonableness of Limitation of Scope of Representation*

Rule 1.2(c) states, "A lawyer may limit the scope of the representation if the limitation is reasonable under the circumstances and the client gives informed consent." When lawyers provide CL representation, they limit the scope of their representation by excluding the possibility of representing CL clients in litigation. * * *

A comment to Rule 1.2 states:

> A limited representation may be appropriate because the client has limited objectives for the representation. In addition, the terms upon which representation is undertaken may exclude specific means that might otherwise be used to accomplish the client's objectives. Such limitations may exclude actions that the client thinks are too costly or that the lawyer regards as repugnant or imprudent.

In CL, lawyers and clients preclude lawyers who sign a participation agreement with a disqualification clause from representing clients in court typically because they believe it would be repugnant to the CL process or imprudent for advancing the client's interests.

* * *

* * * Rule 1.1, entitled "Competence," states that "[a] lawyer shall provide competent representation to a client. Competent representation requires the legal knowledge, skill, thoroughness and preparation reasonably necessary for the representation." A comment to that rule states, "Competent handling of a particular matter includes inquiry into and analysis of the factual and legal elements of the problem, and use of methods and procedures meeting the standards of competent practitioners." A comment to Model Rule 1.5, governing fee agreements, states that "[a]n agreement may not be made whose terms might induce the lawyer improperly to curtail services for the client or perform them in a way contrary to the client's interest."

* * * A 2007 ABA ethics opinion states the "collaborative law and the provisions of the four-way agreement represent a permissible limited scope representation under Model Rule 1.2, with the concomitant duties of competence, diligence, and communication." * * *

The factors regarding appropriateness discussed in Part II all relate to whether a CL process would be constructive and successful. * * * If there is a significant risk that using CL in a case would not realistically advance clients' interests (or prospective clients' interests), it would not be a reasonable limitation of the scope of the lawyers' services to act as a CL lawyer * * * Although Rule 1.2 requires clients to provide informed consent to limited-scope representation, such consent would be insufficient to authorize the representation if it would be unreasonable under the circumstances.

The ethical rules suggest that CL lawyers should continue to assess the appropriateness of CL throughout a case. If, during a CL case, continued use of a limited-scope representation foreseeably becomes unreasonable, CL lawyers may be required to reassess whether the representation is permissible and terminate their representation if no longer reasonable. * * *

B. *Requirement that Lawyers Avoid Conflicts of Interest that Interfere with Competent and Diligent Representation*

In addition to the screening requirement under Rule 1.2, Rule 1.7 requires CL lawyers to screen cases to avoid potential conflicts of interest and obtain clients' informed consent prior to beginning representation. * * *

* * *

C. *Requirement that Lawyers Obtain Informed Consent Regarding Limited Scope Representation and Conflict of Interest*

* * *

* * * [I]nformed consent under Rule 1.2 requires discussion of the limited scope of representation, and informed consent under Rule 1.7 requires discussion of possible conflicts of interest.

* * *

The [ethics] opinions set high standards for informed consent to use a CL process. For example, [a] Kentucky opinion states:

> [B]ecause the relationship between the [CL] lawyer and the client is different from what would normally be expected, the lawyer has a heightened obligation to communicate with the client regarding the representation and the special implications of collaborative law process. . . .

* * *

D. *Potential Malpractice Liability for Failure to Screen Cases for Appropriateness or Obtain Informed Consent*

Although we do not know of any malpractice claims filed against CL lawyers for failing to screen the appropriateness of cases for CL or obtain clients' informed consent, CL lawyers face considerable exposure to such liability. * * * [L]egal ethics rules are often used as evidence in malpractice cases and some courts hold that violation of such rules creates a rebuttable or conclusive presumption of violation of the lawyers' duty of care. * * *

RACHEL REBOUCHÉ, A CASE AGAINST COLLABORATION
76 Md. L. Rev. 547, 551–53 (2017).

* * * [I]ntroducing parties' marital misconduct and focusing on their post-divorce relationship may undercut some of the advantages of no-fault divorce. Collaborative approaches to improving communication and

promoting forgiveness may entrench stereotypes that were common in the fault era. Collaborative materials tend to rely on patterned narratives about how and why marriages end, loosely analogous to the stock explanations of marital failure that pervaded the fault regime. Examples in collaborative handbooks, guides, and manuals—which are designed to instruct professionals on how to conduct a collaborative divorce and to entice clients to participate in a collaborative process—portray bad-behaving men and duped women. And, case studies rarely involve couples of the same sex. Collaborative materials tend to rely on stereotypes about feminine and masculine behavior: women are caretakers concerned mostly about children's well-being during divorce, and men are breadwinners concerned mostly about protecting their assets and future earning potential. Collaboration has the potential to reduce marriage to gendered, heteronormative roles that may sustain rather than subvert gender stereotypes. Even if these stereotypes reflect some realities, collaborative divorce's malleability and client-centered approach can accommodate all manner of relationships and lifestyles.

These characterizations of spousal roles and priorities may have consequences for settlement agreements. Collaborative negotiations could disfavor women who engage in marital misconduct or who do not conform to the conventional expectations of wives or mothers. It may also understate some women's bargaining power, who are not financially vulnerable or disadvantaged compared to their spouses. Further, emphasizing post-divorce relationships will also shape parties' negotiations. The collaborative process might exert pressure on the spouse with less wealth to agree to have a post-divorce relationship in order to receive financial support. It can also induce a spouse to provide spousal support in exchange for forgiveness or friendship when the application of statutory factors (or a state formula) might result in a limited alimony award, or none at all.

It is difficult to evaluate whether collaboration results in empathy and stability or conflict and disappointment—indeed, the private aspects of collaboration make its "success" challenging to assess. Good faith financial disclosure can invite incomplete information and abuse that are hard to measure. Ex-spouses may end up in court after collaboration over modifications to the settlement agreement and custody arrangements. Commitments to conflict resolution and emotional healing during collaborative negotiations may obscure the likelihood of these future disagreements. * * *

NOTES AND QUESTIONS

1. *Practical issues raised by the Lande-Mosten and Rebouché articles.* Assume that after nearly two years of marriage, Melissa and Cheryl Smith-Jones are seeking a divorce. They have an adopted one-year-old daughter. The

couple would like to explore the prospect of mediation or arbitration, but they are also intrigued by friends' descriptions of collaborative law.

As Melissa's lawyer, what advice would you provide her concerning the relative advantages and disadvantages of collaborative law, traditional litigation, negotiation, or mediation? What further information would you seek from Melissa? What if your client expresses concern whether her spouse can be trusted not to hide assets or other information during a collaborative process? What advice would you give concerning the risks of withdrawal from representation, and what steps would you take if withdrawal becomes a reality? Would your advice depend in some measure on the fact that the couple has a young child?

2. *Family lawyers' emotional needs.* Some family lawyers have reportedly embraced collaborative law to help cure their own disillusionment with traditional domestic relations practice marked by clients' emotion and trauma, and by minor dependent children who are often caught in the middle of their parents' tugs-of-war. When the parties choose collaborative law, the lawyer becomes "more of an educator, an adviser and a problem solver, and less of a weapon." Becky Beaupre Gillespie & Hollee Schwartz Temple, *Sometimes the Choice of Practice Can Bring a Better Balance,* 96 A.B.A.J. 27 (June 2010). What ethical pitfalls might lawyers face if they, consciously or unconsciously, steer the client toward collaborative law for the lawyer's sake and not necessarily for the client's?

3. *Cooperative law.* "The cooperative law movement is much smaller than the collaborative law movement, with local groups of practitioners in only a few areas." John Lande & Gregg Herman, *Fitting the Forum to the Family Fuss: Choosing Mediation, Collaborative Law, or Cooperative Law for Negotiating Divorce Cases,* 42 Fam. Ct. Rev. 280, 284 (2004). Cooperative law "involves an agreement by lawyers and parties setting out a negotiation process with a goal of reaching an agreement that is fair for both parties. These agreements vary, and may include terms committing to negotiate in good faith, act respectfully toward each other, disclose all relevant information, use jointly retained experts, protect confidentiality of communications, and refrain from formal discovery and contested litigation during negotiation. Unlike Collaborative law, however, it does not include a disqualification agreement." Lande & Mosten, *supra,* at 377 n.154.

A CONCLUDING NOTE ABOUT A LAWYER'S ETHICAL DUTY TO INFORM CLIENTS ABOUT ADR

Alternative dispute resolution methods have been praised for their potential to reduce acrimony in divorce, but the praise has been tempered with caution depending on the parties' perceptions of their needs and circumstances. But do lawyers have an ethical duty to inform their domestic relations clients about ADR alternatives that may better suit the client?

The ABA Model Rules of Professional Conduct do not clearly impose this duty, in family law cases or otherwise. Model Rule 1.2(a) provides that with limited exceptions, "[a] lawyer shall abide by a client's decisions concerning the objectives of representation and * * * shall consult with the client as to the means by which they are to be pursued." Model Rule 1.4(a)(2) requires the lawyer to "reasonably consult with the client about the means by which the client's objectives are to be accomplished." Model Rule 1.4(b) requires the lawyer to "explain a matter to the extent reasonably necessary to permit the client to make informed decisions regarding the representation." Where litigation is likely, "it may be necessary under Rule 1.4 to inform the client of forms of dispute resolution that might constitute reasonable alternatives to litigation." Model Rule 2.1 cmt.5.

Several states have court rules mandating that lawyers discuss alternatives to litigation with their clients. *See* Andrew Schepard, Kramer v. Kramer *Revisited: A Comment on the Miller Commission Report and the Obligation of Divorce Lawyers for Parents to Discuss Alternative Dispute Resolution with Their Clients*, 27 Pace L. Rev. 677, 679 n.8 (2007). Virginia, for example, mandates that "a lawyer shall advise the client about the advantages, disadvantages, and availability of dispute resolution processes that might be appropriate in pursuing these objectives [of the representation]." Va. Code Ann., S. Ct. R. pt. 6, sec. II, 1.2, cmt. 1 (2018).

A few other states are inching toward imposing a duty to inform the client about ADR, though the standard is only aspirational in most. *See, e.g.,* Colo. Rules of Prof'l Conduct R. 2.1 (2018) ("[i]n a matter involving or expected to involve litigation, a lawyer should advise the client of alternative forms of dispute resolution that might reasonably be pursued to attempt to resolve the legal dispute or to reach the legal objective sought").

PROBLEM 15-5

You are a member of a state bar association task force that is charged with reviewing the state's rules of professional conduct. The task force is considering a proposed rule concerning an obligation of family lawyers, in representations in which litigation may result, to inform clients about ADR options, including collaborative law. The proposed amendment would state that "[a] lawyer has an obligation to recommend alternatives to litigation when an alternative is a reasonable course of action to further the client's interests."

As a family law practitioner, you have been asked to present your views about how such an obligation would affect lawyers who practice in your field. Would you favor the proposed amendment? If not, would you leave as-is the ABA Model Rules quoted in the Concluding Note above, or would you change the proposal? Obligation or not, would you inform your own family law clients and prospective clients about ADR options? In some cases or all?

CHAPTER 16

PRIVATE ORDERING IN MARRIAGE AND DIVORCE: PREMARITAL, POSTNUPTIAL, AND SEPARATION AGREEMENTS

■ ■ ■

Earlier chapters have shown how constitutional, statutory, and common law govern family formation, such as the rules for entering into marriage or becoming recognized as a legal parent. We have also considered some of the rights and responsibilities that flow from the legal status of being married. The contemporary model of marriage differs dramatically from the common law model, which placed husband and wife in a hierarchical relationship with fixed duties and rights; however, marriage still has economic consequences and remains a significant source of benefits and obligations. Earlier chapters have also examined how the law specifies the many consequences that may flow from dissolving a marriage, including property distribution, alimony (spousal maintenance), child support, and custody and visitation.

As explained in Chapter 15, another way to think about this body of family law is as a set of "default rules" that will apply unless the parties agree otherwise through "private ordering," or making their own legally enforceable agreement. The notion of "bargaining in the shadow of the law" captures the idea that statutes and case law continue to influence private bargains by shaping the parties' expectations of how they might fare if they fail to reach agreement and end up in court. *See* Robert H. Mnookin & Lewis Kornhauser, *Bargaining in the Shadow of the Law: The Case of Divorce*, 88 Yale L.J. 950 (1979), which was a principal reading in Chapter 15.

Private ordering is now a central feature of family law practice. As Professor Brian Bix explains, however, this term requires some clarification, since "truly *private* ordering is not the actual focus. Within quite broad limits, consenting adults can act and interact as much as they please in domestic matters." Instead, issues over "private ordering" arise only when those consenting adults "seek recognition by the state of their arrangements or enforcement of their commitments." Brian Bix, *Private Ordering and Family Law*, 23 J. Am. Acad. Matrimonial L. 249, 250 (2010). Parties may ask lawyers to draft or advise them about such contemplated agreements; parties may also enlist lawyers when they seek either to enforce an agreement or to argue against its enforcement.

This Chapter examines the law and practice concerning three kinds of agreements that enable marrying, married, or divorcing parties to bargain against the backdrop of the default rules concerning the economic and other consequences of marriage and divorce. The first is a *premarital agreement* (also referred to as a prenuptial or antenuptial agreement), which the parties may execute before marrying. After they marry, but before their marriage ends or divorce is imminent, in some states the parties may enter into a second kind of agreement, known as a *postnuptial agreement* (also referred to as a postmarital or mid-marriage agreement). Third, when married persons are separating or otherwise contemplating divorce, they may enter into a *separation agreement* (also referred to as a marital settlement agreement). Separation agreements are the most common of the three forms of agreement, since the outcome of most divorces is controlled directly by some agreement of the parties.

The prominent role of private ordering in marriage and divorce represents a recent and significant development in family law. Historically, spouses had little room to alter the legal incidents of marriage. Further, courts categorically refused to enforce premarital or other agreements that contemplated the possibility of divorce. Courts reasoned that by removing uncertainty about the consequences of divorce, enforcement would violate public policy favoring marriage and disfavoring divorce.

Most courts and legislatures no longer view premarital or postnuptial agreements as contrary to public policy. Moreover, statutes in almost all states not only permit, but affirmatively *encourage,* private settlement in divorce.

This Chapter considers the movement toward greater contractual freedom and room for private ordering in family law by examining the legal frameworks that apply to the agreements that the parties negotiate at various stages of adult relationships: before marriage, during marriage, and during divorce. State laws vary significantly concerning the procedural requirements for negotiating an enforceable premarital, postnuptial, or separation agreement, the terms over which parties may (and may not) bargain, and the extent to which courts will police the agreement's procedural and substantive fairness. As you will see, notwithstanding broad consensus about the general permissibility of marriage and divorce-related agreements, significant controversies remain about the extent to which courts should defer to such private ordering.

On the one hand, the pendulum has swung toward permitting greater private ordering in marriage and divorce; on the other, scholars, judges, and law reform groups have voiced reservations about the wisdom of embracing ordinary contract principles in family law. In this sense, debate over public policy limitations on contractual freedom in family formation and dissolution remains very much alive. In addition, lawyers as well as the general public express conflicting views about the desirability and utility of premarital agreements. *See Is a Prenup a Must for Most Couples?: Some See Security, Others An Uneven Playing Field*, Wall St. J. (Mar. 1, 2015).

This Chapter's focus is on private ordering in the context of marital agreements, but Chapter 4 illustrated that, in most states, unmarried partners may also engage in private ordering about the economic consequences of their relationships. These agreements are generally called cohabitation agreements (or sometimes living-together contracts, or palimony agreements). Cohabitation agreements, as elaborated in Chapter 4, follow general contract law principles; courts will look closely to ascertain that the agreement has a lawful objective and that sexual services do not constitute the consideration for the contract. These agreements may indicate whether couples want to keep their assets separate or engage in economic sharing during their relationship, and whether they will have any post-dissolution obligations to each other.

As you read the materials in this Chapter on marriage-related agreements, consider whether courts should treat these types of family agreements just as they would any other contract, or whether the parties' incipient or actual intimate relationship creates interpersonal dynamics or moral obligations that justify distinct rules of judicial review and enforcement.

1. MARRIAGE—CONTRACT OR STATUS?

One puzzle about marriage is its dual nature as a contract and a status. In Chapter 2, you encountered the proposition that marriage is not only an intimate personal relationship into which competent parties choose to enter, but also a social institution in which the public retains great interest. In effect, marriage is a private contract to enter into a public status. The traditional public policy against contracting to modify the terms of marriage undoubtedly reflected the view of marriage as a public institution. Family law supplied the basic terms of the marital contract, such as the spouses' respective duties and rights.

In 1888, the U.S. Supreme Court articulated this public aspect of the marital contract in explaining why a divorce granted over a wife's objection did not constitute a governmental impairment of contract in violation of the Contracts Clause of the federal Constitution:

> [M]arriage * * * is something more than a mere contract. The consent of the parties is of course essential to its existence, but when the contract to marry is executed by the marriage, a relation between the parties is created which they cannot change. Other

contracts may be modified, restricted, or enlarged, or entirely released upon the consent of the parties. Not so with marriage. The relation once formed, the law steps in and holds the parties to various obligations and liabilities.

Maynard v. Hill, 125 U.S. 190, 210–11 (1888).

Until recent decades, the common law tolerated relatively little deviation from the "standard form" marriage. Couples could make enforceable agreements concerning disposition of their property upon either party's death, but contracts that purported to dictate the parties' rights upon divorce were generally held void *ab initio* as contrary to public policy. Perhaps this different treatment of the two types of agreements was because a prenuptial agreement might result in relaxing "obligations imposed by law as incident to the relation of husband and wife," such as the husband's essential and non-negotiable duty to support his wife. *See, e.g., French v. McAnarney*, 195 N.E. 714, 715 (Mass. 1935) (ruling that antenuptial agreement waiving alimony upon divorce was void on this rationale); *Williams v. Williams*, 243 P. 402 (Ariz. 1926) (holding that, just as it would be contrary to public policy to allow a wife to waive, in advance of her marriage, her husband's duty to "provide support for [her] during coverture," it is "equally contrary to public policy" to allow the parties to contract in advance that, if they divorce, the husband will be relieved from providing for his wife's support in an amount the court deems proper).

By the 1960s and 1970s, traditional concerns about facilitating divorce began to seem antiquated amid the expansion of the constitutional privacy doctrine in marital and family matters (recounted in Chapter 1), the introduction of no-fault divorce, and the growing incidence of divorce. The trend in family law toward permitting and even encouraging private agreements may reflect not only the growing emphasis on individual privacy and autonomy in intimate life, but also cultural shifts in the meaning of marriage.

Throughout the 1970s and 1980s, state courts moved steadily toward less state regulation of divorce in the ordinary case of parties negotiating marital dissolution agreements. In effect, the conception of marriage has moved dramatically toward contract. Family law historian Sanford Katz remarks on the transformation of "words of intimacy like love, to the language of commerce * * * and self-interest. Spouses became parties, participation became contribution, and divorce became dissolution." Sanford N. Katz, Family Law in America 37 (2003).

Is the story of the ascendance of private ordering a simple one of the shift from status to contract? *Cf.* Sir Henry Sumner Maine, Ancient Law 163 (1861) (contending that, in "progressive societies," contract, or "the free agreement of individuals," was replacing status, or "those forms of reciprocity in rights and duties which have their origin in the Family").

Certainly, being a family member or spouse today has a less fixed meaning, as a status, and adults (whether married or unmarried) have more room to contract with each other about how to order their private lives. But—as we have seen throughout this course—the family continues to be a relevant unit of regulation, with many legal incidents linked to familial and marital status. Moreover, private contract has limits, both in the bargaining process itself and in the permissible substantive outcomes of such bargaining. On the one hand, arguments favoring private ordering include the anti-paternalist premise that "individuals know better than do other people (including those in government) what is in their own best interests" and that autonomy and consent deserve respect. Bix, *Private Ordering, supra,* at 251–52. On the other hand, possible rationales for putting limits on bargaining include the risk of exploitation, potential for power imbalances between the parties, and the impact of agreements on third parties, such as children. Also relevant is the problem of "bounded rationality," which is the idea that intimates bargaining with each other are "less likely to understand their own interests or to protect them" than parties in other bargaining settings. *Id.* at 256.

Just how far family law should go in embracing contractual freedom remains a matter of lively debate among judges, legislators, and scholars. As you will see, proposed uniform rules about premarital and marital agreements attempt to "find a middle ground" that both protects contractual freedom and requires fair process. Barbara A. Atwood & Brian H. Bix, *A New Uniform Law for Premarital and Marital Agreements,* 46 Fam. L. Q. 313, 318 (2012).

Parties enter into premarital agreements, postnuptial agreements, and separation agreements at different stages of their relationship and for varied reasons. The dilemma is that these agreements are based on contract law, but do not easily fit a model of dispassionate, arms' length bargaining typical of negotiations for commercial and business contracts. How much difference should the marriage context make to the legal rules concerning the standards for forming a valid contract and for enforcing such contracts? Should the legal rules differ depending on whether a couple makes a contract before entering marriage, during an ongoing marriage, or as a prelude to exiting marriage? This Chapter canvasses a range of approaches taken by states as well as uniform laws and proposals for law reform. You will see that some jurisdictions hue closely to treating such agreements as ordinary contracts, but most continue to hold that the marital context requires some limitation on freedom of contract. As we study the various legal frameworks for private ordering through premarital, postmarital, and separation agreements, consider whether these frameworks are sound or whether the law should provide more or less regulation of private agreements by intimate partners.

2.   PREMARITAL AGREEMENTS

Premarital agreements once were predominantly for couples in which at least one partner had substantial wealth. These agreements were used most often in second marriages, when an older, wealthy spouse wanted to ensure that assets would pass on to children of a first marriage. *See* Homer H. Clark, Jr., The Law of Domestic Relations in the United States 1 (2d ed. 1988). When married women had fewer legal protections, wealthy fathers often negotiated prenuptial agreements for their daughters.

Premarital agreements are now a regular part of family law practice, and a far broader range of couples employ them, including same-sex couples. A 2016 survey of members of the American Academy of Matrimonial Lawyers (AAML) indicated that 62% of family lawyers reported an increase in requests for premarital agreements in the prior three years. The survey also reported a growing interest in the use of prenuptial agreements by millennials (persons between 18 and 35). American Academy of Matrimonial Lawyers, *Press Release: Prenuptial Agreements on the Rise, Finds Survey* (Oct. 28, 2016). Noting that as people marry at later ages, they have "more to protect" in the event of divorce, AAML President Joslin Davis observed: "Members of the millennial generation are particularly choosing prenups as the best option to cover separate property holdings, business interests, anticipated family inheritances and potential alimony claims." *Id.* One evident trend among millennials is using prenuptial agreements to protect "intellectual property such as films, songs, screenplays, software, apps, and even ideas for technology concepts yet to be executed." Polly Mosendz, *Prenups for Ideas Are All the Rage With Millennials,* Bloomberg News (Nov. 1, 2016).

Another trend is that an increasing number of women request premarital agreements. AAML Press Release, *Increase of Prenuptial Agreements Reflects Improving Economy and Real Estate Market: Survey of Top Nation's Matrimonial Attorneys Also Cites Rise in Women Requesting Prenups* (Oct. 15, 2013). That increase may be due to women's growing economic power and the fact that a substantial minority of women now earn more than their spouses. Premarital agreements are also sought by couples who are "financial peers," that is, who both have successful careers and significant assets and, in the case of remarriage, obligations to children from prior marriages.

Despite the growing public awareness about—and use of—premarital agreements, research suggests that "most people do not see themselves as needing, or benefitting from, prenuptial agreements." Jerome H. Poliacoff, *What Does Love Have to Do With It?*, 33:3 Fam. Advocate 12 (Winter 2011). Ambivalence about such agreements may explain why more couples do not use them. One study found that, while 28% of Americans "say that prenuptial agreements make smart financial sense for anyone getting married, another fourth (25%) think that such agreements are only for the rich and famous, not 'regular people.' " *Id.* at 13. Nineteen percent of the respondents believed that "a prenuptial agreement is never needed when the two people involved really love each other," and 15% were "convinced that a prenuptial agreement dooms a marriage to failure from the start." *Id.*

Another survey found that 62% of respondents "believed that requiring a prenuptial agreement reflects uncertainty about the success of the marriage." *Id.* at 14. This belief reflects one possible reason that more people do not enter into such agreements: "optimism bias." As elaborated below, couples who are about to marry estimate the likelihood of their own marriage ending in divorce at a far lower rate than the national divorce rate, which makes such agreements seem unnecessary. *Id.* Lawyers themselves express varying views on whether a prenuptial agreement is necessary. *See Is A Prenup A Must for Most Couples?,* Wall St. J. (Mar. 1, 2015) (reporting contrasting views of two family law attorneys). What do you think about the need for a premarital agreement and its likely impact on a marriage?

Premarital agreements may reduce the chance and cost of potential litigation by (1) indicating at the outset the extent to which a couple intends to create marital property during their marriage and whether separate assets will remain separate, (2) clarifying the intended allocation of marital assets, and (3) planning for property distribution and any spousal support at the death of a spouse or upon divorce. Indeed, the "top three items most commonly covered" in recently drafted premarital agreements were "protection of separate property" (noted by 80% of responding attorneys), "alimony/spousal maintenance" (77%), and "division of property" (72%). AAML, *Increase of Prenuptial Agreements, supra.* An additional benefit, some matrimonial lawyers argue, is that such agreements provide couples a "platform to candidly discuss finances prior to marriage," helping to start a marriage with "full financial disclosure and an understanding of the other party's views on money." Rebecca A. Provder, *Insight: Swipe Right for a Prenup,* 44 Family L. Rptr. 1216, Bloomberg BNA (May 15, 2018). Premarital agreements, however, cannot bind the court on child-related issues—support, custody and visitation.

A. MODEL LAWS AND PROPOSED REFORMS

1. The Uniform Premarital Agreement Act

The widespread acceptance of premarital agreements is partly attributable to statutes requiring courts to enforce them. In 1983, the National Conference of Commissioners on Uniform State Laws, also known as the Uniform Law Commission (ULC), promulgated the Uniform

Premarital Agreement Act (UPAA), which facilitates treatment of premarital agreements as essentially ordinary contracts.

The following UPAA provisions are directed at both the agreement's substance and the process by which it is negotiated.

UNIFORM PREMARITAL AGREEMENT ACT
9C U.L.A. 39 (2001).

§ 3. Content.

(a) Parties to a premarital agreement may contract with respect to:

(1) the rights and obligations of each of the parties in any of the property of either or both of them whenever and wherever acquired or located;

(2) the right to buy, sell, use, transfer, exchange, abandon, lease, consume, expend, assign, create a security interest in, mortgage, encumber, dispose of, or otherwise manage and control property;

(3) the disposition of property upon separation, marital dissolution, death, or the occurrence or nonoccurrence of any other event;

(4) the modification or elimination of spousal support;

(5) the making of a will, trust, or other arrangement to carry out the provisions of the agreement;

(6) the ownership rights in and disposition of the death benefit from a life insurance policy;

(7) the choice of law governing construction of the agreement; and

(8) any other matter, including their personal rights and obligations, not in violation of public policy or a statute imposing a criminal penalty.

(b) The right of a child to support may not be adversely affected by a premarital agreement.

* * *

§ 6. Enforcement.

(a) A premarital agreement is not enforceable if the party against whom enforcement is sought proves that:

(1) the party did not execute the agreement voluntarily; or

(2) the agreement was unconscionable when it was executed and, before execution of the agreement, that party:

(i) was not provided a fair and reasonable disclosure of the property or financial obligations of the other party;

(ii) did not voluntarily and expressly waive, in writing, any right to disclosure of the property or financial obligations of the other party beyond the disclosure provided; and

(iii) did not have, or reasonably could not have had, an adequate knowledge of the property or financial obligations of the other party.

(b) If a provision of a premarital agreement modifies or eliminates spousal support and that modification or elimination causes one party to the agreement to be eligible for support under a program of public assistance at the time of separation or marital dissolution, a court, notwithstanding the terms of the agreement, may require the other party to provide support to the extent reasonably necessary to avoid that eligibility.

(c) An issue of unconscionability of a premarital agreement shall be decided by the court as a matter of law.

* * *

9C U.L.A. 43, 48–49.

Similar to traditional contract law, enforcement under the UPAA requires the parties' voluntary consent to contract. In an effort to enhance the likelihood of enforcement, however, the Act departs from traditional contract law principles by allowing for enforcement of an agreement that was unconscionable when executed, provided the affected party received fair and reasonable disclosure, waived disclosure, or reasonably could have had sufficient knowledge of the relevant information. Some commentators have strongly criticized this feature of the UPAA. Laura W. Morgan, *The Uniform Premarital Agreement Act: What the Law Says, and How Courts are Interpreting It*, 24 Fam. Advoc, 13 (Winter 2002). Also drawing criticism is the UPAA provision assessing unconscionability only at the time of execution, and not at the time of divorce.

The UPAA also requires that the agreement be in writing and executed by both parties, but does not require that it be supported by separate consideration other than the marriage itself. 9C U.L.A. 41. Even in states that have not adopted the UPAA, the Statute of Frauds requires that contracts in contemplation of marriage be evidenced in a writing signed by the party against whom contract enforcement is sought. Why is this requirement a good idea?

Some state statutes go further than the UPAA, requiring that premarital agreements be witnessed, notarized, or formally acknowledged. A New York statute, for instance, requires that any marital contract be "in writing, subscribed by the parties, and acknowledged or proven in the manner required to entitle a deed to be recorded." N.Y. Dom. Rel. Law § 236(B)(3) (2019). For lack of these formalities, the New York Court of Appeals denied enforcement of a written marital contract that both parties had signed, acknowledged as authentic in open court, and scrupulously observed during their 13-year marriage. *See Matisoff v. Dobi*, 681 N.E.2d 376, 376–78 (N.Y. 1997). Arkansas requires that premarital agreements "be in writing, signed, and acknowledged by both parties to the agreement." In 2017, the Arkansas legislature amended the statutory law to "clarify" the meaning of "acknowledged" by specifying four ways that parties may "acknowledge their intent to be bound." *See* Ark. Code Ann. § 9–11–401 to –402 (2019) (including a formal declaration before a public officer; a sworn affirmation by the parties' attorneys; an agreement signed and witnessed by a notary public; and an agreement witnessed by two "disinterested parties").

Some states have "softened" the requirement of a writing by applying the rule that partial performance "allows specific enforcement of a contract that lacks the requisite writing." *In re Marriage of Benson*, 116 P.3d 1152, 1159 (Cal. 2005); *see also DewBerry v. George*, 62 P.3d 525 (Wash. Ct. App. 2003).

As of 2019, 25 states and the District of Columbia have adopted all or part of the UPAA. Only thirteen states have adopted it "without substantial revision;" a number of other states have "altered the uniform law in one or more material ways that make it easier to challenge a premarital agreement." J. Thomas Oldham, *With All My Worldly Goods I Thee Endow, or Maybe Not: A Reevaluation of the Uniform Premarital Agreement Act After Three Decades*, 19 Duke J. Gender L. & Pol'y 83 (2011). Examples of alteration include clarifying the meaning of "voluntary" execution, limiting the waiver of spousal support, and permitting courts to assess unconscionability not only at the time of execution, but also when enforcement is sought, that is, at divorce. *Id.* at 85–88.

2. Proposal for Reform: The Uniform Premarital and Marital Agreements Act of 2012

In 2012, the ULC approved a new version of the UPAA, the Uniform Premarital and Marital Agreements Act (UPMAA). One impetus for the UPMAA was the "sharp criticism" directed at the UPAA by the American Law Institute and "numerous commentators." Atwood & Bix, *A New Uniform Law for Premarital and Marital Agreements, supra,* at 314. Another was that, when states adopted the UPAA, many states had diverged from it by strengthening "the procedural and substantive fairness requirements for enforceability." *Id.* at 314–315. Another impetus was to propose a uniform approach to premarital *and* marital agreements, since a number of states applied different standards of enforceability to these two types of agreements. *Id.* at 314.

In light of these considerations, the drafting committee sought to produce a new act that would be widely enacted and would "promote informed decision-making and procedural fairness without undermining interests in contractual autonomy, predictability, and reliance." *Id.* at 315.

The drafters were mindful of criticism that premarital contracts "have disadvantaged women," and that "economic inequality among gender lines" persists. They observed, however, that significant changes in the relative position of women and men since the enactment of the UPAA in 1983 had shifted "the relative value of marriage for men and women." *Id.* at 316. Women have an "equal or higher education level than their husbands" in most marriages, and are the higher wage earner in nearly a quarter of marriages. If such trends continue, they reasoned, then "marriage will carry greater economic value for men than for women, giving women new leverage in this intimate form of contract." *Id.* at 316. (As noted earlier in this Chapter, family lawyers have observed an increase in the frequency of women seeking premarital agreements.) In addition, "the advent of same-sex marriage renders assumptions about gender dynamics in marital contracting somewhat dated." *Id.* As we progress through this Chapter, keep your eyes on the concern over gender dynamics in premarital and postnuptial agreements.

As of 2019, two states (Colorado and North Dakota) have adopted the new UPMAA.

UNIFORM PREMARITAL AND MARITAL AGREEMENTS ACT
9C U.L.A. 12 (Supp. 2015).

§ 9. Enforcement

(a) A premarital agreement or marital agreement is unenforceable if a party against whom enforcement is sought proves:

(1) the party's consent to the agreement was involuntary or the result of duress;

(2) the party did not have access to independent legal representation under subsection (b);

(3) unless the party had independent legal representation at the time the agreement was signed, the agreement did not include a notice of waiver of rights under subsection (c) or an explanation in plain language of the marital rights or obligations being modified or waived by the agreement; or

(4) before signing the agreement, the party did not receive adequate financial disclosure under subsection (d).

(b) A party has access to independent legal representation if:

(1) before signing a premarital or marital agreement, the party has a reasonable time to:

(A) decide whether to retain a lawyer to provide independent legal representation; and

(B) locate a lawyer to provide independent legal representation, obtain the lawyer's advice, and consider the advice provided; and

(2) the other party is represented by a lawyer and the party has the financial ability to retain a lawyer or the other party agrees to pay the reasonable fees and expenses of independent legal representation.

(c) A notice of waiver of rights under this section requires language, conspicuously displayed, substantially similar to the following, as applicable to the premarital agreement or marital agreement:

"If you sign this agreement, you may be:

Giving up your right to be supported by the person you are marrying or to whom you are married.

Giving up your right to ownership or control of money and property.

Agreeing to pay bills and debts of the person you are marrying or to whom you are married.

Giving up your right to money and property if your marriage ends or the person to whom you are married dies.

Giving up your right to have your legal fees paid."

(d) A party has adequate financial disclosure under this section if the party:

(1) receives a reasonably accurate description and good-faith estimate of value of the property, liabilities, and income of the other party;

(2) expressly waives, in a separate signed record, the right to financial disclosure beyond the disclosure provided; or

(3) has adequate knowledge or a reasonable basis for having adequate knowledge of the information described in paragraph (1).

(e) If a premarital agreement or marital agreement modifies or eliminates spousal support and the modification or elimination causes a party to the agreement to be eligible for support under a program of public assistance at the time of separation or marital dissolution, a court, on request of that party, may require the other party to provide support to the extent necessary to avoid that eligibility.

(f) A court may refuse to enforce a term of a premarital agreement or marital agreement if, in the context of the agreement taken as a whole[:]

[(1)] the term was unconscionable at the time of signing[;] or

(2) enforcement of the term would result in substantial hardship for a party because of a material change in circumstances arising after the agreement was signed].

(g) The court shall decide a question of unconscionability [or substantial hardship] under subsection (f) as a matter of law.

Legislative Note:

If your state wants to permit review for "substantial hardship" caused by a premarital agreement or marital agreement at the time of enforcement, Section 9(f), including the bracketed language, should be enacted.

9C ULA 12, § 9.

3. The ALI Principles

As noted above, the American Law Institute (ALI) has criticized the UPAA. Below are excerpts from the ALI's approach to the procedural requirements for premarital agreements and to when a court might decline to enforce an agreement due to "substantial injustice." One important premise behind the ALI's approach is that "[w]hile there are good reasons to respect contracts relating to the consequences of family dissolution, the family context requires some departure from the rules that govern the commercial arena." ALI, Principles of the Law of Family Dissolution § 7.02, cmt. c at 956 (2002). One reason is that "the distinctive expectations that persons planning to marry usually have about one another can disarm their capacity for self-protective judgment, or their inclination to exercise it, as compared to parties negotiating commercial agreements." *Id.*

**AMERICAN LAW INSTITUTE,
PRINCIPLES OF THE LAW OF FAMILY DISSOLUTION:
ANALYSIS AND RECOMMENDATIONS**
2002.

§ 7.04   Procedural Requirements

* * *

(3) A premarital agreement is rebuttably presumed * * * [to satisfy the requirements of informed consent and absence of duress] when the party seeking to enforce the agreement shows that:

(a) it was executed at least 30 days before the parties' marriage;

(b) both parties were advised to obtain independent legal counsel, and had reasonable opportunity to do so, before the agreement's execution; and

(c) in the case of an agreement concluded without the assistance of independent legal counsel for each party, the agreement states, in language easily understandable by an adult of ordinary intelligence with no legal training,

(i) the nature of any rights or claims otherwise arising at dissolution that are altered by the contract, and the nature of that alteration, and

(ii) that the interests of the spouses with respect to the agreement may be adverse.

§ 7.05 When Enforcement Work a Substantial Injustice

(1) A court should not enforce a term in an agreement if, pursuant to Paragraphs (2) and (3) of this section,

(a) The circumstances require it to consider whether enforcement would work a substantial injustice; and

(b) The court finds that enforcement would work a substantial injustice.

(2) A court should consider whether enforcement of an agreement would work a substantial injustice if, and only if, the party resisting its enforcement shows that one or more of the following have occurred since the time of the agreement's execution:

(a) more than a fixed number of years have passed * * * [the commentary suggests 10 years];

(b) a child was born to, or adopted by, the parties, who at the time of execution had no children in common; [or]

(c) there has been a change in circumstances that has a substantial impact on the parties or their children, but when they executed the agreement the parties probably did not anticipate either the change, or its impact.

(3) The party claiming that enforcement of an agreement would work a substantial injustice has the burden of proof on that question. * * *

* * *

ALI, Principles of the Law of Family Dissolution: Analysis and Recommendations § 7.04(3), § 7.05 (2002).

NOTES AND QUESTIONS

1. *Comparisons.* Looking at the UPAA, the UPMAA, and the ALI Principles, what similarities and differences do you see? In comparing them, consider the following questions: (a) When will a premarital agreement be enforced?; (b) What are the procedural requirements?; (c) What are the substantive safeguards?; (d) Who bears the burden of proof?; (e) What other differences do you observe?

2.　*Timing.* Do you agree with the ALI Principles' use of the timing of the agreement as a factor helping to establish a "rebuttable presumption" of informed consent? Would it be better to designate a mandatory timetable, insisting that negotiations commence at least a week—or even a month— before the wedding? A 2001 California law creates a mandatory minimum waiting period by deeming involuntary any prenuptial agreement executed "less than seven calendar days" after it was initially presented. *See* Cal. Fam. Code § 1615(c)(2) (2019).

3.　*A better approach to enforcement?* Is Section 9 of the UPMAA a sound revision to the UPAA? If you were a state legislator, would you support your state adopting the UPMAA? The ALI Principles?

B. ELEMENTS REQUIRED FOR VALID PREMARITAL AGREEMENTS

Nearly half the states have not adopted the UPAA and have developed their own distinct legal standards for determining the validity and enforceability of premarital agreements. For example, the UPAA protects only against unconscionability, and only if there was inadequate disclosure. In many non-UPAA states, by contrast, statutes and common law permit closer regulation by requiring that prenuptial agreements be both procedurally and substantively fair. To be enforceable in most states, an antenuptial agreement must be (1) executed voluntarily or without duress; (2) informed (by adequate financial disclosure); and (3) substantively fair or not unconscionable. Oldham, *With All My Worldly Goods, supra,* at 88–111 (canvassing different states' approaches). State law often permits courts to assess substantive fairness both at the time of execution and at the time enforcement is sought, although the legal standard at these two points may differ. *See, e.g., DeMatteo v. DeMatteo,* 762 N.E.2d 797, 809–810, 813 (Mass. 2002) (premarital agreement must be "fair and reasonable" at time of execution and "conscionable" at the time of enforcement).

The following two decisions are from non-UPAA jurisdictions. The courts employ the same legal test for determining the validity of the challenged premarital agreement. As you read the decisions, consider what might account for their different outcomes about enforceability. Also think about how these cases would be decided under the alternative legal approaches discussed in Section A.

MALLEN V. MALLEN
Supreme Court of Georgia, 2005.
622 S.E.2d 812.

BENHAM, JUSTICE.

At issue in this appeal from a judgment and decree of divorce is the trial court's decision to enforce a prenuptial agreement between the parties. Catherine (Wife) and Peter (Husband) Mallen had lived together unmarried for about four years when Wife got pregnant in 1985. While she was at a clinic to terminate the pregnancy, Husband called to ask her not to have the abortion and to marry him, to both of which requests she agreed. A few days later, nine or ten days before their planned wedding, Husband asked Wife to sign a prenuptial agreement prepared by his attorney. Wife contends Husband told her the agreement was just a formality and he would always take care of her. She took the agreement to an attorney whom she claims Husband paid, who advised her that he did not have time to fully examine it in the days remaining before the wedding. Wife did not consult another attorney or postpone the wedding, but spoke and met with Husband and his counsel about the agreement more than once. She agreed to sign it after a life insurance benefit was increased and the alimony provisions were modified to provide for increases for each year of marriage. The agreement provided that in the event of a divorce, Wife would receive a basic alimony amount to be adjusted for the number of years of marriage, and assets would belong to whomever owned the property originally or received it during the marriage. At the time the agreement was executed, Wife had a high school education and was working as a restaurant hostess, while Husband had a college degree and owned and operated a business. Wife had a net worth of approximately $10,000 and Husband's net worth at the time of the agreement's execution was at least $8,500,000. The record shows that Husband's net worth, as of 2002, appeared to be approximately $22,700,000. After 18 years of marriage and the birth of four children, Husband filed an action for divorce in 2003 and sought to enforce the prenuptial agreement. The trial court held the prenuptial agreement enforceable and incorporated that holding in its final judgment, ruling in accordance with the agreement that Wife was entitled to $2900 per month in alimony for four years and Husband was entitled to all the assets with which he entered the marriage and all assets accumulated during the marriage. This appeal is from that judgment.

Three factors are to be considered in deciding the validity of a prenuptial agreement: "(1) [W]as the agreement obtained through fraud, duress or mistake, or through misrepresentation or nondisclosure of material facts? (2) [I]s the agreement unconscionable? (3) Have the facts and circumstances changed since the agreement was executed, so as to make its enforcement unfair and unreasonable?" *Scherer v. Scherer*, 292

S.E.2d 662, 666 (Ga. 1982). "Whether an agreement is enforceable in light of these criteria is a decision made in the trial court's sound discretion." *Alexander v. Alexander*, 610 S.E.2d 48, 49 (Ga. 2005).

1. With regard to the first factor, Wife claims the agreement is infected with fraud, duress, and nondisclosure of material facts.

A. Fraud. The alleged misrepresentation forming the basis of the fraud claim was a statement Wife avers Husband made to induce her to enter into the agreement, an assertion that the agreement was just a formality and a promise that he would "take care" of her. To avoid the general rule that "in the absence of special circumstances one must exercise ordinary diligence in making an independent verification of contractual terms and representations," Wife asserts that by virtue of their engagement, she and Husband had a confidential relationship which excused her from the duty to verify Husband's statement. While it is true that spouses enjoy a confidential relationship entitling one to repose confidence and trust in the other, Georgia law has not recognized the existence of a confidential relationship between persons who have agreed to marry. A majority of jurisdictions which have addressed the issue have recognized a special relationship between persons engaged to be married that imposes a higher duty with regard to contracts between the parties than exists between other contracting parties. However, we believe Georgia law to be more consistent with the states that have rejected such a protective stance. In deciding that prenuptial agreements should not be considered void as against public policy, this Court in *Scherer v. Scherer*, *supra*, put into place the factors quoted above which are to be considered in judging the validity to such agreements, but did not impose the additional burden of acting in "the utmost good faith," as would be required of persons in confidential relationships. [Ga. Code Ann.] § 23–2–58. Accordingly, we reject Wife's contention that there existed when the agreement was executed a confidential relationship between the parties which would relieve her of responsibility to verify representations regarding the meaning and content of the agreement.

Applying the rule requiring ordinary diligence in making an independent verification of contractual terms and representations, Husband's alleged statement that the agreement was a mere formality cannot serve as a basis for a claim of fraud since Wife could ascertain from the clear terms of the agreement that her rights in the event of divorce would be extremely limited. * * * Husband's alleged promise to take care of Wife is likewise insufficient as a basis for a claim of fraud because it amounts to no more than a promise regarding future action, which is not actionable.

B. Duress. The duress Wife asserts was applied to compel her to execute the agreement was that the marriage would not occur in the absence of the prenuptial agreement and she would be left pregnant and unmarried. * * * [W]e conclude that insistence on a prenuptial agreement as a condition of marriage "does not rise to the level of duress required to void an otherwise valid contract." [*Alexander*, 610 S.E.2d at 50 (Sears, J., concurring)]. *See also Doig v. Doig*, 787 So.2d 100, 102–103 (Fla. Dist. Ct. App. 2001) (ultimatum that without the agreement there would be no wedding does not, in itself, constitute duress). Compare *Holler v. Holler*, 612 S.E.2d 469, 475–76 (S.C. Ct. App. 2005) (pregnant, non-English-speaking wife without employment or funds or ability to consult with counsel, and with expiring visa signed agreement written only in English under duress). * * * Nothing in the record of this case suggests that Wife's free will was overcome by the "threat" of not going through with the wedding. In fact, Wife exercised her free will and declined to sign the agreement in the form it was presented to her, acquiescing only when changes were made improving her position in the event of divorce or Husband's death. The fact of Wife's pregnancy does not make Husband's insistence on the agreement rise to the level of duress. She had already demonstrated her willingness to terminate the pregnancy, so she cannot credibly claim the pregnancy put such pressure on her as to overcome her will.

C. Nondisclosure of material facts. Attached to the prenuptial agreement executed by the parties were financial disclosure forms on which each party set out their assets and liabilities. Neither form listed income. Citing foreign authority based on the existence of a confidential relationship between persons engaged to be married, Wife asserts the absence of Husband's income from the financial statement constituted the nondisclosure of a material fact which would render the agreement unenforceable. In *Posner v. Posner*, 257 So.2d 530 (Fla. 1972), the Florida Supreme Court held that in light of the confidential relationship of parties to a prenuptial agreement and the inadequate provision for the wife in the agreement under review, the husband's failure to disclose significant sources of income rendered the agreement unenforceable. However, as we held above, parties to prenuptial agreements in Georgia are not by virtue of their planned marriage in a confidential relationship. Wife also cited *DeLorean v. DeLorean*, 511 A.2d 1257 (N.J. Super. Ct. 1986), for the statement in that case that New Jersey law would require a complete written disclosure of all assets and all income. We find that case more persuasive for its holding that under California law, which the agreement specified would be applied and which does not consider persons planning marriage to be in a confidential relationship, a prenuptial agreement is enforceable "[s]o long as the spouse seeking to set aside such an agreement has a general idea of the character and extent of the financial assets and income of the other. . . . Indeed, absent fraud or misrepresentation, there appears to be a duty to make some inquiry to ascertain the full nature and extent of the financial resources of the other." *Id.* [at 1262]. That statement of law is consistent with our holding above that persons planning marriage are not in a confidential relationship that will excuse a party from the duty to "exercise ordinary diligence in making an independent verification of contractual terms and representations[.]" In the present case, although the financial statement did not include income, it did reveal Husband to be a wealthy individual with significant income-producing assets, including an 80% ownership share of a business bearing his name. Wife had lived with Husband for four years and was aware from the standard of living they enjoyed that he received significant income from his business and other sources. Under those circumstances and in light of the authority cited above, Wife cannot be said to have demonstrated that the absence from Husband's financial statement of precise income data constituted the nondisclosure of material facts which would render the prenuptial agreement unenforceable.

2.   Concerning the second inquiry to be made pursuant to *Scherer v. Scherer, supra*, Wife asserts that the disparity in financial situation and business experience rendered the prenuptial agreement unconscionable when executed. "An unconscionable contract is one abhorrent to good morals and conscience ... where one of the parties takes a fraudulent advantage of another[,] an agreement that no sane person not acting under a delusion would make and that no honest person would take advantage of." *William J. Cooney, P.C. v. Rowland*, 524 S.E.2d 730, 732 (Ga. Ct. App. 1999). We do not believe the agreement involved here fits that description.

* * * Given our conclusion above that the agreement is not infected with fraud, and given the absence of any suggestion that Wife suffered from any delusion, the disparities between Wife and Husband in financial status and business experience do not demand a conclusion that the agreement was unconscionable.

3.   The remaining factor to be considered is whether circumstances have changed since the execution of the agreement so as to render its enforcement unfair and unreasonable. The changed circumstance which Wife contends in her brief renders enforcement of the agreement unfair and unreasonable is that Husband's net worth increased by 14 million dollars during the marriage.

Since this Court's adoption in *Scherer v. Scherer, supra*, of the factors to consider in determining the enforceability of prenuptial agreements, we have not had occasion to address directly the question of what changes in circumstance might render a prenuptial agreement unfair and unreasonable. However, in *Curry v. Curry*, 392 S.E.2d 879, 881 n.2 (Ga. 1990), in considering a trial court's application of those same factors to uphold a reconciliation agreement, this Court found no error in the trial court's holding that there "has been no change in circumstances that [was] not foreseeable at the time that the agreement was entered into. . . ." That element of foreseeability has been recognized by other states as a key element in consideration of changed circumstances. In *Reed v. Reed*, 693 N.W.2d 825, 836 (Mich. Ct. App. 2005), the court held that a significant growth of assets over many years "can hardly be considered an unforeseeable changed circumstance that justifies voiding the . . . prenuptial agreement." The Supreme Court of South Carolina, in *Hardee v. Hardee*, 585 S.E.2d 501, 505 (S.C. 2003), agreed with the lower court's holding that the wife's becoming totally disabled was not a change in circumstance that would render the prenuptial agreement unenforceable because "[t]he premarital agreement specifically noted Wife's health problems [and i]t was completely foreseeable to Wife that her health would worsen."

In the present case, Wife was familiar with Husband's financial circumstances from living with him for four years prior to marriage and must have anticipated that his wealth would grow over the ensuing years. Since the continued disparity in their financial situations was plainly foreseeable from the terms of the prenuptial agreement, Wife cannot rely on that as a change in circumstance which renders the agreement unfair.

Because the record in this case supports a finding that none of the factors set forth in *Scherer v. Scherer*, *supra*, call[s] for a judicial repudiation of the prenuptial agreement signed by the parties, we conclude the trial court did not abuse its discretion in enforcing the agreement.

Judgment affirmed.

SEARS, CHIEF JUSTICE, dissenting.

* * *

In *Scherer v. Scherer*, this Court held that a prenuptial agreement is unenforceable if there was a "nondisclosure of material facts" when the agreement was entered. Thus, under *Scherer*, parties entering a prenuptial agreement have a duty to disclose material facts even absent the presence of a confidential relationship. By necessity, whether a fact is material to a prenuptial agreement will depend on the property and alimony issues that are addressed in the agreement. In the present case, Mr. Mallen's attorney prepared a prenuptial agreement that significantly limited Ms. Mallen's right to alimony. The agreement provides that, in the event of a divorce, Ms. Mallen would be entitled to $1,000 per month in alimony, to be increased $100 a month for each year of the parties' marriage, with Ms. Mallen's right to alimony to terminate four years after the date of the parties' divorce decree. Because a party's income is a critical factor in determining the appropriate amount of alimony, Mr. Mallen's income was material to the prenuptial agreement. In this regard, it is undisputed that, at the time the parties entered the prenuptial agreement, Mr. Mallen did not disclose his income to Ms. Mallen and that his income was approximately $560,000 per year.

Because this material fact was not disclosed to Ms. Mallen, I conclude that the parties' prenuptial agreement is unenforceable. I therefore dissent to the majority opinion. * * *

NOTES AND QUESTIONS

1. *Confidential relationship.* As *Mallen* illustrates, the determination whether parties negotiating a premarital agreement stand in a "confidential relationship" may be relevant to more than one aspect of enforceability. The presence or absence of a confidential relationship may help determine whether the agreement was truly "voluntary," or was instead induced by fraud, and whether each party's consent is sufficiently "informed." As *Mallen* indicates, whether the parties stand in a "confidential relationship" also affects the scope of their disclosure obligations: the fiduciary duties that spring from a "confidential relationship" ordinarily require much fuller sharing of financial data than is required of other contracting parties.

Deciding when the "confidential relationship" begins is thus a matter of some importance. In Georgia and a handful of other states—including, prominently, California—the "confidential relationship" commences only upon marriage. *See In re Marriage of Bonds,* 5 P.3d 815 (Cal. 2000); *In re Marriage of Hill and Dittmer,* 136 Cal. Rptr. 3d 700, 705 (Cal. Ct. App. 2011). As *Mallen* concedes, however, the strong majority rule is that an engaged couple negotiating a premarital agreement occupies a confidential relationship. *See, e.g., McNamara v. McNamara,* 40 So. 3d 78 (Fla. Dist. Ct. App. 2010); *Ex parte Brown,* 26 So.3d 1222 (Ala. 2009); *Bratton v. Bratton,* 136 S.W.3d 595 (Tenn. 2004); *DeMatteo v. DeMatteo,* 762 N.E.2d 797 (Mass. 2002). Authorities disagree about whether a confidential relationship exists when parties negotiate a prenuptial agreement before they are actually engaged. *Compare Cannon v. Cannon,* 865 A.2d 563, 573–74 (Md. 2005) (yes), *with Lightman v. Magid,* 394 S.W.2d 151, 156–57 (Tenn. Ct. App. 1965) (no).

2. *Change of circumstances and foreseeability.* Do you agree with *Mallen's* conclusion about the foreseeability of the husband's increased wealth? If you were representing the wife, what other arguments might you have made about change in circumstances? What type of financial changes are foreseeable? In *Finkelstein v. Finkelstein,* 2012 WL 1252680 (N.M. Ct. App. 2012), the court reversed a ruling that a prenuptial agreement governed by Georgia law was unenforceable due to a change in circumstances that rendered it unfair and unreasonable, including the disparity in the husband's and wife's assets at the time of the divorce. Citing *Mallen* as "instructive," *Finkelstein* stated that the wife was "aware at the time the Agreement was executed" of the "large disparity" between their assets—the husband's net worth was approximately $805,000, and the wife's was approximately $37,000—and "there was no reason for her not to anticipate that the value of Husband's business and other assets would also grow over time." *Id.* at *4. However, the

dissent also enlisted *Mallen* to criticize the majority's "limited" analysis of foreseeability. It argued that the wife could not foresee that the husband would "intentionally" widen the disparity in their assets by entirely depleting her separate assets to zero while building up his own and minimizing any community property through his "complete control and management of *all* assets during the marriage." *Id.* at *7 (emphasis original).

3.   *Overreaching and duress. Mallen* found nothing in the circumstances of the premarital negotiation that impeded the parties' "free will" and rendered the agreement involuntary, including Catherine Mallen's pregnancy. Do you agree? Should the overbearing destruction of "free will" be the measure of "voluntariness"?

In *Newell v. Newell,* 2017 WL 2591348 (Nev. Ct. App. 2017), the court upheld a lower court ruling that a prenuptial agreement limiting spousal support was unenforceable because of duress (citing *Mallen*). Applying Georgia law's definition of "duress" ("threats of bodily or other harms, or other means amounting to coercion, or tending to coerce the will of another, and actually inducing him to do an act contrary to his free will"), the lower court found that the wife credibly testified that she signed the agreement "only because [husband] had previously committed acts of domestic violence against her, threatened to take the couple's son away from her, and was holding a pending criminal investigation over her head with threats to file charges against her if she did not sign the agreement." *Id.* at *2.

Various jurisdictions offer different tests for "overreaching" when determining voluntariness. In *Stewart v. Stewart,* 76 A.3d 1221, 1227–1230 (Md. Ct. Spec. App. 2013), for example, the court explained that overreaching has both a "substantive prong" (whether the agreement was "fair and equitable under the circumstances") and a "procedural prong" (whether the person seeking to avoid the contract entered into it "freely and understandingly"). In *Vanderbilt v. Vanderbilt,* an Ohio appellate court explained that courts should "look to the totality of the surrounding circumstances when considering the existence of duress, coercion, fraud, or overreaching, including knowledge of the nature of the agreement and whether the agreement was presented for signature in close proximity to the scheduled wedding." 2013 WL 1286012, *4 (Ohio Ct. App. 2013).

In contrast to *Mallen,* the court in the following decision refused to enforce an agreement concluded shortly before a wedding because the circumstances of the negotiation rendered the wife's consent "involuntary." Like Georgia, New Hampshire has not adopted the UPAA.

IN RE ESTATE OF HOLLETT
Supreme Court of New Hampshire, 2003.
834 A.2d 348.

DUGGAN, J.

The petitioner, Erin Hollett, appeals an order by the Merrimack County Probate Court (Patten, J.) declaring the prenuptial agreement made between Erin and the decedent, John Hollett, to be valid. Erin argues that the agreement should be set aside because of duress, undue influence, insufficient financial disclosure, and lack of effective independent counsel. The respondents, Kathryn Hollett, the decedent's first wife, and their five children, argue that the agreement is valid and the probate court's order should be affirmed. We reverse and remand.

The following facts were found by the trial court or are evident from the record. John and Erin married on August 18, 1990. Their courtship had begun in 1984, when John was fifty-two and Erin was twenty-two. John was a successful real estate investor and developer who regularly bought and sold property in New Hampshire and Florida. He had considerable experience with attorneys and accountants because of his business dealings. Erin had dropped out of high school in the eleventh grade, and had no work or business experience aside from several low level jobs. Throughout their relationship and marriage, Erin had almost no involvement in or understanding of John's business.

John had previously been married to Kathryn C. Hollett, with whom he had five children. Under the terms of their divorce, John owed Kathryn a substantial property settlement, and still owed her millions of dollars at the time of his death. Erin was unaware of this property settlement.

In 1988, the same year that John and Erin became engaged, Erin found a newspaper article about prenuptial agreements that John had left on the kitchen counter. When Erin confronted John with the article, he explained that his first wife had given it to him, and stated that he would not get married without a prenuptial agreement. This statement provoked a "heated and unpleasant" discussion during which Erin said she would not sign such an agreement, particularly because John's first wife had insisted upon it. John said nothing to Erin about a prenuptial agreement again until several days before the August 18, 1990 wedding.

In May 1990, apparently in anticipation of the impending marriage, John sent a statement of his net worth to his attorneys in the law firm of McLane, Graf, Raulerson, and Middleton. After meeting with John on July 18, 1990, his lawyers drafted a prenuptial agreement that was sent to him on July 26. Erin testified that she did not learn about the agreement until the evening of August 16, less than forty-eight hours before the wedding. Under the original draft, Erin was to renounce any claim to alimony or a property settlement in the event of a divorce, and would receive only $25,000 and an automobile.

Several days before the wedding, John's lawyers contacted Brian Shaughnessy, a recent law school graduate, and requested that he counsel Erin regarding the prenuptial agreement. The lawyers told Shaughnessy that John would pay his fee. Shaughnessy first called Erin on August 16 to obtain her consent to act as counsel and to set up a meeting at the McLane law firm office the next day. Shaughnessy had never before negotiated a prenuptial agreement, but prior to the meeting he studied the law of prenuptial agreements and reviewed the draft agreement.

Erin, accompanied by her mother, met with Shaughnessy in person for the first and only time at the McLane law firm on August 17, the day before the wedding. At that time, all of the plans and arrangements for the elaborate wedding, at which over 200 guests were expected, had already been made and paid for; Erin's mother and father had already flown in from Thailand. During the meeting and subsequent negotiations with John's attorneys, Shaughnessy noted that Erin was under considerable emotional distress, sobbing throughout the three or four hours he was with her and at times so distressed that he was unable to speak with her. Erin testified that she remembered almost nothing about the conference. Shaughnessy, however, testified that he carefully reviewed John's financial disclosure and draft of the agreement with Erin, explained their legal significance, and asked her what she sought to obtain from the agreement. He testified that he advised her that the settlement offer in the draft was inadequate, and reminded her that the wedding could be put off if necessary.

Shaughnessy also testified that he believed the financial disclosure provided by John, which had not been audited or reviewed by any other party, was inadequate. Shaughnessy, however, had no time to independently verify any of John's finances. In any case, he believed that any failure to disclose was John's problem, as it could lead to the invalidation of the agreement.

At the end of the negotiations, the prenuptial agreement was considerably more favorable to Erin, allowing her to obtain as much as one-sixth of John's estate in the event of a divorce or John's death. John's lawyers prepared a final version of the agreement, which John and Erin signed on the morning of August 18, the day of their wedding.

The parties remained married until John's death on April 30, 2001. John was survived by Erin, his first wife, and his children from his first marriage. Erin subsequently petitioned the probate court to invalidate the prenuptial agreement, while John's first wife and children argued in favor of upholding it. After four days of hearings, the probate court concluded that the prenuptial agreement was valid and enforceable.

On appeal, Erin argues that the prenuptial agreement was invalid for three reasons: (1) the agreement was not voluntary because it was the product of duress and undue influence; (2) John's financial disclosures were inadequate; and (3) she did not have independent counsel. We need only address the issue of duress. * * *

RSA 460:2–a (1997)[a] permits a man and a woman to enter into a written contract "in contemplation of marriage." A prenuptial agreement is presumed valid unless the party seeking the invalidation of the agreement proves that: (1) the agreement was obtained through fraud, duress or mistake, or through misrepresentation or nondisclosure of a material fact; (2) the agreement is unconscionable; or (3) the facts and circumstances have so changed since the agreement was executed as to make the agreement unenforceable. *See In the Matter of Yannalfo and Yannalfo*, 794 A.2d 795, 797 (N.H. 2002).

"As a practical matter, the claim of undue duress is essentially a claim that the agreement was not signed voluntarily." 3 C. Douglas, New Hampshire Practice, Family Law § 1.05, at 12 (2002). To establish duress, a party must ordinarily "show that it involuntarily accepted the other party's terms, that the coercive circumstances were the result of the other party's acts, that the other party exerted pressure wrongfully, and that under the circumstances the party had no alternative but to accept the terms set out by the other party." *Yannalfo*, [794 A.2d at 797]. However, "the State has a special interest in the subject matter" of prenuptial agreements and "courts tend to scrutinize [them] more closely than ordinary commercial contracts." *MacFarlane v. Rich (MacFarlane)*, 567 A.2d 585, 589 (N.H. 1989). Moreover, because such agreements often involve persons in a confidential relationship, "the parties must exercise the highest degree of good faith, candor and sincerity in all matters bearing on the terms and execution of the proposed agreement, with fairness being the ultimate measure."

Under the heightened scrutiny afforded to prenuptial agreements, the timing of the agreement is of paramount importance in assessing whether it was voluntary. Fairness demands that the party presented with the agreement have "an opportunity to seek independent advice and a reasonable time to reflect on the proposed terms." * * * Some States, in fact, automatically invalidate any prenuptial agreement signed immediately before a wedding. *See, e.g.*, Minn. Stat. § 519.11 (2002) (agreement "must be entered into and executed prior to the day of solemnization of marriage").

---

[a] *Editors' Note:* Section 460:2–a of the New Hampshire Revised States, N.H. Rev. Stat. Ann. § 460:2–a (2007), is the governing statute for antenuptial agreements, which is not based on the UPAA.

In arguing for the validity of the Holletts' agreement, the respondents rely upon *In the Matter of Yannalfo and Yannalfo*, [*supra*]. In that case, the husband and wife, each of whom was employed by the United States Postal Service, signed a prenuptial agreement a "day or so" before their wedding. The agreement was limited to a house that the husband and wife had purchased one month before the wedding, for which the husband had contributed $70,000 as a down payment, and the wife had provided $5,000 for closing costs. The agreement stated that the first $70,000 of equity in the house was the property of the husband, and that in the event of a divorce, the house would be sold and $70,000 would be paid to the husband. The agreement did not concern any property other than the $70,000 contribution.

In upholding the agreement in *Yannalfo*, we rejected a *per se* invalidation of agreements signed immediately before the wedding. Instead, we established that each case must be decided upon the totality of its own circumstances. Citing cases from other jurisdictions, however, we suggested that "additional circumstances coupled with [such] timing" may compel a finding that a prenuptial agreement was involuntary.

Several important circumstances distinguish the present case from *Yannalfo*. First, the agreement in *Yannalfo* did not involve the entire estates of the parties. Rather, it only concerned money used in a transaction that both parties had participated in one month before the wedding. The agreement in this case, by contrast, involves the post-marriage disbursement of an estate that totaled over six million dollars at the time of the agreement, and the relinquishment of marital rights such as alimony. Such a complicated and important agreement will require more time for negotiation and reflection than the agreement in *Yannalfo*.

Second, unlike the parties in *Yannalfo*, Erin's bargaining position was vastly inferior to that of her husband. John was much older than Erin, and he had already been married. According to their financial disclosures, John had approximately six million dollars in assets, while Erin owned approximately five thousand dollars' worth of personal property at the time of the agreement. Erin's work experience during the relationship was limited to stints as a bartender and a grocery store cashier. She had little understanding of and no real involvement in John's business ventures. According to Erin, in fact, John had encouraged Erin to stop working after they began their relationship. If Erin refused to sign the agreement, she thus not only stood to face the embarrassment of canceling a two hundred guest wedding, but also stood to lose her means of support. Prenuptial agreements that result from such a vast disparity in bargaining power must meet a high standard of procedural fairness.

Finally, John's conduct before the wedding raises serious questions regarding his good faith in dealing with Erin. John had contemplated a prenuptial agreement at least two years before the wedding, as evidenced by his argument with Erin in 1988. Despite Erin's opposition to the idea, however, he did not discuss the agreement with her again. Moreover, although John's lawyers had drafted a prenuptial agreement almost a month before the wedding, John did not obtain counsel for his wife or even inform her of the agreement until several days before the ceremony. * * *

* * *

* * * [In upholding the validity of the prenuptial contract,] the trial court focused upon the assistance Erin received from Brian Shaughnessy before the execution of the agreement. The respondents, in fact, suggest that the presence of counsel should be dispositive of the issue of voluntariness. We note that the trial court itself found that the time constraints limited the quality of Shaughnessy's representation: for example, he was unable to verify the accuracy of John's disclosures. Even assuming, however, that Shaughnessy provided Erin with effective independent counsel, and that the financial representations upon which he relied were accurate, we cannot agree that his counsel by itself was sufficient to validate this agreement.

Independent counsel is useless without the ability and the time to make effective use of such counsel. * * *

In this case, it would be unreasonable to conclude that Erin had "sufficient time" or a "reasonable opportunity" to make use of Brian Shaughnessy's advice. Given the complexity of John's finances and the agreement, and the disparity in the parties' bargaining power, Erin needed more than one day to negotiate and reflect upon his draft proposal. Without such time, we conclude as a matter of law that her signing of the agreement was involuntary under the heightened standard applied to prenuptial agreements.

Reversed and remanded.

QUESTIONS

1.   *Why the different outcomes?* Given that *Mallen* and *Hollett,* both from non-UPAA jurisdictions, articulate the same legal test for determining the validity of a premarital agreement, what accounts for their different outcomes? Were contrasting facts really determinative—such as the timing of contract negotiations or the different nature of the wedding plans? Or are the decisions best understood as driven by differing legal conceptions of voluntariness, or by whether the parties stood in a confidential relationship?

2.   *Applying different tests.* In either of these cases, do you think a court would reach a different result if it applied the UPA, the UPMAA, or the ALI Principles?

3.   *Why treat premarital contracts differently from other contracts?* The *Hollett* court asserts that heightened scrutiny of prenuptial agreements stems both from the state's "special interest" in them and from the confidential relationship between the parties. Do you agree? To help evaluate whether the law should impose special duties of fair dealing upon couples about to enter into marriage, consider the dynamics of bargaining within an intimate relationship. When couples embark on marriage, they bargain not only in "the shadow of the law," *see* Mnookin & Kornhauser, *Bargaining in the Shadow of the Law, supra,* but also in "the shadow of love." Brian Bix, *Bargaining in the Shadow of Love: The Enforcement of Premarital Agreements and How We Think About Marriage,* 40 Wm. & Mary L. Rev. 145 (1998). The term "bounded rationality" captures some of the psychological impediments to effective, clear-eyed bargaining in this context, in which persons are "less likely to understand their own interests or to protect them." *Bix, Private Ordering and Family Law, supra,* at 256. Classical contract law assumed the "rational-actor model of psychology," under which "actors are fully knowledgeable, know the law, and act rationally to further their economic self-interest." Melvin A. Eisenberg, *Why There Is No Law of Relational Contracts,* 94 Nw. U. L. Rev. 805, 808 (2000). This model "accounts in part for the rule that bargains would not be reviewed for fairness: if actors always act rationally in their own self-interest, then, in the absence of fraud, duress, or the like, all bargains must be fair." *Id.* These assumptions about rational actors may be imperfect even in ordinary commercial settings, but, the argument goes, are especially inapt in premarital negotiations. In this excerpt, Professor Eisenberg explains why:

> The limits of cognition have an obvious bearing on the enforceability of prenuptial agreements. To begin with, individuals who plan to marry are often likely to be unduly optimistic about the fate of their marriage. Two people in love are likely to heavily discount the possibility of divorce, because they will overemphasize the concrete evidence of their currently thriving relationship and underemphasize abstract divorce statistics; and because divorce is a risk that, like other risks, people systematically underestimate. As a result, prospective spouses are likely to heavily discount the probability that their prenuptial agreement will come into play.

Melvin A. Eisenberg, *The Limits of Cognition and the Limits of Contract,* 47 Stan. L. Rev. 211, 254 (1995).

Indeed, survey results illustrate this "optimism bias": most respondents contemplating marriage estimate their chance of divorce as zero, despite awareness that a significant percentage of all marriages ended in divorce. *See* Lynn A. Baker & Robert E. Emery, *When Every Relationship Is Above Average: Perceptions and Expectations of Divorce at the Time of Marriage,* 17 Law & Hum. Behav. 439, 443 (1993); Heather Mahar, *Why Are There So Few Prenuptial Agreements?,* John M. Olin Center for Law, Economics, and Business Discussion Paper No. 436 (Sept. 2003).

Do the problems of "optimism bias" and "bounded rationality" and support classifying premarital relationships as "confidential"? Is it realistic to expect intended spouses, in the weeks or months before a wedding, to investigate each other's finances and to challenge or express skepticism about assurances about the future? How should knowledge of such problems inform a lawyer's representation of a party negotiating a premarital agreement?

C. SPECIFIC FACTORS IN EVALUATING THE VALIDITY OF PREMARITAL AGREEMENTS

In addition to the general rules governing the enforceability of contracts, antenuptial agreements must satisfy heightened scrutiny. In most jurisdictions, (1) each party must enter the agreement voluntarily and with full knowledge of the meaning and effect of its terms, (2) each party must truthfully disclose his or her assets, and (3) the agreement's terms must be substantively fair and equitable.

1. Voluntariness

Most courts apply some form of heightened scrutiny to determine a premarital agreement's voluntariness, but courts often differ about how to apply or weigh the relevant factors. In addition to circumstances that might be considered coercive, courts often look to the timing of negotiations, the role of counsel, and disparities in the parties' sophistication. *Hollett* viewed the timing of contract negotiations as a "paramount" consideration, but declined to adopt a *per se* rule.

When evaluating timing, many courts consider the nature of the planned wedding ceremony, and other factors. In Ohio, for instance, "presentation of an agreement a very short time before the wedding ceremony will create a presumption of overreaching or coercion if * * * postponement of the wedding would cause significant hardship, embarrassment or emotional stress." *Fletcher v. Fletcher*, 628 N.E.2d 1343, 1348 (Ohio 1994). *Cf. In re Marriage of Murphy*, 834 N.E.2d 56, 67–68 (Ill. App. Ct. 2005) (enforcing agreement presented by husband one week before wedding where wife had time to negotiate terms; noting that "[t]he period of time between the execution of the antenuptial agreement and the marriage ceremony is only one factor among many that is considered when determining the validity of the agreement"). Where the planned ceremony is small and informal, courts may be more tolerant of agreements signed on short notice. *See In re Marriage of Bonds*, 5 P.3d 815 (Cal. 2000). Courts may consider an agreement voluntary when, "despite the agreement being signed shortly before the wedding, the parties had agreed to the material terms substantially earlier." Oldham, *With All My Worldly Goods, supra,* at 96.

The timing of the agreement also bears on other elements of establishing voluntariness, such as the opportunity to consult an attorney and the good faith of the parties. In *Kremer v. Kremer*, the appellate court affirmed a lower court's conclusion that a premarital agreement had a "fatal" lack of procedural fairness, which requires "full disclosure of financial condition" and "opportunity to consult independently with counsel," when the future husband presented a signed premarital agreement to his future wife a few days before their flights to the Cayman Islands for a "destination wedding" with family and friends. 889 N.W.2d 41, 45, 48 (Minn. Ct. App. 2017), *aff'd,* 912 N.W.2d 617 (Minn. 2018). The future husband, without the future wife's knowledge, had been meeting with his attorney to draft a premarital agreement for two months. When he presented the agreement to her, he told her to "talk to an attorney" and "made clear that there would be no wedding if she did not sign the agreement." By then, friends and family "had paid for their lodging and airfare to the Cayman Islands, and some of them had started their travels." *Id.* The court of appeals found that the husband "used the wedding deadline to create an atmosphere of pressure that resulted in the [wife] not having an adequate opportunity to negotiate any of the terms of the premarital agreement." *Id.* The wife consulted with an attorney and signed the agreement the same day. The agreement "foreclosed any claims to spousal maintenance and provided that marital property would be divided 'in proportion to the actual monetary consideration provided by each [party].' " *Id.*

All jurisdictions agree that access to advice of independent counsel is an important factor in determining the voluntariness of any premarital agreement. Many jurisdictions agree with the view of the California Supreme Court that "the best assurance of enforceability is independent representation of both parties." *Marriage of Bonds*, 5 P.3d at 833; *accord Binek v. Binek*, 673 N.W.2d 594, 598 (N.D. 2004) ("[A]dequate legal representation will often be the best evidence that a spouse signed a premarital agreement knowledgeably and voluntarily"). Nevertheless, *Bonds* and many other decisions have enforced agreements signed by a party who opted to forgo counsel, or who met only with an attorney retained by the other spouse. In such cases, courts sometimes emphasize that the unrepresented spouse was advised to seek legal counsel or was given concessions even without counsel.

In response to *Bonds*, which held that access to independent counsel was just one factor in assessing the voluntariness of prenuptial agreements, the California legislature amended the state's version of the UPAA in 2001 to mandate that a premarital agreement will be deemed involuntary unless, among other things, "[t]he party against whom enforcement is sought was represented by independent legal counsel at the time of signing the agreement or, after being advised to seek independent legal counsel, expressly waived, in a separate writing, representation by independent legal counsel." Cal. Fam. Code § 1615(c)(1) (2019). Where the issue is waiver of spousal support, the statute strictly requires independent representation for enforceability. *See* Cal. Fam. Code § 1612(c) (2019).

The UPMAA does not require independent representation, but it does require that each party must have had "access to independent legal representation." UPMAA, 9C ULA 12, at § 9(a)(2). To satisfy this new requirement, it must be shown that before the agreement was signed, the objecting party had a reasonable time (a) to decide whether to retain a lawyer to provide independent legal representation; and (b) to locate a lawyer, obtain advice, and consider the advice provided. *Id.* § 9(b). In addition to considering the timing of negotiations and each party's access to counsel, courts often consider, as *Mallen* and *Hollett* did, whether one party has significantly more education, experience or business sophistication than the other. Disparity alone does not necessarily establish lack of voluntariness, but it may be relevant in evaluating the coercive pressure created by timing or other circumstances.

Most often, courts find lack of voluntariness when some combination of these factors is present. For example, in *In re Marriage of Tamraz*, 2005 WL 1524199 (Cal. Ct. App. 2005), the court found a lack of voluntary assent where the future husband, an experienced attorney, unexpectedly faxed his fiancée a draft agreement late in the afternoon on the day before the wedding and led her to believe that the agreement's terms were more limited than they actually were. Similar facts led the reviewing court, in *In re Marriage of Porter*, to affirm the trial court's ruling that the premarital agreement was unenforceable because the wife did not enter it voluntarily. 381 P.3d 873 (Or. App. 2016), *review dismissed*, 389 P.3d 1135 (Or. 2017). When the future husband initially mentioned such an agreement, he said he "just wanted to make sure that [his future wife] wasn't in this relationship for his money." He did not mention the agreement again, and the future wife did not see it, until they were running errands when he "suddenly pulled up to a bank and said, 'We are going to the bank to sign the prenuptial agreement.'" (They became engaged that evening, after she signed the agreement.) The wife testified that she "did not understand" most of the document, including its provision that, in the event of divorce, she "would not be entitled to spousal support or to any portion of husband's property." *Id.* at 875. Nonetheless, the agreement recited that both parties had ample opportunity to consult independent legal counsel and had "complete understanding of such legal effects" of the agreement. *Id.* at 876. The reviewing court observed: "Wife [who grew up and was educated in Germany] was considerably disadvantaged by her lack of familiarity with divorce in the United States and with English legal terminology; husband took advantage of that circumstance by implying that the document was relatively inconsequential and by presenting it to her suddenly, without sufficient time to review it or to have it reviewed by a lawyer." *Id.* at 880.

In *Owen v. Owen,* 759 S.E.2d 468 (W.Va. 2014), the court explained that for a presumption of validity to apply to a prenuptial agreement, "both parties * * * must be represented by independent counsel." Where one party is unrepresented, "the burden of proof is on the party seeking its enforcement." *Id.* at 473. In *Owen,* the wife did not have independent counsel. The husband argued that she was a "reasonably-intelligent adult" who could understand what she was signing and should be "deemed to have read it," but the court concluded the husband did not satisfy his burden to show validity. The wife had "no specific explanation of the rights she was waiving, especially those associated with property acquired during the course of the marriage that would be deemed marital property, subject to equitable distribution." The husband's attorney (who drafted the agreement) discussed with her "only the general concepts of a prenuptial agreement." *Id.* at 474.

Courts may uphold some, but not all, provisions of an agreement. In *Large v. Large,* 2012 WL 1057598 (Ariz. Ct. App. 2012), the court focused on procedural unconscionability to hold invalid an attorney fee shifting provision in the event suit was brought about the agreement. The circumstances included that: (1) the wife was a high school graduate without business experience, who had lived with the husband since she was 15 years old; (2) the husband did not offer to get her independent legal advice; (3) there was "no evidence" that the provision was explained to the wife or that she understood it; and (4) the husband, a doctor with his own business, "was in control of virtually all of the couple's finances, such that the wife was " 'not in a position to bargain,' " although he made her pay half the fee charged by his attorney to draft the agreement. *Id.* at *5. Notably, the court upheld the wife's waiver of spousal maintenance because she "testified that she signed the agreement voluntarily because she wanted to marry" him and was aware of his property and debts, meeting the "statutory threshold for enforceability" under Arizona's version of the UPAA. *Id.* at *6.

2. Financial Disclosure

Courts widely agree that parties to a prenuptial agreement must fairly disclose to one another material information about their financial status and prospects. Yet jurisdictions often disagree about precisely how much disclosure is required. As *Mallen* notes, part of the disagreement hinges on whether the parties are regarded as occupying a "confidential relationship" that triggers greater disclosure obligations.

Even in most jurisdictions that do regard engaged partners as fiduciaries, requirements concerning the scope and specificity of disclosure are not uniform. A few jurisdictions insist that each party provide a detailed listing of assets and income. Most, however, take a more flexible view, requiring only that each spouse have reasonably clear general knowledge of the other's financial status. The ALI Principles take this flexible position, considering it sufficient that "the other party knew, at least approximately, the moving party's assets and income, or was provided by the moving party with a written statement containing that information." *Principles*, § 7.04(5).

The UPAA requires a "fair and reasonable disclosure of the property or financial obligations of the other party." UPAA, 9C ULA 39, at § 6(a)(2)(i). The UPMAA additionally requires that each party fairly and reasonably disclose their income. *See* UPMAA, 9C ULA 12, at § 9(d)(1). Financial disclosure, under the UPMAA, must be "reasonably accurate;" "an estimate of value of property, liabilities, and income made in good faith [will] satisfy the act even if it were later found to be inaccurate." *Id.* at § 9, Reporter's cmt.

Aside from differences in the applicable legal standards, it is not easy to predict whether a court will find disclosure sufficient as a factual matter. In North Dakota, for example—a jurisdiction where parties to a prenuptial agreement are considered fiduciaries—the state supreme court found adequate disclosure where a wife "testified that before she signed the agreement she knew Theodore Binek owned the Binek coal mine and the equipment thereon, guessed he owned his house, and had been told by her family that he was worth over a million dollars." *Binek*, 673 N.W.2d at 599. Yet, in California—a state in which premarital partners are not considered fiduciaries—a court found inadequate disclosure where the parties had been living together for ten years before the marriage, reasoning that:

> Although respondent was aware of appellant's interest in the condominium, that he had his own law practice and that he owned three cars, she testified that she did not know anything "about the rest of his financial life" [and] that appellant never disclosed to her all of his assets and debts, * * * never shared any information about any investments he had * * * or about the balances in his bank accounts and * * * never gave her access to "the books" at his law firm. Appellant admitted that prior to their marriage he never provided respondent with copies of his personal tax returns.

In re Marriage of Tamraz, supra, 2005 WL 1524199, at *6.

In *McLeod v. McLeod*, 145 So. 3d 1246 (Miss. Ct. App. 2014), the court reversed a decision that a premarital agreement was invalid due to the lack of full financial disclosure to the wife of the husband's assets. At the time of the agreement, the parties had lived together for a few years, and she worked in his office, managed his business (including some of his rental property), signed many checks, and had taken records to his accountant for tax-return purposes.

3.   Review for "Substantive Fairness" or "Unconscionability"

Mallen and *Hollett* both state that courts must undertake some review of the substantive fairness of prenuptial agreements. Jurisdictions differ, however, about the nature and timing of this review. The differences mostly cluster around two issues: first, the *time* at which the agreement's fairness should be measured, and second, how *fairness* should be defined for these purposes.

a.   Timing of Review: One Look or Two?

In cases that turn on unconscionability, ordinary contract law measures it only at the time of contract formation. The UPAA takes this approach with respect to premarital contracts. Some UPAA jurisdictions (for example, New Jersey and North Dakota) focus on unconscionability only at the time of signing. Oldham, *With My World Goods, supra,* at 104.

As in *Mallen* and *Hollett,* some jurisdictions also take a "second look" to assess unconscionability or substantive fairness by considering whether circumstances at the time of divorce would make enforcement offensive to public policy. These jurisdictions include some states that, in otherwise enacting the UPAA, specifically added language to require an assessment of unconscionability at the time of enforcement. *See, e.g.,* Conn. Gen. Stat. § 46b–36g (2019) ("premarital agreement * * * shall not be enforceable if * * * the agreement was unconscionable when it was executed or when enforcement is sought").

The UPMAA (as excerpted in Section 2.A, above) includes an optional provision permitting states to authorize challenges to a term in a premarital agreement when "enforcement of the term would result in substantial hardship for a party because of a material change in circumstances arising since the agreement was signed." § 9(f)(2).

The ALI Principles endorse a middle-ground position, which (as also excerpted above) would permit courts to deny enforcement of a premarital agreement because of changed circumstances during the marriage under three limited circumstances where enforcement could work "a substantial injustice." Section 7.05(2). The drafters of the ALI Principles explain the need for taking this second look because "[p]remarital agreements, with potential long-term application, raise a different kind of fairness concern * * * which is not addressed by the [traditional] unconscionability doctrine":

> A premarital agreement that at the time of execution is fair on its face, and is entered into by parties whose consent is truly mutual, may have a very different significance in the parties' lives when enforcement is sought 15 years later, after they have borne and nurtured children. The law's usual assumption that contracting parties are capable judges of their own self-interest is put in doubt

when the judgment is so distant in time and circumstance from its consequences. This capability problem is exacerbated by another uncommon feature of premarital agreements: its principal terms speak exclusively to a marital dissolution that the parties do not expect to occur, and so the agreement has no expected application.

Principles, § 1 at 38.

b.   Standards for Reviewing Premarital Agreements

Once a court resolves the timing issue, a second issue is what sort of review a court should undertake to determine whether a premarital agreement is unenforceable as substantively unfair or unconscionable. Ordinary contracts are unenforceable where the terms are unconscionable, but what should unconscionability mean in the context of premarital agreements? The UPAA, for example, does not define "unconscionability." As noted earlier in this Chapter, it also specifies that a court may deny enforcement of an unconscionable agreement only where the challenging party has been denied "fair and reasonable disclosure of the property or financial obligations of the other party," "did not voluntarily and expressly waive" such disclosure, and "reasonably could not have had, an adequate knowledge" of the other party's property or financial obligations. UPAA § 6(a)(2), 9C U.L.A. 49. Some states (for example, Rhode Island) have embraced this feature of the UPAA, but others (for example, Connecticut and Iowa) have not. *Principles,* § 7.04, Reporter's Notes to cmt. g., 981. (citing decisions).

The UPMAA rejects this "controversial" feature of the UPAA, making unconscionability at the time of signing sufficient by itself to invalidate an agreement, without any need to show inadequate financial disclosure. *See* Atwood & Bix, *A New Uniform Law, supra,* at 332.

States vary considerably in what tests they use to determine substantive (as distinct from procedural) unconscionability or unfairness. *See* Oldham, *Would Enactment of the Uniform Premarital and Marital Agreements Act in All Fifty States Change U.S. Law Regarding Premarital Agreements?,* 46 Fam. L. Q. 367, 378–79 (2012).

Some jurisdictions stake out a very narrow role for judicial review on the ground that premarital agreements should be treated like ordinary contracts. In *Simeone v. Simeone,* 581 A.2d 162 (Pa. 1990), for example, the court held that courts should undertake no heightened scrutiny to ensure the "reasonableness" of prenuptial terms because such efforts would "interfere with the power of persons contemplating marriage to agree upon, and to act in reliance upon, what they regard as an acceptable distribution scheme for their property":

> A court should not ignore the parties' expressed intent by proceeding to determine whether a prenuptial agreement was, in the court's view, reasonable at the time of its inception or the time of divorce. These are exactly the sorts of judicial determinations that such agreements are designed to avoid.

Id. at 166; *accord Stoner v. Stoner*, 819 A.2d 529, 532 (Pa. 2003) (affirming that "prenuptial agreements should be evaluated under the same standards as [a]re other contracts, and * * * that '[a]bsent fraud, misrepresentation, or duress, spouses should be bound by the terms of their agreements' ").

Other jurisdictions affirm the importance of respecting "the parties' freedom to contract," but place some restrictions upon a party's ability to waive or limit rights because "[m]arriage is not a mere contract between two parties, but a legal status from which certain rights and obligations arise." *DeMatteo, supra,* 762 N.E.2d at 808–09. In Massachusetts, an enforceable premarital agreement must be "fair and reasonable" at the time of execution and "not unconscionable" at the time of divorce. *Id.* at 809. To be "fair and reasonable," the agreement "need not approximate an alimony award and property division ruling a judge would be required to make" under Massachusetts' statutory factors, lest the "parties' right to settle their assets as they wish * * * be meaningless." *Id.* Instead, even a "one-sided agreement" leaving the contesting party with "considerably fewer assets" and "a far different lifestyle after divorce than he or she may enjoy during the marriage" is fair and reasonable unless "the contesting party is essentially stripped of substantially all marital interests." *Id.* (internal citation omitted).

Should the court's evaluation of fairness be limited to circumstances that were not reasonably foreseeable by the parties when they made the agreement? In *Hardee v. Hardee*, 585 S.E.2d 501, 505 (S.C. 2003), the wife waived alimony and agreed to keep separate property separate, but did not waive equitable division of any property acquired during the marriage. The appellate court reversed the family court's holding that the waiver was unenforceable due to the change of circumstances that left the wife "totally disabled and unable to support herself," so that she "would be a public charge if substantial support were not given." *Id.* at 505. The appellate court concluded that it was "completely foreseeable" to the wife that the "serious health problems" she had at the time of signing would "worsen." Thus, it would be "unfair and inequitable to permit a party who, fully aware of serious health issues and declining health, knowingly signs a prenuptial agreement against the advice of her attorney, to thereafter recover alimony and/or support." *Id.*

As noted above, the ALI Principles permit broader fairness review, at least in cases falling within one of the three categories that qualify for review at enforcement (*see Principles*, § 7.05(2)). In these cases, courts could enforce only contract terms that did not impose a "substantial injustice"; that judgment, in turn, would depend on such factors as "the magnitude of the disparity between the outcome under the agreement and the outcome under otherwise prevailing legal principles," and whether the agreement was intended to make reasonable provision for "children from a prior relationship." *Principles*, § 7.05(3)(a), (c).

NOTES AND QUESTIONS

1. *Disclosure.* What sort of financial disclosure should be required? Do you favor the UPA, UPMAA, or ALI approach? If you favor the flexible "general knowledge" approach taken in some jurisdictions, do you agree that the disclosure in *Mallen* or *Binek* enabled the party to make an "informed" decision about whether to waive future claims to maintenance or property?

2. *Evaluating waivers.* Would the UPAA permit enforcement of the *Hardee* waiver agreement? What about the UPMAA?

3. *One look or two?* Do you think that the ALI's middle-ground approach about when to assess enforceability is preferable (a) on the one hand, to the UPAA's approach of looking only at the time of execution and (b) on the other, to requiring a second look at the time of enforcement in all cases?

PROBLEM 16-1

Judy and John Moore were married in June 1994, when Judy was 24 and John was 36. She was a new schoolteacher earning $13,000 annually, and he was an attorney with his own practice and an average annual income of $80,000.

As a condition of the marriage, John asked Judy to sign a premarital agreement drafted by his lawyer. During the course of negotiation, Judy and John disclosed assets of $5,000 and $529,607, respectively. Judy's first lawyer refused to approve of the agreement because he found the terms were one-sided, and he resigned as her counsel because she would not take his advice to reject the terms. Judy retained new counsel who acquiesced to her wish to sign the agreement.

The agreement, which the parties signed six months before the wedding, provided that in the event of divorce: (1) each party would waive any right to alimony beyond that provided under the terms of the agreement, (2) maintenance terms would consist of John's obligation to make a lump-sum payment to Judy of $2,000 for each year of their marriage up to a maximum of $50,000, and (3) each party would retain all separate property owned before the marriage, and each person's earnings from employment during the marriage would remain his or her separate property. The agreement also provided (1) that at execution, Judy would receive $10,000, (2) that John would pay Judy's attorneys' fees to cover the negotiation of the premarital agreement, and (3) that during each year of the marriage, John would contribute $2,000 to an IRA in Judy's name.

Three children were born during the Moores' 21-year marriage. Judy stayed at home to raise the children, and John became the principal shareholder and chief executive officer of his family's successful construction business.

On the parties' cross-petitions for divorce, the court found that the premarital agreement was conscionable and that the parties had entered into it knowingly and with full disclosure. The court enforced the agreement and awarded John $3,551,650 in separate and marital property and Judy $434,454 in property. The court denied separate maintenance for both parties, and ordered John to pay Judy $42,000, or $2,000 for each year of their 21-year marriage.

You are a judge of the state's court of appeals, which has just heard argument on the conscionability of the premarital agreement. If your state has enacted the UPAA, would you find the agreement enforceable? Would your answer be different if your state has enacted the UPMAA? What if it follows the ALI Principles?

If there were no binding case law or statutes in your state, which standard would you choose to reach the most equitable result?

PROBLEM 16-2

Willie and Maggie married in a relatively informal wedding attended by about 30 family members and friends. The day before the wedding, Willie took Maggie to see a lawyer that he had hired for her. Maggie knew that Willie worked as a delivery truck driver and approximately what he made. The lawyer presented Maggie with a fully drafted antenuptial agreement, explained each of its provisions, and asked her to sign it. Maggie complied. Under the agreement, both parties waived all claims to alimony and property division. In addition, the agreement specifically provided that Willie would retain as his sole and separate property a 19-acre parcel of land in a neighboring county that he had previously purchased "together with any house or structure which may be situated upon said property." There was no house or structure on the property when the parties married, but Willie had hidden away $150,000 in cash that he planned to use to build a home there after the wedding. Willie never told Maggie about the $150,000 in cash, and she had no knowledge of the money from any other source.

After eight years of marriage, Willie files for divorce and seeks to enforce the antenuptial agreement. Maggie contends that the agreement is unenforceable and asks the court to divide the couple's marital property. What advice would you give Maggie on her prospects for avoiding enforcement of the agreement in a jurisdiction in which *Mallen* governs?

D. PROVISIONS OF PREMARITAL AGREEMENTS

Parties to a premarital agreement may seek to include a variety of terms concerning their respective financial and nonfinancial obligations. The following material discusses a range of subjects that arise in the context of drafting and enforcing prenuptial agreements, including child support, waiver of alimony, and terms governing personal behavior and other nonfinancial matters.

1. Modification of Child-Related Support Obligations

All authorities agree that parties may not contractually waive or limit the court's authority either to award child support or to ensure that custody or visitation arrangements remain consistent with the best interests of children. *See, e.g., Principles*, §§ 7.06–7.07; *In re Marriage of Best*, 901 N.E.2d 967, 970 (Ill. 2009) ("Illinois law per se rejects marital agreements that impair child-custody support rights or specify custody").

Section 3(b) of the UPAA prohibits premarital agreements from adversely affecting the right to child support, which belongs to the child. So, too, does Section 10 of the UPMAA, which also specifies that a contractual term "which defines the rights or duties of the parties regarding custodial responsibility is not binding on the court." However, premarital agreements can be powerful tools to set forth a more meaningful understanding of the specific contributions each parent intends to provide to their child. Of course, child support issues may also arise in negotiations between parents who are not married to each other, as well as in negotiations pursuant to divorce.

The validity of child-related provisions negotiated prior to marriage depends on ordinary contract law, as well as the provisions' positive or negative effect on the children. Courts "will generally uphold agreements for the benefit of children that provide a higher level of support or a longer duration than state law requires, or support for a stepchild for whom the obligor would otherwise have no legal obligation." Linda J. Ravdin, *Prenups to Protect Children*, 24 Fam. Advoc. 32, 33 (Winter 2002). They will also protect children from agreements providing too little support. Additionally, parties may validly agree to child support obligations continuing after the obligor's death by way of a trust or other instrument. *Id.* at 33, 36.

Parties may agree to pay post-majority support or college and graduate school tuition. *See, e.g., Shortt v. Damron*, 649 S.E.2d 283 (W. Va. 2007) (enforcing terms of separation agreement obligating father to pay children's college expenses). Such a provision might limit payment to savings accrued prior to college, and could change form depending on the exact terms of the prenup. For example, a parent might contract to have some role in school choice or only pay up to a certain tuition level. Ravdin, *supra*, at 35. Enforcement of these obligations depends on a court order;

otherwise, "the parent receiving payments for the child may obtain a money judgment for breach of contract, specific performance, or other contract remedies." *Id.* at 36.

As Chapter 12 explained, the law concerning how courts should decide custody claims for pets, or animal companions, when a couple divorces is shifting in some states from a property analysis to a "best interest of the pet" or "best for all concerned" standard. A related trend is that some couples are now including provisions in their premarital agreement about care and custody of an animal companion in the event of divorce, including designating a veterinarian to make medical decisions if they are unable to agree. Alexandra Anastasio, *Who Gets the Dog in the Divorce? Enter the Pet Prenup*, ABC News (Dec. 12, 2018).

2. Waivers of Spousal Support

Traditionally, courts were especially hostile to contractual waivers of future rights to alimony (or maintenance). Under the common law model of marriage, as Section 1 introduced, the husband's duty to support his wife—and in its original form, the support duty was indeed gender-specific—was viewed as inherent in marriage and unalterable by any agreement of the parties. So, too, was the wife's reciprocal duty to provide services.

Even after the law in all states changed to embrace premarital and marital bargaining about property rights, many jurisdictions treated waivers of spousal support as void, or subject to more searching scrutiny for "fairness." This has changed. Both the UPAA and UPMAA allow for waiver under most circumstances. Indeed, most jurisdictions have abandoned the traditional bar against spousal support waivers. *See Sanford v. Sanford*, 694 N.W.2d 283, 288 n.2 (S.D. 2005) (noting 41 states permit such waivers); Cal. Fam. Code § 1612(c) (2019) (permitting waiver of spousal support, provided that waiver is not "unconscionable at the time of enforcement").

Courts take different approaches to when such a waiver is unconscionable or unfair. One relevant factor may be whether the premarital agreement makes any other financial provision for the spouse who seeks enforcement. In *Austin v. Austin*, 839 N.E.2d 837, 841 (Mass. 2005), the court upheld a premarital agreement waiving alimony and interest in the husband's separate property, because, at divorce, the wife was not "stripped of substantially all assets" (applying *DeMatteo, supra*): she had the "marital home worth $1,275,000, many of home's contents, and was awarded $525,000 in cash." In *Lane v. Lane*, 202 S.W.2d 577, 580 (Ky. 2006), the court struck as unconscionable a waiver of maintenance in light of several factors, including that the "significant disparity" in the parties' income at the time of execution "grew exponentially during the marriage in large part because the husband was able to concentrate on his career while the wife stayed home to care for the children and the home"—a contribution by the wife that was "not of nominal value." That factor, along with the parties' "affluent lifestyle maintained during the marriage," should render the maintenance waiver unconscionable. *Id.* at 580.

On the other hand, in *Hudson v. Hudson,* 757 S.E.2d 727, 731 (S.C. Ct. App. 2014), the court held that the wife's waiver of alimony was not unconscionable even though she also waived a right to equitable distribution of property. The wife argued the change of the parties' circumstances rendered the agreement unfair, but the court disagreed: the wife entered the marriage unemployed and "with insignificant assets" and, at the time of the separation, "was employed and had substantially the same assets as when she entered the marriage." *Id.* at 732.

Against this strong current, a handful of jurisdictions still refuse to enforce spousal support waivers. *See, e.g., Sanford,* 694 N.W.2d at 288–89; Iowa Code Ann. § 596.5(2) (2019) ("The right of a spouse or child to support shall not be adversely affected by a premarital agreement"); Oldham, *Would Enactment of the Uniform Premarital and Marital Agreements Act in All Fifty States Change U.S. Law, supra,* at 381 (observing that "a significant minority of states * * * consider any restriction on spousal support to be unenforceable").

QUESTIONS

1. *Why allow waivers?* On what bases might courts or legislatures consider spousal support rights entirely or partially nonwaivable? To help formulate your answer, reconsider the rationales for alimony discussed in Chapter 10. Consider also the different functions of family law introduced in Chapter 1.

2. *Rich spouse, poor spouse.* How do the UPAA and UPMAA differ on the permissibility of spousal support waivers?

3. Nonmonetary Terms

The UPAA expressly permits parties to negotiate about at least some "personal rights and obligations." UPAA § 3(a)(8), 9C U.L.A. 43.The UMPAA has a section listing "unenforceable terms" that include provisions either in premarital or postnuptial agreements that courts generally decline to enforce on public policy grounds. These include, for example, a term that that "limits or restricts a remedy available to a victim of domestic violence" under state law or "penalize[s] a party for initiating a legal proceeding leading to a court-decreed separation or marital dissolution." UMPAA § 10, 9C ULA 12. Otherwise, because courts generally refuse to enforce "provisions relating to topics beyond the parties' financial obligations"—including terms that "purport to regulate or attach financial penalties to conduct during the marriage"—the UPMAA "does not expressly deal with such provisions." Atwood & Bix, *A New Uniform Law, supra,* at 344. Such nonmonetary terms may include, for example, provisions that "dictate conduct within the marriage, including the division of labor, cohabitation, or sexual relations; restrict the right to seek a divorce; govern child custody; or specify children's religious training in the event of a divorce." Katharine B. Silbaugh, *Marriage Contracts and the Family Economy,* 93 Nw. U. L. Rev. 65, 78 (1998). As a result of this judicial reluctance, provisions concerning the nonmonetary rights and obligations of the parties occupy, at best, a "legal limbo." Barbara Stark, *Marriage Proposals: From One-Size-Fits-All to Postmodern Marriage Law,* 89 Cal. L. Rev. 1479, 1496–97 (2001).

What do you think accounts for this judicial reluctance to enforce provisions relating to nonmonetary rights and obligations? Professor Katharine Silbaugh contends that this "selective enforcement" generally disadvantages women because they "contribute more nonmonetary wealth [to marriage] than men, and men more money than women, on average." *See* Silbaugh, *supra,* at 99–101. Is this observation still accurate, given the growing number of households with women as the primary earners? If this observation is accurate, should the law help achieve gender equality by enforcing nonmonetary terms more strongly? *See also* Katharine B. Silbaugh, *Gender and Nonfinancial Matters in the ALI Principles of the Law of Family Dissolution,* 8 Duke J. Gender L. & Pol'y 203 (2001).

A news story reported that prominent matrimonial lawyers were seeing an increase in "lifestyle clause" requests to include in premarital agreements, including these:

"No piano playing while the husband is home";

"Wife not allowed to cut her hair";

"If husband is rude or cruel to wife's parents, husband agrees to pay $10,000 for each infraction";

"In the event that Husband's weight exceeds 240, he agrees to pay Wife $10,000"; and "if the wife's weight exceeds 170 pounds, she forfeits her $10,000 'allowance' "; and

"We're going to have a smoke-free household."

Doree Lewak, *New York's Craziest Prenups,* N.Y. Post (Sept. 25, 2012).

Some couples include provisions about sexual fidelity and reproductive conduct during marriage. Reportedly, Rosie O'Donnell's prenuptial agreement included a clause that if her partner, Michelle Rounds, "were to cheat, she'd get nothing in a divorce." *Id.* In *Brown v. Brown,* 2013 WL 12108656 at * 1 (Tenn. Ct. App. Sept. 12, 2013), the premarital agreement included a term that waived alimony, but gave the wife $80,000 if their marriage lasted several years; the husband did not owe the payment if

"Wife has a sexual affair or commits adultery during the marriage or without grounds."

NOTES AND QUESTIONS

1. *The role of law?* Do you think that the law should permit parties who marry to contract about how they conduct themselves in marriage, as in some of the terms discussed above? Does such private ordering require availability of judicial remedies? Do divorce laws already provide such a remedy?

2. *Enforcing fidelity?* Should courts enforce a premarital agreement provision that adulterous conduct reduces a financial award or triggers a financial penalty at divorce? Conversely, what about an agreement to have a consensually non-monogamous marriage and to forego adultery as a ground for divorce?

3. *Promises not to procreate?* Could a court enforce a "no children" provision agreeing never to have children, and requiring a spouse to have an abortion if she became pregnant or to incur a financial penalty at divorce? *See* Lewak, *New York's Craziest Prenups, supra;* Jill Brooke, *A Promise To Love, Honor and Bear No Children,* N.Y. Times, Oct. 13, 2002, at § 9–1 (reporting on trend of including "no children" clauses, especially in marriages involving wealthy divorced fathers and younger second wives). *See also* Joline F. Sikaitis, *A New Form of Family Planning?: The Enforceability of No-Child Provisions in Prenuptial Agreements,* 54 Cath. U. L. Rev. 335 (2004) (contending that judicial enforcement would impinge upon fundamental privacy interests in childbearing).

4. Enforcing Terms of Religious Marriage Contracts

Courts are regularly called upon to enforce terms of marital contracts that are entered in connection with religious marriages. This Section provides only a brief introduction to this complex topic. *See generally* Allison Gerli, *Living Happily Ever After in A Land of Separate Church and State: Treatment of Islamic Marriage Contracts,* 26 J. Am. Acad. Matrimonial Law 113 (2013). Under Jewish law, even if the couple divorces under civil authority, the wife may not remarry under Jewish law until her husband gives her a certificate of divorce (a *get*). Jewish couples may make a premarital agreement concerning the dissolution of their marriage, including that they agree to submit to the jurisdiction of a rabbinical tribunal or rabbinic arbitration panel to resolve matters concerning their Jewish divorce. Such agreements are one mechanism used to ensure that a husband gives his wife a *get*. Michael J. Broyde, *New York's Regulation of Jewish Marriage: Covenant, Contract, or Statute?, in* Marriage and Divorce in a Multicultural Context 138, 156 (Joel A. Nichols, ed. 2012). These couples may also include such terms in their marriage contract, or *ketubah*.

In *Avitzur v. Avitzur*, 446 N.E.2d 136 (N.Y. 1983), the court upheld an agreement in the couple's *ketubah* to appear before a Jewish religious tribunal that would "advise and counsel the parties" about their marriage; the court concluded (drawing on U.S. Supreme Court First Amendment cases) that it could apply "neutral principles of contract law" without having to interpret religious doctrine. *Id.* at 138. In this way, the court concluded, it could avoid triggering any First Amendment problems by excessively entangling itself with religion. Professor Ann Estin explains the constitutional concerns: "Denying enforcement of a marital agreement signed by two individuals in a religious context might infringe their free exercise rights, but interpreting and enforcing such an agreement on the basis of religious law verges dangerously on an establishment of religion." Ann Laquer Estin, *Embracing Tradition: Pluralism in American Family Law*, 63 Md. L. Rev. 540 (2004).

The same constitutional concerns arise in the context of civil enforcement of terms of Islamic marriage contracts. A required element of such contracts is the husband's promise to pay the wife *mahr*, a wedding gift. A contractual provision typically defers payment of most of this gift until a specified event, such as the termination of the marriage by death or divorce. *See* Julie Macfarlane, Islamic Divorce in North America (2012). Similar to *Avitzur*, some courts have enforced such agreements under a "neutral principles" approach, reasoning that they can enforce the agreement by applying state contract law rather than religious doctrine. *See Odatalla v. Odatalla*, 810 A.2d 93 (N.J. Super. Ct. 2002) (applying New Jersey contract law); *Akileh v. Elchahal*, 666 So. 246 (Fla. Dist. App. 1996) (applying Florida contract law).

On the other hand, some courts have also declined to enforce these marriage agreements for various reasons, including failure to satisfy general contract principles; the court's inability to interpret the contract without recourse to religious doctrine; and violation of public policy. *See generally* Macfarlane, *supra*, at 210–239; *Dajani v. Dajani*, 251 Cal. Rptr. 871 (Ct. App. 1988) (declining to enforce a husband's deferred payment due upon the dissolution of the marriage or the husband's death on the ground that the agreement "clearly provided for [the] wife to profit by a divorce"). In declining enforcement, courts sometimes draw on rules concerning premarital agreements, finding that an agreement was unenforceable because it was the result of "overreaching or coercion." *See Zawahiri v. Alwattar*, 2008 WL 2698679 (Ohio Ct. App. 2008) (declining to enforce agreement when the husband testified that he did not have a chance to consult an attorney, was presented with the *mahr* agreement a few hours before the ceremony, and signed only because he was "embarrassed and stressed").

Some courts have distinguished religious marriage agreements and premarital or postmarital agreements when declining to enforce the former on public policy grounds. In *Aleem v. Aleem*, 931 A.2d 1123, 1134 (Md. Ct. Spec. App. 2007), *aff'd*, 947 A.2d 489 (Md. 2008), the court concluded that it should not equate a Pakistani marriage contract concerning payment to wife of *mahr* with "a premarital or postmarital agreement that validly relinquished, under Maryland law, rights in marital property." The court observed that the two legal systems had different "default" rules about the economic consequences of marriage and that, in light of Maryland's public policy about property distribution, the marriage contract, entered into in Pakistan many years before the couple settled in the United States, did not preclude the court from making equitable distribution of the couple's assets or ordering spousal support. *See also* Linda C. McClain, *The Intersection of Civil and Religious Family Law in the U.S. Constitutional Order: A Mild Legal Pluralism, in* Religion, Secularism & Constitutional Democracy 379–99 (Jean L. Cohen & Cécile Laborde, eds. 2016) (discussing judicial considerations of public policy).

In *In re Marriage of Iqbal and Khan*, 11 N.E.3d 1, 9 (Ill. App. Ct. 2014), the court held that a postnuptial agreement was unenforceable as contrary to public policy because it designated a third party to be the "Religious and Marital Counselor and Arbiter of [the spouses'] Marital Affairs" and specified that "his authorization and approval was required for any major decisions, including but not limited to . . . financial matters, matters of the Children, work and travel, and any contemplated divorce or separation." The Counselor agreed to "reasonably follow Islamic law" in his decisions. *Id.* at 10. The agreement, for example, gave the "Marital Counselor" sole authority to deny custody to one parent if they brought an "unreasonable divorce" action (without defining the term). *Id.* at 14. The court held that this agreement violated Illinois's public policy because "parties may not make the child-related terms of their agreements nonmodifiable" or immune from judicial approval. *Id.* at 13.

In the last decade or so, several states have prohibited courts from employing "foreign or international law" in legal disputes, including in family law matters (sometimes called "anti-shari'a law bans"). These statutes affect how courts handle religious marriage contracts. For example, in *Soleimani v. Soleimani*, 2012 WL 3729939 (Kan. Dist. Ct. 2012), a court invoked Kansas's new ban on judicial enforcement of foreign law in declining to enforce a *mahr* agreement. The court rejected the "neutral principles" approach, contending that the agreement was negotiated in the "shadow" of Islamic law and that features of Islamic law violated public policy. On the impact of these foreign law bans on how civil courts address religious family law, *see* Ann Laquer Estin, *Foreign and Religious Family Law: Comity, Contract, and the Constitution*, 41 Pepp. L. Rev. 1029 (2014). Such foreign law bans may also have an adverse impact on the long-standing practice (discussed in Chapter 15) of allowing parties to submit their disputes to religious arbitration and for that resolution to have binding force in U.S. law. *See* Michael A. Helfand, *Religious Arbitration and the New Multiculturalism: Negotiating Conflicting Legal Orders*, 86 NYU L. Rev. 1231 (2011).

PROBLEM 16-3

You are a well-established family law practitioner who has accepted the state bar association's invitation to speak at a continuing legal education training program on premarital agreements. The organizers ask you to address such questions as: (1) who should have a premarital agreement?; (2) should matrimonial lawyers routinely advise clients or potential clients to enter into one?; (3) what are the advantages and disadvantages of having a premarital agreement?; (4) what accounts for the mixed feelings that the public seems to have about premarital agreements, and how can an attorney address the emotions that may arise when persons planning to marry discuss or negotiate such an agreement?; and (5) what are the most important do's and don'ts for drafting premarital agreements?

What will you say in your presentation?

3. POSTNUPTIAL AGREEMENTS

After parties are married, they may enter into a *postnuptial* or *marital* agreement. Such an agreement is entered into by "spouses who plan to continue their marriage" and "alters or confirms the legal rights and obligations that would otherwise arise under * * * [the] law governing marital dissolution." *Ansin v. Craven-Ansin*, 929 N.E.2d 955 (Mass. 2010) (quoting the ALI Principles § 7.01 (b), at 946). When one or both of the spouses wants to preserve a troubled marriage rather than divorce, postnuptial agreements may amount to reconciliation agreements, which allow the marriage to continue and make a mid-course correction.

The timing of these agreements distinguishes them, on the one hand, from premarital agreements and, on the other, from separation agreements, when divorce is imminent. As this Section explores, courts and legislatures take a variety of approaches to the question of what difference the timing of postnuptial agreements should make in assessing their validity and enforceability. Just as with other forms of private ordering in marriage and divorce, family law has shifted away from regarding such agreements as *per se* against public policy.

A. WHY ENTER INTO A POSTNUPTIAL AGREEMENT?

A postnuptial agreement allows a married couple to document their intentions concerning their property, earnings, and financial obligations during marriage and in the event of a future divorce, and for inheritance. A trigger for a postnuptial agreement might be new economic circumstances that arise in one spouse's life (for example, a large gift or inheritance) or in the marriage. Couples may also enter into postnuptial agreements to address points of conflict that have arisen within a marriage or to "codify what is written on the kitchen bulletin board, such as who washes the dishes or who shovels the snow." Patricia Wen, *Sealing a Contract After the Marriage*, Boston Globe, Dec. 19, 2005, at A1.

Postnuptial agreements appear to be "increasingly popular"; one recent AAML survey found that half of its members reported being asked more often to draft postnuptial agreements. Ben Steverman, *Why More Couples Are Signing Postnuptial Agreements*, Bloomberg News, April 28, 2017. Linda Ravdin, a divorce attorney and expert on prenuptial and postnuptial agreements, observes that two common reasons why couples seek such agreements are: (1) that they ran out of time before their wedding to execute a premarital agreement, or (2) that "[a] couple is estranged, but they're willing to take a chance on a reconciliation." *Id. See also* Veronica Daugher, *Why Postnuptial Agreements Are On the Rise*, Wall St. J. (Mar. 10, 2016). One legal scholar predicts that "because of their practical advantages, [postnuptial agreements] will become the dominant form of marital contract" in the years ahead. Sean Hannon Williams, *Postnuptial Agreements*, 2007 Wis. L. Rev. 827, 829.

Such agreements may include both economic and noneconomic terms. Anecdotal evidence suggests that for some couples, concluding a postnuptial agreement can be a positive turning point in a successful marriage. For example, therapists who work with married couples observe that "the process of drafting postnuptial agreements can help trigger sweeping behavioral changes that might keep couples together." Wen, *supra*, at A1.

As we saw earlier with premarital agreements, whether a court will enforce the nonmonetary terms is another issue.

B. WHAT LEGAL STANDARDS SHOULD GOVERN A POSTNUPTIAL AGREEMENT?

If a marriage ultimately fails or if the parties breach any term of the postnuptial agreement, what legal standards determine the enforceability of the agreement? Are postnuptial agreements like ordinary contracts? Should the standards for prenuptial and postnuptial agreements be the same, or do the respective contexts in which parties negotiate each of these agreements call for different legal standards? This Section explores a range of answers to these questions.

The UPAA facially applies only to premarital agreements. By court decisions, several states have extended its application to postnuptial agreements. Other state courts have held that postnuptial agreements are not subject to statutory standards governing premarital agreements. By contrast, the UPMAA covers both types of agreements. Similarly, the ALI

Principles assert that "the principles applicable to marital and premarital agreements are the same," a position that is "consistent with the law in many states." *Principles* § 7.01. Reporter's Notes, cmt. e, 953. New York, for example, permits parties to enter into agreements "before or during the marriage" concerning "provision for the amount and duration of maintenance or other terms and conditions of the marriage relationship * * * provided that such terms were fair and reasonable at the time of the agreement and not unconscionable at the time of entry of final judgment." N.Y. Dom. Rel. L. § 236 (B) (3) (2019).

What standards should govern the enforceability of postnuptial agreements if they fall outside the scope of existing statutes governing premarital agreements or separation agreements? The following opinion addresses that question. As you read it, consider whether sound policy reasons support distinguishing between the enforcement of premarital and postnuptial agreements.

BEDRICK V. BEDRICK
Supreme Court of Connecticut, 2011.
17 A.3d 17.

MCLACHLAN, J.

This appeal involves a dissolution of marriage action in which the defendant, Bruce L. Bedrick, seeks to enforce a postnuptial agreement. Today we are presented for the first time with the issue of whether a postnuptial agreement is valid and enforceable in Connecticut.

The defendant appeals from the trial court's judgment in favor of the plaintiff, Deborah Bedrick. The defendant claims that the trial court improperly relied upon principles of fairness and equity in concluding that the postnuptial agreement was unenforceable and, instead, should have applied only ordinary principles of contract law. We conclude that postnuptial agreements are valid and enforceable and generally must comply with contract principles. We also conclude, however, that the terms of such agreements must be both fair and equitable at the time of execution and not unconscionable at the time of dissolution. Because the terms of the present agreement were unconscionable at the time of dissolution, we affirm the judgment of the trial court.

The record reveals the following undisputed facts and procedural history. In August, 2007, the plaintiff initiated this action, seeking dissolution of the parties' marriage, permanent alimony, an equitable distribution of the parties' real and personal property and other relief. The defendant filed a cross complaint, seeking to enforce a postnuptial agreement that the parties executed on December 10, 1977, and modified by way of handwritten addenda on five subsequent occasions, most recently on May 18, 1989.

The agreement provides that in the event of dissolution, neither party will pay alimony. Instead, the plaintiff will receive a cash settlement in an amount to be "reviewed from time to time." The May 18, 1989 addendum to the agreement provides for a cash settlement of $75,000. The agreement further provides that the plaintiff will waive her interests in the defendant's car wash business, and that the plaintiff will not be held liable for the defendant's personal and business loans.

In its memorandum of decision, the trial court stated that, although "[t]here is scant case law addressing the enforcement of postnuptial agreements in Connecticut . . . it is clear that a court may not enforce a postnuptial agreement if it is not fair and equitable. . . . [C]ourts have refused to enforce postnuptial agreements for lack of consideration, failure to disclose financial information, or an improper purpose." Concluding that the agreement was not fair and equitable, the trial court declined to enforce it. The court found that the value of the parties' combined assets was approximately $927,123, and ordered, inter alia, the defendant to pay lump sum alimony in the amount of $392,372 to the plaintiff. The defendant filed a motion to reargue claiming that the court should have applied principles of contract law in determining the enforceability of the agreement.

* * *

The trial court also opined that enforcement of the agreement would have been unjust and was "not . . . a fair and equitable distribution of the parties' assets" because the financial circumstances of the parties had changed dramatically since the agreement was last modified in 1989. Since 1989, the parties had had a child together and the defendant's car wash business had both prospered and deteriorated. This appeal followed.

The defendant contends that the trial court improperly applied equitable principles in determining whether the postnuptial agreement was enforceable and, instead, should have applied only principles of contract law. * * * Although we agree with the defendant that principles of contract law generally apply in determining the enforceability of a postnuptial agreement, we conclude that postnuptial agreements are subject to special scrutiny and the terms of such agreements must be both fair and equitable at the time of execution and not unconscionable at the time of dissolution. Because the terms of the present postnuptial agreement were unconscionable at the time of dissolution, the trial court properly concluded that the agreement was unenforceable.

* * * We begin our analysis of postnuptial agreements by considering the public policies served by the recognition of agreements regarding the dissolution of marriage, including prenuptial, postnuptial and separation agreements.

Historically, we have stated that "[t]he state does not favor divorces. * * *" Accordingly, prenuptial agreements were generally held to violate public policy if they promoted, facilitated or provided an incentive for separation or divorce. Similarly, a separation agreement is not necessarily contrary to public policy unless it is made to facilitate divorce or is concealed from the court. * * *

More recently, our court has acknowledged that the government has an interest in encouraging the incorporation of separation agreements into decrees for dissolution. * * * Postnuptial agreements may also encourage the private resolution of family issues. In particular, they may allow couples to eliminate a source of emotional turmoil—usually, financial uncertainty—and focus instead on resolving other aspects of the marriage that may be problematic. By alleviating anxiety over uncertainty in the determination of legal rights and obligations upon dissolution, postnuptial agreements do not encourage or facilitate dissolution; in fact, they harmonize with our public policy favoring enduring marriages. * * *

Postnuptial agreements are consistent with public policy; they realistically acknowledge the high incidence of divorce and its effect upon our population. We recognize "the reality of the increasing rate of divorce and remarriage." *Heuer v. Heuer,* 704 A.2d 913, 917 (1998). * * * Postnuptial agreements are no different than prenuptial agreements in this regard.

* * * To aid in our analysis of the enforceability of postnuptial agreements, we review our law on the enforceability of prenuptial agreements.[4] Two different sets of principles govern decisions as to the enforceability of a prenuptial agreement; the date of the execution of the agreement determines which set of principles controls.

Prenuptial agreements entered into on or after October 1, 1995, are governed by the Connecticut Premarital Agreement Act.[b] * * *

Prenuptial agreements entered into prior to October 1, 1995, however, are governed by the common law. * * * [I]n *McHugh v. McHugh* (1980), * * * we explicitly determined that, although a prenuptial agreement "is a type of contract and must, therefore, comply with ordinary principles of contract law" the validity of such a contract depends on the circumstances of the particular case. * * *

---

[4]   We do not review our law on the enforceability of separation agreements, which are distinct from both prenuptial and postnuptial agreements and are entered into when spouses have determined to dissolve their marriage. [*Editors' Note:* The court explains that separation agreements are governed by Conn. Gen. Stat. § 46b–66 (a) ("where the parties have submitted to the court an agreement concerning . . . alimony or the disposition of property, the court shall . . . determine whether the agreement of the spouses is fair and equitable under all the circumstances. . . .").]

[b]   *Editors' Note:* This is Connecticut's version of the UPAA and departs from it in certain respects, as discussed earlier in this Chapter.

We further note that "* * * the party seeking to challenge the enforceability of the [prenuptial] contract bears a heavy burden. . . . [W]here the economic status of [the] parties has changed dramatically between the date of the agreement and the dissolution, literal enforcement of the agreement may work injustice. Absent such unusual circumstances, however, [prenuptial] agreements freely and fairly entered into will be honored and enforced by the courts as written. . . . This heavy burden comports with the well settled general principle that [c]ourts of law must allow parties to make their own contracts."

Although we view postnuptial agreements as encouraging the private resolution of family issues, we also recognize that spouses do not contract under the same conditions as either prospective spouses or spouses who have determined to dissolve their marriage. * * *

The Appellate Division of the New Jersey Superior Court has also recognized this "contextual difference" and has noted that a wife "face[s] a more difficult choice than [a] bride who is presented with a demand for a pre-nuptial agreement. The cost to [a wife is] . . . the destruction of a family and the stigma of a failed marriage." *Pacelli v. Pacelli,* 725 A.2d 56, 59 (App. Div.), cert. denied, 735 A.2d 572 (1999). A spouse who bargains [over] a settlement agreement, on the other hand, "recogniz[es] that the marriage is over, can look to his or her economic rights; the relationship is adversarial." *Id.* at 60. Thus, a spouse enters a postnuptial agreement under different conditions than a party entering either a prenuptial or a separation agreement. * * *

Other state courts have not only observed that spouses contract under different conditions; they have also observed that postnuptial agreements "should not be treated as mere 'business deals.'" * * * "Ordinarily and presumptively, a confidential relation or a relationship of special confidence exists between husband and wife. It includes, but is not limited to, a fiduciary duty between the spouses, of the highest degree." * * *

Prospective spouses share a "confidential relationship"; but spouses share the institution of marriage, "one of the most fundamental of human relationships. . . ." *Davis v. Davis,* 175 A. 574, 577 (1934). * * * Courts simply should not countenance either party to such a unique human relationship dealing with each other at arms' length." * * *

Because of the nature of the marital relationship, the spouses to a postnuptial agreement may not be as cautious in contracting with one another as they would be with prospective spouses, and they are certainly less cautious than they would be with an ordinary contracting party. With lessened caution comes greater potential for one spouse to take advantage of the other. This leads us to conclude that postnuptial agreements require stricter scrutiny than prenuptial agreements. In applying special scrutiny, a court may enforce a postnuptial agreement only if it complies with applicable contract principles, and the terms of the agreement are both fair and equitable at the time of execution and not unconscionable at the time of dissolution.

We further hold that the terms of a postnuptial agreement are fair and equitable at the time of execution if the agreement is made voluntarily, and without any undue influence, fraud, coercion, duress or similar defect. Moreover, each spouse must be given full, fair and reasonable disclosure of the amount, character and value of property, both jointly and separately held, and all of the financial obligations and income of the other spouse. This mandatory disclosure requirement is a result of the deeply personal marital relationship.

Just as "[t]he validity of a [prenuptial] contract depends upon the circumstances of the particular case," in determining whether a particular postnuptial agreement is fair and equitable at the time of execution, a court should consider the totality of the circumstances surrounding execution. A court may consider various factors, including "the nature and complexity of the agreement's terms, the extent of and disparity in assets brought to the marriage by each spouse, the parties' respective age, sophistication, education, employment, experience, prior marriages, or other traits potentially affecting the ability to read and understand an agreement's provisions, and the amount of time available to each spouse to reflect upon the agreement after first seeing its specific terms . . . [and] access to independent counsel prior to consenting to the contract terms." * * *.

With regard to the determination of whether a postnuptial agreement is unconscionable at the time of dissolution, "* * * [t]he question of unconscionability is a matter of law to be decided by the court based on all the facts and circumstances of the case." *Crews v. Crews,* supra, 989 A.2d at 1065 * * * Unfairness or inequality alone does not render a postnuptial agreement unconscionable; spouses may agree on an unequal distribution of assets at dissolution. "[T]he mere fact that hindsight may indicate the provisions of the agreement were improvident does not render the agreement unconscionable." Instead, the question of whether enforcement of an agreement would be unconscionable is analogous to determining whether enforcement of an agreement would work an injustice. Marriage, by its very nature, is subject to unforeseeable developments, and no agreement can possibly anticipate all future events. Unforeseen changes in the relationship, such as having a child, loss of employment or moving to another state, may render enforcement of the agreement unconscionable.

II

Now * * * we turn to the present case * * * must apply the legal standards described in this opinion, namely, whether the terms of the agreement were fair and equitable at the time of execution and not unconscionable at the time of dissolution, to the underlying facts. * * *

We therefore provide the following additional facts. Although the value of the parties combined assets is $927,123, the last addendum to the agreement, dated May 18, 1989, provides that the plaintiff will receive a cash settlement of only $75,000. This addendum was written prior to the initial success of the car wash business in the early 1990s, the birth of the parties' son in 1991, when the parties were forty-one years old, and the subsequent deterioration of the business in the 2000s. At the time of trial, the parties were both fifty-seven years old. Neither had a college degree. The defendant had been steadily employed by the car wash business since 1973. The plaintiff had worked for that business for thirty-five years, providing administrative and bookkeeping support, and since approximately 2001, when the business began to deteriorate, the plaintiff had managed all business operations excluding maintenance. In 2004, the plaintiff also had worked outside of the business in order to provide the family with additional income. Since approximately 2007, when the plaintiff stopped working for the business, the defendant had not been able to complete administrative or bookkeeping tasks, and had not filed taxes.

The trial court found that "[t]he economic circumstances of the parties had changed dramatically since the execution of the agreement" and that "enforcement of the postnuptial agreement would have worked injustice." It, therefore, concluded that the agreement was unenforceable. * * * The facts and circumstances of the present case clearly support the findings of the trial court that, as a matter of law, enforcement of the agreement would be unconscionable. * * * Accordingly, we hold that the trial court properly concluded that the agreement was unenforceable.

The judgment is affirmed.

NOTES AND QUESTIONS

1.   *Public policy.* Why does the *Bedrick* opinion conclude that postnuptial agreements are not against public policy? What public policies do such agreements serve? In *Devney v. Devney*, 886 N.W.2d 61, 68 (Neb. 2016), the Nebraska Supreme Court held that a postnuptial property agreement entered into five months after marriage was void, citing its own prior decision affirming "Nebraska's public policy against postnuptial property agreements because of the deleterious effect such agreements have on marriages." *Id.* at 69. It pointed out that while the Nebraska legislature had authorized premarital agreements (by adopting the UPAA) and separation agreements (by adopting the UMDA), it had "not yet seen fit" to adopt the UPMAA.

2.   *Dynamics of bargaining and legal standards.* Do you agree with the *Bedrick* court's analysis that the bargaining context for a postnuptial agreement calls for different enforcement standards than those for a prenuptial agreement or a separation agreement? How do the problems of bounded rationality and optimism bias, discussed earlier in the context of premarital negotiations, apply to married couples negotiating a postnuptial

agreement? Do you agree that prospective spouses are likely to be warier of their partners—and less in need of court protection—than are spouses?

Professor Sean Hannon Williams argues that "spousal bargaining dynamics severely limit the extent to which one spouse can take advantage of the other." In contrast to premarital partners, he reasons, spouses have better information about their bargaining partner's preferences, are less likely to be clouded by excessive optimism about the relationship, and are typically less financially vulnerable to threats by a partner to walk away. Williams, *Postnuptial Agreements, supra,* at 830. Do you agree? Or does *Bedrick* correctly apply closer scrutiny of postnuptial agreements than prenuptial agreements on the rationale that partners are *more* vulnerable to overbearing tactics and deceit after marriage than before?

3. *Treating postmarital agreements as separation agreements.* In *Marriage of Traster,* 291 P.3d 494, 507 (Kan. Ct. App. 2012), the court drew both on *Bedrick* and *Ansin, supra,* to hold that postmarital agreements, because of the particular dynamics in which parties negotiate them, require a distinct enforceability standard. The Kansas Supreme Court reversed in part, holding that "all agreements entered into during marriage that provide for a spouse's property rights in the event of divorce or separation" fall within the meaning of "separation agreement" as used in the Kansas statute, "regardless of whether the parties intend to remain married at the time of execution." *In re Marriage of Traster,* 339 P.3d 778, 789 (Kan. 2014). Under that statute, the court must determine whether the separation agreement is "valid, just, and equitable." *Id.*

4. *Consideration.* In a part of the opinion not reprinted above, *Bedrick* indicated that postmarital agreements must have adequate consideration to satisfy contract principles. Such consideration was present in the agreement before it, the court concluded, because both husband and wife released certain economic rights and interests: "Consideration consists of a benefit to the party promising, or a loss or detriment to the party to whom the promise is made." 17 A.3d at 704 n.5 (quoting an earlier Connecticut decision). By statute, premarital agreements in Connecticut are enforceable without consideration. Why treat these two types of agreements differently with respect to the issue of consideration?

Applying the *Bedrick* test, a subsequent Connecticut case held that there was no consideration for a postnuptial agreement in which the spouses each released "all marital rights which he/she may acquire by reason of the marriage in the property of the other." *Centmehaiey v. Centmehaiey,* 2014 WL 5097788 (Conn. Sup. Ct. 2014). The husband released any claim on the wife's two assets: a nine-year old Pontiac and her $400-a-month disability income; the wife released any claims to alimony as well as to a 50% interest in their marital home, and a possible inheritance by husband. The court stated that the wife "gained only the minimal benefit of having her limited assets not available" to the husband "in the event of marital discord," but "gave up her valuable right to claim any alimony or property settlement" from the husband's assets. *Id.* at *4. Do you agree that there was insufficient consideration for this agreement?

5.   *Is the threat to leave a marriage coercion? Bedrick* observes that "the circumstances surrounding [postnuptial] agreements," in contrast both to premarital and separation agreements, are "pregnant with the opportunity for one party to use the threat of dissolution to bargain themselves into positions of advantage." As an example, it mentions *Pacelli v. Pacelli*, 725 A.2d 56 (N.J. Super. Ct. 1999). In that case, midway through a 20-year marriage, the husband, a highly successful entrepreneur with approximately $4.7 million in assets, presented his wife, who had been a 20-year-old immigrant at the time of the marriage, with a nonnegotiable demand that she sign an agreement waiving her rights to any property distribution or alimony in the event of divorce. Against the advice of independent counsel, the wife signed the agreement because the husband had threatened to end the marriage if she did not sign and "she wanted to preserve the marriage and did not want her children to grow up in a broken family." The court declined to enforce the agreement because its economic provisions were "not fair and just." *Id.* at 58, 62. *See also Centmehaiey*, 2014 WL 097788, at *4 (ruling that there was "duress" when "a 36-year old woman with physical problems, who is unable to be employed, is told by her husband to 'sign or get out' ").

Courts generally hold that threats not to marry without a prenuptial agreement are not coercive. *See, e.g., In re Marriage of Barnes*, 755 N.E.2d 522, 527 (Ill. App. Ct. 2001) (the parties "could have remained single. Nothing was legally or morally wrong with either of them conditioning marriage upon the execution of a premarital agreement."). Is there a sound reason for distinguishing between prenuptial and postnuptial agreements?

6.   *May courts enforce a prenuptial or postnuptial agreement while the marriage remains intact?* To the extent that agreements cover the parties' behavior and financial dealings during the marriage, the agreements are treated like any other contract, requiring enforcement through a civil suit. Would you advise a client on an ongoing marriage to file a complaint to enforce the terms of a marital agreement? Why or why not?

7.   *Penalties for marital misconduct.* As noted in Section 2.D, premarital agreements sometimes include provisions about marital misconduct. Should a court enforce a postnuptial agreement that imposes a financial penalty for adultery or other misconduct during the marriage? A Wyoming trial court enforced a provision forfeiting a contingent $100,000 payment to the wife who committed adultery. *See Bradley v. Bradley*, 118 P.3d 984 (Wyo. 2005) (reversing the judgment on other grounds).

The ALI Principles would condition enforceability of misconduct clauses on whether the state permits courts to consider marital fault in dividing property or awarding maintenance. *See Principles,* § 7.08(2). The official commentary notes:

Modern no-fault divorce laws reflect, among other things, a policy of limiting the role of legal institutions in monitoring and policing the details of intimate relationships, and it would defeat that purpose if parties were permitted, by their own agreement, to require courts to decide if either of them was at fault for their relationship's decline.

Id. at cmt. a. Do you agree with this approach?

PROBLEM 16-4

Dan and Dora married in 1984. Dan has been a practicing attorney since 1988; Dora graduated from law school but never sat for the bar or practiced law. She has had limited employment during their marriage because of a traumatic brain injury she received in 1987 in a car accident. In 2014, after 30 years of marriage, Dan drafted a postnuptial agreement. The agreement stated that he did so because Dora "does not have Dan's practical experience with and knowledge about drafting and enforcing agreements. Dora is relying on Dan's legal expertise and advice."

The agreement included the following provisions:

- "We have experienced problems and difficulties during the marriage, but neither of us has current plans to seek a dissolution."

- "If our marriage does fail, Dan will receive his personal belongings and effects, tools, and guns, and Dora will receive all other assets, including but not limited to our home, vehicles, personal property, accounts, funds, stocks, bonds, and investments."

- "Dora's parents have directly or indirectly provided nearly all of our marital assets and their generosity and the opportunities they have given have made possible the accumulation of our marital assets. Any assets contributed by Dan from his employment have been, and will continue to be, during the marriage, used by the parties to maintain their lifestyle."

- "The parties agree that they are both aware of the full extent of the assets of the parties. They expressly waive any right to further disclosure of the property or financial obligations of the other party."

In 2019, Dan filed for divorce on the ground of irretrievable breakdown and asked the court to equitably divide the marital property. Dora did not contest that the marriage was broken, but asked the court to enforce the postnuptial agreement because it controlled the disposition of any personal and real property. Dan responded that the agreement was invalid and unenforceable because it "ran counter to public policy by promoting and encouraging divorce." The lower court ruled in his favor.

You are a law clerk for the judge hearing the case. What position will you recommend on the enforceability of Dan's and Dora's postnuptial agreement?

PROBLEM 16-5

In December 2005, Jan worked as an attorney for a prestigious law firm. She met and fell in love with Tom, who had just sailed around the world and wanted to start a forensic consulting business. They discussed marriage. Jan said she wanted to keep her law practice as separate property if she married and Tom agreed.

Weeks after their meeting, Tom was diagnosed with leukemia. Lacking insurance for medical treatment, he decided "to go off sailing again and just die." However, after Jan urged Tom to undergo a bone marrow transplant and proposed to marry him so that he could be placed on her medical insurance, he agreed. In January 2006, they married.

Within days of the marriage, Tom told his attorney, Sharon Spivak, that he wanted to protect Jan from his creditors if he did not survive the medical treatment, which was a distinct possibility. On January 30, 2006, he and Jan met with Spivak, who suggested a postnuptial agreement providing that their individual income, business property, and debts would be separate property and not community property (they married and reside in a community property state). Spivak explained that she was representing Tom and that Jan would have to retain separate counsel or represent herself.

Jan made changes to the postnuptial agreement, which were incorporated into the final draft. They both signed on March 30, 2006. To protect against medical creditors, Tom gifted his boat to Jan.

Tom underwent a bone marrow transplant and fully recovered. During the marriage, the parties maintained separate bank accounts and separate businesses. Jan started her own law practice but also helped Tom in his fledgling business. Tom's business flourished beyond his and Jan's dreams, becoming enormously valuable.

In mid-2016, the parties experienced marital problems. Jan told Tom to "get rid" of the postnuptial agreement and that she did not want "that postnuptial agreement hanging over my head anymore." He did not agree to do so.

On September 1, 2019, Jan filed a petition for marital dissolution. Tom argued that, under the postnuptial agreement, the forensic consulting business was not community property. Jan claimed that the agreement was invalid. She argued that it was not voluntary because she was not represented by independent counsel and because of the circumstances when they entered into the agreement—the specter of Tom's life-threatening illness.

Should a court uphold this postnuptial agreement under *Bedrick*? Under the UPMAA? What additional facts would you want to know in evaluating Jan's argument?

C. RECONCILIATION AGREEMENTS AS A
FORM OF POSTMARITAL AGREEMENT

Courts have enforced reconciliation agreements negotiated by married couples having marital strife and based on the parties' mutual promises to continue the marriage. *See, e.g., Hodge v. Parks*, 844 N.W.2d 189 (Mich. Ct. App. 2014) (enforcing a reconciliation agreement that treated a sailboat as marital property and observing that "if a postnuptial agreement seeks to promote marriage by keeping a husband and wife together, Michigan courts may enforce the agreement if it is equitable to do so"). One issue that sometimes arises in determining whether a postnuptial agreement is a reconciliation agreement is whether there was sufficient consideration for the agreement. Is a promise to remain married and forebear from bringing a dissolution action sufficient consideration for a postnuptial agreement? Should it matter whether the promise is made when separation or divorce is imminent?

In *Hall v. Hall*, 27 N.E.3d 281, 283 (Ind. Ct. App. 2015), the court rejected the husband's argument that his postnuptial agreement with his wife was unenforceable due to a lack of adequate consideration. The court affirmed a trial court's conclusion that the agreement, which the parties entered into—at the husband's suggestion—after the wife conveyed her "adamant" desire to dissolve the marriage, was a "valid and enforceable reconciliation agreement." Eight months after the parties married, husband was incarcerated and the wife, after seeking legal counsel, informed him she sought to dissolve the marriage "due to his untruthfulness because of his finances and criminal history" and the separation caused by his incarceration. He sought to preserve the marriage and to "do anything to make her more comfortable with him," including drafting an agreement to provide her "financial protection in the event of a future divorce." *Id.* She agreed that she would not pursue a divorce in exchange for the agreement, which provided that they would keep separate any properties or assets that either brought to the marriage or acquired during the marriage as separate property. After his release from prison in 2006, they lived together until 2013, when she filed for divorce. Explaining that the proper test was whether the agreement "was executed in order to preserve and extend a marriage that otherwise would have been dissolved but for the execution of the agreement," the appellate court concluded that there was "adequate consideration to support a reconciliation agreement." *Id.* at 284–86.

By contrast, in *Bratton v. Bratton*, 136 S.W.3d 595, 598 (Tenn. 2004), the court held that the parties' postnuptial agreement was not a reconciliation agreement. The husband, it concluded, received no valuable consideration when he made the following promise:

In the event the Husband is guilty of statutory grounds for divorce * * *, all property jointly owned by the parties, real, personal, or mixed, shall be divided equally between the parties [and * * * the Husband shall pay to the Wife, one-half (1/2) of all of the Husband's net gross income (after deduction for state and federal income taxes).

Bratton stated that while marriage itself is consideration for a premarital agreement, it "cannot act as sufficient consideration" for a postnuptial agreement "because past consideration cannot support a current promise." *Id.* at 600. The court observed that while it was clear that "there is consideration flowing from the husband to the wife," in the form of providing her with property and his income, the agreement did not "specify what act or forbearance is to be undertaken by the wife as consideration for the contract." The wife's promise not to leave the marriage if the husband signed the agreement was not consideration for the agreement because the parties were not having marital difficulties when they made the agreement. If separation or divorce were imminent, then "the wife's promise to remain in the marriage" would be "a meaningful act" and provide consideration for a valid reconciliation agreement. *Id.* at 603. The majority also concluded that, even if a promise to stay in a marriage and not carry out a threat to leave "were to constitute adequate consideration," the agreement before it would be invalid due to the taint of coercion and duress." *Id.*

In 2007, an Illinois appellate court distinguished *Bratton* and upheld a postnuptial agreement negotiated after the wife discovered that her husband had been having an affair. It found sufficient consideration for the husband's waiver of property rights in the wife's agreement to remain in the marriage because the parties negotiated the contract in the midst of genuine "marital difficulties" even though they had not yet separated or filed for divorce. *In re Marriage of Tabassum and Younis,* 881 N.E.2d 396, 407–08 (Ill. App. Ct. 2007).

4. SEPARATION AGREEMENTS

The third type of agreement this Chapter examines is by far the most common—a separation agreement (also called a "marital settlement agreement"). This agreement arises when a spouse has filed or is about to file for divorce. A separation agreement may resolve all issues between the divorcing spouses, ranging from economic matters, such as property division, alimony, and child support, to child custody and visitation (or parenting time). Because approximately 90% of divorces are ultimately uncontested proceedings, these agreements are a prominent feature of contemporary family law practice. As Chapter 1 discussed, in many divorces, either one or both of the parties is self-represented and does not have an attorney. Some state court websites provide "self-help" or "self-representation" guidance to such parties on how to draft a separation or settlement agreement. *See, e.g., Default Case with Written Agreement: Writing Up Your Agreement,* California Courts, https://www.courts.ca.gov/ 8410.htm (how to write separation agreement to dissolve marriage or domestic partnership); Dissolution of Marriage—Petitioner's Forms, Missouri Courts, https://www.selfrepresent.mo.gov/page.jsp?id=3832 (providing form for proposed separation agreement).

As with premarital and postnuptial agreements, negotiating and bargaining about separation agreements takes place in "the shadow of the law," that is, the "default rules" that will shape a judicially-imposed settlement if the parties cannot agree. Chapter 15 discussed such negotiation. A separation agreement has two distinct aspects: the agreement declares the spouses' physical separation and settles the rights and obligations arising out of the marriage relationship.

Legislatures and courts now strongly favor separation agreements. These agreements are seen to reduce litigation costs, time, and emotional anguish. In addition, such agreements may reduce "the overburdened docket of the family courts." Bix, *Private Ordering and Family Law, supra,* at 261. Also, these agreements may promote the interests of divorcing spouses and their children in ways that a judicial resolution cannot. As a result, the parties may be more likely to abide by the terms of an agreement they have helped to craft. *Id.*

In most jurisdictions today, courts must treat terms in separation agreements concerning alimony or property distribution with great deference. Agreements about child support, custody, and visitation are subject to greater judicial scrutiny to help assure that children's interests are protected.

If parties draft a marital settlement agreement, but then reconcile and continue in the marriage, this does not automatically rescind their agreement. For example, in *N.B.M. v. J.M.,* 68 N.Y.S.3d 681 (N.Y. Sup. Ct. 2017), the court rejected the wife's argument that a separation agreement concerning property and maintenance entered into with her husband two years after their marriage was invalid because they subsequently reconciled and lived together for twelve years. The husband argued that the separation agreement remained enforceable because (1) it included a clause stating that it "shall not be invalidated or otherwise affected by a reconciliation between the parties hereto, or a resumption of marital relations between them," and (2) specified that the agreement "shall not be amended, modified, discharged, or terminated except by a writing * * *." *Id.* at 685. The court agreed.

The following provision of the Uniform Marriage and Divorce Act reflects the modern consensus favoring separation agreements.

A. THE UNIFORM MARRIAGE AND DIVORCE ACT

UNIFORM MARRIAGE AND DIVORCE ACT
9A U.L.A. 248–49 (1998).

§ 306. [Separation Agreement].

(a) To promote amicable settlement of disputes between parties to a marriage attendant upon their separation or the dissolution of their marriage, the parties may enter into a written separation agreement containing provisions for disposition of any property owned by either of them, maintenance of either of them, and support, custody, and visitation of their children.

(b) In a proceeding for dissolution of marriage or for legal separation, the terms of the separation agreement, except those providing for the support, custody, and visitation of children, are binding upon the court unless it finds, after considering the economic circumstances of the parties and any other relevant evidence produced by the parties, on their own motion or on request of the court, that the separation agreement is unconscionable.

(c) If the court finds the separation agreement unconscionable, it may request the parties to submit a revised separation agreement or may make orders for the disposition of property, maintenance, and support.

(d) If the court finds that the separation agreement is not unconscionable as to disposition of property or maintenance, and not unsatisfactory as to support:

(1) unless the separation agreement provides to the contrary, its terms shall be set forth in the decree of dissolution or legal separation and the parties shall be ordered to perform them, or

(2) if the separation agreement provides that its terms shall not be set forth in the decree, the decree shall identify the separation agreement and state that the court has found the terms not unconscionable.

(e) Terms of the agreement set forth in the decree are enforceable by all remedies available for enforcement of a judgment, including contempt, and are enforceable as contract terms.

(f) Except for terms concerning the support, custody, or visitation of children, the decree may expressly preclude or limit modification of terms set forth in the decree if the separation agreement so provides. Otherwise, terms of a separation agreement set forth in the decree are automatically modified by modification of the decree.

B. ENFORCEMENT AND MODIFICATION OF SEPARATION AGREEMENTS

As UMDA section 306(d) suggests, when a court accepts a separation agreement as valid, it will set forth the agreement's terms in some manner in the divorce decree. Depending on the jurisdiction and the court's procedural rules, separation agreements may be approved, incorporated, or merged into the divorce judgment.

Where the court approves or "ratifies" a separation agreement, the court endorses it as valid under state law and as reasonable. However, the agreement is not part of the judgment and thus is enforceable only under contract principles. "Incorporation" permits the agreement to be part of the judgment, while it also remains contractually binding. An incorporation clause in a separation agreement might provide, for example that the agreement:

> is intended to be and remain effective as a contract and shall not be extinguished by merger as a result of incorporation in any decree or order or judgment, irrespective of any court decree, order or judgment to the contrary stating that it shall merge. This Agreement shall in all events survive such decree, order or judgment and be forever binding upon the parties.

Lalchandani v. Roddy, 22 N.E.3d 166, 167 n. 3 (Mass. App. Div. 2015) (quoting divorcing couple's agreement).

"Merger" means that the agreement becomes fully a part of the judgment and may no longer be enforced as a separate contract. A court may enforce a merged agreement, like other judgments, by contempt of court. *See, e.g., Custis v. Custis*, 2008 WL 2338499 (Va. Ct. App. 2008).

Whether the court or the parties may modify the terms of a marital separation agreement depends on whether the agreement has been approved, incorporate, or merged into a final judgment. Absent a provision barring modification, an incorporated or merged agreement may be modified after entry of the judgment on the same limited grounds permitted for modification of other court orders. If a separation agreement is not incorporated into the decree, the parties may later modify its terms in accordance with general contract law. *See* Doris Del Tosto Brogan, *Divorce Settlement Agreements: The Problem of Merger or Incorporation and the Status of the Agreement in Relation to the Decree*, 67 Neb. L. Rev. 235 (1988).

Nearly all jurisdictions follow the approach of UMDA section 306(f), which enables parties to bar or limit future modification of contract terms, except terms relating to child custody, visitation or support. As discussed in the Chapters 11, 12, and 13, terms relating to minor children's support and custody are always subject to judicial scrutiny and modification. With respect to other terms, if the separation agreement bars modification, courts honor that directive notwithstanding a later change of circumstances. *See Richardson v. Richardson*, 218 S.W.3d 426 (Mo. 2007) (declining to modify an ex-husband's obligation to pay alimony even though his ex-wife attempted to hire a hit man to kill him). In a small handful of states, however, judicial authority to modify spousal support, like authority to modify child support, may not be divested by the parties' agreement. *See Toni v. Toni*, 636 N.W.2d 396, 400–401 (N.D. 2001) (collecting decisions). In *Miles v. Miles*, 711 S.E.2d 880, 885 (S.C. 2011), the court clarified that, while the burden to prove entitlement to a modification of spousal or child support due to changed circumstances is a "substantial one," that burden is not higher when a party seeks to do so in the context of a court-approved separation agreement.

C. VOIDING A SEPARATION AGREEMENT

Court review of separation agreements is normally minimal. Under the prevailing legal standard, reflected in UMDA section 306(b), the parties' agreement concerning alimony or property rights is presumptively "binding" on the court, absent proof of fraud, duress, or unconscionability. Some jurisdictions, however, do require a more "searching inquiry" to assure that an agreement is "fair and reasonable" in light of various factors. *See Ansin, supra,* 929 N.E.2d at 968–969 (stating that the court should use the same factors to evaluate postmarital and separation agreements). As in the case reprinted below, some courts articulate that "separation agreements are subject to closer judicial scrutiny than other contracts because of the fiduciary relationship between spouses." *Tuzzolino v. Tuzzolino,* 67 N.Y.S.3d 740, 742 (N.Y. App. Div. 2017).

With respect to child-related provisions concerning child support and custody and visitation (or, to use the more contemporary terminology, parenting time), courts are required to review such provisions more closely to make sure they are consistent with the best interests of the child. However, "[b]y all accounts, * * * courts tend to rubber-stamp" even the child-related provisions of separation agreements "with comparable lack of supervision." Bix, *Private Ordering and Family Law, supra,* at 262. On the other hand, some scholars criticize this "best interests" review power as being too intrusive on parental decision making. For example, Kimberly Emery and Robert Emery propose that judges should be *more* deferential to agreements by parents about post-dissolution parenting, treating such an agreement as the primary factor in a "best interests of the child" determination. Kimberly C. Emery & Robert E. Emery, *Who Knows What Is Best For Children? Honoring Agreements and Contracts Between Parents Who Live Apart,* 77 Law and Cont. Prob. 151 (2014).

Courts may *sua sponte* probe the parties' economic circumstances to ensure conscionability, but they ordinarily rely on the parties' representations. Appellate courts have rejected the suggestion that trial courts have a duty of independent investigation. *See, e.g., Grigsby v. Grigsby*, 2007 WL 1378460 (Ky. Ct. App. 2007); *Swank v. Swank*, 865 S.W.2d 841, 845 (Mo. Ct. App. 1993). Accordingly, in the great majority of cases, court approval of a separation agreement is, as noted above, minimal and "a required formality." Eleanor E. Maccoby & Robert H. Mnookin, Dividing the Child: Social and Legal Dilemmas of Custody 40 (1992). Occasionally, however, as in the following decision, a court denies enforcement of a separation agreement.

IN RE MARRIAGE OF THORNHILL

Colorado Court of Appeals, 2008.
200 P.3d 1083.

TERRY, J.

[Antoinette Thornhill executed a separation agreement with her husband, Chuck Thornhill, but later changed her mind and sought to avoid the agreement at the time the trial court granted the divorce. The trial court concluded that the agreement was valid, notwithstanding the wife's change of mind, and divided the couple's property according to its terms. She appealed.] * * *

Wife first argues that the trial court erred in finding the separation agreement conscionable. We agree.

Parties to a marriage, attendant upon their separation or dissolution of the marriage, may enter into a written separation agreement providing for maintenance and the disposition of property. Such provisions are binding on the court unless it finds, after considering the economic circumstances of the parties and any other relevant evidence produced by the parties, that the agreement is unconscionable.

* * *

" '[B]ecause of the fiduciary relationship between husband and wife, separation agreements generally are closely scrutinized by the courts, and such agreements are more readily set aside in equity under circumstances that would be insufficient to nullify an ordinary contract.' " *In re Marriage of Manzo*, 659 P.2d 669, 674 (Colo. 1983).

A court reviewing a separation agreement for conscionability should first review the provisions for fraud, overreaching, concealment of assets, or sharp dealing not consistent with the obligations of marital partners to deal fairly with each other. However, even where the trial court finds no fraud, overreaching, concealment of assets, or sharp dealing, we are still required to review the agreement to determine whether it is "fair, just and reasonable." We do this by looking at the economic circumstances of the parties which result from the agreement.

Here, the parties were married for 27 years before they separated. During most of the marriage, wife cared for the children and held several low-wage jobs while husband worked in the oil business. The family lived for many years in various oil field camps in desolate parts of Wyoming. Although husband earned a sufficient amount to meet his family's needs, his income during most of that time did not approach the substantial sums he began to earn after starting an oil and gas equipment sales and servicing business (the business) in 2001. At the time of the permanent orders hearing, husband's business valuation expert valued his 70.5% ownership share of the business at $1,625,000, after applying a 33% marketability discount. Husband also signed a financial disclosure stating that his total monthly income before expenses was nearly $15,000. Wife's disclosure showed her total monthly income before expenses was less than $5,000.

The parties entered into a separation agreement providing for maintenance to wife and dividing the marital property. However, by the time of the scheduled court hearing to enter a decree based on the agreement, wife realized that at the time she signed the agreement, she had not had a good understanding of the value of the marital assets, and therefore she disavowed the agreement as unfair to her.

Because of wife's disavowal of the agreement, the matter was set for a permanent orders hearing. In its findings after that hearing, the trial court did not find fraud, overreaching, concealment of assets, or sharp dealing. Instead, it found the agreement to be "both enforceable and equitable."

After considering the totality of the circumstances, we conclude the property disposition is not fair, just, or reasonable, and we set it aside and remand for a new permanent orders hearing. The following facts support our conclusion that the agreement is unconscionable:

- Importantly, despite the fact that the parties had more than one million dollars in marital assets, wife was not represented by counsel at the time the separation agreement was negotiated and signed. Although in recent years she earned a graduate degree in occupational therapy, the record does not indicate she is sophisticated in legal or financial matters. *See In re Marriage of Seely*, 689 P.2d 1154, 1160 (Colo.App.1984) (court closely scrutinizes separation agreement where one party was not represented by counsel).

- Wife's father, who was chief financial officer of the business, had assisted in negotiating the separation agreement, and in the trial court's ruling following the permanent orders hearing, the court based its determination of conscionability largely on the father's testimony. However, purely by virtue of his role as chief financial officer, the father was required to attempt preservation of the business assets, which necessarily resulted in dual loyalties under the circumstances presented here.

• Wife testified to her lack of mathematical ability, her need to rely on her father to explain financial details of the settlement, her repeated statements that she did not understand the details, and the fact that she was never presented with the promissory note referenced in the agreement concerning payment of husband's obligation to her.

Thus, even accepting the court's implicit finding that there was no fraud, overreaching, concealment of assets, or sharp dealing, we conclude that the agreement is unconscionable. To accomplish the parties' avowed purpose of dividing equally the marital assets that existed at the time of the agreement, it provided that husband would pay wife $752,692, half of what was represented to be the marital assets at the time the agreement was entered into. However, he was not required to pay that sum to wife immediately. Rather, the parties' agreement called for him to pay it in equal monthly installments of $6,272 over ten years, and failed to require him to pay her interest on the total sum or to secure the obligation.

Accordingly, wife lost the ability to obtain the full use and enjoyment, as well as the investment value, of the entire sum, while husband, whose income is substantially greater than wife's, obtained the considerable benefit of retaining the use, enjoyment, and investment value of the unpaid balance. Thus, the present value of the payments to wife was considerably less than $756,692. As wife testified, "[husband] wants me to be [his] bank." Even applying a modest interest rate, the accumulated interest on $752,692 over ten years would be a considerable sum.

We conclude that this combination of factors—wife's lack of understanding of the value of the marital assets; her lack of legal representation and independent financial advice; her father's conflicting roles as her financial advisor and chief financial officer of the business in which husband was majority shareholder; and the failure to provide for interest on such a large obligation over such a lengthy period—results in a property distribution that is not "fair, just and reasonable."

* * *

Because the issues of property, maintenance, and the payment of attorney fees and costs, are inextricably intertwined, we remand to the trial court with directions to vacate the property settlement and to enter new permanent orders. * * *

* * *

NOTES AND QUESTIONS

1. *Rescuing people from bad bargains?* Do you agree with the outcome in *Thornhill?* Courts are usually unwilling to rescue parties from ill-advised bargains. *See* Judith T. Younger, *Across Curricular Boundaries: Searching for a Confluence Between Marital Agreements and Indian Land Transactions,* 26 Law & Inequality 495, 511–12 (2008) (concluding that courts are inclined to enforce even draconian marital agreements, and that recent decisions "display a lamentable disregard for the spouse who, in the interest of the relationship, gives up the production of income to devote herself to the family enterprise"). A New York appellate court expresses this sentiment: " 'An agreement will not be overturned merely because, in retrospect, some of its provisions were improvident or one-sided' or because 'a party had a change of heart.' " *Brennan-Duffy v. Duffy,* 804 N.Y.S.2d 399, 400 (App. Div. 2005).

If the bargain is exceptionally one-sided, however, courts may withhold enforcement. The Kentucky Supreme Court invalidated as unconscionable a separation agreement in which a divorcing psychiatrist agreed to pay his former wife $5,500 per month in maintenance and $8,000 per month in child support (under a formula by which each figure would be gradually reduced over time), and to cover his children's educational and insurance costs. "Under the agreement, [the wife] was entitled to remain in the marital residence with the children [though she was obligated to pay the $5,200 monthly mortgage payment] and to receive most of the household goods and a vehicle. [The husband] was to receive his medical practice, his retirement account, an automobile, and a $30,000 wine collection." *Shraberg v. Shraberg,* 939 S.W.2d 330, 331 (Ky. 1997). The court emphasized that "the single most important fact is that while [the husband] had a pre-tax income of about $200,000 annually, by the agreement he obligated himself to pay in excess of $160,000 annually for the support of his children and former wife." *Id.* at 333. Two judges dissented, arguing that the case involved nothing more than "the striking of a bad bargain entered into by a highly educated professional spouse, who was unrepresented by counsel." *Id.* at 335 (Stumbo, J., dissenting).

2. *Not just on ordinary contract—more on unconscionability.* The *Thornhill* court emphasizes the fiduciary relationship between the spouses in the context of negotiating a separation agreement. Two recent New York cases similarly emphasized this duty in distinguishing an ordinary contract and in holding that a particular separation agreement was unconscionable. Both courts defined an unconscionable agreement as one that "no person in his or her senses and not under delusion would make on the one hand, and as no honest and fair person would accept on the other, the inequality being so strong and manifest as to shock the conscience and confound the judgment of any person of common sense." *Gardella v. Remizov,* 42 N.Y.S.3d 225, 227 (N.Y. App. Div. 2d 2016).

In *Gardella,* the court concluded that the husband had raised "triable issues" as to whether the parties' separation agreement was unconscionable. The husband was not represented by legal counsel when he executed the agreement, which provided that he would "have no interest in any of the assets acquired during the parties' marriage, included six parcels of real property, the [wife's] partnership in a neurological practice, and [the wife's] bank and brokerage accounts, and that he waived his right to spousal maintenance." Id. at 227. The husband was a wine salesman, earning $40,000 per year, and the wife was a neurologist, earning $600,000 per year. He also had a medical condition limiting his future earning capacity. *Id.* at 229. In *Tuzzolino v. Tuzzolino, supra,* the court agreed with the husband's argument that a separation agreement and subsequent modification agreement were "unfair and unconscionable and should be set aside." 67 N.Y.S.3d at 742. As in *Gardella*, the husband was not represented by counsel, while the wife was. Although the wife's assets were approximately $799,000 and the husband's assets were approximately $77,000, the initial agreement provided him no maintenance; the modification provided it, but required him to transfer his interest in the marital residence to the wife. The court set aside the agreement as the "product of overreaching" by the wife. *Id.*

3. *Disclosure obligations and the parties' confidential relationship.* Like most jurisdictions, Colorado holds that the "confidential relationship" occasioned by marriage continues until the court formally dissolves the marriage. Under the majority rule, "[p]arties to a separation agreement stand as fiduciaries to each other, and will be held to the highest standards of good faith and fair dealing in the performance of their contractual obligations." *Krapf v. Krapf*, 786 N.E.2d 318, 323 (Mass. 2003). These standards include an affirmative obligation to disclose all material information relating to one's financial assets and income. Breach of this duty constitutes fraud, which under ordinary civil procedure rules exposes even a settled judgment accepting a separation agreement to potential reopening when the injured party discovers the fraud. *See, e.g., In re Marriage of Palacios*, 656 N.E.2d 107, 112 (Ill. App. Ct. 1995) (voiding a separation agreement when the husband, while negotiating the agreement, fraudulently concealed from his wife, who waived maintenance, the "material fact" that he had won $5.38 million in the lottery four days before filing for divorce). In *McNeil v. Hoskyns*, 337 P. 3d 46 (Ariz. Ct. App. 2014), the court modified a spousal maintenance term of a divorce decree even though, by statute, a court lacks jurisdiction to modify a dissolution decree that approves the parties' agreement that spousal support may not be modified. The reason? The wife knew but failed to disclose either to the husband or to the court that, at the time the settlement agreement specified the term and amount of husband's future spousal support payments to wife, he had accidently paid her double payments for 17 months. She signed an agreement stating that husband was in arrears, when he actually had overpaid by $85,000. The court stated that the wife had committed "fraud on the court" not only by failing to disclose the double payments but by making false statement under oath. *Id.* at 50. Under such circumstances, the court had equitable power to modify the support obligation and grant the husband appropriate relief. *Id.* at 51.

In *Brown v. Brown*, 2013 Tenn. App. LEXIS 596 (Tenn. Ct. App. Sept. 12, 2013), fraud was the basis for vacating a portion of a divorce decree. As mentioned above, in Section 2, the premarital agreement included a term that if the marriage lasted more than four years, the husband would pay the wife $80,000 unless she had a "sexual affair or commits adultery during the marriage." *Id.* at *3–*4. The parties included that payment in their marital settlement agreement, which was incorporated into the divorce decree. However, when the wife gave birth to a child six and a half months after the divorce decree was entered, the husband was "alerted to the fact that Wife must have had a sexual affair while they were married." *Id.* at *5. The husband moved to vacate that provision of the divorce decree for nondisclosure and concealment. He stated that, given the confidential relationship between the parties, the wife had a duty to disclose the pertinent facts that would eliminate his payment obligation. *Id.* at *6. The trial court denied relief, but the reviewing court reversed and vacated the relevant portion of the decree in light of the "clear and convincing evidence of misrepresentation and misconduct by Wife." *Id.* at *17.

By contrast, some jurisdictions hold that the spouses' confidential relationship may end before entry of the divorce judgment, removing any heightened duties of disclosure when a separation agreement is brokered. A North Carolina court explained that:

> [W]hile a husband and wife generally share a confidential relationship, this relationship ends when the parties become adversaries. It is well established that when one party to a marriage hires an attorney to begin divorce proceedings, the confidential relationship is usually over, although the mere involvement of an attorney does not automatically end the confidential relationship. Further, when one party moves out of the marital home, this too is evidence that the confidential relationship is over, although it is not controlling.

Lancaster v. Lancaster, 530 S.E.2d 82, 84–85 (N.C. Ct. App. 2000). Without a confidential relationship, the divorcing parties are not obligated to volunteer material financial information, but must respond truthfully to specific inquiries. *See Daughtry v. Daughtry*, 497 S.E.2d 105, 107 (N.C. Ct. App. 1998).

Should parties also be required to disclose material nonfinancial information? In *Barnes v. Barnes*, 340 S.E.2d 803 (Va. 1986), an ex-husband sought to repudiate a separation agreement because his ex-wife had not disclosed that she had twice committed adultery during the marriage. The court rejected the husband's challenge on the ground that, because the spouses negotiated the agreement when they were separated and represented by independent counsel, they were no longer in a confidential relationship. *Id.* at 804–05. What would result if the parties resided in a jurisdiction that considers spouses to be fiduciaries until entry of the final divorce decree? Does it make sense to apply a stricter fiduciary duty to married persons who are estranged than to engaged persons who are arguably at the height of their commitment to each other?

4. *Terms fixing parental rights and obligations.* When a settlement agreement provides for greater child support than the amount required by the child support guidelines, courts generally grant or enforce the greater obligation, unless evidence of involuntariness or manifest unfairness appears. By comparison, courts are unlikely to permit agreed terms that set a child support obligation at an amount lower than prevailing law would otherwise impose. *See Upchurch v. Upchurch*, 624 S.E.2d 643, 647 (S.C. 2006) (holding that "an agreement between the parents may not affect the basic support rights of minor children," and that "[n]otwithstanding any provisions of a separation agreement, the family court retains jurisdiction to do whatever is in the best interest of the children"). What if one party agrees to give the other substantially more marital property in exchange for a lower child support obligation? *See Hammack v. Hammack*, 60 P.3d 663 (Wash. Ct. App. 2003) (holding exchange to be void as against public policy, but acknowledging that parties may characterize a disproportionate award of community property as an "advance payment" of child support if they establish that it is tailored to meet the amount due under prevailing child support guidelines).

Courts often give substantial deference to parental agreements about visitation and child custody, even though courts must similarly ensure their consistency with the child's best interests. As Chapter 12 discussed, contemporary family law encourages parents to reach agreement about parenting time through such devices as parenting plans, instead of relying on courts to decide custody. Is there a compelling reason to be less deferential with respect to child support?

5. *Coercion and duress.* In the separation agreement context, common factors that determine coercion and duress include whether both parties had the assistance of independent counsel, had read and understood the agreement's terms and obligations, and had negotiated changes in the draft agreement. No one factor is determinative. Indeed, courts have upheld agreements where each of these factors would tend to suggest coercion or duress. In *Morand v. Morand*, 767 N.Y.S.2d 523, 525 (App. Div. 2003), for example, the court found that there was no duress even though wife signed a separation agreement after only a "cursory review" and without advice of counsel. Although the husband presented her with the agreement as she was going out for the night, and "ma[d]e a scene" in front of the children about her signing it before going out, "at no time was she fearful or stressed by his behavior." The court concluded: "While her decision to hastily sign the agreement may have been unwise, her claim of duress is unsupported." Id.

6. *Contrast with other marital agreements.* Case law often reflects a greater willingness to enforce separation agreements than premarital agreements or postnuptial agreements. The ALI Principles suggests that the difference "may * * * reflect the different negotiating context":

The parties to a premarital agreement are contracting about a speculative contingent future event (dissolution), in a setting dominated by a quite different and immediate event (marriage). By contrast, in an impending family dissolution, the parties are contracting for the event at hand and are better able to anticipate the circumstances within which the agreement will be enforced, and thus to understand the significance of the terms of the agreement. It may also generally be assumed that each party is less naive about the beneficent intentions of the other party and, given the demise of the relationship, is bargaining at arm's length.

Principles, § 7.09 cmt. B. Do these considerations support enforcement of agreements like the one in *Thornhill?*?

7. *Comparing enforceability under the UMDA and the Principles.* Like the UMDA, section 7.09(1) of the ALI Principles generally would make agreed financial terms "binding" on the court if the parties voluntarily entered into a written separation agreement with a "full and fair opportunity to be informed" about each party's financial assets and earning potential. In contrast to the UMDA's open-ended provision against "unconscionable" bargains, section 7.09(2) of the ALI Principles provides:

Except as provided in the last sentence of this Paragraph, the terms of a separation agreement providing for the disposition of property or for compensatory payments are unenforceable if they substantially limit or augment property rights or compensatory payments otherwise due under law, and enforcement of those terms would substantially impair the economic well-being of a party who has or will have

(a) primary or dual residential responsibility for a child or

(b) substantially fewer economic resources than the other party.

Nevertheless, the court may enforce such terms if it finds, under the particular circumstances of the case, that enforcement of the terms would not work an injustice.

Does section 7.09(2) differ in substance from the understanding of "unconscionability" reflected in the UMDA? If a divorcing spouse enters into an onerous agreement freely and knowingly, what policy rationale supports overriding the parties' free choice? The official commentary to section 7.09(2) states:

When a residential parent's economic well-being is substantially impaired by contractual relinquishment of legal rights, the interests of a child with whom that parent shares a household are equally impaired. When the economic well-being of a spouse with substantially fewer economic resources than the other spouse is similarly impaired, the public-policy purposes underlying the law of property distribution and compensatory payments [*i.e.,* spousal support] may be completely frustrated.

Are you persuaded?

CHAPTER 17

LOCATIONS OF FAMILY LAW LITIGATION

■ ■ ■

This Chapter considers a number of complex issues that determine which court has authority to issue orders in actions for divorce, property distribution, child support, and child custody. Questions concerning the appropriate forum for family law litigation begin with where a party may make an initial filing, and continue in actions seeking to modify an earlier order. This Chapter brings together issues of subject matter and personal jurisdiction, full faith and credit, and related constitutional issues. Because we live in a mobile society, jurisdictional issues are pervasive in domestic relations cases.

1. INTRODUCTION

As in other civil litigation, domestic relations litigants may proceed only in a court that has personal and subject matter jurisdiction under constitutional prescriptions, applicable statutes, and court rules. As you know from Civil Procedure, personal jurisdiction, which limits who may be sued in a particular geographic location, may rest on domicile, consent, physical presence, or another basis. *International Shoe Co. v. Washington*, 326 U.S. 310, 316, 319 (1945), established that personal jurisdiction extends to a state in which the defendant's "minimum contacts" make issuance of a binding judgment fair. For its part, subject matter jurisdiction concerns the court's constitutional and statutory authority to hear and decide the particular claims raised in the case.

This Chapter considers the differing standards for initial and continuing jurisdiction in various types of domestic relations proceedings you studied in earlier chapters, namely, divorce, property distribution, alimony, child support, and child custody and visitation. You will learn an alphabet soup of state and federal law: the state-based UCCJEA (Uniform Child Custody Jurisdiction and Enforcement Act) and the federal PKPA (Parental Kidnapping Prevention Act) for child custody jurisdiction, and the state-based UIFSA (Uniform Interstate Family Support Act) and the federal FFCSO (Full Faith and Credit for Child Support Orders) for support jurisdiction. Finally, the Chapter introduces unified family courts, which hear a variety of family law issues in one forum in jurisdictions that maintain these tribunals.

goals w/ the proper jurisdiction

Throughout, it is important to remember that all of this common law, state law, and federal law seeks to accomplish two primary goals in family law litigation: first, to ensure that courts rule only where they have authority over the litigants and their claims; and second, to avoid overlapping jurisdiction, so that only one state has authority to rule in each case on any particular issue.

Family law issues are in state court

Indeed, federal courts rarely hear traditional family law disputes. To be sure, Congress has conferred federal diversity-of-citizenship jurisdiction in civil cases or controversies between citizens of different states where the amount in controversy exceeds $75,000. 28 U.S.C. § 1332(a) (2018). Under the court-created "domestic relations exception," however, federal courts will not exercise diversity jurisdiction to grant or deny a divorce, alimony, property distribution, or child custody or visitation. Consequently, these issues are left to the state courts. *See Ankenbrandt v. Richards*, 504 U.S. 689 (1992) (reaffirming the domestic relations exception to diversity jurisdiction); *Aldmyr Sys. v. Friedman*, 215 F. Supp. 3d 440, 454 (2016) (dismissing case and "deem[ing] the present action for alleged copyright infringement and theft of trade secrets as nothing more than a thinly veiled, too-clever-by-half effort to gain an unfair advantage in a state divorce proceeding").

The following excerpt, from a classic 1995 article, introduces some of the complicated jurisdictional issues that can arise in domestic relations cases, including the complexity of having different jurisdictional rules govern various claims in the same action. The excerpt shows that jurisdiction has always been a difficult yet crucial aspect of family law.

RHONDA WASSERMAN,
PARENTS, PARTNERS, AND PERSONAL JURISDICTION
1995 U. Ill. L. Rev. 813, 813–15 (1995).

The intersection between family law and jurisdiction is messy. If a married couple with children decides to divorce, a court may be asked to resolve at least three different sets of family law issues: whether to grant the divorce itself; how to resolve financial matters (such as alimony, child support and division of marital property); and how to allocate child custody and visitation rights. Although often it would make sense to resolve all of these issues in a single proceeding, each set of issues is governed by a unique set of jurisdictional principles. With respect to the divorce itself, a state has power, consistent with the Due Process Clause, to enter a divorce decree as long as one of the spouses is domiciled there, even if the state lacks *in personam* jurisdiction over the other spouse. But a state cannot resolve the financial matters of alimony or child support without first acquiring *in personam* jurisdiction over the spouse charged with payment. Yet it can adjudicate child custody disputes as long as it is the child's "home

messy issues

state," regardless of whether the child or either parent is domiciled there or whether it has *in personam* jurisdiction over the parents.

What explains this smorgasbord of jurisdictional rules governing family matters? Why are alimony, child support, and marital property matters governed by standard jurisdictional rules—*International Shoe's* minimum contacts test—while divorce and child custody issues are not?

[handwritten: & financial matters = governed by standard jurisdictional rules]

It is easy to understand why financial matters—alimony, child support and marital property—are governed by standard jurisdictional rules. After all, the minimum contacts test was devised to assure that defendants were not deprived of *property* without due process of law, and money and marital assets are clearly property. But the Due Process Clause protects against deprivations of liberty as well as property, and the rights to marry and to bear and raise children are constitutionally protected liberty interests. Why then are divorce and child custody suits not governed by the same jurisdictional rules as alimony actions?

NOTE AND QUESTION

1. *Family law differences?* As Professor Wasserman's article makes clear, a state may have authority to grant a divorce, but not to distribute property. How do jurisdictional rules affect substantive family law issues?

2. *Basis for the domestic relations exception.* Commentators have struggled to define a solid basis for the domestic relations exception to diversity jurisdiction because nothing in Article III of the Constitution or in the diversity statute explicitly creates the exception. Are domestic relations cases inherently matters of state concern?

Ankenbrandt justified recognition of the domestic relations exception partly on the basis of the relative lack of expertise of federal judges in these matters, as compared to state judges. However, commentators have pointed out that expertise is not unattainable by federal judges, and that expertise is merely one factor among many—including the countervailing potential for bias against particular individuals or families in state courts. *See* Joseph Carroll, *Family Law is not "Civil": The Faulty Foundation of the Domestic Relations Exception to Federal Jurisdiction*, American Bar Ass'n 1, 16 (2017). The Framers may have included diversity jurisdiction in Article III based on a concern that out-of-state parties would suffer discrimination if they were forced to litigate in state court. Think about how states might approach this issue in family law cases.

3. *Scope.* In light of the domestic relations exception, why did a federal district court, a federal circuit court, and the Supreme Court hear and decide *Obergefell v. Hodges,* which you read as a lead case in Chapter 2? 135 S. Ct. 2584 (2015). Indeed, in his dissent, Chief Justice Roberts referred to the extensive scope of state power over domestic relations. *Obergefell*, 135 S. Ct. at 2613–14 (Roberts, C.J., dissenting); *see* Meredith Johnson Harbach, *Is the Family a Federal Question?*, 66 Wash. & Lee L. Rev. 131 (2009).

PROBLEM 17-1

Lisa and Janet met at a party, and it was love at first sight. They married in Vermont and decided to have a child through artificial insemination. Lisa volunteered to carry the child so that Janet could pursue various business ventures. Both women actively participated in the pregnancy process, and Lisa gave birth to a baby girl named Inez. Lisa stayed home with Inez while Janet worked and took care of the family's finances. Inez called Janet "mommy" and Lisa "mammy." Both women involved themselves in their child's life.

After almost five years of marriage, Janet and Lisa separated. Lisa moved to Virginia with Inez. The week after Lisa and Inez moved, Janet filed for divorce and custody in Vermont. A month later, the Vermont Family Court entered divorce and custody judgments that granted Lisa custody of the child and Janet visitation rights and distributed the couple's property equally. Because Lisa and Inez were no longer both resident in Vermont, Lisa then filed for custody in Virginia, seeking to void the Vermont order and deny visitation to Janet. What should the Virginia court do about the divorce, custody, and property distribution orders?

Although you have not yet studied the jurisdictional rules that govern this case, think about when one state should accord full faith and credit to another state's family law judgments. Should it matter for the divorce judgment itself as opposed to custody?

PROBLEM 17-2

Carol Anderson, a citizen of Missouri, has sued Jon Richard, her former husband and a citizen of Louisiana, in federal court based on diversity of citizenship. Anderson claims that Richard committed physical and sexual abuse against their two joint children during visitation periods. She sought half a million dollars in monetary damages. Richard has moved to dismiss, based on the domestic relations exception. You are the law clerk to the judge hearing this case. Should the case go forward or be dismissed? Why?

2. DIVORCE JURISDICTION

By reaffirming the domestic relations exception to diversity jurisdiction, *Ankenbrandt* explains why state courts hear most domestic relations proceedings, including divorce. Before granting a divorce, of course, the state court must have both subject matter and personal jurisdiction. Subject matter jurisdiction is generally established by statute; parties can consent to personal jurisdiction, but they cannot consent to subject matter jurisdiction or waive objection to its absence.

The court must also decide whether the marriage is recognized in its state. As you learned in Chapter 2, the general rule is that marriages that are valid in the state where they are celebrated are valid in all other states, just as marriages that are void where celebrated are void everywhere else.

Citing the *Williams I* opinion (discussed below), *Obergefell's* majority stated that "being married in one State but having that valid marriage denied in another is one of " 'the most perplexing and distressing complication[s]' in the law of domestic relations."135 S. Ct. at 2607.

If the state will recognize the marriage (at least for purposes of getting a divorce) and both parties are domiciled in the same state, then it seems clear that the state may assert both subject matter and personal jurisdiction to grant a divorce. But does a court have subject matter jurisdiction if only one party is domiciled in the state?

This question became particularly significant during World War II. The 1940s witnessed a divorce boom, which yielded "increasingly frequent conflict of law issues" that were "exacerbated by the fact that state divorce laws varied widely, as some states severely restricted access to divorce while states at the other end of the legal spectrum competed for the migratory divorce trade." Jessica Miles, *We Are Never Ever Getting Back Together: Domestic Violence Victims, Defendants, and Due Process*, 35 Card. L. Rev. 141, 168–69 (2013). Nevada's requirement of a six-week residency period before a litigant could file for divorce was the shortest in the country, followed by Florida's 90-day residency requirement. Some divorcing couples obtained fast divorces in the courts of other countries, including Mexico and the Dominican Republic. Because of the confusion caused by out-of-state divorce decrees during these years, the Supreme Court decided a number of cases involving complex issues of federalism and family law. Spouses today are less likely to forum shop for a quick divorce, but our society has high rates of mobility, and spouses who separate may move to different states.

A. *EX PARTE* DIVORCE: *WILLIAMS I* AND *WILLIAMS II*

In two landmark decisions reviewing the consequences of the same divorce, the Supreme Court held that states may exercise subject matter jurisdiction over the marital status of individuals in dissolving marriages and could grant divorces on an *ex parte* basis, that is, by having personal jurisdiction over only one party.

In *Williams v. North Carolina*, 317 U.S. 287 (1942) ("*Williams I*"), the Court determined the validity of a Nevada divorce decree issued to O. B. Williams. He married Carrie Wyke in 1916 in North Carolina and lived with her until May 1940, when he went to Las Vegas. Coincidentally, Lillie Shaver Hendrix, who had married Thomas Hendrix in 1920, and who also lived in North Carolina, also moved to Las Vegas in May 1940.

Williams and Hendrix each filed for divorce in Nevada in June 1940. Williams was granted a divorce in August, and, on October 4, 1940, the same day that Hendrix was granted her decree, Williams and Hendrix married each other. A North Carolina court subsequently convicted both of

NC court rejection

bigamous cohabitation, rejecting their defense based on the Nevada divorce decrees. The Supreme Court reversed:

> * * * Each state as a sovereign has a rightful and legitimate concern in the marital status of persons domiciled within its borders. [I]t is plain that each state by virtue of its command over its domiciliaries and its large interest in the institution of marriage can alter within its own borders the marriage status of the spouse domiciled there, even though the other spouse is absent. * * *

Cons held that NC was bound to accept the nevada divorce as lawful

Id. at 298–99. The Court held that North Carolina was bound to accept the Nevada divorces as lawful: "[I]f decrees of a state altering the marital status of its domiciliaries are not valid throughout the Union even though the requirements of procedural due process are wholly met, a rule would be fostered which could not help but bring 'considerable disaster to innocent persons' and 'bastardize children hitherto supposed to be the offspring of lawful marriage.'" *Id.* at 299–301 (quoting *Haddock v. Haddock*, 201 U.S. 562, 628 (1906) (Holmes, J., dissenting)). Relying on the Full Faith and Credit Clause of the U.S. Constitution,[a] *Williams I* held that any state had jurisdiction to grant a divorce to an individual who was legally domiciled in that state *and* that all other states must recognize these divorces. Following remand to the North Carolina Supreme Court, the parties were again convicted of bigamy and sentenced to prison terms. Again they appealed.

(Reasoning = full faith + credit clause of constitution)

key Holding

Williams v. North Carolina, 325 U.S. 226 (1945) ("*Williams II*"), considered the validity of the spouses' Nevada domicile, an issue that had not been addressed in *Williams I*. The North Carolina Supreme Court had held that the Nevada court did not have jurisdiction. The U.S. Supreme Court affirmed:

> The fact that the Nevada court found that they were domiciled there is entitled to respect, and more. The burden of undermining the verity which the Nevada decrees import rests heavily upon the assailant. But simply because the Nevada court found that it had power to award a divorce decree cannot, we have seen, foreclose reexamination by another State. Otherwise, as was pointed out long ago, a court's record would establish its power and the power would be proved by the record. Such circular reasoning would give one State a control over all the other States which the Full Faith and Credit Clause certainly did not confer. * * *

---

[a] *Editors' Note:* The Full Faith and Credit Clause provides that "Full Faith and Credit shall be given in each State to the public Acts, Records, and judicial Proceedings of every other State. And the Congress may by general Laws prescribe the Manner in which such Acts, Records and Proceedings shall be proved, and the Effect thereof." U.S. Const. Art. IV, § 1.

[T]he existence of domicil in Nevada [is] the decisive issue. * * * If the jury found, as they were told, that petitioners had domicils in North Carolina and went to Nevada "simply and solely for the purpose of obtaining" divorces, intending to return to North Carolina on obtaining them, they never lost their North Carolina domicils nor acquired new domicils in Nevada. Domicil, the jury was instructed, was that place where a person "has voluntarily fixed his abode * * * not for a mere special or temporary purpose, but with a present intention of making it his home, either permanently or for an indefinite or unlimited length of time."

* * *

Id. at 233–36. *Williams II* upheld the convictions of Williams and Hendrix for bigamous cohabitation because the Nevada court did not have subject matter jurisdiction; Williams "never lost" his North Carolina domicile. Note that the divorce decree could be valid in the issuing state but not been titled to full faith and credit.

Williams II concerned the validity of an *ex parte* divorce decree, that is, a decree issued when only one spouse was present. Three years after *Williams II,* the Supreme Court considered a challenge to a decree issued when both spouses were present before the divorce court.

In *Sherrer v. Sherrer,* 334 U.S. 343 (1948), Edward Sherrer alleged that his wife's petition for a Florida divorce was invalid because she had never been domiciled in Florida. After 14 years of marriage, Margaret Sherrer left the couple's Massachusetts home in 1944 for what she claimed was a Florida vacation with the parties' two children. Once in Florida, Margaret informed her husband that she intended to remain there. She found housing there, sent their older daughter to school, worked as a waitress, and filed for divorce 93 days after arriving in Florida, three days beyond the state's 90-day minimum residency requirement for filing divorce actions.

Margaret's complaint alleged that she was domiciled in Florida. Edward retained a Florida attorney and filed a general appearance in the divorce action. He denied the allegations of the complaint, including that Margaret was domiciled in Florida. The Florida court granted the divorce, finding that Margaret was, in fact, a Florida resident and that the court had subject matter jurisdiction. Three days later, Margaret married Henry Phelps, who had followed her to Florida from Massachusetts. They lived in Florida for two months before returning together to Massachusetts.

Edward did not appeal the Florida divorce decree. In a later action to clear title to land in Massachusetts, however, he alleged that Margaret had deserted him. The lower courts held that the Florida divorce decree was not entitled to full faith and credit in the Massachusetts courts because

Margaret had not validly established domicile in Florida. Margaret appealed to the U.S. Supreme Court, which reversed on the ground that the Florida divorce judgment was entitled to full faith and credit.

The Court distinguished *Sherrer* from *Williams I* and *II* because Edward was involved in the divorce proceedings and, consequently, had had the opportunity to challenge domicile at that time. The "obligation of full faith and credit" required that Massachusetts respect the Florida judgment. Margaret's actions might indicate that she never intended to remain in Florida, but Edward could not challenge the domicile issue in a second action.

NOTES AND QUESTIONS

1. *Domicile and the Nevada decree's validity.* Domicile is generally defined as the place where a person resides with the intent to remain indefinitely. Did O.B. Williams and Lillie Shaver Hendrix establish domicile in Nevada? What if they moved back to Nevada?

Williams I and *II* were decided during the fault-based era of divorce, when states were concerned that a spouse unable to prove fault in a state with strict divorce laws would establish domicile elsewhere to obtain a divorce, and then would return to the home state. What purposes, if any, does the domicile rule serve today under a no-fault regime? Does it matter that many jurisdictions retain both fault and no-fault regimes?

2. *Uniformity among states.* Should states enact a uniform divorce jurisdiction statute that would accord full faith and credit to *ex parte* divorce decrees where the petitioner satisfied a brief residency requirement, such as 90 days? Pursuant to the Full Faith and Credit Clause, should Congress enact legislation establishing such a requirement as a federal standard? If an individual has an *ex parte* divorce decree from one state, under what circumstances should that individual be able to remarry?

3. *The long view.* These cases involve state efforts to control their citizens' status. Do the Supreme Court's opinions allow individuals themselves, rather than the state, "the ability to choose which jurisdiction would control their marital status"? Ann Laquer Estin, *Family Law Federalism: Divorce and the Constitution,* 16 Wm. & Mary Bill Rts. J. 381, 383 (2007). If you were addressing a continuing legal education audience of family lawyers, what rule(s) of decision would you glean from the Supreme Court's two *Williams* decisions and *Sherrer*?

B. RESIDENCY AND SERVICE REQUIREMENTS

In addition to the domicile requirement, almost all states have enacted statutes requiring residency for a specified period before a court may issue a divorce decree (as you learned in Chapter 8). *See Chart 4: Grounds for Divorce and Residency Requirements,* 51 Fam. L.Q. 565, 560–67 (2018). The two words (domicile and residency) may often be used interchangeably in casual communication, but they have different legal significance. Intent *[Residency vs. Domicile]* distinguishes residency (simply the physical habitation of a place) from domicile (the place a person considers his or her permanent home).

1.   Residency: In the following case, the Supreme Court considered whether the Constitution allows states to deny access to their courts for a party seeking a divorce.   *[→ yes]*

SOSNA V. IOWA
Supreme Court of the United States, 1975.
419 U.S. 393.

[1 year residency requirement]

MR. JUSTICE REHNQUIST delivered the opinion of the Court.

Appellant Carol Sosna married Michael Sosna on September 5, 1964, in Michigan. They lived together in New York between October 1967 and August 1971, after which date they separated but continued to live in New York. In August 1972, appellant moved to Iowa with her three children, *[facts]* and the following month she petitioned the District Court of Jackson County, Iowa, for a dissolution of her marriage. Michael Sosna, who had been personally served with notice of the action when he came to Iowa to visit his children, made a special appearance to contest the jurisdiction of the Iowa court. The Iowa court dismissed the petition for lack of jurisdiction, finding that Michael Sosna was not a resident of Iowa and appellant had not been a resident of the State of Iowa for one year preceding the filing of her petition. In so doing the Iowa court applied the provisions of Iowa Code § 598.6 (1973) requiring that the petitioner in such an action be "for the last year a resident of the state."

* * *

II

The durational residency requirement under attack in this case is a part of Iowa's comprehensive statutory regulation of domestic relations, an area that has long been regarded as a virtually exclusive province of the States. * * *

* * *

[Carol Sosna's argument]

Appellant contends that the Iowa requirement of one year's residence is unconstitutional for two separate reasons: *first*, because it establishes two classes of persons and discriminates against those who have recently exercised their right to travel to Iowa, thereby contravening the Court's holdings in [prior cases]; and, *second*, because it denies a litigant the opportunity to make an individualized showing of bona fide residence and therefore denies such residents access to the only method of legally dissolving their marriage.

State statutes imposing durational residency requirements were, of course, invalidated when imposed by States as a qualification for [welfare payments, for voting,] and for medical care. But none of those cases intimated that the States might never impose durational residency requirements, and such a proposition was in fact expressly disclaimed. What those cases had in common was that the durational residency requirements they struck down were justified on the basis of budgetary or recordkeeping considerations which were held insufficient to outweigh the constitutional claims of the individuals. But Iowa's divorce residency requirement is of a different stripe. Appellant was not irretrievably foreclosed from obtaining some part of what she sought[.] * * * She would eventually qualify for the same sort of adjudication which she demanded virtually upon her arrival in the State. Iowa's requirement delayed her access to the courts, but, by fulfilling it, she could ultimately have obtained the same opportunity for adjudication which she asserts ought to have been hers at an earlier point in time.

Iowa's residency requirement may reasonably be justified on grounds other than purely budgetary considerations or administrative convenience. A decree of divorce is not a matter in which the only interested parties are the State as a sort of "grantor," and a divorce petitioner such as appellant in the role of "grantee." Both spouses are obviously interested in the proceedings, since it will affect their marital status and very likely their property rights. Where a married couple has minor children, a decree of divorce would usually include provisions for their custody and support. With consequences of such moment riding on a divorce decree issued by its courts, Iowa may insist that one seeking to initiate such a proceeding have the modicum of attachment to the State required here.

Such a requirement additionally furthers the State's parallel interests both in avoiding officious intermeddling in matters in which another State has a paramount interest, and in minimizing the susceptibility of its own divorce decrees to collateral attack. A State such as Iowa may quite reasonably decide that it does not wish to become a divorce mill for unhappy spouses who have lived there as short a time as appellant had when she commenced her action in the state court after having long resided elsewhere. Until such time as Iowa is convinced that appellant intends to remain in the State, it lacks the "nexus between person and place of such permanence as to control the creation of legal relations and responsibilities of the utmost significance." [*Williams II*.] Perhaps even more important, Iowa's interests extend beyond its borders and include the recognition of its divorce decrees by other States under the Full Faith and Credit Clause of the Constitution, Art. IV, § 1. For that purpose, this Court has often stated that "judicial power to grant a divorce—jurisdiction, strictly speaking—is founded on domicil." [*Williams II*.] Where a divorce decree is entered after a finding of domicile in *ex parte* proceedings, this Court has held that the finding of domicile is not binding upon another State and may be disregarded in the face of "cogent evidence" to the contrary. [*Williams II.*] For that reason, the State asked to enter such a decree is entitled to insist that the putative divorce petitioner satisfy something more than the bare minimum of constitutional requirements before a divorce may be granted. The State's decision to exact a one-year residency requirement as a matter of policy is therefore buttressed by a quite permissible inference that this requirement not only effectuates state substantive policy but likewise provides a greater safeguard against successful collateral attack than would a requirement of bona fide residence alone. * * *

↑ 1-year residency is allowed

We therefore hold that the state interest in requiring that those who seek a divorce from its courts be genuinely attached to the State, as well as a desire to insulate divorce decrees from the likelihood of collateral attack, requires a different resolution of the constitutional issue presented than [those cases invalidating state statutes imposing durational requirements in the contexts of welfare payments, voting, and medical care].

Nor are we of the view that the failure to provide an individualized determination of residency violates the Due Process Clause of the Fourteenth Amendment. * * *

In *Boddie v. Connecticut* [401 U.S. 371 (1971)], this Court held that Connecticut might not deny access to divorce courts to those persons who could not afford to pay the required fee. Because of the exclusive role played by the State in the termination of marriages, it was held that indigents could not be denied an opportunity to be heard "absent a countervailing state interest of overriding significance." [*Id.*] at 377. But the gravamen of appellant Sosna's claim is not total deprivation, as in *Boddie*, but only delay. The operation of the filing fee in *Boddie* served to exclude forever a certain segment of the population from obtaining a divorce in the courts of Connecticut. No similar total deprivation is present in appellant's case, and the delay which attends the enforcement of the one-year durational residency requirement is, for the reasons previously stated, consistent with the provisions of the United States Constitution.

Affirmed.

* * *

[The dissenting opinion of WHITE, J., is omitted.]

MR. JUSTICE MARSHALL, with whom MR. JUSTICE BRENNAN joins, dissenting.

* * *

As we have made clear in *Shapiro* [*v. Thompson*, 394 U.S. 618 (1969)], and subsequent cases, any classification that penalizes exercise of the constitutional right to travel is invalid unless it is justified by a compelling governmental interest. * * *

* * *

I

The Court omits altogether what should be the first inquiry: whether the right to obtain a divorce is of sufficient importance that its denial to recent immigrants constitutes a penalty on interstate travel. In my view, it clearly meets that standard. The previous decisions of this Court make it plain that the right of marital association is one of the most basic rights conferred on the individual by the State. The interests associated with marriage and divorce have repeatedly been accorded particular deference, and the right to marry has been termed "one of the vital personal rights essential to the orderly pursuit of happiness by free men." *Loving v. Virginia,* 388 U.S. 1, 12 (1967). * * *

II

Having determined that the interest in obtaining a divorce is of substantial social importance, I would scrutinize Iowa's durational residency requirement to determine whether it constitutes a reasonable means of furthering important interests asserted by the State. * * *

The Court proposes three defenses for the Iowa statute: first, the residency requirement merely delays receipt of the benefit in question—it does not deprive the applicant of the benefit altogether; second, since significant social consequences may follow from the conferral of a divorce, the State may legitimately regulate the divorce process; and third, the State has interests both in protecting itself from use as a "divorce mill" and in protecting its judgments from possible collateral attack in other States. In my view, the first two defenses provide no significant support for the statute in question here. Only the third has any real force.

A

With the first justification, the Court seeks to distinguish [earlier] cases. Yet the distinction the Court draws seems to me specious. Iowa's residency requirement, the Court says, merely forestalls access to the courts; applicants seeking welfare payments, medical aid, and the right to vote, on the other hand, suffer unrecoverable losses throughout the waiting period. This analysis, however, ignores the severity of the deprivation suffered by the divorce petitioner who is forced to wait a year for relief. *See Stanley v. Illinois,* 405 U.S. 645, 647 (1972). The injury accompanying that delay is not directly measurable in money terms like the loss of welfare benefits, but it cannot reasonably be argued that when the year has elapsed, the petitioner is made whole. The year's wait prevents remarriage and locks both partners into what may be an intolerable, destructive relationship. * * *

B

I find the majority's second argument no more persuasive. The Court forgoes reliance on the usual justifications for durational residency requirements—budgetary considerations and administrative convenience. * * * The critical importance of the divorce process, however, weakens the argument for a long residency requirement rather than strengthens it. The impact of the divorce decree only underscores the necessity that the State's regulation be evenhanded.

* * * * I fail to see how any legitimate objective of Iowa's divorce regulations would be frustrated by granting equal access to new state residents. To draw on an analogy, the States have great interests in the local voting process and wide latitude in regulating that process. Yet one regulation that the States may not impose is an unduly long residency requirement. * * *

C

The Court's third justification seems to me the only one that warrants close consideration. Iowa has a legitimate interest in protecting itself against invasion by those seeking quick divorces in a forum with relatively lax divorce laws, and it may have some interest in avoiding collateral attacks on its decree in other States. These interests, however, would adequately be protected by a simple requirement of domicile—physical presence plus intent to remain—which would remove the rigid one-year barrier while permitting the State to restrict the availability of its divorce process to citizens who are genuinely its own.

* * *

* * * In sum, concerns about the need for a long residency requirement to defray collateral attacks on state judgments seem more fanciful than real. If, as the majority assumes, Iowa is interested in assuring itself that its divorce petitioners are legitimately Iowa citizens, requiring petitioners to provide convincing evidence of bona fide domicile should be more than adequate to the task.

* * *

NOTES AND QUESTIONS

1. *Reasons for residency requirements.* Residency is only one element of domicile, so satisfying durational residency requirements does not necessarily establish domiciliary status. Given the full faith and credit requirements of domicile, why do states retain distinct residency periods for divorce? Do you agree with the *Sosna* majority or the dissent? Should states retain their residency requirements for divorce? Why or why not?

2. *Iowa or Nevada?* Many mid-twentieth century decisions concerning divorce jurisdiction involve a spouse who ran to Nevada for a divorce because, unlike other states, it required only a short residency period. Nevada's six-week residency requirement is still viewed as fairly short, but that state is no longer the quickest place for divorce. Alaska, Louisiana, South Dakota, and Washington do not impose any minimum period of residency before divorce. *Chart 4: Grounds for Divorce and Residency Requirements,* 51 Fam. L.Q. 560–67 (2018). Absence of a durational residency requirement essentially means that a spouse with money can travel to one of these states, instantly declare domicile, file for divorce, and then re-establish domicile in the original state. While a number of states have eliminated the residency requirement or implemented more lenient requirements, some states continue to impose stringent residency requirements. For example, in *Barth v. Barth*, 862 N.E.2d 496, 500 (Ohio 2007), the court held that a wife seeking a divorce did not meet the state's six-month residency requirement when she had moved to California for a little over a month to join her husband, returned to Ohio, and then immediately filed for divorce.

3. *Relocated parties.* Does a court retain authority to render further binding rulings in a case after each divorced party has relocated to another state? The Rhode Island Supreme Court held that the state's courts retained authority over a woman who had filed for divorce (and soon moved to Pennsylvania) and her husband, who lived in New Jersey. The court reasoned that the wife had satisfied Rhode Island's domicile and residency requirements, and that the state's divorce jurisdiction statute "does not require that the party remain a domiciled inhabitant or resident of the state for the petition to be granted;" otherwise, future plaintiffs who were dissatisfied with the divorce proceedings in Rhode Island could "forum shop" their complaints in another state. *Rogers v. Rogers*, 18 A.3d 491, 494 (R.I. 2011).

———

2. *Service of process.* As in all civil litigation, to obtain jurisdiction, the plaintiff must serve the defendant in accordance with the applicable statutory and rules requirements. In most states, service of process may be made on an individual outside the jurisdiction either by personal service or by mailing a copy of the summons and complaint to the individual by registered or certified mail, return receipt requested. At a minimum, due process requires that notice be reasonably calculated, under all the circumstances, to apprise interested parties of the pendency of the action and afford them an opportunity to be heard.

Some jurisdictions explicitly allow service by publication in domestic relations cases when the defendant cannot be located. For example, the Washington statute provides:

> When the defendant cannot be found within the state, and upon the filing of an affidavit of the plaintiff * * * stating that he or she believes that the defendant is not a resident of the state, or cannot

be found therein, and that he or she has deposited a copy of the summons * * * and complaint in the post office, directed to the defendant at his or her place of residence, unless it is stated in the affidavit that such residence is not known to the affiant * * * the service may be made by publication [in an action] for (a) establishment or modification of a parenting plan or residential schedule; or (b) dissolution of marriage, legal separation, or declaration of invalidity * * *.

Wash. Rev. Code § 4.28 100 (2018). Consider whether this statute adequately protect the interests at stake in divorce.

A few courts have approved service of process for divorce proceedings by email, Facebook, or other social networking sites as an alternative to notice by publication; *see Baidoo v. Blood-Dzraku*, 5 N.Y.S.3d 709, 716 (Sup. Ct. 2015) ("plaintiff is granted permission to serve defendant with the divorce summons using a private message through Facebook"). It remains unclear whether such service is constitutional and whether, as due process requires, it "is reasonably calculated to reach interested parties." *Mullane v. Cent. Hanover Bank & Tr. Co.*, 339 U.S. 306, 318 (1950).

It has been argued that "social media provides new avenues of achieving constitutionally sufficient notice." Angela Upchurch, *'Hacking' Service of Process: Using Social Media to Provide Constitutionally Sufficient Service of Process*, 38 U. Ark. Little Rock L. Rev. 559, 559–60 (2016).

PROBLEM 17-3

You are a member of your state legislature, which is considering whether to expand service of process to permit various social media methods. What will you decide?

C. COVENANT MARRIAGE

Under covenant marriage statutes in Louisiana, Arizona and Arkansas, a small number of couples have agreed to a marriage with strong restraints against divorce (discussed in Chapter 8). The question then arises as to whether one spouse may file for conventional divorce in a state that has not enacted a covenant marriage statute.

Running to another state to obtain a divorce seems to resemble a full faith and credit *Williams*-type dilemma, but establishing residency and domicile in the second state is not the problem in covenant marriage cases. The problem instead concerns the specific provisions of the covenant marriage itself; for example, in Louisiana, the couples agree that Louisiana law will control their marriage. Nonetheless, regardless of the couple's intent to create a covenant marriage with strict requirements for divorce, covenant marriage still may not prevent one spouse from traveling to another state to invoke that state's no-fault divorce laws. The second state, because of its connection to the divorce petitioner, appears likely to apply its own laws instead of the covenant marriage laws. *See Blackburn v. Blackburn*, 180 So.3d 16 (Ala. Civ. App. 2015) (applying divorce law of Alabama, where parties were domiciled, to Louisiana covenant marriage).

NOTES AND QUESTIONS

1.   *Interstate recognition revisited.* In applying its divorce laws, should a state be required to respect other states' conceptions of covenant marriage? As discussed earlier, this was an important issue for same-sex married couples until the Supreme Court's 2015 decision in *Obergefell, supra.*

2.   *Comity.* Would Louisiana recognize another state's decree dissolving a covenant marriage? One state may use the principle of comity to recognize another state's judicial decisions. The doctrine of comity is based on respect for the sovereignty of other states or countries. Even when the forum state is not required to recognize a judgment issued by a foreign jurisdiction, the forum state may do so pursuant to the principles of comity. As a matter of respect, convenience, and expediency, there is respect for recognizing appropriately-rendered foreign judicial decrees. 44B Am. Jur. 2d, Int'l Law § 9 (2018).

Comity does not require deference to another state or country's determination, but " 'it is an expression of one State's entirely voluntary decision to defer to the policy of another. Such a decision may be perceived as promoting uniformity of decision [or] as encouraging harmony among participants in a system of cooperative federalism.' " *Debra H. v. Janice R.*, 930 N.E.2d 184, 196 (N.Y. 2010).

3. APPROPRIATE LOCATIONS FOR LITIGATING ALIMONY AND PROPERTY DISTRIBUTION

A court can issue a divorce decree without personal jurisdiction over both parties, but litigation concerning alimony awards and distribution of property present different jurisdictional issues.

A. PERSONAL JURISDICTION REQUIREMENT FOR ALIMONY AND PROPERTY DISTRIBUTION

Divorce is available based on one spouse's domicile, regardless of whether a court has personal jurisdiction over the other spouse. A court may award alimony or property distribution, however, only where it has personal jurisdiction over both spouses.

Estin v. Estin, 334 U.S. 541 (1948), was the Supreme Court's first discussion of personal jurisdiction in the alimony-property distribution context. Gertrude and Joseph Estin married and then separated in New York. Gertrude Estin sued her husband in a New York court which, after he appeared, granted the wife a separation decree that included an award of permanent alimony. The husband subsequently moved to Nevada, obtained an absolute divorce that did not provide for alimony, and he stopped paying alimony. The Supreme Court upheld the validity of the husband's Nevada divorce judgment, but held that only a court with personal jurisdiction over the wife could change the New York alimony decree's effect:

> * * * New York evinced a concern with this broken marriage when both parties were domiciled in New York and before Nevada had any concern with it. New York was rightly concerned lest the abandoned spouse be left impoverished and perhaps become a public charge. The problem of her livelihood and support is plainly a matter in which her community had a legitimate interest. The New York court, having jurisdiction over both parties, undertook to protect her by granting her a judgment of permanent alimony. Nevada, however, apparently follows the rule that dissolution of the marriage puts an end to a support order. But the question is whether Nevada could under any circumstances adjudicate rights of respondent under the New York judgment when she was not personally served or did not appear in the proceeding.
>
> * * *
>
> The New York judgment is a property interest of respondent, created by New York in a proceeding in which both parties were present.

Id. at 547–48. *Estin* thus recognized the jurisdictional concept of "divisible divorce," which treats property, support, and custodial rights arising from marriage differently than the marital status itself.

In 1957, the Court extended the divisible divorce doctrine to instances in which support rights had not been established by a support order prior to the divorce. In *Vanderbilt v. Vanderbilt*, 354 U.S. 416 (1957), the Court held that a state with the requisite jurisdictional contacts may grant support to an ex-spouse, even after another state had issued a valid divorce decree. The couple had resided in California during the marriage, and the wife moved to New York after the parties separated. Mr. Vanderbilt secured a final divorce in Nevada, without serving process on his wife and without her appearance. Mrs. Vanderbilt then sued in New York for separation and maintenance, sequestering Mr. Vanderbilt's New York property to satisfy personal jurisdiction. The Court rejected the husband's argument that New York had no jurisdiction to order support after dissolution of the spouses' marriage:

> * * * Since the wife was not subject to its jurisdiction, the Nevada divorce court had no power to extinguish any right which she had under the law of New York to financial support from her husband.

It has long been the constitutional rule that a court cannot adjudicate a personal claim or obligation unless it has jurisdiction over the person of the defendant. Here, the Nevada divorce court was as powerless to cut off the wife's support right as it would have been to order the husband to pay alimony if the wife had brought the divorce action and he had not been subject to the divorce court's jurisdiction.

Id. at 418–19.

As the following decision shows, state courts continue to use the principles enunciated in *Estin* and *Vanderbilt* to decide cases involving "divisible divorces."

GABOURY V. GABOURY
Superior Court of Pennsylvania, 2009.
988 A.2d 672.

OPINION BY BOWES, J.:

Lisa Gaboury ("Wife") appeals from the August 29, 2008 order granting her divorce from Christopher Gaboury ("Husband"). On June 3, 2008, the trial court dismissed all economic claims against Husband, determining that it had jurisdiction to dissolve the parties' marriage but lacked the necessary personal jurisdiction over Husband to adjudicate related economic claims. For the following reasons, we affirm.

Husband and Wife met on an Internet site while Husband was living in Texas, and Wife was living in Canada. In April 2004, the parties moved from their respective locations to Pennsylvania and married a year later on April 21, 2005, in Lancaster, Pennsylvania. They resided in Pennsylvania in rental housing until Husband's job transfer in December 2006, when they relocated to Wisconsin and lived in a rented apartment. The couple separated, and Wife moved to Beaver County, Pennsylvania, in August 2007. Husband remained in the marital residence in Wisconsin.

Wife filed a divorce complaint in Pennsylvania on March 12, 2008, alleging an irretrievable breakdown of the marriage pursuant to [Pennsylvania law]. In her complaint, Wife set forth economic claims for equitable distribution, counsel fees, expenses, spousal support, alimony *pendente lite*, alimony, and permanent alimony. On April 9, 2008, Husband filed preliminary objections challenging the court's personal jurisdiction over him. Wife filed an answer [ ] on April 28, 2008. Following a hearing on May 19, 2008, the trial court concluded that it had jurisdiction to dissolve the bonds of matrimony, but it did not have the requisite personal jurisdiction over Husband to decide any economic claims. * * *

* * *

Our Divorce Code requires a six-month residency period in order to maintain an action for divorce, and domiciliary intent is inferred from the residency. Instantly, since Wife moved to Pennsylvania seven months before initiating divorce proceedings, she satisfied the residency requirement and was able to obtain a divorce in this Commonwealth. In order to resolve the parties' ancillary economic claims, however, the trial court required personal jurisdiction over Husband. *See Shaffer v. Heitner*, 433 U.S. 186 (1977) (economic claims that may be joined pursuant to authority of Divorce Code require *in personam* jurisdiction).

In declining to find the existence of personal jurisdiction over Husband, the trial court explained:

> The Due Process Clause of the Fourteenth Amendment operates as a limitation on the jurisdiction of state courts. A valid judgment imposing a personal obligation or duty in favor of the plaintiff may be entered only by a court having jurisdiction over the person of the defendant. *Pennoyer v. Neff*, 95 U.S. 714 (1877). Due process requires that in order to subject a defendant to a judgment *in personam*, if he is not present within the territory of the forum, he [must] have certain minimum contacts with it such that the maintenance of the suit does not offend traditional notions of fair play and substantial justice. *International Shoe Co. v. Washington*, 326 U.S. 310 (1945).

There were no children born of this marriage, and any marital property if it exists, is located in Wisconsin. The parties have acquired no real estate during the term of the marriage, in either Pennsylvania or Wisconsin. Unilateral conduct of the Plaintiff/Wife by moving to Pennsylvania cannot satisfy the requirement of sufficient contact with Pennsylvania for this Court to have personal jurisdiction over the Defendant. This Court believes that the Defendant of his own volition must do a purposeful act that provides the minimum contact necessary for personal jurisdiction.

The result herein, the court's grant of a party's request for dissolution of a marriage and the concomitant dismissal of economic claims, effected a "divisible divorce." In *Estin v. Estin*, 334 U.S. 541 (1948), the United States Supreme Court held that a foreign divorce decree, although entitled to full faith and credit regarding the divorce itself, is not necessarily dispositive of the economic aspects of the divorce. Where a foreign decree has failed to address the economic aspects of the divorce, the divorce is "divisible," leaving such questions open for determination in other jurisdictions. The "divisible divorce" concept is recognized in Pennsylvania.

As the *Estin* Court explained, "The requirements of procedural due process [are] satisfied and the domicile" of one party in the forum state is the "foundation for a decree effecting a change in the marital capacity of both parties in all the other States of the Union. . . ." *Estin v. Estin, supra* at 544. That same court, however, lacks jurisdiction to address issues of alimony and equitable distribution if it does not possess personal jurisdiction over the defendant. *Vanderbilt v. Vanderbilt*, 354 U.S. 416 (1957). In such a case, the inability of the court to address ancillary economic claims results in a divisible divorce.

Although concluding that it had subject matter jurisdiction to enter a divorce decree, the trial court herein determined that it could not resolve the economic claims due to a lack of personal jurisdiction over Husband. The court could have acquired *in personam* jurisdiction over Husband if he had been present in Pennsylvania at the time process was served, if he was a domiciliary of Pennsylvania at the time process was served, if he had consented to personal jurisdiction, or if there existed sufficient minimum contacts with Pennsylvania to support the exercise of *in personam* jurisdiction by extraterritorial service.

While personal jurisdiction over non-resident defendants may be conferred by 42 Pa. C.S. § 5322, the Pennsylvania Long-Arm Statute, certain conditions must be met:

> The Pennsylvania Long-Arm Statute, 42 Pa. C.S. § 5322, is basically divided into two sections. Section (a) contains ten subsections, which specify particular types of contact with Pennsylvania which will be deemed sufficient to warrant the exercise of long-arm personal jurisdiction. Section (b) is a catchall provision which authorizes the exercise of personal jurisdiction over persons who do not come within one of the express provisions of the ten subsections of section (a) so long as the minimum requisites of federal constitutional law are met. * * *

* * *

* * * [Wife] contends that Husband's actions in Pennsylvania prior to Wife's filing for divorce satisfy the minimum contacts requirement of 42 Pa. C.S. § 5322(b). In support, she emphasizes that the parties were married in Pennsylvania, they resided here for two years and eight months before relocating to Wisconsin, where they lived for six months before separating, and that prior to moving to Wisconsin, Husband had worked in Pennsylvania. * * *

* * * Wife suggests that "if the court has jurisdiction over a divorce, it has jurisdiction over the economic issues," maintaining it "would be very odd for a Pennsylvania court to be able to decide a divorce, but not be able to divide the parties' marital property. . . ." Odd or not, that is exactly the outcome in a divisible divorce.

* * *

As to Wife's contention that the record reveals the requisite minimum contacts to establish personal jurisdiction over Husband, we do not agree. Husband was not served in Pennsylvania, he has not consented to the jurisdiction of the court, and the requisite minimum contacts under the long-arm statute do not exist. The purpose of the minimum-contacts test is to protect a defendant from having to litigate a matter in a distant forum unless his contacts with that forum "make it just to force him to defend there." *Phillips Petroleum Co. v. Shutts*, 472 U.S. 797 (1985). The standard of minimum contacts, set out by Pennsylvania's long-arm statute, is reasonableness. * * *

* * *

In the present case, it is undisputed that the parties left Pennsylvania and established their marital residence in Wisconsin. Indeed, Wife admitted that Wisconsin was the last marital domicile. Wife asserted that the parties relocated to Wisconsin in December 2006 due to Husband's job transfer and lived there together until August 2007 when she unilaterally moved from the marital residence to Pennsylvania. Thus, in the case at bar, there is no contention that Pennsylvania, not Wisconsin, is the last marital domicile.

* * *

In the case at bar, the trial court correctly noted that there were no children born of the marriage, the parties have acquired no real estate in either Pennsylvania or Wisconsin, and any existing marital property was located in Wisconsin, the place of the last marital domicile, where Husband remained. Husband's only contacts with Pennsylvania occurred prior to the couple's relocation to Wisconsin.

Thus, the trial court's determination that Husband did not satisfy the requisite minimum contacts to support *in personam* jurisdiction is supported by the record. As there were insufficient contacts between the nonresident Husband and Pennsylvania, the exercise of personal jurisdiction over him would violate both the Pennsylvania Long-Arm Statute and the Due Process Clause of the Fourteenth Amendment to the United States Constitution. Viewing Husband's contacts in the light most favorable to Wife, the nonmoving party, the granting of Husband's preliminary objections to the trial court's jurisdiction over the economic claims, which resulted in the dismissal of those claims for lack of personal jurisdiction, was proper.

Order affirmed.

NOTES AND QUESTIONS

1. *When? Gaboury* explains the circumstances under which the court could have awarded alimony. Why would these circumstances have supported jurisdiction?

2. *Divisible divorce: what happens next?* An *ex parte* divorce ends the marriage, but what happens to the economic issues? Where alimony otherwise appears appropriate, courts tend to award it even after one spouse obtains a foreign *ex parte* divorce.

In *Scharer v. Scharer*, 2001 WL 1203408 (Conn. Super. Ct. Sept. 17, 2001) (unpublished opinion), for example, the court upheld the husband's California *ex parte* divorce decree because he had established domicile there and thus could file for divorce in the state. However, because California lacked personal jurisdiction over the wife, the Connecticut court did not recognize the California court's alimony order, and held that Connecticut courts, which had personal jurisdiction over both spouses, provided the appropriate forum for considering alimony. Many state statutes recognize the authority of the state courts to award alimony or divide property after another court, which lacked personal jurisdiction over the person seeking alimony, has granted a divorce. *See, e.g.*, MD Code, Family Law § 11–105 (2018) (alimony); S.C. Code § 20–3–620 (2018) (distribute property).

What is the justification for awarding alimony or dividing property after a court in another state has validly dissolved the marriage?

3. *Different standards for divorce and property.* Why should a court have jurisdiction to dissolve a marriage *ex parte*, but be required to have personal jurisdiction over both parties before dividing marital assets and debts?

A NOTE ON OBTAINING PERSONAL JURISDICTION THROUGH LONG-ARM STATUTES

State long-arm statutes expand the availability of personal jurisdiction over parties who are not physically present within the state. Some long-arm statutes apply specifically to domestic relations matters. For example, New York provides for personal jurisdiction over a non-resident defendant in divorce cases:

> [N]otwithstanding the fact that he or she no longer is a resident or domiciliary of this state, * * * if the party seeking support is a resident of or domiciled in this state at the time such demand is made, provided that this state was the matrimonial domicile of the parties before their separation, or the defendant abandoned the plaintiff in this state, or the claim for support, alimony, maintenance, distributive awards or special relief in matrimonial actions accrued under the laws of this state or under an agreement executed in this state.

N.Y. C.P.L.R. § 302(b) (2018). In addition, all states have enacted the Uniform Interstate Family Support Act (UIFSA), discussed in Section 5, which applies to alimony and child support claims. Long-arm statutes are often more restrictive than what would be permissible under the Due Process Clause.

NOTE AND QUESTIONS

How far? Should spousal support long-arm statutes be more restrictive than general long-arm statutes? Should the state court be able to assert jurisdiction over a party who is no longer a resident, cannot be found in that state, or does not own property in the state?

B. LIMITS ON OUT-OF-STATE PROPERTY DISTRIBUTION

The Constitution requires states to give full faith and credit to decisions entered in the courts of other states, but this requirement does not extend to judgments over real property located in other states. Because property distribution is central to many domestic relations cases, this jurisdictional restriction is crucial in dissolution proceedings.

The Supreme Court first addressed this real property issue in *Fall v. Eastin*, 215 U.S. 1 (1909). After the husband and wife jointly acquired real property in Nebraska, they moved to Washington state where they separated a few years later. The Washington court had personal jurisdiction over both parties, but could not convey land that the couple owned in another state.

Later decisions, however, have held that a court may affect disposition of real property located outside the state, provided that the judgment is directed at the person rather than the property: courts distinguish judgments calculated to affect title to property itself from orders directing owners subject to their jurisdiction to take certain actions concerning property located outside the jurisdiction. *Roberts v. Locke*, 304 P.3d 116, 120 (Wyo. 2013); *see Johnson v. Johnson*, 891 N.Y.S.2d 848, 850 (App. Div. 2009).

In *Breitenstine v. Breitenstine*, 62 P.3d 587 (Wyo. 2003), for example, the court struggled with its limited jurisdiction over property when it sought to divide the marital estate, including real property. The court could not require the husband to transfer his out-of-state property directly to the wife because it did not have jurisdiction over the real property. Instead, the court held that property must be divided "to the extent necessary to satisfy the judgment hereby awarded in favor of the [wife], provide for the alimony payments herein ordered, provide for the child support payments herein ordered, or to comply otherwise with the orders of this Court." *Id.* at 595. Without directly disposing of the out-of-state property, the court nonetheless made a determination affecting it.

Similarly, in *In re Marriage of Kowalewski*, 182 P.3d 959 (Wash. 2008). the court upheld an award of title to an apartment and farm located in Poland. It observed that while "a court in one state does not have power directly to affect title to real property located outside the state" based on the principle that "jurisdiction in rem (directly over the thing itself) exists only in the state where the real property is located," a court may nonetheless "indirectly affect title by means of an in personam decree operating on the person over whom it has jurisdiction." *Id.* at 962. You may remember similar contentious issues from Chapter 9 concerning equitable distribution of marital property.

PROBLEM 17-4

Sally and James have been married for 15 years, and are now seeking a divorce. They have lived in Michigan during the entire marriage. Ten years ago, the couple bought a condominium in Florida as an investment, which they have rented out to families visiting the Orlando area. Sally and James have not been to their condo in seven years, and all their rentals take place through an agent located in Michigan. Can a Michigan court order a change in title to the Florida condo, and what laws would govern that determination?

4. CHILD CUSTODY JURISDICTION

Child custody jurisdiction raises a series of issues, including where a decree may be entered, when other states must respect that decree, and which state may modify that decree. Chapter 13 discusses the international impact of these decisions.

A. WHICH STATE HAS JURISDICTION TO ISSUE A CUSTODY ORDER?

1.   The Constitutional Context for Jurisdiction

The traditional view of custody jurisdiction was that only a court of the state where the child was domiciled could enter a custody decree. *See* Restatement of Conflict of Laws §§ 1, 17 (1934). Because a custody proceeding was viewed as being in rem, jurisdiction followed the child's location. Barbara Ann Atwood, *Child Custody Jurisdiction and Territoriality*, 52 Ohio St. L.J. 369, 377 (1991). This domicile rule was based on the theory that only the child's domiciliary state could issue a binding judgment. In the following case, the Supreme Court considered issues of child custody jurisdiction in a case involving an order issued by a court that did not have personal jurisdiction over the mother. As you read the opinions, consider which bases might be appropriate for a court to exercise jurisdiction over a child custody dispute.

MAY v. ANDERSON

Supreme Court of the United States, 1953.
345 U.S. 528.

MR. JUSTICE BURTON delivered the opinion of the Court.

The question presented is whether, in a habeas corpus proceeding attacking the right of a mother to retain possession of her minor children, an Ohio court must give full faith and credit to a Wisconsin decree awarding custody of the children to their father when that decree is obtained by the father in an *ex parte* divorce action in a Wisconsin court which had no personal jurisdiction over the mother. For the reasons hereafter stated, our answer is no.

This proceeding began July 5, 1951, when Owen Anderson, here called the appellee, filed a petition for a writ of habeas corpus in the Probate Court of Columbiana County, Ohio. He alleged that his former wife, Leona Anderson May, here called the appellant, was illegally restraining the liberty of their children, Ronald, Sandra and James, aged, respectively, 12, 8 and 5, by refusing to deliver them to him in response to a decree issued by the County Court of Waukesha County, Wisconsin [ ]. * * *

* * * [T]he Probate Court decided that it was obliged by the Full Faith and Credit Clause of the Constitution of the United States to accept the Wisconsin decree as binding upon the mother. Accordingly, proceeding to the merits of the case upon the issues presented by the stipulations of counsel, it ordered the children discharged from further restraint by her. That order has been held in abeyance and the children are still with her. * * *

* * *

The parties were married in Wisconsin and, until 1947, both were domiciled there. After marital troubles developed, they agreed in December, 1946, that appellant should take their children to Lisbon, Columbiana County, Ohio, and there think over her future course. By New Year's Day, she had decided not to return to Wisconsin and, by telephone, she informed her husband of that decision.

Within a few days he filed suit in Wisconsin, seeking both an absolute divorce and custody of the children. The only service of process upon appellant consisted of the delivery to her personally, in Ohio, of a copy of the Wisconsin summons and petition. Such service is authorized by a Wisconsin statute for use in an action for a divorce but that statute makes no mention of its availability in a proceeding for the custody of children. Appellant entered no appearance and took no part in this Wisconsin proceeding which produced not only a decree divorcing the parties from the bonds of matrimony but a decree purporting to award the custody of the children to their father, subject to a right of their mother to visit them at reasonable times. Appellant contests only the validity of the decree as to custody.

Armed with a copy of the decree and accompanied by a local police officer, appellee, in Lisbon, Ohio, demanded and obtained the children from their mother. The record does not disclose what took place between 1947 and 1951, except that the children remained with their father in Wisconsin until July 1, 1951. He then brought them back to Lisbon and permitted them to visit their mother. This time, when he demanded their return, she refused to surrender them.

Relying upon the Wisconsin decree, he promptly filed in the Probate Court of Columbiana County, Ohio, the petition for a writ of habeas corpus now before us. * * *

* * *

* * * [W]e have before us the elemental question whether a court of a state, where a mother is neither domiciled, resident nor present, may cut off her immediate right to the care, custody, management and companionship of her minor children without having jurisdiction over her *in personam*. Rights far more precious to appellant than property rights will be cut off if she is to be bound by the Wisconsin award of custody.

* * *

In [earlier cases], this Court upheld the validity of a Nevada divorce obtained *ex parte* by a husband, resident in Nevada, insofar as it dissolved the bonds of matrimony. At the same time, we held Nevada powerless to cut off, in that proceeding, a spouse's right to financial support under the prior decree of another state. In the instant case, we recognize that a mother's right to custody of her children is a personal right entitled to at least as much protection as her right to alimony.

In the instant case, the Ohio courts gave weight to appellee's contention that the Wisconsin award of custody binds appellant because, at the time it was issued, her children had a technical domicile in Wisconsin, although they were neither resident nor present there. We find it unnecessary to determine the children's legal domicile because, even if it be with their father, that does not give Wisconsin, certainly as against Ohio, the personal jurisdiction that it must have in order to deprive their mother of her personal right to their immediate possession.[8]

---

8   * * *

The instant case does not present the special considerations that arise where a parent, with or without minor children, leaves a jurisdiction for the purpose of escaping process or otherwise evading jurisdiction, and we do not have here the considerations that arise when children are unlawfully or surreptitiously taken by one parent from the other.

The judgment of the Supreme Court of Ohio, accordingly, is reversed and the cause is remanded to it for further proceedings not inconsistent with this opinion.

Reversed and remanded.

MR. JUSTICE CLARK, not having heard oral argument, took no part in the consideration or decision of this case.

MR. JUSTICE FRANKFURTER, concurring.

* * *

What is decided—the only thing the Court decides—is that the Full Faith and Credit Clause does not require Ohio, in disposing of the custody of children in Ohio, to accept, in the circumstances before us, the disposition made by Wisconsin. The Ohio Supreme Court felt itself so bound. This Court does not decide that Ohio would be precluded from recognizing, as a matter of local law, the disposition made by the Wisconsin court. For Ohio to give respect to the Wisconsin decree would not offend the Due Process Clause. Ohio is no more precluded from doing so than a court of Ontario or Manitoba would be, were the mother to bring the children into one of these provinces.

Property, personal claims, and even the marriage status (see, *e.g.*, *Sherrer v. Sherrer*, 334 U.S. 343), generally give rise to interests different from those relevant to the discharge of a State's continuing responsibility to children within her borders. Children have a very special place in life which law should reflect. Legal theories and their phrasing in other cases readily lead to fallacious reasoning it uncritically transferred to determination of a State's duty towards children. There are, of course, adjudications other than those pertaining to children, as for instance decrees of alimony, which may not be definitive even in the decreeing State, let alone binding under the Full Faith and Credit Clause. * * * But the child's welfare in a custody case has such a claim upon the State that its responsibility is obviously not to be foreclosed by a prior adjudication reflecting another State's discharge of its responsibility at another time. Reliance on opinions regarding out-of-State adjudications of property rights, personal claims or the marital status is bound to confuse analysis when a claim to the custody of children before the courts of one State is based on an award previously made by another State. Whatever light may be had from such opinions, they cannot give conclusive answers.

MR. JUSTICE JACKSON, whom MR. JUSTICE REED joins, dissenting.

The Court apparently is holding that the Federal Constitution prohibits Ohio from recognizing the validity of this Wisconsin divorce decree insofar as it settles custody of the couple's children. In the light of settled and unchallenged precedents of this Court, such a decision can only rest upon the proposition that Wisconsin's courts had no jurisdiction to make such a decree binding upon appellant.

* * *

The Court's decision holds that the state in which a child and one parent are domiciled and which is primarily concerned about his welfare cannot constitutionally adjudicate controversies as to his guardianship. The state's power here is defeated by the absence of the other parent for a period of two months. The convenience of a leave-taking parent is placed above the welfare of the child, but neither party is greatly aided in obtaining a decision. The Wisconsin courts cannot bind the mother, and the Ohio courts cannot bind the father. A state of the law such as this, where possession apparently is not merely nine points of the law but all of them and self-help the ultimate authority, has little to commend it in legal logic or as a principle of order in a federal system.

Nor can I agree on principle with the Court's treatment of the question of personal jurisdiction of the wife. I agree with its conclusion and that of the Ohio courts that Wisconsin never obtained jurisdiction of the person of the appellant in this action and therefore the jurisdiction must be rested on domicile of the husband and children. And I have heretofore expressed the view that such personal jurisdiction is necessary in cases where the domicile is obviously a contrived one or the claim of it a sham. But here the Court requires personal service upon a spouse who decamps before the State of good-faith domicile can make provision for custody and support of the children still legally domiciled within it. Wisconsin had a far more real concern with the transactions here litigated than have many of the divorce-mill forums whose judgments we have commanded their sister states to recognize.

In spite of the fact that judges and law writers long have recognized the similarity between the jurisdictional requirements for divorce and for custody, this decision appears to equate the jurisdictional requirements for a custody decree to those for an *in personam* money judgment. One reads the opinion in vain to discover reasons for this choice, unless it is found in the remark that for the wife "rights far more precious than property will be cut off" in the custody proceeding. The force of this cardiac consideration is self-evident, but it seems to me to reflect a misapprehension as to the nature of a custody proceeding or a revision of the views that have heretofore prevailed. * * *

The difference between a proceeding involving the status, custody and support of children and one involving adjudication of property rights is too apparent to require elaboration. In the former, courts are no longer concerned primarily with the proprietary claims of the contestants for the "*res*" before the court, but with the welfare of the "*res*" itself. Custody is viewed not with the idea of adjudicating rights *in* the children, as if they were chattels, but rather with the idea of making the best disposition possible for the welfare of the children. To speak of a court's "cutting off" a mother's right to custody of her children, as if it raised problems similar to those involved in "cutting off" her rights in a plot of ground, is to obliterate these obvious distinctions. Personal jurisdiction of all parties to be affected by a proceeding is highly desirable, to make certain that they have had valid notice and opportunity to be heard. But the assumption that it overrides all other considerations and in its absence a state is constitutionally impotent to resolve questions of custody flies in the face of our own cases. The wife's marital ties may be dissolved without personal jurisdiction over her by a state where the husband has a genuine domicile because the concern of that state with the welfare and marital status of its domiciliary is felt to be sufficiently urgent. * * *

* * *

I fear this decision will author new confusions. The interpretative concurrence, if it be a true interpretation, seems to reduce the law of custody to a rule of seize-and-run. I would affirm the decision of the Ohio courts that they should respect the judgment of the Wisconsin court, until it or some other court with equal or better claims to jurisdiction shall modify it.

[The dissenting opinion of MINTON, J. is omitted.]

NOTES AND QUESTIONS

1. *Jurisdictional concerns in practice.* Five justices joined the *May* majority opinion; one of them, Justice Frankfurter, also wrote a separate concurrence distinguishing between the requirements of the Due Process and Full Faith and Credit Clauses. According to the various opinions, what was the effect of the father's Wisconsin court decree? Based on *May*, when must a second state honor a first state's custody decree? To issue a custody decree that is valid in a second state, must the issuing court have personal jurisdiction over both parties?

2. *Lingering effects of* May. *May* led to considerable debate and criticism, just as Justice Jackson predicted. Moreover, many courts appeared to reject the plurality's holding in *May's* that personal jurisdiction was required. Indeed, the 1997 Uniform Child Custody Jurisdiction and Enforcement Act (UCCJEA) (which is discussed in the next Section) explains that "jurisdiction to make a child custody determination is subject matter jurisdiction." UCCJEA § 201, cmt. 2, 9 U.L.A., pt. IA, 649, 673 (1999). Personal jurisdiction over a child or a parent is not necessarily required under the UCCJEA. *Id.*

2. State Courts and Subject Matter Jurisdiction

Following *May v. Anderson*, a parent unhappy with one state's custody decree could move to another state and seek relitigation of the custody decision. The search for a legislative solution to achieve consistency in interstate jurisdictional child custody disputes resulted in promulgation of the Uniform Child Custody Jurisdiction Act (UCCJA) by the National Conference of Commissioners on Uniform State Law (NCCUSL) in 1968.[b] All 50 states, the District of Columbia, and the U.S. Virgin Islands adopted the Act. UCCJEA, prefatory note.

Despite widespread state adoption of the UCCJA, differing interpretations of its provisions produced uncertainty regarding enforcement of custody decisions.

In response to the problems that arose when courts did not feel compelled to give full faith and credit to other states' custody decrees under the UCCJA, Congress enacted the Parental Kidnapping Prevention Act (PKPA) in 1980. Pub. L. No. 96–611, 94 Stat. 3568 (1980) (codified at 28 U.S.C. § 1738A (2018). Despite its name, the Act is not limited to parental kidnapping cases, but applies to all interstate custody disputes.

The PKPA mandates that states give full faith and credit to a custody order that substantially complies with the statute's provisions. The PKPA clearly gives preference to home state jurisdiction, and allows another state to exercise jurisdiction only where no state qualifies as a home state. The PKPA further authorizes continuing exclusive jurisdiction in the state where the custody order was issued as long as one parent or the child remains there. The PKPA's provisions are still in effect today and are discussed in more detail later in the Chapter.

The PKPA did not settle all interstate jurisdictional problems. To resolve remaining issues, the NCCUSL promulgated the Uniform Child Custody Jurisdiction and Enforcement Act (UCCJEA) in 1997. Uniform Law Commission, UCCJEA (1997). The PKPA is federal legislation, focused on full faith and credit; the UCCJEA is state-focused, setting out when a court may assert initial jurisdiction, when a court must enforce a custody order from another state, and when a court has jurisdiction to modify a custody order.

Exclusive, continuing jurisdiction is a feature of both the PKPA and the UCCJEA. This concept deters forum shopping by granting subject matter jurisdiction to one court and then making it difficult for another court to assume authority. *See* Kevin Wessel, Comment, *Home Is Where the Court Is: Determining Residence for Child Custody Matters Under the UCCJEA*, 79 U. Chi. L. Rev. 1141, 1145 (2012).

---

[b]   *Editors' Note:* NCCUSL is now known as the Uniform Law Commission.

The UCCJEA is designed to: (1) prioritize home-state subject matter jurisdiction; (2) clarify emergency jurisdictional issues; (3) specify the meaning of exclusive continuing jurisdiction for the state that entered the child custody decree; and (4) specify the types of custody proceedings that are subject to the act. UCCJEA, prefatory note As of 2019, 49 states (all but Massachusetts) have adopted the UCCJEA. Uniform Law Commission, *Child Custody Jurisdiction and Enforcement Act* (2019).

a.　The UCCJEA

Portions of the UCCJEA are set out below. The Act relies firmly on the home state's initial and continuing subject matter jurisdiction, and does not require personal jurisdiction over the parents. Nonetheless, as the decisions in this Section show, even the UCCJEA and the PKPA together have not yet resolved all conflicts.

**UNIFORM CHILD CUSTODY JURISDICTION
AND ENFORCEMENT ACT**
9 U.L.A., pt. IA, 649 (1999).

§ 102.　Definitions.

* * *

(7)　"Home State" means the State in which a child lived with a parent or a person acting as a parent for at least six consecutive months immediately before the commencement of a child-custody proceeding. In the case of a child less than six months of age, the term means the State in which the child lived from birth with any of the persons mentioned. A period of temporary absence of any of the mentioned persons is part of the period.

* * *

§ 201.　Initial Child-Custody Jurisdiction.

(a)　* * * [A] court of this State has jurisdiction to make an initial child-custody determination only if:

(1)　this State is the home State of the child on the date of the commencement of the proceeding, or was the home State of the child within six months before the commencement of the proceeding and the child is absent from this State but a parent or person acting as a parent continues to live in this State;

(2)　a court of another State does not have jurisdiction under paragraph (1), or a court of the home State of the child has declined to exercise jurisdiction on the ground that this State is the more appropriate forum under Section 207 or 208, and:

(A) the child and the child's parents, or the child and at least one parent or a person acting as a parent, have a significant connection with this State other than mere physical presence; and

(B) substantial evidence is available in this State concerning the child's care, protection, training, and personal relationships;

(3) all courts having jurisdiction under paragraph (1) or (2) have declined to exercise jurisdiction on the ground that a court of this State is the more appropriate forum to determine the custody of the child under [other provisions of this Act]; or

(4) no court of any other State would have jurisdiction under the criteria specified in paragraph (1), (2), or (3).

(b) Subsection (a) is the exclusive jurisdictional basis for making a child-custody determination by a court of this State.

(c) Physical presence of, or personal jurisdiction over, a party or a child is not necessary or sufficient to make a child-custody determination.

§ 202.   Exclusive, Continuing Jurisdiction.

(a) Except as otherwise provided in Section 204, a court of this State which has made a child-custody determination consistent with Section 201 or 203 has exclusive, continuing jurisdiction over the determination until:

(1) a court of this State determines that neither the child, nor the child and one parent, nor the child and a person acting as a parent have a significant connection with this State and that substantial evidence is no longer available in this State concerning the child's care, protection, training, and personal relationships; or

(2) a court of this State or a court of another State determines that the child, the child's parents, and any person acting as a parent do not presently reside in this State.

(b) A court of this State which has made a child-custody determination and does not have exclusive, continuing jurisdiction under this section may modify that determination only if it has jurisdiction to make an initial determination under Section 201.

§ 204.   Temporary Emergency Jurisdiction.

(a) A court of this State has temporary emergency jurisdiction if the child is present in this State and the child has been abandoned or it is necessary in an emergency to protect the child because the child, or a sibling or parent of the child, is subjected to or threatened with mistreatment or abuse.

* * *

§ 206.   Simultaneous Proceedings.

(a) Except as otherwise provided in Section 204, a court of this State may not exercise its jurisdiction under this [article] if, at the time of the commencement of the proceeding, a proceeding concerning the custody of the child has been commenced in a court of another State having jurisdiction substantially in conformity with this [Act], unless the proceeding has been terminated or is stayed by the court of the other State because a court of this State is a more convenient forum [ ].

* * *

(c) In a proceeding to modify a child-custody determination, a court of this State shall determine whether a proceeding to enforce the determination has been commenced in another State. If a proceeding to enforce a child-custody determination has been commenced in another State, the court may:

> (1) stay the proceeding for modification pending the entry of an order of a court of the other State enforcing, staying, denying, or dismissing the proceeding for enforcement;

> (2) enjoin the parties from continuing with the proceeding for enforcement; or

> (3) proceed with the modification under conditions it considers appropriate.

NOTES AND QUESTIONS

1.   *The Uniform Deployed Parents Custody and Visitation Act.* The unique circumstances that face parents who are armed services members led to development of the Uniform Deployed Parents Custody and Visitation Act (UDPCVA) in July 2012. As of 2018, it had been enacted in 14 states. Many states do not have any specific provisions for handling the custody matters of deployed parents, so the UDPCVA creates a model act for dealing with these issues. A court may issue an order on custody under the UDPCVA only if it has jurisdiction under the UCCJEA. *See* Uniform Law Commission, Uniform Deployed Parents Custody and Visitation Act § 104 (2012). An essential jurisdictional point of the UDPCVA is that the deploying parent's residence does not change simply by reason of the deployment itself. *Id.*

2.   *Unresolved issues: the difficulty of uniformly defining residence.* The ambiguity of the term "residence" presents unresolved issues under the UCCJEA. Unlike domicile, residence has no specific, concrete intent or time requirements. The Second Restatement of Conflict of Laws notes: "Residence is an ambiguous word whose meaning in a legal phrase must be determined in each case." Restatement (Second) of Conflict of Laws § 11, cmt. K (1971). The UCCJEA standard of "presently reside" creates even further ambiguity. The UCCJEA official comment explains that parties "no longer presently reside" in

a state when they "physically leave the State to live elsewhere[.]" UCCJEA § 202 cmt. 2. However, the UCCJEA does not qualify how long the physical absence must be. This ambiguity has produced contradictory results among the states. *See* Wessel, *supra*, at 1151–62.

3.   *Specifying the jurisdictional basis.* To reinforce a court's proper assumption of jurisdiction, the parties may want to include an appropriate provision in the parenting plans they submit for court approval. *See, e.g., Child Custody*, 35-SPG Fam. Advoc. 14 (2013).

PROBLEM 17-5

Harper and Ryan were married in Kansas in 2010. Their child, Tyler, was born in Kansas in 2014. In June, 2018, Harper and Tyler moved to Missouri; Ryan, who remained in Kansas, visited Tyler in Missouri each weekend. In January, 2019, Ryan filed for divorce and custody in Kansas. When Harper received service, Harper then filed in Missouri. Which state has authority to decide the divorce and custody proceedings?

———

In the following case, the court had to decide whether Montana had initial child custody subject matter jurisdiction, even though the child had not lived there for a substantial period of time. Consider the effect of the preceding UCCJEA sections on the appellate court's reasoning.

IN RE MYRLAND

Supreme Court of Montana, 2010.
248 P.3d 290.

JUSTICE W. WILLIAM LEAPHART delivered the Opinion of the Court.

Carl Myrland (Carl) appeals from the 2009 Order dismissing his Petition for Dissolution and Parenting Plan for lack of subject matter jurisdiction. * * *

FACTUAL AND PROCEDURAL BACKGROUND

Carl and Heather were married March 28, 1998, in Helena, Montana. Heather and Carl had one child (ANM), born in Lewiston, Montana. Carl and Heather both lived with ANM in Lewiston. Thereafter, Carl and Heather moved to North Carolina for work. Then, Heather moved to Las Vegas, leaving ANM and Carl in North Carolina. Carl and ANM moved back to Montana and remained in the state from 2002–2006. Heather made no attempt to contact ANM during this time period and alleges that she was living in Texas.

In March, 2006, Heather came to Helena along with her partner whom she introduced as her common law husband. They were living in the cab of a semi truck that they parked in front of the house where Carl and ANM were living in Helena, Montana. Heather requested to take ANM "for her Birthday" and offered to return her in a month. Heather took ANM and never returned. Heather filed an action for dissolution of marriage in Texas on May 26, 2006.

Carl claims that he was unaware of the whereabouts of Heather and ANM. Carl filed for a dissolution action in Montana on October 2, 2006. Carl attempted to serve Heather in Nevada, but to no avail. Carl effectively served Heather in Texas on about March 23, 2009.

* * *

The court issued the Decree on April 30, 2009, without actual knowledge of Heather's appearance on file at the courthouse. Heather then, through counsel, moved to have the default and dissolution set aside. Heather's motion was granted. * * *

* * *

DISCUSSION

* * *

Both Montana and Texas have adopted the Uniform Child Custody Jurisdiction and Enforcement Act (UCCJEA), which outlines the jurisdictional requirements for custodial determinations:

* * * [T]he pertinent date for purposes of determining jurisdiction is the date of commencement, that is, the date the first pleading was filed. The Commissioners' Note explains how the UCCJEA should address potential jurisdictional conflicts by reason of conduct:

> [I]f a parent takes the child from the home State and seeks an original custody determination elsewhere, the stay-at-home parent has six months to file a custody petition under the extended home state jurisdictional provision of Section 201, which will ensure that the case is retained in the home State.

The facts in this case are identical to the scenario described in the Commissioners' Note. Heather left Montana with ANM and immediately sought an original custody determination elsewhere. ANM had resided in Montana for four years when Heather removed her from the State on or about April 24, 2006. Therefore, Montana was ANM's home state for purposes of jurisdiction until at least October 24, 2006. When Heather filed in Texas on May 26, 2006, ANM could have been in Texas for a few weeks. A few weeks are clearly insufficient to establish Texas as the home state. When Carl filed in Montana, on October 2, 2006, Montana was still the home state of ANM and his petition was filed within six months of Heather's petition. Despite a delay in service and subsequent judicial proceedings, Montana is the only home state of ANM for purposes of jurisdiction.

* * * The home state for purposes of jurisdiction is the home state of the child within six months before commencement of the proceeding. The home state is not, as the District Court's logic would suggest, any state where the child has resided for six months or for "the last" six months. Next, the District Court states that since ANM had been in Texas for nearly six months by the time Carl filed, the time ANM was in Texas is "close enough" to establish jurisdiction. However, this interpretation disregards that the pertinent date is the filing of the first pleading. The first pleading in this case was Heather's May 26, 2006, petition. At the time that Heather filed, ANM may have been in Texas for a few weeks. A few weeks are not at all "close enough" to the six month minimum requirement for home state jurisdiction. Finally, the fact that ANM has been in Texas for the last three years is not at all significant to our jurisdictional inquiry because according to [the UCCJEA], physical presence of the child is neither necessary nor sufficient to establish jurisdiction.

Dismissing the case for lack of subject matter jurisdiction does not comport with the purpose of the UCCJEA to "deter abductions of children" and is a misapplication of the statute. * * * Montana was the only home state of ANM at the time Heather filed her Petition for Dissolution and thus is the only State with jurisdiction over the custody of ANM.

* * *

Under the UCCJEA, even where Montana is the home state, a district court may decide to decline jurisdiction at any time if it determines that it is an inconvenient forum. * * *

* * *

* * *Although the time the child has spent in another state is one of the many factors outlined in [the statute], the District Court has not considered whether Montana is an inconvenient forum for that reason or any of the other reasons established in [Montana law].

CONCLUSION

* * *

* * *[S]ince Montana is the home state of ANM, the court had to either exercise its jurisdiction of the custody proceedings or determine that Montana is not a convenient forum for those proceedings. In the event the court determines that Montana is an inconvenient forum, the court must stay the proceedings so that custody proceedings may be promptly commenced in another state. Accordingly, we affirm the setting aside of the Decree of Dissolution and, as to the custody proceedings, we reverse and remand for the court to address the inconvenient forum factors under [Montana law].

NOTES AND QUESTIONS

1. *Inconvenient to whom?* On remand, should the court decide that Montana is an inconvenient forum? The UCCJEA allows a court to consider a variety of factors, including the location of relevant evidence, how long the child has lived in the other state, the distance between the states, the parties' comparative financial situations, and, if there has been domestic violence, which state can better protect the child. UCCJEA Sec. 207. If you were representing the parties, what other factors might you ask the court to consider?

2. *Defining a "custody proceeding."* The UCCJEA sets out a comprehensive definition of custody proceedings that "includes a proceeding for divorce, separation, neglect, abuse, dependency, guardianship, paternity, termination of parental rights, and protection from domestic violence, in which the issue may appear." UCCJEA § 102(4). A Texas court found that a court-ratified agreement between two men and a surrogate qualified as a custody order, triggering the UCCJEA. *Berwick v. Wagner*, 336 S.W.3d 805, 814 (Tex. Ct. App. 2011). The UCCJEA explicitly excludes juvenile delinquency actions and adoption cases. Juvenile delinquency actions are not "custody proceedings" because they do not relate to civil aspects of access to a child, and adoption cases are excluded because adoption is a specialized area covered by the Uniform Adoption Act promulgated in 1994.

3. *Notice.* Under Section 205 of the UCCJEA, a child custody determination is enforceable only where notice and opportunity to be heard have been given to any parent whose parental rights have not been terminated, anyone who has physical custody of the child, or anyone else entitled to notice in child custody proceedings under state law. Section 108(a) of the Act requires that notice to parties outside the state "must be given in a manner reasonably calculated to give actual notice but may be made by publication if other means are not effective." Because the notice provisions also require that respondents be given an opportunity to be heard, *ex parte* orders (including temporary protection orders related to domestic violence) do not satisfy the UCCJEA's notice provision.

4. *Common law marriage.* Texas allows "informal marriage." Tex. Family Law § 2.401 (2018). Given the requirements for a valid marriage discussed in Chapter 2, was Ms. Myrland accurate about her new partner's status?

b. Special Situations Involving Jurisdiction Under the UCCJEA

Notwithstanding home state priority, the UCCJEA recognizes some situations in which a court may need to exercise authority—or decline to do so—regardless of whether it is the home state.

1. *Emergency jurisdiction.* Section 204 allows courts to assert emergency jurisdiction where the child is subjected to or threatened with

"mistreatment or abuse." The section allows a court to assume jurisdiction even without either home state or significant connection jurisdiction. This emergency jurisdiction protects victims who flee across state lines and seek legal relief, even where the children have not been abused. However, the UCCJEA limits emergency jurisdiction to temporary orders, which protect the child until a state with initial and exclusive jurisdiction enters an order. Where there is no existing child custody decree and no custody proceeding has been filed in the home state (or other state with jurisdiction under Sections 201–203), then an emergency custody determination can become final when the issuing state becomes the child's home state and the order so provides. UCCJEA § 204, cmt.

In *In re E.D.*, 812 N.W.2d 712, 717 (Iowa Ct. App. 2012), the Iowa Court of Appeals held that the trial court properly exercised emergency jurisdiction based on reports of the mother's drug abuse and inadequate supervision. The court affirmed that these reports established "mistreatment or abuse."

In *In re Ruff*, 275 P.3d 1175, 1181 (Wash. Ct. App. 2012), the court held that a father's attempt to take a child from daycare after the provider refused to release the child to him did not warrant exercising temporary emergency jurisdiction over the mother's motion. The court found the father's "conduct and the circumstances [to be] troubling," but did not find that this constituted such abuse required for exercising emergency jurisdiction. Where should this fine line between "troubling" and "mistreatment and abuse" be drawn?

In *Baker v. Tunney*, 201 So.3d 1235, 1239 (Fla. 2016), the mother, father, and child lived together in Florida for the first two weeks of the child's life, at which point the mother and child moved to New York because of the father's domestic violence. Both parents then filed custody petitions, and courts in both states proceeded. The Florida court determined that it was the home state under the UCCJEA, even though New York could exercise emergency jurisdiction based on the violence. Nonetheless, the court held that unless Florida relinquished jurisdiction to New York, the child custody proceeding should continue in Florida. How should the mother's behavior in *Myrland* affect jurisdiction?

2. *Domestic violence and the UCCJEA.* Victims of domestic violence confront challenges beyond those relating to their safety, particularly in the realm of child custody. Many states have implemented "address confidentiality programs" (ACPs), which help domestic violence victims maintain the confidentiality of their address to ensure their safety. Jonathan Grant, Note, *Address Confidentiality and Real Property Records: Safeguarding Interests in Land While Protecting Battered Women*, 100 Minn. L. Rev. 2577, 2578 (2016). The UCCJEA defines a custody proceeding to include those seeking protection from domestic violence.

Additionally, UCCJEA § 207 permits a court to consider "whether domestic violence has occurred and is likely to continue in the future and which State could best protect the parties and the child" as one factor for declining jurisdiction due to an inconvenient forum, even if the court would otherwise have jurisdiction under the UCCJEA.

In *S.K.C. v. J.L.C.*, 94 A.3d 402, 414–15 (Pa. Super. Ct. 2014), for example, the court determined that an occurrence of domestic violence was one factor that made the Pennsylvania court a convenient forum because it was in a better position to protect the mother from future domestic violence.

3.   *Unclean hands and no relief.* Section 208 of the UCCJEA requires a court to decline to hear a case when a person seeking to invoke jurisdiction has "engaged in unjustifiable conduct." This provision, codifying the equitable "clean hands doctrine," was designed to ensure that parents who kidnap their children do not subsequently benefit from the abduction. The UCCJEA's exclusive, continuing jurisdiction provision ensures that one state will retain jurisdiction, and reduces the likelihood that one parent will take the child to another jurisdiction in an effort to find a more favorable forum. How should the mother's behavior in *Myrland* affect jurisdiction?

The clean hands doctrine does not apply in emergency jurisdiction cases. Thus, when a parent flees a state based on a threat of abuse to the child and violates an existing custody decree, the refuge state may not decline jurisdiction if the requirements for emergency jurisdiction have been met.

4.   *The Uniform Child Abduction Prevention Act (UCAPA).* The UCAPA was promulgated in 2006 to provide courts with a means to prevent child abduction even before a custody decree is issued. The court may, on its own, direct that specified child abduction prevention measures be taken; one party or a prosecutor may also petition the court for such measures. The court must have jurisdiction pursuant to the UCCJEA (including emergency jurisdiction). Upon a finding that a "credible risk" of abduction exists, section 8 of the UCAPA allows courts to order a range of possible abduction prevention measures, including travel or visitation restrictions, Uniform Law Commission, UCAPA § 8 (2008). As of 2018, fourteen states and the District of Columbia had enacted the UCAPA.

PROBLEM 17-6

Susan and Brad were married in New York and had a daughter, Mary. The two were later divorced by a New York court, which awarded Susan sole physical and legal custody of Mary, and granted Brad reasonable visitation rights. Susan moved to Wyoming with Mary, while Brad remained in New York. Several years later, a New York trial court modified the original custody order and awarded Brad sole physical and legal custody of Mary, based on the mother's refusal to encourage Mary to visit her father. Susan then sought custody in a Wyoming court. Under the UCCJEA, how should the Wyoming court handle the case?

PROBLEM 17-7

Alison feared that her child's father, Daniel, would abuse both her and their daughter. Alison, Daniel and their child all lived in Kentucky, where a court entered a temporary order for protection from abuse and a temporary custody award to Alison. Alison fled to Maine after Daniel threatened to kill her and their child. As soon as she arrived in Maine, Alison filed a complaint for determination of parental rights and child support. In Kentucky, Daniel filed his own motion to establish physical and legal custody. The Maine court issued a temporary custody order to Alison, who later sought a permanent order.

Did Maine have jurisdiction to issue the temporary custody order? Does Maine have jurisdiction to issue a permanent order? If you were Alison's lawyer, what arguments would you make that Maine has jurisdiction? If you were Daniel's lawyer, what arguments would you make that Kentucky retained jurisdiction? What additional information might you want to have?

PROBLEM 17-8

Carol and Juan were married in Arizona. When Carol was seven months pregnant, she moved to Texas. Within a month of Carol's departure, Juan sued her in Arizona, seeking custody of the child in advance of her birth. The baby, Dana, was subsequently born in Texas, and, when Dana was four months old, Carol filed a custody action in Texas. What arguments might the mother and father each make in the Texas courts? In the Arizona courts? Does it matter that Dana was born in Texas rather than Arizona?

B. ENFORCING AND MODIFYING ANOTHER STATE'S CUSTODY DECREE

A custody order validly issued in one state should be enforceable in other states. Indeed, federal law seemingly requires enforcement of custody determinations under the PKPA. Moreover, the UCCJEA requires that states enforce a custody determination that is consistent with the PKPA. UCCJEA § 303, cmt. As mentioned earlier, however, notwithstanding the PKPA and the UCCJEA, jurisdictional conflicts may still occur. Courts in two states can each assert that it is appropriately exercising jurisdiction, with each asserting that another state must give full faith and credit to the resulting custody decree.

1. The Parental Kidnapping Prevention Act

As discussed above, the Parental Kidnapping Prevention Act (PKPA) requires states to give full faith and credit to other states' child custody determinations. Pub. L. No. 96–611, 94 Stat. 3568 (1980) (codified at 28 U.S.C. § 1738A (2018)). The PKPA establishes a hierarchy of jurisdictional bases; requires states to enforce orders issued by the court in the state with preferred jurisdiction; and prohibits a court from exercising initial jurisdiction when a valid custody proceeding is pending in another state. It is substantially similar to the UCCJEA.

2. The UCCJEA's Modification and Enforcement Provisions

The UCCJEA limits a second state's authority to modify another state's child custody decree, and it creates a duty to enforce a first state's judgment.

**UNIFORM CHILD CUSTODY JURISDICTION
AND ENFORCEMENT ACT**

(1999).

§ 203. Jurisdiction to Modify Determination.

* * * [A] court of this State may not modify a child-custody determination made by a court of another State unless a court of this State has jurisdiction to make an initial determination under Section 201(a)(1) or (2) and:

(1) the court of the other State determines it no longer has exclusive, continuing jurisdiction under Section 202 or that a court of this State would be a more convenient forum under Section 207; or

(2) a court of this State or a court of the other State determines that the child, the child's parents, and any person acting as a parent do not presently reside in the other State.

* * *

§ 303. Duty To Enforce.

(a) A court of this State shall recognize and enforce a child-custody determination of a court of another State if the latter court exercised jurisdiction in substantial conformity with this [Act] or the determination was made under factual circumstances meeting the jurisdictional standards of this [Act] and the determination has not been modified in accordance with this [Act].

* * *

Thus, under the UCCJEA, a state is not required to enforce a custody determination of another state where the issuing state exercised custody jurisdiction that did not comport with the UCCJEA.

In addition, the UCCJEA provides five enforcement remedies: (1) a simplified process for registration of custody orders issued by another state; (2) authorization for courts to issue temporary visitation or parenting time orders; (3) authorization for a state to take physical custody of a child in imminent danger of being harmed or removed from the state; (4) a swift enforcement mechanism for violations of custody and visitation provisions, and (5) authorization of public officials to assist in enforcement of child custody determinations. UCCJEA, Art. 3.

NOTES AND QUESTIONS

1. *No federal cause of action.* In *Thompson v. Thompson*, 484 U.S. 174 (1988), the Court considered whether the PKPA created an implied right of action in federal courts to determine which of two conflicting state custody statutes is valid. In July 1978, Susan Clay (then Thompson) filed a petition in Los Angeles Superior Court for divorce against David Thompson, asking for custody of their son, Matthew. The court initially awarded joint custody, but awarded Susan full custody after she obtained a job in Louisiana. This custody arrangement was supposed to be temporary until an investigator reported back to the court.

After moving to Louisiana, however, Susan filed a petition there to enforce the California custody decree and to modify visitation rights; the Louisiana court subsequently awarded Susan sole custody of Matthew in April 1981. In June 1981, the California court, after receiving its investigatory report, awarded sole custody to David. In August 1983, David brought an action in California federal district court seeking a declaration that the Louisiana order was invalid, and enforcement of the new California order. The district court rejected David's claims, and the Ninth Circuit held that the PKPA did not create a private right of action in federal court to determine the validity of competing custody orders. *Thompson v. Thompson*, 798 F.2d 1547, 1552–59 (9th Cir. 1986).

The Supreme Court affirmed, stating that the PKPA's context, language, and legislative history did not support a private right of action in federal courts. *Thompson*, 484 U.S. at 187. The Court observed that the problem of jurisdictional deadlocks among states in custody cases, and a national problem of interstate parental abductions at the time of the PKPA's passage, suggested congressional intent only to extend the Full Faith and Credit clause to custody decisions, not to create an entirely new cause of action. The Act's language and legislative history likewise did not support David's claim. In response to the contention that failure to imply a cause of action would diminish the force of the Act, Justice Marshall, writing for the Court, explained:

> State courts faithfully administer the Full Faith and Credit Clause every day; now that Congress has extended full faith and credit requirements to child custody orders, we can think of no reason why the courts' administration of federal law in custody disputes will be

any less vigilant. Should state courts prove as obstinate as petitioner predicts, Congress may choose to revisit the issue.

Id. Should Congress revisit the issue?

2. *Not following the PKPA.* What are the consequences if one court acts contrary to the PKPA by modifying an earlier custody decree from another state?

3. *An example of continuing jurisdiction.* As noted earlier in the Chapter, the UCCJEA provides that a state in which the decree was issued normally has exclusive, continuing jurisdiction over future disputes. UCCJEA § 201(a)(2). This jurisdiction can continue even when the child no longer lives in the state so long as one parent still has a significant connection with the state.

White v. Harrison-White, 760 N.W.2d 691 (Mich. Ct. App. 2008), analyzed the definition of "significant connection" under the UCCJEA. A Michigan court issued a divorce and custody order. About a year later, the mother, who had moved to Canada with the child, challenged Michigan's continuing jurisdiction. The court interpreted the UCCJEA's "significant connection" clause to refer to situations in which one parent still lives in the state, and has "a meaningful relationship with the child, and, in maintaining the relationship, exercises parenting time in the state." *Id.* at 698. The court held that a significant connection with Michigan existed because the plaintiff father stayed in Michigan and maintained a meaningful relationship with the child through telephone contact, visits during alternating weekends, and vacation time.

PROBLEM 17-9

A California court awarded Jack and Shawna joint legal custody of their son, Michael, and awarded Shawna primary physical custody. Shawna and Michael moved to Norway for two years so Shawna could pursue an education, while Jack remained in California. At the end of the two-year period, Shawna informed Jack that she wished to remain in Norway permanently with Michael. A year later, when Michael returned to California to visit his father, Jack filed a motion to modify custody to award him sole custody of Michael. Shawna argued that California lacked jurisdiction to consider the motion because California was no longer Michael's home state. How should a California court rule?

PROBLEM 17-10

During their marriage, John and Nancy had two children and lived in Illinois for six years. In 2015, the couple divorced and an Illinois court issued a custody order providing for shared parental rights and responsibilities, giving Nancy primary physical custody of the children. In 2013, the children moved to Colorado to live with their father, who had remarried. Nancy claims that this arrangement was temporary, while John claims that the relocation was permanent. The children lived with John until 2019, when John moved to modify the Illinois custody judgment in a Colorado court, arguing that Illinois no longer had jurisdiction under the UCCJEA. Nancy later filed a similar modification motion in a court in Illinois, where she continued to reside. John moved to dismiss the Illinois action claiming that Colorado was the proper jurisdiction and that Illinois no longer had continuing, exclusive jurisdiction.

If you were the judge in Colorado, how would you handle the situation? If you were the judge in Illinois, how would you rule? According to the UCCJEA, did Illinois retain continuing, exclusive jurisdiction over the children? Would you want any further information before deciding?

PROBLEM 17-11

Eric and Arlene lived in Maine, and a Maine court issued a divorce decree granting Arlene shared custody, with primary residence to Arlene. Two years later, the court modified the decree, transferring primary residential custody to Eric, who was now living in Pennsylvania. Eric moved to confirm his custody in Pennsylvania, and that court issued an order confirming custody in him. Arlene then filed in Maine court, seeking a return of custody to her. How should the Maine court handle this? *See Fitzpatrick v. McCrary*, 182 A.3d 737 (Me. 2018).

C. INTERNATIONAL CHILD ABDUCTION

Chapter 13 includes an extensive discussion of the 1980 Hague Convention on the Civil Aspects of International Child Abduction. The Convention governs all civil cases of international child abduction where the petitioning parent and the child are in different countries, so long as the countries are parties to the Convention and have executed reciprocal agreements. Hague Convention, Oct. 25, 1980, 1343 U.N.T.S. 89 (1983). Just as the UCCJEA and PKPA ensure that only one state has jurisdiction, the Hague Convention ensures that only one country has jurisdiction over a child custody dispute.

In 1988, the United States became a signatory state, ratified the Convention, and implemented it through the International Child Abduction Remedies Act (ICARA), 22 U.S.C. §§ 9001 *et seq.* (2018). ICARA authorizes a party seeking return of a child to file a petition in a court of appropriate jurisdiction where the child is located. ICARA grants state and federal courts concurrent jurisdiction to hear Hague Convention cases.

NOTES AND QUESTIONS

1.   *How do courts respond when countries have not signed the Hague Convention?* The Hague Convention has been widely adopted, but it is not in force in many countries where religious courts exercise jurisdiction over child custody matters. One such country is Israel, where religious courts do decide custody issues. Under United States law and the Convention, respect for a foreign court's jurisdiction and custody is not affected by whether the court

applies secular or religious law. American courts are often wary of foreign custody decrees that appear to be based solely on religious principles or rules because such decrees may not appropriately weigh the best interests of the child.

    2.   *The International Parental Kidnapping Crime Act (IPKCA).* In 1993, Congress enacted the International Parental Kidnapping Crime Act (IPKCA), 18 U.S.C. § 1204 (2018). The IPKCA makes it a crime to "remove" or "retain" a child outside of the United States to obstruct another person's lawful exercise of parental rights.

    The IPKCA supplements the Hague Convention, and applies regardless of whether the abducting parent is located in a country that is a party to it.

> By making parental abduction a federal offense, the IPKCA increases the chances that an abductor may be extradited, and strengthens diplomatic efforts to bring about a child's return. The IPKCA also was intended to act as a deterrent, and to "verify [Congress's] serious concern over international parental kidnapping." As a practical matter, the IPKCA has little value as a tool for seeking return of a child from a foreign country. Even in cases where the abductor is successfully extradited and prosecuted, the child is not necessarily returned. The IPKCA is relevant to the analysis of international relocation mainly because it represents the clear intent of Congress to preserve the parent-child relationship against international abduction—including parental abduction.

Maryl Sattler, *Note: The Problem of Parental Relocation: Closing the Loophole in the Law of International Child Abduction*, 67 Wash. & Lee L. Rev. 1709, 1718 (2010).

5.   SUPPORT JURISDICTION

    As with custody decisions, alimony and child support determinations must comply with due process. The most significant decision concerning due process and personal jurisdiction over modification and enforcement of interstate support obligations remains *Kulko v. Superior Court of California*, set out below.

A. WHICH STATE HAS JURISDICTION TO ISSUE A SUPPORT ORDER?

1. Constitutional Limits

    As you learned in first year civil procedure, a court must have personal jurisdiction to decide an individual's financial obligations. The next case explicitly applies this general rule to issues of intrafamilial support.

KULKO V. SUPERIOR COURT

Supreme Court of the United States, 1978.
436 U.S. 84.

MR. JUSTICE MARSHALL delivered the opinion of the Court.

The issue before us is whether, in this action for child support, the California state courts may exercise *in personam* jurisdiction over a nonresident, nondomiciliary parent of minor children domiciled within the State. For reasons set forth below, we hold that the exercise of such jurisdiction would violate the Due Process Clause of the Fourteenth Amendment.

I

Appellant Ezra Kulko married appellee Sharon Kulko Horn in 1959, during appellant's three-day stopover in California en route from a military base in Texas to a tour of duty in Korea. At the time of this marriage, both parties were domiciled in and residents of New York State. Immediately following the marriage, Sharon Kulko returned to New York, as did appellant after his tour of duty. Their first child, Darwin, was born to the Kulkos in New York in 1961, and a year later their second child, Ilsa, was born, also in New York. The Kulkos and their two children resided together as a family in New York City continuously until March 1972, when the Kulkos separated.

Following the separation, Sharon Kulko moved to San Francisco, Cal. A written separation agreement was drawn up in New York; in September 1972, Sharon Kulko flew to New York City in order to sign this agreement. The agreement provided, *inter alia*, that the children would remain with their father during the school year but would spend their Christmas, Easter, and summer vacations with their mother. While Sharon Kulko waived any claim for her own support or maintenance, Ezra Kulko agreed to pay his wife $3,000 per year in child support for the periods when the children were in her care, custody, and control. Immediately after execution of the separation agreement, Sharon Kulko flew to Haiti and procured a divorce there; the divorce decree incorporated the terms of the agreement. She then returned to California, where she remarried and took the name Horn.

The children resided with appellant during the school year and with their mother on vacations, as provided by the separation agreement, until December 1973. At this time, just before Ilsa was to leave New York to spend Christmas vacation with her mother, she told her father that she wanted to remain in California after her vacation. Appellant bought his daughter a one-way plane ticket, and Ilsa left, taking her clothing with her. Ilsa then commenced living in California with her mother during the school year and spending vacations with her father. In January 1976, appellant's other child, Darwin, called his mother from New York and advised her that he wanted to live with her in California. Unbeknownst to appellant, appellee Horn sent a plane ticket to her son, which he used to fly to California where he took up residence with his mother and sister.

Less than one month after Darwin's arrival in California, appellee Horn commenced this action against appellant in the California Superior Court. She sought to establish the Haitian divorce decree as a California judgment; to modify the judgment so as to award her full custody of the children; and to increase appellant's child-support obligations. Appellant appeared specially and moved to quash service of the summons on the ground that he was not a resident of California and lacked sufficient "minimum contacts" with the State under *International Shoe Co. v. Washington*, 326 U.S. 310 (1945), to warrant the State's assertion of personal jurisdiction over him.

[The lower California courts rejected appellant's claims.]

* * *

The California Supreme Court granted appellant's petition for review, and in a 4–2 decision sustained the rulings of the lower state courts. It noted first that the California Code of Civil Procedure demonstrated an intent that the courts of California utilize all bases of *in personam* jurisdiction "not inconsistent with the Constitution." [Cal. Civ. Proc. Code § 410.10 (1973).] Agreeing with the court below, the Supreme Court stated that, where a nonresident defendant has caused an effect in the State by an act or omission outside the State, personal jurisdiction over the defendant in causes arising from that effect may be exercised whenever "reasonable." It went on to hold that such an exercise was "reasonable" in this case because appellant had "purposely availed himself of the benefits and protections of the laws of California" by sending Ilsa to live with her mother in California. While noting that appellant had not, "with respect to his other child, Darwin, caused an effect in [California]"—since it was appellee Horn who had arranged for Darwin to fly to California in January 1976—the court concluded that it was "fair and reasonable for defendant to be subject to personal jurisdiction for the support of both children, where he has committed acts with respect to one child which confers [*sic*] personal jurisdiction and has consented to the permanent residence of the other child in California."

* * *

* * * [W]e hereby grant the petition and reverse the judgment below.

II

* * *

Like any standard that requires a determination of "reasonableness," the "minimum contacts" test of *International Shoe* is not susceptible of mechanical application; rather, the facts of each case must be weighed to determine whether the requisite "affiliating circumstances" are present. *Hanson v. Denckla*, 357 U.S. 235, 246 (1958). * * *

A

In reaching its result, the California Supreme Court did not rely on appellant's glancing presence in the State some 13 years before the events that led to this controversy, nor could it have. Appellant has been in California on only two occasions, once in 1959 for a three-day military stopover on his way to Korea, and again in 1960 for a 24-hour stopover on his return from Korean service. To hold such temporary visits to a State a basis for the assertion of *in personam* jurisdiction over unrelated actions arising in the future would make a mockery of the limitations on state jurisdiction imposed by the Fourteenth Amendment. Nor did the California court rely on the fact that appellant was actually married in California on one of his two brief visits. We agree that where two New York domiciliaries, for reasons of convenience, marry in the State of California and thereafter spend their entire married life in New York, the fact of their California marriage by itself cannot support a California court's exercise of jurisdiction over a spouse who remains a New York resident in an action relating to child support.

Finally, in holding that personal jurisdiction existed, the court below carefully disclaimed reliance on the fact that appellant had agreed at the time of separation to allow his children to live with their mother three months a year and that he had sent them to California each year pursuant to this agreement. As was noted below, to find personal jurisdiction in a State on this basis, merely because the mother was residing there, would discourage parents from entering into reasonable visitation agreements. Moreover, it could arbitrarily subject one parent to suit in any State of the Union where the other parent chose to spend time while having custody of their offspring pursuant to a separation agreement. * * *

* * *

The "purposeful act" that the California Supreme Court believed did warrant the exercise of personal jurisdiction over appellant in California was his "actively and fully consent[ing] to Ilsa living in California for the school year . . . and . . . sen[ding] her to California for that purpose." We cannot accept the proposition that appellant's acquiescence in Ilsa's desire to live with her mother conferred jurisdiction over appellant in the California courts in this action. A father who agrees, in the interests of family harmony and his children's preferences, to allow them to spend more time in California than was required under a separation agreement can hardly be said to have "purposefully availed himself" of the "benefits and protections" of California's laws.[7]

Nor can we agree with the assertion of the court below that the exercise of *in personam* jurisdiction here was warranted by the financial benefit appellant derived from his daughter's presence in California for nine months of the year. This argument rests on the premise that, while appellant's liability for support payments remained unchanged, his yearly expenses for supporting the child in New York decreased. But this circumstance, even if true, does not support California's assertion of jurisdiction here. Any diminution in appellant's household costs resulted, not from the child's presence in California, but rather from her absence from appellant's home. Moreover, an action by appellee Horn to increase support payments could now be brought, and could have been brought when Ilsa first moved to California, in the State of New York; a New York court would clearly have personal jurisdiction over appellant and, if a judgment were entered by a New York court increasing appellant's child-support obligations, it could properly be enforced against him in both New York and California. Any ultimate financial advantage to appellant thus results not from the child's presence in California, but from appellee's failure earlier to seek an increase in payments under the separation agreement. The argument below to the contrary, in our view, confuses the question of appellant's liability with that of the proper forum in which to determine that liability.

B

* * *

The circumstances in this case clearly render "unreasonable" California's assertion of personal jurisdiction. There is no claim that appellant has visited physical injury on either property or persons within the State of California. The cause of action herein asserted arises, not from the defendant's commercial transactions in interstate commerce, but rather from his personal, domestic relations. It thus cannot be said that appellant has sought a commercial benefit from solicitation of business from a resident of California that could reasonably render him liable to suit in state court; appellant's activities cannot fairly be analogized to an insurer's sending an insurance contract and premium notices into the State to an insured resident of the State. *Cf. McGee v. International Life Insurance Co.*, 355 U.S. 220 (1957). Furthermore, the controversy between the parties arises from a separation that occurred in the State of New York; appellee Horn seeks modification of a contract that was negotiated in New

---

[7] The court below stated that the presence in California of appellant's daughter gave appellant the benefit of California's "police and fire protection, its school system, its hospital services, its recreational facilities, its libraries and museums. . . ." But, in the circumstances presented here, these services provided by the State were essentially benefits to the child, not the father, and in any event were not benefits that appellant purposefully sought for himself.

York and that she flew to New York to sign. As in *Hanson v. Denckla*, 357 U.S. at 252, the instant action involves an agreement that was entered into with virtually no connection with the forum State.

Finally, basic considerations of fairness point decisively in favor of appellant's State of domicile as the proper forum for adjudication of this case, whatever the merits of appellee's underlying claim. It is appellant who has remained in the State of the marital domicile, whereas it is appellee who has moved across the continent. *Cf. May v. Anderson*, 345 U.S. 528, 534–35, n.8 (1953). * * *. * * * As noted above, appellant did no more than acquiesce in the stated preference of one of his children to live with her mother in California. This single act is surely not one that a reasonable parent would expect to result in the substantial financial burden and personal strain of litigating a child-support suit in a forum 3,000 miles away, and we therefore see no basis on which it can be said that appellant could reasonably have anticipated being "haled before a [California] court," *Shaffer v. Heitner*, 433 U.S. [186, 216 (1977)]. To make jurisdiction in a case such as this turn on whether appellant bought his daughter her ticket or instead unsuccessfully sought to prevent her departure would impose an unreasonable burden on family relations, and one wholly unjustified by the "quality and nature" of appellant's activities in or relating to the State of California. *International Shoe Co. v. Washington*, 326 U.S. at 319.

III

In seeking to justify the burden that would be imposed on appellant were the exercise of *in personam* jurisdiction in California sustained, appellee argues that California has substantial interests in protecting the welfare of its minor residents and in promoting to the fullest extent possible a healthy and supportive family environment in which the children of the State are to be raised. These interests are unquestionably important. But while the presence of the children and one parent in California arguably might favor application of California law in a lawsuit in New York, the fact that California may be the " 'center of gravity' " for choice-of-law purposes does not mean that California has personal jurisdiction over the defendant. * * *

California's legitimate interest in ensuring the support of children resident in California without unduly disrupting the children's lives, moreover, is already being served by the State's participation in the Revised Uniform Reciprocal Enforcement of Support Act of 1968. This statute provides a mechanism for communication between court systems in different States, in order to facilitate the procurement and enforcement of child-support decrees where the dependent children reside in a State that cannot obtain personal jurisdiction over the defendant. * * *

* * *

Reversed.

MR. JUSTICE BRENNAN, with whom MR. JUSTICE WHITE and MR. JUSTICE POWELL join, dissenting.

* * * I cannot say that the Court's determination against state-court *in personam* jurisdiction is implausible, but, though the issue is close, my independent weighing of the facts leads me to conclude, in agreement with the analysis and determination of the California Supreme Court, that appellant's connection with the State of California was not too attenuated, under the standards of reasonableness and fairness implicit in the Due Process Clause, to require him to conduct his defense in the California courts. I therefore dissent.

NOTE AND QUESTIONS

Physical presence and purposeful act. Given the location of the children and relevant evidence in California, as well as California's interest in children living there, why didn't the Supreme Court hold that the California courts had ruled correctly? How does sending a child to live in another state differ from sending an insurance contract to another state? Should there be an exception to normal rules of personal jurisdiction for child custody and support cases?

2. State Laws

The Uniform Interstate Family Support Act (UIFSA), first promulgated in 1992, provides uniform rules for enforcement and modification of family support orders by setting jurisdictional standards for state courts, determining the basis for a state to exercise exclusive jurisdiction over a child support proceeding, and creating rules for determining which state issues a controlling order if proceedings are commenced in multiple jurisdictions. In 1996, Congress mandated that states enact some parts of UIFSA as a condition of remaining eligible for federal funding of child support enforcement. By 1998, all U.S. jurisdictions had complied. UIFSA, prefatory note (2008).

UIFSA is only the most recent effort to develop uniform state laws on support jurisdiction. In 1950, the National Conference of Commissioners on Uniform State Laws (NCCUSL) drafted the Uniform Reciprocal Enforcement of Support Act (URESA). In *Kulko*, the Court relied on a revised version of URESA to reach its decision.

UIFSA provides procedural and jurisdictional rules for establishing, enforcing, and modifying family support orders, including the ability to determine parentage in the interstate litigation. Only one state has continuing jurisdiction to modify a support order. Unlike the UCCJEA, which governs only subject matter jurisdiction, UIFSA addresses both personal and subject matter jurisdiction. For example, Section 202, reproduced below, provides that personal jurisdiction continues as long as a tribunal has continuing, exclusive jurisdiction to modify or enforce an order.

UNIFORM INTERSTATE FAMILY SUPPORT ACT[c]
(2008).

§ 102.   Definitions.

* * *

(4)   "Home state" means the state or foreign country in which a child lived with a parent or a person acting as parent for at least six consecutive months immediately preceding the time of filing of a [petition] or comparable pleading for support and, if a child is less than six months old, the state or foreign country in which the child lived from birth with any of them. A period of temporary absence of any of them is counted as part of the six-month or other period.

* * *

§ 201.   Bases For Jurisdiction Over Nonresident.

(a)   In a proceeding to establish or enforce a support order or to determine parentage of a child, a tribunal of this state may exercise personal jurisdiction over a nonresident individual [or the individual's guardian or conservator] if:

     (1)   the individual is personally served with [citation, summons, notice] within this state;

     (2)   the individual submits to the jurisdiction of this state by consent in a record, by entering a general appearance, or by filing a responsive document having the effect of waiving any contest to personal jurisdiction;

     (3)   the individual resided with the child in this state;

     (4)   the individual resided in this state and provided prenatal expenses or support for the child;

     (5)   the child resides in this state as a result of the acts or directives of the individual;

     (6)   the individual engaged in sexual intercourse in this state and the child may have been conceived by that act of intercourse;

     (7)   the individual asserted parentage of a child in the [putative father registry] maintained in this state by the [appropriate agency]; or

     (8)   there is any other basis consistent with the constitutions of this state and the United States for the exercise of personal jurisdiction.

---

[c]   *Editors' Note:* Brackets are reproduced as they appear in the original material.

* * *

§ 202.   Duration Of Personal Jurisdiction.

Personal jurisdiction acquired by a tribunal of this state in a proceeding under this [act] or other law of this state relating to a support order continues as long as a tribunal of this state has continuing, exclusive jurisdiction to modify its order or continuing jurisdiction to enforce its order as provided by Sections 205, 206, and 211.

NOTES AND QUESTIONS

1.   *Long-arm jurisdiction.* UIFSA contains a broad provision for asserting long-arm jurisdiction over an absent respondent in the state of residence of the other parent, the child's custodian, or the child who is entitled to support. Sections 201 and 202 of UIFSA (reproduced above) allow an issuing state to assert long-arm jurisdiction over a nonresident respondent to establish a support order or to determine parentage. UIFSA § 201, cmt. Such jurisdiction ensures that child support can be established through a one-state proceeding. Where the long-arm statute can be satisfied, the petitioner (either the obligor or obligee) can: (1) use the long-arm statute to obtain personal jurisdiction over the respondent; or (2) initiate a two-state proceeding seeking to establish a support order in the respondent's state of residence. *Id.*

2.   Kulko *and UIFSA.* Are all of the provisions in Section 201 of UIFSA concerning personal jurisdiction constitutional under *Kulko*?

B. MODIFYING AND ENFORCING A CHILD SUPPORT ORDER

As in the child custody jurisdiction area, both federal and state laws control child support subject matter jurisdiction.

1. FFCCSOA

Congress enacted the Full Faith and Credit for Child Support Orders Act (FFCCSOA) in 1994. 28 U.S.C. § 1738B (2018). The legislation, which is similar to the PKPA, is designed: (1) to facilitate enforcement of child support orders among the states; (2) to discourage continuing interstate controversies over child support to ensure greater financial stability and secure family relationships for the child; and (3) to avoid jurisdictional competition and conflict among the state courts in establishing child support orders.

The FFCCSOA requires a state to give full faith and credit to any valid child support order. A support order is valid if: (1) it was issued by a court pursuant to the laws of the state in which the court was located; (2) the court had subject matter jurisdiction to hear and resolve the matter; and

(3) the court had personal jurisdiction over the parties, provided that the parties had reasonable notice and an opportunity to be heard.

The FFCCSOA also limits one state's authority to modify a support order issued by another state. A second state can modify the order if it has been properly registered in that state under the Act and either: (1) the issuing court no longer has continuing, exclusive jurisdiction because neither the child nor any individual contestant resides there, and the parties have not consented to having that court continue to exercise its jurisdiction to modify; or (2) each contestant has filed written consent with the state that has continuing, exclusive jurisdiction for a second state's court to assume jurisdiction. Note that a state loses continuing, exclusive jurisdiction if it is no longer the resident state of the child or any contestant, unless all the contestants have filed written consents for that state to retain jurisdiction. 28 U.S.C. § 1738B(d),(e); see Margaret Campbell Haynes & Susan Friedman Paikin, *"Reconciling" FFCSOA and UIFSA*, 49 Fam. L.Q. 331, 340 (2015).

NOTE AND QUESTIONS

The FFCCSOA contains several choice-of-law provisions that courts must apply. First, the Act states that the forum state's law applies in proceedings to establish, modify or enforce a child support order unless otherwise provided. 28 U.S.C. § 1738B(h)(1). Second, the law of the issuing court's state applies in interpreting a child support order, such as determining the duration of current payments and other obligations. 28 U.S.C. § 1738B(h)(2). However, the court must apply the statute of limitations that provides the longer period of limitation of either the forum state or the issuing state. 28 U.S.C. § 1738B(h)(3). What policies support these choice-of-law provisions?

PROBLEM 17-12

Susan and Michael were married and had three children, ages 25, 21, and 19. The couple, who lived in New York throughout their marriage, recently divorced, and a New York court issued a child support order. Under New York law, a child is eligible for child support until she reaches the age of 21, and therefore the youngest child was eligible for support. Susan and the youngest child moved to Virginia, where the law mandates child support only until the age of 18. Does the Virginia court have the authority to enforce the New York support order? Is the youngest child entitled to child support in Virginia?

2.   UIFSA

Under UIFSA, a party who requests another state's tribunal to modify an existing child support order must register the original order in the other state. Because UIFSA provides continuing, exclusive authority in the court exercising original jurisdiction, generally only that court may modify the support order. However, if modification jurisdiction is no longer appropriate in the issuing court, a second tribunal may become vested with the continuing, exclusive jurisdiction necessary to modify the order. This vesting can occur when neither the individual parties nor the child reside in the issuing state, or when the parties agree that another tribunal may assume modification jurisdiction. Section 205 allows parties to agree that the issuing tribunal will continue to exercise its continuing, exclusive jurisdiction even if the parties and child have moved from that state.

Together, UIFSA and the FFCCSOA have simplified issues involving modification and enforcement. A second state must "enforce according to its terms" a child support order from another state according to the first state's law. "For example, the duration of the obligation to pay support is determined by the law of the rendering state (F1), even if the law of the recognizing state (F2) provides for a shorter duration, such as when it provides for an earlier age of majority or emancipation." Symeon C. Symeonides, *Choice of Law in the American Courts in 2009: Twenty-Third Annual Survey*, 58 Am. J. Comp. L. 227, 285 (2010).

PROBLEM 17-13

In 2012, a California trial court ordered Father to pay Mother $700.00 per month in child support for their son. In 2016, Mother moved with their son from California to Texas. In June 2018, Father moved from California to Nevada.

On June 14, 2019, Father filed a request in California court to modify the amount of his child support payments based on his reduced income. Mother opposed his request, arguing that the matter should be heard in the state of their son's residence (i.e., Texas) because none of the trio lived in California.

You are the law clerk to the California state court judge who is assigned to hear this case, and the judge asks for your recommendation about how to proceed.

As you research the legal issues, you find the following in the Comments to Section 205 of the UIFSA:

> This section is perhaps the most crucial provision in UIFSA. [T]he issuing tribunal retains continuing, exclusive jurisdiction over a child-support order [so] long as one of the individual parties or the child continues to reside in the issuing state, and as long as the parties do not agree to the contrary, the issuing tribunal has continuing, exclusive jurisdiction over its child-support order—which in practical terms means that it may modify its order. . .
>
> The other side of the coin follows logically. Just as subsection (a) defines the retention of continuing, exclusive jurisdiction, by clear implication the subsection also identifies how jurisdiction to modify may be lost. That is, if all the relevant persons—the obligor, the individual obligee, and the child—have permanently left the issuing

state, absent an agreement the issuing tribunal no longer has an appropriate nexus with the parties or child to justify the exercise of jurisdiction to modify its child-support order. Further, the issuing tribunal will have no current evidence readily available to it about the factual circumstances of anyone involved, and the taxpayers of that state will have no reason to expend public funds on the process. Note, however, that the original order of the issuing tribunal remains valid and enforceable. That order is in effect not only in the issuing state, but also in those states in which the order has been registered.

UIFSA Section 205, Comments.

What advice would you deliver to your judge?

NOTES AND QUESTIONS

1. *Enforcing a support order.* A keystone of UIFSA is that authority to enforce the issuing state's order is not "exclusive" to that state. Instead, if requested, one or more states may also enforce the order. UIFSA provides two direct enforcement procedures that do not require court assistance. First, section 501 permits a notice to be sent directly to the obligor's employer in another state, triggering income withholding by the employer, without a hearing unless the employee objects. Second, Section 507 provides for direct administrative enforcement by the support enforcement agency in the obligor's state.

When enforcing a support order in another state requires court involvement, the obligee must first register the existing support order in the responding state. The responding state must enforce the order except in a few limited circumstances in which modification is permitted.

2. *Modification jurisdiction.* Why are the requirements for initial subject matter jurisdiction and modification jurisdiction different? Should UIFSA be amended "to allow custodial parents to file for modification of child support orders in their state of residence if all interested persons have moved from the issuing jurisdiction, provided th[e] jurisdiction also has personal jurisdiction over the non-custodial parent," aside from 'cases of extreme hardship to the non-custodial parent' "? Stephen K. Berenson, *Home Court Advantage Revisited: Interstate Modification of Child Support Orders Under UIFSA and FFCCSOA*, 45 Gonz. L. Rev. 479, 497 (2010).

3. *Knock, knock.* Can you think of any reason why the parties might request that the issuing tribunal retain jurisdiction even if no litigant remains in the state? Why would the UIFSA drafters have added this provision to the original Act?

4. *States' UIFSA and federal FFCCSOA.* If the original state court has lost continuing, exclusive jurisdiction under the FFCCSOA, this loss does not automatically confer jurisdiction on another state. Under the FFCCSOA, the new court must have jurisdiction to modify a child support order *in addition to* the original state's loss of continuing jurisdiction. A state's UIFSA provisions

set out the circumstances under which a state has jurisdiction to modify another state's support order. Thus, the FFCCSOA works with a state's UIFSA provisions rather than preempting them.

PROBLEM 17-14

New Mexico issued a support order requiring John Vincent to pay $2000 monthly to his ex-wife to support their child. John has resided in California for three years since the issuance of this order because he was assigned to active Air Force duty there. If John filed his income tax returns in New Mexico and intended to return to New Mexico after he retired from the military, does that state retain continuing, exclusive jurisdiction over child support? Does California have jurisdiction to modify New Mexico's order? Under what circumstances would California have jurisdiction? What further information would you need to make your decision? Does California have jurisdiction to enforce the order? What information would you need to make that determination?

PROBLEM 17-15

In 2013, Mark and Tammy were divorced in Colorado, where a court issued a child support order for their two children. The Colorado court later modified this order three times. In 2019, Tammy and the children moved to Washington State, where she filed a petition seeking to modify the child support order. Mark moved to dismiss for lack of subject matter jurisdiction under UIFSA. If you were Mark's lawyer, what arguments would you make that Washington does not have jurisdiction? If you were the judge, what further information would you need to make your decision?

PROBLEM 17-16

Ten years ago, Ashley gave birth to a nonmarital child in Kansas. A Kansas court ordered Kyle, the child's biological father, to pay child support. Two years ago, Ashley moved to Hong Kong and married. The child later received a Hong Kong identity card and began attending school in Hong Kong. Kyle then moved and became a resident of Missouri. Ashley recently filed a motion with the Kansas court to increase Kyle's child support payments. Ashley argues that while she currently lives in Hong Kong and married a Hong Kong resident, Kansas is still her domicile as she maintains a Kansas driver's license, voter's registration, and intends to return to Kansas one day.

Is domicile enough for residence under UIFSA, which exclusively uses the term residence? Would it matter if Ashley's driver's license lists an address that she no longer has in Kansas, or if she hasn't voted in any Kansas elections since moving? May the Kansas court increase Kyle's child support payments under these circumstances?

6. UNIFIED FAMILY COURTS

Domestic relations cases are the largest and fastest growing segment of state court caseloads. Approximately 30% of the civil cases in state courts involve family problems, a percentage exceeded only by that for traffic offenses. Courts that hear family matters, however, are often overburdened and inefficient. The late nineteenth-century innovation of juvenile courts, which were designed to provide a supportive atmosphere for adjudicating cases involving delinquency, abuse and neglect, status offenses and (in most states) adoption, ironically turned out to be one source of inefficiency. Legal scholars have long observed that a court that treats a range of family problems "as a series of single separate controversies may often not do justice to the whole or the several separate parts." Roscoe Pound, *The Place of the Family Court in the Judicial System*, 5 Nat'l Probation & Parole Ass'n J. 161, 164 (1959).

In an effort to avoid the delays, duplication, and unnecessary expenses that frequently arise when families must proceed in both juvenile court and general jurisdiction court, many jurisdictions have created unified family courts. Unified family courts have existed since the early twentieth-century, but gained prominence in a few states, such as Rhode Island and Hawaii, starting in the 1960s. "The American Bar Association has long endorsed [broad] jurisdiction for unified family courts." Catherine J. Ross, *The Failure of Fragmentation: The Promise of A System of Unified Family Courts*, 32 Fam. L.Q. 3, 15 (1998). In 1991, the National Council of Juvenile and Family Court Judges developed recommendations for a model family court.

In addition to the children's cases traditionally heard in juvenile court, the family court's subject matter jurisdiction typically includes divorce proceedings, paternity suits, emancipation proceedings, proceedings for protective orders under child abuse and adult abuse statutes, and, in some jurisdictions, criminal prosecutions charging abuse or neglect or domestic violence. They allow for ongoing case management, and can connect litigants to the "appropriate nonlegal services, all under the supervision of specially trained and interested judges." Barbara A. Babb, *Another Look at the Need for Family Law Education Reform: One Law School's Innovations*, 55 Fam. Ct. Rev. 59, 61 (2017).

Proponents also assert that unified family courts can produce consistency and efficiency that serve the best interests of children, families, and courts. *See* Barbara Babb, *Family Courts are Here to Stay, So Let's Improve Them*, 53 Fam. Ct. Rev. 642 (2014). Families and the judicial system save time, effort and resources when one decision maker remains familiar with the family's circumstances and resolves all family-related matters. Family members are spared the ordeal of appearing in multiple courts that determine frequently interrelated factual and legal issues.

Children are spared the discomfort of testifying in multiple proceedings. Consider, for example, the plight of a young child allegedly molested by her father. In a jurisdiction without a unified family court, the child may be forced to testify about the same or similar events in multiple proceedings if the mother files for divorce after learning of the sexual assault, if child protective authorities file a civil abuse proceeding to remove the child from the home, and if the prosecutor files criminal charges.

Proponents argue that the one-judge-one-family approach enables family courts to treat family distress efficiently while minimizing the risk of inconsistent judgments or of multiple initiatives that each overlook a basic need. Indeed, new approaches to family law conflicts view disputes as continuing social and emotional processes rather than as a single encounter with the legal system. Jane Murphy & Jana B. Singer, Divorced From Reality: Rethinking Family Dispute Resolution, ch. 3 (2015). A unified family court fits in with this approach.

A successful unified family court system has the following characteristics: "(1) comprehensive jurisdiction; (2) efficient administration designed to support the concept of 'one family, one team'; (3) broad training for all court personnel; and (4) comprehensive services." Ross *supra*, at 15.

Some states do not have unified family courts, nor plans to create them. Approximately two-thirds of states and the District of Columbia have one of the following: a statewide family court system, family courts in some parts of the state, family court pilot programs, or plans to establish a family court system.

Additional innovations include: "(1) family resource centers," which help families resolve issues outside of court (the HFI Resource Center for Separating and Divorcing Families at the University of Denver is an example), and "(2) informal family law trials, which streamline clogged calendars and provide an empowering and efficient forum" by, for example, relaxing the rules of evidence. William J. Howe, III & Elizabeth Potter Scully, *Redesigning the Family Law System to Promote Healthy Families*, 53 Fam. Ct. Rev. 361 (2015).

In jurisdictions without a unified family court, divorce actions and various other family-related cases may be heard in a general jurisdiction court or in a family court with more limited jurisdiction. Cases within the four traditional categories of juvenile court jurisdiction, recited above, are heard in that specialized court.

NOTES AND QUESTIONS

1.   *The good and the bad.* Significant questions remain about whether unified family courts are feasible or can live up to expectations. While "families may benefit from the capacity-building and problem-solving approaches embraced in the new paradigm, most courts are not equipped to provide these

services." Murphy and Singer, *supra* at 57. However, when a unified court is not a realistic option for a jurisdiction, there may be alternative measures to facilitate informed judicial decision-making, such as developing written protocols to expand the exchange of information between multiple judges hearing cases concerning one family. *See* Gabrielle Davis, Nancy Ver Steegh, & Loretta Fredrick, *An Appeal for Autonomy, Access, and Accountability in Family Court Reform Efforts*, Family Court Rev. J. (2014).

2.   *Criminal matters.* Most unified family courts have jurisdiction over juvenile delinquency cases, but only about half have jurisdiction over criminal matters that charge adults. What reasons support including adult family criminal matters in unified family courts? Why might states have chosen not to include these matters? Andrea L. Dennis, *Criminal Law as Family Law*, 33 Ga. L. Rev. 285 (2017).

3.   *Model unified court.* Vermont has provided a model for unified family courts since 1990. As the Chief Administrative Judge for the Vermont Trial Courts explained, " 'parents may be divorcing while at the same time a protective order is issued because there is domestic violence. Then you have the 12-year-old child running away from home * * *. Having the same judge see all of these cases could be critical for that child.' " Andrea S. Glenn, *Crisis in the Family Court*, 93 Judicature 253, 254 (2010).

On the other hand, this "pure" notion of unified family courts, that all cases relating to one family are assigned to one judge, may present substantial legal barriers. For example, juvenile dependency proceedings may be confidential, but the unified family court judge has access to that file as she considers other family-related issues. *See* John M. Greacen, *Confidentiality, Due Process, and Judicial Disqualification in the Unified Family Court: Report to the Honorable Stephanie Domitrovich*, 46 Fam. Ct. Rev. 340, 340 (2008). Indeed, a survey of stakeholders in Baltimore's family courts found that the primary concern was that judges might allow earlier decisions concerning the family to affect later decisions. Corey Shdaimah & Alicia Summers, *Baltimore City's Model Court: Professional Stakeholders' Experience with Baltimore City's One Family, One Judge Docketing*, 51 Fam. Ct. Rev. 286, 295 (2013). How might courts deal with such issues?

POSTSCRIPT: YOUR FUTURE
IN FAMILY LAW

■ ■ ■

The Preface to this casebook advised that now is an exciting time to practice family law. Chapters 1 and 14 describe family law practice and ethics, and Chapter 15 addresses the role of alternative dispute resolution in that practice. Now that you have nearly completed the course, ponder this final Problem as you consider whether practicing family law might lead to professional fulfillment.

PROBLEM

You teach family law as an adjunct at State University School of Law, and you make yourself readily available to students who wish to discuss their future career plans. A student stops by your office to talk with you about whether to accept an offer to become an associate in a leading local firm that practices family law exclusively. The student is not certain about whether to make a commitment to a long-term career practicing family law. What advice will you provide? What might you want to know about the student's motivations, career goals, and life aspirations?

INDEX

References are to Pages